21st-CENTURY (

M000197894

GENERAL EDITOR

SEAMUS PERRY

This volume in the 21st-Century Oxford Authors series offers students and readers a comprehensive selection of the work of Samuel Johnson (1709–1784). Accompanied by full scholarly apparatus, the edition enables students to study Johnson's work in the order in which it was written, and, wherever possible, using the text of the first published version.

The volume presents a selection of Johnson's most important writings, drawn from all periods of his life. It reflects almost completely the range of literary forms in which Johnson wrote, including poetic translation, biographical sketches, literary criticism, and letters. It includes a broad selection from *The Rambler* (1750–1752) and *The Idler* (1758–1760), along with the travel narrative *A Journey to the Western Islands of Scotland* (1775), and a selection from *The Lives of the Poets* (1781). David Womersley's introduction explores how Johnson's mastery of style enabled him to adopt various personae, sometimes simultaneously, in order to communicate through many different genres and registers. Johnson is shown to be an active participant in the philosophical and social currents of his time. This selection reveals an author driven by deeply-held principles, concerned with how the ethical, political, and affective dimensions of language go beyond vocabulary and reach into the lives of its users.

Explanatory notes and commentary are included to enhance the study, understanding, and enjoyment of these works, and the edition includes an Introduction to the life of Johnson, and a Chronology.

David Womersley is the Thomas Warton Professor of English Literature at the University of Oxford, and a fellow of St. Catherine's College.

Seamus Perry is the General Editor of the 21st-Century Oxford Authors series. He is Massey Fellow in English Literature, Balliol College, and Professor in the English Faculty, University of Oxford. His publications include *Coleridge and the Uses of Division, Coleridge's Notebooks: A Selection*, and, co-edited with Robert Douglas-Fairhurst, *Tennyson Among the Poets* (all OUP).

21st-CENTURY OXFORD AUTHORS

Samuel Johnson

EDITED BY

DAVID WOMERSLEY

OXFORD
UNIVERSITY PRESS

OXFORD

UNIVERSITY PRESS

Great Clarendon Street, Oxford, OX2 6DP,
United Kingdom

Oxford University Press is a department of the University of Oxford.
It furthers the University's objective of excellence in research, scholarship,
and education by publishing worldwide. Oxford is a registered trade mark of
Oxford University Press in the UK and in certain other countries

First published 2018
First published in paperback 2020

Impression: 2

Published in the United States of America by Oxford University Press
198 Madison Avenue, New York, NY 10016, United States of America

British Library Cataloguing in Publication Data
Data available

Library of Congress Cataloging in Publication Data
Data available

ISBN 978-0-19-960951-2 (Hbk.)
ISBN 978-0-19-885924-6 (Pbk.)

Printed and bound by
CPI Group (UK) Ltd, Croydon, CR0 4YY

CONTENTS

LIST OF ILLUSTRATIONS

LIST OF ABBREVIATIONS

ALC   D. A. Russell and M. Winterbottom (eds), *Ancient Literary Criticism* (Oxford: Clarendon Press, 1972)

Anecdotes   Hester Lynch Piozzi, *Anecdotes of the Late Samuel Johnson, LL.D.* (1786)

Bacon, *Essayes* Sir Francis Bacon, *The Essayes or Counsels, Ciuill and Morall*, ed. Michael Kiernan (Oxford: Clarendon Press, 1985)

Brief Lives   *Aubrey's Brief Lives*, ed. Oliver Lawson Dick (Harmondsworth: Penguin Books, 1962)

DF   Edward Gibbon, *The History of the Decline and Fall of the Roman Empire*, ed. David Womersley, 3 vols (London: Penguin Books, 1995)

Diaries   E. L. McAdam Jr. and Donald and Mary Hyde (eds), *Diaries, Prayers, and Annals* (New Haven, CT: Yale University Press, 1958)

Early Biographies *The Early Biographies of Samuel Johnson*, ed. O.M. Brack Jr. and Robert E. Kelley (Iowa City, IA: University of Iowa Press, 1974)

GT   Jonathan Swift, *Gulliver's Travels*, ed. David Womersley (Cambridge: Cambridge University Press, 2012)

Hawkins   Sir John Hawkins, *The Life of Samuel Johnson*, second edition (1787)

Hebrides   James Boswell, *The Journal of a Tour to the Hebrides* (1785)

Hooker   Richard Hooker, *Works* (1705)

Journey   Samuel Johnson, *A Journey to the Western Islands of Scotland*, ed. J. D. Fleeman (Oxford: Clarendon Press, 1985)

Life   James Boswell, *The Life of Johnson*, ed. David Womersley (London: Penguin Books, 2008)

Lonsdale   Samuel Johnson, *The Lives of the Poets*, ed. Roger Lonsdale, 4 vols (Oxford: Clarendon Press, 2006)

Miscellanies   *Johnsonian Miscellanies*, ed. G. Birkbeck Hill, 2 vols (Oxford: Clarendon Press, 1897)

Montaigne   Michel de Montaigne, *The Complete Essays*, tr. M. Screech (Harmondsworth: Penguin Books, 1991)

Nichol Smith   D. Nichol Smith (ed.), *Eighteenth Century Essays on Shakespeare*, 2nd edn (Oxford: Clarendon Press, 1963)

Poems   *Samuel Johnson: The Complete English Poems*, ed. J. D. Fleeman (Harmondsworth: Penguin Books, 1971)

Quotations   *The Concise Oxford Dictionary of Quotations*, 3rd edn (Oxford: Oxford University Press, 1993)

Reddick   Allen Reddick, *The Making of Johnson's Dictionary 1746–1773*, rev. edn (Cambridge: Cambridge University Press, 1996)

Redford   *The Letters of Samuel Johnson,* ed. Bruce Redford, 'The Hyde Edition', 5 vols (Oxford: Clarendon Press, 1992–94)

Shakespeare   *Selections from Johnson on Shakespeare,* ed. Bertrand H. Bronson and Jean M. O'Meara (New Haven, CT: Yale University Press, 1986)

Thraliana   *Thraliana: the Diary of Mrs. Hester Lynch Thrale (later Mrs. Piozzi) 1776–1809,* ed. K. C. Balderston, 2nd edn, 2 vols (Oxford: Clarendon Press, 1951)

V&P   *Extracts from the Votes and Proceedings of the American Continental Congress* (1774)

Wright   Richard Wright (ed.), *An Account of the Life of Dr. Samuel Johnson* (1805)

INTRODUCTION

In the opening paragraphs of the 'Preface' to his *Dictionary*, Johnson presents the toil of the lexicographer as a Herculean labour of cleansing, ordering, and stabilizing a language which had been suffered to sprawl in waste fertility:

> When I took the first survey of my undertaking, I found our speech copious without order, and energetick without rules: wherever I turned my view, there was perplexity to be disentangled, and confusion to be regulated; choice was to be made out of boundless variety, without any established principle of selection; adulterations were to be detected, without a settled test of purity; and modes of expression to be rejected or received, without the suffrages of any writers of classical reputation or acknowledged authority.[1]

Notwithstanding such adversity, Johnson claimed to have 'reduced [the language] to method'.[2] Johnson's career as a writer did indeed coincide with a transformation in English literature and the usage of the English language: a transformation towards refinement, regularity, and elegance. It was a development which Johnson himself helped to bring about through the *Dictionary* itself, through scholarly projects such as the *Harleian Miscellany*, the edition of Shakespeare, and the *Lives of the Poets*, through his periodical essays and fictions which impregnated those literary forms with moral substance, and not least through his poetry.

Nevertheless, Johnson viewed the 'improvements' in English of his own day with distinctly mixed feelings. Later in the 'Preface' he identified 'the writers before the restoration' as 'the wells of English undefiled'.[3] It was a considered judgement which reflected critically on the language and literature of his own day; for from the authors of a period as remote as the reign of Elizabeth, he believed, might be extracted a speech 'adequate to all the purposes of use and elegance'.[4] Every language, he ruefully noted, 'has a time of rudeness antecedent to perfection, as well as of false refinement and declension.'[5] False refinement, in all its guises and wherever it might lurk, was something Johnson was resolutely determined to expose and explode, as his scything review of Soame Jenyns's blithe essay in the moral refinement of heartless theodicy amply shows.[6]

So, although Johnson had soon dismissed as a fantasy his initial dream that his *Dictionary* might fix the language in perpetuity (for that lexicographer may be 'derided' who 'shall imagine that his dictionary can embalm his language, and secure it from corruption and decay, that it is in his power to change sublunary nature, or clear the world at once from folly, vanity, and

---

[1] See below, p. 491.   [2] See below, p. 491.   [3] See below, p. 501.
[4] See below, p. 501.   [5] See below, p. 501.   [6] See below, pp. 549–68.

affectation'), he was far from therefore welcoming the volatility he saw in the language and literature of his own day. He recognised that linguistic changes could arise from things which were in themselves good, such as economic and intellectual progress. Only the language of a people 'raised a little, and but a little, above barbarity' might achieve stability and 'continue long without alteration':

> But no such constancy can be expected in a people polished by arts, and classed by subordination, where one part of the community is sustained and accommodated by the labour of the other. Those who have much leisure to think, will always be enlarging the stock of ideas, and every increase of knowledge, whether real or fancied, will produce new words, or combinations of words.[7]

Yet these new words or combinations of words, although generated by the welcome progress of society, might nevertheless threaten to degrade the language. The inevitable fact of linguistic change puts the lexicographer at bay, in a characteristically Johnsonian stance of guarded defiance before insuperable odds:

> If the changes we fear be thus irresistible, what remains but to acquiesce with silence, as in the other insurmountable distresses of humanity? it remains that we retard what we cannot repel, that we palliate what we cannot cure. Life may be lengthened by care, though death cannot be ultimately defeated: tongues, like governments, have a natural tendency to degeneration; we have long preserved our constitution, let us make some struggles for our language.[8]

In that distinctively Johnsonian conjunction of realism and resistance, we see also how the deepest questions of language, of morals, and of politics were merged in Johnson's mind, just as they shaped his career as a writer.

* * *

Johnson was born in Lichfield on 18 September 1709, the son of Michael Johnson, a bookseller. In 1717 he entered Lichfield Grammar School, proceeding in 1728 to Pembroke College, Oxford. However, Johnson remained in Oxford for barely a year, leaving in December 1729. After the death of his father in 1731 he spent the early 1730s teaching and pursuing a literary career in the midlands; for instance, in 1733 he translated Lobo's *Voyage to Abyssinia*, a work eventually published in 1735.[9] This was also the year in which Johnson married Elizabeth Jervis, a widow with three children. In the following year he opened his own school at Edial near Lichfield, and began work on *Irene*, a moral tragedy set in

---

[7] See below, p. 506.
[8] See below, p. 507. For another celebrated image of Johnson *agonistes*, cf. *Life*, p. 315.
[9] For the 'Preface', see below, pp. 15–17.

Constantinople after its fall to the Turks (although the play was not to be performed until January 1749). Meanwhile, the school at Edial seems never to have flourished. It closed in 1737, and in March of that year Johnson, accompanied by David Garrick, moved to London and committed himself to a career as a man of letters. The late 1730s and early 1740s were thus for Johnson a period of Grub-Street hackery,[10] interspersed with some brighter triumphs, such as the publication in 1738 of his Juvenalian imitation, 'London'.[11] He began writing for *The Gentleman's Magazine*, contributing miscellaneous essays and the 'Debates in the Senate of Lilliput' which, in a period when it was forbidden to report the debates in the House of Commons directly, were a mock-Swiftian vehicle for disseminating awareness of what was happening in Parliament.[12] It was at this time, too, that Johnson composed two anti-government pamphlets, the anti-Walpolean *Marmor Norfolciense* and *A Compleat Vindication of the Licensers of the Stage*.[13] In both these works he revealed his antipathy to the prevailing politics of whiggism, as well as a streak of literary inventiveness.

The other literary form Johnson pursued during these years was biography. He composed lives of his friend the poet Richard Savage, of the historian Paolo Sarpi, and of the physician Herman Boerhaave, as well as a series of shorter biographical sketches which he contributed to *The Gentleman's Magazine*.[14] Now, too, he began to frame larger literary projects. He contributed to the *Harleian Miscellany*, and compiled the catalogue of the Harleian library.[15] He proposed an edition of Shakespeare, and in 1746 signed the contract for the *Dictionary* (finally to be published in 1755). In 1747 he published the *Plan of an English Dictionary*, dedicated to Lord Chesterfield, and in 1749 there appeared a second Juvenalian imitation, *The Vanity of Human Wishes*.

* * *

In *The Life of Johnson* Boswell records Johnson's memory that, at some time early in 1750 and after the publication of a few *Ramblers*, his wife Tetty had confessed that these most recent writings had transformed her understanding of Johnson. They had revealed in him unsuspected powers: 'I thought very well of you before; but I did not imagine you could have written any thing equal to this.'[16] Some two years later, on 13 March 1752, Johnson presented his wife with the four duodecimo volumes of the collected *Rambler*. A few

---

[10] In 1739 Lord Gower, in the course of supplying a testimonial to assist Johnson in his candidacy for the headmastership of Appleby School, reported that Johnson would prefer 'to die upon the road, *than be starved to death in translating for booksellers*; which has been his only subsistence for some time past' (*Life*, p. 77).

[11] Below, pp. 19–26. For Pope's 'candid and liberal' praise of the poem, see *Life*, p. 75.

[12] See below, pp. 26–32.

[13] The second of which is reprinted below, pp. 50–61.

[14] Below, pp. 35–50, 79–111.   [15] Below, pp. 71–7, 145–50.

[16] *Life*, p. 117.

days later she was dead. As Allen Reddick has said with compassionate insight of this episode: 'The timing of her epiphanic comment—the discovery of the extent of her husband's genius just as her own decline began to hasten—and Johnson's touching and desperate attempt to reach her through a gift of his own work that she had valued are simply further sad and ironical elements characteristic of the Johnsons' marriage.'[17] The common view of Tetty—that she was a slothful woman of unleavenable ordinariness, who took no interest in the work of her husband, and who killed herself with drink and opium[18]— might encourage us to see her surprise at *The Rambler* as just another instance of her inability to understand her own experience. But would anyone have guessed in the early months of 1750 that Johnson would be able to write, not only anything as good as *The Rambler*, but even anything like it?

Even those who in 1750 knew Johnson well might have seen few clues. When the first *Rambler* appeared anonymously in 1750, even had its readers known that the author was Samuel Johnson, that name would have identified a jobbing journalist and political pamphleteer; an accomplished if not prolific poet; and a professional writer who had recently branched out into lexicography, textual editing, and antiquarianism. It would not have suggested a master of moral wisdom. Yet in a few years, it would be these moral essays that formed Johnson's surest claim to regard. When in 1755 the Earl of Arran wrote to the Vice-Chancellor of Oxford to request that the degree of M.A. be conferred on Johnson, he emphasized that the honorand had 'very eminently distinguished himself by the publication of a series of essays, excellently calculated to form the manners of the people, and in which the cause of religion and morality is every where maintained by the strongest powers of argument and language'.[19] Johnson was resolved to make even technical scholarship active in the work of improving the moral sense of his readers. In the 'Preface' to his edition of Shakespeare he stated the principle most clearly: 'it is always a writer's duty to make the world better.'[20] So even the quotations used in the *Dictionary* to illustrate the meanings of words were selected with an eye to their potency for a broader instruction: 'When first I collected these authorities, I was desirous that every quotation should be useful to some other end than the illustration of a word; I therefore extracted from philosophers principles of science; from historians remarkable facts; from chymists complete processes; from divines striking exhortations; and from poets beautiful descriptions.'[21]

The periodical essay was a well-established form before Johnson wrote *The Rambler*, and towards the end of his life, when writing his 'Life' of Addison,

---

[17] Reddick, p. 68.

[18] See the clipped and unsympathetic judgement of Robert Levet (*Thraliana*, vol. I, p. 178). This was not a view shared by Johnson himself, as his affliction after Tetty's death sufficiently shows (below, pp. 431–2).

[19] *Life*, p. 153.   [20] Below, p. 734.   [21] Below, p. 500.

he explained what he saw as its particular strengths. In his view, the periodical essay derived from conduct books such as Casa's *Il Galatheo*, Castiglione's *Il libro del cortegiano*, and La Bruyère's *Les caractères, ou les moeurs de ce siècle*. These works, according to Johnson, had set themselves to 'teach the minuter decencies and inferior duties, to regulate the practice of daily conversation, to correct those depravities which are rather ridiculous than criminal, and remove those grievances which, if they produce no lasting calamities, impress hourly vexation.'[22] But, in Johnson's opinion, before the publication of *The Tatler* and *The Spectator* in 1709–11 and 1711–12 respectively, 'England had no masters of common life':

> No writers had yet undertaken to reform either the savageness of neglect or the impertinence of civility; to shew when to speak, or to be silent; how to refuse, or how to comply. We had many books to teach us our more important duties, and to settle opinions in philosophy or politicks; but an *Arbiter elegantiarum*, a judge of propriety, was yet wanting, who should survey the track of daily conversation and free it from thorns and prickles, which teaze the passer, though they do not wound him.[23]

Yet this important function is discharged by nothing so well as 'the frequent publication of short papers, which we read not as study, but amusement. If the subject be slight, the treatise is short. The busy may find time, and the idle may find patience.'[24] Johnson was, in fact, wrong when he suggested that *The Tatler* and *The Spectator* had been first in the field. The periodical format went back as far as the 1660s and Henry Muddiman's *Oxford Gazette*, while (as Angus Ross has pointed out) 'it is no exaggeration to say that every form of writing, every topic of discussion or method of circulation (save the issue of collected papers by subscription) characteristic of *The Tatler* and *The Spectator* had been seen in some periodical or other before they appeared.'[25]

Moreover, when Johnson came to write *The Rambler*, he aspired to a much graver character than that of an *arbiter elegantiarum*. Instead, he chose to move the periodical form back towards those 'more important duties' which in the 'Life of Addison' he considered had been already adequately covered. Johnson wished 'to reach the same audience the *Spectator* had so successfully entertained, but to encourage in it a more rigorously *critical* kind of thinking.'[26] What may have impelled Johnson in the direction of rigour and moral seriousness?

Johnson's moral seriousness has a double aspect. On the one hand, he was a collector of instances of moral heroism, particularly if that heroism had not been exercised in the full glare of public renown. Examples of this occur in

---

[22] Below, p. 1015.   [23] Below, p. 1015.   [24] Below, p. 1016.
[25] A. Ross (ed.), *Selections from The Tatler and The Spectator* (Harmondsworth: Penguin Books, 1982), p. 22.
[26] Leo Damrosch, 'Johnson's Manner of Proceeding in the *Rambler*', *ELH*, 40 (1973), p. 72.

the short essay 'Of Epitaphs', and also at greater length in the biography of the physician Boerhaave, where Johnson's admiration was captured by a combination of unshakeable and undogmatic inward piety ('He worshipped God as he is in himself, without attempting to enquire into his Nature'), and an equally unshakeable determination to be useful to his fellow-man.[27] It was this admiration which dictated Johnson's final portrait of his subject:

> Thus died *Boerhaave*, a Man formed by Nature for great Designs, and guided by Religion in the Exertion of his Abilities. He was of a robust and athletic Constitution of Body, so harden'd by early Severities, and wholesome Fatigue, that he was insensible of any Sharpness of Air, or Inclemency of Weather. He was tall, and remarkable for extraordinary Strength. There was in his Air and Motion something rough and artless, but so majestick and great at the same time, that no Man ever looked upon him without Veneration, and a kind of tacit Submission to the Superiority of his Genius.[28]

Images of moral heroism may inspire; but they may equally discourage, by suggesting the impossibility of emulation. Certainly the emphasis Johnson laid on particular details of Boerhaave's moral constitution—for instance, his unbroken habit of early rising—occasionally corresponded to parallel weaknesses of his own. The moral instructor must be a master both of chiding and encouraging, and so must possess a sympathetic understanding of the condition of moral imbecillity prevalent amongst those he hopes to improve. Accordingly, as well as being invigorated by instances of moral heroism, Johnson was also compassionately fascinated by conditions of moral adversity, whether of the ordinary kind composed of mild misfortunes and feebleness of will, or of the more operatic kind which afflicted his friend Richard Savage, in which it is hard to say whether Johnson was more appalled by Savage's persecutors, or astonished by Savage's ability to remain uncrushed.[29] Johnson's moral curiosity was sharpened by the paradoxical interplay he observed in human affairs between resolution and recidivism, courage and capitulation. The scene of human moral conduct in this resembles the 'mingled drama' of Shakespeare, which Johnson so relished, and which he defended conclusively against the cavils of 'the rules of criticism'.[30]

But it was surely also the work for the *Dictionary of the English Language*, on which Johnson had embarked during the later 1740s, which both made the periodical essay an attractive form, and induced him to give that form a graver turn. At one level, the composition of brief essays must have seemed to offer relief after the unremitting reading required by the *Dictionary*. At the same time, that very reading may have suggested to Johnson both the perennial moral topics which form the heart of *The Rambler*, and also how to treat them. In part, that was because work on the *Dictionary* was equipping

---

[27] Below, p. 48.   [28] Below, p. 46.   [29] Below, pp. 79–111.   [30] Below, p. 732.

Johnson with a philosophical vocabulary in which he could give weighty expression to his judgements on the topics of common life.[31] The programme of reading which Johnson had set himself in order to assemble his illustrative quotations was in itself an education, involving as it did 'incessant reading' of 'the best authors in our language.'[32]

Just as Johnson was politically an internal exile (a stubborn Tory obliged to live under Hanoverian monarchs and in a world of which the politics, irrespective of which particular party happened to be in or out, were fundamentally shaped by the 'Revolution Principles' of 1688) so, too, he was estranged from the most fashionable ethical theories of his time, the spokesman for a conscious ethics of the will at a time when a contrary theory of morals was dominant. The two positions were elegantly formulated by Hume, in his *Enquiry Concerning the Principles of Morals* (1751):

> There has been a controversy started of late...concerning the general foundation of Morals; whether they be derived from Reason, or from Sentiment; whether we attain the knowledge of them by a chain of argument and induction, or by an immediate feeling and finer internal sense; whether, like all sound judgement of truth and falsehood, they should be the same to every rational intelligent being; or whether, like the perception of beauty and deformity, they be founded entirely on the particular fabric and constitution of the human species.[33]

In the terms of this opposition, Johnson was an opponent of affective theories of ethics (that is to say, theories which located the origin of moral discriminations in involuntary sentiments, rather than in conscious and reasoned judgements). The very holders of such views were probably enough to blacken them irredeemably in Johnson's eyes: Shaftesbury, the arch-Whig and freethinker; Hume, the religious sceptic against whom Johnson repeatedly ranged and defined himself; Adam Smith, a leading figure of that Scottish Enlightenment which Johnson would emphatically slight in his *Journey to the Western Islands*.

In conversation with Boswell, however, Johnson expanded on his opposition to the ethical theories of Shaftesbury, Hume, and Smith, and made clear that his suspicion of those theories was not simply transferred suspicion of the men who disseminated them:

---

[31] W. K. Wimsatt, *Philosophic Words: A Study of Style and Meaning in the Rambler and Dictionary of Samuel Johnson* (New Haven, CT: Yale University Press, 1948). A. Reddick, *The Making of Johnson's Dictionary 1746–1773*, rev. edn (Cambridge: Cambridge University Press, 1996). See, too, the coda to *Rambler*, no. 208 (below, pp. 413–14).

[32] Hawkins, p. 175. Although Thomas Percy dissents from Hawkins's account of the physical process whereby the illustrative quotations for the *Dictionary* were assembled and collated, he endorses what Hawkins says about the trawl of reading which underpropped the whole enterprise: 'He began his task by devoting his first care to a diligent perusal of all such English writers as were most correct in their language' (*Miscellanies*, vol. II, p. 214). For the manner in which the *Dictionary* was compiled, see Reddick, esp. pp. 27–41.

[33] David Hume, *Enquiry Concerning the Principles of Morals* (1751), Section 1, para. 134.

We can have no dependence upon that instinctive, that constitutional goodness which is not founded upon principle. I grant you that such a man may be a very amiable member of society. I can conceive him placed in such a situation that he is not much tempted to deviate from what is right; and as every man prefers virtue, when there is not some strong incitement to transgress its precepts, I can conceive him doing nothing wrong. But if such a man stood in need of money, I should not like to trust him; and I should certainly not trust him with young ladies, for *there* there is always temptation.[34]

This conviction, that a morality based upon the affections might not serve to support us in those hard cases which are the test of any moral position, led Johnson also to oppose speculative theories which tended to diminish man's responsibility for his moral health – for example, fashionable theories which related morals to climate, or which located the cause of moral degeneration in broad social phenomena such as luxury. A good example of Johnson's resistance to anything which suggested that moral judgements were not peculiarly human, and rooted in the conscious will, is his refusal even to entertain one of Boswell's experiences while on the Grand Tour:

I told him that I had several times, when in Italy, seen the experiment of placing a scorpion within a circle of burning coals; that it ran round and round in extreme pain; and finding no way to escape, retired to the centre, and like a true Stoick philosopher, darted its sting into its head, and thus at once freed itself from its woes. . . . I said, this was a curious fact, as it shewed deliberate suicide in a reptile.[35]

Johnson refused point blank to accept the possibility of a reptile's committing suicide, because he could admit neither that animals possess a moral sense, nor that an ethical act could be a reflex, without sacrificing the essence of his moral position; namely, that our moral sense is the product of our waking judgement.

Given that Johnson was such an advocate for an ethics of conscious principle, one would expect his ethical language to be overt and declaratory; that is to say, conscious, stated and argued for. But the experience of reading Johnson is not like that. Sir John Hawkins caught well how the impact of Johnson's writing is not one of propositional clarity:

In all Johnson's disquisitions, whether argumentative or critical, there is a certain even-handed justice that leaves the mind in a strange perplexity.[36]

'A strange perplexity': it is precisely that sense of being moved at a level beyond or beneath the level of language which, I think, characterizes the experience of reading Johnson's best moral writing. To understand why this

---

[34] *Life*, p. 234.   [35] *Life*, pp. 290–1.   [36] Hawkins, p. 482.

should be so, we need to consider the theory of language which exerted the greatest influence over Johnson, namely the theory developed by Locke in Book III of *An Essay Concerning Human Understanding*.

The importance of language for Locke was that, since words represent ideas and not objects, they can transmit knowledge from one person to another:

it was further necessary that he [man] should be *able to use these sounds as signs of internal conceptions*, and to make them stand as marks for the *ideas* within his own mind, whereby they might be made known to others, and the thoughts of men's minds be conveyed from one to another.[37]

According to Locke, the ideas that language can convey are of two kinds, simple and complex. An example of a simple idea would be 'goat'. Simple ideas, Locke insisted, cannot be defined. However, in practice this is not a great problem since they can be demonstrated, or pointed out. By contrast, an example of a complex idea (or 'mixed mode', as Locke more often calls it) would be 'ingratitude' (and indeed the ideas represented by all ethical language fall into this category of 'mixed modes'). For mixed modes, the reverse holds true. They cannot be demonstrated because, in Locke's words, 'they are the creatures of the understanding rather than the works of nature.'[38] However, the compensation for this is that they can be *defined* with perfect precision:

the signification of their names [those of mixed modes] cannot be made known, as those of simple *ideas*, by any showing, but, in recompense thereof, may be perfectly and exactly *defined*. For they being combinations of several *ideas* that the mind of man has arbitrarily put together, without reference to any archetypes [i.e. things existing in nature which form the original patterns of those ideas], men may, if they please, exactly know the *ideas* that go to each composition, and so both use these words in a certain and undoubted signification, and perfectly declare, when there is occasion, what they stand for.[39]

For Locke, this is a source of great comfort, because from it he deduces that moral language can be made more precise than any other kind of language:

This, if well considered, would lay great blame on those who make not their discourses about moral things very clear and distinct. For since the precise signification of the names of mixed modes...is to be known, they being not of nature's but man's making, it is a great negligence and perverseness to discourse of moral things with uncertainty and obscurity....Upon this ground it is that I am bold to think that *morality is capable of demonstration*, as well as mathematics: since the precise real essence of the things

[37] John Locke, *An Essay Concerning Human Understanding*, III, 1.2.
[38] Ibid, III, 5.12   [39] Ibid, III, 11.15.

moral words stand for may be perfectly known, and so the congruity or incongruity of the things themselves be certainly discovered, in which consists perfect knowledge.[40]

Johnson's famous comment—'words are the daughters of earth, and . . . things are the sons of heaven. Language is only the instrument of science, and words are but the signs of ideas'—shows his subscription to Locke's theory of language.[41] But on this point of the demonstrability of morality, he is at the opposite pole from his philosophical predecessor. What Locke saw as a source of encouragement—that moral terms are susceptible of exact definition—Johnson, as a practical rather than a speculative moralist, found a cause of disquiet. It may be that such moral *terms* can be precisely defined. But those precise definitions may not help in the practical business of grasping the substantive essence of moral *ideas*.

The point can be clarified if we compare definitions from the *Dictionary* of what Locke would have called simple ideas with mixed modes. First, two definitions of simple ideas:

Horse] A neighing quadruped, used in war, in draught, and in carriage.
Ink]   The black liquor with which men write.

These definitions follow on from Locke's insistence on the demonstrability of a simple idea, in that they take the form of a set of instructions as to where to look. If you want to know what ink is, you find a man who is writing, and look at the black liquor he is using. Johnson's definitions of mixed modes are quite different:

Virtue]   Moral goodness: opposed to vice.
Vice]   The course of action opposite to virtue.
Good]   Not bad; not ill.
Ill]   Not well.

It is quite clear that, considered purely as *definitions*, these have a formal precision which the definitions of 'horse' and 'ink' lack. But it is hard to see what use they would be to someone who wishes to lead a moral life, and therefore needs to know the content of the ideas terms such as 'virtue', 'vice', 'good', and 'ill' represent. Locke had assumed that, because these words could be precisely defined, we could have exact knowledge of the essence of the idea. But for Johnson, it is possible to have a precision of moral language, but nothing else, as he shows in the character of the philosopher in chapter twenty-two of *Rasselas*:

To live according to nature, is to act always with due regard to the fitness arising from the relations and qualities of causes and effects; to concur with the great and

---

[40] Ibid, III, 11.15–16.   [41] Below, p. 494.

unchangeable scheme of universal felicity; to cooperate with the general disposition and tendency of the present system of things.[42]

For Johnson, to live a moral life was less a question of possessing a vocabulary than of adhering to a certain standard of conduct. In *The Rambler* no. 14 he acknowledged the power of moral theory: 'In moral discussions it is to be remembered that many impediments obstruct our practice, which very easily give way to theory.'[43] But that power will be only a snare and a delusion unless it be also remembered that 'human experience, which is constantly contradicting theory, is the great test of truth.'[44] How can language lay hold on the substance of morality, instead of merely shadowing the world of moral action with a self-regarding and futile precision?[45]

It is here that Johnson's notion of the special virtue of poetic language is important. In *The Idler* no. 60 Johnson amusingly mocked Dick Minim's 'enactment' theory of poetic language. He was obliged to do so in order to distinguish that crassness from a notion of poetic language which he took very seriously: namely, that 'the force of poetry...calls new powers into being', which powers are capable of 'embodying sentiment', including moral sentiment.[46] Johnson's own elegy on Robert Levet is an example of that force and of those powers at work.[47] The neo-classical decorations of Milton's 'Lycidas' had, a few years before Levet's death, roused Johnson's indignation: 'In this poem there is no nature, for there is no truth; there is no art, for there is nothing new. Its form is that of a pastoral, easy, vulgar, and therefore disgusting: whatever images it can supply, are long ago exhausted; and its inherent improbability always forces dissatisfaction on the mind.'[48] Yet this severe verdict on 'Lycidas' also implies a brighter corollary. The elegy could be invigorated by nature and art, and could still give satisfaction, provided it was refreshed with truth, novelty, and probability.

Boswell gave a disdainful sketch of Levet: 'he was of a strange grotesque appearance, stiff and formal in his manner, and seldom said a word while any company was present.'[49] From this unpromising raw material, Johnson made a moral poem of extraordinary force. In his essay 'Of Epitaphs', he had written:

The best subject for epitaphs is private virtue; virtue exerted in the same circumstances in which the bulk of mankind are placed, and which, therefore, may admit of many imitators...he that has repelled the temptations of poverty, and disdained to free

---

[42] Below, p. 670.   [43] Below, p. 205.   [44] *Life*, pp. 238–9.

[45] Cf. the remark of Leo Damrosch, that 'the heart of Johnson's mission as a moralist is to make us stop parroting the precepts of moralists and start thinking for ourselves' ('Johnson's Manner of Proceeding in the *Rambler*', *ELH*, 40 (1973), p. 81).

[46] From *Rambler* no. 168 (below, p. 381).   [47] Below, pp. 1146–7.

[48] 'Life of Milton' (below, p. 959).   [49] *Life*, p. 133.

himself from distress, at the expense of his virtue, may animate multitudes by his example, to the same firmness of heart and steadiness of resolution.[50]

It takes no very profound reading of 'On the Death of Dr. Robert Levet' to see that its surface meaning is very much concerned with rectifying the neglect of society, and of paying due accord to the virtues of the obscure and the petty.

But, beneath that, there is also a more searching moral aspect to the poem, where it engages with the consideration that Johnson felt should always inform a person's moral conduct; that is to say, the certainty of death. *Rambler* no. 78 states the principle:

the remembrance of death ought to predominate in our minds, as an habitual and settled principle, always operating, though not always perceived.... [for] the great incentive to virtue is the reflection that we must die.

Yet the fact of our own eventual death, as Johnson conceded in that same paper, is a certainty from which the repetitious nature of daily life perpetually distracts us. In his elegy for Levet Johnson employed what he had, as a grammarian, considered a flaw in the English language to penetrate the reader afresh with the knowledge that, while virtually everything else can happen to us many times, or may not happen to us at all, we will certainly encounter death, and will encounter it only once.

For the first eight stanzas of this poem, Johnson is concerned with repeated actions: our daily toil in hope's delusive mine, Levet's toil of every day which met the needs of every day, the narrow round of his habitual exercise of his single talent. And in the penultimate stanza Johnson also alludes to the inattention engendered by the repetitive nature of our quotidian existence:

> The busy day, the peaceful night,
> Unfelt, uncounted, glided by;

But in the last stanza the verbs do not describe repeated actions. They become instead true preterites, referring to single, accomplished actions:

> Death broke at once the vital chain,
> And freed his soul the nearest way.

In the 'Preface' to the *Dictionary*, Johnson had sighed over the haphazard way in which English verbs conjugate the past tense:

---

[50] Below, p. 67.

I have been careful to insert and elucidate the anomalous...preterites of verbs, which in the *Teutonick* dialects are very frequent, and, though familiar to those who have always used them, interrupt and embarrass the learners of our language.[51]

It is a feature of 'the anomalous...preterites of verbs' in English that two distinct functions of the past tense (that of referring to repeated action in the past, and also of referring to single, accomplished past actions) are not distinguished by grammatical inflection: exactly the same word has to serve for both. Had, for instance, Johnson decided to write the elegy for Levet in Latin (as he was well capable of doing),[52] the terminations of the verbs would clearly have distinguished the separate kinds of past event to which they refer, because Latin (like French) has two separate past tenses, one for repeated actions and the other for single completed actions. So in a Latin elegy for Levet, 'Glided' might have been rendered by 'surrepebant'; 'broke' and 'freed' by 'fregit' and 'liberavit'. This hypothetical Latin poem, by virtue of the more regular and intricate formation of past tenses in that language, would have discriminated the two types of past event to which the poem refers more scrupulously than does, or could, the English poem which we possess.

But this hypothetical Latin poem would also, I believe, be a lesser poem. For it is in the 'strange perplexity' (to return to Hawkins's phrase) which every reader must, for a moment, feel as we move, without preparation or warning, from imperfect to perfect tense in the final stanza, and so from repeated to single events, that the poem achieves its moral impact. The irregular identity of imperfect and perfect tenses in English, deplored by Johnson the grammarian as an anomaly, is here made the vehicle for a vivid expression of the reflection which Johnson the moralist wished to place in the foundations of our ethical existence: namely, the 'reflection that we must die.' The tenses of our hypothetical Latin poem could register clearly and directly the different event which is death. It could shock us with it. It could not, as Johnson's English poem does, ambush us with it. For the moral impact of the elegy for Levet is more subtle, and more profound because more subtle, than that of any translation could be, except a translation into a language as casual as is English in forming its past tenses. Only in such a language could what Johnson does in this poem be duplicated. Surprised by death at the end of the poem, we are prompted to acknowledge, before our habitual state of moral distractedness resumes, that we too will die, and to reflect, albeit momentarily, on whether or not death will be for us a true emancipation, as it was for Levet. In the strange perplexity of that final moment, Johnson's poem achieves its moral stature, triumphs over the solipsism which lies in wait for moral language, and administers to its reader an impetus to moral reformation. At

---

[51] See below, p. 494.   [52] See, e.g., Γνωθι σεαυτον (below, pp. 791–2).

the same time, Johnson comes close to his subject: he, too, displays 'the power of art without the show.'

In *The Idler* no. 41 Johnson, recently smitten by the death of his mother, had already reflected on the paradoxes arising from our habitual distraction from the inevitability of death:

That it is vain to shrink from what cannot be avoided, and to hide that from ourselves which must some time be found, is a truth which we all know, but which all neglect...Nothing is more evident than that the decays of age must terminate in death; yet there is no man, says Tully, who does not believe that he may yet live another year.[53]

The purpose of moral writing is forcibly to awaken us from this condition of ineffective awareness. It is therefore a kind of assault upon us—in just the way that Johnson reported to Boswell that he himself had been assaulted and awakened, when a young man, from an unexpected quarter. The 'religious progress' of the young Johnson had it seems been fitful and uneven:

I fell into an inattention to religion, or an indifference about it, in my ninth year. The church at Lichfield, in which we had a seat, wanted reparation, so I was to go and find a seat in other churches; and having bad eyes, and being awkward about this, I used to go and read in the fields on Sunday. This habit continued till my fourteenth year; and still I find a great reluctance to go to church. I then became a sort of lax *talker* against religion, for I did not much *think* against it; and this lasted till I went to Oxford, where it would not be *suffered*. When at Oxford, I took up Law's 'Serious Call to a Holy Life', expecting to find it a dull book, (as such books generally are), and perhaps to laugh at it. But I found Law quite an overmatch for me; and this was the first occasion of my thinking in earnest of religion, after I became capable of rational enquiry.[54]

When Johnson says that Law was an 'overmatch' for him, he draws a metaphor from wrestling, which hints to us that the benefit which flowed from Johnson's reading of Law's *Serious Call* arose precisely from the energy of its attack upon the dullness of his spiritual apprehension. Johnson was always liable to fall back into religious torpor, and his private prayers and diary entries show the vigour with which he tried to resist such backsliding.[55] The intensity of Johnson's inner torments vindicate his moral writings from any charge of complacent dogmatism.

Such writing is like ethical sandpaper. By means of literary surprise it outmanoeuvres readerly expectation, and resensitizes us to the moral realities from which the carapace of daily life will surely separate us unless it is vigorously challenged. It is a kind of writing which Johnson himself could achieve in *The Rambler*, as the conclusion of the second essay shows:

---

[53] Below, p. 597–8. [54] *Life*, p. 43. [55] e.g. below, pp. 725–6, 759–60, 907.

But, though it should happen that an author is capable of excelling, yet his merit may pass without notice, huddled in the variety of things, and thrown into the general miscellany of life. He that endeavours after fame by writing, solicits the regard of a multitude fluctuating in pleasures, or immersed in business, without time for intellectual amusements; he appeals to judges prepossessed by passions, or corrupted by prejudices, which preclude their approbation of any new performance. Some are too indolent to read any thing, till its reputation is established; others too envious to promote that fame, which gives them pain by its increase. What is new is opposed, because most are unwilling to be taught; and what is known is rejected, because it is not sufficiently considered, that men more frequently require to be reminded than informed. The learned are afraid to declare their opinion early, lest they should put their reputation in hazard; the ignorant always imagine themselves giving some proof of delicacy, when they refuse to be pleased: and he that finds his way to reputation, through all these obstructions, must acknowledge that he is indebted to other causes besides his industry, his learning, or his wit.[56]

The paragraph opens with the proposition that fame is elusive, and then goes on to offer a series of particular reasons why this is so. At this point, then, Johnson seems to be offering consolation to the obscure. However, the final limb of the concluding sentence springs the mine: 'and he that finds his way to reputation, through all these obstructions, must acknowledge that he is indebted to other causes besides his industry, his learning, or his wit.' The shift in perspective, from consoling the obscure to mortifying the proud, is abrupt and complete, and arises from Johnson's astute perception of the further implication hidden within the instances explaining the elusiveness of fame. For what is balm to the overlooked may be wormwood to the celebrated. The startling pivot jolts the complacent reader, and reminds us that the conditions of our moral life are more surprising and reticulated than we slackly suppose them to be. As a result, all readers should be unsettled by this writing: the lowly should feel less securely tethered to their lowliness, the eminent more precarious in their elevation. In *The Adventurer* no. 111 Johnson revealingly misremembered one of Robert South's sermons.[57] South had proposed that men would find 'a Continuall unintermitted Pleasure' intolerable. Johnson characteristically substituted idleness for South's pleasure. Notwithstanding—indeed, perhaps because of—all his temptations to sloth, Johnson recognised that for men work was a condition of happiness.[58] The resistances and abrasions of his own moral style create for his reader an opportunity of healthily laborious struggle, in which they may find that Johnson is an overmatch for them, just as William Law had been for Johnson.

---

[56] Below, p. 183–4.
[57] See below, p. 475 for the text, and p. 1207, for the relevant quotation from South's sermon.
[58] Consider Johnson's many resolutions to rise early in the morning - resolutions frequently made, because frequently broken (below, pp. 790, 907).

The Rambler did not sell well.[59] This may have been due to the unexpected seriousness of its moral appeal. However, there is also evidence to suggest that Johnson's style was difficult or even repugnant for some readers.[60] Like any literary manner, it could be guyed. 'The ludicrous imitators of Johnson's style are innumerable', as Boswell pointed out.[61] Bonnell Thornton's parody shows that imitation could be done with insight and affection.[62] A sharper emotion, however, seems to have prompted Horace Walpole's strictures on Johnson's style. The *Journey to the Western Islands* he dismissed as verbose: 'What a heap of words to express very little! and though it is the least cumbrous of any style he ever used, how far from easy and natural!'[63] But the much more cumbrous style of *The Rambler* inspired Walpole to a freak of satiric imagination. Writing to the Countess of Ossory on 1 February 1779, he began by distancing himself from the popular mania for David Garrick, before moving on to Johnson himself:

I have always thought that he [Garrick] was just the counterpart of Shakespeare; this, the first of writers, and an indifferent actor; that, the first of actors, and a woeful author. Posterity would believe me, who will see only his writings; and who will see those of another modern idol, far less deservedly enshrined, Dr. Johnson. I have been saying this morning, that the latter deals so much in triple tautology, or the fault of repeating the same sense in three different phrases, that I believe it would be possible, taking the ground-work for all three, to make one of his 'Ramblers' into three different papers, that should all have exactly the same purport and meaning, but in different phrases. It would be a good trick for somebody to produce one and read it; a second would say, "Bless me, I have this very paper in my pocket, but in quite another diction"; and so a third...[64]

If one recollects the conclusion of *The Rambler* no. 2 quoted above, it is easy to see what prompted this Walpolean fantasy. The very premise of Johnson's

[59] R. M. Wiles, 'The Contemporary Distribution of Johnson's *Rambler*', *ECS*, 2 (1968), pp. 155–71. However, unless we recall that it was widely reprinted in provincial newspapers we are likely seriously to underestimate its contemporary readership.

[60] For the history of the reception of Johnson's writings, see *Johnson: The Critical Heritage*, ed. J. T. Boulton (London: Routledge and Kegan Paul, 1971).

[61] *Life*, p. 980. An interesting and neglected instance of such imitation is to be found in Philip Parsons, *Dialogues of the Dead with the Living* (1779), in which dialogue VII is between Johnson and Addison.

[62] See Appendix C (below, pp. 1161–2).

[63] To the Countess of Ossory, 19 January 1775; *The Yale Edition of Horace Walpole's Correspondence*, ed. W. S. Lewis, vol. 32 (London: Oxford University Press, and New Haven, CT: Yale University Press, 1965), p. 225.

[64] To the Countess of Ossory, 1 February 1779; *The Yale Edition of Horace Walpole's Correspondence*, ed. W. S. Lewis, vol. 33 (London: Oxford University Press, and New Haven, CT: Yale University Press, 1965), pp. 88–9.

moral essays, that men more often require to be reminded than informed, perhaps by itself drives their author towards an iterative style.[65]

Moreover, it may be that Johnson himself after a while found the character and prose style of the 'Rambler' constricting. If, when he first forged that persona it offered release by allowing him to give voice to the fund of information and reflection which he had accumulated as a result of earlier study and the labours of the *Dictionary*, it was also a character he found it increasingly hard to shake off. Certainly towards the end of his life Johnson was troubled by thoughts of the path not taken:

Johnson, however, had a noble ambition floating in his mind, and had, undoubtedly, often speculated on the possibility of his supereminent powers being rewarded in this great and liberal country by the highest honours of the state. Sir William Scott informs me, that upon the death of the late Lord Lichfield, who was Chancellor of the University of Oxford, he said to Johnson, 'What a pity it is, Sir, that you did not follow the profession of the law. You might have been Lord Chancellor of Great Britain, and attained to the dignity of the peerage; and now that the title of Lichfield, your native city, is extinct, you might have had it.' Johnson, upon this, seemed much agitated; and, in an angry tone, exclaimed, 'Why will you vex me by suggesting this, when it is too late?'[66]

This reluctance to contemplate possibilities not grasped surely accompanies a measure of restiveness – an agitation even – concerning the life that has been lived. Certainly the literary *personae* that Johnson created for himself in *The Idler* and *The Adventurer* seem partly to have been chosen to contrast with that of *The Rambler* by trimming back some of the moral seriousness associated with Johnson's first set of periodical essays. And as *The Rambler* itself progressed, it sometimes seems as if the author is attempting to increase the tonal range and formal variety of the papers. In addition to the moral disquisitions, we have a series of moral case studies (sometimes amounting almost to a compressed novel, as in the story of 'Misella' in *The Rambler* nos. 170 and 171), stories continued over some distance, as with *The Rambler* nos. 132 and 194, and also *contes* set in the Orient and even Greenland.

But to step aside from the character of the 'Rambler' was for Johnson a difficult task. Once dead, and when the advent of the French Revolution had turned Johnson from a recently-deceased author to the embodiment of a pugnacious Englishness and a bulwark against the democratical principles then ravaging France, it was impossible. In the 'Advertisement' to the second edition of the *Life of Johnson*, published after the execution of Louis XVI in 1793, Boswell presented his dead friend to a new group of readers in precisely these terms:

His strong, clear, and animated enforcement of religion, morality, loyalty, and subordination, while it delights and improves the wise and the good, will, I trust,

---

[65] Below, p. 183.   [66] *Life*, pp. 690–91.

prove an effectual antidote to that detestable sophistry which has been lately imported from France, under the false name of *Philosophy*, and with a malignant industry has been employed against the peace, good order, and happiness of society, in our free and prosperous country; but thanks be to GOD, without producing the pernicious effects which were hoped for by its propagators.[67]

This Johnson seems distant from the exuberant and disaffected political ventriloquist of *A Compleat Vindication of the Licensers of the Stage*, or the mordant author of the essays severely critical of the government's conduct of the Seven Years' War, or the bleak satirist of the suppressed *Idler* no. 22.[68]

This selection of Johnson's writings has been made in part with a view to displaying his variety, and the virtue of the chronological order generally adopted in this series is that it allows us to see how the different facets of Johnson's literary character existed simultaneously, and interacted with one another.

[67] *Life*, p. 7 [italic and roman reversed].   [68] See below, pp. 50–61, 535–42, 574–6.

A CHRONOLOGY OF SAMUEL JOHNSON

1709	Born on 18 September in Lichfield; son of Michael and Sarah Johnson.
1712	Touched for the king's evil by Queen Anne.
1717-25	Attends Lichfield Grammar School.
1728	Enters Pembroke College Oxford in October.
1729	Leaves Oxford in December.
1731	Death of his father, Michael Johnson.
1732	Works as an usher at Market Bosworth school.
1733	Translates Lobo's *Voyage to Abyssinia*; contributes essays to the *Birmingham Journal*.
1735	Marries Elizabeth Porter; opens school at Edial.
1737	Leaves for London in March, accompanied by one of his pupils, David Garrick; begins working for the publisher Edward Cave, and contributes to *The Gentleman's Magazine*.
1738	Publication of *London*.
1739	Publication of *Compleat Vindication of the Licensers of the Stage*.
1744	Publication of *Life of Mr. Richard Savage*, and *Harleian Miscellany*.
1746	*Dictionary* undertaken.
1747	Publication of the 'Plan' of the *Dictionary*.
1749	Publication of *Vanity of Human Wishes*; Garrick produces *Irene*.
1750	Begins *The Rambler*.
1752	Death of Elizabeth Johnson; *The Rambler* concludes.
1753	Begins contributing to *The Adventurer* in March.
1754	Ceases to contribute to *The Adventurer* in March; publishes biography of Cave.
1755	M.A., Oxford; publication of the *Dictionary*.
1758	Begins *The Idler*, published in the *Universal Chronicle*.
1759	Death of his mother, Sarah Johnson; publication of *Rasselas*.
1760	*The Idler* concludes.
1762	Receives pension of £300 per annum from George III.
1763	Meets James Boswell.
1764	Founding of 'The Club'.
1765	LL.D., Dublin; publication of *The Dramatic Works of William Shakespeare*. Meets the Thrales.
1770	Publication of *The False Alarm*.

1771	Publication of *Thoughts on the late Transactions Respecting Falkland's Islands.*
1773	Tour of the highlands of Scotland and the Hebrides.
1774	Publication of *The Patriot*; tour of Wales with the Thrales.
1775	D.C.L., Oxford; visits Paris with the Thrales; publication of *A Journey to the Western Islands of Scotland* and *Taxation No Tyranny.*
1777	Begins work on the *Lives of the Poets.*
1779	Publication of first instalment of the *Lives of the Poets.*
1781	Publication of second instalment of the *Lives of the Poets.*
1783	Founding of the Essex Head Club.
1784	Dies on 13 December.

NOTE ON THE TEXTS

The endnotes to the texts reprinted in this edition specify the copy-text which has been followed. Evident slips and errors have been silently corrected; otherwise, the handling of the copy-texts has been deliberately conservative. The annotation draws the reader's attention to variants of particular interest; any systematic historical collation would be inappropriate in an edition such as this. However, where reliable and scholarly editions exist (such as Lonsdale's edition of *The Lives of the Poets*, or Fleeman's edition of *A Journey to the Western Islands of Scotland*) they are noted, and the curious reader is encouraged to consult them.

EARLY POETRY AND
PROSE TO 1750

Translation of Horace, *Odes*, I.xxii

The man, my friend, whose conscious heart
 With virtue's sacred ardour glows,
Nor taints with death th'envenom'd dart,
 Nor needs the guard of Moorish bows.

Tho' Scythia's icy cliffs he treads
 Or torrid Africk's faithless sands;
Or where the fam'd Hydaspes spreads
 His liquid wealth o'er barb'rous lands.

For while by Chloe's image charm'd,
 Too far in Sabine woods I stray'd,   10
Me singing, careless and unarm'd,
 A grizly wolf surpris'd, and fled.

No savage more portentous stain'd
 Apulia's spacious wilds with gore;
None fiercer Juba's thirsty land,
 Dire nurse of raging lions, bore.

Place me where no soft summer gale
 Among the quivering branches sighs;
Where clouds condens'd for ever veil,
 With horrid gloom the frowning skies.   20

Place me beneath the burning line,
 A clime deny'd to human race;
I'll sing of Chloe's charms divine,
 Her heavenly voice, and beautious face.

Translation of Horace, *Epodes*, II

Blest as th'immortal Gods is he
Who lives from toilsome bus'ness free,
Like the first race in Saturns reign
When floods of Nectar stain'd the main,

Manuring with laborious hand
His own hereditary Land,
Whome no contracted debts molest
No griping Creditors infesst.
No trumpets sound, no Soldiers cries,
Drive the soft Slumbers from his eyes,   10
He sees no boist'rous Tempests sweep
The Surface of the boiling Deep,
Him no contentious suits in law
From his belov'd retirement draw,
He ne'er with forc'd Submission waits
Obsequious, at his Patrons gates;
But round the lofty Poplar twines
With artfull hand the teeming vines,
Or prunes the barren boughs away;
[Or] sees from far his Bullocks play   20
Or drains the Labour of the Bees,
Or sheers the Lambkins snowy fleece.
Or when with golden Apples crown'd
Autumn o'er looks the smiling Ground
When rip'ning fruits perfume the year,
Plucking the blushing Grape and Pear,
Gratefull, rewards the Deities,
That, fav'ring, listen to his cries.
Beneath some spreading Ilex Shade
On some green bank supinely Laid,   30
Where Riv'lets gently purl along
And, murm'ring, balmy Sleep prolong,
Whilst each Musician of the Grove
Lamenting, warbles out his love,
In pleasing Dreams he cheats the Day
Unhurt by Phœbus fi'ry ray.
But when increas'd by Winter shours
Down cliffs the roaring Torrent pours
The grizly foaming Boar surrounds
With twisted toils, and op'ning hounds;   40
[So]me times the greedy Thrush to kill
[He] sets his nets, employs his skill.
With secret springes oft ensnares
The screaming Cranes and fearfull Hares.
Would not these pleasures soon remove
The bitter pangs of slighted love?

If to compleat this heav'nly Life
A frugal, chast, industrious, Wife,
Such as the Sun-burnt Sabines were,
Divide the burden of his care,   50
And heap the fire, and milk the Kine
And crown the bowl with new-prest wine
And waiting for her weary lord
With unbought dainties load the board;
I should behold with scornfull eye
The studied arts of Luxury:
No fish from the Carpathian coast
By Eastern Tempests hither tost,
Nor Lybian fowls, nor Snipes of Greece,
So much my Appetite would please   60
As herbs of which the forrests nigh
Wholsome variety supply.
Then to the Gods, on solemn days,
The farmer annuall honours pays
Or feasts on Kids the Wolves had kill'd
And frighted, left upon the field,
How pleas'd he sees his Cattle come,
Their dugs with milk distended, home!
How pleas'd beholds his Oxen bow
And faintly draw th'inverted Plow.   70
His chearfull Slaves, a num'rous band,
Around in beauteous order stand.

Thus did the Us'rer Alphius praise,
With transports kindled, rural ease,
His money he collected strait,
Resolv'd to purchase a retreat.
But still desires of sordid gain   )
Fix'd in his canker'd breast remain: }
Next Month he sets it out again.   )

Translation of Horace, Odes, *II.xiv*

Alass, dear Friend, the fleeting years
In everlasting Circles run,
In vain you spend your vows and prayers,
They roll, and ever will roll on.

Should Hecatombs each rising Morn
On cruel Pluto's Altar dye,
Should costly Loads of incense burn,
Their fumes ascending to the Skie;

You could not gain a Moments breath,
Or move the haughty King below   10
Nor would inexorable Death
Defer an hour the fatal blow.

In vain we shun the Din of war,
And terrours of the Stormy Main,
In vain with anxious breasts we fear
Unwholesome Sirius' sultry reign;

We all must view the Stygian flood
That silent cuts the dreary plains,
And cruel Danaus' bloody Brood
Condemn'd to everduring pains.   20

Your shady Groves, your pleasing wife,
And fruitfull fields, my dearest Friend,
You'll leave together with your life,
Alone the Cypress shall attend.

After your death, the lavish heir
Will quickly drive away his woe,
The wine you kept with so much care
Along the marble floor shall flow.

Translation of Horace, Odes, *II.xx*

Now with no weak unballast wing
A Poet double-form'd I rise,
From th'envious world with scorn I spring,
And cut with joy the wond'ring Skies.

Though from no Princes I descend,
Yet shall I see the blest abodes,
Yet, great Mæcenas, shall your friend
Quaff Nectar with th'immortal Gods.

See! how the mighty Change is wrought!
See! how whate'er remain'd of Man   10

By plumes is viel'd; see! quick as thought
I pierce the Clouds a tunefull Swan.

Swifter than Icarus Ill flie
Where Lybia's swarthy offspring burns,
And where beneath th'inclement Skie
The hardy Scythian ever mourns.

My Works shall propagate my fame,
To distant realms and climes unknown,
Nations shall celebrate my Name
That drink the Phasis or the Rhône.   20

Restrain your tears and cease your cries,
Nor grace with fading flours my Herse,
I without fun'ral elegies
Shall live for ever in my verse.

Festina Lente

Whatever course of Life great Jove allots,
Whether you sit on thrones, or dwell in cots,
Observe your steps; be carefull to command
Your passions; guide the reins with steady hand,
Nor down steep cliffs precipitately move
Urg'd headlong on by hatred or by love:
Let Reason with superiour force controul
The floods of rage, and calm thy rufled soul.
Rashness! thou spring from whence misfortunes flow!
Parent of ills! and source of all our woe!   10
Thou to a scene of bloodshed turn'st the Ball,
By thee wholl citys burn, wholl nations fall!
By thee Orestes plung'd his vengefull dart
Into his supplicating mothers heart.
Hurry'd to death by thee, Flaminius fell,
And crowds of godlike Romans sunk to hell.
But cautious Fabius from impending fate
Preserv'd the reliques of the Latian state
From bold invaders clear'd th'Italian lands
And drove the swarthy troops to their own barren sands.   20

The Young Author

When first the peasant, long inclin'd to roam,
Forsakes his rural seats and peaceful home,
Charm'd with the scene the smiling ocean yields,
He scorns the flow'ry vales and verdant fields;
Jocund he dances o'er the wat'ry way,
While the breeze whispers and the streamers play.
Joys insincere! thick clouds invade the skies,
Loud roars the tempest, high the billows rise,
Sick'ning with fear he longs to view the shore,
And vows to trust the faithless deep no more.   10
  So the young author panting for a name,
And fir'd with pleasing hope of endless fame,
Intrusts his happiness to human kind,
More false, more cruel than the seas and wind.
'Toil on, dull croud, in extacy, he cries,
'For wealth or title, perishable prize;
'While I these transitory blessings scorn,
'Secure of praise from nations yet unborn.
This thought once form'd, all counsel comes too late,
He plies the press, and hurries on his fate;   20
Swiftly he sees the imagin'd laurels spread,
He feels th'unfading wreath surround his head;
Warn'd by another's fate, vain youth, be wise,
These dreams were Settle's once and Ogilby's.
  The pamphlet spreads, incessant hisses rise,
To some retreat the baffled writer flies,
Where no sour criticks damn, nor sneers molest,
Safe from the keen lampoon and stinging jest;
There begs of heav'n a less distinguish'd lot;
Glad to be hid, and proud to be forgot.   30

Annals

1. 1709–10

SEPT. 7, 1709, I was born at Lichfield. My mother had a very difficult and dangerous labour, and was assisted by George Hector, a man-midwife of great reputation. I was born almost dead, and could not cry for some time. When he had me in his arms, he said, "Here is a brave boy."

In a few weeks an inflammation was discovered on my buttock, which was at first, I think, taken for a burn; but soon appeared to be a natural disorder. It swelled, broke, and healed.

My Father being that year Sheriff of Lichfield, and to ride the circuit of the County next day, which was a ceremony then performed with great pomp; he was asked by my mother, "Whom he would invite to the Riding?" and answered, "All the town now." He feasted the citizens with uncommon magnificence, and was the last but one that maintained the splendour of the Riding.

I was, by my father's persuasion, put to one Marclew, commonly called Bellison, the servant, or wife of a servant of my father, to be nursed in George Lane, where I used to call when I was a bigger boy, and eat fruit in the garden, which was full of trees. Here it was discovered that my eyes were bad; and an issue was cut in my left arm, of which I took no great notice, as I think my mother has told me, having my little hand in a custard. How long this issue was continued I do not remember. I believe it was suffered to dry when I was about six years old.

It is observable, that, having been told of this operation, I always imagined that I remembered it, but I laid the scene in the wrong house. Such confusions of memory I suspect to be common.

My mother visited me every day, and used to go different ways, that her assiduity might not expose her to ridicule; and often left her fan or glove behind her, that she might have a pretence to come back unexpected; but she never discovered any token of neglect. Dr. Swinfen told me, that the scrofulous sores which afflicted me proceeded from the bad humours of the nurse, whose son had the same distemper, and was likewise short-sighted, but both in a less degree. My mother thought my diseases derived from her family.

In ten weeks I was taken home, a poor, diseased infant, almost blind.

I remember my aunt Nath. Ford told me, when I was about...years old, that she would not have picked such a poor creature up in the street.

In...67, when I was at Lichfield, I went to look for my nurse's house; and, inquiring somewhat obscurely, was told "this is the house in which you were nursed." I saw my nurse's son, to whose milk I succeeded, reading a large Bible, which my nurse had bought, as I was then told, some time before her death.

Dr. Swinfen used to say, that he never knew any child reared with so much difficulty.

2. 1710–11

In the second year I know not what happened to me. I believe it was then that my mother carried me to Trysul, to consult Dr. Atwood, an oculist of Worcester. My father and Mrs. Harriots, I think, never had much kindness for each other. She was my mother's relation; and he had none so high to whom he could send any of his family. He saw her seldom himself, and willingly disgusted her, by sending his horses from home on Sunday; which she considered, and with reason, as a breach of duty. My father had much vanity, which his adversity hindered from being fully exerted. I remember, that, mentioning her legacy in the humility of distress, he called her *our good Cousin Harriots*. My mother had no value for his relations; those indeed whom we knew of were much lower than hers. This contempt began, I know not on which side, very early: but, as my father was little at home, it had not much effect.

My father and mother had not much happiness from each other. They seldom conversed; for my father could not bear to talk of his affairs; and my mother, being unacquainted with books, cared not to talk of any thing else. Had my mother been more literate, they had been better companions. She might have sometimes introduced her unwelcome topick with more success, if she could have diversified her conversation. Of business she had no distinct conception; and therefore her discourse was composed only of complaint, fear, and suspicion. Neither of them ever tried to calculate the profits of trade, or the expenses of living. My mother concluded that we were poor, because we lost by some of our trades; but the truth was, that my father, having in the early part of his life contracted debts, never had trade sufficient to enable him to pay them, and maintain his family; he got something, but not enough.

It was not till about 1768, that I thought to calculate the returns of my father's trade, and by that estimate his probable profits. This, I believe, my parents never did.

3. 1711–12

This year, in Lent—12, I was taken to London, to be touched for the evil by Queen Anne. My mother was at Nicholson's, the famous bookseller, in Little Britain. My mother, then with child, concealed her pregnancy, that she might not be hindered from the journey. I always retained some memory of this journey, though I was then but thirty months old. I remembered a little dark room behind the kitchen, where the jack-weight fell through a hole in the floor, into which I once slipped my leg. I seem to remember, that I played with a string and a bell, which my cousin Isaac Johnson gave me; and that there was a cat with a white collar, and a dog, called Chops, that leaped over a stick: but I know not whether I remember the thing, or the talk of it.

I remember a boy crying at the palace when I went to be touched. Being asked "on which side of the shop was the counter?" I answered, "on the left from the entrance," many years after, and spoke, not by guess, but by memory. We went in the stage-coach, and returned in the waggon, as my mother said, because my cough was violent. The hope of saving a few shillings was no slight motive; for she, not having been accustomed to money, was afraid of such expenses as now seem very small. She sewed two guineas in her petticoat, lest she should be robbed.

We were troublesome to the passengers; but to suffer such inconveniences in the stage-coach was common in those days to persons in much higher rank. I was sick; one woman fondled me, the other was disgusted. She bought me a small silver cup and spoon, marked SAM. I. lest if they had been marked S. I. which was her name, they should, upon her death, have been taken from me. She bought me a speckled linen frock, which I knew afterwards by the name of my London frock. The cup was one of the last pieces of plate which dear Tetty sold in our distress. I have now the spoon. She bought at the same time two teaspoons, and till my manhood she had no more.

My father considered tea as very expensive, and discouraged my mother from keeping company with the neighbours, and from paying visits or receiving them. She lived to say, many years after, that, if the time were to pass again, she would not comply with such unsocial injunctions.

I suppose that in this year I was first informed of a future state. I remember, that being in bed with my mother one morning, I was told by her of the two places to which the inhabitants of this world were received after death; one a fine place filled with happiness, called Heaven; the other a *sad* place, called Hell. That this account much affected my imagination, I do not remember. When I was risen, my mother bade me repeat what she had told me to Thomas Jackson. When I told this afterwards to my mother, she seemed to wonder that she should begin such talk so late as that the first time could be remembered.

[Here there is a chasm of thirty-eight pages in the manuscript.]

examination. We always considered it as a day of ease; for we made no preparation, and indeed were asked commonly such questions as we had been asked often before, and could regularly answer. But I believe it was of use at first.

On Thursday night a small portion of Aesop was learned by heart, and on Friday morning the lessons in Aesop were repeated; I believe, not those in Helvicus. On Friday afternoon we learned *Quae Genus*; I suppose that other boys might say their repetition, but of this I have now no distinct remembrance. To learn *Quae Genus* was to me always pleasing; and *As in Praesenti* was, I know not why, always disgusting.

When we learned our Accidence we had no parts, but, I think, two lessons. The boys that came to school untaught read the Accidence twice through before they learned it by heart.

When we learned *Propria quae Maribus*, our parts were in the Accidence; when we learned *As in Praesenti*, our parts were in the Accidence and *Propria quae Maribus*; when we learned *Syntaxis*, in the former three. *Propria quae Maribus* I could repeat without any effort of recollection. I used to repeat it to my mother and Tom Johnson; and remember, that I once went as far as the middle of the paragraph, "Mascula dicuntur monosyllaba," in a dream.

On Saturday, as on Thursday, we were examined. We were sometimes, on one of those days, asked our Catechism, but with no regularity or constancy. G. Hector never had been taught his Catechism.

The progress of examination was this. When we learned *Propria quae Maribus*, we were examined in the Accidence; particularly we formed Verbs, that is, went through the same person in all the Moods and Tenses. This was very difficult to me; and I was once very anxious about the next day, when this exercise was to be performed, in which I had failed till I was discouraged. My mother encouraged me, and I proceeded better. When I told her of my good escape, "We often," said she, dear mother! "come off best, when we are most afraid." She told me, that, once when she asked me about forming verbs, I said, "I did not form them in an ugly shape." "You could not," said she, "speak plain; and I was proud that I had a boy who was forming verbs." These little memorials sooth my mind. Of the parts of Corderius or Aesop, which we learned to repeat, I have not the least recollection, except of a passage in one of the Morals, where it is said of some man, that, when he hated another, he made him rich; this I repeated emphatically in my mother's hearing, who could never conceive that riches could bring any evil. She remarked it, as I expected.

I had the curiosity, two or three years ago, to look over Garretson's Exercises, Willymot's Particles, and Walker's Exercises; and found very few sentences that I should have recollected if I had found them in any other books. That which is read without pleasure is not often recollected nor infixed by conversation, and therefore in a great measure drops from the memory. Thus it happens that those who are taken early from school, commonly lose all that they had learned.

When we learned *As in Praesenti*, we parsed *Propria quae Maribus* by Hool's Terminations; and, when we learned *Syntaxis*, we parsed *As in Praesenti*; and afterwards *Quae Genus*, by the same book; sometimes, as I remember, proceeding in order of the rules, and sometimes, particularly in *As in Praesenti*, taking words as they occurred in the Index.

The whole week before we broke up, and the part of the week in which we broke up, were spent wholly, I know not why, in examination; and were therefore easy to both us and the master. The two nights before the vacation were free from exercise.

This was the course of the school, which I remember with pleasure; for I was indulged and caressed by my master, and, I think, really excelled the rest.

I was with Hawkins but two years, and perhaps four months. The time, till I had computed it, appeared much longer by the multitude of novelties which it supplied, and of incidents, then in my thoughts important, it produced. Perhaps it is not possible that any other period can make the same impression on the memory.

10. 1719

In the Spring of 1719, our class consisting of eleven, the number was always fixed in my memory, but one of the names I have forgotten, was removed to the upper school, and put under Holbrook, a peevish and ill-tempered man. We were removed sooner than had been the custom; for the head-master, intent upon his boarders, left the town-boys long in the lower school. Our removal was caused by a reproof from the Town-clerk; and Hawkins complained that he had lost half his profit. At this removal I cried. The rest were indifferent. My exercise in Garretson was somewhere about the Gerunds. Our places in Aesop and Helvicus I have totally forgotten.

At Whitsuntide Mrs. Longworth brought me a "Hermes Garretsoni," of which I do not remember that I ever could make much use. It was afterwards lost, or stolen at school. My exercise was then in the end of the Syntax. Hermes furnished me with the word *inliciturus*, which I did not understand, but used it.

This task was very troublesome to me; I made all the twenty-five exercises, others made but sixteen. I never shewed all mine; five lay long after in a drawer in the shop. I made an exercise in a little time, and shewed it my mother; but the task being long upon me, she said, "Though you could make an exercise in so short a time, I thought you would find it difficult to make them all as soon as you should."

This Whitsuntide, I and my brother were sent to pass some time at Birmingham; I believe, a fortnight. Why such boys were sent to trouble other houses, I cannot tell. My mother had some opinion that much improvement was to be had by changing the mode of life. My uncle Harrison was a widower; and his house was kept by Sally Ford, a young woman of such sweetness of temper, that I used to say she had no fault. We lived most at uncle Ford's, being much caressed by my aunt, a good-natured, coarse woman, easy of converse, but willing to find something to censure in the absent. My uncle Harrison did not much like us, nor did we like him. He was a very mean and vulgar man, drunk every night, but drunk with little drink, very peevish, very proud, very ostentatious, but, luckily, not rich. At my aunt Ford's I eat so much of a boiled leg of mutton, that she used to talk of it. My mother, who had lived in a narrow sphere, and was then affected by little things, told me seriously that it would hardly ever be forgotten. Her mind, I think, was afterwards much enlarged, or greater evils wore out the care of less.

I staid after the vacation was over some days; and remember, when I wrote home, that I desired the horses to come on Thursday of the first school week; and then, and not till then, they should be welcome to go. I was much pleased with a rattle to my whip, and wrote of it to my mother.

When my father came to fetch us home, he told the ostler, that he had twelve miles home, and two boys under his care. This offended me. He had then a watch, which he returned when he was to pay for it.

In making, I think, the first exercise under Holbrook, I perceived the power of continuity of attention, of application not suffered to wander or to pause. I was writing at the kitchen windows, as I thought, alone, and turning my head saw Sally dancing. I went on without notice, and had finished almost without perceiving that any time had elapsed. This close attention I have seldom in my whole life obtained.

In the upper-school, I first began to point my exercise, which we made noon's business. Of the method I have not so distinct a remembrance as of the foregoing system. On Thursday morning we had a lesson, as on other mornings. On Thursday afternoon, and on Saturday morning, we commonly made examples to the Syntax.

We were soon raised from Aesop to Phaedrus, and then said our repetition on Friday afternoon to Hunter. I remember the fable of the wolf and lamb, *to my draught—that I may drink*. At what time we began Phaedrus, I know not. It was the only book which we learned to the end. In the latter part thirty lines were expected for a lesson. What reconciles masters to long lessons is the pleasure of tasking.

Helvicus was very difficult: the dialogue *Vestitus*, Hawkins directed us to omit, as being one of the hardest in the book. As I remember, there was another upon food, and another upon fruits, which we began, and were ordered not to pursue. In the dialogue of Fruits, we perceived that Holbrook did not know the meaning of *Uvae Crispae*. That lesson gave us great trouble. I observed that we learned Helvicus a long time with very little progress. We learned it in the afternoon on Monday and Wednesday.

Gladiolus Scriptorius.—A little lapse, we quitted it. I got an English Erasmus.

In Phaedrus we tried to use the interpretation, but never attempted the notes. Nor do I remember that the interpretation helped us.

In Phaedrus we were sent up twice to the upper master to be punished. The second time we complained that we could not get the passage. Being told that we should ask, we informed him that we had asked, and that the assistant would not tell us.

Letter to Edward Cave

MONDAY 25 NOVEMBER 1734

Sir: [Lichfield] Novr. 25th 1734

As You appear no less sensible than Your Readers of the defects of your Poetical Article, You will not be displeased, if, in order to the improvement of it, I communicate to You the sentiments of a person, who will undertake on reasonable terms sometimes to fill a column.

His opinion is, that the Publick would not give You a bad reception, if beside the current Wit of the Month, which a critical examination would generally reduce to a narrow Compass, You admitted not only Poems, Inscriptions etc. never printed before, which he will sometimes supply You with; but likewise short literary Dissertations in Latin or English, Critical Remarks on Authors Ancient or Modern, forgotten Poems that deserve Revival, or loose pieces, like Floyers, worth preserving. By this Method your Literary Article, for so it might be call'd, will, he thinks, be better recommended to the Publick, than by low Jests, awkward Buffoonery, or the dull Scurrilities of either Party.

If such a Correspondence will be agreable to You, be pleased to inform me in two posts, what the Conditions are on which You shall expect it. Your late offer gives me no reason to distrust your Generosity. If You engage in any Literary projects besides this Paper, I have other designs to impart if I could be secure from having others reap the advantage of what I should hint.

Your letter, by being directed to S. Smith to be left at the Castle in Birmingham, Warwackshire, will reach Your humble Servant.

Preface to Lobo's Voyage to Abyssinia

THE following Relation is so Curious and Entertaining, and the Dissertations that Accompany it so Judicious and Instructive, that the Translator is confident his Attempt stands in need of no Apology, whatever Censures may fall on the Performance.

THE Portuguese Traveller, contrary to the general Vein of his Countrymen, has amused his Reader with no Romantick Absurdities or Incredible Fictions, whatever he relates, whether true or not, is at least probable, and he who tells nothing exceeding the bounds of probability, has a right to demand, that they should believe him, who cannot contradict him.

HE appears by his modest and unaffected Narration to have described Things as he saw them, to have copied Nature from the Life, and to have consulted his Senses not his Imagination; He meets with no Basilisks that destroy with their Eyes, his Crocodiles devour their Prey without Tears, and his Cataracts fall from the Rock without Deafening the Neighbouring Inhabitants.

THE Reader will here find no Regions cursed with irremediable Barrenness, or bless'd with Spontaneous Fecundity, no perpetual Gloom or unceasing Sunshine; nor are the Nations here described either devoid of all Sense of Humanity, or consummate in all private and social Virtues, here are no Hottentots without Religion, Polity, or Articulate Language, no Chinese perfectly Polite, and compleatly skill'd in all Sciences: He will discover, what will always be discover'd by a diligent and impartial Enquirer, that wherever Human Nature is to be found, there is a mixture of Vice and Virtue, a contest of Passion and Reason, and that the Creator doth not appear Partial in his Distributions, but has balanced in most Countries their particular Inconveniences by particular Favours.

IN *his Account of the Mission, where his Veracity is most to be suspected, He neither exaggerates overmuch the Merits of the Jesuits, if we consider the partial Regard paid by the* Portuguese *to their Countrymen, by the* Jesuits *to their Society, and by the* Papists *to their Church, nor aggravates the Vices of the* Abyssins, *but if the Reader will not be satisfied with a Popish Account of a Popish Mission, he may have recourse to the History of the Church of* Abyssinia, *written by Dr.* Geddes, *in which he will find the Actions and Sufferings of the Missionaries placed in a different Light, though the same in which Mr.* Le Grand, *with all his Zeal for the Roman Church, appears to have seen them.*

THIS *Learned Dissertator however valuable for his Industry and Erudition, is yet more to be esteem'd for having dared so freely in the midst of* France *to declare his Disapprobation of the Patriarch* Oviedo's *Sanguinary Zeal, who was continually importuning the* Portuguese *to beat up their Drums for Missionaries, who might preach the Gospel with Swords in their Hands, and propagate by Desolation and Slaughter the true Worship of the God of Peace.*

IT *is not easy to forbear reflecting with how little Reason these Men profess themselves the Followers of* JESUS, *who left this great Characteristick to his Disciples, that they should be known* by loving one another, *by universal and unbounded Charity and Benevolence.*

LET *us suppose an Inhabitant of some remote and superiour Region, yet unskill'd in the Ways of Men, having read and considered the Precepts of the Gospel, and the Example of our Saviour, to come down in search of the* True Church: *If he would not enquire after it among the Cruel, the Insolent, and the Oppressive; among those who are continually grasping at Dominion over Souls as well as Bodies; among those who are employed in procuring to themselves impunity for the most enormous Villanies, and studying methods of destroying their Fellow-creatures, not for their Crimes but their Errors; if he would not expect to meet* Benevolence, *engage in Massacres, or to find* Mercy *in a Court of Inquisition, he would not look for the* True Church *in the Church of* Rome.

Mr. LE GRAND *has given in one Dissertation an Example of great Moderation, in deviating from the Temper of his Religion, but in the others has left Proofs, that Learning and Honesty are often too weak to oppose Prejudice. He has made no scruple of preferring the Testimony of Father* du Bernat, *to the Writings of all the* Portuguese *Jesuits, to whom he allows great Zeal, but little Learning, without giving any other Reason than that his Favourite was a Frenchman. This is writing only to Frenchmen and to Papists: A Protestant would be desirous to know why he must imagine that Father* du Bernat *had a cooler Head or more Knowledge; and why one Man whose account is singular, is not more likely to be mistaken than many agreeing in the same Account.*

IF *the* Portuguese *were byass'd by any particular Views, another byass equally powerful may have deflected the Frenchman from the Truth, for they evidently write with contrary Designs; the* Portuguese, *to make their Mission seem more necessary, endeavour'd to place in the strongest light the Differences between the* Abyssinian *and* Roman *Church, but the Great* Ludolfus *laying hold on the Advantage, reduced these later Writers to prove their Conformity.*

UPON the whole, the Controversy seems of no great Importance to those who believe the Holy Scriptures sufficient to teach the way of Salvation, out of whatever Moment it may be thought, there are not proofs sufficient to decide it.

HIS Discourses on indifferent Subjects, will divert as well as instruct, and if either in these or in the Relation of Father Lobo, *any Argument shall appear unconvincing, or description obscure, they are defects incident to all Mankind, which, however, are not too rashly to be imputed to the Authors, being, sometimes, perhaps more justy chargeable on the Translator.*

IN this Translation (if it may be so call'd) great Liberties have been taken, which, whether justifiable or not, shall be fairly confess'd, and let the Judicious part of Mankind pardon or condemn them.

IN the first part the greatest Freedom has been used, in reducing the Narration into a narrow Compass. So that it is by no Means a Translation but an Epitome, in which whether every thing either useful or entertaining be comprised, the compiler is least qualified to determine.

IN the Account of Abyssinia, *and the Continuation, the Authors have been follow'd with more exactness, and as few Passages appeared either insignificant or tedious, few have been either shortened or omitted.*

THE Dissertations are the only part in which an exact Translation has been attempted, and even in those, Abstracts are sometimes given instead of literal Quotations particularly in the first; and sometimes other parts have been contracted.

SEVERAL Memorials and Letters, which are printed at the end of the Dissertations to secure the credit of the foregoing Narrative, are entirely left out.

IT IS hoped, that, after this Confession, whoever shall compare this Attempt with the Original, if he shall find no Proofs of Fraud or Partiality, will candidly overlook any failure of Judgment.

Letter to Edward Cave

TUESDAY 12 JULY 1737

Sir:

Greenwich, next door to the golden Heart,
Church Street, July 12th 1737

Having observed in Your papers very uncommon offers of encouragement to Men of Letters, I have chosen, being a Stranger in London, to communicate to You the following design, which, I hope, if You join in it, will be of advantage to both of us.

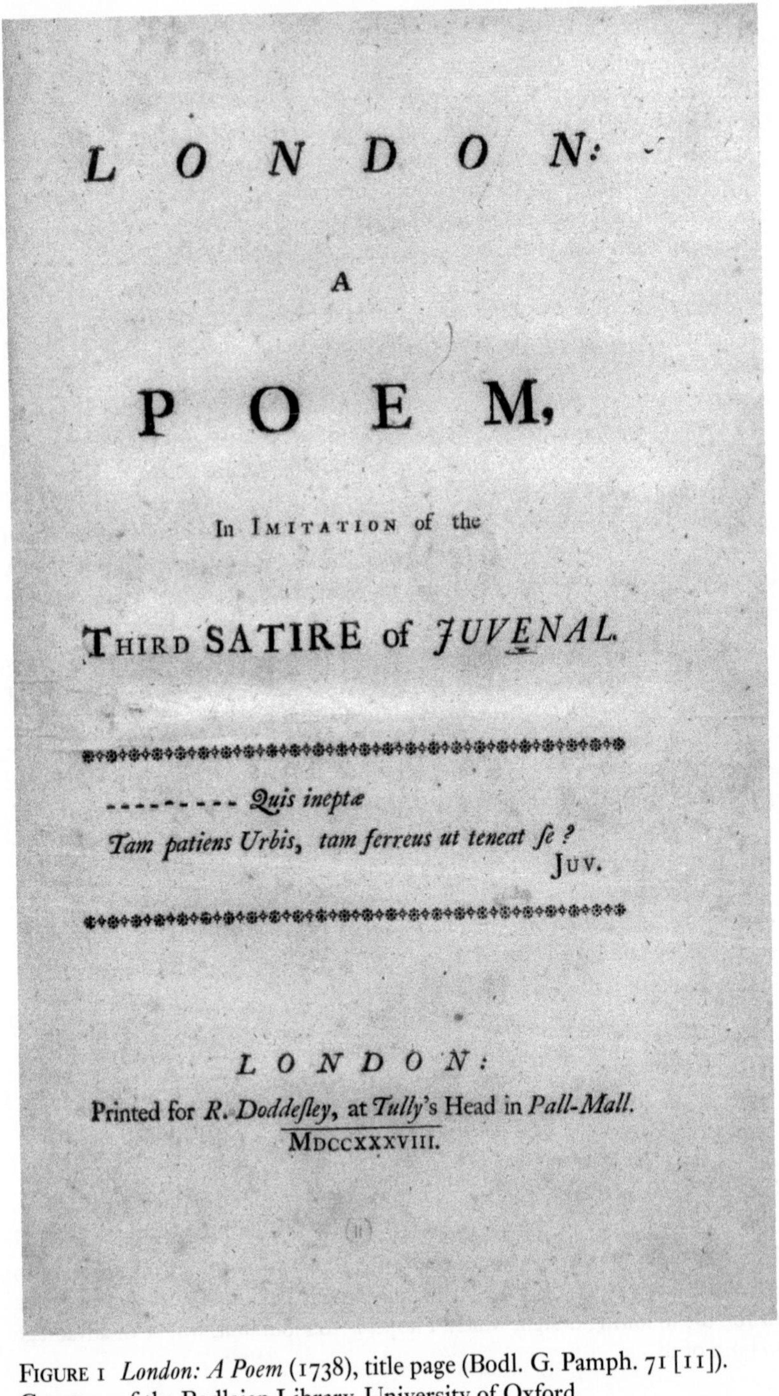

LONDON:

A

POEM,

In IMITATION of the

THIRD SATIRE of JUVENAL.

- - - - - - - - - *Quis ineptæ*
Tam patiens Urbis, tam ferreus ut teneat se ?
JUV.

LONDON:

Printed for R. Doddesley, at *Tully*'s Head in *Pall-Mall.*
MDCCXXXVIII.

FIGURE 1 *London: A Poem* (1738), title page (Bodl. G. Pamph. 71 [11]).
Courtesy of the Bodleian Library, University of Oxford.

The History of the council of Trent having been lately translated into French, and published with large Notes by Dr. Le Courayer, The Reputation of that Book is so much revived in England, that it is presumed, a new translation of it from the Italian, together with Le Courayer's Notes from the French, could not fail of a favourable Reception.

If it be answered that the History is already in English, it must be remembred, that there was the same objection against Le Courayer's Undertaking, with this disadvantage, that the French had a version by one of their best translators, whereas You cannot read three Pages of the English History, without discovering that the Stile is capable of great Improvements, but whether those improvements are to be expected from this attempt, You must judge from the Specimen which, if You approve the Proposal, I shall submit to your examination.

Suppose the merit of the Versions equal, we may hope that the Addition of the Notes will turn the Ballance in our Favour, considering the Reputation of the Annotator.

Be pleas'd to favour me with a speedy Answer, if You are not willing to engage in this Scheme, and appoint me a day to wait upon You, if You are. I am, Sir, Your humble Servant,

SAM. JOHNSON

London: A Poem in Imitation of the Third Satire of Juvenal

THO' Grief and Fondness in my Breast rebel,
When injur'd THALES bids the Town farewell,
Yet still my calmer Thoughts his Choice commend,
I praise the Hermit, but regret the Friend,
Who now resolves, from Vice and LONDON far,
To breathe in distant Fields a purer Air,
And, fix'd on CAMBRIA's solitary Shore,
Give to St DAVID one *true Briton* more.

For who would leave, unbrib'd, *Hibernia*'s Land,
Or change the Rocks of *Scotland* for the *Strand?*   10
There none are swept by sudden Fate away,
But all whom Hunger spares, with Age decay:
Here Malice, Rapine, Accident, conspire,
And now a Rabble rages, now a Fire;
Their Ambush here relentless Ruffians lay,
And here the fell Attorney prowls for Prey;

Here falling Houses thunder on your Head,
And here a female Atheist talks you dead.

While THALES waits the Wherry that contains
Of dissipated Wealth the small Remains,   20
On *Thames*'s Banks, in silent Thought we stood,
Where GREENWICH smiles upon the silver Flood:
Struck with the Seat that gave ELIZA Birth,
We kneel, and kiss the consecrated Earth;
In pleasing Dreams the blissful Age renew,
And call BRITANNIA'*s* Glories back to view;
Behold her Cross triumphant on the Main,
The Guard of Commerce, and the Dread of *Spain*,
Ere Masquerades debauch'd, Excise oppress'd,
Or *English* Honour grew a standing Jest.   30

A transient Calm the happy Scenes bestow,
And for a Moment lull the Sense of Woe.
At length awaking, with contemptuous Frown,
Indignant THALES eyes the neighb'ring Town.

SINCE Worth, he cries, in these degen'rate Days,
Wants ev'n the cheap Reward of empty Praise;
In those curst Walls, devote to Vice and Gain;
Since unrewarded Science toils in vain;
Since Hope but sooths to double my Distress,
And ev'ry Moment leaves my Little less;   40
While yet my steady Steps no Staff sustains,
And Life still vig'rous revels in my Veins;
Grant me, kind Heaven, to find some happier Place,
Where Honesty and Sense are no Disgrace;
Some pleasing Bank where verdant Osiers play,
Some peaceful Vale with Nature's Paintings gay;
Where once the harrass'd BRITON found Repose,
And safe in Poverty defy'd his Foes;
Some secret Cell, ye Pow'rs, indulgent give.
Let - - - - live here, for - - - - has learn'd to live.   50
Here let those reign, whom Pensions can incite
To vote a Patriot black, a Courtier white;
Explain their Country's dear-bought Rights away,
And plead for Pirates in the Face of Day;
With slavish Tenets taint our poison'd Youth,
And lend a Lye the Confidence of Truth.

Let such raise Palaces, and Manors buy,
Collect a Tax, or farm a Lottery,
With warbling Eunuchs fill our silenc'd Stage,
And lull to Servitude a thoughtless Age.   60

Heroes, proceed! What Bounds your Pride shall hold?
What Check restrain your Thirst of Pow'r and Gold?
Behold rebellious Virtue quite o'erthrown,
Behold our Fame, our Wealth, our Lives your own.

To such the Plunder of a Land is giv'n,
When publick Crimes inflame the Wrath of Heav'n:
But what, my Friend, what Hope remains for me,
Who start at Theft, and blush at Perjury?
Who scarce forbear, tho' BRITAIN's Court he sing,
To pluck a titled Poet's borrow'd Wing;   70
A Statesman's Logic, unconvinc'd can hear,
And dare to slumber o'er the *Gazetteer*;
Despise a Fool in half his Pension drest,
And strive in vain to laugh at *H - - - y*'s Jest.

Others with softer Smiles, and subtler Art,
Can sap the Principles, or taint the Heart;
With more Address a Lover's Note convey,
Or bribe a Virgin's Innocence away.
Well may they rise, while I, whose Rustic Tongue
Ne'er knew to puzzle Right, or varnish Wrong,   80
Spurn'd as a Beggar, dreaded as a Spy,
Live unregarded, unlamented die.

For what but social Guilt the Friend endears?
Who shares *Orgilio*'s Crimes, his Fortune shares.
But thou, should tempting Villainy present
All *Marlb'rough* hoarded, or all *Villiers* spent;
Turn from the glitt'ring Bribe thy scornful Eye,
Nor sell for Gold, what Gold could never buy,
The peaceful Slumber, self-approving Day,
Unsullied Fame, and Conscience ever gay.   90

The cheated Nation's happy Fav'rites see!
Mark whom the Great caress, who frown on me!
LONDON! the needy Villain's gen'ral Home,
The Common Shore of *Paris* and of *Rome*;
With eager Thirst, by Folly or by Fate,

Sucks in the Dregs of each corrupted State.
Forgive my Transports on a Theme like this,
I cannot bear a *French* Metropolis.

Illustrious EDWARD ! from the Realms of Day,
The Land of Heroes and of Saints survey;   100
Nor hope the *British* Lineaments to trace,
The rustic Grandeur, or the surly Grace;
But lost in thoughtless Ease, and empty Show,
Behold the Warriour dwindled to a Beau;
Sense, Freedom, Piety, refin'd away,
Of FRANCE the Mimic, and of SPAIN the Prey.

All that at home no more can beg or steal,
Or like a Gibbet better than a Wheel;
Hiss'd from the Stage, or hooted from the Court,
Their Air, their Dress, their Politicks import;   110
Obsequious, artful, voluble and gay,
On *Britain*'s fond Credulity they prey.
No gainful Trade their Industry can 'scape,
They sing, they dance, clean Shoes, or cure a Clap;
All Sciences a fasting Monsieur knows,
And bid him go to Hell, to Hell he goes.

Ah! what avails it, that, from Slav'ry far,
I drew the Breath of Life in *English* Air;
Was early taught a *Briton*'s Right to prize,
And lisp the Tale of HENRY'*s* Victories;   120
If the gull'd Conqueror receives the Chain,
And what their Armies lost, their Cringes gain?

Studious to please, and ready to submit,
The supple *Gaul* was born a Parasite:
Still to his Int'rest true, where'er he goes,
Wit, Brav'ry, Worth, his lavish Tongue bestows;
In ev'ry Face a Thousand Graces shine,
From ev'ry Tongue flows Harmony divine.
These Arts in vain our rugged Natives try, ⎫
Strain out with fault'ring Diffidence a Lye, ⎬   130
And gain a Kick for awkward Flattery. ⎭

Besides, with Justice, this discerning Age
Admires their wond'rous Talents for the Stage:
Well may they venture on the Mimic's Art,
Who play from Morn to Night a borrow'd Part;
Practis'd their Master's Notions to embrace,

Repeat his Maxims, and reflect his Face;
With ev'ry wild Absurdity comply,
And view each Object with another's Eye;
To shake with Laughter ere the Jest they hear,   140
To pour at Will the counterfeited Tear;
And as their Patron hints the Cold or Heat,
To shake in Dog-days, in *December* sweat.

How, when Competitors like these contend,
Can surly Virtue hope to fix a Friend?
Slaves that with serious Impudence beguile,
And lye without a Blush, without a Smile;
Exalt each Trifle, ev'ry Vice adore,
Your Taste in Snuff, your Judgment in a Whore;
Can *Balbo*'s Eloquence applaud, and swear   150
He gropes his Breeches with a Monarch's Air.

For Arts like these preferr'd, admir'd, carest,
They first invade your Table, then your Breast;
Explore your Secrets with insidious Art,
Watch the weak Hour, and ransack all the Heart;
Then soon your ill-plac'd Confidence repay,
Commence your Lords, and govern or betray.
By Numbers here from Shame or Censure free,
All Crimes are safe, but hated Poverty.
This, only this, the rigid Law persues,   160
This, only this, provokes the snarling Muse;
The sober Trader at a tatter'd Cloak,
Wakes from his Dream, and labours for a Joke;
With brisker Air the silken Courtiers gaze,
And turn the varied Taunt a thousand Ways.
Of all the Griefs that harrass the Distrest,
Sure the most bitter is a scornful Jest;
Fate never wounds more deep the gen'rous Heart,
Than when a Blockhead's Insult points the Dart.

Has Heaven reserv'd, in Pity to the Poor,   170
No pathless Waste, or undiscover'd Shore?
No secret Island in the boundless Main?
No peaceful Desart yet unclaim'd by SPAIN?
Quick let us rise, the happy Seats explore,
And bear Oppression's Insolence no more.

This mournful Truth is ev'ry where confest,
SLOW RISES WORTH, BY POVERTY DEPREST:

But here more slow, where all are Slaves to Gold,
Where Looks are Merchandise, and Smiles are sold,
Where won by Bribes, by Flatteries implor'd,   180
The Groom retails the Favours of his Lord.

But hark! th' affrighted Crowd's tumultuous Cries
Roll thro' the Streets, and thunder to the Skies;
Rais'd from some pleasing Dream of Wealth and Pow'r,
Some pompous Palace, or some blissful Bow'r,
Aghast you start, and scarce with aking Sight,
Sustain th' approaching Fire's tremendous Light;
Swift from pursuing Horrors take your Way,
And Leave your little ALL to Flames a Prey;
Then thro' the World a wretched Vagrant roam,   190
For where can starving Merit find a Home?
In vain your mournful Narrative disclose,
While all neglect, and most insult your Woes.

Should Heaven's just Bolts *Orgilio*'s Wealth confound,
And spread his flaming Palace on the Ground,
Swift o'er the Land the dismal Rumour flies,
And publick Mournings pacify the Skies;
The Laureat Tribe in venal Verse relate,
How Virtue wars with persecuting Fate;
With well-feign'd Gratitude the pension'd Band   200
Refund the Plunder of the begger'd Land.
See! while he builds, the gaudy Vassals come,
And crowd with sudden Wealth the rising Dome;
The Price of Boroughs and of Souls restore,
And raise his Treasures higher than before.
Now bless'd with all the Baubles of the Great,
The polish'd Marble, and the shining Plate,
Orgilio sees the golden Pile aspire,
And hopes from angry Heav'n another Fire.

Could'st thou resign the Park and Play content,   210
For the fair Banks of *Severn* or of *Trent*;
There might'st thou find some elegant Retreat,
Some hireling Senator's deserted Seat;
And stretch thy Prospects o'er the smiling Land,
For less than rent the Dungeons of the *Strand*;
There prune thy Walks, support thy drooping Flow'rs,
Direct thy Rivulets, and twine thy Bow'rs;
And, while thy Beds a cheap Repast afford,

Despise the Dainties of a venal Lord:
There ev'ry Bush with Nature's Music rings,   220
There ev'ry Breeze bears Health upon its Wings;
On all thy Hours Security shall smile,
And bless thine Evening Walk and Morning Toil.

    Prepare for Death, if here at Night you roam,
And sign your Will before you sup from Home.
Some fiery Fop, with new Commission vain,
Who sleeps on Brambles till he kills his Man;
Some frolick Drunkard, reeling from a Feast,
Provokes a Broil, and stabs you for a Jest.
Yet ev'n these Heroes, mischievously gay,   230
Lords of the Street, and Terrors of the Way;
Flush'd as they are with Folly, Youth and Wine,
Their prudent Insults to the Poor confine;
Afar they mark the Flambeau's bright Approach,
And shun the shining Train, and golden Coach.

    In vain, these Dangers past, your Doors you close,
And hope the balmy Blessings of Repose:
Cruel with Guilt, and daring with Despair,
The midnight Murd'rer bursts the faithless Bar;
Invades the sacred Hour of silent Rest,   240
And plants, unseen, a Dagger in your Breast.

    Scarce can our Fields, such Crowds at *Tyburn* die,
With Hemp the Gallows and the Fleet supply.
Propose your Schemes, ye Senatorian Band,
Whose *Ways and Means* support the sinking Land;
Lest Ropes be wanting in the tempting Spring,
To rig another Convoy for the K—g.

    A single Jail, in ALFRED's golden Reign,
Could half the Nation's Criminals contain;
Fair Justice then, without Constraint ador'd,   250
Sustain'd the Ballance, but resign'd the Sword;
No Spies were paid, no *Special Juries* known,
Blest Age ! But ah! how diff'rent from our own!

    Much could I add, —— but see the Boat at hand,
The Tide retiring, calls me from the Land:
Farewell! —— When Youth, and Health, and Fortune spent,
Thou fly'st for Refuge to the Wilds of *Kent*;
And tir'd like me with Follies and with Crimes,

In angry Numbers warn'st succeeding Times;
Then shall thy Friend, nor thou refuse his Aid,   260
Still Foe to Vice forsake his *Cambrian* Shade;
In Virtue's Cause once more exert his Rage.
Thy Satire point, and animate thy Page.

FINIS.

Debates in the Senate of Magna Lilliputia

THE Publick several Years ago received a great deal of Entertainment and Instruction from Capt. *Gulliver*'s elaborate and curious Account of the newly discovered Empire of LILIPUT; a Relation, which (however rejected at its first Appearance, by some, as incredible, and criticis'd by others, as partial or ostentatious) has, with the Success almost always attendant on Probity and Truth, triumphed over all Opposition, gain'd Belief from the most obstinate Incredulity, and established a Reputation in the World, which can fear no Diminution, nor admit of any Increase.

It is much to be regretted, that the ingenious Traveller was diverted from his Design of compleating a full and accurate Description of that unknown Country; by bringing down its History from the earliest Ages, explaining the Laws and Customs of the Inhabitants, and delineating the Works of Art, and Productions of Nature, peculiar to that Soil and People. Happy had it been for Mankind, had so noble and instructive a Subject been cultivated and adorn'd by the Genius of LEMUEL GULLIVER, a Genius equally sublime and extensive, acute and sagacious, worthy to display the Policy of the most refined, and celebrate the Atchievements of the most warlike Nation. Then might the Legislators of *Lilliput* have been produced as Rivals in Fame to *Numa* or *Lycurgus*; and its Heroes have shone with no less Lustre than *Cadmus* and *Theseus*.

Felix tanto Argumento Ingenium, felix tanto Ingenio Argumentum!

But as the Hope conceived by the Publick of seeing this immense Undertaking successfully compleated, has been frustrated by Indolence, Business, or perhaps by the unexpected Stroke of sudden Death; we doubt not but our Readers will be much pleased with an Appendix to Capt. GULLIVER's Account, which we received last Month, and which the late Resolution of the House of Commons, whereby we are forbidden to insert any Account of the Proceedings of the *British Parliament*, gives us an Opportunity of communicating in their Room.

Some Years after the Publication of Capt. GULLIVER's Discoveries, in the midst of the Clamour raised against them by Ignorance, Misapprehension, and Malice, a Grandson of the Captain, fired with Resentment at the Indignities offered to his Ancestor's Character, by Men, who, without the least Regard to his celebrated Veracity, dared to charge his Relation with no less than premeditated, deliberate Falshood, resolved, as the most effectual Method of vindicating his Memory, to undertake a Voyage to *Lilliput*, that he might be able at his Return to confirm his Grandfather's Reports by ocular Testimony, and for ever silence those Aspersions, which were, in his Opinion, founded on nothing but extreme Ignorance of both Geography and human Nature.

This Voyage, by the Assistance of some Charts and Observations which he found amongst his Grandfather's Papers, he successfully performed in the Ship named the *Confidence*, and met, upon his discovering his Name and Family, with such a Reception at the Court of *Lilliput*, as sufficiently shewed that the Memory of the *Man-Mountain* was far from being obliterated among them; and that Time had in *Lilliput* the Effect which it is observ'd to have on our Side of the Globe, of preserving and increasing a Reputation built on great and illustrious Actions, and of dissipating the Whispers of Malice and Calumnies of Faction. The Accusations brought against the Captain by his Enemies were cleared up, or forgot; and the Grandson, at his Arrival, found the Preservation of MILDENDO from the Flames, and the Conquest of the formidable Navy of *Blefuscu*, the Subject of Epic Poems, and annual Orations, the old Man's constant Topic of Discourse, and the Example by which their Youth were animated to Fidelity, Presence of Mind, and military Prowess.

The hospitable and generous Reception he found in the Country, gave him Opportunities of informing himself more fully of the State of that Part of the World; for which he came prepared by his Grandfather's Conversation, and a tolerable Knowledge of the *Lilliputian* Tongue, attain'd by the Help of a Grammar and a Vocabulary, which, with other Writings in that Language, Captain GULLIVER had left behind him.

Enabled by these concurrent Advantages to make a speedy Progress in his Enquiries, he returned at the End of 3 Years, not with a Cargo of Gold, or Silk, or Diamonds, but with Histories, Memoirs, Tracts, Speeches, Treaties, Debates, Letters and Instructions, which will be a sufficient Compensation to Mankind for the Loss they have sustained by the Negligence or untimely Death of Capt. GULLIVER; and establish'd a Correspondence between *Lilliput* and the *English* Colonies in the *East-Indies*, by which all the valuable Writings published there, and all historical and political Novelties, are to be annually transmitted to him.

This Gentleman, notwithstanding that Veneration for his Grandfather which engaged him to take so long and tedious a Voyage, upon no other Motive than a Desire of obliging the World to do Justice to his Character, has given the highest Testimonies that Truth is yet dearer to him than the Reputation of his Family, and that no mistaken Piety can prevail upon him to palliate the Mistakes, or conceal the Errors which were the necessary Effects of Capt. GULLIVER's short Stay, difficult Situation, formidable Appearance, and perplex'd Affairs.

The ready Access to the great Men of *Lilliput*, and Familiarity with the Emperor himself, which the traditional Regard paid to his Grandfather's Merit procured him, rendered it easy for him to make greater Discoveries in three Days, than Capt. *Gulliver* had been able to do during his whole Stay. He was particularly surprized in his first Conference with the Emperor, to hear him mention many States and Empires beside those of *Lilliput* and *Blefuscu*; and, upon observing that in his Grandfather's Account no other Nations are taken Notice of, he was told with great Condescension by his Majesty, that there had been lately discovered, in an old Repository of Archives, an Edict of those Times, absolutely forbidding, under the Pain and Penalty of Death, any Person or Persons to give the *Man-Mountain* the least Information relating to the State of any other Country; lest his Ambition might prompt him to seize upon some defenseless Part, either of his *Lilliputian* Majesty's Dominions, or of some weak Prince, or petty State, and to erect an absolute Dominion, which might in time perhaps become formidable to the State of *Lilliput* itself. Nor do I believe, said his Majesty, that your Ancestor would have heard the Name of *Blefuscu*, had not the Necessities of State obliged the Court unwillingly to discover it; and even in that Emergence of Affairs, they gave him so imperfect an Account, that he has represented *Blefuscu* as an Island; whereas it is a very large Empire on the Continent, confining on other Empires, Kingdoms, and States, of which I'll order my Geographer to communicate to you an accurate Description.

He had immediately recourse to the Royal Professor of Geography, and found upon Inspection, that the Maps of *Lilliput* and *Blefuscu*, and the neighbouring Islands, Kingdoms and Empires, were a perfect Epitome of the Map of *Europe*, and that these petty Regions, with their Dependencies, constitute a Resemblance or Compendium of our great World, just as the Model of a Building contains all the Parts in the same Disposition as the principal Design.

This Observation engaged him closely to his Geographical Studies, and the farther he advanced, the more he was convinced of the Justness of the Notion he had conceived of a World in Miniature, inhabited by this Pigmy Race —— In it he found all the four Parts of our Earth represented by correspondent Countries, excepting that the *Lilliputian* World is not Spherical, but must be considered as bearing the Form which the Ancients attributed to our own. Neither need I acquaint the Mathematical Reader, that being enlightened by our Sun, it does not admit of any Diversity of Zones, or Climates, but bears an exact Analogy to our Earth in its Lands and Seas, Chains of Mountains, Tracts of Desarts, and Diversity of Nations.

The People of *Degulia*, or the *Lilliputian Europe*, which Name is derived from DEGUL, *illustrious,* (a Word now obsolete, and only known to Antiquaries and Etymologists) are, above those of the other Parts of the World, famous for Arts, Arms, and Navigation, and, in consequence of this Superiority, have made Conquests, and settled Colonies in very distant Regions, the Inhabitants of which they look upon as barbarous, tho' in Simplicity of Manners, Probity, and Temperance superior to themselves; and seem to think that they have a Right to treat them as Passion, Interest or Carprice shall direct, without much Regard to the Rules of Justice or Humanity; they have carried this imaginary Sovereignty so far, that they have sometimes proceeded to Rapine, Bloodshed and Desolation. If you endeavour to examine the Foundation of this Authority, they neither produce any Grant from a superior Jurisdiction, nor plead the Consent of the People whom they govern in this tyrannical Manner; but either threaten you with Punishment for abridging the Emperor's Sovereignty, or pity your Stupidity, or tell you in positive Terms, that *Power is Right*. Some indeed pretend to a Grant from a Pontiff, to whom, as they happen to be inclined, they sometimes pay an absolute Submission, and as often deny common Respect; but this Grant is not worth Examination, the Pontiff from whom it is derived, being equally at a loss to fix his own Authority upon any solid Ground; so that at best the *Degulians* Claim to these Settlements, is like the Mahometan World, which rests upon an Elephant, which is supported by a Stone, which is supported by nothing.

It is observable, that their Conquests and Acquisitions in *Columbia*, (which is the *Lilliputian* Name for the Country that answers our *America*,) have very little contributed to the Power of those Nations, which have, to obtain them, broke thro' all the Ties of human Nature. They have indeed added Extent to their Territories, and procured new Titles for their Princes, but at the same time have exhausted their Mother Country of its Inhabitants, and subjected themselves to a thousand Insults, by possessing vast Tracts of Land, which are too spacious to be constantly garrison'd, and too remote to be occasionally and duly supply'd.

Even *Iberia*, a Country at the Southwest Point of *Degulia*, whose Inhabitants were the first Discoverers of *Columbia*, tho' she boasts herself Mistress of the richest and most fertile part of that Quarter of the World, which she secured to herself by the most dreadful Massacres and Devastations, has not yet, in all the Gold she has imported, received an Equivalent for the Numbers of her Natives sent out to people those Kingdoms her Sword has wasted; so that the whole Advantage of her mighty Conquests, is Bulk without Strength, and Pride without Power.

It must be observed to the Honour of the *Lilliputians*, who have in all Ages been famous for their Politicks, that they have the Art of civilizing their remote Dominions without doing much Injury to their Native Country; for when any of their People have forfeited the Rights of Society, by Robberies, Seditions, or any other Crimes, which make it not safe to suffer them to live, and yet are esteemed scarce heinous enough to be punished with Death, they send them to some distant Colony for a certain Number of Years proportionate to their Crimes. Of these Mr. *Gulliver*, during his Stay, saw ten thousand convey'd from the Prisons of *Mildendo* in close Lighters to Ships that lay at Anchor in the River to carry them to *Columbia*, where they were disposed among the Inhabitants, undoubtedly very much to the Propagation of Knowledge and Virtue, and no less to the Honour of their native Country.

Another Inconvenience of these new Claims, is, that they are a constant Source of Discord and Debate among the *Degulian* Powers, some of which are perpetually disputing their Titles to Countries, which neither has a Right to, and which sometimes are defended by the Natives against both. There not long since arose a Quarrel of this Kind, between the *Lilliputians* and *Iberians*, who contested the Limits of their *Columbian* (or *American*) Acquisitions. The *Lilliputians*, contrary to the ancient Genius of that martial People, made very liberal Concessions, such as rather drew upon them the Imputation of Cowardice, than procured them the Praise of Moderation; but the *Iberians*, insatiable in their Ambition, resolved to insist on nothing less than the absolute uninterrupted Possession of that whole Quarter of the World. In pursuance of this Resolution they seiz'd, upon various Pretences, all the *Lilliputian* Shipping that ventured or were drove near their Shores in the *Columbian* Seas, confiscated their Lading, and imprisoned, tortured, and starved their Seamen. The *Lilliputians* were patient under all these Insults for a long time, but being at length awakened by frequent Injuries, were making, at Mr. *Gulliver*'s Departure, Preparations for War; the Event of which is not yet come to his Knowledge.

Our Author having satisfied his Curiosity, with regard to the Geography of this petty World, began to enquire more nearly into the Constitution and Laws of *Lilliput:* But how great was his Suprize, when he found it so nearly to resemble our own! The Executive Power being lodged wholly in the Emperor; as the Legislative is in the Emperor, the House of *Hurgos*, or Lords, whose Honours and Privileges are Hereditary, and the House of *Clinabs*, or Commons, Representatives elect of the Body of the People, whose Assemblies are continued by several Sessions and Adjournments, or Prorogations, for the space of seven *Moons*, after which their Authority determines, and Writs are issued for new Elections.

Mr GULLIVER, astonish'd at this wonderful Conformity between the Constitution of *England* and *Lilliput*, consulted *Flibo Quibus*, the Royal *Historiographer*, upon that Subject, who gave him the following Account:

''Tis now, according to the best Chronologers, more than 392 Moons since the Arrival of your illustrious Ancestor *Quinbus Flestrin*, or the *Man-Mountain* upon the Confines of *Lilliput*, where he performed those Atchievements still recorded in our Histories, and celebrated by our Poets; but alas! he was at last disgraced and banished by the Effects of the most undeserved Calumny and Malice.

'After his Departure, the People, who had been irritated against him by false Reports, finding the same evil Measures that were imputed to his Advice still pursued, and all the Calamities still subsisting which had been describ'd as the Effects of his Stay amongst them, were on the sudden, not only convinc'd of his Innocence, but so exasperated against his Enemies by the Remembrance of his Wisdom, Clemency, and Valour, that they surrounded the Royal Palace, and demanded the Heads of the *Man-Mountain's* Accusers. The Ministers, according to Custom, ran for Shelter to the Royal Authority; but far from appeasing the People by that Artifice, they involved their Master in the common Destruction.

'The People having set fire to the Palace, and buried the whole Royal Family in its Ruins, placed one *Mulgo Malvin*, who had been Secretary to the *Man-Mountain*, upon the Throne of *Lilliput*. This Man new-modelled the Form of Government, according to the Plan which his Master had delivered to him, and affirm'd to be an exact Account of the *British* Constitution.

'Our Government (continued the *Lilliputian*) has in some Particulars varied from its Original. The *Clinabs* were at first elected every Moon, but now continue in Office 7 Moons; to which Alteration many attribute the present Venality and Dependency discovered in their Assemblies. They were likewise anciently paid by the People they represented for their Attendance on the Publick Business; but of late it is more common for the *Clinabs* to pay the People for admitting them to attend. Our Ancestors, in ancient Times, had some Regard to the moral Character of the Person sent to represent them in their national Assemblies, and would have shewn some Degree of Resentment, or Indignation, had their Votes been asked for a Murderer, an Adulterer, a known Oppressor, an hireling Evidence, an Attorney, a Gamester, or a Pimp. They demanded likewise in those who stood Candidates for the Power of making Laws, some Knowledge of the Laws already made; but now neither the most flagrant Immorality, nor the grossest Ignorance, are, amongst some Electors, any Objections to the Character of a Man who solicits Voices with Gold in his Hand.'

Such was the Answer of the learned *Lilliputian*, which incited Mr GULLIVER to pursue his Search into their Laws, Customs, and History; if haply he might discover, since human Nature generally operates alike in all Parts of the World, by what Means the Government of *Lilliput*, which had been once establish'd on so excellent a Plan, became so miserably degenerate; while the Government of *Britain*, its Original, maintained inviolate the Purity and Vigour of its primitive Constitution.

As we propose to publish every Month such Part of Mr GULLIVER's Papers as shall seem most proper to bring our Readers acquainted with the History and present State of *Lilliput*, we have chosen for this half Year's Entertainment, the DEBATES of the *Lilliputian* Senate, and shall begin with a very important one upon Occasion of the *Iberian* Depredations already mentioned, and the

Measures to be pursued for Redress, which Debate, as indeed all others on
such high Affairs, was carried on with the greatest Eloquence and Spirit,
in the 4th Session of the 8th Senate (or Parliament) of *Magna Lilliputia*,
held at *Belfaborac* in the 11th Moon of the Reign of the Emperor GORGENTI
the Second.

A Prayer on My Birth-Day

SEPT. 7TH 1738. O God the Creatour and preserver of all Mankind, Father of
all mercies, I thine unworthy servant do give thee most humble thanks, for
all thy goodness and lovingkindness to me. I bless Thee for my Creation,
Preservation and Redemption, for the Knowledge of thy Son Jesus Christ, for
the means of Grace, and the Hope of Glory. In the days of Childhood and
Youth, in the midst of weakness, blindness, and danger, Thou hast protected
me; amidst Afflictions of Mind, Body, and Estate thou hast supported me;
and amidst vanity and Wickedness thou hast spared me. Grant, O merciful
Father, that I may have a lively sense of thy mercies. Create in me a contrite
Heart, that I may worthily lament my Sins, acknowledge my wickedness, and
obtain Remission and forgiveness through the Satisfaction of Jesus Christ.
And O Lord, enable me by thy Grace to use all diligence in redeeming the
time which I have spent in Sloth, Vanity, and wickedness; to make use of thy
Gifts to the honour of thy Name; to lead a new life in thy Faith, Fear, and
Love; and finally to obtain everlasting Life. Grant this, Almighty Lord, for
the merits and through the meditation of our most holy and blessed Saviour,
Jesus Christ, to whom with Thee and the Holy Ghost, three Persons and one
God be all honour and Glory World without end. Amen.

   This is the first solemn prayer of which I have a copy. Whether I composed
any before this, I question.

On Gay's Epitaph

Mr URBAN,
Matters of very small Consequence in themselves, are often made important
by the Circumstances that attend them. Little Follies, and petty Weaknesses,
of no Moment in common Life, may, when they enter into the Characters
of Men in high Stations, obstruct the Happiness of a great Part of Mankind.
A barbarous Inscription, or disproportion'd Busto, deserves no Notice on
account of the Statuary who carv'd it, or the Writer who compos'd it; they
were only private Follies in the Study or the Shop, but erected in a Temple, or
engrav'd on a Column, they are considered as publick Works, and censured

as a Disgrace to a Nation. For this Reason I have been often offended with the trifling Distich upon Mr *Gay*'s Monument in *Westminster Abbey*:

> *Life is a Jest, and all Things show it;*
> *I thought so once, but now I know it.*

I never heard when, or where this wonderful Couplet was composed, or to what happy Genius we are indebted for it: The miserable Poetry of the first Line makes it unlikely that it could be a studied Production, unless it were one of the first Efforts of a Romantick Girl, or some dapper School boy's Imitation of

Παντα γελως, καὶ παντα κονις, και παντα το μηδεν.

If I might be indulged in making Conjectures on a Question of such Weight, I should conceive it to have been a drunken Sally, which was, perhaps, after Midnight, applauded as a lively Epigram, and might have preserv'd its Reputation, had it, instead of being engraved on a Monument at *Westminster*, been scribed in its proper Place, the Window of a Brothel.

There are very different Species of Wit appropriated to particular Persons and Places; the Smartness of a Shoeboy would not be extremely agreeable in a Chancellor, and a Tavern Joke sounds but ill in a Church, from which it ought to be banish'd, if for no other Reason, at least for that which forbids a drunken Man to be introduced into sober Company.

Yet, lest this Epigram should have any secret Merit, which, tho' it has escaped the Observation of negligent and vulgar Readers, has intitled it to the Place I have found it in Possession of, we will consider it with a little more Attention than I fear we shall discover it to deserve.

The Design of Epitaphs is rational and moral, being generally to celebrate the Virtues of the Dead, and to excite and awaken the Reader to the Imitation of those Excellencies which he sees thus honoured and distinguished, of which Kind almost every Sepulchral Monument affords us an Example.

There is another Kind, in which the Person departed is represented, as delivering some Precept to those whom he has left behind him, or uttering some important Sentence suitable to his present State, from which the Reader is prepared to receive very strong Impressions by the Silence and Solemnity of the Place where such Inscriptions are generally found, and by the serious and affecting Thoughts which naturally arise, at the Sight of the Receptacles of the Dead, upon the transitory and uncertain Nature of human Pleasure, Vanity and Greatness. Of this Sort the most ancient and the best that I have met with, is that ordered (if I forget not) by the great *Sesostris* to be inscrib'd on his Tomb,

> Εις εμε τις οραων, ευσεβης εστω.
> *Let every Man who looks upon me learn to be pious.*

On this Monument perhaps no Man ever look'd without being, at least for some Time, wiser and better, and doubtless, by so striking an Instruction, the Libertine has been often check'd in the Height of his Debaucheries, and the Oppressor softened in the midst of his Tyranny. Perhaps, as long Life is often the Effect of Virtue, the Tomb of *Sesostris* may have more than repair'd the Ravages of his Arms. Of this latter Kind is the important Distich we are considering. Mr *Gay*, like the *Ægyptian* King, calls upon us from the Habitations of the Dead; but in such a Manner, and for such Ends, as shews, what was anciently believed, that departed Souls still preserve the Characters they supported on Earth, and that the Author of the *Beggar's Opera* is not yet on the level with *Sesostris*. I cannot help thinking upon the Dialogue on this Occasion between *Oedipus* and his *Jocasta:*

> *Was* Laius *us'd to lye?*
> Joc. *O no! the most sincere, plain, honest Man; one that abhorr'd a Lye.*
> Oed. *Then he has got that Quality in Hell.*   DRYDEN.

Mr *Gay* has returned from the Regions of Death, not much improved in his Poetry, and very much corrupted in his Morals; for he is come back with a Lye in his Mouth, *Life is a Jest.*

Mankind, with regard to their Notions of Futurity, are divided into two Parties: A very small one, that believes, or pretends to believe, that the present is the only State of Existence; and another, which acknowledges, that in some Life to come, Men will meet Rewards or Punishments according to their Behaviour in this World.

In one of the Classes our Poet must be ranked: If he properly belonged to the first, he might indeed think Life a Jest, and might live as if he thought so; but I must leave it to acuter Reasoners to explain how he could in that Case *know* it after Death, being for my Part inclined to believe that Knowledge ceases with Existence.

If he was of the latter Opinion, he must think Life more than a Jest, unless he thought Eternity a Jest too; and if these were his Sentiments, he is by this Time most certainly undeceived. These Lines, therefore, are impious in the Mouth of a Christian, and Nonsense in that of an Atheist.

But whether we consider them as ludicrous or wicked, they ought not to stand where they are at present; Buffoonery appears with a very ill Grace, and Impiety with much worse, in Temples and on Tombs. A childish Levity has of late infected our Conversation and Behaviour, but let it not make its Way into our Churches. ——— Irreligion has corrupted the present Age, but let us not inscribe it on Marble, to be the Ruin or Scorn of another Generation. Let us have some Regard to our Reputation amongst Foreigners, who do not hold either Fools or Atheists in high Veneration, and will imagine that they can justify themselves in terming us such from our own Monuments. Let us therefore review our publick Edifices, and, where Inscriptions like this appear, spare our Posterity the Trouble of erasing them.

PAMPHILUS.

The Life of Dr Herman Boerhaave

The following ACCOUNT *of the late Dr* BOERHAAVE, *so loudly celebrated, and so universally lamented thro' the whole learned World, will, we hope, be not unacceptable to our Readers: We could have made it much larger, by adopting flying Reports, and inserting unattested Facts; a close Adherence to Certainty has contracted our Narrative, and hindred it from swelling to that Bulk, at which modern Histories generally arrive.*

The LIFE *of Dr* HERMAN BOERHAAVE, *late Professor of Physick in the University of* Leyden *in* Holland.

DR *Herman Boerhaave* was born on yᵉ last Day of *December*, 1668, about One in the Morning, at *Voorhout*, a Village two Miles distant from *Leyden:* His Father, *James Boerhaave*, was Minister of *Voorhout*, of whom his Son, in a small Account of his own Life, has given a very amiable Character, for the Simplicity and Openness of his Behaviour, for his exact Frugality in the Management of a narrow Fortune, and the Prudence, Tenderness and Diligence, with which he educated a numerous Family of nine Children. He was eminently skill'd in History and Genealogy, and versed in the *Latin*, *Greek* and *Hebrew* Languages.

His Mother was *Hagar Daelder*, a Tradesman's Daughter of *Amsterdam*, from whom he might, perhaps, derive an hereditary Inclination to the Study of Physick, in which she was very inquisitive, and had obtained a Knowledge of it not common in Female Students.

This Knowledge, however, she did not live to communicate to her Son, for she died in 1673, ten Years after her Marriage.

His Father, finding himself encumber'd with the Care of seven Children, thought it necessary to take a second Wife, and in *July*, 1674, was married to *Eve du Bois*, Daughter of a Minister of *Leyden*, who, by her prudent and impartial Conduct, so endear'd herself to her Husband's Children, that they all regarded her as their own Mother.

Herman Boerhaave was always design'd by his Father for the Ministry, and with that View instructed by him in Grammatical Learning, and the first Elements of Languages; in which he made such a Proficiency, that he was, at the Age of eleven Years, not only Master of the Rules of Grammar, but capable of translating with tolerable Accuracy, and not wholly ignorant of critical Niceties.

At Intervals, to recreate his Mind and strengthen his Constitution, it was his Father's Custom to send him into the Fields, and employ him in Agriculture, and such kind of rural Occupations, which he continued thro' all his Life to love and practise; and by this Vicissitude of Study and Exercise, preserv'd himself, in a great Measure, from those Distempers and Depressions which are frequently the Consequences of indiscreet Diligence, and uninterrupted Application; and from which, Students, not well acquainted with the Constitution of the human Body, sometimes fly for Relief to Wine instead of Exercise, and purchase temporary Ease by the Hazard of the most dreadful Consequences.

The Studies of young *Boerhaave* were, about this time, interrupted by an Accident, which deserves a particular Mention, as it first inclin'd him to that Science, to which he was by Nature so well adapted, and which he afterwards carried to so great Perfection.

In the twelfth Year of his Age a stubborn, painful, and malignant Ulcer, broke out upon his left Thigh; which, for near five Years, defeated all the Art of the Surgeons and Physicians, and not only afflicted him with most excruciating Pains, but exposed him to such sharp and tormenting Applications, that the Disease and Remedies were equally insufferable. Then it was that his own Pain taught him to compassionate others, and his Experience of the Inefficacy of the Methods then in Use incited him to attempt the Discovery of others more certain.

He began to practise at least honestly, for he began upon himself; and his first Essay was a Prelude to his future Success, for, having laid aside all the Prescriptions of his Physicians, and all the Applications of his Surgeons, he, at last, by fomenting the Part with Salt and Urine, effected a Cure.

That he might, on this Occasion, obtain the Assistance of Surgeons with less Inconvenience and Expence, he was brought, by his Father, at Fourteen, to *Leyden*, and placed in the fourth Class of the publick School, after being examined by the Master: Here his Application and Abilities were equally conspicuous. In six Months, by gaining the first Prize in the fourth Class, he was raised to the fifth; and in six Months more, upon the same Proof of the Superiority of his Genius; rewarded with another Prize, and translated to the sixth; from whence it is usual in six Months more to be removed to the University.

Thus did our young Student advance in Learning and Reputation, when, as he was within View of the University, a sudden and unexpected Blow threaten'd to defeat all his Expectations.

On the 12th of *November*, in 1682, his Father died, and left behind him a very slender Provision for his Widow and nine Children, of which the Eldest was not yet seventeen Years old.

This was a most afflicting Loss to the young Scholar, whose Fortune was by no means sufficient to bear the Expences of a learned Education, and who therefore seem'd to be now summon'd by Necessity to some Way of Life more immediately and certainly lucrative; but with a Resolution equal to his Abilities, and a Spirit not so depress'd or shaken, he determined to break thro' the Obstacles of Poverty, and supply, by Diligence, yᵉ Want of Fortune.

He therefore ask'd and obtained the Consent of his Guardians to prosecute his Studies as long as his Patrimony would support him, and continuing his wonted Industry gained another Prize.

He was now to quit the School for the University, but on Account of the Weakness yet remaining in his Thigh, was at his own Entreaty continued six Months longer under the Care of his Master, the learned *Wynschotan*, where he once more was honoured with the Prize.

At his Removal to the University, the same Genius and Industry met with the same Encouragement and Applause. The learned *Triglandius*, one of his Father's Friends, made soon after Professor of Divinity at *Leiden*, distinguished him in a particular Manner and recommended him to the Friendship of Mr *Van Apphen*, in whom he found a generous and constant Patron.

He became now a diligent Hearer of the most celebrated Professors, and made great Advances in all the Sciences, still regulating his Studies with a View principally to Divinity, for which he was originally intended by his Father, and for that Reason exerted his utmost Application to attain an exact Knowledge of the *Hebrew* Tongue.

Being convinced of the Necessity of Mathematical Learning, he began to study those Sciences in 1687, but without that intense Industry with which the Pleasure he found in that Kind of Knowledge induced him afterwards to cultivate them.

In 1690, having perform'd the Exercises of the University with uncommon Reputation, he took his Degree in Philosophy; and on that Occasion discuss'd the important and arduous Subject of the distinct Natures of the Soul and Body, with such Accuracy, Perspicuity and Subtilty, that he entirely confuted all the Sophistry of *Epicurus*, *Hobbes* and *Spinosa*, and equally raised the Characters of his Piety and Erudition.

Divinity was still his great Employment, and the chief Aim of all his Studies. He read the Scriptures in their original Languages, and when Difficulties occur'd, consulted the Interpretations of the most antient Fathers, whom he read in order of Time, beginning with *Clemens Romanus*.

In the Perusal of these early Writers, he was struck with the profoundest Veneration of the Simplicity and Purity of their Doctrine, the Holiness of their Lives, and the Sanctity of the Discipline practised by them; but as he descended to the lower Ages, found the Peace of Christianity broken by useless Controversies, and its Doctrines sophisticated by the Subtilties of the Schools. He found the holy Writers interpreted according to the Notions of Philosophers, and the Chimera's of Metaphysicians adopted as Articles of Faith. He found Difficulties raised by Niceties, and fomented to Bitterness and Rancour. He saw the Simplicity of the Christian Doctrine corrupted by the private Fancies of particular Parties, while each adhered to its own Philosophy and Orthodoxy was confined to the Sect in Power.

* * *

HAVING now exhausted his Fortune in the Pursuit of his Studies, he found the Necessity of applying to some Profession, that, without engrossing all his Time, might enable him to support himself, and having obtained a very uncommon Knowledge of the Mathematick, he read Lectures in those Sciences to a select Number of young Gentlemen in the University.

At length, his Propension to the Study of Physick grew too violent to be resisted, and, though he still intended to make Divinity the great Employment of his Life, he could not deny himself the Satisfaction of spending some Time upon the Medical Writers, for the Perusal of which he was so well qualified by his Acquaintance with the Mathematicks and Philosophy.

But this Science corresponded so much with his natural Genius, that he could not forbear making that his Business which he intended only as his Diversion, and still growing more eager, as he advanced further, he at length determined wholly to master that Profession, and to take his Degree in Physick, before he engaged in the Duties of the Ministry.

It is, I believe, a very just Observation, that Men's Ambition is generally proportioned to their Capacity. Providence seldom sends any into the World with an Inclination to attempt great Things, who have not Abilities likewise to perform them. To have formed the Design of gaining a compleat Knowledge of Medicine by way of digression from Theological Studies, would have been little less than Madness in most Men, and would have only exposed them to Ridicule and Contempt. But *Boerhaave* was one of those mighty Geniuses, to whom scarce any thing appears impossible, and who think nothing worthy of their Efforts but what appears insurmountable to common Understandings.

He begun this new Course of Study by a diligent Perusal of *Vesalius, Bartholine* and *Fallopius*; and to acquaint himself more fully with the Structure of Bodies, was a constant Attendant upon *Nuck*'s publick Dissections in the Theatre, and himself very accurately inspected the Bodies of different Animals.

Having furnish'd himself with this preparatory Knowledge, he began to read the ancient Physicians in the order of Time, pursuing his Enquiries downwards from *Hippocrates* thro' all the *Greek* and *Latin* Writers.

Finding, as he tells us himself, that *Hippocrates* was the original Source of all Medical Knowledge, and that all the later Writers were little more than Transcribers from him, he returned to him with more Attention, and spent much Time in making Extracts from him, digesting his Treatises into Method, and fixing them in his Memory.

He then descended to the Moderns, among whom none engaged him longer, or improved him more, than *Sydenham*, to whose Merit he has left this Attestation, *that he frequently perused him, and always with greater Eagerness.*

His insatiable Curiosity after Knowledge engaged him now in the Practice of Chymistry, which he prosecuted with all the Ardour of a Philosopher, whose Industry was not to be wearied, and whose Love of Truth was too strong to suffer him to acquiesce in the Reports of others.

Yet did he not suffer one Branch of Science to withdraw his Attention from others: Anatomy did not withhold him from Chymistry, nor Chymistry, enchanting as it is, from the Study of *Botany*, in which he was no less skilled than in other Parts of Physick. He was not only a careful Examiner of all the Plants in the Garden of the University, but made Excursions for his further Improvement, into the Woods and Fields, and left no Place unvisited where any Increase of Botanical Knowledge could be reasonably hoped for.

In conjunction to all these Enquiries he still pursued his Theological Studies, *and still*, as we are informed by himself, *proposed, when he had made himself Master of the whole Art of Physick, and obtained the Honour of a Degree in that Science, to petition regularly for a Licence to preach, and to engage in the Cure of Souls*, and intended in his Theological Exercise to discuss this Question, *Why so many were formerly converted to Christianity by illiterate Persons, and so few at present by Men of Learning.*

In pursuance of this Plan, he went to *Hardewich*, in order to take the Degree of Doctor in Physick, which he obtained in *July* 1693, having performed a publick Disputation, *de utilitate explorandorum excrementorum in agris, ut signorum.*

Then returning to *Leiden*, full of his pious Design of undertaking the Ministry, he found to his surprise unexpected Obstacles thrown in his Way, and an Insinuation dispersed through the University, that made him suspected, not of any slight Deviation from received Opinions, not of any pertinacious Adherence to his own Notions in doubtful and disputable Matters, but of no less than *Spinosism*, or in plainer Terms of Atheism itself.

How so injurious a Report came to be raised, circulated and credited will be doubtless very eagerly inquired: We shall therefore give the Relation, not only to satisfy the Curiosity of Mankind, but to shew that no Merit, however exalted, is exempt from being not only attacked but wounded by the most contemptible Whispers. Those who cannot strike with force, can however poyson their Weapon, and, weak as they are, give mortal Wounds, and bring a Hero to the Grave: So true is that Observation, that many are able to do hurt, but few to do good.

This detestable Calumny owed its Rise to an Incident from which no Consequence of Importance could be possibly apprehended. As *Boerhaave* was sitting in a common Boat, there arose a Conversation among the Passengers upon the impious and pernicious Doctrine of *Spinosa*, which, as they all agreed, tends to the utter Overthrow of all Religion. *Boerhaave* sat, and attended silently to this Discourse for some time, till one of the Company, willing to distinguish himself by his Zeal, instead of confuting yᵉ Positions of *Spinosa* by Argument, begun to give a loose to contumelious Language, and virulent Invectives, which *Boerhaave* was so little pleased with, that at last he could not forbear asking him, whether he had ever read the Author he declaimed against.

The Orator, not being able to make much Answer, was checked in the midst of his Invectives, but not without feeling a secret Resentment against the Person who had at once interrupted his Harangue, and exposed his Ignorance.

This was observed by a Stranger who was in the Boat with them; he enquired of his Neighbour the Name of the young Man, whose Question had put an End to the Discourse, and having learned it, set it down in his Pocketbook, as it appears, with a malicious Design, for in a few Days, it was the common Conversation at *Leiden*, that *Boerhaave* had revolted to *Spinosa*.

It was in vain that his Advocates and Friends pleaded his learned and unanswerable Confutation of all atheistical Opinions, and particularly of the System of *Spinosa*, in his Discourse of the Distinction between Soul and Body. Such Calumnies are not easily suppress'd, when they are once become general. They are kept alive and supported by the Malice of bad, and sometimes by the Zeal of good Men, who, though they do not absolutely believe them, think it yet the securest Method to keep not only guilty but suspected Men out of publick Employments, upon this Principle, That the Safety of Many is to be preferred before the Advantage of Few.

Boerhaave finding this formidable Opposition raised against his Pretensions to Ecclesiastical Honours or Preferments, and even against his Design of assuming the Character of a Divine, thought it neither necessary nor prudent to struggle with the Torrent of popular Prejudice, as he was equally qualified for a Profession, not indeed of equal Dignity or Importance, but which must undoubtedly claim the second Place among those which are of the greatest Benefit to Mankind.

He therefore applied himself to his Medical Studies with new Ardour and Alacrity, reviewed all his former Observations and Enquiries, and was continually employed in making new Acquisitions.

* * *

HAVING now qualified himself for the Practice of Physick, he began to visit Patients, but without that Encouragement which others, not equally deserving, have sometimes met with. His Business was, at first, not great, and his Circumstances by no means easy; but still superiour to any Discouragement, he continued his Search after Knowledge, and determined that Prosperity, if ever he was to enjoy it, should be the Consequence, not of mean Art, or disingenuous Solicitations, but of real Merit, and solid Learning.

His steady Adherence to his Resolutions appears yet more plainly from this Circumstance: He was, while he yet remained in this unpleasing Situation, invited by one of the first Favourites of K. *William* III. to settle at the *Hague*, upon very advantageous Conditions; but declined the Offer. For having no Ambition but after Knowledge, he was desirous of living at liberty, without any Restraint upon his Looks, his Thoughts, or his Tongue, and at the utmost Distance from all Contentions, and State-Parties. His Time was wholly taken up in visiting the Sick, Studying, making Chymical Experiments, searching into every part of Medicine with the utmost Diligence, teaching the Mathematicks, and reading the Scriptures, and those Authors who profess to teach a certain Method of loving God.

This was his Method of living to the Year 1701, when he was recommended by Mr *Van Berg* to the University, as a proper Person to succeed *Drelincurtius* in the Professorship of Physick, and elected without any Solicitation on his part, and almost without his Consent, on the 18th of *May*.

On this Occasion, having observed, with Grief, that *Hippocrates*, whom he regarded not only as the Father but as the Prince of Physicians, was not sufficiently read or esteemed by young Students, he pronounced an Oration, *de commendando Studio Hippocratico*; by which he restored that great Author to his just and antient Reputation.

He now began to read publick Lectures with great Applause, and was prevailed upon by his Audience to enlarge his original Design, and instruct them in Chymistry.

This he undertook, not only to the great Advantage of his Pupils, but to the great Improvement of the Art itself, which had been hitherto treated only in a confused and irregular Manner, and was little more than a History of particular Experiments, not reduced to certain Principles, nor connected one with another: this vast Chaos he reduced to Order, and made that clear and easy, which was before to the last degree difficult and obscure.

His Reputation began now to bear some Proportion to his Merit, and extended itself to distant Universities; so that in 1703, the Professorship of Physick being vacant at *Groningen*, he was invited thither; but he refused to leave *Leiden*, and chose to continue his present Course of Life.

This Invitation and Refusal being related to the Governors of the University of *Leiden*, they had so grateful a Sense of his Regard for them, that they immediately voted an Honorary Increase of his Salary, and promised him the first Professorship that should be vacant.

On this Occasion he pronounced an Oration upon *the Use of Mechanicks in the Science of Physick*, in which he endeavour'd to recommend a rational and mathematical Enquiry into the Causes of Diseases, and the Structure of Bodies; and to shew the Follies and Weaknesses of the Jargon introduced by *Paracelsus*, *Helmont*, and other chymical Enthusiasts, who have obtruded upon the World the most airy Dreams, and instead of enlightening their

Readers with Explications of Nature have darken'd the plainest Appearances, and bewilder'd Mankind in Error and Obscurity.

Boerhaave had now for nine Years read physical Lectures, but without the Title or Dignity of a Professor, when by the Death of Professor *Hotten*, the Professorship of Physick and Botany fell to him of course.

On this Occasion he asserted the Simplicity and Facility of the Science of Physick, in opposition to those that think Obscurity contributes to the Dignity of Learning, and that to be admired it is necessary not to be understood.

His Profession of Botany made it part of his Duty to superintend the physical Garden, which improved so much by the immense Number of new Plants which he procured, that it was enlarged to twice its original Extent.

In 1714 he was deservedly advanced to the highest Dignities of the University, and in the same Year made Physician of *St Augustin*'s Hospital in *Leiden*, into which the Students are admitted twice a Week to learn the Practice of Physick.

This was of equal Advantage to the Sick and to the Students, for the Success of his Practice was the best Demonstration of the Soundness of his Principles.

When he laid down his Office of Governor of the University in 1715, he made an Oration upon the Subject of *attaining to Certainty in natural Philosophy*; in which he declares, in the strongest Terms, in favour of Experimental Knowledge, and reflects with just Severity upon those arrogant Philosophers, who are too easily disgusted with the slow Methods of obtaining true Notions by frequent Experiments, and who, possest with too high an Opinion of their own Abilities, rather chuse to consult their own Imaginations, than enquire into Nature, and are better pleased with the charming Amusement of forming Hypotheses, than the toilsome Drudgery of making Observations.

The Emptiness and Uncertainty of all those Systems, whether venerable for their Antiquity, or agreeable for their Novelty, he has evidently shown; and not only declared, but proved, that we are entirely ignorant of the Principles of Things, and that all the Knowledge we have is of such Qualities alone as are discoverable by Experience, or such as may be deduced from them by Mathematical Demonstration.

This Discourse, filled as it was with Piety, and a true Sense of the Greatness of the Supreme Being, and the Incomprehensibility of his Works, gave such Offence to a Professor of *Franeker*, who professed the utmost Esteem for *Des Cartes*, and considered his Principles as the Bulwark of Orthodoxy, that he appeared in vindication of his darling Author, and spoke of the Injury done him with the utmost Vehemence, declaring little less than that the *Cartesian* System and the Christian must inevitably stand and fall together, and that to say we were ignorant of the Principles of Things, was not only to enlist among the Sceptics but sink into Atheism itself.

So far can Prejudice darken the Understanding, as to make it consider precarious Systems as the chief Support of sacred and unvariable Truth.

This Treatment of *Boerhaave* was so far resented by the Governors of his University, that they procured from *Franeker* a Recantation of the Invective that had been thrown out against him; this was not only complied with, but Offers were made him of more ample Satisfaction; to which he return'd an Answer not less to his Honour than the Victory he gain'd, "That he should think himself sufficiently compensated, if his Adversary received no farther Molestation on his Account."

* * *

So far was this weak and injudicious Attack from shaking a Reputation, not casually raised by Fashion or Caprice, but founded upon solid Merit, that the same Year his Correspondence was desired upon Botany and Natural Philosophy by the Academy of Sciences at *Paris*, of which he was, upon the Death of Count *Marsigli*, in the Year 1728, elected a Member.

Nor were the *French* the only Nation by which this great Man was courted and distinguished, for two Years after he was elected Fellow of our Royal Society.

It cannot be doubted, but thus caress'd, and honoured with the highest and most publick Marks of Esteem by other Nations, he became more celebrated in the University; for *Boerhaave* was not one of those learned Men, of whom the World has seen too many, that disgrace their Studies by their Vices, and by unaccountable Weakness make themselves ridiculous at home, while their Writings procure them the Veneration of distant Countries, where their Learning is known, but not their Follies.

Not that his Countrymen can be charged with being insensible of his Excellencies till other Nations taught them to admire him; for in 1718 he was chosen to succeed *Le Mort* in the Professorship of *Chemistry*, on which Occasion he pronounced an Oration *De Chemia errores suos expurgante*, in which he treated that Science with an Elegance of Stile not often to be found in chemical Writers, who seem generally to have affected not only a barbarous, but unintelligible Phrase, and to have, like the *Pythagoreans* of old, wrapt up their Secrets in Symbols and Ænigmatical Expressions, either because they believed that Mankind would reverence most what they least understood, or because they wrote not from Benevolence but Vanity, and were desirous to be praised for their Knowledge, though they could not prevail upon themselves to communicate it.

In 1722, his Course both of Lectures and Practice was interrupted by the Gout, which, as he relates it in his Speech after his Recovery, he brought upon himself, by an imprudent Confidence in the Strength of his own Constitution, and by transgressing those Rules which he had a thousand times inculcated to his Pupils and Acquaintance. Rising in the Morning before Day, he went immediately, hot and sweating, from his Bed into the open Air, and exposed himself to the cold Dews.

The History of his Illness can hardly be read without Horror: He was for five Months confined to his Bed, where he lay upon his Back without daring to attempt the least Motion, because any Effort renewed his Torments, which were so exquisite, that he was at length not only deprived of Motion but of Sense. Here Art was at a stand, nothing could be attempted, because nothing could be proposed with the least Prospect of Success. At length having, in the sixth Month of his Illness, obtained some Remission, he took simple Medicines in large Quantities, and at length wonderfully recovered.

His Recovery, so much desired, and so unexpected, was celebrated on *Jan.* 11, 1723, when he open'd his School again with general Joy and publick Illuminations.

It would be an Injury to the Memory of *Boerhaave* not to mention what was related by himself to one of his Friends, That when he lay whole Days and Nights without Sleep, he found no Method of diverting his Thoughts so effectual as Meditation upon his Studies, and that he often relieved and mitigated the Sense of his Torments, by the Recollection of what he had read, and by reviewing those Stores of Knowledge which he had reposited in his Memory.

This is perhaps an Instance of Fortitude and steady Composure of Mind, which would have been for ever the Boast of the Stoick Schools, and increased the Reputation of *Seneca* or *Cato.* The Patience of *Boerhaave,* as it was more rational, was more lasting than theirs; it was that *Patientia Christiana* which *Lipsius,* the great Master of the Stoical Philosophy, begged of God in his last Hours; it was founded on Religion, not Vanity, not on vain Reasonings, but on Confidence in God.

In 1727 he was seized with a violent Burning Fever, which continued so long that he was once more given up by his Friends.

From this time he was frequently afflicted with Returns of his Distemper, which yet did not so far subdue him, as to make him lay aside his Studies or his Lectures, till in 1729 he found himself so worn out, that it was improper for him to continue any longer the Professorships of Botany and Chymistry, which he therefore resigned *April* 28, and upon his Resignation spoke a *Sermo Academicus,* or Oration, in which he asserts the Power and Wisdom of the Creator from the wonderful Fabric of the Human Body; and confutes all those idle Reasoners who pretend to explain the Formation of Parts, or the animal Operations, to which he proves that Art can produce nothing equal, nor any thing parallel. One Instance I shall mention, which is produced by him, of the Vanity of any Attempt to rival the Work of God. Nothing is more boasted by the Admirers of Chemistry, than that they can, by artificial Heats and Digestion, imitate the Productions of Nature. *Let all these Heroes of Science meet together,* says Boerhaave, *let them take Bread and Wine, the Food that forms the Blood of Man, and by Assimilation contributes to the Growth of the Body: Let them try all their Arts, they shall not be able from these Materials to produce a single Drop of Blood.* So much is the most common Act of Nature beyond the utmost Efforts of the most extended Science!

From this Time *Boerhaave* lived with less publick Employment indeed, but not an idle or an useless Life; for, besides his Hours spent in instructing his Scholars, a great Part of his Time was taken up by Patients which came, when the Distemper would admit it, from all Parts of *Europe* to consult him, or by Letters which, in more urgent Cases, were continually sent to enquire his Opinion, and ask his Advice.

Of his Sagacity, and the wonderful Penetration with which he often discover'd and describ'd, at the first Sight of a Patient, such Distempers as betray themselves by no Symptoms to common Eyes, such wonderful Relations have been spread over ye World, as, though attested beyond doubt, can scarcely be credited. I mention none of them, because I have no Opportunity of collecting Testimonies, or distinguishing between those Accounts which are well proved, and those which owe their Rise to Fiction and Credulity.

Yet I cannot but implore, with the greatest Earnestness, such as have been conversant with this great Man, that they will not so far neglect the common Interest of Mankind, as to suffer any of these Circumstances to be lost to Posterity. Men are generally idle, and ready to satisfy themselves, and intimidate the Industry of others, by calling that impossible which is only difficult. The Skill to which *Boerhaave* attained, by a long and unwearied Observation of Nature, ought therefore to be transmitted in all its Particulars to future Ages, that his Successors may be ashamed to fall below him, and that none may hereafter excuse his Ignorance by pleading the Impossibility of clearer Knowledge.

Yet so far was this great Master from presumptuous Confidence in his Abilities, that in his Examinations of the Sick he was remarkably circumstantial and particular. He well knew that the Originals of Distempers are often at a Distance from their visible Effects, that to conjecture where Certainty may be obtained, is either Vanity or Negligence, and that Life is not to be sacrificed, either to an Affectation of quick Discernment, or of crowded Practice, but may be required, if trifled away, at the Hand of the Physician.

About the Middle of the Year 1737, he felt the first Approaches of that fatal Illness that brought him to the Grave, of which we have inserted an Account written by himself *Sept.* 8, 1738, to a Friend at *London*; which deserves not only to be preserved as an Historical Relation of the Disease which deprived us of so great a Man, but as a Proof of his Piety and Resignation to the divine Will.

In this last Illness, which was to the last degree lingering, painful and afflictive, his Constancy and Firmness did not forsake him. He neither intermitted the necessary Cares of Life, nor forgot the proper Preparations for Death. Tho Dejection and Lowness of Spirit was, as he himself tells us, Part of his Distemper, yet even this, in some measure, gave way to that Vigour which the Soul receives from a Consciousness of Innocence.

About three Weeks before his Death he received a Visit at his Country House from the Rev. Mr *Schultens*, his intimate Friend, who found him sitting without Door, with his Wife, Sister, and Daughter: After the Compliments of Form, the Ladies withdrew, and left them to private Conversation; when *Boerhaave* took Occasion to tell him what had been, during his Illness, the chief Subject of his Thoughts. He had never doubted of the spiritual and immaterial Nature of the Soul, but declared that he had lately had a kind of experimental Certainty of the Distinction between Corporeal and Thinking Substances, which mere Reason and Philosophy cannot afford, and Opportunities of contemplating the wonderful and inexplicable Union of Soul and Body, which nothing but long Sickness can give. This he illustrated by a Description of the Effects which the Infirmities of his Body had upon his Faculties, which yet they did not so oppress or vanquish, but his Soul was always Master of itself, and always resigned to the Pleasure of its Maker.

He related, with great Concern, that once his Patience so far gave way to Extremity of Pain, that, after having lain fifteen Hours in exquisite Tortures, he prayed to God that he might be set free by Death.

Mr *Schultens*, by way of Consolation, answered, That he thought such Wishes, when forced by continued and excessive Torments, unavoidable in the present State of human Nature; that the best Men, even *Job* himself, were not able to refrain from such Starts of Impatience. This he did not deny, but said, "He that loves God, ought to think nothing desirable but what is most pleasing to the supreme Goodness."

Such were his Sentiments, and such his Conduct in this State of Weakness and Pain: As Death approached nearer, he was so far from Terror or Confusion, that he seemed even less sensible of Pain, and more chearful under his Torments, which continued till the 23d Day of *September* 1738, on which he died, between Four and Five in the Morning, in the 70th Year of his Age.

Thus died *Boerhaave*, a Man formed by Nature for great Designs, and guided by Religion in the Exertion of his Abilities. He was of a robust and athletic Constitution of Body, so harden'd by early Severities, and wholesome Fatigue, that he was insensible of any Sharpness of Air, or Inclemency of Weather. He was tall, and remarkable for extraordinary Strength. There was in his Air and Motion something rough and artless, but so majestick and great at the same time, that no Man ever looked upon him without Veneration, and a kind of tacit Submission to the Superiority of his Genius.

The Vigour and Activity of his Mind sparkled visibly in his Eyes, nor was it ever observed, that any Change of his Fortune, or Alteration in his Affairs, whether happy or unfortunate, affected his Countenance.

He was always chearful, and desirous of promoting Mirth by a facetious and humourous Conversation; he was never soured by Calumny and Detraction, nor ever thought it necessary to confute them; for *they are Sparks*, said he, *which, if you do not blow them, will go out of themselves.*

Yet he took Care never to provoke Enemies by Severity of Censure, for he never dwelt on the Faults or Defects of others, and was so far from inflaming the Envy of his Rivals by dwelling on his own Excellencies, that he rarely mentioned himself or his Writings.

He was not to be over-aw'd or depress'd by the Presence, Frowns, or Insolence of Great Men, but persisted on all Occasions in the Right, with a Resolution always present and always calm. He was modest, but not timorous, and firm without Rudeness.

He could, with uncommon Readiness and Certainty, make a Conjecture of Mens Inclinations and Capacity by their Aspect.

His Method of Life was, to study in the Morning and Evening, and to allot the middle of the Day to his publick Business. His usual Exercise was Riding, till, in his latter Years, his Distempers made it more proper for him to walk; when he was weary, he amused himself with playing on the Violin.

His greatest Pleasure was to retire to his House in the Country, where he had a Garden stored with all the Herbs and Trees which the Climate would bear; here he used to enjoy his Hours unmolested, and prosecute his Studies without Interruption.

The Diligence with which he pursued his Studies, is sufficiently evident from his success. Statesmen and Generals may grow great by unexpected Accidents, and a fortunate Concurrence of Circumstances, neither procured, nor foreseen by themselves: But Reputation in the Learned World must be the effect of Industry and Capacity. *Boerhaave* lost none of his Hours, but when he had attained one Science, attempted another: He added Physic to Divinity, Chemistry to the Mathematicks, and Anatomy to Botany. He examined Systems by Experiments, and formed Experiments into Systems. He neither neglected the Observations of others, nor blindly submitted to celebrated Names. He neither thought so highly of himself as to imagine he could receive no Light from Books, nor so meanly as to believe he could discover nothing but what was to be learned from them. He examined the Observations of other Men, but trusted only to his own.

Nor was he unacquainted with the Art of recommending Truth by Elegance, and embellishing the Philosopher with polite Literature; he knew that but a small part of Mankind will sacrifice their Pleasure to their Improvement, and those Authors, who would find many Readers, must endeavour to please while they instruct.

He knew the Importance of his own Writings to Mankind, and lest he might by a Roughness and Barbarity of Stile, too frequent among Men of great Learning, disappoint his own Intentions, and make his Labours less useful, he did not neglect the politer Arts of Eloquence and Poetry. Thus was his Learning at once various and exact, profound and agreeable.

But his Knowledge, however uncommon, holds, in his Character, but the second Place; his Virtue was yet much more uncommon than his Learning. He was an admirable Example of Temperance, Fortitude, Humility and Devotion. His Piety, and a religious Sense of his Dependence on God, was the Basis of all his Virtues, and the Principle of his whole Conduct. He was too sensible of his Weakness to ascribe any thing to himself, or to conceive that he could subdue Passion, or withstand Temptation by his own natural Power; he attributed every good Thought, and every laudable Action to the Father of Goodness. Being once asked by a Friend, who had often admired his Patience under great Provocations, whether he knew what it was to be angry, and by what means he had so entirely suppressed that impetuous and ungovernable Passion? He answer'd, with ye utmost Frankness and Sincerity, that he was naturally quick of Resentment, but that he had, by daily Prayer and Meditation, at length attained to this Mastery over himself.

As soon as he rose in the Morning, it was, throughout his whole Life, his daily Practice to retire for an Hour to private Prayer and Meditation; this, he often told his Friends, gave him Spirit and Vigour in the Business of the Day, and this he therefore commended as the best Rule of Life; for nothing, he knew, could support the Soul in all Distresses but a Confidence in the Supreme Being, nor can a steady and rational Magnanimity flow from any other Source than a Consciousness of the divine Favour.

He asserted on all Occasions the divine Authority, and sacred Efficacy of the Holy Scriptures, and maintained that they alone taught the Way of Salvation, and that they only could give Peace of Mind. The Excellency of the Christian Religion was the frequent Subject of his Conversation. A strict Obedience to the Doctrine, and a diligent Imitation of the Example of our blessed Saviour he often declared to be the Foundation of true Tranquillity. He recommended to his Friends a careful Observation of the Precept of *Moses* concerning the Love of God and Man. He worshipped God as he is in himself, without attempting to enquire into his Nature. He desired only to think of God, what God knows of himself. There he stopped, lest by indulging his own Ideas, he should form a Deity from his own Imagination, and sin by falling down before him. To the Will of God he paid an absolute Submission, without endeavouring to discover ye Reason of his Determinations; and this he accounted the first and most inviolable Duty of a Christian. When he heard of a Criminal condemned to die, he used to think, Who can tell whether this Man is not better than I? Or, if I am better, it is not to be ascribed to myself but to the Goodness of God.

Such were the Sentiments of *Boerhaave*, whose Words we have added in y^e *Note*. So far was this Man from being made impious by Philosophy, or vain by Knowledge, or by Virtue, that he ascribed all his Abilities to the Bounty, and

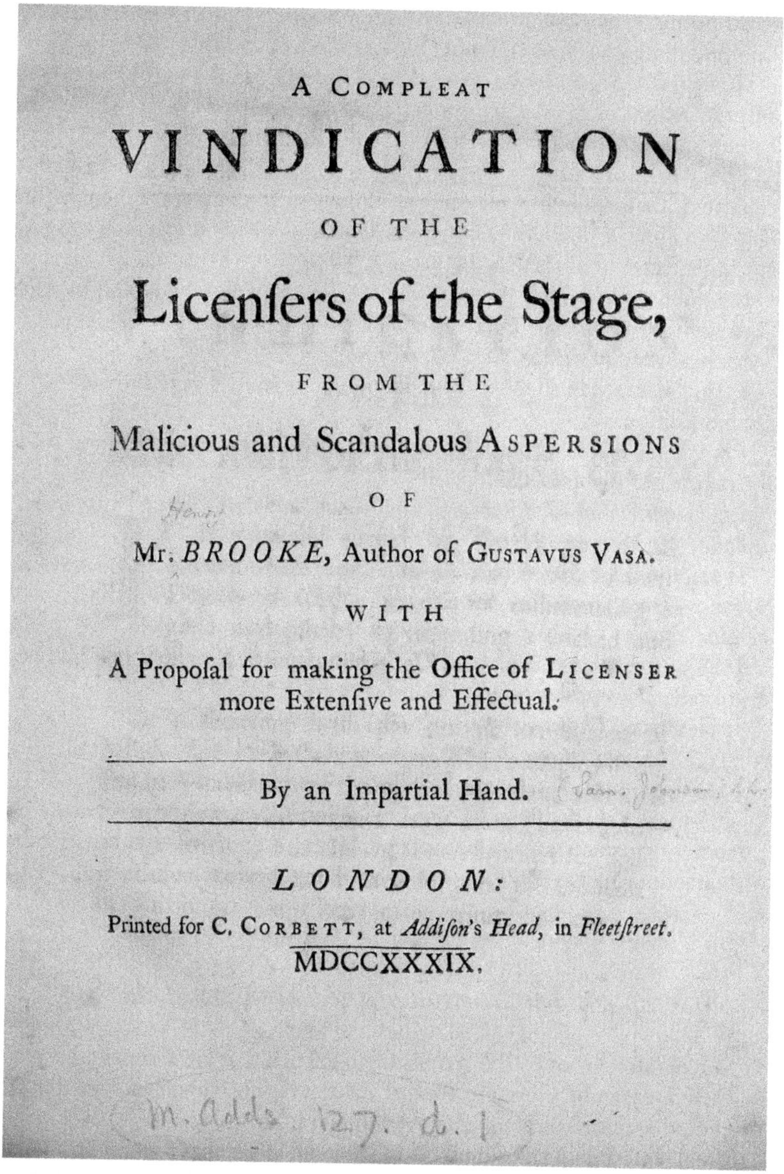

A COMPLEAT

VINDICATION

OF THE

Licensers of the Stage,

FROM THE

Malicious and Scandalous ASPERSIONS

O F

Henry

Mr. *BROOKE,* Author of GUSTAVUS VASA.

WITH

A Propofal for making the Office of LICENSER
more Extenfive and Effectual.

By an Impartial Hand. *Sam. Johnson*

L O N D O N :

Printed for C. CORBETT, at *Addifon's Head,* in *Fleetftreet.*
MDCCXXXIX.

FIGURE 2 *A Compleat Vindication of the Licensers of the Stage* (1739), title
page (Bodl. Vet. A4 d. 111). Courtesy of the Bodleian Library, University
of Oxford.

all his Goodness to the Grace of God. May his Example extend its Influence to his Admirers and Followers! May those who study his Writings imitate his Life, and those who endeavour after his Knowledge aspire likewise to his Piety!

He married, *September* 17, 1710, *Mary Drolenveaux*, the only Daughter of a Burgo-master of *Leyden*, by whom he had *Joanna Maria*, who survives her Father, and three other Children who died in their Infancy.

The Works of this great Writer are so generally known, and so highly esteemed, that, though it may not be improper to enumerate them in the Order of Time in which they were published, it is wholly unnecessary to give any other Account of them.

He published in 1707 *Institutiones Medicæ*, to which he added in 1708 *Aphorismi de cognoscendis & curandis morbis.*

1710, *Index Stirpium in Horto Academico.*

1719, *De Materia Medica, & Remediorum formulis Liber*; and in 1727 a second Edition.

1720, *Alter Index Stirpium*, &c. adorned with Plates, and containing twice the number of Plants as the former.

1722, *Epistola ad Cl. Ruischium, qua sententiam Malpighianam de glandulis defendit.*

1724, *Atrocis nec prius descripti Morbi Historia Illustrissimi Baronis Wassenariae.*

1725, *Opera Anatomica & Chirurgica Andreæ Vesalii*, with the Life of *Vesalius.*

1728, *Altera atrocis rarissimique Morbi Marchionis de Sancto Albano Historia. Auctores de lue Aphrodisiaca, cum tractatu præfixo.*

1731, *Aretaei Cappadocis nova Editio.*

1732, *Elementa Chemiæ.*

1734, *Observata de Argento vivo, ad Reg. Soc. & Acad. Scient.*

These are the Writings of the great *Boerhaave*, which have made all Encomiums useless and vain, since no Man can attentively peruse them without admiring the Abilities, and reverencing the Virtue of the Author.

A Compleat Vindication of the Licensers of the Stage

IT is generally agreed by the Writers of all Parties, that few Crimes are equal, in their Degree of Guilt, to that of calumniating a good and gentle, or defending a wicked and oppressive Administration.

IT is therefore with the utmost Satisfaction of Mind, that I reflect how often I have employ'd my Pen in Vindication of the present Ministry, and their Dependents and Adherents, how often I have detected the specious Fallacies of the Advocates for Independence, how often I have softened the Obstinacy of Patriotism, and how often triumphed over the Clamour of Opposition.

I HAVE, indeed, observed but one Set of Men upon whom all my Arguments have been thrown away, which neither Flattery can draw to Compliance, not Threats reduce to Submission, and who have, notwithstanding all Expedients that either Invention or Experience could suggest, continued to exert their Abilities in a vigorous and constant Opposition of all our Measures.

THE unaccountable Behaviour of these Men, the enthusiastick Resolution with which, after a hundred successive Defeats, they still renewed their Attacks, the Spirit with which they continued to repeat their Arguments in the Senate, though they found a Majority determined to condemn them, and the Inflexibility with which they rejected all Offers of Places and Preferments at last excited my Curiosity so far, that I applied myself to enquire with great Diligence into the real Motives of their Conduct, and to discover what Principle it was that had Force to inspire such unextinguishable Zeal, and to animate such unwearied Efforts.

FOR this Reason I attempted to cultivate a nearer Acquaintance with some of the Chiefs of that Party, and imagined that it would be necessary for some Time to dissemble my Sentiments that I might learn theirs.

DISSIMULATION to a true Politician is not difficult, and therefore I readily assumed the Character of a Proselyte, but found that their Principle of Action was no other, than that which they make no Scruple of avowing in the most publick Manner, notwithstanding the Contempt and Ridicule to which it every Day exposes them, and the Loss of those Honours and Profits from which it excludes them.

THIS wild Passion, or Principle, is a kind of Fanaticism by which they distinguish those of their own Party, and which they look upon as a certain Indication of a great Mind. *We* have no Name for it *at Court*, but among themselves, they term it by a kind of *Cant-phrase*, A REGARD FOR POSTERITY.

THIS Passion seems to predominate in all their Conduct, to regulate every Action of their Lives, and Sentiment of their Minds; I have heard *L*—— and *P*——, when they have made a vigorous Opposition, or blasted the Blossom of some ministerial Scheme, cry out, in the Height of their Exultations, *This will deserve the Thanks of Posterity!* And when their Adversaries, as it much more frequently falls out, have out-number'd and overthrown them, they will say with an Air of Revenge, and a kind of gloomy Triumph, *Posterity will curse you for this.*

IT is common among Men under the Influence of any kind of Frenzy, to believe that all the World has the same odd Notions that disorder their own Imaginations. Did these unhappy Men, these deluded Patriots, know how little we are concerned about Posterity, they would never attempt to fright us with their Curses, or tempt us to a Neglect of our own Interest by a Prospect of their Gratitude.

BUT so strong is their Infatuation, that they seem to have forgotten even the primary Law of Self-preservation, for they sacrifice without scruple every flattering Hope, every darling Enjoyment, and every Satisfaction of Life to this *ruling Passion*, and appear in every Step to consult not so much their own Advantage as that of *Posterity*.

Strange Delusion! that can confine all their Thoughts to a Race of Men whom they neither know, nor can know; from whom nothing is to be feared, nor any Thing expected; who cannot even bribe a special Jury, nor have so much as a single Riband to bestow.

THIS Fondness for Posterity is a kind of Madness which at *Rome* was once almost epidemical, and infected even the Women and the Children. It reigned there till the entire Destruction of *Carthage*, after which it began to be less general, and in a few Years afterwards a Remedy was discovered, by which it was almost entirely extinguished.

IN *England* it never prevailed in any such Degree, some few of the ancient Barons seem indeed to have been disorder'd by it, but the Contagion has been for the most part timely checked, and our Ladies have been generally free.

BUT there has been in every Age a Set of Men much admired and reverenced, who have affected to be always talking of Posterity, and have laid out their Lives upon the Composition of Poems for the Sake of being applauded by this imaginary Generation.

THE present Poets I reckon amongst the most inexorable Enemies of our most excellent Ministry, and much doubt whether any Method will effect the Cure of a Distemper which in this Class of Men may be termed not an accidental Disease, but a Defect in their original Frame and Constitution.

MR. *Brooke*, a Name I mention with all the Detestation suitable to my Character, could not forbear discovering this Depravity of his Mind in his very Prologue, which is filled with Sentiments so wild, and so much unheard of among those who frequent Levees and Courts, that I much doubt, whether the zealous Licenser proceeded any further in his Examination of his Performance.

HE might easily perceive that a Man, *Who bade his moral Beam through every Age,* was too much a Bigot to exploded Notions, to compose a Play which he could license without manifest Hazard of his Office, a Hazard which no Man would incur untainted with the Love of Posterity.

WE cannot therefore wonder that an Author, wholly possessed by this Passion, should vent his Resentment for the Licenser's just Refusal, in virulent Advertisements, insolent Complaints, and scurrilous Assertions of his Rights and Privileges, and proceed in Defiance of Authority to solicite a Subscription.

THIS Temper which I have been describing is almost always complicated with Ideas of the high Prerogatives of human Nature, of a sacred unalienable Birthright, which no Man has conferr'd upon us, and which neither Kings can take, nor Senates give away, which we may justly assert whenever and by whomsoever it is attacked, and which, if ever it should happen to be lost, we may take the first Opportunity to recover.

THE natural Consequence of these Chimeras is Contempt of Authority, and an Irreverence for any Superiority but what is founded upon Merit, and their Notions of Merit are very peculiar, for it is among them no great Proof of Merit to be wealthy and powerful, to wear a Garter or a Star, to command a Regiment or a Senate, to have the Ear of the Minister or of the King, or to possess any of those Virtues and Excellencies which among us intitle a Man to little less than Worship and Prostration.

WE may therefore easily conceive that Mr. *Brooke* thought himself intitled to be importunate for a License, because, in his own Opinion, he deserved one, and to complain thus loudly at the Repulse he met with.

HIS Complaints will have, I hope, but little Weight with the Publick, since the Opinions of the Sect in which he is inlisted are exposed and shewn to be evidently and demonstrably opposite to that System of Subordination and Dependence to which we are indebted for the present Tranquillity of the Nation, and that Chearfulness and Readiness with which the two Houses concur in all our Designs.

I SHALL however, to silence him intirely, or at least to shew those of our Party, that he ought to be silent, consider singly every Instance of Hardship and Oppression which he has dared to publish in the Papers, and to publish in such a Manner that I hope no Man will condemn me for Want of Candour in becoming an Advocate for the Ministry, if I can consider his Advertisements as nothing less than AN APPEAL TO HIS COUNTRY.

LET me be forgiven if I cannot speak with Temper of such Insolence as this: Is a Man without Title, Pension, or Place, to suspect the Impartiality or the Judgment of those who are intrusted with the Administration of publick Affairs? Is he, when the Law is not strictly observed in Regard to him, to think himself *aggrieved*, to tell his Sentiments in Print, assert his Claim to better Usage, and fly for Redress to another Tribunal?

IF such Practices are permitted, I will not venture to foretell the Effects of them, the Ministry may soon be convinced that such Sufferers will find Compassion, and that it is safer not to bear hard upon them than to allow them to complain.

THE Power of Licensing in general, being firmly established by an Act of Parliament, our Poet has not attempted to call in Question, but contents himself with censuring the Manner in which it has been executed, so that I am not now engaged to assert the Licenser's Authority, but to defend his Conduct.

THE Poet seems to think himself aggrieved, because the Licenser kept his Tragedy in his Hands one and twenty Days, whereas the Law allows him to detain it only fourteen.

WHERE will the Insolence of the Malecontents end? Or how are such unreasonable Expectations possibly to be satisfied? Was it ever known that a Man exalted into a high Station dismissed a Suppliant in the Time limited by Law?

Ought not Mr. *Brooke* to think himself happy that his Play was not detained longer? If he had been kept a Year in Suspense, what Redress could he have obtained? Let the Poets remember when they appear before the Licenser, or his Deputy, that they stand at the Tribunal from which there is no Appeal permitted, and where nothing will so well become them as Reverence and Submission.

MR. *Brooke* mentions in his Preface his Knowledge of the Laws of his own Country, had he extended his Enquiries to the Civil Law, he could have found a full Justification of the Licenser's Conduct, *Boni Judicis est ampliare suam auctoritatem.*

IF then it be *the Business of a good Judge to enlarge his Authority*, was it not in the Licenser the utmost Clemency and Forbearance, to extend fourteen Days only to twenty one.

I SUPPOSE *this great* Man's Inclination to perform at least this Duty of a good Judge, is not questioned by any, either of his Friends or Enemies, I may therefore venture to hope that he will extend his Power by proper Degrees, and that I shall live to see a Malecontent Writer earnestly soliciting for the Copy of a Play, which he had delivered to the Licenser twenty Years before.

I waited, says he, *often on the Licenser, and with the utmost Importunity entreated an Answer.* Let Mr *Brooke* consider, whether that Importunity was not a sufficient Reason for the Disappointment. Let him reflect how much more decent it had been to have waited the Leisure of a great Man, than to have pressed upon him with repeated Petitions, and to have intruded upon those precious Moments which he has dedicated to the Service of his Country.

MR. *Brooke* was doubtless led into this improper Manner of acting, by an erroneous Notion that the Grant of a License was not an Act of Favour but of Justice, a Mistake into which he could not have fallen, but from a supine Inattention to the Design of the Statute, which was only to bring Poets into Subjection and Dependence, not to encourage good Writers, but to discourage all.

THERE lies no Obligation upon the Licenser to grant his Sanction to a Play, however excellent, nor can Mr. *Brooke* demand any Reparation, whatever Applause his Performance may meet with.

ANOTHER Grievance is, that the Licenser assigned no Reason for his Refusal. This is a higher Strain of Insolence than any of the former. Is it for a Poet to demand a Licenser's Reason for his Proceedings? Is he not rather to acquiesce in the Decision of Authority, and conclude that there are Reasons which he cannot comprehend?

UNHAPPY would it be for Men in Power, were they always obliged to publish the Motives of their Conduct. What is Power but the Liberty of acting without being accountable? The Advocates for the Licensing Act have alledged, that the Lord Chamberlain has always had Authority to prohibit the

Representation of a Play for just Reasons. Why then did we call in all our Force to procure an Act of Parliament? Was it to enable him to do what he has always done, to confirm an Authority which no Man attempted to impair, or pretended to dispute; no certainly: Our Intention was to invest him with new Privileges, and to empower him to do that *without* Reason, which *with* Reason he could do before.

WE have found by long Experience, that to lie under a Necessity of assigning Reasons, is very troublesome, and that many an excellent Design has miscarried by the Loss of Time spent unnecessarily in examining Reasons.

ALWAYS to call for Reasons, and always to reject them, shews a strange Degree of Perverseness, yet such is the daily Behaviour of our Adversaries, who have never yet been satisfied with any Reasons that have been offered by us.

THEY have made it their Practice to demand once a Year the Reasons for which we maintain a Standing Army.

ONE Year we told them that it was necessary, because all the Nations round us were involved in War; this had no Effect upon them, and therefore resolving to do our utmost for their Satisfaction, we told them the next Year that it was necessary, because all the Nations round us were at Peace.

THIS Reason finding no better Reception than the other, we had Recourse to our Apprehensions of an Invasion from the Pretender, of an Insurrection in Favour of *Gin*, and of a general Disaffection among the People.

BUT as they continue still impenetrable, and oblige us still to assign our annual Reasons, we shall spare no Endeavours to procure such as may be more satisfactory than any of the former.

THE Reason we once gave for building Barracks was for fear of the Plague, and we intend next Year to propose the Augmentation of our Troops for fear of a Famine.

THE Committee, by which the Act for Licensing the Stage was drawn up, had too long known the Inconvenience of giving Reasons, and were too well acquainted with the Characters of great Men, to lay the Lord Chamberlain, or his Deputy, under any such tormenting Obligation.

YET lest Mr. *Brooke* should imagine that a License was refused him without just Reasons, I shall condescend to treat him with more Regard than he can reasonably expect, and point out such Sentiments as not only justly exposed him to that Refusal, but would have provoked any Ministry less merciful than the present to have inflicted some heavier Penalties upon him.

HIS Prologue is filled with such Insinuations as no Friend of our excellent Government can read without Indignation and Abhorrence, and cannot but be owned to be a proper Introduction to such Scenes as seem designed to kindle in the Audience a Flame of Opposition, Patriotism, publick Spirit, and Independency, that Spirit which we have so long endeavoured to suppress, and which cannot be revived without the entire Subversion of all our Schemes.

THIS seditious Poet not content with making an open Attack upon us, by declaring in plain Terms, that he looks upon Freedom as the only Source of publick Happiness and national Security, has endeavoured with Subtlety, equal to his Malice, to make us suspicious of our firmest Friends, to infect our Consultations with Distrust, and to ruin us by disuniting us.

THIS indeed will not be easily effected, an Union founded upon Interest and cemented by Dependance is naturally lasting: But Confederacies which owe their Rise to Virtue or mere Conformity of Sentiments are quickly dissolved, since no Individual has any Thing either to hope or fear for himself, and publick Spirit is generally too weak to combat with private Passions.

THE Poet has, however, attempted to weaken our Combination by an artful and sly Assertion, which, if suffered to remain unconfuted, may operate by Degrees upon our Minds in the Days of Leisure and Retirement which are now approaching, and perhaps fill us with such Surmises as may at least very much embarrass our Affairs.

THE Law by which the *Swedes* justified their Opposition to the Incroachments of the King of *Denmark* he not only calls

Great Nature's Law, the Law within the Breast

But proceeds to tells us that it is

———*Stamp'd by Heav'n upon th' unletter'd Mind.*

By which he evidently intends to insinuate a Maxim which is, I hope, as false as it is pernicious, that Men are naturally fond of Liberty till those unborn Ideas and Desires are effaced by Literature.

THE Author, if he be not a Man mew'd up in his solitary Study and entirely unacquainted with the Conduct of the present Ministry, must know that we have hitherto acted upon different Principles. We have always regarded *Letters* as great Obstructions to our Scheme of Subordination, and are therefore, when we have heard of any Man remarkably *unletter'd*, carefully noted him down as the most proper Person for any Employments of Trust or Honour, and considered him as a Man in whom we could safely repose our most important Secrets.

FROM among the uneducated and *unletter'd* we have chosen not only our Embassadors and other Negotiators, but even our Journalists and Pamphleteers, nor have we had any Reason to change our Measures or to repent of the Confidence which we have placed in Ignorance.

ARE we now therefore to be told that this Law is

Stamp'd upon th' unletter'd Mind?

Are we to suspect our Place-men, our Pensions, our Generals, our Lawyers, our best Friends in both Houses, all our Adherents among the Atheists and Infidels, and our very Gazetteers, Clarks, and Court-pages, as Friends to Independency? Doubtless this is the Tendency of his Assertion; but we have known them too long to be thus imposed upon, the *unletter'd* have been our warmest and most constant Defenders, nor have we omitted any Thing to deserve their Favour, but have always endeavoured to raise their Reputation, extend their Influence, and encrease their Number.

IN his first Act he abounds with Sentiments very inconsistent with the Ends for which the Power of Licensing was granted; to enumerate them all would be to transcribe a great Part of his Play, a Task which I shall very willingly leave to others, who, tho' true Friends to the Government, are not inflamed with Zeal so fiery and impatient as mine, and therefore do not feel the same Emotions of Rage and Resentment at the Sight of those infamous Passages, in which Venality and Dependance are represented as mean in themselves, and productive of Remorse and Infelicity.

ONE Line which ought, in my Opinion, to be erased from every Copy by a special Act of Parliament, is mentioned by *Anderson*, as pronounced by the Hero in his Sleep,

> O Sweden, *O my Country, yet I'll save thee.*

This Line I have Reason to believe thrown out as a kind of a Watch-word for the opposing Faction, who, when they meet in their seditious Assemblies, have been observed to lay their Hands upon their Breasts; and cry out with great Vehemence of Accent,

> *O B——, O my Country, yet I'll save thee.*

IN the second Scene he endeavours to fix Epithets of Contempt upon those Passions and Desires which have been always found most useful to the Ministry, and most opposite to the Spirit of Independency.

> *Base Fear, the Laziness of Lust; gross Appetites,*
> *These are the Ladders and the grov'ling Foot-stool*
> *From whence the Tyrant rises ——*
> *Secure and scepter'd in the Soul's Servility*
> *He has debauched the Genius of our Country*
> *And rides triumphant, while her captive Sons*
> *Await his Nod, the silken Slaves of Pleasure,*
> *Or fetter'd in their Fears.——*

Thus is that decent Submission to our Superiors, and that proper Awe of Authority which we are taught in Courts, termed *base Fear* and the *Servility of the Soul*. Thus are those Gayeties and Enjoyments, those elegant Amusements, and lulling Pleasures which the Followers of a Court are blessed with, as the just Rewards of their Attendance and Submission, degraded to *Lust, Grossness,* and *Debauchery*. The Author ought to be told, that Courts are not to be mentioned with so little Ceremony, and that though Gallantries and Amours are admitted there, it is almost Treason to suppose them infected with Debauchery or Lust.

IT is observable that when this hateful Writer has conceived any Thought of an uncommon Malignity, a Thought which tends in a more particular Manner to excite the Love of Liberty, animate the Heat of Patriotism, or degrade the Majesty of Kings, he takes Care to put it in the Mouth of his Hero, that it may be more forcibly impressed upon his Reader. Thus *Gustavus*, speaking of his Tatters, cries out,

> —— *Yes, my* Arvida,
> *Beyond the Sweeping of the proudest Train*
> *That shades a Monarch's Heel, I prize these Weeds,*
> *For they are sacred to my Country's Freedom.*

Here this abandoned Son of Liberty makes a full Discovery of his execrable Principles, the Tatters of *Gustavus*, the usual Dress of the Assertors of these Doctrines, are of more Divinity, because they are sacred to Freedom than the sumptuous and magnificent Robes of Regality itself. Such Sentiments are truly detestable, nor could any Thing be an Aggravation of the Author's Guilt, except his ludicrous Manner of mentioning a Monarch.

THE *Heel of a Monarch*, or even the Print of his *Heel* is a Thing too venerable and sacred to be treated with such Levity, and placed in Contrast with Rags and Poverty. He, that will speak contemptuously of the *Heel* of a *Monarch*, will, whenever he can with Security, speak contemptuously of his Head.

THESE are the most glaring Passages which have occurr'd, in the Perusal of the first Pages; my Indignation will not suffer me to proceed farther, and I think much better of the Licenser, than to believe he went so far.

IN the few Remarks which I have set down, the Reader will easily observe that I have strained no Expression beyond its natural Import, and have divested myself of all Heat, Partiality, and Prejudice.

So far therefore is Mr. *Brooke* from having received any hard or unwarrantable Treatment, that the Licenser has only acted in Pursuance of that Law to which he owes his Power, a Law which every Admirer of the Administration must own to be very necessary, and to have produced very salutary Effects.

I am indeed surprised that this great Office is not drawn out into a longer Series of Deputations, since it might afford a gainful and reputable Employment to a great Number of the Friends of the Government; and I should think instead of having immediate Recourse to the Deputy-licenser himself, it might be sufficient Honour for any Poet, except the Laureat, to stand bareheaded in the Presence of the Deputy of the Deputy's Deputy in the nineteenth Subordination.

Such a Number cannot but be thought necessary if we take into Consideration the great Work of drawing up an Index *Expurgatorius* to all the old Plays; which is, I hope, already undertaken, or if it has been hitherto unhappily neglected, I take this Opportunity to recommend.

THE Productions of our old Poets are crouded with Passages very unfit for the Ears of an *English* Audience, and which cannot be pronounced without irritating the Minds of the People.

THIS Censure I do not confine to those Lines in which Liberty, natural Equality, wicked Ministers, deluded Kings, mean Arts of Negotiation, venal Senates, mercenary Troops, oppressive Officers, servile and exorbitant Taxes, universal Corruption, the Luxuries of a Court, the Miseries of the People, the Decline of Trade, or the Happiness of Independency are directly mentioned. These are such glaring Passages as cannot be suffered to pass without the most supine and criminal Negligence. I hope the Vigilance of the Licensers will extend to all such Speeches and Soliloquies as tend to recommend the Pleasures of Virtue, the Tranquillity of an uncorrupted Head, and the Satisfactions of conscious Innocence; for though such Strokes as these do not appear to a common Eye to threaten any Danger to the Government, yet it is well known to more penetrating Observers that they have such Consequences as cannot be too diligently obviated, or too cautiously avoided.

A MAN, who becomes once enamour'd of the Charms of Virtue, is apt to be very little concerned about the Acquisition of Wealth or Titles, and is therefore not easily induced to act in a Manner contrary to his real Sentiments, or to vote at the Word of Command; by contracting his Desires, and regulating his Appetites, he wants much less than other Men, and every one versed in the Arts of Government can tell; that Men are more easily influenced in Proportion as they are more necessitous.

THIS is not the only Reason why Virtue should not receive too much Countenance from a licensed Stage, her Admirers and Followers are not only naturally independent, but learn such an uniform and consistent Manner of speaking and acting, that they frequently by the mere Force of artless Honesty surmount all the Obstacles which Subtlety and Politicks can throw in their Way, and obtain their Ends in spite of the most profound and sagacious Ministry.

SUCH then are the Passages to be expunged by the Licensers: In many Parts indeed the Speeches will be imperfect, and the Action appear not regularly conducted, but the Poet Laureat may easily supply these Vacuities by inserting some of his own Verses in Praise of Wealth, Luxury, and Venality.

BUT alas! all those pernicious Sentiments which we shall banish from the Stage, will be vented from the Press, and more studiously read because they are prohibited.

I CANNOT but earnestly implore the Friends of the Government to leave no Art untry'd by which we may hope to succeed in our Design of extending the Power of the Licenser to the Press, and of making it criminal to publish any Thing without an *Imprimatur*.

How much would this single Law lighten the mighty Burden of State Affairs? With how much Security might our Ministers enjoy their Honours, their Places, their Reputations, and their Admirers, could they once suppress those malicious Invectives which are at present so industriously propagated, and so eagerly read, could they hinder any Arguments but their own from coming to the Ears of the People, and stop effectually the Voice of Cavil and Enquiry.

I CANNOT but indulge myself a little while by dwelling on this pleasing Scene, and imagining those *Halcyon-days* in which no Politicks shall be read but those of the *Gazetteer*, nor any Poetry but that of the Laureat; when we shall hear of nothing but the successful Negotiations of our Ministers, and the great Actions of ——

How much happier would this State be, than those perpetual Jealousies and Contentions which are inseparable from Knowledge and Liberty, and which have for many Years kept this Nation in perpetual Commotions.

BUT these are Times rather to be wished for than expected, for such is the Nature of our unquiet Countrymen, that if they are not admitted to the Knowledge of Affairs, they are always suspecting their Governors of Designs prejudicial to their Interest, they have not the least Notion of the pleasing Tranquillity of Ignorance, nor can be brought to imagine that they are kept in the Dark, lest too much Light should hurt their Eyes. They have long claimed a Right of directing their Superiors, and are exasperated at the least Mention of Secrets of State.

THIS Temper makes them very readily encourage any Writer or Printer, who, at the Hazard of his Life or Fortune, will give them any Information; and while this Humour prevails there never will be wanting some daring Adventurer who will write in Defence of Liberty, and some zealous or avaricious Printer who will disperse his Papers.

IT has never yet been found that any Power, however vigilant or despotick, has been able to prevent the Publication of seditious Journals, Ballads, Essays and Dissertations, *Considerations on the present State of Affairs, and Enquiries into the Conduct of the Administration*.

YET I must confess, that considering the Success with which the present Ministry has hitherto proceeded in their Attempts to drive out of the World the old Prejudices of Patriotism and publick Spirit, I cannot but entertain some Hopes that what has been so often attempted by their Predecessors, is reserved to be accomplished by their superior Abilities.

IF I might presume to advise them upon this great Affair, I should dissuade them from any direct Attempt upon the Liberty of the Press, which is the Darling of the common People, and therefore cannot be attacked without immediate Danger. They may proceed by a more sure and silent Way, and attain the desired End without Noise, Detraction, or Opposition.

THERE are scatter'd over this Kingdom several little Seminaries in which the lower Ranks of People, and the younger Sons of our Nobility and Gentry are taught, from their earliest Infancy, the pernicious Arts of Spelling and Reading, which they afterwards continue to practise very much to the Disturbance of their own Quiet, and the Interruption of ministerial Measures.

THESE Seminaries may, by an Act of Parliament, be at once suppressed, and that our Posterity be deprived of all Means of reviving this corrupt Method of Education, it may be made Felony to teach to read, without a License from the Lord Chamberlain.

THIS Expedient, which I hope will be carefully concealed from the Vulgar, must infallibly answer the great End proposed by it, and set the Power of the Court not only above the Insults of the Poets, but in a short Time above the Necessity of providing against them. The Licenser having his Authority thus extended will in Time enjoy the Title and the Salary without the Trouble of exercising his Power, and the Nation will rest at length in Ignorance and Peace.

FINIS.

Prologue to Garrick's Lethe

Prodigious Madness of the writing Race!
Ardent of Fame, yet fearless of Disgrace.
　　Without a boding Tear, or anxious Sigh,
The Bard obdurate sees his Brother die.
Deaf to the Critick, Sullen to the Friend,
Not One takes Warning, by another's End.
　　Oft has our Bard in this disastrous Year,
Beheld the Tragic Heroes taught to fear.
Oft has he seen the indignant Orange fly,
And heard th'ill Omen'd Catcall's direful Cry. 　　10
Yet dares to venture on the dangerous Stage,
And weakly hopes to 'scape the Critick's Rage.
　　This Night he hopes to shew that Farce may charm,
Tho' no lewd Hint the mantling Virgin warm,
That useful Truth with Humour may unite,
That Mirth may mend, and Innocence delight.

An Epitaph on Claudy Philips, a Musician

An EPITAPH *upon the celebrated* CLAUDY
PHILIPS, *Musician, who died very poor.*

P*Hilips*, whose touch harmonious could remove
   The pangs of guilty pow'r and hapless love,
Rest here, distress'd by poverty no more,
Here find that calm, thou gav'st so oft before,
Sleep, undisturb'd within this peaceful shrine,
Till angels wake thee, with a note like thine.

An Essay on Epitaphs

THO' Criticism has been cultivated in every Age of Learning, by Men of great Abilities and extensive Knowledge, till the Rules of Writing are become rather burthensome than instructive to the Mind; tho' almost every Species of Composition has been the Subject of particular Treatises, and given Birth to Definitions, Distinctions, Precepts and Illustrations; yet no Critic of Note, that has fallen within my Observation, has hitherto thought *Sepulchral Inscriptions* worthy of a minute Examination, or pointed out with proper Accuracy their Beauties and Defects.

The Reasons of this Neglect it is useless to enquire, and perhaps impossible to discover; it might be justly expected that this Kind of Writing would have been the favourite Topic of Criticism, and that Self-Love might have produced some Regard for it, in those Authors that have crowded Libraries with elaborate Dissertations upon *Homer*; since to afford a Subject for heroick Poems is the Privilege of very few, but every Man may expect to be recorded in an Epitaph, and, therefore, finds some Interest in providing that his Memory may not suffer by an unskilful Panegyrick.

If our Prejudices in favour of Antiquity deserve to have any Part in the Regulation of our Studies, EPITAPHS seem intitled to more than common Regard, as they are probably of the same Age with the Art of Writing. The most ancient Structures in the World, the Pyramids, are supposed to be Sepulchral Monuments, which either Pride or Gratitude erected, and the same Passions which incited Men to such laborious and expensive Methods of preserving their own Memory, or that of their Benefactors, would doubtless incline them not to neglect any easier Means by which ye same Ends might be obtained. Nature and Reason have dictated to every Nation, that to preserve good Actions from Oblivion, is both the Interest and Duty of Mankind; and therefore we find no People acquainted with the Use of Letters, that omitted to grace the Tombs of their Heroes and wise Men with panegyrical Inscriptions.

To examine, therefore, in what the Perfection of EPITAPHS consists, and what Rules are to be observed in composing them, will be at least of as much Use as other critical Enquiries; and for assigning a few Hours to such Disquisitions, great Examples at least, if not strong Reasons may be pleaded.

An EPITAPH, as the Word itself implies, is an *Inscription on a Tomb*, and in its most extensive Import may admit indiscriminately Satire or Praise. But as Malice has seldom produced Monuments of Defamation, and the Tombs hitherto raised have been the Work of Friendship and Benevolence, Custom has contracted the Original Latitude of the *Word*, so that it signifies in the general Acceptation an *Inscription engraven on a Tomb in Honour of the Person deceased*.

As Honours are paid to the Dead in order to incite others to the Imitation of their Excellencies, the principal Intention of EPITAPHS is to perpetuate the Examples of Virtue, that the Tomb of a good Man may supply the Want of his Presence, and Veneration for his Memory produce the same Effect as the Observation of his Life. Those EPITAPHS are, therefore, the most perfect, which set Virtue in the strongest Light, and are best adapted to exalt the Reader's Ideas and rouse his Emulation.

To this End it is not always necessary to recount the Actions of a Hero, or enumerate the Writings of a Philosopher; to imagine such Informations necessary, is to detract from their Characters, or to suppose their Works mortal; or their Atchievements in danger of being forgotten. The bare Name of such Men answers every Purpose of a long Inscription.

Had only the Name of Sir ISAAC NEWTON been subjoined to the Design upon his Monument, instead of a long Detail of his Discoveries, which no Philosopher can want, and which none but a Philosopher can understand, those, by whose Direction it was raised, had done more Honour both to him and to themselves.

This indeed is a Commendation which it requires no Genius to bestow, but which can never become vulgar or contemptible, if bestow'd with Judgment; because no single Age produces many Men of Merit superior to Panegyrick. None but the first Names can stand unassisted against the Attacks of Time, and if Men raised to Reputation by Accident or Caprice, have nothing but their Names engraved on their Tombs, there is Danger left in a few Years the Inscription require an Interpreter. Thus have their Expectations been disappointed who honoured *Picus* of *Mirandola*, with this pompous Epitaph,

> *Hic situs est* PICUS MIRANDOLA, *cætera norunt*
> *Et* Tagus *et* Ganges, *forsan et* Antipodes.

His Name then celebrated in the remotest Corners of the Earth is now almost forgotten, and his Works, then studied, admired and applauded, are now mouldering in Obscurity.

Next in Dignity to the bare Name is a short Character simple and unadorned, without Exaggeration, Superlatives, or Rhetoric. Such were the Inscriptions in Use among the *Romans*, in which the Victories gained by their Emperors were commemorated by a single Epithet; as Cæsar *Germanicus*, Cæsar *Dacicus*, *Germanicus, Illyricus*. Such would be this Epitaph, ISAACUS NEWTONUS, *Naturæ Legibus investigatis, hic quiescit*.

But to far the greatest Part of Mankind a longer Encomium is necessary for the Publication of their Virtues, and the Preservation of their Memories, and in the Composition of these it is that Art is principally required, and Precepts therefore may be useful.

In writing EPITAPHS one Circumstance is to be considered, which affects no other Composition; the Place in which they are now commonly found restrains them to a particular Air of Solemnity, and debars them from the Admission of all lighter or gayer Ornaments. In this it is that the Stile of an EPITAPH necessarily differs from that of an ELEGY. The Custom of burying our Dead either in or near our Churches, perhaps originally founded on a rational Design of fitting the Mind for religious Exercises, by laying before it the most affecting Proofs of the Uncertainty of Life, makes it proper to exclude from our EPITAPHS all such Allusions as are contrary to the Doctrines for the Propagation of which the Churches are erected, and to the End for which those who peruse the Monuments must be supposed to come thither. Nothing is, therefore, more ridiculous than to copy the *Roman* Inscriptions which were engraven on Stones by the Highway, and composed by those who generally reflected on Mortality only to excite in themselves and others a quicker Relish of Pleasure, and a more luxurious Enjoyment of Life, and whose Regard for the Dead extended no farther than a Wish that *the Earth might be light upon them*.

All Allusions to the Heathen Mythology are therefore absurd, and all Regard for the senseless Remains of a dead Man impertinent and superstitious. One of the first Distinctions of the primitive Christians, was their Neglect of bestowing Garlands on the Dead, in which they are very rationally defended by their Apologist in *Minutius Felix. We lavish no Flowers nor Odours on the Dead*, says he, *because they have no Sense of Fragrance or of Beauty*. We profess to Reverence the Dead not for their Sake but for our own. It is therefore always with Indignation or Contempt that I read the Epitaph on *Cowley*, a Man, whose Learning and Poetry were his lowest Merits.

> *Aurea dum late volitant tua Scripta per Orbem*
> *Et fama eternum vivis, divine Poeta,*
> *Hic placida jaceas requie, custodiat urnam*
> *Cana, Fides, vigilentque perenni Lampade Musæ!*
> *Sit sacer ille locus, nec quis temerarius ausit*

Sacrilega turbare manu venerabile bustum,
Intacti maneant, maneant per sæcula dulces
COWLEII *cineres, serventq; immobile Saxum.*

To pray, that ye Ashes of a Friend may lie undisturbed, and that the Divinities that favoured him in his Life, may watch for ever round him to preserve his Tomb from Violation and drive Sacrilege away, is only rational in him who believes the Soul interested in the Repose of the Body, and the Powers which he invokes for its Protection able to preserve it. To censure such Expressions as contrary to Religion, or as Remains of Heathen Superstition, would be too great a Degree of Severity. I condemn them only as uninstructive and unaffecting, as too ludicrous for Reverence or Grief, for Christianity and a Temple.

That the Designs and Decorations of Monuments, ought likewise to be formed with the same Regard to the Solemnity of the Place, cannot be denied: It is an established Principle that all Ornaments owe their Beauty to their Propriety. The same Glitter of Dress that adds Graces to Gayety and Youth, would make Age and Dignity contemptible. CHARON with his Boat is far from heightening the awful Grandeur of the universal Judgment, tho' drawn by *Angelo* himself; nor is it easy to imagine a greater Absurdity than that of gracing the Walls of a Christian Temple with the Figure of *Mars* leading a Hero to Battle, or *Cupids* sporting round a Virgin. The Pope who defaced the Statues of the Deities, at the Tomb of *Sannazarius* is, in my Opinion, more easily to be defended, than he that erected them.

It is for the same Reason improper to address the EPITAPH to the Passenger, a Custom which an injudicious Veneration for Antiquity introduced again at the Revival of Letters, and which, among many others, *Passeratius* suffered to mislead him in his EPITAPH upon the Heart of *Henry* King of *France*, who was stabbed by *Clement* the Monk, which yet deserves to be inserted, for the Sake of shewing how beautiful even Improprieties may become, in the Hands of a good Writer.

Adsta, Viator, et dole regum vices.
Cor Regis isto conditur sub marmore,
Qui jura Gallis, *jura* Sarmatis *dedit.*
Tectus Cucullo hunc sustulit Sicarius.
Abi, Viator, et dole regum vices.

In the Monkish Ages, however ignorant and unpolished, the EPITAPHS were drawn up with far greater Propriety than can be shown in those, which more enlightened Times have produced.

Orate pro Anima —— miserrimi Peccatoris

was an Address to the last Degree striking and solemn, as it flowed naturally from the Religion then believed, and awakened in the Reader Sentiments of Benevolence for the Deceased, and of Concern for his own Happiness. There was Nothing trifling or ludicrous, Nothing that did not tend to the noblest End, the Propagation of Piety and the Increase of Devotion.

It may seem very superfluous to lay it down as the first Rule for writing Epitaphs, that the Name of the Deceased is not to be omitted; nor should I have thought such a Precept necessary, had not the Practice of the greatest Writers shewn, that it has not been sufficiently regarded. In most of the Poetical Epitaphs, the Names for whom they were composed may be sought to no Purpose, being only prefixed on the Monument. To expose yᵉ Absurdity of this Omission, it is only necessary to ask how the Epitaphs, which have outlived the Stones on which they were inscribed, would have contributed to the Information of Posterity, had they wanted the Names of those whom they celebrated.

In drawing the Character of the Deceased, there are no Rules to be observ'd which do not equally relate to other Compositions. The Praise ought not to be general, because the Mind is lost in the Extent of any indefinite Idea, and cannot be affected with what it cannot comprehend. When we hear only of a good or great Man, we know not in what Class to place him, nor have any Notion of his Character, distinct from that of a thousand others; his Example can have no Effect upon our Conduct, as we have nothing remarkable or eminent to propose to our Imitation. The Epitaph composed by *Ennius* for his own Tomb, has both the Faults last mentioned,

> *Nemo me decoret lacrumis, nec funera, fletu*
> *Faxit. Cur? volito vivu' per ora virum.*

The Reader of this Epitaph receives scarce any Idea from it; he neither conceives any Veneration for the Man to whom it belongs, nor is instructed by what Methods this boasted Reputation is to be obtained.

Tho' a sepulchral Inscription is professedly a Panegyric, and, therefore, not confined to historical Impartiality, yet it ought always to be written with regard to Truth. No Man ought to be commended for Virtues which he never possessed, but whoever is curious to know his Faults must enquire after them in other Places; the Monuments of the Dead are not intended to perpetuate the Memory of Crimes, but to exhibit Patterns of Virtue. On the Tomb of *Mæcenas*, his Luxury is not to be mentioned with his Munificence, nor is the Proscription to find a Place on the Monument of *Augustus*.

The best Subject for Epitaphs is private Virtue; Virtue exerted in the same Circumstances in which the Bulk of Mankind are placed, and which, therefore, may admit of many Imitators. He that has delivered his Country from

Oppression, or freed the World from Ignorance and Error, can excite the Emulation of a very small Number; but he that has repell'd the Temptations of Poverty, and disdained to free himself from Distress at the Expence of his Virtue, may animate Multitudes, by his Example, to the same Firmness of Heart and Steadiness of Resolution.

Of this Kind I cannot forbear the Mention of two *Greek* Inscriptions; one upon a Man whose Writings are well known, the other upon a Person whose Memory is preserved only in her EPITAPH, who both lived in Slavery; the most calamitous Estate in human Life.

> Ζωσιμη ἡ π̅ξιν εουσα μονω τω Σωματι δουλη,
> Και τω σωματι νυν ἑυρεν ἑλευθεριην.

> Zosima, *quæ solo fuit olim Corpore Serva,*
> *Corpore nunc etiam libera facta fuit.*

> 'Zosima, *who in her Life could only have*
> *her Body enslaved, now finds her Body*
> *likewise set at Liberty.'*

It is impossible to read this EPITAPH without being animated to bear the Evils of Life with Constancy, and to support the Dignity of Human Nature under the most pressing Afflictions, both by the Example of the Heroine, whose Grave we behold, and the Prospect of that State in which, to use the Language of the inspired Writers, *The Poor cease from their Labours, and the Weary be at rest.* ——

The other is upon *Epictetus,* the Stoic Philosopher.

> Δουλος Επικτητος γενομην, και Σωμ'αναπηρος;
> Και πενιην Ιρος, και φιλος Ἀθανατοις.

> *Servus* Epictetus, *mutilatus corpore, vixi*
> *Pauperieque Irus, Curaque prima Deum.*

> 'Epictetus, *who lies here, was a Slave and a Cripple, poor as the*
> *Begger in the Proverb, and the Favourite of Heaven.*

In this Distich is comprised the noblest Panegyric, and the most important Instruction. We may learn from it that Virtue is impracticable in no Condition, since *Epictetus* could recommend himself to the Regard of Heaven, amidst the Temptations of Poverty and Slavery: Slavery, which has always been found so destructive to Virtue, that in many Languages a Slave and a Thief are expressed by the same Word. And we may be likewise admonished by it, not to lay any Stress on a Man's outward Circumstances in making an Estimate of his real Value, since *Epictetus* the Begger, the Cripple, and the Slave, was the Favourite of Heaven.

Review of the Memoirs of the Duchess of Marlborough

SIR,   March 9,

THE *Account of the Conduct of the Dutchess of* Marlborough, *having been so eagerly received, and so attentively considered, as to become even at this Time of Business, Contests, Wars and Revolutions, the most popular Topic of Conversation, you may perhaps willingly admit into your Collection this short Essay upon it, which does not appear written with an Intention to please or offend any Party.*

THE universal Regard, which is paid by Mankind to such Accounts of publick Transactions as have been written by those who were engaged in them, may be, with great Probability ascribed to that ardent Love of Truth, which Nature has kindled in the Breast of Man, and which remains even where every other laudable Passion is extinguished. We cannot but read such Narratives with uncommon Curiosity, because we consider the Writer as indubitably possessed of the Ability to give us just Representations, and do not always reflect, that, very often, proportionate to the Opportunities of knowing the Truth, are the Temptations to disguise it.

Authors of this Kind, have at least an incontestable Superiority over those whose Passions are the same, and whose Knowledge is less. It is evident that those who write in their own Defence, discover often more Impartiality, and less Contempt of Evidence, than the Advocates which Faction or Interest have raised in their Favour.

It is, however to be remembred, that the Parent of all Memoirs, is the Ambition of being distinguished from the Herd of Mankind, and the Fear of either Infamy or Oblivion, Passions which cannot but have some Degree of Influence, and which may at least affect the Writers Choice of Facts, though they may not prevail upon him to advance known Falshoods. He may aggravate or extenuate particular Circumstances, though he preserves the grand Transaction; as the general Likeness may be preserved in painting, though a Blemish is hid or a Beauty improved.

Every Man that is sollicitous about the Esteem of others, is in a greater Degree desirous of his own, and makes by Consequence his first Apology for his Conduct to himself, and when he has once deceived his own Heart, which is for the greatest Part too easy a Task, he propagates the Deceit in the World, without Reluctance or Consciousness of Falshood.

But to what Purpose, it may be asked, are such Reflections, except to produce a general Incredulity and to make History of no Use? The Man who knows not the Truth *cannot*, and he who knows it *will not* tell it; what then remains, but to distrust every Relation, and live in perpetual Negligence of past Events; or, what is still more disagreeable, in perpetual Suspense.

That by such Remarks, some Incredulity is indeed produced, cannot be denied, but Distrust is a necessary Qualification of a Student in History. Distrust quickens his Discernment of different Degrees of Probability, animates his Search after Evidence, and perhaps heightens his Pleasure at the Discovery of Truth; for Truth, though not always obvious, is generally discoverable, nor is it any where more likely to be found than in private Memoirs, which are generally published at a Time when any gross Falshood may be detected by living Witnesses, and which always contain a thousand Incidents, of which the Writer could not but have acquired a certain Knowledge, and which he has no Reason for disguising.

Such is the Account lately published by the Dutchess of *Marlborough*, of her own Conduct, by which those who are very little concerned about the Character which it is principally intended to preserve or to retrieve, may be entertained and instructed. By the Perusal of this Account, the Enquirer into Human Nature may obtain an intimate Acquaintance with the Characters of those whose Names have crouded the latest Histories, and discover the Relation between their Minds and their Actions. The Historian may trace the Progress of great Transactions, and discover the secret Causes of important Events. And, to mention one Use more, the polite Writer may learn an unaffected Dignity of Stile, and an artful Simplicity of Narration.

The Method of confirming her Relation, by inserting at length the Letters that every Transaction occasioned, has not only set the greatest Part of the Work, above the Danger of Confutation, but has added to the Entertainment of the Reader, who has now the Satisfaction of forming to himself the Characters of the Actors, and judging how nearly such as have hitherto been given of them agree with these which they now give of themselves.

Even of those whose Letters could not be made publick, we have a more exact Knowledge than can be expected from general Histories, because we see them in their private Apartments, in their careless Hours, and observe these Actions in which they indulged their own Inclinations, without any Regard to Censure or Applause.

Thus it is, that we are made acquainted with the Disposition of King *William*, of whom it may be collected from various Instances that he was arbitrary, insolent, gloomy, rapacious, and brutal, that he was at all Times disposed to play the Tyrant, *that he had neither in great Things nor in small the Manners of a Gentleman*, that he was capable of gaining Money by mean Artifices, and that he only regarded his Promise when it was his Interest to keep it.

There are doubtless great Numbers who will be offended with this Delineation of the Mind of the immortal *William*, but they whose Honesty or Sense enables them to consider impartially the Events of his Reign, will now be enabled to discover the Reason of the frequent Oppositions, which he encountred, and of the personal Affronts which he was sometimes forced to endure. They will observe that it is not always sufficient to do Right, and that it is often necessary to add Gracefulness to Virtue. They will recollect how vain it is to endeavour to gain Men by great Qualities, while our cursory Behaviour is insolent and offensive, and that those may be disgusted by little Things, who can scarcely be pleased with great.

Charles the Second by his Affability and Politeness, made himself the Idol of the Nation, which he betrayed and sold. *William* the Third was for his Insolence and Brutality, hated by that People which he protected and enriched; had the best Part of these two Characters been united in one Prince, the House of *Bourbon* had fallen before him.

It is not without Pain, that the Reader observes a Shade encroaching upon the Light, with which the Memory of Queen *Mary* has been hitherto invested. The popular, the beneficent, the pious, the celestial Queen *Mary*, from whose Presence none ever withdrew without an Addition to his Happiness. What can be charged upon this Delight of Human Kind? Nothing less than that *she wanted Bowels*, and was insolent with her Power, that she was resentful and pertinacious in her Resentment, that she descended to mean Acts of Revenge, when heavier Vengeance was not in her Power. That she was desirous of controuling where she had no Authority, and backward to forgive, even when she had no real Injury to complain of.

This is a Character so different from all those that have been hitherto given of this celebrated Princess, that the Reader stands in Suspense, till he considers the Inconsistencies in human Conduct, remembers that no Virtue is without its Weakness, and considers that Q. *Mary's* Character has hitherto had this great Advantage, that it has only been compared with those of Kings.

The greatest Number of the Letters inserted in this Account, were written by Q. *Anne*, of which it may be truly observed, that they will be equally useful for the Confutation of those who have exalted or depressed her Character. They are written with great Purity and Correctness, without any forced Expressions, affected Phrases, or unnatural Sentiments, and show uncommon Clearness of Understanding, Tenderness of Affection, and Rectitude of Intention; but discover at the same Time, a Temper timorous, anxious, and impatient of Misfortune, a Tendency to burst into Complaints, helpless Dependence on the Affection of others, and a weak Desire of moving Compassion. There is indeed nothing insolent or over-bearing, but then there is nothing great, or firm, or regal; nothing that enforces Obedience and Respect, or which does not rather invite Opposition and Petulance. She seems born for Friendship, not for Government, and to be unable to regulate the Conduct of others, otherwise than by her own Example.

That this Character is just, appears from the Occurrences in her Reign, in which the Nation was governed for many Years, by a Party whose Principles she detested, but whose Influence she knew not how to obviate, and to whose Schemes she was subservient against her Inclination.

The Charge of tyrannising over her, which was made by Turns against each Party, proves that, in the Opinion of both, she was easily to be governed; and tho' it may be supposed that the Letters here publish'd were selected with some Regard to Respect and Ceremony, it appears plainly enough from them, that she was what she has been represented, little more than *the Slave of the* Marlborough *Family*.

The inferior Characters, as they are of less Importance, are less accurately delineated; the Picture of *Harley* is at least partially drawn, all the Deformities are heighten'd, and the Beauties, for Beauties of Mind he certainly had, are entirely omitted.

An Account of the Harleian Library

To solicit a SUBSCRIPTION for a Catalogue of Books exposed to Sale, is an Attempt for which some Apology cannot but be necessary, for Few would willingly contribute to the Expence of Volumes, by which neither Instruction nor Entertainment could be afforded, from which only the Bookseller could expect Advantage, and of which the only Use must cease, at the Dispersion of the Library.

NOR could the Reasonableness of an universal Rejection of our Proposal be denied, if this Catalogue were to be compiled with no other View, than that of promoting the Sale of the Books which it enumerates, and drawn up with that Inaccuracy and Confusion which may be found in those that are daily published.

BUT our Design, like our Proposal, is uncommon, and to be prosecuted at a very uncommon Expence, it being intended, that the Books shall be distributed into their distinct Classes, and every Class ranged with some Regard to the Age of the Writers; that every Book shall be accurately described; that the Peculiarities of Editions shall be remarked, and Observations from the Authors of Literary History occasionally interspersed, that, by this Catalogue, we may inform Posterity, of the Excellence and Value of this great Collection, and promote the Knowledge of scarce Books, and elegant Editions. For this Purpose, Men of Letters are engaged, who cannot even be supplied with Amanuenses, but at an Expence above that of a common Catalogue.

To shew that this Collection deserves a particular Degree of Regard from the Learned and the Studious, that it excels any Library that was ever yet offered to public Sale, in the Value as well as Number of the Volumes which it contains, and that therefore this Catalogue will not be of less Use to Men of Letters, than those of the *Thuanian, Heinsian,* or *Barberinian* Libraries, it may not be improper to exhibit a general Account of the different Classes as they are naturally divided by the several Sciences.

By this Method we can indeed exhibit only a general Idea, at once, magnificent and confused; an Idea of the Writings of many Nations, collected from distant Parts of the World, discovered sometimes by Chance, and sometimes by Curiosity, amidst the Rubbish of forsaken Monasteries, and the Repositories of ancient Families, and brought hither from every Part, as to the universal Receptacle of Learning.

It will be no unpleasing Effect of this Account, if those, that shall happen to peruse it, should be inclined by it, to reflect on the Character of the late Proprietors, and to pay some Tribute of Veneration to their Ardor for Literature, to that generous and exalted Curiosity which they gratified with incessant Searches and immense Expence, and to which they dedicated that Time and that Superfluity of Fortune which many others of their Rank employ in the Pursuit of contemptible Amusements, or the Gratification of guilty Passions. And, surely, every Man, who considers Learning as ornamental and advantageous to the Community, must allow them the Honour of public Benefactors, who have introduced amongst us Authors not hitherto well known, and added to the Literary Treasures of their Native Country.

That our Catalogue will excite any other Man to emulate the Collectors of this Library, to prefer Books and Manuscripts to Equipage and Luxury, and to forsake Noise and Diversion for the Conversation of the Learned, and the Satisfaction of extensive Knowledge, we are very far from presuming to hope, but shall make no Scruple to assert, that, if any Man should happen to be seized with such laudable Ambition, he may find in this Catalogue Hints and Informations which are not easily to be met with; he will discover, that the boasted *Bodleian* Library is very far from a perfect Model, and that even the learned *Fabricius* cannot compleatly instruct him in the early Editions of the Classic Writers.

But the Collectors of Libraries cannot be numerous, and, therefore, Catalogues could not very properly be recommended to the Public, if they had not a more general and frequent Use, an Use which every Student has experienced, or neglected to his Loss. By the Means of Catalogues only can it be known, what has been written on every Part of Learning, and the Hazard avoided of encountering Difficulties which have already been cleared, discussing Questions which have already been decided, and digging in Mines of Literature which former Ages have exhausted.

How often this has been the Fate of Students, every Man of Letters can declare, and, perhaps, there are very few who have not sometimes valued as new Discoveries, made by themselves, those Observations, which have long since been published, and of which the World therefore will refuse them the Praise; nor can that Refusal be censured as any enormous Violation of Justice; for, why should they not forfeit by their Ignorance, what they might claim by their Sagacity?

To illustrate this Remark, by the Mention of obscure Names, would not much confirm it, and to vilify for this Purpose the Memory of Men truly great would be to deny them the Reverence which they may justly claim from those whom their Writings have instructed. May the Shade at least of one great *English* Critic rest without Disturbance, and may no Man presume to insult his Memory who wants his Learning, his Reason, or his Wit.

FROM the vexatious Disappointment of meeting Reproach, where Praise is expected, every Man will certainly desire to be secured, and therefore that Book will have some Claim to his Regard from which he may receive Informations of the Labours of his Predecessors, such as a Catalogue of the *Harleian* Library will copiously afford him.

NOR is the Use of Catalogues of less Importance to those whom Curiosity has engaged in the Study of Literary History, and who think the intellectual Revolutions of the World more worthy of their Attention, than the Ravages of Tyrants, the Desolation of Kingdoms, the Rout of Armies, and the Fall of Empires. Those who are pleased with observing the first Birth of new Opinions, their Struggles against Opposition, their silent Progress under Persecution, their general Reception, and their gradual Decline, or sudden Extinction; those that amuse themselves with remarking the different Periods of human Knowledge, and observe how Darkness and Light succeed each other, by what Accident the most gloomy Nights of Ignorance have given Way to the Dawn of Science, and how Learning has languished and decayed for Want of Patronage and Regard, or been overborne by the Prevalence of fashionable Ignorance, or lost amidst the Tumults of Invasion and the Storms of Violence. All those, who desire any Knowledge of the Literary Transactions of past Ages, may find in Catalogues, like this, at least, such an Account as is given by Annalists and Chronologers of Civil History.

How the Knowledge of the Sacred Writings has been diffused, will be observed from the Catalogue of the various Editions of the Bible, from the first Impression by *Fust*, in 1462, to the present Time, in which will be contained the Polyglot Editions of *Spain*, *France*, and *England*, those of the Original *Hebrew*, the *Greek Septuagint*, and the *Latin Vulgate*, with the Versions which are now used in the remotest Parts of *Europe*, in the Country of the *Grisons*, in *Lithuania*, *Bohemia*, *Finland*, and *Iceland*.

WITH regard to the Attempts of the same Kind made in our own Country, there are few whose Expectations will not be exceeded by the Number of *English* Bibles, of which not one is forgotten, whether valuable for the Pomp and Beauty of the Impression, or for the Notes with which the Text is accompanied, or for any Controversy or Persecution that it produced, or for the Peculiarity of any single Passage. With the same Care have the various Editions of the Book of Common Prayer been selected, from which all the Alterations which have been made in it may be easily remarked.

AMONGST a great Number of *Roman* Missals and Breviaries, remarkable for the Beauty of their Cuts and Illuminations, will be found the *Masarabic* Missal and Breviary, that raised such Commotions in the Kingdom of *Spain*.

THE Controversial Treatises written in *England*, about the Time of the Reformation, have been diligently collected, with a Multitude of remarkable Tracts, single Sermons, and small Treatises, which, however worthy to be preserved, are perhaps to be found in no other Place.

THE Regard which was always paid, by the Collectors of this Library, to that remarkable Period of Time, in which the Art of Printing was invented, determined them to accumulate the ancient Impressions of the Fathers of the Church, to which the later Editions are added, lest Antiquity should have seemed more worthy of Esteem than Accuracy.

HISTORY has been considered with the Regard due to that Study by which the Manners are most easily formed, and from which the most efficacious Instruction is received, nor will the most extensive Curiosity fail of Gratification in this Library, from which no Writers have been excluded that relate either the Religious or Civil Affairs of any Nation.

NOT only those Authors of Ecclesiastical History have been procured, that treat of the State of Religion in general, or deliver Accounts of Sects or Nations, but those likewise who have confined themselves to particular Orders of Men in every Church, who have related the Original, and the Rules of every Society, or recounted the Lives of its Founder and its Members; those who have deduced in every Country the Succession of Bishops, and those who have employed their Abilities in celebrating the Piety of particular Saints, or Martyrs, or Monks, or Nuns.

THE Civil History of all Nations has been amassed together, nor is it easy to determine, which has been thought most worthy of Curiosity.

OF *France*, not only the general Histories and ancient Chronicles, the Accounts of celebrated Reigns, and Narratives of remarkable Events, but even the Memorials of single Families, the Lives of private Men, the Antiquities of particular Cities, Churches, and Monasteries, the Topography of Provinces, and the Accounts of Laws, Customs, and Prescriptions, are here to be found.

THE several States of *Italy* have, in this Treasury, their particular Historians, whose Accounts are, perhaps, generally more exact, by being less extensive, and more interesting, by being more particular.

NOR has less Regard been paid to the different Nations of the *Germanic* Empire, of which, neither the *Bohemians*, nor *Hungarians*, nor *Austrians*, nor *Bavarians*, have been neglected; nor have their Antiquities, however generally disregarded, been less studiously searched, than their present State.

THE Northern Nations have supplied this Collection, not only with History, but Poetry, with *Gothic* Antiquities, and *Runic* Inscriptions; which at least have this Claim to Veneration, above the Remains of the *Roman* Magnificence, that they are the Works of those Heroes, by whom the *Roman* Empire was destroyed, and which may plead, at least in this Nation, that they ought not to be neglected by those that owe to the Men whose Memories they preserve, their Constitution, their Properties, and their Liberties.

THE Curiosity of these Collectors extended equally to all Parts of the World; nor did they forget to add to the Northern the Southern Writers, or to adorn their Collection with Chronicles of *Spain*, and the Conquest of *Mexico*.

EVEN of those Nations with which we have less Intercourse, whose Customs are less accurately known, and whose History is less distinctly recounted, there are in this Library reposited such Accounts, as the *Europeans* have been hitherto able to obtain; nor are the *Mogul*, the *Tartar*, the *Turk*, and the *Saracen*, without their Historians.

THAT Persons so inquisitive, with regard to the Transactions of other Nations, should enquire yet more ardently after the History of their own, may be naturally expected, and, indeed, this Part of the Library is no common Instance of Diligence and Accuracy. Here are to be found with the ancient Chronicles, and larger Histories of *Britain*, the Narratives of single Reigns, and the Accounts of remarkable Revolutions, the topographical Histories of Counties, the Pedigrees of Families, the Antiquities of Churches and Cities, the Proceedings of Parliaments, the Records of Monasteries, and the Lives of particular Men, whether eminent in the Church or the State, or remarkable in private Life; whether exemplary for their Virtues, or detestable for their Crimes; whether persecuted for Religion, or executed for Rebellion.

THAT memorable Period of the *English* History, which begins with the Reign of King *Charles* the First, and ends with the Restoration, will almost furnish a Library alone, such is the Number of Volumes, Pamphlets, and Papers, which were published by either Party, and such is the Care with which they have been preserved.

NOR is History without the necessary Preparatives and Attendants, Geography and Chronology; of Geography, the best Writers and Delineators have been procured, and Pomp and Accuracy have both been regarded. The Student of Chronology may here find likewise those Authors who searched the Records of Time, and fixed the Periods of History.

WITH the Historians and Geographers, may be ranked the Writers of Voyages and Travels, which may be read here in the *Latin*, *English*, *Dutch*, *German*, *French*, *Italian*, and *Spanish* Languages.

THE Laws of different Countries, as they are in themselves equally worthy of Curiosity with their History, have, in this Collection, been justly regarded; and the Rules, by which the various Communities of the World are governed, may be here examined and compared. Here are the ancient Editions of the Papal Decretals, and the Commentators on the Civil Law, the Edicts of *Spain*, and the Statutes of *Venice*.

BUT, with particular Industry, have the various Writers on the Laws of our own Country been collected, from the most ancient to the present Time, from the Bodies of the Statutes to the minutest Treatise; not only the Reports, Precedents, and Readings of our own Courts, but even the Laws of our *West-Indian* Colonies will be exhibited in our Catalogue.

But neither History nor Law have been so far able to engross this Library, as to exclude Physic, Philosophy, or Criticism. These have been thought, with Justice, worthy of a Place, who have examined the different Species of Animals, delineated their Form, or described their Properties and Instincts, or who have penetrated the Bowels of the Earth, treated on its different *Strata*, and analysed its Metals; or who have amused themselves with less laborious Speculations, and planted Trees, or cultivated Flowers.

Those that have exalted their Thoughts above the minuter Parts of the Creation, who have observed the Motions of the Heavenly Bodies, and attempted Systems of the Universe, have not been denied the Honour which they deserved by so great an Attempt, whatever has been their Success. Nor have those Mathematicians been rejected, who have applied their Science to the common Purposes of Life, or those that have deviated into the kindred Arts, of Tactics, Architecture, and Fortification.

Even Arts of far less Importance have found their Authors, nor have these Authors been despised by the boundless Curiosity of the Proprietors of the *Harleian* Library. The Writers on Horsemanship and Fencing are more numerous, and more bulky, than could be expected, by those who reflect how seldom those excel in either, whom their Education has qualified to compose Books.

The Admirer of *Greek* and *Roman* Literature will meet, in this Collection, with Editions little known to the most inquisitive Critics, and which have escaped the Observation of those whose great Employment has been the Collation of Copies; nor will he find only the most ancient Editions of *Faustus*, *Jenson*, *Spira*, *Sweynheim*, and *Pannartz*, but the most accurate likewise and beautiful of *Colinæus*, the *Juntæ*, *Plantin*, *Aldus*, the *Stephens*, and *Elzevir*, with the Commentaries and Observations of the most learned Editors.

Nor are they accompanied only with the Illustrations of those who have confined their Attempts to particular Writers, but of those likewise who have treated on any Part of the *Greek* or *Roman* Antiquities, their Laws, their Customs, their Dress, their Buildings, their Wars, their Revenues, or the Rites and Ceremonies of their Worship, and those that have endeavoured to explain any of their Authors from their Statues or their Coins.

Next to the Ancients, those Writers deserve to be mentioned, who, at the Restoration of Literature, imitated their Language and their Stile with so great Success, or who laboured with so much Industry to make them understood: Such were *Philelphus* and *Politian*, *Scaliger* and *Buchanan*, and the Poets of the Age of *Leo* the Tenth; these are likewise to be found in this Library, together with the *Deliciæ*, or Collections of all Nations.

Painting is so nearly allied to Poetry, that it cannot be wondered that those who have so much esteemed the one, have paid an equal Regard to the other; and therefore it may be easily imagined, that the Collection of Prints is numerous in an uncommon Degree; but surely the Expectation of every Man will be exceeded, when he is informed that there are more than forty thousand engraven from *Raphael*, *Titian*, *Guido*, the *Carraches*, and a thousand others, by *Nautueil*, *Hollar*, *Callet*, *Edelinck*, and *Dorigny*, and other Engravers of equal Reputation.

THERE is also a great Collection of original Drawings of which three seem to deserve a particular Mention, the first exhibits a Representation of the Inside of St. *Peter*'s Church at *Rome*, the second, of that of St. *John Lateran*, and the third, of the high Altar of St. *Ignatius*, all painted with the utmost Accuracy in their proper Colours.

As the Value of this great Collection may be conceived from this Account, however imperfect, as the Variety of Subjects must engage the Curiosity of Men of different Studies, Inclinations, and Employments, it may be thought of very little Use to mention any slighter Advantages, or to dwell on the Decorations and Embellishments which the Generosity of the Proprietors has bestowed upon it; yet, since the Compiler of the *Thuanian* Catalogue thought not even that Species of Elegance below his Observation, it may not be improper to observe, that the *Harleian* Library, perhaps, excels all others, not more in the Number and Excellence, than in the Splendor of its Volumes.

WE may now surely be allowed to hope, that our Catalogue will be thought not unworthy of the Public Curiosity; that it will be purchased as a Record of this great Collection, and preserved as one of the Memorials of Learning.

THE Patrons of Literature will forgive the Purchaser of this Library, if he presumes to assert some Claim to their Protection and Encouragement, as he may have been instrumental in continuing to this Nation the Advantage of it. The Sale of *Vossius*'s Collection into a Foreign Country is, to this Day, regretted by Men of Letters; and, if this Effort for the Prevention of another Loss of the same Kind should be disadvantageous to him, no Man will hereafter willingly risque his Fortune in the Cause of Learning.

As it is imagined that the approaching Sale of so great and eminent a Collection will excite, in an uncommon Degree, the Curiosity of the Public, it is intended not only to receive Subscriptions, as already mentioned, but to publish this Catalogue in Twelve Numbers, by five Sheets a Week, at One Shilling each Number, of which the first will be delivered on *Saturday* the Fourth of *December*.

Letter to Edward Cave

AUTUMN 1743

Sir:

I believe I am going to write a long Letter, and have therefore taken a whole Sheet of Paper. The first thing to be written about is our Historical Design.

You mentioned the proposal of printing in Numbers as an alteration in the Scheme, but I believe You mistook some way or other, my meaning, I had no other view than that You might rather print too many of five Sheets than of five and thirty.

With regard to what I shall say on the manner of proceeding, I would have it understood as wholly indifferent to me, and my opinion only not my Resolution. *Emptoris sit eligere.*

I think the insertion of the exact dates of the most important events in the margin or of so many events as may enable the reader to regulate the order of facts with sufficient exactness the proper medium between a Journal which has regard only to time, and a history which ranges facts according to their dependence on each other, and postpones or anticipates according to the convenience of narration. I think our work ought to partake of the spirit of History which is contrary to minute exactness, and of the regularity of a Journal which is inconsistent with Spirit. For this Reason I neither admit numbers or dates nor reject them.

I am of your opinion with regard to placing most of the resolutions etc. in the Margin, and think we shall give the most complete account of Parliamentary proceedings that [can] be contrived. The Naked Papers without an Historical treatise interwoven, require some other Book to make them understood. I will date the succeeding parts with some exactness but, I think in the margin. You told me on Saturday that I had received money on this work and I find set down 13£, 2–6. reckoning the half Guinea, of last Saturday, as You hinted to me that you had many calls for Money, I would *not* press You too hard, and therefore shall desire only as I send it in two Guineas for a Sheet of Copy the rest You may pay me when it may be more convenient, and even by this Sheet payment I shall for some time be very expensive.

The Life of Savage I am ready to go upon and in great Primer and Pica Notes reckon on sending in half a Sheet a day, but the money for that shall likewise lye by in your hands till it is done.

With the debates shall I not have business enough? If I had but good Pens.—Towards Mr. Savage's Life what more have You got? I would willingly have his tryal etc. and know whether his Defence be at Bristol, and would have his Collection of Poems on account of the Preface—The Plain Dealer—All the Magazins that have any thing of his or relating to him. I thought my Letter would be long but it is now, ended and I am, Sir, Your etc.

SAM. JOHNSON

The Boy found me writing this, almost in the dark, when I could not quite easily read yours, I have reade the Latin—nothing in it is well.—

I had no notion of having any thing for the Inscription, I hope You don't think I kept it to extort a price. I could think on Nothing till today. If You could spare me another Guinea for the Hist. I should take it very kindly tonight, but if You do not shall not think it an injury—I am almost well again—

An Account of the Life of Mr Richard Savage

IT has been observed in all Ages, that the Advantages of Nature or of Fortune have contributed very little to the Promotion of Happiness; and that those whom the Splendor of their Rank, or the Extent of their Capacity, have placed upon the Summits of human Life, have not often given any just Occasion to Envy in those who look up to them from a lower Station. Whether it be that apparent Superiority incites great Designs, and great Designs are naturally liable to fatal Miscarriages, or that the general Lot of Mankind is Misery, and the Misfortunes of those whose Eminence drew upon them an universal Attention, have been more carefully recorded, because they were more generally observed, and have in reality been only more conspicuous than those of others, not more frequent, or more severe.

That Affluence and Power, Advantages extrinsic and adventitious, and therefore easily separable from those by whom they are possessed, should very often flatter the Mind with Expectations of Felicity which they cannot give, raises no Astonishment; but it seems rational to hope, that intellectual Greatness should produce better Effects, that Minds qualified for great Attainments should first endeavour their own Benefit, and that they who are most able to teach others the Way to Happiness, should with most Certainty follow it themselves.

But this Expectation, however plausible, has been very frequently disappointed. The Heroes of literary as well as civil History have been very often no less remarkable for what they have suffered, than for what they have atchieved; and Volumes have been written only to enumerate the Miseries of the Learned, and relate their unhappy Lives, and untimely Deaths.

To these mournful Narratives, I am about to add the Life of *Richard Savage*, a Man whose Writings entitle him to an eminent Rank in the Classes of Learning, and whose Misfortunes claim a Degree of Compassion, not always due to the unhappy, as they were often the Consequences of the Crimes of others, rather than his own.

In the Year 1697, *Anne* Countess of *Macclesfield* having lived for some Time upon very uneasy Terms with her Husband, thought a public Confession of Adultery the most obvious and expeditious Method of obtaining her Liberty, and therefore declared, that the Child, with which she was then great, was begotten by the Earl *Rivers*. This, as may be easily imagined, made her Husband no less desirous of a Separation than herself, and he prosecuted his Design in the most effectual Manner; for he applied not to the Ecclesiastical Courts for a Divorce, but to the Parliament for an Act, by which his Marriage might be dissolved, the nuptial Contract totally annulled, and the Children of his Wife illegitimated. This Act, after the usual Deliberation, he obtained, tho' without the Approbation of some, who considered Marriage as an Affair only

A N

ACCOUNT

OF THE

LIFE

OF

Mr *Richard Savage,*

Son of the Earl R I V E R S.

LONDON:

Printed for J. Roberts in *Warwick-Lane.*
M.DCC.XLIV.

FIGURE 3 *An Account of the Life of Mr Richard Savage,* title page (Bodl. 12 Θ 977). Courtesy of the Bodleian Library, University of Oxford.

cognizable by Ecclesiastical Judges; and on *March* 3d was separated from his Wife, whose Fortune, which was very great, was repaid her; and who having as well as her Husband the Liberty of making another Choice, was in a short Time married to Colonel *Bret*.

While the Earl of *Macclesfield* was prosecuting this Affair, his Wife was, on the tenth of *January* 1697–8, delivered of a Son, and the Earl *Rivers*, by appearing to consider him as his own, left none any Reason to doubt of the Sincerity of her Declaration; for he was his Godfather, and gave him his own Name, which was by his Direction inserted in the Register of *St. Andrew*'s Parish in *Holbourn*, but unfortunately left him to the Care of his Mother, whom, as she was now set free from her Husband, he probably imagined likely to treat with great Tenderness the Child that had contributed to so pleasing an Event. It is not indeed easy to discover what Motives could be found to over-balance that natural Affection of a Parent, or what Interest could be promoted by Neglect or Cruelty. The Dread of Shame or of Poverty, by which some Wretches have been incited to abandon or to murder their Children, cannot be supposed to have affected a Woman who had proclaimed her Crimes and solicited Reproach, and on whom the Clemency of the Legislature had undeservedly bestowed a Fortune, which would have been very little diminished by the Expences which the Care of her Child could have brought upon her. It was therefore not likely that she would be wicked without Temptation, that she would look upon her Son from his Birth with a kind of Resentment and Abhorrence; and instead of supporting, assisting, and defending him, delight to see him struggling with Misery, or that she would take every Opportunity of aggravating his Misfortunes, and obstructing his Resources, and with an implacable and restless Cruelty continue her Persecution from the first Hour of his Life to the last.

But whatever were her Motives, no sooner was her Son born, than she discovered a Resolution of disowning him; and in a very short Time removed him from her Sight, by committing him to the Care of a poor Woman, whom she directed to educate him as her own, and injoined never to inform him of his true Parents.

Such was the Begining of the Life of *Richard Savage:* Born with a legal Claim to Honour and to Affluence, he was in two Months illegitimated by the Parliament, and disowned by his Mother, doomed to Poverty and Obscurity, and launched upon the Ocean of Life, only that he might be swallowed by its Quicksands, or dashed upon its Rocks.

His Mother could not indeed infect others with the same Cruelty. As it was impossible to avoid the Inquiries which the Curiosity or Tenderness of her Relations made after her Child, she was obliged to give some Account of the Measures that she had taken, and her Mother, the Lady *Mason*, whether in Approbation of her Design, or to prevent more criminal Contrivances, engaged to transact with the Nurse, to pay her for her Care, and to superintend the Education of the Child.

In this charitable Office she was assisted by his Godmother Mrs. *Loyd*, who while she lived always looked upon him with that Tenderness, which the Barbarity of his Mother made peculiarly necessary; but her Death, which happened in his tenth Year, was another of the Misfortunes of his Childhood; for though she kindly endeavoured to alleviate his Loss by a Legacy of three hundred Pounds, yet as he had none to prosecute his Claim, to shelter him from Oppression, or call in Law to the Assistance of Justice, her Will was eluded by the Executors, and no Part of the Money was ever paid.

He was however not yet wholly abandoned. The Lady *Mason* still continued her Care, and directed him to be placed at a small Grammar School near St. *Alban*'s, where he was called by the Name of his Nurse, without the least Intimation that he had a Claim to any other.

Here he was initiated in Literature, and passed through several of the Classes, with what Rapidity or what Applause cannot now be known. As he always spoke with Respect of his Master, it is probable that the mean Rank, in which he then appeared, did not hinder his Genius from being distinguished, or his Industry from being rewarded, and if in so low a State he obtained Distinction and Rewards, it is not likely that they were gained but by Genius and Industry.

It is very reasonable to conjecture, that his Application was equal to his Abilities, because his Improvement was more than proportioned to the Opportunities which he enjoyed; nor can it be doubted, that if his earliest Productions had been preserved, like those of happier Students, we might in some have found vigorous Sallies of that sprightly Humour, which distinguishes the *Author to be let*, and in others, strong Touches of that ardent Imagination which painted the solemn Scenes of *the Wanderer*.

While he was thus cultivating his Genius, his Father the Earl *Rivers* was seized with a Distemper, which in a short Time put an End to his Life. He had frequently inquired after his Son, and had always been amused with fallacious and evasive Answers; but being now in his own Opinion on his Death-bed, he thought it his Duty to provide for him among his other natural Children, and therefore demanded a positive Account of him, with an Importunity not to be diverted or denied. His Mother, who could no longer refuse an Answer, determined at least to give such as should cut him off for ever from that Happiness which Competence affords, and therefore declared that he was dead; which is perhaps the first Instance of a Lie invented by a Mother to deprive her Son of a Provision which was designed him by another, and which she could not expect herself, though he should lose it.

This was therefore an Act of Wickedness which could not be defeated, because it could not be suspected; the Earl did not imagine, that there could exist in a human Form a Mother that would ruin her Son without enriching herself, and therefore bestowed upon some other Person six thousand Pounds, which he had in his Will bequeathed to *Savage*.

The same Cruelty which incited his Mother to intercept this Provision which had been intended him, prompted her in a short Time to another Project, a Project worthy of such a Disposition. She endeavoured to rid herself from the Danger of being at any Time made known to him, by sending him secretly to the *American* Plantations.

By whose Kindness this Scheme was counteracted, or by what Interposition she was induced to lay aside her Design, I know not; it is not improbable that the Lady *Mason* might persuade or compel her to desist, or perhaps she could not easily find Accomplices wicked enough to concur in so cruel an Action; for it may be conceived, that those who had by a long Gradation of Guilt hardened their Hearts against the Sense of common Wickedness, would yet be shocked at the Design of a Mother to expose her Son to Slavery and Want, to expose him without Interest, and without Provocation; and *Savage* might on this Occasion find Protectors and Advocates among those who had long traded in Crimes, and whom Compassion had never touched before.

Being hindered, by whatever Means, from banishing him into another Country, she formed soon after a Scheme for burying him in Poverty and Obscurity in his own; and that his Station of Life, if not the Place of his Residence, might keep him for ever at a Distance from her, she ordered him to be placed with a Shoemaker in *Holbourn*, that after the usual Time of Trial, he might become his Apprentice.

It is generally reported, that this Project was for some time successful, and that *Savage* was employed at the Awl longer than he was willing to confess; nor was it perhaps any great Advantage to him, that an unexpected Discovery determined him to quit his Occupation.

About this Time his Nurse, who had always treated him as her own Son, died; and it was natural for him to take Care of those Effects which by her Death were, as he imagined, become his own; he therefore went to her House, opened her Boxes, and examined her Papers, among which he found some Letters written to her by the Lady *Mason*, which informed him of his Birth, and the Reasons for which it was concealed.

He was now no longer satisfied with the Employment which had been allotted him, but thought he had a Right to share the Affluence of his Mother, and therefore without Scruple applied to her as her Son, and made use of every Art to awaken her Tenderness, and attract her Regard. But neither his Letters, nor the Interposition of those Friends which his Merit or his Distress procured him, made any Impression upon her Mind: She still resolved to neglect, though she could no longer disown him.

It was to no Purpose that he frequently solicited her to admit him to see her; she avoided him with the most vigilant Precaution, and ordered him to be excluded from her House, by whomsoever he might be introduced, and what Reason soever he might give for entering it.

Savage was at the same Time so touched with the Discovery of his real Mother, that it was his frequent Practice to walk in the dark Evenings for several Hours before her Door, in Hopes of seeing her as she might come by Accident to the Window, or cross her Apartment with a Candle in her Hand.

But all his Assiduity and Tenderness were without Effect, for he could neither soften her Heart, nor open her Hand, and was reduced to the utmost Miseries of Want, while he was endeavouring to awaken the Affection of a Mother: He was therefore obliged to seek some other Means of Support, and having no Profession, became, by Necessity, an Author.

At this Time the Attention of all the literary World was engrossed by the *Bangorian* Controversy, which filled the Press with Pamphlets, and the Coffee-houses with Disputants. Of this Subject, as most popular, he made Choice for his first Attempt, and without any other Knowledge of the Question, than he had casually collected from Conversation, published a Poem against the Bishop.

What was the Success or Merit of this Performance I know not, it was probably lost among the innumerable Pamphlets to which that Dispute gave Occasion. Mr. *Savage* was himself in a little time ashamed of it, and endeavoured to suppress it, by destroying all the Copies that he could collect.

He then attempted a more gainful Kind of Writing, and in his eighteenth Year offered to the Stage a Comedy borrowed from a *Spanish* Plot, which was refused by the Players, and was therefore given by him to Mr. *Bullock*, who having more Interest, made some slight Alterations, and brought it upon the Stage, under the Title of *Woman's a Riddle*, but allowed the unhappy Author no Part of the Profit.

Not discouraged however at his Repulse, he wrote two Years afterwards *Love in a Veil*, another Comedy, borrowed likewise from the *Spanish*, but with little better Success than before; for though it was received and acted, yet it appeared so late in the Year, that the Author obtained no other Advantage from it, than the Acquaintance of Sir *Richard Steele*, and Mr. *Wilks*; by whom he was pitied, caressed, and relieved.

Sir *Richard Steele* having declared in his Favour with all the Ardour of Benevolence which constituted his Character, promoted his Interest with the utmost Zeal, related his Misfortunes, applauded his Merit, took all Opportunities of recommending him, and asserted that *the Inhumanity of his Mother had given him a Right to find every good Man his Father*.

Nor was Mr. *Savage* admitted to his Acquaintance only, but to his Confidence, of which he sometimes related an Instance too extraordinary to be omitted, as it affords a very just Idea of his Patron's Character.

He was once desired by Sir *Richard*, with an Air of the utmost Importance, to come very early to his House the next Morning. Mr. *Savage* came as he had promised, found the Chariot at the Door, and Sir *Richard* waiting for him, and ready to go out. What was intended, and whither they were to go,

Savage could not conjecture, and was not willing to enquire; but immediately seated himself with Sir *Richard*; the Coachman was ordered to drive, and they hurried with the utmost Expedition to *Hyde-park Corner*, where they stopped at a petty Tavern, and retired to a private Room. Sir *Richard* then informed him, that he intended to publish a Pamphlet, and that he had desired him to come thither that he might write for him. They soon sat down to the Work, Sir *Richard* dictated, and *Savage* wrote, till the Dinner that had been ordered was put upon the Table. *Savage* was surprised at the Meanness of the Entertainment, and after some Hesitation, ventured to ask for Wine, which Sir *Richard*, not without Reluctance, ordered to be brought. They then finished their Dinner, and proceeded in their Pamphlet, which they concluded in the Afternoon.

Mr. *Savage* then imagined his Task over, and expected that Sir *Richard* would call for the Reckoning, and return home; but his Expectations deceived him, for Sir *Richard* told him, that he was without Money, and that the Pamphlet must be sold before the Dinner could be paid for; and *Savage* was therefore obliged to go and offer their new Production to Sale for two Guineas, which with some Difficulty he obtained. Sir *Richard* then returned home, having retired that Day only to avoid his Creditors, and composed the Pamphlet only to discharge his Reckoning.

Mr. *Savage* related another Fact equally uncommon, which, though it has no Relation to his Life, ought to be preserved. Sir *Richard Steele* having one Day invited to his House a great Number of Persons of the first Quality, they were surprised at the Number of Liveries which surrounded the Table; and after Dinner, when Wine and Mirth had set them free from the Observation of rigid Ceremony, one of them enquired of Sir *Richard*, how such an expensive Train of Domestics could be consistent with his Fortune. Sir *Richard* very frankly confessed, that they were Fellows of whom he would very willingly be rid. And being then asked, why he did not discharge them, declared that they were Bailiffs who had introduced themselves with an Execution, and whom, since he could not send them away, he had thought it convenient to embellish with Liveries, that they might do him Credit while they staid.

His Friends were diverted with the Expedient, and by paying the Debt discharged their Attendance, having obliged Sir *Richard* to promise that they should never again find him graced with a Retinue of the same Kind.

Under such a Tutor, Mr. *Savage* was not likely to learn Prudence or Frugality, and perhaps many of the Misfortunes which the Want of those Virtues brought upon him in the following Parts of his Life, might be justly imputed to so unimproving an Example.

Nor did the Kindness of Sir *Richard* end in common Favours. He proposed to have established him in some settled Scheme of Life, and to have contracted a Kind of Alliance with him, by marrying him to a natural Daughter; on whom he intended to bestow a thousand Pounds. But though he was always lavish of future Bounties, he conducted his Affairs in such a Manner, that he was very seldom able to keep his Promises, or execute his own Intentions; and as he was never able to raise the Sum which he had offered, the Marriage was delayed. In the mean time he was officiously informed that Mr. *Savage* had ridiculed him; by which he was so much exasperated, that he withdrew the Allowance which he had paid him, and never afterwards admitted him to his House.

It is not indeed unlikely that *Savage* might by his Imprudence expose himself to the Malice of a Tale-bearer; for his Patron had many Follies, which as his Discernment easily discovered, his Imagination might sometimes incite him to mention too ludicrously. A little Knowledge of the World is sufficient to discover that such Weakness is very common, and that there are few who do not sometimes in the Wantonness of thoughtless Mirth, or the Heat of transient Resentment, speak of their Friends and Benefactors with Levity and Contempt, though in their cooler Moments, they want neither Sense of their Kindness, nor Reverence for their Virtue. The Fault therefore of Mr. *Savage* was rather Negligence than Ingratitude; but Sir *Richard* must likewise be acquitted of Severity, for who is there that can patiently bear Contempt from one whom he has relieved and supported, whose Establishment he has laboured, and whose Interest he has promoted?

He was now again abandoned to Fortune, without any other Friend than Mr. *Wilks*; a Man, who, whatever were his Abilities or Skill as an Actor, deserves at least to be remembered for his Virtues, which are not often to be found in the World, and perhaps less often in his Profession than in others. To be humane, generous and candid, is a very high Degree of Merit in any State; but those Qualities deserve still greater Praise, when they are found in that Condition, which makes almost every other Man, for whatever Reason, contemptuous, insolent, petulant, selfish, and brutal.

As Mr. *Wilks* was one of those to whom Calamity seldom complained without Relief, he naturally took an unfortunate Wit into his Protection, and not only assisted him in any casual Distresses, but continued an equal and steady Kindness to the Time of his Death.

By his Interposition Mr. *Savage* once obtained from his Mother fifty Pounds, and a Promise of one hundred and fifty more; but it was the Fate of this unhappy Man, that few Promises of any Advantage to him were performed. His Mother was infected among others with the general Madness of the *South-Sea* Traffick, and having been disappointed in her Expectations, refused to pay what perhaps nothing but the Prospect of sudden Affluence prompted her to promise.

Being thus obliged to depend upon the Friendship of Mr. *Wilks*, he was consequently an assiduous Frequenter of the Theatres, and in a short Time the Amusements of the Stage took such Possession of his Mind, that he never was absent from a Play in several Years.

This constant Attendance naturally procured him the Acquaintance of the Players, and among others, of Mrs. *Oldfield*, who was so much pleased with his Conversation, and touched with his Misfortunes, that she allowed him a settled Pension of fifty Pounds a Year, which was during her Life regularly paid.

That this Act of Generosity may receive it's due Praise, and that the good Actions of Mrs. *Oldfield* may not be sullied by her general Character, it is proper to mention what Mr. *Savage* often declared in the strongest Terms, that he never saw her alone, or in any other Place than behind the Scenes.

At her Death, he endeavoured to shew his Gratitude in the most decent Manner, by wearing Mourning as for a Mother, but did not celebrate her in Elegies, because he knew that too great Profusion of Praise would only have revived those Faults which his natural Equity did not allow him to think less, because they were committed by one who favoured him; but of which, though his Virtue would not endeavour to palliate them, his Gratitude would not suffer him to prolong the Memory, or diffuse the Censure.

In his *Wanderer*, he has indeed taken an Opportunity of mentioning her, but celebrates her not for her Virtue, but her Beauty, an Excellence which none ever denied her: This is the only Encomium with which he has rewarded her Liberality, and perhaps he has even in this been too lavish of his Praise. He seems to have thought that never to mention his Benefactress, would have an Appearance of Ingratitude, though to have dedicated any particular Performance to her Memory, would have only betrayed an officious Partiality, that without exalting her Character, would have depressed his own.

He had sometimes, by the Kindness of Mr. *Wilks*, the Advantage of a Benefit, on which Occasions he often received uncommon Marks of Regard and Compassion; and was once told by the Duke of *Dorset*, that it was just to consider him as an injured Nobleman, and that in his Opinion the Nobility ought to think themselves obliged without Solicitation to take every Opportunity of supporting him by their Countenance and Patronage. But he had generally the Mortification to hear that the whole Interest of his Mother was employed to frustrate his Applications, and that she never left any Expedient untried, by which he might be cut off from the Possibility of supporting Life. The same Disposition she endeavoured to diffuse among all those over whom Nature or Fortune gave her any Influence, and indeed succeeded too well in her Design; but could not always propagate her Effrontery with her Cruelty, for some of those whom she incited against him, were ashamed of their own Conduct, and boasted of that Relief which they never gave him.

In this Censure I do not indiscriminately involve all his Relations; for he has mentioned with Gratitude the Humanity of one Lady, whose Name I am now unable to recollect, and to whom therefore I cannot pay the Praises which she deserves for having acted well in Opposition to Influence, Precept, and Example.

The Punishment which our Laws inflict upon those Parents who murder their Infants, is well known, nor has its Justice ever been contested; but if they deserve Death who destroy a Child in it's Birth, what Pains can be severe enough for her who forbears to destroy him only to inflict sharper Miseries upon him; who prolongs his Life only to make it miserable; and who exposes him without Care and without Pity, to the Malice of Oppression, the Caprices of Chance, and the Temptations of Poverty; who rejoices to see him overwhelmed with Calamities; and when his own Industry, or the Charity of others, has enabled him to rise for a short Time above his Miseries, plunges him again into his former Distress?

The Kindness of his Friends not affording him any constant Supply, and the Prospect of improving his Fortune, by enlarging his Acquaintance, necessarily leading him to Places of Expence, he found it necessary to endeavour once more at dramatic Poetry, for which he was now better qualified by a more extensive Knowledge, and longer Observation. But having been unsuccessful in Comedy, though rather for Want of Opportunities than Genius, he resolved now to try whether he should not be more fortunate in exhibiting a Tragedy.

The Story which he chose for the Subject, was that of Sir *Thomas Overbury*, a Story well adapted to the Stage, though perhaps not far enough removed from the present Age, to admit properly the Fictions necessary to complete the Plan; for the Mind which naturally loves Truth is always most offended with the Violation of those Truths of which we are most certain, and we of course conceive those Facts most certain which approach nearest to our own Time.

Out of this Story he formed a Tragedy, which, if the Circumstances in which he wrote it be considered, will afford at once an uncommon Proof of Strength of Genius, and Evenness of Mind, of a Serenity not to be ruffled, and an Imagination not to be suppressed.

During a considerable Part of the Time, in which his was employed upon this Performance, he was without Lodging, and often without Meat; nor had he any other Conveniences for Study than the Fields or the Street allowed him, there he used to walk and form his Speeches, and afterwards step into a Shop, beg for a few Moments the Use of the Pen and Ink, and write down what he had composed upon Paper which he had picked up by Accident.

If the Performance of a Writer thus distressed is not perfect, its Faults ought surely to be imputed to a Cause very different from Want of Genius, and must rather excite Pity than provoke Censure.

But when under these Discouragements the Tragedy was finished, there yet remained the Labour of introducing it on the Stage, an Undertaking which to an ingenuous Mind was in a very high Degree vexatious and disgusting; for having little Interest or Reputation, he was obliged to submit himself wholly to the Players, and admit, with whatever Reluctance, the Emendations of Mr. *Cibber*, which he always considered as the Disgrace of his Performance.

He had indeed in Mr. *Hill* another Critic of a very different Class, from whose Friendship he received great Assistance on many Occasions, and whom he never mentioned but with the utmost Tenderness and Regard. He had been for some Time distinguished by him with very particular Kindness, and on this Occasion it was natural to apply to him as an Author of an established Character. He therefore sent this Tragedy to him with a short Copy of Verses in which he desired his Correction. Mr. *Hill*, whose Humanity and Politeness are generally known, readily complied with his Request; but as he is remarkable for singularity of Sentiment, and bold Experiments in Language, Mr. *Savage* did not think his Play much improved by his Innovation, and had even at that Time the Courage to reject several Passages which he could not approve, and what is still more laudable, Mr. *Hill* had the Generosity not to resent the Neglect of his Alterations, but wrote the Prologue and Epilogue, in which he touches on the Circumstances of the Author with great Tenderness.

After all these Obstructions and Compliances, he was only able to bring his Play upon the Stage in the Summer, when the chief Actors had retired, and the rest were in Possession of the House for their own Advantage. Among these Mr. *Savage* was admitted to play the Part of Sir *Thomas Overbury*, by which he gained no great Reputation, the Theatre being a Province for which Nature seemed not to have designed him; for neither his Voice, Look, nor Gesture, were such as are expected on the Stage, and he was himself so much ashamed of having been reduced to appear as a Player, that he always blotted out his Name from the List, when a Copy of his Tragedy was to be shown to his Friends.

In the Publication of his Performance he was more successful, for the Rays of Genius that glimmered in it, that glimmered through all the Mists which Poverty and *Cibber* had been able to spread over it, procured him the Notice and Esteem of many Persons eminent for their Rank, their Virtue, and their Wit.

Of this Play, acted, printed, and dedicated, the accumulated Profits arose to an hundred Pounds, which he thought at that Time a very large Sum, having been never Master of so much before.

In the Dedication, for which he received ten Guineas, there is nothing remarkable. The Preface contains a very liberal Encomium on the blooming Excellencies of Mr. *Theophilus Cibber*, which Mr. *Savage* could not in the latter Part of his Life see his Friends about to read without snatching the Play out of their Hands.

The Generosity of Mr. *Hill* did not end on this Occasion; for afterwards when Mr. *Savage*'s Necessities returned, he encouraged a Subscription to a Miscellany of Poems in a very extraordinary Manner, by publishing his Story in the *Plain Dealer*, with some affecting Lines, which he asserts to have been written by Mr. *Savage* upon the Treatment received by him from his Mother, but of which he was himself the Author, as Mr. *Savage* afterwards declared.

These Lines, and the Paper in which they were inserted, had a very powerful Effect upon all but his Mother, whom by making her Cruelty more publick, they only hardened in her Aversion.

Mr. *Hill* not only promoted the Subscription to the Miscellany, but furnished likewise the greatest Part of the Poems of which it is composed, and particularly *the Happy Man*, which he published as a Specimen.

The Subscriptions of those whom these Papers should influence to patronise Merit in Distress, without any other Solicitation, were directed to be left at *Button*'s Coffee-house, and Mr. *Savage* going thither a few Days afterwards, without Expectation of any Effect from his Proposal, found to his Surprise seventy Guineas, which had been sent him in Consequence of the Compassion excited by Mr. *Hill*'s pathetic Representation.

To this Miscellany he wrote a Preface, in which he gives an Account of his Mother's Cruelty in a very uncommon Strain of Humour, and with a Gaiety of Imagination, which the Success of his Subscription probably produced.

The Dedication is addressed to the Lady *Mary Wortley Montague*, whom he flatters without Reserve, and, to confess the Truth, with very little Art. The same Observation may be extended to all his Dedications: his Compliments are constrained and violent, heaped together without the Grace of Order, or the Decency of Introduction: he seems to have written his Panegyrics for the Perusal only of his Patrons, and to have imagined that he had no other Task than to pamper them with Praises however gross, and that Flattery would make it's Way to the Heart, without the Assistance of Elegance or Invention.

Soon afterwards the Death of the King furnished a general Subject for a poetical Contest, in which Mr. *Savage* engaged, and is allowed to have carried the Prize of Honour from his Competitors; but I know not whether he gained by his Performance any other Advantage than the Increase of his Reputation; though it must certainly have been with farther Views that he prevailed upon himself to attempt a Species of Writing of which all the Topics had been long before exhausted, and which was made at once difficult by the Multitudes that had failed in it, and those that had succeeded.

He was now advancing in Reputation, and though frequently involved in very distressful Perplexities, appeared however to be gaining upon Mankind, when both his Fame and his Life were endangered by an Event, of which it is not yet determined, whether it ought to be mentioned as a Crime or a Calamity.

On the 20th of *November* 1727. Mr. *Savage* came from *Richmond*, where he then lodged that he might persue his Studies with less Interruption, with an Intent to discharge another Lodging which he had in *Westminster*, and accidentally meeting two Gentlemen his Acquaintances, whose Names were *Merchant* and *Gregory*, he went in with them to a neighbouring Coffee-house, and sat drinking till it was late, it being in no Time of Mr. *Savage*'s Life any Part of his Character to be the first of the Company that desired to separate.

He would willingly have gone to Bed in the same House, but there was not Room for the whole Company, and therefore they agreed to ramble about the Streets, and divert themselves with such Amusements as should offer themselves till Morning.

In their Walk they happened unluckily to discover Light in *Robinson*'s Coffee-house, near *Charing-Cross*, and therefore went in. *Merchant* with some Rudeness, demanded a Room, and was told that there was a good Fire in the next Parlour, which the Company were about to leave, being then paying their Reckoning. *Merchant* not satisfied with this Answer, rushed into the Room, and was followed by his Companions. He then petulantly placed himself between the Company and the Fire, and soon after kicked down the Table. This produced a Quarrel, Swords were drawn on both Sides, and one Mr. *James Sinclair* was killed. *Savage* having wounded likewise a Maid that held him, forced his way with *Merchant* out of the House; but being intimidated and confused, without Resolution either to fly or stay, they were taken in a back Court by one of the Company and some Soldiers, whom he had called to his Assistance.

Being secured and guarded that Night, they were in the Morning carried before three Justices, who committed them to the *Gatehouse*, from whence, upon the Death of Mr. *Sinclair*, which happened the same Day, they were removed in the Night to *Newgate*, where they were however treated with some Distinction, exempted from the Ignominy of Chains, and confined, not among the common Criminals, but in the *Press-Yard*.

When the Day of Trial came, the Court was crouded in a very unusual manner, and the Publick appeared to interest itself as in a Cause of general Concern. The Witnesses against Mr. *Savage* and his Friends were, the Woman who kept the House, which was a House of ill Fame, and her Maid, the Men who were in the Room with Mr. *Sinclair*, and a Woman of the Town, who had been drinking with them, and with whom one of them had been seen in Bed. They swore in general, that *Merchant* gave the Provocation, which *Savage* and *Gregory* drew their Swords to justify; that *Savage* drew first, and that he stabbed *Sinclair* when he was not in a Posture of Defence, or while *Gregory* commanded his Sword; that after he had given the Thrust he turned pale, and would have retired, but that the Maid clung round him, and one of the Company endeavoured to detain him, from whom he broke, by cutting the Maid on the Head, but was afterwards taken in a Court.

There was some Difference in their Depositions; one did not see *Savage* give the Wound, another saw it given when *Sinclair* held his Point towards the Ground; and the Woman of the Town asserted, that she did not see *Sinclair*'s Sword at all: This Difference however was very far from amounting to Inconsistency, but it was sufficient to shew, that the Hurry of the Dispute was such, that it was not easy to discover the Truth with relation to particular Circumstances, and that therefore some Deductions were to be made from the Credibility of the Testimonies.

Sinclair had declared several times before his Death, that he received his Wound from *Savage*, nor did *Savage* at his Trial deny the Fact, but endeavoured partly to extenuate it by urging the Suddenness of the whole Action, and the Impossibility of any ill Design, or premeditated Malice, and partly to justify it by the Necessity of Self-Defence, and the Hazard of his own Life, if he had lost that Opportunity of giving the Thrust: He observed, that neither Reason nor Law obliged a Man to wait for the Blow which was threatned, and which, if he should suffer it, he might never be able to return; that it was always allowable to prevent an Assault, and to preserve Life by taking away that of the Adversary, by whom it was endangered.

With regard to the Violence with which he endeavoured his Escape, he declared, that it was not his Design to fly from Justice, or decline a Trial, but to avoid the Expences and Severities of a Prison, and that he intended to have appeared at the Bar without Compulsion.

This Defence, which took up more than an Hour, was heard by the Multitude that thronged the Court with the most attentive and respectful Silence: Those who thought he ought not to be acquitted owned that Applause could not be refused him; and those who before pitied his Misfortunes, now reverenced his Abilities.

The Witnesses which appeared against him were proved to be Persons of Characters which did not entitle them to much Credit; a common Strumpet, a Woman by whom Strumpets were entertained, and a Man by whom they were supported; and the Character of *Savage* was by several Persons of Distinction asserted, to be that of a modest inoffensive Man, not inclined to Broils, or to Insolence, and who had, to that Time, been only known for his Misfortunes and his Wit.

Had his Audience been his Judges, he had undoubtedly been acquitted; but Mr. *Page*, who was then upon the Bench, treated him with his usual Insolence and Severity, and when he had summed up the Evidence, endeavoured to exasperate the Jury, as Mr. *Savage* used to relate it, with this eloquent Harangue.

"Gentlemen of the Jury, you are to consider, that Mr. *Savage* is a very great Man, a much greater Man than you or I, Gentlemen of the Jury; that he wears very fine Clothes, much finer Clothes than you or I, Gentlemen of the Jury; that he has abundance of Money in his Pocket, much more Money than you or I, Gentlemen of the Jury; but, Gentlemen of the Jury, is it not a very hard Case, Gentlemen of the Jury, that Mr. *Savage* should therefore kill you or me, Gentlemen of the Jury?"

Mr. *Savage* hearing his Defence thus misrepresented, and the Men who were to decide his Fate incited against him by invidious Comparisons, resolutely asserted, that his Cause was not candidly explained, and began to recapitulate what he had before said with regard to his Condition and the Necessity of endeavouring to escape the Expences of Imprisonment; but the

Judge having ordered him to be silent, and repeated his Orders without Effect, commanded that he should be taken from the Bar by Force.

The Jury then heard the Opinion of the Judge, that good Characters were of no Weight against positive Evidence, though they might turn the Scale, where it was doubtful; and that though when two Men attack each other, the Death of either is only Manslaughter; but where one is the Aggressor, as in the Case before them, and in Pursuance of his first Attack, kills the other, the Law supposes the Action, however sudden, to be malicious. They then deliberated upon their Verdict, and determined that Mr. *Savage* and Mr. *Gregory* were guilty of Murder, and Mr. *Merchant*, who had no Sword, only of Manslaughter.

Thus ended this memorable Trial, which lasted eight Hours. Mr. *Savage* and Mr. *Gregory* were conducted back to Prison, where they were more closely confined, and loaded with Irons of fifty Pounds Weight: Four Days afterwards they were sent back to the Court to receive Sentence; on which Occasion Mr. *Savage* made, as far as it could be retained in Memory, the following Speech.

"It is now, my Lord, too late to offer any Thing by way of Defence, or Vindication; nor can we expect ought from your Lordships, in this Court, but the Sentence which the Law requires you, as Judges, to pronounce against Men of our calamitous Condition.——But we are also persuaded, that as mere Men, and out of this Seat of rigorous Justice, you are susceptive of the tender Passions, and too humane, not to commiserate the unhappy Situation of those, whom the Law sometimes perhaps——exacts —— from you to pronounce upon. No doubt you distinguish between Offences, which arise out of Premeditation, and a Disposition habituated to Vice or Immorality, and Transgressions, which are the unhappy and unforeseen Effects of a casual Absence of Reason, and sudden Impulse of Passion: We therefore hope you will contribute all you can to an Extension of that Mercy, which the Gentlemen of the Jury have been pleased to shew Mr. *Merchant*, who (allowing Facts as sworn against us by the Evidence) has led us into this our Calamity. I hope, this will not be construed as if we meant to reflect upon that Gentleman, or remove any Thing from us upon him, or that we repine the more at our Fate, because he has no Participation of it: No, my Lord! For my Part, I declare nothing could more soften my Grief, than to be without any Companion in so great a Misfortune."

Mr. *Savage* had now no Hopes of Life, but from the Mercy of the Crown, which was very earnestly solicited by his Friends, and which, with whatever Difficulty the Story may obtain Belief, was obstructed only by his Mother.

To prejudice the Queen against him, she made use of an Incident, which was omitted in the order of Time, that it might be mentioned together with the Purpose which it was made to serve. Mr. *Savage*, when he had discovered his Birth, had an incessant Desire to speak to his Mother, who always avoided him in publick, and refused him Admission into her House. One Evening walking, as it was his Custom, in the Street that she inhabited, he saw the Door of her House by Accident open; he entered it, and finding no Persons in the Passage, to hinder him, went up Stairs to salute her. She discovered him before he could enter her Chamber, alarmed the Family with the most distressful Outcries, and when she had by her Screams gathered them about her, ordered them to drive out of the House that Villain, who had forced himself in upon her, and endeavoured to murder her. *Savage*, who had attempted with the most submissive Tenderness to soften her Rage, hearing her utter so detestable an Accusation, thought it prudent to retire, and, I believe, never attempted afterwards to speak to her.

But shocked as he was with her Falshood and her Cruelty, he imagined that she intended no other Use of her Lie, than to set herself free from his Embraces and Solicitations, and was very far from suspecting that she would treasure it in her Memory, as an Instrument of future Wickedness, or that she would endeavour for this fictitious Assault to deprive him of his Life.

But when the Queen was solicited for his Pardon, and informed of the severe Treatments which he had suffered from his Judge, she answered, that however unjustifiable might be the Manner of his Trial, or whatever Extenuation the Action for which he was condemned might admit, she could not think that Man a proper Object of the King's Mercy, who had been capable of entering his Mother's House in the Night, with an Intent to murder her.

By whom this atrocious Calumny had been transmitted to the Queen, whether she that invented, had the Front to relate it; whether she found any one weak enough to credit it, or corrupt enough to concur with her in her hateful Design, I know not; but Methods had been taken to persuade the Queen so strongly of the Truth of it, that she for a long Time refused to hear any of those who petitioned for his Life.

Thus had *Savage* perished by the Evidence of a Bawd, a Strumpet, and his Mother, had not Justice and Compassion procured him an Advocate of Rank too great to be rejected unheard, and of Virtue too eminent to be heard without being believed. His Merit and his Calamities happened to reach the Ear of the Countess of *Hertford*, who engaged in his Support with all the Tenderness that is excited by Pity, and all the Zeal which is kindled by Generosity, and demanding an Audience of the Queen, laid before her the whole Series of his Mother's Cruelty, exposed the Improbability of an Accusation by which he was charged with an Intent to commit a Murder, that could produce no Advantage, and soon convinced her how little his former Conduct could deserve to be mentioned as a Reason for extraordinary Severity.

The Interposition of this Lady was so successful, that he was soon after admitted to Bail, and on the 9th of *March* 1728, pleaded the King's Pardon.

It is natural to enquire upon what Motives his Mother could persecute him in a Manner so outragious and implacable; for what Reason she could employ all the Acts of Malice and all the Snares of Calumny, to take away the Life of her own Son, of a Son who never injured her, who was never supported by her Expence, nor obstructed any Prospect of Pleasure or Advantage; why she should endeavour to destroy him by a Lie; a Lie which could not gain Credit, but must vanish of itself at the first Moment of Examination, and of which only this can be said to make it probable, that it may be observed from her Conduct, that the most execrable Crimes are sometimes committed without apparent Temptation.

This Mother is still alive, and may perhaps even yet, though her Malice was so often defeated, enjoy the Pleasure of reflecting, that the Life which she often endeavoured to destroy, was at least shortened by her maternal Offices; that though she could not transport her Son to the Plantations, bury him in the Shop of a Mechanick, or hasten the Hand of the publick Executioner, she has yet had the Satisfaction of imbittering all his Hours, and forcing him into Exigencies, that hurried on his Death.

It is by no Means necessary to aggravate the Enormity of this Woman's Conduct, by placing it in Opposition to that of the Countess of *Hertford*; no one can fail to observe how much more amiable it is to relieve, than to oppress, and to rescue Innocence from Destruction, than to destroy without an Injury.

Mr. *Savage*, during his Imprisonment, his Trial, and the Time in which he lay under Sentence of Death, behaved with great Firmness and Equality of Mind, and confirmed by his Fortitude the Esteem of those, who before admired him for his Abilities. The peculiar Circumstances of his Life were made more generally known by a short Account, which was then published, and of which several thousands were in a few Weeks dispersed over the Nation; and the Compassion of Mankind operated so powerfully in his Favour, that he was enabled, by frequent Presents, not only to support himself, but to assist Mr. *Gregory* in Prison; and when he was pardoned and released he found the Number of his Friends not lessened.

The Nature of the Act for which he had been tried was in itself doubtful; of the Evidences which appeared against him, the Character of the Man was not unexceptionable, that of the Women notoriously infamous; she whose Testimony chiefly influenced the Jury to condemn him, afterwards retracted her Assertions. He always himself denied that he was drunk, as had been generally reported. Mr. *Gregory*, who is now Collector of *Antegua*, is said to declare him far less criminal than he was imagined, even by some who favoured him: And *Page* himself afterwards confessed, that he had treated him with uncommon Rigour. When all these Particulars are rated together, perhaps the Memory of *Savage* may not be much sullied by his Trial.

Some Time after he had obtained his Liberty, he met in the Street the Woman that had sworn with so much Malignity against him. She informed him, that she was in Distress, and, with a Degree of Confidence not easily attainable, desired him to relieve her. He, instead of insulting her Misery, and taking Pleasure in the Calamities of one who had brought his Life into Danger, reproved her gently for her Perjury, and changing the only Guinea that he had, divided it equally between her and himself.

This is an Action which in some Ages would have made a Saint, and perhaps in others a Hero, and which, without any hyperbolical Encomiums, must be allowed to be an Instance of uncommon Generosity, an Act of complicated Virtue; by which he at once relieved the Poor, corrected the Vicious, and forgave an Enemy; by which he at once remitted the strongest Provocations, and exercised the most ardent Charity.

Compassion was indeed the distinguishing Quality of *Savage*; he never appeared inclined to take Advantage of Weakness, to attack the defenceless, or to press upon the falling: whoever was distressed was certain at least of his Good-Wishes; and when he could give no Assistance, to extricate them from Misfortunes he endeavoured to sooth them by Sympathy and Tenderness.

But when his Heart was not softened by the Sight of Misery, he was sometimes obstinate in his Resentment, and did not quickly lose the Remembrance of an Injury. He always continued to speak with Anger of the Insolence and Partiality of *Page*, and a short Time before his Death revenged it by a Satire.

It is natural to enquire in what Terms Mr. *Savage* spoke of this fatal Action, when the Danger was over, and he was under no Necessity of using any Art to set his Conduct in the fairest Light. He was not willing to dwell upon it, and if he transiently mentioned it, appeared neither to consider himself as a Murderer, nor as a Man wholly free from the Guilt of Blood. How much and how long he regretted it, appeared in a Poem which he published many Years afterwards. On Occasion of a Copy of Verses in which the Failings of good Men were recounted, and in which the Author had endeavoured to illustrate his Position, that *the best may sometimes deviate from Virtue*, by an Instance of Murder committed by *Savage* in the Heat of Wine, *Savage* remarked, that it was no very just Representation of a good Man, to suppose him liable to Drunkenness, and disposed in his Riots to cut Throats.

He was now indeed at Liberty, but was, as before, without any other Support than accidental Favours and uncertain Patronage afforded him; Sources by which he was sometimes very liberally supplied, and which at other Times were suddenly stopped; so that he spent his Life between Want and Plenty, or what was yet worse, between Beggary and Extravagance; for as whatever he received was the Gift of Chance, which might as well favour him at one Time as another, he was tempted to squander what he had, because he always hoped to be immediately supplied.

Another Cause of his Profusion was the absurd Kindness of his Friends, who at once rewarded and enjoyed his Abilities, by treating him at Taverns, and habituated him to Pleasures which he could not afford to enjoy, and which he was not able to deny himself, though he purchased the Luxury of a single Night by the Anguish of Cold and Hunger for a Week.

The Experience of these Inconveniences determined him to endeavour after some settled Income, which, having long found Submission and Intreaties fruitless, he attempted to extort from his Mother by rougher Methods. He had now, as he acknowledged, lost that Tenderness for her, which the whole Series of her Cruelty had not been able wholly to repress, till he found, by the Efforts which she made for his Destruction, that she was not content with refusing to assist him, and being neutral in his Struggles with Poverty, but was as ready to snatch every Opportunity of adding to his Misfortunes, and that she was to be considered as an Enemy implacably malicious, whom nothing but his Blood could satisfy. He therefore threatned to harass her with Lampoons, and to publish a copious Narrative of her Conduct, unless she consented to purchase an Exemption from Infamy, by allowing him a Pension.

This Expedient proved successful. Whether Shame still survived, though Virtue was extinct, or whether her Relations had more Delicacy than herself, and imagined that some of the Darts which Satire might point at her would glance upon them: Lord *Tyrconnel*, whatever were his Motives, upon his Promise to lay aside his Design of exposing the Cruelty of his Mother, received him into his Family, treated him as his Equal, and engaged to allow him a Pension of two hundred Pounds a Year.

This was the Golden Part of Mr. *Savage*'s Life; and for some Time he had no Reason to complain of Fortune; his Appearance was splendid, his Expences large, and his Acquaintance extensive. He was courted by all who endeavoured to be thought Men of Genius, and caressed by all who valued themselves upon a refined Taste. To admire Mr. *Savage* was a Proof of Discernment, and to be acquainted with him was a Title to poetical Reputation. His Presence was sufficient to make any Place of publick Entertainment popular; and his Approbation and Example constituted the Fashion. So powerful is Genius, when it is invested with the Glitter of Affluence; Men willingly pay to Fortune that Regard which they owe to Merit, and are pleased when they have an Opportunity at once of gratifying their Vanity, and practising their Duty.

This Interval of Prosperity furnished him with Opportunities of enlarging his Knowledge of human Nature, by contemplating Life from it's highest Gradations to it's lowest, and had he afterwards applied to Dramatic Poetry, he would perhaps not have had many Superiors; for as he never suffered any Scene to pass before his Eyes without Notice, he had treasured in his Mind all the different Combinations of Passions, and the innumerable Mixtures of Vice and Virtue, which distinguish one Character from another; and as his Conception was strong, his Expressions were clear, he easily received Impressions from Objects, and very forcibly transmitted them to others.

Of his exact Observations on human Life he has left a Proof, which would do Honour to the greatest Names, in a small Pamphlet, called, *The Author to be let*, where he introduces *Iscariot Hackney*, a prostitute Scribler, giving an Account of his Birth, his Education, his Disposition and Morals, Habits of

Life and Maxims of Conduct. In the Introduction are related many secret Histories of the petty Writers of that Time, but sometimes mixed with ungenerous Reflections on their Birth, their Circumstances, or those of their Relations; nor can it be denied, that some Passages are such as *Iscariot Hackney* might himself have produced.

He was accused likewise of living in an Appearance of Friendship with some whom he satirised, and of making use of the Confidence which he gained by a seeming Kindness to discover Failings and expose them; it must be confessed, that Mr. *Savage*'s Esteem was no very certain Possession, and that he would lampoon at one Time those whom he had praised at another.

It may be alledged, that the same Man may change his Principles, and that he who was once deservedly commended, may be afterwards satirised with equal Justice, or that the Poet was dazzled with the Appearance of Virtue, and found the Man whom he had celebrated, when he had an Opportunity of examining him more nearly, unworthy of the Panegyric which he had too hastily bestowed; and that as a false Satire ought to be recanted, for the sake of him whose Reputation may be injured, false Praise ought likewise to be obviated, lest the Distinction between Vice and Virtue should be lost, lest a bad Man should be trusted upon the Credit of his Encomiast or lest others should endeavour to obtain the like Praises by the same Means.

But though these Excuses may be often plausible, and sometimes just, they are very seldom satisfactory to Mankind; and the Writer, who is not constant to his Subject, quickly sinks into Contempt, his Satire loses its Force, and his Panegyric its Value, and he is only considered at one Time as a Flatterer, and as a Calumniator at another.

To avoid these Imputations, it is only necessary to follow the Rules of Virtue, and to preserve an unvaried Regard to Truth. For though it is undoubtedly possible, that a Man, however cautious, may be sometimes deceived by an artful Appearance of Virtue, or by false Evidences of Guilt, such Errors will not be frequent; and it will be allowed, that the Name of an Author would never have been made contemptible, had no Man ever said what he did not think, or misled others, but when he was himself deceived.

The *Author to be let* was first published in a single Pamphlet, and afterwards inserted in a Collection of Pieces relating to the *Dunciad*, which were addressed by Mr. *Savage* to the Earl of *Middlesex*, in a Dedication, which he was prevailed upon to sign, though he did not write it, and in which there are some Positions, that the true Author would perhaps not have published under his own Name; and on which Mr. *Savage* afterwards reflected with no great Satisfaction.

The Enumeration of the bad Effects of the *uncontrolled Freedom of the Press*, and the Assertion that the *Liberties taken by the Writers of Journals with their Superiors were exorbitant and unjustifiable*, very ill became Men, who have themselves not always shewn the exactest Regard to the Laws of Subordination in their Writings, and who have often satirised those that at least thought themselves their Superiors, as they were eminent for their hereditary Rank, and employed in the highest Offices of the Kingdom. But this is only an Instance of that Partiality which almost every Man indulges with Regard to himself; the Liberty of the Press is a Blessing when we are inclined to write against others, and a Calamity when we find ourselves overborn by the Multitude of our Assailants; as the Power of the Crown is always thought too great by those who suffer by it's Influence, and too little by those in whose Favour it is exerted; and a Standing Army is generally accounted necessary by those who command, and dangerous and oppressive by those who support it.

Mr. *Savage* was likewise very far from believing, that the Letters annexed to each Species of bad Poets in the *Bathos*, were, as he was directed to assert, *set down at Random*; for when he was charged by one of his Friends with putting his Name to such an Improbability, he had no other Answer to make, than that *he did not think of it*, and his Friend had too much Tenderness to reply, that next to the Crime of writing contrary to what he thought, was that of writing without thinking.

After having remarked what is false in this Dedication, it is proper that I observe the Impartiality which I recommend, by declaring what *Savage* asserted, that the Account of the Circumstances which attended the Publication of the *Dunciad*, however strange and improbable, was exactly true.

The Publication of this Piece at this Time raised Mr. *Savage* a great Number of Enemies among those that were attacked by Mr. *Pope*, with whom he was considered as a Kind of Confederate, and whom he was suspected of supplying with private Intelligence and secret Incidents: So that the Ignominy of an Informer was added to the Terror of a Satirist.

That he was not altogether free from literary Hypocrisy, and that he sometimes spoke one thing, and wrote another, cannot be denied, because he himself confessed, that when he lived in great Familiarity with *Dennis*, he wrote an Epigram against him.

Mr. *Savage* however set all the Malice of all the pigmy Writers at Defiance, and thought the Friendship of Mr. *Pope* cheaply purchased by being exposed to their Censure and their Hatred; nor had he any Reason to repent of the Preference, for he found Mr. *Pope* a steady and unalienable Friend almost to the End of his Life.

About this Time, notwithstanding his avowed Neutrality with regard to Party, he published a Panegyric on Sir *Robert Walpole*, for which he was rewarded by him with twenty Guineas, a Sum not very large, if either the Excellence of the Performance, or the Affluence of the Patron be considered; but greater than he afterwards obtained from a Person of yet higher Rank, and more desirous in Appearance of being distinguished as a Patron of Literature.

As he was very far from approving the Conduct of Sir *Robert Walpole*, and in Conversation mentioned him sometimes with Acrimony, and generally with Contempt, as he was one of those who were always zealous in their Assertions of the Justice of the late Opposition, jealous of the Rights of the People, and alarmed by the long continued Triumph of the Court; it was natural to ask him what could induce him to employ his Poetry in Praise of that Man who was, in his Opinion, an Enemy to Liberty, and an Oppressor of his Country? He alleged, that he was then dependent upon the Lord *Tyrconnel*, who was an implicite Follower of the Ministry, and that being enjoined by him not without Menaces, to write in Praise of his Leader, he had not Resolution sufficient to sacrifice the Pleasure of Affluence to that of Integrity.

On this and on many other Occasions he was ready to lament the Misery of living at the Tables of other Men, which was his Fate from the Beginning to the End of his Life for I know not whether he ever had, for three Months together, a settled Habitation in which he could claim a Right of Residence.

To this unhappy State it is just to impute much of the Inconstancy of his Conduct; for though a Readiness to comply with the Inclination of others was no Part of his natural Character, yet he was sometimes obliged to relax his Obstinacy, and submit his own Judgment and even his Virtue to the Government of those by whom he was supported: So that if his Miseries were sometimes the Consequences of his Faults, he ought not yet to be wholly excluded from Compassion, because his Faults were very often the Effects of his Misfortunes.

In this gay Period of his Life, while he was surrounded by Affluence and Pleasure, he published the *Wanderer*, a moral Poem of which the Design is comprised in these Lines:

> I fly all public Care, all venal Strife,
> To try the *still* compar'd with *active Life*,
> To prove by these, the Sons of Men may owe
> The Fruits of Bliss to bursting Clouds of Woe;
> That even Calamity by Thought refin'd
> Inspirits and adorns the thinking Mind.

and more distinctly in the following Passage;

> By Woe the Soul to daring Action swells,
> By Woe in plaintless Patience it excels;
> From Patience prudent, clear Experience springs,
> And traces Knowledge through the Course of Things.
> Thence Hope is form'd, thence Fortitude, Success
> Renown—whate'er Men covet and caress.

This Performance was always considered by himself as his Master-piece, and Mr. *Pope* when he asked his Opinion of it, told him, that he read it once over, and was not displeased with it, that it gave him more Pleasure at the second Perusal, and delighted him still more at the third.

It has been generally objected to the *Wanderer*, that the Disposition of the Parts is irregular, that the Design is obscure, and the Plan perplexed, that the Images, however beautiful, succeed each other without Order; and that the whole Performance is not so much a regular Fabric as a Heap of shining Materials thrown together by Accident, which strikes rather with the solemn Magnificence of a stupendous Ruin, than the elegant Grandeur of a finished Pile.

This Criticism is universal, and therefore it is reasonable to believe it at least in a great Degree just; but Mr. *Savage* was always of a contrary Opinion, and thought his Drift could only be missed by Negligence or Stupidity, and that the whole Plan was regular, and the Parts distinct.

It was never denied to abound with strong Representations of Nature, and just Observations upon Life, and it may easily be observed, that most of his Pictures have an evident Tendency to illustrate his first great Position, *that Good is the Consequence of Evil.* The Sun that burns up the Mountains, fructifies the Vales, the Deluge that rushes down the broken Rocks with dreadful Impetuosity, is separated into purling Brooks; and the Rage of the Hurricane purifies the Air.

Even in this Poem he has not been able to forbear one Touch upon the Cruelty of his Mother, which though remarkably delicate and tender, is a Proof how deep an Impression it had made upon his Mind.

This must be at least acknowledged, which ought to be thought equivalent to many other Excellencies, that this Poem can promote no other Purposes than those of Virtue, and that it is written with a very strong Sense of the Efficacy of Religion.

But my Province is rather to give the History of Mr. *Savage*'s Performances, than to display their Beauties, or to obviate the Criticisms, which they have occasioned, and therefore I shall not dwell upon the particular Passages which deserve Applause: I shall neither show the Excellence of his Descriptions, nor expatiate on the terrific Portrait of *Suicide*, nor point out the artful Touches, by which he has distinguished the intellectual Features of the Rebels, who suffer Death in his last Canto. It is, however, proper to observe, that Mr. *Savage* always declared the Characters wholly fictitious, and without the least Allusion to any real Persons or Actions.

From a Poem so diligently laboured, and so successfully finished, it might be reasonably expected that he should have gained considerable Advantage; nor can it, without some Degree of Indignation and Concern, be told that he sold the Copy for ten Guineas, of which he afterwards returned two, that the two last Sheets of the Work might be reprinted, of which he had in his Absence intrusted the Correction to a Friend, who was too indolent to perform it with Accuracy.

A superstitious Regard to the Correction of his Sheets was one of Mr. *Savage*'s Peculiarities; he often altered, revised, recurred to his first Reading or Punctuation, and again adopted the Alteration; he was dubious and irresolute without End, as on a Question of the last Importance, and at last was seldom satisfied; the Intrusion or Omission of a Comma was sufficient to discompose him, and he would lament an Error of a single Letter as a heavy Calamity. In one of his Letters relating to an Impression of some Verses he remarks, that he had with regard to the Correction of the Proof *a Spell upon him*, and indeed the Anxiety, with which he dwelt upon the minutest and most trifling Niceties, deserved no other Name than that of Fascination.

That he sold so valuable a Performance for so small a Price was not to be imputed either to Necessity by which the Learned and Ingenious are often obliged to submit to very hard Conditions, or to Avarice by which the Booksellers are frequently incited to oppress that Genius by which they are supported, but to that intemperate Desire of Pleasure, and habitual Slavery to his Passions, which involved him in many Perplexities; he happened at that Time to be engaged in the Pursuit of some trifling Gratification, and being without Money for the present Occasion, sold his Poem to the first Bidder, and perhaps for the first Price that was proposed, and would probably have been content with less, if less had been offered him.

This Poem was addressed to the Lord *Tyrconnel* not only in the first Lines, but in a formal Dedication filled with the highest Strains of Panegyric, and the warmest Professions of Gratitude, but by no Means remarkable for Delicacy of Connection or Elegance of Stile.

These Praises in a short Time he found himself inclined to retract, being discarded by the Man on whom he had bestowed them, and whom he then immediately discovered not to have deserved them. Of this Quarrel, which every Day made more bitter, Lord *Tyrconnel* and Mr. *Savage* assigned very different Reasons, which might perhaps all in Reality concur, though they were not all convenient to be alleged by either Party. Lord *Tyrconnel* affirmed, that it was the constant Practice of Mr. *Savage*, to enter a Tavern with any Company that proposed it, drink the most expensive Wines, with great Profusion, and when the Reckoning was demanded, to be without Money: If, as it often happened, his Company were willing to defray his Part, the Affair ended, without any ill Consequences; but if they were refractory, and expected that the Wine should be paid for by him that drank it, his Method of Composition was, to take them with him to his own Apartment, assume the Government of the House, and order the Butler in an imperious Manner to set the best Wine in the Cellar before his Company, who often drank till they forgot the Respect due to the House in which they were entertained, indulged themselves in the utmost Extravagance of Merriment, practised the most licentious Frolics, and committed all the Outrages of Drunkenness.

Nor was this the only Charge which Lord *Tyrconnel* brought against him: Having given him a Collection of valuable Books, stamped with his own Arms, he had the Mortification to see them in a short Time exposed to Sale upon the Stalls, it being usual with Mr. *Savage*, when he wanted a small Sum, to take his Books to the Pawnbroker.

Whoever was acquainted with Mr. *Savage*, easily credited both these Accusations; for having been obliged from his first Entrance into the World to subsist upon Expedients, Affluence was not able to exalt him above them; and so much was he delighted with Wine and Conversation, and so long had he been accustomed to live by Chance, that he would at any time go to the Tavern, without Scruple, and trust for his Reckoning to the Liberality of his Company, and frequently of Company to whom he was very little known. This Conduct indeed very seldom drew upon him those Inconveniences that might be feared by any other Person, for his Conversation was so entertaining, and his Address so pleasing, that few thought the Pleasure which they received from him dearly purchased by paying for his Wine. It was his peculiar Happiness, that he scarcely ever found a Stranger, whom he did not leave a Friend; but it must likewise be added, that he had not often a Friend long, without obliging him to become a Stranger.

Mr. *Savage*, on the other Hand, declared, that Lord *Tyrconnel* quarrelled with him, because he would substract from his own Luxury and Extravagance what he had promised to allow him, and that his Resentment was only a Plea for the Violation of his Promise: He asserted that he had done nothing that ought to exclude him from that Subsistence which he thought not so much a Favour, as a Debt, since it was offered him upon Conditions, which he had never broken; and that his only Fault was, that he could not be supported with nothing.

He acknowledged, that Lord *Tyrconnel* often exhorted him to regulate his Method of Life, and not to spend all his Nights in Taverns, and that he appeared very desirous, that he would pass those Hours with him which he so freely bestowed upon others. This Demand Mr. *Savage* considered as a Censure of his Conduct, which he could never patiently bear; and which in the latter and cooler Part of his Life was so offensive to him, that he declared it as his Resolution, *to spurn that Friend who should presume to dictate to him*; and it is not likely, that in his earlier Years he received Admonitions with more Calmness.

He was likewise inclined to resent such Expectations, as tending to infringe his Liberty, of which he was very jealous when it was necessary to the Gratification of his Passions, and declared, that the Request was still more unreasonable, as the Company to which he was to have been confined was insupportably disagreeable. This Assertion affords another Instance of that Inconsistency of his Writings with his Conversation, which was so often to be observed. He forgot how lavishly he had, in his Dedication to the WANDERER, extolled the Delicacy and Penetration, the Humanity and Generosity, the Candour and Politeness of the Man, whom, when he no longer loved him, he declared to be a Wretch without Understanding, without Good-Nature, and without Justice; of whose Name he thought himself obliged to leave no Trace in any future Edition of his Writings; and accordingly blotted it out of that Copy of the *Wanderer* which was in his Hands.

During his Continuance with the Lord *Tyrconnel* he wrote *The Triumph of Health and Mirth*, on the Recovery of Lady *Tyrconnel* from a languishing Illness. This Performance is remarkable, not only for the Gayety of the Ideas, and the Melody of the Numbers, but for the agreeable Fiction upon which it is formed. *Mirth* overwhelmed with Sorrow, for the Sickness of her Favourite, takes a Flight in Quest of her Sister *Health*, whom she finds reclined upon the Brow of a lofty Mountain, amidst the Fragrance of perpetual Spring, with the Breezes of the Morning sporting about her. Being solicited by her Sister *Mirth*, she readily promises her Assistance, flies away in a Cloud, and impregnates the Waters of *Bath* with new Virtues, by which the Sickness of *Belinda* is relieved.

As the Reputation of his Abilities, the particular Circumstances of his Birth and Life, the Splendour of his Appearance, and the Distinction which was for some Time paid him by Lord *Tyrconnel*, intitled him to Familiarity with Persons of higher Rank, than those to whose Conversation he had been before admitted, he did not fail to gratify that Curiosity, which induced him to take a nearer View of those whom their Birth, their Employments, or their Fortunes, necessarily place at a Distance from the greatest Part of Mankind, and to examine, whether their Merit was magnified or diminished by the Medium through which it was contemplated; whether the Splendour with which they dazzled their Admirers, was inherent in themselves, or only reflected on them by the Objects that surrounded them; and whether great Men were selected for high Stations, or high Stations made great Men.

For this Purpose, he took all Opportunities of conversing familiarly with those who were most conspicuous at that Time, for their Power, or their Influence; he watched their looser Moments, and examined their domestic Behaviour, with that Acuteness which Nature had given him, and which the uncommon Variety of his Life had contributed to increase, and that Inquisitiveness which must always be produced in a vigorous Mind by an absolute Freedom from all pressing or domestic Engagements. His Discernment was quick, and therefore he soon found in every Person, and in every Affair, something that deserved Attention; he was supported by others, without any Care for himself, and was therefore at Leisure to pursue his Observations.

More Circumstances to constitute a Critic on human Life could not easily concur, nor indeed could any Man who assumed from accidental Advantages more Praise than he could justly claim from his real Merit, admit an Acquaintance more dangerous than that of *Savage*; of whom likewise it must be confessed, that Abilities really exalted above the common Level, or Virtue refined from

Passion, or Proof against Corruption could not easily find an abler Judge, or a warmer Advocate.

What was the Result of Mr. *Savage*'s Enquiry, though he was not much accustomed to conceal his Discoveries, it may not be entirely safe to relate, because the Persons whose Characters he criticised are powerful; and Power and Resentment are seldom Strangers; nor would it perhaps be wholly just, because what he asserted in Conversation might, though true in general, be heightened by some momentary Ardour of Imagination, and as it can be delivered only from Memory, may be imperfectly represented; so that the Picture at first aggravated, and then unskilfully copied, may be justly suspected to retain no great Resemblance of the Original.

It may however be observed, that he did not appear to have formed very elevated Ideas of those to whom the Administration of Affairs, or the Conduct of Parties, has been intrusted; who have been considered as the Advocates of the Crown, or the Guardians of the People, and who have obtained the most implicit Confidence, and the loudest Applauses. Of one particular Person, who has been at one Time so popular as to be generally esteemed, and at another so formidable as to be universally detested, he observed, that his Acquisitions had been small, or that his Capacity was narrow, and that the whole Range of his Mind was from Obscenity to Politics, and from Politics to Obscenity.

But the Opportunity of indulging his Speculations on great Characters was now at an End. He was banished from the Table of Lord *Tyrconnel*, and turned again adrift upon the World, without Prospect of finding quickly any other Harbour. As Prudence was not one of the Virtues by which he was distinguished, he had made no Provision against a Misfortune like this. And though it is not to be imagined, but that the Separation must for some Time have been preceded by Coldness, Peevishness, or Neglect, though it was undoubtedly the Consequence of accumulated Provocations on both Sides, yet every one that knew *Savage* will readily believe, that to him it was sudden as a Stroke of Thunder; that though he might have transiently suspected it, he had never suffered any Thought so unpleasing to sink into his Mind, but that he had driven it away by Amusements, or Dreams of future Felicity and Affluence, and had never taken any Measures by which he might prevent a Precipitation from Plenty to Indigence.

This Quarrel and Separation, and the Difficulties to which Mr. *Savage* was exposed by them, were soon known both to his Friends and Enemies; nor was it long before he perceived, from the Behaviour of both, how much is added to the Lustre of Genius, by the Ornaments of Wealth.

His Condition did not appear to excite much Compassion; for he had not always been careful to use the Advantages which he enjoyed with that Moderation, which ought to have been with more than usual Caution preserved by him, who knew, if he had reflected, that he was only a Dependant on the Bounty of another, whom he could expect to support him no longer than he endeavoured to preserve his Favour, by complying with his Inclinations, and whom he nevertheless set at Defiance, and was continually irritating by Negligence or Encroachments.

Examples need not be sought at any great Distance to prove that Superiority of Fortune has a natural Tendency to kindle Pride, and that Pride seldom fails to exert itself in Contempt and Insult; and if this is often the Effect of hereditary Wealth, and of Honours enjoyed only by the Merit of others, it is some Extenuation of any indecent Triumphs to which this unhappy Man may have been betrayed, that his Prosperity was heightened by the Force of Novelty, and made more intoxicating by a Sense of the Misery in which he had so long languished, and perhaps of the Insults which he had formerly born, and which he might now think himself entitled to revenge. It is too common for those who have unjustly suffered Pain, to inflict it likewise in their Turn, with the same Injustice, and to imagine that they have a Right to treat others as they have themselves been treated.

That Mr. *Savage* was too much elevated by any good Fortune is generally known; and some Passages of his Introduction to the *Author to be let* sufficiently shew, that he did not wholly refrain from such Satire as he afterwards thought very unjust, when he was exposed to it himself; for when he was afterwards ridiculed in the Character of a distressed Poet, he very easily discovered, that Distress was not a proper Subject for Merriment, or Topic of Invective. He was then able to discern that if Misery be the Effect of Virtue, it ought to be reverenced; if of Ill-Fortune, to be pitied; and if of Vice, not to be insulted, because it is perhaps itself a Punishment adequate to the Crime by which it was produced. And the Humanity of that Man can deserve no Panegyric, who is capable of reproaching a Criminal in the Hands of the Executioner.

But these Reflections, though they readily occurred to him in the first and last Parts of his Life, were, I am afraid, for a long Time forgotten; at least they were, like many other Maxims, treasured up in his Mind, rather for Shew than Use, and operated very little upon his Conduct, however elegantly he might sometimes explain, or however forcibly he might inculcate them.

His Degradation therefore from the Condition which he had enjoyed with such wanton Thoughtlessness, was considered by many as an Occasion of Triumph. Those who had before paid their Court to him, without Success, soon returned the Contempt which they had suffered, and they who had received Favours from him, for of such Favours as he could bestow he was very liberal, did not always remember them. So much more certain are the Effects of Resentment than of Gratitude: It is not only to many more pleasing to recollect those Faults which place others below them, than those Virtues by which they are themselves comparatively depressed; but it is likewise more easy to neglect, than to recompense; and though there are few who will practise a laborious Virtue, there will never be wanting Multitudes that will indulge an easy Vice.

Savage however was very little disturbed at the Marks of Contempt which his Ill-Fortune brought upon him, from those whom he never esteemed, and with whom he never considered himself as levelled by any Calamities; and though it was not without some Uneasiness, that he saw some, whose Friendship he valued, change their Behaviour; he yet observed their Coldness without much Emotion, considered them as the Slaves of Fortune and the Worshippers of Prosperity; and was more inclined to despise them, than to lament himself.

It does not appear, that after this Return of his Wants, he found Mankind equally favourable to him, as at his first Appearance in the World. His Story, though in Reality not less melancholy, was less affecting, because it was no longer new; it therefore procured him no new Friends, and those that had formerly relieved him thought they might now consign him to others. He was now likewise considered by many rather as criminal, than as unhappy; for the Friends of Lord *Tyrconnel* and of his Mother were sufficiently industrious to publish his Weaknesses, which were indeed very numerous, and nothing was forgotten that might make him either hateful or ridiculous.

It cannot but be imagined, that such Representations of his Faults must make great Numbers less sensible of his Distress; many who had only an Opportunity to hear one Part made no Scruple to propagate the Account which they received; many assisted their Circulation from Malice or Revenge, and perhaps many pretended to credit them, that they might with a better Grace withdraw their Regard, or withhold their Assistance.

Savage however was not one of those, who suffered himself to be injured without Resistance, nor was less diligent in exposing the Faults of Lord *Tyrconnel*, over whom he obtained at least this Advantage, that he drove him first to the Practice of Outrage and Violence; for he was so much provoked by the Wit and Virulence of *Savage*, that he came with a Number of Attendants, that did no Honour to his Courage, to beat him at a Coffee-House. But it happened that he had left the Place a few Minutes, and his Lordship had without Danger the Pleasure of boasting, how he would have treated him. Mr. *Savage* went next Day to repay his Visit at his own House, but was prevailed on by his Domestics, to retire without insisting upon seeing him.

Lord *Tyrconnel* was accused by Mr. *Savage* of some Actions, which scarcely any Provocations will be thought sufficient to justify; such as seizing what he had in his Lodgings, and other Instances of wanton Cruelty, by which he encreased the Distress of *Savage*, without any Advantage to himself.

These mutual Accusations were retorted on both Sides for many Years, with the utmost Degree of Virulence and Rage, and Time seemed rather to augment than diminish their Resentment; that the Anger of Mr. *Savage* should be kept alive is not strange, because he felt every Day the Consequences of the Quarrel, but it might reasonably have been hoped, that Lord *Tyrconnel* might have relented, and at length have forgot those Provocations, which, however they might have once inflamed him, had not in Reality much hurt him.

The Spirit of Mr. *Savage* indeed never suffered him to solicite a Reconciliation; he returned Reproach for Reproach, and Insult for Insult; his Superiority of Wit supplied the Disadvantages of his Fortune, and inabled him to form a Party, and prejudice great Numbers in his Favour.

But though this might be some Gratification of his Vanity, it afforded very little Relief to his Necessities, and he was very frequently reduced to uncommon Hardships, of which, however, he never made any mean or importunate Complaints, being formed rather to bear Misery with Fortitude, than enjoy Prosperity with Moderation.

He now thought himself again at Liberty to expose the Cruelty of his Mother, and therefore, I believe, about this Time, published *The Bastard*, a Poem remarkable for the vivacious Sallies of Thought in the Beginning, where he makes a pompous Enumeration of the imaginary Advantages of base Birth, and the pathetic Sentiments at the End, where he recounts the real Calamities which he suffered by the Crime of his Parents.

The Vigour and Spirit of the Verses, the peculiar Circumstances of the Author, the Novelty of the Subject, and the Notoriety of the Story, to which the Allusions are made, procured this Performance a very favourable Reception; great Numbers were immediately dispersed, and Editions were multiplied with unusual Rapidity.

One Circumstance attended the Publication, which *Savage* used to relate with great Satisfaction. His Mother, to whom the Poem was *with due Reverence* inscribed, happened then to be at *Bath*, where she could not conveniently retire from Censure, or conceal herself from Observation; and no sooner did the Reputation of the Poem begin to spread, than she heard it repeated in all Places of Concourse, nor could she enter the Assembly Rooms, or cross the Walks, without being saluted with some Lines from *The Bastard*.

This was perhaps the first Time that ever she discovered a Sense of Shame, and on this Occasion the Power of Wit was very conspicuous; the Wretch who had, without Scruple, proclaimed herself an Adulteress, and who had first endeavoured to starve her Son, then to transport him, and afterwards to hang him, was not able to bear the Representation of her own Conduct, but fled from Reproach, though she felt no Pain from Guilt, and left *Bath* with the utmost Haste, to shelter herself among the Crouds of *London*.

Thus *Savage* had the Satisfaction of finding, that though he could not reform his Mother, he could punish her, and that he did not always suffer alone.

The Pleasure which he received from this Increase of his poetical Reputation, was sufficient for some Time to over-balance the Miseries of Want, which this Performance did not much alleviate, for it was sold for a very trivial Sum to a Bookseller, who, though the Success was so uncommon, that five Impressions were sold, of which many were undoubtedly very numerous, had not Generosity sufficient to admit the unhappy Writer to any Part of the Profit.

The Sale of this Poem was always mentioned by Mr. *Savage* with the utmost Elevation of Heart, and referred to by him as an incontestable Proof of a general Acknowledgement of his Abilities. It was indeed the only Production of which he could justly boast a general Reception.

But though he did not lose the Opportunity which Success gave him of setting a high Rate on his Abilities, but paid due Deference to the Suffrages of Mankind when they were given in his Favour, he did not suffer his Esteem of himself to depend upon others, nor found anything sacred in the Voice of the People when they were inclined to censure him; he then readily shewed the Folly of expecting that the Publick should judge right, observed how slowly poetical Merit had often forced its Way into the World, he contented himself with the Applause of Men of Judgment; and was somewhat disposed to exclude all those from the Character of Men of Judgment, who did not applaud him.

But he was at other Times more favourable to Mankind, than to think them blind to the Beauties of his Works, and imputed the Slowness of their Sale to other Causes; either they were published at a Time when the Town was empty, or when the Attention of the Publick was engrossed by some Struggle in the Parliament, or some other Object of general Concern; or they were by the Neglect of the Publisher not diligently dispersed, or by his Avarice not advertised with sufficient Frequency. Address, or Industry, or Liberality, was always wanting; and the Blame was laid rather on any other Person than the Author.

By Arts like these, Arts which every Man practises in some Degree, and to which too much of the little Tranquillity of Life is to be ascribed, *Savage* was always able to live at Peace with himself. Had he indeed only made use of these Expedients to alleviate the Loss or Want of Fortune or Reputation, or any other Advantages, which it is not in Man's Power to bestow upon himself, they might have been justly mentioned as Instances of a philosophical Mind, and very properly proposed to the Imitation of Multitudes, who, for want of diverting their Imaginations with the same Dexterity, languish under Afflictions which might be easily removed.

It were doubtless to be wished, that Truth and Reason were universally prevalent; that every thing were esteemed according to its real Value; and that Men would secure themselves from being disappointed in their Endeavours after Happiness, by placing it only in Virtue, which is always to be obtained; but if adventitious and foreign Pleasures must be persued, it would be perhaps of some Benefit, since that Persuit must frequently be fruitless, if the Practice of *Savage* could be taught, that Folly might be an Antidote to Folly, and one Fallacy be obviated by another.

But the Danger of this pleasing Intoxication must not be concealed; nor indeed can any one, after having observed the Life of *Savage*, need to be cautioned against it. By imputing none of his Miseries to himself, he continued to act upon the same Principles, and to follow the same Path; was never made wiser by his Sufferings, nor preserved by one Misfortune from falling into another. He proceeded throughout his Life to tread the same Steps on the same Circle; always applauding his past Conduct, or at least forgetting it, to amuse himself with Phantoms of Happiness, which were dancing before him; and willingly turned his Eyes from the Light of Reason, when it would have discovered the Illusion, and shewn him, what he never wished to see, his real State.

He is even accused, after having lulled his Imagination with those ideal Opiates, of having tried the same Experiment upon his Conscience; and having accustomed himself to impute all Deviations from the right to foreign Causes, it is certain that he was upon every Occasion too easily reconciled to himself, and that he appeared very little to regret those Practices which had impaired his Reputation. The reigning Error of his Life was, that he mistook the Love for the Practice of Virtue, and was indeed not so much a good Man, as the Friend of Goodness.

This at least must be allowed him, that he always preserved a strong Sense of the Dignity, the Beauty and the Necessity of Virtue, and that he never contributed deliberately to spread Corruption amongst Mankind; his Actions, which were generally precipitate, were often blameable, but his Writings being the Productions of Study, uniformly tended to the Exaltation of the Mind, and the Propagation of Morality and Piety.

These Writings may improve Mankind, when his Failings shall be forgotten, and therefore he must be considered upon the whole as a Benefactor to the World; nor can his personal Example do any hurt, since whoever hears of his Faults, will hear of the Miseries which they brought upon him, and which would deserve less Pity, had not his Condition been such as made his Faults pardonable. He may be considered as a Child *exposed* to all the Temptations of Indigence, at an Age when Resolution was not yet strengthened by Conviction, nor Virtue confirmed by Habit; a Circumstance which in his *Bastard* he laments in a very affecting Manner.

> ——No Mother's Care
> Shielded my Infant Innocence with Prayer:
> No Father's guardian Hand my Youth maintain'd,
> Call'd forth my Virtues, and from Vice restrain'd.

The *Bastard*, however it might provoke or mortify his Mother, could not be expected to melt her to Compassion, so that he was still under the same Want of the Necessaries of Life, and he therefore exerted all the Interest, which his Wit, or his Birth, or his Misfortunes could procure, to obtain upon the Death of *Eusden* the Place of Poet Laureat, and prosecuted his Application with so much Diligence, that the King publickly declared it his Intention to bestow it upon him; but such was the Fate of *Savage*, that even the King, when he intended his Advantage, was disappointed in his Schemes; for the Lord Chamberlain, who has the Disposal of the Laurel as one of the Appendages of his Office, either did not know the King's Design, or did not approve it, or thought the Nomination of the Laureat an Encroachment upon his Rights, and therefore bestowed the Laurel upon *Colly Cibber*.

Mr. *Savage* thus disappointed took a Resolution of applying to the Queen, that having once given him Life, she would enable him to support it, and therefore published a short Poem on her Birth-Day, to which he gave the odd Title of *Volunteer Laureat*. The Event of this Essay he has himself related in the following Letter, which he prefixed to the Poem, when he afterwards reprinted it in the *Gentleman's Magazine*, from whence I have copied it intire, as this was one of the few Attempts in which Mr. *Savage* succeeded.

Mr. *Urban*,

In your Magazine for *February* you published the last *Volunteer Laureat*, written on a very melancholy Occasion, the Death of the Royal Patroness of Arts and Literature in general, and of the Author of that Poem in particular; I now send you the first that Mr. *Savage* wrote under that Title.——This Gentleman, notwithstanding a very considerable Interest, being, on the Death of Mr. *Eusden*, disappointed of the Laureat's Place, wrote the following Verses; which were no sooner published, but the late Queen sent to a Bookseller for them: The Author had not at that Time a Friend either to get him introduced, or his Poem presented at Court; yet such was the unspeakable Goodness of that Princess, that, notwithstanding this Act of Ceremony was wanting, in a few Days after Publication, Mr. *Savage* received a Bank-Bill of fifty Pounds, and a gracious Message from her Majesty, by the Lord *North* and *Guilford*, to this Effect: "That her Majesty was highly pleased with the Verses; that she took particularly kind his Lines there relating to the King; that he had Permission to write annually on the same Subject; and that he should yearly receive the like Present, till something better (which was her Majesty's Intention) could be done for him." After this he was permitted to present one of his annual Poems to her Majesty, had the Honour of kissing her Hand, and met with the most gracious Reception.

Your's, &*c*.

The *Volunteer Laureat*.

A Poem: On the Queen's Birth-Day. *Humbly addressed to her Majesty*.

Twice twenty tedious Moons have roll'd away,
Since Hope, kind Flatt'rer! tun'd my pensive Lay,
Whisp'ring, that you, who rais'd me from Despair,
Meant, by your Smiles, to make Life worth my Care;

With pitying Hand an Orphan's Tears to screen,
And o'er the motherless extend the Queen.
'Twill be—the Prophet guides the Poet's Strain!
Grief never touch'd a Heart like your's in vain:
Heav'n gave you Power, because you love to bless,
And pity, when you feel it, is Redress.   10
 Two Fathers join'd to rob my Claim of one!
My Mother too thought fit to have no Son!
The Senate next, whose Aid the helpless own,
Forgot my Infant Wrongs, and mine alone!
Yet Parents pitiless, nor Peers unkind,
Nor Titles lost, nor Woes mysterious join'd,
Strip me of Hope — by Heav'n thus lowly laid,
To find a *Pharoah*'s Daughter in the Shade.
 You cannot hear unmov'd, when Wrongs implore,
Your Heart is Woman, though your Mind be more;   20
Kind, like the Pow'r who gave you to our Pray'rs,
You would not lengthen Life to sharpen Cares:
They who a barren Leave to live bestow,
Snatch but from Death to sacrifice to Woe.
Hated by her, from whom my Life I drew,
Whence should I hope, if not from Heav'n and you?
Nor dare I groan beneath Affliction's Rod,
My Queen, my Mother; and my Father, God.
 The pitying Muses saw me Wit pursue,
A *Bastard Son*, alas! on that Side too,   30
Did not your Eyes exalt the Poet's Fire,
And what the Muse denies, the Queen inspire;
While rising thus your heavenly Soul to view,
I learn, how Angels think, by copying you.
 Great Princess! 'tis decreed—once ev'ry Year
I march uncall'd your Laureat Volunteer;
Thus shall your Poet his low Genius raise,
And charm the World with Truths too vast for Praise.
Nor need I dwell on Glories all your own,
Since surer Means to tempt your Smiles are known;   40
Your Poet shall allot your Lord his Part,
And paint him in his noblest Throne, your Heart.
 Is there a Greatness that adorns him best,
A rising Wish that ripens in his Breast?
Has he fore-meant some distant Age to bless,
Disarm Oppression, or expel Distress?
Plans he some Scheme to reconcile Mankind,

People the Seas, and busy ev'ry Wind?
Would he, by Pity, the deceiv'd reclaim,
And smile contending Factions into Shame?   50
Would his Example lend his Laws a Weight,
And breathe his own soft Morals o'er his State?
The Muse shall find it all, shall make it seen,
And teach the World his Praise, to charm his Queen.
    Such be the annual Truths my Verse imparts,
Nor frown, fair *Fav'rite* of a People's Hearts!
Happy if plac'd, perchance, beneath your Eye,
My Muse unpension'd might her Pinions try,
Fearless to fail, while you indulge her Flame,
And bid me proudly boast your Laureat's Name;   60
Renobled thus by Wreaths my Queen bestows,
I lose all Memory of Wrongs and Woes.

Such was the Performance, and such its Reception; a Reception which, though by no Means unkind, was yet not in the highest Degree generous: To chain down the Genius of a Writer to an annual Panegyric, shewed in the Queen too much Desire of hearing her own Praises, and a greater Regard to herself than to him on whom her Bounty was conferred. It was a kind of avaricious Generosity, by which Flattery was rather purchased than Genius rewarded.

Mrs. *Oldfield* had formerly given him the same Allowance with much more heroic Intention; she had no other View than to enable him to prosecute his Studies, and to set himself above the Want of Assistance, and was contented with doing good without stipulating for Encomiums.

Mr. *Savage* however was not at Liberty to make Exceptions, but was ravished with the Favours which he had received, and probably yet more with those which he was promised; he considered himself now as a Favourite of the Queen, and did not doubt but a few annual Poems would establish him in some profitable Employment.

He therefore assumed the Title of *Volunteer Laureat*, not without some Reprehensions from *Cibber*, who informed him, that the Title of *Laureat* was a Mark of Honour conferred by the King, from whom all Honour is derived, and which therefore no Man has a Right to bestow upon himself; and added, that he might with equal Propriety stile himself a Volunteer Lord, or Volunteer Baronet. It cannot be denied that the Remark was just, but *Savage* did not think any Title, which was conferred upon Mr. *Cibber*, so honourable as that the Usurpation of it could be imputed to him as an Instance of very exorbitant Vanity, and therefore continued to write under the same Title, and received every Year the same Reward.

He did not appear to consider these Encomiums as Tests of his Abilities, or as anything more than annual Hints to the Queen of her Promise, or Acts of

Ceremony, by the Performance of which he was intitled to his Pension, and therefore did not labour them with great Diligence, or print more than fifty each Year, except that for some of the last Years he regularly inserted them in the *Gentleman's Magazine*, by which they were dispersed over the Kingdom.

Of some of them he had himself so low an Opinion, that he intended to omit them in the Collection of Poems, for which he printed Proposals, and solicited Subscriptions; nor can it seem strange, that being confined to the same Subject, he should be at some times indolent, and at others unsuccessful, that he should sometimes delay a disagreeable Task, till it was too late to perform it well; or that he should sometimes repeat the same Sentiment on the same Occasion, or at others be misled by an Attempt after Novelty to forced Conceptions, and far-fetched Images.

He wrote indeed with a double Intention, which supplied him with some Variety, for his Business was to praise the Queen for the Favours which he had received, and to complain to her of the Delay of those which she had promised: In some of his Pieces, therefore, Gratitude is predominant, and in some Discontent; in some he represents himself as happy in her Patronage, and in others as disconsolate to find himself neglected.

Her Promise, like other Promises made to this unfortunate Man, was never performed, though he took sufficient Care that it should not be forgotten. The Publication of his *Volunteer Laureat* procured him no other Reward than a regular Remittance of fifty Pounds.

He was not so depressed by his Disappointments as to neglect any Opportunity that was offered of advancing his Interest. When the Princess *Anne* was married, he wrote a Poem upon her Departure, only, as he declared, *because it was expected from him*, and he was not willing to bar his own Prospects by any Appearance of Neglect.

He never mentioned any Advantage gain'd by this Poem, or any Regard that was paid to it, and therefore it is likely that it was considered at Court as an Act of Duty to which he was obliged by his Dependence, and which it was therefore not necessary to reward by any new Favour: Or perhaps the Queen really intended his Advancement, and therefore thought it superfluous to lavish Presents upon a Man whom she intended to establish for Life.

About this Time not only his Hopes were in Danger of being frustrated, but his Pension likewise of being obstructed by an accidental Calumny. The Writer of the *Daily Courant*, a Paper then published under the Direction of the Ministry, charged him with a Crime, which though not very great in itself, would have been remarkably invidious in him, and might very justly have incensed the Queen against him. He was accused by Name of influencing Elections against the Court, by appearing at the Head of a Tory Mob; nor did the Accuser fail to aggravate his Crime, by representing it as the Effect of the most atrocious Ingratitude, and a kind of Rebellion against the Queen, who had first preserved him from an infamous Death, and afterwards distinguished him by her Favour, and supported him by her Charity. The Charge, as it was open and confident, was likewise by good Fortune very particular. The Place of the Transaction was mentioned, and the whole Series of the Rioter's Conduct related. This Exactness made Mr. *Savage*'s Vindication easy, for he never had in his Life seen the Place which was declared to be the Scene of his Wickedness, nor ever had been present in any Town when its Representatives were chosen. This Answer he therefore made haste to publish, with all the Circumstances necessary to make it credible, and very reasonably demanded, that the Accusation should be retracted in the same Paper, that he might no longer suffer the Imputation of Sedition and Ingratitude. This Demand was likewise pressed by him in a private Letter to the Author of the Paper, who either trusting to the Protection of those whose Defence he had undertaken, or having entertained some personal Malice against Mr. *Savage*, or fearing left, by retracting so confident an Assertion, he should impair the Credit of his Paper, refused to give him that Satisfaction.

Mr. *Savage* therefore thought it necessary, to his own Vindication, to prosecute him in the King's Bench; but as he did not find any ill Effects from the Accusation, having sufficiently cleared his Innocence, he thought any farther Procedure would have the Appearance of Revenge, and therefore willingly dropped it.

He saw soon afterwards a Process commenced in the same Court against himself, on an Information in which he was accused of writing and publishing an obscene Pamphlet.

It was always Mr. *Savage*'s Desire to be distinguished, and when any Controversy became popular, he never wanted some Reason for engaging in it with great Ardour, and appearing at the Head of the Party which he had chosen. As he was never celebrated for his Prudence, he had no sooner taken his Side, and informed himself of the chief Topics of the Dispute, than he took all Opportunities of asserting and propagating his Principles, without much Regard to his own Interest, or any other visible Design than that of drawing upon himself the Attention of Mankind.

The Dispute between the Bishop of *London* and the Chancellor is well known to have been for some Time the chief Topic of political Conversation, and therefore Mr. *Savage*, in Pursuance of his Character, endeavoured to become conspicuous among the Controvertists with which every Coffee-House was filled on that Occasion. He was an indefatigable Opposer of all the Claims of Ecclesiastical Power, though he did not know on what they were founded, and was therefore no Friend to the Bishop of *London*. But he had another Reason for appearing as a warm Advocate for Dr. *Rundle*, for he was the Friend of Mr. *Foster* and Mr. *Thompson*, who were the Friends of Mr. *Savage*.

Thus remote was his Interest in the Question, which however, as he imagined, concerned him so nearly, that it was not sufficient to harangue and dispute, but necessary likewise to write upon it.

He therefore engaged with great Ardour in a new Poem, called by him, *The Progress of a Divine*, in which he conducts a profligate Priest by all the Gradations of Wickedness from a poor Curacy in the Country, to the highest Preferments of the Church, and describes with that Humour which was natural to him, and that Knowledge which was extended to all the Diversities of human Life, his Behaviour in every Station, and insinuates, that this Priest thus accomplished found at last a Patron in the Bishop of *London*.

When he was asked by one of his Friends, on what Pretence he could charge the Bishop with such an Action, he had no more to say, than that he had only inverted the Accusation, and that he thought reasonable to believe, that he, who obstructed the Rise of a good Man without Reason, would for bad Reasons promote the Exaltation of a Villain.

The Clergy were universally provoked by this Satire, and *Savage*, who, as was his constant Practice, had set his Name to his Performance, was censured in the *Weekly Miscellany* with Severity, which he did not seem inclined to forget.

But a Return of Invective was not thought a sufficient Punishment. The Court of *King's Bench* was therefore moved against him, and he was obliged to return an Answer to a Charge of Obscenity. It was urged in his Defence, that Obscenity was criminal when it was intended to promote the Practice of Vice, but that Mr. *Savage* had only introduced obscene Ideas with the View of exposing them to Detestation, and of amending the Age by shewing the Deformity of Wickedness. This Plea was admitted, and Sir *Philip Yorke*, who then presided in that Court, dismissed the Information with Encomiums upon the Purity and Excellence of Mr. *Savage*'s Writings.

The Prosecution however answered in some Measure the Purpose of those by whom it was set on Foot, for Mr. *Savage* was so far intimidated by it, that when the Edition of his Poem was sold, he did not venture to reprint it, so that it was in a short Time forgotten, or forgotten by all but those whom it offended.

It is said, that some Endeavours were used to incense the Queen against him, but he found Advocates to obviate at least Part of their Effect; for though he was never advanced, he still continued to receive his Pension.

This Poem drew more Infamy upon him than any incident of his Life, and as his Conduct cannot be vindicated, it is proper to secure his Memory from Reproach, by informing those whom he made his Enemies, that he never intended to repeat the Provocation; and that, though whenever he thought he had any Reason to complain of the Clergy, he used to threaten them with a new Edition of *The Progress of a Divine*, it was his calm and settled Resolution to suppress it for ever.

He once intended to have made a better Reparation for the Folly or Injustice with which he might be charged, by writing another Poem, called, *The Progress of a Free-Thinker*, whom he intended to lead through all the

Stages of Vice and Folly, to convert him from Virtue to Wickedness, and from Religion to Infidelity by all the modish Sophistry used for that Purpose; and at last to dismiss him by his own Hand into the other World.

That he did not execute this Design is a real Loss to Mankind, for he was too well acquainted with all the Scenes of Debauchery to have failed in his Representations of them, and too zealous for Virtue not to have represented them in such a Manner as should expose them either to Ridicule or Detestation.

But this Plan was like others, formed and laid aside, till the Vigour of his Imagination was spent, and the Effervescence of Invention had subsided, but soon gave Way to some other Design which pleased by its Novelty for a while, and then was neglected like the former.

He was still in his usual Exigencies, having no certain Support but the Pension allowed him by the Queen, which though it might have kept an exact Oeconomist from Want, was very far from being sufficient for Mr. *Savage*, who had never been accustomed to dismiss any of his Appetites without the Gratification which they solicited, and whom nothing but Want of Money withheld from partaking of every Pleasure that fell within his View.

His Conduct with regard to his Pension was very particular. No sooner had he changed the Bill, than he vanished from the Sight of all his Acquaintances, and lay for some Time out of the Reach of all the Enquiries that Friendship or Curiosity could make after him; at length he appeared again pennyless as before, but never informed even those whom he seemed to regard most, where he had been, nor was his Retreat ever discovered.

This was his constant Practice during the whole Time that he received the Pension from the Queen: He regularly disappeared and returned. He indeed affirmed, that he retired to study, and that the Money supported him in Solitude for many Months; but his Friends declared, that the short Time in which it was spent sufficiently confuted his own Account of his Conduct.

His Politeness and his Wit still raised him Friends, who were desirous of setting him at length free from that Indigence by which he had been hitherto oppressed, and therefore solicited Sir *Robert Walpole* in his Favour with so much Earnestness, that they obtained a Promise of the next Place that should become vacant, not exceeding two hundred Pounds a Year. This Promise was made with an uncommon Declaration, *that it was not the Promise of a Minister to a Petitioner, but of a Friend to his Friend.*

Mr. *Savage* now concluded himself set at Ease for ever, and as he observes in a Poem written on that Incident of his Life, *trusted* and *was trusted*, but soon found that his Confidence was ill-grounded, and this *friendly* Promise was not inviolable. He spent a long Time in Solicitations, and at last despaired and desisted.

He did not indeed deny that he had given the Minister some Reason to believe that he should not strengthen his own Interest by advancing him, for he had taken Care to distinguish himself in Coffee-Houses as an Advocate for

the Ministry of the last Years of Queen *Anne*, and was always ready to justify
the Conduct, and exalt the Character of Lord *Bolingbroke*, whom he mentions
with great Regard in an Epistle upon Authors, which he wrote about that
Time, but was too wise to publish, and of which only some Fragments have
appeared, inserted by him in the Magazine after his Retirement.

To despair was not, however, the Character of *Savage*, when one Patronage
failed, he had recourse to another. The Prince was now extremely popular,
and had very liberally rewarded the Merit of some Writers whom Mr. *Savage*
did not think superior to himself, and therefore he resolved to address a Poem
to him.

For this Purpose he made Choice of a Subject, which could regard only
Persons of the highest Rank and greatest Affluence, and which was therefore
proper for a Poem intended to procure the Patronage of a Prince; and having
retired for some Time to *Richmond*, that he might prosecute his Design in full
Tranquillity, without the Temptations of Pleasure, or the Solicitations of
Creditors, by which his Meditations were in equal Danger of being disconcerted, he produced *a Poem On public Spirit, with regard to public Works*.

The Plan of this Poem is very extensive, and comprises a Multitude of
Topics, each of which might furnish Matter sufficient for a long Performance,
and of which some have already employed more eminent Writers; but as he
was perhaps not fully acquainted with the whole Extent of his own Design,
and was writing to obtain a Supply of Wants too pressing to admit of long
or accurate Enquiries, he passes negligently over many public Works, which,
even in his own Opinion, deserved to be more elaborately treated.

But though he may sometimes disappoint his Reader by transient Touches
upon these Subjects, which have often been considered, and therefore naturally
raise Expectations, he must be allowed amply to compensate his Omissions
by expatiating in the Conclusion of his Work upon a Kind of Beneficence not
yet celebrated by any eminent Poet, though it now appears more susceptible
of Embellishments, more adapted to exalt the Ideas, and affect the Passions,
than many of those which have hitherto been thought most worthy of the
Ornaments of Verse. The Settlement of Colonies in uninhabited Countries,
the Establishment of those in Security whose Misfortunes have made their
own Country no longer pleasing or safe, the Acquisition of Property without
Injury to any, the Appropriation of the waste and luxuriant Bounties of
Nature, and the Enjoyment of those Gifts which Heaven has scattered upon
Regions uncultivated and unoccupied, cannot be considered without giving
Rise to a great Number of pleasing Ideas, and bewildering the Imagination in
delightful Prospects; and, therefore, whatever Speculations they may produce in those who have confined themselves to political Studies, naturally fixed
the Attention, and excited the Applause of a Poet. The Politician, when he
considers Men driven into other Countries for Shelter, and obliged to retire
to Forests and Deserts, and pass their Lives and fix their Posterity in the

remotest Corners of the World, to avoid those Hardships which they suffer or fear in their native Place, may very properly enquire why the Legislature does not provide a Remedy for these Miseries, rather than encourage an Escape from them. He may conclude, that the Flight of every honest Man is a Loss to the Community, that those who are unhappy without Guilt ought to be relieved, and the Life which is overburthened by accidental Calamities, set at Ease by the Care of the Publick, and that those, who have by Misconduct forfeited their Claim to Favour, ought rather to be made useful to the Society which they have injured, than be driven from it. But the Poet is employed in a more pleasing Undertaking than that of proposing Laws, which, however just or expedient, will never be made, or endeavouring to reduce to rational Schemes of Government Societies which were formed by Chance, and are conducted by the private Passions of those who preside in them. He guides the unhappy Fugitive from Want and Persecution, to Plenty, Quiet, and Security, and seats him in Scenes of peaceful Solitude, and undisturbed Repose.

Savage has not forgotten amidst the pleasing Sentiments which this Prospect of Retirement suggested to him to censure those Crimes which have been generally committed by the Discoverers of new Regions, and to expose the enormous Wickedness of making War upon barbarous Nations because they cannot resist, and of invading Countries because they are fruitful; of extending Navigation only to propagate Vice, and of visiting distant Lands only to lay them waste. He has asserted the natural Equality of Mankind, and endeavoured to suppress that Pride which inclines Men to imagine that Right is the Consequence of Power.

His Description of the various Miseries which force Men to seek for Refuge in distant Countries affords another Instance of his Proficiency in the important and extensive Study of human Life, and the Tenderness with which he recounts them, another Proof of his Humanity and Benevolence.

It is observable, that the Close of this Poem discovers a Change which Experience had made in Mr. *Savage*'s Opinions. In a Poem written by him in his Youth, and published in his Miscellanies, he declares his Contempt of the contracted Views and narrow Prospects of the middle State of Life, and declares his Resolution either to tower like the Cedar, or be trampled like the Shrub; but in this Poem, though addressed to a Prince, he mentions this State of Life as comprising those who ought most to attract Reward, those who merit most the Confidence of Power, and the Familiarity of Greatness, and accidentally mentioning this Passage to one of his Friends, declared that in his Opinion all the Virtue of Mankind was comprehended in that State.

In describing Villas and Gardens he did not omit to condemn that absurd Custom which prevails among the *English* of permitting Servants to receive Money from Strangers for the Entertainment that they receive, and therefore inserted in his Poem these Lines:

But what the flow'ring Pride of Gardens rare,
However royal, or however fair:
If Gates which to access should still give Way,
Ope but, like *Peter*'s Paradise, for Pay.
If perquisited Varlets frequent stand,
And each new Walk must a new Tax demand?
What foreign Eye but with Contempt surveys?
What Muse shall from Oblivion snatch their Praise?

But before the Publication of his Performance he recollected, that the Queen allowed her Garden and Cave at *Richmond* to be shewn for Money, and that she so openly countenanced the Practice, that she had bestowed the Privilege of shewing them as a Place of Profit on a Man whose Merit she valued herself upon rewarding, though she gave him only the Liberty of disgracing his Country.

He therefore thought, with more Prudence than was often exerted by him, that the Publication of these Lines might be officiously represented as an Insult upon the Queen to whom he owed his Life and his Subsistence, and that the Propriety of his Observation would be no Security against the Censures which the Unseasonableness of it might draw upon him; he therefore suppressed the Passage in the first Edition, but after the Queen's Death thought the same Caution no longer necessary, and restored it to the proper Place.

The Poem was therefore published without any political Faults, and inscribed to the Prince, but Mr. *Savage* having no Friend upon whom he could prevail to present it to him, had no other Method of attracting his Observation than the Publication of frequent Advertisements, and therefore received no Reward from his Patron, however generous on other Occasions.

This Disappointment he never mentioned without Indignation, being by some Means or other confident that the Prince was not ignorant of his Address to him, and insinuated, that if any Advances in Popularity could have been made by distinguishing him, he had not written without Notice, or without Reward.

He was once inclined to have presented his Poem in Person, and sent to the Printer for a Copy with that Design; but either his Opinion changed, or his Resolution deserted him, and he continued to resent Neglect without attempting to force himself into Regard.

Nor was the Public much more favourable than his Patron, for only seventy-two were sold, though the Performance was much commended by some whose Judgment in that Kind of Writing is generally allowed. But *Savage* easily reconciled himself to Mankind without imputing any Defect to his Work, by observing that his Poem was unluckily published two Days after the Prorogation of the Parliament, and by Consequence at a Time when all those who could be expected to regard it were in the Hurry of preparing for their Departure, or engaged in taking Leave of others upon their Dismission from public Affairs.

It must be however allowed, in Justification of the Public, that this Performance is not the most excellent of Mr. *Savage*'s Works, and that though it cannot be denied to contain many striking Sentiments, majestic Lines, and just Observations, it is in general not sufficiently polished in the Language, or enlivened in the Imagery, or digested in the Plan.

Thus his Poem contributed nothing to the Alleviation of his Poverty, which was such as very few could have supported with equal Patience, but to which it must likewise be confessed, that few would have been exposed who received punctually fifty Pounds a Year; a Salary which though by no Means equal to the Demands of Vanity and Luxury, is yet found sufficient to support Families above Want, and was undoubtedly more than the Necessities of Life require.

But no sooner had he received his Pension, than he withdrew to his darling Privacy, from which he return'd in a short Time to his former Distress, and for some Part of the Year, generally lived by Chance, eating only when he was invited to the Tables of his Acquaintances, from which the Meanness of his Dress often excluded him, when the Politeness and Variety of his Conversation would have been thought a sufficient Recompence for his Entertainment.

He lodged as much by Accident as he dined and passed the Night, sometimes in mean Houses, which are set open at Night to any casual Wanderers, sometimes in Cellars among the Riot and Filth of the meanest and most profligate of the Rabble; and sometimes, when he had not Money to support even the Expences of these Receptacles, walked about the Streets till he was weary, and lay down in the Summer upon a Bulk, or in the Winter with his Associates in Poverty, among the Ashes of a Glass-house.

In this Manner were passed those Days and those Nights, which Nature had enabled him to have employed in elevated Speculations, useful Studies, or pleasing Conversation. On a Bulk, in a Cellar, or in a Glass-house among Thieves and Beggers, was to be found the Author of the *Wanderer*, the Man of exalted Sentiments, extensive Views and curious Observations, the Man whose Remarks on Life might have assisted the Statesman, whose Ideas of Virtue might have enlightned the Moralist, whose Eloquence might have influenced Senates, and whose Delicacy might have polished Courts.

It cannot be imagined that such Necessities might sometimes force him upon disreputable Practices, and it is probable that these Lines in the *Wanderer* were occasioned by his Reflections on his own Conduct.

> Though Mis'ry leads to Fortitude and Truth,
> Unequal to the Load this languid Youth,
> (O! let none Censure if untried by Grief,
> Or amidst Woes untempted by Relief,)

He stoop'd, reluctant, to mean Acts of Shame,
Which then, ev'n then, he scorn'd, and blush'd to name.

Whoever was acquainted with him, was certain to be solicited for small
Sums, which the Frequency of the Request made in Time considerable, and
he was therefore quickly shunned by those who were become familiar enough
to be trusted with his Necessities; but his rambling Manner of Life, and
constant Appearance at Houses of public Resort, always procured him a new
Succession of Friends, whose Kindness had not been exhausted by repeated
Requests, so that he was seldom absolutely without Resources, but had in
his utmost Exigences this Comfort, that he always imagined himself sure of
speedy Relief.

It was observed that he always asked Favours of this Kind without the least
Submission or apparent Consciousness of Dependence, and that he did not
seem to look upon a Compliance with his Request as an Obligation that
deserved any extraordinary Acknowledgments, but a Refusal was resented by
him as an Affront, or complained of as an Injury; nor did he readily reconcile
himself to those who either denied to lend, or gave him afterwards any
Intimation, that they expected to be repaid.

He was sometimes so far compassionated by those who knew both his
Merit and his Distresses, that they received him into their Families, but they
soon discovered him to be a very incommodious Inmate; for being always
accustomed to an irregular Manner of Life, he could not confine himself to
any stated Hours, or pay any Regard to the Rules of a Family, but would prolong his Conversation till Midnight, without considering that Business might
require his Friend's Application in the Morning; and when he had persuaded
himself to retire to Bed, was not, without equal Difficulty, called up to Dinner;
it was therefore impossible to pay him any Distinction without the entire
Subversion of all Oeconomy, a Kind of Establishment which, wherever he
went, he always appeared ambitious to overthrow.

It must therefore be acknowledged, in Justification of Mankind, that it was
not always by the Negligence or Coldness of his Friends that *Savage* was distressed, but because it was in reality very difficult to preserve him long in a
State of Ease. To supply him with Money was a hopeless Attempt, for no
sooner did he see himself Master of a Sum sufficient to set him free from
Care for a Day, than he became profuse and luxurious. When once he had
entred a Tavern, or engaged in a Scheme of Pleasure, he never retired till
Want of Money obliged him to some new Expedient. If he was entertained in
a Family, nothing was any longer to be regarded there but Amusements and
Jollity; wherever *Savage* entered he immediately expected that Order and
Business should fly before him, that all should thence-forward be left to Hazard,
and that no dull Principle of domestic Management should be opposed to his
Inclination, or intrude upon his Gaiety.

His Distresses, however afflictive, never dejected him; in his lowest State he wanted not Spirit to assert the natural Dignity of Wit, and was always ready to repress that Insolence which Superiority of Fortune incited, and to trample that Reputation which rose upon any other Basis than that of Merit: He never admitted any gross Familiarities, or submitted to be treated otherwise than as an equal. Once when he was without Lodging, Meat, or Cloaths, one of his Friends, a Man not indeed remarkable for Moderation in his Prosperity, left a Message, that he desired to see him about nine in the Morning. *Savage* knew that his Intention was to assist him, but was very much disgusted, that he should presume to prescribe the Hour of his Attendance, and, I believe, refused to visit him, and rejected his Kindness.

The same invincible Temper, whether Firmness or Obstinacy, appeared in his Conduct to the Lord *Tyrconnel*, from whom he very frequently demanded that the Allowance which was once paid him should be restored, but with whom he never appeared to entertain for a Moment the Thought of soliciting a Reconciliation, and whom he treated at once with all the Haughtiness of Superiority, and all the Bitterness of Resentment. He wrote to him not in a Stile of Supplication or Respect, but of Reproach, Menace, and Contempt, and appeared determined, if he ever regained his Allowance, to hold it only by the Right of Conquest.

As many more can discover, that a Man is richer than that he is wiser than themselves, Superiority of Understanding is not so readily acknowledged as that of Fortune; nor is that Haughtiness, which the Consciousness of great Abilities incites, borne with the same Submission as the Tyranny of Affluence; and therefore *Savage*, by asserting his Claim to Deference and Regard, and by treating those with Contempt whom better Fortune animated to rebel against him, did not fail to raise a great Number of Enemies in the different Classes of Mankind. Those who thought themselves raised above him by the Advantages of Riches, hated him because they found no Protection from the Petulance of his Wit. Those who were esteemed for their Writings feared him as a Critic, and maligned him as a Rival, and almost all the smaller Wits were his professed Enemies.

Among these Mr. *Millar* so far indulged his Resentment as to introduce him in a Farce, and direct him to be personated on the Stage in a Dress like that which he then wore; a mean Insult which only insinuated, that *Savage* had but one Coat, and which was therefore despised by him rather than resented; for though he wrote a Lampoon against *Millar*, he never printed it: and as no other Person ought to prosecute that Revenge from which the Person who was injured desisted, I shall not preserve what Mr. *Savage* suppressed; of which the Publication would indeed have been a Punishment too severe for so impotent an Assault.

The great Hardships of Poverty were to *Savage* not the Want of Lodging or of Food, but the Neglect and Contempt which it drew upon him. He complained that as his Affairs grew desperate he found his Reputation for Capacity visibly decline, that his Opinion in Questions of Criticism was no longer regarded, when his Coat was out of Fashion; and that those who in the Interval of his Prosperity were always encouraging him to great Undertakings by Encomiums on his Genius and Assurances of Success, now received any Mention of his Designs with Coldness, thought that the Subjects on which he proposed to write were very difficult; and were ready to inform him, that the Event of a Poem was uncertain, that an Author ought to employ much Time in the Consideration of his Plan, and not presume to sit down to write in Confidence of a few cursory Ideas, and a superficial Knowledge; Difficulties were started on all Sides, and he was no longer qualified for any Performance but the *Volunteer Laureat.*

Yet even this Kind of Contempt never depressed him; for he always preserved a steady Confidence in his own Capacity, and believed nothing above his Reach which he should at any Time earnestly endeavour to attain. He formed Schemes of the same Kind with regard to Knowledge and to Fortune, and flattered himself with Advances to be made in Science, as with Riches to be enjoyed in some distant Period of his Life. For the Acquisition of Knowledge he was indeed far better qualified than for that of Riches; for he was naturally inquisitive and desirous of the Conversation of those from whom any Information was to be obtained, but by no Means solicitous to improve those Opportunities that were sometimes offered of raising his Fortune; and he was remarkably retentive of his Ideas, which, when once he was in Possession of them, rarely forsook him; a Quality which could never be communicated to his Money.

While he was thus wearing out his Life in Expectation that the Queen would some time recollect her Promise, he had Recourse to the usual Practice of Writers, and published Proposals for printing his Works by Subscription, to which he was encouraged by the Success of many who had not a better Right to the Favour of the Public; but whatever was the Reason, he did not find the World equally inclined to favour him, and he observed with some Discontent, that though he offered his Works at half a Guinea, he was able to procure but a small Number in Comparison with those who subscribed twice as much to *Duck.*

Nor was it without Indignation that he saw his Proposals neglected by the Queen, who patronised Mr. *Duck*'s with uncommon Ardour, and incited a Competition among those who attended the Court, who should most promote his Interest, and who should first offer a Subscription. This was a Distinction to which Mr. *Savage* made no Scruple of asserting that his Birth, his Misfortunes, and his Genius gave him a fairer Title, than could be pleaded by him on whom it was conferred.

Savage's Applications were however not universally unsuccessful; for some of the Nobility countenanced his Design, encouraged his Proposals, and subscribed with great Liberality. He related of the Duke of *Chandos* particularly, that, upon receiving his Proposals, he sent him ten Guineas.

But the Money which his Subscriptions afforded him was not less volatile than that which he received from his other Schemes; whenever a Subscription was paid him he went to a Tavern, and as Money so collected is necessarily received in small Sums, he never was able to send his Poems to the Press, but for many Years continued his Solicitation, and squandered whatever he obtained.

This Project of printing his Works was frequently revived, and as his Proposals grew obsolete, new ones were printed with fresher Dates. To form Schemes for the Publication was one of his favourite Amusements, nor was he ever more at Ease than when with any Friend who readily fell in with his Schemes, he was adjusting the Print, forming the Advertisements, and regulating the Dispersion of his new Edition, which he really intended some time to publish, and which, as long Experience had shewn him the Impossibility of printing the Volume together, he at last determined to divide into weekly or monthly Numbers, that the Profits of the first might supply the Expences of the next.

Thus he spent his Time in mean Expedients and tormenting Suspense, living for the greatest Part in Fear of Prosecutions from his Creditors, and consequently skulking in obscure Parts of the Town, of which he was no Stranger to the remotest Corners. But wherever he came his Address secured him Friends, whom his Necessities soon alienated, so that he had perhaps a more numerous Acquaintance than any Man ever before attained, there being scarcely any Person eminent on any Account to whom he was not known, or whose Character he was not in some Degree able to delineate.

To the Acquisition of this extensive Acquaintance every Circumstance of his Life contributed. He excelled in the Arts of Conversation, and therefore willingly practised them: He had seldom any Home, or even a Lodging in which he could be private, and therefore was driven into public Houses for the common Conveniences of Life, and Supports of Nature. He was always ready to comply with every Invitation, having no Employment to withhold him, and often no Money to provide for himself; and by dining with one Company, he never failed of obtaining an Introduction into another.

Thus dissipated was his Life, and thus casual his Subsistence; yet did not the Distraction of his Views hinder him from Reflection, nor the Uncertainty of his Condition depress his Gaiety. When he had wandered about without any fortunate Adventure, by which he was led into a Tavern, he sometimes retired into the Fields, and was able to employ his Mind in Study to amuse it with pleasing Imaginations; and seldom appeared to be melancholy, but when some sudden Misfortune had just fallen upon him, and even then in a few Moments he would disentangle himself from his Perplexity, adopt the Subject of Conversation, and apply his Mind wholly to the Objects that others presented to it.

This Life, unhappy as it may be already imagined, was yet imbitter'd in 1738, with new Calamities. The Death of the Queen deprived him of all the Prospects of Preferment with which he had so long entertained his Imagination; and as Sir *Robert Walpole* had before given him Reason to believe that he never intended the Performance of his Promise, he was now abandoned again to Fortune.

He was, however at that time, supported by a Friend; and as it was not his Custom to look out for distant Calamities, or to feel any other Pain than that which forced itself upon his Senses, he was not much afflicted at his Loss, and perhaps comforted himself that his Pension would be now continued without the annual Tribute of a Panegyric.

Another Expectation contributed likewise to support him; he had taken a Resolution to write a second Tragedy upon the Story of Sir *Thomas Overbury*, in which he preserved a few Lines of his former Play; but made a total Alteration of the Plan, added new Incidents, and introduced new Characters; so that it was a new Tragedy, not a Revival of the former.

Many of his Friends blamed him for not making Choice of another Subject; but in Vindication of himself, he asserted, that it was not easy to find a better; and that he thought it his Interest to extinguish the Memory of the first Tragedy, which he could only do by writing one less defective upon the same Story; by which he should entirely defeat the Artifice of the Booksellers, who after the Death of any Author of Reputation, are always industrious to swell his Works, by uniting his worst Productions with his best.

In the Execution of this Scheme however, he proceeded but slowly, and probably only employed himself upon it when he could find no other Amusement; but he pleased himself with counting the Profits, and perhaps imagined, that the theatrical Reputation which he was about to acquire, would be equivalent to all that he had lost by the Death of his Patroness.

He did not in Confidence of his approaching Riches neglect the Measures proper to secure the Continuance of his Pension, though some of his Favourers thought him culpable for omitting to write on her Death; but on her Birth Day next Year, he gave a Proof of the Solidity of his Judgment, and the Power of his Genius. He knew that the Track of Elegy had been so long beaten, that it was impossible to travel in it without treading in the Footsteps of those who had gone before him; and that therefore it was necessary that he might distinguish himself from the Herd of Encomiasts, to find out some new Walk of funeral Panegyric.

This difficult Task he performed in such a Manner, that his Poem may be justly ranked among the best Pieces that the Death of Princes has produced. By transferring the Mention of her Death to her Birth Day, he has formed a happy Combination of Topics which any other Man would have thought it very difficult to connect in one View; but which he has united in such a Manner, that the Relation between them appears natural; and it may be justly said that what no other Man would have thought on, it now appears scarcely possible for any Man to miss.

The Beauty of this peculiar Combination of Images is so masterly, that it is sufficient to set this Poem above Censure; and therefore it is not necessary to mention many other delicate Touches which may be found in it, and which would deservedly be admired in any other Performance.

To these Proofs of his Genius may be added, from the same Poem, an Instance of his Prudence, an Excellence for which he was not so often distinguished; he does not forget to remind the King in the most delicate and artful Manner of continuing his Pension.

With regard to the Success of this Address he was for some Time in Suspense; but was in no great Degree sollicitous about it; and continued his Labour upon his new Tragedy with great Tranquillity, till the Friend, who had for a considerable time supported him, removing his Family to another Place, took Occasion to dismiss him. It then became necessary to enquire more diligently what was determined in his Affair, having Reason to suspect that no great Favour was intended him, because he had not received his Pension at the usual Time.

It is said, that he did not take those Methods of retrieving his Interest which were most likely to succeed; and some of those who were employed in the Exchequer, cautioned him against too much Violence in his Proceedings; but Mr. *Savage* who seldom regulated his Conduct by the Advice of others, gave way to his Passion, and demanded of Sir *Robert Walpole*, at his Levee, the Reason of the Distinction that was made between him and the other Pensioners of the Queen, with a Degree of Roughness which perhaps determined him to withdraw what had been only delayed.

Whatever was the Crime of which he was accused or suspected, and whatever Influence was imployed against him, he received soon after an Account that took from him all Hopes of regaining his Pension; and he had now no Prospect of Subsistence but from his Play, and he knew no Way of Living for the Time required to finish it.

So peculiar were the Misfortunes of this Man, deprived of an Estate and Title by a particular Law, exposed and abandoned by a Mother, defrauded by a Mother of a Fortune which his Father had allotted him, he enter'd the World without a Friend; and though his Abilities forced themselves into Esteem and Reputation, he was never able to obtain any real Advantage, and whatever Prospects arose, were always intercepted as he began to approach them. The King's Intentions in his Favour were frustrated; his Dedication to the Prince, whose Generosity on every other Occasion was eminent, procured him no Reward; Sir *Robert Walpole* who valued himself upon keeping his Promise to others, broke it to him without Regret; and the Bounty of the Queen was, after her Death, withdrawn from him, and from him only.

Such were his Misfortunes, which yet he bore not only with Decency, but with Cheerfulness, nor was his Gaiety clouded even by his last Disappointments, though he was in a short Time reduced to the lowest Degree of Distress; and often wanted both Lodging and Food. At this Time he gave another Instance of the insurmountable Obstinacy of his Spirit; his Cloaths were worn out, and he received Notice that at a Coffee-House some Cloaths and Linen were left for him; the Person who sent them, did not, I believe, inform him to whom he was to be obliged, that he might spare the Perplexity of acknowledging the Benefit; but though the Offer was so far generous, it was made with some Neglect of Ceremonies, which Mr. *Savage* so much resented, that he refused the Present, and declined to enter the House, till the Cloaths that had been designed for him were taken away.

His Distress was now publickly known, and his Friends, therefore, thought it proper to concert some Measures for his Relief; and one of them wrote a Letter to him, in which he expressed his Concern *for the miserable withdrawing of his Pension*; and gave him Hopes that in a short Time, he should find himself supplied with a Competence, *without any Dependence on those little Creatures which we are pleased to call the Great.*

The Scheme proposed for this happy and independent Subsistence, was, that he should retire into *Wales*, and receive an Allowance of fifty Pounds a Year, to be raised by a Subscription, on which he was to live privately in a cheap Place, without aspiring any more to Affluence, or having any farther Care of Reputation.

This Offer Mr. *Savage* gladly accepted, tho' with Intentions very different from those of his Friends; for they proposed, that he should continue an Exile from *London* for ever, and spend all the remaining Part of his Life at *Swansea*; but he designed only to take the Opportunity, which their Scheme offered him, of retreating for a short Time, that he might prepare his Play for the Stage, and his other Works for the Press, and then to return to *London* to exhibit his Tragedy, and live upon the Profits of his own Labour.

With regard to his Works, he proposed very great Improvements, which would have required much Time, or great Application; and when he had finish'd them, he designed to do Justice to his Subscribers, by publishing them according to his Proposals.

As he was ready to entertain himself with future Pleasures, he had planned out a Scheme of Life for the Country, of which he had no Knowledge but from Pastorals and Songs. He imagined that he should be transported to Scenes of flow'ry Felicity, like those which one Poet has reflected to another, and had projected a perpetual Round of innocent Pleasures, of which he suspected no Interruption from Pride, or Ignorance, or Brutality.

With these Expectations he was so enchanted, that when he was once gently reproach'd by a Friend for submitting to live upon a Subscription, and advised rather by a resolute Exertion of his Abilities to support himself, he could not bear to debar himself from the Happiness which was to be found in the Calm of a Cottage, or lose the Opportunity of listening without Intermission, to the Melody of the Nightingale, which he believ'd was to be heard from every Bramble, and which he did not fail to mention as a very important Part of the Happiness of a Country Life.

While this Scheme was ripening, his Friends directed him to take a Lodging in the Liberties of the Fleet, that he might be secure from his Creditors, and sent him every Monday a Guinea, which he commonly spent before the next Morning, and trusted, after his usual Manner, the remaining Part of the Week to the Bounty of Fortune.

He now began very sensibly to feel the Miseries of Dependence: Those by whom he was to be supported, began to prescribe to him with an Air of Authority, which he knew not how decently to resent, nor patiently to bear; and he soon discovered from the Conduct of most of his Subscribers, that he was yet in the Hands of *Little Creatures*.

Of the Insolence that he was obliged to suffer, he gave many Instances, of which none appeared to raise his Indignation to a greater Height, than the Method which was taken of furnishing him with Cloaths. Instead of consulting him and allowing him to send to a Taylor his Orders for what they thought proper to allow him, they proposed to send for a Taylor to take his Measure, and then to consult how they should equip him.

This Treatment was not very delicate, nor was it such as *Savage*'s Humanity would have suggested to him on a like Occasion; but it had scarcely deserved mention, had it not, by affecting him in an uncommon Degree, shewn the Peculiarity of his Character. Upon hearing the Design that was formed, he came to the Lodging of a Friend with the most violent Agonies of Rage; and being asked what it could be that gave him such Disturbance, he replied with the utmost Vehemence of Indignation, "That they had sent for a Taylor to measure him."

How the Affair ended, was never enquired, for fear of renewing his Uneasiness. It is probable that, upon Recollection, he submitted with a good Grace to what he could not avoid, and that he discovered no Resentment where he had no Power.

He was, however, not humbled to implicit and universal Compliance; for when the Gentleman, who had first informed him of the Design to support him by a Subscription, attempted to procure a Reconciliation with the Lord *Tyrconnel*, he could by no Means be prevailed upon to comply with the Measures that were proposed.

A Letter was written for him to Sir *William Lemon*, to prevail upon him to interpose his good Offices with Lord *Tyrconnel*, in which he solicited Sir *William*'s Assistance, *for a Man who really needed it as much as any Man could well do*; and informed him, that he was retiring *for ever to a Place where he should no more trouble his Relations, Friends, or Enemies*; he confessed, that his

Passion had *betrayed* him to some Conduct, with Regard to Lord *Tyrconnel*, *for which he could not but heartily ask his Pardon*; and as he imagined Lord *Tyrconnel's* Passion might be yet so high, that he would not *receive a Letter from him*, begg'd that Sir *William* would endeavour to soften him; and expressed his Hopes, that he would comply with his Request, and that *so small a Relation would not harden his Heart against him.*

That any Man should presume to dictate a Letter to him, was not very agreeable to Mr. *Savage*; and therefore he was, before he had opened it, not much inclined to approve it. But when he read it, he found it contained Sentiments entirely opposite to his own, and, as he asserted, to the Truth, and therefore instead of copying it, wrote his Friend a Letter full of masculine Resentment and warm Expostulations. He very justly observed, that the Style was too supplicatory, and the Representation too abject, and that he ought at least to have made him complain with *the Dignity of a Gentleman in Distress*. He declared that he would not write the Paragraph in which he was to ask Lord *Tyrconnel's* Pardon; for *he despised his Pardon, and therefore could not heartily, and would not hypocritically ask it*. He remarked, that his Friend made a very unreasonable Distinction between himself and him; for, says he, when you mention Men of high Rank *in your own Character*, they are *those little Creatures whom we are pleased to call the Great*; but when you address them *in mine*, no Servility is sufficiently humble. He then with great Propriety explained the ill Consequences might be expected from such a Letter, which his Relations would print in their own Defence, and which would for ever be produced as a full Answer to all that he should allege against them; for he always intended to publish a minute Account of the Treatment which he had received. It is to be remembered to the Honour of the Gentleman by whom this Letter was drawn up, that he yielded to Mr. *Savage's* Reasons, and agreed that it ought to be suppressed.

After many Alterations and Delays, a Subscription was at length raised which did not amount to fifty Pounds a Year, though twenty were paid by one Gentleman; such was the Generosity of Mankind, that what had been done by a Player without Solicitation, could not now be effected by Application and Interest; and *Savage* had a great Number to court and to obey for a Pension less than that which Mrs. *Oldfield* paid him without exacting any Servilities.

Mr. *Savage* however was satisfied, and willing to retire, and was convinced that the Allowance, though scanty, would be more than sufficient for him, being now determined to commence a rigid Oeconomist, and to live according to the exactest Rules of Frugality; for nothing was in his Opinion more contemptible than a Man, who, when he knew his Income, exceeded it, and yet he confessed that Instances of such Folly, were too common, and lamented, that some Men were not to be trusted with their own Money.

Full of these salutary Resolutions, he left *London*, in *July* 1739, having taken Leave with great Tenderness of his Friends, and parted from the Author of this Narrative with Tears in his Eyes. He was furnished with fifteen Guineas, and informed, that they would be sufficient, not only for the Expence of his Journey, but for his Support in *Wales* for some Time; and that there remained but little more of the first Collection. He promised a strict Adherence to his Maxims of Parsimony, and went away in the Stage Coach; nor did his Friends expect to hear from him, till he informed them of his Arrival at *Swansea*.

But when they least expected, arrived a Letter dated the fourteenth Day after his Departure, in which he sent them Word, that he was yet upon the Road, and without Money; and that he therefore could not proceed without a Remittance. They then sent him the Money that was in their Hands, with which he was enabled to reach *Bristol*, from whence he was to go to *Swansea* by Water.

At *Bristol* he found an Embargo laid upon the Shipping, so that he could not immediately obtain a Passage; and being therefore obliged to stay there some Time, he, with his usual Felicity, ingratiated himself with many of the principal Inhabitants, was invited to their Houses, distinguished at their pub-lick Feasts, and treated with a Regard that gratify'd his Vanity, and therefore easily engaged his Affection.

He began very early after his Retirement to complain of the Conduct of his Friends in *London*, and irritated many of them so much by his Letters, that they withdrew, however honourably, their Contributions; and it is believed, that little more was paid him than the twenty Pounds a Year, which were allowed him by the Gentleman who proposed the Subscription.

After some Stay at *Bristol*, he retired to *Swansea*, the Place *originally* proposed for his Residence, where he lived about a Year very much dissatis-fied with the Diminution of his Salary; but contracted, as in other Places, Acquaintance with those who were most distinguished in that Country, among whom he has celebrated Mr *Powel* and Mrs. *Jones*, by some Verses which he inserted in the *Gentleman's Magazine*.

Here he completed his Tragedy, of which two Acts were wanting when he left *London*, and was desirous of coming to Town to bring it upon the Stage. This Design was very warmly opposed, and he was advised by his chief Benefactor to put it into the Hands of Mr *Thomson* and Mr *Mallet*, that it might be fitted for the Stage, and to allow his Friends to receive the Profits, out of which an annual Pension should be paid him.

This Proposal he rejected with the utmost Contempt. He was by no Means convinced that the Judgment of those to whom he was required to submit, was superior to his own. He was now determined, as he expressed it, to be *no longer kept in Leading-strings*, and had no elevated Idea of *his Bounty*, who proposed to *pension him out of the Profits of his own Labours*.

He attempted in *Wales* to promote a Subscription for his Works, and had once Hopes of Success; but in a short Time afterwards, formed a Resolution of leaving that Part of the Country, to which he thought it not reasonable to be confined, for the Gratification of those, who having promised him a liberal Income, had no sooner banished him to a remote Corner, than they reduced his Allowance to a Salary scarcely equal to the Necessities of Life.

His Resentment of this Treatment, which, in his own Opinion, at least, he had not deserved, was such that he broke off all Correspondence with most of his Contributors, and appeared to consider them as Persecutors and Oppressors, and in the latter Part of his Life, declared, that their Conduct toward him, since his Departure from *London, had been Perfidiousness improving on Perfidiousness, and Inhumanity on Inhumanity*.

It is not to be supposed, that the Necessities of Mr *Savage* did not sometimes incite him to satirical Exaggerations of the Behaviour of those by whom he thought himself reduced to them. But it must be granted, that the Diminution of his Allowance was a great Hardship, and, that those who withdrew their Subscription from a Man, who, upon the Faith of their Promise, had gone into a Kind of Banishment, and abandoned all those by whom he had been before relieved in his Distresses, will find it no easy Task to vindicate their Conduct.

It may be alleged, and, perhaps, justly, that he was petulant and contemptuous, that he more frequently reproached his Subscribers for not giving him more, than thanked them for what he received; but it is to be remembred, that this Conduct, and this is the worst Charge that can be drawn up against him, did them no real Injury; and that it, therefore, ought rather to have been pitied than resented, at least, the Resentment that it might provoke ought to have been generous and manly; Epithets which his Conduct will hardly deserve, that starves the Man whom he has persuaded to put himself into his Power.

It might have been reasonably demanded by *Savage*, that they should, before they had taken away what they promised, have replaced him in his former State, that they should have taken no Advantages from the Situation to which the Appearance of their Kindness had reduced him, and that he should have been re-called to *London*, before he was abandoned. He might justly represent, that he ought to have been considered as a Lion in the Toils, and demand to be released before the Dogs should be loosed upon him.

He endeavoured, indeed, to release himself, and with an Intent to return to *London*, went to *Bristol*, where a Repetition of the Kindness which he had formerly found, invited him to stay. He was not only carressed and treated, but had a Collection made for him of about thirty Pounds, with which it had been happy if he had immediately departed for *London*; but his Negligence did not suffer him to consider, that such Proofs of Kindness were not often to be expected, and that this Ardour of Benevolence was in a great Degree, the Effect of Novelty, and might, probably, be every Day less; and, therefore, he took no Care to improve the happy Time, but was encouraged by one Favour to hope for another, till at length Generosity was exhausted, and Officiousness wearied.

Another Part of his Misconduct was the Practice of prolonging his Visits, to unseasonable Hours, and disconcerting all the Families into which he was admitted. This was an Error in a Place of Commerce which all the Charms of his Conversation could not compensate; for what Trader would purchase such airy Satisfaction by the Loss of solid Gain, which must be the Consequence of Midnight Merriment, as those Hours which were gained at Night, were generally lost in the Morning?

Thus Mr *Savage*, after the Curiosity of the Inhabitants was gratified, found the Number of his Friends daily decreasing, perhaps without suspecting for what Reason their Conduct was altered, for he still continued to harrass, with his nocturnal Intrusions, those that yet countenanced him, and admitted him to their Houses.

But he did not spend all the Time of his Residence at *Bristol*, in Visits or at Taverns; for he sometimes returned to his Studies, and began several considerable Designs. When he felt an Inclination to write, he always retired from the Knowledge of his Friends, and lay hid in an obscure Part of the Suburbs, till he found himself again desirous of Company, to which it is likely that Intervals of Absence made him more welcome.

He was always full of his Design of returning to *London* to bring his Tragedy upon the Stage; but having neglected to depart with the Money that was raised for him, he could not afterwards procure a Sum sufficient to defray the Expences of his Journey; nor, perhaps, would a fresh Supply have had any other Effect, than, by putting immediate Pleasures in his Power, to have driven the Thoughts of his Journey out of his Mind.

While he was thus spending the Day in contriving a Scheme for the Morrow, Distress stole upon him by imperceptible Degrees. His Conduct had already wearied some of those who were at first enamoured of his Conversation; but he might, perhaps, still have devolved to others, whom he might have entertained with equal Success, had not the Decay of his Cloaths made it no longer consistent with their Vanity to admit him to their Tables, or to associate with him in publick Places. He now began to find every Man from home at whose House he called; and was, therefore, no longer able to procure the Necessaries of Life, but wandered about the Town slighted and neglected, in quest of a Dinner, which he did not always obtain.

To complete his Misery, he was persued by the Officers for small Debts which he had contracted; and was, therefore, obliged to withdraw from the small Number of Friends from whom he had still Reason to hope for Favours. His Custom was to lye in Bed the greatest Part of the Day, and to go out in the Dark with the utmost Privacy, and after having paid his Visit, return again before Morning to his Lodging, which was in the Garret of an obscure Inn.

Being thus excluded on one hand, and confined on the other, he suffered the utmost Extremities of Poverty, and often fasted so long, that he was seized with Faintness, and had lost his Appetite, not being able to bear the smell of Meat, 'till the Action of his Stomach was restored by a Cordial.

In this Distress he received a Remittance of five Pounds from *London*, with which he provided himself a decent Coat, and determined to go to *London*, but unhappily spent his Money at a favourite Tavern. Thus was he again confined to *Bristol*, where he was every Day hunted by Bailiffs. In this Exigence he once more found a Friend, who sheltered him in his House, though at the usual Inconveniences with which his Company was attended for he could neither be persuaded to go to bed in the Night, nor to rise in the Day.

It is observable, that in these various Scenes of Misery, he was always disengaged and cheerful; he at some Times persued his Studies, and at others continued or enlarged his epistolary Correspondence, nor was he ever so far dejected as to endeavour to procure an Encrease of his Allowance, by any other Methods than Accusations and Reproaches.

He had now no longer any Hopes of Assistance from his Friends at *Bristol*, who as Merchants, and by Consequence sufficiently studious of Profit, cannot be supposed to have look'd with much Compassion upon Negligence and Extravagance, or to think any Excellence equivalent to a Fault of such Consequence as Neglect of Oeconomy. It is natural to imagine, that many of those who would have relieved his real Wants, were discouraged from the Exertion of their Benevolence, by Observation of the Use which was made of their Favours, and Conviction that Relief would only be momentary, and that the same Necessity would quickly return.

At last he quitted the House of his Friend, and returned to his Lodging at the Inn, still intending to set out in a few Days for *London*, but on the tenth of *January* 1742–3, having been at Supper with two of his Friends, he was at his Return to his Lodgings arrested for a Debt of about eight Pounds, which he owed at a Coffee-House, and conducted to the House of a Sheriff's Officer. The Account which he gives of this Misfortune in a Letter to one of the Gentlemen with whom he had supped, is too remarkable to be omitted.

"It was not a little unfortunate for me, that I spent yesterday's Evening with you; because the Hour hindered me from entering on my new Lodging; however, I have now got one; but such an one, as I believe Nobody would chuse.

"I was arrested at the Suit of Mrs *Read*, just as I was going up Stairs to Bed, at Mr *Bowyer*'s; but taken in so private a Manner, that I believe Nobody at the *White Lyon* is apprised of it. Tho' I let the Officers know the Strength (or rather Weakness of my Pocket) yet they treated me with the utmost Civility, and even when they conducted me to Confinement, 'twas in such a Manner, that I verily believe I could have escaped, which I would rather be ruined than have done; notwithstanding the whole Amount of my Finances was but three Pence halfpenny.

"In the first Place I must insist, that you will industriously conceal this from Mrs S————————s; because I would not have her good Nature suffer that Pain, which, I know, she would be apt to feel on this Occasion.

"Next I conjure you, dear Sir, by all the Ties of Friendship, by no Means to have one uneasy Thought on my Account; but to have the same Pleasantry of Countenance and unruffled Serenity of Mind, which (God be praised!) I have in this, and have had in a much severer Calamity. Furthermore, I charge you, if you value my Friendship as truly as I do yours, *not* to utter, or even harbour the least Resentment against Mrs *Read*. I believe she has ruin'd me, but I freely forgive her; and (tho' I will never more have any Intimacy with her) would, at a due Distance, rather do her an Act of Good, than ill Will. Lastly, (pardon the Expression) I *absolutely command* you not to offer me any pecuniary Assistance, nor to attempt getting me any from any one of your Friends. At another Time, or on any other Occasion, you may, dear Friend, be well assured, I would rather write to you in the submissive Stile of a Request, than that of a peremptory Command.

"However, that my truly valuable Friend may not think I am too proud to ask a Favour, let me entreat you to let me have your Boy to attend me for this Day, not only for the Sake of saving me the Expence of Porters; but for the Delivery of some Letters to People, whose Names I would not have known to Strangers.

"The civil Treatment I have thus far met from those, whose Prisoner I am, makes me thankful to the Almighty, that, tho' He has thought fit to visit me (on my Birth-night) with Affliction; yet (such is his great Goodness!) my Affliction is not without alleviating Circumstances. I murmur not, but am all Resignation to the *divine Will*. As to the World, I hope that I shall be endued by Heaven with that Presence of Mind, that serene Dignity in Misfortune, that constitutes the Character of a true Nobleman; a Dignity far beyond that of Coronets; a Nobility arising from the just Principles of Philosophy, refined and exalted, by those of Christianity.

He continued five Days at the Officer's, in Hopes that he should be able to procure Bail, and avoid the Necessity of going to Prison. The State in which he passed his Time, and the Treatment which he received, are very justly expressed by him in a Letter which he wrote to a Friend; "The whole Day, *says he*, has been employed in various People's filling my Head with their fool-ish chimerical Systems, which has obliged me coolly (as far as Nature will admit) to digest, and accommodate myself to, every different Person's Way of thinking; hurried from one wild System to another, 'till it has quite made a Chaos of my Imagination, and nothing done—Promised—disappointed—Order'd to send every hour, from one part of the Town to the other."————

When his Friends, who had hitherto caressed and applauded, found that to give Bail and pay the Debt was the same, they all refused to preserve him from a Prison, at the Expence of eight Pounds; and therefore after having been for some Time at the Officer's House, *at an immense Expence*, as he observes in his Letter, he was at length removed to *Newgate*.

This Expence he was enabled to support, by the Generosity of Mr *Nash* at *Bath*, who upon receiving from him an Account of his Condition, immediately sent him five Guineas, and promised to promote his Subscription at *Bath*, with all his Interest.

By his Removal to *Newgate*, he obtained at least a Freedom from Suspense, and Rest from the disturbing Vicissitudes of Hope and Disappointment; he now found that his Friends were only Companions, who were willing to share his Gaiety, but not to partake of his Misfortunes; and therefore he no longer expected any Assistance from them.

It must however be observed of one Gentleman, that he offered to relase him by paying the Debt, but that Mr *Savage* would not consent, I suppose, because he thought he had been before too burthensome to him.

He was offered by some of his Friends, that a Collection should be made for his Enlargement, but he *treated the Proposal*, and declared, *that he should again treat it, with Disdain. As to writing any mendicant Letters, he had too high a Spirit, and determined only to write to some Ministers of State, to try to regain his Pension.*

He continued to complain of those that had sent him into the Country, and objected to them, that he had *lost the Profits of his Play which had been finished three Years*, and in another Letter declares his Resolution to publish a Pamphlet, that the World might know how *he had been used*.

This Pamphlet was never written, for he in a very short Time recover'd his usual Tranquillity, and chearfully applied himself to more inoffensive Studies. He indeed steadily declared, that he was promised a yearly Allowance of fifty Pounds, and never received half the Sum, but he seemed to resign himself to that as well as to other Misfortunes, and lose the Remembrance of it in his Amusements, and Employments.

The Chearfulness with which he bore his Confinement, appears from the following Letter which he wrote *Jan.* 30th, to one of his Friends in *London*.

I Now write to you from my Confinement in *Newgate*, where I have been ever since Monday last was Sev'n-night; and where I enjoy myself with much more Tranquillity than I have known for upwards of a twelve-month past; having a Room entirely to myself, and persuing the Amusement of my poetical Studies, uninterrupted and agreeable to my Mind. I thank the Almighty, I am now all collected in myself, and tho' my Person is in Confinement, my Mind can expatiate on ample and useful Subjects, with all the Freedom imaginable. I am now more conversant with the Nine than ever; and if, instead of a *Newgate* Bird, I may be allowed to be a Bird of the Muses, I assure you, Sir, I sing very freely in my Cage; sometimes indeed in the plaintive Notes of the Nightingale; but, at others, in the chearful Strains of the Lark.——

In another Letter he observes, that he ranges from one Subject to another without confining himself to any particular Task, and that he was employed one Week upon one Attempt, and the next upon another.

Surely the Fortitude of this Man deserves, at least, to be mentioned with Applause, and whatever Faults may be imputed to him, the Virtue of *suffering well* cannot be denied him. The two Powers which, in the Opinion of *Epictetus*, constituted a wise Man, are those of *bearing* and *forbearing*, which it cannot indeed be affirmed to have been equally possessed by *Savage*, and indeed the Want of one obliged him very *frequently* to practise the other.

He was treated by Mr *Dagg*, the Keeper of the Prison, with great Humanity; was supported by him at his own Table without any certainty of Recompense, had a Room to himself, to which he could at any Time retire from all Disturbance, was allowed to stand at the Door of the Prison, and sometimes taken out into the Fields; so that he suffered fewer Hardships in the Prison, than he had been accustomed to undergo in the greatest part of his Life.

The Keeper did not confine his Benevolence to a gentle Execution of his Office, but made some Overtures to the Creditor for his Release, but without Effect; and continued, during the whole Time of his Imprisonment to treat him with the utmost Tenderness and Civility.

Virtue is undoubtedly most laudable in that State which makes it most difficult; and therefore the Humanity of a Gaoler, certainly deserves this publick Attestation; and the Man whose Heart has not been hardened by such an Employment, may be justly proposed as a Pattern of Benevolence. If an Inscription was once engraved to the *honest Toll-gatherer*, less Honours ought not to be paid *to the tender Gaoler*.

Mr. *Savage* very frequently received Visits, and sometimes Presents from his Acquaintances, but they did not amount to a Subsistence, for the greater Part of which he was indebted to the Generosity of this Keeper; but these Favours, however they might endear to him the particular Persons, from whom he received them, were very far from impressing upon his Mind any advantageous Ideas of the People of *Bristol*, and therefore he thought he could not more properly employ himself in Prison, than in writing the following Poem.

LONDON *and* BRISTOL *delineated.*

Two Sea-port Cities mark *Britannia*'s Fame,
And these from Commerce different Honours claim.
What different Honours shall the Muses pay,
While one inspires and one untunes the Lay?
    Now silver *Isis* bright'ning flows along,
Echoing from *Oxford*'s Shore each classic Song;

Then weds with *Thame*; and these, O *London*, see
Swelling with naval Pride, the Pride of Thee!
Wide deep unsullied *Thames* meand'ring glides
And bears thy Wealth on mild majestic Tides.   10
Thy Ships, with gilded Palaces that vie,
In glitt'ring Pomp, strike wond'ring *China*'s Eye;
And thence returning bear, in splendid State,
To *Britain*'s Merchants, *India*'s eastern Freight.
India, her Treasures from her western Shores,
Due at thy Feet, a willing Tribute pours;
Thy warring Navies distant Nations awe,
And bid the World obey thy righteous Law.
Thus shine thy manly Sons of lib'ral Mind;
Thy Change deep-busied, yet as Courts refin'd;   20
Councils, like Senates that enforce Debate
With fluent Eloquence and Reason's Weight.
Whose Patriot Virtue, lawless Pow'r controuls;
Their *British* emulating *Roman* Souls.
Of these the worthiest still selected stand,
Still lead the Senate, and still save the Land:
Social, not selfish, here, O Learning trace
Thy Friends, the Lovers of all human Race!

    In a dark Bottom sunk, O *Bristol* now,
With native Malice, lift thy low'ring Brow!   30
Then as some Hell-born Sprite, in mortal Guise,
Borrows the Shape of Goodness and belies,
All fair, all smug to yon proud Hall invite,
To feast all Strangers ape an Air polite!
From *Cambria* drain'd, or *England*'s western Coast,
Not elegant yet costly Banquets boast!
Revere, or seem the Stranger to revere;
Praise, fawn, profess, be all Things but sincere;
Insidious now, our bosom Secrets steal,
And these with sly sarcastic Sneer reveal.   40
Present we meet thy sneaking treach'rous Smiles;
The harmless Absent still thy Sneer reviles;
Such as in Thee all Parts superior find;
The Sneer that marks the Fool and Knave combin'd.
When melting Pity wou'd afford Relief,
The ruthless Sneer that Insult adds to Grief.
What Friendship can'st thou boast? what Honours claim?
To Thee each Stranger owes an injur'd Name.
What Smiles thy Sons must in their Foes excite?

Thy Sons to whom all Discord is Delight; 50
From whom eternal mutual Railing flows;
Who in each others Crimes, their own expose;
Thy Sons, tho' crafty, deaf to Wisdom's Call;
Despising all Men and despis'd by all.
Sons, while thy Clifs a ditch-like River laves,
Rude as thy Rocks, and muddy as thy Waves;
Of Thoughts as narrow as of Words immense;
As full of Turbulence as void of Sense:
Thee, Thee what senatorial Souls adorn?
Thy Natives sure wou'd prove a Senate's Scorn. 60
Do Strangers deign to serve Thee? what their Praise?
Their gen'rous Services thy Murmurs raise.
What Fiend malign, that o'er thy Air presides,
Around from Breast to Breast inherent glides,
And, as he glides, there scatters in a Trice
The lurking Seeds of ev'ry rank Device?
Let foreign Youths to thy Indentures run!
Each, each will prove, in thy adopted Son,
Proud, pert and dull—Tho' brilliant once from Schools,
Will scorn all Learning's as all Virtue's Rules; 70
And, tho' by Nature friendly, honest, brave,
Turn a sly, selfish, simp'ring, sharping Knave.
Boast petty-Courts, where 'stead of fluent Ease;
Of cited Precedents and learned Pleas;
'Stead of sage Council in the dubious Cause,
Attorneys chatt'ring wild, burlesque the Laws.
So shameless Quacks, who Doctor's Rights invade,
Of Jargon and of Poison form a Trade.
So canting Coblers, while from Tubs they teach,
Buffoon the Gospel they pretend to preach. 80
Boast petty Courts, whence Rules new Rigour draw;
Unknown to Nature's and to Statute Law;
Quirks that explain all saving Rights away,
To give th'Attorney and the Catch-poll Prey.
Is there where Law too rig'rous may descend?
Or Charity her kindly Hand extend?
Thy Courts, that shut when Pity wou'd redress,
Spontaneous open to inflict Distress.
Try Misdemeanours !—all thy Wiles employ,
Not to chastise the Offender but destroy; 90
Bid the large lawless Fine his Fate foretell;
Bid it beyond his Crime and Fortune swell.

Cut off from Service due to kindred Blood
To private Welfare and to public Good,
Pitied by all, but thee, he sentenc'd lies;
Imprison'd languishes, imprison'd dies,

****

Boast swarming Vessels, whose *Plœbeian* State
Owes not to Merchants but Mechanics Freight.
Boast nought but Pedlar Fleets—In War's Alarms,
Unknown to Glory, as unknown to Arms.
Boast thy base *Tolsey*, and thy turn-spit Dogs;
Thy *Hallier*'s Horses and thy human Hogs;
Upstarts and Mushrooms, proud, relentless Hearts;
Thou Blank of Sciences! Thou Dearth of Arts!
Such Foes as Learning once was doom'd to see;   10
Huns, *Goths*, and *Vandals* were but Types of Thee.

Proceed, great *Bristol*, in all-righteous Ways,
And let one Justice heighten yet thy Praise;
Still spare the Catamite and swinge the Whore,
And be, whate'er *Gomorrah* was before.

When he had brought this Poem to its present State, which, without considering the Chasm, is not perfect, he wrote to *London* an Account of his
Design, and informed his Friend, that he was determined to print it with
his Name; but enjoined him not to communicate his Intention to his *Bristol*
Acquaintance. The Gentleman surprised at his Resolution, endeavoured
to dissuade him from publishing it, at least, from prefixing his Name, and
declared, that he could not reconcile the Injunction of Secrecy with his
Resolution to own it at its first Appearance. To this Mr *Savage* returned an
Answer agreeable to his Character in the following Terms.

"I received yours this Morning and not without a little Surprize at the
Contents. To answer a Question with a Question, you ask me concerning
London and *Bristol*, *Why will I add* delineated? Why did Mr *Woolaston* add the
same Word to his Religion of Nature? I suppose that it was his Will and
Pleasure to add it in his Case; and it is mine to do so in my Own. You are
pleased to tell me, that you understand not, why Secrecy is injoin'd, and yet
I intend to set my Name to it. My Answer is—I have my private Reasons;
which I am not obliged to explain to any One. You doubt, my Friend Mr
S——— would not approve of it—And what is it to me whether he does or
not? Do you imagine, that Mr *S*——— is to dictate to me? If any Man, who
calls himself my Friend, should assume such an Air, I would spurn at his
Friendship with Contempt. You say, I seem to think so by not letting him
know it—And suppose I do, what then? Perhaps I can give Reasons for that
Disapprobation, very foreign from what you would imagine. You go on in

saying, suppose, I should not put my Name to it—My Answer is, that I will not suppose any such Thing, being determined to the contrary; neither, Sir, would I have you suppose, that I applied to you for Want of another Press: Nor would I have you imagine, that I owe Mr S——— Obligations which I do not."

Such was his Imprudence and such his obstinate Adherence to his own Resolutions, however absurd. A Prisoner! supported by Charity! and, whatever Insults he might have received during the latter Part of his Stay in *Bristol*, once caressed, esteemed, and presented with a liberal Collection, he could forget on a sudden his Danger, and his Obligations, to gratify the Petulance of his Wit, or the Eagerness of his Resentment, and publish a Satire by which he might reasonably expect, that he should alienate those who then supported him, and provoke those whom he could neither resist nor escape.

This Resolution, from the Execution of which, it is probable, that only his Death could have hindered him, is sufficient to show, how much he disregarded all Considerations that opposed his present Passions, and how readily he hazarded all future Advantages for any immediate Gratifications. Whatever was his predominant Inclination, neither Hope nor Fear hinder'd him from complying with it, nor had Opposition any other Effect than to heighten his Ardour and irritate his Vehemence.

This Performance was however laid aside, while he was employed in soliciting Assistance from several great Persons, and one Interruption succeeding another hinder'd him from supplying the Chasm, and perhaps from retouching the other Parts, which he can hardly be imagined to have finished, in his own Opinion; for it is very unequal, and some of the Lines are rather inserted to rhyme to others than to support or improve the Sense; but the first and last Parts are worked up with great Spirit and Elegance.

His Time was spent in the Prison for the most part in Study, or in receiving Visits; but sometimes he descended to lower Amusements, and diverted himself in the Kitchen with the Conversation of the Criminals; for it was not pleasing to him to be much without Company, and though he was very capable of a judicious Choice, he was often contented with the first that offered; for this he was sometimes reproved by his Friends who found him surrounded with Felons; but the Reproof was on that as on other Occasions thrown away; he continued to gratify himself, and to set very little Value on the Opinion of others.

But here, as in every other Scene of his Life, he made use of such Opportunities as occur'd of benefiting those who were more miserable than himself, and was always ready to perform any Offices of Humanity to his fellow Prisoners.

He had now ceased from corresponding with any of his Subscribers except one, who yet continued to remit him the twenty Pounds a Year which he had promised him, and by whom it was expected, that he would have been in a very short Time enlarged, because he had directed the Keeper to enquire after the State of his Debts.

However he took Care to enter his Name according to the Forms of the Court, that the Creditor might be obliged to make him some Allowance, if he was continued a Prisoner, and when on that Occasion he appeared in the Hall was treated with very unusual Respect.

But the Resentment of the City was afterwards raised by some Accounts that had been spread of the Satire, and he was informed that some of the Merchants intended to pay the Allowance which the Law required, and to detain him a Prisoner at their own Expence. This he treated as an empty Menace, and perhaps might have hasten'd the Publication, only to shew how much he was superior to their Insults, had not all his Schemes been suddenly destroyed.

When he had been six Months in Prison he received from one of his Friends in whose Kindness he had the greatest Confidence, and on whose Assistance he chiefly depended, a Letter that contained a Charge of very atrocious Ingratitude, drawn up in such Terms as sudden Resentment dictated. Mr *Savage* returned a very solemn Protestation of his Innocence, but however appeared much disturbed at the Accusation. Some Days afterwards he was seized with a Pain in his Back and Side, which as it was not violent was not suspected to be dangerous; but growing daily more languid and dejected, on the 25th of *July* he confined himself to his Room, and a Fever seized his Spirits. The Symptoms grew every Day more formidable, but his Condition did not enable him to procure any Assistance. The last Time that the Keeper saw him was on *July* the 31st, when *Savage* seeing him at his Bed-side said, with an uncommon Earnestness, *I have something to say to you, Sir*, but after a Pause, moved his Hand in a melancholy Manner, and finding himself unable to recollect what he was going to communicate, said *'Tis gone*. The Keeper soon after left him, and the next Morning he died. He was buried in the Church-yard of St *Peter*, at the Expence of the Keeper.

Such were the Life and Death of *Richard Savage*, a Man equally distinguished by his Virtues and Vices, and at once remarkable for his Weaknesses and Abilities.

He was of a middle Stature, of a thin Habit of Body, a long Visage, coarse Features, and melancholy Aspect; of a grave and manly Deportment, a solemn Dignity of Mien, but which upon a nearer Acquaintance softened into an engaging Easiness of Manners. His Walk was slow, and his Voice tremulous and mournful. He was easily excited to Smiles, but very seldom provoked to Laughter.

His Mind was in an uncommon Degree vigorous and active. His Judgment was accurate, his Apprehension quick, and his Memory so tenacious, that he was frequently observed to know what he had learned from others in a short Time better than those by whom he was informed, and could frequently recollect Incidents, with all their Combination of Circumstances, which few would have regarded at the present Time; but which the Quickness of his Apprehension impressed upon him. He had the peculiar Felicity, that his Attention never deserted him; he was present to every Object, and regardful of the most trifling Occurrences. He had the Art of escaping from his own Reflections and accomodating himself to every new Scene.

To this Quality is to be imputed the Extent of his Knowledge compared with the small Time which he spent in visible Endeavours to acquire it. He mingled in cursory Conversation with the same Steadiness of Attention as others apply to a Lecture, and, amidst the Appearance of thoughtless Gayety, lost no new Idea that was started, nor any Hint that could be improved. He had therefore made in Coffee-houses the same Proficiency as others in Studies; and it is remarkable, that the Writings of a Man of little Education and little Reading have an Air of Learning scarcely to be found in any other Performances, but which perhaps as often obscures as embellishes them.

His Judgment was eminently exact both with regard to Writings and to Men. The Knowledge of Life was indeed his chief Attainment, and it is not without some Satisfaction, that I can produce the Suffrage of *Savage* in favour of human Nature, of which he never appeared to entertain such odious Ideas, as some who perhaps had neither his Judgment nor Experience have published, either in Ostentation of their Sagacity, Vindication of their Crimes, or Gratification of their Malice.

His Method of Life particularly qualified him for Conversation, of which he knew how to practise all the Graces. He was never vehement or loud, but at once modest and easy, open and respectful, his Language was vivacious and elegant, and equally happy upon grave or humorous Subjects. He was generally censured for not knowing when to retire, but that was not the Defect of his Judgment, but of his Fortune; when he left his Company he was frequently to spend the remaining Part of the Night in the Street, or at least was abandoned to gloomy Reflections, which it is not strange that he delayed as long as he could, and sometimes forgot that he gave others Pain to avoid it himself.

It cannot be said, that he made Use of his Abilities for the Direction of his own Conduct; an irregular and dissipated Manner of Life had made him the Slave of every Passion that happened to be excited by the Presence of its Object, and that Slavery to his Passions reciprocally produced a Life irregular and dissipated. He was not Master of his own Motions, nor could promise any Thing for the next Day.

With Regard to his Oeconomy, nothing can be added to the Relation of his Life: he appeared to think himself born to be supported by others, and dispensed from all Necessity of providing for himself; he therefore never prosecuted any Scheme of Advantage, nor endeavoured even to secure the Profits which his Writings might have afforded him.

His Temper was in consequence of the Dominion of his Passions uncertain and capricious; he was easily engaged, and easily disgusted; but he is accused of retaining his Hatred more tenaciously than his Benevolence.

He was compassionate both by Nature and Principle, and always ready to perform Offices of Humanity; but when he was provoked, and very small Offences were sufficient to provoke him, he would prosecute his Revenge with the utmost Acrimony till his Passion had subsided.

His Friendship was therefore of little Value; for though he was zealous in the Support or Vindication of those whom he loved, yet it was always dangerous to trust him, because he considered himself as discharged by the first Quarrel, from all Ties of Honour or Gratitude; and would betray those Secrets which in the Warmth of Confidence had been imparted to him. This Practice drew upon him an universal Accusation of Ingratitude; nor can it be denied that he was very ready to set himself free from the Load of an Obligation; for he could not bear to conceive himself in a State of Dependence, his Pride being equally powerful with his other Passions, and appearing in the Form of Insolence at one time and of Vanity at another. Vanity the most innocent Species of Pride, was most frequently predominant: he could not easily leave off when he had once began to mention himself or his Works, nor ever read his Verses without stealing his Eyes from the Page, to discover in the Faces of his Audience, how they were affected with any favourite Passage.

A kinder Name than that of Vanity ought to be given to the Delicacy with which he was always careful to separate his own Merit from every other Man's; and to reject that Praise to which he had no Claim. He did not forget, in mentioning his Performances, to mark every Line that had been suggested or amended, and was so accurate as to relate that he owed *three Words* in *THE WANDERER*, to the Advice of his Friends.

His Veracity was questioned but with little reason; his Accounts, tho' not indeed always the same, were generally consistent. When he loved any Man, he suppress'd all his Faults, and when he had been offended by him, concealed all his Virtues: but his Characters were generally true, so far as he proceeded; tho' it cannot be denied that his Partiality might have sometimes the Effect of Falsehood.

In Cases indifferent he was zealous for Virtue, Truth and Justice; he knew very well the Necessity of Goodness to the present and future Happiness of Mankind; nor is there perhaps any Writer, who has less endeavoured to please by flattering the Appetites or perverting the Judgment.

As an Author, therefore, and he now ceases to influence Mankind in any other Character, if one Piece which he had resolved to suppress be excepted, he has very little to fear from the strictest moral or religious Censure. And though he may not be altogether secure against the Objections of the Critic, it must however be acknowledged, that his Works are the Productions of a Genius truly poetical; and, what many Writers who have been more lavishly applauded cannot boast, that they have an original Air, which has no Resemblance of any foregoing Writer; that the Versification and Sentiments have a Cast peculiar to themselves, which no Man can imitate with Success, because what was Nature in *Savage* would in another be Affectation. It must be confessed that his Descriptions are striking, his Images animated, his Fictions justly imagined, and his Allegories artfully persued; that his Diction is elevated, though sometimes forced, and his Numbers sonorous and majestick, though frequently sluggish and encumbered. Of his Stile the general Fault is Harshness, and its general Excellence is Dignity; of his Sentiments the prevailing Beauty is Sublimity, and Uniformity the prevailing Defect.

For his Life, or for his Writings, none who candidly consider his Fortune, will think an Apology either necessary or difficult. If he was not always sufficiently instructed in his Subject, his Knowledge was at least greater than could have been attained by others in the same State. If his Works were sometimes unfinished, Accuracy cannot reasonably be exacted from a Man oppressed with Want, which he has no Hope of relieving but by a speedy Publication. The Insolence and Resentment of which he is accused, were not easily to be avoided by a great Mind, irritated by perpetual Hardships and constrained hourly to return the Spurns of Contempt, and repress the Insolence of Prosperity; and Vanity may surely readily be pardoned in him, to whom Life afforded no other Comforts than barren Praises, and the Consciousness of deserving them.

Those are no proper Judges of his Conduct who have slumber'd away their Time on the Down of Affluence, nor will any wise Man presume to say, "Had I been in *Savage*'s Condition, I should have lived, or written, better than *Savage*."

This Relation will not be wholly without its Use, if those, who languish under any Part of his Sufferings, shall be enabled to fortify their Patience by reflecting that they feel only those Afflictions from which the Abilities of *Savage* did not exempt him; or those, who in Confidence of superior Capacities or Attainments disregard the common Maxims of Life, shall be reminded that nothing will supply the Want of Prudence, and that Negligence and Irregularity, long continued, will make Knowledge useless, Wit ridiculous, and Genius contemptible.

FINIS.

Introduction to the Harleian Miscellany

THOUGH the Scheme of the following *Miscellany* is so obvious, that the Title alone is sufficient to explain it; and though several Collections have been formerly attempted upon Plans, as to the Method, very little, but, as to the

Capacity and Execution, very different from Ours; we, being possessed of the greatest Variety for such a Work, hope for a more general Reception than those confined Schemes had the Fortune to meet with; and, therefore, think it not wholly unnecessary to explain our Intentions, to display the Treasure of Materials, out of which this *Miscellany* is to be compiled, and to exhibit a general Idea of the Pieces which we intend to insert in it.

THERE is, perhaps, no Nation, in which it is so necessary, as in our own to assemble, from Time to Time, the *small* Tracts and *fugitive* Pieces, which are occasionally published: For, besides the general Subjects of Enquiry, which are cultivated by us in common with every other learned Nation, our Constitution in Church and State naturally gives Birth to a Multitude of Performances, which would either not have been written, or could not have been made publick in any other Place.

THE *Form* of our *Government*, which gives every Man, that has Leisure, or Curiosity, or Vanity, the Right of enquiring into the Propriety of publick Measures; and, by Consequence, obliges those, who are intrusted with the Administration of *National* Affairs, to give an Account of their Conduct, to almost every Man, who demands it, may be reasonably imagined to have occasioned *innumerable* Pamphlets, which would never have appeared under *arbitrary* Governments, where every Man lulls himself in Indolence under Calamities, of which he cannot promote the Redress, or thinks it prudent to conceal the Uneasiness of which he cannot complain without Danger.

THE Multiplicity of *Religious Sects* tolerated among us, of which every one has found Opponents and Vindicators, is another Source of unexhaustible Publication, almost peculiar to ourselves; for, *Controversies* cannot be long continued, nor frequently revived, where an *Inquisitor* has a Right to shut up the Disputants in Dungeons, or where Silence can be imposed on either Party, by the Refusal of a *License*.

NOT that it should be inferred from hence, that *Political* or *Religious* Controversies are the *only* Products of the *Liberty* of the *British Press*; the Mind once let loose to Enquiry, and suffered to operate without Restraint, necessarily deviates into peculiar Opinions, and wanders in new Tracks, where she is indeed sometimes lost in a Labyrinth, from which, tho' she cannot return, and scarce knows how to proceed; yet, sometimes, makes useful Discoveries, or finds out nearer Paths to Knowledge.

THE boundless Liberty, with which every Man may write his own Thoughts, and the Opportunity of conveighing new Sentiments to the Publick, without Danger of suffering either Ridicule or Censure, which every Man may enjoy, whose Vanity does not incite him too hastily to own his Performances, natur-ally invites those, who employ themselves in Speculation, to try how their Notions will be received by a Nation, which exempts Caution from Fear, and Modesty from Shame; and it is no Wonder, that where Reputation may be gained, but needs not be lost, Multitudes are willing to try their Fortune, and thrust their Opinions into the Light, sometimes with unsuccessful Haste, and sometimes with happy Temerity.

It is observed, that, among the Natives of *England*, is to be found a greater Variety of Humour, than in any other Country; and, doubtless, where every Man has a full Liberty to propagate his Conceptions, Variety of Humour must produce Variety of Writers; and, where the Number of Authors is so great, there cannot but be some worthy of Distinction.

All these and many other Causes, too tedious to be enumerated, have contributed to make *Pamphlets* and *small Tracts* a very *important* Part of an *English* Library; nor are there any Pieces, upon which those, who aspire to the Reputation of *judicious* Collectors of Books, bestow more Attention, or greater Expence; because many Advantages may be expected from the Perusal of these small Productions, which are scarcely to be found in that of larger Works.

If we regard *History*, it is well known, that most *Political* Treatises have for a long Time appeared in this Form, and that the first Relations of Transactions, while they are yet the Subject of Conversation, divide the Opinions, and employ the Conjectures of Mankind, are delivered by these *petty* Writers, who have Opportunities of collecting the different Sentiments of Disputants, of enquiring the Truth from living Witnesses, and of copying their Representations from the Life; and, therefore, they preserve a Multitude of particular Incidents, which are forgotten in a short Time, or omitted in formal Relations, and which are yet to be considered as Sparks of Truth, which, when united, may afford Light in some of the darkest Scenes of State, as, we doubt not, will be sufficiently proved in the Course of this *Miscellany*; and which it is, therefore, the *Interest* of the Publick to preserve unextinguished.

The same Observation may be extended to Subjects of yet more Importance. In Controversies that relate to the Truths of Religion, the first Essays of Reformation are generally timorous; and those, who have Opinions to offer, which they expect to be opposed, produce their Sentiments, by Degrees; and for the most Part in *small Tracts:* By Degrees, that they may not shock their Readers with too many Novelties at once; and in *small Tracts*, that they may be easily dispersed, or privately printed; almost every Controversy, therefore, has been, for a Time, carried on in Pamphlets, nor has swelled into larger Volumes, till the first Ardor of the Disputants has subsided, and they have recollected their Notions with Coolness enough to digest them into Order, consolidate them into Systems, and fortify them with Authorities.

From *Pamphlets*, consequently, are to be learned the *Progress* of every Debate; the various State, to which the Questions have been changed; the Artifices and Fallacies, which have been used; and the Subterfuges, by which Reason has been eluded: In such Writings may be seen how the Mind has been opened by Degrees, how one Truth has led to another, how Error has been disentangled, and Hints improved to Demonstration. Which Pleasure, and many others are lost by him, that only reads the *larger Writers*, by whom these scattered Sentiments are collected, who will see none of the Changes of Fortune, which every Opinion has passed through, will have no Opportunity of remarking the transient Advantages, which Error, may sometimes obtain, by the Artifices of its Patron, or the successful Rallies, by which Truth regains the Day, after a Repulse; but will be to him, who traces the Dispute through, into particular Gradations, as he that hears of a Victory, to him that sees the Battle.

SINCE the Advantages of preserving these *small Tracts* are so numerous; our Attempt to unite them in Volumes cannot be thought either *useless* or *unseasonable*; for there is *no other* Method of securing them from Accidents; and they have already been so long neglected, that this Design cannot be delayed, without hazarding the Loss of many Pieces, which deserve to be transmitted to another Age.

THE Practice of publishing Pamphlets, on the most important Subjects, has now prevailed more than *two Centuries* among us; and, therefore, it cannot be doubted, but that, as no large Collections have been yet made, many curious Tracts must have perished; but it is too late to lament that Loss; nor ought we to reflect upon it, with any other View, than that of quickening our Endeavours, for the Preservation of those that yet remain, of which we have now a *greater Number*, than was, perhaps, ever amassed by any *one* Person.

THE first Appearance of Pamphlets among us is generally thought to be at the new Opposition raised against the Errors and Corruptions of the Church of *Rome*. Those, who were first convinced of the Reasonableness of the *New Learning*, as it was *then* called, propagated their Opinions in small Pieces, which were cheaply printed; and, what was then of great Importance, easily concealed. These Treatises were generally printed in foreign Countries, and are not, therefore, always very correct. There was not then that Opportunity of Printing in *private*, for, the Number of Printers was small, and the Presses were easily overlooked by the Clergy, who spared no Labour or Vigilance for the Suppression of *Heresy*. There is, however, Reason to suspect, that some Attempts were made to carry on the Propagation of Truth by a *secret* Press; for one of the first Treatises, in Favour of the Reformation, is said, at the End, to be printed at *Greenwich, by the Permission of the Lord of Hosts.*

IN the Time of King *Edward the Sixth*, the Presses were employed in Favour of the *Reformed* Religion, and *small Tracts* were dispersed over the Nation, to reconcile them to the new Forms of Worship. In this Reign, likewise, *Political* Pamphlets may be said to have been begun, by the Address of the Rebels of *Devonshire*; all which Means propagating the Sentiments of the People so disturbed the Court, that no sooner was Queen *Mary* resolved to reduce her Subjects to the *Romish* Superstition; but she artfully, by a *Charter* granted to certain Freemen of *London*, in whose Fidelity, no doubt, she confided, intirely prohibited all Presses, but what should be licensed by them; which Charter is that by which the Corporation of *Stationers*, in *London*, is at this Time incorporated.

UNDER the Reign of Queen *Elizabeth*, when Liberty again began to flourish, the Practice of writing Pamphlets became more general; Presses were multiplied, and Books more dispersed; and, I believe, it may properly be said, that the *Trade of Writing* began at this Time, and that it has ever since gradually increased in the Number, though, perhaps, not in the Stile of those that followed it.

IN this Reign, was erected the first *secret* Press against the Church as now Established, of which I have found any certain Account. It was employed by the *Puritans*, and conveighed from one Part of the Nation to another, by them, as they found themselves in Danger of Discovery. From this Press issued most of the Pamphlets against *Whitgift*, and his Associates, in the Ecclesiastical Government; and, when it was at last seized at *Manchester*, it was employed upon a Pamphlet, called, *MORE WORK FOR A COOPER*.

IN the peaceable Reign of King *James*, those Minds, which might, perhaps, with less Disturbance, of the World, have been engrossed by War, were employed in Controversy; and Writings of all Kinds were multiplied among us. The Press, however, was not wholly engaged in Polemical Performances, for more innocent Subjects were sometimes treated; and it deserves to be remarked, because it is not generally known, that the Treatises of *Husbandry* and *Agriculture*, which were published about that Time, are so numerous, that it can scarcely be imagined by whom they were written, or to whom they were sold.

THE next Reign is too well known to have been a Time of Confusion, and Disturbance, and Disputes of every Kind; and the Writings, which were produced, bear a natural Proportion to the Number of the Questions that were discussed at that Time; each Party had its Authors, and its Presses, and no Endeavours were omitted to gain Proselytes to every Opinion. I know not whether this may not properly be called, *The Age of Pamphlets*; for, though they, perhaps, may not arise to such Multitudes as Mr. *Rawlinson* imagined, they were, undoubtedly, more numerous than can be conceived by any who have not had an Opportunity of examining them.

AFTER the Restoration, the same differences, in Religious Opinions, are well known to have subsisted, and the same Political Struggles to have been frequently renewed; and, therefore, a great Number of Pens were employed, on different Occasions, till, at length, all other Disputes were absorbed in the *Popish* Controversy.

FROM the Pamphlets which these different Periods of Time produced, it is proposed, that this *Miscellany* shall be compiled; for which it cannot be supposed that Materials will be wanting, and, therefore, the only Difficulty will be in what Manner to dispose them.

THOSE who have gone before us, in Undertakings of this Kind, have ranged the Pamphlets, which Chance threw into their Hands, without any Regard either to the Subject on which they treated, or the Time in which they were written; a Practice, in no wise, to be imitated by us, who want for no Materials; of which we shall chuse those we think best for the *particular* Circumstances of *Times* and *Things*, and most instructing and entertaining to the Reader.

OF the different Methods which present themselves, upon the first View of the great Heaps of Pamphlets, which the *Harleian Library* exhibits, the two which merit most Attention, are to distribute the Treatises according to their *Subjects* or their *Dates*; but neither of these Ways can be conveniently followed. By ranging our Collection in *Order of Time*, we must necessarily publish those Pieces first, which least engage the Curiosity of the Bulk of Mankind, and our Design must fall to the Ground for Want of Encouragement, before it can be so far advanced as to obtain general Regard: By confining ourselves for any long Time to any *single Subject*, we shall reduce our Readers to one Class, and, as we shall lose all the Grace of Variety, shall disgust all those who read chiefly to be diverted. There is likewise one Objection of equal Force, against both these Methods, that we shall preclude ourselves from the Advantage of any future Discoveries, and we cannot hope to assemble at once all the Pamphlets which have been written in any Age or on any Subject.

IT may be added, in Vindication of our intended Practice, that it is the same with that of *Photius*, whose Collections are no less Miscellaneous than ours, and who declares, that he leaves it to his Reader, to reduce his Extracts under their proper Heads.

MOST of the Pieces, which shall be offered in this Collection to the Publick, will be introduced by short Prefaces, in which will be given some Account of the Reasons for which they are inserted; Notes will be sometimes adjoined for the Explanation of obscure Passages, or obsolete Expressions; and Care will be taken to mingle Use and Pleasure through the whole Collection. Notwithstanding *every Subject* may not be relished by *every Reader*; yet the Buyer may be assured that each Number will repay his generous Subscription.

To Miss — on Her Playing upon the Harpsichord in a Room Hung with Some Flower-Pieces of Her Own Painting

When Stella strikes the tuneful String
In Scenes of imitated Spring,
Where Beauty lavishes her Powers
On Beds of never-fading Flowers;
And Pleasure propagates around
Each Charm of modulated Sound;
Ah! think not, in the dang'rous hour,

The Nymph fictitious as the Flower;
But shun, rash Youth, the gay Alcove,
Nor tempt the Snares of wily Love.   10
    When Charms thus press on every Sense,
What Thought of Flight, or of Defence?
Deceitful Hope, and vain Desire,
Forever flutter o'er her Lyre;
Delighting, as the Youth draws nigh,
To point the Glances of her Eye;
And forming with unerring Art,
New Chains to hold the Captive-Heart.
    But on those Regions of Delight,
Might *Truth* intrude, with daring Flight,   20
Could Stella, sprightly, fair, and young,
One Moment hear the Moral Song,
Instruction with her Flowers might spring,
And *Wisdom* warble from her String.
    Mark, when from thousand mingled Dyes
Thou seest one pleasing Form arise;
How active Light, and thoughtful Shade,
In greater Scenes each other aid;
Mark, when the diff'rent Notes agree
In friendly Contrariety;   30
How Passion's well-accorded Strife
Gives all the Harmony of Life:
Thy Pictures shall thy Conduct frame,
Consistent still, tho' not the same;
Thy Musick teach the nobler Art,
To tune the regulated Heart.

Prologue Spoken by Mr Garrick at the Opening of the Theatre in Drury-Lane

WHEN Learning's Triumph o'er her barb'rous Foes
First rear'd the Stage, immortal SHAKESPEAR rose;
Each Change of many-colour'd Life he drew,
Exhausted Worlds, and then imagin'd new:
Existence saw him spurn her bounded Reign,
And panting Time toil'd after him in vain:
His pow'rful Strokes presiding Truth impress'd,
And unresisted Passion storm'd the Breast.

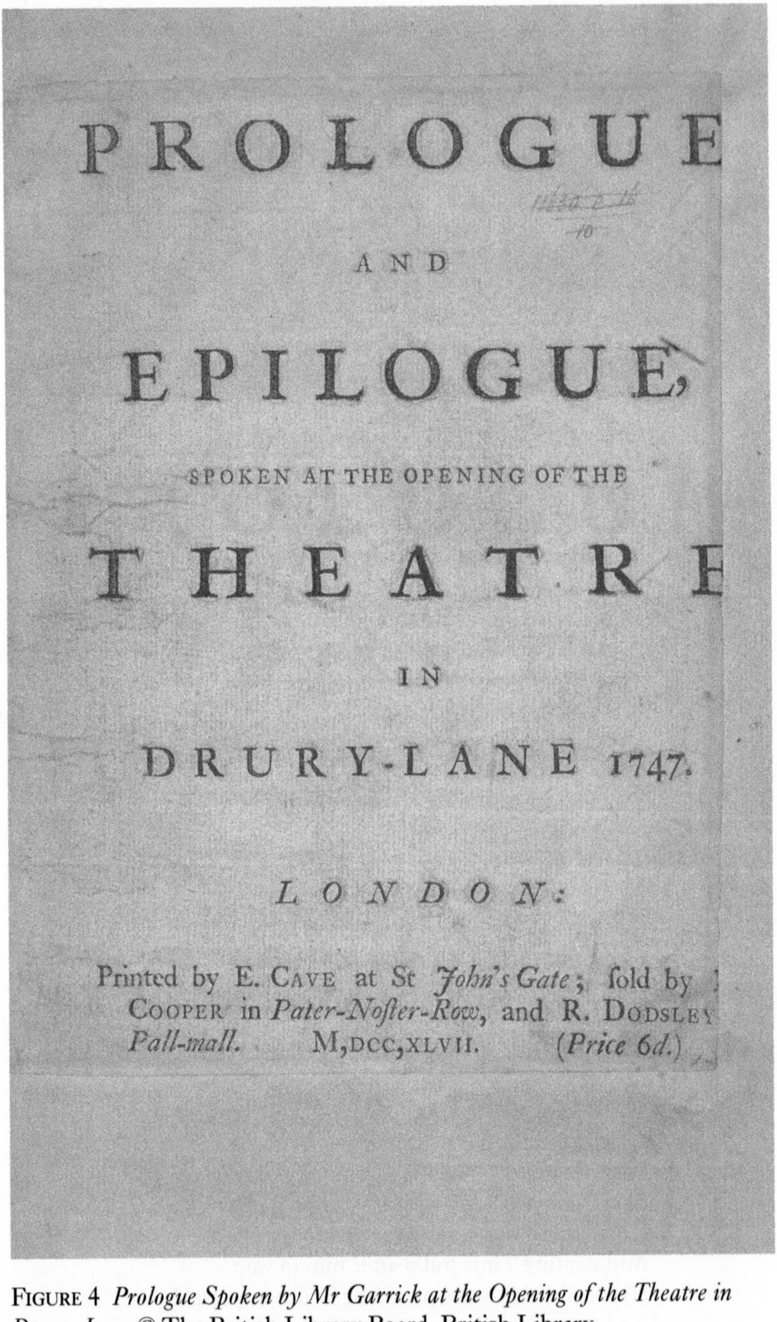

PROLOGUE

AND

EPILOGUE,

SPOKEN AT THE OPENING OF THE

THEATRE

IN

DRURY-LANE 1747.

LONDON:

Printed by E. CAVE at St *John's Gate* ; fold by
COOPER in *Pater-Noster-Row*, and R. DODSLEY
Pall-mall. M,DCC,XLVII. (*Price 6d.*)

FIGURE 4 *Prologue Spoken by Mr Garrick at the Opening of the Theatre in Drury-Lane* © The British Library Board, British Library.

Then JOHNSON came, instructed from the School,
To please in Method, and invent by Rule;   10
His studious Patience, and laborious Art,
By regular Approach essay'd the Heart;
Cold Approbation gave the ling'ring Bays,
For those who durst not censure, scarce cou'd praise.
A Mortal born he met the general Doom,
But left, like *Egypt*'s Kings, a lasting Tomb.

The Wits of *Charles* found easier Ways to Fame,
Nor wish'd for JOHNSON's Art, or SHAKESPEAR's Flame,
Themselves they studied, as they felt, they writ,
Intrigue was Plot, Obscenity was Wit.   20
Vice always found a sympathetick Friend;
They pleas'd their Age, and did not aim to mend.
Yet Bards like these aspir'd to lasting Praise,
And proudly hop'd to pimp in future Days.
Their Cause was gen'ral, their Supports were strong,
Their Slaves were willing, and their Reign was long;
Till Shame regain'd the Post that Sense betray'd,
And Virtue call'd Oblivion to her Aid.

Then crush'd by Rules, and weaken'd as refin'd,
For Years the Pow'r of Tragedy declin'd;   30
From Bard, to Bard, the frigid Caution crept,
Till Declamation roar'd, while Passion slept.
Yet still did Virtue deign the Stage to tread,
Philosophy remain'd, though Nature fled.
But forc'd at length her antient Reign to quit,
She saw great *Faustus* lay the Ghost of Wit:
Exulting Folly hail'd the joyful Day,
And Pantomime, and Song, confirm'd her Sway.

But who the coming Changes can presage,
And mark the future Periods of the Stage?—   40
Perhaps if Skill could distant Times explore,
New *Behns*, new *Durfeys*, yet remain in Store.
Perhaps, where *Lear* has rav'd, and *Hamlet* dy'd,
On flying Cars new Sorcerers may ride.
Perhaps, for who can guess th' Effects of Chance?
Here *Hunt* may box, or *Mahomet* may dance.

Hard is his Lot, that here by Fortune plac'd,
Must watch the wild Vicissitudes of Taste;
With ev'ry Meteor of Caprice must play,

And chase the new-blown Bubbles of the Day.   50
Ah! let not Censure term our Fate our Choice,
The Stage but echoes back the publick Voice.
The Drama's Laws the Drama's Patrons give,
For we that live to please, must please to live.

    Then prompt no more the Follies you decry,
As Tyrants doom their Tools of Guilt to die;
'Tis yours this Night to bid the Reign commence
Of rescu'd Nature, and reviving Sense;
To chase the Charms of Sound, the Pomp of Show,
For useful Mirth, and salutary Woe;   60
Bid scenic Virtue form the rising Age,
And Truth diffuse her Radiance from the Stage.

The Vision of Theodore, the Hermit of Teneriffe, found in his Cell

SON of Perseverance, whoever thou art, whose Curiosity has led thee hither, read and be wise. He that now calls upon thee is *Theodore* the Hermit of *Teneriffe*, who in the fifty-seventh Year of his Retreat left this Instruction to Mankind, lest his solitary Hours should be spent in vain.

I was once what thou art now, a Groveller on the Earth, and a Gazer at the Sky; I traffick'd and heaped Wealth together, I loved and was favoured, I wore the Robe of Honour, and heard the Musick of Adulation; I was ambitious, and rose to Greatness; I was unhappy, and retired. I sought for some time what I at length found here, a Place where all real Wants might be easily supplied, and where I might not be under the Necessity of purchasing the Assistance of Men by the Toleration of their Follies. Here I saw Fruits and Herbs and Water, and here determined to wait the Hand of Death, which I hope, when at last it comes, will fall lightly upon me.

Forty-eight Years had I now passed in Forgetfulness of all mortal Cares, and without any Inclination to wander farther than the Necessity of procuring Sustenance required; but as I stood one Day beholding the Rock that overhangs my Cell, I found in myself a Desire to climb it; and when I was on its Top, was in the same manner determined to scale the next, till by Degrees I conceived a Wish to view the Summit of the Mountain, at the Foot of which I had so long resided. This Motion of my Thoughts I endeavoured to suppress, not because it appeared criminal, but because it was new; and all Change, not evidently for the better, alarms a Mind taught by Experience to distrust itself. I was often afraid that my Heart was deceiving me, that my

Impatience of Confinement rose from some earthly Passion, and that my Ardour to survey the Works of Nature, was only a hidden Longing to mingle once again in the Scenes of Life. I therefore endeavoured to settle my Thoughts into their former State, but found their Distraction every Day greater. I was always reproaching myself with the Want of Happiness within my Reach; and at last began to question whether it was not Laziness rather than Caution, that restrained me from climbing to the Summit of *Teneriffe*.

I rose therefore before the Day, and began my Journey up the Steep of the Mountain; but I had not advanced far, old as I was and burthened with provisions, when the Day began to shine upon me; the Declivities grew more precipitous, and the Sand slided from beneath my Feet; at last, fainting with Labour, I arrived at a small Plain, almost inclosed by Rocks and open only to the East. I sat down to rest a while, in full Persuasion that when I had recovered my Strength, I should proceed on my Design; but when once I had tasted Ease, I found many Reasons against disturbing it. The Branches spread a Shade over my Head, and the Gales of Spring wafted Odours to my Bosom.

As I sat thus forming alternately Excuses for Delay, and Resolutions to go forward, an irresistable Heaviness suddenly surprized me; I laid my Head upon the Bank and resigned myself to Sleep: when methought I heard a Sound as of the Flight of Eagles, and a Being of more than human Dignity stood before me. While I was deliberating how to address him, he took me by the Hand with an Air of Kindness, and asked me solemnly, but without Severity, '*Theodore*, whither art thou going?' I am climbing, answered I, to the Top of the Mountain, to enjoy a more extensive Prospect of the Works of Nature. 'Attend first (said he) to the Prospect which this Place affords, and what thou dost not understand I will explain. I am one of the benevolent Beings who watch over the Children of the Dust, to preserve them from those Evils which will not ultimately terminate in Good, and which they do not, by their own Faults, bring upon themselves. Look round therefore without Fear: observe, contemplate, and be instructed.'

Encouraged by this Assurance, I looked and beheld a Mountain higher than *Teneriffe*, to the Summit of which the Human Eye could never reach; when I had tired myself with gazing upon its Height, I turned my Eyes towards its Foot, which I could easily discover, but was amazed to find it without Foundation, and placed inconceiveably in Emptiness and Darkness. Thus I stood terrified and confused; above were Tracts inscrutable, and below was total Vacuity. But my Protector, with a Voice of Admonition, cried out, *Theodore*, be not affrighted, but raise thy Eyes again, the *Mountain* of *Existence* is before thee, survey it and be wise.

I then looked with more deliberate Attention, and observed the Bottom of the Mountain to be of gentle Rise, and overspread with Flowers; the Middle to be more steep, embarrassed with Crags, and interrupted by Precipices, over which hung Branches loaded with Fruits, and among which were scattered Palaces and Bowers. The Tracts which my Eye could reach nearest the Top were generally barren; but there were among the Clefts of the Rocks, a few hardy Evergreens, which though they did not give much Pleasure to the Sight or Smell, yet seemed to cheer the Labour and facilitate the Steps of those who were clambering among them.

Then beginning to examine more minutely the different Parts, I observed, at a great Distance a Multitude of both Sexes issuing into View from the Bottom of the Mountain. Their first Actions I could not accurately discern; but as they every Moment approached nearer, I found that they amused themselves with gathering Flowers under the Superintendance of a modest Virgin in a white Robe, who seemed not over solicitous to confine them to any settled Pace, or certain Track; for she knew that the whole Ground was smooth and solid, and that they could not easily be hurt or bewildered. When, as it often happened, they plucked a Thistle for a Flower, *Innocence*, so was she called, would smile at the Mistake. Happy said I, are they who are under so gentle a Government, and yet are safe. But I had no Opportunity to dwell long on the Consideration of their Felicity; for I found that *Innocence* continued her Attendance but a little Way, and seemed to consider only the flowery Bottom of the Mountain as her proper Province. Those whom she abandoned scarcely knew that they were left, before they perceived themselves in the Hands of *Education*, a Nymph more severe in her Aspect and imperious in her Commands, who confined them to certain Paths, in their Opinion, too narrow and too rough. These they were continually solicited to leave by *Appetite*, whom *Education* could never fright away, though she sometimes awed her to such Timidity, that the Effects of her Presence were scarcely perceptible. Some went back to the first Part of the Mountain, and seemed desirous of continuing busied in plucking Flowers, but were no longer guarded by *Innocence*; and such as *Education* could not force back, proceeded up the Mountain by some miry Road, in which they were seldom seen, and scarcely ever regarded.

As *Education* led her Troop up the Moutain, nothing was more observable than that she was frequently giving them Cautions to beware of *Habits*; and was calling out to one or another at every Step, that a *Habit* was ensnaring them; that they would be under the Dominion of *Habit* before they perceived their Danger; and that those whom a *Habit* should once subdue, had little hope of regaining their Liberty.

Of this Caution, so frequently repeated, I was very solicitous to know the Reason, when my Protector directed my Regard to a Troop of Pygmies, which appeared to walk silently before those that were climbing the Mountain, and each to smooth the Way before her Follower. I found that I had missed the Notice of them before, both because they were so minute as not easily to be discerned, and because they grew every Moment nearer in their Colour to the

Objects with which they were surrounded. As the Followers of *Education* did not appear to be sensible of the Presence of these dangerous Associates, or, ridiculing their diminutive Size, did not think it possible that human Beings should ever be brought into Subjection by such feeble Enemies, they generally heard her Precepts of Vigilance with Wonder; and, when they thought her Eye withdrawn, treated them with Contempt. Nor could I myself think her Cautions so necessary as her frequent Inculcation seemed to suppose, till I observed that each of these petty Beings held secretly a Chain in her Hand, with which she prepared to bind those whom she found within her Power. Yet these *Habits* under the Eye of *Education* went quietly forward, and seemed very little to encrease in Bulk or Strength; for though they were always willing to join with *Appetite*, yet when *Education* kept them apart from her, they would very punctually obey Command, and make the narrow Roads in which they were confin'd easier and smoother.

It was observable, that their Stature was never at a Stand, but continually growing or decreasing, yet not always in the same Proportions; nor could I forbear to express my Admiration, when I saw in how much less Time they generally gained than lost Bulk. Though they grew slowly in the Road of *Education*, it might however be perceived that they grew; but if they once deviated at the Call of *Appetite*, their Stature soon became gigantic, and their Strength was such, that *Education* pointed out to her Tribe many that were led in Chains by them, whom she could never more rescue from their Slavery. She pointed them out, but with little Effect; for all her Pupils appeared confident of their own Superiority to the strongest *Habit*, and some seemed in secret to regret that they were hindred from following the Triumph of *Appetite*.

It was the peculiar Artifice of *Habit* not to suffer her Power to be felt at first. Those whom she led, she had the Address of appearing only to attend, but was continually doubling her Chains upon her Companions, which were so slender in themselves, and so silently fastened, that while the Attention was engaged by other Objects, they were not easily perceived. Each Link grew tighter as it had been longer worn, and when by continual Additions they became so heavy as to be felt, they were very frequently too strong to be broken.

When *Education* had proceeded in this Manner to the Part of the Mountain where the Declivity began to grow craggy, she resigned her Charge to two Powers of superior Aspect. The meaner of them appeared capable of presiding in Senates or governing Nations, and yet watched the Steps of the other with the most anxious Attention, and was visibly confounded and perplexed if ever she suffered her Regard to be drawn away. The other seemed to approve her Submission as pleasing, but with such a Condescension as plainly shewed that she claimed it as due; and indeed so great was her Dignity and Sweetness, that he who would not reverence, must not behold her.

"*Theodore*," said my Protector, "be fearless, and be wise; approach these Powers, whose Dominion extends to all the remaining Part of the *Mountain* of *Existence*." I trembled, and ventured to address the inferior Nymph, whose Eyes though piercing and awful, I was not unable to sustain. "Bright Power, said I, by whatever Name it is lawful to address thee, tell me, thou who presidest here, on what Condition thy Protection will be granted." "It will be granted! said she, only to Obedience. *I* am *Reason*, of all subordinate Beings the noblest and the greatest; who, if thou wilt receive my Laws, will reward thee like the rest of my Votaries, by conducting thee to *Religion*." Charmed by her Voice and Aspect, I professed my Readiness to follow her. She then presented me to her *Mistress*, who looked upon me with Tenderness. I bowed before her, and she smil'd.

When *Education* delivered up those for whose Happiness she had been so long solicitous, she seemed to expect that they should express some Gratitude for her Care, or some Regret at the Loss of that Protection which she had hitherto afforded them. But it was easy to discover, by the Alacrity which broke out at her Departure, that her Presence had been long displeasing, and that she had been teaching those who felt in themselves no want of Instruction. They all agreed in rejoicing that they should no longer be subject to her Caprices, or disturb'd by her Documents, but should be now under the Direction only of *Reason*, to whom they made no doubt of being able to recommend themselves by a steady Adherence to all her Precepts. *Reason* counselled them at their first Entrance upon her Province, to inlist themselves among the Votaries of *Religion*; and informed them, that if they trusted to her alone, they would find the same Fate with her other Admirers, whom she had not been able to secure against *Appetites* and *Passions*, and who having been seized by *Habits* in the Regions of *Desire*, had been dragged away to the Caverns of *Despair*. Her Admonition was vain, the greater Number declared against any other Direction, and doubted not but by her Superintendency they should climb with Safety up the *Mountain* of *Existence*. "My Power, said *Reason*, is to advise, not to compel; I have already told you the Danger of your Choice. The Path now seems plain and even, but there are Asperities and Pitfals, over which *Religion* only can conduct you. Look upwards, and you perceive a Mist before you settled upon the highest visible Part of the Mountain, a Mist by which my Prospect is terminated, and which is pierced only by the Eyes of *Religion*. Beyond it are the Temples of *Happiness*, in which those who climb the Precipice by her Direction, after the Toil of their Pilgrimages repose for ever. I know not the Way, and therefore can only conduct you to a better Guide. *Pride* has sometimes reproached me with the Narrowness of my View, but when she endeavoured to extend it, could only shew me, below the Mist, the Bowers of *Content*; even they vanished as I fix'd my Eyes upon them; and those whom she persuaded to travel towards them were inchained by *Habits*, and ingulfed by *Despair*, a cruel Tyrant, whose

Caverns are beyond the Darkness on the right Side and on the left, from whose Prisons none can escape, and whom I cannot teach you to avoid."

Such was the Declaration of *Reason* to those who demanded her Protection. Some that recollected the Dictates of *Education*, finding them now seconded by another Authority, submitted with Reluctance to the strict Decree, and engaged themselves among the Followers of *Religion*, who were distinguished by the Uniformity of their March, though many of them were Women, and by their continual Endeavours to move upwards, without appearing to regard the Prospects which at every Step courted their Attention.

All those who determined to follow either *Reason* or *Religion* were continually importuned to forsake the Road, sometimes by *Passions*, and sometimes by *Appetites*, of whom both had reason to boast the Success of their Artifices; for so many were drawn into By-paths, that any way was more populous than the right. The Attacks of the *Appetites* were more impetuous, those of the *Passions* longer continued. The *Appetites* turned their Followers directly from the true Way, but the *Passions* marched at first in a Path nearly in the same Direction with that of *Reason* and *Religion*; but deviated by slow Degrees, till at last they entirely changed their Course. *Appetite* drew aside the Dull, and *Passion* the Sprightly. Of the *Appetites Lust* was the strongest, and of the *Passions Vanity*. The most powerful Assault was to be feared, when a *Passion* and an *Appetite* joined their Enticements; and the Path of *Reason* was best followed, when a Passion called to one Side, and an Appetite to the other.

These Seducers had the greatest Success upon the Followers of *Reason*, over whom they scarcely ever failed to prevail, except when they counteracted one another. They had not the same Triumphs over the Votaries of *Religion*; for though they were often led aside for a Time, *Religion* commonly recalled them by her Emissary *Conscience*, before *Habit* had Time to enchain them. But they that professed to obey *Reason*, if once they forsook her, seldom returned; for she had no Messenger to summon them but *Pride*, who generally betrayed her Confidence, and imployed all her Skill to support *Passion*; and if ever she did her Duty, was found unable to prevail, if *Habit* had interposed.

I soon found that the great Danger to the Followers of *Religion* was only from *Habit*; every other Power was easily resisted, nor did they find any Difficulty when they inadvertently quitted her, to find her again by the Direction of *Conscience*, unless they had given Time to *Habit* to draw her Chain behind them and bar up the Way by which they had wandered. Of some of those the Condition was justly to be pitied, who turned at every Call of *Conscience*, and tried, but without Effect, to burst the Chains of *Habit:* saw *Religion* walking forward at a Distance, saw her with Reverence, and longed to join her; but were, when ever they approached her, withheld by *Habit*, and languished in sordid Bondage which they could not escape, though they scorned and hated it.

It was evident that the *Habits* were so far from growing weaker by these repeated Contests, that if they were not totally overcome, every Struggle enlarged their Bulk and increased their Strength; and a *Habit* oppos'd and victorious was more than twice as strong as before the Contest. The Manner in which those who were weary of their Tyranny endeavoured to escape from them, appeared by the Event to be generally wrong; they tried to loose their Chains one by one, and to retreat by the same Degrees as they advanced; but before the Deliverance was compleated, *Habit* always threw new Chains upon her Fugitive; nor did any escape her but those who by an Effort sudden and violent, burst their Shackles at once, and left her at a Distance; and even of these many rushing too precipitately forward, and hindered by their Terrors from stopping where they were safe, were fatigued with their own Vehemence, and resigned themselves again to that Power from whom an Escape must be so dearly bought, and whose Tyranny was little felt, except when it was resisted.

Some however there always were, who, when they found *Habit* prevailing over them, called upon *Reason* or *Religion* for Assistance; each of them willingly came to the Succour of her Suppliant; but neither with the same Strength nor the same Success. *Habit*, insolent with her Power would often presume to parley with *Reason*, and offer to loose some of her Chains if the rest might remain. To this *Reason*, who was never certain of Victory, frequently consented, but always found her Concession destructive, and saw the Captive led away by *Habit* to his former Slavery. *Religion* never submitted to Treaty, but held out her Hand with Certainty of Conquest; and if the Captive to whom she gave it did not quit his Hold, always led him away in Triumph, and placed him in the direct Path to the Temple of *Happiness*, where *Reason* never failed to congratulate his Deliverance, and encourage his Adherence to that Power to whose timely Succour he was indebted for it.

When the Traveller was again placed in the Road of *Happiness*, I saw *Habit* again gliding before him, but reduced to the Stature of a Dwarf, without Strength and without Activity; but when the *Passions* or *Appetites* which had before seduced him, made their Approach, *Habit* would on a sudden start into Size, and with unexpected Violence push him towards them. The Wretch thus impelled on one Side, and allured on the other, too frequently quitted the Road of *Happiness*, to which, after his second Deviation from it, he rarely returned. But if by a timely Call upon *Religion*, the Force of *Habit* was eluded, her Attacks grew fainter, and at last her Correspondence with the Enemy was entirely destroyed. She then began to employ those restless Faculties, in compliance with the Power which she could not overcome; and as she grew again in Stature and in Strength, cleared away the Asperities of the Road to *Happiness*.

From this Road I could not easily withdraw my Attention, because all who travelled it appeared chearful and satisfied; and the farther they proceeded, the greater appeared their Alacrity, and the stronger their Conviction of the Wisdom of their Guide. Some who had never deviated but by short Excursions, had *Habit* in the Middle of their Passage, vigorously supporting them and driving off their *Appetites* and *Passions*, which attempted to interrupt their Progress. Others, who had entered this Road late, or had long forsaken it, were toiling on without her Help at least, and commonly against her Endeavours. But I observed, when they approached to the barren Top, that few were able to proceed without some Support from *Habit*, and that those whose *Habits* were strong, advanced toward the Mists with little Emotion, and entered them at last with Calmness and Confidence; after which they were seen only by the Eye of *Religion*, and though *Reason* looked after them with the most earnest Curiosity, she could only obtain a faint Glimpse, when her Mistress, to enlarge her Prospect, raised her from the Ground. *Reason* however, discerned that they were safe, but *Religion* saw that they were happy.

'Now, *Theodore*, said my Protector, withdraw thy View from the Regions of Obscurity, and see the Fate of those who, when they were dismissed by *Education*, would admit no Direction but that of *Reason*. Survey their Wanderings, and be wise.'

I looked then upon the Road of *Reason*, which was indeed, so far as it reached, the same with that of *Religion*, nor had *Reason* discovered it but by her Instructions. Yet when she had once been taught it, she clearly saw that it was right; and *Pride* had sometimes incited her to declare that she discovered it herself, and persuaded her to offer herself as a Guide to *Religion*; whom after many vain Experiments she found it her highest Privilege to follow. *Reason* was however at last well instructed in Part of the Way, and appeared to teach it with some Success, when her Precepts were not misrepresented by *Passion*, or her Influence overborn by *Appetite*. But neither of these Enemies was she able to resist. When *Passion* seized upon her Votaries, she seldom attempted Opposition; she seemed indeed to contend with more Vigour against *Appetite*, but was generally overwearied in the Contest; and if either of her Opponents had confederated with *Habit*, her Authority was wholly at an End. When *Habit* endeavoured to captivate the Votaries of *Religion*, she grew by slow Degrees, and gave time to escape; but in seizing the unhappy Followers of *Reason*, she proceeded as one that had nothing to fear, and enlarged her Size, and doubled her Chains without Intermission, and without Reserve.

Of those who forsook the Directions of *Reason*, some were led aside by the Whispers of *Ambition*, who was perpetually pointing to stately Palaces, situated on Eminences on either side, recounting the Delights of Affluence, and boasting the Security of Power. They were easily persuaded to follow her, and *Habit* quickly threw her Chains upon them; they were soon convinced of the Folly of their Choice, but few of them attempted to return. *Ambition* led them forward from Precipice to Precipice, where many fell and were seen no more. Those that escaped, were, after a long Series of Hazards, generally delivered over to *Avarice*, and enlisted by her in the Service of *Tyranny*, where they continued to heap up Gold, till their Patrons or their Heirs pushed them headlong at last into the Caverns of *Despair*.

Others were inticed by *Intemperance* to ramble in search of those Fruits that hung over the Rocks, and filled the Air with their Fragrance. I observed, that the *Habits* which hovered about these soon grew to an enormous Size, nor were there any who less attempted to return to *Reason*, or sooner sunk into the Gulphs that lay before them. When these first quitted the Road, *Reason* looked after them with a Frown of Contempt, but had little Expectations of being able to reclaim them; for the Bowl of Intoxication was of such Qualities, as to make them lose all Regard but for the present Moment; neither *Hope* nor *Fear* could enter their Retreats, and *Habit* had so absolute a Power, that even *Conscience*, if *Religion* had employed her in their Favour, would not have been able to force an Entrance.

There were others whose Crime it was rather to neglect *Reason*, than to disobey her, and who retreated from the Heat and Tumult of the Way, not to the Bowers of *Intemperance*, but to the Maze of *Indolence*. They had this Peculiarity in their Condition, that they were always in sight of the Road of *Reason*, always wishing for her Presence, and always resolving to return to-morrow. In these was most eminently conspicuous the Subtlety of *Habit*, who hung imperceptible Shackles upon them, and was every Moment leading them farther from the Road, which they always imagined that they had the Power of reaching. They wandered on from one Double of the Labyrinth to another with the Chains of Habit hanging secretly upon them, till as they advanced, the Flowers grew paler, and the Scents fainter: they proceeded in their dreary March without Pleasure in their Progress, yet without Power to return; and had this Aggravation above all others, that they were criminal but not delighted. The Drunkard for a Time laughed over his Wine; the ambitious Man triumphed in the Miscarriage of his Rival; but the Captives of *Indolence* had neither Superiority nor Merriment. *Discontent* lowered in their Looks, and *Sadness* hovered round their Shades; yet they crawled on reluctant and gloomy, till they arrived at the Depth of the Recess, varied only with Poppies and Nightshade, where the Dominion of *Indolence* terminates, and the hopeless Wanderer is delivered up to *Melancholy:* the Chains of *Habit* are rivetted for ever, and *Melancholy* having tortured her Prisoner for a Time, consigns him at last to the Cruelty of *Despair*.

While I was musing on this miserable Scene, my Protector called out to me, 'Remember, *Theodore*, and be wise, and let not HABIT prevail against thee.' I started, and beheld myself surrounded by the Rocks of *Teneriffe*; the Birds of Light were singing in the Trees, and the Glances of the Morning darted upon me.

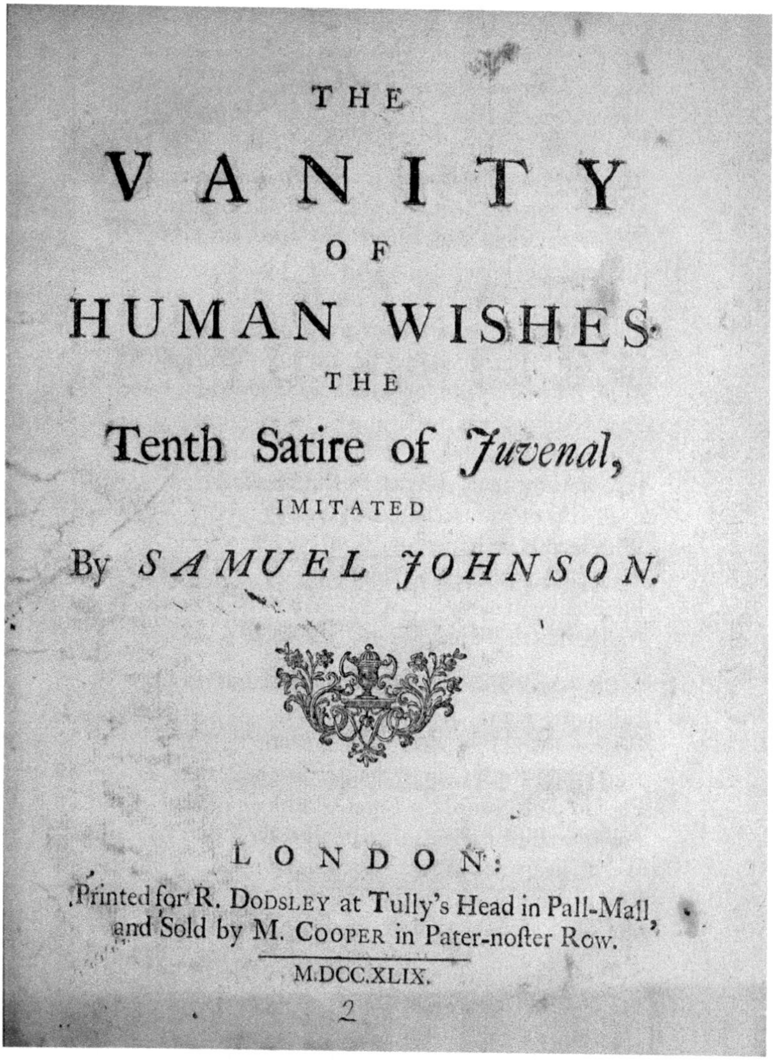

THE
VANITY
OF
HUMAN WISHES.
THE
Tenth Satire of *Juvenal*,
IMITATED
By *SAMUEL JOHNSON.*

LONDON:
Printed for R. DODSLEY at Tully's Head in Pall-Mall,
and Sold by M. COOPER in Pater-noster Row.

M.DCC.XLIX.

2

FIGURE 5 *The Vanity of Human Wishes* (1749), title page (Bodl. G. Pamph. 1732 [2]). Courtesy of the Bodleian Library, University of Oxford.

The Vanity of Human Wishes: The Tenth Satire of Juvenal Imitated

LET Observation with extensive View,
Survey Mankind, from *China* to *Peru*;
Remark each anxious Toil, each eager Strife,
And watch the busy Scenes of crouded Life;
Then say how Hope and Fear, Desire and Hate,
O'erspread with Snares the clouded Maze of Fate,
Where wav'ring Man, betray'd by vent'rous Pride,
To tread the dreary Paths without a Guide;
As treach'rous Phantoms in the Mist delude,
Shuns fancied Ills, or chases airy Good.   10
How rarely Reason guides the stubborn Choice,
Rules the bold Hand, or prompts the suppliant Voice,
How Nations sink, by darling Schemes oppress'd,
When Vengeance listens to the Fool's Request.
Fate wings with ev'ry Wish th'afflictive Dart,
Each Gift of Nature, and each Grace of Art,
With fatal Heat impetuous Courage glows,
With fatal Sweetness Elocution flows,
Impeachment stops the Speaker's pow'rful Breath,
And restless Fire precipitates on Death.   20

　　But scarce observ'd the Knowing and the Bold,
Fall in the gen'ral Massacre of Gold;
Wide-wasting Pest! that rages unconfin'd,
And crouds with Crimes the Records of Mankind,
For Gold his Sword the Hireling Ruffian draws,
For Gold the hireling Judge distorts the Laws;
Wealth heap'd on Wealth, nor Truth nor Safety buys,
The Dangers gather as the Treasures rise.

　　Let Hist'ry tell where rival Kings command,
And dubious Title shakes the madded Land,   30
When Statutes glean the Refuse of the Sword,
How much more safe the Vassal than the Lord,
Low sculks the Hind beneath the Rage of Pow'r,
And leaves the *bonny Traytor* in the *Tow'r*,
Untouch'd his Cottage, and his Slumbers sound,
Tho' Confiscation's Vulturs clang around.

The needy Traveller, serene and gay,
Walks the wild Heath, and sings his Toil away.
Does Envy seize thee? crush th'upbraiding Joy,
Encrease his Riches and his Peace destroy,   40
New Fears in dire Vicissitude invade,
The rustling Brake alarms, and quiv'ring Shade,
Nor Light nor Darkness bring his Pain Relief,
One shews the Plunder, and one hides the Thief.

Yet still the gen'ral Cry the Skies assails
And Gain and Grandeur load the tainted Gales;
Few know the toiling Statesman's Fear or Care,
Th'insidious Rival and the gaping Heir.

Once more, *Democritus*, arise on Earth,
With chearful Wisdom and instructive Mirth,   50
See motley Life in modern Trappings dress'd,
And feed with varied Fools th'eternal Jest:
Thou who couldst laugh where Want enchain'd Caprice,
Toil crush'd Conceit, and Man was of a Piece;
Where Wealth unlov'd without a Mourner dy'd;
And scarce a Sycophant was fed by Pride;
Where ne'er was known the Form of mock Debate,
Or seen a new-made Mayor's unwieldy State;
Where change of Fav'rites made no Change of Laws,
And Senates heard before they judg'd a Cause;   60
How wouldst thou shake at *Britain*'s modish Tribe,
Dart the quick Taunt, and edge the piercing Gibe?
Attentive Truth and Nature to descry,
And pierce each Scene with Philosophic Eye,
To thee were solemn Toys or empty Shew,
The Robes of Pleasure and the Veils of Woe:
All aid the Farce, and all thy Mirth maintain,
Whose Joys are causeless, or whose Griefs are vain.

Such was the Scorn that fill'd the Sage's Mind,
Renew'd at ev'ry Glance on Humankind;   70
How just that Scorn ere yet thy Voice declare,
Search every State, and canvass ev'ry Pray'r.

Unnumber'd Suppliants croud Preferment's Gate,
Athirst for Wealth, and burning to be great;
Delusive Fortune hears th'incessant Call,
They mount, they shine, evaporate, and fall.
On ev'ry Stage the Foes of Peace attend,

Hate dogs their Flight, and Insult mocks their End.
Love ends with Hope, the sinking Statesman's Door
Pours in the Morning Worshiper no more;   80
For growing Names the weekly Scribbler lies,
To growing Wealth the Dedicator flies,
From every Room descends the painted Face,
That hung the bright *Palladium* of the Place,
And smoak'd in Kitchens, or in Auctions sold,
To better Features yields the Frame of Gold;
For now no more we trace in ev'ry Line
Heroic Worth, Benevolence Divine:
The Form distorted justifies the Fall,
And Detestation rids th'indignant Wall.   90

But will not *Britain* hear the last Appeal,
Sign her Foes Doom, or guard her Fav'rites Zeal;
Through Freedom's Sons no more Remonstrance rings,
Degrading Nobles and controuling Kings;
Our supple Tribes repress their Patriot Throats,
And ask no Questions but the Price of Votes;
With Weekly Libels and Septennial Ale,
Their Wish is full to riot and to rail.

In full-blown Dignity, see *Wolsey* stand,
Law in his Voice, and Fortune in his Hand: 100
To him the Church, the Realm, their Pow'rs consign,
Thro' him the Rays of regal Bounty shine,
Turn'd by his Nod the Stream of Honour flows,
His Smile alone Security bestows:
Still to new Heights his restless Wishes tow'r,
Claim leads to Claim, and Pow'r advances Pow'r;
Till Conquest unresisted ceas'd to please,
And Rights submitted, left him none to seize.
At length his Sov'reign frowns—the Train of State
Mark the keen Glance, and watch the Sign to hate.   110
Where-e'er he turns he meets a Stranger's Eye,
His Suppliants scorn him, and his Followers fly;
Now drops at once the Pride of aweful State,
The golden Canopy, the glitt'ring Plate,
The regal Palace, the luxurious Board,
The liv'ried Army, and the menial Lord.
With Age, with Cares, with Maladies oppress'd,
He seeks the Refuge of Monastic Rest.

Grief aids Disease, remember'd Folly stings,
And his last Sighs reproach the Faith of Kings. 120

Speak thou, whose Thoughts at humble Peace repine,
Shall *Wolsey*'s Wealth, with *Wolsey*'s End be thine?
Or liv'st thou now, with safer Pride content,
The richest Landlord on the Banks of *Trent?*
For why did *Wolsey* by the Steps of Fate,
On weak Foundations raise th' enormous Weight?
Why but to sink beneath Misfortune's Blow,
With louder Ruin to the Gulphs below?

What gave great *Villiers* to th' Assassin's Knife,
And fix'd Disease on *Harley*'s closing Life? 130
What murder'd *Wentworth*, and what exil'd *Hyde*,
By Kings protected and to Kings ally'd?
What but their Wish indulg'd in Courts to shine,
And Pow'r too great to keep or to resign?

When first the College Rolls receive his Name,
The young Enthusiast quits his Ease for Fame;
Resistless burns the Fever of Renown,
Caught from the strong Contagion of the Gown;
O'er *Bodley*'s Dome his future Labours spread,
And *Bacon*'s Mansion trembles o'er his Head; 140
Are these thy Views? proceed, illustrious Youth,
And Virtue guard thee to the Throne of Truth,
Yet should thy Soul indulge the gen'rous Heat,
Till captive Science yields her last Retreat;
Should Reason guide thee with her brightest Ray,
And pour on misty Doubt resistless Day;
Should no false Kindness lure to loose Delight,
Nor Praise relax, nor Difficulty fright;
Should tempting Novelty thy Cell refrain,
And Sloth's bland Opiates shed their Fumes in vain; 150
Should Beauty blunt on Fops her fatal Dart,
Nor claim the Triumph of a letter'd Heart;
Should no Disease thy torpid Veins invade,
Nor Melancholy's Phantoms haunt thy Shade;
Yet hope not Life from Grief or Danger free,
Nor think the Doom of Man revers'd for thee:
Deign on the passing World to turn thine Eyes,
And pause awhile from Learning to be wise;
There mark what Ills the Scholar's Life assail,

Toil, Envy, Want, the Garret, and the Jail.   160
See Nations slowly wise, and meanly just,
To buried Merit raise the tardy Bust.
If Dreams yet flatter, once again attend,
Hear *Lydiat*'s Life, and *Galileo*'s End.

Nor deem, when Learning her last Prize bestows
The glitt'ring Eminence exempt from Foes;
See when the Vulgar 'scap'd, despis'd or aw'd,
Rebellion's vengeful Talons seize on *Laud*.
From meaner Minds, tho' smaller Fines content
The plunder'd Palace or sequester'd Rent;   170
Mark'd out by dangerous Parts he meets the Shock,
And fatal Learning leads him to the Block:
Around his Tomb let Art and Genius weep,
But hear his Death, ye Blockheads, hear and sleep.

The festal Blazes, the triumphal Show,
The ravish'd Standard, and the captive Foe,
The Senate's Thanks, the Gazette's pompous Tale,
With Force resistless o'er the Brave prevail.
Such Bribes the rapid *Greek* o'er *Asia* whirl'd,
For such the steady *Romans* shook the World;   180
For such in distant Lands the *Britons* shine,
And stain with Blood the *Danube* or the *Rhine*;
This Pow'r has Praise, that Virtue scarce can warm,
Till Fame supplies the universal Charm.
Yet Reason frowns on War's unequal Game,
Where wasted Nations raise a single Name,
And mortgag'd States their Grandsires Wreaths regret
From Age to Age in everlasting Debt;
Wreaths which at last the dear-bought Right convey
To rust on Medals, or on Stones decay.   190

On what Foundation stands the Warrior's Pride?
How just his Hopes let *Swedish Charles* decide;
A Frame of Adamant, a Soul of Fire,
No Dangers fright him, and no Labours tire;
O'er Love, o'er Force, extends his wide Domain,
Unconquer'd Lord of Pleasure and of Pain;
No Joys to him pacific Scepters yield,
War sounds the Trump, he rushes to the Field;
Behold surrounding Kings their Pow'r combine,
And One capitulate, and One resign;   200

Peace courts his Hand, but spread her Charms in vain;
"Think Nothing gain'd, he cries, till nought remain,
On *Moscow*'s Walls till *Gothic* Standards fly,
And all is Mine beneath the Polar Sky."
The March begins in Military State,
And Nations on his Eye suspended wait;
Stern Famine guards the solitary Coast,
And Winter barricades the Realms of Frost;
He comes, nor Want nor Cold his Course delay;—
Hide, blushing Glory, hide *Pultowa*'s Day: 210
The vanquish'd Hero leaves his broken Bands,
And shews his Miseries in distant Lands;
Condemn'd a needy Supplicant to wait,
While Ladies interpose, and Slaves debate.
But did not Chance at length her Error mend?
Did no subverted Empire mark his End?
Did rival Monarchs give the fatal Wound?
Or hostile Millions press him to the Ground?
His Fall was destin'd to a barren Strand,
A petty Fortress, and a dubious Hand;   220
He left the Name, at which the World grew pale,
To point a Moral, or adorn a Tale.

All Times their Scenes of pompous Woes afford,
From *Persia*'s Tyrant to *Bavaria*'s Lord.
In gay Hostility, and barb'rous Pride,
With half Mankind embattled at his Side,
Great *Xerxes* comes to seize the certain Prey,
And starves exhausted Regions in his Way;
Attendant Flatt'ry counts his Myriads o'er,
Till counted Myriads sooth his Pride no more;   230
Fresh Praise is try'd till Madness fires his Mind,
The Waves he lashes, and enchains the Wind;
New Pow'rs are claim'd, new Pow'rs are still bestow'd,
Till rude Resistance lops the spreading God;
The daring *Greeks* deride the Martial Shew,
And heap their Vallies with the gaudy Foe;
Th'insulted Sea with humbler Thoughts he gains,
A single Skiff to speed his Flight remains;
Th' incumber'd Oar scarce leaves the dreaded Coast
Through purple Billows and a floating Host.   240

The bold *Bavarian*, in a luckless Hour,
Tries the dread Summits of *Cesarean* Pow'r,

With unexpected Legions bursts away,
And sees defenceless Realms receive his Sway;
Short Sway! fair *Austria* spreads her mournful Charms,
The Queen, the Beauty, sets the World in Arms;
From Hill to Hill the Beacons rousing Blaze
Spreads wide the Hope of Plunder and of Praise;
The fierce *Croatian*, and the wild *Hussar*,
And all the Sons of Ravage croud the War;   250
The baffled Prince in Honour's flatt'ring Bloom
Of hasty Greatness finds the fatal Doom,
His Foes Derision, and his Subjects Blame,
And steals to Death from Anguish and from Shame.

Enlarge my Life with Multitude of Days,
In Health, in Sickness, thus the Suppliant prays;
Hides from himself his State, and shuns to know,
That Life protracted is protracted Woe.
Time hovers o'er, impatient to destroy,
And shuts up all the Passages of Joy: 260
In vain their Gifts the bounteous Seasons pour,
The Fruit Autumnal, and the Vernal Flow'r,
With listless Eyes the Dotard views the Store,
He views, and wonders that they please no more;
Now pall the tastless Meats, and joyless Wines,
And Luxury with Sighs her Slave resigns.
Approach, ye Minstrels, try the soothing Strain,
And yield the tuneful Lenitives of Pain:
No Sounds alas would touch th' impervious Ear,
Though dancing Mountains witness'd *Orpheus* near;   270
Nor Lute nor Lyre his feeble Pow'rs attend,
Nor sweeter Musick of a virtuous Friend,
But everlasting Dictates croud his Tongue,
Perversely grave, or positively wrong.
The still returning Tale, and ling'ring Jest,
Perplex the fawning Niece and pamper'd Guest,
While growing Hopes scarce awe the gath'ring Sneer,
And scarce a Legacy can bribe to hear;
The watchful Guests still hint the last Offence,
The Daughter's Petulance, the Son's Expence,   280
Improve his heady Rage with treach'rous Skill,
And mould his Passions till they make his Will.

Unnumber'd Maladies each Joint invade,
Lay Siege to Life and press the dire Blockade;

But unextinguish'd Av'rice still remains,
And dreaded Losses aggravate his Pains;
He turns, with anxious Heart and cripled Hands,
His Bonds of Debt, and Mortgages of Lands;
Or views his Coffers with suspicious Eyes,
Unlocks his Gold, and counts it till he dies.   290

But grant, the Virtues of a temp'rate Prime
Bless with an Age exempt from Scorn or Crime;
An Age that melts in unperceiv'd Decay,
And glides in modest Innocence away;
Whose peaceful Day Benevolence endears,
Whose Night congratulating Conscience cheers;
The gen'ral Fav'rite as the gen'ral Friend:
Such Age there is, and who could wish its End?

Yet ev'n on this her Load Misfortune flings,
To press the weary Minutes flagging Wings: 300
New Sorrow rises as the Day returns,
A Sister sickens, or a Daughter mourns.
Now Kindred Merit fills the sable Bier,
Now lacerated Friendship claims a Tear.
Year chases Year, Decay pursues Decay,
Still drops some Joy from with'ring Life away;
New Forms arise, and diff'rent Views engage,
Superfluous lags the Vet'ran on the Stage,
Till pitying Nature signs the last Release,
And bids afflicted Worth retire to Peace.   310

But few there are whom Hours like these await,
Who set unclouded in the Gulphs of Fate.
From *Lydia*'s Monarch should the Search descend,
By *Solon* caution'd to regard his End,
In Life's last Scene what Prodigies surprise,
Fears of the Brave, and Follies of the Wise?
From *Marlb'rough*'s Eyes the Streams of Dotage flow,
And *Swift* expires a Driv'ler and a Show.

The teeming Mother, anxious for her Race,
Begs for each Birth the Fortune of a Face: 320
Yet *Vane* could tell what Ills from Beauty spring;
And *Sedley* curs'd the Form that pleas'd a King.
Ye Nymphs of rosy Lips and radiant Eyes,
Whom Pleasure keeps too busy to be wise,
Whom Joys with soft Varieties invite

By Day the Frolick, and the Dance by Night,
Who frown with Vanity, who smile with Art,
And ask the latest Fashion of the Heart,
What Care, what Rules your heedless Charms shall save,
Each Nymph your Rival, and each Youth your Slave?   330
An envious Breast with certain Mischief glows,
And Slaves, the Maxim tells, are always Foes.
Against your Fame with Fondness Hate combines,
The Rival batters, and the Lover mines.
With distant Voice neglected Virtue calls,
Less heard, and less the faint Remonstrance falls;
Tir'd with Contempt, she quits the slipp'ry Reign,
And Pride and Prudence take her Seat in vain.
In croud at once, where none the Pass defend,
The harmless Freedom, and the private Friend.   340
The Guardians yield, by Force superior ply'd;
By Int'rest, Prudence; and by Flatt'ry, Pride.
Here Beauty falls betray'd, despis'd, distress'd,
And hissing Infamy proclaims the rest.

   Where then shall Hope and Fear their Objects find?
Must dull Suspence corrupt the stagnant Mind?
Must helpless Man, in Ignorance sedate,
Swim darkling down the Current of his Fate?
Must no Dislike alarm, no Wishes rise,
No Cries attempt the Mercies of the Skies?   350
Enquirer, cease, Petitions yet remain,
Which Heav'n may hear, nor deem Religion vain.
Still raise for Good the supplicating Voice,
But leave to Heav'n the Measure and the Choice.
Safe in his Pow'r, whose Eyes discern afar
The secret Ambush of a specious Pray'r,
Implore his Aid, in his Decisions rest,
Secure whate'er he gives, he gives the best.
Yet with the Sense of sacred Presence prest,
When strong Devotion fills thy glowing Breast,   360
Pour forth thy Fervours for a healthful Mind,
Obedient Passions, and a Will resign'd;
For Love, which scarce collective Man can fill;
For Patience sov'reign o'er transmuted Ill;
For Faith, that panting for a happier Seat,
Thinks Death kind Nature's Signal of Retreat:
These Goods for Man the Laws of Heav'n ordain,

These Goods he grants, who grants the Pow'r to gain;
With these celestial Wisdom calms the Mind,
And makes the Happiness she does not find.   370
                    FINIS.

The Vanity of Wealth: An Ode
To a Friend

No more thus brooding o'er yon heap,
With Av'rice painful vigils keep.
Still unenjoy'd the present store,
Still endless sighs are breath'd for more.
O! quit the shadow, catch the prize,
Which not all *India*'s treasure buys!
　　To purchase heav'n, has gold the pow'r?
Can gold remove the mortal hour?
In life, can *Love* be bought with gold?
Are *Friendship*'s pleasures to be sold?   10
No—all that's worth a wish, a thought,
Fair *Virtue* gives, unbrib'd, unbought.
Cease, then, on trash thy hopes to bind,
Let nobler views engage thy mind.
　　With *Science* tread the wond'rous way,
Or learn the *Muse*'s moral lay;
In social hours indulge thy soul,
Where *Mirth* and *Temp'rance* mix the bowl,
To virtuous *Love* resign thy breast,
And be, by blessing *Beauty*, blest.   20
　　Thus taste the feast by Nature spread,
Ere Youth and all its joys are fled;
Come, taste with me the balm of life,
Secure from pomp, and wealth, and strife.
I boast whate'er for man was meant,
In health, and *Stella*, and content:
And scorn, oh! let that scorn be thine!
Mere things of clay, that dig the mine.

'DICTIONARY' JOHNSON

The Rambler

No. 1. Tuesday, 20 March 1750.

Cur tamen hoc libeat potius decurrere campo,
Per quem magnus equos Auruncæ flexit alumnus,
Si vacat, et placidi rationem admittitis, edam.

Juv.

Why to expatiate in this beaten field,
Why arms, oft us'd in vain, I mean to wield;
If time permit, and candour will attend,
Some satisfaction this essay may lend.

Elphinston.*

The difficulty of the first address on any new occasion, is felt by every man in his transactions with the world, and confessed by the settled and regular forms of salutation which necessity has introduced into all languages. Judgment was wearied with the perplexity of being forced upon choice, where there was no motive to preference; and it was found convenient that some easy method of introduction should be established, which, if it wanted the allurement of novelty, might enjoy the security of prescription.

Perhaps few authors have presented themselves before the public, without wishing that such ceremonial modes of entrance had been anciently established, as might have freed them from those dangers which the desire of pleasing is certain to produce, and precluded the vain expedients of softening censure by apologies, or rousing attention by abruptness.

The epic writers have found the proemial part of the poem such an addition to their undertaking, that they have almost unanimously adopted the first lines of Homer, and the reader needs only be informed of the subject to know in what manner the poem will begin.

But this solemn repetition is hitherto the peculiar distinction of heroic poetry; it has never been legally extended to the lower orders of literature, but

---

* Mr. Elphinston, to whom the author of these papers is indebted for many elegant translations of the mottos which are inserted from the Edinburgh edition, now keeps an academy for young gentlemen, at Brompton, near Kensington.

seems to be considered as an hereditary privilege, to be enjoyed only by those who claim it from their alliance to the genius of Homer.

The rules which the injudicious use of this prerogative suggested to Horace, may indeed be applied to the direction of candidates for inferior fame; it may be proper for all to remember, that they ought not to raise expectation which it is not in their power to satisfy, and that it is more pleasing to see smoke brightening into flame, than flame sinking into smoke.

This precept has been long received both from regard to the authority of Horace and its conformity to the general opinion of the world, yet there have been always some, that thought it no deviation from modesty to recommend their own labours, and imagined themselves entitled by indisputable merit to an exemption from general restraints, and to elevations not allowed in common life. They, perhaps, believed that when, like Thucydides, they bequeathed to mankind κτῆμα ἐς ἀεὶ, *an estate for ever*, it was an additional favour to inform them of its value.

It may, indeed, be no less dangerous to claim, on certain occasions, too little than too much. There is something captivating in spirit and intrepidity, to which we often yield, as to a resistless power; nor can he reasonably expect the confidence of others, who too apparently distrusts himself.

Plutarch, in his enumeration of the various occasions, on which a man may without just offence proclaim his own excellencies, has omitted the case of an author entering the world; unless it may be comprehended under his general position, that a man may lawfully praise himself for those qualities which cannot be known but from his own mouth; as when he is among strangers, and can have no opportunity of an actual exertion of his powers. That the case of an author is parallel will scarcely be granted, because he necessarily discovers the degree of his merit to his judges, when he appears at his trial. But it should be remembered, that unless his judges are inclined to favour him, they will hardly be persuaded to hear the cause.

In love, the state which fills the heart with a degree of solicitude next that of an author, it has been held a maxim, that success is most easily obtained by indirect and unperceived approaches; he who too soon professes himself a lover, raises obstacles to his own wishes, and those whom disappointments have taught experience, endeavour to conceal their passion till they believe their mistress wishes for the discovery. The same method, if it were practicable to writers, would save many complaints of the severity of the age, and the caprices of criticism. If a man could glide imperceptibly into the favour of the publick, and only proclaim his pretensions to literary honours when he is sure of not being rejected, he might commence author with better hopes, as his failings might escape contempt, though he shall never attain much regard.

But since the world supposes every man that writes ambitious of applause, as some ladies have taught themselves to believe that every man intends love, who expresses civility, the miscarriage of any endeavour in learning raises an unbounded contempt, indulged by most minds without scruple, as an honest triumph over unjust claims, and exorbitant expectations. The artifices of those who put themselves in this hazardous state, have therefore been multiplied in proportion to their fear as well as their ambition; and are to be looked upon with more indulgence, as they are incited at once by the two great movers of the human mind, the desire of good, and the fear of evil. For who can wonder that, allured on one side, and frightned on the other, some should endeavour to gain favour by bribing the judge with an appearance of respect which they do not feel, to excite compassion by confessing weakness of which they are not convinced, and others to attract regard by a shew of openness and magnanimity, by a daring profession of their own deserts, and a publick challenge of honours and rewards.

The ostentatious and haughty display of themselves has been the usual refuge of diurnal writers, in vindication of whose practice it may be said, that what it wants in prudence is supplied by sincerity, and who at least may plead, that if their boasts deceive any into the perusal of their performances, they defraud them of but little time.

> ——Quid enim? Concurritur—horae
> Momento cita mors venit, aut victoria laeta.

> The battle joins, and, in a moment's flight,
> Death, or a joyful conquest, ends the fight.
> FRANCIS.

The question concerning the merit of the day is soon decided, and we are not condemned to toil thro' half a folio, to be convinced that the writer has broke his promise.

It is one among many reasons for which I purpose to endeavour the entertainment of my countrymen by a short essay on Tuesday and Saturday, that I hope not much to tire those whom I shall not happen to please; and if I am not commended for the beauty of my works, to be at least pardoned for their brevity. But whether my expectations are most fixed on pardon or praise, I think it not necessary to discover; for having accurately weighed the reasons for arrogance and submission, I find them so nearly equiponderant, that my impatience to try the event of my first performance will not suffer me to attend any longer the trepidations of the balance.

There are, indeed, many conveniencies almost peculiar to this method of publication, which may naturally flatter the author, whether he be confident or timorous. The man to whom the extent of his knowledge, or the sprightliness of his imagination, has, in his own opinion, already secured the praises of the world, willingly takes that way of displaying his abilities which will soonest give him an opportunity of hearing the voice of fame; it heightens his alacrity to think in how many places he shall hear what he is now writing, read with ecstasies to morrow. He will often please himself with reflecting, that the author of a large treatise must proceed with anxiety, lest, before the completion of his work, the attention of the publick may have changed its object; but that he who is confined to no single topick, may follow the national taste through all its variations, and catch the *Aura popularis*, the gale of favour, from what point soever it shall blow.

Nor is the prospect less likely to ease the doubts of the cautious, and the terrours of the fearful, for to such the shortness of every single paper is a powerful encouragement. He that questions his abilities to arrange the dissimilar parts of an extensive plan, or fears to be lost in a complicated system, may yet hope to adjust a few pages without perplexity; and if, when he turns over the repositories of his memory, he finds his collection too small for a volume, he may yet have enough to furnish out an essay. He that would fear to lay out too much time upon an experiment of which he knows not the event, persuades himself that a few days will shew him what he is to expect from his learning and his genius. If he thinks his own judgment not sufficiently enlightned, he may, by attending the remarks which every paper will produce, rectify his opinions. If he should with too little premeditation encumber himself by an unwieldly subject, he can quit it without confessing his ignorance, and pass to other topicks less dangerous, or more tractable. And if he finds, with all his industry, and all his artifices, that he cannot deserve regard, or cannot attain it, he may let the design fall at once, and, without injury to others or himself, retire to amusements of greater pleasure, or to studies of better prospect.

No. 2. Saturday, 24 March 1750.

Stare loco nescit, pereunt vestigia mille
Ante fugam, absentemque ferit gravis ungula campum.
                                        STATIUS.

Th'impatient courser pants in ev'ry vein,
And pawing seems to beat the distant plain;
Hills, vales, and floods, appear already crost,
And, ere he starts, a thousand steps are lost.
                                        POPE.

That the mind of man is never satisfied with the objects immediately before it, but is always breaking away from the present moment, and losing itself in schemes of future felicity; and that we forget the proper use of the time now in our power, to provide for the enjoyment of that which, perhaps, may never be granted us, has been frequently remarked; and as this practice is a commodious subject of raillery to the gay, and of declamation to the serious, it has been ridiculed with all the pleasantry of wit, and exaggerated with all the amplifications of rhetoric. Every instance, by which its absurdity might appear most flagrant, has been studiously collected; it has been marked with every epithet of contempt, and all the tropes and figures have been called forth against it.

Censure is willingly indulged, because it always implies some superiority; men please themselves with imagining that they have made a deeper search, or wider survey, than others, and detected faults and follies, which escape vulgar observation. And the pleasure of wantoning in common topicks is so tempting to a writer, that he cannot easily resign it; a train of sentiments generally received enables him to shine without labour, and to conquer without a contest. It is so easy to laugh at the folly of him who lives only in idea, refuses immediate ease for distant pleasures, and, instead of enjoying the blessings of life, lets life glide away in preparations to enjoy them. It affords such opportunities of triumphant exultation, to exemplify the uncertainty of the human state, to rouse mortals from their dream, and inform them of the silent celerity of time, that we may believe authors willing rather to transmit than examine so advantageous a principle, and more inclined to pursue a track so smooth and so flowery, than attentively to consider whether it leads to truth.

This quality of looking forward into futurity seems the unavoidable condition of a being, whose motions are gradual, and whose life is progressive: as his powers are limited, he must use means for the attainment of his ends, and intend first what he performs last; as, by continual advances from his first stage of existence, he is perpetually varying the horizon of his prospects, he must always discover new motives of action, new excitements of fear, and allurements of desire.

The end therefore which at present calls forth our efforts will be found, when it is once gained, to be only one of the means to some remoter end. The natural flights of the human mind are not from pleasure to pleasure, but from hope to hope.

He that directs his steps to a certain point, must frequently turn his eyes to that place which he strives to reach; he that undergoes the fatigue of labour, must solace his weariness with the contemplation of its reward. In agriculture, one of the most simple and necessary employments, no man turns up the ground but because he thinks of the harvest, that harvest which blights may intercept, which inundations may sweep away, or which death or calamity may hinder him from reaping.

Yet as few maxims are widely received or long retained but for some conformity with truth and nature, it must be confessed, that this caution against keeping our view too intent upon remote advantages is not without its propriety or usefulness, though it may have been recited with too much levity, or enforced with too little distinction: for, not to speak of that vehemence of desire which presses through right and wrong to its gratification, or that anxious inquietude which is justly chargeable with distrust of heaven, subjects too solemn for my present purpose; it frequently happens that, by indulging early the raptures of success, we forget the measures necessary to secure it, and suffer the imagination to riot in the fruition of some possible good, till the time of obtaining it has slipped away.

There would however be few enterprises of great labour or hazard undertaken, if we had not the power of magnifying the advantages which we persuade ourselves to expect from them. When the knight of La Mancha gravely recounts to his companion the adventures by which he is to signalize himself in such a manner that he shall be summoned to the support of empires, solicited to accept the heiress of the crown which he has preserved, have honours and riches to scatter about him, and an island to bestow on his worthy squire, very few readers, amidst their mirth or pity, can deny that they have admitted visions of the same kind; though they have not, perhaps, expected events equally strange, or by means equally inadequate. When we pity him, we reflect on our own disappointments; and when we laugh, our hearts inform us that he is not more ridiculous than ourselves, except that he tells what we have only thought.

The understanding of a man, naturally sanguine, may, indeed, be easily vitiated by the luxurious indulgence of hope, however necessary to the production of every thing great or excellent, as some plants are destroyed by too open exposure to that sun which gives life and beauty to the vegetable world.

Perhaps no class of the human species requires more to be cautioned against this anticipation of happiness, than those that aspire to the name of authors. A man of lively fancy no sooner finds a hint moving in his mind, than he makes momentaneous excursions to the press, and to the world, and, with a little encouragement from flattery, pushes forward into future ages, and prognosticates the honours to be paid him, when envy is extinct, and faction forgotten, and those, whom partiality now suffers to obscure him, shall have given way to other triflers of as short duration as themselves.

Those, who have proceeded so far as to appeal to the tribunal of succeeding times, are not likely to be cured of their infatuation; but all endeavours ought to be used for the prevention of a disease, for which, when it has attained its height, perhaps no remedy will be found in the gardens of philosophy, however she may boast her physick of the mind, her catharticks of vice, or lenitives of passion.

I shall, therefore, while I am yet but lightly touched with the symptoms of the writer's malady, endeavour to fortify myself against the infection, not without some weak hope, that my preservatives may extend their virtue to others, whose employment exposes them to the same danger:

Laudis amore tumes? Sunt certa piacula, quæ te
Ter pure lecto poterunt recreare libello.

Is fame your passion? Wisdom's pow'rful charm,
If thrice read over, shall its force disarm.

FRANCIS.

It is the sage advice of Epictetus, that a man should accustom himself often to think of what is most shocking and terrible, that by such reflexions he may be preserved from too ardent wishes for seeming good, and from too much dejection in real evil.

There is nothing more dreadful to an author than neglect, compared with which reproach, hatred, and opposition, are names of happiness; yet this worst, this meanest fate every man who dares to write has reason to fear.

I nunc, et versus tecum meditare canoros.

Go now, and meditate thy tuneful lays.

ELPHINSTON.

It may not be unfit for him who makes a new entrance into the lettered world, so far to suspect his own powers as to believe that he possibly may deserve neglect; that nature may not have qualified him much to enlarge or embellish knowledge, nor sent him forth entitled by indisputable superiority to regulate the conduct of the rest of mankind; that, though the world must be granted to be yet in ignorance, he is not destined to dispel the cloud, nor to shine out as one of the luminaries of life. For this suspicion, every catalogue of a library will furnish sufficient reason, as he will find it crouded with names of men, who, though now forgotten, were once no less enterprising or confident than himself, equally pleased with their own productions, equally caressed by their patrons, and flattered by their friends.

But, though it should happen that an author is capable of excelling, yet his merit may pass without notice, huddled in the variety of things, and thrown into the general miscellany of life. He that endeavours after fame by writing, solicits the regard of a multitude fluctuating in pleasures, or immersed in business, without time for intellectual amusements; he appeals to judges prepossessed by passions, or corrupted by prejudices, which preclude their approbation of any new performance. Some are too indolent to read any thing, till its reputation is established; others too envious to promote that fame, which gives them pain by its increase. What is new is opposed, because most are unwilling to be taught; and what is known is rejected, because it is not sufficiently considered, that men more frequently require to be reminded than informed. The learned are afraid to declare their opinion early, lest they should put their reputation in hazard; the ignorant always imagine themselves giving some proof of delicacy, when they refuse to be pleased: and he that finds his way to reputation, through all these obstructions, must acknowledge that he is indebted to other causes besides his industry, his learning, or his wit.

No. 4. Saturday, 31 March 1750.

Simul et jucunda et idonea dicere Vitæ.
     Hor.

And join both profit and delight in one.
     Creech.

The works of fiction, with which the present generation seems more particularly delighted, are such as exhibit life in its true state, diversified only by accidents that daily happen in the world, and influenced by passions and qualities which are really to be found in conversing with mankind.

This kind of writing may be termed not improperly the comedy of romance, and is to be conducted nearly by the rules of comic poetry. Its province is to bring about natural events by easy means, and to keep up curiosity without the help of wonder: it is therefore precluded from the machines and expedients of the heroic romance, and can neither employ giants to snatch away a lady from the nuptial rites, nor knights to bring her back from captivity; it can neither bewilder its personages in desarts, nor lodge them in imaginary castles.

I remember a remark made by Scaliger upon Pontanus, that all his writings are filled with the same images; and that if you take from him his lillies and his roses, his satyrs and his dryads, he will have nothing left that can be called poetry. In like manner, almost all the fictions of the last age will vanish, if you deprive them of a hermit and a wood, a battle and a shipwreck.

Why this wild strain of imagination found reception so long, in polite and learned ages, it is not easy to conceive; but we cannot wonder that, while readers could be procured, the authors were willing to continue it: for when a man had by practice gained some fluency of language, he had no further care than to retire to his closet, let loose his invention, and heat his mind with incredibilities; a book was thus produced without fear of criticism, without the toil of study, without knowledge of nature, or acquaintance with life.

The task of our present writers is very different; it requires, together with that learning which is to be gained from books, that experience which can never be attained by solitary diligence, but must arise from general converse, and accurate observation of the living world. Their performances have, as Horace expresses it, *plus oneris quantum veniæ minus*, little indulgence, and therefore more difficulty. They are engaged in portraits of which every one knows the original, and can detect any deviation from exactness of resemblance. Other writings are safe, except from the malice of learning, but these are in danger from every common reader; as the slipper ill executed was censured by a shoemaker who happened to stop in his way at the Venus of Apelles.

But the fear of not being approved as just copyers of human manners, is not the most important concern that an author of this sort ought to have before him. These books are written chiefly to the young, the ignorant, and the idle, to whom they serve as lectures of conduct, and introductions into life. They are the entertainment of minds unfurnished with ideas, and therefore easily susceptible of impressions; not fixed by principles, and therefore easily following the current of fancy; not informed by experience, and consequently open to every false suggestion and partial account.

That the highest degree of reverence should be paid to youth, and that nothing indecent should be suffered to approach their eyes or ears; are precepts extorted by sense and virtue from an ancient writer, by no means eminent for chastity of thought. The same kind, tho' not the same degree of caution, is required to every thing which is laid before them, to secure them from unjust prejudices, perverse opinions, and incongruous combinations of images.

In the romances formerly written, every transaction and sentiment was so remote from all that passes among men, that the reader was in very little danger of making any applications to himself; the virtues and crimes were equally beyond his sphere of activity; and he amused himself with heroes and with traitors, deliverers and persecutors, as with beings of another species, whose actions were regulated upon motives of their own, and who had neither faults nor excellencies in common with himself.

But when an adventurer is levelled with the rest of the world, and acts in such scenes of the universal drama, as may be the lot of any other man; young spectators fix their eyes upon him with closer attention, and hope by observing his behaviour and success to regulate their own practices, when they shall be engaged in the like part.

For this reason these familiar histories may perhaps be made of greater use than the solemnities of professed morality and convey the knowledge of vice and virtue with more efficacy than axioms and definitions. But if the power of example is so great, as to take possession of the memory by a kind of violence, and produce effects almost without the intervention of the will, care ought to be taken that, when the choice is unrestrained, the best examples only should be exhibited; and that which is likely to operate so strongly, should not be mischievous or uncertain in its effects.

The chief advantage which these fictions have over real life is, that their authors are at liberty, tho' not to invent, yet to select objects, and to cull from the mass of mankind, those individuals upon which the attention ought most to be employ'd; as a diamond, though it cannot be made, may be polished by art, and placed in such a situation, as to display that lustre which before was buried among common stones.

It is justly considered as the greatest excellency of art, to imitate nature; but it is necessary to distinguish those parts of nature, which are most proper for imitation: greater care is still required in representing life, which is so often discoloured by passion, or deformed by wickedness. If the world be promiscuously described, I cannot see of what use it can be to read the account; or why it may not be as safe to turn the eye immediately upon mankind, as upon a mirror which shows all that presents itself without discrimination.

It is therefore not a sufficient vindication of a character, that it is drawn as it appears, for many characters ought never to be drawn; nor of a narrative, that the train of events is agreeable to observation and experience, for that observation which is called knowledge of the world, will be found much more frequently to make men cunning than good. The purpose of these writings is surely not only to show mankind, but to provide that they may be seen hereafter with less hazard; to teach the means of avoiding the snares which are laid by TREACHERY for INNOCENCE, without infusing any wish for that superiority with which the betrayer flatters his vanity; to give the power of counteracting fraud, without the temptation to practise it; to initiate youth by mock encounters in the art of necessary defence, and to increase prudence without impairing virtue.

Many writers, for the sake of following nature, so mingle good and bad qualities in their principal personages, that they are both equally conspicuous; and as we accompany them through their adventures with delight, and are led by degrees to interest ourselves in their favour, we lose the abhorrence of their faults, because they do not hinder our pleasure, or, perhaps, regard them with some kindness for being united with so much merit.

There have been men indeed splendidly wicked, whose endowments threw a brightness on their crimes, and whom scarce any villainy made perfectly detestable, because they never could be wholly divested of their excellencies; but such have been in all ages the great corrupters of the world, and their resemblance ought no more to be preserved, than the art of murdering without pain.

Some have advanced, without due attention to the consequences of this notion, that certain virtues have their correspondent faults, and therefore that to exhibit either apart is to deviate from probability. Thus men are observed by Swift to be "grateful in the same degree as they are resentful." This principle, with others of the same kind, supposes man to act from a brute impulse, and persue a certain degree of inclination, without any choice of the object; for, otherwise, though it should be allowed that gratitude and resentment arise from the same constitution of the passions, it follows not that they will be equally indulged when reason is consulted; yet unless that consequence be admitted, this sagacious maxim becomes an empty sound, without any relation to practice or to life.

Nor is it evident, that even the first motions to these effects are always in the same proportion. For pride, which produces quickness of resentment, will obstruct gratitude, by unwillingness to admit that inferiority which obligation implies; and it is very unlikely, that he who cannot think he receives a favour will acknowledge or repay it.

It is of the utmost importance to mankind, that positions of this tendency should be laid open and confuted; for while men consider good and evil as springing from the same root, they will spare the one for the sake of the other, and in judging, if not of others at least of themselves, will be apt to estimate their virtues by their vices. To this fatal error all those will contribute, who confound the colours of right and wrong, and instead of helping to settle their boundaries, mix them with so much art, that no common mind is able to dis-unite them.

In narratives, where historical veracity has no place, I cannot discover why there should not be exhibited the most perfect idea of virtue; of virtue not angelical, nor above probability, for what we cannot credit we shall never imi-tate, but the highest and purest that humanity can reach, which, exercised in such trials as the various revolutions of things shall bring upon it, may, by conquering some calamities, and enduring others, teach us what we may hope, and what we can perform. Vice, for vice is necessary to be shewn, should always disgust; nor should the graces of gaiety, or the dignity of courage, be so united with it, as to reconcile it to the mind. Wherever it appears, it should raise hatred by the malignity of its practices, and contempt by the meanness of its stratagems; for while it is supported by either parts or spirit, it will be seldom heartily abhorred. The Roman tyrant was content to be hated, if he was but feared; and there are thousands of the readers of romances willing to be thought wicked, if they may be allowed to be wits. It is therefore to be steadily inculcated, that virtue is the highest proof of understanding, and the only solid basis of greatness; and that vice is the natural consequence of nar-row thoughts, that it begins in mistake, and ends in ignominy.

No. 6. Saturday, 7 April 1750.

Strenua nos exercet inertia, navibus atque
Quadrigis petimus bene vivere: quod petis, hic est;
Est Ulubris, animus si te non deficit æquus.

HOR.

Active in indolence, abroad we roam
In quest of happiness, which dwells at home:
With vain persuits fatigu'd, at length you'll find,
No place excludes it from an equal mind.

ELPHINSTON.

That man should never suffer his happiness to depend upon external cir-cumstances, is one of the chief precepts of the Stoical philosophy; a pre-cept, indeed, which that lofty sect has extended beyond the condition of human life, and in which some of them seem to have comprised an utter exclusion of all corporal pain and pleasure, from the regard or attention of a wise man.

Such *sapientia insaniens* as Horace calls the doctrine of another sect, such extravagance of philosophy, can want neither authority nor argument for its confutation; it is overthrown by the experience of every hour, and the powers of nature rise up against it. But we may very properly enquire, how near to this exalted state it is in our power to approach, how far we can exempt ourselves from outward influences, and secure to our minds a state of tranquillity: For, though the boast of absolute independence is ridiculous and vain, yet a mean flexibility to every impulse, and a patient submission to the tyranny of casual troubles, is below the dignity of that mind, which, however depraved or weakened, boasts its derivation from a celestial original, and hopes for an union with infinite goodness, and unvariable felicity.

> *Ni vitiis pejora fovens*
> *Proprium deserat ortum.*

> Unless the soul, to vice a thrall,
> Desert her own original.

The necessity of erecting ourselves to some degree of intellectual dignity, and of preserving resources of pleasure, which may not be wholly at the mercy of accident, is never more apparent than when we turn our eyes upon those whom fortune has let loose to their own conduct; who not being chained down by their condition to a regular and stated allotment of their hours, are obliged to find themselves business or diversion, and having nothing within that can entertain or employ them, are compelled to try all the arts of destroying time.

The numberless expedients practised by this class of mortals to alleviate the burthen of life, is not less shameful, nor, perhaps, much less pitiable, than those to which a trader on the edge of bankruptcy is reduced. I have seen melancholy overspread a whole family at the disappointment of a party for cards; and when, after the proposal of a thousand schemes, and the dispatch of the footman upon a hundred messages, they have submitted, with gloomy resignation, to the misfortune of passing one evening in conversation with each other, on a sudden, such are the revolutions of the world, an unexpected visiter has brought them relief, acceptable as provision to a starving city, and enabled them to hold out till the next day.

The general remedy of those, who are uneasy without knowing the cause, is change of place; they are willing to imagine that their pain is the consequence of some local inconvenience, and endeavour to fly from it, as children from their shadows; always hoping for more satisfactory delight from every new scene, and always returning home with disappointment and complaints.

Who can look upon this kind of infatuation, without reflecting on those that suffer under the dreadful symptom of canine madness, termed by physicians the "dread of water"? These miserable wretches, unable to drink, though burning with thirst, are sometimes known to try various contortions, or inclinations of the body, flattering themselves that they can swallow in one posture that liquor, which they find in another to repel their lips.

Yet such folly is not peculiar to the thoughtless or ignorant, but sometimes seizes those minds which seem most exempted from it, by the variety of attainments, quickness of penetration, or severity of judgment; and, indeed, the pride of wit and knowledge is often mortified by finding, that they confer no security against the common errors, which mislead the weakest and meanest of mankind.

These reflexions arose in my mind upon the remembrance of a passage in Cowley's preface to his poems, where, however exalted by genius, and enlarged by study, he informs us of a scheme of happiness to which the imagination of a girl, upon the loss of her first lover, could have scarcely given way; but which he seems to have indulged till he had totally forgotten its absurdity, and would probably have put in execution, had he been hindered only by his reason.

"My desire," says he, "has been for some years past, though the execution has been accidentally diverted, and does still vehemently continue, to retire myself to some of our American plantations, not to seek for gold, or enrich myself with the traffic of those parts, which is the end of most men that travel thither; but to forsake this world for ever, with all the vanities and vexations of it, and to bury myself there in some obscure retreat, but not without the consolation of letters and philosophy."

Such was the chimerical provision which Cowley had made, in his own mind, for the quiet of his remaining life, and which he seems to recommend to posterity, since there is no other reason for disclosing it. Surely no stronger instance can be given of a persuasion that content was the inhabitant of particular regions, and that a man might set sail with a fair wind, and leave behind him all his cares, incumbrances, and calamities.

If he travelled so far with no other purpose than to "bury himself in some obscure retreat," he might have found, in his own country, innumerable coverts sufficiently dark to have concealed the genius of Cowley; for, whatever might be his opinion of the importunity with which he should be summoned back into publick life, a short experience would have convinced him, that privation is easier than acquisition, and that it would require little continuance to free himself from the intrusion of the world. There is pride enough in the human heart to prevent much desire of acquaintance with a man by whom we are sure to be neglected, however his reputation for science or virtue may excite our curiosity or esteem; so that the lover of retirement needs not be afraid lest the respect of strangers should overwhelm him with visits. Even those to whom he has formerly been known will very patiently support his absence, when they have tried a little to live without him, and found new diversions for those moments which his company contributed to exhilarate.

It was, perhaps, ordained by providence, to hinder us from tyrannising over one another, that no individual should be of such importance, as to cause, by his retirement or death, any chasm in the world. And Cowley had conversed to little purpose with mankind, if he had never remarked, how soon the useful friend, the gay companion, and the favoured lover, when once they are removed from before the sight, give way to the succession of new objects.

The privacy, therefore, of his hermitage might have been safe enough from violation, though he had chosen it within the limits of his native island; he might have found here preservatives against the *vanities* and *vexations* of the world, not less efficacious than those which the woods or fields of America could afford him: but having once his mind imbittered with disgust, he conceived it impossible to be far enough from the cause of his uneasiness; and was posting away with the expedition of a coward, who, for want of venturing to look behind him, thinks the enemy perpetually at his heels.

When he was interrupted by company, or fatigued with business, he so strongly imaged to himself the happiness of leisure and retreat, that he determined to enjoy them for the future without interruption, and to exclude for ever all that could deprive him of his darling satisfaction. He forgot, in the vehemence of desire, that solitude and quiet owe their pleasures to those miseries, which he was so studious to obviate; for such are the vicissitudes of the world, through all its parts, that day and night, labour and rest, hurry and retirement, endear each other; such are the changes that keep the mind in action; we desire, we pursue, we obtain, we are satiated; we desire something else, and begin a new persuit.

If he had proceeded in his project, and fixed his habitation in the most delightful part of the new world, it may be doubted, whether his distance from the *vanities* of life would have enabled him to keep away the *vexations*. It is common for a man, who feels pain, to fancy that he could bear it better in any other part. Cowley having known the troubles and perplexities of a particular condition, readily persuaded himself that nothing worse was to be found, and that every alteration would bring some improvement; he never suspected that the cause of his unhappiness was within, that his own passions were not sufficiently regulated, and that he was harrassed by his own impatience, which could never be without something to awaken it, would accompany him over the sea, and find its way to his American elysium. He would, upon the tryal, have been soon convinced, that the fountain of content must spring up in the mind; and that he, who has so little knowledge of human nature, as to seek happiness by changing any thing, but his own dispositions, will waste his life in fruitless efforts, and multiply the griefs which he purposes to remove.

No. 7. Tuesday, 10 April 1750.

O qui perpetuâ mundum ratione gubernas,
Terrarum cœlique sator!——

Disjice terrenæ nebulas & pondera molis,
Atque tuo splendore mica! Tu namque serenum,
Tu requies tranquilla piis. Te cernere, finis,
Principium, vector, dux, semita, terminus, idem.
BOETHIUS.

O Thou whose pow'r o'er moving worlds presides,
Whose voice created, and whose wisdom guides,
On darkling man in pure effulgence shine,
And chear the clouded mind with light divine.
'Tis thine alone to calm the pious breast
With silent confidence and holy rest;
From thee, great God, we spring, to thee we tend,
Path, motive, guide, original and end.

The love of RETIREMENT has, in all ages, adhered closely to those minds, which have been most enlarged by knowledge, or elevated by genius. Those who enjoyed every thing generally supposed to confer happiness, have been forced to seek it in the shades of privacy. Though they possessed both power and riches, and were, therefore, surrounded by men, who considered it as their chief interest to remove from them every thing that might offend their ease, or interrupt their pleasure, they have soon felt the languors of satiety, and found themselves unable to pursue the race of life without frequent respirations of intermediate solitude.

To produce this disposition nothing appears requisite but quick sensibility, and active imagination; for, though not devoted to virtue, or science, the man, whose faculties enable him to make ready comparisons of the present with the past, will find such a constant recurrence of the same pleasures, and troubles, the same expectations, and disappointments, that he will gladly snatch an hour of retreat, to let his thoughts expatiate at large, and seek for that variety in his own ideas, which the objects of sense cannot afford him.

Nor will greatness, or abundance, exempt him from the importunities of this desire, since, if he is born to think, he cannot restrain himself from a thousand enquiries and speculations, which he must persue by his own reason, and which the splendour of his condition can only hinder; for those who are most exalted above dependance or controul, are yet condemned to pay so large a tribute of their time to custom, ceremony, and popularity, that, according to the *Greek* proverb, no man in the house is more a slave than the master.

When a king asked Euclid the mathematician, whether he could not explain his art to him in a more compendious manner, he was answered, that there was no royal way to geometry. Other things may be seized by might, or purchased with money, but knowledge is to be gained only by study, and study to be prosecuted only in retirement.

These are some of the motives which have had power to sequester kings and heroes from the crouds that soothed them with flatteries, or inspirited them with acclamations; but their efficacy seems confined to the higher mind, and to operate little upon the common classes of mankind, to whose conceptions the present assemblage of things is adequate, and who seldom range beyond those entertainments and vexations, which solicit their attention by pressing on their senses.

But there is an universal reason for some stated intervals of solitude, which the institutions of the church call upon me, now especially, to mention; a reason, which extends as wide as moral duty, or the hopes of divine favour in a future state; and which ought to influence all ranks of life, and all degrees of intellect; since none can imagine themselves not comprehended in its obligation, but such as determine to set their maker at defiance by obstinate wickedness, or whose enthusiastick security of his approbation places them above external ordinances, and all human means of improvement.

The great task of him, who conducts his life by the precepts of religion, is to make the future predominate over the present, to impress upon his mind so strong a sense of the importance of obedience to the divine will, of the value of the reward promised to virtue, and the terrors of the punishment denounced against crimes, as may overbear all the temptations which temporal hope or fear can bring in his way, and enable him to bid equal defiance to joy and sorrow, to turn away at one time from the allurements of ambition, and push forward at another against the threats of calamity.

It is not without reason that the apostle represents our passage through this stage of our existence by images drawn from the alarms and solicitude of a military life; for we are placed in such a state, that almost every thing about us conspires against our chief interest. We are in danger from whatever can get possession of our thoughts; all that can excite in us either pain or pleasure has a tendency to obstruct the way that leads to happiness, and either to turn us aside, or retard our progress.

Our senses, our appetites, and our passions, are our lawful and faithful guides, in most things that relate solely to this life; and, therefore, by the hourly necessity of consulting them, we gradually sink into an implicit submission, and habitual confidence. Every act of compliance with their motions facilitates a second compliance, every new step towards depravity is made with less reluctance than the former, and thus the descent to life merely sensual is perpetually accelerated.

The senses have not only that advantage over conscience, which things necessary must always have over things chosen, but they have likewise a kind of prescription in their favour. We feared pain much earlier than we apprehended guilt, and were delighted with the sensations of pleasure, before we had capacities to be charmed with the beauty of rectitude. To this power, thus early established, and incessantly increasing, it must be remembered, that almost every man has, in some part of his life, added new strength by a voluntary or negligent subjection of himself; for who is there that has not instigated his appetites by indulgence, or suffered them by an unresisting neutrality to enlarge their dominion, and multiply their demands?

From the necessity of dispossessing the sensitive faculties of the influence which they must naturally gain by this preoccupation of the soul, arises that conflict between opposite desires, in the first endeavours after a religious life; which, however enthusiastically it may have been described, or however contemptuously ridiculed, will naturally be felt in some degree, though varied without end, by different tempers of mind, and innumerable circumstances of health or condition, greater or less fervour, more or fewer temptations to relapse.

From the perpetual necessity of consulting the animal faculties, in our provision for the present life, arises the difficulty of withstanding their impulses, even in cases where they ought to be of no weight; for the motions of sense are instantaneous, its objects strike unsought, we are accustomed to follow its directions, and therefore often submit to the sentence without examining the authority of the judge.

Thus it appears, upon a philosophical estimate, that, supposing the mind, at any certain time, in an equipoise between the pleasures of this life, and the hopes of futurity, present objects falling more frequently into the scale would in time preponderate, and that our regard for an invisible state would grow every moment weaker, till at last it would lose all its activity, and become absolutely without effect.

To prevent this dreadful event, the balance is put into our own hands, and we have power to transfer the weight to either side. The motives to a life of holiness are infinite, not less than the favour or anger of omnipotence, not less than eternity of happiness or misery. But these can only influence our conduct as they gain our attention, which the business, or diversions, of the world are always calling off by contrary attractions.

The great art therefore of piety, and the end for which all the rites of religion seem to be instituted, is the perpetual renovation of the motives to virtue, by a voluntary employment of our mind in the contemplation of its excellence, its importance, and its necessity, which, in proportion as they are more frequently and more willingly revolved, gain a more forcible and permanent influence, 'till in time they become the reigning ideas, the standing principles of action, and the test by which every thing proposed to the judgment is rejected or approved.

To facilitate this change of our affections, it is necessary that we weaken the temptations of the world, by retiring at certain seasons from it; for its influence arising only from its presence, is much lessened when it becomes the object of solitary meditation. A constant residence amidst noise and pleasure inevitably obliterates the impressions of piety, and a frequent abstraction of ourselves into a state, where this life, like the next, operates only upon the reason, will reinstate religion in its just authority, even without those irradiations from above, the hope of which I have yet no intention to withdraw from the sincere and the diligent.

This is that conquest of the world and of ourselves, which has been always considered as the perfection of human nature; and this is only to be obtained by fervent prayer, steady resolutions, and frequent retirement from folly and vanity, from the cares of avarice, and the joys of intemperance, from the lulling sounds of deceitful flattery, and the tempting sight of prosperous wickedness.

No. 8. Saturday, 14 April 1750.

——Patitur poenas peccandi sola voluntas;
Nam scelus intra se tacitum qui cogitat ullum,
Facti crimen habet.

JUV.

For he that but conceives a crime in thought,
Contracts the danger of an actual fault.

CREECH.

If the most active and industrious of mankind was able, at the close of life, to recollect distinctly his past moments, and distribute them, in a regular account, according to the manner in which they have been spent, it is scarcely to be imagined how few would be marked out to the mind, by any permanent or visible effects, how small a proportion his real action would bear to his seeming possibilities of action, how many chasms he would find of wide and continued vacuity, and how many interstitial spaces unfilled, even in the most tumultuous hurries of business, and the most eager vehemence of persuit.

It is said by modern philosophers, that not only the great globes of matter are thinly scattered thro' the universe, but the hardest bodies are so porous, that, if all matter were compressed to perfect solidity, it might be contained in a cube of a few feet. In like manner, if all the employment of life were crowded into the time which it really occupied, perhaps a few weeks, days, or hours, would be sufficient for its accomplishment, so far as the mind was engaged in the performance. For such is the inequality of our corporeal to our intellectual faculties, that we contrive in minutes what we execute in years, and the soul often stands an idle spectator of the labour of the hands, and expedition of the feet.

For this reason, the antient generals often found themselves at leisure to persue the study of philosophy in the camp; and Lucan, with historical veracity, makes Cæsar relate of himself, that he noted the revolutions of the stars in the midst of preparations for battle.

———*Media inter prælia semper*
Sideribus, cælique plagis, superisque vacavi.

Amid the storms of war, with curious eyes
I trace the planets and survey the skies.

That the soul always exerts her peculiar powers, with greater or less force, is very probable, though the common occasions of our present condition require but a small part of that incessant cogitation; and by the natural frame of our bodies, and general combination of the world, we are so frequently condemned to inactivity, that as through all our time we are thinking, so for a great part of our time we can only think.

Lest a power so restless should be either unprofitably, or hurtfully employed, and the superfluities of intellect run to waste, it is no vain speculation to consider how we may govern our thoughts, restrain them from irregular motions, or confine them from boundless dissipation.

How the understanding is best conducted to the knowledge of science, by what steps it is to be led forwards in its persuit, how it is to be cured of its defects, and habituated to new studies, has been the inquiry of many acute and learned men, whose observations I shall not either adopt or censure; my purpose being to consider the moral discipline of the mind, and to promote the increase of virtue rather than of learning.

This inquiry seems to have been neglected for want of remembering that all action has its origin in the mind, and that therefore to suffer the thoughts to be vitiated, is to poison the fountains of morality: Irregular desires will produce licentious practices; what men allow themselves to wish they will soon believe, and will be at last incited to execute what they please themselves with contriving.

For this reason the casuists of the Romish church, who gain, by confession, great opportunities of knowing human nature, have generally determined that what it is a crime to do, it is a crime to think. Since by revolving with pleasure, the facility, safety or advantage of a wicked deed, a man soon begins to find his constancy relax, and his detestation soften; the happiness of success glittering before him, withdraws his attention from the atrociousness of the guilt, and acts are at last confidently perpetrated, of which the first conception only crept into the mind, disguised in pleasing complications, and permitted rather than invited.

No man has ever been drawn to crimes, by love or jealousy, envy or hatred, but he can tell how easily he might at first have repelled the temptation, how readily his mind would have obeyed a call to any other object, and how weak his passion has been after some casual avocation, 'till he has recalled it again to his heart, and revived the viper by too warm a fondness.

Such, therefore, is the importance of keeping reason a constant guard over imagination, that we have otherwise no security for our own virtue, but may corrupt our hearts in the most recluse solitude, with more pernicious and tyrannical appetites and wishes, than the commerce of the world will generally produce; for we are easily shocked by crimes which appear at once in their full magnitude, but the gradual growth of our own wickedness, endeared by interest, and palliated by all the artifices of self-deceit, gives us time to form distinctions in our own favour, and reason by degrees submits to absurdity, as the eye is in time accommodated to darkness.

In this disease of the soul, it is of the utmost importance to apply remedies at the beginning; and, therefore, I shall endeavour to shew what thoughts are to be rejected or improved, as they regard the past, present, or future; in hopes that some may be awakened to caution and vigilance, who, perhaps, indulge themselves in dangerous dreams, so much the more dangerous, because being yet only dreams they are concluded innocent.

The recollection of the past is only useful by way of provision for the future; and therefore, in reviewing all occurrences that fall under a religious consideration, it is proper that a man stop at the first thoughts, to remark how he was led thither, and why he continues the reflexion. If he is dwelling with delight upon a stratagem of successful fraud, a night of licentious riot, or an intrigue of guilty pleasure, let him summon off his imagination as from an unlawful persuit, expel those passages from his remembrance, of which, though he cannot seriously approve them, the pleasure overpowers the guilt, and refer them to a future hour, when they may be considered with greater safety. Such an hour will certainly come; for the impressions of past pleasure are always lessening, but the sense of guilt, which respects futurity, continues the same.

The serious and impartial retrospect of our conduct is indisputably necessary to the confirmation or recovery of virtue, and is, therefore, recommended under the name of self-examination, by divines, as the first act previous to repentance. It is, indeed, of so great use, that without it we should always be to begin life, be seduced for ever by the same allurements, and misled by the same fallacies. But in order that we may not lose the advantage of our experience, we must endeavour to see every thing in its proper form, and excite in ourselves those sentiments which the great author of nature has decreed the concomitants or followers of good or bad actions.

> Μηδ' ὕ;πνον μαλακοῖσιν ἐπ' ὄμμασι προσδέξασθαι,
> Πρὶν τῶν ἡμερινῶν ἔργων τρὶς ἕκαστον ἐπελθεῖν·
> Πῆ παρέβην; τί δ'ἔρεξα; τί μὸι δέον οὐκ ἐτελέσθη;
> Ἀρξάμενος δ' ἀπὸ πρώτου ἐπέξιθι· καὶ μετέπειτα,
> Δειλὰ μὲν ἐκπρήξας, ἐπιπλήσσεο, χρηστὰ δὲ, τέρπου.

Let not sleep, says Pythagoras, *fall upon thy eyes till thou hast thrice reviewed the transactions of the past day. Where have I turned aside from rectitude? What have I been doing? What have I left undone, which I ought to have done? Begin thus from the first act, and proceed; and in conclusion, at the ill which thou hast done be troubled, and rejoice for the good.*

Our thoughts on present things being determined by the objects before us, fall not under those indulgences, or excursions, which I am now considering. But I cannot forbear, under this head, to caution pious and tender minds, that are disturbed by the irruptions of wicked imaginations, against too great dejection, and too anxious alarms; for thoughts are only criminal, when they are first chosen, and then voluntarily continued.

> *Evil into the mind of god or man*
> *May come and go, so unapprov'd, and leave*
> *No spot or stain behind.*
>
> MILTON.

In futurity chiefly are the snares lodged, by which the imagination is intangled. Futurity is the proper abode of hope and fear, with all their train and progeny of subordinate apprehensions and desires. In futurity events and chances are yet floating at large, without apparent connexion with their causes, and we therefore easily indulge the liberty of gratifying ourselves with a pleasing choice. To pick and cull among possible advantages is, as the civil law terms it, *in vacuum venire*, to take what belongs to nobody; but it has this hazard in it, that we shall be unwilling to quit what we have seized, though an owner should be found. It is easy to think on that which may be gained, till at last we resolve to gain it, and to image the happiness of particular conditions till we can be easy in no other. We ought, at least, to let our desires fix upon nothing in another's power for the sake of our quiet, or in another's possession for the sake of our innocence. When a man finds himself led, though by a train of honest sentiments, to a wish for that to which he has no right, he should start back as from a pitfal covered with flowers. He that fancies he should benefit the publick more in a great station than the man that fills it, will in time imagine it an act of virtue to supplant him; and, as opposition readily kindles into hatred, his eagerness to do that good, to which he is not called, will betray him to crimes, which in his original scheme were never purposed.

He therefore that would govern his actions by the laws of virtue, must regulate his thoughts by those of reason; he must keep guilt from the recesses of his heart, and remember that the pleasures of fancy, and the emotions of desire are more dangerous as they are more hidden, since they escape the awe of observation, and operate equally in every situation, without the concurrence of external opportunities.

No. 9. Tuesday, 17 April 1750.

Quod sis esse velis, nihilque malis.
MART.

Chuse what you are; no other state prefer.
ELPHINSTON.

It is justly remarked by Horace, that, howsoever every man may complain occasionally of the hardships of his condition, he is seldom willing to change it for any other on the same level: for whether it be that he, who follows an employment, made choice of it at first on account of its suitableness to his inclination; or that when accident, or the determination of others, have placed him in a particular station, he, by endeavouring to reconcile himself to it, gets the custom of viewing it only on the fairest side; or whether every man thinks that class to which he belongs the most illustrious, merely because he has honoured it with his name; it is certain that, whatever be the reason, most men have a very strong and active prejudice in favour of their own vocation, always working upon their minds, and influencing their behaviour.

This partiality is sufficiently visible in every rank of the human species; but it exerts itself more frequently and with greater force among those who have never learned to conceal their sentiments for reasons of policy, or to model their expressions by the laws of politeness; and therefore the chief contests of wit among artificers and handicraftsmen arise from a mutual endeavour to exalt one trade by depreciating another.

From the same principle are derived many consolations to alleviate the inconveniences to which every calling is peculiarly exposed. A blacksmith was lately pleasing himself at his anvil, with observing that, though his trade was hot and sooty, laborious and unhealthy, yet he had the honour of living by his hammer, he got his bread like a man, and if his son should rise in the world, and keep his coach, no body could reproach him that his father was a taylor.

A man, truly zealous for his fraternity, is never so irresistibly flattered, as when some rival calling is mentioned with contempt. Upon this principle a linen-draper boasted that he had got a new customer, whom he could safely trust, for he could have no doubt of his honesty, since it was known, from unquestionable authority, that he was now filing a bill in chancery to delay payment for the cloaths which he had worn the last seven years; and he himself had heard him declare, in a publick coffee-house, that he looked upon the whole generation of woollen-drapers to be such despicable wretches, that no gentleman ought to pay them.

It has been observed that physicians and lawyers are no friends to religion; and many conjectures have been formed to discover the reason of such a combination between men who agree in nothing else, and who seem less to be affected, in their own provinces, by religious opinions, than any other part of the community. The truth is, very few of them have thought about religion; but they have all seen a parson, seen him in a habit different from their own, and therefore declared war against him. A young student from the inns of court, who has often attacked the curate of his father's parish with such arguments as his acquaintances could furnish, and returned to town without success, is now gone down with a resolution to destroy him; for he has learned at last how to manage a prig, and if he pretends to hold him again to syllogism, he has a catch in reserve, which neither logic nor metaphysics can resist.

> *I laugh to think how your unshaken* Cato
> *Will look aghast, when unforeseen destruction*
> *Pours in upon him thus.*

The malignity of soldiers and sailors against each other has been often experienced at the cost of their country; and, perhaps, no orders of men have an enmity of more acrimony, or longer continuance. When, upon our late successes at sea, some new regulations were concerted for establishing the rank of the naval commanders, a captain of foot very acutely remarked, that nothing was more absurd than to give any honorary rewards to seamen, "for honour," says he, "ought only to be won by bravery, and all the world knows that in a sea-fight there is no danger, and therefore no evidence of courage."

But although this general desire of aggrandizing themselves by raising their profession, betrays men to a thousand ridiculous and mischievous acts of supplantation and detraction, yet as almost all passions have their good as well as bad effects, it likewise excites ingenuity, and sometimes raises an honest and useful emulation of diligence. It may be observed in general that no trade had ever reached the excellence to which it is now improved, had its professors looked upon it with the eyes of indifferent spectators; the advances, from the first rude essays, must have been made by men who valued themselves for performances, for which scarce any other would be persuaded to esteem them.

It is pleasing to contemplate a manufacture rising gradually from its first mean state by the successive labours of innumerable minds; to consider the first hollow trunk of an oak, in which, perhaps, the shepherd could scarce venture to cross a brook swelled with a shower, enlarged at last into a ship of war, attacking fortresses, terrifying nations, setting storms and billows at defiance, and visiting the remotest parts of the globe. And it might contribute to dispose us to a kinder regard for the labours of one another, if we were to consider from what unpromising beginnings the most useful productions of art have probably arisen. Who, when he saw the first sand or ashes, by a casual intenseness of heat melted into a metalline form, rugged with excrescences, and clouded with impurities, would have imagined, that in this shapeless lump lay concealed so many conveniencies of life, as would in time constitute a great part of the happiness of the world? Yet by some such fortuitous lique-faction was mankind taught to procure a body at once in a high degree solid and transparent, which might admit the light of the sun, and exclude the vio-lence of the wind; which might extend the sight of the philosopher to new ranges of existence, and charm him at one time with the unbounded extent of the material creation, and at another with the endless subordination of animal life; and, what is yet of more importance, might supply the decays of nature, and succour old age with subsidiary sight. Thus was the first artificer in glass employed, though without his own knowledge or expectation. He was facilitat-ing and prolonging the enjoyment of light, enlarging the avenues of science, and conferring the highest and most lasting pleasures; he was enabling the student to contemplate nature, and the beauty to behold herself.

This passion for the honour of a profession, like that for the grandeur of our own country, is to be regulated not extinguished. Every man, from the highest to the lowest station, ought to warm his heart and animate his endeav-ours with the hopes of being useful to the world, by advancing the art which it is his lot to exercise; and for that end he must necessarily consider the whole extent of its application, and the whole weight of its importance. But let him not too readily imagine that another is ill employed, because, for want of fuller knowledge of his business, he is not able to comprehend its dignity. Every man ought to endeavour at eminence, not by pulling others down, but by raising himself, and enjoy the pleasure of his own superiority, whether imaginary or real, without interrupting others in the same felicity. The phil-osopher may very justly be delighted with the extent of his views, and the artificer with the readiness of his hands; but let the one remember, that, with-out mechanical performances, refined speculation is an empty dream, and the other, that, without theoretical reasoning, dexterity is little more than a brute instinct.

No. 13. Tuesday, 1 May 1750.

Commissumque teges & vino tortus & irâ.
HOR.

And let not wine or anger wrest
Th' intrusted secret from your breast.
FRANCIS.

It is related by Quintus Curtius, that the Persians always conceived an invin-cible contempt of a man, who had violated the laws of secrecy; for they thought, that, however he might be deficient in the qualities requisite to actual excellence, the negative virtues at least were in his power, and though he perhaps could not speak well if he was to try, it was still easy for him not to speak.

In forming this opinion of the easiness of secrecy, they seem to have consider'd it as opposed, not to treachery, but loquacity, and to have conceived the man, whom they thus censured, not frighted by menaces to reveal, or bribed by promises to betray, but incited by the mere pleasure of talking, or some other motive equally trifling, to lay open his heart without reflection, and to let whatever he knew slip from him, only for want of power to retain it. Whether, by their settled and avowed scorn of thoughtless talkers, the Persians were able to diffuse to any great extent the virtue of taciturnity, we are hindered by the distance of those times from being able to discover, there being very few memoirs remaining of the court of Persepolis, nor any distinct accounts handed down to us of their office clerks, their ladies of the bedchamber, their attorneys, their chamber-maids, or their footmen.

In these latter ages, though the old animosity against a prattler is still retained, it appears wholly to have lost its effects upon the conduct of mankind; for secrets are so seldom kept, that it may with some reason be doubted, whether the antients were not mistaken in their first postulate, whether the quality of retention be so generally bestowed, and whether a secret has not some subtle volatility, by which it escapes imperceptibly at the smallest vent, or some power of fermentation, by which it expands itself so as to burst the heart that will not give it way.

Those that study either the body or the mind of man, very often find the most specious and pleasing theory falling under the weight of contrary experience; and instead of gratifying their vanity by inferring effects from causes, they are always reduced at last to conjecture causes from effects. That it is easy to be secret the speculatist can demonstrate in his retreat, and therefore thinks himself justified in placing confidence; the man of the world knows, that, whether difficult or not, it is uncommon, and therefore finds himself rather inclined to search after the reason of this universal failure in one of the most important duties of society.

The vanity of being known to be trusted with a secret is generally one of the chief motives to disclose it; for however absurd it may be thought to boast an honour by an act which shews that it was conferred without merit, yet most men seem rather inclined to confess the want of virtue than of importance, and more willingly shew their influence, though at the expense of their probity, than glide through life with no other pleasure than the private consciousness of fidelity; which, while it is preserved, must be without praise, except from the single person who tries and knows it.

There are many ways of telling a secret, by which a man exempts himself from the reproaches of his conscience, and gratifies his pride without suffering himself to believe that he impairs his virtue. He tells the private affairs of his patron, or his friend, only to those from whom he would not conceal his own; he tells them to those, who have no temptation to betray the trust, or with a denunciation of a certain forfeiture of his friendship, if he discovers that they become public.

Secrets are very frequently told in the first ardour of kindness, or of love, for the sake of proving, by so important a sacrifice, sincerity, or tenderness; but with this motive, though it be strong in itself, vanity concurs, since every man desires to be most esteemed by those whom he loves, or with whom he converses, with whom he passes his hours of pleasure, and to whom he retires from business and from care.

When the discovery of secrets is under consideration, there is always a distinction carefully to be made between our own and those of another; those of which we are fully masters as they affect only our own interest, and those which are reposited with us in trust, and involve the happiness or convenience of such as we have no right to expose to hazard. To tell our own secrets is generally folly, but that folly is without guilt; to communicate those with which we are intrusted is always treachery, and treachery for the most part combined with folly.

There have, indeed, been some enthusiastick and irrational zealots for friendship, who have maintained, and perhaps believed, that one friend has a right to all that is in possession of another; and that therefore it is a violation of kindness to exempt any secret from this boundless confidence. Accordingly a late female minister of state has been shameless enough to inform the world, that she used, when she wanted to extract any thing from her sovereign, to remind her of Montaigne's reasoning, who has determined, that to tell a secret to a friend is no breach of fidelity, because the number of persons trusted is not multiplied, a man and his friend being virtually the same.

That such a fallacy could be imposed upon any human understanding, or that an author could have advanced a position so remote from truth and reason, any otherwise than as a declaimer, to shew to what extent he could stretch his imagination, and with what strength he could press his principle, would scarcely have been credible, had not this lady kindly shewn us how far weakness may be deluded, or indolence amused. But since it appears, that even this sophistry has been able, with the help of a strong desire to repose in quiet upon the understanding of another, to mislead honest intentions, and an understanding not contemptible, it may not be superfluous to remark, that those things which are common among friends are only such as either possesses in his own right, and can alienate or destroy without injury to any other person. Without this limitation, confidence must run on without end, the second person may tell the secret to the third upon the same principle as he received it from the first, and the third may hand it forward to a fourth, till at last it is told in the round of friendship to them from whom it was the first intention chiefly to conceal it.

The confidence which Caius has of the faithfulness of Titius is nothing more than an opinion which himself cannot know to be true, and which

Claudius, who first tells his secret to Caius may know to be false; and therefore the trust is transferred by Caius, if he reveal what has been told him, to one from whom the person originally concerned would have withheld it; and, whatever may be the event, Caius has hazarded the happiness of his friend, without necessity and without permission, and has put that trust in the hand of fortune which was given only to virtue.

All the arguments upon which a man who is telling the private affairs of another may ground his confidence of security, he must upon reflection know to be uncertain, because he finds them without effect upon himself. When he is imagining that Titius will be cautious from a regard to his interest, his reputation, or his duty, he ought to reflect that he is himself at that instant acting in opposition to all these reasons, and revealing what interest, reputation, and duty direct him to conceal.

Every one feels that in his own case he should consider the man incapable of trust, who believed himself at liberty to tell whatever he knew to the first whom he should conclude deserving of his confidence; therefore Caius, in admitting Titius to the affairs imparted only to himself, must know that he violates his faith, since he acts contrary to the intention of Claudius, to whom that faith was given. For promises of friendship are, like all others, useless and vain, unless they are made in some known sense, adjusted and acknowledged by both parties.

I am not ignorant that many questions may be started relating to the duty of secrecy, where the affairs are of publick concern; where subsequent reasons may arise to alter the appearance and nature of the trust; that the manner in which the secret was told may change the degree of obligation; and that the principles upon which a man is chosen for a confident may not always equally constrain him. But these scruples, if not too intricate, are of too extensive consideration for my present purpose, nor are they such as generally occur in common life; and though casuistical knowledge be useful in proper hands, yet it ought by no means to be carelessly exposed, since most will use it rather to lull than awaken their own consciences; and the threads of reasoning, on which truth is suspended, are frequently drawn to such subtility, that common eyes cannot perceive, and common sensibility cannot feel them.

The whole doctrine as well as practice of secrecy, is so perplexing and dangerous, that, next to him who is compelled to trust, I think him unhappy who is chosen to be trusted; for he is often involved in scruples without the liberty of calling in the help of any other understanding; he is frequently drawn into guilt, under the appearance of friendship and honesty; and sometimes subjected to suspicion by the treachery of others, who are engaged without his knowledge in the same schemes; for he that has one confident has generally more, and when he is at last betrayed, is in doubt on whom he shall fix the crime.

The rules therefore that I shall propose concerning secrecy, and from which I think it not safe to deviate, without long and exact deliberation, are—Never to solicit the knowledge of a secret. Not willingly, nor without many limitations, to accept such confidence when it is offered. When a secret is once admitted, to consider the trust as of a very high nature, important as society, and sacred as truth, and therefore not to be violated for any incidental convenience, or slight appearance of contrary fitness.

No. 14. Saturday, 5 May 1750.

———————— *Nil fuit unquam*
Sic dispar sibi————————
                                        HOR.

Sure such a various creature ne'er was known.
                                        FRANCIS.

Among the many inconsistencies which folly produces, or infirmity suffers in the human mind, there has often been observed a manifest and striking contrariety between the life of an author and his writings; and Milton, in a letter to a learned stranger, by whom he had been visited, with great reason congratulates himself upon the consciousness of being found equal to his own character, and having preserved in a private and familiar interview that reputation which his works had procured him.

Those whom the appearance of virtue, or the evidence of genius, have tempted to a nearer knowledge of the writer in whose performances they may be found, have indeed had frequent reason to repent their curiosity; the bubble that sparkled before them has become common water at the touch; the phantom of perfection has vanished when they wished to press it to their bosom. They have lost the pleasure of imagining how far humanity may be exalted, and, perhaps, felt themselves less inclined to toil up the steeps of virtue, when they observe those who seem best able to point the way, loitering below, as either afraid of the labour, or doubtful of the reward.

It has been long the custom of the oriental monarchs to hide themselves in gardens and palaces, to avoid the conversation of mankind, and to be known to their subjects only by their edicts. The same policy is no less necessary to him that writes, than to him that governs; for men would not more patiently submit to be taught, than commanded, by one known to have the same follies and weaknesses with themselves. A sudden intruder into the closet of an author would perhaps feel equal indignation with the officer, who having long solicited admission into the presence of Sardanapalus, saw him not consulting upon laws, enquiring into grievances, or modelling armies, but employed in feminine amusements, and directing the ladies in their work.

It is not difficult to conceive, however, that for many reasons a man writes much better than he lives. For, without entering into refined speculations, it may be shown much easier to design than to perform. A man proposes his schemes of life in a state of abstraction and disengagement, exempt from the enticements of hope, the solicitations of affection, the importunities of appetite, or the depressions of fear, and is in the same state with him that teaches upon land the art of navigation, to whom the sea is always smooth, and the wind always prosperous.

The mathematicians are well acquainted with the difference between pure science, which has to do only with ideas, and the application of its laws to the use of life, in which they are constrained to submit to the imperfection of matter and the influence of accidents. Thus, in moral discussions it is to be remembred that many impediments obstruct our practice, which very easily give way to theory. The speculatist is only in danger of erroneous reasoning, but the man involved in life has his own passions, and those of others, to encounter, and is embarrassed with a thousand inconveniences, which confound him with variety of impulse, and either perplex or obstruct his way. He is forced to act without deliberation, and obliged to choose before he can examine; he is surprised by sudden alterations of the state of things, and changes his measures according to superficial appearances; he is led by others, either because he is indolent, or because he is timorous; he is sometimes afraid to know what is right, and sometimes finds friends or enemies diligent to deceive him.

We are, therefore, not to wonder that most fail, amidst tumult, and snares, and danger, in the observance of those precepts, which they laid down in solitude, safety, and tranquillity, with a mind unbiassed, and with liberty unobstructed. It is the condition of our present state to see more than we can attain, the exactest vigilance and caution can never maintain a single day of unmingled innocence, much less can the utmost efforts of incorporated mind reach the summits of speculative virtue.

It is, however, necessary for the idea of perfection to be proposed, that we may have some object to which our endeavours are to be directed; and he that is most deficient in the duties of life, makes some atonement for his faults, if he warns others against his own failings, and hinders, by the salubrity of his admonitions, the contagion of his example.

Nothing is more unjust, however common, than to charge with hypocrisy him that expresses zeal for those virtues, which he neglects to practise; since he may be sincerely convinced of the advantages of conquering his passions, without having yet obtained the victory, as a man may be confident of the advantages of a voyage, or a journey, without having courage or industry to undertake it, and may honestly recommend to others, those attempts which he neglects himself.

The interest which the corrupt part of mankind have in hardening themselves against every motive to amendment, has disposed them to give to these contradictions, when they can be produced against the cause of virtue, that weight which they will not allow them in any other case. They see men act in opposition to their interest, without supposing, that they do not know it; those who give way to the sudden violence of passion, and forsake the most important persuits for petty pleasures, are not supposed to have changed their opinions, or to approve their own conduct. In moral or religious questions alone, they determine the sentiments by the actions, and charge every man with endeavouring to impose upon the world, whose writings are not confirmed by his life. They never consider that they themselves neglect, or practise something every day, inconsistently with their own settled judgment, nor discover that the conduct of the advocates for virtue can little increase, or lessen, the obligations of their dictates; argument is to be invalidated only by argument, and is in itself of the same force, whether or not it convinces him by whom it is proposed.

Yet since this prejudice, however unreasonable, is always likely to have some prevalence, it is the duty of every man to take care lest he should hinder the efficacy of his own instructions. When he desires to gain the belief of others, he should shew that he believes himself; and when he teaches the fitness of virtue by his reasonings, he should, by his example, prove its possibility: Thus much at least may be required of him, that he shall not act worse than others because he writes better, nor imagine that, by the merit of his genius, he may claim indulgence beyond mortals of the lower classes, and be excused for want of prudence, or neglect of virtue.

BACON, in his History of the winds, after having offered something to the imagination as desirable, often proposes lower advantages in its place to the reason as attainable. The same method may be sometimes pursued in moral endeavours, which this philosopher has observed in natural enquiries; having first set positive and absolute excellence before us, we may be pardoned though we sink down to humbler virtue, trying, however, to keep our point always in view, and struggling not to lose ground, though we cannot gain it.

It is recorded of Sir Matthew Hale, that he, for a long time, concealed the consecration of himself to the stricter duties of religion, lest, by some flagitious and shameful action, he should bring piety into disgrace. For the same reason, it may be prudent for a writer, who apprehends that he shall not inforce his own maxims by his domestic character, to conceal his name that he may not injure them.

There are, indeed, a greater number whose curiosity to gain a more familiar knowledge of successful writers, is not so much prompted by an opinion of their power to improve as to delight, and who expect from them not arguments against vice, or dissertations on temperance or justice, but flights of wit, and sallies of pleasantry, or, at least, acute remarks, nice distinctions, justness of sentiment, and elegance of diction.

This expectation is, indeed, specious and probable, and yet, such is the fate of all human hopes, that it is very often frustrated, and those who raise admiration by their books, disgust by their company. A man of letters for the most part spends, in the privacies of study, that season of life in which the manners are to be softened into ease, and polished into elegance, and, when he has gained knowledge enough to be respected, has neglected the minuter acts by which he might have pleased. When he enters life, if his temper be soft and timorous, he is diffident and bashful, from the knowledge of his defects; or if he was born with spirit and resolution, he is ferocious and arrogant from the consciousness of his merit: he is either dissipated by the awe of company, and unable to recollect his reading, and arrange his arguments; or he is hot, and dogmatical, quick in opposition, and tenacious in defence, disabled by his own violence, and confused by his haste to triumph.

The graces of writing and conversation are of different kinds, and though he who excels in one might have been with opportunities and application equally successful in the other, yet as many please by extemporary talk, though utterly unacquainted with the more accurate method, and more laboured beauties, which composition requires; so it is very possible that men, wholly accustomed to works of study, may be without that readiness of conception, and affluence of language, always necessary to colloquial entertainment. They may want address to watch the hints which conversation offers for the display of their particular attainments, or they may be so much unfurnished with matter on common subjects, that discourse not professedly literary glides over them as heterogeneous bodies, without admitting their conceptions to mix in the circulation.

A transition from an author's books to his conversation, is too often like an entrance into a large city, after a distant prospect. Remotely, we see nothing but spires of temples, and turrets of palaces, and imagine it the residence of splendor, grandeur, and magnificence; but, when we have passed the gates, we find it perplexed with narrow passages, disgraced with despicable cottages, embarrassed with obstructions, and clouded with smoke.

No. 16. Saturday, 12 May 1750.

―― *Multis dicendi copia torrens,*
Et sua mortifera est facundia ――
JUV.

Some who the depths of eloquence have found,
In that unnavigable stream were drown'd.
DRYDEN.

SIR,

I am the modest young man whom you favoured with your advice, in a late paper; and, as I am very far from suspecting that you foresaw the numberless inconveniences which I have, by following it, brought upon myself, I will lay my condition open before you, for you seem bound to extricate me from the perplexities, in which your counsel, however innocent in the intention, has contributed to involve me.

You told me, as you thought, to my comfort, that a writer might easily find means of introducing his genius to the world, for the *presses of England were open*. This I have now fatally experienced; the press is, indeed, open.

>——*Facilis descensus Averni,*
>*Noctes atque dies patet atri janua Ditis.*

>The gates of hell are open night and day;
>Smooth the descent, and easy is the way.
>   DRYDEN.

The means of doing hurt to ourselves are always at hand. I immediately sent to a printer, and contracted with him for an impression of several thousands of my pamphlet. While it was at the press, I was seldom absent from the printing-house, and continually urged the workmen to haste, by solicitations, promises, and rewards. From the day all other pleasures were excluded, by the delightful employment of correcting the sheets; and from the night sleep was generally banished, by anticipations of the happiness, which every hour was bringing nearer.

At last the time of publication approached, and my heart beat with the raptures of an author. I was above all little precautions, and, in defiance of envy or of criticism, set my name upon the title, without sufficiently considering, that what has once passed the press is irrevocable, and that though the printing-house may properly be compared to the infernal regions, for the facility of its entrance, and the difficulty with which authors return from it; yet there is this difference, that a great genius can never return to his former state, by a happy draught of the waters of oblivion.

I am now, Mr. Rambler, known to be an author, and am condemned, irreversibly condemned, to all the miseries of high reputation. The first morning after publication my friends assembled about me; I presented each, as is usual, with a copy of my book. They looked into the first pages, but were hindered, by their admiration, from reading farther. The first pages are, indeed, very elaborate. Some passages they particularly dwelt upon, as more eminently beautiful than the rest; and some delicate strokes, and secret elegancies, I pointed out to them, which had escaped their observation. I then begged of them to forbear their compliments, and invited them, I could not do less, to dine with me at a tavern. After dinner, the book was resumed; but their praises very often so much overpowered my modesty, that I was forced to put about the glass, and had often no means of repressing the clamours of their admiration, but by thundering to the drawer for another bottle.

Next morning another set of my acquaintance congratulated me upon my performance, with such importunity of praise, that I was again forced to obviate their civilities by a treat. On the third day I had yet a greater number of applauders to put to silence in the same manner; and, on the fourth, those whom I had entertained the first day came again, having, in the perusal of the remaining part of the book, discovered so many forcible sentences and masterly touches, that it was impossible for me to bear the repetition of their commendations. I, therefore, persuaded them once more to adjourn to the tavern, and choose some other subject, on which I might share in the conversation. But it was not in their power to withold their attention from my performance, which had so entirely taken possession of their minds, that no intreaties of mine could change their topick, and I was obliged to stifle, with claret, that praise, which neither my modesty could hinder, nor my uneasiness repress.

The whole week was thus spent in a kind of literary revel, and I have now found that nothing is so expensive as great abilities, unless there is join'd with them an insatiable eagerness of praise; for to escape from the pain of hearing myself exalted above the greatest names dead and living of the learned world, it has already cost me two hogsheads of port, fifteen gallons of arrack, ten dozen of claret, and five and forty bottles of champagne.

I was resolved to stay at home no longer, and, therefore, rose early and went to the coffee-house; but found that I had now made myself too eminent for happiness, and that I was no longer to enjoy the pleasure of mixing, upon equal terms, with the rest of the world. As soon as I enter the room, I see part of the company raging with envy, which they endeavour to conceal, sometimes with the appearance of laughter, and sometimes with that of contempt; but the disguise is such, that I can discover the secret rancour of their hearts, and as envy is deservedly its own punishment, I frequently indulge myself in tormenting them with my presence.

But, though there may be some slight satisfaction received from the mortification of my enemies, yet my benevolence will not suffer me to take any pleasure in the terrors of my friends. I have been cautious, since the appearance of my work, not to give myself more premeditated airs of superiority, than the most rigid humility might allow. It is, indeed, not impossible that I may sometimes have laid down my opinion, in a manner that shewed a consciousness of my ability to maintain it, or interrupted the conversation, when I saw its tendency, without suffering the speaker to waste his time in explaining his sentiments; and, indeed, I did indulge myself for two days in a custom of drumming with my fingers, when the company began to lose themselves in absurdities, or to encroach upon subjects which I knew them unqualified to discuss. But I generally acted with great appearance of respect, even to those whose stupidity I pitied in my heart. Yet, notwithstanding this exemplary moderation, so universal is the dread of uncommon powers, and such the unwillingness of mankind to be made wiser, that I have now for some days found myself shunned by all my acquaintance. If I knock at a door, no body is at home; if I enter a coffee-house, I have the box to myself. I live in the town like a lion in his desart, or an eagle on his rock, too great for friendship or society, and condemned to solitude, by unhappy elevation, and dreaded ascendency.

Nor is my character only formidable to others, but burdensome to myself. I naturally love to talk without much thinking, to scatter my merriment at random, and to relax my thoughts with ludicrous remarks and fanciful images; but such is now the importance of my opinion, that I am afraid to offer it, lest, by being established too hastily into a maxim, it should be the occasion of error to half the nation; and such is the expectation with which I am attended, when I am going to speak, that I frequently pause to reflect whether what I am about to utter is worthy of myself.

This, Sir, is sufficiently miserable, but there are still greater calamities behind. You must have read in Pope and Swift how men of parts have had their closets rifled, and their cabinets broke open at the instigation of piratical booksellers, for the profit of their works; and it is apparent, that there are many prints now sold in the shops, of men whom you cannot suspect of sitting for that purpose, and whose likenesses must have been certainly stolen when their names made their faces vendible. These considerations at first put me on my guard, and I have, indeed, found sufficient reason for my caution, for I have discovered many people examining my countenance, with a curiosity that shewed their intention to draw it; I immediately left the house, but find the same behaviour in another.

Others may be persecuted, but I am haunted; I have good reason to believe that eleven painters are now dogging me, for they know that he who can get my face first will make his fortune. I often change my wig, and wear my hat over my eyes, by which I hope somewhat to confound them; for you know it is not fair to sell my face, without admitting me to share the profit.

I am, however, not so much in pain for my face as for my papers, which I dare neither carry with me nor leave behind. I have, indeed, taken some measures for their preservation, having put them in an iron chest, and fixed a padlock upon my closet. I change my lodgings five times a week, and always remove at the dead of night.

Thus I live, in consequence of having given too great proofs of a predominant genius, in the solitude of a hermit, with the anxiety of a miser, and the caution of an outlaw; afraid to shew my face, lest it should be copied; afraid to speak, lest I should injure my character, and to write lest my correspondents should publish my letters; always uneasy lest my servants should steal my papers for the sake of money, or my friends for that of the publick. This it is to soar above the rest of mankind; and this representation I lay before you, that I may be informed how to divest myself of the laurels which are so cumbersome to the wearer, and descend to the enjoyment of that quiet from which I find a writer of the first class so fatally debarred.

MISELLUS.

No. 17. Tuesday, 15 May 1750.

——*Me non oracula certum,*
Sed mors certa facit.

LUCAN.

Let those weak minds, who live in doubt and fear,
To juggling priests for oracles repair;
One certain hour of death to each decreed,
My fixt, my certain soul from doubt has freed.

ROWE.

It is recorded of some eastern monarch, that he kept an officer in his house, whose employment it was to remind him of his mortality, by calling out every morning, at a stated hour: *Remember, prince, that thou shalt die.* And the contemplation of the frailness and uncertainty of our present state appeared of so much importance to Solon of Athens, that he left this precept to future ages: *Keep thine eye fixed upon the end of life.*

A frequent and attentive prospect of that moment, which must put a period to all our schemes, and deprive us of all our acquisitions, is, indeed, of the utmost efficacy to the just and rational regulation of our lives; nor would ever any thing wicked, or often any thing absurd, be undertaken or prosecuted by him who should begin every day with a serious reflection, that he is born to die.

The disturbers of our happiness, in this world, are our desires, our griefs, and our fears, and to all these, the consideration of mortality is a certain and adequate remedy. Think, says Epictetus, frequently on poverty, banishment, and death, and thou wilt then never indulge violent desires, or give up thy heart to mean sentiments, οὐδὲν οὐδέποτε ταπεινὸν ἐνθυμήσῃ, οὔτε ἄγαν ἐπιθυμήσεις τινός.

That the maxim of Epictetus is founded on just observation will easily be granted, when we reflect, how that vehemence of eagerness after the common objects of persuit is kindled in our minds. We represent to ourselves the pleasures of some future possession, and suffer our thoughts to dwell attentively upon it, till it has wholly ingrossed the imagination, and permits us not to conceive any happiness but its attainment, or any misery but its loss; every other satisfaction which the bounty of providence has scattered over life is neglected as inconsiderable, in comparison of the great object which we have placed before us, and is thrown from us as incumbering our activity, or trampled under foot as standing in our way.

Every man has experienced, how much of this ardour has been remitted, when a sharp or tedious sickness has set death before his eyes. The extensive influence of greatness, the glitter of wealth, the praises of admirers, and the attendance of supplicants, have appeared vain and empty things, when the last hour seemed to be approaching; and the same appearance they would always have, if the same thought was always predominant. We should then find the absurdity of stretching out our arms incessantly to grasp that which we cannot keep, and wearing out our lives in endeavours to add new turrets to the fabrick of ambition, when the foundation itself is shaking, and the ground on which it stands is mouldering away.

All envy is proportionate to desire; we are uneasy at the attainments of another, according as we think our own happiness would be advanced by the addition of that which he witholds from us; and, therefore, whatever depresses immoderate wishes, will, at the same time, set the heart free from the corrosion of envy, and exempt us from that vice which is, above most others, tormenting to ourselves, hateful to the world, and productive of mean artifices, and sordid projects. He that considers how soon he must close his life, will find nothing of so much importance as to close it well; and will, therefore, look with indifference upon whatever is useless to that purpose. Whoever reflects frequently upon the uncertainty of his own duration, will find out, that the state of others is not more permanent, and that what can confer nothing on himself very desirable, cannot so much improve the condition of a rival, as to make him much superior to those from whom he has carried the prize, a prize too mean to deserve a very obstinate opposition.

Even grief, that passion to which the virtuous and tender mind is particularly subject, will be obviated, or alleviated, by the same thoughts. It will be obviated, if all the blessings of our condition are enjoyed with a constant sense of this uncertain tenure. If we remember, that whatever we possess is to be in our hands but a very little time, and that the little, which our most lively hopes can promise us, may be made less, by ten thousand accidents; we shall not much repine at a loss, of which we cannot estimate the value, but of which, though we are not able to tell the least amount, we know, with sufficient certainty, the greatest, and are convinced that the greatest is not much to be regretted.

But, if any passion has so much usurped our understanding, as not to suffer us to enjoy advantages with the moderation prescribed by reason, it is not too late to apply this remedy, when we find ourselves sinking under sorrow, and inclined to pine for that which is irrecoverably vanished. We may then usefully revolve the uncertainty of our own condition, and the folly of lamenting that from which, if it had stayed a little longer, we should ourselves have been taken away.

With regard to the sharpest and most melting sorrow, that which arises from the loss of those whom we have loved with tenderness, it may be observed, that friendship between mortals can be contracted on no other terms, than that one must sometime mourn for the other's death: And this grief will always yield to the surviver one consolation proportionate to his affliction; for the pain, whatever it be, that he himself feels, his friend has escaped.

Nor is fear, the most overbearing and resistless of all our passions, less to be temperated by this universal medicine of the mind. The frequent contemplation of death, as it shows the vanity of all human good, discovers likewise the lightness of all terrestrial evil, which, certainly, can last no longer than the subject upon which it acts, and, according to the old observation, must be shorter, as it is more violent. The most cruel calamity, which misfortune can produce, must, by the necessity of nature, be quickly at an end. The soul cannot long be held in prison, but will fly away, and leave a lifeless body to human malice.

———— *Ridetque sui ludibria trunci.*

And soaring mocks the broken frame below.

The utmost that we can threaten to one another is that death, which, indeed, we may precipitate, but cannot retard, and from which, therefore, it cannot become a wise man to buy a reprieve at the expense of virtue, since he knows not how small a portion of time he can purchase, but knows that, whether short or long, it will be made less valuable by the remembrance of the price at which it has been obtained. He is sure that he destroys his happiness, but is not sure that he lengthens his life.

The known shortness of life, as it ought to moderate our passions, may likewise, with equal propriety, contract our designs. There is not time for the most forcible genius, and most active industry, to extend its effects beyond a certain sphere. To project the conquest of the world, is the madness of mighty princes; to hope for excellence in every science, has been the folly of literary heroes; and both have found, at last, that they have panted for a height of eminence denied to humanity, and have lost many opportunities of making themselves useful and happy, by a vain ambition of obtaining a species of honour, which the eternal laws of providence have placed beyond the reach of man.

The miscarriages of the great designs of princes are recorded in the histories of the world, but are of little use to the bulk of mankind, who seem very little interested in admonitions against errors which they cannot commit. But the fate of learned ambition is a proper subject for every scholar to consider; for who has not had occasion to regret the dissipation of great abilities in a boundless multiplicity of persuits, to lament the sudden desertion of excellent designs, upon the offer of some other subject, made inviting by its novelty, and to observe the inaccuracy and deficiencies of works left unfinished by too great an extension of the plan?

It is always pleasing to observe, how much more our minds can conceive, than our bodies can perform; yet it is our duty, while we continue in this complicated state, to regulate one part of our composition by some regard to the other. We are not to indulge our corporeal appetites with pleasures that impair our intellectual vigour, nor gratify our minds with schemes which we know our lives must fail in attempting to execute. The uncertainty of our duration ought at once to set bounds to our designs, and add incitements to our industry; and when we find ourselves inclined either to immensity in our schemes, or sluggishness in our endeavours, we may either check, or animate, ourselves, by recollecting, with the father of physic, *that art is long, and life is short.*

No. 18. Saturday, 19 May 1750.

Illic matre carentibus
Privignis mulier temperat innocens,
Nec dotata regit virum
Conjux, nec nitido fidit adultero:
  Dos est magna parentium
Virtus, et metuens alterius tori
  Certo fœdere castitas.

HOR.

Not there the guiltless step-dame knows
The baleful draught for orphans to compose;
  No wife high-portion'd rules her spouse,
Or trusts her essenc'd lover's faithless vows:
  The lovers there for dowr'y claim,
The father's virtue, and the spotless fame,
  Which dares not break the nuptial tie.

FRANCIS.

There is no observation more frequently made by such as employ themselves in surveying the conduct of mankind, than that marriage, though the dictate of nature, and the institution of providence, is yet very often the cause of misery, and that those who enter into that state can seldom forbear to express their repentance, and their envy of those whom either chance or caution has witheld from it.

This general unhappiness has given occasion to many sage maxims among the serious, and smart remarks among the gay; the moralist and the writer of epigrams have equally shown their abilities upon it; some have lamented, and some have ridiculed it; but as the faculty of writing has been chiefly a masculine endowment, the reproach of making the world miserable has been always thrown upon the women, and the grave and the merry have equally thought themselves at liberty to conclude either with declamatory complaints, or satirical censures, of female folly or fickleness, ambition or cruelty, extravagance or lust.

Led by such a number of examples, and incited by my share in the common interest, I sometimes venture to consider this universal grievance, having endeavoured to divest my heart of all partiality, and place myself as a kind of neutral being between the sexes, whose clamours, being equally vented on both sides with all the vehemence of distress, all the apparent confidence of justice, and all the indignation of injured virtue, seem entitled to equal regard. The men have, indeed, by their superiority of writing, been able to collect the evidence of many ages, and raise prejudices in their favour by the venerable testimonies of philosophers, historians and poets; but the pleas of the ladies appeal to passions of more forcible operation than the reverence of antiquity. If they have not so great names on their side, they have stronger arguments; it is to little purpose that Socrates, or Euripides, are produced against the sighs of softness, and the tears of beauty. The most frigid and inexorable judge would, at least, stand suspended between equal powers, as Lucan was perplexed in the determination of the cause, where the deities were on one side, and Cato on the other.

But I, who have long studied the severest and most abstracted philosophy, have now, in the cool maturity of life, arrived to such command over my passions, that I can hear the vociferations of either sex without catching any of the fire from those that utter them. For I have found, by long experience, that a man will sometimes rage at his wife, when in reality his mistress has offended him; and a lady complain of the cruelty of her husband, when she has no other enemy than bad cards. I do not suffer myself to be any longer imposed upon by oaths on one side, or fits on the other; nor when the husband hastens to the tavern, and the lady retires to her closet, am I always confident that they are driven by their miseries; since I have sometimes reason to believe, that they purpose not so much to sooth their sorrows, as to animate their fury. But how little credit soever may be given to particular accusations, the general accumulation of the charge shews, with too much evidence, that married persons are not very often advanced in felicity; and, therefore, it may be proper to examine at what avenues so many evils have made their way into the world. With this purpose, I have reviewed the lives of my friends, who have been least successful in connubial contracts, and attentively considered by what motives they were incited to marry, and by what principles they regulated their choice.

One of the first of my acquaintances that resolved to quit the unsettled thoughtless condition of a batchelor, was Prudentius, a man of slow parts, but not without knowledge or judgment in things which he had leisure to consider gradually before he determined them. Whenever we met at a tavern, it was his province to settle the scheme of our entertainment, contract with the cook, and inform us when we had called for wine to the sum originally proposed. This grave considerer found by deep meditation that a man was no loser by marrying early, even though he contented himself with a less fortune; for estimating the exact worth of annuities, he found that, considering the constant diminution of the value of life, with the probable fall of the interest of money, it was not worse to have ten thousand pounds at the age of two and twenty years, than a much larger fortune at thirty; for many opportunities, says he, occur of improving money, which if a man misses, he may not afterwards recover.

Full of these reflections, he threw his eyes about him, not in search of beauty, or elegance, dignity, or understanding, but of a woman with ten thousand pounds. Such a woman, in a wealthy part of the kingdom, it was not very difficult to find; and by artful management with her father, whose ambition was to make his daughter a gentlewoman, my friend got her, as he boasted to us in confidence two days after his marriage, for a settlement of seventy three pounds a year less than her fortune might have claimed, and less than he would himself have given, if the fools had been but wise enough to delay the bargain.

Thus, at once delighted with the superiority of his parts, and the augmentation of his fortune, he carried Furia to his own house, in which he never afterwards enjoyed one hour of happiness. For Furia was a wretch of mean intellects, violent passions, a strong voice, and low education, without any sense of happiness but that which consisted in eating, and counting money. Furia was a scold. They agreed in the desire of wealth, but with this difference, that Prudentius was for growing rich by gain, Furia by parsimony. Prudentius would venture his money with chances very much in his favour; but Furia very wisely observing that what they had was, while they had it, *their own*, thought all traffick too great a hazard, and was for putting it out at low interest, upon good security. Prudentius ventured, however, to insure a ship, at a very unreasonable price, but happening to lose his money, was so tormented with the clamours of his wife, that he never durst try a second experiment. He has now grovelled seven and forty years under Furia's direction, who never once mentioned him, since his bad luck, by any other name than that of *the insurer*.

The next that married from our society was Florentius. He happened to see Zephyretta in a chariot at a horse-race, danced with her at night, was confirmed in his first ardour, waited on her next morning, and declared himself her lover. Florentius had not knowledge enough of the world, to distinguish between the flutter of coquetry, and the sprightliness of wit, or between the smile of allurement, and that of chearfulness. He was soon waked from his rapture by conviction that his pleasure was but the pleasure of a day. Zephyretta had in four and twenty hours spent her stock of repartee, gone round the circle of her airs, and had nothing remaining for him but childish insipidity, or for herself, but the practice of the same artifices upon new men.

Melissus was a man of parts, capable of enjoying, and of improving life. He had passed through the various scenes of gayety with that indifference and possession of himself, natural to men who have something higher and nobler in their prospect. Retiring to spend the summer in a village little frequented, he happened to lodge in the same house with Ianthe, and was unavoidably drawn to some acquaintance, which her wit and politeness soon invited him to improve. Having no opportunity of any other company, they were always together; and, as they owed their pleasures to each other, they began to forget that any pleasure was enjoyed before their meeting. Melissus, from being delighted with her company, quickly began to be uneasy in her absence, and being sufficiently convinced of the force of her understanding, and finding, as he imagined, such a conformity of temper as declared them formed for each other, addressed her as a lover, after no very long courtship obtained her for his wife, and brought her next winter to town in triumph.

Now began their infelicity. Melissus had only seen her in one scene, where there was no variety of objects, to produce the proper excitements to contrary desires. They had both loved solitude and reflection, where there was nothing but solitude and reflection to be loved; but when they came into publick life, Ianthe discovered those passions which accident rather than hypocrisy had hitherto concealed. She was, indeed, not without the power of thinking, but was wholly without the exertion of that power, when either gayety, or splendour, played on her imagination. She was expensive in her diversions, vehement in her passions, insatiate of pleasure however dangerous to her reputation, and eager of applause by whomsoever it might be given. This was the wife which Melissus the philosopher found in his retirement, and from whom he expected an associate in his studies, and an assistant to his virtues.

Prosapius, upon the death of his younger brother, that the family might not be extinct, married his housekeeper, and has ever since been complaining to his friends that mean notions are instilled into his children, that he is ashamed to sit at his own table, and that his house is uneasy to him for want of suitable companions.

Avaro, master of a very large estate, took a woman of bad reputation, recommended to him by a rich uncle, who made that marriage the condition on which he should be his heir. Avaro now wonders to perceive his own fortune, his wife's, and his uncle's, insufficient to give him that happiness which is to be found only with a woman of virtue.

I intend to treat in more papers on this important article of life, and shall, therefore, make no reflexion upon these histories, except that all whom I have mentioned failed to obtain happiness, for want of considering that marriage is the strictest tye of perpetual friendship; that there can be no friendship without confidence, and no confidence without integrity; and that he must expect to be wretched, who pays to beauty, riches, or politeness, that regard which only virtue and piety can claim.

No. 22. Saturday, 2 June 1750.

——*Ego nec studium sine divite venâ,*
Nec rude quid prosit video ingenium, alterius sic
Altera poscit opem res, & conjurat amice.
HOR.

Without a genius learning soars in vain;
And without learning genius sinks again:
Their force united crowns the sprightly reign.
ELPHINSTON.

WIT and LEARNING were the children of Apollo, by different mothers; WIT was the offspring of EUPHROSYNE, and resembled her in chearfulness and vivacity; LEARNING was born of SOPHIA, and retained her seriousness and caution. As their mothers were rivals, they were bred up by them, from their birth, in habitual opposition, and all means were so incessantly employed to impress upon them a hatred and contempt of each other, that though Apollo, who foresaw the ill effects of their discord, endeavoured to soften them, by dividing his regard equally between them, yet his impartiality and kindness were without effect; the maternal animosity was deeply rooted, having been intermingled with their first ideas, and was confirmed every hour, as fresh opportunities occurred of exerting it. No sooner were they of age to be received into the apartments of the other celestials, than WIT began to entertain Venus at her toilet, by aping the solemnity of LEARNING, and LEARNING to divert Minerva at her loom, by exposing the blunders and ignorance of WIT.

Thus they grew up, with malice perpetually increasing, by the encouragement which each received from those whom their mothers had persuaded to patronise and support them; and longed to be admitted to the table of Jupiter, not so much for the hope of gaining honour, as of excluding a rival from all pretensions to regard, and of putting an everlasting stop to the progress of that influence which either believed the other to have obtained by mean arts and false appearances.

At last the day came, when they were both, with the usual solemnities, received into the class of superior deities, and allowed to take nectar from the hand of Hebe. But from that hour CONCORD lost her authority at the table of Jupiter. The rivals, animated by their new dignity, and incited by the alternate applauses of the associate powers, harrassed each other by incessant contests, with such a regular vicissitude of victory, that neither was depressed.

It was observable, that at the beginning of every debate, the advantage was on the side of WIT; and that, at the first sallies, the whole assembly sparkled, according to Homer's expression, with unextinguishable merriment. But LEARNING would reserve her strength till the burst of applause was over, and the languor with which the violence of joy is always succeeded, began to promise more calm and patient attention. She then attempted her defence, and, by comparing one part of her antagonist's objections with another, commonly made him confute himself; or, by shewing how small a part of the question he had taken into his view, proved that his opinion could have no weight. The audience began gradually to lay aside their prepossessions, and rose, at last, with great veneration for LEARNING, but with greater kindness for WIT.

Their conduct was, whenever they desired to recommend themselves to distinction, entirely opposite. WIT was daring and adventurous; LEARNING cautious and deliberate. WIT thought nothing reproachful but dulness; LEARNING was afraid of no imputation, but that of error. WIT answered before he understood, lest his quickness of apprehension should be questioned; LEARNING paused, where there was no difficulty, lest any insidious sophism should lie undiscovered. WIT perplexed every debate by rapidity and confusion; LEARNING tired the hearers with endless distinctions, and prolonged the dispute without advantage, by proving that which never was denied. WIT, in hopes of shining, would venture to produce what he had not considered, and often succeeded beyond his own expectation, by following the train of a lucky thought; LEARNING would reject every new notion, for fear of being intangled in consequences which she could not foresee, and was often hindered, by her caution, from pressing her advantages, and subduing her opponent.

Both had prejudices, which in some degree hindered their progress towards perfection, and left them open to attacks. Novelty was the darling of WIT, and antiquity of LEARNING. To WIT, all that was new, was specious; to LEARNING, whatever was antient, was venerable. WIT, however, seldom failed to divert those whom he could not convince, and to convince was not often his ambition; LEARNING always supported her opinion with so many collateral truths, that, when the cause was decided against her, her arguments were remembered with admiration.

Nothing was more common, on either side, than to quit their proper characters, and to hope for a compleat conquest by the use of the weapons which had been employed against them. WIT would sometimes labour a syllogism, and LEARNING distort her features with a jest; but they always suffered by the experiment, and betrayed themselves to confutation or contempt. The seriousness of WIT was without dignity, and the merriment of LEARNING without vivacity.

Their contests, by long continuance, grew at last important, and the divinities broke into parties. WIT was taken into the protection of the laughter-loving Venus, had a retinue allowed him of SMILES and JESTS, and was often permitted to dance among the GRACES. LEARNING still continued the favourite of Minerva, and seldom went out of her palace, without a train of the severer virtues, CHASTITY, TEMPERANCE, FORTITUDE, and LABOUR. WIT, cohabiting with MALICE, had a son named SATYR, who followed him, carrying a quiver filled with poisoned arrows, which, where they once drew blood, could by no skill ever be extracted. These arrows he frequently shot at LEARNING, when she was most earnestly or usefully employed, engaged in abstruse inquiries, or giving instructions to her followers. Minerva, therefore, deputed CRITICISM to her aid, who generally broke the point of SATYR's arrows, turned them aside, or retorted them on himself.

Jupiter was at last angry, that the peace of the heavenly regions should be in perpetual danger of violation, and resolved to dismiss these troublesome antagonists to the lower world. Hither therefore they came, and carried on their antient quarrel among mortals, nor was either long without zealous votaries. WIT, by his gaiety, captivated the young; and LEARNING, by her authority, influenced the old. Their power quickly appeared by very eminent effects, theatres were built for the reception of WIT, and colleges endowed for the residence of LEARNING. Each party endeavoured to outvy the other in cost and magnificence, and to propagate an opinion, that it was necessary, from the first entrance into life, to enlist in one of the factions; and that none could hope for the regard of either divinity, who had once entered the temple of the rival power.

There were indeed a class of mortals, by whom WIT and LEARNING were equally disregarded: These were the devotees of Plutus, the god of riches; among these it seldom happened that the gaiety of WIT could raise a smile, or the eloquence of LEARNING procure attention. In revenge of this contempt, they agreed to incite their followers against them; but the forces that were sent on those expeditions frequently betrayed their trust; and, in contempt of the orders which they had received, flattered the rich in public, while they scorned them in their hearts; and when, by this treachery, they had obtained the favour of Plutus, affected to look with an air of superiority on those who still remained in the service of WIT and LEARNING.

Disgusted with these desertions, the two rivals, at the same time, petitioned Jupiter for re-admission to their native habitations, Jupiter thundered on the right hand, and they prepared to obey the happy summons. WIT readily spread his wings, and soared aloft, but not being able to see far, was bewildered in the pathless immensity of the ethereal spaces. LEARNING, who knew the way, shook her pinions; but for want of natural vigour could only take short flights: so, after many efforts, they both sunk again to the ground, and learned, from their mutual distress, the necessity of union. They therefore joined their hands, and renewed their flight: LEARNING was borne up by the vigour of WIT, and WIT guided by the perspicacity of LEARNING. They soon reached the dwellings of Jupiter, and were so endeared to each other, that they lived afterwards in perpetual concord. WIT persuaded LEARNING to converse with the GRACES, and LEARNING engaged WIT in the service of the VIRTUES.

They were now the favourites of all the powers of heaven, and gladdened every banquet by their presence. They soon after married, at the command of Jupiter, and had a numerous progeny of ARTS and SCIENCES.

No. 23. Tuesday, 5 June 1750.

Tres mihi convivæ prope dissentire videntur;
Poscentur vario multum diversa palato.

HOR.

Three guests I have, dissenting at my feast,
Requiring each to gratify his taste
With different food.

FRANCIS.

That every man should regulate his actions by his own conscience, without any regard to the opinions of the rest of the world, is one of the first precepts of moral prudence; justified not only by the suffrage of reason, which declares that none of the gifts of heaven are to lie useless, but by the voice likewise of experience, which will soon inform us that, if we make the praise or blame of others the rule of our conduct, we shall be distracted by a boundless variety of irreconcileable judgments, be held in perpetual suspense between contrary impulses, and consult for ever without determination.

I know not whether, for the same reason, it is not necessary for an author to place some confidence in his own skill, and to satisfy himself in the knowledge that he has not deviated from the established law of composition, without submitting his works to frequent examinations before he gives them to the publick, or endeavouring to secure success by a solicitous conformity to advice and criticism.

It is, indeed, quickly discoverable, that consultation and compliance can conduce little to the perfection of any literary performance; for whoever is so doubtful of his own abilities as to encourage the remarks of others, will find himself every day embarrassed with new difficulties, and will harrass his mind, in vain, with the hopeless labour of uniting heterogeneous ideas, digesting independent hints, and collecting into one point the several rays of borrowed light, emitted often with contrary directions.

Of all authors, those who retail their labours in periodical sheets would be most unhappy, if they were much to regard the censures or the admonitions of their readers; for, as their works are not sent into the world at once, but by small parts in gradual succession, it is always imagined, by those who think themselves qualified to give instructions, that they may yet redeem their former failings by hearkening to better judges, and supply the deficiencies of their plan, by the help of the criticisms which are so liberally afforded.

I have had occasion to observe, sometimes with vexation, and sometimes with merriment, the different temper with which the same man reads a printed and manuscript performance. When a book is once in the hands of the public, it is considered as permanent and unalterable; and the reader, if he be free from personal prejudices, takes it up with no other intention than of pleasing or instructing himself; he accommodates his mind to the author's design; and, having no interest in refusing the amusement that is offered him, never interrupts his own tranquillity by studied cavils, or destroys his satisfaction in that which is already well, by an anxious enquiry how it might be better; but is often contented without pleasure, and pleased without perfection.

But if the same man be called to consider the merit of a production yet unpublished, he brings an imagination heated with objections to passages, which he has yet never heard; he invokes all the powers of criticism, and stores his memory with Taste and Grace, Purity and Delicacy, Manners and Unities, sounds which, having been once uttered by those that understood them, have been since re-echoed without meaning, and kept up to the disturbance of the world, by a constant repercussion from one coxcomb to another. He considers himself as obliged to shew, by some proof of his abilities, that he is not consulted to no purpose, and, therefore, watches every opening for objection, and looks round for every opportunity to propose some specious alteration. Such opportunities a very small degree of sagacity will enable him to find; for, in every work of imagination, the disposition of parts, the insertion of incidents, and use of decorations, may be varied a thousand ways with equal propriety; and as, in things nearly equal, that will always seem best to every man which he himself produces, the critic, whose business is only to propose, without the care of execution, can never want the satisfaction of believing that he has suggested very important improvements, nor the power of enforcing his advice by arguments, which, as they appear convincing to himself, either his kindness, or his vanity, will press obstinately and importunately, without suspicion that he may possibly judge too hastily in favour of his own advice, or enquiry whether the advantage of the new scheme be proportionate to the labour.

It is observed, by the younger Pliny, that an orator ought not so much to select the strongest arguments which his cause admits, as to employ all which his imagination can afford; for, in pleading, those reasons are of most value, which will most affect the judges; and the judges, says he, will be always most touched with that which they had before conceived. Every man, who is called to give his opinion of a performance, decides upon the same principle; he first suffers himself to form expectations, and then is angry at his disappointment. He lets his imagination rove at large, and wonders that another, equally unconfined in the boundless ocean of possibility, takes a different course.

But, though the rule of Pliny be judiciously laid down, it is not applicable to the writer's cause, because there always lies an appeal from domestick criticism to a higher judicature, and the publick, which is never corrupted, nor often deceived, is to pass the last sentence upon literary claims.

Of the great force of preconceived opinions I had many proofs, when I first entered upon this weekly labour. My readers having, from the performances of my predecessors, established an idea of unconnected essays, to which they believed all future authors under a necessity of conforming, were impatient of the least deviation from their system, and numerous remonstrances were accordingly made by each, as he found his favourite subject omitted or delayed. Some were angry that the RAMBLER did not, like the SPECTATOR, introduce himself to the acquaintance of the publick, by an account of his own birth and studies, an enumeration of his adventures, and a description of his physiognomy. Others soon began to remark that he was a solemn, serious, dictatorial writer, without sprightliness or gaiety, and called out with vehemence for mirth and humour. Another admonished him to have a special eye upon the various clubs of this great city, and informed him that much of the Spectator's vivacity was laid out upon such assemblies. He has been censured for not imitating the politeness of his predecessors, having hitherto neglected to take the ladies under his protection, and give them rules for the just opposition of colours, and the proper dimensions of ruffles and pinners. He has been required by one to fix a particular censure upon those matrons who play at cards with spectacles. And another is very much offended whenever he meets with a speculation, in which naked precepts are comprised, without the illustration of examples and characters.

I make not the least question that all these monitors intend the promotion of my design, and the instruction of my readers; but they do not know, or do not reflect that an author has a rule of choice peculiar to himself, and selects those subjects which he is best qualified to treat, by the course of his studies, or the accidents of his life; that some topicks of amusement have been already treated with too much success to invite a competition; and that he who endeavours to gain many readers, must try various arts of invitation, essay every avenue of pleasure, and make frequent changes in his methods of approach.

I cannot but consider myself amidst this tumult of criticism, as a ship in a poetical tempest, impelled at the same time by opposite winds, and dashed by the waves from every quarter, but held upright by the contrariety of the assailants, and secured, in some measure, by multiplicity of distress. Had the opinion of my censurers been unanimous, it might, perhaps, have overset my resolution; but since I find them at variance with each other, I can, without scruple, neglect them, and endeavour to gain the favour of the publick, by following the direction of my own reason, and indulging the sallies of my own imagination.

No. 24. Saturday, 9 June 1750.

Nemo in sese tentat descendere.
PERSIUS.

None, none descends into himself.
DRYDEN.

Among the precepts, or aphorisms, admitted by general consent, and inculcated by frequent repetition, there is none more famous among the masters of antient wisdom, than that compendious lesson, Γνῶθι σεαυτὸν, *Be acquainted with thyself*; ascribed by some to an oracle, and by others to Chilo of Lacedemon.

This is, indeed, a dictate, which, in the whole extent of its meaning, may be said to comprise all the speculation requisite to a moral agent. For what more can be necessary to the regulation of life, than the knowledge of our original, our end, our duties, and our relation to other beings?

It is however very improbable that the first author, whoever he was, intended to be understood in this unlimited and complicated sense; for of the inquiries, which, in so large an acceptation, it would seem to recommend, some are too extensive for the powers of man, and some require light from above, which was not yet indulged to the heathen world.

We might have had more satisfaction concerning the original import of this celebrated sentence, if history had informed us, whether it was uttered as a general instruction to mankind, or as a particular caution to some private inquirer; whether it was applied to some single occasion, or laid down as the universal rule of life.

There will occur, upon the slightest consideration, many possible circumstances, in which this monition might very properly be inforced; for every error in human conduct must arise from ignorance in ourselves, either perpetual or temporary; and happen either because we do not know what is best and fittest, or because our knowledge is at the time of action not present to the mind.

When a man employs himself upon remote and unnecessary subjects, and wastes his life upon questions, which cannot be resolved, and of which the solution would conduce very little to the advancement of happiness; he, when he lavishes his hours in calculating the weight of the terraqueous globe, or in adjusting successive systems of worlds beyond the reach of the telescope; he may be very properly recalled from his excursions by this precept, and reminded that there is a nearer being with which it is his duty to be more acquainted; and from which, his attention has hitherto been witheld, by studies, to which he has no other motive, than vanity or curiosity.

The great praise of Socrates is, that he drew the wits of Greece, by his instruction and example, from the vain persuit of natural philosophy to moral inquiries, and turned their thoughts from stars and tides, and matter and motion, upon the various modes of virtue, and relations of life. All his lectures were but commentaries upon this saying; if we suppose the knowledge of ourselves recommended by Chilo, in opposition to other inquiries less suitable to the state of man.

The great fault of men of learning is still, that they offend against this rule, and appear willing to study any thing rather than themselves; for which reason they are often despised by those, with whom they imagine themselves above comparison; despised, as useless to common purposes, as unable to conduct the most trivial affairs, and unqualified to perform those offices by which the concatenation of society is preserved, and mutual tenderness excited and maintained.

Gelidus is a man of great penetration, and deep researches. Having a mind naturally formed for the abstruser sciences, he can comprehend intricate combinations without confusion, and being of a temper naturally cool and equal, he is seldom interrupted by his passions in the persuit of the longest chain of unexpected consequences. He has, therefore, a long time indulged hopes, that the solution of some problems, by which the professors of science have been hitherto baffled, is reserved for his genius and industry. He spends his time in the highest room of his house, into which none of his family are suffered to enter; and when he comes down to his dinner, or his rest, he walks about like a stranger that is there only for a day, without any tokens of regard or tenderness. He has totally divested himself of all human sensations; he has neither eye for beauty, nor ear for complaint; he neither rejoices at the good fortune of his nearest friend, nor mourns for any publick or private calamity. Having once received a letter, and given it his servant to read, he was informed, that it was written by his brother, who, being shipwrecked, had swam naked to land, and was destitute of necessaries in a foreign country. Naked and destitute! says Gelidus, reach down the last volume of meteorological observations, extract an exact account of the wind, and note it carefully in the diary of the weather.

The family of Gelidus once broke into his study, to shew him that a town at a small distance was on fire, and in a few moments a servant came up to tell him, that the flame had caught so many houses on both sides, that the inhabitants were confounded, and began to think rather of escaping with their lives, than saving their dwellings. What you tell me, says Gelidus, is very probable, for fire naturally acts in a circle.

Thus lives this great philosopher, insensible to every spectacle of distress, and unmoved by the loudest call of social nature, for want of considering that men are designed for the succour and comfort of each other; that, though there are hours which may be laudably spent upon knowledge not immediately useful, yet the first attention is due to practical virtue; and that he may be justly driven out from the commerce of mankind, who has so far abstracted himself from the species, as to partake neither of the joys nor griefs of others, but neglects the endearments of his wife, and the caresses of his children, to count the drops of rain, note the changes of the wind, and calculate the eclipses of the moons of Jupiter.

I shall reserve to some future paper the religious and important meaning of this epitome of wisdom, and only remark, that it may be applied to the gay and light, as well as to the grave and solemn parts of life; and that not only the philosopher may forfeit his pretences to real learning, but the wit, and the beauty, may miscarry in their schemes, by the want of this universal requisite, the knowledge of themselves.

It is surely for no other reason, that we see such numbers resolutely struggling against nature, and contending for that which they never can attain, endeavouring to unite contradictions, and determined to excel in characters inconsistent with each other; that stock-jobbers affect dress, gaiety, and elegance, and mathematicians labour to be wits; that the soldier teazes his acquaintance with questions in theology, and the academick hopes to divert the ladies by a recital of his gallantries. That absurdity of pride could proceed only from ignorance of themselves, by which Garth attempted criticism, and Congreve waved his title to dramatick reputation, and desired to be considered only as a gentleman.

Euphues, with great parts, and extensive knowledge, has a clouded aspect, and ungracious form; yet it has been his ambition, from his first entrance into life, to distinguish himself by particularities in his dress, to outvie beaus in embroidery, to import new trimmings, and to be foremost in the fashion. Euphues has turned on his exterior appearance, that attention, which would always have produced esteem had it been fixed upon his mind; and, though his virtues, and abilities, have preserved him from the contempt which he has so diligently solicited, he has, at least, raised one impediment to his reputation; since all can judge of his dress, but few of his understanding; and many who discern that he is a fop, are unwilling to believe that he can be wise.

There is one instance in which the ladies are particularly unwilling to observe the rule of Chilo. They are desirous to hide from themselves the advances of age, and endeavour too frequently to supply the sprightliness and bloom of youth by artificial beauty, and forced vivacity. They hope to inflame the heart by glances which have lost their fire, or melt it by languor which is no longer delicate; they play over the airs which pleased at a time when they were expected only to please, and forget that airs ought in time to give place to virtues. They continue to trifle, because they could once trifle agreeably, till those who shared their early pleasures are withdrawn to more serious engagements; and are scarcely awakened from their dream of perpetual youth, but by the scorn of those whom they endeavour to rival.

No. 25. Tuesday, 12 June 1750.

Possunt quia posse videntur.
VIRGIL.

For they can conquer who believe they can.
DRYDEN.

There are some vices and errors, which, though often fatal to those in whom they are found, have yet, by the universal consent of mankind, been considered as entitled to some degree of respect, or have, at least, been exempted from contemptuous infamy, and condemned by the severest moralists with pity rather than detestation.

A constant and invariable example of this general partiality will be found in the different regard which has always been shown to rashness and cowardice, two vices, of which, though they may be conceived equally distant from the middle point, where true fortitude is placed, and may equally injure any publick or private interest, yet the one is never mentioned without some kind of veneration, and the other always considered as a topick of unlimited and licentious censure, on which all the virulence of reproach may be lawfully exerted.

The same distinction is made, by the common suffrage, between profusion and avarice, and, perhaps, between many other opposite vices: and, as I have found reason to pay great regard to the voice of the people, in cases where knowledge has been forced upon them by experience, without long deductions or deep researches, I am inclined to believe that this distribution of respect, is not without some agreement with the nature of things; and that in the faults, which are thus invested with extraordinary privileges, there are generally some latent principles of merit, some possibilities of future virtue, which may, by degrees, break from obstruction, and by time and opportunity be brought into act.

It may be laid down as an axiom, that it is more easy to take away superfluities than to supply defects; and, therefore, he that is culpable, because he has passed the middle point of virtue, is always accounted a fairer object of hope, than he who fails by falling short. The one has all that perfection requires, and more, but the excess may be easily retrenched; the other wants the qualities requisite to excellence, and who can tell how he shall obtain them? We are certain that the horse may be taught to keep pace with his fellows, whose fault is that he leaves them behind. We know that a few strokes of the axe will lop a cedar; but what arts of cultivation can elevate a shrub?

To walk with circumspection and steadiness in the right path, at an equal distance between the extremes of error, ought to be the constant endeavour of every reasonable being; nor can I think those teachers of moral wisdom much to be honoured as benefactors to mankind, who are always enlarging upon the difficulty of our duties, and providing rather excuses for vice, than incentives to virtue.

But, since to most it will happen often, and to all sometimes, that there will be a deviation towards one side or the other, we ought always to employ our vigilance, with most attention, on that enemy from which there is greatest danger, and to stray, if we must stray, towards those parts from whence we may quickly and easily return.

Among other opposite qualities of the mind, which may become dangerous, though in different degrees, I have often had occasion to consider the contrary effects of presumption and despondency; of heady confidence, which promises victory without contest, and heartless pusillanimity, which shrinks back from the thought of great undertakings, confounds difficulty with impossibility, and considers all advancement towards any new attainment as irreversibly prohibited.

Presumption will be easily corrected. Every experiment will teach caution, and miscarriages will hourly shew, that attempts are not always rewarded with success. The most precipitate ardour will, in time, be taught the necessity of methodical gradation, and preparatory measures; and the most daring confidence be convinced that neither merit, nor abilities, can command events.

It is the advantage of vehemence and activity, that they are always hastening to their own reformation; because they incite us to try whether our expectations are well grounded, and therefore detect the deceits which they are apt to occasion. But timidity is a disease of the mind more obstinate and fatal; for a man once persuaded, that any impediment is insuperable, has given it, with respect to himself, that strength and weight which it had not before. He can scarcely strive with vigour and perseverance, when he has no hope of gaining the victory; and since he never will try his strength, can never discover the unreasonableness of his fears.

There is often to be found in men devoted to literature, a kind of intellectual cowardice, which whoever converses much among them, may observe frequently to depress the alacrity of enterprise, and, by consequence, to retard the improvement of science. They have annexed to every species of knowledge some chimerical character of terror and inhibition, which they transmit, without much reflexion, from one to another; they first fright themselves, and then propagate the panic to their scholars and acquaintance. One study is inconsistent with a lively imagination, another with a solid judgment; one is improper in the early parts of life, another requires so much time, that it is not to be attempted at an advanced age; one is dry and contracts the sentiments, another is diffuse and overburdens the memory; one is insufferable to taste and delicacy, and another wears out life in the study of words, and is useless to a wise man, who desires only the knowledge of things.

But of all the bugbears by which the *Infantes barbati*, boys both young and old, have been hitherto frighted from digressing into new tracts of learning, none has been more mischievously efficacious than an opinion that every kind of knowledge requires a peculiar genius, or mental constitution, framed for the reception of some ideas, and the exclusion of others; and that to him whose genius is not adapted to the study which he prosecutes, all labour shall be vain and fruitless, vain as an endeavour to mingle oil and water, or, in the language of chemistry, to amalgamate bodies of heterogeneous principles.

This opinion we may reasonably suspect to have been propagated, by vanity, beyond the truth. It is natural for those who have raised a reputation by any science, to exalt themselves as endowed by heaven with peculiar powers, or marked out by an extraordinary designation for their profession; and to fright competitors away by representing the difficulties with which they must contend, and the necessity of qualities which are supposed to be not generally conferred, and which no man can know, but by experience, whether he enjoys.

To this discouragement it may be possibly answered, that since a genius, whatever it be, is like fire in the flint, only to be produced by collision with a proper subject, it is the business of every man to try whether his faculties may not happily cooperate with his desires; and since they whose proficiency he admires, knew their own force only by the event, he needs but engage in the same undertaking, with equal spirit, and may reasonably hope for equal success.

There is another species of false intelligence, given by those who profess to shew the way to the summit of knowledge, of equal tendency to depress the mind with false distrust of itself, and weaken it by needless solicitude and dejection. When a scholar, whom they desire to animate, consults them at his entrance on some new study, it is common to make flattering representations of its pleasantness and facility. Thus they generally attain one of two ends almost equally desirable; they either incite his industry by elevating his hopes, or produce a high opinion of their own abilities, since they are supposed to relate only what they have found, and to have proceeded with no less ease than they promise to their followers.

The student, inflamed by this encouragement, sets forward in the new path, and proceeds a few steps with great alacrity, but he soon finds asperities and intricacies of which he has not been forewarned, and imagining that none ever were so entangled or fatigued before him, sinks suddenly into despair, and desists as from an expedition in which fate opposes him. Thus his terrors are multiplied by his hopes, and he is defeated without resistance, because he had no expectation of an enemy.

Of these treacherous instructors, the one destroys industry, by declaring that industry is vain, the other by representing it as needless; the one cuts away the root of hope, the other raises it only to be blasted. The one confines his pupil to the shore, by telling him that his wreck is certain, the other sends him to sea, without preparing him for tempests.

False hopes and false terrors are equally to be avoided. Every man, who proposes to grow eminent by learning, should carry in his mind, at once, the difficulty of excellence, and the force of industry; and remember that fame is not conferred but as the recompense of labour, and that labour, vigorously continued, has not often failed of its reward.

No. 28. Saturday, 23 June 1750.

Illi mors gravis incubat,
Qui, notus nimis omnibus,
Ignotus moritur sibi.
    SENECA.

To him, alas, to him, I fear,
The face of death will terrible appear,
Who in his life, flatt'ring his senseless pride,
By being known to all the world beside,
Does not himself, when he is dying know,
Nor what he is, nor whither he's to go.
    COWLEY.

I have shewn, in a late essay, to what errors men are hourly betrayed by a mistaken opinion of their own powers, and a negligent inspection of their own character. But as I then confined my observations to common occurrences, and familiar scenes, I think it proper to enquire how far a nearer acquaintance with ourselves is necessary to our preservation from crimes as well as follies, and how much the attentive study of our own minds may contribute to secure to us the approbation of that being, to whom we are accountable for our thoughts and our actions, and whose favour must finally constitute our total happiness.

If it be reasonable to estimate the difficulty of any enterprise by frequent miscarriages, it may justly be concluded that it is not easy for a man to know himself; for wheresoever we turn our view, we shall find almost all with whom we converse so nearly as to judge of their sentiments, indulging more favourable conceptions of their own virtue than they have been able to impress upon others, and congratulating themselves upon degrees of excellence, which their fondest admirers cannot allow them to have attained.

Those representations of imaginary virtue are generally considered as arts of hypocrisy, and as snares laid for confidence and praise. But I believe the suspicion often unjust; those who thus propagate their own reputation, only extend the fraud by which they have been themselves deceived; for this failing is incident to numbers, who seem to live without designs, competitions, or persuits; it appears on occasions which promise no accession of honour or of profit, and to persons from whom very little is to be hoped or feared. It is, indeed, not easy to tell how far we may be blinded by the love of ourselves, when we reflect how much a secondary passion can cloud our judgment, and how few faults a man, in the first raptures of love, can discover in the person or conduct of his mistress.

To lay open all the sources from which error flows in upon him who contemplates his own character, would require more exact knowledge of the human heart, than, perhaps, the most acute and laborious observers have acquired. And, since falsehood may be diversified without end, it is not unlikely that every man admits an imposture in some respect peculiar to himself, as his views have been accidentally directed, or his ideas particularly combined.

Some fallacies, however, there are, more frequently insidious, which it may, perhaps, not be useless to detect, because though they are gross they may be fatal, and because nothing but attention is necessary to defeat them.

One sophism by which men persuade themselves that they have those virtues which they really want, is formed by the substitution of single acts for habits. A miser who once relieved a friend from the danger of a prison, suffers his imagination to dwell for ever upon his own heroick generosity; he yields his heart up to indignation at those who are blind to merit, or insensible to misery, and who can please themselves with the enjoyment of that wealth, which they never permit others to partake. From any censures of the world, or reproaches of his conscience, he has an appeal to action and to knowledge; and though his whole life is a course of rapacity and avarice, he concludes himself to be tender and liberal, because he has once performed an act of liberality and tenderness.

As a glass which magnifies objects by the approach of one end to the eye, lessens them by the application of the other, so vices are extenuated by the inversion of that fallacy, by which virtues are augmented. Those faults which we cannot conceal from our own notice, are considered, however frequent, not as habitual corruptions, or settled practices, but as casual failures, and single lapses. A man who has, from year to year, set his country to sale, either for the gratification of his ambition or resentment, confesses that the heat of party now and then betrays the severest virtue to measures that cannot be seriously defended. He that spends his days and nights in riot and debauchery, owns that his passions oftentimes overpower his resolution. But each comforts himself that his faults are not without precedent, for the best and the wisest men have given way to the violence of sudden temptations.

There are men who always confound the praise of goodness with the practice, and who believe themselves mild and moderate, charitable and faithful, because they have exerted their eloquence in commendation of mildness, fidelity, and other virtues. This is an error almost universal among those that converse much with dependents, with such whose fear or interest disposes them to a seeming reverence for any declamation, however enthusiastick, and submission to any boast, however arrogant. Having none to recall their attention to their lives, they rate themselves by the goodness of their opinions, and forget how much more easily men may shew their virtue in their talk than in their actions.

The tribe is likewise very numerous of those who regulate their lives, not by the standard of religion, but the measure of other men's virtue; who lull their own remorse with the remembrance of crimes more atrocious than their own, and seem to believe that they are not bad while another can be found worse.

For escaping these and a thousand other deceits, many expedients have been proposed. Some have recommended the frequent consultation of a wise friend, admitted to intimacy, and encouraged to sincerity. But this appears a remedy by no means adapted to general use: for in order to secure the virtue of one, it presupposes more virtue in two than will generally be found. In the first, such a desire of rectitude and amendment, as may incline him to hear his own accusation from the mouth of him whom he esteems, and by whom, therefore, he will always hope that his faults are not discovered; and in the second such zeal and honesty, as will make him content for his friend's advantage to lose his kindness.

A long life may be passed without finding a friend in whose understanding and virtue we can equally confide, and whose opinion we can value at once for its justness and sincerity. A weak man, however honest, is not qualified to judge. A man of the world, however penetrating, is not fit to counsel. Friends are often chosen for similitude of manners, and therefore each palliates the other's failings, because they are his own. Friends are tender and unwilling to give pain, or they are interested, and fearful to offend.

These objections have inclined others to advise, that he who would know himself, should consult his enemies, remember the reproaches that are vented to his face, and listen for the censures that are uttered in private. For his great business is to know his faults, and those malignity will discover, and resentment will reveal. But this precept may be often frustrated; for it seldom happens that rivals or opponents are suffered to come near enough to know our conduct with so much exactness as that conscience should allow and reflect the accusation. The charge of an enemy is often totally false, and commonly so mingled with falsehood, that the mind takes advantage from the failure of one part to discredit the rest, and never suffers any disturbance afterward from such partial reports.

Yet it seems that enemies have been always found by experience the most faithful monitors; for adversity has ever been considered as the state in which a man most easily becomes acquainted with himself, and this effect it must produce by withdrawing flatterers, whose business it is to hide our weaknesses from us, or by giving loose to malice, and licence to reproach; or at least by cutting off those pleasures which called us away from meditation on our conduct, and repressing that pride which too easily persuades us, that we merit whatever we enjoy.

Part of these benefits it is in every man's power to procure to himself, by assigning proper portions of his life to the examination of the rest, and by putting himself frequently in such a situation by retirement and abstraction, as may weaken the influence of external objects. By this practice he may obtain the solitude of adversity without its melancholy, its instructions without its censures, and its sensibility without its perturbations.

The necessity of setting the world at a distance from us, when we are to take a survey of ourselves, has sent many from high stations to the severities of a monastick life; and indeed, every man deeply engaged in business, if all regard to another state be not extinguished, must have the conviction, tho', perhaps, not the resolution of Valdesso, who, when he solicited Charles the fifth to dismiss him, being asked, whether he retired upon disgust, answered that he laid down his commission, for no other reason but because *there ought to be some time for sober reflection between the life of a soldier and his death.*

There are few conditions which do not entangle us with sublunary hopes and fears, from which it is necessary to be at intervals disencumbered, that we may place ourselves in his presence who views effects in their causes, and actions in their motives; that we may, as Chillingworth expresses it, consider things as if there were no other beings in the world but God and ourselves; or, to use language yet more awful, *may commune with our own hearts, and be still.*

Death, says Seneca, falls heavy upon him who is too much known to others, and too little to himself; and Pontanus, a man celebrated among the early restorers of literature, thought the study of our own hearts of so much importance, that he has recommended it from his tomb. *Sum* Joannes Jovianus Pontanus, *quem amaverunt bonæ musæ, suspexerunt viri probi, honestaverunt reges domini; jam scis qui sim, vel qui potius fuerim; ego vero te, hospes, noscere in tenebris nequeo, sed teipsum ut noscas rogo.* "I am Pontanus, beloved by the powers of literature, admired by men of worth, and dignified by the monarchs of the world. Thou knowest now who I am, or more properly who I was. For thee, stranger, I who am in darkness cannot know thee, but I intreat thee to know thyself."

I hope every reader of this paper will consider himself as engaged to the observation of a precept, which the wisdom and virtue of all ages have concurred to enforce, a precept dictated by philosophers, inculcated by poets, and ratified by saints.

No. 29. Tuesday, 26 June 1750.

Prudens futuri temporis exitum
Caliginosa nocte premit deus,
Ridetque si mortalis ultra
Fas trepidet———

HOR.

> But God has wisely hid from human sight
>   The dark decrees of future fate,
> And sown their seeds in depth of night;
> He laughs at all the giddy turns of state,
>   When mortals search too soon, and fear too late.
>
> Dryden.

There is nothing recommended with greater frequency among the gayer poets of antiquity, than the secure possession of the present hour, and the dismission of all the cares which intrude upon our quiet, or hinder, by importunate perturbations, the enjoyment of those delights which our condition happens to set before us.

The antient poets are, indeed, by no means unexceptionable teachers of morality; their precepts are to be always considered as the sallies of a genius, intent rather upon giving pleasure than instruction, eager to take every advantage of insinuation, and provided the passions can be engaged on its side, very little solicitous about the suffrage of reason.

The darkness and uncertainty through which the heathens were compelled to wander in the persuit of happiness, may, indeed, be alleged as an excuse for many of their seducing invitations to immediate enjoyment, which the moderns, by whom they have been imitated, have not to plead. It is no wonder that such as had no promise of another state should eagerly turn their thoughts upon the improvement of that which was before them; but surely those who are acquainted with the hopes and fears of eternity, might think it necessary to put some restraint upon their imagination, and reflect that by echoing the songs of the ancient bacchanals, and transmitting the maxims of past debauchery, they not only prove that they want invention, but virtue, and submit to the servility of imitation only to copy that of which the writer, if he was to live now, would often be ashamed.

Yet as the errors and follies of a great genius are seldom without some radiations of understanding, by which meaner minds may be enlightened, the incitements to pleasure are, in these authors, generally mingled with such reflections upon life, as well deserve to be considered distinctly from the purposes for which they are produced, and to be treasured up as the settled conclusions of extensive observation, acute sagacity, and mature experience.

It is not without true judgment that on these occasions they often warn their readers against enquiries into futurity, and solicitude about events which lie hid in causes yet unactive, and which time has not brought forward into the view of reason. An idle and thoughtless resignation to chance, without any struggle against calamity, or endeavour after advantage, is indeed below the dignity of a reasonable being, in whose power providence has put a great part even of his present happiness; but it shews an equal ignorance of our proper sphere, to harrass our thoughts with conjectures about things not yet in being. How can we regulate events, of which we yet know not whether they will ever happen? And why should we think, with painful anxiety, about that on which our thoughts can have no influence?

It is a maxim commonly received, that a wise man is never surprised; and perhaps, this exemption from astonishment may be imagined to proceed from such a prospect into futurity, as gave previous intimation of those evils which often fall unexpected upon others that have less foresight. But the truth is, that things to come, except when they approach very nearly, are equally hidden from men of all degrees of understanding; and if a wise man is not amazed at sudden occurrences, it is not that he has thought more, but less upon futurity. He never considered things not yet existing as the proper objects of his attention; he never indulged dreams till he was deceived by their phantoms, nor ever realized nonentities to his mind. He is not surprised because he is not disappointed, and he escapes disappointment because he never forms any expectations.

The concern about things to come, that is so justly censured, is not the result of those general reflections on the variableness of fortune, the uncertainty of life, and the universal insecurity of all human acquisitions, which must always be suggested by the view of the world; but such a desponding anticipation of misfortune, as fixes the mind upon scenes of gloom and melancholy, and makes fear predominate in every imagination.

Anxiety of this kind is nearly of the same nature with jealousy in love, and suspicion in the general commerce of life; a temper which keeps the man always in alarms, disposes him to judge of every thing in a manner that least favours his own quiet, fills him with perpetual stratagems of counteraction, wears him out in schemes to obviate evils which never threatened him, and at length, perhaps, contributes to the production of those mischiefs of which it had raised such dreadful apprehensions.

It has been usual in all ages for moralists to repress the swellings of vain hope by representations of the innumerable casualties to which life is subject, and by instances of the unexpected defeat of the wisest schemes of policy, and sudden subversions of the highest eminences of greatness. It has, perhaps, not been equally observed, that all these examples afford the proper antidote to fear as well as to hope, and may be applied with no less efficacy as consolations to the timorous, than as restraints to the proud.

Evil is uncertain in the same degree as good, and for the reason that we ought not to hope too securely, we ought not to fear with too much dejection. The state of the world is continually changing, and none can tell the result of the next vicissitude. Whatever is afloat in the stream of time, may, when it is very near us, be driven away by an accidental blast, which shall happen to cross the general course of the current. The sudden accidents by which the powerful are depressed, may fall upon those whose malice we fear; and the greatness by which we expect to be overborn, may become another proof of the false flatteries of fortune. Our enemies may become weak, or we grow strong before our encounter, or we may advance against each other without ever meeting. There are, indeed, natural evils which we can flatter ourselves with no hopes of escaping, and with little of delaying; but of the ills which are apprehended from human malignity, or the opposition of rival interests, we may always alleviate the terror by considering that our persecutors are weak and ignorant, and mortal like ourselves.

The misfortunes which arise from the concurrence of unhappy incidents should never be suffered to disturb us before they happen; because, if the breast be once laid open to the dread of mere possibilities of misery, life must be given a prey to dismal solicitude, and quiet must be lost for ever.

It is remarked by old Cornaro, that it is absurd to be afraid of the natural dissolution of the body; because it must certainly happen, and can, by no caution or artifice, be avoided. Whether this sentiment be entirely just, I shall not examine; but certainly, if it be improper to fear events which must happen, it is yet more evidently contrary to right reason to fear those which may never happen, and which, if they should come upon us, we cannot resist.

As we ought not to give way to fear any more than indulgence to hope, because the objects both of fear and hope are yet uncertain, so we ought not to trust the representations of one more than of the other, because they are both equally fallacious; as hope enlarges happiness, fear aggravates calamity. It is generally allowed, that no man ever found the happiness of possession proportionate to that expectation which incited his desire, and invigorated his pursuit; nor has any man found the evils of life so formidable in reality, as they were described to him by his own imagination; every species of distress brings with it some peculiar supports, some unforeseen means of resisting, or power of enduring. Taylor justly blames some pious persons, who indulge their fancies too much, set themselves, by the force of imagination, in the place of the ancient martyrs and confessors, and question the validity of their own faith because they shrink at the thoughts of flames and tortures. It is, says he, sufficient that you are able to encounter the temptations which now assault you; when God sends trials, he may send strength.

All fear is in itself painful, and when it conduces not to safety is painful without use. Every consideration, therefore, by which groundless terrors may be removed, adds something to human happiness. It is likewise not unworthy of remark, that in proportion as our cares are imployed upon the future, they are abstracted from the present, from the only time which we can call our own, and of which if we neglect the duties, to make provision against visionary attacks, we shall certainly counteract our own purpose; for he, doubtless, mistakes his true interest, who thinks that he can increase his safety, when he impairs his virtue.

No. 31. Tuesday, 3 July 1750.

Non ego mendosos ausim defendere mores,
Falsaque pro vitiis arma tenere meis.
OVID.

Corrupted manners I shall ne'er defend,
Nor, falsely witty, for my faults contend.
ELPHINSTON.

Though the fallibility of man's reason, and the narrowness of his knowledge, are very liberally confessed, yet the conduct of those who so willingly admit the weakness of human nature, seems to discern that this acknowledgement is not altogether sincere; at least, that most make it with a tacit reserve in favour of themselves, and that with whatever ease they give up the claims of their neighbours, they are desirous of being thought exempt from faults in their own conduct, and from error in their opinions.

The certain and obstinate opposition, which we may observe made to confutation, however clear, and to reproof however tender, is an undoubted argument, that some dormant privilege is thought to be attacked; for as no man can lose what he neither possesses, nor imagines himself to possess, or be defrauded of that to which he has no right, it is reasonable to suppose that those who break out into fury at the softest contradiction, or the slightest censure, since they apparently conclude themselves injured, must fancy some antient immunity violated, or some natural prerogative invaded. To be mistaken, if they thought themselves liable to mistake, could not be considered as either shameful or wonderful, and they would not receive with so much emotion intelligence which only informed them of what they knew before, nor struggle with such earnestness against an attack that deprived them of nothing to which they held themselves entitled.

It is related of one of the philosophers, that when an account was brought him of his son's death, he received it only with this reflexion, *I knew that my son was mortal.* He that is convinced of an error, if he had the same knowledge of his own weakness, would, instead of straining for artifices, and brooding malignity, only regard such oversights as the appendages of humanity, and pacify himself with considering that he had always known man to be a fallible being.

If it be true that most of our passions are excited by the novelty of objects, there is little reason for doubting that to be considered as subject to fallacies of ratiocination, or imperfection of knowledge, is to a great part of mankind entirely new; for it is impossible to fall into any company where there is not some regular and established subordination, without finding rage and vehemence produced only by difference of sentiments about things in which neither of the disputants have any other interest than what proceeds from their mutual unwillingness to give way to any opinion that may bring upon them the disgrace of being wrong.

I have heard of one that, having advanced some erroneous doctrines in philosophy, refused to see the experiments by which they were confuted: and the observation of every day will give new proofs with how much industry subterfuges and evasions are sought to decline the pressure of resistless arguments, how often the state of the question is altered, how often the antagonist is wilfully misrepresented, and in how much perplexity the clearest positions are involved by those whom they happen to oppose.

Of all mortals none seem to have been more infected with this species of vanity, than the race of writers, whose reputation arising solely from their understanding, gives them a very delicate sensibility of any violence attempted on their literary honour. It is not unpleasing to remark with what solicitude men of acknowledged abilities will endeavour to palliate absurdities and reconcile contradictions, only to obviate criticisms to which all human performances must ever be exposed, and from which they can never suffer, but when they teach the world by a vain and ridiculous impatience to think them of importance.

DRYDEN, whose warmth of fancy, and haste of composition very frequently hurried him into inaccuracies, heard himself sometimes exposed to ridicule for having said in one of his tragedies,

I follow fate, which does too fast persue.

That no man could at once follow and be followed was, it may be thought, too plain to be long disputed; and the truth is, that DRYDEN was apparently betrayed into the blunder by the double meaning of the word FATE, to which in the former part of the verse he had annexed the idea of FORTUNE, and in the latter that of DEATH; so that the sense only was, *though persued by* DEATH, *I will not resign myself to despair, but will follow* FORTUNE, *and do and suffer what is appointed.* This however was not completely expressed, and DRYDEN being determined not to give way to his critics, never confessed that he had been surprised by an ambiguity; but finding luckily in *Virgil* an account of a man moving in a circle, with this expression, *Et se sequiturque fugitque,* "Here, says he, is the passage in imitation of which I wrote the line that my critics were pleased to condemn as nonsense; not but I may sometimes write nonsense, though they have not the fortune to find it."

Every one sees the folly of such mean doublings to escape the persuit of criticism; nor is there a single reader of this poet, who would not have paid him greater veneration, had he shewn consciousness enough of his own superiority to set such cavils at defiance, and owned that he sometimes slipped into errors by the tumult of his imagination, and the multitude of his ideas.

It is happy when this temper discovers itself only in little things, which may be right or wrong without any influence on the virtue or happiness of mankind. We may, with very little inquietude, see a man persist in a project, which he has found to be impracticable, live in an inconvenient house because it was contrived by himself, or wear a coat of a particular cut, in hopes by perseverance to bring it into fashion. These are indeed follies, but they are only follies, and, however wild or ridiculous, can very little affect others.

But such pride, once indulged, too frequently operates upon more important objects, and inclines men not only to vindicate their errors, but their vices; to persist in practices which their own hearts condemn, only lest they should seem to feel reproaches, or be made wiser by the advice of others; or to search for sophisms tending to the confusion of all principles, and the evacuation of all duties, that they may not appear to act what they are not able to defend.

Let every man, who finds vanity so far predominant, as to betray him to the danger of this last degree of corruption, pause a moment to consider what will be the consequences of the plea which he is about to offer for a practice to which he knows himself not led at first by reason, but impelled by the violence of desire, surprized by the suddenness of passion, or seduced by the soft approaches of temptation, and by imperceptible gradations of guilt. Let him consider what he is going to commit by forcing his understanding to patronise those appetites, which it is its chief business to hinder and reform.

The cause of virtue requires so little art to defend it, and good and evil, when they have been once shewn, are so easily distinguished, that such apologists seldom gain proselytes to their party, nor have their fallacies power to deceive any but those whose desires have clouded their discernment. All that the best faculties thus employed can perform is, to persuade the hearers that the man is hopeless whom they only thought vitious, that corruption has passed from his manners to his principles, that all endeavours for his recovery are without prospect of success, and that nothing remains but to avoid him as infectious, or hunt him down as destructive.

But if it be supposed that he may impose on his audience by partial representations of consequences, intricate deductions of remote causes, or perplexed combinations of ideas, which having various relations appear different as viewed on different sides; that he may sometimes puzzle the weak and well-meaning, and now and then seduce, by the admiration of his abilities, a young mind still fluctuating in unsettled notions, and neither fortified by instruction nor enlightened by experience; yet what must be the event of such a triumph? A man cannot spend all this life in frolick: age, or disease, or solitude will bring some hours of serious consideration, and it will then afford no comfort to think, that he has extended the dominion of vice, that he has loaded himself with the crimes of others, and can never know the extent of his own wickedness, or make reparation for the mischief that he has caused.

There is not perhaps in all the stores of ideal anguish, a thought more painful, than the consciousness of having propagated corruption by vitiating principles, of having not only drawn others from the paths of virtue, but blocked up the way by which they should return, of having blinded them to every beauty but the paint of pleasure, and deafened them to every call but the alluring voice of the syrens of destruction.

There is yet another danger in this practice: men who cannot deceive others, are very often successful in deceiving themselves; they weave their sophistry till their own reason is entangled, and repeat their positions till they are credited by themselves; by often contending they grow sincere in the cause, and by long wishing for demonstrative arguments they at last bring themselves to fancy that they have found them. They are then at the uttermost verge of wickedness, and may die without having that light rekindled in their minds, which their own pride and contumacy have extinguished.

The men who can be charged with fewest failings, either with respect to abilities or virtue, are generally most ready to allow them; for not to dwell on things of solemn and awful consideration, the humility of confessors, the tears of saints, and the dying terrors of persons eminent for piety and innocence, it is well known that Caesar wrote an account of the errors committed by him in his wars of Gaul, and that Hippocrates, whose name is perhaps in rational estimation greater than Caesar's, warned posterity against a mistake into which he had fallen. *So much*, says Celsus, *does the open and artless confession of an error become a man conscious that he has enough remaining to support his character.*

As all error is meanness, it is incumbent on every man who consults his own dignity, to retract it as soon as he discovers it, without fearing any censure so much as that of his own mind. As justice requires that all injuries should be repaired, it is the duty of him who has seduced others by bad practices, or false notions, to endeavour that such as have adopted his errors should know his retraction, and that those who have learned vice by his example, should by his example be taught amendment.

No. 32. Saturday, 7 July 1750.

Ὅσσά τε δαιμονίῃσι τύχαις βροτοὶ ἄλγε᾽ ἔχουσιν,
Ὧν ἂν μοῖραν ἔχῃς, πρᾴως φέρε, μηδ᾽ ἀγανάκτει·
Ἰᾶσθαι δὲ πρέπει κάθοσον δύνῃ.

PYTHAG.

Of all the woes that load the mortal state,
Whate'er thy portion, mildly meet thy fate;
But ease it as thou can'st————

ELPHINSTON.

So large a part of human life passes in a state contrary to our natural desires, that one of the principal topics of moral instruction is the art of bearing calamities. And such is the certainty of evil, that it is the duty of every man to furnish his mind with those principles that may enable him to act under it with decency and propriety.

The sect of ancient philosophers, that boasted to have carried this necessary science to the highest perfection, were the stoics, or scholars of Zeno, whose wild enthusiastick virtue pretended to an exemption from the sensibilities of unenlightened mortals, and who proclaimed themselves exalted, by the doctrines of their sect, above the reach of those miseries, which embitter life to the rest of the world. They therefore removed pain, poverty, loss of friends, exile, and violent death, from the catalogue of evils; and passed, in their haughty stile, a kind of irreversible decree, by which they forbad them to be counted any longer among the objects of terror or anxiety, or to give any disturbance to the tranquillity of a wise man.

This edict was, I think, not universally observed, for though one of the more resolute, when he was tortured by a violent disease, cried out, that let pain harrass him to its utmost power, it should never force him to consider it as other than indifferent and neutral; yet all had not stubbornness to hold out against their senses: for a weaker pupil of *Zeno* is recorded to have confessed in the anguish of the gout, that *he now found pain to be an evil.*

It may however be questioned, whether these philosophers can be very properly numbered among the teachers of patience; for if pain be not an evil, there seems no instruction requisite how it may be borne; and therefore when they endeavour to arm their followers with arguments against it, they may be thought to have given up their first position. But such inconsistencies are to be expected from the greatest understandings, when they endeavour to grow eminent by singularity, and employ their strength in establishing opinions opposite to nature.

The controversy about the reality of external evils is now at an end. That life has many miseries, and that those miseries are, sometimes at least, equal to all the powers of fortitude, is now universally confessed; and therefore it is useful to consider not only how we may escape them, but by what means those which either the accidents of affairs, or the infirmities of nature must bring upon us, may be mitigated and lightened; and how we may make those hours less wretched, which the condition of our present existence will not allow to be very happy.

The cure for the greatest part of human miseries is not radical, but palliative. Infelicity is involved in corporeal nature, and interwoven with our being; all attempts therefore to decline it wholly are useless and vain: the armies of pain send their arrows against us on every side, the choice is only between those which are more or less sharp, or tinged with poison of greater or less malignity; and the strongest armour which reason can supply, will only blunt their points, but cannot repel them.

The great remedy which heaven has put in our hands is patience, by which, though we cannot lessen the torments of the body, we can in a great measure preserve the peace of the mind, and shall suffer only the natural and genuine force of an evil, without heightening its acrimony, or prolonging its effects.

There is indeed nothing more unsuitable to the nature of man in any calamity than rage and turbulence, which, without examining whether they are not sometimes impious, are at least always offensive, and incline others rather to hate and despise than to pity and assist us. If what we suffer has been brought upon us by ourselves, it is observed by an ancient poet, that patience is eminently our duty, since no one should be angry at feeling that which he has deserved.

> *Leniter ex merito quicquid patiare ferendum est.*
>
> Let pain deserv'd without complaint be borne.

And surely, if we are conscious that we have not contributed to our own sufferings, if punishment fall upon innocence, or disappointment happens to industry and prudence, patience, whether more necessary or not, is much easier, since our pain is then without aggravation, and we have not the bitterness of remorse to add to the asperity of misfortune.

In those evils which are allotted to us by providence, such as deformity, privation of any of the senses, or old age, it is always to be remembred, that impatience can have no present effect, but to deprive us of the consolations which our condition admits, by driving away from us those by whose conversation or advice we might be amused or helped; and that with regard to futurity it is yet less to be justified, since, without lessening the pain, it cuts off the hope of that reward, which he by whom it is inflicted will confer upon them that bear it well.

In all evils which admit a remedy, impatience is to be avoided, because it wastes that time and attention in complaints, that, if properly applied, might remove the cause. Turenne, among the acknowledgments which he used to pay in conversation to the memory of those by whom he had been instructed in the art of war, mentioned one with honour, who taught him not to spend his time in regretting any mistake which he had made, but to set himself immediately and vigorously to repair it.

Patience and submission are very carefully to be distinguished from cowardice and indolence. We are not to repine, but we may lawfully struggle; for the calamities of life, like the necessities of nature, are calls to labour, and exercises of diligence. When we feel any pressure of distress, we are not to conclude that we can only obey the will of heaven by languishing under it, any more than when we perceive the pain of thirst we are to imagine that water is prohibited. Of misfortune it never can be certainly known whether, as proceeding from the hand of GOD, it is an act of favour, or of punishment: but since all the ordinary dispensations of providence are to be interpreted according to the general analogy of things, we may conclude, that we have a right to remove one inconvenience as well as another; that we are only to take care lest we purchase ease with guilt; and that our Maker's purpose, whether of reward or severity, will be answered by the labours which he lays us under the necessity of performing.

This duty is not more difficult in any state, than in diseases intensely painful, which may indeed suffer such exacerbations as seem to strain the powers of life to their utmost stretch, and leave very little of the attention vacant to precept or reproof. In this state the nature of man requires some indulgence, and every extravagance but impiety may be easily forgiven him. Yet, lest we should think ourselves too soon entitled to the mournful privileges of irresistible misery, it is proper to reflect that the utmost anguish which human wit can contrive, or human malice can inflict, has been borne with constancy; and that if the pains of disease be, as I believe they are, sometimes greater than those of artificial torture, they are therefore in their own nature shorter, the vital frame is quickly broken, or the union between soul and body is for a time suspended by insensibility, and we soon cease to feel our maladies when they once become too violent to be born. I think there is some reason for questioning whether the body and mind are not so proportioned, that the one can bear all which can be inflicted on the other, whether virtue cannot stand its ground as long as life, and whether a soul well principled will not be separated sooner than subdued.

In calamities which operate chiefly on our passions, such as diminution of fortune, loss of friends, or declension of character, the chief danger of impatience is upon the first attack, and many expedients have been contrived, by which the blow may be broken. Of these the most general precept is, not to take pleasure in any thing, of which it is not in our power to secure the possession to ourselves. This counsel, when we consider the enjoyment of any terrestrial advantage, as opposite to a constant and habitual solicitude for future felicity, is undoubtedly just, and delivered by that authority which cannot be disputed; but in any other sense, is it not like advice, not to walk lest we should stumble, or not to see lest our eyes should light upon deformity? It seems to me reasonable to enjoy blessings with confidence as well as to resign them with submission, and to hope for the continuance of good which we possess without insolence or voluptuousness, as for the restitution of that which we lose without despondency or murmurs.

The chief security against the fruitless anguish of impatience, must arise from frequent reflection on the wisdom and goodness of the GOD of nature, in whose hands are riches and poverty, honour and disgrace, pleasure and pain, and life and death. A settled conviction of the tendency of every thing to our good, and of the possibility of turning miseries into happiness, by receiving them rightly, will incline us to *bless the name of the* LORD, *whether he gives or takes away.*

No. 33. Tuesday, 10 July 1750.

Quod caret alternâ requie durabile non est.
OVID.

Alternate rest and labour long endure.

In the early ages of the world, as is well known to those who are versed in antient traditions, when innocence was yet untainted, and simplicity unadulterated, mankind was happy in the enjoyment of continual pleasure, and constant plenty, under the protection of REST; a gentle divinity, who required of her worshippers neither altars nor sacrifices, and whose rites were only performed by prostrations upon tufts of flowers in shades of jasmine and myrtle, or by dances on the banks of rivers flowing with milk and nectar.

Under this easy government the first generations breathed the fragrance of perpetual spring, eat the fruits, which, without culture, fell ripe into their hands, and slept under bowers arched by nature, with the birds singing over their heads, and the beasts sporting about them. But by degrees they began to lose their original integrity; each, though there was more than enough for all, was desirous of appropriating part to himself. Then entered violence and fraud, and theft and rapine. Soon after pride and envy broke into the world, and brought with them a new standard of wealth; for men, who till then thought themselves rich when they wanted nothing, now rated their demands, not by the calls of nature, but by the plenty of others; and began to consider themselves as poor when they beheld their own possessions exceeded by those of their neighbours. Now only one could be happy, because only one could have most, and that one was always in danger, lest the same arts by which he had supplanted others should be practised upon himself.

Amidst the prevalence of this corruption, the state of the earth was changed; the year was divided into seasons; part of the ground became barren, and the rest yielded only berries, acorns, and herbs. The summer and autumn indeed furnished a coarse and inelegant sufficiency, but winter was without any relief; FAMINE, with a thousand diseases, which the inclemency of the air invited into the upper regions, made havock among men, and there appeared to be danger lest they should be destroyed before they were reformed.

To oppose the devastations of FAMINE, who scattered the ground every where with carcases, LABOUR came down upon earth. LABOUR was the son of NECESSITY, the nurseling of HOPE, and the pupil of ART; he had the strength of his mother, the spirit of his nurse, and the dexterity of his governess. His face was wrinkled with the wind, and swarthy with the sun; he had the implements of husbandry in one hand, with which he turned up the earth; in the other he had the tools of architecture, and raised walls and towers at his pleasure. He called out with a rough voice, "Mortals! see here the power to whom you are consigned, and from whom you are to hope for all your pleasures, and all your safety. You have long languished under the dominion of REST, an impotent and deceitful goddess, who can neither protect nor relieve you, but resigns you to the first attacks of either FAMINE or DISEASE, and suffers her shades to be invaded by every enemy, and destroyed by every accident."

"Awake therefore to the call of LABOUR. I will teach you to remedy the sterility of the earth, and the severity of the sky; I will compel summer to find provisions for the winter; I will force the waters to give you their fish, the air its fowls, and the forest its beasts; I will teach you to pierce the bowels of the earth, and bring out from the caverns of the mountains metals which shall give strength to your hands, and security to your bodies, by which you may be covered from the assaults of the fiercest beasts, and with which you shall fell the oak, and divide rocks, and subject all nature to your use and pleasure."

Encouraged by this magnificent invitation, the inhabitants of the globe considered LABOUR as their only friend, and hasted to his command. He led them out to the fields and mountains, and shewed them how to open mines, to level hills, to drain marshes, and change the course of rivers. The face of things was immediately transformed; the land was covered with towns and villages, encompassed with fields of corn, and plantations of fruit-trees; and nothing was seen but heaps of grain, and baskets of fruit, full tables, and crouded storehouses.

Thus LABOUR and his followers added every hour new acquisitions to their conquests, and saw FAMINE gradually dispossessed of his dominions; till at last, amidst their jollity and triumphs, they were depressed and amazed by the approach of LASSITUDE, who was known by her sunk eyes, and dejected countenance. She came forward trembling and groaning: at every groan the hearts of all those that beheld her lost their courage, their nerves slackened, their hands shook, and the instruments of labour fell from their grasp.

Shocked with this horrid phantom they reflected with regret on their easy compliance with the solicitations of LABOUR, and began to wish again for the golden hours which they remembered to have passed under the reign of REST, whom they resolved again to visit, and to whom they intended to dedicate the remaining part of their lives. REST had not left the world; they quickly found her, and to attone for their former desertion, invited her to the enjoyment of those acquisitions which LABOUR had procured them.

REST therefore took leave of the groves and vallies, which she had hitherto inhabited, and entered into palaces, reposed herself in alcoves, and slumbered away the winter upon beds of down, and the summer in artificial grottos with cascades playing before her. There was indeed always something wanting to complete her felicity, and she could never lull her returning fugitives to that serenity, which they knew before their engagements with LABOUR: Nor was her dominion entirely without controul, for she was obliged to share it with LUXURY, tho' she always looked upon her as a false friend, by whom her influence was in reality destroyed, while it seemed to be promoted.

The two soft associates, however, reigned for some time without visible disagreement, till at last LUXURY betrayed her charge, and let in DISEASE to seize upon her worshippers. REST then flew away, and left the place to the usurpers; who employed all their arts to fortify themselves in their possession, and to strengthen the interest of each other.

REST had not always the same enemy: in some places she escaped the incursions of DISEASE; but had her residence invaded by a more slow and subtle intruder, for very frequently when every thing was composed and quiet, when there was neither pain within, nor danger without, when every flower was in bloom, and every gale freighted with perfumes, SATIETY would enter with a languishing and repining look, and throw herself upon the couch placed and adorned for the accommodation of REST. No sooner was she seated than a general gloom spread itself on every side, the groves immediately lost their verdure, and their inhabitants desisted from their melody, the breeze sunk in sighs, and the flowers contracted their leaves and shut up their odours. Nothing was seen on every side but multitudes wandering about they knew not whither, in quest they knew not of what; no voice was heard but of complaints that mentioned no pain, and murmurs that could tell of no misfortune.

REST had now lost her authority. Her followers again began to treat her with contempt; some of them united themselves more closely to LUXURY, who promised by her arts to drive SATIETY away, and others that were more wise or had more fortitude, went back again to LABOUR, by whom they were indeed protected from SATIETY, but delivered up in time to LASSITUDE, and forced by her to the bowers of REST.

Thus REST and LABOUR equally perceived their reign of short duration and uncertain tenure, and their empire liable to inrodes from those who were alike enemies to both. They each found their subjects unfaithful, and ready to desert them upon every opportunity. LABOUR saw the riches which he had given always carried away as an offering to REST, and REST found her votaries in every exigence flying from her to beg help of LABOUR. They, therefore, at last determined upon an interview, in which they agreed to divide the world between them, and govern it alternately, allotting the dominion of the day to one, and that of the night to the other, and promised to guard the frontiers of each other, so that, whenever hostilities were attempted, SATIETY should be intercepted by LABOUR, and LASSITUDE expelled by REST. Thus the antient quarrel was appeased, and as hatred is often succeeded by its contrary, REST afterwards became pregnant by Labour, and was delivered of Health, a benevolent goddess, who consolidated the union of her parents, and contributed to the regular vicissitudes of their reign, by dispensing her gifts to those only who shared their lives in just proportions between Rest and Labour.

No. 36. Saturday, 21 July 1750.

Ἄμ' ἕποντο νομῆες
Τερπόμενοι σύριγξι· δόλον δ' οὔτι προνόησαν.
HOMER.

——Piping on their reeds, the shepherds go,
Nor fear an ambush, nor suspect a foe.
POPE.

There is scarcely any species of poetry, that has allured more readers, or excited more writers, than the pastoral. It is generally pleasing, because it entertains the mind with representations of scenes familiar to almost every imagination, and of which all can equally judge whether they are well described. It exhibits a life, to which we have been always accustomed to associate peace, and leisure, and innocence: and therefore we readily set open the heart, for the admission of its images, which contribute to drive away cares and perturbations, and suffer ourselves, without resistance, to be transported to elysian regions, where we are to meet with nothing but joy, and plenty, and contentment; where every gale whispers pleasure, and every shade promises repose.

It has been maintained by some, who love to talk of what they do not know, that pastoral is the most antient poetry; and, indeed, since it is probable, that poetry is nearly of the same antiquity with rational nature, and since the life of the first men was certainly rural, we may reasonably conjecture, that, as their ideas would necessarily be borrowed from those objects with which they were acquainted, their composures, being filled chiefly with such thoughts on the visible creation as must occur to the first observers, were pastoral hymns like those which *Milton* introduces the original pair singing, in the day of innocence, to the praise of their Maker.

For the same reason that pastoral poetry was the first employment of the human imagination, it is generally the first literary amusement of our minds. We have seen fields, and meadows, and groves from the time that our eyes opened upon life; and are pleased with birds, and brooks, and breezes, much earlier than we engage among the actions and passions of mankind. We are therefore delighted with rural pictures, because we know the original at an age when our curiosity can be very little awakened, by descriptions of courts which we never beheld, or representations of passion which we never felt.

The satisfaction received from this kind of writing not only begins early, but lasts long; we do not, as we advance into the intellectual world, throw it away among other childish amusements and pastimes, but willingly return to it in any hour of indolence and relaxation. The images of true pastoral have always the power of exciting delight, because the works of nature, from which they are drawn, have always the same order and beauty, and continue to force themselves upon our thoughts, being at once obvious to the most careless regard, and more than adequate to the strongest reason, and severest contemplation. Our inclination to stillness and tranquillity is seldom much lessened by long knowledge of the busy and tumultuary part of the world. In childhood we turn our thoughts to the country, as to the region of pleasure, we recur to it in old age as a port of rest, and perhaps with that secondary and adventitious gladness, which every man feels on reviewing those places, or recollecting those occurrences, that contributed to his youthful enjoyments, and bring him back to the prime of life, when the world was gay with the bloom of novelty, when mirth wantoned at his side, and hope sparkled before him.

The sense of this universal pleasure has invited *numbers without number* to try their skill in pastoral performances, in which they have generally succeeded after the manner of other imitators, transmitting the same images in the same combination from one to another, till he that reads the title of a poem, may guess at the whole series of the composition; nor will a man, after the perusal of thousands of these performances, find his knowledge enlarged with a single view of nature not produced before, or his imagination amused with any new application of those views to moral purposes.

The range of pastoral is indeed narrow, for though nature itself, philosophically considered, be inexhaustible, yet its general effects on the eye and on the ear are uniform, and incapable of much variety of description. Poetry cannot dwell upon the minuter distinctions, by which one species differs from another, without departing from that simplicity of grandeur which fills the imagination; nor dissect the latent qualities of things, without losing its general power of gratifying every mind by recalling its conceptions. However, as each age makes some discoveries, and those discoveries are by degrees generally known, as new plants or modes of culture are introduced, and by little and little become common, pastoral might receive, from time to time, small augmentations, and exhibit once in a century a scene somewhat varied.

But pastoral subjects have been often, like others, taken into the hands of those that were not qualified to adorn them, men to whom the face of nature was so little known, that they have drawn it only after their own imagination, and changed or distorted her features, that their portraits might appear something more than servile copies from their predecessors.

Not only the images of rural life, but the occasions on which they can be properly produced, are few and general. The state of a man confined to the employments and pleasures of the country, is so little diversified, and exposed to so few of those accidents which produce perplexities, terrors and surprises, in more complicated transactions, that he can be shewn but seldom in such circumstances as attract curiosity. His ambition is without policy, and his love without intrigue. He has no complaints to make of his rival, but that he is richer than himself; nor any disasters to lament, but a cruel mistress, or a bad harvest.

The conviction of the necessity of some new source of pleasure induced *Sannazarius* to remove the scene from the fields to the sea, to substitute fishermen for shepherds, and derive his sentiments from the piscatory life; for which he has been censured by succeeding criticks, because the sea is an object of terrour, and by no means proper to amuse the mind, and lay the passions asleep. Against this objection he might be defended by the established maxim, that the poet has a right to select his images, and is no more obliged to shew the sea in a storm, than the land under an inundation; but may display all the pleasures, and conceal the dangers of the water, as he may lay his shepherd under a shady beech, without giving him an ague, or letting a wild beast loose upon him.

There are however two defects in the piscatory eclogue, which perhaps cannot be supplied. The sea, though in hot countries it is considered by those who live, like *Sannazarius*, upon the coast, as a place of pleasure and diversion, has notwithstanding much less variety than the land, and therefore will be sooner exhausted by a descriptive writer. When he has once shewn the sun rising or setting upon it, curled its waters with the vernal breeze, rolled the waves in gentle succession to the shore, and enumerated the fish sporting in the shallows, he has nothing remaining but what is common to all other poetry, the complaint of a nymph for a drowned lover, or the indignation of a fisher that his oysters are refused, and Mycon's accepted.

Another obstacle to the general reception of this kind of poetry, is the ignorance of maritime pleasures, in which the greater part of mankind must always live. To all the inland inhabitants of every region, the sea is only known as an immense diffusion of waters, over which men pass from one country to another, and in which life is frequently lost. They have, therefore, no opportunity of tracing, in their own thoughts, the descriptions of winding shores, and calm bays, nor can look on the poem in which they are mentioned, with other sensations, than on a sea-chart, or the metrical geography of *Dionysius*.

This defect *Sannazarius* was hindered from perceiving, by writing in a learned language to readers generally acquainted with the works of nature; but if he had made his attempt in any vulgar tongue, he would soon have discovered how vainly he had endeavoured to make that loved, which was not understood.

I am afraid it will not be found easy to improve the pastorals of antiquity, by any great additions or diversifications. Our descriptions may indeed differ from those of Virgil, as an English from an Italian summer, and, in some respects, as modern from ancient life; but as nature is in both countries nearly the same, and as poetry has to do rather with the passions of men, which are uniform, than their customs, which are changeable, the varieties, which time or place can furnish, will be inconsiderable: and I shall endeavour to shew, in the next paper, how little the latter ages have contributed to the improvement of the rustick muse.

No. 37. Tuesday, 24 July 1750.

Canto quæ solitus, si quando armenta vocabat,
Amphion Dircæus.
                                                  VIRG.

Such strains I sing as once *Amphion* play'd,
When list'ning flocks the pow'rful call obey'd.
                                                  ELPHINSTON.

In writing or judging of pastoral poetry, neither the authors nor criticks of latter times seem to have paid sufficient regard to the originals left us by antiquity, but have entangled themselves with unnecessary difficulties, by advancing principles, which, having no foundation in the nature of things, are wholly to be rejected from a species of composition in which, above all others, mere nature is to be regarded.

It is, therefore, necessary to enquire after some more distinct and exact idea of this kind of writing. This may, I think, be easily found in the pastorals of Virgil, from whose opinion it will not appear very safe to depart, if we consider that every advantage of nature, and of fortune, concurred to complete his productions; that he was born with great accuracy and severity of judgment, enlightened with all the learning of one of the brightest ages, and embellished with the elegance of the Roman court; that he employed his powers rather in improving, than inventing, and therefore must have endeavoured to recompense the want of novelty by exactness; that taking Theocritus for his original, he found pastoral far advanced towards perfection, and that having so great a rival, he must have proceeded with uncommon caution.

If we search the writings of Virgil, for the true definition of a pastoral, it will be found *a poem in which any action or passion is represented by its effects upon a country life.* Whatsoever therefore may, according to the common course of things, happen in the country, may afford a subject for a pastoral poet.

In this definition, it will immediately occur to those who are versed in the writings of the modern criticks, that there is no mention of the golden age. I cannot indeed easily discover why it is thought necessary to refer descriptions of a rural state to remote times, nor can I perceive that any writer has consistently preserved the Arcadian manners and sentiments. The only reason, that I have read, on which this rule has been founded, is, that, according to the customs of modern life, it is improbable that shepherds should be capable of harmonious numbers, or delicate sentiments; and therefore the reader must exalt his ideas of the pastoral character, by carrying his thoughts back to the age in which the care of herds and flocks was the employment of the wisest and greatest men.

These reasoners seem to have been led into their hypothesis, by considering pastoral, not in general, as a representation of rural nature, and consequently as exhibiting the ideas and sentiments of those, whoever they are, to whom the country affords pleasure or employment, but simply as a dialogue, or narrative of men actually tending sheep, and busied in the lowest and most laborious offices; from whence they very readily concluded, since characters must necessarily be preserved, that either the sentiments must sink to the level of the speakers, or the speakers must be raised to the height of the sentiments.

In consequence of these original errors, a thousand precepts have been given, which have only contributed to perplex and to confound. Some have thought it necessary that the imaginary manners of the golden age should be universally preserved, and have therefore believed, that nothing more could be admitted in pastoral, than lilies and roses, and rocks and streams, among which are heard the gentle whispers of chaste fondness, or the soft complaints of amorous impatience. In pastoral, as in other writings, chastity of sentiment ought doubtless to be observed, and purity of manners to be represented; not because the poet is confined to the images of the golden age, but because, having the subject in his own choice, he ought always to consult the interest of virtue.

These advocates for the golden age lay down other principles, not very consistent with their general plan; for they tell us, that, to support the character of the shepherd, it is proper that all refinement should be avoided, and that some slight instances of ignorance should be interspersed. Thus the shepherd in Virgil is supposed to have forgot the name of Anaximander, and in Pope the term Zodiack is too hard for a rustick apprehension. But if we place our shepherds in their primitive condition, we may give them learning among their other qualifications; and if we suffer them to allude at all to things of later existence, which, perhaps, cannot with any great propriety be allowed, there can be no danger of making them speak with too much accuracy, since they conversed with divinities, and transmitted to succeeding ages the arts of life.

Other writers, having the mean and despicable condition of a shepherd always before them, conceive it necessary to degrade the language of pastoral, by obsolete terms and rustick words, which they very learnedly call Dorick, without reflecting, that they thus become authors of a mingled dialect, which no human

being ever could have spoken, that they may as well refine the speech as the sentiments of their personages, and that none of the inconsistencies which they
endeavour to avoid, is greater than that of joining elegance of thought with
coarseness of diction. Spenser begins one of his pastorals with studied barbarity;

> Diggon Davie, *I bid her good-day:*
> Or, Diggon *her is, or I missay.*
> Dig. *Her was her while it was day-light,*
> *But now her is a most wretched wight.*

What will the reader imagine to be the subject on which speakers like these
exercise their eloquence? Will he not be somewhat disappointed, when he
finds them met together to condemn the corruptions of the church of Rome?
Surely, at the same time that a shepherd learns theology, he may gain some
acquaintance with his native language.

Pastoral admits of all ranks of persons, because persons of all ranks inhabit
the country. It excludes not, therefore, on account of the characters necessary
to be introduced, any elevation or delicacy of sentiment; those ideas only are
improper, which, not owing their original to rural objects, are not pastoral.
Such is the exclamation in Virgil,

> *Nunc scio quid sit Amor, duris in cautibus illum*
> *Ismarus, aut Rhodope, aut extremi Garamantes,*
> *Nec generis nostri puerum nec sanguinis, edunt;*

> I know thee, love, in desarts thou wert bred,
> And at the dugs of savage tygers fed:
> Alien of birth, usurper of the plains.
>
> Dryden.

which Pope endeavouring to copy, was carried to still greater impropriety.

> *I know thee, Love, wild as the raging main,*
> *More fierce than tigers on the Libyan plain;*
> *Thou wert from Ætna's burning entrails torn,*
> *Begot in tempests, and in thunders born!*

Sentiments like these, as they have no ground in nature, are indeed of little
value in any poem, but in pastoral they are particularly liable to censure,
because it wants that exaltation above common life, which in tragick or heroick writings often reconciles us to bold flights and daring figures.

Pastoral being the *representation of an action or passion, by its effects upon a
country life,* has nothing peculiar but its confinement to rural imagery, without

which it ceases to be pastoral. This is its true characteristick, and this it cannot lose by any dignity of sentiment, or beauty of diction. The Pollio of Virgil, with all its elevation, is a composition truly bucolic, though rejected by the criticks; for all the images are either taken from the country, or from the religion of the age common to all parts of the empire.

The Silenus is indeed of a more disputable kind, because though the scene lies in the country, the song being religious and historical, had been no less adapted to any other audience or place. Neither can it well be defended as a fiction, for the introduction of a god seems to imply the golden age, and yet he alludes to many subsequent transactions, and mentions Gallus, the poet's contemporary.

It seems necessary, to the perfection of this poem, that the occasion which is supposed to produce it, be at least not inconsistent with a country life, or less likely to interest those who have retired into places of solitude and quiet, than the more busy part of mankind. It is therefore improper to give the title of a pastoral to verses, in which the speakers, after the slight mention of their flocks, fall to complaints of errors in the church, and corruptions in the government, or to lamentations of the death of some illustrious person, whom when once the poet has called a shepherd, he has no longer any labour upon his hands, but can make the clouds weep, and lilies wither, and the sheep hang their heads, without art or learning, genius or study.

It is part of Claudian's character of his rustick, that he computes his time not by the succession of consuls, but of harvests. Those who pass their days in retreats distant from the theatres of business, are always least likely to hurry their imagination with publick affairs.

The facility of treating actions or events in the pastoral stile, has incited many writers, from whom more judgment might have been expected, to put the sorrow or the joy which the occasion required into the mouth of Daphne or of Thyrsis, and as one absurdity must naturally be expected to make way for another, they have written with an utter disregard both of life and nature, and filled their productions with mythological allusions, with incredible fictions, and with sentiments which neither passion nor reason could have dictated, since the change which religion has made in the whole system of the world.

No. 39. Tuesday, 31 July 1750.

Infelix——nulli bene nupta marito.
AUSONIUS.

Unblest, still doom'd to wed with misery.

The condition of the female sex has been frequently the subject of compassion to medical writers, because their constitution of body is such, that every state of life brings its peculiar diseases: they are placed, according to the proverb, between Scylla and Charybdis, with no other choice than of dangers equally formidable; and whether they embrace marriage, or determine upon a single life, are exposed, in consequence of their choice, to sickness, misery, and death.

It were to be wished that so great a degree of natural infelicity might not be increased by adventitious and artificial miseries; and that beings whose beauty we cannot behold without admiration, and whose delicacy we cannot contemplate without tenderness, might be suffered to enjoy every alleviation of their sorrows. But, however it has happened, the custom of the world seems to have been formed in a kind of conspiracy against them, though it does not appear but they had themselves an equal share in its establishment; and prescriptions which, by whomsoever they were begun, are now of long continuance, and by consequence of great authority, seem to have almost excluded them from content, in whatsoever condition they shall pass their lives.

If they refuse the society of men, and continue in that state which is reasonably supposed to place happiness most in their own power, they seldom give those that frequent their conversation, any exalted notions of the blessing of liberty; for whether it be that they are angry to see with what inconsiderate eagerness other heedless females rush into slavery, or with what absurd vanity the married ladies boast the change of their condition, and condemn the heroines who endeavour to assert the natural dignity of their sex; whether they are conscious that like barren countries they are free, only because they were never thought to deserve the trouble of a conquest, or imagine that their sincerity is not always unsuspected, when they declare their contempt of men; it is certain, that they generally appear to have some great and incessant cause of uneasiness, and that many of them have at last been persuaded, by powerful rhetoricians, to try the life which they had so long contemned, and put on the bridal ornaments at a time when they least became them.

What are the real causes of the impatience which the ladies discover in a virgin state, I shall perhaps take some other occasion to examine. That it is not to be envied for its happiness, appears from the solicitude with which it is avoided; from the opinion universally prevalent among the sex, that no woman continues long in it but because she is not invited to forsake it; from the disposition always shewn to treat old maids as the refuse of the world; and from the willingness with which it is often quitted at last, by those whose experience has enabled them to judge at leisure, and decide with authority.

Yet such is life, that whatever is proposed, it is much easier to find reasons for rejecting than embracing. Marriage, though a certain security from the reproach and solitude of antiquated virginity, has yet, as it is usually conducted, many disadvantages, that take away much from the pleasure which society promises, and might afford, if pleasures and pains were honestly shared, and mutual confidence inviolably preserved.

The miseries, indeed, which many ladies suffer under conjugal vexations, are to be considered with great pity, because their husbands are often not taken by them as objects of affection, but forced upon them by authority and violence, or by persuasion and importunity, equally resistless when urged by those whom they have been always accustomed to reverence and obey; and it very seldom appears, that those who are thus despotick in the disposal of their children, pay any regard to their domestick and personal felicity, or think it so much to be enquired whether they will be happy, as whether they will be rich.

It may be urged, in extenuation of this crime, which parents, not in any other respect to be numbered with robbers and assassins, frequently commit, that, in their estimation, riches and happiness are equivalent terms. They have passed their lives with no other wish than that of adding acre to acre, and filling one bag after another, and imagine the advantage of a daughter sufficiently considered, when they have secured her a large jointure, and given her reasonable expectations of living in the midst of those pleasures, with which she had seen her father and mother solacing their age.

There is an oeconomical oracle received among the prudential part of the world, which advises fathers *to marry their daughters lest they should marry themselves*; by which I suppose it is implied that women left to their own conduct, generally unite themselves with such partners as can contribute very little to their felicity. Who was the author of this maxim, or with what intention it was originally uttered, I have not yet discovered; but imagine that however solemnly it may be transmitted, or however implicitly received, it can confer no authority which nature has denied; it cannot license Titius to be unjust, lest Caia should be imprudent; nor give right to imprison for life, lest liberty should be ill employed.

That the ladies have sometimes incurred imputations which might naturally produce edicts not much in their favour, must be confessed by their warmest advocates; and I have indeed seldom observed, that when the tenderness or virtue of their parents has preserved them from forced marriage, and left them at large to chuse their own path in the labyrinth of life, they have made any great advantage of their liberty: They commonly take the opportunity of independence to trifle away youth and lose their bloom in a hurry of diversions, recurring in a succession too quick to leave room for any settled reflection; they see the world without gaining experience, and at last regulate their choice by motives trifling as those of a girl, or mercenary as those of a miser.

Melanthia came to town upon the death of her father, with a very large fortune, and with the reputation of a much larger; she was therefore followed and caressed by many men of rank, and by some of understanding; but having an insatiable desire of pleasure, she was not at leisure, from the park, the gardens, the theatres, visits, assemblies, and masquerades, to attend seriously to any proposal, but was still impatient for a new flatterer, and neglected marriage as always in her power; till in time her admirers fell away, wearied with expence, disgusted at her folly, or offended by her inconstancy; she heard of concerts to which she was not invited, and was more than once forced to sit still at an assembly, for want of a partner. In this distress, chance threw in her way Philotryphus, a man vain, glittering, and thoughtless as herself, who had spent a small fortune in equipage and dress, and was shining in the last suit for which his taylor would give him credit. He had been long endeavouring to retrieve his extravagance by marriage, and therefore soon paid his court to Melanthia, who after some weeks of insensibility saw him at a ball, and was wholly overcome by his performance in a minuet. They married; but a man cannot always dance, and Philotryphus had no other method of pleasing; however, as neither was in any great degree vitious, they live together with no other unhappiness, than vacuity of mind, and that tastelessness of life, which proceeds from a satiety of juvenile pleasures, and an utter inability to fill their place by nobler employments. As they have known the fashionable world at the same time, they agree in their notions of all those subjects on which they ever speak, and being able to add nothing to the ideas of each other, are not much inclined to conversation, but very often join in one wish, "That they could sleep more, and think less."

Argyris, after having refused a thousand offers, at last consented to marry Cotylus, the younger brother of a duke, a man without elegance of mien, beauty of person, or force of understanding; who, while he courted her, could not always forbear allusions to her birth, and hints how cheaply she would purchase an alliance to so illustrious a family. His conduct from the hour of his marriage has been insufferably tyrannical, nor has he any other regard to her than what arises from his desire that her appearance may not disgrace him. Upon this principle, however, he always orders that she should be gaily dressed, and splendidly attended; and she has, among all her mortifications, the happiness to take place of her eldest sister.

No. 41. Tuesday, 7 August 1750.

Nulla recordanti lux est ingrata gravisque,
Nulla fuit cujus non meminisse velit.
Ampliat ætatis spatium sibi vir bonus, hoc est
Vivere bis, vitâ posse priore frui.
                                                    MART.

No day's remembrance shall the good regret,
Nor wish one bitter moment to forget;
They stretch the limits of this narrow span,
And, by enjoying, live past life again.
                                                    F. LEWIS.

So few of the hours of life are filled up with objects adequate to the mind of man, and so frequently are we in want of present pleasure or employment, that we are forced to have recourse every moment to the past and future for supplemental satisfactions, and relieve the vacuities of our being, by recollection of former passages, or anticipation of events to come.

I cannot but consider this necessity of searching on every side for matter on which the attention may be employed, as a strong proof of the superior and celestial nature of the soul of man. We have no reason to believe that other creatures have higher faculties, or more extensive capacities, than the preservation of themselves, or their species, requires; they seem always to be fully employed, or to be completely at ease without employment, to feel few intellectual miseries or pleasures, and to have no exuberance of understanding to lay out upon curiosity or caprice, but to have their minds exactly adapted to their bodies, with few other ideas than such as corporal pain or pleasure impress upon them.

Of memory, which makes so large a part of the excellence of the human soul, and which has so much influence upon all its other powers, but a small portion has been allotted to the animal world. We do not find the grief, with which the dams lament the loss of their young, proportionate to the tenderness with which they caress, the assiduity with which they feed, or the vehemence with which they defend them. Their regard for their offspring, when it is before their eyes, is not, in appearance, less than that of a human parent; but when it is taken away, it is very soon forgotten, and, after a short absence, if brought again, wholly disregarded.

That they have very little remembrance of any thing once out of the reach of their senses, and scarce any power of comparing the present with the past, and regulating their conclusions from experience, may be gathered from this, that their intellects are produced in their full perfection. The sparrow that was hatched last spring makes her first nest the ensuing season, of the same materials, and with the same art, as in any following year; and the hen conducts and shelters her first brood of chickens with all the prudence that she ever attains.

It has been asked by men who love to perplex any thing that is plain to common understandings, how reason differs from instinct; and Prior has with no great propriety made Solomon himself declare, that, to distinguish them is *the fool's ignorance, and the pedant's pride*. To give an accurate answer to a question, of which the terms are not compleatly understood, is impossible; we do not know in what either reason or instinct consist, and therefore cannot tell with exactness how they differ; but surely he that contemplates a ship and a bird's nest, will not be long without finding out, that the idea of the one was impressed at once, and continued through all the progressive descents of the species, without variation or improvement; and that the other is the result of experiments compared with experiments, has grown, by accumulated observation, from less to greater excellence, and exhibits the collective knowledge of different ages, and various professions.

Memory is the purveyor of reason, the power which places those images before the mind upon which the judgment is to be exercised, and which treasures up the determinations that are once passed, as the rules of future action, or grounds of subsequent conclusions.

It is, indeed, the faculty of remembrance, which may be said to place us in the class of moral agents. If we were to act only in consequence of some immediate impulse, and receive no direction from internal motives of choice, we should be pushed forward by an invincible fatality, without power or reason for the most part to prefer one thing to another, because we could make no comparison but of objects which might both happen to be present.

We owe to memory not only the increase of our knowledge, and our progress in rational enquiries, but many other intellectual pleasures. Indeed, almost all that we can be said to enjoy is past or future; the present is in perpetual motion, leaves us as soon as it arrives, ceases to be present before its presence is well perceived, and is only known to have existed by the effects which it leaves behind. The greatest part of our ideas arises, therefore, from the view before or behind us, and we are happy or miserable, according as we are affected by the survey of our life, or our prospect of future existence.

With regard to futurity, when events are at such a distance from us, that we cannot take the whole concatenation into our view, we have generally power enough over our imagination to turn it upon pleasing scenes, and can promise ourselves riches, honours, and delights, without intermingling those vexations and anxieties, with which all human enjoyments are polluted. If fear breaks in on one side, and alarms us with dangers and disappointments, we can call in hope on the other, to solace us with rewards, and escapes, and victories; so that we are seldom without means of palliating remote evils, and can generally sooth ourselves to tranquillity, whenever any troublesome presage happens to attack us.

It is therefore, I believe, much more common for the solitary and thoughtful, to amuse themselves with schemes of the future, than reviews of the past. For the future is pliant and ductile, and will be easily moulded by a strong fancy into any form. But the images which memory presents are of a stubborn and untractable nature, the objects of remembrance have already existed, and left their signature behind them impressed upon the mind, so as to defy all attempts of rasure, or of change.

As the satisfactions, therefore, arising from memory are less arbitrary, they are more solid, and are, indeed, the only joys which we can call our own. Whatever we have once reposited, as Dryden expresses it, *in the sacred treasure of the past,* is out of the reach of accident, or violence, nor can be lost either by our own weakness, or another's malice:

——————— *Non tamen irritum*
Quodcunque retro est efficiet, neque
Diffinget, infectumque reddet,
Quod fugiens semel hora vexit.

Be fair or foul or rain or shine,
  The joys I have possess'd in spite of fate are mine.
Not heav'n itself upon the past has pow'r,
But what has been has been, and I have had my hour.
                                                                  DRYDEN.

There is certainly no greater happiness, than to be able to look back on a life usefully and virtuously employed, to trace our own progress in existence, by such tokens as excite neither shame nor sorrow. Life, in which nothing has been done or suffered to distinguish one day from another, is to him that has passed it, as if it had never been, except that he is conscious how ill he has husbanded the great deposit of his Creator. Life, made memorable by crimes, and diversified thro' its several periods by wickedness, is indeed easily reviewed, but reviewed only with horror and remorse.

The great consideration which ought to influence us in the use of the present moment, is to arise from the effect, which, as well or ill applied, it must have upon the time to come; for though its actual existence be inconceivably short, yet its effects are unlimited, and there is not the smallest point of time but may extend its consequences, either to our hurt or our advantage, through all eternity, and give us reason to remember it for ever, with anguish or exultation.

The time of life, in which memory seems particularly to claim predominance over the other faculties of the mind, is our declining age. It has been remarked by former writers, that old men are generally narrative, and fall easily into recitals of past transactions, and accounts of persons known to them in their youth. When we approach the verge of the grave it is more eminently true;

Vitæ summa brevis spem nos vetat inchoare longam.

Life's span forbids thee to extend thy cares,
  And stretch thy hopes beyond thy years.
                                                                  CREECH.

We have no longer any possibility of great vicissitudes in our favour; the changes which are to happen in the world will come too late for our accommodation; and those who have no hope before them, and to whom their present state is painful and irksome, must of necessity turn their thoughts back to try what retrospect will afford. It ought, therefore, to be the care of those who wish to pass the last hours with comfort, to lay up such a treasure of pleasing ideas, as shall support the expences of that time, which is to depend wholly upon the fund already acquired.

> —— *Petite hinc juvenesque senesque*
> *Finem animo certum, miserisque viatica canis.*

Seek here, ye young, the anchor of your mind;
Here, suff'ring age, a bless'd provision find.
ELPHINSTON.

In youth, however unhappy, we solace ourselves with the hope of better fortune, and, however vicious, appease our consciences with intentions of repentance; but the time comes at last, in which life has no more to promise, in which happiness can be drawn only from recollection, and virtue will be all that we can recollect with pleasure.

No. 45. Tuesday, 21 August 1750.

Ἥπερ μεγίστη γίγνεται σωτηρία,
Ὅταν γύνη πρὸς ἄνδρα μὴ διχοστατῇ,
Νῦν δ' ἐχθρὰ πάντα.
EURIP.

This is the chief felicity of life,
That concord smile on the connubial bed;
But now 'tis hatred all ——————

To the RAMBLER.

SIR,
   Though, in the dissertations which you have given us on marriage, very just cautions are laid down against the common causes of infelicity, and the necessity of having, in that important choice, the first regard to virtue is carefully inculcated; yet I cannot think the subject so much exhausted, but that a little reflection would present to the mind many questions in the discussion of which great numbers are interested, and many precepts which deserve to be more particularly and forcibly impressed.

   You seem, like most of the writers that have gone before you, to have allowed, as an uncontested principle, that *Marriage is generally unhappy*: but I know not whether a man who professes to think for himself, and concludes from his own observations, does not depart from his character when he follows the crowd thus implicitly, and receives maxims without recalling them to a new examination, especially when they comprise so wide a circuit of life, and include such variety of circumstances. As I have an equal right with others to give my opinion of the objects about me, and a better title to determine concerning that state which I have tried, than many who talk of it without experience, I am unwilling to be restrained by mere authority from advancing what, I believe, an accurate view of the world will confirm, that marriage is not commonly unhappy, otherwise than as life is unhappy; and that most of those who complain of connubial miseries, have as much satisfaction as their nature would have admitted, or their conduct procured in any other condition.

It is, indeed, common to hear both sexes repine at their change, relate the happiness of their earlier years, blame the folly and rashness of their own choice, and warn those whom they see coming into the world against the same precipitance and infatuation. But it is to be remembred, that the days which they so much wish to call back, are the days not only of celibacy but of youth, the days of novelty and improvement, of ardour and of hope, of health and vigour of body, of gayety and lightness of heart. It is not easy to surround life with any circumstances in which youth will not be delightful; and I am afraid that whether married or unmarried, we shall find the vesture of terrestrial existence more heavy and cumbrous, the longer it is worn.

That they censure themselves for the indiscretion of their choice, is not a sufficient proof that they have chosen ill, since we see the same discontent at every other part of life which we cannot change. Converse with almost any man, grown old in a profession, and you will find him regretting that he did not enter into some different course, to which he too late finds his genius better adapted, or in which he discovers that wealth and honour are more easily attained. "The merchant," says Horace, "envies the soldier, and the soldier recounts the felicity of the merchant; the lawyer when his clients harrass him, calls out for the quiet of the countryman; and the countryman, when business calls him to town, proclaims that there is no happiness but amidst opulence and crouds." Every man recounts the inconveniencies of his own station, and thinks those of any other less, because he has not felt them. Thus the married praise the ease and freedom of a single state, and the single fly to marriage from the weariness of solitude. From all our observations we may collect with certainty, that misery is the lot of man, but cannot discover in what particular condition it will find most alleviations; or whether all external appendages are not, as we use them, the causes either of good or ill.

Whoever feels great pain naturally hopes for ease from change of posture; he changes it, and finds himself equally tormented: and of the same kind are the expedients by which we endeavour to obviate or elude those uneasinesses, to which mortality will always be subject. It is not likely that the married state is eminently miserable, since we see such numbers, whom the death of their partners has set free from it, entering it again.

Wives and husbands are, indeed, incessantly complaining of each other; and there would be reason for imagining that almost every house was infested with perverseness or oppression beyond human sufferance, did we not know upon how small occasions some minds burst out into lamentations and reproaches, and how naturally every animal revenges his pain upon those who happen to be near, without any nice examination of its cause. We are always willing to fancy ourselves within a little of happiness, and when, with repeated efforts, we cannot reach it, persuade ourselves that it is intercepted by an ill-paired mate, since, if we could find any other obstacle, it would be our own fault that it was not removed.

Anatomists have often remarked, that though our diseases are sufficiently numerous and severe, yet when we enquire into the structure of the body, the tenderness of some parts, the minuteness of others, and the immense multi-plicity of animal functions that must concur to the healthful and vigorous exercise of all our powers, there appears reason to wonder rather that we are preserved so long, than that we perish so soon, and that our frame subsists for a single day, or hour, without disorder, rather than that it should be broken or obstructed by violence of accidents, or length of time.

The same reflection arises in my mind, upon observation of the manner in which marriage is frequently contracted. When I see the avaricious and crafty taking companions to their tables, and their beds, without any enquiry, but after farms and money; or the giddy and thoughtless uniting themselves for life to those whom they have only seen by the light of tapers at a ball; when parents make articles for their children, without enquiring after their consent; when some marry for heirs to disappoint their brothers, and others throw themselves into the arms of those whom they do not love, because they have found themselves rejected where they were more solicitous to please; when some marry because their servants cheat them, some because they squander their own money, some because their houses are pestered with company, some because they will live like other people, and some only because they are sick of themselves, I am not so much inclined to wonder that marriage is sometimes unhappy, as that it appears so little loaded with calamity; and cannot but conclude that society has something in itself eminently agreeable to human nature, when I find its pleasures so great that even the ill choice of a companion can hardly over-balance them.

By the ancient custom of the Muscovites the men and women never saw each other till they were joined beyond the power of parting. It may be sus-pected that by this method many unsuitable matches were produced, and many tempers associated that were not qualified to give pleasure to each other. Yet, perhaps, among a people so little delicate, where the paucity of gratifica-tions, and the uniformity of life gave no opportunity for imagination to inter-pose its objections, there was not much danger of capricious dislike, and while they felt neither cold nor hunger they might live quietly together, without any thought of the defects of one another.

Amongst us, whom knowledge has made nice, and affluence wanton, there are, indeed, more cautions requisite to secure tranquillity; and yet if we observe the manner in which those converse, who have singled out each other for mar-riage, we shall, perhaps, not think that the Russians lost much by their restraint.

For the whole endeavour of both parties, during the time of courtship, is to hinder themselves from being known, and to disguise their natural temper, and real desires, in hypocritical imitation, studied compliance, and continued affectation. From the time that their love is avowed, neither sees the other but in a mask, and the cheat is managed often on both sides with so much art, and discovered afterwards with so much abruptness, that each has reason to suspect that some transformation has happened on the wedding-night, and that by a strange imposture one has been courted, and another married.

I desire you, therefore, Mr. RAMBLER, to question all who shall hereafter come to you with matrimonial complaints, concerning their behaviour in the time of courtship, and inform them that they are neither to wonder nor repine, when a contract begun with fraud has ended in disappointment.

I AM, &C.

No. 47. Tuesday, 28 August 1750.

Quanquam his solatiis acquiescam, debilitor & frangor eadem illa humanitate quæ me, ut hoc ipsum permitterem, induxit, non ideo tamen velim durior fieri: nec ignoro alios hujusmodi casus nihil amplius vocare quam damnum; eoque sibi magnos homines & sapientes videri. Qui an magni sapientesque sint, nescio: homines non sunt. Hominis est enim affici dolore, sentire: resistere tamen, & solatia admittere; non solatiis non egere.

PLIN.

These proceedings have afforded me some comfort in my distress; notwithstanding which, I am still dispirited, and unhinged by the same motives of humanity that induced me to grant such indulgences. However, I by no means wish to become less susceptible of tenderness. I know these kind of misfortunes would be estimated by other persons only as common losses, and from such sensations they would conceive themselves great and wise men. I shall not determine either their greatness or their wisdom; but I am certain they have no humanity. It is the part of a man to be affected with grief; to feel sorrow, at the same time, that he is to resist it, and to admit of comfort.

EARL OF ORRERY.

Of the passions with which the mind of man is agitated, it may be observed, that they naturally hasten towards their own extinction by inciting and quickening the attainment of their objects. Thus fear urges our flight, and desire animates our progress; and if there are some which perhaps may be indulged till they out-grow the good appropriated to their satisfaction, as is frequently observed of avarice and ambition, yet their immediate tendency is to some means of happiness really existing, and generally within the prospect. The miser always imagines that there is a certain sum that will fill his heart to the brim; and every ambitious man, like king Pyrrhus, has an acquisition in his thoughts that is to terminate his labours, after which he shall pass the rest of his life in ease or gayety, in repose or devotion.

Sorrow is perhaps the only affection of the breast that can be excepted from this general remark, and it therefore deserves the particular attention of those who have assumed the arduous province of preserving the balance of the mental constitution. The other passions are diseases indeed, but they necessarily direct us to their proper cure. A man at once feels the pain, and knows the medicine, to which he is carried with greater haste as the evil which requires it is more excruciating, and cures himself by unerring instinct, as the wounded stags of Crete are related by Ælian to have recourse to vulnerary herbs. But for sorrow there is no remedy provided by nature; it is often occasioned by accidents irreparable, and dwells upon objects that have lost or changed their existence; it requires what it cannot hope, that the laws of the universe should be repealed; that the dead should return, or the past should be recalled.

Sorrow is not that regret for negligence or error which may animate us to future care or activity, or that repentance of crimes for which, however irrevocable, our Creator has promised to accept it as an attonement; the pain which arises from these causes has very salutary effects, and is every hour extenuating itself by the reparation of those miscarriages that produce it. Sorrow is properly that state of the mind in which our desires are fixed upon the past, without looking forward to the future, an incessant wish that something were otherwise than it has been, a tormenting and harrassing want of some enjoyment or possession which we have lost, and which no endeavours can possibly regain. Into such anguish many have sunk upon some sudden diminution of their fortune, an unexpected blast of their reputation, or the loss of children or of friends. They have suffered all sensibility of pleasure to be destroyed by a single blow, have given up for ever the hopes of substituting any other object in the room of that which they lament, resigned their lives to gloom and despondency, and worn themselves out in unavailing misery.

Yet so much is this passion the natural consequence of tenderness and endearment, that, however painful and however useless, it is justly reproachful not to feel it on some occasions; and so widely and constantly has it always prevailed, that the laws of some nations, and the customs of others, have limited a time for the external appearances of grief caused by the dissolution of close alliances, and the breach of domestic union.

It seems determined, by the general suffrage of mankind, that sorrow is to a certain point laudable, as the offspring of love, or at least pardonable as the effect of weakness; but that it ought not to be suffered to increase by indulgence, but must give way, after a stated time, to social duties, and the common avocations of life. It is at first unavoidable, and therefore must be allowed, whether with or without our choice; it may afterwards be admitted as a decent and affectionate testimony of kindness and esteem; something will be extorted by nature, and something may be given to the world. But all beyond the bursts of passion, or the forms of solemnity, is not only useless, but culpable; for we have no right to sacrifice, to the vain longings of affection, that time which providence allows us for the task of our station.

Yet it too often happens that sorrow, thus lawfully entering, gains such a firm possession of the mind, that it is not afterwards to be ejected; the mournful ideas, first violently impressed, and afterwards willingly received, so much engross the attention, as to predominate in every thought, to darken gayety, and perplex ratiocination. An habitual sadness seizes upon the soul, and the faculties are chained to a single object, which can never be contemplated but with hopeless uneasiness.

From this state of dejection it is very difficult to rise to chearfulness and alacrity, and therefore many who have laid down rules of intellectual health, think preservatives easier than remedies, and teach us not to trust ourselves with favourite enjoyments, not to indulge the luxury of fondness, but to keep our minds always suspended in such indifference, that we may change the objects about us without emotion.

An exact compliance with this rule might, perhaps, contribute to tranquillity, but surely it would never produce happiness. He that regards none so much as to be afraid of losing them, must live for ever without the gentle pleasures of sympathy and confidence; he must feel no melting fondness, no warmth of benevolence, nor any of those honest joys which nature annexes to the power of pleasing. And as no man can justly claim more tenderness than he pays, he must forfeit his share in that officious and watchful kindness which love only can dictate, and those lenient endearments by which love only can soften life. He may justly be overlooked and neglected by such as have more warmth in their heart; for who would be the friend of him, whom, with whatever assiduity he may be courted, and with whatever services obliged, his principles will not suffer to make equal returns, and who, when you have exhausted all the instances of good will, can only be prevailed on not to be an enemy?

An attempt to preserve life in a state of neutrality and indifference, is unreasonable and vain. If by excluding joy we could shut out grief, the scheme would deserve very serious attention; but since, however we may debar ourselves from happiness, misery will find its way at many inlets, and the assaults of pain will force our regard, though we may withhold it from the invitations of pleasure, we may surely endeavour to raise life above the middle point of apathy at one time, since it will necessarily sink below it at another.

But though it cannot be reasonable not to gain happiness for fear of losing it, yet it must be confessed, that in proportion to the pleasure of possession, will be for some time our sorrow for the loss; it is therefore the province of the moralist to enquire whether such pains may not quickly give way to mitigation. Some have thought, that the most certain way to clear the heart from its embarrassment is to drag it by force into scenes of merriment. Others imagine, that such a transition is too violent, and recommend rather to sooth it into tranquillity, by making it acquainted with miseries more dreadful and afflictive, and diverting to the calamities of others the regard which we are inclined to fix too closely upon our own misfortunes.

It may be doubted whether either of those remedies will be sufficiently powerful. The efficacy of mirth it is not always easy to try, and the indulgence of melancholy may be suspected to be one of those medicines, which will destroy, if it happens not to cure.

The safe and general antidote against sorrow, is employment. It is commonly observed, that among soldiers and seamen, though there is much kindness, there is little grief; they see their friend fall without any of that lamentation which is indulged in security and idleness, because they have no leisure to spare from the care of themselves; and whoever shall keep his thoughts equally busy, will find himself equally unaffected with irretrievable losses.

Time is observed generally to wear out sorrow, and its effects might doubtless be accelerated by quickening the succession, and enlarging the variety of objects.

> *Si tempore longo*
> *Leniri poterit luctus, tu sperne morari,*
> *Qui sapiet sibi tempus erit.——*
> GROTIUS.

> 'Tis long e'er time can mitigate your grief;
> To wisdom fly, she quickly brings relief.
> F. LEWIS.

Sorrow is a kind of rust of the soul, which every new idea contributes in its passage to scour away. It is the putrefaction of stagnant life, and is remedied by exercise and motion.

No. 49. Tuesday, 4 September 1750.

> *Non omnis moriar, multaque pars mei*
> *Vitabit Libitinam, usque ego posterâ*
> *Crescam laude recens.*
> HOR.

> Whole *Horace* shall not die; his songs shall save
> The greatest portion from the greedy grave.
> CREECH.

The first motives of human actions are those appetites which providence has given to man, in common with the rest of the inhabitants of the earth.

Immediately after our birth, thirst and hunger incline us to the breast, which we draw by instinct, like other young creatures, and, when we are satisfied, we express our uneasiness by importunate and incessant cries, till we have obtained a place or posture proper for repose.

The next call that rouses us from a state of inactivity, is that of our passions; we quickly begin to be sensible of hope and fear, love and hatred, desire and aversion; these arising from the power of comparison and reflexion, extend their range wider, as our reason strengthens, and our knowledge enlarges. At first we have no thought of pain, but when we actually feel it; we afterwards begin to fear it, yet not before it approaches us very nearly; but by degrees we discover it at a greater distance, and find it lurking in remote consequences. Our terror in time improves into caution, and we learn to look round with vigilance and solicitude, to stop all the avenues at which misery can enter, and to perform or endure many things in themselves toilsome and unpleasing, because we know by reason, or by experience, that our labour will be overbalanced by the reward, that it will either procure some positive good, or avert some evil greater than itself.

But as the soul advances to a fuller exercise of its powers, the animal appetites, and the passions immediately arising from them, are not sufficient to find it employment; the wants of nature are soon supplied, the fear of their return is easily precluded, and something more is necessary to relieve the long intervals of inactivity, and to give those faculties, which cannot lie wholly quiescent, some particular direction. For this reason, new desires, and artificial passions are by degrees produced; and, from having wishes only in consequence of our wants, we begin to feel wants in consequence of our wishes; we persuade ourselves to set a value upon things which are of no use, but because we have agreed to value them; things which can neither satisfy hunger, nor mitigate pain, nor secure us from any real calamity, and which, therefore, we find of no esteem among those nations whose artless and barbarous manners keep them always anxious for the necessaries of life.

This is the original of avarice, vanity, ambition, and generally of all those desires which arise from the comparison of our condition with that of others. He that thinks himself poor, because his neighbour is richer; he that, like Caesar, would rather be the first man of a village, than the second in the capital of the world, has apparently kindled in himself desires which he never received from nature, and acts upon principles established only by the authority of custom.

Of those adscititious passions, some, as avarice and envy, are universally condemned; some, as friendship and curiosity, generally praised; but there are others about which the suffrages of the wise are divided, and of which it is doubted, whether they tend most to promote the happiness, or increase the miseries of mankind.

Of this ambiguous and disputable kind is the love of fame, a desire of filling the minds of others with admiration, and of being celebrated by generations to come with praises which we shall not hear. This ardour has been considered by some, as nothing better than splendid madness, as a flame kindled by pride, and fanned by folly; for what, say they, can be more remote from wisdom, than to direct all our actions by the hope of that which is not to exist till we ourselves are in the grave? To pant after that which can never be possessed, and of which the value thus wildly put upon it, arises from this particular condition, that, during life, it is not to be obtained? To gain the favour, and hear the applauses of our contemporaries, is indeed equally desirable with any other prerogative of superiority, because fame may be of use to smooth the paths of life, to terrify opposition, and fortify tranquillity; but to what end shall we be the darlings of mankind, when we can no longer receive any benefits from their favour? It is more reasonable to wish for reputation, while it may yet be enjoyed, as Anacreon calls upon his companions to give him for present use the wine and garlands which they purpose to bestow upon his tomb.

The advocates for the love of fame allege in its vindication, that it is a passion natural and universal; a flame lighted by heaven, and always burning with greatest vigour in the most enlarged and elevated minds. That the desire of being praised by posterity implies a resolution to deserve their praises, and that the folly charged upon it, is only a noble and disinterested generosity, which is not felt, and therefore not understood by those who have been always accustomed to refer every thing to themselves, and whose selfishness has contracted their understandings. That the soul of man, formed for eternal life, naturally springs forward beyond the limits of corporeal existence, and rejoices to consider herself as co-operating with future ages, and as co-extended with endless duration. That the reproach urged with so much petulance, the reproach of labouring for what cannot be enjoyed, is founded on an opinion which may with great probability be doubted; for since we suppose the powers of the soul to be enlarged by its separation, why should we conclude that its knowledge of sublunary transactions is contracted or extinguished?

Upon an attentive and impartial review of the argument, it will appear that the love of fame is to be regulated, rather than extinguished; and that men should be taught not to be wholly careless about their memory, but to endeavour that they may be remembered chiefly for their virtues, since no other reputation will be able to transmit any pleasure beyond the grave.

It is evident that fame, considered merely as the immortality of a name, is not less likely to be the reward of bad actions than of good; he therefore has no certain principle for the regulation of his conduct, whose single aim is not to be forgotten. And history will inform us, that this blind and undistinguishing appetite of renown has always been uncertain in its effects, and directed by accident or opportunity, indifferently to the benefit or devastation of the world. When Themistocles complained that the trophies of Miltiades hindered him from sleep, he was animated by them to perform the same services in the same cause. But Cæsar, when he wept at the sight of Alexander's picture, having no honest opportunities of action, let his ambition break out to the ruin of his country.

If, therefore, the love of fame is so far indulged by the mind as to become independent and predominant, it is dangerous and irregular; but it may be usefully employed as an inferior and secondary motive, and will serve sometimes to revive our activity, when we begin to languish and lose sight of that more certain, more valuable, and more durable reward, which ought always to be our first hope and our last. But it must be strongly impressed upon our minds, that virtue is not to be persued as one of the means to fame, but fame to be accepted as the only recompence which mortals can bestow on virtue; to be accepted with complacence, but not sought with eagerness. Simply to be remembered is no advantage; it is a privilege which satire as well as panegyric can confer, and is not more enjoyed by Titus or Constantine, than by Timocreon of Rhodes, of whom we only know from his epitaph, *that he had eaten many a meal, drank many a flaggon, and uttered many a reproach.*

> Πολλὰ φαγὼν, καὶ πολλὰ πιὼν, καὶ πολλὰ κακ᾽ εἰπὼν
> Ἀνθρώπους, κεῖμαι Τιμοκρέων Ῥόδιος.

The true satisfaction which is to be drawn from the consciousness that we shall share the attention of future times, must arise from the hope, that, with our name, our virtues will be propagated; and that those whom we cannot benefit in our lives, may receive instruction from our examples, and incitement from our renown.

No. 60. Saturday, 13 October 1750.

—*Quid sit pulchrum, quid turpe, quid utile, quid non,*
Plenius et melius Chrysippo et Crantore dicit.

Hor.

Whose works the beautiful and base contain;
Of vice and virtue more instructive rules,
Than all the sober sages of the schools.

Francis.

All joy or sorrow for the happiness or calamities of others is produced by an act of the imagination, that realises the event however fictitious, or approximates it however remote, by placing us, for a time, in the condition of him whose fortune we contemplate; so that we feel, while the deception lasts, whatever motions would be excited by the same good or evil happening to ourselves.

Our passions are therefore more strongly moved, in proportion as we can more readily adopt the pains or pleasure proposed to our minds, by recognising them as once our own, or considering them as naturally incident to our state of life. It is not easy for the most artful writer to give us an interest in happiness or misery, which we think ourselves never likely to feel, and with which we have never yet been made acquainted. Histories of the downfal of kingdoms, and revolutions of empires, are read with great tranquillity; the imperial tragedy pleases common auditors only by its pomp of ornament, and grandeur of ideas; and the man whose faculties have been engrossed by business, and whose heart never fluttered but at the rise or fall of stocks, wonders how the attention can be seized, or the affections agitated by a tale of love.

Those parallel circumstances, and kindred images, to which we readily conform our minds, are, above all other writings, to be found in narratives of the lives of particular persons; and therefore no species of writing seems more worthy of cultivation than biography, since none can be more delightful or more useful, none can more certainly enchain the heart by irresistible interest, or more widely diffuse instruction to every diversity of condition.

The general and rapid narratives of history, which involve a thousand fortunes in the business of a day, and complicate innumerable incidents in one great transaction, afford few lessons applicable to private life, which derives its comforts and its wretchedness from the right or wrong management of things which nothing but their frequency makes considerable, *Parva, si non fiunt quotidie*, says Pliny, and which can have no place in those relations which never descend below the consultation of senates, the motions of armies, and the schemes of conspirators.

I have often thought that there has rarely passed a life of which a judicious and faithful narrative would not be useful. For, not only every man has, in the mighty mass of the world, great numbers in the same condition with himself, to whom his mistakes and miscarriages, escapes and expedients, would be of immediate and apparent use; but there is such an uniformity in the state of man, considered apart from adventitious and separable decorations and disguises, that there is scarce any possibility of good or ill, but is common to human kind. A great part of the time of those who are placed at the greatest distance by fortune, or by temper, must unavoidably pass in the same manner; and though, when the claims of nature are satisfied, caprice, and vanity, and accident, begin to produce discriminations and peculiarities, yet the eye is not very heedful, or quick, which cannot discover the same causes still terminating their influence in the same effects, though sometimes accelerated, sometimes retarded, or perplexed by multiplied combinations. We are all prompted by the same motives, all deceived by the same fallacies, all animated by hope, obstructed by danger, entangled by desire, and seduced by pleasure.

It is frequently objected to relations of particular lives, that they are not distinguished by any striking or wonderful vicissitudes. The scholar who passed his life among his books, the merchant who conducted only his own affairs, the priest, whose sphere of action was not extended beyond that of his duty, are considered as no proper objects of publick regard, however they might have excelled in their several stations, whatever might have been their learning, integrity, and piety. But this notion arises from false measures of excellence and dignity, and must be eradicated by considering, that, in the esteem of uncorrupted reason, what is of most use is of most value.

It is, indeed, not improper to take honest advantages of prejudice, and to gain attention by a celebrated name; but the business of the biographer is often to pass slightly over those performances and incidents, which produce vulgar greatness, to lead the thoughts into domestick privacies, and display the minute details of daily life, where exterior appendages are cast aside, and men excel each other only by prudence and by virtue. The account of Thuanus is, with great propriety, said by its author to have been written, that it might lay open to posterity the private and familiar character of that man, *cujus ingenium et candorem ex ipsius scriptis sunt olim semper miraturi*, whose candour and genius will to the end of time be by his writings preserved in admiration.

There are many invisible circumstances which, whether we read as enquirers after natural or moral knowledge, whether we intend to enlarge our science, or increase our virtue, are more important than publick occurrences. Thus Salust, the great master of nature, has not forgot, in his account of Catiline, to remark that *his walk was now quick, and again slow*, as an indication of a mind revolving something with violent commotion. Thus the story of Melancthon affords a striking lecture on the value of time, by informing us, that when he made an appointment, he expected not only the hour, but the minute to be fixed, that the day might not run out in the idleness of suspense; and all the plans and enterprizes of De Wit are now of less importance to the world, than that part of his personal character which represents him as *careful of his health, and negligent of his life*.

But biography has often been allotted to writers who seem very little acquainted with the nature of their task, or very negligent about the performance. They rarely afford any other account than might be collected from publick papers, but imagine themselves writing a life when they exhibit a chronological series of actions or preferments; and so little regard the manners or behaviour of their heroes, that more knowledge may be gained of a man's real character, by a short conversation with one of his servants, than from a formal and studied narrative, begun with his pedigree, and ended with his funeral.

If now and then they condescend to inform the world of particular facts, they are not always so happy as to select the most important. I know not well what advantage posterity can receive from the only circumstance by which Tickell has distinguished Addison from the rest of mankind, *the irregularity of his pulse*: nor can I think myself overpaid for the time spent in reading the life of Malherb, by being enabled to relate, after the learned biographer, that Malherb had two predominant opinions; one, that the looseness of a single woman might destroy all her boast of ancient descent; the other, that the French beggars made use very improperly and barbarously of the phrase *noble Gentleman*, because either word included the sense of both.

There are, indeed, some natural reasons why these narratives are often written by such as were not likely to give much instruction or delight, and why most accounts of particular persons are barren and useless. If a life be delayed till interest and envy are at an end, we may hope for impartiality, but must expect little intelligence; for the incidents which give excellence to biography are of a volatile and evanescent kind, such as soon escape the memory, and are rarely transmitted by tradition. We know how few can portray a living acquaintance, except by his most prominent and observable particularities, and the grosser features of his mind; and it may be easily imagined how much of this little knowledge may be lost in imparting it, and how soon a succession of copies will lose all resemblance of the original.

If the biographer writes from personal knowledge, and makes haste to gratify the publick curiosity, there is danger lest his interest, his fear, his gratitude, or his tenderness, overpower his fidelity, and tempt him to conceal, if not to invent. There are many who think it an act of piety to hide the faults or failings of their friends, even when they can no longer suffer by their detection; we therefore see whole ranks of characters adorned with uniform panegyrick, and not to be known from one another, but by extrinsick and casual circumstances. "Let me remember, says Hale, when I find myself inclined to pity a criminal, that there is likewise a pity due to the country." If we owe regard to the memory of the dead, there is yet more respect to be paid to knowledge, to virtue, and to truth.

No. 63. Tuesday, 23 October 1750.

——*Habebat sæpe ducentos,*
Sæpe decem servos; modò reges atque tetrarchas,
Omnia magna loquens: modò, sit mihi mensa tripes, et
Concha salis puri, et toga, quæ defendere frigus,
Quamvis crassa, queat.

HOR.

Now with two hundred slaves he crowds his train;
Now walks with ten. In high and haughty strain
At morn, of kings and governors he prates:
At night —— "A frugal table, O ye fates,
A little shell the sacred salt to hold,
And clothes, tho' coarse, to keep me from the cold."

FRANCIS.

It has been remarked, perhaps, by every writer, who has left behind him observations upon life, that no man is pleased with his present state, which proves equally unsatisfactory, says Horace, whether fallen upon by chance or chosen with deliberation; we are always disgusted with some circumstance or other of our situation, and imagine the condition of others more abundant in blessings, or less exposed to calamities.

This universal discontent has been generally mentioned with great severity of censure, as unreasonable in itself, since of two, equally envious of each other, both cannot have the larger share of happiness, and as tending to darken life with unnecessary gloom, by withdrawing our minds from the contemplation and enjoyment of that happiness which our state affords us, and fixing our attention upon foreign objects, which we only behold to depress ourselves, and increase our misery by injurious comparisons.

When this opinion of the felicity of others predominates in the heart, so as to excite resolutions of obtaining, at whatever price, the condition to which such transcendent privileges are supposed to be annexed; when it bursts into action, and produces fraud, violence, and injustice, it is to be persued with all the rigour of legal punishments. But while operating only upon the thoughts, it disturbs none but him who has happened to admit it, and, however it may interrupt content, makes no attack on piety or virtue, I cannot think it so far criminal or ridiculous, but that it may deserve some pity, and admit some excuse.

That all are equally happy, or miserable, I suppose none is sufficiently enthusiastical to maintain; because, though we cannot judge of the condition of others, yet every man has found frequent vicissitudes in his own state, and must therefore be convinced that life is susceptible of more or less felicity. What then shall forbid us to endeavour the alteration of that which is capable of being improved, and to grasp at augmentations of good, when we know it possible to be increased, and believe that any particular change of situation will increase it?

If he that finds himself uneasy may reasonably make efforts to rid himself from vexation, all mankind have a sufficient plea for some degree of restlessness, and the fault seems to be little more than too much temerity of conclusion, in favour of something not yet experienced, and too much readiness to believe, that the misery which our own passions and appetites produce, is brought upon us by accidental causes, and external efficients.

It is, indeed, frequently discovered by us, that we complained too hastily of peculiar hardships, and imagined ourselves distinguished by embarrassments, in which other classes of men are equally entangled. We often change a lighter for a greater evil, and wish ourselves restored again to the state from which we thought it desirable to be delivered. But this knowledge, though it is easily gained by the trial, is not always attainable any other way; and that error cannot justly be reproached, which reason could not obviate, nor prudence avoid.

To take a view at once distinct and comprehensive of human life, with all its intricacies of combination, and varieties of connexion, is beyond the power of mortal intelligences. Of the state with which practice has not acquainted us, we snatch a glimpse, we discern a point, and regulate the rest by passion, and by fancy. In this enquiry every favourite prejudice, every innate desire, is busy to deceive us. We are unhappy, at least less happy than our nature seems to admit; we necessarily desire the melioration of our lot; what we desire, we very reasonably seek, and what we seek we are naturally eager to believe that we have found. Our confidence is often disappointed, but our reason is not convinced, and there is no man who does not hope for something which he has not, though perhaps his wishes lie unactive, because he foresees the difficulty of attainment. As among the numerous students of Hermetick philosophy, not one appears to have desisted from the task of transmutation, from conviction of its impossibility, but from weariness of toil, or impatience of delay, a broken body, or exhausted fortune.

Irresolution and mutability are often the faults of men, whose views are wide, and whose imagination is vigorous and excursive, because they cannot confine their thoughts within their own boundaries of action, but are continually ranging over all the scenes of human existence, and consequently, are often apt to conceive that they fall upon new regions of pleasure, and start new possibilities of happiness. Thus they are busied with a perpetual succession of schemes, and pass their lives in alternate elation and sorrow, for want of that calm and immoveable acquiescence in their condition, by which men of slower understandings are fixed for ever to a certain point, or led on in the plain beaten track, which their fathers, and grandsires, have trod before them.

Of two conditions of life equally inviting to the prospect, that will always have the disadvantage which we have already tried; because the evils which we have felt we cannot extenuate; and tho' we have, perhaps from nature, the power as well of aggravating the calamity which we fear, as of heightening the blessing we expect, yet in those meditations which we indulge by choice, and which are not forced upon the mind by necessity, we have always the art of fixing our regard upon the more pleasing images, and suffer hope to dispose the lights by which we look upon futurity.

The good and ill of different modes of life are sometimes so equally opposed, that perhaps no man ever yet made his choice between them upon a full conviction, and adequate knowledge; and therefore fluctuation of will is not more wonderful, when they are proposed to the election, than oscillations of a beam charged with equal weights. The mind no sooner imagines itself determined by some prevalent advantage, than some convenience of equal weight is discovered on the other side, and the resolutions which are suggested by the nicest examination, are often repented as soon as they are taken.

Eumenes, a young man of great abilities, inherited a large estate from a father, long eminent in conspicuous employments. His father, harrassed with competitions, and perplexed with multiplicity of business, recommended the quiet of a private station with so much force, that Eumenes for some years resisted every motion of ambitious wishes; but being once provoked by the sight of oppression, which he could not redress, he began to think it the duty of an honest man to enable himself to protect others, and gradually felt a desire of greatness, excited by a thousand projects of advantage to his country. His fortune placed him in the senate, his knowledge and eloquence advanced him at court, and he possessed that authority and influence which he had resolved to exert for the happiness of mankind.

He now became acquainted with greatness, and was in a short time convinced, that in proportion as the power of doing well is enlarged, the temptations to do ill are multiplied and enforced. He felt himself every moment in danger of being either seduced or driven from his honest purposes. Sometimes a friend was to be gratified, and sometimes a rival to be crushed, by means which his conscience could not approve. Sometimes he was forced to comply with the prejudices of the publick, and sometimes with the schemes of the ministry. He was by degrees wearied with perpetual struggles to unite policy and virtue, and went back to retirement as the shelter of innocence, persuaded that he could only hope to benefit mankind by a blameless example of private virtue. Here he spent some years in tranquillity and beneficence; but finding that corruption increased, and false opinions in government prevailed, he thought himself again summoned to posts of publick trust, from which new evidence of his own weakness again determined him to retire.

Thus men may be made inconstant by virtue and by vice, by too much or too little thought; yet inconstancy, however dignified by its motives, is always to be avoided, because life allows us but a small time for enquiry and experiment, and he that steadily endeavours at excellence, in whatever employment, will more benefit mankind than he that hesitates in choosing his part till he is called to the performance. The traveller that resolutely follows a rough and winding path, will sooner reach the end of his journey, than he that is always changing his direction, and wastes the hours of daylight in looking for smoother ground, and shorter passages.

No. 64. Saturday, 27 October 1750.

Idem velle, et idem nolle, ea demum firma amicitia est.
Salust.

To live in friendship, is to have the same desires and the same aversions.

When Socrates was building himself a house at Athens, being asked by one that observed the littleness of the design, why a man so eminent would not have an abode more suitable to his dignity? he replied, that he should think himself sufficiently accommodated, if he could see that narrow habitation filled with real friends. Such was the opinion of this great master of human life, concerning the infrequency of such an union of minds as might deserve the name of friendship, that among the multitudes whom vanity or curiosity, civility or veneration, crouded about him, he did not expect, that very spacious apartments would be necessary to contain all that should regard him with sincere kindness, or adhere to him with steady fidelity.

So many qualities are indeed requisite to the possibility of friendship, and so many accidents must concur to its rise and its continuance, that the greatest part of mankind content themselves without it, and supply its place as they can, with interest and dependance.

Multitudes are unqualified for a constant and warm reciprocation of benevolence, as they are incapacitated for any other elevated excellence, by perpetual attention to their interest, and unresisting subjection to their passions. Long habits may superinduce inability to deny any desire, or repress by superior motives, the importunities of any immediate gratification, and an inveterate selfishness will imagine all advantages diminished in proportion as they are communicated.

But not only this hateful and confirmed corruption, but many varieties of disposition, not inconsistent with common degrees of virtue, may exclude friendship from the heart. Some ardent enough in their benevolence, and defective neither in officiousness, nor liberality, are mutable and uncertain, soon attracted by new objects, disgusted without offence, and alienated without enmity. Others are soft and flexible, easily influenced by reports or whispers, ready to catch alarms from every dubious circumstance, and to listen to every suspicion which envy and flattery shall suggest, to follow the opinion of every confident adviser, and move by the impulse of the last breath. Some are impatient of contradiction, more willing to go wrong by their own judgment, than to be indebted for a better or a safer way to the sagacity of another, inclined to consider counsel as insult, and enquiry as want of confidence, and to confer their regard on no other terms than unreserved submission, and implicit compliance. Some are dark and involved, equally careful to conceal good and bad purposes; and pleased with producing effects by invisible means, and shewing their design only in its execution. Others are universally communicative, alike open to every eye, and equally profuse of their own secrets and those of others, without the necessary vigilance of caution, or the honest arts of prudent integrity, ready to accuse without malice, and to betray without treachery. Any of these may be useful to the community, and pass through the world with the reputation of good purposes and uncorrupted morals, but they are unfit for close and tender intimacies. He cannot properly be chosen for a friend, whose kindness is exhaled by its own warmth, or frozen by the first blast of slander; he cannot be a useful counsellor, who will hear no opinion but his own; he will not much invite confidence whose principal maxim is to suspect; nor can the candour and frankness of that man be much esteemed, who spreads his arms to humankind, and makes every man, without distinction, a denizon of his bosom.

That friendship may be at once fond and lasting, there must not only be equal virtue on each part, but virtue of the same kind; not only the same end must be proposed, but the same means must be approved by both. We are often, by superficial accomplishments and accidental endearments, induced to love those whom we cannot esteem; we are sometimes, by great abilities and incontestable evidences of virtue, compelled to esteem those whom we cannot love. But friendship, compounded of esteem and love, derives from one its tenderness, and its permanence from the other; and therefore requires not only that its candidates should gain the judgement, but that they should attract the affections; that they should not only be firm in the day of distress, but gay in the hour of jollity; not only useful in exigences, but pleasing in familiar life; their presence should give chearfulness as well as courage, and dispel alike the gloom of fear and of melancholy.

To this mutual complacency is generally requisite an uniformity of opinions, at least of those active and conspicuous principles which discriminate parties in government, and sects in religion, and which every day operate more or less on the common business of life. For though great tenderness has, perhaps, been sometimes known to continue between men eminent in contrary factions; yet such friends are to be shewn rather as prodigies than examples, and it is no more proper to regulate our conduct by such instances, than to leap a precipice, because some have fallen from it and escaped with life.

It cannot but be extremely difficult to preserve private kindness in the midst of publick opposition, in which will necessarily be involved a thousand incidents, extending their influence to conversation and privacy. Men engaged, by moral or religious motives, in contrary parties, will generally look with different eyes upon every man, and decide almost every question upon different principles. When such occasions of dispute happen, to comply is to betray our cause, and to maintain friendship by ceasing to deserve it; to be silent, is to lose the happiness and dignity of independence, to live in perpetual constraint, and to desert, if not to betray: and who shall determine which of two friends shall yield, where neither believes himself mistaken, and both confess the importance of the question? What then remains but contradiction and debate? and from those what can be expected, but acrimony and vehemence, the insolence of triumph, the vexation of defeat, and, in time, a weariness of contest, and an extinction of benevolence? Exchange of endearments and intercourse of civility may continue, indeed, as boughs may for a while be verdant, when the root is wounded; but the poison of discord is infused, and though the countenance may preserve its smile, the heart is hardening and contracting.

That man will not be long agreeable, whom we see only in times of seriousness and severity; and therefore, to maintain the softness and serenity of benevolence, it is necessary that friends partake each others pleasures as well as cares, and be led to the same diversions by similitude of taste. This is, however, not to be considered as equally indispensable with conformity of principles, because any man may honestly, according to the precepts of Horace, resign the gratifications of taste to the humour of another, and friendship may well deserve the sacrifice of pleasure, though not of conscience.

It was once confessed to me, by a painter, that no professor of his art ever loved another. This declaration is so far justified by the knowledge of life, as to damp the hopes of warm and constant friendship, between men whom their studies have made competitors, and whom every favourer and every censurer are hourly inciting against each other. The utmost expectation that experience can warrant, is, that they should forbear open hostilities and secret machinations, and when the whole fraternity is attacked, be able to unite against a common foe. Some however, though few, may perhaps be found, in whom emulation has not been able to overpower generosity, who are distinguished from lower beings by nobler motives than the love of fame, and can preserve the sacred flame of friendship from the gusts of pride, and the rubbish of interest.

Friendship is seldom lasting but between equals, or where the superiority on one side is reduced by some equivalent advantage on the other. Benefits which cannot be repaid, and obligations which cannot be discharged, are not commonly found to increase affection; they excite gratitude indeed, and heighten veneration, but commonly take away that easy freedom, and familiarity of intercourse, without which, though there may be fidelity, and zeal, and admiration, there cannot be friendship. Thus imperfect are all earthly blessings; the great effect of friendship is beneficence, yet by the first act of uncommon kindness it is endangered, like plants that bear their fruit and die. Yet this consideration ought not to restrain bounty, or repress compassion; for duty is to be preferred before convenience, and he that loses part of the pleasures of friendship by his generosity, gains in its place the gratulation of his conscience.

No. 70. Saturday, 17 November 1750.

———— *Argentea proles,*
Auro deterior, fulvo pretiosior ære.
OVID.

Succeeding times a silver age behold,
Excelling brass, but more excell'd by gold.
DRYDEN.

Hesiod, in his celebrated distribution of mankind, divides them into three orders of intellect. "The first place, says he, belongs to him that can by his own powers discern what is right and fit, and penetrate to the remoter motives of action. The second is claimed by him that is willing to hear instruction, and can perceive right and wrong when they are shewn him by another; but he that has neither acuteness nor docility, who can neither find the way by himself, nor will be led by others, is a wretch without use or value."

If we survey the moral world, it will be found, that the same division may be made of men, with regard to their virtue. There are some whose principles are so firmly fixed, whose conviction is so constantly present to their minds, and who have raised in themselves such ardent wishes for the approbation of God, and the happiness with which he has promised to reward obedience and perseverance, that they rise above all other cares and considerations, and uniformly examine every action and desire, by comparing it with the divine commands. There are others in a kind of equipoise between good and ill; who are moved on one part by riches or pleasure, by the gratifications of passion, and the delights of sense; and, on the other, by laws of which they own the obligation, and rewards of which they believe the reality, and whom a very small addition of weight turns either way. The third class consists of beings immersed in pleasure, or abandoned to passion, without any desire of higher good, or any effort to extend their thoughts beyond immediate and gross satisfactions.

The second class is so much the most numerous, that it may be considered as comprising the whole body of mankind. Those of the last are not very many, and those of the first are very few; and neither the one nor the other fall much under the consideration of the moralist, whose precepts are intended chiefly for those who are endeavouring to go forward up the steeps of virtue, not for those who have already reached the summit, or those who are resolved to stay for ever in their present situation.

To a man not versed in the living world, but accustomed to judge only by speculative reason, it is scarcely credible that any one should be in this state of indifference, or stand undetermined and unengaged, ready to follow the first call to either side. It seems certain, that either a man must believe that virtue will make him happy, and resolve therefore to be virtuous, or think that he may be happy without virtue, and therefore cast off all care but for his present interest. It seems impossible that conviction should be on one side, and practice on the other; and that he who has seen the right way, should voluntarily shut his eyes, that he may quit it with more tranquillity. Yet all these absurdities are every hour to be found; the wisest and best men deviate from known and acknowledged duties, by inadvertency or surprise; and most are good no longer than while temptation is away, than while their passions are without excitements, and their opinions are free from the counteraction of any other motive.

Among the sentiments which almost every man changes as he advances into years, is the expectation of uniformity of character. He that without acquaintance with the power of desire, the cogency of distress, the complications of affairs, or the force of partial influence, has filled his mind with the excellence of virtue, and having never tried his resolution in any encounters with hope or fear, believes it able to stand firm whatever shall oppose it, will be always clamorous against the smallest failure, ready to exact the utmost punctualities of right, and to consider every man that fails in any part of his duty, as without conscience and without merit; unworthy of trust, or love, of pity, or regard; as an enemy whom all should join to drive out of society, as a pest which all should avoid, or as a weed which all should trample.

It is not but by experience, that we are taught the possibility of retaining some virtues, and rejecting others, or of being good or bad to a particular degree. For it is very easy to the solitary reasoner to prove that the same arguments by which the mind is fortified against one crime are of equal force against all, and the consequence very naturally follows, that he whom they fail to move on any occasion, has either never considered them, or has by some fallacy taught himself to evade their validity; and that, therefore, when a man is known to be guilty of one crime, no farther evidence is needful of his depravity and corruption.

Yet such is the state of all mortal virtue, that it is always uncertain and variable, sometimes extending to the whole compass of duty, and sometimes shrinking into a narrow space, and fortifying only a few avenues of the heart, while all the rest is left open to the incursions of appetite, or given up to the dominion of wickedness. Nothing therefore is more unjust than to judge of man by too short an acquaintance, and too slight inspection; for it often happens, that in the loose, and thoughtless, and dissipated, there is a secret radical worth, which may shoot out by proper cultivation; that the spark of heaven, though dimmed and obstructed, is yet not extinguished, but may by the breath of counsel and exhortation be kindled into flame.

To imagine that every one who is not completely good is irrecoverably abandoned, is to suppose that all are capable of the same degrees of excellence; it is indeed to exact, from all, that perfection which none ever can attain. And since the purest virtue is consistent with some vice, and the virtue of the greatest number with almost an equal proportion of contrary qualities, let none too hastily conclude that all goodness is lost, though it may for a time be clouded and overwhelmed; for most minds are the slaves of external circumstances, and conform to any hand that undertakes to mould them, roll down any torrent of custom in which they happen to be caught, or bend to any importunity that bears hard against them.

It may be particularly observed of women, that they are for the most part good or bad, as they fall among those who practise vice or virtue; and that neither education nor reason gives them much security against the influence of example. Whether it be that they have less courage to stand against opposition, or that their desire of admiration makes them sacrifice their principles to the poor pleasure of worthless praise, it is certain, whatever be the cause, that female goodness seldom keeps its ground against laughter, flattery, or fashion.

For this reason, every one should consider himself as entrusted, not only with his own conduct, but with that of others; and as accountable, not only for the duties which he neglects, or the crimes that he commits, but for that negligence and irregularity which he may encourage or inculcate. Every man, in whatever station, has, or endeavours to have his followers, admirers, and imitators, and has therefore the influence of his example to watch with care; he ought to avoid not only crimes but the appearance of crimes, and not only to practise virtue, but to applaud, countenance, and support it. For it is possible that for want of attention we may teach others faults from which ourselves are free, or by a cowardly desertion of a cause which we ourselves approve, may pervert those who fix their eyes upon us, and having no rule of their own to guide their course, are easily misled by the aberrations of that example which they chuse for their direction.

No. 71. Tuesday, 20 November 1750.

Vivere quod propero pauper, nec inutilis annis
Da veniam, properat vivere nemo satis.
MART.

True, sir, to live I haste, your pardon give,
For tell me, who makes haste enough to live?
F. LEWIS.

Many words and sentences are so frequently heard in the mouths of men, that a superficial observer is inclined to believe, that they must contain some primary principle, some great rule of action, which it is proper always to have present to the attention, and by which the use of every hour is to be adjusted. Yet, if we consider the conduct of those sententious philosophers, it will often be found, that they repeat these aphorisms, merely because they have somewhere heard them, because they have nothing else to say, or because they think veneration gained by such appearances of wisdom, but that no ideas are annexed to the words, and that, according to the old blunder of the followers of Aristotle, their souls are mere pipes or organs, which transmit sounds, but do not understand them.

Of this kind is the well known and well attested position, *that life is short*, which may be heard among mankind by an attentive auditor, many times a day, but which never yet within my reach of observation left any impression upon the mind; and perhaps if my readers will turn their thoughts back upon their old friends, they will find it difficult to call a single man to remembrance, who appeared to know that life was short till he was about to lose it.

It is observable that *Horace*, in his account of the characters of men, as they are diversified by the various influence of time, remarks, that the old man is *dilator, spe longus,* given to procrastination, and inclined to extend his hopes to a great distance. So far are we, generally, from thinking what we often say of the shortness of life, that at the time when it is necessarily shortest, we form projects which we delay to execute, indulge such expectations as nothing but a long train of events can gratify, and suffer those passions to gain upon us, which are only excusable in the prime of life.

These reflections were lately excited in my mind, by an evening's conversation with my friend *Prospero,* who at the age of fifty-five, has bought an estate, and is now contriving to dispose and cultivate it with uncommon elegance. His great pleasure is to walk among stately trees, and lye musing in the heat of noon under their shade; he is therefore maturely considering how he shall dispose his walks and his groves, and has at last determined to send for the best plans from *Italy,* and forbear planting till the next season.

Thus is life trifled away in preparations to do what never can be done, if it be left unattempted till all the requisites which imagination can suggest are gathered together. Where our design terminates only in our own satisfaction, the mistake is of no great importance; for the pleasure of expecting enjoyment, is often greater than that of obtaining it, and the completion of almost every wish is found a disappointment; but when many others are interested in an undertaking, when any design is formed, in which the improvement or security of mankind is involved, nothing is more unworthy either of wisdom or benevolence, than to delay it from time to time, or to forget how much every day that passes over us, takes away from our power, and how soon an idle purpose to do an action, sinks into a mournful wish that it had once been done.

We are frequently importuned, by the bacchanalian writers, to lay hold on the present hour, to catch the pleasures within our reach, and remember that futurity is not at our command.

> Τὸ ῥόδον ἀκμάζει βαιὸν χρόνον· ἤν δὲ παρέλθῃ,
> Ζητῶν εὑρήσεις οὐ ῥόδον, ἀλλά βάτον.

> Soon fades the rose; once past the fragrant hour,
> The loiterer finds a bramble for a flow'r.

But surely these exhortations may, with equal propriety, be applied to better purposes; it may be at least inculcated, that pleasures are more safely postponed than virtues, and that greater loss is suffered by missing an opportunity of doing good, than an hour of giddy frolick and noisy merriment.

When *Baxter* had lost a thousand pounds, which he had laid up for the erection of a school, he used frequently to mention the misfortune, as an incitement to be charitable while God gives the power of bestowing, and considered himself as culpable in some degree for having left a good action in the hands of chance, and suffered his benevolence to be defeated for want of quickness and diligence.

It is lamented by *Hearne*, the learned antiquary of *Oxford*, that this general forgetfulness of the fragility of life, has remarkably infected the students of monuments and records; as their employment consists first in collecting and afterwards in arranging or abstracting what libraries afford them, they ought to amass no more than they can digest; but when they have undertaken a work, they go on searching and transcribing, call for new supplies, when they are already overburdened, and at last leave their work unfinished. *It is*, says he, *the business of a good antiquary, as of a good man, to have mortality always before him.*

Thus, not only in the slumber of sloth, but in the dissipation of ill directed industry, is the shortness of life generally forgotten. As some men lose their hours in laziness, because they suppose, that there is time enough for the reparation of neglect; others busy themselves in providing that no length of life may want employment; and it often happens, that sluggishness and activity are equally surprised by the last summons, and perish not more differently from each other, than the fowl that received the shot in her flight, from her that is killed upon the bush.

Among the many improvements, made by the last centuries in human knowledge, may be numbered the exact calculations of the value of life; but whatever may be their use in traffick, they seem very little to have advanced morality. They have hitherto been rather applied to the acquisition of money, than of wisdom; the computer refers none of his calculations to his own tenure, but persists, in contempt of probability, to foretel old age to himself, and believes that he is marked out to reach the utmost verge of human existence, and see thousands and ten thousands fall into the grave.

So deeply is this fallacy rooted in the heart, and so strongly guarded by hope and fear against the approach of reason, that neither science nor experience can shake it, and we act as if life were without end, though we see and confess its uncertainty and shortness.

Divines have, with great strength and ardour, shewn the absurdity of delaying reformation and repentance; a degree of folly indeed, which sets eternity to hazard. It is the same weakness in proportion to the importance of the neglect, to transfer any care, which now claims our attention, to a future time; we subject ourselves to needless dangers from accidents which early diligence would have obviated, or perplex our minds by vain precautions, and make provision for the execution of designs, of which the opportunity once missed never will return.

As he that lives longest lives but a little while, every man may be certain that he has no time to waste. The duties of life are commensurate to its duration, and every day brings its task, which if neglected, is doubled on the morrow. But he that has already trifled away those months and years, in which he should have laboured, must remember that he has now only a part of that of which the whole is little; and that since the few moments remaining are to be considered as the last trust of heaven, not one is to be lost.

No. 72. Saturday, 24 November 1750.

Omnis Aristippum *decuit status, et color, et res,*
Sectantem majora fere; presentibus æquum.

HOR.

Yet *Aristippus* ev'ry dress became;
In ev'ry various change of life the same:
And though he aim'd at things of higher kind,
Yet to the present held an equal mind.

FRANCIS.

To the RAMBLER.

SIR,

Those who exalt themselves into the chair of instruction, without enquiring whether any will submit to their authority, have not sufficiently considered how much of human life passes in little incidents, cursory conversation, slight business, and casual amusements; and therefore they have endeavoured only to inculcate the more awful virtues, without condescending to regard those petty qualities, which grow important only by their frequency, and which though they produce no single acts of heroism, nor astonish us by great events, yet are every moment exerting their influence upon us, and make the draught of life sweet or bitter by imperceptible instillations. They operate unseen and unregarded, as change of air makes us sick or healthy, though we breathe it without attention, and only know the particles that impregnate it by their salutary or malignant effects.

You have shewn yourself not ignorant of the value of those subaltern endowments, yet have hitherto neglected to recommend good humour to the world, though a little reflection will shew you that it is the *balm of being*, the quality to which all that adorns or elevates mankind must owe its power of pleasing. Without good humour, learning and bravery can only confer that superiority which swells the heart of the lion in the desart, where he roars without reply, and ravages without resistance. Without good humour, virtue may awe by its dignity, and amaze by its brightness; but must always be viewed at a distance, and will scarcely gain a friend or attract an imitator.

Good humour may be defined a habit of being pleased; a constant and perennial softness of manner, easiness of approach, and suavity of disposition; like that which every man perceives in himself, when the first transports of new felicity have subsided, and his thoughts are only kept in motion by a slow succession of soft impulses. Good humour is a state between gayety and unconcern; the act or emanation of a mind at leisure to regard the gratification of another.

It is imagined by many, that whenever they aspire to please, they are required to be merry, and to shew the gladness of their souls by flights of pleasantry, and bursts of laughter. But, though these men may be for a time heard with applause and admiration, they seldom delight us long. We enjoy them a little, and then retire to easiness and good humour, as the eye gazes a while on eminences glittering with the sun, but soon turns aching away to verdure and to flowers.

Gayety is to good humour as animal perfumes to vegetable fragrance; the one overpowers weak spirits, and the other recreates and revives them. Gayety seldom fails to give some pain; the hearers either strain their faculties to accompany its towerings, or are left behind in envy and despair. Good humour boasts no faculties which every one does not believe in his own power, and pleases principally by not offending.

It is well known that the most certain way to give any man pleasure, is to persuade him that you receive pleasure from him, to encourage him to freedom and confidence, and to avoid any such appearance of superiority as may overbear and depress him. We see many that by this art only, spend their days in the midst of caresses, invitations, and civilities; and without any extraordinary qualities or attainments, are the universal favourites of both sexes, and certainly find a friend in every place. The darlings of the world will, indeed, be generally found such as excite neither jealousy nor fear, and are not considered as candidates for any eminent degree of reputation, but content themselves with common accomplishments, and endeavour rather to solicit kindness than to raise esteem; therefore in assemblies and places of resort it seldom fails to happen, that though at the entrance of some particular person every face brightens with gladness, and every hand is extended in salutation, yet if you persue him beyond the first exchange of civilities, you will find him of very small importance, and only welcome to the company, as one by whom all conceive themselves admired, and with whom any one is at liberty to amuse himself when he can find no other auditor or companion, as one with whom all are at ease, who will hear a jest without criticism, and a narrative without contradiction, who laughs with every wit, and yields to every disputer.

There are many whose vanity always inclines them to associate with those from whom they have no reason to fear mortification; and there are times in which the wise and the knowing are willing to receive praise without the labour of deserving it, in which the most elevated mind is willing to descend, and the most active to be at rest. All therefore are at some hour or another fond of companions whom they can entertain upon easy terms, and who will relieve them from solitude, without condemning them to vigilance and caution. We are most inclined to love when we have nothing to fear, and he that encourages us to please ourselves, will not be long without preference in our affection to those whose learning holds us at the distance of pupils, or whose wit calls all attention from us, and leaves us without importance and without regard.

It is remarked by prince *Henry*, when he sees Falstaff lying on the ground, that *he could have better spared a better man*. He was well acquainted with the vices and follies of him whom he lamented, but while his conviction compelled him to do justice to superior qualities, his tenderness still broke out at the remembrance of *Falstaff*, of the chearful companion, the loud buffoon, with whom he had passed his time in all the luxury of idleness, who had gladded him with unenvied merriment, and whom he could at once enjoy and despise.

You may perhaps think this account of those who are distinguished for their good humour, not very consistent with the praises which I have bestowed upon it. But surely nothing can more evidently shew the value of this quality, than that it recommends those who are destitute of all other excellencies, and procures regard to the trifling, friendship to the worthless, and affection to the dull.

Good humour is indeed generally degraded by the characters in which it is found; for being considered as a cheap and vulgar quality, we find it often neglected by those that having excellencies of higher reputation and brighter splendor, perhaps imagine that they have some right to gratify themselves at the expense of others, and are to demand compliance, rather than to practise it. It is by some unfortunate mistake that almost all those who have any claim to esteem or love, press their pretensions with too little consideration of others. This mistake my own interest as well as my zeal for general happiness makes me desirous to rectify, for I have a friend, who because he knows his own fidelity, and usefulness, is never willing to sink into a companion. I have a wife whose beauty first subdued me, and whose wit confirmed her conquest, but whose beauty now serves no other purpose than to entitle her to tyranny, and whose wit is only used to justify perverseness.

Surely nothing can be more unreasonable than to lose the will to please, when we are conscious of the power, or show more cruelty than to chuse any kind of influence before that of kindness. He that regards the welfare of others, should make his virtue approachable, that it may be loved and copied; and he that considers the wants which every man feels, or will feel of external assistance, must rather wish to be surrounded by those that love him, than by those that admire his excellencies, or sollicit his favours; for admiration ceases with novelty, and interest gains its end and retires. A man whose great qualities want the ornament of superficial attractions, is like a naked mountain with mines of gold, which will be frequented only till the treasure is exhausted.

I am, &c.

PHILOMIDES.

No. 73. Tuesday, 27 November 1750.

Stulte quid heu votis frustra puerilibus optas
Quæ non ulla tulit, fertve, feretve dies.

OVID.

Why thinks the fool with childish hope to see
What neither is, nor was, nor e'er shall be?

ELPHINSTON.

To the RAMBLER.

SIR,

If you feel any of that compassion, which you recommend to others, you will not disregard a case which I have reason from observation to believe very common, and which I know by experience to be very miserable. And though the querulous are seldom received with great ardour of kindness, I hope to escape the mortification of finding that my lamentations spread the contagion of impatience, and produce anger rather than tenderness. I write not merely to vent the swelling of my heart, but to enquire by what means I may recover my tranquillity; and shall endeavour at brevity in my narrative, having long known that complaint quickly tires, however elegant, or however just.

I was born in a remote county, of a family that boasts alliances with the greatest names in *English* history, and extends its claims of affinity to the *Tudors* and *Plantagenets*. My ancestors, by little and little, wasted their patrimony, till my father had not enough left for the support of a family, without descending to the cultivation of his own grounds, being condemned to pay three sisters the fortunes allotted them by my grandfather, who is suspected to have made his will when he was incapable of adjusting properly the claims of his children, and who, perhaps without design, enriched his daughters by beggaring his son. My aunts being, at the death of their father, neither young nor beautiful, nor very eminent for softness of behaviour, were suffered to live unsolicited, and by accumulating the interest of their portions grew every day richer and prouder. My father pleased himself with foreseeing that the possessions of those ladies must revert at last to the hereditary estate, and, that his family might lose none of its dignity, resolved to keep me untainted with a lucrative employment; whenever therefore I discovered any inclination to the improvement of my condition, my mother never failed to put me in mind of my birth, and charged me to do nothing with which I might be reproached, when I should come to my aunts' estate.

In all the perplexities or vexations which want of money brought upon us, it was our constant practice to have recourse to futurity. If any of our neighbours surpassed us in appearance, we went home and contrived an equipage, with which the death of my aunts was to supply us. If any purse-proud upstart was deficient in respect, vengeance was referred to the time in which our estate was to be repaired. We registered every act of civility and rudeness, enquired the number of dishes at every feast, and minuted the furniture of every house, that we might, when the hour of affluence should come, be able to eclipse all their splendor, and surpass all their magnificence.

Upon plans of elegance and schemes of pleasure the day rose and set, and the year went round unregarded, while we were busied in laying out plantations on ground not yet our own, and deliberating whether the manor-house should be rebuilt or repaired. This was the amusement of our leisure, and the solace of our exigencies; we met together only to contrive how our approaching fortune should be enjoyed; for in this our conversation always ended, on whatever subject it began. We had none of the collateral interests, which diversify the life of others with joys and hopes, but had turned our whole attention on one event, which we could neither hasten nor retard, and had no other object of curiosity, than the health or sickness of my aunts, of which we were careful to procure very exact and early intelligence.

This visionary opulence for a while soothed our imagination, but afterwards fired our wishes, and exasperated our necessities, and my father could not always restrain himself from exclaiming, that *no creature had so many lives as a cat and an old maid*. At last upon the recovery of his sister from an ague, which she was supposed to have caught by sparing fire, he began to lose his stomach, and four months afterwards sunk into the grave.

My mother, who loved her husband, survived him but a little while, and left me the sole heir of their lands, their schemes, and their wishes. As I had not enlarged my conceptions either by books or conversation, I differed only from my father by the freshness of my cheeks, and the vigour of my step; and, like him, gave way to no thoughts but of enjoying the wealth which my aunts were hoarding.

At length the eldest fell ill. I paid the civilities and compliments which sickness requires with the utmost punctuality. I dreamed every night of escutcheons and white gloves, and enquired every morning at an early hour, whether there were any news of my dear aunt. At last a messenger was sent to inform me that I must come to her without the delay of a moment. I went and heard her last advice, but opening her will found that she had left her fortune to her second sister.

I hung my head; the younger sister threatned to be married, and every thing was disappointment and discontent. I was in danger of losing irreparably one third of my hopes, and was condemned still to wait for the rest. Of part of my terror I was soon eased; for the youth, whom his relations would have compelled to marry the old lady, after innumerable stipulations, articles, and settlements, ran away with the daughter of his father's groom; and my aunt, upon this conviction of the perfidy of man, resolved never to listen more to amorous addresses.

Ten years longer I dragged the shackles of expectation, without ever suffering a day to pass, in which I did not compute how much my chance was improved of being rich tomorrow. At last the second lady died, after a short illness, which yet was long enough to afford her time for the disposal of her estate, which she gave to me after the death of her sister.

I was now relieved from part of my misery; a larger fortune, though not in my power, was certain and unalienable; nor was there now any danger, that I might at last be frustrated of my hopes by a fret of dotage, the flatteries of a chambermaid, the whispers of a tale-bearer, or the officiousness of a nurse. But my wealth was yet in reversion, my aunt was to be buried before I could emerge to grandeur and pleasure; and there were yet, according to my father's observation, nine lives between me and happiness.

I however lived on, without any clamours of discontent, and comforted myself with considering, that all are mortal, and they who are continually decaying, must at last be destroyed.

But let no man from this time suffer his felicity to depend on the death of his aunt. The good gentlewoman was very regular in her hours, and simple in her diet, and in walking or sitting still, waking or sleeping, had always in view the preservation of her health. She was subject to no disorder but hypochondriac dejection; by which, without intention, she encreased my miseries, for whenever the weather was cloudy, she would take her bed and send me notice that her time was come. I went with all the haste of eagerness, and sometimes received passionate injunctions to be kind to her maid, and directions how the last offices should be performed; but if before my arrival the sun happened to break out, or the wind to change, I met her at the door, or found her in the garden, bustling and vigilant, with all the tokens of long life.

Sometimes however she fell into distempers, and was thrice given over by the doctor, yet she found means of slipping through the gripe of death, and after having tortured me three months at each time with violent alternations of hope and fear, came out of her chamber without any other hurt than the loss of flesh, which in a few weeks she recovered by broths and jellies.

As most have sagacity sufficient to guess at the desires of an heir, it was the constant practice of those who were hoping at second hand, and endeavoured to secure my favour against the time when I should be rich, to pay their court, by informing me that my aunt began to droop, that she had lately a bad night, that she coughed feebly, and that she could never climb *May* hill; or at least, that the autumn would carry her off. Thus was I flattered in the winter with the piercing winds of *March*, and in summer, with the fogs of *September*. But she lived through spring and fall, and set heat and cold at defiance, till after near half a century, I buried her on the fourteenth of last June, aged ninety-three years, five months, and six days.

For two months after her death I was rich, and was pleased with that obsequiousness and reverence which wealth instantaneously procures. But this joy is now past, and I have returned again to my old habit of wishing. Being accustomed to give the future full power over my mind, and to start away from the scene before me to some expected enjoyment, I deliver up myself to the tyranny of every desire which fancy suggests, and long for a thousand things which I am unable to procure. Money has much less power, than is ascribed to it by those that want it. I had formed schemes which I cannot execute, I had supposed events which do not come to pass, and the rest of my life must pass in craving solicitude, unless you can find some remedy for a mind, corrupted with an inveterate disease of wishing, and unable to think on any thing but wants, which reason tells me will never be supplied.

I am, &c.
CUPIDUS.

No. 76. Saturday, 8 December 1750.

―――― *Silvis ubi passim*
Palantes error certo de tramite pellit,
Ille sinistrorsum, hic dextrorsum abit, unus utrique
Error, sed variis illudit partibus.

HOR.

While mazy error draws mankind astray
From truth's sure path, each takes his devious way:
One to the right, one to the left recedes,
Alike deluded, as each fancy leads.

ELPHINSTON.

It is easy for every man, whatever be his character with others, to find reasons for esteeming himself, and therefore censure, contempt, or conviction of crimes, seldom deprive him of his own favour. Those, indeed, who can see only external facts, may look upon him with abhorrence, but when he calls himself to his own tribunal, he finds every fault, if not absolutely effaced, yet so much palliated by the goodness of his intention, and the cogency of the motive, that very little guilt or turpitude remains; and when he takes a survey of the whole complication of his character, he discovers so many latent excellencies, so many virtues that want but an opportunity to exert themselves in act, and so many kind wishes for universal happiness, that he looks on himself as suffering unjustly under the infamy of single failings, while the general temper of his mind is unknown or unregarded.

It is natural to mean well, when only abstracted ideas of virtue are proposed to the mind, and no particular passion turns us aside from rectitude; and so willing is every man to flatter himself, that the difference between approving laws, and obeying them, is frequently forgotten; he that acknowledges the obligations of morality, and pleases his vanity with enforcing them to others, concludes himself zealous in the cause of virtue, though he has no longer any regard to her precepts, than they conform to his own desires; and counts himself among her warmest lovers, because he praises her beauty, though every rival steals away his heart.

There are, however, great numbers who have little recourse to the refinements of speculation, but who yet live at peace with themselves, by means which require less understanding, or less attention. When their hearts are burthened with the consciousness of a crime, instead of seeking for some remedy within themselves, they look round upon the rest of mankind, to find others tainted with the same guilt: they please themselves with observing, that they have numbers on their side; and that though they are hunted out from the society of good men, they are not likely to be condemned to solitude.

It may be observed, perhaps without exception, that none are so industrious to detect wickedness, or so ready to impute it, as they whose crimes are apparent and confessed. They envy an unblemished reputation, and what they envy they are busy to destroy: they are unwilling to suppose themselves meaner, and more corrupt than others, and therefore willingly pull down from their elevations those with whom they cannot rise to an equality. No man yet was ever wicked without secret discontent, and according to the different degrees of remaining virtue, or unextinguished reason, he either endeavours to reform himself, or corrupt others; either to regain the station which he has quitted, or prevail on others to imitate his defection.

It has been always considered as an alleviation of misery not to suffer alone, even when union and society can contribute nothing to resistance or escape; some comfort of the same kind seems to incite wickedness to seek associates, though indeed another reason may be given, for as guilt is propagated the power of reproach is diminished, and among numbers equally detestable every individual may be sheltered from shame, though not from conscience.

Another lenitive by which the throbs of the breast are assuaged, is, the contemplation, not of the same, but of different crimes. He that cannot justify himself by his resemblance to others, is ready to try some other expedient, and to enquire what will rise to his advantage from opposition and dissimilitude. He easily finds some faults in every human being, which he weighs against his own, and easily makes them preponderate while he keeps the balance in his own hand, and throws in or takes out at his pleasure circumstances that make them heavier or lighter. He then triumphs in his comparative purity, and sets himself at ease, not because he can refute the charges advanced against him, but because he can censure his accusers with equal justice, and no longer fears the arrows of reproach, when he has stored his magazine of malice with weapons equally sharp and equally envenomed.

This practice, though never just, is yet specious and artful, when the censure is directed against deviations to the contrary extreme. The man who is branded with cowardice, may, with some appearance of propriety, turn all his force of argument against a stupid contempt of life, and rash precipitation into unnecessary danger. Every recession from temerity is an approach towards cowardice, and though it be confessed that bravery, like other virtues, stands between faults on either hand, yet the place of the middle point may always be disputed; he may therefore often impose upon careless understandings, by turning the attention wholly from himself, and keeping it fixed invariably on the opposite fault; and by shewing how many evils are avoided by his behaviour, he may conceal for a time those which are incurred.

But vice has not always opportunities or address for such artful subterfuges; men often extenuate their own guilt, only by vague and general charges upon others, or endeavour to gain rest to themselves, by pointing some other prey to the persuit of censure.

Every whisper of infamy is industriously circulated, every hint of suspicion eagerly improved, and every failure of conduct joyfully published, by those whose interest it is, that the eye and voice of the publick should be employed on any rather than on themselves.

All these artifices, and a thousand others equally vain and equally despicable, are incited by that conviction of the deformity of wickedness, from which none can set himself free, and by an absurd desire to separate the cause from the effects, and to enjoy the profit of crimes without suffering the shame. Men are willing to try all methods of reconciling guilt and quiet, and when their understandings are stubborn and uncomplying, raise their passions against them, and hope to over-power their own knowledge.

It is generally not so much the desire of men, sunk into depravity, to deceive the world as themselves, for when no particular circumstances make them dependant on others, infamy disturbs them little, but as it revives their remorse, and is echoed to them from their own hearts. The sentence most dreaded is that of reason and conscience, which they would engage on their side at any price but the labours of duty, and the sorrows of repentance. For this purpose every seducement and fallacy is sought, the hopes still rest upon some new experiment till life is at an end; and the last hour steals on unperceived, while the faculties are engaged in resisting reason, and repressing the sense of the divine disapprobation.

No. 77. Tuesday, 11 December 1750.

Os dignum æterno nitidum quod fulgeat Auro,
Si mallet laudare Deum, cui sordida Monstra
Prætulit, et liquidam temeravit Crimine vocem.
PRUDENT.

A golden statue such a wit might claim,
Had God and virtue rais'd the noble flame;
But ah! how lewd a subject has he sung,
What vile obscenity profanes his tongue.
F. LEWIS.

Among those, whose hopes of distinction or riches, arise from an opinion of their intellectual attainments, it has been, from age to age, an established custom to complain of the ingratitude of mankind to their instructors, and the discouragement which men of genius and study suffer from avarice and ignorance, from the prevalence of false taste, and the encroachment of barbarity.

Men are most powerfully affected by those evils which themselves feel, or which appear before their own eyes; and as there has never been a time of such general felicity, but that many have failed to obtain the rewards to which they had, in their own judgment, a just claim, some offended writer has always declaimed in the rage of disappointment, against his age or nation; nor is there one who has not fallen upon times more unfavourable to learning than any former century, or who does not wish, that he had been reserved in the insensibility of non-existence to some happier hour, when literary merit shall no longer be despis'd, and the gifts and caresses of mankind shall recompence the toils of study, and add lustre to the charms of wit.

Many of these clamours are undoubtedly to be considered only as the bursts of pride never to be satisfied, as the prattle of affectation mimicking distresses unfelt, or as the commonplaces of vanity solicitous for splendour of sentences, and acuteness of remark. Yet it cannot be denied that frequent discontent must proceed from frequent hardships, and tho' it is evident, that not more than one age or people can deserve the censure of being more averse from learning than any other, yet at all times knowledge must have encountered impediments, and wit been mortified with contempt, or harrassed with persecution.

It is not necessary, however, to join immediately in the outcry, or to condemn mankind as pleased with ignorance, or always envious of superior abilities. The miseries of the learned have been related by themselves; and since they have not been found exempt from that partiality with which men look upon their own actions and sufferings, we may conclude that they have not forgotten to deck their cause with the brightest ornaments, and strongest colours. The logician collected all his subtilties when they were to be employed in his own defence; and the master of rhetoric exerted against his adversary all the arts by which hatred is embittered, and indignation inflamed.

To believe no man in his own cause, is the standing and perpetual rule of distributive justice. Since therefore, in the controversy between the learned and their enemies, we have only the pleas of one party, of the party more able to delude our understandings, and engage our passions, we must determine our opinion by facts uncontested, and evidences on each side allowed to be genuine.

By this procedure, I know not whether the students will find their cause promoted, or the compassion which they expect much increased. Let their conduct be impartially surveyed; let them be allowed no longer to direct attention at their pleasure, by expatiating on their own deserts; let neither the dignity of knowledge over-awe the judgment, nor the graces of elegance seduce it. It will then, perhaps, be found, that they were not able to produce claims to kinder treatment, but provoked the calamities which they suffered, and seldom wanted friends, but when they wanted virtue.

That few men, celebrated for theoretic wisdom, live with conformity to their precepts, must be readily confessed; and we cannot wonder that the indignation of mankind rises with great vehemence against those, who neglect the duties which they appear to know with so strong conviction the necessity of performing. Yet since no man has power of acting equal to that of thinking, I know not whether the speculatist may not sometimes incur censures too severe, and by those, who form ideas of his life from their knowledge of his books, be considered as worse than others, only because he was expected to be better.

He, by whose writings the heart is rectified, the appetites counter-acted, and the passions repressed, may be considered as not unprofitable to the great republick of humanity, even though his behaviour should not always exemplify his rules. His instructions may diffuse their influence to regions, in which it will not be inquired, whether the author be *albus an ater*, good or bad; to times, when all his faults and all his follies shall be lost in forgetfulness, among things of no concern or importance to the world; and he may kindle in thousands and ten thousands that flame which burnt but dimly in himself, through the fumes of passion, or the damps of cowardice. The vicious moralist may be considered as a taper, by which we are lighted through the labyrinth of complicated passions; he extends his radiance farther than his heat, and guides all that are within view, but burns only those who make too near approaches.

Yet, since good or harm must be received for the most part from those to whom we are familiarly known, he whose vices over-power his virtues, in the compass to which his vices can extend, has no reason to complain that he meets not with affection or veneration, when those with whom he passes his life are more corrupted by his practice than enlightened by his ideas. Admiration begins where acquaintance ceases; and his favourers are distant, but his enemies at hand.

Yet many have dared to boast of neglected merit, and to challenge their age for cruelty and folly, of whom it cannot be alleged that they have endeavoured to increase the wisdom or virtue of their readers. They have been at once profligate in their lives, and licentious in their compositions; have not only forsaken the paths of virtue, but attempted to lure others after them. They have smoothed the road of perdition, covered with flowers the thorns of guilt, and taught temptation sweeter notes, softer blandishments, and stronger allurements.

It has been apparently the settled purpose of some writers, whose powers and acquisitions place them high in the ranks of literature, to set fashion on the side of wickedness; to recommend debauchery, and lewdness, by associating them with qualities most likely to dazzle the discernment, and attract the affections; and to show innocence and goodness with such attendant weaknesses as necessarily expose them to contempt and derision.

Such naturally found intimates among the corrupt, the thoughtless, and the intemperate; passed their lives amidst the levities of sportive idleness, or the warm professions of drunken friendship; and fed their hopes with the promises of wretches, whom their precepts had taught to scoff at truth. But when fools had laughed away their sprightliness, and the languors of excess could no longer be relieved, they saw their protectors hourly drop away, and wondered and stormed to find themselves abandoned. Whether their companions persisted in wickedness, or returned to virtue, they were left equally without assistance; for debauchery is selfish and negligent, and from virtue the virtuous only can expect regard.

It is said by *Florus* of *Catiline*, who died in the midst of slaughtered enemies, that *his death had been illustrious, had it been suffered for his country*. Of the wits, who have languished away life under the pressures of poverty, or in the restlessness of suspense, caressed and rejected, flattered and despised, as they were of more or less use to those who stiled themselves their patrons, it might be observed, that their miseries would enforce compassion, had they been brought upon them by honesty and religion.

The wickedness of a loose or profane author is more atrocious than that of the giddy libertine, or drunken ravisher, not only because it extends its effects wider; as a pestilence that taints the air is more destructive than poison infused in a draught, but because it is committed with cool deliberation. By the instantaneous violence of desire a good man may sometimes be surprised before reflection can come to his rescue; when the appetites have strengthened their influence by habit, they are not easily resisted or suppress'd; but for the frigid villainy of studious lewdness, for the calm malignity of laboured impiety, what apology can be invented? What punishment can be adequate to the crime of him who retires to solitudes for the refinement of debauchery; who tortures his fancy, and ransacks his memory, only that he may leave the world less virtuous than he found it; that he may intercept the hopes of the rising generation; and spread snares for the soul with more dexterity?

What were their motives, or what their excuses, is below the dignity of reason to examine. If having extinguished in themselves the distinction of right and wrong, they were insensible of the mischief which they promoted, they deserved to be hunted down by the general compact, as no longer partaking of social nature; if influenced by the corruption of patrons, or readers, they sacrificed their own convictions to vanity or interest, they were to be abhorred with more acrimony than he that murders for pay; since they committed greater crimes without greater temptations.

Of him, to whom much is given, much shall be required. Those, whom God has favoured with superiour faculties, and made eminent for quickness of intuition, and accuracy of distinctions, will certainly be regarded as culpable in his eye, for defects and deviations which, in souls less enlightened, may be guiltless. But, surely, none can think without horror on that man's condition, who has been more wicked in proportion as he had more means of excelling in virtue, and used the light imparted from heaven only to embellish folly, and shed lustre upon crimes.

No. 79. Tuesday, 18 December 1750.

Tam sæpe nostrum decipi Fabullum, quid
Miraris, Aule? Semper bonus homo tiro est.
                                        MART.

You wonder I've so little wit,
Friend *John*, so often to be bit,—
None better guard against a cheat
Than he who is a knave compleat.
                    F. LEWIS.

Suspicion, however necessary it may be to our safe passage through ways beset on all sides by fraud and malice, has been always considered, when it exceeds the common measures, as a token of depravity and corruption; and a *Greek* writer of sentences has laid down as a standing maxim, that *he who believes not another on his oath, knows himself to be perjured.*

We can form our opinions of that which we know not, only by placing it in comparison with something that we know: whoever therefore is over-run with suspicion, and detects artifice and stratagem in every proposal, must either have learned by experience or observation the wickedness of mankind, and been taught to avoid fraud by having often suffered or seen treachery, or he must derive his judgment from the consciousness of his own disposition, and impute to others the same inclinations which he feels predominant in himself.

To learn caution by turning our eyes upon life, and observing the arts by which negligence is surprised, timidity overborne, and credulity amused, requires either great latitude of converse and long acquaintance with business, or uncommon activity of vigilance, and acuteness of penetration. When therefore a young man, not distinguished by vigour of intellect, comes into the world full of scruples and diffidence; makes a bargain with many provisional limitations; hesitates in his answer to a common question, lest more should be intended than he can immediately discover; has a long reach in detecting the projects of his acquaintance; considers every caress as an act of hypocrisy, and feels neither gratitude nor affection from the tenderness of his friends, because he believes no one to have any real tenderness but for himself; whatever expectations this early sagacity may raise of his future eminence or riches, I can seldom forbear to consider him as a wretch incapable of generosity or benevolence, as a villain early completed beyond the need of common opportunities and gradual temptations.

Upon men of this class instruction and admonition are generally thrown away, because they consider artifice and deceit as proofs of understanding; they are misled at the same time by the two great seducers of the world, vanity and interest, and not only look upon those who act with openness and confidence, as condemned by their principles to obscurity and want, but as contemptible for narrowness of comprehension, shortness of views, and slowness of contrivance.

The world has been long amused with the mention of policy in publick transactions, and of art in private affairs; they have been considered as the effects of great qualities, and as unattainable by men of the common level: yet I have not found many performances either of art, or policy, that required such stupendous efforts of intellect, or might not have been effected by falshood and impudence, without the assistance of any other powers. To profess what he does not mean, to promise what he cannot perform, to flatter ambition with prospects of promotion, and misery with hopes of relief, to sooth pride with appearances of submission, and appease enmity by blandishments and bribes, can surely imply nothing more or greater than a mind devoted wholly to its own purposes, a face that cannot blush, and a heart that cannot feel.

These practices are so mean and base, that he who finds in himself no tendency to use them, cannot easily believe that they are considered by others with less detestation; he therefore suffers himself to slumber in false security, and becomes a prey to those who applaud their own subtilty, because they know how to steal upon his sleep, and exult in the success which they could never have obtained, had they not attempted a man better than themselves, who was hindered from obviating their stratagems, not by folly, but by innocence.

Suspicion is, indeed, a temper so uneasy and restless, that it is very justly appointed the concomitant of guilt. It is said, that no torture is equal to the inhibition of sleep long continued; a pain, to which the state of that man bears a very exact analogy, who dares never give rest to his vigilance and circumspection, but considers himself as surrounded by secret foes, and fears to entrust his children, or his friend, with the secret that throbs in his breast, and the anxieties that break into his face. To avoid, at this expence, those evils to which easiness and friendship might have exposed him, is surely to buy safety at too dear a rate, and, in the language of the *Roman* satirist, to save life by losing all for which a wise man would live.

When in the diet of the *German* empire, as *Camerarius* relates, the princes were once displaying their felicity, and each boasting the advantages of his own dominions, one who possessed a country not remarkable for the grandeur of its cities, or the fertility of its soil, rose to speak, and the rest listened between pity and contempt, till he declared, in honour of his territories, that he could travel through them without a guard, and if he was weary, sleep in safety upon the lap of the first man whom he should meet; a commendation which would have been ill exchanged for the boast of palaces, pastures, or streams.

Suspicion is not less an enemy to virtue than to happiness: he that is already corrupt is naturally suspicious, and he that becomes suspicious will quickly be corrupt. It is too common for us to learn the frauds by which ourselves have suffered; men who are once persuaded that deceit will be employed against them, sometimes think the same arts justified by the necessity of defence. Even they whose virtue is too well established to give way to example, or be shaken by sophistry, must yet feel their love of mankind diminished with their esteem, and grow less zealous for the happiness of those by whom they imagine their own happiness endangered.

Thus we find old age, upon which suspicion has been strongly impressed by long intercourse with the world, inflexible and severe, not easily softened by submission, melted by complaint, or subdued by supplication. Frequent experience of counterfeited miseries, and dissembled virtue, in time overcomes that disposition to tenderness and sympathy, which is so powerful in our younger years, and they that happen to petition the old for compassion or assistance, are doomed to languish without regard, and suffer for the crimes of men who have formerly been found undeserving or ungrateful.

Historians are certainly chargeable with the depravation of mankind, when they relate without censure those stratagems of war by which the virtues of an enemy are engaged to his destruction. A ship comes before a port, weather-beaten and shattered, and the crew implore the liberty of repairing their breaches, supplying themselves with necessaries, or burying their dead. The humanity of the inhabitants inclines them to consent, the strangers enter the town with weapons concealed, fall suddenly upon their benefactors, destroy those that make resistance, and become masters of the place; they return home rich with plunder, and their success is recorded to encourage imitation.

But surely war has its laws, and ought to be conducted with some regard to the universal interest of man. Those may justly be pursued as enemies to the community of nature, who suffer hostility to vacate the unalterable laws of right, and pursue their private advantage by means, which, if once established, must destroy kindness, cut off from every man all hopes of assistance from another, and fill the world with perpetual suspicion and implacable malevolence. Whatever is thus gained ought to be restored, and those who have conquered by such treachery may be justly denied the protection of their native country.

Whoever commits a fraud is guilty not only of the particular injury to him whom he deceives, but of the diminution of that confidence which constitutes not only the ease but the existence of society. He that suffers by imposture has too often his virtue more impaired than his fortune. But as it is necessary not to invite robbery by supineness, so it is our duty not to suppress tenderness by suspicion; it is better to suffer wrong than to do it, and happier to be sometimes cheated than not to trust.

No. 85. Tuesday, 8 January 1751.

Otia si tollas periere Cupidinis *arcus*
Contemptæque jacent, et sine luce faces.
OVID.

At busy hearts in vain love's arrows fly;
Dim, scorn'd, and impotent, his torches lie.

Many writers of eminence in physick have laid out their diligence upon the consideration of those distempers to which men are exposed by particular states of life, and very learned treatises have been produced upon the maladies of the camp, the sea, and the mines. There are, indeed, few employments which a man accustomed to anatomical enquiries, and medical refinements, would not find reasons for declining as dangerous to health, did not his learning or experience inform him, that almost every occupation, however inconvenient or formidable, is happier and safer than a life of sloth.

The necessity of action is not only demonstrable from the fabrick of the body, but evident from observation of the universal practice of mankind, who for the preservation of health, in those whose rank or wealth exempts them from the necessity of lucrative labour, have invented sports and diversions, though not of equal use to the world with manual trades, yet of equal fatigue to those that practise them, and differing only from the drudgery of the husbandman or manufacturer, as they are acts of choice, and therefore performed without the painful sense of compulsion. The huntsman rises early, persues his game through all the dangers and obstructions of the chase, swims rivers, and scales precipices, till he returns home no less harrassed than the soldier, and has, perhaps, sometimes incurred as great hazard of wounds or death: Yet he has no motive to incite his ardour; he is neither subject to the commands of a general, nor dreads any penalties for neglect and disobedience; he has neither profit or honour to expect from his perils and his conquests, but toils without the hope of mural or civick garlands, and must content himself with the praise of his tenants and companions.

But such is the constitution of man, that labour may be stiled its own reward; nor will any external incitements be requisite, if it be considered how much happiness is gained, and how much misery escaped by frequent and violent agitation of the body.

Ease is the utmost that can be hoped from a sedentary and unactive habit; ease, a neutral state between pain and pleasure. The dance of spirits, the bound of vigour, readiness of enterprize, and defiance of fatigue, are reserved for him that braces his nerves, and hardens his fibres, that keeps his limbs pliant with motion, and by frequent exposure fortifies his frame against the common accidents of cold and heat.

With ease, however, if it could be secured, many would be content; but nothing terrestrial can be kept at a stand. Ease, if it is not rising into pleasure, will be falling towards pain; and whatever hope the dreams of speculation may suggest of observing the proportion between nutriment and labour, and keeping the body in a healthy state by supplies exactly equal to its waste, we know that, in effect, the vital powers unexcited by motion, grow gradually languid; that as their vigour fails, obstructions are generated; and that from obstructions proceed most of those pains which wear us away slowly with periodical tortures, and which, though they sometimes suffer life to be long, condemn it to be useless, chain us down to the couch of misery, and mock us with the hopes of death.

Exercise cannot secure us from that dissolution to which we are decreed; but while the soul and body continue united, it can make the association pleasing, and give probable hopes that they shall be disjoined by an easy separation. It was a principle among the ancients, that acute diseases are from heaven, and chronical from ourselves; the dart of death indeed falls from heaven, but we poison it by our own misconduct; to die is the fate of man, but to die with lingering anguish is generally his folly.

It is necessary to that perfection of which our present state is capable, that the mind and body should both be kept in action; that neither the faculties of the one nor of the other be suffered to grow lax or torpid for want of use; that neither health be purchased by voluntary submission to ignorance, nor knowledge cultivated at the expence of that health, which must enable it either to give pleasure to its possessor or assistance to others. It is too frequently the pride of students to despise those amusements and recreations which give to the rest of mankind strength of limbs and cheerfulness of heart. Solitude and contemplation are indeed seldom consistent with such skill in common exercises or sports as is necessary to make them practised with delight, and no man is willing to do that of which the necessity is not pressing and immediate, when he knows that his aukwardness must make him ridiculous.

> *Ludere qui nescit, campestribus abstinet armis,*
> *Indoctusque Pilæ, Discive, Trochive quiescit,*
> *Ne spissæ risum tollant impunè Coronæ.*

> He that's unskilful will not toss a ball,
> Nor run, nor wrestle, for he fears the fall;
> He justly fears to meet deserv'd disgrace,
> And that the *ring* will hiss the baffled ass.
>   CREECH.

Thus the man of learning is often resigned, almost by his own consent, to languor and pain; and while in the prosecution of his studies he suffers the weariness of labour, is subject by his course of life to the maladies of idleness.

It was, perhaps, from the observation of this mischievous omission in those who are employed about intellectual objects, that *Locke* has, in his *System of Education*, urged the necessity of a trade to men of all ranks and professions, that when the mind is weary with its proper task, it may be relaxed by a slighter attention to some mechanical operation; and that while the vital functions are resuscitated and awakened by vigorous motion, the understanding may be restrained from that vagrance and dissipation by which it relieves itself after a long intenseness of thought, unless some allurement be presented that may engage application without anxiety.

There is so little reason for expecting frequent conformity to *Locke*'s precept, that it is not necessary to enquire whether the practice of mechanical arts might not give occasion to petty emulation, and degenerate ambition; and whether, if our divines and physicians were taught the lathe and the chizzel, they would not think more of their tools than their books; as *Nero* neglected the care of his empire for his chariot and his fiddle. It is certainly dangerous to be too much pleased with little things; but what is there which may not be perverted? Let us remember how much worse employment might have been found for those hours, which a manual occupation appears to engross; let us compute the profit with the loss, and when we reflect how often a genius is allured from his studies, consider likewise that perhaps by the same attractions he is sometimes withheld from debauchery, or recalled from malice, from ambition, from envy, and from lust.

I have always admired the wisdom of those by whom our female education was instituted, for having contrived, that every woman of whatever condition should be taught some arts of manufacture, by which the vacuities of recluse and domestick leisure may be filled up. These arts are more necessary as the weakness of their sex and the general system of life debar ladies from many employments which by diversifying the circumstances of men, preserve them from being cankered by the rust of their own thoughts. I know not how much of the virtue and happiness of the world may be the consequence of this judicious regulation. Perhaps, the most powerful fancy might be unable to figure the confusion and slaughter that would be produced by so many piercing eyes and vivid understandings, turned loose at once upon mankind, with no other business than to sparkle and intrigue, to perplex and to destroy.

For my part, whenever chance brings within my observation a knot of misses busy at their needles, I consider myself as in the school of virtue; and though I have no extraordinary skill in plain work or embroidery, look upon their operations with as much satisfaction as their governess, because I regard them as providing a security against the most dangerous ensnarers of the soul, by enabling themselves to exclude idleness from their solitary moments, and with idleness her attendant train of passions, fancies, and chimeras, fears, sorrows and desires. *Ovid* and *Cervantes* will inform them that love has no power but over those whom he catches unemployed; and *Hector*, in the *Iliad*, when he sees *Andromache* overwhelmed with terrors, sends her for consolation to the loom and the distaff.

It is certain that any wild wish or vain imagination never takes such firm possession of the mind, as when it is found empty and unoccupied. The old peripatetick principle, that *Nature abhors a Vacuum*, may be properly applied to the intellect, which will embrace any thing, however absurd or criminal, rather than be wholly without an object. Perhaps every man may date the predominance of those desires that disturb his life and contaminate his conscience, from some unhappy hour when too much leisure exposed him to their incursions; for he has lived with little observation either on himself or others, who does not know that to be idle is to be vicious.

No. 87. Tuesday, 15 January 1751.

Invidus, iracundus, iners, vinosus, amator,
Nemo adeo ferus est, ut non mitescere possit,
Si modo culturæ patientem commodet aurem.

Hor.

The slave to envy, anger, wine or love,
The wretch of sloth, its excellence shall prove:
Fierceness itself shall hear its rage away,
When list'ning calmly to th' instructive lay.

Francis.

That few things are so liberally bestowed, or squandered with so little effect, as good advice, has been generally observed; and many sage positions have been advanced concerning the reasons of this complaint, and the means of removing it. It is, indeed, an important and noble enquiry, for little would be wanting to the happiness of life, if every man could conform to the right as soon as he was shown it.

This perverse neglect of the most salutary precepts, and stubborn resistance of the most pathetic persuasion, is usually imputed to him by whom the counsel is received, and we often hear it mentioned as a sign of hopeless depravity, that though good advice was given, it has wrought no reformation.

Others who imagine themselves to have quicker sagacity and deeper penetration, have found out, that the inefficacy of advice is usually the fault of the counsellor, and rules have been laid down, by which this important duty may be successfully performed: We are directed by what tokens to discover the favourable moment at which the heart is disposed for the operation of truth and reason, with what address to administer and with what vehicles to disguise *the catharticks of the soul.*

But, notwithstanding this specious expedient, we find the world yet in the same state; advice is still given, but still received with disgust; nor has it appeared that the bitterness of the medicine has been yet abated, or its power encreased by any methods of preparing it.

If we consider the manner in which those who assume the office of directing the conduct of others execute their undertaking, it will not be very wonderful that their labours, however zealous or affectionate, are frequently useless. For what is the advice that is commonly given? A few general maxims, enforced with vehemence and inculcated with importunity, but failing for want of particular reference, and immediate application.

It is not often that any man can have so much knowledge of another, as is necessary to make instruction useful. We are sometimes not ourselves conscious of the original motives of our actions, and when we know them, our first care is to hide them from the sight of others, and often from those most diligently, whose superiority either of power or understanding may intitle them to inspect our lives; it is therefore very probable that he who endeavours the cure of our intellectual maladies, mistakes their cause; and that his prescriptions avail nothing, because he knows not which of the passions or desires is vitiated.

Advice, as it always gives a temporary appearance of superiority, can never be very grateful, even when it is most necessary or most judicious. But for the same reason every one is eager to instruct his neighbours. To be wise or to be virtuous, is to buy dignity and importance at a high price; but when nothing is necessary to elevation but detection of the follies or the faults of others, no man is so insensible to the voice of fame as to linger on the ground.

> —*Tentanda via est, qua me quoque possim*
> *Tollere humo, victorque virûm volitare per ora.*

> New ways I must attempt, my groveling name
> To raise aloft, and wing my flight to fame.
> DRYDEN.

Vanity is so frequently the apparent motive of advice, that we, for the most part, summon our powers to oppose it without any very accurate enquiry whether it is right. It is sufficient that another is growing great in his own eyes at our expence, and assumes authority over us without our permission; for many would contentedly suffer the consequences of their own mistakes, rather than the insolence of him who triumphs as their deliverer.

It is, indeed, seldom found that any advantages are enjoyed with that moderation which the uncertainty of all human good so powerfully enforces; and therefore the adviser may justly suspect, that he has inflamed the opposition which he laments by arrogance and superciliousness. He may suspect, but needs not hastily to condemn himself, for he can rarely be certain, that the softest language or most humble diffidence would have escaped resentment; since scarcely any degree of circumspection can prevent or obviate the rage with which the slothful, the impotent, and the unsuccessful, vent their discontent upon those that excel them. Modesty itself, if it is praised, will be envied; and there are minds so impatient of inferiority, that their gratitude is a species of revenge, and they return benefits, not because recompence is a pleasure, but because obligation is a pain.

The number of those whom the love of themselves has thus far corrupted, is perhaps not great; but there are few so free from vanity as not to dictate to those who will hear their instructions with a visible sense of their own beneficence; and few to whom it is not unpleasing to receive documents, however tenderly and cautiously delivered, or who are not willing to raise themselves from pupillage, by disputing the propositions of their teacher.

It was the maxim, I think, of *Alphonsus* of *Arragon*, that *dead counsellors are safest*. The grave puts an end to flattery and artifice, and the information that we receive from books is pure from interest, fear, or ambition. Dead counsellors are likewise most instructive; because they are heard with patience and with reverence. We are not unwilling to believe that man wiser than ourselves, from whose abilities we may receive advantage, without any danger of rivalry or opposition, and who affords us the light of his experience, without hurting our eyes by flashes of insolence.

By the consultation of books, whether of dead or living authors, many temptations to petulance and opposition, which occur in oral conferences, are avoided. An author cannot obtrude his advice unasked, nor can be often suspected of any malignant intention to insult his readers with his knowledge or his wit. Yet so prevalent is the habit of comparing ourselves with others, while they remain within the reach of our passions, that books are seldom read with complete impartiality, but by those from whom the writer is placed at such a distance that his life or death is indifferent.

We see that volumes may be perused, and perused with attention, to little effect; and that maxims of prudence, or principles of virtue, may be treasured in the memory without influencing the conduct. Of the numbers that pass their lives among books, very few read to be made wiser or better, apply any general reproof of vice to themselves, or try their own manners by axioms of justice. They purpose either to consume those hours for which they can find no other amusement; to gain or preserve that respect which learning has always obtained; or to gratify their curiosity with knowledge, which, like treasures buried and forgotten, is of no use to others or themselves.

"The preacher, (says a *French* author) may spend an hour in explaining and enforcing a precept of religion, without feeling any impression from his own performance, because he may have no further design than to fill up his hour."

A student may easily exhaust his life in comparing divines and moralists, without any practical regard to morality or religion; he may be learning not to live, but to reason; he may regard only the elegance of stile, justness of argument, and accuracy of method; and may enable himself to criticise with judgment, and dispute with subtilty, while the chief use of his volumes is unthought of, his mind is unaffected, and his life is unreformed.

But though truth and virtue are thus frequently defeated by pride, obstinacy, or folly, we are not allowed to desert them; for whoever can furnish arms which they have not hitherto employed, may enable them to gain some hearts which would have resisted any other method of attack. Every man of genius has some arts of fixing the attention peculiar to himself, by which, honestly exerted, he may benefit mankind; for the arguments for purity of life fail of their due influence, not because they have been considered and confuted, but because they have been passed over without consideration. To the position of *Tully*, that if Virtue could be seen, she must be loved, may be added, that if Truth could be heard, she must be obeyed.

No. 90. Saturday, 26 January 1751.

In tenui labor.
VIRG.

What toil in slender things!

It is very difficult to write on the minuter parts of literature without failing either to please or instruct. Too much nicety of detail disgusts the greatest part of readers, and to throw a multitude of particulars under general heads, and lay down rules of extensive comprehension, is to common understandings of little use. They who undertake these subjects are therefore always in danger, as one or other inconvenience arises to their imagination, of frighting us with rugged science, or amusing us with empty sound.

In criticising the work of *Milton*, there is, indeed, opportunity to intersperse passages that can hardly fail to relieve the languors of attention; and since, in examining the variety and choice of the pauses with which he has diversified his numbers, it will be necessary to exhibit the lines in which they are to be found, perhaps the remarks may be well compensated by the examples, and the irksomeness of grammatical disquisitions somewhat alleviated.

MILTON formed his scheme of versification by the poets of *Greece* and *Rome*, whom he proposed to himself for his models so far as the difference of his language from theirs would permit the imitation. There are indeed many inconveniencies inseparable from our heroick measure compared with that of *Homer* and *Virgil*; inconveniencies, which it is no reproach to *Milton* not to have overcome, because they are in their own nature insuperable; but against which he has struggled with so much art and diligence, that he may at least be said to have deserved success.

The hexameter of the ancients may be considered as consisting of fifteen syllables, so melodiously disposed, that, as every one knows who has examined the poetical authors, very pleasing and sonorous lyrick measures are formed from the fragments of the heroick. It is, indeed, scarce possible to break them in such a manner but that *invenias etiam disjecti membra poetæ*, some harmony will still remain, and the due proportions of sound will always be discovered. This measure therefore allowed great variety of pauses, and great liberties of connecting one verse with another, because wherever the line was interrupted, either part singly was musical. But the ancients seem to have confined this privilege to hexameters; for in their other measures, though longer than the *English* heroick, those who wrote after the refinements of versification venture so seldom to change their pauses, that every variation may be supposed rather a compliance with necessity than the choice of judgment.

MILTON was constrained within the narrow limits of a measure not very harmonious in the utmost perfection; the single parts, therefore, into which it was to be sometimes broken by pauses, were in danger of losing the very form of verse. This has, perhaps, notwithstanding all his care, sometimes happened.

As harmony is the end of poetical measures, no part of a verse ought to be so separated from the rest as not to remain still more harmonious than prose, or to shew, by the disposition of the tones, that it is part of a verse. This rule in the old hexameter might be easily observed, but in *English* will very frequently be in danger of violation; for the order and regularity of accents cannot well be perceived in a succession of fewer than three syllables, which will confine the *English* poet to only five pauses; it being supposed, that, when he connects one line with another, he should never make a full pause at less distance than that of three syllables from the beginning or end of a verse.

That this rule should be universally and indispensably established, perhaps cannot be granted; something may be allowed to variety, and something to the adaptation of the numbers to the subject; but it will be found generally necessary, and the ear will seldom fail to suffer by its neglect.

Thus when a single syllable is cut off from the rest, it must either be united to the line with which the sense connects it, or be sounded alone. If it be united to the other line, it corrupts its harmony; if disjoined, it must stand alone and with regard to musick, be superfluous; for there is no harmony in a single sound, because it has no proportion to another.

> Hypocrites austerely talk,
> Defaming as impure what God declares
> *Pure*; and commands to some, leaves free to all.

When two syllables likewise are abscinded from the rest, they evidently want some associate sounds to make them harmonious.

> ——Eyes——
> ——more wakeful than to drouze,
> Charm'd with arcadian pipe, the past'ral reed
> Of *Hermes*, or his opiate rod. *Meanwhile*
> To re-salute the world with sacred light
> *Leucothea* wak'd.

> He ended, and the Son gave signal high
> To the bright minister that watch'd: *he blew*
> His trumpet

> First in his east the glorious lamp was seen,
> Regent of day; and all th' horizon round
> Invested with bright rays, jocund to run
> His longitude through heav'n's high road; *the gray*
> Dawn, and the pleiades, before him danc'd,
> Shedding sweet influence.

The same defect is perceived in the following lines, where the pause is at the second syllable from the beginning.

> The race
> Of that wild rout that tore the *Thracian* bard
> In *Rhodope*, where woods and rocks had ears,
> To rapture, 'till the savage clamour drown'd
> Both harp and voice; nor could the muse defend
> *Her son*. So fail not thou, who thee implores.

When the pause falls upon the third syllable or the seventh, the harmony is better preserved; but as the third and seventh are weak syllables, the period leaves the ear unsatisfied, and in expectation of the remaining part of the verse.

> He, with his horrid crew,
> Lay vanquish'd, rolling in the fiery gulph,
> Confounded though immor*tal*. But his doom
> Reserv'd him to more wrath; for now the thought
> Both of lost happiness and lasting pain
> Torments *him*.

> God,——with frequent intercourse,
> Thither will send his winged messengers

> On errands of supernal grace. So sung
> The glorious train ascend*ing*.

It may be, I think, established as a rule, that a pause which concludes a period should be made for the most part upon a strong syllable, as the fourth and sixth; but those pauses which only suspend the sense may be placed upon the weaker. Thus the rest in the third line of the first passage satisfies the ear better than in the fourth, and the close of the second quotation better than of the third.

> The evil soon
> Drawn back, redounded (as a flood) on those
> From whom it *sprung*; impossible to mix
> With *blessedness*.

> ———What we by day
> Lop overgrown, or prune, or prop, or bind
> One night or two with wanton growth derides,
> Tending to *wild*.

> The paths and bow'rs doubt not but our joint hands
> Will keep from wilderness with ease as wide
> As we need walk, till younger hands ere long
> Assist *us*.

The rest in the fifth place has the same inconvenience as in the seventh and third, that the syllable is weak.

> Beast now with beast 'gan war, and fowl with fowl,
> And fish with fish, to graze the herb all leaving,
> Devour'd each *other*: Nor stood much in awe
> Of man, but fled *him*, or with countenance grim,
> Glar'd on him pass*ing*.

The noblest and most majestic pauses which our versification admits, are upon the fourth and sixth syllables, which are both strongly sounded in a pure and regular verse, and at either of which the line is so divided, that both members participate of harmony.

> But now at last the sacred influence
> Of light ap*pears*, and from the walls of heav'n
> Shoots far into the bosom of dim night
> A glimmering *dawn*: here nature first begins
> Her farthest verge, and chaos to retire.

But far above all others, if I can give any credit to my own ear, is the rest upon the sixth syllable, which taking in a complete compass of sound, such as is sufficient to constitute one of our lyrick measures, makes a full and solemn close. Some passages which conclude at this stop, I could never read without some strong emotions of delight or admiration.

> Before the hills appear'd, or fountain flow'd,
> Thou with the eternal wisdom didst converse,
> Wisdom thy sister; and with her didst play
> In presence of the almighty father, pleas'd
> With thy celestial *song*.

> Or other worlds they seem'd, or happy isles,
> Like those *Hesperian* gardens fam'd of old,
> Fortunate fields, and groves, and flow'ry vales,
> Thrice happy isles! But who dwelt happy there,
> He staid not to in*quire*.

> He blew
> His trumpet, heard in *Oreb* since, perhaps
> When God descended; and, perhaps, once more
> To sound at general *doom*.

If the poetry of *Milton* be examined, with regard to the pauses and flow of his verses into each other, it will appear, that he has performed all that our language would admit; and the comparison of his numbers with those who have cultivated the same manner of writing, will show that he excelled as much in the lower as the higher parts of his art, and that his skill in harmony was not less than his invention or his learning.

No. 93. Tuesday, 5 February 1751.

———*Experiar quid concedatur in illos*
Quorum Flaminiâ tegitur cinis atque Latinâ.
JUV.

More safely truth to urge her claim presumes,
On names now found alone on books and tombs.

There are few books on which more time is spent by young students, than on treatises which deliver the characters of authors; nor any which oftener deceive the expectation of the reader, or fill his mind with more opinions which the progress of his studies and the encrease of his knowledge oblige him to resign.

Baillet has introduced his collection of the decisions of the learned, by an enumeration of the prejudices which mislead the critick, and raise the passions in rebellion against the judgment. His catalogue, though large, is imperfect; and who can hope to complete it? The beauties of writing have been observed to be often such as cannot in the present state of human knowledge be evinced by evidence, or drawn out into demonstrations; they are therefore wholly subject to the imagination, and do not force their effects upon a mind preoccupied by unfavourable sentiments, nor overcome the counteraction of a false principle or of stubborn partiality.

To convince any man against his will is hard, but to please him against his will is justly pronounced by *Dryden* to be above the reach of human abilities. Interest and passion will hold out long against the closest siege of diagrams and syllogisms, but they are absolutely impregnable to imagery and sentiment; and will for ever bid defiance to the most powerful strains of *Virgil* or *Homer*, though they may give way in time to the batteries of *Euclid* or *Archimedes*.

In trusting therefore to the sentence of a critick, we are in danger not only from that vanity which exalts writers too often to the dignity of teaching what they are yet to learn, from that negligence which sometimes steals upon the most vigilant caution, and that fallibility to which the condition of nature has subjected every human understanding; but from a thousand extrinsick and accidental causes, from every thing which can excite kindness or malevolence, veneration or contempt.

Many of those who have determined with great boldness, upon the various degrees of literary merit, may be justly suspected of having passed sentence, as *Seneca* remarks of *Claudius*,

> *Una tantum Parte audita,*
> *Sæpe et nulla,*

without much knowledge of the cause before them; for it will not easily be imagined of *Langbaine, Borrichitus* or *Rapin*, that they had very accurately perused all the books which they praise or censure; or that, even if nature and learning had qualified them for judges, they could read for ever with the attention necessary to just criticism. Such performances, however, are not wholly without their use; for they are commonly just echoes to the voice of fame, and transmit the general suffrage of mankind when they have no particular motives to suppress it.

Criticks, like all the rest of mankind, are very frequently misled by interest. The bigotry with which editors regard the authors whom they illustrate or correct, has been generally remarked. *Dryden* was known to have written most of his critical dissertations only to recommend the work upon which he then happened to be employed; and *Addison* is suspected to have denied the expediency of poetical justice, because his own *Cato* was condemned to perish in a good cause.

There are prejudices which authors, not otherwise weak or corrupt, have indulged without scruple; and perhaps some of them are so complicated with our natural affections, that they cannot easily be disintangled from the heart. Scarce any can hear with impartiality a comparison between the writers of his own and another country; and though it cannot, I think, be charged equally on all nations, that they are blinded with this literary patriotism, yet there are none that do not look upon their authors with the fondness of affinity, and esteem them as well for the place of their birth, as for their knowledge or their wit. There is, therefore, seldom much respect due to comparative criticism, when the competitors are of different countries, unless the judge is of a nation equally indifferent to both. The *Italians* could not for a long time believe, that there was any learning beyond the mountains; and the *French* seem generally persuaded, that there are no wits or reasoners equal to their own. I can scarcely conceive that if *Scaliger* had not considered himself as allied to *Virgil*, by being born in the same country, he would have found his works so much superior to those of *Homer*, or have thought the controversy worthy of so much zeal, vehemence, and acrimony.

There is, indeed, one prejudice, and only one, by which it may be doubted whether it is any dishonour to be sometimes misguided. Criticism has so often given occasion to the envious and ill-natured of gratifying their malignity, that some have thought it necessary to recommend the virtue of candour without restriction, and to preclude all future liberty of censure. Writers possessed with this opinion are continually enforcing civility and decency, recommending to criticks the proper diffidence of themselves, and inculcating the veneration due to celebrated names.

I am not of opinion that these professed enemies of arrogance and severity, have much more benevolence or modesty than the rest of mankind; or that they feel in their own hearts, any other intention than to distinguish themselves by their softness and delicacy. Some are modest because they are timorous, and some are lavish of praise because they hope to be repaid.

There is indeed some tenderness due to living writers, when they attack none of those truths which are of importance to the happiness of mankind, and have committed no other offence than that of betraying their own ignorance or dulness. I should think it cruelty to crush an insect who had provoked me only by buzzing in my ear; and would not willingly interrupt the dream of harmless stupidity, or destroy the jest which makes its author laugh. Yet I am far from thinking this tenderness universally necessary; for he that writes may be considered as a kind of general challenger, whom every one has a right to attack; since he quits the common rank of life, steps forward beyond the lists, and offers his merit to the publick judgment. To commence author is to claim praise, and no man can justly aspire to honour, but at the hazard of disgrace.

But whatever be decided concerning contemporaries, whom he that knows the treachery of the human heart, and considers how often we gratify our own pride or envy under the appearance of contending for elegance and propriety, will find himself not much inclined to disturb; there can surely be no exemptions pleaded to secure them from criticism, who can no longer suffer by reproach, and of whom nothing now remains but their writings and their names. Upon these authors the critick is, undoubtedly, at full liberty to exercise the strictest severity, since he endangers only his own fame, and, like *Æneas* when he drew his sword in the infernal regions, encounters phantoms which cannot be wounded. He may indeed pay some regard to established reputation; but he can by that shew of reverence consult only his own security, for all other motives are now at an end.

The faults of a writer of acknowledged excellence are more dangerous, because the influence of his example is more extensive; and the interest of learning requires that they should be discovered and stigmatized, before they have the sanction of antiquity conferred upon them, and become precedents of indisputable authority.

It has, indeed, been advanced by *Addison*, as one of the characteristicks of a true critick, that he points out beauties rather than faults. But it is rather natural to a man of learning and genius, to apply himself chiefly to the study of writers who have more beauties than faults to be displayed: for the duty of criticism is neither to depreciate, nor dignify by partial representations, but to hold out the light of reason, whatever it may discover; and to promulgate the determinations of truth, whatever she shall dictate.

No. 101. Tuesday, 5 March 1751.

Mella jubes Hyblæa tibi vel Hymettia nasci,
Et thyma Cecropiæ Corsica ponis api.
MART.

Alas! dear Sir, you try in vain,
Impossibilities to gain;
No bee from *Corsica*'s rank juice,
Hyblæan honey can produce.
F. LEWIS.

To the RAMBLER.

SIR,

Having by several years of continual study treasured in my mind a great number of principles and ideas, and obtained by frequent exercise the power of applying them with propriety, and combining them with readiness, I resolved to quit the university, where I considered myself as a gem hidden in the mine, and to mingle in the croud of publick life. I was naturally attracted by the company of those who were of the same age with myself, and finding that my academical gravity contributed very little to my reputation, applied my faculties to jocularity and burlesque. Thus, in a short time, I had heated my imagination to such a state of activity and ebullition, that upon every occasion it fumed away in bursts of wit, and evaporations of gaiety. I became on a sudden the idol of the coffee-house, was in one winter sollicited to accept the presidentship of five clubs, was dragged by violence to every new play, and quoted in every controversy upon theatrical merit; was in every publick place surrounded by a multitude of humble auditors, who retailed in other places of resort my maxims and my jests, and was boasted as their intimate and companion by many, who had no other pretensions to my acquaintance, than that they had drank chocolate in the same room.

You will not wonder, Mr. RAMBLER, that I mention my success with some appearance of triumph and elevation. Perhaps no kind of superiority is more flattering or alluring than that which is conferred by the powers of conversation, by extemporaneous sprightliness of fancy, copiousness of language, and fertility of sentiment. In other exertions of genius, the greater part of the praise is unknown and unenjoyed; the writer, indeed, spreads his reputation to a wider extent, but receives little pleasure or advantage from the diffusion of his name, and only obtains a kind of nominal sovereignty over regions which pay no tribute. The colloquial wit has always his own radiance reflected on himself, and enjoys all the pleasure which he bestows; he finds his power confessed by every one that approaches him, sees friendship kindling with rapture, and attention swelling into praise.

The desire which every man feels of importance and esteem, is so much gratified by finding an assembly, at his entrance, brightened with gladness and hushed with expectation, that the recollection of such distinctions can scarcely fail to be pleasing whensoever it is innocent. And my conscience does not reproach me with any mean or criminal effects of vanity; since I always employed my influence on the side of virtue, and never sacrificed my understanding or my religion to the pleasure of applause.

There were many whom either the desire of enjoying my pleasantry, or the pride of being thought to enjoy it, brought often into my company; but I was caressed in a particular manner by *Demochares*, a gentleman of a large estate, and a liberal disposition. My fortune being by no means exuberant, enclined me to be pleased with a friend who was willing to be entertained at his own charge. I became by daily invitations habituated to his table, and, as he believed my acquaintance necessary to the character of elegance, which he was desirous of establishing, I lived in all the luxury of affluence, without expence or dependence, and passed my life in a perpetual reciprocation of pleasure with men brought together by similitude of accomplishments, or desire of improvement.

But all power has its sphere of activity, beyond which it produces no effect. *Demochares* being called by his affairs into the country, imagined that he should encrease his popularity by coming among his neighbours accompanied by a man whose abilities were so generally allowed. The report presently spread thro' half the county that *Demochares* was arrived, and had brought with him the celebrated *Hilarius*, by whom such merriment would be excited, as had never been enjoyed or conceived before. I knew, indeed, the purpose for which I was invited, and, as men do not look diligently out for possible miscarriages, was pleased to find myself courted upon principles of interest, and considered as capable of reconciling factions, composing feuds, and uniting a whole province in social happiness.

After a few days spent in adjusting his domestick regulations, *Demochares* invited all the gentlemen of his neighbourhood to dinner, and did not forget to hint how much my presence was expected to heighten the pleasure of the feast. He informed me what prejudices my reputation had raised in my favour, and represented the satisfaction with which he should see me kindle up the blaze of merriment, and should remark the various effects that my fire would have upon such diversity of matter.

This declaration, by which he intended to quicken my vivacity, filled me with solicitude. I felt an ambition of shining, which I never knew before; and was therefore embarrassed with an unusual fear of disgrace. I passed the night in planning out to myself the conversation of the coming day; recollected all my topicks of raillery, proposed proper subjects of ridicule, prepared smart replies to a thousand questions, accommodated answers to imaginary repartees, and formed a magazine of remarks, apophthegms, tales, and illustrations.

The morning broke at last in the midst of these busy meditations. I rose with the palpitations of a champion on the day of combat; and, notwithstanding all my efforts, found my spirits sunk under the weight of expectation. The company soon after began to drop in, and every one, at his entrance was introduced to *Hilarius*. What conception the inhabitants of this region had formed of a wit, I cannot yet discover; but observed that they all seemed, after the regular exchange of compliments, to turn away disappointed, and that while we waited for dinner, they cast their eyes first upon me, and then upon each other, like a theatrical assembly waiting for a shew.

From the uneasiness of this situation, I was relieved by the dinner, and as every attention was taken up by the business of the hour, I sunk quietly to a level with the rest of the company. But no sooner were the dishes removed, than instead of chearful confidence and familiar prattle, an universal silence again shewed their expectation of some unusual performance. My friend endeavoured to rouse them by healths and questions, but they answered him with great brevity, and immediately relapsed into their former taciturnity.

I had waited in hope of some opportunity to divert them, but could find no pass opened for a single sally; and who can be merry without an object of mirth? After a few faint efforts, which produced neither applause nor opposition, I was content to mingle with the mass, to put round the glass in silence, and solace myself with my own contemplations.

My friend looked round him; the guests stared at one another; and if now and then a few syllables were uttered with timidity and hesitation, there was none ready to make any reply. All our faculties were frozen, and every minute took away from our capacity of pleasing, and disposition to be pleased. Thus passed the hours to which so much happiness was decreed; the hours which had, by a kind of open proclamation, been devoted to wit, to mirth, and to *Hilarius*.

At last the night came on, and the necessity of parting freed us from the persecutions of each other. I heard them as they walked along the court murmuring at the loss of the day, and enquiring whether any man would pay a second visit to a house haunted by a wit.

Demochares, whose benevolence is greater than his penetration, having flattered his hopes with the secondary honour which he was to gain by my sprightliness and elegance, and the affection with which he should be followed for a perpetual banquet of gaiety, was not able to conceal his vexation and resentment, nor would easily be convinced, that I had not sacrificed his interest to sullenness and caprice, had studiously endeavoured to disgust his guests, and suppressed my powers of delighting, in obstinate and premeditated silence. I am informed that the reproach of their ill reception is divided by the gentlemen of the country between us; some being of opinion that my friend is deluded by an impostor, who, though he has found some art of gaining his favour, is afraid to speak before men of more penetration; and others concluding, that I think only *London* the proper theatre of my abilities, and disdain to exert my genius for the praise of rusticks.

I believe, Mr. RAMBLER, that it has sometimes happened to others, who have the good or ill fortune to be celebrated for wits, to fall under the same censures upon the like occasions. I hope therefore that you will prevent any misrepresentations of such failures, by remarking that invention is not wholly at the command of its possessor; that the power of pleasing is very often obstructed by the desire; that all expectation lessens surprize, yet some surprize is necessary to gaiety; and that those who desire to partake of the pleasure of wit must contribute to its production, since the mind stagnates without external ventilation, and that effervescence of the fancy, which flashes into transport, can be raised only by the infusion of dissimilar ideas.

No. 106. Saturday, 23 March 1751.

Opinionum commenta delet dies, naturæ judicia confirmat.
CIC.

Time obliterates the fictions of opinion, and confirms the decisions of nature.

It is necessary to the success of flattery, that it be accommodated to particular circumstances or characters, and enter the heart on that side where the passions stand ready to receive it. A lady seldom listens with attention to any praise but that of her beauty; a merchant always expects to hear of his influence at the bank, his importance on the exchange, the height of his credit, and the extent of his traffick: and the author will scarcely be pleased without lamentations of the neglect of learning, the conspiracies against genius, and the slow progress of merit, or some praises of the magnanimity of those who encounter poverty and contempt in the cause of knowledge, and trust for the reward of their labours to the judgment and gratitude of posterity.

An assurance of unfading laurels, and immortal reputation, is the settled reciprocation of civility between amicable writers. To raise *monuments more durable than brass, and more conspicuous than pyramids*, has been long the common boast of literature; but among the innumerable architects that erect columns to themselves, far the greater part, either for want of durable materials, or of art to dispose them, see their edifices perish as they are towering to completion, and those few that for a while attract the eye of mankind, are generally weak in the foundation, and soon sink by the saps of time.

No place affords a more striking conviction of the vanity of human hopes, than a publick library; for who can see the wall crouded on every side by mighty volumes, the works of laborious meditation, and accurate enquiry, now scarcely known but by the catalogue, and preserved only to encrease the pomp of learning, without considering how many hours have been wasted in vain endeavours, how often imagination has anticipated the praises of futurity, how many statues have risen to the eye of vanity, how many ideal converts have elevated zeal, how often wit has exulted in the eternal infamy of his antagonists, and dogmatism has delighted in the gradual advances of his authority, the immutability of his decrees, and the perpetuity of his power?

> ——*Non unquam dedit*
> *Documenta fors majora, quàm fragili loco*
> *Starent superbi.* ——

Insulting chance ne'er call'd with louder voice,
On swelling mortals to be proud no more.

Of the innumerable authors whose performances are thus treasured up in magnificent obscurity, most are forgotten, because they never deserved to be remembered, and owed the honours which they once obtained, not to judgment or to genius, to labour or to art, but to the prejudice of faction, the stratagem of intrigue, or the servility of adulation.

Nothing is more common than to find men whose works are now totally neglected, mentioned with praises by their contemporaries, as the oracles of their age, and the legislators of science. Curiosity is naturally excited, their volumes after long enquiry are found, but seldom reward the labour of the search. Every period of time has produced these bubbles of artificial fame, which are kept up a while by the breath of fashion, and then break at once and are annihilated. The learned often bewail the loss of ancient writers whose characters have survived their works; but, perhaps, if we could now retrieve them, we should find them only the *Granvilles, Montagues, Stepneys,* and *Sheffields* of their time, and wonder by what infatuation or caprice they could be raised to notice.

It cannot, however, be denied, that many have sunk into oblivion, whom it were unjust to number with this despicable class. Various kinds of literary fame seem destined to various measures of duration. Some spread into exuberance with a very speedy growth, but soon wither and decay; some rise more slowly, but last long. Parnassus has its flowers of transient fragrance, as well as its oaks of towering height, and its laurels of eternal verdure.

Among those whose reputation is exhausted in a short time by its own luxuriance, are the writers who take advantage of present incidents or characters which strongly interest the passions, and engage universal attention. It is not difficult to obtain readers, when we discuss a question which every one is desirous to understand, which is debated in every assembly, and has divided the nation into parties; or when we display the faults or virtues of him whose public conduct has made almost every man his enemy or his friend. To the quick circulation of such productions all the motives of interest and vanity concur; the disputant enlarges his knowledge, the zealot animates his passion, and every man is desirous to inform himself concerning affairs so vehemently agitated and variously represented.

It is scarcely to be imagined, through how many subordinations of interest, the ardour of party is diffused; and what multitudes fancy themselves affected by every satire or panegyrick on a man of eminence. Whoever has, at any time, taken occasion to mention him with praise or blame, whoever happens to love or hate any of his adherents, as he wishes to confirm his opinion, and to strengthen his party, will diligently peruse every paper from which he can hope for sentiments like his own. An object, however small in itself, if placed near to the eye, will engross all the rays of light; and a transaction, however trivial, swells into importance, when it presses immediately on our attention. He that shall peruse the political pamphlets of any past reign, will wonder why they were so eagerly read, or so loudly praised. Many of the performances which had power to inflame factions, and fill a kingdom with confusion, have now very little effect upon a frigid critick, and the time is coming, when the compositions of later hirelings shall lie equally despised. In proportion, as those who write on temporary subjects, are exalted above their merit at first, they are afterwards depressed below it; nor can the brightest elegance of diction, or most artful subtilty of reasoning, hope for much esteem from those whose regard is no longer quickened by curiosity or pride.

It is, indeed, the fate of controvertists, even when they contend for philosophical or theological truth, to be soon laid aside and slighted. Either the question is decided, and there is no more place for doubt and opposition; or mankind despair of understanding it, and grow weary of disturbance, content themselves with quiet ignorance, and refuse to be harrassed with labours which they have no hopes of recompensing with knowledge.

The authors of new discoveries may surely expect to be reckoned among those, whose writings are secure of veneration: yet it often happens that the general reception of a doctrine obscures the books in which it was delivered. When any tenet is generally received and adopted as an incontrovertible principle, we seldom look back to the arguments upon which it was first established, or can bear that tediousness of deduction, and multiplicity of evidence, by which its author was forced to reconcile it to prejudice, and fortify it in the weakness of novelty against obstinacy and envy.

It is well known how much of our philosophy is derived from *Boyle*'s discovery of the qualities of the air; yet of those who now adopt or enlarge his theory, very few have read the detail of his experiments. His name is, indeed, reverenced; but his works are neglected; we are contented to know, that he conquered his opponents, without enquiring what cavils were produced against him, or by what proofs they were confuted.

Some writers apply themselves to studies boundless and inexhaustible, as experiments and natural philosophy. These are always lost in successive compilations, as new advances are made, and former observations become more familiar. Others spend their lives in remarks on language, or explanations of antiquities, and only afford materials for lexicographers and commentators, who are themselves overwhelmed by subsequent collectors, that equally destroy the memory of their predecessors by amplification, transposition, or contraction. Every new system of nature gives birth to a swarm of expositors, whose business is to explain and illustrate it, and who can hope to exist no longer than the founder of their sect preserves his reputation.

There are, indeed, few kinds of composition from which an author, however learned or ingenious, can hope a long continuance of fame. He who has carefully studied human nature, and can well describe it, may with most reason flatter his ambition. *Bacon*, among all his pretensions to the regard of posterity, seems to have pleased himself chiefly with his essays, *which come home to mens business and bosoms*, and of which, therefore, he declares his expectation, that they *will live as long as books last*. It may, however, satisfy an honest and benevolent mind to have been useful, though less conspicuous; nor will he that extends his hope to higher rewards, be so much anxious to obtain praise, as to discharge the duty which Providence assigns him.

No. 108. Saturday, 30 March 1751.

Sapere aude,
Incipe. Vivendi recte qui prorogat horam,
Rusticus expectat dum defluat amnis: at ille
Labitur, & labetur in omne volubilis ævum.
HOR.

Begin, be bold, and venture to be wise;
He who defers this work from day to day,
Does on a river's bank expecting stay,
Till the whole stream, which stop'd him, should be gone,
That runs, and as it runs, for ever will run on.

COWLEY.

An ancient poet, unreasonably discontented at the present state of things, which his system of opinions obliged him to represent in its worst form, has observed of the earth, "that its greater part is covered by the uninhabitable ocean; that of the rest some is encumbered with naked mountains, and some lost under barren sands; some scorched with unintermitted heat, and some petrified with perpetual frost; so that only a few regions remain for the production of fruits, the pasture of cattle, and the accommodation of man."

The same observation may be transferred to the time allotted us in our present state. When we have deducted all that is absorbed in sleep, all that is inevitably appropriated to the demands of nature, or irresistibly engrossed by the tyranny of custom; all that passes in regulating the superficial decorations of life, or is given up in the reciprocations of civility to the disposal of others; all that is torn from us by the violence of disease, or stolen imperceptibly away by lassitude and languor; we shall find that part of our duration very small of which we can truly call ourselves masters, or which we can spend wholly at our own choice. Many of our hours are lost in a rotation of petty cares, in a constant recurrence of the same employments; many of our provisions for ease or happiness are always exhausted by the present day; and a great part of our existence serves no other purpose, than that of enabling us to enjoy the rest.

Of the few moments which are left in our disposal, it may reasonably be expected, that we should be so frugal, as to let none of them slip from us without some equivalent; and perhaps it might be found, that as the earth, however streightened by rocks and waters, is capable of producing more than all its inhabitants are able to consume, our lives, though much contracted by incidental distraction, would yet afford us a large space vacant to the exercise of reason and virtue; that we want not time, but diligence, for great performances; and that we squander much of our allowance, even while we think it sparing and insufficient.

This natural and necessary comminution of our lives, perhaps, often makes us insensible of the negligence with which we suffer them to slide away. We never consider ourselves as possessed at once of time sufficient for any great design, and therefore indulge ourselves in fortuitous amusements. We think it unnecessary to take an account of a few supernumerary moments, which, however employed, could have produced little advantage, and which were exposed to a thousand chances of disturbance and interruption.

It is observable, that either by nature or by habit, our faculties are fitted to images of a certain extent, to which we adjust great things by division, and little things by accumulation. Of extensive surfaces we can only take a survey, as the parts succeed one another; and atoms we cannot perceive, till they are united into masses. Thus we break the vast periods of time into centuries and years; and thus, if we would know the amount of moments, we must agglomerate them into days and weeks.

The proverbial oracles of our parsimonious ancestors have informed us, that the fatal waste of fortune is by small expences, by the profusion of sums too little singly to alarm our caution, and which we never suffer ourselves to consider together. Of the same kind is the prodigality of life; he that hopes to look back hereafter with satisfaction upon past years, must learn to know the present value of single minutes, and endeavour to let no particle of time fall useless to the ground.

It is usual for those who are advised to the attainment of any new qualification, to look upon themselves as required to change the general course of their conduct, to dismiss business, and exclude pleasure, and to devote their days and nights to a particular attention. But all common degrees of excellence are attainable at a lower price; he that should steadily and resolutely assign to any science or language those interstitial vacancies which intervene in the most crouded variety of diversion or employment, would find every day new irradiations of knowledge, and discover how much more is to be hoped from frequency and perseverance, than from violent efforts, and sudden desires; efforts which are soon remitted when they encounter difficulty, and desires which, if they are indulged too often, will shake off the authority of reason, and range capriciously from one object to another.

The disposition to defer every important design to a time of leisure, and a state of settled uniformity, proceeds generally from a false estimate of the human powers. If we except those gigantick and stupendous intelligences who are said to grasp a system by intuition, and bound forward from one series of conclusions to another, without regular steps through intermediate propositions, the most successful students make their advances in knowledge by short flights between each of which the mind may lie at rest. For every single act of progression a short time is sufficient; and it is only necessary, that whenever that time is afforded, it be well employed.

Few minds will be long confined to severe and laborious meditation; and when a successful attack on knowledge has been made, the student recreates himself with the contemplation of his conquest, and forbears another incursion, till the new-acquired truth has become familiar, and his curiosity calls upon him for fresh gratifications. Whether the time of intermission is spent in company, or in solitude, in necessary business, or in voluntary levities, the understanding is equally abstracted from the object of enquiry; but, perhaps, if it be detained by occupations less pleasing, it returns again to study with greater alacrity, than when it is glutted with ideal pleasures, and surfeited with intemperance of application. He that will not suffer himself to be discouraged by fancied impossibilities, may sometimes find his abilities invigorated by the necessity of exerting them in short intervals, as the force of a current is encreased by the contraction of its channel.

From some cause like this, it has probably proceeded, that among those who have contributed to the advancement of learning, many have risen to eminence in opposition to all the obstacles which external circumstances could place in their way, amidst the tumult of business, the distresses of poverty, or the dissipations of a wandering and unsettled state. A great part of the life of Erasmus was one continual peregrination; ill supplied with the gifts of fortune, and led from city to city, and from kingdom to kingdom, by the hopes of patrons and preferment, hopes which always flattered and always deceived him; he yet found means by unshaken constancy, and a vigilant improvement of those hours, which, in the midst of the most restless activity, will remain unengaged, to write more than another in the same condition would have hoped to read. Compelled by want to attendance and solicitation, and so much versed in common life, that he has transmitted to us the most perfect delineation of the manners of his age, he joined to his knowledge of the world, such application to books, that he will stand for ever in the first rank of literary heroes. How this proficiency was obtained he sufficiently discovers, by informing us, that the *Praise of Folly*, one of his most celebrated performances, was composed by him on the road to *Italy*; *ne totum illud tempus quo equo fuit insidendum, illiteratis fabulis terreretur*, lest the hours which he was obliged to spend on horseback, should be tattled away without regard to literature.

An *Italian* philosopher expressed in his motto, that *time was his estate*; an estate, indeed, which will produce nothing without cultivation, but will always abundantly repay the labours of industry, and satisfy the most extensive desires, if no part of it be suffered to lie waste by negligence, to be overrun with noxious plants, or laid out for shew rather than for use.

No. 113. Tuesday, 16 April 1751.

——— *Uxorem, Posthume, ducis?*
Dic, quâ Tisiphone, quibus exagitare colubris?
JUVENAL.

A sober man like thee to change his life!
What fury wou'd possess thee with a wife?
DRYDEN.

To the RAMBLER.

SIR,

I know not whether it is always a proof of innocence to treat censure with contempt. We owe so much reverence to the wisdom of mankind, as justly to wish, that our own opinion of our merit may be ratified by the concurrence of other suffrages; and since guilt and infamy must have the same effect upon intelligences unable to pierce beyond external appearance, and influenced often rather by example than precept, we are obliged to refute a false charge, lest we should countenance the crime which we have never committed. To turn away from an accusation with supercilious silence, is equally in the power of him that is hardened by villainy, and inspirited by innocence. The wall of brass which Horace erects upon a clear conscience, may be sometimes raised by impudence or power; and we should always wish to preserve the dignity of virtue by adorning her with graces which wickedness cannot assume.

For this reason I have determined no longer to endure, with either patient or sullen resignation, a reproach, which is, at least in my opinion, unjust; but will lay my case honestly before you, that you or your readers may at length decide it.

Whether you will be able to preserve your boasted impartiality, when you hear, that I am considered as an adversary by half the female world, you may surely pardon me for doubting, notwithstanding the veneration to which you may imagine yourself entitled by your age, your learning, your abstraction, or your virtue. Beauty, Mr. RAMBLER, has often overpowered the resolutions of the firm, and the reasonings of the wise, roused the old to sensibility, and subdued the rigorous to softness.

I am one of those unhappy beings, who have been marked out as husbands for many different women, and deliberated a hundred times on the brink of matrimony. I have discussed all the nuptial preliminaries so often, that I can repeat the forms in which jointures are settled, pin-money secured, and provisions for younger children ascertained; but am at last doomed by general consent to everlasting solitude, and excluded by an irreversible decree from all hopes of connubial felicity. I am pointed out by every mother, as a man whose visits cannot be admitted without reproach; who raises hopes only to embitter disappointment, and makes offers only to seduce girls into a waste of that part of life, in which they might gain advantageous matches, and become mistresses and mothers.

I hope you will think, that some part of this penal severity may justly be remitted, when I inform you, that I never yet professed love to a woman without sincere intentions of marriage; that I have never continued an appearance of intimacy from the hour that my inclination changed, but to preserve her whom I was leaving from the shock of abruptness, or the ignominy of contempt; that I always endeavoured to give the ladies an opportunity of seeming to discard me; and that I never forsook a mistress for larger fortune, or brighter beauty, but because I discovered some irregularity in her conduct, or some depravity in her mind; not because I was charmed by another, but because I was offended by herself.

I was very early tired of that succession of amusements by which the thoughts of most young men are dissipated, and had not long glittered in the splendour of an ample patrimony before I wished for the calm of domestick happiness. Youth is naturally delighted with sprightliness and ardour, and therefore I breathed out the sighs of my first affection at the feet of the gay, the sparkling, the vivacious *Ferocula*. I fancied to myself a perpetual source of happiness in wit never exhausted, and spirit never depressed; looked with veneration on her readiness of expedients, contempt of difficulty, assurance of address, and promptitude of reply; considered her as exempt by some prerogative of nature from the weakness and timidity of female minds; and congratulated myself upon a companion superior to all common troubles and embarrassments. I was, indeed, somewhat disturbed by the unshaken perseverance with which she enforced her demands of an unreasonable settlement; yet I should have consented to pass my life in union with her, had not my curiosity led me to a croud gathered in the street, where I found *Ferocula*, in the presence of hundreds, disputing for six-pence with a chairman. I saw her in so little need of assistance, that it was no breach of the laws of chivalry to forbear interposition, and I spared myself the shame of owning her acquaintance. I forgot some point of ceremony at our next interview, and soon provoked her to forbid me her presence.

My next attempt was upon a lady of great eminence for learning and philosophy. I had frequently observed the barrenness and uniformity of connubial conversation, and therefore thought highly of my own prudence and discernment when I selected from a multitude of wealthy beauties, the deep-read *Misothea*, who declared herself the inexorable enemy of ignorant pertness, and puerile levity; and scarcely condescended to make tea, but for the linguist, the geometrician, the astronomer, or the poet. The queen of the *Amazons* was only to be gained by the hero who could conquer her in single combat; and *Misothea*'s heart was only to bless the scholar who could overpower her by disputation. Amidst the fondest transports of courtship she could call for a definition of terms, and treated every argument with contempt that could not be reduced to regular syllogism. You may easily imagine, that I wished this courtship at an end; but when I desired her to shorten my torments, and fix the day of my felicity, we were led into a long conversation, in which *Misothea* endeavoured to demonstrate the folly of attributing choice and self-direction to any human being. It was not difficult to discover the danger of committing myself for ever to the arms of one who might at any time mistake the dictates of passion, or the calls of appetite, for the decree of fate; or consider cuckoldom as necessary to the general system, as a link in the everlasting chain of successive causes. I therefore told her, that destiny had ordained us to part; and that nothing should have torn me from her but the talons of necessity.

I then solicited the regard of the calm, the prudent, the œconomical *Sophronia*, a lady who considered wit as dangerous, and learning as superfluous; and thought that the woman who kept her house clean, and her accounts exact, took receipts for every payment, and could find them at a sudden call, enquired nicely after the condition of the tenants, read the price of stocks once a week, and purchased every thing at the best market, could want no accomplishments necessary to the happiness of a wise man. She discoursed with great solemnity on the care and vigilance which the superintendence of a family demands; observed how many were ruined by confidence in servants; and told me, that she never expected honesty but from a strong chest, and that the best storekeeper was the mistress's eye. Many such oracles of generosity she uttered, and made every day new improvements in her schemes for the regulation of her servants, and the distribution of her time. I was convinced, that whatever I might suffer from *Sophronia*, I should escape poverty; and we therefore proceeded to adjust the settlements according to her own rule, *fair and softly*. But one morning her maid came to me in tears to intreat my interest for a reconciliation to her mistress, who had turned her out at night for breaking six teeth in a tortoise-shell comb: she had attended her lady from a distant province, and having not lived long enough to save much money, was destitute among strangers, and though of a good family, in danger of perishing in the streets, or of being compelled by hunger to prostitution. I made no scruple of promising to restore her; but upon my first application to *Sophronia* was answered with an air which called for approbation, that if she neglected her own affairs, I might suspect her of neglecting mine; that the comb stood her in three half-crowns; that no servant should wrong her twice; and that indeed, she took the first opportunity of parting with *Phyllida*, because, though she was honest, her constitution was bad, and she thought her very likely to fall sick. Of our conference I need not tell you the effect; it surely may be forgiven, if on this occasion I forgot the decency of common forms.

From two more ladies I was disengaged by finding, that they entertained my rivals at the same time, and determined their choice by the liberality of our settlements. Another I thought myself justified in forsaking, because she gave my attorney a bribe to favour her in the bargain; another, because I could never soften her to tenderness, till she heard that most of my family had died young; and another, because to encrease her fortune by expectations, she represented her sister as languishing and consumptive.

I shall in another letter give the remaining part of my history of courtship. I presume that I should hitherto have injured the majesty of female virtue, had I not hoped to transfer my affection to higher merit.

I am, &c.
HYMENÆUS.

No. 114. Saturday, 20 April 1751.

——————— *Audi,*
Nulla unquam de morte hominis cunctatio longa est.
Juv.

——— When man's life is in debate,
The judge can ne'er too long deliberate.
Dryden.

Power and superiority are so flattering and delightful, that, fraught with temptation and exposed to danger as they are, scarcely any virtue is so cautious, or any prudence so timorous, as to decline them. Even those that have most reverence for the laws of right, are pleased with shewing that not fear, but choice, regulates their behaviour; and would be thought to comply, rather than obey. We love to overlook the boundaries which we do not wish to pass; and, as the *Roman* satirist remarks, he that has no design to take the life of another, is yet glad to have it in his hands.

From the same principle, tending yet more to degeneracy and corruption, proceeds the desire of investing lawful authority with terror, and governing by force rather than persuasion. Pride is unwilling to believe the necessity of assigning any other reason than her own will; and would rather maintain the most equitable claims by violence and penalties, than descend from the dignity of command to dispute and expostulation.

It may, I think, be suspected, that this political arrogance has sometimes found its way into legislative assemblies, and mingled with deliberations upon property and life. A slight perusal of the laws by which the measures of vindictive and coercive justice are established, will discover so many disproportions between crimes and punishments, such capricious distinctions of guilt, and such confusion of remissness and severity, as can scarcely be believed to have been produced by publick wisdom, sincerely and calmly studious of publick happiness.

The learned, the judicious, the pious *Boerhaave* relates, that he never saw a criminal dragged to execution without asking himself, "Who knows whether this man is not less culpable than me?" On the days when the prisons of this city are emptied into the grave, let every spectator of the dreadful procession put the same question to his own heart. Few among those that croud in thousands to the legal massacre, and look with carelessness, perhaps with triumph, on the utmost exacerbations of human misery, would then be able to return without horror and dejection. For, who can congratulate himself upon a life passed without some act more mischievous to the peace or prosperity of others, than the theft of a piece of money?

It has been always the practice, when any particular species of robbery becomes prevalent and common, to endeavour its suppression by capital denunciations. Thus, one generation of malefactors is commonly cut off, and their successors are frighted into new expedients; the art of thievery is augmented with greater variety of fraud, and subtilized to higher degrees of dexterity, and more occult methods of conveyance. The law then renews the persuit in the heat of anger, and overtakes the offender again with death. By this practice, capital inflictions are multiplied, and crimes very different in their degrees of enormity are equally subjected to the severest punishment that man has the power of exercising upon man.

The lawgiver is undoubtedly allowed to estimate the malignity of an offence, not merely by the loss or pain which single acts may produce, but by the general alarm and anxiety arising from the fear of mischief, and insecurity of possession: he therefore exercises the right which societies are supposed to have over the lives of those that compose them, not simply to punish a transgression, but to maintain order, and preserve quiet; he enforces those laws with severity that are most in danger of violation, as the commander of a garrison doubles the guard on that side which is threatned by the enemy.

This method has been long tried, but tried with so little success, that rapine and violence are hourly encreasing; yet few seem willing to despair of its efficacy, and of those who employ their speculations upon the present corruption of the people, some propose the introduction of more horrid, lingering and terrifick punishments; some are inclined to accelerate the executions; some to discourage pardons; and all seem to think that lenity has given confidence to wickedness, and that we can only be rescued from the talons of robbery by inflexible rigour, and sanguinary justice.

Yet since the right of setting an uncertain and arbitrary value upon life has been disputed, and since experience of past times gives us little reason to hope that any reformation will be effected by a periodical havock of our fellow-beings, perhaps it will not be useless to consider what consequences might arise from relaxations of the law, and a more rational and equitable adaptation of penalties to offences.

Death is, as one of the ancients observes, τὸ τῶν φοβερῶν φοβερώτατον, *of dreadful things the most dreadful*; an evil, beyond which nothing can be threatened by sublunary power, or feared from human enmity or vengeance. This terror should, therefore, be reserved as the last resort of authority, as the strongest and most operative of prohibitory sanctions, and placed before the treasure of life, to guard from invasion what cannot be restored. To equal robbery with murder is to reduce murder to robbery, to confound in common minds the gradations of iniquity, and incite the commission of a greater crime to prevent the detection of a less. If only murder were punished with death, very few robbers would stain their hands in blood; but when, by the last act of cruelty no new danger is incurred, and greater security may be obtained, upon what principle shall we bid them forbear?

It may be urged, that the sentence is often mitigated to simple robbery; but surely this is to confess, that our laws are unreasonable in our own opinion; and, indeed, it may be observed, that all but murderers have, at their last hour, the common sensations of mankind pleading in their favour.

From this conviction of the inequality of the punishment to the offence proceeds the frequent solicitation of pardons. They who would rejoice at the correction of a thief, are yet shocked at the thought of destroying him. His crime shrinks to nothing, compared with his misery; and severity defeats itself by exciting pity.

The gibbet, indeed, certainly disables those who die upon it from infesting the community; but their death seems not to contribute more to the reformation of their associates than any other method of separation. A thief seldom passes much of his time in recollection or anticipation, but from robbery hastens to riot, and from riot to robbery; nor, when the grave closes upon his companion, has any other care than to find another.

The frequency of capital punishments therefore rarely hinders the commission of a crime, but naturally and commonly prevents its detection, and is, if we proceed only upon prudential principles, chiefly for that reason to be avoided. Whatever may be urged by casuists or politicians, the greater part of mankind, as they can never think that to pick the pocket and to pierce the heart is equally criminal, will scarcely believe that two malefactors so different in guilt can be justly doomed to the same punishment; nor is the necessity of submitting the conscience to human laws so plainly evinced, so clearly stated, or so generally allowed, but that the pious, the tender, and the just, will always scruple to concur with the community in an act which their private judgment cannot approve.

He who knows not how often rigorous laws produce total impunity, and how many crimes are concealed and forgotten for fear of hurrying the offender to that state in which there is no repentance, has conversed very little with mankind. And whatever epithets of reproach or contempt this compassion may incur from those who confound cruelty with firmness, I know not whether any wise man would wish it less powerful, or less extensive.

If those whom the wisdom of our laws has condemned to die, had been detected in their rudiments of robbery, they might by proper discipline and useful labour, have been disentangled from their habits, they might have escaped all the temptations to subsequent crimes, and passed their days in reparation and penitence; and detected they might all have been, had the prosecutors been certain, that their lives would have been spared. I believe, every thief will confess, that he has been more than once seized and dismissed; and that he has sometimes ventured upon capital crimes, because he knew, that those whom he injured would rather connive at his escape, than cloud their minds with the horrors of his death.

All laws against wickedness are ineffectual, unless some will inform, and some will prosecute; but till we mitigate the penalties for mere violations of property, information will always be hated, and prosecution dreaded. The heart of a good man cannot but recoil at the thought of punishing a slight injury with death; especially when he remembers, that the thief might have procured safety by another crime, from which he was restrained only by his remaining virtue.

The obligations to assist the exercise of publick justice are indeed strong; but they will certainly be overpowered by tenderness for life. What is punished with severity contrary to our ideas of adequate retribution, will be seldom discovered; and multitudes will be suffered to advance from crime to crime, till they deserve death, because if they had been sooner prosecuted, they would have suffered death before they deserved it.

This scheme of invigorating the laws by relaxation, and extirpating wickedness by lenity, is so remote from common practice, that I might reasonably fear to expose it to the publick, could it be supported only by my own observations: I shall, therefore, by ascribing it to its author, Sir *Thomas More*, endeavour to procure it that attention, which I wish always paid to prudence, to justice, and to mercy.

No. 115. Tuesday, 23 April 1751.

Quædam parva quidem, sed non toleranda maritis.
JUV.

Some faults, tho' small, intolerable grow.
DRYDEN.

To the RAMBLER.

SIR,

I sit down in pursuance of my late engagement to recount the remaining part of the adventures that befel me in my long quest of conjugal felicity, which, though I have not yet been so happy as to obtain it, I have at least endeavoured to deserve by unwearied diligence, without suffering from repeated disappointments any abatement of my hope or repression of my activity.

You must have observed in the world a species of mortals who employ themselves in promoting matrimony, and without any visible motive of interest or vanity, without any discoverable impulse of malice or benevolence, without any reason, but that they want objects of attention, and topicks of conversation, are incessantly busy in procuring wives and husbands. They fill the ears of every single man and woman with some convenient match, and when they are informed of your age and fortune, offer a partner of life with the same readiness, and the same indifference, as a salesman, when he has taken measure by his eye, fits his customer with a coat.

It might be expected that they should soon be discouraged from this officious interposition by resentment or contempt; and that every man should determine the choice on which so much of his happiness must depend, by his own judgment and observation: yet it happens, that as these proposals are generally made with a shew of kindness, they seldom provoke anger, but are at worst heard with patience, and forgotten. They influence weak minds to approbation; for many are sure to find in a new acquaintance, whatever qualities report has taught them to expect; and in more powerful and active understandings they excite curiosity, and sometimes by a lucky chance bring persons of similar tempers within the attraction of each other.

I was known to possess a fortune, and to want a wife; and therefore was frequently attended by these hymeneal solicitors, with whose importunity I was sometimes diverted, and sometimes perplexed; for they contended for me as vulturs for a carcase; each employed all his eloquence, and all his artifices, to enforce and promote his own scheme, from the success of which he was to receive no other advantage than the pleasure of defeating others equally eager, and equally industrious.

An invitation to sup with one of those busy friends, made me by a concerted chance acquainted with *Camilla*, by whom it was expected, that I should be suddenly and irresistibly enslaved. The lady, whom the same kindness had brought without her own concurrence into the lists of love, seemed to think me at least worthy of the honour of captivity; and exerted the power, both of her eyes and wit, with so much art and spirit, that though I had been too often deceived by appearances to devote myself irrevocably at the first interview, yet I could not suppress some raptures of admiration, and flutters of desire. I was easily persuaded to make nearer approaches; but soon discovered, that an union with *Camilla* was not much to be wished. *Camilla* professed a boundless contempt for the folly, levity, ignorance, and impertinence of her own sex; and very frequently expressed her wonder, that men of learning or experience could submit to trifle away life, with beings incapable of solid thought. In mixed companies, she always associated with the men, and declared her satisfaction when the ladies retired. If any short excursion into the country was proposed, she commonly insisted upon the exclusion of women from the party; because, where they were admitted, the time was wasted in frothy compliments, weak indulgencies, and idle ceremonies. To shew the greatness of her mind, she avoided all compliance with the fashion; and to boast the profundity of her knowledge, mistook the various textures of silk, confounded tabbies with damasks, and sent for ribbands by wrong names. She despised the commerce of stated visits, a farce of empty form without instruction; and congratulated herself, that she never learned to write message-cards. She often applauded the noble sentiment of *Plato*, who rejoiced that he was born a man rather than a woman; proclaimed her approbation of *Swift*'s opinion, that women are only a higher species of monkies;

and confessed, that when she considered the behaviour, or heard the conversation, of her sex, she could not but forgive the *Turks* for suspecting them to want souls.

It was the joy and pride of *Camilla* to have provoked, by this insolence, all the rage of hatred, and all the persecutions of calumny; nor was she ever more elevated with her own superiority, than when she talked of female anger, and female cunning. Well, says she, has nature provided that such virulence should be disabled by folly, and such cruelty be restrained by impotence.

CAMILLA doubtless expected, that what she lost on one side, she should gain on the other; and imagined that every male heart would be open to a lady, who made such generous advances to the borders of virility. But man, ungrateful man, instead of springing forward to meet her, shrunk back at her approach. She was persecuted by the ladies as a deserter, and at best received by the men only as a fugitive. I, for my part, amused myself a while with her fopperies, but novelty soon gave way to detestation, for nothing out of the common order of nature can be long borne. I had no inclination to a wife who had the ruggedness of man without his force, and the ignorance of woman without her softness; nor could I think my quiet and honour to be entrusted to such audacious virtue as was hourly courting danger, and soliciting assault.

My next mistress was *Nitella*, a lady of gentle mien, and soft voice, always speaking to approve, and ready to receive direction from those with whom chance had brought her into company. In *Nitella* I promised myself an easy friend, with whom I might loiter away the day without disturbance or altercation. I therefore soon resolved to address her, but was discouraged from prosecuting my courtship by observing, that her apartments were superstitiously regular; and that, unless she had notice of my visit, she was never to be seen. There is a kind of anxious cleanliness which I have always noted as the characteristick of a slattern; it is the superfluous scrupulosity of guilt, dreading discovery, and shunning suspicion: it is the violence of an effort against habit, which, being impelled by external motives, cannot stop at the middle point.

NITELLA was always tricked out rather with nicety than elegance; and seldom could forbear to discover by her uneasiness and constraint, that her attention was burdened, and her imagination engrossed: I therefore concluded, that being only occasionally and ambitiously dressed, she was not familiarized to her own ornaments. There are so many competitors for the fame of cleanliness, that it is not hard to gain information of those that fail, from those that desire to excel: I quickly found, that *Nitella* passed her time between finery and dirt; and was always in a wrapper, night-cap, and slippers, when she was not decorated for immediate shew.

I was then led by my evil destiny to *Charybdis*, who never neglected an opportunity of seizing a new prey when it came within her reach. I thought myself quickly made happy by a permission to attend her to publick places; and pleased my own vanity with imagining the envy which I should raise in a thousand hearts, by appearing as the acknowledged favourite of *Charybdis*. She soon after hinted her intention to take a ramble for a fortnight, into a part of the kingdom which she had never seen. I solicited the happiness of accompanying her, which, after a short reluctance, was indulged me. She had no other curiosity in her journey, than after all possible means of expence; and was every moment taking occasion to mention some delicacy, which I knew it my duty upon such notices to procure.

After our return, being now more familiar, she told me, whenever we met, of some new diversion; at night she had notice of a charming company that would breakfast in the gardens; and in the morning had been informed of some new song in the opera, some new dress at the play-house, or some performer at a concert whom she longed to hear. Her intelligence was such, that there never was a shew, to which she did not summon me on the second day; and as she hated a croud, and could not go alone, I was obliged to attend at some intermediate hour, and pay the price of a whole company. When we passed the streets, she was often charmed with some trinket in the toy-shops; and from moderate desires of seals and snuff-boxes, rose, by degrees, to gold and diamonds. I now began to find the smile of *Charybdis* too costly for a private purse, and added one more to six and forty lovers, whose fortune and patience her rapacity had exhausted.

IMPERIA then took possession of my affections; but kept them only for a short time. She had newly inherited a large fortune, and, having spent the early part of her life in the perusal of romances, brought with her into the gay world all the pride of *Cleopatra*; expected nothing less than vows, altars, and sacrifices; and thought her charms dishonoured, and her power infringed, by the softest opposition to her sentiments, or the smallest transgression of her commands. Time might indeed cure this species of pride in a mind not naturally undiscerning, and vitiated only by false representations; but the operations of time are slow; and I therefore left her to grow wise at leisure, or to continue in error at her own expence.

Thus I have hitherto, in spite of myself, passed my life in frozen celibacy. My friends, indeed, often tell me, that I flatter my imagination with higher hopes than human nature can gratify; that I dress up an ideal charmer in all the radiance of perfection, and then enter the world to look for the same excellence in corporeal beauty. But surely, Mr. RAMBLER, it is not madness to hope for some terrestrial lady unstained with the spots which I have been describing; at least, I am resolved to pursue my search; for I am so far from thinking meanly of marriage, that I believe it able to afford the highest happiness decreed to our present state; and if after all these miscarriages I find a woman that fills up my expectation, you shall hear once more from

Yours, &c.
HYMENÆUS.

No. 121. Tuesday, 14 May 1751.

O imitatores, servum pecus!
HOR.

Away, ye imitators, servile herd!
ELPHINSTON.

I have been informed by a letter, from one of the universities, that among the youth from whom the next swarm of reasoners is to learn philosophy, and the next flight of beauties to hear elegies and sonnets, there are many, who, instead of endeavouring by books and meditation to form their own opinions, content themselves with the secondary knowledge, which a convenient bench in a coffee-house can supply; and, without any examination or distinction, adopt the criticisms and remarks, which happen to drop from those, who have risen, by merit or fortune, to reputation and authority.

These humble retailers of knowledge my correspondent stigmatizes with the name of *Echoes*; and seems desirous, that they should be made ashamed of lazy submission, and animated to attempts after new discoveries, and original sentiments.

It is very natural for young men to be vehement, acrimonious, and severe. For, as they seldom comprehend at once all the consequences of a position, or perceive the difficulties by which cooler and more experienced reasoners are restrained from confidence, they form their conclusions with great precipitance. Seeing nothing that can darken or embarrass the question, they expect to find their own opinion universally prevalent, and are inclined to impute uncertainty and hesitation to want of honesty, rather than of knowledge. I may, perhaps, therefore be reproached by my lively correspondent, when it shall be found, that I have no inclination to persecute these collectors of fortuitous knowledge with the severity required; yet, as I am now too old to be much pained by hasty censure, I shall not be afraid of taking into protection those whom I think condemned without a sufficient knowledge of their cause.

He that adopts the sentiments of another, whom he has reason to believe wiser than himself, is only to be blamed, when he claims the honours which are not due but to the author, and endeavours to deceive the world into praise and veneration; for, to learn, is the proper business of youth; and whether we encrease our knowledge by books, or by conversation, we are equally indebted to foreign assistance.

The greater part of students are not born with abilities to construct systems, or advance knowledge; nor can have any hope beyond that of becoming intelligent hearers in the schools of art, of being able to comprehend what others discover, and to remember what others teach. Even those to whom Providence has allotted greater strength of understanding, can expect only to improve a single science. In every other part of learning, they must be content to follow opinions, which they are not able to examine; and, even in that which they claim as peculiarly their own, can seldom add more than some small particle of knowledge, to the hereditary stock devolved to them from ancient times, the collective labour of a thousand intellects.

In science, which being fixed and limited, admits of no other variety than such as arises from new methods of distribution, or new arts of illustration, the necessity of following the traces of our predecessors is indisputably evident; but there appears no reason, why imagination should be subject to the same restraint. It might be conceived, that of those who profess to forsake the narrow paths of truth every one may deviate towards a different point, since though rectitude is uniform and fixed, obliquity may be infinitely diversified. The roads of science are narrow, so that they who travel them, must either follow or meet one another; but in the boundless regions of possibility, which fiction claims for her dominion, there are surely a thousand recesses unexplored, a thousand flowers unplucked, a thousand fountains unexhausted, combinations of imagery yet unobserved, and races of ideal inhabitants not hitherto described.

Yet, whatever hope may persuade, or reason evince, experience can boast of very few additions to ancient fable. The wars of *Troy*, and the travels of *Ulysses*, have furnished almost all succeeding poets with incidents, characters, and sentiments. The *Romans* are confessed to have attempted little more than to display in their own tongue the inventions of the *Greeks*. There is, in all their writings, such a perpetual recurrence of allusions to the tales of the fabulous age, that they must be confessed often to want that power of giving pleasure which novelty supplies; nor can we wonder, that they excelled so much in the graces of diction, when we consider how rarely they were employed in search of new thoughts.

The warmest admirers of the great *Mantuan* poet can extol him for little more than the skill with which he has, by making his hero both a traveller and a warrior, united the beauties of the *Iliad* and *Odyssey* in one composition: yet his judgment was perhaps sometimes overborn by his avarice of the *Homeric* treasures; and, for fear of suffering a sparkling ornament to be lost, he has inserted it where it cannot shine with its original splendor.

When *Ulysses* visited the infernal regions, he found, among the heroes that perished at *Troy*, his competitor *Ajax*, who, when the arms of *Achilles* were adjudged to *Ulysses*, died by his own hand in the madness of disappointment. He still appeared to resent, as on earth, his loss and disgrace. *Ulysses* endeavoured to pacify him with praises and submission; but *Ajax* walked away without reply. This passage has always been considered as eminently beautiful; because *Ajax*, the haughty chief, the unlettered soldier, of unshaken courage, of immoveable constancy, but without the power of recommending his own virtues by eloquence, or enforcing his assertions by any other argument than the sword, had no way of making his anger known, but by gloomy sullenness, and dumb ferocity. His hatred of a man whom he conceived to have defeated him only by volubility of tongue, was therefore naturally shewn by silence more contemptuous and piercing than any words that so rude an orator could have found, and by which he gave his enemy no opportunity of exerting the only power in which he was superior.

When *Æneas* is sent by *Virgil* to the shades, he meets *Dido* the queen of *Carthage*, whom his perfidy had hurried to the grave; he accosts her with tenderness and excuses; but the lady turns away like *Ajax* in mute disdain. She turns away like *Ajax*, but she resembles him in none of those qualities which give either dignity or propriety to silence. She might, without any departure from the tenour of her conduct, have burst out like other injured women into clamour, reproach, and denunciation; but *Virgil* had his imagination full of *Ajax*, and therefore could not prevail on himself to teach *Dido* any other mode of resentment.

If *Virgil* could be thus seduced by imitation, there will be little hope, that common wits should escape; and accordingly we find, that besides the universal and acknowledged practice of copying the ancients, there has prevailed in every age a particular species of fiction. At one time all truth was conveyed in allegory; at another, nothing was seen but in a vision; at one period, all the poets followed sheep, and every event produced a pastoral; at another they busied themselves wholly in giving directions to a painter.

It is indeed easy to conceive why any fashion should become popular, by which idleness is favoured, and imbecillity assisted; but surely no man of genius can much applaud himself for repeating a tale with which the audience is already tired, and which could bring no honour to any but its inventor.

There are, I think, two schemes of writing, on which the laborious wits of the present time employ their faculties. One is the adaptation of sense to all the rhymes which our language can supply to some word, that makes the burden of the stanza; but this, as it has been only used in a kind of amorous burlesque, can scarcely be censured with much acrimony. The other is the imitation of *Spenser*, which, by the influence of some men of learning and genius, seems likely to gain upon the age, and therefore deserves to be more attentively considered.

To imitate the fictions and sentiments of *Spenser* can incur no reproach, for allegory is perhaps one of the most pleasing vehicles of instruction. But I am very far from extending the same respect to his diction or his stanza. His stile was in his own time allowed to be vicious, so darkened with old words and peculiarities of phrase, and so remote from common use, that *Johnson* boldly pronounces him *to have written no language*. His stanza is at once difficult and unpleasing; tiresome to the ear by its uniformity, and to the attention by its length. It was at first formed in imitation of the *Italian* poets, without due regard to the genius of our language. The *Italians* have little variety of termination, and were forced to contrive such a stanza as might admit the greatest number of similar rhymes; but our words end with so much diversity, that it is seldom convenient for us to bring more than two of the same sound together. If it be justly observed by *Milton*, that rhyme obliges poets to express their thoughts in improper terms, these improprieties must always be multiplied, as the difficulty of rhyme is encreased by long concatenations.

The imitators of *Spenser* are indeed not very rigid censors of themselves, for they seem to conclude, that when they have disfigured their lines with a few obsolete syllables, they have accomplished their design, without considering that they ought not only to admit old words, but to avoid new. The laws of imitation are broken by every word introduced since the time of *Spenser*, as the character of *Hector* is violated by quoting *Aristotle* in the play. It would indeed be difficult to exclude from a long poem all modern phrases, though it is easy to sprinkle it with gleanings of antiquity. Perhaps, however, the stile of *Spenser* might by long labour be justly copied; but life is surely given us for higher purposes than to gather what our ancestors have wisely thrown away, and to learn what is of no value, but because it has been forgotten.

No. 129. Tuesday, 11 June 1751.

—— *Nunc, o nunc, Dædale, dixit,*
Materiam, qua sis ingeniosus, habes.
Possidet en terras, et possidet æquora Minos:
Nec tellus nostræ, nec patet unda fugæ.
Restat iter cælo: cælo tentabimus ire.
Da veniam cœpto, Jupiter alte, meo.

OVID.

Now, *Dædalus*, behold, by fate assign'd,
A task proportion'd to thy mighty mind!
Unconquer'd bars on earth and sea withstand;
Thine, *Minos*, is the main, and thine the land.
The skies are open —— let us try the skies:
Forgive, great *Jove*, the daring enterprize.

Moralists, like other writers, instead of casting their eyes abroad in the living world, and endeavouring to form maxims of practice and new hints of theory, content their curiosity with that secondary knowledge which books afford, and think themselves entitled to reverence by a new arrangement of an ancient system, or new illustration of established principles. The sage precepts of the first instructors of the world are transmitted from age to age with little variation, and echoed from one author to another, not perhaps without some loss of their original force at every repercussion.

I know not whether any other reason than this idleness of imitation can be assigned for that uniform and constant partiality, by which some vices have hitherto escaped censure, and some virtues wanted recommendation; nor can I discover why else we have been warned only against part of our enemies, while the rest have been suffered to steal upon us without notice; why the heart has on one side been doubly fortified, and laid open on the other to the incursions of error, and the ravages of vice.

Among the favourite topics of moral declamation, may be numbered the miscarriages of imprudent boldness, and the folly of attempts beyond our power. Every page of every philosopher is crouded with examples of temerity that sunk under burthens which she laid upon herself, and called out enemies to battle by whom she was destroyed.

Their remarks are too just to be disputed, and too salutary to be rejected; but there is likewise some danger lest timorous prudence should be inculcated, till courage and enterprize are wholly repressed, and the mind congealed in perpetual inactivity by the fatal influence of frigorifick wisdom.

Every man should, indeed, carefully compare his force with his undertaking; for though we ought not to live only for our own sakes, and though therefore danger or difficulty should not be avoided merely because we may expose ourselves to misery or disgrace; yet it may be justly required of us, not to throw away our lives, upon inadequate and hopeless designs, since we might by a just estimate of our abilities become more useful to mankind.

There is an irrational contempt of danger which approaches nearly to the folly, if not the guilt, of suicide; there is a ridiculous perseverance in impracticable schemes, which is justly punished with ignominy and reproach. But in the wide regions of probability which are the proper province of prudence and election, there is always room to deviate on either side of rectitude without rushing against apparent absurdity; and according to the inclinations of nature, or the impressions of precept, the daring and the cautious may move in different directions without touching upon rashness or cowardice.

That there is a middle path which it is every man's duty to find, and to keep, is unanimously confessed; but it is likewise acknowledged that this middle path is so narrow, that it cannot easily be discovered, and so little beaten that there are no certain marks by which it can be followed; the care therefore of all those who conduct others has been, that whenever they decline into obliquities, they should tend towards the side of safety.

It can, indeed, raise no wonder that temerity has been generally censured; for it is one of the vices with which few can be charged, and which therefore great numbers are ready to condemn. It is the vice of noble and generous minds, the exuberance of magnanimity, and the ebullition of genius; and is therefore not regarded with much tenderness, because it never flatters us by that appearance of softness and imbecillity which is commonly necessary to conciliate compassion. But if the same attention had been applied to the search of arguments against the folly of presupposing impossibilities, and anticipating frustration, I know not whether many would not have been roused to usefulness, who, having been taught to confound prudence with timidity, never ventured to excel, lest they should unfortunately fail.

It is necessary to distinguish our own interest from that of others, and that distinction will perhaps assist us in fixing the just limits of caution and adventurousness. In an undertaking that involves the happiness, or the safety of many, we have certainly no right to hazard more than is allowed by those who partake the danger; but where only ourselves can suffer by miscarriage, we are not confined within such narrow limits; and still less is the reproach of temerity, when numbers will receive advantage by success, and only one be incommoded by failure.

Men are generally willing to hear precepts by which ease is favoured; and as no resentment is raised by general representations of human folly, even in those who are most eminently jealous of comparative reputation, we confess, without reluctance, that vain man is ignorant of his own weakness, and therefore frequently presumes to attempt what he can never accomplish; but it ought likewise to be remembered, that man is no less ignorant of his own powers, and might perhaps have accomplished a thousand designs, which the prejudices of cowardice restrained him from attempting.

It is observed in the golden verses of *Pythagoras*, that *Power is never far from necessity*. The vigour of the human mind quickly appears, when there is no longer any place for doubt and hesitation, when diffidence is absorbed in the sense of danger, or overwhelmed by some resistless passion. We then soon discover, that difficulty is, for the most part, the daughter of idleness, that the obstacles with which our way seemed to be obstructed were only phantoms, which we believed real because we durst not advance to a close examination; and we learn that it is impossible to determine without experience how much constancy may endure, or perseverance perform.

But whatever pleasure may be found in the review of distresses when art or courage has surmounted them, few will be persuaded to wish that they may be awakened by want or terror to the conviction of their own abilities. Every one should therefore endeavour to invigorate himself by reason and reflection, and determine to exert the latent force that nature may have reposited in him before the hour of exigence comes upon him, and compulsion shall torture him to diligence. It is below the dignity of a reasonable being to owe that strength to necessity which ought always to act at the call of choice, or to need any other motive to industry than the desire of performing his duty.

Reflections that may drive away despair, cannot be wanting to him who considers how much life is now advanced beyond the state of naked, undisciplined, uninstructed nature. Whatever has been effected for convenience or elegance, while it was yet unknown, was believed impossible; and therefore would never have been attempted, had not some, more daring than the rest, adventured to bid defiance to prejudice and censure. Nor is there yet any reason to doubt that the same labour would be rewarded with the same success. There are qualities in the products of nature yet undiscovered, and combinations in the powers of art yet untried. It is the duty of every man to endeavour that something may be added by his industry to the hereditary aggregate of knowledge and happiness. To add much can indeed be the lot of few, but to add something, however little, every one may hope; and of every honest endeavour it is certain, that, however unsuccessful, it will be at last rewarded.

No. 134. Saturday, 29 June 1751.

Quis scit, an adjiciant hodiernæ crastina summæ
Tempora Dî superi!

HOR.

Who knows if Heav'n, with ever-bounteous pow'r,
Shall add to-morrow to the present hour?

FRANCIS.

I sat yesterday morning employed in deliberating on which, among the various subjects that occurred to my imagination, I should bestow the paper of to-day. After a short effort of meditation by which nothing was determined, I grew every moment more irresolute, my ideas wandered from the first intention, and I rather wished to think, than thought, upon any settled subject; till at last I was awakened from this dream of study by a summons from the press: the time was come for which I had been thus negligently purposing to provide, and, however dubious or sluggish, I was now necessitated to write.

Though to a writer whose design is so comprehensive and miscellaneous, that he may accommodate himself with a topick from every scene of life, or view of nature, it is no great aggravation of his task to be obliged to a sudden composition, yet I could not forbear to reproach myself for having so long neglected what was unavoidably to be done, and of which every moment's idleness increased the difficulty. There was however some pleasure in reflecting that I, who had only trifled till diligence was necessary, might still congratulate myself upon my superiority to multitudes, who have trifled till diligence is vain; who can by no degree of activity or resolution recover the opportunities which have slipped away; and who are condemned by their own carelessness to hopeless calamity and barren sorrow.

The folly of allowing ourselves to delay what we know cannot be finally escaped, is one of the general weaknesses, which, in spite of the instruction of moralists, and the remonstrances of reason, prevail to a greater or less degree in every mind: even they who most steadily withstand it, find it, if not the most violent, the most pertinacious of their passions, always renewing its attacks, and though often vanquished, never destroyed.

It is indeed natural to have particular regard to the time present, and to be most solicitous for that which is by its nearness enabled to make the strongest impressions. When therefore any sharp pain is to be suffered, or any formidable danger to be incurred, we can scarcely exempt ourselves wholly from the seducements of imagination; we readily believe that another day will bring some support or advantage which we now want; and are easily persuaded, that the moment of necessity which we desire never to arrive, is at a great distance from us.

Thus life is languished away in the gloom of anxiety, and consumed in collecting resolution which the next morning dissipates; in forming purposes which we scarcely hope to keep, and reconciling ourselves to our own cowardice by excuses, which, while we admit them, we know to be absurd. Our firmness is by the continual contemplation of misery hourly impaired; every submission to our fear enlarges its dominion; we not only waste that time in which the evil we dread might have been suffered and surmounted, but even where procrastination produces no absolute encrease of our difficulties, make them less superable to ourselves by habitual terrors. When evils cannot be avoided, it is wise to contract the interval of expectation; to meet the mischiefs which will overtake us if we fly; and suffer only their real malignity without the conflicts of doubt and anguish of anticipation.

To act is far easier than to suffer, yet we every day see the progress of life retarded by the *vis inertiae*, the mere repugnance to motion, and find multitudes repining at the want of that which nothing but idleness hinders them from enjoying. The case of *Tantalus*, in the region of poetick punishment, was somewhat to be pitied, because the fruits that hung about him retired from his hand; but what tenderness can be claimed by those who though perhaps they suffer the pains of *Tantalus* will never lift their hands for their own relief?

There is nothing more common among this torpid generation than murmurs and complaints; murmurs at uneasiness which only vacancy and suspicion expose them to feel, and complaints of distresses which it is in their own power to remove. Laziness is commonly associated with timidity. Either fear originally prohibits endeavours by infusing despair of success; or the frequent failure of irresolute struggles, and the constant desire of avoiding labour, impress by degrees false terrors on the mind. But fear, whether natural or acquired, when once it has full possession of the fancy, never fails to employ it upon visions of calamity, such as if they are not dissipated by useful employment, will soon overcast it with horrors, and imbitter life not only with those miseries by which all earthly beings are really more or less tormented, but with those which do not yet exist, and which can only be discerned by the perspicacity of cowardice.

Among all who sacrifice future advantage to present inclination, scarcely any gain so little as those that suffer themselves to freeze in idleness. Others are corrupted by some enjoyment of more or less power to gratify the passions; but to neglect our duties, merely to avoid the labour of performing them, a labour which is always punctually rewarded, is surely to sink under weak temptations. Idleness never can secure tranquillity; the call of reason and of conscience will pierce the closest pavilion of the sluggard, and, though it may not have force to drive him from his down, will be loud enough to hinder him from sleep. Those moments which he cannot resolve to make useful by devoting them to the great business of his being, will still be usurped by powers that will not leave them to his disposal; remorse and vexation will seize upon them, and forbid him to enjoy what he is so desirous to appropriate.

There are other causes of inactivity incident to more active faculties and more acute discernment. He to whom many objects of persuit arise at the same time, will frequently hesitate between different desires, till a rival has precluded him, or change his course as new attractions prevail, and harrass himself without advancing. He who sees different ways to the same end, will, unless he watches carefully over his own conduct, lay out too much of his attention upon the comparison of probabilities, and the adjustment of expedients, and pause in the choice of his road, till some accident intercepts his journey. He whose penetration extends to remote consequences, and who, whenever he applies his attention to any design, discovers new prospects of advantage, and possibilities of improvement, will not easily be persuaded that his project is ripe for execution; but will superadd one contrivance to another, endeavour to unite various purposes in one operation, multiply complications, and refine niceties, till he is entangled in his own scheme, and bewildered in the perplexity of various intentions. He that resolves to unite all the beauties of situation in a new purchase, must waste his life in roving to no purpose from province to province. He that hopes in the same house to obtain every convenience, may draw plans and study *Palladio*, but will never lay a stone. He will attempt a treatise on some important subject, and amass materials, consult authors, and study all the dependent and collateral parts of learning, but never conclude himself qualified to write. He that has abilities to conceive perfection, will not easily be content without it; and since perfection cannot be reached, will lose the opportunity of doing well in the vain hope of unattainable excellence.

The certainty that life cannot be long, and the probability that it will be much shorter than nature allows, ought to awaken every man to the active prosecution of whatever he is desirous to perform. It is true that no diligence can ascertain success; death may intercept the swiftest career; but he who is cut off in the execution of an honest undertaking, has at least the honour of falling in his rank, and has fought the battle, though he missed the victory.

No. 135. Tuesday, 2 July 1751.

Cœlum, non animum mutant.

HOR.

Place may be chang'd; but who can change his mind?

It is impossible to take a view on any side, or observe any of the various classes that form the great community of the world, without discovering the influence of example; and admitting with new conviction the observation of *Aristotle*, that *man is an imitative being*. The greater, far the greater, number follow the track which others have beaten, without any curiosity after new discoveries, or ambition of trusting themselves to their own conduct. And, of those who break the ranks and disorder the uniformity of the march, most return in a short time from their deviation, and prefer the equal and steady satisfaction of security before the frolicks of caprice and the honours of adventure.

In questions difficult or dangerous it is indeed natural to repose upon authority, and, when fear happens to predominate, upon the authority of those whom we do not in general think wiser than ourselves. Very few have abilities requisite for the discovery of abstruse truth; and of those few some want leisure and some resolution. But it is not so easy to find the reason of the universal submission to precedent where every man might safely judge for himself; where no irreparable loss can be hazarded, nor any mischief of long continuance incurred. Vanity might be expected to operate where the more powerful passions are not awakened; the mere pleasure of acknowledging no superior might produce slight singularities, or the hope of gaining some new degree of happiness awaken the mind to invention or experiment.

If in any case the shackles of prescription could be wholly shaken off, and the imagination left to act without controul, on what occasion should it be expected, but in the selection of lawful pleasure? Pleasure, of which the essence is choice; which compulsion dissociates from every thing to which nature has united it; and which owes not only its vigour but its being to the smiles of liberty. Yet we see that the senses, as well as the reason, are regulated by credulity; and that most will feel, or say that they feel, the gratifications which others have taught them to expect.

At this time of universal migration, when almost every one, considerable enough to attract regard, has retired, or is preparing with all the earnestness of distress to retire, into the country; when nothing is to be heard but the hopes of speedy departure, or the complaints of involuntary delay; I have often been tempted to enquire what happiness is to be gained, or what inconvenience to be avoided, by this stated recession. Of the birds of passage, some follow the summer, and some the winter, because they live upon sustenance which only summer or winter can supply; but of the annual flight of human rovers it is much harder to assign the reason, because they do not appear either to find or seek any thing which is not equally afforded by the town and country.

I believe, that many of these fugitives may have heard of men whose continual wish was for the quiet of retirement, who watched every opportunity to steal away from observation, to forsake the croud, and delight themselves with

the society of solitude. There is indeed scarcely any writer who has not celebrated the happiness of rural privacy, and delighted himself and his reader
with the melody of birds, the whisper of groves, and the murmur of rivulets;
nor any man eminent for extent of capacity, or greatness of exploits, that has
not left behind him some memorials of lonely wisdom, and silent dignity.

But almost all absurdity of conduct arises from the imitation of those
whom we cannot resemble. Those who thus testified their weariness of tumult
and hurry, and hasted with so much eagerness to the leisure of retreat, were
either men overwhelmed with the pressure of difficult employments, harrassed with importunities, and distracted with multiplicity; or men wholly
engrossed by speculative sciences, who having no other end of life but to learn
and teach, found their searches interrupted by the common commerce of
civility, and their reasonings disjointed by frequent interruptions. Such men
might reasonably fly to that ease and convenience which their condition
allowed them to find only in the country. The statesman who devoted the
greater part of his time to the publick, was desirous of keeping the remainder
in his own power. The general ruffled with dangers, wearied with labours, and
stunned with acclamations, gladly snatched an interval of silence and relaxation. The naturalist was unhappy where the works of providence were not
always before him. The reasoner could adjust his systems only where his
mind was free from the intrusion of outward objects.

Such examples of solitude very few of those who are now hastening from
the town, have any pretensions to plead in their own justification, since they
cannot pretend either weariness of labour, or desire of knowledge. They purpose nothing more than to quit one scene of idleness for another, and after
having trifled in publick, to sleep in secrecy. The utmost that they can hope to
gain is the change of ridiculousness to obscurity, and the privilege of having
fewer witnesses to a life of folly. He who is not sufficiently important to be
disturbed in his pursuits, but spends all his hours according to his own inclination, and has more hours than his mental faculties enable him to fill either
with enjoyment or desires, can have nothing to demand of shades and valleys.
As bravery is said to be a panoply, insignificancy is always a shelter.

There are however pleasures and advantages in a rural situation, which are
not confined to philosophers and heroes. The freshness of the air, the verdure
of the woods, the paint of the meadows, and the unexhausted variety which
summer scatters upon the earth, may easily give delight to an unlearned spectator. It is not necessary that he who looks with pleasure on the colours of a
flower should study the principles of vegetation, or that the *Ptolemaick* and
Copernican system should be compared before the light of the sun can gladden, or its warmth invigorate. Novelty is itself a source of gratification, and
Milton justly observes, that to him who has been long pent up in cities no
rural object can be presented, which will not delight or refresh some of his
senses.

Yet even these easy pleasures are missed by the greater part of those who waste their summer in the country. Should any man pursue his acquaintances to their retreats, he would find few of them listening to *Philomel*, loitering in woods, or plucking daisies, catching the healthy gale of the morning, or watching the gentle coruscations of declining day. Some will be discovered at a window by the road side, rejoicing when a new cloud of dust gathers towards them, as at the approach of a momentary supply of conversation, and a short relief from the tediousness of unideal vacancy. Others are placed in the adjacent villages, where they look only upon houses as in the rest of the year, with no change of objects but what a remove to any new street in *London* might have given them. The same set of acquaintances still settle together, and the form of life is not otherwise diversified than by doing the same things in a different place. They pay and receive visits in the usual form, they frequent the walks in the morning, they deal cards at night, they attend to the same tattle, and dance with the same partners; nor can they at their return to their former habitation congratulate themselves on any other advantage, than that they have passed their time like others of the same rank; and have the same right to talk of the happiness and beauty of the country, of happiness which they never felt, and beauty which they never regarded.

To be able to procure its own entertainments, and to subsist upon its own stock, is not the prerogative of every mind. There are indeed understandings so fertile and comprehensive, that they can always feed reflection with new supplies, and suffer nothing from the preclusion of adventitious amusements; as some cities have within their own walls enclosed ground enough to feed their inhabitants in a siege. But others live only from day to day, and must be constantly enabled, by foreign supplies, to keep out the encroachments of languor and stupidity. Such could not indeed be blamed for hovering within reach of their usual pleasures, more than any other animal for not quitting its native element, were not their faculties contracted by their own fault. But let not those who go into the country, merely because they dare not be left alone at home, boast their love of nature, or their qualifications for solitude; nor pretend that they receive instantaneous infusions of wisdom from the *Dryads*, and are able, when they leave smoke and noise behind, to act, or think, or reason for themselves.

No. 137. Tuesday, 9 July 1751.

Dum vitant stulti vitia, in contraria currunt.
HOR.

——— Whilst fools one vice condemn,
They run into the opposite extreme.
CREECH.

That wonder is the effect of ignorance, has been often observed. The awful stillness of attention, with which the mind is overspread at the first view of an unexpected effect, ceases when we have leisure to disentangle complications and investigate causes. Wonder is a pause of reason, a sudden cessation of the mental progress, which lasts only while the understanding is fixed upon some single idea, and is at an end when it recovers force enough to divide the object into its parts, or mark the intermediate gradations from the first agent to the last consequence.

It may be remarked with equal truth, that ignorance is often the effect of wonder. It is common for those who have never accustomed themselves to the labour of enquiry, nor invigorated their confidence by conquests over difficulty, to sleep in the gloomy quiescence of astonishment, without any effort to animate enquiry or dispel obscurity. What they cannot immediately conceive, they consider as too high to be reached, or too extensive to be comprehended; they therefore content themselves with the gaze of folly, forbear to attempt what they have no hopes of performing, and resign the pleasure of rational contemplation to more pertinacious study or more active faculties.

Among the productions of mechanic art, many are of a form so different from that of their first materials, and many consist of parts so numerous and so nicely adapted to each other, that it is not possible to view them without amazement. But when we enter the shops of artificers, observe the various tools by which every operation is facilitated, and trace the progress of a manufacture thro' the different hands that, in succession to each other, contribute to its perfection, we soon discover that every single man has an easy task, and that the extremes however remote of natural rudeness and artificial elegance, are joined by a regular concatenation of effects, of which every one is introduced by that which precedes it, and equally introduces that which is to follow.

The same is the state of intellectual and manual performances. Long calculations or complex diagrams affright the timorous and unexperienced from a second view; but if we have skill sufficient to analise them into simple principles, it will be discovered that our fear was groundless. *Divide and conquer*, is a principle equally just in science as in policy. Complication is a species of confederacy, which, while it continues united, bids defiance to the most active and vigorous intellect; but of which every member is separately weak, and which may therefore be quickly subdued if it can once be broken.

The chief art of learning, as *Locke* has observed, is to attempt but little at a time. The widest excursions of the mind are made by short flights frequently repeated; the most lofty fabricks of science are formed by the continued accumulation of single propositions.

It often happens, whatever be the cause, that impatience of labour or dread of miscarriage, seizes those who are most distinguished for quickness of apprehension; and that they who might with greatest reason promise themselves victory, are least willing to hazard the encounter. This diffidence, where the attention is not laid asleep by laziness or dissipated by pleasures, can arise only from confused and general views, such as negligence snatches in haste, or from the disappointment of the first hopes formed by arrogance without reflection. To expect that the intricacies of science will be pierced by a careless glance, or the eminences of fame ascended without labour, is to expect a peculiar privilege, a power denied to the rest of mankind; but to suppose that the maze is inscrutable to diligence, or the heights inaccessible to perseverance, is to submit tamely to the tyranny of fancy, and enchain the mind in voluntary shackles.

It is the proper ambition of the heroes in literature to enlarge the boundaries of knowledge by discovering and conquering new regions of the intellectual world. To the success of such undertakings perhaps some degree of fortuitous happiness is necessary, which no man can promise or procure to himself; and therefore doubt and irresolution may be forgiven in him that ventures into the unexplored abysses of truth, and attempts to find his way through the fluctuations of uncertainty, and the conflicts of contradiction. But when nothing more is required, than to pursue a path already beaten, and to trample obstacles which others have demolished, why should any man so much distrust his own intellect as to imagine himself unequal to the attempt?

It were to be wished that they who devote their lives to study would at once believe nothing too great for their attainment, and consider nothing as too little for their regard; that they would extend their notice alike to science and to life, and unite some knowledge of the present world to their acquaintance with past ages and remote events.

Nothing has so much exposed men of learning to contempt and ridicule, as their ignorance of things which are known to all but themselves. Those who have been taught to consider the institutions of the schools, as giving the last perfection to human abilities, are surprised to see men wrinkled with study, yet wanting to be instructed in the minute circumstances of propriety, or the necessary forms of daily transaction; and quickly shake off their reverence for modes of education, which they find to produce no ability above the rest of mankind.

BOOKS, says Bacon, *can never teach the use of books.* The student must learn by commerce with mankind to reduce his speculations to practice, and accommodate his knowledge to the purposes of life.

It is too common for those who have been bred to scholastic professions, and passed much of their time in academies where nothing but learning confers honours, to disregard every other qualification, and to imagine that they shall find mankind ready to pay homage to their knowledge, and to crowd about them for instruction. They, therefore, step out from their cells into the open world, with all the confidence of authority and dignity of importance; they look round about them at once with ignorance and scorn on a race of beings to whom they are equally unknown and equally contemptible, but whose manners they must imitate, and with whose opinions they must comply, if they desire to pass their time happily among them.

To lessen that disdain with which scholars are inclined to look on the common business of the world, and the unwillingness with which they condescend to learn what is not to be found in any system of philosophy, it may be necessary to consider that though admiration is excited by abstruse researches and remote discoveries, yet pleasure is not given, nor affection conciliated, but by softer accomplishments, and qualities more easily communicable to those about us. He that can only converse upon questions, about which only a small part of mankind has knowledge sufficient to make them curious, must lose his days in unsocial silence, and live in the crowd of life without a companion. He that can only be useful in great occasions, may die without exerting his abilities, and stand a helpless spectator of a thousand vexations which fret away happiness, and which nothing is required to remove but a little dexterity of conduct and readiness of expedients.

No degree of knowledge attainable by man is able to set him above the want of hourly assistance, or to extinguish the desire of fond endearments, and tender officiousness; and therefore, no one should think it unnecessary to learn those arts by which friendship may be gained. Kindness is preserved by a constant reciprocation of benefits or interchange of pleasures; but such benefits only can be bestowed, as others are capable to receive, and such pleasures only imparted, as others are qualified to enjoy.

By this descent from the pinacles of art no honour will be lost; for the condescensions of learning are always overpaid by gratitude. An elevated genius employed in little things, appears, to use the simile of *Longinus*, like the sun in his evening declination, he remits his splendor but retains his magnitude, and pleases more, though he dazzles less.

No. 142. Saturday, 27 July 1751.

Ἔνθα δ' ἀνὴρ ἐνίαυε πελώριος——οὐδὲ, μετ' ἀλλούς
Πωλεῖτ', ἀλλ' ἀπάνευθεν ἐὼν ἀθεμίστια ᾔδη·
Καὶ γὰρ θαῦμ' ἐτέτυκτο πελώριον, οὐδὲ ἐῴκει
Ἀνδρί σιτοφάγῳ·

HOM.

A giant shepherd here his flock maintains
Far from the rest, and solitary reigns,
In shelter thick of horrid shade reclin'd;
And gloomy mischiefs labour in his mind.
A form enormous! far unlike the race
Of human birth, in stature or in face.

POPE.

To the RAMBLER.

SIR,

Having been accustomed to retire annually from the town, I lately accepted the invitation of *Eugenio*, who has an estate and seat in a distant county. As we were unwilling to travel without improvement, we turned often from the direct road to please ourselves with the view of nature or of art; we examined every wild mountain and medicinal spring, criticised every edifice, contemplated every ruin, and compared every scene of action with the narratives of historians. By this succession of amusements we enjoyed the exercise of a journey without suffering the fatigue, and had nothing to regret but that by a progress so leisurely and gentle, we missed the adventures of a post chaise, and the pleasure of alarming villages with the tumult of our passage, and of disguising our insignificancy by the dignity of hurry.

The first week after our arrival at *Eugenio*'s house was passed in receiving visits from his neighbours, who crowded about him with all the eagerness of benevolence; some impatient to learn the news of the court and town, that they might be qualified by authentick information to dictate to the rural politicians on the next bowling day; others desirous of his interest to accommodate disputes, or of his advice in the settlement of their fortunes and the marriage of their children.

The civilities which we had received were soon to be returned; and I passed some time with great satisfaction in roving through the country, and viewing the seats, gardens and plantations which are scattered over it. My pleasure would indeed have been greater had I been sometimes allowed to wander in a park or wilderness alone, but to appear as the friend of *Eugenio* was an honour not to be enjoyed without some inconveniences; so much was every one solicitous for my regard, that I could seldom escape to solitude, or steal a moment from the emulation of complaisance, and the vigilance of officiousness.

In these rambles of good neighbourhood, we frequently passed by a house of unusual magnificence. While I had my curiosity yet distracted among many novelties, it did not much attract my observation; but in a short time I could not forbear surveying it with particular notice; for the length of the wall which enclosed the gardens, the disposition of the shades that waved over it, and the canals, of which I could obtain some glimpses through the trees from our own windows, gave me reason to expect more grandeur and beauty than I had yet seen in that province. I therefore enquired, as we rode by it, why we never amongst our excursions spent an hour where there was such appearance of splendor and affluence. *Eugenio* told me that the seat which I so much admired, was commonly called in the country the *haunted house*, and that no visits were paid there by any of the gentlemen whom I had yet seen. As the haunts of incorporeal beings are generally ruinous, neglected and desolate, I easily conceived that there was something to be explained, and told him that I supposed it only fairy ground, on which we might venture by day-light without danger. The danger, says he, is indeed only that of appearing to solicit the acquaintance of a man, with whom it is not possible to converse without infamy, and who has driven from him, by his insolence or malignity, every human being who can live without him.

Our conversation was then accidentally interrupted; but my inquisitive humour being now in motion, could not rest without a full account of this newly discovered prodigy. I was soon informed that the fine house and spacious gardens were haunted by squire *Bluster*, of whom it was very easy to learn the character, since nobody had regard for him sufficient to hinder them from telling whatever they could discover.

Squire *Bluster* is descended of an ancient family. The estate which his ancestors had immemorially possessed was much augmented by Captain *Bluster*, who served under *Drake* in the reign of *Elizabeth*; and the *Blusters*, who were before only petty gentlemen, have from that time frequently represented the shire in parliament, been chosen to present addresses, and given laws at hunting-matches and races. They were eminently hospitable and popular, till the father of this gentleman died of an election. His lady went to the grave soon after him, and left the heir, then only ten years old, to the care of his grandmother, who would not suffer him to be controlled, because she could not bear to hear him cry; and never sent him to school, because she was not able to live without his company. She taught him however very early to inspect the steward's accounts, to dog the butler from the cellar, and to catch the servants at a junket; so that he was at the age of eighteen a complete master of all the lower arts of domestick policy, had often on the road detected combinations between the coachman and the ostler, and procured the discharge of nineteen maids for illicit correspondence with cottagers and charwomen.

By the opportunities of parsimony which minority affords, and which the probity of his guardians had diligently improved, a very large sum of money was accumulated, and he found himself, when he took his affairs into his own hands, the richest man in the county. It has been long the custom of this family to celebrate the heir's completion of his twenty-first year, by an entertainment, at which the house is thrown open to all that are inclined to enter it, and the whole province flocks together as to a general festivity. On this occasion young *Bluster* exhibited the first tokens of his future eminence, by shaking his purse at an old gentleman, who had been the intimate friend of his father, and offering to wager a greater sum than he could afford to venture; a practice with which he has at one time or other insulted every freeholder within ten miles round him.

His next acts of offence were committed in a contentious and spiteful vindication of the privileges of his manors, and a rigorous and relentless prosecution of every man that presumed to violate his game. As he happens to have no estate adjoining equal to his own, his oppressions are often borne without resistance, for fear of a long suit, of which he delights to count the expences without the least solicitude about the event; for he knows, that where nothing but an honorary right is contested, the poorer antagonist must always suffer, whatever shall be the last decision of the law.

By the success of some of these disputes, he has so elated his insolence, and by reflection upon the general hatred which they have brought upon him, so irritated his virulence, that his whole life is spent in meditating or executing mischief. It is his common practice to procure his hedges to be broken in the night, and then to demand satisfaction for damages which his grounds have suffered from his neighbour's cattle. An old widow was yesterday soliciting *Eugenio* to enable her to replevin her only cow then in the pound by squire *Bluster*'s order, who had sent one of his agents to take advantage of her calamity, and persuade her to sell the cow at an under rate. He has driven a day-labourer from his cottage, for gathering blackberries in a hedge for his children; and has now an old woman in the county-jail for a trespass which she committed, by coming into his grounds to pick up acorns for her hog.

Money, in whatever hands, will confer power. Distress will fly to immediate refuge, without much consideration of remote consequences. *Bluster* has therefore a despotick authority in many families, whom he has assisted, on pressing occasions, with larger sums than they can easily repay. The only visits that he makes are to these houses of misfortune, where he enters with the insolence of absolute command, enjoys the terrors of the family, exacts their obedience, riots at their charge, and in the height of his joy insults the father with menaces, and the daughters with obscenity.

He is of late somewhat less offensive; for one of his debtors, after gentle expostulations, by which he was only irritated to grosser outrage, seized him by the sleeve, led him trembling into the court-yard, and closed the door upon him in a stormy night. He took his usual revenge next morning by a writ, but the debt was discharged by the assistance of *Eugenio*.

It is his rule to suffer his tenants to owe him rent, because by this indulgence, he secures to himself the power of seizure whenever he has an inclination to amuse himself with calamity, and feast his ears with entreaties and lamentations. Yet as he is sometimes capriciously liberal to those whom he happens to adopt as favourites, and lets his lands at a cheap rate, his farms are never long unoccupied; and when one is ruined by oppression, the possibility of better fortune quickly lures another to supply his place.

Such is the life of squire *Bluster*; a man in whose power fortune has liberally placed the means of happiness, but who has defeated all her gifts of their end by the depravity of his mind. He is wealthy without followers; he is magnificent without witnesses; he has birth without alliance, and influence without dignity. His neighbours scorn him as a brute; his dependents dread him as an oppressor; and he has only the gloomy comfort of reflecting, that if he is hated, he is likewise feared.

I am, Sir, &c.
Vagulus.

No. 145. Tuesday, 6 August 1751.

Non si priores Mæonius tenet
Sedes Homerus, Pindaricæ latent,
  Ceæque & Alcæi minaces
  Stesichorique graves Camœnæ.

Hor.

What though the muse her *Homer* thrones
  High above all th' immortal quire;
Nor *Pindar*'s rapture she disowns,
  Nor hides the plaintive *Cæan* lyre:
Alcæus strikes the tyrant's soul with dread,
Nor yet is grave *Stesichorus* unread.

Francis.

It is allowed, that vocations and employments of least dignity are of the most apparent use; that the meanest artisan or manufacturer contributes more to the accommodation of life, than the profound scholar and argumentative theorist; and that the publick would suffer less present inconvenience from the banishment of philosophers than from the extinction of any common trade.

Some have been so forcibly struck with this observation, that they have, in the first warmth of their discovery, thought it reasonable to alter the common distribution of dignity, and ventured to condemn mankind of universal ingratitude. For justice exacts that those by whom we are most benefited should be most honoured. And what labour can be more useful than that which procures to families and communities those necessaries which supply the wants of nature, or those conveniencies by which ease, security, and elegance are conferred?

This is one of the innumerable theories which the first attempt to reduce them into practice certainly destroys. If we estimate dignity by immediate usefulness, agriculture is undoubtedly the first and noblest science; yet we see the plow driven, the clod broken, the manure spread, the seeds scattered, and the harvest reaped, by men whom those that feed upon their industry will never be persuaded to admit into the same rank with heroes, or with sages; and who, after all the confessions which truth may extort in favour of their occupation, must be content to fill up the lowest class of the commonwealth, to form the base of the pyramid of subordination, and lie buried in obscurity themselves, while they support all that is splendid, conspicuous, or exalted.

It will be found, upon a closer inspection, that this part of the conduct of mankind is by no means contrary to reason or equity. Remuneratory honours are proportioned at once to the usefulness and difficulty of performances, and are properly adjusted by comparison of the mental and corporeal abilities, which they appear to employ. That work, however necessary, which is carried on only by muscular strength and manual dexterity, is not of equal esteem, in the consideration of rational beings, with the tasks that exercise the intellectual powers, and require the active vigour of imagination, or the gradual and laborious investigations of reason.

The merit of all manual occupations seems to terminate in the inventor; and surely the first ages cannot be charged with ingratitude; since those who civilized barbarians, and taught them how to secure themselves from cold and hunger were numbered amongst their deities. But these arts once discovered by philosophy, and facilitated by experience, are afterwards practised with very little assistance from the faculties of the soul; nor is any thing necessary to the regular discharge of these inferior duties, beyond that rude observation which the most sluggish intellect may practise, and that industry which the stimulations of necessity naturally enforce.

Yet, though the refusal of statues and panegyrics to those who employ only their hands and feet in the service of mankind may be easily justified, I am far from intending to incite the petulance of pride, to justify the superciliousness of grandeur, or to intercept any part of that tenderness and benevolence which by the privilege of their common nature one man may claim from another.

That it would be neither wise nor equitable to discourage the husbandman, the labourer, the miner, or the smith, is generally granted; but there is another race of beings equally obscure and equally indigent, who because their usefulness is less obvious to vulgar apprehensions, live unrewarded and die unpitied, and who have been long exposed to insult without a defender, and to censure without an apologist.

The authors of *London* were formerly computed by *Swift* at several thousands, and there is not any reason for suspecting that their number has decreased. Of these only a very few can be said to produce, or endeavour to produce new ideas, to extend any principle of science, or gratify the imagination with any uncommon train of images or contexture of events; the rest, however laborious, however arrogant, can only be considered as the drudges of the pen, the manufacturers of literature, who have set up for authors, either with or without a regular initiation, and like other artificers, have no other care than to deliver their tale of wares at the stated time.

It has been formerly imagined, that he who intends the entertainment or instruction of others, must feel in himself some peculiar impulse of genius; that he must watch the happy minute in which his natural fire is excited, in which his mind is elevated with nobler sentiments, enlightened with clearer views, and invigorated with stronger comprehension; that he must carefully select his thoughts and polish his expressions; and animate his efforts with the hope of raising a monument of learning, which neither time nor envy shall be able to destroy.

But the authors whom I am now endeavouring to recommend have been too long *hackneyed in the ways of men* to indulge the chimerical ambition of immortality; they have seldom any claim to the trade of writing, but that they have tried some other without success; they perceive no particular summons to composition, except the sound of the clock; they have no other rule than the law or the fashion for admitting their thoughts or rejecting them; and about the opinion of posterity they have little solicitude, for their productions are seldom intended to remain in the world longer than a week.

That such authors are not to be rewarded with praise is evident, since nothing can be admired when it ceases to exist; but surely though they cannot aspire to honour, they may be exempted from ignominy, and adopted into that order of men which deserves our kindness though not our reverence. These papers of the day, the *Ephemeræ* of learning, have uses more adequate to the purposes of common life than more pompous and durable volumes. If it is necessary for every man to be more acquainted with his contemporaries than with past generations, and to rather know the events which may immediately affect his fortune or quiet, than the revolutions of antient kingdoms, in which he has neither possessions nor expectations; if it be pleasing to hear of the preferment and dismission of statesmen, the birth of heirs, and the marriage of beauties, the humble author of journals and gazettes must be considered as a liberal dispenser of beneficial knowledge.

Even the abridger, compiler and translator, though their labours cannot be ranked with those of the diurnal historiographer, yet must not be rashly doomed to annihilation. Every size of readers requires a genius of correspondent capacity; some delight in abstracts and epitomes because they want room in their memory for long details, and content themselves with effects, without enquiry after causes; some minds are overpowered by splendor of sentiment, as some eyes are offended by a glaring light; such will gladly contemplate an author in an humble imitation, as we look without pain upon the sun in the water.

As every writer has his use, every writer ought to have his patrons; and since no man, however high he may now stand, can be certain that he shall not be soon thrown down from his elevation by criticism or caprice, the common interest of learning requires that her sons should cease from intestine hostilities, and instead of sacrificing each other to malice and contempt, endeavour to avert persecution from the meanest of their fraternity.

No. 146. Saturday, 10 August 1751.

Sunt illic duo, tresve, qui revolvant
Nostrarum tineas ineptiarum:
Sed cum sponsio, fabulæque lassæ
De scorpo fuerint et Incitato.

MART.

'Tis possible that one or two
These fooleries of mine may view;
But then the bettings must be o'er,
Nor *Crab* or *Childers* talk'd of more.

F. LEWIS.

None of the projects or designs which exercise the mind of man, are equally subject to obstructions and disappointments with the pursuit of fame. Riches cannot easily be denied to them who have something of greater value to offer in exchange; he whose fortune is endangered by litigation, will not refuse to augment the wealth of the lawyer; he whose days are darkened by languor, or whose nerves are excruciated by pain, is compelled to pay tribute to the science of healing. But praise may be always omitted without inconvenience. When once a man has made celebrity necessary to his happiness, he has put it in the power of the weakest and most timorous malignity, if not to take away his satisfaction, at least to withhold it. His enemies may indulge their pride by airy negligence, and gratify their malice by quiet neutrality. They that could never have injured a character by invectives may combine to annihilate it by silence; as the women of *Rome* threatened to put an end to conquest and dominion, by supplying no children to the commonwealth.

When a writer has with long toil produced a work intended to burst upon mankind with unexpected lustre, and withdraw the attention of the learned world from every other controversy or enquiry, he is seldom contented to wait long without the enjoyment of his new praises. With an imagination full of his own importance, he walks out like a monarch in disguise, to learn the various opinions of his readers. Prepared to feast upon admiration; composed to encounter censures without emotion; and determined not to suffer his quiet to be injured by a sensibility too exquisite of praise or blame, but to laugh with equal contempt at vain objections and injudicious commendations, he enters the places of mingled conversation, sits down to his tea in an obscure corner, and while he appears to examine a file of antiquated journals, catches the conversation of the whole room. He listens, but hears no mention of his book, and therefore supposes that he has disappointed his curiosity by delay, and that as men of learning would naturally begin their conversation with such a wonderful novelty, they had digressed to other subjects before his arrival. The company disperses, and their places are supplied by others equally ignorant, or equally careless. The same expectation hurries him to another place, from which the same disappointment drives him soon away. His impatience then grows violent and tumultuous; he ranges over the town with restless curiosity, and hears in one quarter of a cricket-match, in another of a pick-pocket; is told by some of an unexpected bankrupcy, by others of a turtle feast; is sometimes provoked by importunate enquiries after the white bear, and sometimes with praises of the dancing dog; he is afterwards entreated to give his judgment upon a wager about the height of the monument; invited to see a foot race in the adjacent villages; desired to read a ludicrous advertisement; or consulted about the most effectual method of making enquiry after a favourite cat. The whole world is busied in affairs, which he thinks below the notice of reasonable creatures, and which are nevertheless sufficient to withdraw all regard from his labours and his merits.

He resolves at last to violate his own modesty, and to recal the talkers from their folly by an enquiry after himself. He finds every one provided with an answer; one has seen the work advertised, but never met with any that had read it; another has been so often imposed upon by specious titles, that he never buys a book till its character is established; a third wonders what any man can hope to produce after so many writers of greater eminence; the next has enquired after the author, but can hear no account of him, and therefore suspects the name to be fictitious; and another knows him to be a man condemned by indigence to write too frequently what he does not understand.

Many are the consolations with which the unhappy author endeavours to allay his vexation, and fortify his patience. He has written with too little indulgence to the understanding of common readers; he has fallen upon an age in which solid knowledge, and delicate refinement, have given way to low merriment and idle buffoonry, and therefore no writer can hope for distinction, who has any higher purpose than to raise laughter. He finds that his enemies, such as superiority will always raise, have been industrious, while his performance was in the press, to vilify and blast it; and that the bookseller, whom he had resolved to enrich, has rivals that obstruct the circulation of his copies. He at last reposes upon the consideration, that the noblest works of learning and genius have always made their way slowly against ignorance and prejudice; and that reputation which is never to be lost, must be gradually obtained, as animals of longest life are observed not soon to attain their full stature and strength.

By such arts of voluntary delusion does every man endeavour to conceal his own unimportance from himself. It is long before we are convinced of the small proportion which every individual bears to the collective body of mankind; or learn how few can be interested in the fortune of any single man; how little vacancy is left in the world for any new object of attention; to how small extent the brightest blaze of merit can be spread amidst the mists of business and of folly; and how soon it is clouded by the intervention of other novelties. Not only the writer of books, but the commander of armies, and the deliverer of nations, will easily outlive all noisy and popular reputation: he may be celebrated for a time by the public voice, but his actions and his name will soon be considered as remote and unaffecting, and be rarely mentioned but by those whose alliance gives them some vanity to gratify by frequent commemoration.

It seems not to be sufficiently considered how little renown can be admitted in the world. Mankind are kept perpetually busy by their fears or desires, and have not more leisure from their own affairs, than to acquaint themselves with the accidents of the current day. Engaged in contriving some refuge from calamity, or in shortening the way to some new possession, they seldom suffer their thoughts to wander to the past or future; none but a few solitary students have leisure to enquire into the claims of antient heroes or sages, and names which hoped to range over kingdoms and continents shrink at last into cloisters or colleges.

Nor is it certain, that even of these dark and narrow habitations, these last retreats of fame, the possession will be long kept. Of men devoted to literature very few extend their views beyond some particular science, and the greater part seldom enquire, even in their own profession, for any authors but those whom the present mode of study happens to force upon their notice; they desire not to fill their minds with unfashionable knowledge, but contentedly resign to oblivion those books which they now find censured or neglected.

The hope of fame is necessarily connected with such considerations as must abate the ardour of confidence, and repress the vigour of pursuit. Whoever claims renown from any kind of excellence, expects to fill the place which is now possessed by another, for there are already names of every class sufficient to employ all that will desire to remember them; and surely he that is pushing his predecessors into the gulph of obscurity, cannot but sometimes suspect, that he must himself sink in like manner, and as he stands upon the same precipice, be swept away with the same violence.

It sometimes happens, that fame begins when life is at an end; but far the greater number of candidates for applause have owed their reception in the world to some favourable casualties, and have therefore immediately sunk into neglect, when death stripped them of their casual influence, and neither fortune nor patronage operated in their favour. Among those who have better claims to regard, the honour paid to their memory is commonly proportionate to the reputation which they enjoyed in their lives, though still growing fainter, as it is at a greater distance from the first emission; and since it is so difficult to obtain the notice of contemporaries, how little is to be hoped from future times? What can merit effect by its own force, when the help of art or friendship can scarcely support it?

No. 148. Saturday, 17 August 1751.

Me pater sævis oneret catenis
Quod viro clemens misero peperci,
Me vel extremis Numidarum in oris
    Classe releget.

HOR.

Me let my father load with chains,
Or banish to *Numidia*'s farthest plains;
My crime, that I a loyal wife,
In kind compassion spar'd my husband's life.

FRANCIS.

Politicians remark that no oppression is so heavy or lasting as that which is inflicted by the perversion and exorbitance of legal authority. The robber may be seized, and the invader repelled whenever they are found; they who pretend no right but that of force, may by force be punished or suppressed. But when plunder bears the name of impost, and murder is perpetrated by a judicial sentence, fortitude is intimidated and wisdom confounded; resistance shrinks from an alliance with rebellion, and the villain remains secure in the robes of the magistrate.

Equally dangerous and equally detestable are the cruelties often exercised in private families, under the venerable sanction of parental authority; the power which we are taught to honour from the first moments of reason; which is guarded from insult and violation by all that can impress awe upon the mind of man; and which therefore may wanton in cruelty without controul, and trample the bounds of right with innumerable transgressions, before duty and piety will dare to seek redress, or think themselves at liberty to recur to any other means of deliverance than supplications by which insolence is elated, and tears by which cruelty is gratified.

It was for a long time imagined by the *Romans*, that no son could be the murderer of his father, and they had therefore no punishment appropriated to parricide. They seem likewise to have believed with equal confidence that no father could be cruel to his child, and therefore they allowed every man the supreme judicature in his own house, and put the lives of his offspring into his hands. But experience informed them by degrees, that they had determined too hastily in favour of human nature; they found that instinct and habit were not able to contend with avarice or malice; that the nearest relation might be violated; and that power, to whomsoever entrusted, might be ill employed. They were therefore obliged to supply and to change their institutions; to deter the parricide by a new law, and to transfer capital punishments from the parent to the magistrate.

There are indeed many houses which it is impossible to enter familiarly, without discovering that parents are by no means exempt from the intoxications of dominion; and that he who is in no danger of hearing remonstrances but from his own conscience, will seldom be long without the art of controlling his convictions, and modifying justice by his own will.

If in any situation the heart were inaccessible to malignity, it might be supposed to be sufficiently secured by parental relation. To have voluntarily become to any being the occasion of its existence, produces an obligation to make that existence happy. To see helpless infancy stretching out her hands and pouring out her cries in testimony of dependance, without any powers to alarm jealousy, or any guilt to alienate affection, must surely awaken tenderness in every human mind; and tenderness once excited will be hourly encreased by the natural contagion of felicity, by the repercussion of communicated pleasure, and the consciousness of the dignity of benefaction. I believe no generous or benevolent man can see the vilest animal courting his regard, and shrinking at his anger, playing his gambols of delight before him, calling on him in distress, and flying to him in danger, without more kindness than he can persuade himself to feel for the wild and unsocial inhabitants of the air and water. We naturally endear to ourselves those to whom we impart any kind of pleasure, because we imagine their affection and esteem secured to us by the benefits which they receive.

There is indeed another method by which the pride of superiority may be likewise gratified. He that has extinguished all the sensations of humanity, and has no longer any satisfaction in the reflection that he is loved as the distributor of happiness, may please himself with exciting terror as the inflicter of pain; he may delight his solitude with contemplating the extent of his power and the force of his commands, in imagining the desires that flutter on the tongue which is forbidden to utter them, or the discontent which preys on the heart in which fear confines it; he may amuse himself with new contrivances of detection, multiplications of prohibition, and varieties of punishment; and swell with exultation when he considers how little of the homage that he receives he owes to choice.

That princes of this character have been known, the history of all absolute kingdoms will inform us; and since, as *Aristotle* observes, ἡ ὀικονομική μοναρχία, *the government of a family is naturally monarchical*, it is like other monarchies too often arbitrarily administered. The regal and parental tyrant differ only in the extent of their dominions, and the number of their slaves. The same passions cause the same miseries; except that seldom any prince, however despotick, has so far shaken off all awe of the publick eye as to venture upon those freaks of injustice, which are sometimes indulged under the secrecy of a private dwelling. Capricious injunctions, partial decisions, unequal allotments, distributions of reward not by merit but by fancy, and punishments regulated not by the degree of the offence, but by the humour of the judge, are too frequent where no power is known but that of a father.

That he delights in the misery of others no man will confess, and yet what other motive can make a father cruel? The king may be instigated by one man to the destruction of another; he may sometimes think himself endangered by the virtues of a subject; he may dread the successful general or the popular orator; his avarice may point out golden confiscations; and his guilt may whisper that he can only be secure, by cutting off all power of revenge.

But what can a parent hope from the oppression of those who were born to his protection, of those who can disturb him with no competition, who can enrich him with no spoils? Why cowards are cruel may be easily discovered; but for what reason not more infamous than cowardice can that man delight in oppression who has nothing to fear?

The unjustifiable severity of a parent is loaded with this aggravation, that those whom he injures are always in his sight. The injustice of a prince is often exercised upon those of whom he never had any personal or particular knowledge; and the sentence which he pronounces, whether of banishment, imprisonment, or death, removes from his view the man whom he condemns. But the domestick oppressor dooms himself to gaze upon those faces which he clouds with terror and with sorrow; and beholds every moment the effects of his own barbarities. He that can bear to give continual pain to those who surround him, and can walk with satisfaction in the gloom of his own presence; he that can see submissive misery without relenting, and meet without emotion the eye that implores mercy, or demands justice, will scarcely be amended by remonstrance or admonition; he has found means of stopping the avenues of tenderness, and arming his heart against the force of reason.

Even though no consideration should be paid to the great law of social beings, by which every individual is commanded to consult the happiness of others, yet the harsh parent is less to be vindicated than any other criminal, because he less provides for the happiness of himself. Every man, however little he loves others, would willingly be loved; every man hopes to live long, and therefore hopes for that time at which he shall sink back to imbecillity, and must depend for ease and chearfulness upon the officiousness of others. But how has he obviated the inconveniences of old age, who alienates from him the assistance of his children, and whose bed must be surrounded in his last hours, in the hours of languor and dejection, of impatience and of pain, by strangers to whom his life is indifferent, or by enemies to whom his death is desirable?

Piety will indeed in good minds overcome provocation, and those who have been harrassed by brutality will forget the injuries which they have suffered so far as to perform the last duties with alacrity and zeal. But surely no resentment can be equally painful with kindness thus undeserved, nor can severer punishment be imprecated upon a man not wholly lost in meanness and stupidity, than through the tediousness of decrepitude, to be reproached by the kindness of his own children, to receive not the tribute but the alms of attendance, and to owe every relief of his miseries not to gratitude but to mercy.

No. 151. Tuesday, 27 August 1751.

Ἀμφὶ δ'ἀνθρώ—
πων φρεσὶν ἀμπλακίαι
ἀναρίθμητοι κρέμανται.
τοῦτο δ'ἀμήχανον εὑρεῖν
Ὅτι νῦν, καὶ ἐν τελευ—
τᾷ φέρτατον ἀνδρὶ τυχεῖν.

PIND.

But wrapt in error is the human mind,
　And human bliss is ever insecure:
Know we what fortune yet remains behind?
Know we how long the present shall endure?

WEST.

The writers of medicine and physiology have traced with great appearance of accuracy, the effects of time upon the human body, by marking the various periods of the constitution, and the several stages by which animal life makes its progress from infancy to decrepitude. Though their observations have not enabled them to discover how manhood may be accelerated, or old age retarded, yet surely if they be considered only as the amusements of curiosity, they are of equal importance with conjectures on things more remote, with catalogues of the fixed stars, and calculations of the bulk of planets.

It had been a task worthy of the moral philosophers to have considered with equal care the climactericks of the mind; to have pointed out the time at which every passion begins and ceases to predominate, and noted the regular variations of desire, and the succession of one appetite to another.

The periods of mental change are not to be stated with equal certainty: Our bodies grow up under the care of nature, and depend so little on our own management, that something more than negligence is necessary to discompose their structure, or impede their vigour. But our minds are committed in a great measure first to the direction of others, and afterwards of ourselves. It would be difficult to protract the weakness of infancy beyond the usual time, but the mind may be very easily hindered from its share of improvement, and the bulk and strength of manhood must, without the assistance of education and instruction, be informed only with the understanding of a child.

Yet amidst all the disorder and inequality which variety of discipline, example, conversation, and employment produce in the intellectual advances of different men, there is still discovered by a vigilant spectator such a general and remote similitude as may be expected in the same common nature affected by external circumstances indefinitely varied. We all enter the world in equal ignorance, gaze round about us on the same objects, and have our first pains and pleasures, our first hopes and fears, our first aversions and desires from the same causes; and though, as we proceed farther, life opens wider prospects to our view, and accidental impulses determine us to different paths, yet as every mind, however vigorous or abstracted, is necessitated in its present state of union, to receive its informations, and execute its purposes by the intervention of the body, the uniformity of our corporeal nature communicates itself to our intellectual operations; and those whose abilities or knowledge incline them most to deviate from the general round of life, are recalled from excentricity by the laws of their existence.

If we consider the exercises of the mind, it will be found that in each part of life some particular faculty is more eminently employed. When the treasures of knowledge are first opened before us, while novelty blooms alike on either hand, and every thing equally unknown and unexamined seems of equal value, the power of the soul is principally exerted in a vivacious and desultory curiosity. She applies by turns to every object, enjoys it for a short time, and flies with equal ardour to another. She delights to catch up loose and unconnected ideas, but starts away from systems and complications which would obstruct the rapidity of her transitions, and detain her long in the same pursuit.

When a number of distinct images are collected by these erratick and hasty surveys, the fancy is busied in arranging them; and combines them into pleasing pictures with more resemblance to the realities of life as experience advances, and new observations rectify the former. While the judgment is yet uninformed and unable to compare the draughts of fiction with their originals, we are delighted with improbable adventures, impracticable virtues, and inimitable characters: But, in proportion as we have more opportunities of acquainting ourselves with living nature, we are sooner disgusted with copies in which there appears no resemblance. We first discard absurdity and impossibility, then exact greater and greater degrees of probability, but at last become cold and insensible to the charms of falshood, however specious, and from the imitations of truth, which are never perfect, transfer our affection to truth itself.

Now commences the reign of judgment or reason; we begin to find little pleasure, but in comparing arguments, stating propositions, disentangling perplexities, clearing ambiguities, and deducing consequences. The painted vales of imagination are deserted, and our intellectual activity is exercised in winding through the labyrinths of fallacy, and toiling with firm and cautious steps up the narrow tracks of demonstration. Whatever may lull vigilance, or mislead attention, is contemptuously rejected, and every disguise in which error may be concealed, is carefully observed, till by degrees a certain number of incontestable or unsuspected propositions are established, and at last concatenated into arguments, or compacted into systems.

At length weariness succeeds to labour, and the mind lies at ease in the contemplation of her own attainments, without any desire of new conquests or excursions. This is the age of recollection and narrative; the opinions are settled, and the avenues of apprehension shut against any new intelligence; the days that are to follow must pass in the inculcation of precepts already collected, and assertion of tenets already received; nothing is henceforward so odious as opposition, so insolent as doubt, or so dangerous as novelty.

In like manner the passions usurp the separate command of the successive periods of life. To the happiness of our first years nothing more seems necessary than freedom from restraint: Every man may remember that if he was left to himself, and indulged in the disposal of his own time, he was once content without the superaddition of any actual pleasure. The new world is itself a banquet, and till we have exhausted the freshness of life, we have always about us sufficient gratifications: The sunshine quickens us to play, and the shade invites us to sleep.

But we soon become unsatisfied with negative felicity, and are solicited by our senses and appetites to more powerful delights, as the taste of him who has satisfied his hunger must be excited by artificial stimulations. The simplicity of natural amusement is now past, and art and contrivance must improve our pleasures; but in time art, like nature, is exhausted, and the senses can no longer supply the cravings of the intellect.

The attention is then transferred from pleasure to interest, in which pleasure is perhaps included, though diffused to a wider extent, and protracted through new gradations. Nothing now dances before the eyes but wealth and power, nor rings in the ear but the voice of fame; wealth, to which, however variously denominated, every man at some time or other aspires; power, which all wish to obtain within their circle of action; and fame, which no man, however high or mean, however wise or ignorant, was yet able to despise. Now prudence and foresight exert their influence: no hour is devoted wholly to any present enjoyment, no act or purpose terminates in itself, but every motion is referred to some distant end; the accomplishment of one design begins another, and the ultimate wish is always pushed off to its former distance.

At length fame is observed to be uncertain, and power to be dangerous; the man whose vigour and alacrity begin to forsake him, by degrees contracts his designs, remits his former multiplicity of persuits, and extends no longer his regard to any other honour than the reputation of wealth, or any other influence than its power. Avarice is generally the last passion of those lives of which the first part has been squandered in pleasure, and the second devoted to ambition. He that sinks under the fatigue of getting wealth, lulls his age with the milder business of saving it.

I have in this view of life considered men as actuated only by natural desires, and yielding to their own inclinations without regard to superior principles by which the force of external agents may be counteracted, and the temporary prevalence of passions restrained. Nature will indeed always operate, human desires will be always ranging; but these motions; though very powerful, are not resistless; nature may be regulated, and desires governed; and to contend with the predominance of successive passions, to be endangered first by one affection, and then by another, is the condition upon which we are to pass our time, the time of our preparation for that state which shall put an end to experiment, to disappointment, and to change.

No. 156. Saturday, 14 September 1751.

Nunquam aliud natura, aliud sapientia dicit.
Juv.

For wisdom ever echoes nature's voice.

Every government, say the politicians, is perpetually degenerating towards corruption, from which it must be rescued at certain periods by the resuscitation of its first principles, and the re-establishment of its original constitution. Every animal body, according to the methodick physicians, is, by the predominance of some exuberant quality, continually declining towards disease and death, which must be obviated by a seasonable reduction of the peccant humour to the just equipoise which health requires.

In the same manner the studies of mankind, all at least which, not being subject to rigorous demonstration, admit the influence of fancy and caprice, are perpetually tending to error and confusion. Of the great principles of truth which the first speculatists discovered, the simplicity is embarrassed by ambitious additions, or the evidence obscured by inaccurate argumentation; and as they descend from one succession of writers to another, like light transmitted from room to room, they lose their strength and splendour, and fade at last in total evanescence.

The systems of learning therefore must be sometimes reviewed, complications analised into principles, and knowledge disentangled from opinion. It is not always possible, without a close inspection, to separate the genuine shoots of consequential reasoning, which grow out of some radical postulate, from the branches which art has engrafted on it. The accidental prescriptions of authority, when time has procured them veneration, are often confounded with the laws of nature, and those rules are supposed coeval with reason, of which the first rise cannot be discovered.

Criticism has sometimes permitted fancy to dictate the laws by which fancy ought to be restrained, and fallacy to perplex the principles by which fallacy is to be detected; her superintendance of others has betrayed her to negligence of herself; and, like the antient *Scythians*, by extending her conquests over distant regions, she has left her throne vacant to her slaves.

Among the laws of which the desire of extending authority, or ardour of promoting knowledge has prompted the prescription, all which writers have received, had not the same original right to our regard. Some are to be considered as fundamental and indispensable, others only as useful and convenient; some as dictated by reason and necessity, others as enacted by despotick antiquity; some as invincibly supported by their conformity to the order of nature and operations of the intellect; others as formed by accident, or instituted by example, and therefore always liable to dispute and alteration.

That many rules have been advanced without consulting nature or reason, we cannot but suspect, when we find it peremptorily decreed by the antient masters, that *only three speaking personages should appear at once upon the stage*; a law which, as the variety and intricacy of modern plays has made it impossible to be observed, we now violate without scruple, and, as experience proves, without inconvenience.

The original of this precept was merely accidental. Tragedy was a monody or solitary song in honour of *Bacchus*, improved afterwards into a dialogue by the addition of another speaker; but the antients, remembering that the tragedy was at first pronounced only by one, durst not for some time venture beyond two; at last when custom and impunity had made them daring, they extended their liberty to the admission of three, but restrained themselves by a critical edict from further exorbitance.

By what accident the number of acts was limited to five, I know not that any author has informed us; but certainly it is not determined by any necessity arising either from the nature of action or propriety of exhibition. An act is only the representation of such a part of the business of the play as proceeds in an unbroken tenor, or without any intermediate pause. Nothing is more evident than that of every real, and by consequence of every dramatick action, the intervals may be more or fewer than five; and indeed the rule is upon the *English* stage every day broken in effect, without any other mischief than that which arises from an absurd endeavour to observe it in appearance. Whenever the scene is shifted the act ceases, since some time is necessarily supposed to elapse while the personages of the drama change their place.

With no greater right to our obedience have the criticks confined the dramatic action to a certain number of hours. Probability requires that the time of action should approach somewhat nearly to that of exhibition, and those plays will always be thought most happily conducted which croud the greatest variety into the least space. But since it will frequently happen that some delusion must be admitted, I know not where the limits of imagination can be fixed. It is rarely observed that minds not prepossessed by mechanical criticism feel any offence from the extension of the intervals between the acts; nor can I conceive it absurd or impossible, that he who can multiply three hours into twelve or twenty-four, might image with equal ease a greater number.

I know not whether he that professes to regard no other laws than those of nature, will not be inclined to receive tragi-comedy to his protection, whom, however generally condemned, her own laurels have hitherto shaded from the fulminations of criticism. For what is there in the mingled drama which impartial reason can condemn? The connexion of important with trivial incidents, since it is not only common but perpetual in the world, may surely be allowed upon the stage, which pretends only to be the mirrour of life. The impropriety of suppressing passions before we have raised them to the intended agitation, and of diverting the expectation from an event which we keep suspended only to raise it, may be speciously urged. But will not experience shew this objection to be rather subtle than just? is it not certain that the tragic and comic affections have been moved alternately with equal force, and that no plays have oftner filled the eye with tears, and the breast with palpitation, than those which are variegated with interludes of mirth?

I do not however think it safe to judge of works of genius merely by the event. These resistless vicissitudes of the heart, this alternate prevalence of merriment and solemnity, may sometimes be more properly ascribed to the vigour of the writer than the justness of the design: and instead of vindicating tragicomedy by the success of *Shakespear*, we ought perhaps to pay new honours to that transcendent and unbounded genius that could preside over the passions in sport; who, to actuate the affections, needed not the slow gradation of common means, but could fill the heart with instantaneous jollity or sorrow, and vary our disposition as he changed his scenes. Perhaps the effects even of *Shakespeare*'s poetry might have been yet greater, had he not counteracted himself; and we might have been more interested in the distresses of his heroes had we not been so frequently diverted by the jokes of his buffoons.

There are other rules more fixed and obligatory. It is necessary that of every play the chief action should be single; for since a play represents some transaction, through its regular maturation to its final event, two actions equally important must evidently constitute two plays.

As the design of tragedy is to instruct by moving the passions, it must always have a hero, a personage apparently and incontestably superior to the rest, upon whom the attention may be fixed, and the anxiety suspended. For though of two persons opposing each other with equal abilities and equal virtue, the auditor will inevitably in time choose his favourite, yet as that choice must be without any cogency of conviction, the hopes or fears which it raises will be faint and languid. Of two heroes acting in confederacy against a common enemy, the virtues or dangers will give little emotion, because each claims our concern with the same right, and the heart lies at rest between equal motives.

It ought to be the first endeavour of a writer to distinguish nature from custom, or that which is established because it is right, from that which is right only because it is established; that he may neither violate essential principles by a desire of novelty, nor debar himself from the attainment of beauties within his view by a needless fear of breaking rules which no literary dictator had authority to enact.

No. 158. Saturday, 21 September 1751.

Grammatici certant, et adhuc sub Judice lis est.

HOR.

———— Criticks yet contend,
And of their vain disputings find no end.

FRANCIS.

Criticism, though dignified from the earliest ages by the labours of men eminent for knowledge and sagacity; and, since the revival of polite literature, the favourite study of *European* scholars, has not yet attained the certainty and stability of science. The rules hitherto received, are seldom drawn from any settled principle or self-evident postulate, or adapted to the natural and invariable constitution of things; but will be found upon examination the arbitrary edicts of legislators, authorised only by themselves, who, out of various means by which the same end may be attained, selected such as happened to occur to their own reflexion, and then by a law which idleness and timidity were too willing to obey, prohibited new experiments of wit, restrained fancy from the indulgence of her innate inclination to hazard and adventure, and condemned all future flights of genius to pursue the path of the *Meonian* eagle.

This authority may be more justly opposed, as it is apparently derived from them whom they endeavour to controul; for we owe few of the rules of writing to the acuteness of criticks, who have generally no other merit than that having read the works of great authors with attention, they have observed the arrangement of their matter, or the graces of their expression, and then expected honour and reverence for precepts which they never could have invented: so that practice has introduced rules, rather than rules have directed practice.

For this reason the laws of every species of writing have been settled by the ideas of him who first raised it to reputation, without enquiry whether his performances were not yet susceptible of improvement. The excellencies and faults of celebrated writers have been equally recommended to posterity; and so far has blind reverence prevailed, that even the number of their books has been thought worthy of imitation.

The imagination of the first authors of lyrick poetry was vehement and rapid, and their knowledge various and extensive. Living in an age when science had been little cultivated, and when the minds of their auditors, not being accustomed to accurate inspection, were easily dazzled by glaring ideas, they applied themselves to instruct, rather by short sentences and striking thoughts, than by regular argumentation; and finding attention more successfully excited by sudden sallies and unexpected exclamations, than by the more artful and placid beauties of methodical deduction, they loosed their genius to its own course, passed from one sentiment to another without expressing the intermediate ideas, and roved at large over the ideal world with such lightness and agility that their footsteps are scarcely to be traced.

From this accidental peculiarity of the ancient writers the criticks deduce the rules of lyrick poetry, which they have set free from all the laws by which other compositions are confined, and allow to neglect the niceties of transition, to start into remote digressions, and to wander without restraint from one scene of imagery to another.

A writer of later times has, by the vivacity of his essays, reconciled mankind to the same licentiousness in short dissertations; and he therefore who wants skill to form a plan, or diligence to pursue it, needs only entitle his performance an essay, to acquire the right of heaping together the collections of half his life, without order, coherence, or propriety.

In writing, as in life, faults are endured without disgust when they are associated with transcendent merit, and may be sometimes recommended to weak judgments by the lustre which they obtain from their union with excellence; but it is the business of those who presume to superintend the taste or morals of mankind, to separate delusive combinations, and distinguish that which may be praised from that which can only be excused. As vices never promote happiness, though when overpowered by more active and more numerous virtues, they cannot totally destroy it; so confusion and irregularity produce no beauty, though they cannot always obstruct the brightness of genius and learning. To proceed from one truth to another, and connect distant propositions by regular consequences, is the great prerogative of man. Independent and unconnected sentiments flashing upon the mind in quick succession, may, for a time, delight by their novelty, but they differ from systematical reasoning, as single notes from harmony, as glances of lightening from the radiance of the sun.

When rules are thus drawn, rather from precedents than reason, there is danger not only from the faults of an author, but from the errors of those who criticise his works; since they may often mislead their pupils by false representations, as the *Ciceronians* of the sixteenth century were betrayed into barbarisms by corrupt copies of their darling writer.

It is established at present, that the proemial lines of a poem, in which the general subject is proposed, must be void of glitter and embellishment. "The first lines of *Paradise Lost*," says *Addison*, "are perhaps as plain, simple, and unadorned as any of the whole poem, in which particular the author has conformed himself to the example of *Homer* and the precept of *Horace*."

This observation seems to have been made by an implicit adoption of the common opinion, without consideration either of the precept or example. Had *Horace* been consulted, he would have been found to direct only what should be comprised in the proposition, not how it should be expressed, and to have commended *Homer* in opposition to a meaner poet, not for the gradual elevation of his diction, but the judicious expansion of his plan; for displaying unpromised events, not for producing unexpected elegancies.

> ——*Speciosa dehinc miracula promit,*
> *Antiphaten Scyllamque, & cum Cyclope Charybdim.*

> But from a cloud of smoke he breaks to light,
> And pours his specious miracles to sight;
> *Antiphates* his hideous feast devours,
> *Charybdis* barks, and *Polyphemus* roars.
>
> FRANCIS.

If the exordial verses of *Homer* be compared with the rest of the poem, they will not appear remarkable for plainness or simplicity, but rather eminently adorned and illuminated.

> Ἄνδρα μοι ἔννεπε Μοῦσα πολύτροπον, ὅς μάλα πολλὰ
> Πλάγχθη, ἐπεὶ Τροίης ἱερὸν πτολίεθρον ἔπερσε·
> Πολλῶν δ᾽ ἀνθρώπων ἴδεν ἄστεα, καὶ νόον ἔγνω.
> Πολλὰ δ᾽ ὅγ᾽ ἐν πόντῳ πάθεν ἄλγεα ὅν κατὰ θυμόν,
> Ἀρνύμενος ἥν τε ψυχὴν καὶ νόστον ἑταίρων·
> Ἀλλ᾽ οὐδ᾽ ὡς ἑτάρους ἐρρύσατο ἱέμενός περ·
> Αὐτῶν γὰρ σφετέρῃσιν ὄλοντο,
> Νήπιοι οἵ κατὰ βοῦς ὑπερίονος ἠελίοιο
> Ἤσθιον· αὐτὰρ ὅ τοῖσιν ἀφείλετο νόστιμον ἦμαρ·
> Τῶν ἁμόθεν γε, θεά, θύγατερ Διός, εἰπὲ καὶ ἡμῖν.

> The man, for wisdom's various arts renown'd,
> Long exercis'd in woes, O muse! resound.
> Who, when his arms had wrought the destin'd fall
> Of sacred *Troy*, and raz'd her heav'n-built wall,
> Wand'ring from clime to clime, observant stray'd,
> Their manners noted, and their states survey'd.
> On stormy seas unnumber'd toils he bore,
> Safe with his friends to gain his natal shore:
> Vain toils! their impious folly dar'd to prey
> On herds devoted to the god of day;
> The god vindictive doom'd them never more
> (Ah men unbless'd) to touch that natal shore.

O snatch some portion of these acts from fate,
Celestial muse! and to our world relate.

POPE.

The first verses of the *Iliad* are in like manner particularly splendid, and
the proposition of the *Eneid* closes with dignity and magnificence not often to
be found even in the poetry of *Virgil*.

The intent of the introduction is to raise expectation, and suspend it;
something therefore must be discovered, and something concealed; and the
poet, while the fertility of his invention is yet unknown, may properly recommend himself by the grace of his language.

He that reveals too much, or promises too little; he that never irritates the
intellectual appetite, or that immediately satiates it, equally defeats his own
purpose. It is necessary to the pleasure of the reader, that the events should
not be anticipated, and how then can his attention be invited, but by grandeur
of expression?

No. 159. Tuesday, 24 September 1751.

Sunt verba et voces, quibus hunc lenire dolorem
Possis, et magnam morbi deponere partem.

HOR.

The pow'r of words, and soothing sounds appease
The raging pain, and lessen the disease.

FRANCIS.

The imbecillity with which *Verecundulus* complains that the presence of a
numerous assembly freezes his faculties, is particularly incident to the studious part of mankind, whose education necessarily secludes them in their earlier years from mingled converse, till at their dismission from schools and
academies they plunge at once into the tumult of the world, and coming forth
from the gloom of solitude are overpowered by the blaze of publick life.

It is perhaps kindly provided by nature that, as the feathers and strength of a
bird grow together, and her wings are not completed till she is able to fly, so some
proportion should be preserved in the human kind between judgment and courage; the precipitation of inexperience is therefore restrained by shame, and we
remain shackled by timidity, till we have learned to speak and act with propriety.

I believe few can review the days of their youth, without recollecting temptations, which shame, rather than virtue, enabled them to resist; and opinions
which, however erroneous in their principles, and dangerous in their consequences, they have panted to advance at the hazard of contempt and hatred,
when they found themselves irresistibly depressed by a languid anxiety,

which seized them at the moment of utterance, and still gathered strength from their endeavours to resist it.

It generally happens that assurance keeps an even pace with ability, and the fear of miscarriage, which hinders our first attempts, is gradually dissipated as our skill advances towards certainty of success. That bashfulness therefore which prevents disgrace, that short and temporary shame, which secures us from the danger of lasting reproach, cannot be properly counted among our misfortunes.

Bashfulness, however it may incommode for a moment, scarcely ever produces evils of long continuance; it may flush the cheek, flutter in the heart, deject the eyes, and enchain the tongue, but its mischiefs soon pass off without remembrance. It may sometimes exclude pleasure, but seldom opens any avenue to sorrow or remorse. It is observed somewhere, that *few have repented of having forborn to speak.*

To excite opposition and inflame malevolence is the unhappy privilege of courage made arrogant by consciousness of strength. No man finds in himself any inclination to attack or oppose him who confesses his superiority by blushing in his presence. Qualities exerted with apparent fearfulness, receive applause from every voice, and support from every hand. Diffidence may check resolution and obstruct performance, but compensates its embarrassments by more important advantages; it conciliates the proud, and softens the severe, averts envy from excellence, and censure from miscarriage.

It may indeed happen that knowledge and virtue remain too long congealed by this frigorifick power, as the principles of vegetation are sometimes obstructed by lingering frosts. He that enters late into a publick station, though with all the abilities requisite to the discharge of his duty, will find his powers at first impeded by a timidity which he himself knows to be vitious, and must struggle long against dejection and reluctance, before he obtains the full command of his own attention, and adds the gracefulness of ease to the dignity of merit.

For this disease of the mind, I know not whether any remedies of much efficacy can be found. To advise a man unaccustomed to the eyes of multitudes to mount a tribunal without perturbation, to tell him whose life has passed in the shades of contemplation, that he must not be disconcerted or perplexed in receiving and returning the compliments of a splendid assembly, is to advise an inhabitant of *Brasil* or *Sumatra*, not to shiver at an *English* winter, or him who has always lived upon a plain to look from a precipice without emotion. It is to suppose custom instantaneously controlable by reason, and to endeavour to communicate by precept that which only time and habit can bestow.

He that hopes by philosophy and contemplation alone to fortify himself against that awe which all, at their first appearance on the stage of life, must feel from the spectators, will, at the hour of need, be mocked by his resolution; and I doubt whether the preservatives which *Plato* relates *Alcibiades* to have received from *Socrates*, when he was about to speak in publick, proved sufficient to secure him from the powerful fascination.

Yet as the effects of time may by art and industry be accelerated or retarded, it cannot be improper to consider how this troublesome instinct may be opposed when it exceeds its just proportion, and instead of repressing petulance and temerity, silences eloquence, and debilitates force; since, though it cannot be hoped that anxiety should be immediately dissipated, it may be at least somewhat abated; and the passions will operate with less violence, when reason rises against them, than while she either slumbers in neutrality, or, mistaking her interest, lends them her assistance.

No cause more frequently produces bashfulness than too high an opinion of our own importance. He that imagines an assembly filled with his merit, panting with expectation, and hushed with attention, easily terrifies himself with the dread of disappointing them, and strains his imagination in pursuit of something that may vindicate the veracity of fame, and shew that his reputation was not gained by chance. He considers, that what he shall say or do will never be forgotten; that renown or infamy are suspended upon every syllable, and that nothing ought to fall from him which will not bear the test of time. Under such solicitude, who can wonder that the mind is overwhelmed, and by struggling with attempts above her strength, quickly sinks into languishment and despondency.

The most useful medicines are often unpleasing to the taste. Those who are oppressed by their own reputation, will perhaps not be comforted by hearing that their cares are unnecessary. But the truth is, that no man is much regarded by the rest of the world. He that considers how little he dwells upon the condition of others, will learn how little the attention of others is attracted by himself. While we see multitudes passing before us, of whom perhaps not one appears to deserve our notice, or excites our sympathy, we should remember, that we likewise are lost in the same throng, that the eye which happens to glance upon us is turned in a moment on him that follows us, and that the utmost which we can reasonably hope or fear is to fill a vacant hour with prattle, and be forgotten.

No. 161. Tuesday, 1 October 1751.

Οἴη γαϱ φύλλων γενέη, τοίηδε καὶ Ἄνδϱων.
HOM.

Frail as the leaves that quiver on the sprays,
Like them man flourishes, like them decays.

Mr. RAMBLER,

SIR,

You have formerly observed that curiosity often terminates in barren knowledge, and that the mind is prompted to study and enquiry rather by the uneasiness of ignorance, than the hope of profit. Nothing can be of less importance to any present interest than the fortune of those who have been long lost in the grave, and from whom nothing now can be hoped or feared. Yet to rouse the zeal of a true antiquary little more is necessary than to mention a name which mankind have conspired to forget; he will make his way to remote scenes of action thro' obscurity and contradiction, as *Tully* sought amidst bushes and brambles the tomb of *Archimedes*.

It is not easy to discover how it concerns him that gathers the produce or receives the rent of an estate, to know through what families the land has passed, who is registered in the Conqueror's survey as its possessor, how often it has been forfeited by treason, or how often sold by prodigality. The power or wealth of the present inhabitants of a country cannot be much encreased by an enquiry after the names of those barbarians, who destroyed one another twenty centuries ago, in contests for the shelter of woods or convenience of pasturage. Yet we see that no man can be at rest in the enjoyment of a new purchase till he has learned the history of his grounds from the antient inhabitants of the parish, and that no nation omits to record the actions of their ancestors, however bloody, savage and rapacious.

The same disposition, as different opportunities call it forth, discovers itself in great or little things. I have always thought it unworthy of a wise man to slumber in total inactivity only because he happens to have no employment equal to his ambition or genius; it is therefore my custom to apply my attention to the objects before me, and as I cannot think any place wholly unworthy of notice that affords a habitation to a man of letters, I have collected the history and antiquities of the several garrets in which I have resided.

> *Quantulacunque estis, vos ego magna voco.*
>
> How small to others, but how great to me!

Many of these narratives my industry has been able to extend to a considerable length; but the woman with whom I now lodge has lived only eighteen months in the house, and can give no account of its ancient revolutions; the plaisterer, having, at her entrance, obliterated by his white-wash, all the smoky memorials which former tenants had left upon the cieling, and perhaps drawn the veil of oblivion over politicians, philosophers, and poets.

When I first cheapened my lodgings, the landlady told me, that she hoped I was not an author, for the lodgers on the first floor had stipulated that the upper rooms should not be occupied by a noisy trade. I very readily promised to give no disturbance to her family, and soon dispatched a bargain on the usual terms.

I had not slept many nights in my new apartment before I began to enquire after my predecessors, and found my landlady, whose imagination is filled chiefly with her own affairs, very ready to give me information.

Curiosity, like all other desires, produces pain as well as pleasure. Before she began her narrative, I had heated my head with expectations of adventures and discoveries, of elegance in disguise, and learning in distress; and was somewhat mortified when I heard, that the first tenant was a taylor, of whom nothing was remembered but that he complained of his room for want of light; and, after having lodged in it a month, and paid only a week's rent, pawned a piece of cloth which he was trusted to cut out, and was forced to make a precipitate retreat from this quarter of the town.

The next was a young woman newly arrived from the country, who lived for five weeks with great regularity, and became by frequent treats very much the favourite of the family, but at last received visits so frequently from a cousin in *Cheapside*, that she brought the reputation of the house into danger, and was therefore dismissed with good advice.

The room then stood empty for a fortnight; my landlady began to think that she had judged hardly, and often wished for such another lodger. At last an elderly man of a grave aspect, read the bill, and bargained for the room, at the very first price that was asked. He lived in close retirement, seldom went out till evening, and then returned early, sometimes chearful, and at other times dejected. It was remarkable, that whatever he purchased, he never had small money in his pocket, and tho' cool and temperate on other occasions, was always vehement and stormy till he received his change. He paid his rent with great exactness, and seldom failed once a week to requite my landlady's civility with a supper. At last, such is the fate of human felicity, the house was alarm'd at midnight by the constable, who demanded to search the garrets. My landlady assuring him that he had mistaken the door, conducted him up stairs, where he found the tools of a coiner; but the tenant had crawled along the roof to an empty house, and escaped; much to the joy of my landlady, who declares him a very honest man, and wonders why any body should be hanged for making money when such numbers are in want of it. She however confesses that she shall for the future always question the character of those who take her garret without beating down the price.

The bill was then placed again in the window, and the poor woman was teazed for seven weeks by innumerable passengers, who obliged her to climb with them every hour up five stories, and then disliked the prospect, hated the noise of a publick street, thought the stairs narrow, objected to a low cieling, required the walls to be hung with fresher paper, asked questions about the neighbourhood, could not think of living so far from their acquaintance, wished the window had looked to the south rather than the west, told how the door and chimney might have been better disposed, bid her half the price that she asked, or promised to give her earnest the next day, and came no more.

At last, a short meagre man, in a tarnish'd waistcoat, desired to see the garret, and when he had stipulated for two long shelves and a larger table, hired it at a low rate. When the affair was completed, he looked round him with great satisfaction, and repeated some words which the woman did not understand. In two days he brought a great box of books, took possession of his room, and lived very inoffensively, except that he frequently disturbed the inhabitants of the next floor by unseasonable noises. He was generally in bed at noon, but from evening to midnight he sometimes talked aloud with great vehemence, sometimes stamped as in rage, sometimes threw down his poker, then clattered his chairs, then sat down in deep thought, and again burst out into loud vociferations; sometimes he would sigh as oppressed with misery, and sometimes shake with convulsive laughter. When he encountered any of the family he gave way or bowed, but rarely spoke, except that as he went up stairs he often repeated,

—— Ὅς ὑπέρτατα δώματα ναίει.

This habitant th' aerial regions boast.

hard words, to which his neighbours listened so often, that they learned them without understanding them. What was his employment she did not venture to ask him, but at last heard a printer's boy enquire for the author.

My landlady was very often advised to beware of this strange man, who, tho' he was quiet for the present, might perhaps become outrageous in the hot months; but as she was punctually paid, she could not find any sufficient reason for dismissing him, till one night he convinced her by setting fire to his curtains, that it was not safe to have an author for her inmate.

She had then for six weeks a succession of tenants, who left the house on Saturday, and instead of paying their rent, stormed at their landlady. At last she took in two sisters, one of whom had spent her little fortune in procuring remedies for a lingering disease, and was now supported and attended by the other: she climbed with difficulty to the apartment, where she languished eight weeks, without impatience or lamentation, except for the expence and fatigue which her sister suffered, and then calmly and contentedly expired. The sister followed her to the grave, paid the few debts which they had contracted, wiped away the tears of useless sorrow, and returning to the business of common life, resigned to me the vacant habitation.

Such, Mr. *Rambler*, are the changes which have happened in the narrow space where my present fortune has fixed my residence. So true is it that amusement and instruction are always at hand for those who have skill and willingness to find them; and so just is the observation of *Juvenal*, that a single house will shew whatever is done or suffered in the world.

I am, Sir, &c.

No. 165. Tuesday, 15 October 1751.

Ἦν νέος, ἀλλὰ πένης· νῦν γηρῶν, πλούσιός εἰμι.
Ὦ μόνος ἐκ πάντων οἰκτρὸς ἐν ἀμφοτέροις,

Ὅς τότε μὲν χρῆσθαι δυνάμην, ὁπότ᾽ οὐδὲ ἐν εἶχον.
Νῦν δ᾽ ὁπότε χρῆσθαι μή δύναμαι, τότ᾽ ἔχω.
ANTIPHILUS.

Young was I once and poor, now rich and old;
A harder case than mine was never told;
Blest with the pow'r to use them — I had none;
Loaded with *riches* now, the pow'r is gone.
F. LEWIS.

To the RAMBLER.

SIR,

The writers who have undertaken the unpromising task of moderating desire, exert all the power of their eloquence, to shew that happiness is not the lot of man, and have by many arguments and examples proved the instability of every condition by which envy or ambition are excited. They have set before our eyes all the calamities to which we are exposed from the frailty of nature, the influence of accident, or the stratagems of malice; they have terrified greatness with conspiracies, and riches with anxieties, wit with criticism, and beauty with disease.

All the force of reason and all the charms of language are indeed necessary to support positions which every man hears with a wish to confute them. Truth finds an easy entrance into the mind when she is introduced by desire, and attended by pleasure; but when she intrudes uncalled, and brings only fear and sorrow in her train, the passes of the intellect are barred against her by prejudice and passion; if she sometimes forces her way by the batteries of argument, she seldom long keeps possession of her conquests, but is ejected by some favoured enemy, or at best obtains only a nominal sovereignty, without influence and without authority.

That life is short we are all convinced, and yet suffer not that conviction to repress our projects or limit our expectations; that life is miserable we all feel, and yet we believe that the time is near when we shall feel it no longer. But to hope happiness and immortality is equally vain. Our state may indeed be more or less imbittered, as our duration may be more or less contracted; yet the utmost felicity which we can ever attain, will be little better than alleviation of misery, and we shall always feel more pain from our wants than pleasure from our enjoyments. The incident which I am going to relate will shew, that to destroy the effect of all our success, it is not necessary that any signal calamity should fall upon us, that we should be harrassed by implacable persecution, or excruciated by irremediable pains; the brightest hours of prosperity have their clouds, and the stream of life, if it is not ruffled by obstructions, will grow putrid by stagnation.

My father resolving not to imitate the folly of his ancestors, who had hitherto left the younger sons encumbrances on the eldest, destined me to a lucrative profession, and I being careful to lose no opportunity of improvement, was at the usual time in which young men enter the world, well qualified for the exercise of the business which I had chosen.

My eagerness to distinguish myself in publick, and my impatience of the narrow scheme of life to which my indigence confined me, did not suffer me to continue long in the town where I was born. I went away as from a place of confinement, with a resolution to return no more, till I should be able to dazzle with my splendor those who now looked upon me with contempt, to reward those who had paid honours to my dawning merit, and to show all who had suffered me to glide by them unknown and neglected, how much they mistook their interest in omitting to propitiate a genius like mine.

Such were my intentions when I sallied forth into the unknown world, in quest of riches and honours, which I expected to procure in a very short time; for what could withold them from industry and knowledge? He that indulges hope will always be disappointed. Reputation I very soon obtained, but as merit is much more cheaply acknowledged than rewarded, I did not find myself yet enriched in proportion to my celebrity.

I had however in time surmounted the obstacles by which envy and competition obstruct the first attempts of a new claimant, and saw my opponents and censurers tacitly confessing their despair of success, by courting my friendship and yielding to my influence. They who once persued me, were now satisfied to escape from me; and they who had before thought me presumptuous in hoping to overtake them, had now their utmost wish, if they were permitted at no great distance quietly to follow me.

My wants were not madly multiplied as my acquisitions encreased, and the time came at length when I thought myself enabled to gratify all reasonable desires, and when, therefore, I resolved to enjoy that plenty and serenity which I had been hitherto labouring to procure, to enjoy them while I was yet neither crushed by age into infirmity, nor so habituated to a particular manner of life as to be unqualified for new studies or entertainments.

I now quitted my profession, and to set myself at once free from all importunities to resume it, changed my residence, and devoted the remaining part of my time to quiet and amusement. Amidst innumerable projects of pleasure which restless idleness incited me to form, and of which most, when they came to the moment of execution, were rejected for others of no longer continuance, some accident revived in my imagination the pleasing ideas of my native place. It was now in my power to visit those from whom I had been so long absent, in such a manner as was consistent with my former resolution, and I wondered how it could happen that I had so long delayed my own happiness.

Full of the admiration which I should excite, and the homage which I should receive, I dressed my servants in a more ostentatious livery, purchased a magnificent chariot, and resolved to dazzle the inhabitants of the little town with an unexpected blaze of greatness.

While the preparations that vanity required were made for my departure, which, as workmen will not easily be hurried beyond their ordinary rate, I thought very tedious, I solaced my impatience with imaging the various censures that my appearance would produce, the hopes which some would feel from my bounty, the terror which my power would strike on others; the aukward respect with which I should be accosted by timorous officiousness; and the distant reverence with which others less familiar to splendour and dignity would be contented to gaze upon me. I deliberated a long time, whether I should immediately descend to a level with my former acquaintances, or make my condescension more grateful by a gentle transition from haughtiness and reserve. At length I determined to forget some of my companions, till they discovered themselves by some indubitable token, and to receive the congratulations of others upon my good fortune with indifference, to show that I always expected what I had now obtained. The acclamations of the populace I purposed to reward with six hogsheads of ale, and a roasted ox, and then recommend to them to return to their work.

At last all the trappings of grandeur were fitted, and I began the journey of triumph, which I could have wished to have ended in the same moment, but my horses felt none of their master's ardour, and I was shaken four days upon rugged roads. I then entered the town, and having graciously let fall the glasses, that my person might be seen, passed slowly through the street. The noise of the wheels brought the inhabitants to their doors, but I could not perceive that I was known by them. At last I alighted, and my name, I suppose, was told by my servants, for the barber stept from the opposite house, and seized me by the hand with honest joy in his countenance, which, according to the rule that I had prescribed to myself, I repressed with a frigid graciousness. The fellow, instead of sinking into dejection, turned away with contempt, and left me to consider how the second salutation should be received. The next friend was better treated, for I soon found that I must purchase by civility that regard which I had expected to enforce by insolence.

There was yet no smoak of bonfires, no harmony of bells, no shout of crouds, nor riot of joy; the business of the day went forward as before, and after having ordered a splendid supper, which no man came to partake, and which my chagrin hindered me from tasting, I went to bed, where the vexation of disappointment overpowered the fatigue of my journey, and kept me from sleep.

I rose so much humbled by those mortifications, as to enquire after the present state of the town, and found that I had been absent too long to obtain the triumph which had flattered my expectation. Of the friends whose compliments I expected, some had long ago moved to distant provinces, some had lost in the maladies of age all sense of another's prosperity, and some had forgotten our former intimacy amidst care and distresses. Of three whom I had resolved to punish for their former offences by a longer continuance of neglect, one was, by his own industry, raised above my scorn, and two were sheltered from it in the grave. All those whom I loved, feared, or hated, all whose envy or whose kindness I had hopes of contemplating with pleasure, were swept away, and their place was filled by a new generation with other views and other competitions; and among many proofs of the impotence of wealth, I found that it conferred upon me very few distinctions in my native place.

I am, Sir, &c.
SEROTINUS.

No. 167. Tuesday, 22 October 1751.

Candida perpetuo reside concordia lecto,
Tamque pari semper sit Venus æqua jugo.
Diligat ipsa senem quondam, sed et ipsa marito
Tum quoque cum fuerit, non videatur anus.
MART.

Their nuptial bed may smiling concord dress,
And *Venus* still the happy union bless!
Wrinkled with age, may mutual love and truth
To their dim eyes recall the bloom of youth.
F. LEWIS.

To the RAMBLER.

SIR,

It is not common to envy those with whom we cannot easily be placed in comparison. Every man sees without malevolence the progress of another in the tracks of life, which he has himself no desire to tread, and hears without inclination to cavils or contradiction the renown of those whose distance will not suffer them to draw the attention of mankind from his own merit. The sailor never thinks it necessary to contest the lawyer's abilities; nor would the *Rambler*, however jealous of his reputation, be much disturbed by the success of rival wits at *Agra* or *Ispahan*.

We do not therefore ascribe to you any superlative degree of virtue, when we believe that we may inform you of our change of condition without danger of malignant fascination; and that when you read of the marriage of your correspondents *Hymenæus* and *Tranquilla*, you will join your wishes to those of their other friends for the happy event of an union in which caprice and self-ishness had so little part.

There is at least this reason why we should be less deceived in our connubial hopes than many who enter into the same state, that we have allowed our minds to form no unreasonable expectations, nor vitiated our fancies in the soft hours of courtship, with visions of felicity which human power cannot bestow, or of perfection which human virtue cannot attain. That impartiality with which we endeavoured to inspect the manners of all whom we have known was never so much overpowered by our passion, but that we discovered some faults and weaknesses in each other; and joined our hands in conviction, that as there are advantages to be enjoyed in marriage, there are inconveniencies likewise to be endured; and that, together with confederate intellects and auxiliar virtues, we must find different opinions and opposite inclinations.

We however flatter ourselves, for who is not flattered by himself as well as by others on the day of marriage, that we are eminently qualified to give mutual pleasure. Our birth is without any such remarkable disparity as can give either an opportunity of insulting the other with pompous names and splendid alliances, or of calling in upon any domestick controversy the over-bearing assistance of powerful relations. Our fortune was equally suitable, so that we meet without any of those obligations which always produce reproach or suspicion of reproach, which, though they may be forgotten in the gaieties of the first month, no delicacy will always suppress, or of which the suppression must be considered as a new favour, to be repaid by tameness and sub-mission, till gratitude takes the place of love, and the desire of pleasing degenerates by degrees into the fear of offending.

The settlements caused no delay; for we did not trust our affairs to the negotiation of wretches who would have paid their court by multiplying stipulations. *Tranquilla* scorned to detain any part of her fortune from him into whose hands she delivered up her person; and *Hymenæus* thought no act of baseness more criminal than his who enslaves his wife by her own generos-ity, who by marrying without a jointure condemns her to all the dangers of accident and caprice, and at last boasts his liberality by granting what only the indiscretion of her kindness enabled him to withhold. He therefore received on the common terms the portion which any other woman might have brought him, and reserved all the exuberance of acknowledgment for those excellencies which he has yet been able to discover only in *Tranquilla*.

We did not pass the weeks of courtship like those who consider themselves as taking the last draught of pleasure, and resolve not to quit the bowl without a surfeit, or who know themselves about to set happiness to hazard, and endeavour to lose their sense of danger in the ebriety of perpetual amuse-ment, and whirl round the gulph before they sink. *Hymenæus* often repeated a medical axiom, that *the succours of sickness ought not to be wasted in health*. We know that however our eyes may yet sparkle, and our hearts bound at the presence of each other, the time of listlessness and satiety, of peevishness and discontent must come at last, in which we shall be driven for relief to shews and recreations; that the uniformity of life must be sometimes diversified, and the vacuities of conversation sometimes supplied. We rejoice in the reflection that we have stores of novelty yet unexhausted, which may be opened when repletion shall call for change, and gratifications yet untasted, by which life when it shall become vapid or bitter may be restored to its former sweetness and sprightliness, and again irritate the appetite, and again sparkle in the cup.

Our time will probably be less tasteless than that of those whom the authority and avarice of parents unites almost without their consent in their early years, before they have accumulated any fund of reflection, or collected materials for mutual entertainment. Such we have often seen rising in the morning to cards, and retiring in the afternoon to dose, whose happiness was celebrated by their neighbours, because they happened to grow rich by parsimony, and to be kept quiet by insensibility, and agreed to eat and to sleep together.

We have both mingled with the world, and are therefore no strangers to the faults and virtues, the designs and competitions, the hopes and fears of our contemporaries. We have both amused our leisure with books, and can therefore recount the events of former times, or cite the dictates of antient wisdom. Every occurrence furnishes us with some hint which one or the other can improve, and if it should happen that memory or imagination fail us, we can retire to no idle or unimproving solitude.

Tho' our characters beheld at a distance, exhibit this general resemblance, yet a nearer inspection discovers such a dissimilitude of our habitudes and sentiments, as leaves each some peculiar advantages, and affords that *concordia discors*, that suitable disagreement which is always necessary to intellectual harmony. There may be a total diversity of ideas which admits no participation of the same delight, and there may likewise be such a conformity of notions, as leaves neither any thing to add to the decisions of the other. With such contrariety there can be no peace, with such similarity there can be no pleasure. Our reasonings, though often formed upon different views, terminate generally in the same conclusion. Our thoughts like rivulets issuing from distant springs, are each impregnated in its course with various mixtures, and tinged by infusions unknown to the other, yet at last easily unite into one stream, and purify themselves by the gentle effervescence of contrary qualities.

These benefits we receive in a greater degree as we converse without reserve, because we have nothing to conceal. We have no debts to be paid by imperceptible deductions from avowed expences, no habits to be indulged by the private subserviency of a favoured servant, no private interviews with needy relations, no intelligence with spies placed upon each other. We considered marriage as the most solemn league of perpetual friendship, a state from which artifice and concealment are to be banished for ever, and in which every act of dissimulation is a breach of faith.

The impetuous vivacity of youth, and that ardor of desire, which the first sight of pleasure naturally produces, have long ceased to hurry us into irregularity and vehemence; and experience has shewn us that few gratifications are too valuable to be sacrificed to complaisance. We have thought it convenient to rest from the fatigue of pleasure, and now only continue that course of life into which we had before entered, confirmed in our choice by mutual approbation, supported in our resolution by mutual encouragement, and assisted in our efforts by mutual exhortation.

Such, Mr. *Rambler*, is our prospect of life, a prospect which as it is beheld with more attention, seems to open more extensive happiness, and spreads by degrees into the boundless regions of eternity. But if all our prudence has been vain, and we are doomed to give one instance more of the uncertainty of human discernment, we shall comfort ourselves amidst our disappointments, that we were not betrayed but by such delusions as caution could not escape, since we sought happiness only in the arms of virtue. We are,

  SIR,

        Your humble Servants,
        HYMENÆUS,
        TRANQUILLA.

No. 168. Saturday, 26 October 1751.

—————————*Decipit*
Frons prima multos, rara mens intelligit
Quod interiore condidit cura angulo.
     PHÆDRUS.

The tinsel glitter, and the specious mein,
Delude the most; few pry behind the scene.

It has been observed by *Boileau*, that "a mean or common thought expressed in pompous diction, generally pleases more than a new or noble sentiment delivered in low and vulgar language; because the number is greater of those whom custom has enabled to judge of words, than whom study has qualified to examine things."

This solution might satisfy, if such only were offended with meanness of expression as are unable to distinguish propriety of thought, and to separate propositions or images from the vehicles by which they are conveyed to the understanding. But this kind of disgust is by no means confined to the ignorant or superficial; it operates uniformly and universally upon readers of all classes; every man, however profound or abstracted, perceives himself irresistibly alienated by low terms; they who profess the most zealous adherence to truth are forced to admit that she owes part of her charms to her ornaments, and loses much of her power over the soul, when she appears disgraced by a dress uncouth or ill-adjusted.

We are all offended by low terms, but are not disgusted alike by the same compositions, because we do not all agree to censure the same terms as low. No word is naturally or intrinsically meaner than another; our opinion therefore of words, as of other things arbitrarily and capriciously established, depends wholly upon accident and custom. The cottager thinks those apartments splendid and spacious, which an inhabitant of palaces will despise for their inelegance; and to him who has passed most of his hours with the delicate and polite, many expressions will seem sordid, which another, equally acute, may hear without offence; but a mean term never fails to displease him to whom it appears mean, as poverty is certainly and invariably despised, though he who is poor in the eyes of some, may by others be envied for his wealth.

Words become low by the occasions to which they are applied, or the general character of them who use them; and the disgust which they produce, arises from the revival of those images with which they are commonly united. Thus if, in the most solemn discourse, a phrase happens to occur which has been successfully employed in some ludicrous narrative, the gravest auditor finds it difficult to refrain from laughter, when they who are not prepossessed by the same accidental association, are utterly unable to guess the reason of his merriment. Words which convey ideas of dignity in one age, are banished from elegant writing or conversation in another, because they are in time debased by vulgar mouths, and can be no longer heard without the involuntary recollection of unpleasing images.

When *Mackbeth* is confirming himself in the horrid purpose of stabbing his king, he breaks out amidst his emotions into a wish natural to a murderer,

> —— —— Come, thick night!
> And pall thee in the dunnest smoke of hell,
> That my keen knife see not the wound it makes;
> Nor heav'n peep through the blanket of the dark,
> To cry, hold, hold! —— ——

In this passage is exerted all the force of poetry, that force which calls new powers into being, which embodies sentiment, and animates matter; yet perhaps scarce any man now peruses it without some disturbance of his attention from the counteraction of the words to the ideas. What can be more dreadful than to implore the presence of night, invested not in common obscurity, but in the smoke of hell? Yet the efficacy of this invocation is destroyed by the insertion of an epithet now seldom heard but in the stable, and *dun* night may come or go without any other notice than contempt.

If we start into raptures when some hero of the Iliad tells us that δόρυ μάινεται, his lance rages with eagerness to destroy; if we are alarmed at the terror of the soldiers commanded by *Cæsar* to hew down the sacred grove, who dreaded, says *Lucan*, lest the axe aimed at the oak should fly back upon the striker,

> ———— *Si robora sacra ferirent,*
> *In sua credebant redituras membra secures,*

> None dares with impious steel the grove to rend,
> Lest on himself the destin'd stroke descend.

we cannot surely but sympathise with the horrors of a wretch about to murder his master, his friend, his benefactor, who suspects that the weapon will refuse its office, and start back from the breast which he is preparing to violate. Yet this sentiment is weakened by the name of an instrument used by butchers and cooks in the meanest employments; we do not immediately conceive that any crime of importance is to be committed with a *knife*; or who does not, at last, from the long habit of connecting a knife with sordid offices, feel aversion rather than terror?

Macbeth proceeds to wish, in the madness of guilt, that the inspection of heaven may be intercepted, and that he may in the involutions of infernal darkness escape the eye of providence. This is the utmost extravagance of determined wickedness; yet this is so debased by two unfortunate words, that while I endeavour to impress on my reader the energy of the sentiment, I can scarce check my risibility, when the expression forces itself upon my mind; for who, without some relaxation of his gravity, can hear of the avengers of guilt *peeping through a blanket?*

These imperfections of diction are less obvious to the reader, as he is less acquainted with common usages; they are therefore wholly imperceptible to a foreigner, who learns our language from books, and will strike a solitary academick less forcibly than a modish lady.

Among the numerous requisites that must concur to complete an author, few are of more importance than an early entrance into the living world. The seeds of knowledge may be planted in solitude, but must be cultivated in publick. Argumentation may be taught in colleges, and theories formed in retirement, but the artifice of embellishment, and the powers of attraction, can be gained only by general converse.

An acquaintance with prevailing customs and fashionable elegance is necessary likewise for other purposes. The injury that grand imagery suffers from unsuitable language, personal merit may fear from rudeness and indelicacy. When the success of *Æneas* depended on the favour of the queen upon whose coasts he was driven, his celestial protectress thought him not sufficiently secured against rejection by his piety or bravery, but decorated him for the interview with preternatural beauty. Whoever desires, for his writings or himself, what none can reasonably contemn, the favour of mankind, must add grace to strength, and make his thoughts agreeable as well as useful. Many complain of neglect who never tried to attract regard. It cannot be expected that the patrons of science or virtue should be solicitous to discover excellencies which they who possess them shade and disguise. Few have abilities so much needed by the rest of the world as to be caressed on their own terms; and he that will not condescend to recommend himself by external embellishments, must submit to the fate of just sentiments meanly expressed, and be ridiculed and forgotten before he is understood.

No. 170. Saturday, 2 November 1751.

Confiteor; si quid prodest delicta fateri.
Ovid.

I grant the charge; forgive the fault confess'd.

To the RAMBLER.

SIR,

I am one of those beings, from whom many, that melt at the sight of all other misery, think it meritorious to withhold relief; one whom the rigour of virtuous indignation dooms to suffer without complaint, and perish without regard; and whom I myself have formerly insulted in the pride of reputation and security of innocence.

I am of a good family, but my father was burthened with more children than he could decently support. A wealthy relation, as he travelled from *London* to his country seat, condescending to make him a visit, was touched with compassion of his narrow fortune, and resolved to ease him of part of his charge, by taking the care of a child upon himself. Distress on one side and ambition on the other, were too powerful for parental fondness, and the little family passed in review before him, that he might make his choice. I was then ten years old, and without knowing for what purpose, I was called to my great cousin, endeavoured to recommend myself by my best courtesy, sung him my prettiest song, told the last story that I had read, and so much endeared myself by my innocence, that he declared his resolution to adopt me, and to educate me with his own daughters.

My parents felt the common struggles at the thought of parting, and *some natural tears they dropp'd, but wip'd them soon.* They considered, not without that false estimation of the value of wealth which poverty long continued always produces, that I was raised to higher rank than they could give me, and to hopes of more ample fortune than they could bequeath. My mother sold some of her ornaments to dress me in such a manner as might secure me from contempt at my first arrival; and when she dismissed me, pressed me to her bosom with an embrace that I still feel, gave me some precepts of piety which, however neglected, I have not forgotten, and uttered prayers for my final happiness, of which I have not yet ceased to hope, that they will at last be granted.

My sisters envied my new finery, and seemed not much to regret our separation; my father conducted me to the stagecoach with a kind of chearful tenderness; and in a very short time, I was transported to splendid apartments, and a luxurious table, and grew familiar to show, noise and gaiety.

In three years my mother died, having implored a blessing on her family with her last breath. I had little opportunity to indulge a sorrow, which there was none to partake with me, and therefore soon ceased to reflect much upon my loss. My father turned all his care upon his other children, whom some fortunate adventures and unexpected legacies enabled him, when he died four years after my mother, to leave in a condition above their expectations.

I should have shared the encrease of his fortune, and had once a portion assigned me in his will; but my cousin assuring him that all care for me was needless, since he had resolved to place me happily in the world, directed him to divide my part amongst my sisters.

Thus I was thrown upon dependance without resource. Being now at an age in which young women are initiated in company, I was no longer to be supported in my former character but at considerable expence; so that partly lest I should waste money, and partly lest my appearance might draw too many compliments and assiduities, I was insensibly degraded from my equality, and enjoyed few privileges above the head servant, but that of receiving no wages.

I felt every indignity, but knew that resentment would precipitate my fall. I therefore endeavoured to continue my importance by little services and active officiousness, and for a time preserved myself from neglect, by withdrawing all pretences to competition, and studying to please rather than to shine. But my interest, notwithstanding this expedient, hourly declined, and my cousin's favourite maid began to exchange repartees with me, and consult me about the alterations of a cast gown.

I was now completely depressed, and though I had seen mankind enough to know the necessity of outward chearfulness, I often withdrew to my chamber to vent my grief, or turn my condition in my mind, and examine by what means I might escape from perpetual mortification. At last, my schemes and sorrows were interrupted by a sudden change of my relation's behaviour, who one day took an occasion when we were left together in a room, to bid me suffer myself no longer to be insulted, but assume the place which he always intended me to hold in the family. He assured me, that his wife's preference of her own daughters should never hurt me; and, accompanying his professions with a purse of gold, ordered me to bespeak a rich suit at the mercer's, and to apply privately to him for money when I wanted it, and insinuate that my other friends supplied me, which he would take care to confirm.

By this stratagem, which I did not then understand, he filled me with tenderness and gratitude, compelled me to repose on him as my only support, and produced a necessity of private conversation. He often appointed interviews at the house of an acquaintance, and sometimes called on me with a coach, and carried me abroad. My sense of his favour, and the desire of retaining it, disposed me to unlimited complaisance, and though I saw his kindness grow every day more fond, I did not suffer any suspicion to enter my thoughts. At last the wretch took advantage of the familiarity which he enjoyed as my relation, and the submission which he exacted as my benefactor, to complete the ruin of an orphan whom his own promises had made indigent, whom his indulgence had melted, and his authority subdued.

I know not why it should afford subject of exultation, to overpower on any terms the resolution, or surprise the caution of a girl; but of all the boasters that deck themselves in the spoils of innocence and beauty, they surely have the least pretensions to triumph, who submit to owe their success to some casual influence. They neither employ the graces of fancy, nor the force of understanding, in their attempts; they cannot please their vanity with the art of their approaches, the delicacy of their adulations, the elegance of their address, or the efficacy of their eloquence; nor applaud themselves as possessed of any qualities, by which affection is attracted. They surmount no obstacles, they defeat no rivals, but attack only those who cannot resist, and are often content to possess the body without any solicitude to gain the heart.

Many of these despicable wretches does my present acquaintance with infamy and wickedness enable me to number among the heroes of debauchery. Reptiles whom their own servants would have despised, had they not been their servants, and with whom beggary would have disdained intercourse, had she not been allured by hopes of relief. Many of the beings which are now rioting in taverns, or shivering in the streets, have been corrupted not by arts of gallantry which stole gradually upon the affections and laid prudence asleep, but by the fear of losing benefits which were never intended, or of incurring resentment which they could not escape; some have been frighted by masters, and some awed by guardians into ruin.

Our crime had its usual consequence, and he soon perceived that I could not long continue in his family. I was distracted at the thought of the reproach which I now believed inevitable. He comforted me with hopes of eluding all discovery, and often upbraided me with the anxiety, which perhaps none but himself saw in my countenance; but at last mingled his assurances of protection and maintenance with menaces of total desertion, if in the moments of perturbation I should suffer his secret to escape, or endeavour to throw on him any part of my infamy.

Thus passed the dismal hours till my retreat could no longer be delayed. It was pretended that my relations had sent for me to a distant country, and I entered upon a state which shall be described in my next letter.

I am, SIR, &c.
Misella.

No. 171. Tuesday, 5 November 1751.

Tædet cœli convexa tueri.
Virg.

Dark is the sun, and loathsome is the day.

To the Rambler.

SIR,
Misella now sits down to continue her narrative. I am convinced that nothing would more powerfully preserve youth from irregularity, or guard inexperience from seduction, than a just description of the condition into which the wanton plunges herself, and therefore hope that my letter may be a sufficient antidote to my example.

After the distraction, hesitation and delays which the timidity of guilt naturally produces, I was removed to lodgings in a distant part of the town, under one of the characters commonly assumed upon such occasions. Here being, by my circumstances, condemned to solitude, I passed most of my hours in bitterness and anguish. The conversation of the people with whom I was placed, was not at all capable of engaging my attention or dispossessing the reigning ideas. The books which I carried to my retreat were such as heightened my abhorrence of myself; for I was not so far abandoned as to sink voluntarily into corruption, or endeavour to conceal from my own mind the enormity of my crime.

My relation remitted none of his fondness, but visited me so often that I was sometimes afraid lest his assiduity should expose him to suspicion. Whenever he came he found me weeping, and was therefore less delightfully entertained than he expected. After frequent expostulations upon the unreasonableness of my sorrow, and innumerable protestations of everlasting regard, he at last found that I was more affected with the loss of my innocence, than the danger of my fame, and that he might not be disturbed by my remorse, began to lull my conscience with the opiates of irreligion. His arguments were such as my course of life has since exposed me often to the necessity of hearing, vulgar, empty and fallacious; yet they at first confounded me by their novelty, filled me with doubt and perplexity, and interrupted that peace which I began to feel from the sincerity of my repentance, without substituting any other support. I listened a while to his impious gabble, but its influence was soon overpowered by natural reason and early education, and the convictions which this new attempt gave me of his baseness completed my abhorrence. I have heard of barbarians, who, when tempests drive ships upon their coast, decoy them to the rocks that they may plunder their lading, and have always thought that wretches thus merciless in their depredations, ought to be destroyed by a general insurrection of all social beings; yet how light is this guilt to the crime of him, who in the agitations of remorse cuts away the anchor of piety, and when he has drawn aside credulity from the paths of virtue, hides the light of heaven which would direct her to return. I had hitherto considered him as a man equally betrayed with myself by the concurrence of appetite and opportunity; but I now saw with horror that he was contriving to perpetuate his gratification, and was desirous to fit me to his purpose by complete and radical corruption.

To escape, however, was not yet in my power. I could support the expences of my condition, only by the continuance of his favour. He provided all that was necessary, and in a few weeks, congratulated me upon my escape from the danger which we had both expected with so much anxiety. I then began to remind him of his promise to restore me with my fame uninjured to the world. He promised me in general terms, that nothing should be wanting which his power could add to my happiness, but forbore to release me from my confinement. I knew how much my reception in the world depended upon my speedy return, and was therefore outragiously impatient of his delays, which I now perceived to be only artifices of lewdness. He told me, at last, with an appearance of sorrow, that all hopes of restoration to my former state were for ever precluded; that chance had discovered my secret, and malice divulged it; and that nothing now remained, but to seek a retreat more private, where curiosity or hatred could never find us.

The rage, anguish, and resentment, which I felt at this account, are not to be expressed. I was in so much dread of reproach and infamy, which he represented as pursuing me with full cry, that I yielded myself implicitly to his disposal, and was removed with a thousand studied precautions through byways and dark passages, to another house, where I harrassed him with perpetual solicitations for a small annuity, that might enable me to live in the country with obscurity and innocence.

This demand he at first evaded with ardent professions, but in time appeared offended at my importunity and distrust; and having one day endeavoured to sooth me with uncommon expressions of tenderness, when he found my discontent immoveable, left me with some inarticulate murmurs of anger. I was pleased that he was at last roused to sensibility, and expecting that at his next visit, he would comply with my request, lived with great tranquility upon the money in my hands, and was so much pleased with this pause of persecution, that I did not reflect how much his absence had exceeded the usual intervals, till I was alarmed with the danger of wanting subsistence. I then suddenly contracted my expences, but was unwilling to supplicate for assistance. Necessity, however, soon overcame my modesty or my pride, and I applied to him by a letter, but had no answer. I writ in terms more pressing, but without effect. I then sent an agent to enquire after him, who informed me, that he had quitted his house, and was gone with his family to reside for some time upon his estate in *Ireland*.

However shocked at this abrupt departure, I was yet unwilling to believe that he could wholly abandon me, and therefore by the sale of my cloaths I supported myself, expecting that every post would bring me relief. Thus I passed seven months between hope and dejection, in a gradual approach to poverty and distress, emaciated with discontent and bewildered with uncertainty. At last, my landlady, after many hints of the necessity of a new lover, took the opportunity of my absence to search my boxes, and missing some of my apparel, seized the remainder for rent, and led me to the door.

To remonstrate against legal cruelty, was vain; to supplicate obdurate brutality, was hopeless. I went away I knew not whither, and wandered about without any settled purpose, unacquainted with the usual expedients of misery, unqualified for laborious offices, afraid to meet an eye that had seen me before, and hopeless of relief from those who were strangers to my former condition. Night came on in the midst of my distraction, and I still continued to wander till the menaces of the watch obliged me to shelter myself in a covered passage.

Next day, I procured a lodging in the backward garret of a mean house, and employed my landlady to enquire for a service. My applications were generally rejected for want of a character. At length, I was received at a draper's; but when it was known to my mistress that I had only one gown, and that of silk, she was of opinion, that I looked like a thief, and without warning, hurried me away. I then tried to support myself by my needle, and by my landlady's recommendation, obtained a little work from a shop, and for three weeks lived without repining; but when my punctuality had gained me so much reputation, that I was trusted to make up a head of some value, one of my fellow-lodgers stole the lace, and I was obliged to fly from a prosecution.

Thus driven again into the streets, I lived upon the least that could support me, and at night accommodated myself under pent-houses as well as I could. At length I became absolutely pennyless; and having strolled all day without sustenance, was at the close of evening accosted by an elderly man, with an invitation to a tavern. I refused him with hesitation; he seized me by the hand, and drew me into a neighbouring house, where when he saw my face pale with hunger, and my eyes swelling with tears, he spurned me from him, and bad me cant and whine in some other place; he for his part would take care of his pockets.

I still continued to stand in the way, having scarcely strength to walk farther, when another soon addressed me in the same manner. When he saw the same tokens of calamity, he considered that I might be obtained at a cheap rate, and therefore quickly made overtures, which I had no longer firmness to reject. By this man I was maintained four months in penurious wickedness, and then abandoned to my former condition, from which I was delivered by another keeper.

In this abject state I have now passed four years, the drudge of extortion and the sport of drunkenness; sometimes the property of one man, and sometimes the common prey of accidental lewdness; at one time tricked up for sale by the mistress of a brothel, at another begging in the streets to be relieved from hunger by wickedness; without any hope in the day but of finding some whom folly or excess may expose to my allurements, and without any reflections at night, but such as guilt and terror impress upon me.

If those who pass their days in plenty and security, could visit for an hour the dismal receptacles to which the prostitute retires from her nocturnal excursions, and see the wretches that lie crowded together, mad with intemperance, ghastly with famine, nauseous with filth, and noisome with disease; it would not be easy for any degree of abhorrence to harden them against compassion, or to repress the desire which they must immediately feel to rescue such numbers of human beings from a state so dreadful.

It is said that in *France* they annually evacuate their streets, and ship their prostitutes and vagabonds to their colonies. If the women that infest this city had the same opportunity of escaping from their miseries, I believe very little force would be necessary; for who among them can dread any change? Many of us indeed are wholly unqualified for any but the most servile employments, and those perhaps would require the care of a magistrate to hinder them from following the same practices in another country; but others are only precluded by infamy from reformation, and would gladly be delivered on any terms from the necessity of guilt and the tyranny of chance. No place but a populous city can afford opportunities for open prostitution, and where the eye of justice can attend to individuals, those who cannot be made good may be restrained from mischief. For my part I should exult at the privilege of banishment, and think myself happy in any region that should restore me once again to honesty and peace.

I am, Sir, &c.
Misella.

No. 176. Saturday, 23 November 1751.

—— *Naso suspendere adunco.*
Hor.

On me you turn the nose ——

There are many vexatious accidents and uneasy situations which raise little compassion for the sufferer, and which no man but those whom they immediately distress, can regard with seriousness. Petty mischiefs, that have no influence on futurity, nor extend their effects to the rest of life, are always seen with a kind of malicious pleasure. A mistake or embarrasment, which for the present moment fills the face with blushes, and the mind with confusion, will have no other effect upon those who observe it than that of convulsing them with irresistible laughter. Some circumstances of misery are so powerfully ridiculous, that neither kindness nor duty can withstand them; they bear down love, interest, and reverence, and force the friend, the dependent, or the child, to give way to instantaneous motions of merriment.

Among the principal of comick calamities, may be reckoned the pain which an author, not yet hardened into insensibility, feels at the onset of a furious critick, whose age, rank or fortune gives him confidence to speak without reserve; who heaps one objection upon another, and obtrudes his remarks, and enforces his corrections without tenderness or awe.

The author, full of the importance of his work, and anxious for the justification of every syllable, starts and kindles at the slightest attack; the critick, eager to establish his superiority, triumphing in every discovery of failure, and zealous to impress the cogency of his arguments, pursues him from line to line without cessation or remorse. The critick, who hazards little, proceeds with vehemence, impetuosity and fearlessness; the author, whose quiet and fame, and life and immortality are involved in the controversy, tries every art of subterfuge and defence; maintains modestly what he resolves never to yield, and yields unwillingly what cannot be maintained. The critick's purpose is to conquer, the author only hopes to escape; the critick therefore knits his brow, and raises his voice, and rejoices whenever he perceives any tokens of pain excited by the pressure of his assertions, or the point of his sarcasms. The author, whose endeavour is at once to mollify and elude his persecutor, composes his features, and softens his accent, breaks the force of assault by retreat, and rather steps aside than flies or advances.

As it very seldom happens that the rage of extemporary criticism inflicts fatal or lasting wounds, I know not that the laws of benevolence entitle this distress to much sympathy. The diversion of baiting an author has the sanction of all ages and nations, and is more lawful than the sport of teizing other animals, because for the most part he comes voluntarily to the stake, furnished, as he imagines, by the patron powers of literature, with resistless weapons, and impenetrable armour, with the mail of the boar of *Erymanth*, and the paws of the lion of *Nemea*.

But the works of genius are sometimes produced by other motives than vanity; and he whom necessity or duty enforces to write, is not always so well satisfied with himself, as not to be discouraged by censorious impudence. It may therefore be necessary to consider how they, whom publication lays open to the insults of such as their obscurity secures against reprisals, may extricate themselves from unexpected encounters.

Vida, a man of considerable skill in the politicks of literature, directs his pupil wholly to abandon his defence, and even when he can irrefragably refute all objections, to suffer tamely the exultations of his antagonist.

This rule may perhaps be just, when advice is asked, and severity solicited, because no man tells his opinion so freely as when he imagines it received with implicit veneration; and critics ought never to be consulted but while errors may yet be rectified or insipidity suppressed. But when the book has once been dismissed into the world, and can be no more retouched, I know not whether a very different conduct should not be prescribed, and whether firmness and spirit may not sometimes be of use to overpower arrogance and repel brutality. Softness, diffidence and moderation will often be mistaken for imbecility and dejection; they lure cowardice to the attack by the hopes of easy victory, and it will soon be found that he whom every man thinks he can conquer, shall never be at peace.

The animadversions of criticks are commonly such as may easily provoke the sedatest writer to some quickness of resentment and asperity of reply. A man who by long consideration has familiarised a subject to his own mind, carefully surveyed the series of his thoughts, and planned all the parts of his composition into a regular dependance on each other, will often start at the sinistrous interpretations, or absurd remarks of haste and ignorance, and wonder by what infatuation they have been led away from the obvious sense, and upon what peculiar principles of judgment they decide against him.

The eye of the intellect, like that of the body, is not equally perfect in all, nor equally adapted in any to all objects; the end of criticism is to supply its defects; rules are the instruments of mental vision, which may indeed assist our faculties when properly used, but produce confusion and obscurity by unskilful application.

Some seem always to read with the microscope of criticism, and employ their whole attention upon minute elegance, or faults scarcely visible to common observation. The dissonance of a syllable, the recurrence of the same sound, the repetition of a particle, the smallest deviation from propriety, the slightest defect in construction or arrangement, swell before their eyes into enormities. As they discern with great exactness, they comprehend but a narrow compass, and know nothing of the justness of the design, the general spirit of the performance, the artifice of connection, or the harmony of the parts; they never conceive how small a proportion that which they are busy in contemplating bears to the whole, or how the petty inaccuracies with which they are offended, are absorbed and lost in general excellence.

Others are furnished by criticism with a telescope. They see with great clearness whatever is too remote to be discovered by the rest of mankind, but are totally blind to all that lies immediately before them. They discover in every passage some secret meaning, some remote allusion, some artful allegory, or some occult imitation which no other reader ever suspected, but they have no perception of the cogency of arguments, the force of pathetick sentiments, the various colours of diction, or the flowery embellishments of fancy; of all that engages the attention of others, they are totally insensible, while they pry into worlds of conjecture, and amuse themselves with phantoms in the clouds.

In criticism, as in every other art, we fail sometimes by our weakness, but more frequently by our fault. We are sometimes bewildered by ignorance, and sometimes by prejudice, but we seldom deviate far from the right, but when we deliver ourselves up to the direction of vanity.

No. 181. Tuesday, 10 December 1751.

——— *Neu fluitem dubiæ spe pendulus horæ.*
HOR.

Nor let me float in fortune's pow'r,
Dependant on the future hour.
FRANCIS.

To the RAMBLER.

SIR,

As I have passed much of my life in disquiet and suspense, and lost many opportunities of advantage by a passion which I have reason to believe prevalent in different degrees over a great part of mankind, I cannot but think myself well qualified to warn those who are yet uncaptivated, of the danger which they incur by placing themselves within its influence.

I served an apprenticeship to a linen-draper with uncommon reputation for diligence and fidelity; and at the age of three and twenty opened a shop for myself, with a large stock, and such credit among all the merchants who were acquainted with my master, that I could command whatever was imported curious or valuable. For five years I proceeded with success proportionate to close application and untainted integrity; was a daring bidder at every sale; always paid my notes before they were due; and advanced so fast in commercial reputation, that I was proverbially marked out as the model of young traders, and every one expected that a few years would make me an alderman.

In this course of even prosperity, I was one day persuaded to buy a ticket in the lottery. The sum was inconsiderable, part was to be repaid though fortune might fail to favour me, and therefore my established maxims of frugality did not restrain me from so trifling an experiment. The ticket lay almost forgotten till the time at which every man's fate was to be determined; nor did the affair even then seem of any importance, till I discovered by the publick papers that the number next to mine had conferred the great prize.

My heart leaped at the thought of such an approach to sudden riches, which I considered myself, however contrarily to the laws of computation, as having missed by a single chance; and I could not forbear to revolve the consequences which such a bounteous allotment would have produced, if it had happened to me. This dream of felicity, by degrees took possession of my imagination. The great delight of my solitary hours was to purchase an estate, and form plantations with money which once might have been mine, and I never met my friends but I spoiled all their merriment by perpetual complaints of my ill luck.

At length another lottery was opened, and I had now so heated my imagination with the prospect of a prize, that I should have pressed among the first purchasers, had not my ardour been with-held by deliberation upon the probability of success from one ticket rather than another. I hesitated long between even and odd; considered the square and cubick numbers through the lottery; examined all those to which good luck had been hitherto annexed; and at last fixed upon one which by some secret relation to the events of my life I thought predestined to make me happy. Delay in great affairs is often mischievous; the ticket was sold, and its possessor could not be found.

I returned to my conjectures, and after many arts of prognostication, fixed upon another chance, but with less confidence. Never did captive, heir, or lover feel so much vexation from the slow pace of time, as I suffered between the purchase of my ticket and the distribution of the prizes. I solaced my uneasiness as well as I could, by frequent contemplations of approaching happiness; when the sun rose I knew it would set, and congratulated myself at night that I was so much nearer to my wishes. At last the day came, my ticket appeared, and rewarded all my care and sagacity with a despicable prize of fifty pounds.

My friends, who honestly rejoiced upon my success, were very coldly received; I hid myself a fortnight in the country, that my chagrin might fume away without observation, and then returning to my shop, began to listen after another lottery.

With the news of a lottery I was soon gratified, and having now found the vanity of conjecture and inefficacy of computation, I resolved to take the prize by violence, and therefore bought forty tickets, not omitting however to divide them between the even and odd numbers, that I might not miss the lucky class. Many conclusions did I form, and many experiments did I try to determine from which of those tickets I might most reasonably expect riches. At last, being unable to satisfy myself by any modes of reasoning, I wrote the numbers upon dice, and allotted five hours every day to the amusement of throwing them in a garret; and, examining the event by an exact register, found, on the evening before the lottery was drawn, that one of my numbers had been turned up five times more than any of the rest in three hundred and thirty thousand throws.

This experiment was fallacious; the first day presented the hopeful ticket, a detestable blank. The rest came out with different fortune, and in conclusion I lost thirty pounds by this great adventure.

I had now wholly changed the cast of my behaviour and the conduct of my life. The shop was for the most part abandoned to my servants, and, if I entered it, my thoughts were so engrossed by my tickets, that I scarcely heard or answered a question, but considered every customer as an intruder upon my meditations, whom I was in haste to dispatch. I mistook the price of my goods, committed blunders in my bills, forgot to file my receipts, and neglected to regulate my books. My acquaintances by degrees began to fall away, but I perceived the decline of my business with little emotion, because whatever deficiency there might be in my gains I expected the next lottery to supply.

Miscarriage naturally produces diffidence; I began now to seek assistance against ill luck, by an alliance with those that had been more successful. I enquired diligently, at what office any prize had been sold, that I might purchase of a propitious vender; solicited those who had been fortunate in former lotteries, to partake with me in my new tickets; and, whenever I met with one that had in any event of his life been eminently prosperous, I invited him to take a larger share. I had, by this rule of conduct, so diffused my interest, that I had a fourth part of fifteen tickets, an eighth of forty and a sixteenth of ninety.

I waited for the decision of my fate with my former palpitations, and looked upon the business of my trade with the usual neglect. The wheel at last was turned, and its revolutions brought me a long succession of sorrows and disappointments. I indeed often partook of a small prize, and the loss of one day was generally balanced by the gain of the next; but my desires yet remained unsatisfied, and when one of my chances had failed, all my expectation was suspended on those which remained yet undetermined. At last a prize of five thousand pounds was proclaimed; I caught fire at the cry, and enquiring the number found it to be one of my own tickets, which I had divided among those on whose luck I depended, and of which I had retained only a sixteenth part.

You will easily judge, with what detestation of himself, a man thus intent upon gain reflected that he had sold a prize which was once in his possession. It was to no purpose, that I represented to my mind, the impossibility of recalling the past, or the folly of condemning an act, which only its event, an event which no human intelligence could foresee, proved to be wrong. The prize which, though put in my hands, had been suffered to slip from me, filled me with anguish; and knowing that complaint would only expose me to ridicule, I gave myself up silently to grief, and lost by degrees my appetite and my rest.

My indisposition soon became visible; I was visited by my friends, and among them by *Eumathes*, a clergyman, whose piety and learning gave him such an ascendant over me, that I could not refuse to open my heart. There are, said he, few minds sufficiently firm to be trusted in the hands of chance. Whoever finds himself inclined to anticipate futurity, and exalt possibility to certainty, should avoid every kind of casual adventure, since his grief must be always proportionate to his hope. You have long wasted that time which, by a proper application, would have certainly, though moderately, encreased your fortune, in a laborious and anxious persuit of a species of gain, which no labour or anxiety, no art or expedient can secure or promote. You are now fretting away your life in repentance of an act, against which repentance can give no caution, but to avoid the occasion of committing it. Rouse from this lazy dream of fortuitous riches, which, if obtained you could scarcely have enjoyed, because they could confer no consciousness of desert; return to rational and manly industry, and consider the meer gift of luck as below the care of a wise man.

No. 183. Tuesday, 17 December 1751.

Nulla fides regni sociis, omnisque potestas
Impatiens consortis erat.

LUCAN.

No faith of partnership dominion owns;
Still discord hovers o'er divided thrones.

The hostility perpetually exercised between one man and another, is caused by the desire of many for that which only few can possess. Every man would be rich, powerful, and famous; yet fame, power, and riches, are only the names of relative conditions, which imply the obscurity, dependance, and poverty of greater numbers.

This universal and incessant competition, produces injury and malice by two motives, interest, and envy; the prospect of adding to our possessions what we can take from others, and the hope of alleviating the sense of our disparity by lessening others, though we gain nothing to ourselves.

Of these two malignant and destructive powers, it seems probable at the first view, that interest has the strongest and most extensive influence. It is easy to conceive that opportunities to seize what has been long wanted, may excite desires almost irresistible; but surely, the same eagerness cannot be kindled by an accidental power of destroying that which gives happiness to another. It must be more natural to rob for gain, than to ravage only for mischief.

Yet I am inclined to believe, that the great law of mutual benevolence is oftner violated by envy than by interest, and that most of the misery which the defamation of blameless actions, or the obstruction of honest endeavours brings upon the world, is inflicted by men that propose no advantage to themselves but the satisfaction of poisoning the banquet which they cannot taste, and blasting the harvest which they have no right to reap.

Interest can diffuse itself but to a narrow compass. The number is never large of those who can hope to fill the posts of degraded power, catch the fragments of shattered fortune, or succeed to the honours of depreciated beauty. But the empire of envy has no limits, as it requires to its influence very little help from external circumstances. Envy may always be produced by idleness and pride, and in what place will not they be found?

Interest requires some qualities not universally bestowed. The ruin of another will produce no profit to him, who has not discernment to mark his advantage, courage to seize, and activity to pursue it; but the cold malignity of envy may be exerted in a torpid and quiescent state, amidst the gloom of stupidity, in the coverts of cowardice. He that falls by the attacks of interest, is torn by hungry tigers; he may discover and resist his enemies. He that perishes in the ambushes of envy, is destroyed by unknown and invisible assailants, and dies like a man suffocated by a poisonous vapour, without knowledge of his danger, or possibility of contest.

Interest is seldom pursued but at some hazard. He that hopes to gain much, has commonly something to lose, and when he ventures to attack superiority, if he fails to conquer, is irrecoverably crushed. But envy may act without expence, or danger. To spread suspicion, to invent calumnies, to propagate scandal, requires neither labour nor courage. It is easy for the author of a lye, however malignant, to escape detection, and infamy needs very little industry to assist its circulation.

Envy is almost the only vice which is practicable at all times, and in every place; the only passion which can never lie quiet for want of irritation; its effects therefore are every where discoverable, and its attempts always to be dreaded.

It is impossible to mention a name which any advantageous distinction has made eminent, but some latent animosity will burst out. The wealthy trader, however he may abstract himself from publick affairs, will never want those who hint, with *Shylock*, that ships are but boards. The beauty, adorned only with the unambitious graces of innocence and modesty, provokes, whenever she appears, a thousand murmurs of detraction. The genius, even when he endeavours only to entertain or instruct, yet suffers persecution from innumerable criticks, whose acrimony is excited merely by the pain of seeing others pleased, and of hearing applauses which another enjoys.

The frequency of envy makes it so familiar, that it escapes our notice; nor do we often reflect upon its turpitude or malignity, till we happen to feel its influence. When he that has given no provocation to malice, but by attempting to excel, finds himself pursued by multitudes whom he never saw with all the implacability of personal resentment; when he perceives clamour and malice let loose upon him as a publick enemy, and incited by every stratagem of defamation; when he hears the misfortunes of his family, or the follies of his youth exposed to the world; and every failure of conduct, or defect of nature aggravated and ridiculed; he then learns to abhor those artifices at which he only laughed before, and discovers how much the happiness of life would be advanced by the eradication of envy from the human heart.

Envy is, indeed, a stubborn weed of the mind, and seldom yields to the culture of philosophy. There are, however, considerations, which if carefully implanted and diligently propagated, might in time overpower and repress it, since no one can nurse it for the sake of pleasure, as its effects are only shame, anguish, and perturbation.

It is above all other vices inconsistent with the character of a social being, because it sacrifices truth and kindness to very weak temptations. He that plunders a wealthy neighbour, gains as much as he takes away, and may improve his own condition in the same proportion as he impairs another's; but he that blasts a flourishing reputation, must be content with a small dividend of additional fame, so small as can afford very little consolation to balance the guilt by which it is obtained.

I have hitherto avoided that dangerous and empirical morality, which cures one vice by means of another. But envy is so base and detestable, so vile in its original, and so pernicious in its effects, that the predominance of almost any other quality is to be preferred. It is one of those lawless enemies of society, against which poisoned arrows may honestly be used. Let it, therefore, be constantly remembered, that whoever envies another, confesses his superiority, and let those be reformed by their pride who have lost their virtue.

It is no slight aggravation of the injuries which envy incites, that they are committed against those who have given no intentional provocation; and that the sufferer is often marked out for ruin, not because he has failed in any duty, but because he has dared to do more than was required.

Almost every other crime is practised by the help of some quality which might have produced esteem or love, if it had been well employed; but envy is mere unmixed and genuine evil; it pursues a hateful end by despicable means, and desires not so much its own happiness as another's misery. To avoid depravity like this, it is not necessary that any one should aspire to heroism or sanctity, but only, that he should resolve not to quit the rank which nature assigns him, and wish to maintain the dignity of a human being.

No. 184. Saturday, 21 December 1751.

Permittes ipsis expendere numinibus, quid
Conveniat nobis, rebusque sit utile nostris.
                                          JUV.

Intrust thy fortune to the pow'rs above:
Leave them to manage for thee, and to grant
What their unerring wisdom sees thee want.
                                          DRYDEN.

As every scheme of life, so every form of writing has its advantages and inconveniencies, though not mingled in the same proportions. The writer of essays, escapes many embarrassments to which a large work would have exposed him; he seldom harrasses his reason with long trains of consequence, dims his eyes with the perusal of antiquated volumes, or burthens his memory with great accumulations of preparatory knowledge. A careless glance upon a favourite author, or transient survey of the varieties of life, is sufficient to supply the first hint or seminal idea, which enlarged by the gradual accretion of matter stored in the mind, is by the warmth of fancy easily expanded into flowers, and sometimes ripened into fruit.

The most frequent difficulty, by which the authors of these petty compositions are distressed, arises from the perpetual demand of novelty and change. The compiler of a system of science lays his invention at rest, and employs only his judgment, the faculty exerted with least fatigue. Even the relator of feigned adventures, when once the principal characters are established, and the great events regularly connected, finds incidents and episodes crouding upon his mind; every change opens new views, and the latter part of the story grows without labour out of the former. But he that attempts to entertain his reader with unconnected pieces, finds the irksomeness of his task rather encreased than lessened by every production. The day calls afresh upon him for a new topick, and he is again obliged to choose, without any principle to regulate his choice.

It is indeed true, that there is seldom any necessity of looking far, or enquiring long for a proper subject. Every diversity of art or nature, every public blessing or calamity, every domestick pain or gratification, every sally of caprice, blunder of absurdity, or stratagem of affectation may supply matter to him whose only rule is to avoid uniformity. But it often happens, that the judgment is distracted with boundless multiplicity, the imagination ranges from one design to another, and the hours pass imperceptibly away till the composition can be no longer delayed, and necessity enforces the use of those thoughts which then happen to be at hand. The mind rejoicing at deliverance on any terms from perplexity and suspense, applies herself vigorously to the work before her, collects embellishments and illustrations, and sometimes finishes with great elegance and happiness what in a state of ease and leisure she never had begun.

It is not commonly observed, how much, even of actions considered as particularly subject to choice, is to be attributed to accident, or some cause out of our own power, by whatever name it be distinguished. To close tedious deliberations with hasty resolves, and after long consultations with reason to refer the question to caprice, is by no means peculiar to the essayist. Let him that peruses this paper, review the series of his life, and enquire how he was placed in his present condition. He will find that of the good or ill which he has experienced, a great part came unexpected, without any visible gradations of approach; that every event has been influenced by causes acting without his intervention; and that whenever he pretended to the prerogative of foresight, he was mortified with new conviction of the shortness of his views.

The busy, the ambitious, the inconstant, and the adventurous, may be said to throw themselves by design into the arms of fortune, and voluntarily to quit the power of governing themselves; they engage in a course of life in which little can be ascertained by previous measures; nor is it any wonder that their time is past between elation and despondency, hope and disappointment.

Some there are who appear to walk the road of life with more circumspection, and make no step till they think themselves secure from the hazard of a precipice; when neither pleasure nor profit can tempt them from the beaten path; who refuse to climb lest they should fall, or to run lest they should stumble, and move slowly forward without any compliance with those passions by which the heady and vehement are seduced and betrayed.

Yet even the timorous prudence of this judicious class is far from exempting them from the dominion of chance, a subtle and insidious power, who will intrude upon privacy and embarrass caution. No course of life is so prescribed and limited, but that many actions must result from arbitrary election. Every one must form the general plan of his conduct by his own reflections; he must resolve whether he will endeavour at riches or at content; whether he will exercise private or publick virtues; whether he will labour for the general benefit of mankind, or contract his beneficence to his family and dependents.

This question has long exercised the schools of philosophy, but remains yet undecided; and what hope is there that a young man, unacquainted with the arguments on either side, should determine his own destiny otherwise than by chance?

When chance has given him a partner of his bed, whom he prefers to all other women, without any proof of superior desert, chance must again direct him in the education of his children; for, who was ever able to convince himself by arguments, that he had chosen for his son that mode of instruction to which his understanding was best adapted, or by which he would most easily be made wise or virtuous?

Whoever shall enquire by what motives he was determined on these important occasions, will find them such, as his pride will scarcely suffer him to confess; some sudden ardour of desire, some uncertain glimpse of advantage, some petty competition, some inaccurate conclusion, or some example implicitly reverenced. Such are often the first causes of our resolves; for it is necessary to act, but impossible to know the consequences of action, or to discuss all the reasons which offer themselves on every part to inquisitiveness and solicitude.

Since life itself is uncertain, nothing which has life for its basis, can boast much stability. Yet this is but a small part of our perplexity. We set out on a tempestuous sea, in quest of some port, where we expect to find rest, but where we are not sure of admission; we are not only in danger of sinking in the way, but of being misled by meteors mistaken for stars, of being driven from our course by the changes of the wind, and of losing it by unskilful steerage; yet it sometimes happens, that cross winds blow us to a safer coast, that meteors draw us aside from whirlpools, and that negligence or error contributes to our escape from mischiefs to which a direct course would have exposed us. Of those that by precipitate conclusions, involve themselves in calamities without guilt, very few, however they may reproach themselves, can be certain that other measures would have been more successful.

In this state of universal uncertainty, where a thousand dangers hover about us, and none can tell whether the good that he persues is not evil in disguise, or whether the next step will lead him to safety or destruction, nothing can afford any rational tranquillity, but the conviction that, however we amuse ourselves with unideal sounds, nothing in reality is governed by chance, but that the universe is under the perpetual superintendence of him who created it; that our being is in the hands of omnipotent goodness, by whom what appears casual to us is directed for ends ultimately kind and merciful; and that nothing can finally hurt him who debars not himself from the divine favour.

No. 188. Saturday, 4 January 1752.

———— *Si te colo*, Sexte, *non amabo*.
MART.

The more I honour thee, the less I love.

None of the desires dictated by vanity is more general, or less blameable, than that of being distinguished for the arts of conversation. Other accomplishments may be possessed without opportunity of exerting them, or wanted without danger that the defect can often be remarked; but as no man can live otherwise than in an hermitage, without hourly pleasure or vexation, from the fondness or neglect of those about him, the faculty of giving pleasure is of continual use. Few are more frequently envied than those who have the power of forcing attention wherever they come, whose entrance is considered as a promise of felicity, and whose departure is lamented, like the recess of the sun from northern climates, as a privation of all that enlivens fancy, or inspirits gaiety.

It is apparent, that to excellence in this valuable art, some peculiar qualifications are necessary; for every one's experience will inform him, that the pleasure which men are able to give in conversation, holds no stated proportion to their knowledge or their virtue. Many find their way to the tables and the parties of those who never consider them as of the least importance in any other place; we have all, at one time or other, been content to love those whom we could not esteem, and been persuaded to try the dangerous experiment of admitting him for a companion whom we knew to be too ignorant for a counsellor, and too treacherous for a friend.

I question whether some abatement of character is not necessary to general acceptance. Few spend their time with much satisfaction under the eye of uncontestable superiority; and therefore, among those whose presence is courted at assemblies of jollity, there are seldom found men eminently distinguished for powers or acquisitions. The wit whose vivacity condemns slower tongues to silence, the scholar whose knowledge allows no man to fancy that he instructs him, the critick who suffers no fallacy to pass undetected, and the reasoner who condemns the idle to thought, and the negligent to attention, are generally praised and feared, reverenced and avoided.

He that would please must rarely aim at such excellence as depresses his hearers in their own opinion, or debars them from the hope of contributing reciprocally to the entertainment of the company. Merriment, extorted by sallies of imagination, sprightliness of remark, or quickness of reply, is too often what the *Latins* call, the *Sardinian Laughter*, a distortion of the face without gladness of heart.

For this reason, no stile of conversation is more extensively acceptable than the narrative. He who has stored his memory with slight anecdotes, private incidents, and personal particularities, seldom fails to find his audience favourable. Almost every man listens with eagerness to contemporary history; for almost every man has some real or imaginary connection with a celebrated character, some desire to advance, or oppose a rising name. Vanity often co-operates with curiosity. He that is a hearer in one place qualifies himself to become a speaker in another; for though he cannot comprehend a series of argument, or transport the volatile spirit of wit without evaporation, he yet thinks himself able to treasure up the various incidents of a story, and pleases his hopes with the information which he shall give to some inferior society.

Narratives are for the most part heard without envy, because they are not supposed to imply any intellectual qualities above the common rate. To be acquainted with facts not yet echoed by plebeian mouths, may happen to one man as well as to another, and to relate them when they are known, has in appearance so little difficulty, that every one concludes himself equal to the task.

But it is not easy, and in some situations of life not possible, to accumulate such a stock of materials as may support the expence of continual narration; and it frequently happens, that they who attempt this method of ingratiating themselves, please only at the first interview; and, for want of new supplies of intelligence, wear out their stories by continual repetition.

There would be, therefore, little hope of obtaining the praise of a good companion, were it not to be gained by more compendious methods; but such is the kindness of mankind to all, except those who aspire to real merit and rational dignity, that every understanding may find some way to excite benevolence; and whoever is not envied, may learn the art of procuring love. We are willing to be pleased, but are not willing to admire; we favour the mirth or officiousness that solicits our regard, but oppose the worth or spirit that enforces it.

The first place among those that please, because they desire only to please, is due to the *merry fellow*, whose laugh is loud, and whose voice is strong; who is ready to echo every jest with obstreperous approbation, and countenance every frolick with vociferations of applause. It is not necessary to a merry fellow to have in himself any fund of jocularity, or force of conception; it is sufficient that he always appears in the highest exaltation of gladness, for the greater part of mankind are gay or serious by infection, and follow without resistance the attraction of example.

Next to the merry fellow is the *good-natured man*, a being generally without benevolence, or any other virtue, than such as indolence and insensibility confer. The characteristick of a good-natured man is to bear a joke; to sit unmoved and unaffected amidst noise and turbulence, profaneness and obscenity; to hear every tale without contradiction; to endure insult without reply; and to follow the stream of folly, whatever course it shall happen to take. The good-natured man is commonly the darling of the petty wits, with whom they exercise themselves in the rudiments of raillery; for he never takes advantage of failings, nor disconcerts a puny satirist with unexpected sarcasms; but while the glass continues to circulate, contentedly bears the expence of uninterrupted laughter, and retires rejoicing at his own importance.

The *modest man* is a companion of a yet lower rank, whose only power of giving pleasure is not to interrupt it. The modest man satisfies himself with peaceful silence, which all his companions are candid enough to consider as proceeding not from inability to speak, but willingness to hear.

Many, without being able to attain any general character of excellence, have some single art of entertainment which serves them as a passport through the world. One I have known for fifteen years the darling of a weekly club, because every night, precisely at eleven, he begins his favourite song, and during the vocal performance by correspondent motions of his hand, chalks out a giant upon the wall. Another has endeared himself to a long succession of acquaintances by sitting among them with his wig reversed; another by contriving to smut the nose of any stranger who was to be initiated in the club; another by purring like a cat, and then pretending to be frighted; and another by yelping like a hound, and calling to the drawers to drive out the dog.

Such are the arts by which cheerfulness is promoted, and sometimes friendship established; arts, which those who despise them should not rigorously blame, except when they are practised at the expence of innocence; for it is always necessary to be loved, but not always necessary to be reverenced.

No. 191. Tuesday, 14 January 1752.

Cereus in Vitium flecti, Monitoribus asper.
                                                    HOR.

The youth ——
Yielding like wax, th' impressive folly bears;
Rough to reproof, and slow to future cares.
                                            FRANCIS.

To the RAMBLER.

Dear Mr. RAMBLER,

I have been four days confined to my chamber by a cold, which has already kept me from three plays, nine sales, five shows, and six card-tables, and put me seventeen visits behindhand; and the doctor tells my mamma, that if I fret and cry, it will settle in my head, and I shall not be fit to be seen these six weeks. But, dear Mr. *Rambler*, how can I help it? at this very time *Melissa* is dancing with the prettiest gentleman;—she will breakfast with him to-morrow, and then run to two auctions, and hear compliments, and have presents; then she will be drest, and visit, and get a ticket to the play; then go to cards, and win, and come home with two flambeaus before her chair. Dear Mr. *Rambler*, who can bear it?

My aunt has just brought me a bundle of your papers for my amusement. She says, you are a philosopher, and will teach me to moderate my desires, and look upon the world with indifference. But, dear sir, I do not wish, nor intend to moderate my desires, nor can I think it proper to look upon the world with indifference, till the world looks with indifference on me. I have been forced, however, to sit this morning a whole quarter of an hour with your paper before my face; but just as my aunt came in, *Phyllida* had brought me a letter from Mr. *Trip*, which I put within the leaves, and read about *absence* and *inconsolableness*, and *ardour*, and *irresistible passion*, and *eternal constancy*, while my aunt imagined, that I was puzzling myself with your philosophy, and often cried out, when she saw me look confused, "If there is any word that you do not understand, child, I will explain it."

Dear soul! how old people that think themselves wise may be imposed upon! But it is fit that they should take their turn, for I am sure, while they can keep poor girls close in the nursery, they tyrannize over us in a very shameful manner, and fill our imaginations with tales of terror, only to make us live in quiet subjection, and fancy that we can never be safe but by their protection.

I have a mamma and two aunts, who have all been formerly celebrated for wit and beauty, and are still generally admired by those that value themselves upon their understanding, and love to talk of vice and virtue, nature and simplicity, and beauty, and propriety; but if there was not some hope of meeting me, scarcely a creature would come near them that wears a fashionable coat. These ladies, Mr. *Rambler*, have had me under their government fifteen years and a half, and have all that time been endeavouring to deceive me by such representations of life as I now find not to be true; but I knew not whether I ought to impute them to ignorance or malice, as it is possible the world may be much changed since they mingled in general conversation.

Being desirous that I should love books, they told me, that nothing but knowledge could make me an agreeable companion to men of sense, or qualify me to distinguish the superficial glitter of vanity from the solid merit of understanding; and that a habit of reading would enable me to fill up the vacuities of life without the help of silly or dangerous amusements, and preserve me from the snares of idleness and the inroads of temptation.

But their principal intention was to make me afraid of men, in which they succeeded so well for a time, that I durst not look in their faces, or be left alone with them in a parlour; for they made me fancy, that no man ever spoke but to deceive, or looked but to allure; that the girl who suffered him that had once squeezed her hand, to approach her a second time was on the brink of ruin; and that she who answered a billet, without consulting her relations, gave love such power over her, that she would certainly become either poor or infamous.

From the time that my leading-strings were taken off, I scarce heard any mention of my beauty but from the milliner, the mantua-maker, and my own maid; for my mamma never said more, when she heard me commended, but "The girl is very well," and then endeavoured to divert my attention by some enquiry after my needle, or my book.

It is now three months since I have been suffered to pay and receive visits, to dance at publick assemblies, to have a place kept for me in the boxes, and to play at Lady *Racket*'s rout; and you may easily imagine what I think of those who have so long cheated me with false expectations, disturbed me with fictitious terrors, and concealed from me all that I have found to make the happiness of woman.

I am so far from perceiving the usefulness or necessity of books, that if I had not dropped all pretensions to learning, I should have lost Mr. *Trip*, whom I once frighted into another box, by retailing some of *Dryden*'s remarks upon a tragedy; for Mr. *Trip* declares, that he hates nothing like hard words, and I am sure, there is not a better partner to be found; his very walk is a dance. I have talked once or twice among ladies about principles and ideas, but they put their fans before their faces, and told me, I was too wise for them, who for their part, never pretended to read any thing but the play-bill, and then asked me the price of my best head.

Those vacancies of time which are to be filled up with books, I have never yet obtained; for, consider, Mr. *Rambler*, I go to bed late, and therefore cannot rise early; as soon as I am up, I dress for the gardens; then walk in the park;

then always go to some sale or show, or entertainment at the little theatre; then must be dressed for dinner; then must pay my visits; then walk in the park; then hurry to the play; and from thence to the card-table. This is the general course of the day, when there happens nothing extraordinary; but sometimes I ramble into the country and come back again to a ball; sometimes I am engaged for a whole day and part of the night. If, at any time, I can gain an hour by not being at home, I have so many things to do, so many orders to give to the milliner, so many alterations to make in my cloaths, so many visitants names to read over, so many invitations to accept or refuse, so many cards to write, and so many fashions to consider, that I am lost in confusion, forced at last to let in company or step into my chair, and leave half my affairs to the direction of my maid.

This is the round of my day; and when shall I either stop my course, or so change it as to want a book? I suppose it cannot be imagined, that any of these diversions will be soon at an end. There will always be gardens, and a park, and auctions, and shows, and play-houses, and cards; visits will always be paid, and cloaths always be worn; and how can I have time unemployed upon my hands?

But I am most at a loss to guess for what purpose they related such tragick stories of the cruelty, perfidy, and artifices of men, who, if they ever were so malicious and destructive, have certainly now reformed their manners. I have not, since my entrance into the world, found one who does not profess himself devoted to my service, and ready to live or die, as I shall command him. They are so far from intending to hurt me, that their only contention is, who shall be allowed most closely to attend, and most frequently to treat me; when different places of entertainment, or schemes of pleasure are mentioned, I can see the eyes sparkle and the cheeks glow of him whose proposals obtain my approbation; he then leads me off in triumph, adores my condescension, and congratulates himself that he has lived to the hour of felicity. Are these, Mr. *Rambler*, creatures to be feared? Is it likely that any injury will be done me by those who can enjoy life only while I favour them with my presence?

As little reason can I yet find to suspect them of stratagems and fraud. When I play at cards, they never take advantage of my mistakes, nor exact from me a rigorous observation of the game. Even Mr. *Shuffle*, a grave gentleman, who has daughters older than myself, plays with me so negligently, that I am sometimes inclined to believe he loses his money by design, and yet he is so fond of play, that he says, he will one day take me to his house in the country; that we may try by ourselves who can conquer. I have not yet promised him; but when the town grows a little empty, I shall think upon it, for I want some trinkets, like *Letitia*'s, to my watch. I do not doubt my luck, but must study some means of amusing my relations.

For all these distinctions I find myself indebted to that beauty which I was never suffered to hear praised, and of which, therefore, I did not before know the full value. This concealment was certainly an intentional fraud, for my aunts have eyes like other people, and I am every day told, that nothing but blindness can escape the influence of my charms. Their whole account of that world which they pretend to know so well, has been only one fiction entangled with another; and though the modes of life oblige me to continue some appearances of respect, I cannot think that they, who have been so clearly detected in ignorance or imposture, have any right to the esteem, veneration, or obedience of,

SIR, Yours,
BELLARIA.

No. 196. Saturday, 1 February 1752.

Multa ferunt anni venientes commoda secum
Multa recedentes adimunt. ——

HOR.

The blessings flowing in with life's full tide,
Down with our ebb of life decreasing glide.

FRANCIS.

Baxter, in the narrative of his own life, has enumerated several opinions, which, though he thought them evident and incontestable at his first entrance into the world, time and experience disposed him to change.

Whoever reviews the state of his own mind from the dawn of manhood to its decline, and considers what he pursued or dreaded, slighted or esteemed at different periods of his age, will have no reason to imagine such changes of sentiment peculiar to any station or character. Every man, however careless and inattentive, has conviction forced upon him; the lectures of time obtrude themselves upon the most unwilling or dissipated auditor; and, by comparing our past with our present thoughts, we perceive that we have changed our minds, though perhaps we cannot discover when the alteration happened, or by what causes it was produced.

This revolution of sentiments occasions a perpetual contest between the old and young. They who imagine themselves entitled to veneration by the prerogative of longer life, are inclined to treat the notions of those whose conduct they superintend with superciliousness and contempt, for want of considering that the future and the past have different appearances; that the disproportion will always be great between expectation and enjoyment, between new possession and satiety; that the truth of many maxims of age, gives too little pleasure to be allowed till it is felt; and that the miseries of life would be encreased beyond all human power of endurance, if we were to enter the world with the same opinions as we carry from it.

We naturally indulge those ideas that please us. Hope will predominate in every mind, till it has been suppressed by frequent disappointments. The youth has not yet discovered how many evils are continually hovering about us, and when he is set free from the shackles of discipline, looks abroad into the world with rapture; he sees an elysian region open before him, so variegated with beauty, and so stored with pleasure, that his care is rather to accumulate good, than to shun evil; he stands distracted by different forms of delight, and has no other doubt than which path to follow of those which all lead equally to the bowers of happiness.

He who has seen only the superficies of life believes every thing to be what it appears, and rarely suspects that external splendor conceals any latent sorrow or vexation. He never imagines that there may be greatness without safety, affluence without content, jollity without friendship, and solitude without peace. He fancies himself permitted to cull the blessings of every condition, and to leave its inconveniencies to the idle and the ignorant. He is inclined to believe no man miserable but by his own fault, and seldom looks with much pity upon failings or miscarriages, because he thinks them willingly admitted, or negligently incurred.

It is impossible, without pity and contempt, to hear a youth of generous sentiments and warm imagination, declaring in the moment of openness and confidence his designs and expectations; because long life is possible, he considers it as certain, and therefore promises himself all the changes of happiness, and provides gratifications for every desire. He is, for a time, to give himself wholly to frolick and diversion, to range the world in search of pleasure, to delight every eye, to gain every heart, and to be celebrated equally for his pleasing levities and solid attainments, his deep reflections, and his sparkling repartees. He then elevates his views to nobler enjoyments, and finds all the scattered excellencies of the female world united in a woman, who prefers his addresses to wealth and titles; he is afterwards to engage in business, to dissipate difficulty, and over-power opposition; to climb by the mere force of merit to fame and greatness; and reward all those who countenanced his rise, or paid due regard to his early excellence. At last he will retire in peace and honour; contract his views to domestick pleasures; form the manners of children like himself; observe how every year expands the beauty of his daughters, and how his sons catch ardour from their father's history; he will give laws to the neighbourhood; dictate axioms to posterity; and leave the world an example of wisdom and of happiness.

With hopes like these, he sallies jocund into life; to little purpose is he told, that the condition of humanity admits no pure and unmingled happiness; that the exuberant gaiety of youth ends in poverty or disease; that uncommon qualifications and contrarieties of excellence, produce envy equally with applause; that whatever admiration and fondness may promise him, he must marry a wife like the wives of others, with some virtues and some faults, and be as often disgusted by her vices, as delighted by her elegance; that if he adventures into the circle of action, he must expect to encounter men as artful, as daring, as resolute as himself; that of his children, some may be deformed, and others vicious; some may disgrace him by their follies, some offend him by their insolence, and some exhaust him by their profusion. He hears all this with obstinate incredulity, and wonders by what malignity old age is influenced, that it cannot forbear to fill his ears with predictions of misery.

Among other pleasing errors of young minds, is the opinion of their own importance. He that has not yet remarked, how little attention his contemporaries can spare from their own affairs, conceives all eyes turned upon himself, and imagines every one that approaches him to be an enemy or a follower, an admirer or a spy. He therefore considers his fame as involved in the event of every action. Many of the virtues and vices of youth proceed from this quick sense of reputation. This it is that gives firmness and constancy, fidelity and disinterestedness, and it is this that kindles resentment for slight injuries, and dictates all the principles of sanguinary honour.

But as time brings him forward into the world, he soon discovers that he only shares fame or reproach with innumerable partners; that he is left unmarked in the obscurity of the croud; and that what he does, whether good or bad, soon gives way to new objects of regard. He then easily sets himself free from the anxieties of reputation, and considers praise or censure as a transient breath, which, while he hears it, is passing away, without any lasting mischief or advantage.

In youth, it is common to measure right and wrong by the opinion of the world, and in age to act without any measure but interest, and to lose shame without substituting virtue.

Such is the condition of life, that something is always wanting to happiness. In youth we have warm hopes, which are soon blasted by rashness and negligence, and great designs which are defeated by inexperience. In age we have knowledge and prudence without spirit to exert, or motives to prompt them; we are able to plan schemes and regulate measures, but have not time remaining to bring them to completion.

No. 207. Tuesday, 10 March 1752.

Solve senescentem mature sanus equum, ne
Peccet ad extremum ridendus.

HOR.

The voice of reason cries with winning force,
Loose from the rapid car your aged horse,
Lest, in the race derided, left behind,
He drag his jaded limbs and burst his wind.

FRANCIS.

Such is the emptiness of human enjoyment, that we are always impatient of the present. Attainment is followed by neglect, and possession by disgust; and the malicious remark of the *Greek* epigrammatist on marriage may be applied to every other course of life, that its two days of happiness are the first and the last.

Few moments are more pleasing than those in which the mind is concerting measures for a new undertaking. From the first hint that wakens the fancy, till the hour of actual execution, all is improvement and progress, triumph and felicity. Every hour brings additions to the original scheme, suggests some new expedient to secure success, or discovers consequential advantages not hitherto foreseen. While preparations are made, and materials accumulated, day glides after day through elysian prospects, and the heart dances to the song of hope.

Such is the pleasure of projecting, that many content themselves with a succession of visionary schemes, and wear out their allotted time in the calm amusement of contriving what they never attempt or hope to execute.

Others, not able to feast their imagination with pure ideas, advance somewhat nearer to the grossness of action, with great diligence collect whatever is requisite to their design, and, after a thousand researches and consultations, are snatched away by death, as they stand *in procinctu* waiting for a proper opportunity to begin.

If there were no other end of life, than to find some adequate solace for every day, I know not whether any condition could be preferred to that of the man who involves himself in his own thoughts, and never suffers experience to shew him the vanity of speculation; for no sooner are notions reduced to practice, than tranquillity and confidence forsake the breast; every day brings its task, and often without bringing abilities to perform it: Difficulties embarrass, uncertainty perplexes, opposition retards, censure exasperates, or neglect depresses. We proceed, because we have begun; we complete our design, that the labour already spent may not be vain: but as expectation gradually dies away, the gay smile of alacrity disappears, we are compelled to implore severer powers, and trust the event to patience and constancy.

When once our labour has begun, the comfort that enables us to endure it is the prospect of its end; for though in every long work there are some joyous intervals of self-applause, when the attention is recreated by unexpected facility, and the imagination soothed by incidental excellencies; yet the toil with which performance struggles after idea, is so irksome and disgusting, and so frequent is the necessity of resting below that perfection which we imagined within our reach, that seldom any man obtains more from his endeavours than a painful conviction of his defects, and a continual resuscitation of desires which he feels himself unable to gratify.

So certainly is weariness the concomitant of our undertakings, that every man, in whatever he is engaged, consoles himself with the hope of change; if he has made his way by assiduity to publick employment, he talks among his friends of the delight of retreat; if by the necessity of solitary application he is secluded from the world, he listens with a beating heart to distant noises, longs to mingle with living beings, and resolves to take hereafter his fill of diversions, or display his abilities on the universal theatre, and enjoy the pleasure of distinction and applause.

Every desire, however innocent, grows dangerous, as by long indulgence it becomes ascendent in the mind. When we have been much accustomed to consider any thing as capable of giving happiness, it is not easy to restrain our ardour, or to forbear some precipitation in our advances, and irregularity in our persuits. He that has cultivated the tree, watched the swelling bud and opening blossom, and pleased himself with computing how much every sun and shower add to its growth, scarcely stays till the fruit has obtained its maturity, but defeats his own cares by eagerness to reward them. When we have diligently laboured for any purpose, we are willing to believe that we have attained it, and, because we have already done much, too suddenly conclude that no more is to be done.

All attraction is encreased by the approach of the attracting body. We never find ourselves so desirous to finish, as in the latter part of our work, or so impatient of delay, as when we know that delay cannot be long. This unseasonable importunity of discontent may be partly imputed to languor and weariness, which must always oppress those more whose toil has been longer continued; but the greater part usually proceeds from frequent contemplation of that ease which is now considered as within reach, and which, when it has once flattered our hopes, we cannot suffer to be withheld.

In some of the noblest compositions of wit, the conclusion falls below the vigour and spirit of the first books; and as a genius is not to be degraded by the imputation of human failings, the cause of this declension is commonly sought in the structure of the work, and plausible reasons are given why in the defective part less ornament was necessary, or less could be admitted. But, perhaps, the author would have confessed, that his fancy was tired, and his perseverance broken; that he knew his design to be unfinished, but that, when he saw the end so near, he could no longer refuse to be at rest.

Against the instillations of this frigid opiate, the heart should be secured by all the considerations which once concurred to kindle the ardour of enterprize. Whatever motive first incited action, has still greater force to stimulate perseverance; since he that might have lain still at first in blameless obscurity, cannot afterwards desist but with infamy and reproach. He, whom a doubtful promise of distant good, could encourage to set difficulties at defiance, ought not to remit his vigour, when he has almost obtained his recompence. To faint or loiter, when only the last efforts are required, is to steer the ship through tempests, and abandon it to the winds in sight of land; it is to break the ground and scatter the seed, and at last to neglect the harvest.

The masters of rhetorick direct, that the most forcible arguments be produced in the latter part of an oration, lest they should be effaced or perplexed by supervenient images. This precept may be justly extended to the series of life: Nothing is ended with honour, which does not conclude better than it begun. It is not sufficient to maintain the first vigour; for excellence loses its effect upon the mind by custom, as light after a time ceases to dazzle. Admiration must be continued by that novelty which first produced it, and how much soever is given, there must always be reason to imagine that more remains.

We not only are most sensible of the last impressions, but such is the unwillingness of mankind to admit transcendent merit, that, though it be difficult to obliterate the reproach of miscarriages by any subsequent atchievement, however illustrious, yet the reputation raised by a long train of success, may be finally ruined by a single failure, for weakness or error will be always remembered by that malice and envy which it gratifies.

For the prevention of that disgrace, which lassitude and negligence may bring at last upon the greatest performances, it is necessary to proportion carefully our labour to our strength. If the design comprises many parts, equally essential, and therefore not to be separated, the only time for caution is before we engage; the powers of the mind must be then impartially estimated, and it must be remembered, that not to complete the plan, is not to have begun it; and, that nothing is done, while any thing is omitted.

But, if the task consists in the repetition of single acts, no one of which derives its efficacy from the rest, it may be attempted with less scruple, because there is always opportunity to retreat with honour. The danger is only lest we expect from the world the indulgence with which most are disposed to treat themselves; and in the hour of listlessness imagine, that the diligence of one day will atone for the idleness of another, and that applause begun by approbation will be continued by habit.

He that is himself weary will soon weary the public. Let him therefore lay down his employment, whatever it be, who can no longer exert his former activity or attention; let him not endeavour to struggle with censure, or obstinately infest the stage till a general hiss commands him to depart.

No. 208. Saturday, 14 March 1752.

Ἡράκλειτος ἐγώ· τί μεῶ κάτω ἕλκετ᾽ ἄμουσοι;
Οὐχ᾽ ὑμῖν ἐπόνουν, τοῖς δέ μ᾽ ἐπισταμένοις.
Εἷς ἐμοὶ ἄνθρωπος τρισμύριοι οἱ δ᾽ ἀνάριθμοι
Οὐδείς· ταῦτ᾽ αὐδῶ καὶ παρὰ Περσεφόνῃ.
DIOG. LAERT.

Be gone, ye blockheads, *Heraclitus* cries,
And leave my labours to the learn'd and wise:
By wit, by knowledge, studious to be read,
I scorn the multitude, alive and dead.

Time, which puts an end to all human pleasures and sorrows, has likewise concluded the labours of the RAMBLER. Having supported, for two years, the anxious employment of a periodical writer, and multiplied my essays to four volumes, I have now determined to desist.

The reasons of this resolution it is of little importance to declare, since justification is unnecessary when no objection is made. I am far from supposing, that the cessation of my performances will raise any inquiry, for I have never been much a favourite of the publick, nor can boast that, in the progress of my undertaking, I have been animated by the rewards of the liberal, the caresses of the great, or the praises of the eminent.

But I have no design to gratify pride by submission, or malice by lamentation; nor think it reasonable to complain of neglect from those whose regard I never solicited. If I have not been distinguished by the distributers of literary honours, I have seldom descended to the arts by which favour is obtained. I have seen the meteors of fashion rise and fall, without any attempt to add a moment to their duration. I have never complied with temporary curiosity, nor enabled my readers to discuss the topick of the day; I have rarely exemplified my assertions by living characters; in my papers, no man could look for censures of his enemies, or praises of himself; and they only were expected to peruse them, whose passions left them leisure for abstracted truth, and whom virtue could please by its naked dignity.

To some, however, I am indebted for encouragement, and to others for assistance. The number of my friends was never great, but they have been such as would not suffer me to think that I was writing in vain, and I did not feel much dejection from the want of popularity.

My obligations having not been frequent, my acknowledgements may be soon dispatched. I can restore to all my correspondents their productions, with little diminution of the bulk of my volumes, though not without the loss of some pieces to which particular honours have been paid.

The parts from which I claim no other praise than that of having given them an opportunity of appearing, are the four billets in the tenth paper, the second letter in the fifteenth, the thirtieth, the forty-fourth, the ninety-seventh, and the hundredth papers, and the second letter in the hundred and seventh.

Having thus deprived myself of many excuses which candor might have admitted for the inequality of my compositions, being no longer able to alledge the necessity of gratifying correspondents, the importunity with which publication was solicited, or obstinacy with which correction was rejected, I must remain accountable for all my faults, and submit, without subterfuge, to the censures of criticism, which, however, I shall not endeavour to soften by a formal deprecation, or to overbear by the influence of a patron. The supplications of an author never yet reprieved him a moment from oblivion; and, though greatness has sometimes sheltered guilt, it can afford no protection to ignorance or dulness. Having hitherto attempted only the propagation of truth, I will not at last violate it by the confession of terrors which I do not feel: Having laboured to maintain the dignity of virtue, I will not now degrade it by the meanness of dedication.

The seeming vanity with which I have sometimes spoken of myself, would perhaps require an apology, were it not extenuated by the example of those who have published essays before me, and by the privilege which every nameless writer has been hitherto allowed. "A mask," says *Castiglione*, "confers a right of acting and speaking with less restraint, even when the wearer happens to be known." He that is discovered without his own consent, may claim some indulgence, and cannot be rigorously called to justify those sallies or frolicks which his disguise must prove him desirous to conceal.

But I have been cautious lest this offence should be frequently or grossly committed; for, as one of the philosophers directs us to live with a friend, as with one that is some time to become an enemy, I have always thought it the duty of an anonymous author to write, as if he expected to be hereafter known.

I am willing to flatter myself with hopes, that, by collecting these papers, I am not preparing for my future life, either shame or repentance. That all are happily imagined, or accurately polished, that the same sentiments have not sometimes recurred, or the same expressions been too frequently repeated, I have not confidence in my abilities sufficient to warrant. He that condemns himself to compose on a stated day, will often bring to his task an attention dissipated, a memory embarrassed, an imagination overwhelmed, a mind distracted with anxieties, a body languishing with disease: He will labour on a barren topick, till it is too late to change it; or in the ardour of invention, diffuse his thoughts into wild exuberance, which the pressing hour of publication cannot suffer judgment to examine or reduce.

Whatever shall be the final sentence of mankind, I have at least endeavoured to deserve their kindness. I have laboured to refine our language to grammatical purity, and to clear it from colloquial barbarisms, licentious idioms, and irregular combinations. Something, perhaps, I have added to the elegance of its construction, and something to the harmony of its cadence. When common words were less pleasing to the ear, or less distinct in their signification, I have familiarized the terms of philosophy by applying them to popular ideas, but have rarely admitted any word not authorized by former writers; for I believe that whoever knows the *English* tongue in its present extent, will be able to express his thoughts without further help from other nations.

As it has been my principal design to inculcate wisdom or piety, I have allotted few papers to the idle sports of imagination. Some, perhaps, may be found, of which the highest excellence is harmless merriment, but scarcely any man is so steadily serious, as not to complain, that the severity of dictatorial instruction has been too seldom relieved, and that he is driven by the sternness of the Rambler's philosophy to more chearful and airy companions.

Next to the excursions of fancy are the disquisitions of criticism, which, in my opinion, is only to be ranked among the subordinate and instrumental arts. Arbitrary decision and general exclamation I have carefully avoided, by asserting nothing without a reason, and establishing all my principles of judgment on unalterable and evident truth.

In the pictures of life I have never been so studious of novelty or surprize, as to depart wholly from all resemblance; a fault which writers deservedly celebrated frequently commit, that they may raise, as the occasion requires, either mirth or abhorrence. Some enlargement may be allowed to declamation, and some exaggeration to burlesque; but as they deviate farther from reality, they become less useful, because their lessons will fail of application. The mind of the reader is carried away from the contemplation of his own manners; he finds in himself no likeness to the phantom before him; and though he laughs or rages, is not reformed.

The essays professedly serious, if I have been able to execute my own intentions, will be found exactly conformable to the precepts of Christianity, without any accommodation to the licentiousness and levity of the present age. I therefore look back on this part of my work with pleasure, which no blame or praise of man shall diminish or augment. I shall never envy the honours which wit and learning obtain in any other cause, if I can be numbered among the writers who have given ardour to virtue, and confidence to truth.

Αὐτῶν ἐκ μακάρων ἀντάξιος εἴη ἀμοιβή.

Celestial pow'rs! that piety regard,
From you my labours wait their last reward.

The Life of Dr Francis Cheynel

THERE is always this advantage in contending with illustrious adversaries, that the combatant is equally immortalized by conquest or defeat. He that dies by the sword of a hero, will always be mentioned, when the acts of his enemy are mentioned. The man, of whose life the following account is offered to the public, was indeed eminent among his own party, and had qualities, which, employed in a good cause, would have given him some claim to distinction; but no one is now so much blinded with bigotry, as to imagine him equal, either to HAMMOND or CHILLINGWORTH, nor would his memory perhaps have been preserved, had he not, by being conjoined with such illustrious names, become the object of public curiosity.

FRANCIS CHEYNEL was born in 1608, at *Oxford*, where his father Dr. JOHN CHEYNEL, who had been fellow of *Corpus-Christi* College, practised physic with great reputation. He was educated in one of the grammar schools of his native city, and in the beginning of the year 1623, became a member of the University.

It is probable that he lost his father, when he was very young; for it appears, that before 1629, his mother had married Dr. ABBOT, bishop of *Salisbury*, whom she had likewise buried. From this marriage he received great advantage; for his mother being now allied to Dr. BRENT then warden of *Merton* College, exerted her interest so vigorously, that he was admitted there a *Probationer*, and afterwards obtained a fellowship.

Having taken the degree of master of arts, he was admitted to orders according to the rites of the *Church* of *England*, and held a curacy near *Oxford*, together with his Fellowship. He continued in his college 'till he was qualified by his years of residence for the degree of batchelor of divinity, which he attempted to take in 1641, but was denied his *grace* for disputing concerning predestination, contrary to the king's injunctions.

This refusal of his degree he mentions in his dedication to his account of Mr. CHILLINGWORTH; "Do not conceive that I snatch up my pen in an angry mood, that I might vent my dangerous wit, and ease my overburden'd spleen. No, no, I have almost forgot the *visitation at* Merton *college, and the denial of my grace, the plundering of my house, and little library:* I know when, and where, and of whom, to demand satisfaction for all these injuries, and indignities. I have learnt *centum plagas Spartana nobilitate concoquere.* I have not learnt how to plunder others of goods, or living, and make my self amends, by force of arms. I will not take a living which belonged to any civil, studious, learned delinquent; unless it be the much neglected *commendam* of some lordly prelate, condemned by the known laws of the land, and the highest court of the kingdom, for some offence of the first magnitude."

It is observable that he declares himself to have almost forgot his injuries and indignities, tho' he recounts them with an appearance of acrimony, which is no proof that the impression is much weakened; and insinuates his design of demanding, at a proper time, satisfaction for them.

These vexations were the consequence rather of the abuse of learning, than the want of it; no one that reads his works can doubt, that he was turbulent, obstinate and petulant, and ready to instruct his superiors when he most needed information from them. Whatever he believ'd (and the warmth of his imagination naturally made him precipitate in forming his opinions) he thought himself oblig'd to profess; and what he profess'd, he was ready to defend, without that modesty which is always prudent, and generally necessary; and which, tho' it was not agreeable to Mr. CHEYNEL's temper, and therefore readily condemn'd by him, is a very useful associate to truth, and often introduces her by degrees, where she never could have forced her way by argument, or declamation.

A temper of this kind is generally inconvenient and offensive in any society; but in a place of education, is least to be tolerated; for as authority is necessary to instruction, whoever endeavours to destroy subordination, by weakening that reverence which is claimed by those to whom the guardianship of youth is committed by their country, defeats at once the institution; and may be justly driven from a society, by which he thinks himself too wise to be governed, and in which he is too young to teach, and too opinionative to learn.

This may be readily suppos'd to have been the case of CHEYNEL; and I know not how those can be blamed for censuring his conduct, or punishing his disobedience, who had a right to govern him, and who might certainly act with equal sincerity, and with greater knowledge.

With regard to the visitation of *Merton* college, the account is equally obscure; visitors are well known to be generally called to regulate the affairs of colleges, when the members disagree with their head, or with one another; and the temper that Dr. CHEYNEL discovers, will easily incline his readers to suspect, that he could not long live in any place without finding some occasion for debate; nor debate any question without carrying his opposition to such a length as might make a moderator necessary. Whether this was his conduct at *Merton*, or whether an appeal to the visitor's authority was made by him, or his adversaries, or any other member of the college, is not to be known; it appears only, that there was a visitation; that he suffered by it, and resented his punishment.

He was afterwards presented to a living of great value, near *Banbury*, where he had some dispute with Archbishop LAUD. Of this dispute I have found no particular account. CALAMY only says, *he had a ruffle with Bishop* LAUD, *while at his height.*

Had CHEYNEL been equal to his adversary in greatness and learning, it had not been easy to have found either a more proper opposite; for they were both to the last degree zealous, active and pertinacious, and would have afforded mankind a spectacle of resolution, and boldness, not often to be seen. But the amusement of beholding the struggle, would hardly have been without danger, as they were too fiery not to have communicated their heat, tho' it should have produc'd a conflagration of their country.

About the year 1641, when the whole nation was engag'd in the controversy about the rights of the church and necessity of episcopacy, he declared himself a presbyterian, and an enemy to bishops, liturgies, ceremonies, and was consider'd as one of the most learned and acute of his party; for having spent much of his life in a college, it cannot be doubted, that he had a considerable knowledge of books, which the vehemence of his temper enabled him often to display when a more timorous man would have been silent, though in learning not his inferiour.

When the war broke out, Mr. CHEYNEL in consequence of his principles declared himself for the parliament, and as he appears to have held it, as a first principle, that all great and noble spirits abhor neutrality, there is no doubt, but that he exerted himself to gain proselytes and to promote the interest of that party, which he had thought it his duty to espouse. These endeavours were so much regarded by the parliament, that, having taken the covenant, he was nominated one of the assembly of divines, who were to meet at *Westminster* for the settlement of the new discipline.

This distinction drew necessarily upon him the hatred of the cavaliers; and his living being not far distant from the king's head quarters, he received a visit from some of the troops, who, as he affirms, plundered his house, and drove him from it. His living, which was, I suppose, consider'd as forfeited by his absence, (though he was not suffered to continue upon it) was given to a clergyman, of whom he says, that he would become a stage better than a pulpit, a censure, which I can neither confute, nor admit; because I have not discovered, who was his successor. He then retir'd into *Sussex* to exercise his ministry among his friends, *in a place where*, as he observes, *there had been little of the power of religion either known, or practised.* As no reason can be given, why the inhabitants of *Sussex* should have less knowledge or virtue, than those of other places, it may be suspected that he means nothing more than a place where the presbyterian discipline or principles had never been received. We now observe, that the methodists, where they scatter their opinions, represent themselves as preaching the gospel to unconverted nations. And enthusiasts of all kinds have been inclined to disguise their particular tenets with pompous appellations, and to imagine themselves the great instruments of salvation. Yet it must be confessed that all places are not equally enlightned; that in the most civilized nations there are many corners, which may yet be called barbarous, where neither politeness, nor religion, nor the common arts of life have yet been cultivated; and it is likewise certain, that the inhabitants of *Sussex* have been sometimes mentioned as remarkable for brutality.

From *Sussex* he went often to *London*, where, in 1643, he preached three times before the parliament, and returning in *November* to *Colchester* to keep the monthly fast there, as was his custom, he obtained a convoy of sixteen soldiers, whose bravery or good fortune was such, that they faced and put to flight more than two hundred of the king's forces.

In this journey, he found Mr. CHILLINGWORTH in the hands of the parliament's troops, of whose sickness and death he gave the account which has been sufficiently made known to the learned world by Dr. MAIZEAUX, in his life of CHILLINGWORTH.

With regard to this relation, it may be observed, that it is written with an air of fearless veracity, and with the spirit of a man who thinks his cause just, and his behaviour without reproach; nor does there appear any reason for doubting, that CHEYNEL spoke and acted as he relates. For he does not publish an apology, but a challenge, and writes not so much to obviate calumnies, as to gain from others that applause, which he seems to have bestowed very liberally upon himself, for his behaviour on that occasion.

Since therefore, this relation is credible, a great part of it being supported by evidence, which cannot be refused, Dr. MAIZEAUX seems very justly in his life of Mr. CHILLINGWORTH to oppose the common report, that his life was shortened by the inhumanity of those, to whom he was a prisoner; for CHEYNEL appears to have preserved amidst all his detestation of the opinions, which he imputed to him, a great kindness to his person, and veneration for his capacity; nor does he appear to have been cruel to him otherwise than by that incessant importunity of disputation, to which he was doubtless incited, by a sincere belief of the danger of his soul, if he should die without renouncing some of his opinions.

The same kindness, which made him desirous to convert him before his death, would incline him to preserve him from dying before he was converted; and accordingly we find, that, when the castle was yielded, he took care to procure him a commodious lodging; when he was to have been unseasonably removed, he attempted to shorten a journey, which he knew would be dangerous; when the physician was disgusted by CHILLINGWORTH's distrust, he prevail'd upon him, as the symptoms grew more dangerous, to renew his visits; and when death left no other act of kindness to be practised, procured him the rites of burial which some would have denied him.

Having done thus far justice to the humanity of CHEYNEL, it is proper to enquire, how far he deserves blame. He appears to have extended none of that kindness to the opinions of CHILLINGWORTH, which he shewed to his person; for he interprets every word in the worst sense, and seems industrious to discover in every line heresies which might have escaped for ever any other apprehension, he appears always suspicious of some latent malignity, and ready to persecute what he only suspects, with the same violence, as if it had been openly avowed; in all his procedure he shews himself sincere, but without candour.

About this time CHEYNEL, in pursuance of his natural ardour, attended the army under the command of the Earl of Essex, and added the praise of valour, to that of learning; for he distinguished himself so much by his personal bravery, and obtained so much skill in the science of war, that his commands were obeyed by the colonels with as much respect, as those of the general. He seems indeed to have been born a soldier; for he had an intrepidity, which was never to be shaken by any danger, and a spirit of enterprize not to be discouraged by difficulty; which were supported by an unusual degree of bodily strength. His services of all kinds were thought of so much importance by the parliament, that they bestowed upon him the living of *Petworth* in *Sussex*. This living was of the value of 700l. per annum, from which, they had ejected a man remarkable for his loyalty; and therefore, in their opinion, not worthy of such revenues. And it may be enquir'd, whether in accepting this preferment, CHEYNEL did not violate the protestation, which he makes in the passage already recited, and whether, he did not suffer his resolution to be overborn, by the temptations of wealth.

In 1646, when *Oxford* was taken by the forces of the Parliament, and the reformation of the University was resolved, Mr. CHEYNEL was sent with six others, to prepare the way for a visitation; being authorised by the parliament to preach in any of the churches, without regard to the right of the members of the University, that their doctrine might prepare their hearers, for the changes which were intended.

When they arrived at *Oxford*, they began to execute their commission by possessing themselves of the pulpits; but if the relation of WOOD is to be regarded, were heard with very little veneration. Those, who had been accustomed to the preachers of *Oxford*, and the liturgy of the church of *England*, were offended at the emptiness of their discourses, which were noisy and unmeaning; at the unusual gestures, the wild distortions, and the uncouth tone with which they were delivered; at the coldness of their prayers for the king, and the vehemence and exuberance of those, which they did not fail to utter for *the blessed councils*, and actions of the parliament, and army; and, at what was surely not to be remarked without indignation, their omission of the Lord's Prayer.

But power easily supplied the want of reverence, and they proceeded in their plan of reformation; and thinking sermons not so efficacious to conversion as private interrogatories and exhortations, they established a weekly meeting for *freeing tender consciences from scruple*, at a house, that from the business to which it was appropriated, was called the *Scruple-shop*.

With this project they were so well pleased, that they sent to the parliament an account of it, which was afterwards printed and is ascribed by WOOD to Mr. CHEYNEL. They continued for some weeks to hold their meetings regularly, and to admit great numbers, whom curiosity, or a desire of conviction, or compliance with the prevailing party brought thither. But their tranquillity was quickly disturb'd by the turbulence of the independents, whose opinions then prevailed among the soldiers, and was very industriously propagated by the discourses of WILLIAM EARBURY, a preacher of great reputation among them, who one day gathering a considerable number of his most zealous followers went to the house appointed for the resolution of scruples, on a day which was set apart for a disquisition of the dignity and office of a minister, and began to dispute with great vehemence against the presbyterians, whom he denied to have any true ministers among them, and whose assemblies he affirmed not to be the true church. He was opposed with equal heat by the presbyterians, and at length they agreed to examine the point another day, in a regular disputation. Accordingly they appointed the twelfth of *November* for an enquiry, *whether in the christian church the office of minister is committed to any particular persons.*

On the day fixed the antagonists appeared, each attended by great numbers; but when the question was proposed, they began to wrangle, not about the doctrine, which they had engaged to examine, but about the terms of the proposition, which the independent alledged to be changed, since their agreement;

and at length the soldiers insisted, that the question should be, *whether those who call themselves ministers have more right, or power to preach the gospel than any other man, that is a christian.* This question was debated for some time with great vehemence and confusion; but without any prospect of a conclusion. At length one of the soldiers, who thought they had an equal right with the rest to engage in the controversy, demanded of the presbyterians, whence they themselves received their orders, whether from bishops or any other persons. This unexpected interrogatory put them to great difficulties; for it happened that they were all ordain'd by the bishops, which they durst not acknowledge, for fear of exposing themselves to a general censure; and being convicted from their own declarations, in which they had frequently condemned episcopacy, as contrary to christianity; nor durst they deny it, because they might have been confuted, and must at once have sunk into contempt. The soldiers seeing their perplexity, insulted them; and went away boasting of their victory: nor did the presbyterians, for sometime, recover spirit enough, to renew their meetings, or to proceed in the work of easing consciences.

Earbury exulting at the victory, which not his own abilities, but the subtilty of the soldier had procured him, began to vent his notions of every kind without scruple, and at length asserted, that *the Saints had an equal measure of the divine nature with our Saviour, though not equally manifest.* At the same time he took upon him the dignity of a prophet, and began to utter predictions relating to the affairs of *England* and *Ireland.*

His prophecies were not much regarded, but his doctrine was censured by the Presbyterians in their pulpits; and Mr. CHEYNEL challenged him to a disputation to which he agreed, and at his first appearance in St. *Mary*'s church addressed his audience in the following manner:

"Christian friends, kind fellow-soldiers, and worthy students, I, the humble servant of all mankind, am this day drawn, against my will, out of my cell, into this public assembly, by the double chain of accusation and a challenge from the pulpit; I have been charged with heresy, I have been challenged to come hither in a letter written by Mr. FRANCIS CHEYNEL. Here then I stand in defence of myself and my doctrine, which I shall introduce with only this declaration, that I claim not the office of a minister on account of any outward call, though I formerly received ordination, nor do I boast of *illumination*, or the knowledge of our Saviour, though I have been held in esteem by others, and formerly by myself. For I now declare, that I know and am nothing, nothing, nor would I be thought of otherwise than as an enquirer and seeker."

He then advanced his former position in stronger terms, and with additions equally detestable, which CHEYNEL attacked with the vehemence, which, in so warm a temper, such horrid assertions might naturally excite. The dispute, frequently interrupted by the clamours of the audience, and tumults raised to disconcert CHEYNEL, who was very unpopular, continued about four hours, and then both the controvertists grew weary and retired.

The Presbyterians afterwards thought they should more speedily put an end to the heresies of EARBURY by power than by argument; and, by solliciting General FAIRFAX, procured his removal.

Mr. CHEYNEL published an account of this dispute under the title of *Faith triumphing over Error and Heresy in a Revelation*, &c. nor can it be doubted but he had the victory, where his cause gave him so great superiority.

Somewhat before this, his captious and petulant disposition engaged him in a controversy, from which he could not expect to gain equal reputation. Dr. HAMMOND had not long before published his *Practical Catechism*, in which Mr. CHEYNEL, according to his custom, found many errors implied, if not asserted, and therefore, as it was much read, thought it convenient to censure it in the pulpit. Of this Dr. HAMMOND being informed, desired him in a letter to communicate his objections; to which Mr. CHEYNEL returned an answer written with his usual temper, and therefore somewhat perverse. The controversy was drawn out to a considerable length, and the papers on both sides were afterwards made public by Dr. HAMMOND.

In 1647 it was determined by Parliament, that the reformation of *Oxford* should be more vigorously carried on; and Mr. CHEYNEL was nominated one of the visitors. The general process of the visitation, the firmness and fidelity of the students, the address by which the enquiry was delayed, and the steadiness with which it was opposed, which are very particularly related by WOOD, and after him by WALKER, it is not necessary to mention here; as they relate not more to Dr. CHEYNEL's life than to those of his associates.

There is indeed some reason to believe that he was more active and virulent than the rest, because he appears to have been charged in a particular manner with some of their most unjustifiable measures. He was accused of proposing, that the members of the University should be denied the assistance of council, and was lampooned by name, as a madman, in a satire written on the visitation.

One action which shews the violence of his temper, and his disregard both of humanity and decency, when they came into competition with his passions, must not be forgotten. The visitors being offended at the obstinacy of Dr. FELL, Dean of *Christ Church*, and Vice-chancellor of the University, having first deprived him of the Vice-chancellorship, determined afterwards to dispossess him of his deanery; and, in the course of their proceedings, thought it proper to seize upon his chambers in the college. This was an act which most men would willingly have referred to the officers to whom the law assigned it; but CHEYNEL's fury prompted him to a different conduct. He, and three more of the visitors went and demanded admission; which, being steadily refused them, they obtained by the assistance of a file of soldiers, who forced the doors with pick-axes. Then entring, they saw Mrs. FELL in the lodgings, Dr. FELL being in prison at *London*, and ordered her to quit them; but found her not more obsequious than her husband. They repeated their orders with menaces, but were not able to prevail upon her to remove. They then retired, and left her exposed to the brutality of the soldiers, whom they commanded to keep possession; which Mrs. FELL however did not leave. About nine days afterwards she received another visit of the same kind from the new Chancellor, the Earl of PEMBROKE; who having, like the others, ordered her to depart without effect, treated her with reproachful language, and at last commanded the soldiers to take her up in her chair, and carry her out of doors. Her daughters and some other gentlewomen that were with her, were afterwards treated in the same manner; one of whom predicted without dejection, that she should enter the house again with less difficulty, at some other time; nor was she mistaken in her conjecture, for Dr. FELL lived to be restored to his deanery.

At the reception of the Chancellor, CHEYNEL, as the most accomplished of the visitors, had the province of presenting him with the ensigns of his office, some of which were counterfeit, and addressing him with a proper oration. Of this speech, which WOOD has preserved, I shall give some passages by which a judgment may be made of his oratory.

Of the staves of the beadles he observes, that "some are stained with double guilt, that some are pale with fear, and that others have been made use of as crutches, for the support of bad causes and desperate fortunes;" and he remarks of the book of statutes, which he delivers, that "the ignorant may perhaps admire the splendour of the cover, but the learned knew that the real treasure is within." Of these two sentences it is easily discovered, that the first is forced and unnatural, and the second trivial and low.

Soon afterwards Mr. CHEYNEL was admitted to the degree of Batchelor of Divinity for which his grace had been denied him 1641, and as he then suffered for an ill-timed assertion of the Presbyterian doctrines, he obtained that his degree should be dated from the time at which he was refused it; an honour, which however did not secure him from being soon after publicly reproached as a madman.

But the vigour of CHEYNEL was thought by his companions to deserve profit as well as honour; and Dr. BAILEY, the President of St. *John's College*, being not more obedient to the authority of the Parliament than the rest, was deprived of his revenues and authority, with which Mr. CHEYNEL was immediately invested; who, with his usual coolness and modesty, took possession of the lodgings soon after by breaking open the doors.

This preferment being not thought adequate to the deserts or abilities of Mr. CHEYNEL, it was therefore desired by the committee of parliament, that the visitors would recommend him to the lectureship of divinity founded by the Lady MARGARET. To recommend him and to choose was at that time the same; and he had now the pleasure of propagating his darling doctrine of predestination, without interruption and without danger.

Being thus flushed with power and success, there is little reason for doubting, that he gave way to his natural vehemence, and indulged himself in the utmost excesses of raging zeal, by which he was indeed so much distinguished, that, in a satire mentioned by WOOD, he is dignified by the title of Arch-visitor; an appellation which he seems to have been industrious to deserve by severity and inflexibility: For, not contented with the commission which he and his colleagues had already received, he procured six or seven of the members of parliament to meet privately in Mr. ROUSE's lodgings, and assume the stile and authority of a committee, and from them obtained a more extensive and tyrannical power, by which the visitors were enabled to force *the solemn League and Covenant*, and the *negative oath* upon all the members of the University, and to prosecute those for a contempt who did not appear to a citation, at whatever distance they might be, and whatever reasons they might assign for their absence.

By this method he easily drove great numbers from the University, whose places he supplied with men of his own opinion, whom he was very industrious to draw from other parts, with promises of making a liberal provision for them out of the spoils of heretics and malignants.

Having in time almost extirpated those opinions which he found so prevalent at his arrival, or at least obliged those, who would not recant, to an appearance of conformity, he was at leisure for employments which deserve to be recorded with greater commendation. About this time, many Socinian writers began to publish their notions with great boldness, which the Presbyterians considering as heretical and impious, thought it necessary to confute; and therefore CHEYNEL, who had now obtained his Doctor's degree, was desired in 1649 to write a vindication of the doctrine of the Trinity, which he performed, and published the next year.

He drew up likewise a confutation of some Socinian tenets advanced by JOHN FRY, a man who spent great part of his life in ranging from one religion to another, and who sat as one of the judges on the king; but was expelled afterwards from the house of commons, and disabled from sitting in parliament. Dr. CHEYNEL is said to have shewn himself evidently superior to him in the controversy, and was answered by him only with an opprobrious book, against the Presbyterian clergy.

Of the remaining part of his life there is found only an obscure and confused account. He quitted the presidentship of St. *John's*, and the professorship in 1650, as CALAMY relates, because he would not take the engagement; and gave a proof that he could suffer as well as act in a cause which he believed just. We have indeed no reason to question his resolution, whatever occasion might be given to exert it; nor is it probable, that he feared affliction more than danger, or that he would not have born persecution himself for those opinions which inclined him to persecute others.

He did not suffer much on this occasion; for he retained the living of *Petworth*, to which he thence-forward confined his labours, and where he was very assiduous, and, as CALAMY affirms, very successful in the exercise of his ministry; it being his peculiar character to be warm and zealous in all his undertakings.

This heat of his disposition, increased by the uncommon turbulence of the time in which he lived, and by the opposition to which the unpopular nature of some of his employments exposed him, was at last heightened to distraction, so that he was for some time disordered in his understanding, as both WOOD and CALAMY relate, but with such difference, as might be expected from their opposite principles. WOOD appears to think that a tendency to madness was discoverable in a great part of his life; CALAMY, that it was only transient and accidental, though in his additions to his first narrative, he pleads it as an extenuation of that fury with which his kindest friends confess him to have acted on some occasions. WOOD declares that he died little better than distracted; CALAMY, that he was perfectly recovered to a sound mind before the restoration, at which time he retired to *Preston*, a small village in *Sussex*, being turned out of his living of *Petworth*.

It does not appear, that he kept his living till the general ejection of the Nonconformists; and it is not unlikely, that the asperity of his carriage, and the known virulence of his temper might have raised him enemies, who were willing to make him feel the effects of persecution which he had so furiously incited against others; but of this incident of his life there is no particular account.

After his deprivation he lived (till his death, which happened in 1665) at a small village near *Chichester*, upon a paternal estate, not augmented by the large preferments, wasted upon him in the triumphs of his party; having been remarkable throughout his life, for hospitality and contempt of money.

S. J——N.

Sermon for the Funeral of his Wife

THE following SERMON (the Authenticity of which cannot be doubted) came, with many others, into the Hands of the Editor by the Death of Dr. TAYLOR, late Prebendary of WESTMINSTER, &c.

It is now published for two Reasons: First, as it is a Composition that will reflect no Disgrace on the Author; and, Secondly, as it is upon a Subject of the highest Importance to Mankind.

Great Dean's Yard, Westminster,
    March 18th, 1788.

A Sermon, &c.

JOHN, *Ch.* XI. 25, 26 *v.* FORMER PART.

JESUS SAID UNTO HER, I AM THE RESURRECTION, AND THE LIFE: HE THAT BELIEVETH
IN ME, THOUGH HE WERE DEAD, YET SHALL HE LIVE;
AND WHOSOEVER LIVETH, AND BELIEVETH IN ME, SHALL NEVER DIE.

To afford adequate consolations to the last hour, to chear the gloomy passage through the valley of the shadow of death, and to ease that anxiety, to which beings, prescient of their own dissolution, and conscious of their own danger, must be necessarily exposed, is the privilege only of revealed religion. All those to whom the supernatural light of heavenly doctrine has never been imparted, however formidable for power, or illustrious for wisdom, have wanted that knowledge of their future state, which alone can give comfort to misery, or security to enjoyment; and have been forced to rush forwards to the grave, through the darkness of ignorance; or, if they happened to be more refined and inquisitive, to solace their passage with the fallacious and uncertain glimmer of philosophy.

There were, doubtless, at all times, as there are now, many who lived with very little thought concerning their end; many whose time was wholly filled up by public, or domestic business, by the pursuits of ambition, or the desire of riches; many who dissolved themselves in luxurious enjoyments, and, when they could lull their minds by any present pleasure, had no regard to distant events, but withheld their imagination from sallying out into futurity, or catching any terror that might interrupt their quiet; and there were many who rose so little above animal life, that they were completely ingrossed by the objects about them, and had their views extended no farther than to the next hour; in whom the ray of reason was half extinct, and who had neither hopes nor fears, but of some near advantage, or some pressing danger.

But multitudes there must always be, and greater multitudes as arts and civility prevail, who cannot wholly withdraw their thoughts from death. All cannot be distracted with business, or stunned with the clamours of assemblies, or the shouts of armies. All cannot live in the perpetual dissipation of successive diversions, nor will all enslave their understandings to their senses, and seek felicity in the gross gratifications of appetite. Some must always keep their reason and their fancy in action, and seek either honour or pleasure from intellectual operations; and from them, others, more negligent or sluggish, will be in time fixed or awakened; knowledge will be perpetually diffused, and curiosity hourly enlarged.

But, when the faculties were once put in motion, when the mind had broken loose from the shackles of sense, and made excursions to remote consequences, the first consideration that would stop her course, must be the incessant waste of life, the approach of age, and the certainty of death; the approach of that time, in which strength must fail, and pleasure fly away, and the certainty of that dissolution which shall put an end to all the prospects of this world. It is impossible to think, and not sometimes to think on death. Hope, indeed, has many powers of delusion; whatever is possible, however unlikely, it will teach us to promise ourselves; but death no man has escaped, and therefore no man can hope to escape it. From this dreadful expectation no shelter or refuge can be found. Whatever we see, forces it upon us; whatever is, new or old, flourishing or declining, either directly, or by a very short deduction, leads man to the consideration of his end; and accordingly we find, that the fear of death has always been considered as the great enemy of human quiet, the polluter of the feast of happiness, and embitterer of the cup of joy. The young man who rejoices in his youth, amidst his music and his gaiety, has always been disturbed with the thought, that his youth will be quickly at an end. The Monarch, to whom it is said that he is a God, has always been reminded by his own heart, that he shall die like man.

This unwelcome conviction, which is thus continually pressed upon the mind, every art has been employed to oppose. The general remedy, in all ages, has been to chase it away from the present moment, and to gain a suspence of the pain that could not be cured. In the ancient writings, we therefore find the shortness of life frequently mentioned as an excitement to jollity and pleasure; and may plainly discover, that the authors had no other means of relieving that gloom with which the uncertainty of human life clouded their conceptions. Some of the Philosophers, indeed, appear to have sought a nobler, and a more certain remedy, and to have endeavoured to overpower the force of death by arguments, and to dispel the gloom by the light of reason. They inquired into the nature of the soul of man, and shewed, at least probably, that it is a substance distinct from matter, and therefore independent on the body, and exempt from dissolution and corruption. The arguments, whether physical or moral, upon which they established this doctrine, it is not necessary to recount to a Christian audience, by whom it is believed upon more certain proofs, and higher authority; since, though they were such as might determine the calm mind of a Philosopher, inquisitive only after truth, and uninfluenced by external objects; yet they were such as required leisure and capacity, not allowed in general to mankind; they were such as many could never understand, and of which, therefore, the efficacy and comfort were confined to a small number, without any benefit to the unenlightened multitude.

Such has been hitherto the nature of philosophical arguments, and such it must probably for ever remain; for, though, perhaps, the successive industry of the studious may increase the number, or advance the probability, of arguments; and, though continual contemplation of matter will, I believe, shew it, at length, wholly incapable of motion, sensation, or order, by any powers of its own, and therefore necessarily establish the immateriality, and probably the immortality of the soul; yet there never can be expected a time, in which the gross body of mankind can attend to such speculations, or can comprehend them; and therefore there never can be a time, in which this knowledge can be taught in such a manner, as to be generally conducive to virtue, or happiness, but by a messenger from God, from the Creator of the World, and the Father of Spirits.

To persuade common and uninstructed minds to the belief of any fact, we may every day perceive, that the testimony of one man, whom they think worthy of credit, has more force than the arguments of a thousand reasoners, even when the arguments are such as they may be imagined completely qualified to comprehend. Hence it is plain, that the constitution of mankind is such, that abstruse and intellectual truths can be taught no otherwise than by positive assertion, supported by some sensible evidence, by which the assertor is secured from the suspicion of falsehood; and that, if it should please God to inspire a teacher with some demonstration of the immortality of the soul, it would far less avail him for general instruction, than the power of working a miracle in its vindication, unless God should, at the same time, inspire all the hearers with docility and apprehension, and turn, at once, all the sensual, the giddy, the lazy, the busy, the corrupt and the proud, into humble, abstracted and diligent Philosophers.

To bring life and immortality to light, to give such proofs of our future existence, as may influence the most narrow mind, and fill the most capacious intellect, to open prospects beyond the grave, in which the thought may expatiate without obstruction, and to supply a refuge and support to the mind, amidst all the miseries of decaying nature, is the peculiar excellence of the Gospel of Christ. Without this heavenly Instructor, he who feels himself sinking under the weight of years, or melting away by the slow waste of a lingering disease, has no other remedy than obdurate patience, a gloomy resignation to that which cannot be avoided; and he who follows his friend, or whoever there is yet dearer than a friend, to the grave, can have no other consolation than that which he derives from the general misery; the reflection, that he suffers only what the rest of mankind must suffer; a poor consideration, which rather awes us to silence, than sooths us to quiet, and which does not abate the sense of our calamity, though it may sometimes make us ashamed to complain.

But, so much is our condition improved by the Gospel, so much is the sting of death rebated, that we may now be invited to the contemplation of our mortality, as to a pleasing employment of the mind, to an exercise delightful and recreative, not only when calamity and persecution drive us out from the assemblies of men, and sorrow and woe represent the grave as a refuge and an asylum, but even in the hours of the highest earthly prosperity, when our cup is full, and when we have laid up stores for ourselves; for, in him who believes the promise of the Saviour of the World, it can cause no disturbance to remember, that this night his soul may be required of him; and he who suffers one of the sharpest evils which this life can shew, amidst all its varieties of misery; he that has lately been separated from the person whom a long participation of good and evil had endeared to him; he who has seen kindness snatched from his arms, and fidelity torn from his bosom; he whose ear is no more to be delighted with tender instruction, and whose virtue shall be no more awakened by the seasonable whispers of mild reproof, may yet look, without horror, on the tomb which encloses the remains of what he loved and honoured, as upon a place which, if it revives the sense of his loss, may calm him with the hope of that state in which there shall be no more grief or separation.

To Christians the celebration of a funeral is by no means a solemnity of barren and unavailing sorrow, but established by the church for other purposes.

First, for the consolation of sorrow. Secondly, for the enforcement of piety. The mournful solemnity of the burial of the dead is instituted, first, for the consolation of that grief to which the best minds, if not supported and regulated by religion, are most liable. They who most endeavour the happiness of others, who devote their thoughts to tenderness and pity, and studiously maintain the reciprocation of kindness, by degrees mingle their souls, in such a manner, as to feel, from separation, a total destitution of happiness, a sudden abruption of all their prospects, a cessation of all their hopes, schemes and desires. The whole mind becomes a gloomy vacuity, without any image or form of pleasure, a chaos of confused wishes, directed to no particular end, or to that which, while we wish, we cannot hope to obtain; for the dead will not revive; those whom God has called away from the present state of existence, can be seen no more in it; we must go to them; but they cannot return to us.

Yet, to shew that grief is vain, is to afford very little comfort; yet this is all that reason can afford; but religion, our only friend in the moment of distress, in the moment when the help of man is vain, when fortitude and cowardice sink down together, and the sage and the virgin mingle their lamentations; religion will inform us, that sorrow and complaint are not only vain, but unreasonable and erroneous. The voice of God, speaking by his Son, and his apostles, will instruct us, that she, whose departure we now mourn, is not dead, but sleepeth; that only her body is committed to the ground, but that the soul is returned to God, who gave it; that God, who is infinitely merciful, who hateth nothing that he has made, who desireth not the death of a sinner; to that God, who only can compare performance with ability, who alone knows how far the heart has been pure, or corrupted, how inadvertency has surprised, fear has betrayed, or weakness has impeded; to that God, who marks every aspiration after a better state, who hears the prayer which the voice cannot utter, records the purpose that perished without opportunity of action, the wish that vanished away without attainment, who is always ready to receive the penitent, to whom sincere contrition is never late, and who will accept the tears of a returning sinner.

Such are the reflections to which we are called by the voice of truth; and from these we shall find that comfort which philosophy cannot supply, and that peace which the world cannot give. The contemplation of the mercy of God may justly afford some consolation, even when the office of burial is performed to those who have been snatched away without visible amendment of their lives; for, who shall presume to determine the state of departed souls, to lay open what God hath concealed, and to search the counsels of the Most Highest?—But, with more confident hope of pardon and acceptance, may we commit those to the receptacles of mortality, who have lived without any open or enormous crimes; who have endeavoured to propitiate God by repentance, and have died, at last, with hope and resignation. Among these she surely may be remembered whom we have followed hither to the tomb, to pay her the last honours, and to resign her to the grave: she, whom many who now hear me have known, and whom none, who were capable of distinguishing either moral or intellectual excellence, could know, without esteem, or tenderness. To praise the extent of her knowledge, the acuteness of her wit, the accuracy of her judgment, the force of her sentiments, or the elegance of her expression, would ill suit with the occasion.

Such praise would little profit the living, and as little gratify the dead, who is now in a place where vanity and competition are forgotten for ever; where she finds a cup of water given for the relief of a poor brother, a prayer uttered for the mercy of God to those whom she wanted power to relieve, a word of instruction to ignorance, a smile of comfort to misery, of more avail than all those accomplishments which confer honour and distinction among the sons of Folly.—Yet, let it be remembered, that her wit was never employed to scoff at goodness, nor her reason to dispute against truth. In this age of wild opinions, she was as free from scepticism as the cloistered virgin. She never wished to signalize herself by the singularity of paradox. She had a just diffidence of her own reason, and desired to practise rather than to dispute. Her practice was such as her opinions naturally produced. She was exact and regular in her devotions, full of confidence in the divine mercy, submissive to the dispensations of Providence, extensively charitable in her judgments and opinions, grateful for every kindness that she received, and willing to impart assistance of every kind to all whom her little power enabled her to benefit. She passed through many months languor, weakness and decay, without a single murmur of impatience, and often expressed her adoration of that mercy which granted her so long time for recollection and penitence. That she had no failings, cannot be supposed: but she has now appeared before the Almighty Judge; and it would ill become beings like us, weak and sinful as herself, to remember those faults which, we trust, Eternal Purity has pardoned.

Let us therefore preserve her memory for no other end but to imitate her virtues; and let us add her example to the motives to piety which this solemnity was, secondly, instituted to enforce.

It would not indeed be reasonable to expect, did we not know the inattention and perverseness of mankind, that anyone who had followed a funeral, could fail to return home without new resolutions of a holy life: for, who can see the final period of all human schemes and undertakings, without conviction of the vanity of all that terminates in the present state? For, who can see the wise, the brave, the powerful, or the beauteous, carried to the grave, without reflection on the emptiness of all those distinctions which set us here in opposition to each other? And who, when he sees the vanity of all terrestrial advantages, can forbear to wish for a more permanent and certain happiness? Such wishes, perhaps, often arise, and such resolutions are often formed: but, before the resolution can be exerted, before the wish can regulate the conduct, new prospects open before us, new impressions are received; the temptations of the world solicit, the passions of the heart are put into commotion; we plunge again into the tumult, engage again in the contest, and forget, that what we gain cannot be kept, and that the life, for which we are thus busy to provide, must be quickly at an end.

But, let us not be thus shamefully deluded! Let us not thus idly perish in our folly, by neglecting the loudest call of Providence; nor, when we have followed our friends, and our enemies, to the tomb, suffer ourselves to be surprised by the dreadful summons, and die, at last, amazed and unprepared! Let every one whose eye glances on this bier, examine what would have been his condition, if the same hour had called him to judgment, and remember, that, though he is now spared, he may, perhaps, be to-morrow among separate spirits. The present moment is in our power: let us, therefore, from the present moment, begin our repentance! Let us not, any longer, harden our hearts, but hear, this day, the voice of our Saviour and our God, and begin to do, with all our powers, whatever we shall wish to have done, when the grave shall open before us! Let those who came hither weeping and lamenting, reflect, that they have not time for useless sorrow; that their own salvation is to be secured, and that the day is far spent, and the night cometh, when no man can work; that tears are of no value to the dead, and that their own danger may justly claim their whole attention! Let those who entered this place unaffected and indifferent, and whose only purpose was to behold this funeral spectacle, consider, that she, whom they thus behold with negligence, and pass by, was lately partaker of the same nature with themselves; and that they likewise are hastening to their end, and must soon, by others equally negligent, be buried and forgotten! Let all remember, that the day of life is short, and that the day of grace may be much shorter; that this may be the last warning which God will grant us, and that, perhaps, he who looks on this grave unalarmed, may sink unreformed into his own!

Let it, therefore, be our care, when we retire from this solemnity, that we immediately turn from our wickedness, and do that which is lawful and right; that, whenever disease, or violence, shall dissolve our bodies, our souls may be saved alive, and received into everlasting habitations; where, with Angels and Archangels, and all the glorious Host of Heaven, they shall sing glory to God on high, and the Lamb, for ever and ever.

THE END.

Prayers composed by me on the death of My Wife, and reposited among her Memorials, May 8, 1752

Deus exaudi.———*Heu!*

April 24, 1752.

Almighty and most merciful Father, who lovest those whom Thou punishest, and turnest away thy anger from the penitent, look down with pity upon my sorrows, and grant that the affliction which it has pleased Thee to bring upon me, may awaken my conscience, enforce my resolutions of a better life, and impress upon me such conviction of thy power and goodness, that I may place in Thee my only felicity, and endeavour to please Thee in all my thoughts, words, and actions. Grant, O Lord, that I may not languish in fruitless and unavailing sorrow, but that I may consider from whose hand all good and evil is received, and may remember that I am punished for my sins, and hope for comfort only by repentance. Grant, O merciful God, that by the assistance of thy Holy Spirit I may repent, and be comforted, obtain that peace which the world cannot give, pass the residue of my life in humble resignation and cheerful obedience; and when it shall please Thee to call me from this mortal state, resign myself into thy hands with faith and confidence, and finally obtain mercy and everlasting happiness, for the sake of Jesus Christ our Lord. Amen.

April 25, 1752.

O Lord, our heavenly Father, almighty and most merciful God, in whose hands are life and death, who givest and takest away, castest down and raisest up, look with mercy on the affliction of thy unworthy servant, turn away thine anger from me, and speak peace to my troubled soul. Grant me the assistance and comfort of thy Holy Spirit, that I may remember with thankfulness the blessings so long enjoyed by me in the society of my departed wife; make me so to think on her precepts and example, that I may imitate whatever was in her life acceptable in thy sight, and avoid all by which she offended Thee. Forgive me, O merciful Lord, all my sins, and enable me to begin and perfect that reformation which I promised her, and to persevere in that resolution, which she implored Thee to continue, in the purposes which I recorded in thy sight, when she lay dead before me, in obedience to thy laws, and faith in thy word. And now, O Lord, release me from my sorrow, fill me with just hopes, true faith, and holy consolations, and enable me to do my duty in that state of life to which Thou hast been pleased to call me, without disturbance from fruitless grief, or tumultuous imaginations; that in all my thoughts, words, and actions, I may glorify thy Holy Name, and finally obtain, what I hope Thou hast granted to thy departed servant, everlasting joy and felicity, through our Lord Jesus Christ. Amen.

April 26, 1752, being after 12 at night of the 25th.

O LORD, Governor of Heaven and Earth, in whose hands are embodied and departed spirits, if Thou hast ordained the souls of the dead to minister to the living, and appointed my departed wife to have care of me, grant that I may enjoy the good effects of her attention and ministration, whether exercised by appearance, impulses, dreams, or in any other manner agreeable to thy government; forgive my presumption, enlighten my ignorance, and however meaner agents are employed, grant me the blessed influencies of thy Holy Spirit, through Jesus Christ our Lord. Amen.

May 6, 1752.

O Lord, our heavenly Father, without whom all purposes are frustrate, all efforts are vain, grant me the assistance of thy Holy Spirit, that I may not sorrow as one without hope, but may now return to the duties of my present state with humble confidence in thy protection, and so govern my thoughts and actions, that neither business may withdraw my mind from Thee, nor idleness lay me open to vain imaginations; that neither praise may fill me with pride, nor censure with discontent; but that in the changes of this life, I may fix my heart upon the reward which Thou hast promised to them that serve Thee, and that whatever things are true, whatever things are honest, whatever things are just, whatever are pure, whatever are lovely, whatever are of good report, wherein there is virtue, wherein there is praise, I may think upon and do, and obtain mercy and everlasting happiness. Grant this, O Lord, for the sake of Jesus Christ. Amen.

Our Father, &c.—The grace, &c.

May 6. I used this service, written April 24, 25, May 6, as preparatory to my return to life to-morrow.

Μακάριοι οἱ νεκροὶ οἱ ἐν Κυρίῳ ἀποθνήσκοντες ἀπάρτι.   Apoc. xiv. 13.

Prayer on Easter Day

SUNDAY 22 APRIL 1753
On EASTER DAY.

April 22.

O Lord, who givest the grace of repentance, and hearest the prayers of the penitent, grant, that by true contrition, I may obtain forgiveness of all the sins committed, and of all duties neglected, in my union with the wife whom Thou hast taken from me; for the neglect of joint devotion, patient exhortation, and mild instruction. And, O Lord, who canst change evil to good, grant that the loss of my wife may so mortify all inordinate affections in me, that I may henceforth please Thee by holiness of life.

And, O Lord, so far as it may be lawful for me, I commend to thy fatherly goodness the soul of my departed wife; beseeching Thee to grant her whatever is best in her present state, and finally to receive her to eternal happiness. All this I beg, for Jesus Christ's sake, whose death I am now about to commemorate. To whom, &c. Amen.

This I repeated sometimes at church.

Diary entry

SUNDAY 22 APRIL 1753

APRIL 22. 1753. As I purpose to try on Monday to seek a new wife without any derogation from dear Tetty's memory I purpose at sacrament in the morning to take my leave of Tetty in a solemn commendation of her soul to God.

Diary entry

MONDAY 23 APRIL 1753

APR 23. EASTER MONDAY. Yesterday as I purposed I went to Bromley where dear Tetty lies buried & received the sacrament, first praying before I went to the altar according to the prayer precomposed for Tetty and a prayer which I made against unchastity, idleness, & neglect of publick worship. I made it during sermon which I could not perfectly hear. I repeated mentally the commendation of her with the utmost fervour larme à l'oeil before the reception of each element at the altar. I repeated it again in the pew, in the garden before dinner, in the garden before departure, at home at night. I hope I did not sin. Fluunt lacrymae. I likewise ardently applied to her the prayer for the Church militant where the dead are mentioned and commended her again to Eternal Mercy, as in coming out I approached her grave. During the whole service I was never once distracted by any thoughts of any other woman or with my design of a new wife which freedom of mind I remembered with gladness in the Garden. God guide me.

Diary entry
SUNDAY 29 APRIL 1753

APR 29. 1753. I know not whether I do not too much indulge the vain longings of affection; but I hope they intenerate my heart & that when I die like my Tetty this affection will be acknowledged in a happy interview & that in the meantime I am incited by it to piety. I will however not deviate too much from common & received methods of devotion.

The Adventurer
No. 39. Tuesday, 20 March 1753.

―――Ὀδυσεύς φύλλοισι καλύψατο. τῳ δ'ἄϱ' Ἀθήνη
Ὕπνον ἐπ' ὄμμασι χεῦ, ἵνα μιν παύσειε τάχιστα
Δυσπονέος καμάτοιο.

HOM.

―――Pallas pour'd sweet slumbers on his soul;
And balmy dreams, the gift of soft repose,
Calm'd all his pains and banish'd all his woes.

POPE.

If every day did not produce fresh instances of the ingratitude of mankind, we might perhaps be at a loss, why so liberal and impartial a benefactor as SLEEP, should meet with so few historians or panegyrists. Writers are so totally absorbed by the business of the day, as never to turn their attention to that power, whose officious hand so seasonably suspends the burthen of life; and without whose interposition, man would not be able to endure the fatigue of labour however rewarded, or the struggle with opposition however successful.

Night, though she divides to many the longest part of life, and to almost all the most innocent and happy, is yet unthankfully neglected, except by those who pervert her gifts.

The astronomers, indeed, expect her with impatience, and felicitate themselves upon her arrival: FONTENELLE has not failed to celebrate her praises; and to chide the sun for hiding from his view, the worlds which he imagines to appear in every constellation. Nor have the poets been always deficient in her praises: MILTON has observed of the Night, that it is "the pleasant time, the cool, the silent."

These men may, indeed, well be expected to pay particular homage to night; since they are indebted to her, not only for cessation of pain, but increase of pleasure; not only for slumber, but for knowledge. But the greater part of her avowed votaries are the sons of luxury; who appropriate to festivity the hours designed for rest; who consider the reign of pleasure as commencing, when day begins to withdraw her busy multitudes, and ceases to dissipate attention by intrusive and unwelcome variety; who begin to awake to joy, when the rest of the world sinks into insensibility; and revel in the soft effluence of flattering and artificial lights, which "more shadowy set off the face of things."

Without touching upon the fatal consequences of a custom, which, as RAMAZZINI observes, will be for ever condemned, and for ever retained; it may be observed, that however Sleep may be put off from time to time, yet the demand is of so importunate a nature, as not to remain long unsatisfied; and if, as some have done, we consider it as the tax of life, we cannot but observe it is a tax that must be paid, unless we could cease to be men; for Alexander declared, that nothing convinced him that he was not a Divinity, but his not being able to live without Sleep.

To live without Sleep in our present fluctuating state, however desirable it might seem to the lady in CLELIA, can surely be the wish only of the young or the ignorant; to every one else, a perpetual vigil will appear to be a state of wretchedness, second only to that of the miserable beings, whom SWIFT has in his travels so elegantly described, as "supremely cursed with immortality."

Sleep is necessary to the happy, to prevent satiety and to endear life by a short absence; and to the miserable, to relieve them by intervals of quiet. Life is to most, such as could not be endured without frequent intermissions of existence: HOMER, therefore, has thought it an office worthy of the goddess of wisdom, to lay Ulysses asleep when landed on Phæacia.

It is related of BARRETIER, whose early advances in literature scarce any human mind has equalled, that he spent twelve hours of the four and twenty in sleep: yet this appears, from the bad state of his health, and the shortness of his life, to have been too small a respite for a mind so vigorously and intensely employed: it is to be regretted, therefore, that he did not exercise his mind less, and his body more; since by this means it is highly probable, that though he would not then have astonished with the blaze of a comet, he would yet have shone with the permanent radiance of a fixed star.

Nor should it be objected, that there have been many men who daily spent fifteen or sixteen hours in study; for by some of whom this is reported, it has never been done; others have done it for a short time only; and of the rest it appears, that they employed their minds in such operations, as required neither celerity nor strength; in the low drudgery of collating copies, comparing authorities, digesting dictionaries, or accumulating compilations.

Men of study and imagination are frequently upbraided by the industrious and plodding sons of care, with passing too great a part of their life in a state of inaction. But these defiers of Sleep seem not to remember, that though it must be granted them that they are crawling about before the break of day, it can seldom be said that they are perfectly awake; they exhaust no spirits, and require no repairs; but lie torpid as a toad in marble, or at least are known to live only by an inert and sluggish loco-motive faculty, and may be said, like a wounded snake, to "dragg their slow length along."

Man has been long known among philosophers, by the appellation of the microcosm, or epitome of the world: the resemblance between the great and little world, might by a rational observer be detailed to many particulars; and to many more by a fanciful speculatist. I know not in which of these two classes I shall be ranged for observing, that as the total quantity of light and darkness, allotted in the course of the year to every region of the earth, is the same, though distributed at various times and in different portions; so, per-haps, to each individual of the human species, nature has ordained the same quantity of wakefulness and sleep; though divided by some into a total quies-cence and vigorous exertion of their faculties, and blended by others in a kind of twilight of existence, in a state between dreaming and reasoning, in which they either think without action, or act without thought.

The poets are generally well affected to sleep: as men who think with vigour, they require respite from thought; and gladly resign themselves to that gentle power, who not only bestows rest, but frequently leads them to happier regions, where patrons are always kind, and audiences are always candid, where they are feasted in the bowers of imagination, and crowned with flowers divested of their prickles, and laurels of unfading verdure.

The more refined and penetrating part of mankind, who take wide surveys of the wilds of life, who see the innumerable terrors and distresses that are perpetually preying on the heart of man, and discern with unhappy perspicu-ity calamities yet latent in their causes, are glad to close their eyes upon the gloomy prospect, and lose in a short insensibility the remembrance of others miseries and their own. The hero has no higher hope, than that after having routed legions after legions, and added kingdom to kingdom, he shall retire to milder happiness, and close his days in social festivity. The wit or the sage can expect no greater happiness, than that after having harrassed his reason in deep researches, and fatigued his fancy in boundless excursions, he shall sink at night in the tranquillity of Sleep.

The poets among all those that enjoy the blessings of Sleep, have been least ashamed to acknowledge their benefactor. How much STATIUS considered the evils of life as asswaged and softened by the balm of slumber, we may discover by that pathetic invocation, which he poured out in his waking nights: and that COWLEY, among the other felicities of his darling solitude, did not forget to number the privilege of sleeping without disturbance, we may learn from the rank that he assigns among the gifts of nature to the poppy; "which is scattered," says he, "over the fields of corn, that all the needs of man may be easily satisfied, and that bread and sleep may be found together."

> Si quis invisum Cereri benignæ
> Me putat germen, vehementer errat;
> Illa me in partem recipit libenter Fertilis agri.
>
> Meque frumentumque simul per omnes
> Consulens mundo Dea spargit oras;
> Crescite, O! dixit, duo magna sustentacula vitæ.
>
> Carpe, mortalis, mea dona lætus,
> Carpe, nec plantas alias require,
> Sed satur panis, satur et soporis, Cætera sperne.

He widely errs who thinks I yield
Precedence in the well cloth'd field,
   Tho' mix'd with wheat I grow:
Indulgent Ceres knew my worth,
And to adorn the teeming earth,
   She bade the POPPY blow.

Nor vainly gay the sight to please,
But blest with power mankind to ease,
   The Goddess saw me rise:
"Thrive with the life-supporting grain,"
She cry'd, "the solace of the swain,
   The cordial of his eyes."

"Seize, happy mortal, seize the good;
My hand supplies thy sleep and food,
   And makes thee truly blest:
With plenteous meals enjoy the day,
In slumbers pass the night away,
   And leave to fate the rest."

C. B.

Sleep, therefore, as the chief of all earthly blessings, is justly appropriated to industry and temperance; the refreshing rest, and the peaceful night, are the portion only of him, who lies down weary with honest labour, and free from the fumes of indigested luxury: it is the just doom of laziness and gluttony, to be inactive without ease, and drowsy without tranquillity.

Sleep has been often mentioned as the image of death; "so like it," says Sir THOMAS BROWN, "that I dare not trust it without my prayers:" their resemblance is, indeed, apparent and striking; they both, when they seize the body, leave the soul at liberty; and wise is he that remembers of both, that they can be made safe and happy only by VIRTUE.

T

No. 45. Tuesday, 10 April 1753.

Nulla fides regni sociis, omnisque potestas
Impatiens consortis erit.

LUCAN.

No faith of partnership dominion owns;
Still discord hovers o'er divided thrones.

It is well known, that many things appear plausible in speculation, which can never be reduced to practice; and that of the numberless projects that have flattered mankind with theoretical speciousness, few have served any other purpose than to shew the ingenuity of their contrivers. A voyage to the moon, however romantic and absurd the scheme may now appear, since the properties of air have been better understood, seemed highly probable to many of the aspiring wits in the last century, who began to doat upon their glossy plumes, and fluttered with impatience for the hour of their departure:

———*Pereant vestigia mille*
Ante fugam, absentemque ferit gravis ungula campum.

Hills, vales, and floods appear already crost;
And, e'er he starts, a thousand steps are lost.

POPE.

Among the fallacies which only experience can detect, there are some of which scarcely experience itself can destroy the influence; some which, by a captivating shew of indubitable certainty, are perpetually gaining upon the human mind; and which, though every trial ends in disappointment, obtain new credit as the sense of miscarriage wears gradually away, persuade us to try again what we have tried already, and expose us by the same failure to double vexation.

Of this tempting, this delusive kind, is the expectation of great performances by confederated strength. The speculatist, when he has carefully observed how much may be performed by a single hand, calculates by a very easy operation the force of thousands, and goes on accumulating power till resistance vanishes before it; then rejoices in the success of his new scheme, and wonders at the folly or idleness of former ages, who have lived in want of what might so readily be procured, and suffered themselves to be debarred from happiness by obstacles which one united effort would have so easily surmounted.

But this gigantic phantom of collective power vanishes at once into air and emptiness, at the first attempt to put it into action. The different apprehensions, the discordant passions, the jarring interests of men, will scarcely permit that many should unite in one undertaking.

Of a great and complicated design, some will never be brought to discern the end; and of the several means by which it may be accomplished, the choice will be a perpetual subject of debate, as every man is swayed in his determination by his own knowledge or convenience. In a long series of action, some will languish with fatigue, and some be drawn off by present gratifications; some will loiter because others labour, and some will cease to labour because others loiter; and if once they come within prospect of success and profit, some will be greedy and others envious; some will undertake more than they can perform, to enlarge their claims of advantage; some will perform less than they undertake, lest their labours should turn chiefly to the benefit of others.

The history of mankind informs us, that a single power is very seldom broken by a confederacy. States of different interests, and aspects malevolent to each other, may be united for a time by common distress; and in the ardour of self-preservation fall unanimously upon an enemy by whom they are all equally endangered. But if their first attack can be withstood, time will never fail to dissolve their union: success and miscarriage will be equally destructive: after the conquest of a province, they will quarrel in the division; after the loss of a battle, all will be endeavouring to secure themselves by abandoning the rest.

From the impossibility of confining numbers to the constant and uniform prosecution of a common interest, arises the difficulty of securing subjects against the incroachment of governors. Power is always gradually stealing away from the many to the few, because the few are more vigilant and consistent; it still contracts to a smaller number, till in time it centers in a single person.

Thus all the forms of government instituted among mankind, perpetually tend towards monarchy; and power, however diffused through the whole community, is by negligence or corruption, commotion or distress, reposed at last in the chief magistrate.

"There never appear," says SWIFT, "more than five or six men of genius in an age; but if they were united, the world could not stand before them." It is happy, therefore, for mankind, that of this union there is no probability. As men take in a wider compass of intellectual survey, they are more likely to chuse different objects of persuit; as they see more ways to the same end, they will be less easily persuaded to travel together; as each is better qualified to form an independent scheme of private greatness, he will reject with greater obstinacy the project of another; as each is more able to distinguish himself as the head of a party, he will less readily be made a follower or an associate.

The reigning philosophy informs us, that the vast bodies which constitute the universe, are regulated in their progress through the etherial spaces, by the perpetual agency of contrary forces; by one of which they are restrained from deserting their orbits, and losing themselves in the immensity of heaven; and held off by the other from rushing together, and clustering round their centre with everlasting cohesion.

The same contrariety of impulse may be perhaps discovered in the motions of men: we are formed for society, not for combination; we are equally unqualified to live in a close connection with our fellow beings, and in total separation from them: we are attracted towards each other by general sympathy, but kept back from contact by private interests.

Some philosophers have been foolish enough to imagine, that improvements might be made in the system of the universe, by a different arrangement of the orbs of heaven; and politicians, equally ignorant and equally presumptuous, may easily be led to suppose, that the happiness of our world would be promoted by a different tendency of the human mind. It appears, indeed, to a slight and superficial observer, that many things impracticable in our present state, might be easily effected, if mankind were better disposed to union and co-operation: but a little reflection will discover, that if confederacies were easily formed, they would lose their efficacy, since numbers would be opposed to numbers, and unanimity to unanimity; and instead of the present petty competitions of individuals or single families, multitudes would be supplanting multitudes, and thousands plotting against thousands.

There is no class of the human species, of which the union seems to have been more expected, than of the learned: the rest of the world have almost always agreed, to shut scholars up together in colleges and cloisters; surely not without hope, that they would look for that happiness in concord, which they were debarred from finding in variety; and that such conjunctions of intellect would recompense the munificence of founders and patrons, by performances above the reach of any single mind.

But DISCORD, who found means to roll her apple into the banquetting chamber of the Goddesses, has had the address to scatter her laurels in the seminaries of learning. The friendship of students and of beauties is for the most part equally sincere, and equally durable: as both depend for happiness on the regard of others, on that of which the value arises merely from comparison, they are both exposed to perpetual jealousies, and both incessantly employed in schemes to intercept the praises of each other.

I am, however, far from intending to inculcate, that this confinement of the studious to studious companions, has been wholly without advantage to the public: neighbourhood, where it does not conciliate friendship, incites competition; and he that would contentedly rest in a lower degree of excellence, where he had no rival to dread, will be urged by his impatience of inferiority to incessant endeavours after great attainments.

These stimulations of honest rivalry, are, perhaps, the chief effects of academies and societies; for whatever be the bulk of their joint labours, every single piece is always the production of an individual, that owes nothing to his collegues but the contagion of diligence, a resolution to write because the rest are writing, and the scorn of obscurity while the rest are illustrious.

T

No. 50. Saturday, 28 April 1753.

Quicunque turpi fraude semel innotuit,
Etiamsi vera dicit, amittit fidem.

PHÆD.

The wretch that often has deceiv'd,
Though truth he speaks, is ne'er believ'd.

When ARISTOTLE was once asked, what a man could gain by uttering falsehoods; he replied, "not to be credited when he shall tell the truth."

The character of a liar is at once so hateful and contemptible, that even of those who have lost their virtue it might be expected, that from the violation of truth they should be restrained by their pride. Almost every other vice that disgraces human nature, may be kept in countenance by applause and association: the corrupter of virgin innocence sees himself envied by the men, and at least not detested by the women: the drunkard may easily unite with beings, devoted like himself to noisy merriment or silent insensibility, who will celebrate his victories over the novices of intemperance, boast themselves the companions of his prowess, and tell with rapture of the multitudes whom unsuccessful emulation has hurried to the grave: even the robber and the cutthroat have their followers, who admire their address and intrepidity, their stratagems of rapine, and their fidelity to the gang.

The liar, and only the liar, is invariably and universally despised, abandoned, and disowned; he has no domestic consolations, which he can oppose to the censure of mankind; he can retire to no fraternity where his crimes may stand in the place of virtues; but is given up to the hisses of the multitude, without friend and without apologist. It is the peculiar condition of falsehood, to be equally detested by the good and bad: "The devils," says Sir THOMAS BROWN, "do not tell lies to one another; for truth is necessary to all societies; nor can the society of hell subsist without it."

It is natural to expect, that a crime thus generally detested, should be generally avoided; at least, that none should expose himself to unabated and unpitied infamy, without an adequate temptation; and that to guilt so easily detected, and so severely punished, an adequate temptation would not readily be found.

Yet so it is, that in defiance of censure and contempt, truth is frequently violated; and scarcely the most vigilant and unremitted circumspection will secure him that mixes with mankind, from being hourly deceived by men of whom it can scarcely be imagined, that they mean any injury to him, or profit to themselves; even where the subject of conversation could not have been expected to put the passions in motion, or to have excited either hope or fear, or zeal or malignity, sufficient to induce any man to put his reputation in hazard, however little he might value it, or to overpower the love of truth, however weak might be its influence.

The casuists have very diligently distinguished lyes into their several classes, according to their various degrees of malignity: but they have, I think, generally omitted that which is most common, and, perhaps, not least mischievous; which, since the moralists have not given it a name, I shall distinguish as the LYE of VANITY.

To vanity may justly be imputed most of the falsehoods, which every man perceives hourly playing upon his ear, and, perhaps, most of those that are propagated with success. To the lye of commerce, and the lye of malice, the motive is so apparent, that they are seldom negligently or implicitly received: suspicion is always watchful over the practices of interest; and whatever the hope of gain, or desire of mischief, can prompt one man to assert, another is by reasons equally cogent incited to refute. But vanity pleases herself with such slight gratifications, and looks forward to pleasure so remotely consequential, that her practices raise no alarm, and her stratagems are not easily discovered.

Vanity is, indeed, often suffered to pass unpersued by suspicion; because he that would watch her motions, can never be at rest: fraud and malice are bounded in their influence; some opportunity of time and place is necessary to their agency; but scarce any man is abstracted one moment from his vanity; and he, to whom truth affords no gratifications, is generally inclined to seek them in falsehood.

It is remarked by Sir KENELM DIGBY, "that every man has a desire to appear superior to others, though it were only in having seen what they have not seen." Such an accidental advantage, since it neither implies merit, nor confers dignity, one would think should not be desired so much as to be counterfeited: yet even this vanity, trifling as it is, produces innumerable narratives, all equally false; but more or less credible, in proportion to the skill or confidence of the relator. How many may a man of diffusive conversation count among his acquaintances, whose lives have been signalised by numberless escapes; who never cross the river but in a storm, or take a journey into the country without more adventures than befel the knight-errants of antient times, in pathless forests or enchanted castles! How many must he know to whom portents and prodigies are of daily occurrence; and for whom nature is hourly working wonders invisible to every other eye, only to supply them with subjects of conversation!

Others there are that amuse themselves with the dissemination of false-hood, at greater hazard of detection and disgrace; men marked out by some lucky planet for universal confidence and friendship, who have been con-sulted in every difficulty, entrusted with every secret, and summoned to every transaction: it is the supreme felicity of these men, to stun all companies with noisy information; to still doubt, and overbear opposition, with certain know-ledge or authentic intelligence. A liar of this kind, with a strong memory or brisk imagination, is often the oracle of an obscure club, and till time dis-covers his impostures, dictates to his hearers with uncontrouled authority; for if a public question be started, he was present at the debate; if a new fashion be mentioned, he was at court the first day of its appearance; if a new per-formance of literature draws the attention of the public, he has patronised the author, and seen his work in manuscript; if a criminal of eminence be con-demned to die, he often predicted his fate, and endeavoured his reformation: and who that lives at a distance from the scene of action, will dare to contra-dict a man, who reports from his own eyes and ears, and to whom all persons and affairs are thus intimately known?

This kind of falsehood is generally successful for a time, because it is prac-tised at first with timidity and caution: but the prosperity of the liar is of short duration; the reception of one story, is always an incitement to the forgery of another less probable; and he goes on to triumph over tacit credulity, till pride or reason rises up against him, and his companions will no longer endure to see him wiser than themselves.

It is apparent, that the inventors of all these fictions intend some exaltation of themselves, and are led off by the persuit of honour from their attendance upon truth: their narratives always imply some consequence in favour of their courage, their sagacity or their activity, their familiarity with the learned, or their reception among the great; they are always bribed by the present pleasure of seeing themselves superior to those that surround them, and receiving the homage of silent attention and envious admiration.

But vanity is sometimes incited to fiction, by less visible gratifications: the present age abounds with a race of liars, who are content with the conscious-ness of falsehood, and whose pride is to deceive others without any gain or glory to themselves. Of this tribe it is the supreme pleasure to remark a lady in the play-house or the park, and to publish, under the character of a man suddenly enamoured, an advertisement in the news of the next day, contain-ing a minute description of her person and her dress. From this artifice, indeed, no other effect can be expected than perturbations which the writer can never see, and conjectures of which he can never be informed: some mischief, however, he hopes he has done; and to have done mischief, is of some importance. He sets his invention to work again, and produces a narrative of a robbery, or a murder, with all the circumstances of time and place accurately adjusted: this is a jest of greater effect and longer duration: if he fixes his scene at a proper distance, he may for several days keep a wife in terror for her husband, or a mother for her son; and please himself with reflecting, that by his abilities and address, some addition is made to the miseries of life.

There is, I think, an antient law in Scotland, by which LEASING-MAKING was capitally punished. I am, indeed, far from desiring to increase in this kingdom the number of executions: yet I cannot but think, that they who destroy the confidence of society, weaken the credit of intelligence, and interrupt the security of life; harrass the delicate with shame, and perplex the timorous with alarms; might very properly be awakened to a sense of their crimes, by denunciations of a whipping post or pillory: since many are so insensible of right and wrong, that they have no standard of action but the law; nor feel guilt, but as they dread punishment.

T

No. 67. Tuesday, 26 June 1753.

Inventas—vitam excoluere per artes.
VIRG.

They polish life by useful arts.

That familiarity produces neglect, has been long observed. The effect of all external objects, however great or splendid, ceases with their novelty: the courtier stands without emotion in the royal presence; the rustic tramples under his foot the beauties of the spring, with little attention to their colour or their fragrance; and the inhabitant of the coast darts his eye upon the immense diffusion of waters, without awe, wonder, or terror.

Those who have past much of their lives in this great city, look upon its opulence and its multitudes, its extent and variety, with cold indifference; but an inhabitant of the remoter parts of the kingdom is immediately distinguished by a kind of dissipated curiosity, a busy endeavour to divide his attention amongst a thousand objects, and a wild confusion of astonishment and alarm.

The attention of a new-comer is generally first struck by the multiplicity of cries that stun him in the streets, and the variety of merchandise and manufactures which the shopkeepers expose on every hand; and he is apt, by unwary bursts of admiration, to excite the merriment and contempt of those, who mistake the use of their eyes for effects of their understanding, and confound accidental knowledge with just reasoning.

But, surely, these are subjects on which any man may without reproach employ his meditations: the innumerable occupations, among which the thousands that swarm in the streets of London are distributed, may furnish employment to minds of every cast, and capacities of every degree. He that contemplates the extent of this wonderful city, finds it difficult to conceive, by what method plenty is maintained in our markets, and how the inhabitants are regularly supplied with the necessaries of life; but when he examines the shops and warehouses, sees the immense stores of every kind of merchandise piled up for sale, and runs over all the manufactures of art and products of nature, which are every where attracting his eye and solliciting his purse, he will be inclined to conclude, that such quantities cannot easily be exhausted, and that part of mankind must soon stand still for want of employment, till the wares already provided shall be worn out and destroyed.

As SOCRATES was passing through the fair at Athens, and casting his eyes over the shops and customers, "how many things are here," says he, "that I do not want!" The same sentiment is every moment rising in the mind of him that walks the streets of London, however inferior in philosophy to SOCRATES: he beholds a thousand shops crouded with goods, of which he can scarcely tell the use, and which, therefore, he is apt to consider as of no value; and, indeed, many of the arts by which families are supported, and wealth is heaped together, are of that minute and superfluous kind, which nothing but experience could evince possible to be prosecuted with advantage, and which, as the world might easily want, it could scarcely be expected to encourage.

But so it is, that custom, curiosity, or wantonness, supplies every art with patrons, and finds purchasers for every manufacture; the world is so adjusted, that not only bread, but riches may be obtained without great abilities, or arduous performances: the most unskilful hand and unenlightened mind have sufficient incitements to industry; for he that is resolutely busy, can scarcely be in want. There is, indeed, no employment, however despicable, from which a man may not promise himself more than competence, when he sees thousands and myriads raised to dignity, by no other merit than that of contributing to supply their neighbours with the means of sucking smoke through a tube of clay; and others raising contributions upon those, whose elegance disdains the grossness of smoky luxury, by grinding the same materials into a powder, that may at once gratify and impair the smell.

Not only by these popular and modish trifles, but by a thousand unheeded and evanescent kinds of business, are the multitudes of this city preserved from idleness, and consequently from want. In the endless variety of tastes and circumstances that diversify mankind, nothing is so superfluous, but that some one desires it; or so common, but that some one is compelled to buy it. As nothing is useless but because it is in improper hands, what is thrown away by one is gathered up by another; and the refuse of part of mankind furnishes a subordinate class with the materials necessary to their support.

When I look round upon those who are thus variously exerting their qualifications, I cannot but admire the secret concatenation of society, that links together the great and the mean, the illustrious and the obscure; and consider with benevolent satisfaction, that no man, unless his body or mind be totally disabled, has need to suffer the mortification of seeing himself useless or burdensome to the community: he that will diligently labour, in whatever occupation, will deserve the sustenance which he obtains, and the protection which he enjoys; and may lie down every night with the pleasing consciousness, of having contributed something to the happiness of life.

Contempt and admiration are equally incident to narrow minds: he whose comprehension can take in the whole subordination of mankind, and whose perspicacity can pierce to the real state of things through the thin veils of fortune or of fashion, will discover meanness in the highest stations, and dignity in the meanest; and find that no man can become venerable but by virtue, or contemptible but by wickedness.

In the midst of this universal hurry, no man ought to be so little influenced by example, or so void of honest emulation, as to stand a lazy spectator of incessant labour; or please himself with the mean happiness of a drone, while the active swarms are buzzing about him: no man is without some quality, by the due application of which he might deserve well of the world; and whoever he be that has but little in his power, should be in haste to do that little, lest he be confounded with him that can do nothing.

By this general concurrence of endeavours, arts of every kind have been so long cultivated, that all the wants of man may be immediately supplied; idleness can scarcely form a wish which she may not gratify by the toil of others, or curiosity dream of a toy which the shops are not ready to afford her.

Happiness is enjoyed only in proportion as it is known; and such is the state or folly of man, that it is known only by experience of its contrary: we who have long lived amidst the conveniences of a town immensely populous, have scarce an idea of a place where desire cannot be gratified by money. In order to have a just sense of this artificial plenty, it is necessary to have passed some time in a distant colony, or those parts of our island which are thinly inhabited: he that has once known how many trades every man in such situations is compelled to exercise, with how much labour the products of nature must be accommodated to human use, how long the loss or defect of any common utensil must be endured, or by what aukward expedients it must be supplied, how far men may wander with money in their hands before any can sell them what they wish to buy, will know how to rate at its proper value the plenty and ease of a great city.

But that the happiness of man may still remain imperfect, as wants in this place are easily supplied, new wants likewise are easily created: every man, in surveying the shops of London, sees numberless instruments and conveniences, of which, while he did not know them, he never felt the need; and yet, when use has made them familiar, wonders how life could be supported without them. Thus it comes to pass, that our desires always increase with our possessions; the knowledge that something remains yet unenjoyed, impairs our enjoyment of the good before us.

They who have been accustomed to the refinements of science, and multiplications of contrivance, soon lose their confidence in the unassisted powers of nature, forget the paucity of our real necessities, and overlook the easy methods by which they may be supplied. It were a speculation worthy of a philosophical mind, to examine how much is taken away from our native abilities, as well as added to them by artificial expedients. We are so accustomed to give and receive assistance, that each of us singly can do little for himself; and there is scarce any one amongst us, however contracted may be his form of life, who does not enjoy the labour of a thousand artists.

But a survey of the various nations that inhabit the earth will inform us, that life may be supported with less assistance, and that the dexterity, which practice enforced by necessity produces, is able to effect much by very scanty means. The nations of Mexico and Peru erected cities and temples without the use of iron; and at this day the rude Indian supplies himself with all the necessaries of life: sent like the rest of mankind naked into the world, as soon as his parents have nursed him up to strength, he is to provide by his own labour for his own support. His first care is to find a sharp flint among the rocks; with this he undertakes to fell the trees of the forest; he shapes his bow, heads his arrows, builds his cottage, and hollows his canoe, and from that time lives in a state of plenty and prosperity; he is sheltered from the storms, he is fortified against beasts of prey, he is enabled to persue the fish of the sea, and the deer of the mountains; and as he does not know, does not envy the happiness of polished nations, where gold can supply the want of fortitude and skill, and he whose laborious ancestors have made him rich, may lie stretched upon a couch, and see all the treasures of all the elements poured down before him.

This picture of a savage life, if it shews how much individuals may perform, shews likewise how much society is to be desired. Though the perseverance and address of the Indian excite our admiration, they nevertheless cannot procure him the conveniences which are enjoyed by the vagrant begger of a civilized country: he hunts like a wild beast to satisfy his hunger; and when he lies down to rest after a successful chace, cannot pronounce himself secure against the danger of perishing in a few days; he is, perhaps, content with his condition, because he knows not that a better is attainable by man; as he that is born blind does not long for the perception of light, because he cannot conceive the advantages which light would afford him: but hunger, wounds and weariness are real evils, though he believes them equally incident to all his fellow creatures; and when a tempest compels him to lie starving in his hut, he cannot justly be concluded equally happy with those whom art has exempted from the power of chance, and who make the foregoing year provide for the following.

To receive and to communicate assistance, constitutes the happiness of human life: man may indeed preserve his existence in solitude, but can enjoy it only in society: the greatest understanding of an individual, doomed to procure food and cloathing for himself, will barely supply him with expedients to keep off death from day to day; but as one of a large community performing only his share of the common business, he gains leisure for intellectual pleasures, and enjoys the happiness of reason and reflection.

T

No. 69. Tuesday, 3 July 1753.

Ferè libenter homines id quod volunt credunt.

CÆSAR.

Men willingly believe what they wish to be true.

Tully has long ago observed, that no man, however weakened by long life, is so conscious of his own decrepitude, as not to imagine that he may yet hold his station in the world for another year.

Of the truth of this remark every day furnishes new confirmation: there is no time of life, in which men for the most part seem less to expect the stroke of death, than when every other eye sees it impending; or are more busy in providing for another year, than when it is plain to all but themselves, that at another year they cannot arrive. Though every funeral that passes before their eyes, evinces the deceitfulness of such expectations, since every man who is borne to the grave thought himself equally certain of living at least to the next year, the survivor still continues to flatter himself, and is never at a loss for some reason why his life should be protracted, and the voracity of death continue to be pacified with some other prey.

But this is only one of the innumerable artifices practised in the universal conspiracy of mankind against themselves: every age and every condition indulges some darling fallacy; every man amuses himself with projects which he knows to be improbable, and which, therefore, he resolves to persue without daring to examine them. Whatever any man ardently desires, he very readily believes that he shall some time attain: he whose intemperance has overwhelmed him with diseases, while he languishes in the spring, expects vigour and recovery from the summer sun; and while he melts away in the summer, transfers his hopes to the frosts of winter: he that gazes upon elegance or pleasure, which want of money hinders him from imitating or partaking, comforts himself that the time of distress will soon be at an end, and that every day brings him nearer to a state of happiness; though he knows it has passed not only without acquisition of advantage, but perhaps without endeavours after it, in the formation of schemes that cannot be executed, and in the contemplation of prospects which cannot be approached.

Such is the general dream in which we all slumber out our time; every man thinks the day coming, in which he shall be gratified with all his wishes, in which he shall leave all those competitors behind, who are now rejoicing like himself in the expectation of victory; the day is always coming to the servile in which they shall be powerful, to the obscure in which they shall be eminent, and to the deformed in which they shall be beautiful.

If any of my readers has looked with so little attention on the world about him, as to imagine this representation exaggerated beyond probability, let him reflect a little upon his own life; let him consider what were his hopes and prospects ten years ago, and what additions he then expected to be made by ten years to his happiness: those years are now elapsed; have they made good the promise that was extorted from them, have they advanced his fortune, enlarged his knowledge, or reformed his conduct to the degree that was once expected? I am afraid, every man that recollects his hopes, must confess his disappointment; and own, that day has glided unprofitably after day, and that he is still at the same distance from the point of happiness.

With what consolations can those who have thus miscarried in their chief design, elude the memory of their ill success? with what amusements can they pacify their discontent, after the loss of so large a portion of life? they can give themselves up again to the same delusions, they can form new schemes of airy gratifications, and fix another period of felicity; they can again resolve to trust the promise which they know will be broken, they can walk in a circle with their eyes shut, and persuade themselves to think that they go forward.

Of every great and complicated event, part depends upon causes out of our power, and part must be effected by vigour and perseverance. With regard to that which is stiled in common language the work of chance, men will always find reasons for confidence or distrust, according to their different tempers or inclinations; and he that has been long accustomed to please himself with possibilities of fortuitous happiness, will not easily or willingly be reclaimed from his mistake. But the effects of human industry and skill are more easily subjected to calculation; whatever can be completed in a year, is divisible into parts, of which each may be performed in the compass of a day; he, therefore, that has passed the day without attention to the task assigned him, may be certain that the lapse of life has brought him no nearer to his object; for whatever idleness may expect from time, its produce will be only in proportion to the diligence with which it has been used. He that floats lazily down the stream, in persuit of something borne along by the same current, will find himself indeed move forward; but unless he lays his hand to the oar, and increases his speed by his own labour, must be always at the same distance from that which he is following.

There have happened in every age some contingencies of unexpected and undeserved success, by which those who are determined to believe whatever favours their inclinations, have been encouraged to delight themselves with future advantages; they support confidence by considerations, of which the only proper use is to chace away despair: it is equally absurd to sit down in idleness, because some have been enriched without labour; as to leap a precipice because some have fallen and escaped with life, or to put to sea in a storm because some have been driven from a wreck upon the coast to which they were bound.

We are all ready to confess, that belief ought to be proportioned to evidence or probability: let any man, therefore, compare the number of those who have been thus favoured by fortune, and of those who have failed of their expectations; and he will easily determine, with what justness he has registered himself in the lucky catalogue.

But there is no need on these occasions for deep inquiries or laborious calculations; there is a far easier method of distinguishing the hopes of folly from those of reason, of finding the difference between prospects that exist before the eyes, and those that are only painted on a fond imagination. Tom Drowsy had accustomed himself to compute the profit of a darling project, till he had no longer any doubt of its success; it was at last matured by close consideration, all the measures were accurately adjusted, and he wanted only five hundred pounds to become master of a fortune that might be envied by a director of a trading company. Tom was generous and grateful, and was resolved to recompence this small assistance with an ample fortune: he, therefore, deliberated for a time, to whom amongst his friends he should declare his necessities; not that he suspected a refusal, but because he could not suddenly determine which of them would make the best use of riches, and was, therefore, most worthy of his favour. At last his choice was settled; and knowing that in order to borrow he must shew the probability of repayment, he prepared for a minute and copious explanation of his project. But here the golden dream was at an end: he soon discovered the impossibility of imposing upon others the notions by which he had so long imposed upon himself; which way soever he turned his thoughts, impossibility and absurdity rose in opposition on every side; even credulity and prejudice were at last forced to give way, and he grew ashamed of crediting himself what shame would not suffer him to communicate to another.

To this test let every man bring his imaginations, before they have been too long predominant in his mind. Whatever is true will bear to be related, whatever is rational will endure to be explained: but when we delight to brood in secret over future happiness, and silently to employ our meditations upon schemes of which we are conscious that the bare mention would expose us to derision and contempt; we should then remember, that we are cheating ourselves by voluntary delusions; and giving up to the unreal mockeries of fancy, those hours in which solid advantages might be attained by sober thought and rational assiduity.

There is, indeed, so little certainty in human affairs, that the most cautious and severe examiner may be allowed to indulge some hopes, which he cannot prove to be much favoured by probability; since after his utmost endeavours to ascertain events, he must often leave the issue in the hands of chance. And so scanty is our present allowance of happiness, that in many situations life could scarcely be supported, if hope were not allowed to relieve the present hour by pleasures borrowed from futurity; and reanimate the languor of dejection to new efforts, by pointing to distant regions of felicity, which yet no resolution or perseverance shall ever reach.

But these, like all other cordials, though they may invigorate in a small quantity, intoxicate in a greater; these pleasures, like the rest, are lawful only in certain circumstances, and to certain degrees; they may be useful in a due subserviency to nobler purposes, but become dangerous and destructive, when once they gain the ascendant in the heart: to sooth the mind to tranquillity by hope, even when that hope is likely to deceive us, may be sometimes useful; but to lull our faculties in a lethargy, is poor and despicable.

Vices and errors are differently modified, according to the state of the minds to which they are incident: to indulge hope beyond the warrant of reason, is the failure alike of mean and elevated understandings; but its foundation and its effects are totally different: the man of high courage and great abilities, is apt to place too much confidence in himself, and to expect from a vigorous exertion of his powers more than spirit or diligence can attain; between him and his wish he sees obstacles indeed, but he expects to overleap or break them; his mistaken ardour hurries him forward; and though perhaps he misses his end, he nevertheless obtains some collateral good, and performs something useful to mankind and honourable to himself.

The drone of timidity presumes likewise to hope, but without ground and without consequence; the bliss with which he solaces his hours, he always expects from others, though very often he knows not from whom; he folds his arms about him, and sits in expectation of some revolution in the state that shall raise him to greatness, or some golden shower that shall load him with wealth; he dozes away the day in musing upon the morrow; and at the end of life is rouzed from his dream only to discover, that the time of action is past, and that he can now shew his wisdom only by repentance.

T

No. 84. Saturday, 25 August 1753.

——*Tolle periclum,*
Jam vaga prosiliet frænis natura remotis.
HOR.

But take the danger and the shame away,
And vagrant nature bounds upon her prey.
FRANCIS.

To the ADVENTURER.

SIR,

It has been observed, I think, by Sir WILLIAM TEMPLE, and after him by almost every other writer, that England affords a greater variety of characters, than the rest of the world. This is ascribed to the liberty prevailing amongst us, which gives every man the privilege of being wise or foolish his own way, and preserves him from the necessity of hypocrisy, or the servility of imitation.

That the position itself is true, I am not completely satisfied. To be nearly acquainted with the people of different countries can happen to very few; and in life, as in every thing else beheld at a distance, there appears an even uniformity; the petty discriminations which diversify the natural character, are not discoverable but by a close inspection; we, therefore, find them most at home, because there we have most opportunities of remarking them. Much less am I convinced, that this peculiar diversification, if it be real, is the consequence of peculiar liberty: for where is the government to be found, that superintends individuals with so much vigilance, as not to leave their private conduct without restraint? Can it enter into a reasonable mind to imagine, that men of every other nation are not equally masters of their own time or houses with ourselves, and equally at liberty to be parsimonious or profuse, frolic or sullen, abstinent or luxurious? Liberty is certainly necessary to the full play of predominant humours; but such liberty is to be found alike under the government of the many or the few, in monarchies or in commonwealths.

How readily the predominant passion snatches an interval of liberty, and how fast it expands itself when the weight of restraint is taken away, I had lately an opportunity to discover, as I took a journey into the country in a stage coach; which, as every journey is a kind of adventure, may be very properly related to you, though I can display no such extraordinary assembly as CERVANTES has collected at DON QUIXOTE's inn.

In a stage coach the passengers are for the most part wholly unknown to one another, and without expectation of ever meeting again when their journey is at an end; one should therefore imagine, that it was of little importance to any of them, what conjectures the rest should form concerning him. Yet so it is, that as all think themselves secure from detection, all assume that character of which they are most desirous, and on no occasion is the general ambition of superiority more apparently indulged.

On the day of our departure, in the twilight of the morning, I ascended the vehicle, with three men and two women my fellow travellers. It was easy to observe the affected elevation of mien with which every one entered, and the supercilious civility with which they paid their compliments to each other. When the first ceremony was dispatched, we sat silent for a long time, all employed in collecting importance into our faces, and endeavouring to strike reverence and submission into our companions.

It is always observable that silence propagates itself, and that the longer talk has been suspended, the more difficult it is to find any thing to say. We began now to wish for conversation; but no one seemed inclined to descend from his dignity, or first to propose a topic of discourse. At last a corpulent gentleman, who had equipped himself for this expedition with a scarlet surtout, and a large hat with a broad lace, drew out his watch, looked on it in silence, and then held it dangling at his finger. This was, I suppose, understood by all the company as an invitation to ask the time of the day; but no body appeared to heed his overture; and his desire to be talking so far overcame his resentment, that he let us know of his own accord that it was past five, and that in two hours we should be at breakfast.

His condescension was thrown away; we continued all obdurate; the ladies held up their heads; I amused myself with watching their behaviour; and of the other two, one seemed to employ himself in counting the trees as we drove by them, the other drew his hat over his eyes, and counterfeited a slumber. The man of benevolence, to shew that he was not depressed by our neglect, hummed a tune and beat time upon his snuff-box.

Thus universally displeased with one another, and not much delighted with ourselves, we came at last to the little inn appointed for our repast, and all began at once to recompence themselves for the constraint of silence, by innumerable questions and orders to the people that attended us. At last, what every one had called for was got, or declared impossible to be got at that time, and we were persuaded to sit round the same table; when the gentleman in the red surtout looked again upon his watch, told us that we had half an hour to spare, but he was sorry to see so little merriment among us; that all fellow travellers were for the time upon the level, and that it was always his way to make himself one of the company. "I remember," says he, "it was on just such a morning as this that I and my lord Mumble and the duke of Tenterden were out upon a ramble; we called at a little house as it might be this; and my landlady, I warrant you, not suspecting to whom she was talking, was so jocular and facetious, and made so many merry answers to our questions, that we were all ready to burst with laughter. At last the good woman happening to overhear me whisper the duke and call him by his title, was so surprised and confounded that we could scarcely get a word from her: and the duke never met me from that day to this, but he talks of the little house, and quarrels with me for terrifying the landlady."

He had scarcely had time to congratulate himself on the veneration which this narrative must have procured him from the company, when one of the ladies having reached out for a plate on a distant part of the table, began to remark "the inconveniences of travelling, and the difficulty which they who never sat at home without a great number of attendants found in performing for themselves such offices as the road required; but that people of quality often travelled in disguise, and might be generally known from the vulgar by their condescension to poor inn-keepers, and the allowance which they made for any defect in their entertainment: that for her part, while people were civil and meant well, it was never her custom to find fault; for one was not to expect upon a journey all that one enjoyed at one's own house."

A general emulation seemed now to be excited. One of the men, who had hitherto said nothing, called for the last news paper; and having perused it a while with deep pensiveness, "It is impossible," says he, "for any man to guess how to act with regard to the stocks; last week it was the general opinion that they would fall; and I sold out twenty thousand pounds in order to a purchase: they have now risen unexpectedly; and I make no doubt but at my return to London I shall risk thirty thousand pounds amongst them again."

A young man, who had hitherto distinguished himself only by the vivacity of his look, and a frequent diversion of his eyes from one object to another, upon this closed his snuff-box, and told us that "he had a hundred times talked with the chancellor and the judges on the subject of the stocks; that for his part he did not pretend to be well acquainted with the principles on which they were established, but had always heard them reckoned pernicious to trade, uncertain in their produce, and unsolid in their foundation; and that he had been advised by three judges, his most intimate friends, never to venture his money in the funds, but to put it out upon land security, till he could light upon an estate in his own country."

It might be expected that, upon these glimpses of latent dignity, we should all have began to look around us with veneration, and have behaved like the princes of romance, when the enchantment that disguises them is dissolved, and they discover the dignity of each other: yet it happened, that none of these hints made much impression on the company; every one was apparently suspected of endeavouring to impose false appearances upon the rest; all continued their haughtiness, in hopes to enforce their claims; and all grew every hour more sullen, because they found their representations of themselves without effect.

Thus we travelled on four days with malevolence perpetually increasing, and without any endeavour but to outvie each other in superciliousness and neglect; and when any two of us could separate ourselves for a moment, we vented our indignation at the sauciness of the rest.

At length the journey was at an end, and time and chance, that strip off all disguises, have discovered that the intimate of lords and dukes is a nobleman's butler, who has furnished a shop with the money he has saved; the man who deals so largely in the funds, is the clerk of a broker in 'Change-alley; the lady who so carefully concealed her quality, keeps a cookshop behind the Exchange; and the young man, who is so happy in the friendship of the judges, engrosses and transcribes for bread in a garret of the Temple. Of one of the women only I could make no disadvantageous detection, because she had assumed no character, but accommodated herself to the scene before her, without any struggle for distinction or superiority.

I could not forbear to reflect on the folly of practising a fraud, which, as the event shewed, had been already practised too often to succeed, and by the success of which no advantage could have been obtained; of assuming a character, which was to end with the day; and of claiming upon false pretences honours which must perish with the breath that paid them.

But MR. ADVENTURER, let not those who laugh at me and my companions, think this folly confined to a stage coach. Every man in the journey of life takes the same advantage of the ignorance of his fellow travellers, disguises himself in counterfeited merit, and hears those praises with complacency which his conscience reproaches him for accepting. Every man deceives himself, while he thinks he is deceiving others; and forgets that the time is at hand when every illusion shall cease, when fictitious excellence shall be torn away, and ALL must be shown to ALL in their real state.

I am, SIR,
Your humble Servant,
VIATOR.

T

No. 85. Tuesday, 28 August 1753.

Qui cupit optatam cursu contingere metam,
Multa tulit fecitque puer.

HOR.

The youth, who hopes th' Olympic prize to gain,
All arts must try, and every toil sustain.

FRANCIS.

It is observed by BACON, that "reading makes a full man, conversation a ready man, and writing an exact man."

As BACON attained to degrees of knowledge scarcely ever reached by any other man, the directions which he gives for study, have certainly a just claim to our regard; for who can teach an art with so great authority, as he that has practised it with undisputed success?

Under the protection of so great a name, I shall, therefore, venture to inculcate to my ingenious contemporaries, the necessity of reading, the fitness of consulting other understandings than their own, and of considering the sentiments and opinions of those who, however neglected in the present age, had in their own times, and many of them a long time afterwards, such reputation for knowledge and acuteness, as will scarcely ever be attained by those that despise them.

An opinion has of late been, I know not how, propagated among us, that libraries are filled only with useless lumber; that men of parts stand in need of no assistance; and that to spend life in poring upon books, is only to imbibe prejudices, to obstruct and embarrass the powers of nature, to cultivate memory at the expence of judgement, and to bury reason under a chaos of indigested learning.

Such is the talk of many who think themselves wise, and of some who are thought wise by others; of whom part probably believe their own tenets, and part may be justly suspected of endeavouring to shelter their ignorance in multitudes, and of wishing to destroy that reputation which they have no hopes to share. It will, I believe, be found invariably true, that learning was never decried by any learned man; and what credit can be given to those, who venture to condemn that which they do not know?

If reason has the power ascribed to it by its advocates, if so much is to be discovered by attention and meditation, it is hard to believe, that so many millions, equally participating of the bounties of nature with ourselves, have been for ages upon ages meditating in vain: if the wits of the present time expect the regard of posterity, which will then inherit the reason which is now thought superior to instruction, surely they may allow themselves to be instructed by the reason of former generations. When, therefore, an author declares, that he has been able to learn nothing from the writings of his predecessors, and such a declaration has been lately made, nothing but a degree of arrogance unpardonable in the greatest human understanding, can hinder him from perceiving, that he is raising prejudices against his own performance; for with what hopes of success can he attempt that in which greater abilities have hitherto miscarried? or with what peculiar force does he suppose himself invigorated, that difficulties hitherto invincible should give way before him?

Of those whom PROVIDENCE has qualified to make any additions to human knowledge, the number is extremely small; and what can be added by each single mind, even of this superior class, is very little: the greatest part of mankind must owe all their knowledge, and all must owe far the larger part of it, to the information of others. To understand the works of celebrated authors, to comprehend their systems, and retain their reasonings, is a task more than equal to common intellects; and he is by no means to be accounted useless or idle, who has stored his mind with acquired knowledge, and can detail it occasionally to others who have less leisure or weaker abilities.

PERSIUS has justly observed, that knowledge is nothing to him who is not known by others to possess it: to the scholar himself it is nothing with respect either to honour or advantage, for the world cannot reward those qualities which are concealed from it; with respect to others it is nothing, because it affords no help to ignorance or error.

It is with justice, therefore, that in an accomplished character, HORACE unites just sentiments with the power of expressing them; and he that has once accumulated learning, is next to consider, how he shall most widely diffuse and most agreeably impart it.

A ready man is made by conversation. He that buries himself among his manuscripts "besprent," as POPE expresses it, "with learned dust," and wears out his days and nights in perpetual research and solitary meditation, is too apt to lose in his elocution what he adds to his wisdom, and when he comes into the world, to appear overloaded with his own notions, like a man armed with weapons which he cannot wield. He has no facility of inculcating his speculations, of adapting himself to the various degrees of intellect which the accidents of conversation will present; but will talk to most unintelligibly, and to all unpleasantly.

I was once present at the lectures of a profound philosopher, a man really skilled in the science which he professed, who having occasion to explain the terms OPACUM and PELLUCIDUM, told us, after some hesitation, that OPACUM was as one might say OPAKE, and that PELLUCIDUM signified PELLUCID. Such was the dexterity, with which this learned reader facilitated to his auditors the intricacies of science; and so true is it, that a man may know what he cannot teach.

BOERHAAVE complains, that the writers who have treated of chemistry before him, are useless to the greater part of students; because they presuppose their readers to have such degrees of skill as are not often to be found. Into the same error are all men apt to fall, who have familiarized any subject to themselves in solitude: they discourse, as if they thought every other man had been employed in the same inquiries; and expect that short hints and obscure allusions will produce in others, the same train of ideas which they excite in themselves.

Nor is this the only inconvenience which the man of study suffers from a recluse life. When he meets with an opinion that pleases him, he catches it up with eagerness; looks only after such arguments as tend to his confirmation; or spares himself the trouble of discussion, and adopts it with very little proof; indulges it long without suspicion, and in time unites it to the general body of his knowledge, and treasures it up among incontestible truths: but when he comes into the world among men who, arguing upon dissimilar principles, have been led to different conclusions, and being placed in various situations view the same object on many sides; he finds his darling position attacked, and himself in no condition to defend it: having thought always in one train, he is in the state of a man who having fenced always with the same master, is perplexed and amazed by a new posture of his antagonist; he is entangled in unexpected difficulties, he is harrassed by sudden objections, he is unprovided with solutions or replies, his surprize impedes his natural powers of reasoning, his thoughts are scattered and confounded, and he gratifies the pride of airy petulance with an easy victory.

It is difficult to imagine, with what obstinacy truths which one mind perceives almost by intuition, will be rejected by another; and how many artifices must be practised, to procure admission for the most evident propositions into understandings frighted by their novelty, or hardened against them by accidental prejudice: it can scarcely be conceived, how frequently in these extemporaneous controversies, the dull will be subtle, and the acute absurd; how often stupidity will elude the force of argument, by involving itself in its own gloom; and mistaken ingenuity will weave artful fallacies, which reason can scarcely find means to disentangle.

In these encounters the learning of the recluse usually fails him: nothing but long habit and frequent experiments can confer the power of changing a position into various forms, presenting it in different points of view, connecting it with known and granted truths, fortifying it with intelligible arguments, and illustrating it by apt similitudes; and he, therefore, that has collected his knowledge in solitude, must learn its application by mixing with mankind.

But while the various opportunities of conversation invite us to try every mode of argument, and every art of recommending our sentiments, we are frequently betrayed to the use of such as are not in themselves strictly defensible: a man heated in talk, and eager of victory, takes advantage of the mistakes or ignorance of his adversary, lays hold of concessions to which he knows he has no right, and urges proofs likely to prevail on his opponent, though he knows himself that they have no force: thus the severity of reason is relaxed; many topics are accumulated, but without just arrangement or distinction; we learn to satisfy ourselves with such ratiocination as silences others; and seldom recall to a close examination, that discourse which has gratified our vanity with victory and applause.

Some caution, therefore, must be used, lest copiousness and facility be made less valuable by inaccuracy and confusion. To fix the thoughts by writing, and subject them to frequent examinations and reviews, is the best method of enabling the mind to detect its own sophisms, and keep it on guard against the fallacies which it practices on others: in conversation we naturally diffuse our thoughts, and in writing we contract them; method is the excellence of writing, and unconstraint the grace of conversation.

To read, write, and converse in due proportions, is, therefore, the business of a man of letters. For all these there is not often equal opportunity;

excellence, therefore, is not often attainable; and most men fail in one or other of the ends proposed, and are full without readiness, or ready without exactness. Some deficiency must be forgiven all, because all are men; and more must be allowed to pass uncensured in the greater part of the world, because none can confer upon himself abilities, and few have the choice of situations proper for the improvement of those which nature has bestowed: it is, however, reasonable, to have PERFECTION in our eye; that we may always advance towards it, though we know it never can be reached.

T

No. 95. Tuesday, 2 October 1753.

—— *Dulcique animos novitate tenebo.*
OVID.

And with sweet novelty your soul detain.

It is often charged upon writers, that with all their pretensions to genius and discoveries, they do little more than copy one another; and that compositions obtruded upon the world with the pomp of novelty, contain only tedious repetitions of common sentiments, or at best exhibit a transposition of known images, and give a new appearance to truth only by some slight difference of dress and decoration.

The allegation of resemblance between authors, is indisputably true; but the charge of plagiarism, which is raised upon it, is not to be allowed with equal readiness. A coincidence of sentiment may easily happen without any communication, since there are many occasions in which all reasonable men will nearly think alike. Writers of all ages have had the same sentiments, because they have in all ages had the same objects of speculation; the interests and passions, the virtues and vices of mankind, have been diversified in different times, only by unessential and casual varieties; and we must, therefore, expect in the works of all those who attempt to describe them, such a likeness as we find in the pictures of the same person drawn in different periods of his life.

It is necessary, therefore, that before an author be charged with plagiarism, one of the most reproachful, though, perhaps, not the most atrocious of literary crimes, the subject on which he treats should be carefully considered. We do not wonder, that historians, relating the same facts, agree in their narration; or that authors, delivering the elements of science, advance the same theorems, and lay down the same definitions: yet it is not wholly without use to mankind, that books are multiplied, and that different authors lay out their labours on the same subject; for there will always be some reason why one should on particular occasions, or to particular persons, be preferable to another; some will be clear where others are obscure, some will please by their stile and others by their method, some by their embellishments and others by their simplicity, some by closeness and others by diffusion.

The same indulgence is to be shewn to the writers of morality: right and wrong are immutable; and those, therefore, who teach us to distinguish them, if they all teach us right, must agree with one another. The relations of social life, and the duties resulting from them, must be the same at all times and in all nations: some petty differences may be, indeed, produced, by forms of government or arbitrary customs; but the general doctrine can receive no alteration.

Yet it is not to be desired, that morality should be considered as interdicted to all future writers: men will always be tempted to deviate from their duty, and will, therefore, always want a monitor to recall them; and a new book often seizes the attention of the public, without any other claim than that it is new. There is likewise in composition, as in other things, a perpetual vicissitude of fashion; and truth is recommended at one time to regard, by appearances which at another would expose it to neglect; the author, therefore, who has judgement to discern the taste of his contemporaries, and skill to gratify it, will have always an opportunity to deserve well of mankind, by conveying instruction to them in a grateful vehicle.

There are likewise many modes of composition, by which a moralist may deserve the name of an original writer: he may familiarise his system by dialogues after the manner of the ancients, or subtilize it into a series of syllogistic arguments; he may enforce his doctrine by seriousness and solemnity, or enliven it by sprightliness and gayety; he may deliver his sentiments in naked precepts, or illustrate them by historical examples; he may detain the studious by the artful concatenation of a continued discourse, or relieve the busy by short strictures and unconnected essays.

To excel in any of these forms of writing, will require a particular cultivation of the genius; whoever can attain to excellence, will be certain to engage a set of readers, whom no other method would have equally allured; and he that communicates truth with success, must be numbered among the first benefactors to mankind.

The same observation may be extended likewise to the passions: their influence is uniform, and their effects nearly the same in every human breast: a man loves and hates, desires and avoids, exactly like his neighbour; resentment and ambition, avarice and indolence, discover themselves by the same symptoms, in minds distant a thousand years from one another.

Nothing, therefore, can be more unjust, than to charge an author with plagiarism, merely because he assigns to every cause its natural effect; and makes his personages act, as others in like circumstances have always done. There are conceptions in which all men will agree, though each derives them from his own observation: whoever has been in love, will represent a lover impatient of every idea that interrupts his meditations on his mistress, retiring to shades and solitude that he may muse without disturbance on his approaching happiness, or associating himself with some friend that flatters his passion, and talking away the hours of absence upon his darling subject. Whoever has been so unhappy as to have felt the miseries of long continued hatred, will, without any assistance from antient volumes, be able to relate how the passions are kept in perpetual agitation, by the recollection of injury and meditations of revenge; how the blood boils at the name of the enemy, and life is worn away in contrivances of mischief.

Every other passion is alike simple and limited, if it be considered only with regard to the breast which it inhabits: the anatomy of the mind, as that of the body, must perpetually exhibit the same appearances; and though by the continued industry of successive inquirers, new movements will be from time to time discovered, they can affect only the minuter parts, and are commonly of more curiosity than importance.

It will now be natural to inquire, by what arts are the writers of the present and future ages to attract the notice and favour of mankind. They are to observe the alterations which time is always making in the modes of life, that they may gratify every generation with a picture of themselves. Thus love is uniform, but courtship is perpetually varying: the different arts of gallantry, which beauty has inspired, would of themselves be sufficient to fill a volume; sometimes balls and serenades, sometimes tournaments and adventures have been employed to melt the hearts of ladies, who in another century have been sensible of scarce any other merit than that of riches, and listened only to jointures and pin-money. Thus the ambitious man has at all times been eager of wealth and power; but these hopes have been gratified in some countries by supplicating the people, and in others by flattering the prince: honour in some states has been only the reward of military achievements, in others it has been gained by noisy turbulence and popular clamours. Avarice has worn a different form, as she actuated the usurer of Rome, and the stock-jobber of England; and idleness itself, how little soever inclined to the trouble of invention, has been forced from time to time to change its amusements, and contrive different methods of wearing out the day.

Here then is the fund, from which those who study mankind may fill their compositions with an inexhaustible variety of images and allusions; and he must be confessed to look with little attention upon scenes thus perpetually changing, who cannot catch some of the figures before they are made vulgar by reiterated descriptions.

It has been discovered by Sir ISAAC NEWTON, that the distinct and primogenial colours are only seven; but every eye can witness, that from various mixtures in various proportions, infinite diversifications of tints may be produced. In like manner, the passions of the mind, which put the world in motion, and produce all the bustle and eagerness of the busy crouds that swarm upon the earth; the passions, from whence arise all the pleasures and pains that we see and hear of, if we analyze the mind of man, are very few; but those few agitated and combined, as external causes shall happen to operate, and modified by prevailing opinions and accidental caprices, make such frequent alterations on the surface of life, that the show while we are busied in delineating it, vanishes from the view, and a new set of objects succeeds, doomed to the same shortness of duration with the former: thus curiosity may always find employment, and the busy part of mankind will furnish the contemplative with the materials of speculation to the end of time.

The complaint, therefore, that all topics are preoccupied, is nothing more than the murmur of ignorance or idleness, by which some discourage others and some themselves: the mutability of mankind will always furnish writers with new images, and the luxuriance of fancy may always embellish them with new decorations.

T

No. 99. Tuesday, 16 October 1753.

——*Magnis tamen excidit ausis.*
Ovid.

But in the glorious enterprize he dy'd.
Addison.

It has always been the practice of mankind, to judge of actions by the event. The same attempts, conducted in the same manner, but terminated by different success, produce different judgments: they who attain their wishes, never want celebrators of their wisdom and their virtue; and they that miscarry, are quickly discovered to have been defective not only in mental but in moral qualities. The world will never be long without some good reason to hate the unhappy; their real faults are immediately detected, and if those are not sufficient to sink them into infamy, an additional weight of calumny will be superadded: he that fails in his endeavours after wealth or power, will not long retain either honesty or courage.

This species of injustice has so long prevailed in universal practice, that it seems likewise to have infected speculation: so few minds are able to separate the ideas of greatness and prosperity, that even Sir WILLIAM TEMPLE has determined, that "he who can deserve the name of a hero, must not only be virtuous but fortunate."

By this unreasonable distribution of praise and blame, none have suffered oftener than PROJECTORS, whose rapidity of imagination and vastness of design, raise such envy in their fellow mortals, that every eye watches for their fall, and every heart exults at their distresses: yet even a PROJECTOR may gain favour by success; and the tongue that was prepared to hiss, then endeavours to excell others in loudness of applause.

When CORIOLANUS, in SHAKESPEARE, deserted to AUFIDIUS, the Volscian servants at first insulted him, even while he stood under the protection of the houshold Gods: but when they saw that the PROJECT took effect, and the stranger was seated at the head of the table, one of them very judiciously observes, "that he always thought there was more in him than he could think."

MACHIAVEL has justly animadverted on the different notice taken by all succeeding times, of the two great projectors CATILINE and CÆSAR. Both formed the same PROJECT, and intended to raise themselves to power, by subverting the commonwealth: they persued their design, perhaps, with equal abilities, and with equal virtue; but CATILINE perished in the field, and CÆSAR returned from Pharsalia with unlimited authority: and from that time, every monarch of the earth has thought himself honoured by a comparison with CÆSAR; and CATILINE has been never mentioned, but that his name might be applied to traitors and incendiaries.

In an age more remote, XERXES projected the conquest of Greece, and brought down the power of Asia against it: but after the world had been filled with expectation and terror, his army was beaten, his fleet was destroyed, and XERXES has been never mentioned without contempt.

A few years afterwards, Greece likewise had her turn of giving birth to a PROJECTOR; who invading Asia with a small army, went forward in search of adventures, and by his escape from one danger gained only more rashness to rush into another: he stormed city after city, over-ran kingdom after kingdom, fought battles only for barren victory, and invaded nations only that he might make his way through them to new invasions: but having been fortunate in the execution of his projects, he died with the name of ALEXANDER the GREAT.

These are, indeed, events of ancient time; but human nature is always the same, and every age will afford us instances of public censures influenced by events. The great business of the middle centuries, was the holy war; which undoubtedly was a noble PROJECT, and was for a long time prosecuted with a spirit equal to that with which it had been contrived: but the ardour of the European heroes only hurried them to destruction; for a long time they could not gain the territories for which they fought, and, when at last gained, they could not keep them: their expeditions, therefore, have been the scoff of idleness and ignorance, their understanding and their virtue have been equally vilified, their conduct has been ridiculed, and their cause has been defamed.

When COLUMBUS had engaged King Ferdinand in the discovery of the other hemisphere, the sailors with whom he embarked in the expedition had so little confidence in their commander, that after having been long at sea looking for coasts which they expected never to find, they raised a general mutiny, and demanded to return. He found means to sooth them into a permission to continue the same course three days longer, and on the evening of the third day descried land. Had the impatience of his crew denied him a few hours of the time requested, what had been his fate but to have come back with the infamy of a vain PROJECTOR, who had betrayed the king's credulity to useless expences, and risked his life in seeking countries that had no existence? how would those that had rejected his proposals, have triumphed in their acuteness? and when would his name have been mentioned, but with the makers of potable gold and malleable glass?

The last royal PROJECTORS with whom the world has been troubled, were CHARLES of SWEDEN and the CZAR of MUSCOVY. CHARLES, if any judgement may be formed of his designs by his measures and his enquiries, had purposed first to dethrone the CZAR, then to lead his army through pathless desarts into China, thence to make his way by the sword through the whole circuit of Asia, and by the conquest of Turkey to unite Sweden with his new dominions: but this mighty PROJECT was crushed at Pultowa, and CHARLES has since been considered as a madman by those powers, who sent their embassadors to sollicit his friendship, and their generals "to learn under him the art of war."

The CZAR found employment sufficient in his own dominions, and amused himself in digging canals, and building cities; murdering his subjects with insufferable fatigues, and transplanting nations from one corner of his dominions to another, without regretting the thousands that perished on the way: but he attained his end, he made his people formidable, and is numbered by fame among the Demi-gods.

I am far from intending to vindicate the sanguinary projects of heroes and conquerors, and would wish rather to diminish the reputation of their success, than the infamy of their miscarriages: for I cannot conceive, why he that has burnt cities, and wasted nations, and filled the world with horror and desolation, should be more kindly regarded by mankind, than he that died in the rudiments of wickedness; why he that accomplished mischief should be glorious, and he that only endeavoured it should be criminal: I would wish CÆSAR and CATILINE, XERXES and ALEXANDER, CHARLES and PETER, huddled together in obscurity or detestation.

But there is another species of PROJECTORS, to whom I would willingly conciliate mankind; whose ends are generally laudable, and whose labours are innocent; who are searching out new powers of nature, or contriving new works of art; but who are yet persecuted with incessant obloquy, and whom the universal contempt with which they are treated, often debars from that success which their industry would obtain, if it were permitted to act without opposition.

They who find themselves inclined to censure new undertakings, only because they are new, should consider, that the folly of PROJECTION is very seldom the folly of a fool; it is commonly the ebullition of a capacious mind, crouded with variety of knowledge, and heated with intenseness of thought; it proceeds often from the consciousness of uncommon powers, from the confidence of those, who having already done much, are easily persuaded that they can do more: when ROWLEY had completed the Orrery, he attempted the perpetual motion; when BOYLE had exhausted the secrets of vulgar chemistry, he turned his thoughts to the work of transmutation.

A PROJECTOR generally unites those qualities which have the fairest claim to veneration, extent of knowledge and greatness of design: it was said of CATILINE, "immoderata, incredibilia, nimis alta semper cupiebat." Projectors of all kinds agree in their intellects, though they differ in their morals; they all fail by attempting things beyond their power, by despising vulgar attainments, and aspiring to performances, to which, perhaps, nature has not proportioned the force of man: when they fail, therefore, they fail not by idleness or timidity, but by rash adventure and fruitless diligence.

That the attempts of such men will often miscarry, we may reasonably expect; yet from such men, and such only, are we to hope for the cultivation of those parts of nature which lie yet waste, and the invention of those arts which are yet wanting to the felicity of life. If they are, therefore, universally discouraged, art and discovery can make no advances. Whatever is attempted without previous certainty of success, may be considered as a PROJECT, and amongst narrow minds may, therefore, expose its author to censure and contempt; and if the liberty of laughing be once indulged, every man will laugh at what he does not understand, every PROJECT will be considered as madness, and every great or new design will be censured as a PROJECT. Men, unaccustomed to reason and researches, think every enterprise impracticable, which is extended beyond common effects, or comprises many intermediate operations. Many that presume to laugh at PROJECTORS, would consider a flight through the air in a winged chariot, and the movement of a mighty engine by the steam of water, as equally the dreams of mechanic lunacy; and would hear, with equal negligence, of the union of the Thames and Severn by a canal, and the scheme of Albuquerque the viceroy of the Indies, who in the rage of hostility had contrived to make Egypt a barren desart, by turning the Nile into the Red Sea.

Those who have attempted much, have seldom failed to perform more than those who never deviated from the common roads of action: many valuable preparations of chemistry, are supposed to have risen from unsuccessful enquiries after the grand elixir; it is, therefore, just to encourage those who endeavour to enlarge the power of art, since they often succeed beyond expectation; and when they fail, may sometimes benefit the world even by their miscarriages.

T

No. 102. Saturday, 27 October 1753.

——*Quid tam dextro pede concipis, ut te*
Conatus non pœniteat votique peracti?
                                                  Juv.

What in the conduct of our life appears
So well design'd, so luckily begun,
But, when we have our wish, we wish undone.
                                          Dryden.

To the Adventurer.

SIR,

I have been for many years a trader in London. My beginning was narrow,
and my stock small; I was, therefore, a long time brow-beaten and despised by
those, who having more money thought they had more merit than myself.
I did not, however, suffer my resentment to instigate me to any mean arts of
supplantation, nor my eagerness of riches to betray me to any indirect methods
of gain; I persued my business with incessant assiduity, supported by the
hope of being one day richer than those who contemned me; and had upon
every annual review of my books, the satisfaction of finding my fortune
increased beyond my expectation.

In a few years my industry and probity were fully recompensed, my wealth
was really great, and my reputation for wealth still greater. I had large warehouses crouded with goods, and considerable sums in the public funds; I was
caressed upon the Exchange by the most eminent merchants; became the
oracle of the common council; was sollicited to engage in all commercial
undertakings; was flattered with the hopes of becoming in a short time one of
the directors of a wealthy company; and to complete my mercantile honours
enjoyed the expensive happiness of fining for Sheriff.

Riches, you know, easily produce riches: when I had arrived to this degree
of wealth, I had no longer any obstruction or opposition to fear; new acquisitions were hourly brought within my reach, and I continued for some years
longer to heap thousands upon thousands.

At last I resolved to complete the circle of a citizen's prosperity by the purchase of an estate in the country, and to close my life in retirement. From the
hour that this design entered my imagination, I found the fatigues of my
employment every day more oppressive, and persuaded myself that I was no
longer equal to perpetual attention, and that my health would soon be destroyed by the torment and distraction of extensive business. I could image to
myself no happiness, but in vacant jollity, and uninterrupted leisure; nor
entertain my friends with any other topic, than the vexation and uncertainty
of trade, and the happiness of rural privacy.

But notwithstanding these declarations, I could not at once reconcile myself to the thoughts of ceasing to get money; and though I was every day enquiring for a purchase, I found some reason for rejecting all that were offered me; and, indeed, had accumulated so many beauties and conveniencies in my idea of the spot, where I was finally to be happy, that, perhaps, the world might have been travelled over, without discovery of a place which would not have been defective in some particular.

Thus I went on still talking of retirement, and still refusing to retire; my friends began to laugh at my delays, and I grew ashamed to trifle longer with my own inclinations: an estate was at length purchased, I transferred my stock to a prudent young man who had married my daughter, went down into the country, and commenced lord of a spacious manor.

Here for some time I found happiness equal to my expectation. I reformed the old house according to the advice of the best architects, I threw down the walls of the garden and inclosed it with palisades, planted long avenues of trees, filled a greenhouse with exotic plants, dug a new canal, and threw the earth into the old moat.

The fame of these expensive improvements brought in all the country to see the show. I entertained my visitors with great liberality, led them round my gardens, shewed them my apartments, laid before them plans for new decorations, and was gratified by the wonder of some and the envy of others.

I was envied; but how little can one man judge of the condition of another? The time was now coming, in which affluence and splendor could no longer make me pleased with myself. I had built till the imagination of the architect was exhausted; I had added one convenience to another till I knew not what more to wish or to design; I had laid out my gardens, planted my park, and compleated my water-works; and what now remained to be done? what, but to look up to turrets of which when they were once raised I had no farther use, to range over apartments where time was tarnishing the furniture, to stand by the cascade of which I scarcely now perceived the sound, and to watch the growth of woods that must give their shade to a distant generation.

In this gloomy inactivity, is every day begun and ended; the happiness that I have been so long procuring is now at an end, because it has been procured; I wander from room to room till I am weary of myself; I ride out to a neighbouring hill in the centre of my estate, from whence all my lands lie in prospect round me; I see nothing that I have not seen before, and return home disappointed, though I knew that I had nothing to expect.

In my happy days of business I had been accustomed to rise early in the morning, and remember the time when I grieved that the night came so soon upon me, and obliged me for a few hours to shut out affluence and prosperity. I now seldom see the rising sun, but "to tell him," with the fallen angel, "how I hate his beams." I awake from sleep as to languor or imprisonment, and have no employment for the first hour but to consider by what art I shall rid myself of the second. I protract the breakfast as long as I can, because when it is ended I have no call for my attention, till I can with some degree of decency grow impatient for my dinner. If I could dine all my life, I should be happy: I eat not because I am hungry, but because I am idle: but alas! the time quickly comes when I can eat no longer; and so ill does my constitution second my inclination, that I cannot bear strong liquors: seven hours must then be endured before I shall sup; but supper comes at last, the more welcome as it is in a short time succeeded by sleep.

Such, MR. ADVENTURER, is the happiness, the hope of which seduced me from the duties and pleasures of a mercantile life. I shall be told by those who read my narrative, that there are many means of innocent amusement, and many schemes of useful employment which I do not appear ever to have known; and that nature and art have provided pleasures, by which, without the drudgery of settled business, the active may be engaged, the solitary soothed, and the social entertained.

These arts, Sir, I have tried. When first I took possession of my estate, in conformity to the taste of my neighbours, I bought guns and nets, filled my kennel with dogs and my stable with horses; but a little experience shewed me, that these instruments of rural felicity would afford me few gratifications. I never shot but to miss the mark, and, to confess the truth, was afraid of the fire of my own gun. I could discover no music in the cry of the dogs, nor could divest myself of pity for the animal whose peaceful and inoffensive life was sacrificed to our sport: I was not, indeed, always at leisure to reflect upon her danger; for my horse, who had been bred to the chace, did not always regard my choice either of speed or way, but leaped hedges and ditches at his own discretion, and hurried me along with the dogs, to the great diversion of my brother sportsmen: his eagerness of persuit once incited him to swim a river; and I had leisure to resolve in the water, that I would never hazard my life again for the destruction of a hare.

I then ordered books to be procured, and by the direction of the vicar had in a few weeks a closet elegantly furnished. You will, perhaps, be surprized when I shall tell you, that when once I had ranged them according to their sizes, and piled them up in regular gradations, I had received all the pleasure which they could give me. I am not able to excite in myself any curiosity after events which have been long passed, and in which I can, therefore, have no interest: I am utterly unconcerned to know whether TULLY or DEMOSTHENES excelled in oratory, whether HANNIBAL lost Italy by his own negligence or the corruption of his countrymen. I have no skill in controversial learning, nor can conceive why so many volumes should have been written upon questions, which I have lived so long and so happily without understanding. I once resolved to go through the volumes relating to the office of justice of the peace, but found them so crabbed and intricate, that in less than a month I desisted in despair, and resolved to supply my deficiencies by paying a competent salary to a skillful clerk.

I am naturally inclined to hospitality, and for some time kept up a constant intercourse of visits with the neighbouring gentlemen; but though they are easily brought about me by better wine than they can find at any other house, I am not much relieved by their conversation; they have no skill in commerce or the stocks, and I have no knowledge of the history of families or the factions of the county; so that when the first civilities are over, they usually talk to one another, and I am left alone in the midst of the company. Though I cannot drink myself, I am obliged to encourage the circulation of the glass; their mirth grows more turbulent and obstreperous, and before their merriment is at an end, I am sick with disgust, and, perhaps, reproached with my sobriety, or by some sly insinuations insulted as a cit.

Such, Mr. ADVENTURER, is the life to which I am condemned by a foolish endeavour to be happy by imitation; such is the happiness to which I pleased myself with approaching, and which I considered as the chief end of my cares and my labours. I toiled year after year with chearfulness, in expectation of the happy hour in which I might be idle; the privilege of idleness is attained, but has not brought with it the blessing of tranquillity.

I am,

Yours, &c.

MERCATOR.

T

No. 107. Tuesday, 13 November 1753.

——*Sub judice lis est.*

HOR.

And of their vain disputings find no end.

FRANCIS.

It has been sometimes asked by those, who find the appearance of wisdom more easily attained by questions than solutions, how it comes to pass, that the world is divided by such difference of opinion; and why men, equally reasonable, and equally lovers of truth, do not always think in the same manner.

With regard to simple propositions, where the terms are understood, and the whole subject is comprehended at once, there is such an uniformity of sentiment among all human beings, that, for many ages, a very numerous set of notions were supposed to be innate, or necessarily coexistent with the faculty of reason; it being imagined, that universal agreement could proceed only from the invariable dictates of the universal parent.

In questions diffuse and compounded, this similarity of determination is no longer to be expected. At our first sally into the intellectual world, we all march together along one strait and open road; but as we proceed further, and wider prospects open to our view, every eye fixes upon a different scene; we divide into various paths, and, as we move forward, are still at a greater distance from each other. As a question becomes more complicated and involved, and extends to a greater number of relations, disagreement of opinion will always be multiplied; not because we are irrational, but because we are finite beings, furnished with different kinds of knowledge, exerting different degrees of attention, one discovering consequences which escape another, none taking in the whole concatenation of causes and effects, and most comprehending but a very small part, each comparing what he observes with a different criterion, and each referring it to a different purpose.

Where, then, is the wonder, that they, who see only a small part, should judge erroneously of the whole? or that they, who see different and dissimilar parts, should judge differently from each other?

Whatever has various respects, must have various appearances of good and evil, beauty or deformity: thus, the gardener tears up as a weed, the plant which the physician gathers as a medicine; and "a general," says Sir KENELM DIGBY, "will look with pleasure over a plain, as a fit place on which the fate of empires might be decided in battle; which the farmer will despise as bleak and barren, neither fruitful of pasturage, nor fit for tillage."

Two men examining the same question, proceed commonly like the physician and gardener in selecting herbs, or the farmer and hero looking on the plain; they bring minds impressed with different notions, and direct their inquiries to different ends; they form, therefore, contrary conclusions, and each wonders at the other's absurdity.

We have less reason to be surprised or offended when we find others differ from us in opinion, because we very often differ from ourselves: how often we alter our minds, we do not always remark; because the change is sometimes made imperceptibly and gradually, and the last conviction effaces all memory of the former: yet every man, accustomed from time to time to take a survey of his own notions, will by a slight retrospection be able to discover, that his mind has suffered many revolutions, that the same things have in the several parts of his life been condemned and approved, persued and shunned; and that on many occasions, even when his practice has been steddy, his mind has been wavering, and he has persisted in a scheme of action, rather because he feared the censure of inconstancy, than because he was always pleased with his own choice.

Of the different faces shewn by the same objects as they are viewed on opposite sides, and of the different inclinations which they must constantly raise in him that contemplates them, a more striking example cannot easily be found than two Greek Epigrammatists will afford us in their accounts of human life, which I shall lay before the reader in English prose.

POSIDIPPUS, a comic poet, utters this complaint; "Through which of the paths of life is it eligible to pass? In public assemblies are debates and troublesome affairs; domestic privacies are haunted with anxieties; in the country is labour; on the sea is terror; in a foreign land, he that has money must live in fear, he that wants it must pine in distress; are you married? you are troubled with suspicions; are you single? you languish in solitude; children occasion toil, and a childless life is a state of destitution; the time of youth is a time of folly, and grey hairs are loaded with infirmity. This choice only, therefore, can be made, either never to receive being, or immediately to lose it."

Such and so gloomy is the prospect, which POSIDIPPUS has laid before us. But we are not to acquiesce too hastily in his determination against the value of existence, for METRODORUS, a philosopher of Athens, has shewn, that life has pleasures as well as pains; and having exhibited the present state of man in brighter colours, draws, with equal appearance of reason, a contrary conclusion:

"You may pass well through any of the paths of life. In public assemblies are honours, and transactions of wisdom; in domestic privacy, is stilness and quiet; in the country are the beauties of nature; on the sea is the hope of gain; in a foreign land, he that is rich is honoured, he that is poor may keep his poverty secret; are you married? you have a chearful house; are you single? you are unincumbered; children are objects of affection; to be without children is to be without care; the time of youth is the time of vigour; and grey hairs are made venerable by piety. It will, therefore, never be a wise man's choice, either not to obtain existence, or to lose it; for every state of life has its felicity."

In these epigrams are included most of the questions, which have engaged the speculations of the enquirers after happiness; and though they will not much assist our determinations, they may, perhaps, equally promote our quiet, by shewing that no absolute determination ever can be formed.

Whether a public station, or private life be desirable, has always been debated. We see here both the allurements and discouragements of civil employments; on one side there is trouble, on the other honour; the management of affairs is vexatious and difficult, but it is the only duty in which wisdom can be conspicuously displayed: it must then still be left to every man to chuse either ease or glory; nor can any general precept be given, since no man can be happy by the prescription of another.

Thus what is said of children by POSIDIPPUS, "that they are occasions of fatigue," and by METRODORUS, "that they are objects of affection," is equally certain; but whether they will give most pain or pleasure, must depend on their future conduct and dispositions, on many causes over which the parent can have little influence: there is, therefore, room for all the caprices of imagination, and desire must be proportioned to the hope or fear that shall happen to predominate.

Such is the uncertainty, in which we are always likely to remain with regard to questions, wherein we have most interest, and which every day affords us fresh opportunity to examine: we may examine, indeed, but we never can decide, because our faculties are unequal to the subject: we see a little, and form an opinion; we see more, and change it.

This inconstancy and unsteadiness, to which we must so often find ourselves liable, ought certainly to teach us moderation and forbearance towards those, who cannot accommodate themselves to our sentiments: if they are deceived, we have no right to attribute their mistake to obstinacy or negligence, because we likewise have been mistaken: we may, perhaps, again change our own opinion; and what excuse shall we be able to find for aversion and malignity conceived against him, whom we shall then find to have committed no fault, and who offended us only by refusing to follow us into error.

It may likewise contribute to soften that resentment, which pride naturally raises against opposition, if we consider, that he, who differs from us, does not always contradict us; he has one view of an object, and we have another; each describes what he sees with equal fidelity, and each regulates his steps by his own eyes: one man, with POSIDIPPUS, looks on celibacy as a state of gloomy solitude, without a partner in joy or a comforter in sorrow; the other considers it, with METRODORUS, as a state free from incumbrances, in which a man is at liberty to chuse his own gratifications, to remove from place to place in quest of pleasure, and to think of nothing but merriment and diversion; full of these notions, one hastens to chuse a wife, and the other laughs at his rashness, or pities his ignorance; yet it is possible that each is right, but that each is right only for himself.

Life is not the object of science: we see a little, very little; and what is beyond we only can conjecture. If we enquire of those who have gone before us, we receive small satisfaction; some have travelled life without observation, and some willingly mislead us. The only thought, therefore, on which we can repose with comfort, is that which presents to us the care of PROVIDENCE, whose eye takes in the whole of things, and under whose direction all involuntary errors will terminate in happiness.

T

No. 111. Tuesday, 27 November 1753.

——*Quæ non fecimus ipsi,*
Vix ea nostra voco.
                                                    OVID.

The deeds of long descended ancestors
Are but by grace of imputation ours.
                                                    DRYDEN.

The evils inseparably annexed to the present condition of man, are so numerous and afflictive, that it has been, from age to age, the task of some to bewail, and of others to solace them: and he, therefore, will be in danger of seeming a common enemy, who shall attempt to depreciate the few pleasures and felicities which nature has allowed us.

Yet I will confess, that I have sometimes employed my thoughts in examining the pretensions that are made to happiness, by the splendid and envied conditions of life; and have not thought the hour unprofitably spent, when I have detected the imposture of counterfeit advantages, and found disquiet lurking under false appearances of gayety and greatness.

It is asserted by a tragic poet, that "est miser nemo nisi comparatus," "no man is miserable, but as he is compared with others happier than himself:" this position is not strictly and philosophically true. He might have said, with rigorous propriety, that no man is happy, but as he is compared with the miserable; for such is the state of this world, that we find in it absolute misery, but happiness only comparative; we may incur as much pain as we can possibly endure, though we can never obtain as much happiness as we might possibly enjoy.

Yet it is certain likewise, that many of our miseries are merely comparative: we are often made unhappy, not by the presence of any real evil, but by the absence of some fictitious good; of something which is not required by any real want of nature, which has not in itself any power of gratification, and which neither reason nor fancy would have prompted us to wish, did we not see it in the possession of others.

For a mind diseased with vain longings after unattainable advantages, no medicine can be prescribed, but an impartial enquiry into the real worth of that which is so ardently desired. It is well known, how much the mind, as well as the eye, is deceived by distance; and, perhaps, it will be found, that of many imagined blessings it may be doubted, whether he that wants or possesses them has more reason to be satisfied with his lot.

The dignity of high birth and long extraction, no man, to whom nature has denied it, can confer upon himself; and, therefore, it deserves to be considered, whether the want of that which can never be gained, may not easily be endured. It is true, that if we consider the triumph and delight with which most of those recount their ancestors who have ancestors to recount, and the artifices by which some who have risen to unexpected fortune endeavour to insert themselves into an honourable stem, we shall be inclined to fancy, that wisdom or virtue may be had by inheritance, or that all the excellencies of a line of progenitors are accumulated on their descendant. Reason, indeed, will soon inform us, that our estimation of birth is arbitrary and capricious, and that dead ancestors can have no influence but upon imagination: let it then be examined, whether one dream may not operate in the place of another; whether he that owes nothing to fore-fathers, may not receive equal pleasure

474 'DICTIONARY' JOHNSON

from the consciousness of owing all to himself; whether he may not, with a little meditation, find it more honourable to found than to continue a family, and to gain dignity than transmit it; whether, if he receives no dignity from the virtues of his family, he does not likewise escape the danger of being disgraced by their crimes; and whether he that brings a new name into the world, has not the convenience of playing the game of life without a stake, an opportunity of winning much though he has nothing to lose.

There is another opinion concerning happiness, which approaches much more nearly to universality, but which may, perhaps, with equal reason, be disputed. The pretensions to ancestral honours many of the sons of earth easily see to be ill grounded; but all agree to celebrate the advantage of hereditary riches, and to consider those as the minions of fortune, who are wealthy from their cradles; whose estate is "res non parta labore sed relicta," "the acquisition of another, not of themselves;" and whom a father's industry has dispensed from a laborious attention to arts or commerce, and left at liberty to dispose of life as fancy shall direct them.

If every man were wise and virtuous, capable to discern the best use of time, and resolute to practise it; it might be granted, I think, without hesitation, that total liberty would be a blessing; and that it would be desirable to be left at large to the exercise of religious and social duties, without the interruption of importunate avocations.

But since felicity is relative, and that which is the means of happiness to one man may be to another the cause of misery, we are to consider, what state is best adapted to human nature in its present degeneracy and frailty. And, surely, to far the greater number it is highly expedient, that they should by some settled scheme of duties be rescued from the tyranny of caprice, that they should be driven on by necessity through the paths of life, with their attention confined to a stated task, that they may be less at leisure to deviate into mischief at the call of folly.

When we observe the lives of those whom an ample inheritance has let loose to their own direction, what do we discover that can excite our envy? Their time seems not to pass with much applause from others, or satisfaction to themselves; many squander their exuberance of fortune in luxury and debauchery, and have no other use of money than to inflame their passions, and riot in a wider range of licentiousness; others, less criminal indeed, but, surely, not much to be praised, lie down to sleep and rise up to trifle, are employed every morning in finding expedients to rid themselves of the day, chase pleasure through all the places of public resort, fly from London to Bath and from Bath to London, without any other reason for changing place, but that they go in quest of company as idle and as vagrant as themselves, always endeavouring to raise some new desire that they may have something to persue, to rekindle some hope which they know will be disappointed, changing one amusement for another which a few months will make equally insipid, or sinking into languor and disease for want of something to actuate their bodies or exhilarate their minds.

Whoever has frequented those places, where idlers assemble to escape from solitude, knows that this is generally the state of the wealthy; and from this state it is no great hardship to be debarred. No man can be happy in total idleness: he that should be condemned to lie torpid and motionless, "would fly for recreation," says SOUTH, "to the mines and the gallies;" and it is well, when nature or fortune find employment for those, who would not have known how to procure it for themselves.

He, whose mind is engaged by the acquisition or improvement of a fortune, not only escapes the insipidity of indifference, and the tediousness of inactivity; but gains enjoyments wholly unknown to those, who live lazily on the toil of others; for life affords no higher pleasure, than that of surmounting difficulties, passing from one step of success to another, forming new wishes and seeing them gratified. He that labours in any great or laudable undertaking, has his fatigues first supported by hope, and afterwards rewarded by joy; he is always moving to a certain end, and when he has attained it, an end more distant invites him to a new persuit.

It does not, indeed, always happen, that diligence is fortunate; the wisest schemes are broken by unexpected accidents; the most constant perseverance sometimes toils through life without a recompence; but labour, though unsuccessful, is more eligible than idleness: he that prosecutes a lawful purpose by lawful means, acts always with the approbation of his own reason; he is animated through the course of his endeavours by an expectation which though not certain, he knows to be just; and is at last comforted in his disappointment, by the consciousness that he has not failed by his own fault.

That kind of life is most happy which affords us most opportunities of gaining our own esteem; and what can any man infer in his own favour from a condition to which, however prosperous, he contributed nothing, and which the vilest and weakest of the species would have obtained by the same right, had he happened to be the son of the same father?

To strive with difficulties, and to conquer them, is the highest human felicity; the next, is to strive, and deserve to conquer: but he whose life has passed without a contest, and who can boast neither success nor merit, can survey himself only as a useless filler of existence; and if he is content with his own character, must owe his satisfaction to insensibility.

Thus it appears that the satyrist advised rightly, when he directed us to resign ourselves to the hands of HEAVEN, and to leave to superior powers the determination of our lot:

Permittes ipsis expendere Numinibus, quid
Conveniat nobis, rebusque sit utile nostris,
Carior est illis homo quam sibi.

Intrust thy fortune to the pow'rs above:
Leave them to manage for thee, and to grant
What their unerring wisdom sees thee want.
In goodness as in greatness they excell.
Ah! that we lov'd ourselves but half so well.

DRYDEN.

What state of life admits most happiness is uncertain; but that uncertainty ought to repress the petulance of comparison, and silence the murmurs of discontent.

T

No. 119. Tuesday, 25 December 1753.

Latiùs regnes avidum domando
Spiritum, quàm si Lybiam remotis
Gadibus jungas, et uterque Pœnus
Serviat uni.

HOR.

By virtue's precepts to controul
The thirsty cravings of the soul,
Is over wider realms to reign
Unenvied monarch, than if Spain
You could to distant Lybia join,
And both the Carthages were thine.

FRANCIS.

When SOCRATES was asked, "which of mortal men was to be accounted nearest to the GODS in happiness?" he answered, "that man, who is in want of the fewest things."

In this answer, SOCRATES left it to be guessed by his auditors, whether, by the exemption from want which was to constitute happiness, he meant amplitude of possessions or contraction of desire. And, indeed, there is so little difference between them, that ALEXANDER the great confessed the inhabitant of a tub the next man to the master of the world; and left a declaration to future ages, that if he were not ALEXANDER, he should wish to be DIOGENES.

These two states, however, though they resemble each other in their consequence, differ widely with respect to the facility with which they may be attained. To make great acquisitions, can happen to very few; and in the uncertainty of human affairs, to many it will be incident to labour without reward, and to lose what they already possess by endeavours to make it more; some will always want abilities, and others opportunities to accumulate wealth. It is, therefore, happy, that nature has allowed us a more certain and easy road to plenty; every man may grow rich by contracting his wishes, and by quiet acquiescence in what has been given him supply the absence of more.

Yet so far is almost every man from emulating the happiness of the Gods, by any other means than grasping at their power; that it seems to be the great business of life to create wants as fast as they are satisfied. It has been long observed by moralists, that every man squanders or loses a great part of that life, of which every man knows and deplores the shortness; and it may be remarked with equal justness, that though every man laments his own insufficiency to his happiness, and knows himself a necessitous and precarious being, incessantly solliciting the assistance of others, and feeling wants which his own art or strength cannot supply; yet there is no man, who does not, by the superaddition of unnatural cares, render himself still more dependant; who does not create an artificial poverty, and suffer himself to feel pain for the want of that, of which, when it is gained, he can have no enjoyment.

It must, indeed, be allowed, that as we lose part of our time because it steals away silent and invisible, and many an hour is passed before we recollect that it is passing; so unnatural desires insinuate themselves unobserved into the mind, and we do not perceive that they are gaining upon us, till the pain which they give us awakens us to notice. No man is sufficiently vigilant to take account of every minute of his life, or to watch every motion of his heart. Much of our time likewise is sacrificed to custom; we trifle, because we see others trifle: in the same manner we catch from example the contagion of desire; we see all about us busied in persuit of imaginary good, and begin to bustle in the same chace, lest greater activity should triumph over us.

It is true, that to man, as a member of society, many things become necessary, which, perhaps, in a state of nature are superfluous; and that many things, not absolutely necessary, are yet so useful and convenient, that they cannot easily be spared. I will make yet a more ample and liberal concession. In opulent states and regular governments, the temptations to wealth and rank, and to the distinctions that follow them, are such as no force of understanding finds it easy to resist.

If, therefore, I saw the quiet of life disturbed only by endeavours after wealth and honour; by sollicitude, which the world, whether justly or not, considered as important; I should scarcely have had courage to inculcate any precepts of moderation and forbearance. He that is engaged in a persuit, in which all mankind profess to be his rivals, is supported by the authority of all mankind in the prosecution of his design, and will, therefore, scarcely stop to hear the lectures of a solitary philosopher. Nor am I certain, that the accumulation of honest gain ought to be hindered, or the ambition of just honours always to be repressed. Whatever can enable the possessor to confer any benefit upon others, may be desired upon virtuous principles; and we ought not too rashly to accuse any man of intending to confine the influence of his acquisitions to himself.

But if we look round upon mankind, whom shall we find among those that fortune permits to form their own manners, that is not tormenting himself with a wish for something, of which all the pleasure and all the benefit will cease at the moment of attainment? One man is beggering his posterity to build a house, which when finished he never will inhabit; another is levelling mountains to open a prospect, which, when he has once enjoyed it, he can enjoy no more; another is painting cielings, carving wainscot, and filling his apartments with costly furniture, only that some neighbouring house may not be richer or finer than his own.

That splendor and elegance are not desireable, I am not so abstracted from life as to inculcate; but if we enquire closely into the reason for which they are esteemed, we shall find them valued principally as evidences of wealth. Nothing, therefore, can shew greater depravity of understanding, than to delight in the shew when the reality is wanting; or voluntarily to become poor, that strangers may for a time imagine us to be rich.

But there are yet minuter objects and more trifling anxieties. Men may be found, who are kept from sleep by the want of a shell particularly variegated; who are wasting their lives, in stratagems to obtain a book in a language which they do not understand; who pine with envy at the flowers of another man's parterre; who hover like vultures round the owner of a fossil, in hopes to plunder his cabinet at his death; and who would not much regret to see a street in flames, if a box of medals might be scattered in the tumult.

He that imagines me to speak of these sages in terms exaggerated and hyperbolical, has conversed but little with the race of virtuosos. A slight acquaintance with their studies, and a few visits to their assemblies, would inform him, that nothing is so worthless, but that prejudice and caprice can give it value; nor any thing of so little use, but that by indulging an idle competition or unreasonable pride, a man may make it to himself one of the necessaries of life.

Desires like these, I may surely, without incurring the censure of moroseness, advise every man to repel when they invade his mind; or if he admits them, never to allow them any greater influence, than is necessary to give petty employments the power of pleasing, and diversify the day with slight amusements.

An ardent wish, whatever be its object, will always be able to interrupt tranquillity. What we believe ourselves to want, torments us not in proportion to its real value, but according to the estimation by which we have rated it in our own minds: in some diseases, the patient has been observed to long for food, which scarce any extremity of hunger would in health have compelled him to swallow; but while his organs were thus depraved the craving was irresistible, nor could any rest be obtained till it was appeased by compliance. Of the same nature are the irregular appetites of the mind; though they are often excited by trifles, they are equally disquieting with real wants: the Roman, who wept at the death of his lamprey, felt the same degree of sorrow that extorts tears on other occasions.

Inordinate desires, of whatever kind, ought to be repressed upon yet a higher consideration; they must be considered as enemies not only to Happiness but to Virtue. There are men among those commonly reckoned the learned and the wise, who spare no stratagems to remove a competitor at an auction, who will sink the price of a rarity at the expence of truth, and whom it is not safe to trust alone in a library or cabinet. These are faults, which the fraternity seem to look upon as jocular mischiefs, or to think excused by the violence of the temptation: but I shall always fear that he, who accustoms himself to fraud in little things, wants only opportunity to practise it in greater: "he that has hardened himself by killing a sheep," says Pythagoras, "will with less reluctance shed the blood of a man."

To prize every thing according to its REAL use, ought to be the aim of a rational being. There are few things which can much conduce to Happiness, and, therefore, few things to be ardently desired. He that looks upon the business and bustle of the world, with the philosophy with which Socrates surveyed the fair at Athens, will turn away at last with his exclamation, "How many things are here which I do not want!"

T

No. 126. Saturday, 19 January 1754.

——*Steriles nec legit arenas*
Ut caneret paucis, mersitque hoc pulvere verum.
Lucan.

Canst thou believe the vast eternal mind
Was e'er to Syrts and Libyan sands confin'd?
That he would chuse this waste, this barren ground,
To teach the thin inhabitants around,
And leave his truth in wilds and desarts drown'd?

There has always prevailed among that part of mankind that addict their minds to speculation, a propensity to talk much of the delights of retirement; and some of the most pleasing compositions produced in every age, contain descriptions of the peace and happiness of a country life.

I know not whether those who thus ambitiously repeat the praises of solitude, have always considered, how much they depreciate mankind by declaring, that whatever is excellent or desirable is to be obtained by departing from them; that the assistance which we may derive from one another, is not equivalent to the evils which we have to fear; that the kindness of a few is overbalanced by the malice of many; and that the protection of society is too dearly purchased, by encountering its dangers and enduring its oppressions.

These specious representations of solitary happiness, however opprobrious to human nature, have so far spread their influence over the world, that almost every man delights his imagination with the hopes of obtaining some time an opportunity of retreat. Many indeed, who enjoy retreat only in imagination, content themselves with believing, that another year will transport them to rural tranquillity, and die while they talk of doing what if they had lived longer they would never have done. But many likewise there are, either of greater resolution or more credulity, who in earnest try the state which they have been taught to think thus secure from cares and dangers; and retire to privacy, either that they may improve their happiness, increase their knowledge, or exalt their virtue.

The greater part of the admirers of solitude, as of all other classes of mankind, have no higher or remoter view, than the present gratification of their passions. Of these some, haughty and impetuous, fly from society only because they cannot bear to repay to others the regard which themselves exact, and think no state of life eligible, but that which places them out of the reach of censure or controul, and affords them opportunities of living in a perpetual compliance with their own inclinations, without the necessity of regulating their actions by any other man's convenience or opinion.

There are others of minds more delicate and tender, easily offended by every deviation from rectitude, soon disgusted by ignorance or impertinence, and always expecting from the conversation of mankind, more elegance, purity and truth than the mingled mass of life will easily afford. Such men are in haste to retire from grossness, falshood and brutality; and hope to find in private habitations at least a negative felicity, and exemption from the shocks and perturbations with which public scenes are continually distressing them.

To neither of these votaries will solitude afford that content, which she has been taught so lavishly to promise. The man of arrogance will quickly discover, that by escaping from his opponents he has lost his flatterers, that greatness is nothing where it is not seen, and power nothing where it cannot be felt: and he, whose faculties are employed in too close an observation of failings and defects, will find his condition very little mended by transferring his attention from others to himself; he will probably soon come back in quest of new objects, and be glad to keep his captiousness employed on any character rather than his own.

Others are seduced into solitude merely by the authority of great names, and expect to find those charms in tranquillity which have allured statesmen and conquerors to the shades: these likewise are apt to wonder at their disappointment, from want of considering, that those whom they aspire to imitate carried with them to their country seats minds full fraught with subjects of reflection, the consciousness of great merit, the memory of illustrious actions, the knowledge of important events, and the seeds of mighty designs to be ripened by future meditation. Solitude was to such men a release from fatigue, and an opportunity of usefulness. But what can retirement confer upon him, who having done nothing can receive no support from his own importance, who having known nothing can find no entertainment in reviewing the past, and who intending nothing can form no hopes from prospects of the future: he can, surely, take no wiser course, than that of losing himself again in the croud, and filling the vacuities of his mind with the news of the day.

Others consider solitude as the parent of philosophy, and retire in expectation of greater intimacies with science, as NUMA repaired to the groves when he conferred with EGERIA. These men have not always reason to repent. Some studies require a continued prosecution of the same train of thought, such as is too often interrupted by the petty avocations of common life: sometimes, likewise, it is necessary, that a multiplicity of objects be at once present to the mind; and every thing, therefore, must be kept at a distance, which may perplex the memory, or dissipate the attention.

But though learning may be conferred by solitude, its application must be attained by general converse. He has learned to no purpose, that is not able to teach; and he will always teach unsuccessfully, who cannot recommend his sentiments by his diction or address.

Even the acquisition of knowledge is often much facilitated by the advantages of society: he that never compares his notions with those of others, readily acquiesces in his first thoughts, and very seldom discovers the objections which may be raised against his opinions; he, therefore, often thinks himself in possession of truth, when he is only fondling an error long since exploded. He that has neither companions nor rivals in his studies, will always applaud his own progress, and think highly of his performances, because he knows not that others have equalled or excelled him. And I am afraid it may be added, that the student who withdraws himself from the world, will soon feel that ardour extinguished which praise or emulation had enkindled, and take the advantage of secrecy to sleep rather than to labour.

There remains yet another set of recluses, whose intention intitles them to higher respect, and whose motives deserve a more serious consideration. These retire from the world, not merely to bask in ease or gratify curiosity, but that being disengaged from common cares, they may employ more time in the duties of religion, that they may regulate their actions with stricter vigilance, and purify their thoughts by more frequent meditation.

To men thus elevated above the mists of mortality, I am far from presuming myself qualified to give directions. On him that appears "to pass through things temporary," with no other care than "not to lose finally the things eternal," I look with such veneration as inclines me to approve his conduct in the whole, without a minute examination of its parts; yet I could never forbear to wish, that while vice is every day multiplying seducements, and stalking forth with more hardened effrontry, virtue would not withdraw the influence of her presence, or forbear to assert her natural dignity by open and undaunted perseverance in the right. Piety practised in solitude, like the flower that blooms in the desart, may give its fragrance to the winds of heaven, and delight those unbodied spirits that survey the works of GOD and the actions of men; but it bestows no assistance upon earthly beings, and however free from taints of impurity, yet wants the sacred splendor of beneficence.

Our MAKER, who, though he gave us such varieties of temper and such difference of powers yet designed us all for happiness, undoubtedly intended, that we should obtain that happiness by different means. Some are unable to resist the temptations of importunity, or the impetuosity of their own passions incited by the force of present temptations: of these it is undoubtedly the duty, to fly from enemies which they cannot conquer, and to cultivate, in the calm of solitude, that virtue which is too tender to endure the tempests of public life. But there are others, whose passions grow more strong and irregular in privacy; and who cannot maintain an uniform tenor of virtue, but by exposing their manners to the public eye, and assisting the admonitions of conscience with the fear of infamy: for such it is dangerous to exclude all witnesses of their conduct, till they have formed strong habits of virtue, and weakened their passions by frequent victories. But there is a higher order of men so inspirited with ardour, and so fortified with resolution, that the world passes before them without influence or regard: these ought to consider themselves as appointed the guardians of mankind; they are placed in an evil world, to exhibit public examples of good life; and may be said, when they withdraw to solitude, to desert the station which PROVIDENCE assigned them.

T

No. 137. Tuesday, 26 February 1754.

Τίδ'ἔρεξα,
PYTH.

What have I been doing?

As man is a being very sparingly furnished with the power of prescience, he can provide for the future only by considering the past; and as futurity is all in which he has any real interest, he ought very diligently to use the only means by which he can be enabled to enjoy it, and frequently to revolve the experiments which he has hitherto made upon life, that he may gain wisdom from his mistakes and caution from his miscarriages.

Though I do not so exactly conform to the precepts of PYTHAGORAS, as to practise every night this solemn recollection, yet I am not so lost in dissipation as wholly to omit it; nor can I forbear sometimes to enquire of myself, in what employments my life has passed away. Much of my time has sunk into nothing, and left no trace by which it can be distinguished, and of this I now only know, that it was once in my power and might once have been improved.

Of other parts of life memory can give some account: at some hours I have been gay, and at others serious; I have sometimes mingled in conversation, and sometimes meditated in solitude; one day has been spent in consulting the antient sages, and another in writing ADVENTURERS.

At the conclusion of any undertaking, it is usual to compute the loss and profit. As I shall soon cease to write ADVENTURERS, I could not forbear lately to consider what has been the consequence of my labours; and whether I am to reckon the hours laid out in these compositions, as applied to a good and laudable purpose, or suffered to fume away in useless evaporations.

That I have intended well, I have the attestation of my own heart; but good intentions may be frustrated, when they are executed without suitable skill, or directed to an end unattainable in itself.

Some there are, who leave writers very little room for self congratulation; some who affirm, that books have no influence upon the public, that no age was ever made better by its authors, and that to call upon mankind to correct their manners, is, like XERXES, to scourge the wind or shackle the torrent.

This opinion they pretend to support by unfailing experience. The world is full of fraud and corruption, rapine and malignity; interest is the ruling motive of mankind, and every one is endeavouring to increase his own stores of happiness by perpetual accumulation, without reflecting upon the numbers whom his superfluity condemns to want: in this state of things a book of morality is published, in which charity and benevolence are strongly enforced; and it is proved beyond opposition, that men are happy in proportion as they are virtuous, and rich as they are liberal. The book is applauded, and the author is preferred; he imagines his applause deserved, and receives less pleasure from the acquisition of reward, than the consciousness of merit. Let us look again upon mankind: interest is still the ruling motive, and the world is yet full of fraud and corruption, malevolence and rapine.

The difficulty of confuting this assertion, arises merely from its generality and comprehension: to overthrow it by a detail of distinct facts, requires a wider survey of the world than human eyes can take; the progress of reformation is gradual and silent, as the extension of evening shadows; we know that they were short at noon, and are long at sun-set, but our senses were not able to discern their increase; we know of every civil nation that it was once savage, and how was it reclaimed but by precept and admonition?

Mankind are universally corrupt, but corrupt in different degrees; as they are universally ignorant, yet with greater or less irradiations of knowledge. How has knowledge or virtue been increased and preserved in one place beyond another, but by diligent inculcation and rational inforcement.

Books of morality are daily written, yet its influence is still little in the world; so the ground is annually ploughed, and yet multitudes are in want of bread. But, surely, neither the labours of the moralist nor of the husbandman are vain: let them for a while neglect their tasks, and their usefulness will be known; the wickedness that is now frequent would become universal, the bread that is now scarce would wholly fail.

The power, indeed, of every individual is small, and the consequence of his endeavours imperceptible in a general prospect of the world. PROVIDENCE has given no man ability to do much, that something might be left for every man to do. The business of life is carried on by a general co-operation; in which the part of any single man can be no more distinguished, than the effect of a particular drop when the meadows are floated by a summer shower: yet every drop increases the inundation, and every hand adds to the happiness or misery of mankind.

That a writer, however zealous or eloquent, seldom works a visible effect upon cities or nations, will readily be granted. The book which is read most, is read by few, compared with those that read it not; and of those few, the greater part peruse it with dispositions that very little favour their own improvement.

It is difficult to enumerate the several motives, which procure to books the honour of perusal: spite, vanity, and curiosity, hope and fear, love and hatred, every passion which incites to any other action, serves at one time or other to stimulate a reader.

Some are fond to take a celebrated volume into their hands, because they hope to distinguish their penetration, by finding faults which have escaped the public; others eagerly buy it in the first bloom of reputation, that they may join the chorus of praise, and not lag, as FALSTAFF terms it, in "the rear-ward of the fashion."

Some read for stile, and some for argument: one has little care about the sentiment, he observes only how it is expressed; another regards not the conclusion, but is diligent to mark how it is inferred: they read for other purposes, than the attainment of practical knowledge; and are no more likely to grow wise by an examination of a treatise of moral prudence, than an architect to inflame his devotion by considering attentively the proportions of a temple.

Some read that they may embellish their conversation, or shine in dispute; some that they may not be detected in ignorance, or want the reputation of literary accomplishments: but the most general and prevalent reason of study, is the impossibility of finding another amusement equally cheap or constant, equally independent on the hour or the weather. He that wants money to follow the chace of pleasure through her yearly circuit, and is left at home when the gay world rolls to Bath or Tunbridge; he whose gout compells him to hear from his chamber, the rattle of chariots transporting happier beings to plays and assemblies, will be forced to seek in books a refuge from himself.

The author is not wholly useless, who provides innocent amusements for minds like these. There are in the present state of things so many more instigations to evil, than incitements to good, that he who keeps men in a neutral state, may be justly considered as a benefactor to life.

But, perhaps, it seldom happens, that study terminates in mere pastime. Books have always a secret influence on the understanding; we cannot at pleasure obliterate ideas; he that reads books of science, though without any fixed desire of improvement, will grow more knowing; he that entertains himself with moral or religious treatises, will imperceptibly advance in goodness; the ideas which are often offered to the mind, will at last find a lucky moment when it is disposed to receive them.

It is, therefore, urged without reason, as a discouragement to writers, that there are already books sufficient in the world; that all the topics of persuasion have been discussed, and every important question clearly stated and justly decided; and that, therefore, there is no room to hope, that pigmies should conquer where heroes have been defeated, or that the petty copiers of the present time should advance the great work of reformation, which their predecessors were forced to leave unfinished.

Whatever be the present extent of human knowledge, it is not only finite, and therefore in its own nature capable of increase; but so narrow, that almost every understanding may by a diligent application of its powers hope to enlarge it. It is, however, not necessary, that a man should forbear to write, till he has discovered some truth unknown before; he may be sufficiently useful, by only diversifying the surface of knowledge, and luring the mind by a new appearance to a second view of those beauties which it had passed over inattentively before. Every writer may find intellects correspondent to his own, to whom his expressions are familiar, and his thoughts congenial; and, perhaps, truth is often more successfully propagated by men of moderate abilities, who, adopting the opinions of others, have no care but to explain them clearly, than by subtile speculatists and curious searchers, who exact from their readers powers equal to their own, and if their fabrics of science be strong take no care to render them accessible.

For my part, I do not regret the hours which I have laid out on these little compositions. That the world has grown apparently better, since the publication of the ADVENTURER, I have not observed; but am willing to think, that many have been affected by single sentiments, of which it is their business to renew the impression; that many have caught hints of truth, which it is now their duty to persue; and that those who have received no improvement, have wanted not opportunity but intention to improve.

T

No. 138. Saturday, 2 March 1754.

Quid purè tranquillet? honos, an dulce lucellum,
An secretum iter et fallentis semita vitæ?

HOR.

Whether the tranquil mind and pure,
Honours or wealth our bliss insure;
Or down through life unknown to stray,
Where lonely leads the silent way.

FRANCIS.

Having considered the importance of authors to the welfare of the public, I am led by a natural train of thought, to reflect on their condition with regard to themselves; and to enquire, what degree of happiness or vexation is annexed to the difficult and laborious employment, of providing instruction or entertainment for mankind.

In estimating the pain or pleasure of any particular state, every man, indeed, draws his decisions from his own breast, and cannot with certainty determine, whether other minds are affected by the same causes in the same manner. Yet by this criterion we must be content to judge, because no other can be obtained; and, indeed, we have no reason to think it very fallacious, for excepting here and there an anomalous mind, which either does not feel like others, or dissembles its sensibility, we find men unanimously concur in attributing happiness or misery to particular conditions, as they agree in acknowledging the cold of winter and the heat of autumn.

If we apply to authors themselves for an account of their state, it will appear very little to deserve envy; for they have in all ages been addicted to complaint. The neglect of learning, the ingratitude of the present age, and the absurd preference by which ignorance and dulness often obtain favour and rewards, have been from age to age topics of invective; and few have left their names to posterity, without some appeal to future candour from the perverseness and malice of their own times.

I have, nevertheless, been often inclined to doubt, whether authors, however querulous, are in reality more miserable than their fellow mortals. The present life is to all a state of infelicity; every man, like an author, believes himself to merit more than he obtains, and solaces the present with the prospect of the future: others, indeed, suffer those disappointments in silence, of which the writer complains, to shew how well he has learned the art of lamentation.

There is at least one gleam of felicity, of which few writers have missed the enjoyment: he whose hopes have so far overpowered his fears, as that he has resolved to stand forth a candidate for fame, seldom fails to amuse himself, before his appearance, with pleasing scenes of affluence or honour; while his fortune is yet under the regulation of fancy, he easily models it to his wish, suffers no thoughts of critics or rivals to intrude upon his mind, but counts over the bounties of patronage or listens to the voice of praise.

Some there are, that talk very luxuriously of the second period of an author's happiness, and tell of the tumultuous raptures of invention, when the mind riots in imagery, and the choice stands suspended between different sentiments.

These pleasures, I believe, may sometimes be indulged to those, who come to a subject of disquisition with minds full of ideas, and with fancies so vigorous, as easily to excite, select, and arrange them. To write, is, indeed, no unpleasing employment, when one sentiment readily produces another, and both ideas and expressions present themselves at the first summons: but such happiness, the greatest genius does not always obtain; and common writers know it only to such a degree, as to credit its possibility. Composition is, for the most part, an effort of slow diligence and steady perseverance, to which the mind is dragged by necessity or resolution, and from which the attention is every moment starting to more delightful amusements.

It frequently happens, that a design which, when considered at a distance, gave flattering hopes of facility, mocks us in the execution with unexpected difficulties; the mind which, while it considered it in the gross, imagined itself amply furnished with materials, finds sometimes an unexpected barrenness and vacuity, and wonders whither all those ideas are vanished, which a little before seemed struggling for emission.

Sometimes many thoughts present themselves; but so confused and unconnected, that they are not without difficulty reduced to method, or concatenated in a regular and dependent series: the mind falls at once into a labyrinth, of which neither the beginning nor end can be discovered, and toils and struggles without progress or extrication.

It is asserted by HORACE, that "if matter be once got together, words will be found with very little difficulty;" a position which, though sufficiently plausible to be inserted in poetical precepts, is by no means strictly and philosophically true. If words were naturally and necessarily consequential to sentiments, it would always follow, that he who has most knowledge must have most eloquence, and that every man would clearly express what he fully understood: yet we find, that to think, and to discourse, are often the qualities of different persons; and many books might surely be produced, where just and noble sentiments are degraded and obscured by unsuitable diction.

Words, therefore, as well as things, claim the care of an author. Indeed, of many authors, and those not useless or contemptible, words are almost the only care: many make it their study, not so much to strike out new sentiments, as to recommend those which are already known to more favourable notice by fairer decorations; but every man, whether he copies or invents, whether he delivers his own thoughts or those of another, has often found himself deficient in the power of expression, big with ideas which he could not utter, obliged to ransack his memory for terms adequate to his conceptions, and at last unable to impress upon his reader the image existing in his own mind.

It is one of the common distresses of a writer, to be within a word of a happy period, to want only a single epithet to give amplification its full force, to require only a correspondent term in order to finish a paragraph with elegance and make one of its members answer to the other: but these deficiencies cannot always be supplied; and after long study and vexation, the passage is turned anew, and the web unwoven that was so nearly finished.

But when thoughts and words are collected and adjusted, and the whole composition at last concluded, it seldom gratifies the author, when he comes coolly and deliberately to review it, with the hopes which had been excited in the fury of the performance: novelty always captivates the mind; as our thoughts rise fresh upon us, we readily believe them just and original, which, when the pleasure of production is over, we find to be mean and common, or borrowed from the works of others, and supplied by memory rather than invention.

But though it should happen, that the writer finds no such faults in his performance, he is still to remember, that he looks upon it with partial eyes; and when he considers, how much men who could judge of others with great exactness, have often failed in judging of themselves, he will be afraid of deciding too hastily in his own favour, or of allowing himself to contemplate with too much complacence, treasure that has not yet been brought to the test, nor passed the only trial that can stamp its value.

From the public, and only from the public, is he to await a confirmation of his claim, and a final justification of self esteem; but the public is not easily persuaded to favour an author. If mankind were left to judge for themselves, it is reasonable to imagine, that of such writings, at least, as describe the movements of the human passions, and of which every man carries the archetype within him, a just opinion would be formed; but whoever has remarked the fate of books, must have found it governed by other causes, than general consent arising from general conviction. If a new performance happens not to fall into the hands of some, who have courage to tell, and authority to propagate their opinion, it often remains long in obscurity, and perhaps perishes unknown and unexamined. A few, a very few, commonly constitute the taste of the time; the judgment which they have once pronounced, some are too lazy to discuss, and some too timorous to contradict: it may, however, be

I think observed, that their power is greater to depress than exalt, as mankind are more credulous of censure than of praise.

This perversion of the public judgment, is not to be rashly numbered amongst the miseries of an author; since it commonly serves, after miscarriage, to reconcile him to himself. Because the world has sometimes passed an unjust sentence, he readily concludes the sentence unjust by which his performance is condemned; because some have been exalted above their merits by partiality, he is sure to ascribe the success of a rival, not to the merit of his work, but the zeal of his patrons. Upon the whole, as the author seems to share all the common miseries of life, he appears to partake likewise of its lenitives and abatements.

T

Letter to Thomas Warton
TUESDAY 16 JULY 1754

Sir: July 16, 1754

It is but an ill return for the book with which you were pleased to favour me, to have delayed my thanks for it till now. I am too apt to be negligent but I can never deliberately show any disrespect to a man of your character, and I now pay you a very honest ack[n]owledgement for the advancement of the literature of our native Country. You have shown to all who shall hereafter attempt the study of our ancient authours the way to success, by directing them to the perusal of the books which those authours had read. Of this method Hughes and Men much greater than Hughes seem never to have thought. The Reason why the authours which are yet read of the sixteenth Century are so little understood is that they are read alone, and no help is borrowed from those who lived with them or before them. Some part of this ignorance I hope to remove by my book which now draws towards its end, but which I cannot finish to my mind without visiting the libraries of Oxford which I therefore hope to see in about a fortnight. I know not how long I shall stay or where I shall lodge, but shall be sure to look for you at my arrival, and we shall easily settle the rest. I am, Dear Sir, your most obedient and most humble servant,

SAM. JOHNSON

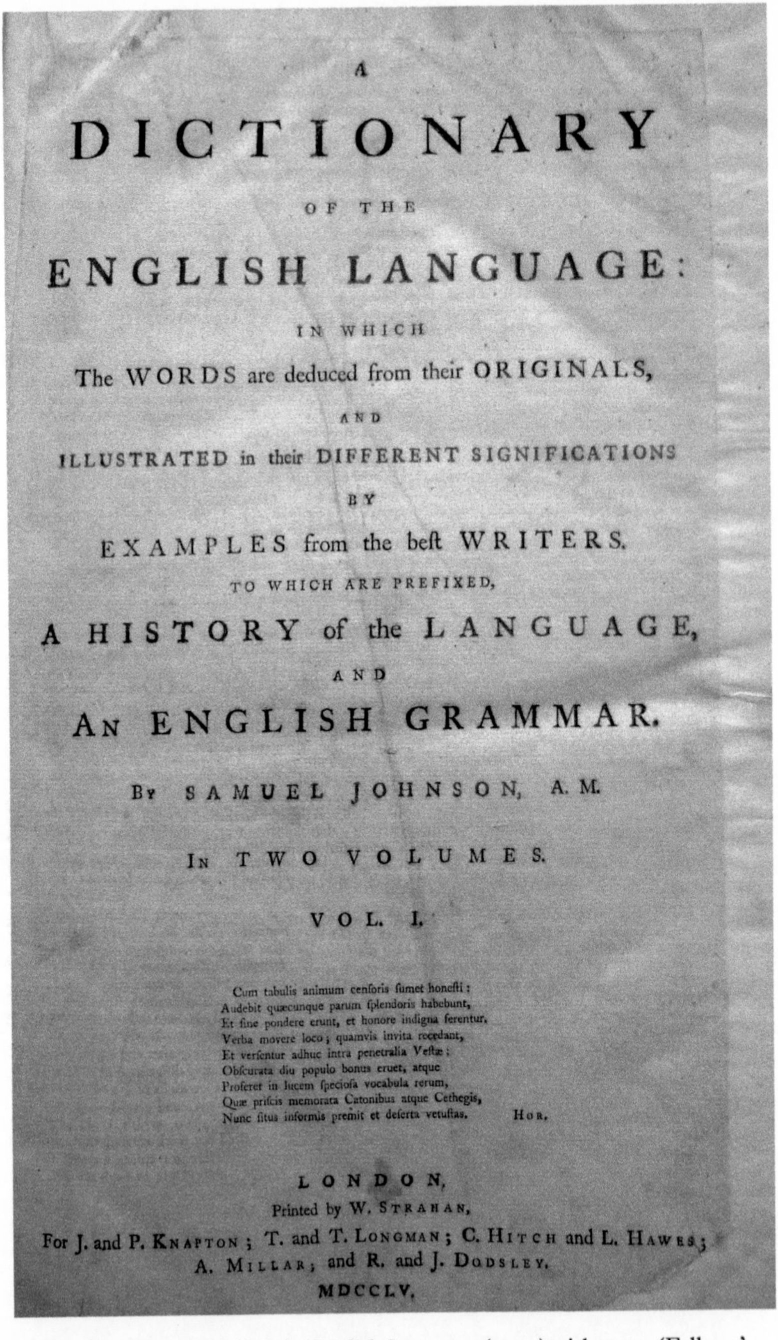

A

DICTIONARY

OF THE

ENGLISH LANGUAGE:

IN WHICH

The WORDS are deduced from their ORIGINALS,

AND

ILLUSTRATED in their DIFFERENT SIGNIFICATIONS

BY

EXAMPLES from the best WRITERS.

TO WHICH ARE PREFIXED,

A HISTORY of the LANGUAGE,

AND

An ENGLISH GRAMMAR.

BY SAMUEL JOHNSON, A.M.

IN TWO VOLUMES.

VOL. I.

Cum tabulis animum cenforis fumet honefti ;
Audebit quæcunque parum fplendoris habebunt,
Et fine pondere erunt, et honore indigna ferentur,
Verba movere loco ; quamvis invita recedant,
Et verfentur adhuc intra penetralia Veftæ ;
Obfcurata diu populo bonus eruet, atque
Proferet in lucem fpeciofa vocabula rerum,
Quæ prifcis memorata Catonibus atque Cethegis,
Nunc fitus informis premit et deferta vetuftas.   HOR.

LONDON,
Printed by W. STRAHAN,
For J. and P. KNAPTON ; T. and T. LONGMAN ; C. HITCH and L. HAWES ;
A. MILLAR ; and R. and J. DODSLEY.
MDCCLV.

FIGURE 6 *A Dictionary of the English Language* (1755), title page (Fellows'
Library, Jesus College, Oxford). Courtesy of the Principal, Fellows, and
Scholars of Jesus College, Oxford.

A Dictionary of the English Language

Preface

It is the fate of those who toil at the lower employments of life, to be rather driven by the fear of evil, than attracted by the prospect of good; to be exposed to censure, without hope of praise; to be disgraced by miscarriage, or punished for neglect, where success would have been without applause, and diligence without reward.

Among these unhappy mortals is the writer of dictionaries; whom mankind have considered, not as the pupil, but the slave of science, the pioneer of literature, doomed only to remove rubbish and clear obstructions from the paths of Learning and Genius, who press forward to conquest and glory, without bestowing a smile on the humble drudge that facilitates their progress. Every other authour may aspire to praise; the lexicographer can only hope to escape reproach, and even this negative recompence has been yet granted to very few.

I have, notwithstanding this discouragement, attempted a dictionary of the *English* language, which, while it was employed in the cultivation of every species of literature, has itself been hitherto neglected, suffered to spread, under the direction of chance, into wild exuberance, resigned to the tyranny of time and fashion, and exposed to the corruptions of ignorance, and caprices of innovation.

When I took the first survey of my undertaking, I found our speech copious without order, and energetick without rules: wherever I turned my view, there was perplexity to be disentangled, and confusion to be regulated; choice was to be made out of boundless variety, without any established principle of selection; adulterations were to be detected, without a settled test of purity, and modes of expression to be rejected or received, without the suffrages of any writers of classical reputation or acknowledged authority.

Having therefore no assistance but from general grammar, I applied myself to the perusal of our writers; and noting whatever might be of use to ascertain or illustrate any word or phrase, accumulated in time the materials of a dictionary, which, by degrees, I reduced to method, establishing to myself, in the progress of the work, such rules as experience and analogy suggested to me; experience, which practice and observation were continually increasing; and analogy, which, though in some words obscure, was evident in others.

In adjusting the ORTHOGRAPHY, which has been to this time unsettled and fortuitous, I found it necessary to distinguish those irregularities that are inherent in our tongue, and perhaps coeval with it, from others which the ignorance or negligence of later writers has produced. Every language has its anomalies, which, though inconvenient, and in themselves once unnecessary, must be tolerated among the imperfections of human things, and which require only to be registred, that they may not be increased, and ascertained, that they may not be confounded: but every language has likewise its improprieties and absurdities, which it is the duty of the lexicographer to correct or proscribe.

As language was at its beginning merely oral, all words of necessary or common use were spoken before they were written; and while they were unfixed by any visible signs, must have been spoken with great diversity, as we now observe those who cannot read to catch sounds imperfectly, and utter them negligently. When this wild and barbarous jargon was first reduced to an alphabet, every penman endeavoured to express, as he could, the sounds which he was accustomed to pronounce or to receive, and vitiated in writing such words as were already vitiated in speech. The powers of the letters, when they were applied to a new language, must have been vague and unsettled, and therefore different hands would exhibit the same sound by different combinations.

From this uncertain pronunciation arise in a great part the various dialects of the same country, which will always be observed to grow fewer, and less different, as books are multiplied; and from this arbitrary representation of sounds by letters, proceeds that diversity of spelling observable in the *Saxon* remains, and I suppose in the first books of every nation, which perplexes or destroys analogy, and produces anomalous formations, which, being once incorporated, can never be afterward dismissed or reformed.

Of this kind are the derivatives *length* from *long, strength* from *strong, darling* from *dear, breadth* from *broad*, from *dry, drought*, and from *high, height*, which *Milton*, in zeal for analogy, writes *highth*; *Quid te exempta juvat spinis de pluribus una*; to change all would be too much, and to change one is nothing.

This uncertainty is most frequent in the vowels, which are so capriciously pronounced, and so differently modified, by accident or affectation, not only in every province, but in every mouth, that to them, as is well known to etymologists, little regard is to be shewn in the deduction of one language from another.

Such defects are not errours in orthography, but spots of barbarity impressed so deep in the *English* language, that criticism can never wash them away; these, therefore, must be permitted to remain untouched: but many words have been altered by accident, or depraved by ignorance, as the pronunciation of the vulgar has been weakly followed; and some still continue to be variously written, as authours differ in their care or skill: of these it was proper to enquire the true orthography, which I have always considered as depending on their derivation, and have therefore referred them to their original languages: thus I write *enchant, enchantment, enchanter*, after the *French*, and *incantation* after the *Latin*; thus *entire* is chosen rather than *intire*, because it passed to us not from the *Latin integer*, but from the *French entier*.

Of many words it is difficult to say whether they were immediately received from the *Latin* or the *French*, since at the time when we had dominions in *France*, we had *Latin* service in our churches. It is, however, my opinion, that the *French* generally supplied us; for we have few *Latin* words, among the terms of domestick use, which are not *French*; but many *French*, which are very remote from *Latin*.

Even in words of which the derivation is apparent, I have been often obliged to sacrifice uniformity to custom; thus I write, in compliance with a numberless majority, *convey* and *inveigh, deceit* and *receipt, fancy* and *phantom*; sometimes the derivative varies from the primitive, as *explain* and *explanation, repeat* and *repetition*.

Some combinations of letters having the same power are used indifferently without any discoverable reason of choice, as in *choak, choke; soap, sope; fewel, fuel*, and many others; which I have sometimes inserted twice, that those who search for them under either form, may not search in vain.

In examining the orthography of any doubtful word, the mode of spelling by which it is inserted in the series of the dictionary, is to be considered as that to which I give, perhaps not often rashly, the preference. I have left, in the examples, to every authour his own practice unmolested, that the reader may balance suffrages, and judge betwixt us: but this question is not always to be determined by reputed or by real learning; some men, intent upon greater things, have thought little on sounds and derivations; some, knowing in the ancient tongues, have neglected those in which our words are commonly to be sought. Thus *Hammond* writes *fecibleness* for *feasibleness*, because I suppose he imagined it derived immediately from the *Latin*; and some words, such as *dependant, dependent; dependance, dependence*, vary their final syllable, as one or other language is present to the writer.

In this part of the work, where caprice has long wantoned without controul, and vanity sought praise by petty reformation, I have endeavoured to proceed with a scholar's reverence for antiquity, and a grammarian's regard to the genius of our tongue. I have attempted few alterations, and among those few, perhaps the greater part is from the modern to the ancient practice; and I hope I may be allowed to recommend to those, whose thoughts have been, perhaps, employed too anxiously on verbal singularities, not to disturb, upon narrow views, or for minute propriety, the orthography of their fathers. It has been asserted, that for the law to be *known*, is of more importance than to be *right*. Change, says *Hooker*, is not made without inconvenience, even from worse to better. There is in constancy and stability a general and lasting advantage, which will always overbalance the slow improvements of gradual correction. Much less ought our written language to comply with the corruptions of oral utterance, or copy that which every variation of time or place makes different from itself, and imitate those changes, which will again be changed, while imitation is employed in observing them.

This recommendation of steadiness and uniformity does not proceed from an opinion, that particular combinations of letters have much influence on human happiness; or that truth may not be successfully taught by modes of spelling fanciful and erroneous: I am not yet so lost in lexicography, as to forget that *words are the daughters of earth, and that things are the sons of heaven.* Language is only the instrument of science, and words are but the signs of ideas: I wish, however, that the instrument might be less apt to decay, and that signs might be permanent, like the things which they denote.

In settling the orthography, I have not wholly neglected the pronunciation, which I have directed, by printing an accent upon the acute or elevated syllable. It will sometimes be found, that the accent is placed by the authour quoted, on a different syllable from that marked in the alphabetical series; it is then to be understood, that custom has varied, or that the authour has, in my opinion, pronounced wrong. Short directions are sometimes given where the sound of letters is irregular; and if they are sometimes omitted, defect in such minute observations will be more easily excused, than superfluity.

In the investigation both of the orthography and signification of words, their ETYMOLOGY was necessarily to be considered, and they were therefore to be divided into primitives and derivatives. A primitive word, is that which can be traced no further to any *English* root; thus *circumspect, circumvent, circumstance, delude, concave,* and *complicate,* though compounds in the *Latin,* are to us primitives. Derivatives, are all those that can be referred to any word in *English* of greater simplicity.

The derivatives I have referred to their primitives, with an accuracy sometimes needless; for who does not see that *remoteness* comes from *remote, lovely* from *love, concavity* from *concave,* and *demonstrative* from *demonstrate?* But this grammatical exuberance the scheme of my work did not allow me to repress. It is of great importance, in examining the general fabrick of a language, to trace one word from another, by noting the usual modes of derivation and inflection; and uniformity must be preserved in systematical works, though sometimes at the expence of particular propriety.

Among other derivatives I have been careful to insert and elucidate the anomalous plurals of nouns and preterites of verbs, which in the *Teutonick* dialects are very frequent, and, though familiar to those who have always used them, interrupt and embarrass the learners of our language.

The two languages from which our primitives have been derived are the *Roman* and *Teutonick:* under the *Roman* I comprehend the *French* and provincial tongues; and under the *Teutonick* range the *Saxon, German,* and all their kindred dialects. Most of our polysyllables are *Roman,* and our words of one syllable are very often *Teutonick.*

In assigning the *Roman* original, it has perhaps sometimes happened that I have mentioned only the *Latin*, when the word was borrowed from the *French*; and considering myself as employed only in the illustration of my own language, I have not been very careful to observe whether the *Latin* word be pure or barbarous, or the *French* elegant or obsolete.

For the *Teutonick* etymologies I am commonly indebted to *Junius* and *Skinner*, the only names which I have forborn to quote when I copied their books; not that I might appropriate their labours or usurp their honours, but that I might spare a perpetual repetition by one general acknowledgment. Of these, whom I ought not to mention but with the reverence due to instructors and benefactors, *Junius* appears to have excelled in extent of learning, and *Skinner* in rectitude of understanding. *Junius* was accurately skilled in all the northern languages, *Skinner* probably examined the ancient and remoter dialects only by occasional inspection into dictionaries; but the learning of *Junius* is often of no other use than to show him a track by which he may deviate from his purpose, to which *Skinner* always presses forward by the shortest way. *Skinner* is often ignorant, but never ridiculous: *Junius* is always full of knowledge; but his variety distracts his judgment, and his learning is very frequently disgraced by his absurdities.

The votaries of the northern muses will not perhaps easily restrain their indignation, when they find the name of *Junius* thus degraded by a disadvantageous comparison; but whatever reverence is due to his diligence, or his attainments, it can be no criminal degree of censoriousness to charge that etymologist with want of judgment, who can seriously derive *dream* from *drama*, because *life is a drama, and a drama is a dream*; and who declares with a tone of defiance, that no man can fail to derive *moan* from μόνος, *monos*, who considers that grief naturally loves to be *alone*.

Our knowledge of the northern literature is so scanty, that of words undoubtedly *Teutonick* the original is not always to be found in any ancient language; and I have therefore inserted *Dutch* or *German* substitutes, which I consider not as radical but parallel, not as the parents, but sisters of the *English*.

The words which are represented as thus related by descent or cognation, do not always agree in sense; for it is incident to words, as to their authours, to degenerate from their ancestors, and to change their manners when they change their country. It is sufficient, in etymological enquiries, if the senses of kindred words be found such as may easily pass into each other, or such as may both be referred to one general idea.

The etymology, so far as it is yet known, was easily found in the volumes where it is particularly and professedly delivered; and, by proper attention to the rules of derivation, the orthography was soon adjusted. But to COLLECT the WORDS of our language was a task of greater difficulty: the deficiency of dictionaries was immediately apparent; and when they were exhausted, what was yet wanting must be sought by fortuitous and unguided excursions into books, and gleaned as industry should find, or chance should offer it, in the boundless chaos of a living speech. My search, however, has been either skilful or lucky; for I have much augmented the vocabulary.

As my design was a dictionary common or appellative, I have omitted all words which have relation to proper names; such as *Arian*, *Socinian*, *Calvinist*, *Benedictine*, *Mahometan*; but have retained those of a more general nature, as *Heathen*, *Pagan*.

Of the terms of art I have received such as could be found either in books of science or technical dictionaries; and have often inserted, from philosophical writers, words which are supported perhaps only by a single authority, and which being not admitted into general use, stand yet as candidates or probationers, and must depend for their adoption on the suffrage of futurity.

The words which our authours have introduced by their knowledge of foreign languages, or ignorance of their own, by vanity or wantonness, by compliance with fashion, or lust of innovation, I have registred as they occurred, though commonly only to censure them, and warn others against the folly of naturalizing useless foreigners to the injury of the natives.

I have not rejected any by design, merely because they were unnecessary or exuberant; but have received those which by different writers have been differently formed, as *viscid*, and *viscidity*, *viscous*, and *viscosity*.

Compounded or double words I have seldom noted, except when they obtain a signification different from that which the components have in their simple state. Thus *highwayman*, *woodman*, and *horsecourser*, require an explication; but of *thieflike* or *coachdriver* no notice was needed, because the primitives contain the meaning of the compounds.

Words arbitrarily formed by a constant and settled analogy, like diminutive adjectives in *ish*, as *greenish*, *bluish*, adverbs in *ly*, as *dully*, *openly*, substantives in *ness*, as *vileness*, *faultiness*, were less diligently sought, and many sometimes have been omitted, when I had no authority that invited me to insert them; not that they are not genuine and regular offsprings of *English* roots, but because their relation to the primitive being always the same, their signification cannot be mistaken.

The verbal nouns in *ing*, such as the *keeping* of the *castle*, the *leading* of the *army*, are always neglected, or placed only to illustrate the sense of the verb, except when they signify things as well as actions, and have therefore a plural number, as *dwelling*, *living*; or have an absolute and abstract signification, as *colouring*, *painting*, *learning*.

The participles are likewise omitted, unless, by signifying rather qualities than action, they take the nature of adjectives; as a *thinking* man, a man of prudence; a *pacing* horse, a horse that can pace: these I have ventured to call *participial adjectives*. But neither are these always inserted, because they are commonly to be understood, without any danger of mistake, by consulting the verb.

Obsolete words are admitted, when they are found in authours not obsolete, or when they have any force or beauty that may deserve revival.

As composition is one of the chief characteristicks of a language, I have endeavoured to make some reparation for the universal negligence of my predecessors, by inserting great numbers of compounded words, as may be found under *after, fore, new, night*, and many more. These, numerous as they are, might be multiplied, but that use and curiosity are here satisfied, and the frame of our language and modes of our combination are amply discovered.

Of some forms of composition, such as that by which *re* is prefixed to note *repetition*, and *un* to signify *contrariety* or *privation*, all the examples cannot be accumulated, because the use of these particles, if not wholly arbitrary, is so little limited, that they are hourly united to new words as occasion requires, or is imagined to require them.

There is another kind of composition more frequent in our language than perhaps in any other, from which arises to foreigners the greatest difficulty. We modify the signification of many verbs by a particle subjoined; as to *come off*, to escape by a fetch; to *fall on*, to attack; to *fall off*, to apostatize; to *break off*, to stop abruptly; to *bear out*, to justify; to *fall in*, to comply; to *give over*, to cease; to *set off*, to embellish; to *set in*, to begin a continual tenour; to *set out*, to begin a course or journey; to *take off*, to copy; with innumerable expressions of the same kind, of which some appear wildly irregular, being so far distant from the sense of the simple words, that no sagacity will be able to trace the steps by which they arrived at the present use. These I have noted with great care; and though I cannot flatter myself that the collection is complete, I have perhaps so far assisted the students of our language, that this kind of phraseology will be no longer insuperable; and the combinations of verbs and particles, by chance omitted, will be easily explained by comparison with those that may be found.

Many words yet stand supported only by the name of *Bailey, Ainsworth, Philips*, or the contracted *Dict.* for *Dictionaries* subjoined: of these I am not always certain that they are seen in any book but the works of lexicographers. Of such I have omitted many, because I had never read them; and many I have inserted, because they may perhaps exist, though they have escaped my notice; they are, however, to be yet considered as resting only upon the credit of former dictionaries. Others, which I considered as useful, or know to be proper, though I could not at present support them by authorities, I have suffered to stand upon my own attestation, claiming the same privilege with my predecessors of being sometimes credited without proof.

The words, thus selected and disposed, are grammatically considered; they are referred to the different parts of speech; traced, when they are irregularly inflected, through their various terminations; and illustrated by observations, not indeed of great or striking importance, separately considered, but necessary to the elucidation of our language, and hitherto neglected or forgotten by *English* grammarians.

That part of my work on which I expect malignity most frequently to fasten, is the *Explanation*; in which I cannot hope to satisfy those, who are perhaps not inclined to be pleased, since I have not always been able to satisfy myself. To interpret a language by itself is very difficult; many words cannot be explained by synonimes, because the idea signified by them has not more than one appellation; nor by paraphrase, because simple ideas cannot be described. When the nature of things is unknown, or the notion unsettled and indefinite, and various in various minds, the words by which such notions are conveyed, or such things denoted, will be ambiguous and perplexed. And such is the fate of hapless lexicography, that not only darkness, but light, impedes and distresses it; things may be not only too little, but too much known, to be happily illustrated. To explain, requires the use of terms less abstruse than that which is to be explained, and such terms cannot always be found; for as nothing can be proved but by supposing something intuitively known, and evident without proof, so nothing can be defined but by supposing some words too plain to admit a definition.

Other words there are, of which the sense is too subtle and evanescent to be fixed in a paraphrase; such are all those which are by the grammarians termed *expletives*, and, in dead languages, are suffered to pass for empty sounds, of no other use than to fill a verse, or to modulate a period, but which are easily perceived in living tongues to have power and emphasis, though it be sometimes such as no other form of expression can convey.

My labour has likewise been much increased by a class of verbs too frequent in the *English* language, of which the signification is so loose and general, the use so vague and indeterminate, and the senses detorted so widely from the first idea, that it is hard to trace them through the maze of variation, to catch them on the brink of utter inanity, to circumscribe them by any limitations, or interpret them by any words of distinct and settled meaning: such are *bear, break, come, cast, full, get, give, do, put, set, go, run, make, take, turn, throw*. If of these the whole power is not accurately delivered, it must be remembered, that while our language is yet living, and variable by the caprice of every tongue that speaks it, these words are hourly shifting their relations, and can no more be ascertained in a dictionary, than a grove, in the agitation of a storm, can be accurately delineated from its picture in the water.

The particles are among all nations applied with so great latitude, that they are not easily reducible under any regular scheme of explication: this difficulty is not less, nor perhaps greater, in *English*, than in other languages. I have laboured them with diligence, I hope with success; such at least as can be expected in a task, which no man, however learned or sagacious, has yet been able to perform.

Some words there are which I cannot explain, because I do not understand them; these might have been omitted very often with little inconvenience, but I would not so far indulge my vanity as to decline this confession; for when *Tully* owns himself ignorant whether *lessus*, in the twelve tables, means a *funeral song*, or *mourning garment*; and *Aristotle* doubts whether οὔρευς, in the Iliad, signifies a *mule*, or *muleteer*, I may freely, without shame, leave some obscurities to happier industry, or future information.

The rigour of interpretative lexicography requires that *the explanation, and the word explained, should be always reciprocal*; this I have always endeavoured, but could not always attain. Words are seldom exactly synonymous; a new term was not introduced, but because the former was thought inadequate: names, therefore, have often many ideas, but few ideas have many names. It was then necessary to use the proximate word, for the deficiency of single terms can very seldom be supplied by circumlocution; nor is the inconvenience great of such mutilated interpretations, because the sense may easily be collected entire from the examples.

In every word of extensive use, it was requisite to mark the progress of its meaning, and show by what gradations of intermediate sense it has passed from its primitive to its remote and accidental signification; so that every foregoing explanation should tend to that which follows, and the series be regularly concatenated from the first notion to the last.

This is specious, but not always practicable; kindred senses may be so interwoven, that the perplexity cannot be disentangled, nor any reason be assigned why one should be ranged before the other. When the radical idea branches out into parallel ramifications, how can a consecutive series be formed of senses in their nature collateral? The shades of meaning sometimes pass imperceptibly into each other; so that though on one side they apparently differ, yet it is impossible to mark the point of contact. Ideas of the same race, though not exactly alike, are sometimes so little different, that no words can express the dissimilitude, though the mind easily perceives it, when they are exhibited together; and sometimes there is such a confusion of acceptations, that discernment is wearied, and distinction puzzled, and perseverance herself hurries to an end, by crouding together what she cannot separate.

These complaints of difficulty will, by those that have never considered words beyond their popular use, be thought only the jargon of a man willing to magnify his labours, and procure veneration to his studies by involution and obscurity. But every art is obscure to those that have not learned it: this uncertainty of terms, and commixture of ideas, is well known to those who have joined philosophy with grammar; and if I have not expressed them very clearly, it must be remembered that I am speaking of that which words are insufficient to explain.

The original sense of words is often driven out of use by their metaphorical acceptations, yet must be inserted for the sake of a regular origination. Thus

I know not whether *ardour* is used for *material heat*, or whether *flagrant*, in *English*, ever signifies the same with *burning*; yet such are the primitive ideas of these words, which are therefore set first, though without examples, that the figurative senses may be commodiously deduced.

Such is the exuberance of signification which many words have obtained, that it was scarcely possible to collect all their senses; sometimes the meaning of derivatives must be sought in the mother term, and sometimes deficient explanations of the primitive may be supplied in the train of derivation. In any case of doubt or difficulty, it will be always proper to examine all the words of the same race; for some words are slightly passed over to avoid repetition, some admitted easier and clearer explanation than others, and all will be better understood, as they are considered in greater variety of structures and relations.

All the interpretations of words are not written with the same skill, or the same happiness: things equally easy in themselves, are not all equally easy to any single mind. Every writer of a long work commits errours, where there appears neither ambiguity to mislead, nor obscurity to confound him; and in a search like this, many felicities of expression will be casually overlooked, many convenient parallels will be forgotten, and many particulars will admit improvement from a mind utterly unequal to the whole performance.

But many seeming faults are to be imputed rather to the nature of the undertaking, than the negligence of the performer. Thus some explanations are unavoidably reciprocal or circular, as *hind, the female of the stag; stag, the male of the hind:* sometimes easier words are changed into harder, as *burial* into *sepulture* or *interment*, *drier* into *desiccative*, *dryness* into *siccity* or *aridity*, *fit* into *paroxysm*; for the easiest word, whatever it be, can never be translated into one more easy. But easiness and difficulty are merely relative, and if the present prevalence of our language should invite foreigners to this dictionary, many will be assisted by those words which now seem only to increase or produce obscurity. For this reason I have endeavoured frequently to join a *Teutonick* and *Roman* interpretation, as to CHEER, to *gladden*, or *exhilarate*, that every learner of *English* may be assisted by his own tongue.

The solution of all difficulties, and the supply of all defects, must be sought in the examples subjoined to the various senses of each word, and ranged according to the time of their authours.

When first I collected these authorities, I was desirous that every quotation should be useful to some other end than the illustration of a word; I therefore extracted from philosophers principles of science; from historians remarkable facts; from chymists complete processes; from divines striking exhortations; and from poets beautiful descriptions. Such is design, while it is yet at a distance from execution. When the time called upon me to range this accumulation of elegance and wisdom into an alphabetical series, I soon discovered that the bulk of my volumes would fright away the student, and was forced to depart from my scheme of including all that was pleasing or useful in *English* literature, and reduce my transcripts very often to clusters of words, in which scarcely any meaning is retained; thus to the weariness of copying, I was condemned to add the vexation of expunging. Some passages I have yet spared, which may relieve the labour of verbal searches, and intersperse with verdure and flowers the dusty desarts of barren philology.

The examples, thus mutilated, are no longer to be considered as conveying the sentiments or doctrine of their authours; the word for the sake of which they are inserted, with all its appendant clauses, has been carefully preserved; but it may sometimes happen, by hasty detruncation, that the general tendency of the sentence may be changed: the divine may desert his tenets, or the philosopher his system.

Some of the examples have been taken from writers who were never mentioned as masters of elegance or models of stile; but words must be sought where they are used; and in what pages, eminent for purity, can terms of manufacture or agriculture be found? Many quotations serve no other purpose, than that of proving the bare existence of words, and are therefore selected with less scrupulousness than those which are to teach their structures and relations.

My purpose was to admit no testimony of living authours, that I might not be misled by partiality, and that none of my cotemporaries might have reason to complain; nor have I departed from this resolution, but when some performance of uncommon excellence excited my veneration, when my memory supplied me, from late books, with an example that was wanting, or when my heart, in the tenderness of friendship, solicited admission for a favourite name.

So far have I been from any care to grace my pages with modern decorations, that I have studiously endeavoured to collect examples and authorities from the writers before the restoration, whose works I regard as *the wells of English undefiled*, as the pure sources of genuine diction. Our language, for almost a century, has, by the concurrence of many causes, been gradually departing from its original *Teutonick* character, and deviating towards a *Gallick* structure and phraseology, from which it ought to be our endeavour to recal it, by making our ancient volumes the ground-work of stile, admitting among the additions of later times, only such as may supply real deficiencies, such as are readily adopted by the genius of our tongue, and incorporate easily with our native idioms.

But as every language has a time of rudeness antecedent to perfection, as well as of false refinement and declension, I have been cautious lest my zeal for antiquity might drive me into times too remote, and croud my book with words now no longer understood. I have fixed *Sidney*'s work for the boundary, beyond which I make few excursions. From the authours which rose in the time of *Elizabeth*, a speech might be formed adequate to all the purposes of use and elegance. If the language of theology were extracted from *Hooker* and the translation of the Bible; the terms of natural knowledge from *Bacon*; the phrases of policy, war, and navigation from *Raleigh*; the dialect of poetry and fiction from *Spenser* and *Sidney*; and the diction of common life from *Shakespeare*, few ideas would be lost to mankind, for want of *English* words, in which they might be expressed.

It is not sufficient that a word is found, unless it be so combined as that its meaning is apparently determined by the tract and tenour of the sentence; such passages I have therefore chosen, and when it happened that any authour gave a definition of a term, or such an explanation as is equivalent to a definition, I have placed his authority as a supplement to my own, without regard to the chronological order, that is otherwise observed.

Some words, indeed, stand unsupported by any authority, but they are commonly derivative nouns or adverbs, formed from their primitives by regular and constant analogy, or names of things seldom occurring in books, or words of which I have reason to doubt the existence.

There is more danger of censure from the multiplicity than paucity of examples; authorities will sometimes seem to have been accumulated without necessity or use, and perhaps some will be found, which might, without loss, have been omitted. But a work of this kind is not hastily to be charged with superfluities: those quotations which to careless or unskilful perusers appear only to repeat the same sense, will often exhibit, to a more accurate examiner, diversities of signification, or, at least, afford different shades of the same meaning: one will shew the word applied to persons, another to things; one will express an ill, another a good, and a third a neutral sense; one will prove the expression genuine from an ancient authour; another will shew it elegant from a modern: a doubtful authority is corroborated by another of more credit; an ambiguous sentence is ascertained by a passage clear and determinate; the word, how often soever repeated, appears with new associates and in different combinations, and every quotation contributes something to the stability or enlargement of the language.

When words are used equivocally, I receive them in either sense; when they are metaphorical, I adopt them in their primitive acceptation.

I have sometimes, tho' rarely, yielded to the temptation of exhibiting a genealogy of sentiments, by shewing how one author copied the thoughts and diction of another: such quotations are indeed little more than repetitions, which might justly be censured, did they not gratify the mind, by affording a kind of intellectual history.

The various syntactical structures occurring in the examples have been carefully noted; the licence or negligence with which many words have been hitherto used, has made our stile capricious and indeterminate; when the different combinations of the same word are exhibited together, the preference is readily given to propriety, and I have often endeavoured to direct the choice.

Thus have I laboured to settle the orthography, display the analogy, regulate the structures, and ascertain the signification of *English* words, to perform all the parts of a faithful lexicographer: but I have not always executed my own scheme, or satisfied my own expectations. The work, whatever proofs of diligence and attention it may exhibit, is yet capable of many improvements: the orthography which I recommend is still controvertible, the etymology which I adopt is uncertain, and perhaps frequently erroneous; the explanations are sometimes too much contracted, and sometimes too much diffused, the significations are distinguished rather with subtilty than skill, and the attention is harrassed with unnecessary minuteness.

The examples are too often injudiciously truncated, and perhaps sometimes, I hope very rarely, alleged in a mistaken sense; for in making this collection I trusted more to memory, than, in a state of disquiet and embarrassment, memory can contain, and purposed to supply at the review what was left incomplete in the first transcription.

Many terms appropriated to particular occupations, though necessary and significant, are undoubtedly omitted; and of the words most studiously considered and exemplified, many senses have escaped observation.

Yet these failures, however frequent, may admit extenuation and apology. To have attempted much is always laudable, even when the enterprize is above the strength that undertakes it: To rest below his own aim is incident to every one whose fancy is active, and whose views are comprehensive; nor is any man satisfied with himself because he has done much, but because he can conceive little. When first I engaged in this work, I resolved to leave neither words nor things unexamined, and pleased myself with a prospect of the hours which I should revel away in feasts of literature, the obscure recesses of northern learning, which I should enter and ransack, the treasures with which I expected every search into those neglected mines to reward my labour, and the triumph with which I should display my acquisitions to mankind. When I had thus enquired into the original of words, I resolved to show likewise my attention to things; to pierce deep into every science, to enquire the nature of every substance of which I inserted the name, to limit every idea by a definition strictly logical, and exhibit every production of art or nature in an accurate description, that my book might be in place of all other dictionaries whether appellative or technical. But these were the dreams of a poet doomed at last to wake a lexicographer. I soon found that it is too late to look for instruments, when the work calls for execution, and that whatever abilities I had brought to my task, with those I must finally perform it. To deliberate whenever I doubted, to enquire whenever I was ignorant, would have protracted the undertaking without end, and, perhaps, without much improvement; for I did not find by my first experiments, that what I had not of my own was easily to be obtained: I saw that one enquiry only gave occasion to another, that book referred to book, that to search was not always to find, and to find was not always to be informed; and that thus to persue perfection, was, like the first inhabitants of Arcadia, to chace the sun, which, when they had reached the hill where he seemed to rest, was still beheld at the same distance from them.

I then contracted my design, determining to confide in myself, and no longer to solicit auxiliaries, which produced more incumbrance than assistance: by this I obtained at least one advantage, that I set limits to my work, which would in time be finished, though not completed.

Despondency has never so far prevailed as to depress me to negligence; some faults will at last appear to be the effects of anxious diligence and persevering activity. The nice and subtile ramifications of meaning were not easily avoided by a mind intent upon accuracy, and convinced of the necessity of disentangling combinations, and separating similitudes. Many of the distinctions which to common readers appear useless and idle, will be found real and important by men versed in the school philosophy, without which no dictionary ever shall be accurately compiled, or skilfully examined.

Some senses however there are, which, though not the same, are yet so nearly allied, that they are often confounded. Most men think indistinctly, and therefore cannot speak with exactness; and consequently some examples might be indifferently put to either signification: this uncertainty is not to be imputed to me, who do not form, but register the language; who do not teach men how they should think, but relate how they have hitherto expressed their thoughts.

The imperfect sense of some examples I lamented, but could not remedy, and hope they will be compensated by innumerable passages selected with propriety, and preserved with exactness; some shining with sparks of imagination, and some replete with treasures of wisdom.

The orthography and etymology, though imperfect, are not imperfect for want of care, but because care will not always be successful, and recollection or information come too late for use.

That many terms of art and manufacture are omitted, must be frankly acknowledged; but for this defect I may boldly allege that it was unavoidable: I could not visit caverns to learn the miner's language, nor take a voyage to perfect my skill in the dialect of navigation, nor visit the warehouses of merchants, and shops of artificers, to gain the names of commodities, utensils, tools and operations, of which no mention is found in books; what favourable accident, or easy enquiry brought within my reach, has not been neglected; but it had been a hopeless labour to glean up words, by courting living information, and contesting with the sullenness of one, and the roughness of another.

To furnish the academicians *della Crusca* with words of this kind, a series of comedies called *la Fiera*, or *the Fair*, was professedly written by *Buonaroti*; but I had no such assistant, and therefore was content to want what they must have wanted likewise, had they not luckily been so supplied.

Nor are all words which are not found in the vocabulary, to be lamented as omissions. Of the laborious and mercantile part of the people, the diction is in a great measure casual and mutable; many of their terms are formed for some temporary or local convenience, and though current at certain times and places, are in others utterly unknown. This fugitive cant, which is always in a state of increase or decay, cannot be regarded as any part of the durable materials of a language, and therefore must be suffered to perish with other things unworthy of preservation.

Care will sometimes betray to the appearance of negligence. He that is catching opportunities which seldom occur, will suffer those to pass by unregarded, which he expects hourly to return; he that is searching for rare and remote things, will neglect those that are obvious and familiar: thus many of the most common and cursory words have been inserted with little illustration, because in gathering the authorities, I forebore to copy those which I thought likely to occur whenever they were wanted. It is remarkable that, in reviewing my collection, I found the word SEA unexemplified.

Thus it happens, that in things difficult there is danger from ignorance, and in things easy from confidence; the mind, afraid of greatness, and disdainful of littleness, hastily withdraws herself from painful searches, and passes with scornful rapidity over tasks not adequate to her powers, sometimes too secure for caution, and again too anxious for vigorous effort; sometimes idle in a plain path, and sometimes distracted in labyrinths, and dissipated by different intentions.

A large work is difficult because it is large, even though all its parts might singly be performed with facility; where there are many things to be done, each must be allowed its share of time and labour, in the proportion only which it bears to the whole; nor can it be expected, that the stones which form the dome of a temple, should be squared and polished like the diamond of a ring.

Of the event of this work, for which, having laboured it with so much application, I cannot but have some degree of parental fondness, it is natural to form conjectures. Those who have been persuaded to think well of my design, require that it should fix our language, and put a stop to those alterations which time and chance have hitherto been suffered to make in it without opposition. With this consequence I will confess that I flattered myself for a while; but now begin to fear that I have indulged expectation which neither reason nor experience can justify. When we see men grow old and die at a certain time one after another, from century to century, we laugh at the elixir that promises to prolong life to a thousand years; and with equal justice may the lexicographer be derided, who being able to produce no example of a nation that has preserved their words and phrases from mutability, shall imagine that his dictionary can embalm his language, and secure it from corruption and decay, that it is in his power to change sublunary nature, or clear the world at once from folly, vanity, and affectation.

With this hope, however, academies have been instituted, to guard the avenues of their languages, to retain fugitives, and repulse intruders; but their vigilance and activity have hitherto been vain; sounds are too volatile and subtile for legal restraints; to enchain syllables, and to lash the wind, are equally the undertakings of pride, unwilling to measure its desires by its strength. The *French* language has visibly changed under the inspection of the academy; the stile of *Amelot*'s translation of father *Paul* is observed by *Le Courayer* to be *un peu passé*; and no *Italian* will maintain, that the diction of any modern writer is not perceptibly different from that of *Boccace*, *Machiavel*, or *Caro*.

Total and sudden transformations of a language seldom happen; conquests and migrations are now very rare: but there are other causes of change, which, though slow in their operation, and invisible in their progress, are perhaps as much superiour to human resistance, as the revolutions of the sky, or intumescence of the tide. Commerce, however necessary, however lucrative, as it depraves the manners, corrupts the language; they that have frequent intercourse with strangers, to whom they endeavour to accommodate themselves, must in time learn a mingled dialect, like the jargon which serves the traffickers on the *Mediterranean* and *Indian* coasts. This will not always be confined to the exchange, the warehouse, or the port, but will be communicated by degrees to other ranks of the people, and be at last incorporated with the current speech.

There are likewise internal causes equally forcible. The language most likely to continue long without alteration, would be that of a nation raised a little, and but a little, above barbarity, secluded from strangers, and totally employed in procuring the conveniencies of life; either without books, or, like some of the *Mahometan* countries, with very few: men thus busied and unlearned, having only such words as common use requires, would perhaps long continue to express the same notions by the same signs. But no such constancy can be expected in a people polished by arts, and classed by subordination, where one part of the community is sustained and accommodated by the labour of the other. Those who have much leisure to think, will always be enlarging the stock of ideas, and every increase of knowledge, whether real or fancied, will produce new words, or combinations of words. When the mind is unchained from necessity, it will range after convenience; when it is left at large in the fields of speculation, it will shift opinions; as any custom is disused, the words that expressed it must perish with it; as any opinion grows popular, it will innovate speech in the same proportion as it alters practice.

As by the cultivation of various sciences, a language is amplified, it will be more furnished with words deflected from their original sense; the geometrician will talk of a courtier's zenith, or the excentrick virtue of a wild hero, and the physician of sanguine expectations and phlegmatick delays. Copiousness of speech will give opportunities to capricious choice, by which some words will be preferred, and others degraded; vicissitudes of fashion will enforce the use of new, or extend the signification of known terms. The tropes of poetry will make hourly encroachments, and the metaphorical will become the current sense: pronunciation will be varied by levity or ignorance, and the pen must at length comply with the tongue; illiterate writers will at one time or other, by publick infatuation, rise into renown, who, not knowing the original import of words, will use them with colloquial licentiousness, confound distinction, and forget propriety. As politeness increases, some expressions will be considered as too gross and vulgar for the delicate, others as too formal and ceremonious for the gay and airy; new phrases are therefore adopted, which must, for the same reasons, be in time dismissed. *Swift*, in his petty treatise on the *English* language, allows that new words must sometimes be introduced, but proposes that none should be suffered to become obsolete. But what makes a word obsolete, more than general agreement to forbear it? and how shall it be continued, when it conveys an offensive idea, or recalled again into the mouths of mankind, when it has once by disuse become unfamiliar, and by unfamiliarity unpleasing.

There is another cause of alteration more prevalent than any other, which yet in the present state of the world cannot be obviated. A mixture of two languages will produce a third distinct from both; and they will always be mixed, where the chief part of education, and the most conspicuous accomplishment, is skill in ancient or in foreign tongues. He that has long cultivated another language, will find its words and combinations croud upon his memory; and haste or negligence, refinement or affectation, will obtrude borrowed terms and exotick expressions.

The great pest of speech is frequency of translation. No book was ever turned from one language into another, without imparting something of its native idiom; this is the most mischievous and comprehensive innovation; single words may enter by thousands, and the fabrick of the tongue continue the same, but new phraseology changes much at once; it alters not the single stones of the building, but the order of the columns. If an academy should be established for the cultivation of our stile, which I, who can never wish to see dependance multiplied, hope the spirit of *English* liberty will hinder or destroy, let them, instead of compiling grammars and dictionaries, endeavour, with all their influence, to stop the licence of translatours, whose idleness and ignorance, if it be suffered to proceed, will reduce us to babble a dialect of *France*.

If the changes we fear be thus irresistible, what remains but to acquiesce with silence, as in the other insurmountable distresses of humanity? it remains that we retard what we cannot repel, that we palliate what we cannot cure. Life may be lengthened by care, though death cannot be ultimately defeated: tongues, like governments, have a natural tendency to degeneration;

we have long preserved our constitution, let us make some struggles for our language.

In hope of giving longevity to that which its own nature forbids to be immortal, I have devoted this book, the labour of years, to the honour of my country, that we may no longer yield the palm of philology without a contest to the nations of the continent. The chief glory of every people arises from its authours: whether I shall add any thing by my own writings to the reputation of *English* literature, must be left to time: much of my life has been lost under the pressures of disease; much has been trifled away; and much has always been spent in provision for the day that was passing over me; but I shall not think my employment useless or ignoble, if by my assistance foreign nations, and distant ages, gain access to the propagators of knowledge, and understand the teachers of truth; if my labours afford light to the repositories of science, and add celebrity to *Bacon*, to *Hooker*, to *Milton*, and to *Boyle*.

When I am animated by this wish, I look with pleasure on my book, however defective, and deliver it to the world with the spirit of a man that has endeavoured well. That it will immediately become popular I have not promised to myself: a few wild blunders, and risible absurdities, from which no work of such multiplicity was ever free, may for a time furnish folly with laughter, and harden ignorance in contempt; but useful diligence will at last prevail, and there never can be wanting some who distinguish desert; who will consider that no dictionary of a living tongue ever can be perfect, since while it is hastening to publication, some words are budding, and some falling away; that a whole life cannot be spent upon syntax and etymology, and that even a whole life would not be sufficient; that he, whose design includes whatever language can express, must often speak of what he does not understand; that a writer will sometimes be hurried by eagerness to the end, and sometimes faint with weariness under a task, which *Scaliger* compares to the labours of the anvil and the mine; that what is obvious is not always known, and what is known is not always present; that sudden fits of inadvertency will surprize vigilance, slight avocations will seduce attention, and casual eclipses will darken learning; and that the writer shall often in vain trace his memory at the moment of need, for that which yesterday he knew with intuitive readiness, and which will come uncalled into his thoughts to-morrow.

In this work, when it shall be found that much is omitted, let it not be forgotten that much likewise is performed; and though no book was ever spared out of tenderness to the authour, and the world is little solicitous to know whence proceeded the faults of that which it condemns; yet it may gratify curiosity to inform it, that the *English Dictionary* was written with little assistance of the learned, and without any patronage of the great; not in the soft obscurities of retirement, or under the shelter of academick bowers, but amidst inconvenience and distraction, in sickness and in sorrow: and it may repress the triumph of malignant criticism to observe, that if our language is not here fully displayed, I have only failed in an attempt which no human powers have hitherto completed. If the lexicons of ancient tongues, now immutably fixed, and comprised in a few volumes, are yet, after the toil of successive ages, inadequate and delusive; if the aggregated knowledge, and co-operating diligence of the *Italian* academicians, did not secure them from the censure of *Beni*; if the embodied criticks of *France*, when fifty years had been spent upon their work, were obliged to change its oeconomy, and give their second edition another form, I may surely be contented without the praise of perfection, which, if I could obtain, in this gloom of solitude, what would it avail me? I have protracted my work till most of those whom I wished to please, have sunk into the grave, and success and miscarriage are empty sounds: I therefore dismiss it with frigid tranquillity, having little to fear or hope from censure or from praise.

Letter to the Earl of Chesterfield

FRIDAY 7 FEBRUARY 1755

My Lord: February 1755

I have been lately informed by the Proprietor of The World that two Papers in which my Dictionary is recommended to the Public were written by your Lordship. To be so distinguished is an honour which, being very little accustomed to favours from the Great, I know not well how to receive, or in what terms to acknowledge.

When upon some slight encouragment I first visited your Lordship I was overpowered like the rest of Mankind by the enchantment of your adress, and could not forbear to wish that I might boast myself Le Vainqueur du Vainqueur de la Terre, that I might obtain that regard for which I saw the world contending, but I found my attendance so little incouraged, that neither pride nor modesty would suffer me to continue it. When I had once adressed your Lordship in public, I had exhausted all the Art of pleasing which a retired and uncourtly Scholar can possess. I had done all that I could, and no Man is well pleased to have his all neglected, be it ever so little.

Seven years, My lord have now past since I waited in your outward Rooms or was repulsed from your Door, during which time I have been pushing on my work through difficulties of which it is useless to complain, and have brought it at last to the verge of Publication without one Act of assistance, one word of encouragement, or one smile of favour. Such treatment I did not expect, for I never had a Patron before.

The Shepherd in Virgil grew at last acquainted with Love, and found him a Native of the Rocks. Is not a Patron, My Lord, one who looks with unconcern on a Man struggling for Life in the water and when he has reached ground encumbers him with help. The notice which you have been pleased to take of my Labours, had it been early, had been kind; but it has been delayed till I am indifferent and cannot enjoy it, till I am solitary and cannot impart it, till I am known and do not want it.

I hope it is no very cinical asperity not to confess obligation where no benefit has been received, or to be unwilling that the Public should consider me as owing that to a Patron, which Providence has enabled me to do for myself.

Having carried on my work thus far with so little obligation to any favourer of Learning I shall not be disappointed though I should conclude it, if less be possible, with less, for I have been long wakened from that Dream of hope, in which I once boasted myself with so much exultation, My lord, Your Lordship's Most humble, most obedient Servant,

S.J.

Letter to Bennet Langton

TUESDAY 6 MAY 1755

Sir: May 6, 1755

It has been long observed that men do not suspect faults which they do not commit; your own Elegance of manners and punctuality of complaisance did not suffer you to impute to me that negligence of which I was guilty, and which I have not since attoned. I received both your Letters and received them with pleasure proportionate to the esteem which so short an acquaintance strongly impressed, and which I hope to confirm by nearer knowledge, though I am afraid that gratification will be for a time witheld.

I have indeed published my Book, of which I beg to know your Fathers Judgement and yours, and I have now staid long enough to watch its progress into the world. It has you see, no patrons, and I think has yet had no opponents except the Criticks of the coffeehouse, whose outcries are soon dispersed into the air, and are thought on no more. From this therefore I am at liberty, and think of taking the opportunity of this interval to make an excursion, and why not then into Lincolnshire, or to mention a stronger attraction why not to dear Mr. Langton? I will give the true reason which I know you will approve. I have a Mother more than eighty years old, who has counted the days to the publication of my book in hopes of seeing me, and to her, if I can disengage myself here, I resolve to go.

As I know, dear Sir, that to delay my visit for a reason like this will not deprive me of your esteem, I beg it may not lessen your kindness. I have very seldom received an offer of Friendship which I so earnestly desire to cultivate and mature. I shall rejoice to hear from you till I can see you, and will see you as soon as I can, for when the duty that calls me to Lichfield is discharged, my inclination will hurry me to Langton. I shall delight to hear the ocean roar or see the stars twinkle, in the company of men to whom nature does not spread her volumes or utter her voice in vain.

Do not, dear Sir, make the slowness of this letter a precedent for delay, or imagine that I approved the incivility that I have committed, for I have known you enough to love you, and sincerely to wish a further knowledge, and I assure you once more that to live in a House which contains such a Father and such a Son will be accounted a very uncommon degree of pleasure by, Dear sir, Your most obliged and most humble servant,

SAM. JOHNSON

Letter to Miss Hill Boothby

WEDNESDAY 31 DECEMBER 1755

My Sweet Angel: Dec. 31

I have read your book, I am afraid you will think without any great improvement, whether you can read my notes I know not. You ought not to be offended, I am perhaps as sincere as the writer. In all things that terminate here I shall be much guided by your influence, and should take or leave by your direction, but I cannot receive my religion from any human hand. I desire however to be instructed and am far from thinking my self perfect.

I beg you to return the book when you have looked into it. I should not have written what is in the margin, had I not had it from you, or had I not intended to show it you.

It affords me a new conviction that in these books there is little new, except new forms of expression, which may be sometimes taken even by the writer, for new doctrines.

I sincerely hope that God whom you so much desire to serve aright will bless you, and restore you to health, if he sees it best. Surely no human understanding can pray for any thing temporal otherwise than conditionally. Dear Angel do not forget me. My heart is full of tenderness.

It has pleased God to permit me to be much better, which I believe will please you.

Give me leave, who have thought much on Medicine, to propose to you an easy and I think a very probable remedy for indigestion and lubricity of the bowels. Dr. Laurence has told me your case. Take an ounce of dried orange peel finely powdered, divide it into scruples, and take one Scruple at a time in any manner; the best way is perhaps to drink it in a glass of hot red port, or to eat it first and drink the wine after it. If you mix cinnamon or nutmeg with the powder it were not worse, but it will be more bulky and so more troublesome. This is a medicine not disgusting, not costly, easily tried, and if not found useful easily left off.

I would not have you offer it to the Doctor as mine. Physicians do not love intruders, yet do not take it without his leave. But do not be easily put off, for it is in my opinion very likely to help you, and not likely to do you harm, do not take too much in haste, a scruple once in three hours or about five scruples a day will be sufficient to begin, or less if you find any aversion. I think using sugar with it might be bad, if Syrup, use old Syrup of Quinces, but even that I do not like. I should think better of conserve of Sloes. Has the Doctor mentioned the bark? in powder you could hardly take it, perhaps you might bear the infusion?

Do not think me troublesome, I am full of care. I love you and honour you, and am very unwilling to lose you. A Dieu Je vous commende. I am, Madam, your most affectionate, humble servant,

SAM. JOHNSON

My compliments to my dear Miss.

Letter to Miss Hill Boothby

THURSDAY 8 JANUARY 1756

Honoured Madam: Jan. 8, 1756

I beg of you to endeavour to live. I have returned your Law which however I earnestly entreat you to give me. I am in great trouble, if you can write three words to me, be pleased to do it. I am afraid to say much, and cannot say nothing when my dearest is in danger.

The Allmercifull God have mercy on You. I am, Madam, your

SAM. JOHNSON

Letter to Samuel Richardson

TUESDAY 16 MARCH 1756

Sir: Gough Square, March 16

I am obliged to entreat your assistance, I am now under an arrest for five pounds eighteen shillings. Mr. Strahan from whom I should have received the necessary help in this case is not at home, and I am afraid of not finding Mr. Millar, if you will be so good as to send me this sum, I will very gratfully repay You, and add it to all former obligations. I am, sir, Your most obedient and most humble servant,

SAM. JOHNSON

An Introduction to the Political State of Great-Britain

As it is intended to exhibit in the following pamphlet an accurate account of every political debate, it appears necessary to lay before the reader a succinct account of *British* affairs, from the time in which our present relations to the continent began, and the competitions which keep us at variance with our neighbours arose. Without this previous knowledge, either recollected or acquired, it is not easy to understand the various opinions which every change in our affairs produces, or the questions which divide the nation into parties, and cause divisions in the parliament, and wars among the pamphleteers.

THE present system of *English* politics may properly be said to have taken rise in the reign of queen *Elizabeth*. At this time the protestant religion was established, which naturally allied us to the reformed state, and made all the popish powers our enemies.

We began in the same reign to extend our trade, by which we made it necessary to ourselves to watch the commercial progress of our neighbours; and, if not to incommode and obstruct their traffick, to hinder them from impairing ours.

We then likewise settled colonies in *America*, which was become the great scene of *European* ambition; for, seeing with what treasures the *Spaniards* were annually inriched from *Mexico* and *Peru*, every nation imagined, that an *American* conquest or plantation would certainly fill the mother country with gold and silver. This produced a large extent of very distant dominions, of which we, at this time, neither knew nor foresaw the advantage or incumbrance: We seem to have snatched them into our hands, upon no very just principles of policy, only because every state, according to a prejudice of long continuance, concludes itself more powerful as its territories become larger.

The discoveries of new regions, which were then every day made, the profit of remote traffick, and the necessity of long voyages, produced, in a few years, a great multiplication of shipping. The sea was considered as the wealthy element; and, by degrees, a new kind of sovereignty arose, called naval dominion.

As the chief trade of the world, so the chief maritime power was at first in the hands of the *Portuguese* and *Spaniards*, who, by a compact, to which the consent of other princes was not asked, had divided the newly discovered countries between them; but the crown of *Portugal* having fallen to the king of *Spain*, or being seized by him, he was master of the ships of the two nations, with which he kept all the coasts of *Europe* in alarm, till the *Armada*, which he had raised at a vast expence for the conquest of *England*, was destroyed, which put a stop, and almost an end, to the naval power of the *Spaniards*.

At this time the *Dutch*, who were oppressed by the *Spaniards*, and feared yet greater evils than they felt, resolved no longer to endure the insolence of their masters; they therefore revolted, and after a struggle, in which they were assisted by the money and forces of *Elizabeth*, erected an independent and powerful commonwealth.

When the inhabitants of the Low-Countries had formed their system of government, and some remission of the war gave them leisure to form schemes of future prosperity, they easily perceived that, as their territories were narrow and their numbers small, they could preserve themselves only by that power which is the consequence of wealth; and that, by a people whose country produced only the necessaries of life, wealth was not to be acquired, but from foreign dominions, and by the transportation of the products of one country into another.

From this necessity, thus justly estimated, arose a plan of commerce, which was for many years prosecuted with industry and success, perhaps never seen in the world before, and by which the poor tenants of mudwalled villages and impassable bogs, erected themselves into high and mighty states, who put the greatest monarchs at defiance, whose alliance was courted by the proudest, and whose power was dreaded by the fiercest nation. By the establishment of this state there arose to *England* a new ally and a new rival.

At this time, which seems to be the period destined for the change of the face of *Europe*, *France* began first to rise into power, and, from defending her own provinces with difficulty and fluctuating success, to threaten her neighbours with incroachments and devastations. *Henry* the fourth having, after a long struggle, obtained the crown, found it easy to govern nobles exhausted and wearied with a long civil war, and having composed the disputes between the protestants and papists, so as to obtain, at least, a truce for both parties, was at leisure to accumulate treasure, and raise forces which he purposed to have employed in a design of settling for ever the balance of *Europe*. Of this great scheme he lived not to see the vanity, or to feel the disappointment; for he was murdered in the midst of his mighty preparations.

The *French* however were in this reign taught to know their own power; and the great designs of a king, whose wisdom they had so long experienced, even though they were not brought to actual experiment, disposed them to consider themselves as masters of the destiny of their neighbours; and, from that time, he that shall nicely examine their schemes and conduct will, I believe, find that they began to take an air of superiority, to which they had never pretended before; and that they have been always employed, more or less openly upon schemes of dominion, though with frequent interruptions from domestic troubles, and with those intermissions which human counsels must always suffer, as men intrusted with great affairs are dissipated in youth and languid in age, are embarrassed by competitors, or, without any external reason, change their minds.

France was now no longer in dread of insults and invasions from *England*. She was not only able to maintain her own territories, but prepared, on all occasions, to invade others, and we had now a neighbour whose interest it was to be an enemy, and who has disturbed us, from that time to this, with open hostility or secret machinations.

Such was the state of *England* and its neighbours, when *Elizabeth* left the crown to *James* of *Scotland*. It has not, I think, been frequently observed by historians at how critical a time the union of the two kingdoms happened. Had *England* and *Scotland* continued separate kingdoms, when *France* was established in the full possession of her natural power, the *Scots*, in continuance of the league, which it would now have been more than ever their interest to observe, would, upon every instigation of the *French* court, have raised an army with *French money*, and harrassed us with an invasion in which they would have thought themselves successful, whatever numbers they might have left behind them. To a people warlike and indigent, an incursion into a rich country is never hurtful. The pay of *France*, and the plunder of the northern counties, would always have tempted them to hazard their lives, and we should have been under a necessity of keeping a line of garrisons along our border.

This trouble, however, we escaped by the accession of king *James*; but it is uncertain, whether his natural disposition did not injure us more than this accidental condition happened to benefit us. He was a man of great theoretical knowledge, but of no practical wisdom; he was very well able to discern the true interest of himself, his kingdom, and his posterity, but sacrificed it, upon all occasions to his present pleasure or his ease; so conscious of his own knowledge and abilities, that he would not suffer a minister to govern and so lax of attention, and timorous of opposition, that he was not able to govern for himself. With this character *James* quietly saw the Dutch invade our commerce; the *French* grew every day stronger and stronger, and the protestant interest, of which he boasted himself the head, was oppressed on every side, while he writ, and hunted, and dispatched ambassadors, who, when their master's weakness was once known, were treated in foreign courts with very little ceremony. *James*, however, took care to be flattered at home, and was neither angry nor ashamed at the appearance that he made in other countries.

Thus *England* grew weaker, or what is in political estimation the same thing, saw her neighbours grow stronger, without receiving proportionable additions to her own power. Not that the mischief was so great as it is generally conceived or represented; for, I believe, it may be made to appear, that the wealth of the nation was, in this reign, very much increased, though that of the crown was lessened. Our reputation for war was impaired, but commerce seems to have been carried on with great industry and vigour, and nothing was wanting, but that we should have defended ourselves from the incroachments of our neighbours.

The inclination to plant colonies in *America* still continued, and this being the only project in which men of adventure and enterprise could exert their qualities in a pacific reign, multitudes, who were discontented with their condition in their native country, and such multitudes there will always be, sought relief, or at least change in the western regions, where they settled in the northern part of the continent, at a distance from the *Spaniards* at that time almost the only nation that had any power or will to obstruct us.

Such was the condition of this country when the unhappy *Charles* inherited the crown. He had seen the errors of his father, without being able to prevent them, and, when he began his reign, endeavoured to raise the nation to its former dignity. The *French* papists had begun a new war upon the protestants: *Charles* sent a fleet to invade *Rhee* and relieve *Rochelle*, but his attempts were defeated, and the protestants were subdued. The *Dutch* grown wealthy and strong, claimed the right of fishing in the *British* seas: this claim the king, who saw the increasing power of the states of *Holland*, resolved to contest. But for this end it was necessary to build a fleet, and a fleet could not be built without expence: he was advised to levy ship-money, which gave occasion to the civil war, of which the events and conclusion are too well known.

While the inhabitants of this island were embroiled among themselves, the power of *France* and *Holland* was every day increasing. The *Dutch* had overcome the difficulties of their infant commonwealth; and as they still retained their vigour and industry, from rich grew continually richer, and from powerful more powerful. They extended their traffick, and had not yet admitted luxury, so that they had the means and the will to accumulate wealth, without any incitement to spend it. The *French*, who wanted nothing to make them powerful, but a prudent regulation of their revenues, and a proper use of their natural advantages, by the successive care of skilful ministers became every day stronger, and more conscious of their strength.

About this time it was, that the *French* first began to turn their thoughts to traffick and navigation, and to desire like other nations an *American* territory. All the fruitful and valuable parts of the western world were already either occupied or claimed, and nothing remained for *France* but the leavings of other navigators, for she was not yet haughty enough to seize what the neighbouring powers had already appropriated.

The *French* therefore contented themselves with sending a colony to *Canada*, a cold uncomfortable uninviting region, from which nothing but furrs and fish were to be had, and where the new inhabitants could only pass a laborious and necessitous life in perpetual regret of the deliciousness and plenty of their native country.

Notwithstanding the opinion which our countrymen have been taught to entertain of the comprehension and foresight of *French* politicians, I am not able to persuade myself, that when this colony was first planted, it was thought of much value, even by those that encouraged it; there was probably nothing more intended than to provide a drain into which the waste of an exuberant nation might be thrown, a place where those who could do no good might live without the power of doing mischief. Some new advantage they undoubtedly saw, or imagined themselves to see, and what more was necessary to the establishment of the colony was supplied by natural inclination to experiments, and that impatience of doing nothing, to which mankind perhaps owe much of what is imagined to be effected by more splendid motives.

In this region of desolate sterility they settled themselves, upon whatever principle; and as they have from that time had the happiness of a government by which no interest has been neglected, nor any part of their subjects overlooked, they have, by continual encouragement and assistance from *France*, been perpetually enlarging their bounds and increasing their numbers.

These were at first, like other nations who invaded *America*, inclined to consider the neighbourhood of the natives, as troublesome and dangerous, and are charged with having destroy'd great numbers, but they are now grown wiser, if not honester, and instead of endeavouring to frighten the *Indians* away, they invite them to intermarriage and cohabitation, and allure them by all practicable methods to become the subjects of the king of *France*.

If the *Spaniards*, when they first took possession of the newly discovered world, instead of destroying the inhabitants by thousands, had either had the humanity or the policy to have conciliated them by kind treatment, and to have united them gradually to their own people, such an accession might have been made to the power of the king of *Spain*, as would have made him far the greatest monarch that ever yet ruled in the globe; but the opportunity was lost by foolishness and cruelty, and now can never be recovered.

When the parliament had finally prevailed over our king and the army over the parliament, the interest of the two commonwealths of *England* and *Holland* soon appeared to be opposite, and the new government declared war against the *Dutch*. In this contest was exerted the utmost power of the two nations, and the *Dutch* were finally defeated, yet not with such evidence of superiority as left us much reason to boast our victory; they were obliged however to solicit peace, which was granted them on easy conditions, and *Cromwell*, who was now possessed of the supreme power, was left at leisure to pursue other designs.

The *European* powers had not yet ceased to look with envy on the *Spanish* acquisitions in *America*, and therefore *Cromwell* thought that, if he gained any part of these celebrated regions, he should exalt his own reputation, and inrich the country. He therefore quarreled with the *Spaniards* upon some such subject of contention, as he that is resolved upon hostility may always find, and sent *Pen* and *Venables* into the western seas. They first landed in *Hispaniola*, whence they were driven off with no great reputation to themselves, and that they might not return without having done something, they afterwards invaded *Jamaica*, where they found less resistance, and obtained that Island, which was afterwards consigned to us, being probably of little value to the *Spaniards*, and continues to this day a place of great wealth and dreadful wickedness, a den of tyrants, and a dungeon of slaves.

Cromwell, who perhaps had not leisure to study foreign politics, was very fatally mistaken with regard to *Spain* and *France*. *Spain* had been the last power in *Europe*, which had openly pretended to give law to other nations, and the memory of this terror remained when the real cause was at an end. We had more lately been frighted by *Spain* than by *France*, and though very few were then alive of the generation that had their sleep broken by the *Armada*, yet the name of the *Spaniards* was still terrible, and a war against them was pleasing to the people.

Our own troubles had left us very little desire to look out upon the continent, and inveterate prejudice hindred us from perceiving, that for more than half a century the power of *France* had been increasing, and that of *Spain* had been growing less; nor does it seem to have been remembered, which, yet required no great depth of policy to discern, that of two monarchs, neither of which could be long our friend, it was our interest to have the weaker near us, or that if a war should happen, *Spain*, however wealthy or strong in herself, was by the dispersion of her territories more obnoxious to the attacks of a naval power, and consequently had more to fear from us, and had it less in her power to hurt us.

All these considerations were overlooked by the wisdom of that age, and *Cromwell* assisted the *French* to drive the *Spaniards* out of *Flanders* at a time when it was our interest to have supported the *Spaniards* against *France*, as formerly the *Hollanders* against *Spain*, by which we might at least have retarded the growth of the *French* power, though I think it must have finally prevailed.

During this time, our colonies which were less disturbed by our commotions than the mother country, naturally increased; it is probable that many who were unhappy at home took shelter in those remote regions, where for the sake of inviting greater numbers, every one was allowed to think and live his own way. The *French* settlement in the mean time went slowly forward, too inconsiderable to raise any jealousy, and too weak to attempt any incroachments.

When *Cromwell* died, the confusions that followed produced the restoration of monarchy, and some time was employed in repairing the ruins of our constitution, and restoring the nation to a state of peace. In every change there will be many that suffer real or imaginary grievances, and therefore many will be dissatisfied. This was, perhaps, the reason why several colonies had their beginning in the reign of *Charles* the second. The *Quakers* willingly sought refuge in *Pensylvania*; and it is not unlikely that *Carolina* owed its inhabitants to the remains of that restless disposition, which had given so much disturbance to our country, and had now no opportunity of acting at home.

The *Dutch* still continuing to increase in wealth and power, either kindled the resentment of their neighbours by their insolence, or raised their envy by their prosperity. *Charles* made war upon them without much advantage; but they were obliged at last to confess him the sovereign of the narrow seas. They were reduced almost to extremities by an invasion from *France*; but soon recovered from their consternation, and, by the fluctuation of war, regained their cities and provinces with the same speed as they had lost them.

During the time of *Charles* the second the power of *France* was every day increasing; and *Charles*, who never disturbed himself with remote consequences, saw the progress of her arms, and the extension of her dominions, with very little uneasiness. He was indeed sometimes driven by the prevailing faction into confederacies against her; but as he had, probably, a secret partiality in her favour, he never persevered long in acting against her, nor ever acted with much vigour: so that, by his feeble resistance, he rather raised her confidence, than hindered her designs.

About this time the *French* first began to perceive the advantage of commerce, and the importance of a naval force; and such encouragement was given to manufactures, and so eagerly was every project received, by which trade could be advanced, that, in a few years, the sea was filled with their ships, and all the parts of the world crowded with their merchants. There is, perhaps, no instance in human story of such a change produced, in so short a time, in the schemes and manners of a people, of so many new sources of wealth opened, and such numbers of artificers and merchants made to start out of the ground, as was seen in the ministry of *Colbert*.

Now it was that the power of *France* became formidable to *England*. Her dominions were large before, and her armies numerous; but her operations were necessarily confined to the continent. She had neither ships for the transportation of her troops, nor money for their support in distant expeditions. *Colbert* saw both these wants, and saw that commerce only would supply them. The fertility of their country furnishes the *French* with commodities; the poverty of the common people keeps the price of labour low. By the obvious practice of selling much and buying little, it was apparent that they would soon draw the wealth of other countries into their own; and, by carrying out their merchandise in their own vessels, a numerous body of sailors would quickly be raised.

This was projected, and this was performed. The king of *France* was soon enabled to bribe those whom he could not conquer, and to terrify with his fleets those whom his armies could not have approached. The influence of *France* was suddenly diffused over all the globe; her arms were dreaded, and her pensions received in remote regions, and those were almost ready to acknowledge her sovereignty, who, a few years before, had scarcely heard her name. She thundered on the coasts of *Africa*, and received ambassadors from *Siam*.

So much may be done by one wise man, endeavouring with honesty the advantage of the public. But that we may not rashly condemn all ministers as wanting wisdom or integrity, whose counsels have produced no such apparent benefits to their country, it must be considered, that *Colbert* had means of acting, which our government does not allow. He could inforce all his orders by the power of an absolute monarch; he could compel individuals to sacrifice their private profit to the general good; he could make one understanding preside over many hands, and remove difficulties by quick and violent expedients. Where no man thinks himself under any obligation to submit to another, and, instead of co-operating in one great scheme, every one hastens through by-paths to private profit, no great change can suddenly be made; nor is superior knowledge of much effect, where every man resolves to use his own eyes and his own judgment, and every one applauds his own dexterity and diligence in proportion as he becomes rich sooner than his neighbour.

Colonies are always the effects and causes of navigation. They who visit many countries find some in which pleasure, profit or safety invite them to settle; and these settlements, when they are once made, must keep a perpetual correspondence with the original country, to which they are subject, and on which they depend for protection in danger, and supplies in necessity. So that a country, once discovered and planted, must always find employment for shipping, more certainly than any foreign commerce, which, depending on casualties, may be sometimes more and sometimes less, and which other nations may contract or suppress. A trade to colonies can never be much impaired, being, in reality, only an intercourse between distant provinces of the same empire, from which intruders are easily excluded; likewise the interest and affection of the correspondent parties, however distant, is the same.

On this reason all nations, whose power has been exerted on the ocean, have fixed colonies in remote parts of the world, and while those colonies subsisted, navigation, if it did not increase, was always preserved from total decay. With this policy the *French* were well acquainted, and therefore improved and augmented the settlements in *America*, and other regions, in proportion as they advanced their schemes of naval greatness.

The exact time in which they made their acquisitions in *America*, or other quarters of the globe, it is not necessary to collect. It is sufficient to observe, that their trade and their colonies increased together; and, if their naval armaments were carried on, as they really were, in greater proportion to their commerce, than can be practised in other countries, it must be attributed to the martial disposition at that time prevailing in the nation, to the frequent wars which *Lewis* the fourteenth made upon his neighbours, and to the extensive commerce of the *English* and *Dutch*, which afforded so much plunder to privateers, that war was more lucrative than traffick.

Thus the naval power of *France* continued to increase during the reign of *Charles* the second, who, between his fondness of ease and pleasure, the struggles of faction, which he could not suppress, and his inclination to the friendship of absolute monarchy, had not much power or desire to repress it. And of *James* the second, it could not be expected that he should act against his neighbours with great vigour, having the whole body of his subjects to oppose. He was not ignorant of the real interest of his country; he desired its power and its happiness, and thought rightly, that there is no happiness without religion; but he thought very erroneously and absurdly, that there is no religion without popery.

When the necessity of self-preservation had impelled the subjects of *James* to drive him from the throne, there came a time in which the passions, as well as interest of the government, acted against the *French*, and in which it may perhaps be reasonably doubted, whether the desire of humbling *France* was not stronger than that of exalting *England*; of this, however, it is not necessary to inquire, since, though the intention may be different, the event will be the same. All mouths were now open to declare what every eye had observed before, that the arms of *France* were become dangerous to *Europe*, and that, if her incroachments were suffered a little longer, resistance would be too late.

It was now determined to reassert the empire of the sea; but it was more easily determined than performed: the *French* made a vigorous defence against the united power of *England* and *Holland*, and were sometimes masters of the ocean, though the two maritime powers were united against them. At length, however, they were defeated at *La Hogue*; a great part of their fleet was destroyed, and they were reduced to carry on the war only with their privateers, from whom there was suffered much petty mischief, though there was no danger of conquest or invasion. They distressed our merchants, and obliged us to the continual expence of convoys and fleets of observation; and, by skulking in little coves and shallow waters, escaped our pursuit.

In this reign began our confederacy with the *Dutch*, which mutual interest has now improved into a friendship, conceived by some to be inseparable, and from that time the states began to be termed, in the stile of politicians, our faithful friends, the allies which nature has given us, our protestant confederates, and by many other names of national endearment. We have, it is true, the same interest, as opposed to *France*, and some resemblance of religion, as opposed to popery; but we have such a rivalry, in respect of commerce, as will always keep us from very close adherence to each other. No mercantile man, or mercantile nation, has any friendship but for money, and alliance between them will last no longer than their common safety or common profit is endangered; no longer than they have an enemy, who threatens to take from each more than either can steal from the other.

We were both sufficiently interested in repressing the ambition, and obstructing the commerce of *France*; and therefore we concurred with as much fidelity and as regular co-operation as is commonly found. The *Dutch* were in immediate danger, the armies of their enemies hovered over their country, and therefore they were obliged to dismiss for a time their love of money, and their narrow projects of private profit, and to do what a trader does not willingly at any time believe necessary, to sacrifice a part for the preservation of the whole.

A peace was at length made, and the *French* with their usual vigour and industry rebuilt their fleets, restored their commerce, and became in a very few years able to contest again the dominion of the sea. Their ships were well built, and always very numerously manned, their commanders having no hopes but from their bravery or their fortune, were resolute, and being very carefully educated for the sea, were eminently skilful.

All this was soon perceived, when queen *Anne*, the then darling of *England*, declared war against *France*. Our success by sea, though sufficient to keep us from dejection, was not such as dejected our enemies. It is, indeed, to be confessed, that we did not exert our whole naval strength; *Marlborough* was the governor of our counsels, and the great view of *Marlborough* was a war by land, which he knew well how to conduct, both to the honour of his country and his own profit. The fleet was therefore starved that the army might be supplied, and naval advantages were neglected for the sake of taking a town in *Flanders*, to be garrisoned by our allies. The *French*, however, were so weakened by one defeat after another, that, though their fleet was never destroyed by any total overthrow, they at last retained it in their harbours, and applied their whole force to the resistance of the confederate army, that now began to approach their frontiers, and threatned to lay waste their provinces and cities.

In the latter years of this war, the danger of their neighbourhood in *America* seems to have been considered, and a fleet was fitted out and supplied with a proper number of land forces to seize *Quebec*, the capital of *Canada*, or *New France*; but this expedition miscarried, like that of *Anson* against the *Spaniards*, by the lateness of the season, and our ignorance of the coasts, on which we were to act. We returned with loss, and only excited our enemies to greater vigilance, and perhaps to stronger fortifications.

When the peace of *Utrecht* was made, which those who clamoured among us most loudly against it, found it their interest to keep, the *French* applied themselves with the utmost industry to the extension of their trade, which we were so far from hindering, that for many years our ministry thought their friendship of such value, as to be cheaply purchased by whatever concession.

Instead therefore of opposing, as we had hitherto professed to do, the boundless ambition of the house of *Bourbon*, we became on a sudden solicitous for its exaltation and studious of its interest. We assisted the schemes of *France* and *Spain* with our fleets, and endeavoured to make these our friends by servility, whom nothing but power will keep quiet, and who must always be our enemies while they are endeavouring to grow greater, and we determine to remain free.

That nothing might be omitted which could testify our willingness to continue on any terms the good friends of *France*, we were content to assist not only their conquests but their traffick; and though we did not openly repeal the prohibitory laws, we yet tamely suffered commerce to be carried on between the two nations, and wool was daily imported to enable them to make cloth, which they carried to our markets and sold cheaper than we.

During all this time, they were extending and strengthening their settlements in *America*, contriving new modes of traffick, and framing new alliances with the *Indian* nations. They began now to find these northern regions barren and desolate as they are, sufficiently valuable to desire at least a nominal possession, that might furnish a pretence for the exclusion of others; they therefore extended their claim to tracts of land, which they could never hope to occupy, took care to give their dominions an unlimited magnitude, have given in their maps the name of *Louisiana* to a country, of which part is claimed by the *Spaniards*, and part by the *English*, without any regard to ancient boundaries or prior discovery.

When the return of *Columbus* from his great voyage had filled all *Europe* with wonder and curiosity, *Henry* the seventh sent *Sebastian Cabot* to try what could be found for the benefit of *England*: he declined the track of *Columbus*, and, steering to the westward, fell upon the island, which, from that time, was called by the *English*, *Newfoundland*. Our princes seem to have considered themselves as intitled by their right of prior seizure to the northern parts of *America*, as the *Spaniards* were allowed by universal consent their claim to the southern region for the same reason, and we accordingly made our principal settlements within the limits of our own discoveries, and, by degrees, planted the eastern coast from *Newfoundland* to *Georgia*.

As we had, according to the *European* principles which allow nothing to the natives of these regions, our choice of situation in this extensive country, we naturally fixed our habitations along the coast, for the sake of traffick and correspondence, and all the conveniencies of navigable rivers. And when one port or river was occupied, the next colony, instead of fixing themselves in the inland parts behind the former, went on southward, till they pleased themselves with another maritime situation. For this reason our colonies have more length than depth; their extent from east to west, or from the sea to the interior country, bears no proportion to their reach along the coast from north to south.

It was, however, understood, by a kind of tacit compact among the commercial powers, that possession of the coast included a right to the inland; and, therefore, the charters granted to the several colonies limit their districts only from north to south, leaving their possessions from east to west unlimited and discretional, supposing that, as the colony increases, they may take lands as they shall want them, the possession of the coasts excluding other navigators, and the unhappy *Indians* having no right of nature or of nations.

This right of the first *European* possessor was not disputed till it became the interest of the *French* to question it. *Canada* or *New-France*, on which they made their first settlement, is situated eastward of our colonies, between which they pass up the great river of *St. Laurence*, with *Newfoundland* on the north, and *Nova Scotia* on the south. Their establishment in this country was neither envied nor hindered; and they lived here, in no great numbers a long time, neither molesting their *European* neighbours, nor molested by them.

But when they grew stronger and more numerous, they began to extend their territories; and, as it is natural for men to seek their own convenience, the desire of more fertile and agreeable habitations tempted them southward. There is land enough to the north and west of their settlements, which they may occupy with as good right as can be shewn by the other *European* usurpers, and which neither the *English* nor *Spaniards* will contest; but of this cold region they have enough already, and their resolution was to get a better country. This was not to be had but by settling to the west of our plantations, on ground which has been hitherto supposed to belong to us.

Hither, therefore, they resolved to remove, and to fix, at their own discretion, the western border of our colonies, which was heretofore considered as unlimited. Thus by forming a line of forts, in some measure parallel to the coast, they inclose us between their garrisons and the sea, and not only hinder our extension westward, but, whenever they have a sufficient navy in the sea, can harrass us on each side, as they can invade us, at pleasure, from one or other of their forts.

This design was not perhaps discovered as soon as it was formed, and was certainly not opposed so soon as it was discovered; we foolishly hoped, that their incroachments would stop, that they would be prevailed on by treaty and remonstrance, to give up what they had taken, or to put limits to themselves. We suffered them to establish one settlement after another, to pass boundary after boundary, and add fort to fort, till at last they grew strong enough to avow their designs, and defy us to obstruct them.

By these provocations long continued, we are at length forced into a war, in which we have had hitherto very ill fortune. Our troops under *Braddock* were dishonourably defeated; our fleets have yet done nothing more than take a few merchant-ships, and have distressed some private families, but have very little weakened the power of *France*. The detention of their seamen makes it indeed less easy for them to fit out their navy; but this deficiency will be easily supplied by the alacrity of the nation, which is always eager for war.

It is unpleasing to represent our affairs to our own disadvantage; yet it is necessary to shew the evils which we desire to be removed; and, therefore, some account may very properly be given of the measures which have given them their present superiority.

They are said to be supplied from *France* with better governors than our colonies have the fate to obtain from *England*. A *French* governor is seldom chosen for any other reason than his qualifications for his trust. To be a bankrupt at home, or to be so infamously vicious that he cannot be decently protected in his own country, seldom recommends any man to the government of a *French* colony. Their officers are commonly skilful either in war or commerce, and are taught to have no expectation of honour or preferment, but from the justice and vigour of their administration.

Their great security is the friendship of the natives, and to this advantage they have certainly an indubitable right; because it is the consequence of their virtue. It is ridiculous to imagine, that the friendship of nations, whether civil or barbarous can be gained and kept but by kind treatment; and surely they who intrude, uncalled, upon the country of a distant people, ought to consider the natives as worthy of common kindness, and content themselves to rob without insulting them. The *French*, as has been already observed, admit the *Indians*, by intermarriage, to an equality with themselves, and those nations, with which they have no such near intercourse, they gain over to their interest by honesty in their dealings. Our factors and traders having no other purpose in view than immediate profit, use all the arts of an *European* counting-house, to defraud the simple hunter of his furs.

These are some of the causes of our present weakness; our planters are always quarreling with their governor, whom they consider as less to be trusted than the *French*; and our traders hourly alienate the *Indians* by their tricks and oppressions, and we continue every day to shew by new proofs, that no people can be great who have ceased to be virtuous.

Review of An Essay on the Writings and Genius of Pope

THIS is a very curious and entertaining miscellany of critical remarks and literary history. Though the book promises nothing but observations on the writings of *Pope*, yet no opportunity is neglected of introducing the character of any other writer, or the mention of any performance or event in which learning is interested. From *Pope*, however, he always takes his hint, and to *Pope* he returns again from his digressions. The facts which he mentions though they are seldom *anecdotes* in a rigorous sense, are often such as are very little known, and such as will delight more readers than naked criticism.

As he examines the works of this great poet in an order nearly chronological, he necessarily begins with his pastorals, which considered as representations of any kind of life, he very justly censures; for there is in them a mixture of *Grecian* and *English*, of ancient and modern images. *Windsor* is coupled with *Hybla*, and *Thames* with *Pactolus*. He then compares some passages which *Pope* has imitated or translated with the imitation or version, and gives the preference to the originals, perhaps not always upon convincing arguments.

Theocritus makes his lover wish to be a bee, that he might creep among the leaves that form the chaplet of his mistress. *Pope*'s enamoured swain longs to be made the captive bird that sings in his fair one's bower, that she might listen to his songs, and reward them with her kisses. The critic prefers the image of *Theocritus* as more wild, more delicate, and more uncommon.

It is natural for a lover to wish that he might be any thing that could come near to his lady. But we more naturally desire to be that which she fondles and caresses, than that which she would avoid, at least would neglect. The superior delicacy of *Theocritus* I cannot discover, nor can indeed find, that either in the one or the other image there is any want of delicacy. Which of the two images was less common in the time of the poet who used it, for on that consideration the merit of novelty depends, I think it is now out of any critic's power to decide.

He remarks, I am afraid with too much justice, that there is not a single new thought in the pastorals, and with equal reason declares, that their chief beauty consists in their *correct and musical versification, which has so influenced the* English *ear, as to render every moderate rhymer harmonious.*

In his examination of the *Messiah*, he justly observes some deviations from the inspired author, which weaken the imagery, and dispirit the expression.

On *Windsor-forest*, he declares, I think without proof, that descriptive poetry was by no means the excellence of *Pope*; he draws this inference from the few images introduced in this poem, which would not equally belong to any other place. He must inquire whether *Windsor-Forest* has in reality any thing peculiar.

The *Stag-chace is not*, he says, *so full, so animated, and so circumstantiated as* Somerville's. Barely to say, that one performance is not so good as another, is to criticise with little exactness. But *Pope* has directed, that we should *in every work regard the author's end.* The *Stag-chace* is the main subject of *Somerville*, and might therefore be properly dilated into all its circumstances; in *Pope* it is only incidental, and was to be dispatched in a few lines.

He makes a just observation, 'that the description of the external beauties of nature, is usually the first effect of a young genius, before he hath studied nature and passions. Some of *Milton*'s most early as well as most exquisite pieces are his *Lycidas*, *l'Allegro*, and *Il penseroso*, if we may except his ode on the nativity of Christ, which is indeed prior in order of time, and in which a penetrating critic might have observed the seeds of that boundless imagination, which was one day to produce the *Paradise Lost*.'

Mentioning *Thomson* and other descriptive poets, he remarks that writers fail in their copies for want of acquaintance with originals, and justly ridicules those who think they can form just ideas of valleys, mountains, and rivers in a garret of the *Strand*. For this reason I cannot regret with this author, that *Pope* laid aside his design of writing *American* pastorals; for as he must have painted scenes which he never saw, and manners he never knew, his performance, though it might have been a pleasing amusement of fancy, would have exhibited no representation of nature or of life.

After the pastorals, the critic considers the lyric poetry of *Pope*, and dwells longest on the ode on St. *Cecilia*'s day, which he, like the rest of mankind, places next to that of *Dryden*, and not much below it. He remarks after Mr. *Spence*, that the first stanza is a perfect concert. The second he thinks a little flat; he justly commends the fourth, but without notice of the best line in that stanza, or in the poem.

> *Transported demigods stood round,*
> *And men grew heroes at the sound.*

In the latter part of the ode he objects to the stanza of triumph.

> *Thus song could reveal*, &c.

As written in a measure *ridiculous and burlesque*, and justifies his answer by observing that *Addison* uses the same numbers in the scene of *Rosamond*, between *Grideline* and Sir *Trusty*.

> *How unhappy is he*, &c.

That the measure is the same in both passages must be confessed, and both poets perhaps chose their numbers properly; for they both meant to express a kind of airy hilarity. The two passions of merriment and exultation are undoubtedly different; they are as different as a gambol and a triumph, but each is a species of joy; and poetical measures have not in any language been so far refined, as to provide for the subdivisions of passion. They can only be adapted to general purposes, but the particular and minuter propriety must be sought only in the sentiment and language. Thus the numbers are the same in *Colin's Complaint*, and in the ballad of *Darby* and *Joan*, though in one sadness is represented, and in the other only tranquillity; so the measure is the same of *Pope*'s *Unfortunate Lady* and the *Praise of Voiture*.

He observes very justly, that the odes both of *Dryden* and *Pope* conclude unsuitably and unnaturally with epigram.

He then spends a page upon Mr. *Handel*'s music to *Dryden*'s ode, and speaks of him with that regard, which he has generally obtain'd among the lovers of sound. He finds something amiss in the air *with ravished ones*, but has overlooked or forgotten the grossest fault in that composition, which is that in this line,

> *Revenge, revenge* Timotheus *cries,*

he has laid much stress upon the two latter words, which are meerly words of connexion, and ought in music to be considered as parenthetical.

From this ode is struck out a digression on the nature of odes, and the comparative excellence of the ancients and moderns. He mentions the chorus which *Pope* wrote for the duke of *Buckingham*, and thence takes occasion to treat of the chorus of the ancients. He then comes to another ode of *the dying Christian to his soul*, in which finding an apparent imitation of *Flatman*, he falls into a pleasing and learned speculation on the resembling passages to be found in different poets.

He mentions, with great regard, *Pope*'s ode on *solitude*, written when he was but twelve years old, but omits to mention the poem on *Silence*, composed, I think, as early, with much greater elegance of diction, music of numbers, extent of observation, and force of thought. If he had happened to think on *Baillet's* chapter of *Enfans celebres*, he might have made, on this occasion, a very entertaining dissertation on early excellence.

He comes next to the *Essay on Criticism*, the stupendous performance of a youth not yet twenty years old, and after having detailed the felicities of condition, to which he imagines *Pope* to have owed his wonderful prematurity of mind, he tells us that he is well informed, this essay was first written in prose: There is nothing improbable in the report, nothing indeed but what is more likely than the contrary; yet I cannot forbear to hint to this writer and all others the danger and weakness of trusting too readily to information. Nothing but experience could evince the frequency of false information, or enable any man to conceive that so many groundless reports should be propagated as every man of eminence may hear of himself. Some men relate what they think as what they know; some men of confused memories and habitual inaccuracy ascribe to one man what belongs to another; and some talk on without thought or care. A few men are sufficient to broach falsehoods, which are afterwards innocently diffused by successive relators.

He proceeds on examining passage after passage of this essay; but we must pass over all these criticisms to which we have not something to add or to object, or where this author does not differ from the general voice of mankind. We cannot agree with him in his censure of the comparison of a student advancing in science with a traveller passing the *Alps*, which is, perhaps, the best simile in our language; that in which the most exact resemblance is traced between things in appearance utterly unrelated to each other. That *the last line conveys* no new IDEA is not true, it makes particular what was before general. Whether the description which he adds from another author be, as he says, more *full and striking*, than that of *Pope*, is not to be inquired. *Pope*'s description is relative, and can admit no greater length than is usually allowed to a simile, nor any other particulars than such as form the correspondence.

Unvaried rhymes, says this writer, *highly disgust readers of a good ear*. It is surely not the ear, but the mind that is offended; the fault rising from the use of common rhymes, is that by reading the past line the second may be guessed, and half the composition loses the grace of novelty.

On occasion of the mention of an alexandrine, the critic observes, that *the alexandrine may be thought a modern measure, but that* Robert *of* Gloucester's *verse is an alexandrine, with the addition of two syllables; and that* Sternhold *and* Hopkins *translated the psalms in the same measure of fourteen syllables, though they are printed otherwise.*

This seems not to be accurately conceived or expressed: an alexandrine, with the addition of two syllables, is no more an alexandrine, than with the detraction of two syllables. *Sternhold* and *Hopkins* did generally write in the alternate measure of eight and six syllables; but *Hopkins* commonly rhymed the first and third, *Sternhold* only the second and fourth: So that *Sternhold* may be considered as writing couplets of long lines; but *Hopkins* wrote regular stanzas. From the practice of printing the long lines of fourteen syllables in two short lines arose the licence of some of our poets, who, though professing to write in stanzas, neglect the rhymes of the first and third lines.

Pope has mentioned *Petronius* among the great names of criticism, as the remarker justly observes without any critical merit. It is to be suspected, that *Pope* had never read his book, and mentioned him on the credit of two or three sentences which he had often seen quoted, imagining that where there was so much there must necessarily be more. Young men in haste to be renowned too frequently talk of books which they have scarcely seen.

The revival of learning, mentioned in this poem, affords an opportunity of mentioning the chief periods of literary history, of which this writer reckons five, that of *Alexander*, of *Ptolemy Philadelphus*, of *Augustus*, of *Leo* the tenth, of queen *Anne*.

These observations are concluded with a remark which deserves great attention: 'In no polished nation, after criticism has been much studied, and the rules of writing established, has any very extraordinary book ever appeared.'

The *Rape of the Lock* was always regarded by *Pope* as the highest production of his genius. On occasion of this work the history of the comic heroic is given, and we are told, that it descended from *Tassoni* to *Boileau*, from *Boileau* to *Garth*, and from *Garth* to *Pope*. *Garth* is mentioned perhaps with too much honour; but all are confessed to be inferior to *Pope*. There is in his remarks on this work no discovery of any latent beauty, nor any thing subtle or striking; he is indeed commonly right, but has discussed no difficult question.

The next pieces to be considered are the *Verses to the Memory of an unfortunate Lady*, the *Prologue to Cato*, and *Epilogue to Jane Shore*. The first piece he commends; on occasion of the second he digresses, according to his custom, into a learned dissertation on tragedies, and compares the *English* and *French* with the *Greek Stage*. He justly censures *Cato* for want of action and of characters, but scarcely does justice to the sublimity of some speeches and the philosophical exactness in the sentiments. *The simile of mount* Atlas, *and that of the* Numidian *traveller smothered in the sands, are indeed, in character*, says the critic, *but sufficiently obvious*. The simile of the mountain is indeed common, but that of the traveller I do not remember that it is obvious, is easy to say, and easy to deny. Many things are obvious when they are taught.

He proceeds to criticise the other works of *Addison*, till the epilogue calls his attention to *Rowe*, whose character he discusses in the same manner with sufficient freedom and sufficient candor.

The translation of the epistle of *Sappho* to *Phaon* is next considered; but *Sappho* and *Ovid* are more the subjects of this disquisition than *Pope*. We shall therefore pass over it to a piece of more importance, the epistle of *Eloisa* to *Abelard*, which may justly be regarded as one of the works on which the reputation of *Pope* will stand in future times.

The critic pursues *Eloisa* through all the changes of passion, produces the passages of her letters to which any allusion is made, and intersperses many agreeable particulars and incidental relations. There is not much profundity of criticism, because the beauties are sentiments of nature, which the learned and the ignorant feel alike. It is justly remarked by him, that the wish of *Eloisa*, for the happy passage of *Abelard* into the other world, is formed according to the ideas of mystic devotion.

These are the pieces examined in this volume; whether the remaining part of the work will be one volume or more, perhaps the writer himself cannot yet inform us. This piece is however a complete work, so far as it goes, and the writer is of opinion, that he has dispatched the chief part of his task; for he ventures to remark, that the reputation of *Pope*, as a poet, among posterity, will be principally founded on his *Windsor-Forest, Rape of the Lock*, and *Eloisa to Abelard*, while the facts and characters alluded to in his late writings will be forgotten and unknown, and their poignancy and propriety little relished; for wit and satire are transitory and perishable, but nature and passion are eternal.

He has interspersed some passages of *Pope*'s life, with which most readers will be pleased. When *Pope* was yet a child, his father, who had been a merchant in *London*, retired to *Binfield*. He was taught to read by an aunt, and learned to write without a master, by copying printed books. His father used to order him to make *English* verses, and would oblige him to correct and retouch them over and over, and at last could say, 'These are good *rhymes*.'

At eight years of age he was committed to one *Taverner* a priest, who taught him the rudiments of the *Latin* and *Greek*. At this time he met with *Ogleby*'s *Homer*, which seized his attention; he fell next upon *Sandys*'s *Ovid*, and remembered these two translations with pleasure to the end of his life.

About ten, being at school near *Hide-park-corner*, he was taken to the playhouse, and was so struck with the splendor of the drama, that he formed a kind of play out of *Ogleby*'s *Homer*, intermixed with verses of his own. He persuaded the head-boys to act this piece, and *Ajax* was performed by his master's gardener; they were habited according to the pictures in *Ogleby*. At twelve he retired with his father to *Windsor-Forest*, and formed himself by the study in the best *English* poets.

In this extract it was thought convenient to dwell chiefly upon such observations as relate immediately to *Pope*, without deviating with the author into incidental inquiries. We intend to kindle, not to extinguish curiosity, by this slight sketch of a work abounding with curious quotations and pleasing disquisitions. He must be much acquainted with literary history both of remote and late times, who does not find in this essay many things which he did not know before; and if there be any too learned to be instructed in facts or opinions, he may yet properly read this book as a just specimen of literary moderation.

Review of Thomas Blackwell, Memoirs of the Court of Augustus

THE first effect which this book has upon the reader is that of disgusting him with the author's vanity. He endeavours to persuade the world, that here are some new treasures of literature spread before his eyes; that something is discovered, which to this happy day had been concealed in darkness; that by his diligence time has been robbed of some valuable monument, which he was on the point of devouring; and that names and facts doomed to oblivion are now restored to fame.

How must the unlearned reader be surprised, when he shall be told that Mr. *Blackwell* has neither digged in the ruins of any demolished city; nor found out the way to the library of *Fez*; nor had a single book in his hands, that has not been in the possession of every man that was inclined to read it, for years and ages; and that his book relates to a people who above all others have furnished employment to the studious, and amusements to the idle, who have scarcely left behind them a coin or a stone, which has not been examined and explained a thousand times, and whose dress, and food, and houshold stuff it has been the pride of learning to understand.

A man need not fear to incur the imputation of vitious diffidence or affected humility, who should have forborn to promise many novelties, when he perceived such multitudes of writers possessed of the same materials, and intent upon the same purpose. Mr. *Blackwell* knows well the opinion of *Horace*, concerning those that open their undertakings with magnificent promises, and he knows likewise the dictates of common sense and common honesty, names of greater authority than that of *Horace*, who direct that no man should promise what he cannot perform.

I do not mean to declare that this volume has nothing new, or that the labours of those who have gone before our author, have made his performance an useless addition to the burden of literature. New works may be constructed with old materials, the disposition of the parts may shew contrivance, the ornaments interspersed may discover elegance.

It is not always without good effect that men of proper qualifications write in succession on the same subject, even when the latter add nothing to the information given to the former; for the same ideas may be delivered more intelligibly or more delightfully by one than by another, or with attractions that may lure minds of a different form. No writer pleases all, and every writer may please some.

But after all, to inherit is not to acquire; to decorate is not to make, and the man who had nothing to do but to read the ancient authors, who mention the *Roman* affairs, and reduce them to common places, ought not to boast himself as a great benefactor to the studious world.

After a preface of boast, and a letter of flattery, in which he seems to imitate the address of *Horace*, in his *vile potabis modicis Sabinum*— he opens his book with telling us, that the '*Roman* republic, after the horrible proscription, was no more at *bleeding Rome*. The regal power of her consuls, the authority of her senate, and the majesty of her people, were now trampled under foot; these [for those] divine laws and hallowed customs, that had been the essence of her constitution—were set at nought, and her best friends were lying exposed in their blood.'

These were surely very dismal times to those who suffered; but I know not why any one but a schoolboy in his declamation should whine over the commonwealth of *Rome*, which grew great only by the misery of the rest of mankind. The *Romans*, like others, as soon as they grew rich grew corrupt, and, in their corruption, sold the lives and freedoms of themselves, and of one another.

'About this time *Brutus* had his patience put to the *highest* trial: he had been married to *Clodia*; but whether the family did not please him, or whether he was dissatisfied with the lady's behaviour, during his absence: he soon entertained thoughts of a separation. *This raised a good deal of talk*, and the women of the *Clodian* family inveighed bitterly against *Brutus*– but he married *Portia*, who was worthy of such a father as *M. Cato*, and such a husband as *M. Brutus*. She had a soul capable of an *exalted passion*, and found a proper object to raise and give it a sanction; she did not only love, but adored her husband; his worth, his truth, his every shining and heroic quality, made her gaze on him like a god, while the indearing returns of esteem and tenderness she met with, brought her joy, her pride, her every wish to centre in her beloved *Brutus*.'

When the reader has been awakened by this rapturous preparation, he hears the whole story of *Portia* in the same luxuriant stile, till she breathed out her last, a little before the *bloody proscription*, and '*Brutus* complained heavily of his friends at *Rome*, as not having paid due attention to his *lady* in the declining state of her health.'

He is a great lover of modern terms. His senators and their wives are *gentlemen* and *ladies*. In this review of *Brutus*'s army, who *was under the command of galant men, not braver officers, than true patriots*, he tells us ' that *Sextus the questor was paymaster, secretary at war, and commissary general*, and that the *sacred discipline* of the *Romans* required the closest connection, like that of father and son, to subsist between the general of an army and his questor. *Cicero* was *general of the cavalry*, and the next *general officer* was *Flavius, master of the artillery*, the elder *Lentulus* was *admiral*, and the younger *rode* in the *band* of *volunteers*; under these the tribunes, *with many others too tedious to name.*' *Lentulus*, however, was but a subordinate officer; for we are informed afterwards, that the *Romans* had made *Sextus Pompeius lord high admiral, in all the seas of their dominions.*

Among other affectations of this writer is a furious and unnecessary zeal for liberty, or rather for one form of government as preferable to another. This indeed might be suffered, because political institution is a subject in which men have always differed, and if they continue to obey their lawful governors, and attempt not to make innovations for the sake of their favourite schemes, they may differ for ever without any just reproach from one another. But who can hear the hardy champion, who ventures nothing? Who in full security undertakes the defence of the assassination of *Cæsar*, and declares his resolution *to speak plain?* Yet let not just sentiments be overlooked: He has justly observed, that the greater part of mankind will be naturally prejudiced against *Brutus*, for all feel the benefits of private friendship; but few can discern the advantages of a well constituted government.

We know not whether some apology may not be necessary for the distance between the first account of this book and its continuation. The truth is that this work not being forced upon our attention by much public applause or censure, was sometimes neglected, and sometimes forgotten, nor would it, perhaps, have been now resumed, but that we might avoid to disappoint our readers by an abrupt desertion of any subject.

It is not our design to criticise the facts of this history but the style; not the veracity, but the address of the writer; for, an account of the ancient *Romans* as it cannot nearly interest any present reader, and must be drawn from writings that have been long known, can owe its value only to the language in which it is delivered, and the reflections with which it is accompanied. Dr. *Blackwell*, however, seems to have heated his imagination so as to be much affected with every event, and to believe that he can affect others. Enthusiasm is indeed sufficiently contagious, but I never found any of his readers much enamoured of the *glorious Pompey, the patriot approv'd*, or much incensed against the *lawless Cæsar*, whom this author probably stabs every day and night in his sleeping or waking dreams.

He is come too late into the world with his fury for freedom, with his *Brutus* and *Cassius*. We have all on this side of the *Tweed* long since settled our opinions, his zeal for *Roman* liberty and declamations against the violators of the republican constitution, only stand now in the reader's way, who wishes to proceed in the narrative without the interruption of epithets and exclamations.

It is not easy to forbear laughter at a man so bold in fighting shadows, so busy in a dispute two thousand years past, and so zealous for the honour of a people who while they were poor robbed mankind, and as soon as they became rich robbed one another. Of these robberies our author seems to have no very quick sense, except when they are committed by *Cæsar's* party, for every act is sanctified by the name of a patriot.

If this author's skill in ancient literature were less generally acknowledged, one might sometimes suspect that he had too frequently consulted the *French* writers. He tells us that *Archelaus* the *Rhodian* made a speech to *Cassius*, and *in so saying* dropt some tears, and that *Cassius* after the reduction of *Rhodes* was *covered with glory.*—*Deiotarus* was a keen and happy spirit.—The ingrate *Castor* kept his court.

His great delight is to shew his universal acquaintance with terms of art, with words that every other polite writer has avoided and despised. When *Pompey* conquered the pirates he destroyed fifteen hundred ships of the line.—The *Xanthian* parapets were tore down.—*Brutus* suspecting that his troops were plundering commanded the trumpets to sound to their colours.—Most people understood the act of attainder passed by the senate.—The *Numidian* troopers were unlikely in their appearance.—The *Numidians* beat up one quarter after another.—*Salvidienus* resolved to pass his men over in boats of leather, and he gave orders for equipping a sufficient number of that sort of small craft—*Pompey* had light agile frigates, and fought in a strait where the current and caverns occasion swirls and a roll—A sharp out-look was kept by the admiral—It is a run of about fifty *Roman* miles—*Brutus* broke *Lipella* in the sight of the army—*Mark Antony* garbled the senate—He was a brave man well qualified for a commodore.

In his choice of phrases he frequently uses words with great solemnity, which every other mouth and pen has appropriated to jocularity and levity! The *Rhodians* gave up the contest and in poor plight fled back to *Rhodes*.—Boys and girls were easily kidnapped—*Deiotarus* was a mighty believer of augury.—*Deiotarus* destroyed his ungracious progeny.—The regularity of the *Romans* was their mortal aversion—They desired the consuls to curb such hainous doings—He had such a shrewd invention that no side of a question came amiss to him—*Brutus* found his mistress a coquettish creature.—

He sometimes with most unlucky dexterity mixes the grand and the burlesque together, *the violation of faith, Sir*, says Cassius, *lies at the door of the* Rhodians *by reiterated acts of perfidy*.—The iron grate fell down, crushed those under it to death, and catched the rest as in a trap—When the *Xanthians* heard the military shout and saw the flame mount they concluded there would be no mercy. It was now about sun-set and they had been at hot work since noon.

He has often words or phrases with which our language has hitherto had no knowledge.—One was a heart friend to the republic. A deed was expeded. The *Numidians* begun to reel and were in hazard of falling into confusion—

The tutor embraced his pupil close in his arms—Four hundred women were taxed who have no doubt been the wives of the best *Roman* citizens.—Men not born to action are inconsequential in government—collectitious troops.— The foot by their violent attack began the fatal break in the *Pharsaliac* field. He and his brother with a politic common to other countries had taken opposite sides.

His epithets are of the gaudy or hyperbolical kind. The glorious news— Eager hopes and dismal fears.—Bleeding *Rome*—divine laws and hallowed customs—Merciless war—intense anxiety.

Sometimes the reader is suddenly ravished with a sonorous sentence, of which when the noise is past the meaning does not long remain. When *Brutus* set his legions to fill a moat, instead of heavy dragging and slow toil, they set about it with huzzas and racing, as if they had been striving at the *Olympic* games. They hurled impetuous down the huge trees and stones and with shouts forced them into the water, so that the work expected to continue half the campaign was with rapid toil completed in a few days. *Brutus*'s soldiers fell to the gate with resistless fury, it gave way at last with hideous crash— This great and good man, doing his duty to his country, received a mortal wound, and glorious fell in the cause of *Rome*; may his memory be ever dear to all lovers of liberty, learning and humanity!—This promise ought ever to embalm his memory—The queen of nations was torn by no foreign invader. *Rome* fell a sacrifice to her own sons, and was ravaged by her unnatural off- spring, all the great men of the state, all the good, all the holy were openly murdered by the wickedest and worst.—Little islands cover the harbour of *Brindisi*, and form the narrow outlet from the numerous creeks that compose its capacious port.—At the appearance of *Brutus* and *Cassius* a shout of joy rent the heavens from the surrounding multitudes.—

Such are the flowers which may be gathered by every hand in every part of this garden of eloquence. But having thus freely mentioned our author's faults, it remains that we acknowledge his merit, and confess that this book is the work of a man of letters, that it is full of events displayed with accuracy and related with vivacity, and though it is sufficiently defective to crush the vanity of its author, it is sufficiently entertaining to invite readers.

Observations on the present State of Affairs

THE time is now come in which every *Englishman* expects to be informed of the national affairs, and in which he has a right to have that expectation gratified. For whatever may be urged by ministers, or those whom vanity or interest make the followers of ministers, concerning the necessity of confidence in our governors, and the presumption of prying with profane eyes into the recesses of policy, it is evident, that this reverence can be claimed only by counsels yet unexecuted, and projects suspended in deliberation. But when a design has ended in miscarriage or success, when every eye and every ear is witness to general discontent, or general satisfaction, it is then a proper time to disintangle confusion and illustrate obscurity, to shew by what causes every event was produced, and in what effects it is likely to terminate: to lay down with distinct particularity what rumour always huddles in general exclamations, or perplexes by undigested narratives; to shew whence happiness or calamity is derived, and whence it may be expected, and honestly to lay before the people what inquiry can gather of the past, and conjecture can estimate of the future.

The general subject of the present war is sufficiently known. It is allowed on both sides, that hostilities began in *America*, and that the *French* and *English* quarrelled about the boundaries of their settlements, about grounds and rivers to which, I am afraid, neither can shew any other right than that of power, and which neither can occupy but by usurpation, and the dispossession of the natural lords and original inhabitants. Such is the contest that no honest man can heartily wish success to either party.

It may indeed be alleged, that the Indians have granted large tracts of land both to one and to the other; but these grants can add little to the validity of our titles, till it be experienced how they were obtained: for if they were extorted by violence, or induced by fraud; by threats, which the miseries of other nations had shewn not to be vain, or by promises of which no performance was ever intended, what are they but new modes of usurpation, but new instances of cruelty and treachery?

And indeed what but false hope, or resistless terror can prevail upon a weaker nation to invite a stronger into their country, to give their lands to strangers whom no affinity of manners, or similitude of opinion can be said to recommend, to permit them to build towns from which the natives are excluded, to raise fortresses by which they are intimidated, to settle themselves with such strength, that they cannot afterwards be expelled, but are for ever to remain the masters of the original inhabitants, the dictators of their conduct, and the arbiters of their fate?

When we see men acting thus against the precepts of reason, and the instincts of nature, we cannot hesitate to determine, that by some means or other they were debarred from choice; that they were lured or frighted into compliance; that they either granted only what they found impossible to keep, or expected advantages upon the faith of their new inmates, which there was no purpose to confer upon them. It cannot be said, that the Indians originally invited us to their coasts; we went uncalled and unexpected to nations who had no imagination that the earth contained any inhabitants so distant and so different from themselves. We astonished them with our ships, with our arms, and with our general superiority. They yielded to us as to beings of another and higher race, sent among them from some unknown regions, with power which naked Indians could not resist, and which they were therefore, by every act of humility, to propitiate, that they, who could so easily destroy, might be induced to spare.

To this influence, and to this only, are to be attributed all the cessions and submissions of the Indian princes, if indeed any such cessions were ever made, of which we have no witness but those who claim from them, and there is no great malignity in suspecting, that those who have robbed have also lied.

Some colonies indeed have been established more peaceably than others. The utmost extremity of wrong has not always been practised; but those that have settled in the new world on the fairest terms, have no other merit than that of a scrivener who ruins in silence over a plunderer that seizes by force; all have taken what had other owners, and all have had recourse to arms, rather than quit the prey on which they had fastened.

The *American* dispute between the *French* and us is therefore only the quarrel of two robbers for the spoils of a passenger, but as robbers have terms of confederacy, which they are obliged to observe as members of the gang, so the *English* and *French* may have relative rights, and do injustice to each other, while both are injuring the Indians. And such, indeed, is the present contest: they have parted the northern continent of *America* between them, and are now disputing about their boundaries, and each is endeavouring the destruction of the other by the help of the Indians, whose interest it is that both should be destroyed.

Both nations clamour with great vehemence about infraction of limits, violation of treaties, open usurpation, insidious artifices, and breach of faith. The *English* rail at the perfidious *French*, and the *French* at the encroaching *English*; they quote treaties on each side, charge each other with aspiring to universal monarchy, and complain on either part of the insecurity of possession near such turbulent neighbours.

Through this mist of controversy it can raise no wonder, that the truth is not easily discovered. When a quarrel has been long carried on between individuals, it is often very hard to tell by whom it was begun. Every fact is darkened by distance, by interest, and by multitudes. Information is not easily procured from far; those whom the truth will not favour, will not step voluntarily forth to tell it, and where there are many agents, it is easy for every single action to be concealed.

All these causes concur to the obscurity of the question, by whom were hostilities in *America* commenced? Perhaps there never can be remembered a time in which hostilities had ceased. Two powerful colonies enflamed with immemorial rivalry, and placed out of the superintendence of the mother nations, were not likely to be long at rest. Some opposition was always going forward, some mischief was every day done or meditated, and the borderers were always better pleased with what they could snatch from their neighbours, than what they had of their own.

In this disposition to reciprocal invasion a cause of dispute never could be wanting. The forests and desarts of *America* are without land-marks, and therefore cannot be particularly specified in stipulations; the appellations of those wide extended regions have in every mouth a different meaning, and are understood on either side as inclination happens to contract or extend them. Who has yet pretended to define how much of *America* is included in *Brazil*, *Mexico*, or *Peru?* It is almost as easy to divide the *Atlantic* ocean by a line, as clearly to ascertain the limits of those uncultivated, uninhabitable, unmeasured regions.

It is likewise to be considered, that contracts concerning boundaries are often left vague and indefinite without necessity, by the desire of each party, to interpret the ambiguity to its own advantage when a fit opportunity shall be found. In forming stipulations, the commissaries are often ignorant, and often negligent; they are sometimes weary with debate, and contract a tedious discussion into general terms, or refer it to a former treaty, which was never understood. The weaker part is always afraid of requiring explanations, and the stronger always has an interest in leaving the question undecided: thus it will happen without great caution on either side, that after long treaties solemnly ratified, the rights that had been disputed are still equally open to controversy.

In *America* it may easily be supposed, that there are tracts of land yet claimed by neither party, and therefore mentioned in no treaties, which yet one or the other may be afterwards inclined to occupy; but to these vacant and unsettled countries each nation may pretend, as each conceives itself intitled to all that is not expresly granted to the other.

Here then is a perpetual ground of contest, every enlargement of the possessions of either will be considered as something taken from the other, and each will endeavour to regain what had never been claimed, but that the other occupied it.

Thus obscure in its original is the *American* contest. It is difficult to find the first invader, or to tell where invasion properly begins; but I suppose it is not to be doubted, that after the last war, when the *French* had made peace with such apparent superiority, they naturally began to treat us with less respect in distant parts of the world, and to consider us as a people from whom they had nothing to fear, and who could no longer presume to contravene their designs, or to check their progress.

The power of doing wrong with impunity seldom waits long for the will, and it is reasonable to believe, that in *America* the *French* would avow their purpose of aggrandising themselves with at least as little reserve as in *Europe*. We may therefore readily believe, that they were unquiet neighbours, and had no great regard to right which they believed us no longer able to enforce.

That in forming a line of forts behind our colonies, if in no other part of their attempt, they had acted against the general intention, if not against the literal terms of treaties, can scarcely be denied; for it never can be supposed, that we intended to be inclosed between the sea and the *French* garrisons, or preclude ourselves from extending our plantations backwards to any length that our convenience should require.

With dominion is conferred every thing that can secure dominion. He that has the coast, has likewise the sea to a certain distance; he that possesses a fortress, has the right of prohibiting another fortress to be built within the command of its cannon. When therefore we planted the coast of *North-America* we supposed the possession of the inland region granted to an indefinite extent, and every nation that settled in that part of the world, seems, by the permission of every other nation, to have made the same supposition in its own favour.

Here then, perhaps, it will be safest to fix the justice of our cause; here we are apparently and indisputably injured, and thus injury may, according to the practice of nations, be justly resented. Whether we have not in return made some incroachments upon them, must be left doubtful, till our practices on the *Ohio* shall be stated and vindicated. There are no two nations confining on each other, between whom a war may not always be kindled with plausible pretences on either part, as there is always passing between them a reciprocation of injuries and fluctuation of incroachments.

From the conclusion of the last peace perpetual complaints of the supplantations and invasions of the *French* have been sent to *Europe* from our colonies, and transmitted to our ministers at *Paris*, where good words were sometimes given us, and the practices of the *American* commanders were sometimes disowned, but no redress was ever obtained, nor is it probable that any prohibition was sent to *America*. We were still amused with such doubtful promises as those who are afraid of war are ready to interpret in their own favour, and the *French* pushed forward their line of fortresses, and seemed to resolve that before our complaints were finally dismissed, all remedy should be hopeless.

We likewise endeavour'd at the same time to form a barrier against the *Canadians* by sending a colony to *New-Scotland*, a cold uncomfortable tract of ground, of which we had long the nominal possession before we really began to occupy it. To this those were invited whom the cessation of war deprived of employment, and made burdensom to their country, and settlers were allured thither by many fallacious descriptions of fertile vallies and clear skies. What effect these pictures of *American* happiness had upon my countrymen I was never informed, but I suppose very few sought provision in those frozen regions, whom guilt or poverty did not drive from their native country. About the boundaries of this new colony there were some disputes, but as there was nothing yet worth a contest, the power of the *French* was not much exerted on that side: some disturbance was however given and some skirmishes ensued. But perhaps being peopled chiefly with soldiers, who would rather live by plunder than by agriculture, and who consider war as their best trade, *New-Scotland* would be more obstinately defended than some settlements of far greater value, and the *French* are too well informed of their own interest, to provoke hostility for no advantage, or to select that country for invasion, where they must hazard much, and can win little. They therefore pressed on southward behind our ancient and wealthy settlements, and built fort after fort at such distances that they might conveniently relieve one another, invade our colonies with sudden incursions, and retire to places of safety before our people could unite to oppose them.

This design of the *French* has been long formed, and long known, both in *America* and *Europe*, and might at first have been easily repressed had force been used instead of expostulation. When the *English* attempted a settlement upon the Island of St. *Lucia*, the *French*, whether justly or not, considering it as neutral and forbidden to be occupied by either nation, immediately landed upon it, and destroyed the houses, wasted the plantations, and drove or carried away the inhabitants. This was done in the time of peace, when mutual professions of friendship were daily exchanged by the two courts, and was not considered as any violation of treaties, nor was any more than a very soft remonstrance made on our part.

The *French* therefore taught us how to act, but an *Hanoverian* quarrel with the house of *Austria* for some time induced us to court, at any expence, the alliance of a nation whose very situation makes them our enemies. We suffered them to destroy our settlements, and to advance their own, which we had an equal right to attack. The time however came at last, when we ventured to quarrel with *Spain*, and then *France* no longer suffered the appearance of peace to subsist between us, but armed in defence of her ally.

The events of the war are well known, we pleased ourselves with a victory at *Dettingen*, where we left our wounded men to the care of our enemies, but our army was broken at *Fontenoy* and *Val*; and though after the disgrace which we suffered in the *Mediterranean* we had some naval success, and an accidental dearth made peace necessary for the *French*, yet they prescribed the conditions, obliged us to give hostages, and acted as conquerors, though as conquerors of moderation.

In this war the *Americans* distinguished themselves in a manner unknown and unexpected. The *New English* raised an army, and under the command of *Pepperel* took *Cape-Breton*, with the assistance of the fleet. This is the most important fortress in *America*. We pleased ourselves so much with the acquisition, that we could not think of restoring it, and among the arguments used to inflame the people against *Charles Stuart*, it was very clamorously urged, that if he gained the kingdom, he would give *Cape-Breton* back to the *French*.

The *French* however had a more easy expedient to regain *Cape-Breton* than by exalting *Charles Stuart* to the *English* throne, they took in their turn fort St. *George*, and had our *East-India* company wholly in their power, whom they restored at the peace to their former possessions, that they may continue to export our silver.

Cape-Breton therefore was restored, and the *French* were re-established in *America*, with equal power and greater spirit, having lost nothing by the war which they had before gained.

To the general reputation of their arms, and that habitual superiority which they derive from it, they owe their power in *America*, rather than to any real strength, or circumstances of advantage. Their numbers are yet not great; their trade, though daily improved, is not very extensive; their country is barren, their fortresses, though numerous, are weak, and rather shelters from wild beasts, or savage nations, than places built for defence against bombs or cannons. *Cape-Breton* has been found not to be impregnable; nor, if we consider the state of the places possessed by the two nations in *America*, is there any reason upon which the *French* should have presumed to molest us; but that they thought our spirit so broken that we durst not resist them, and in this opinion our long forbearance easily confirmed them.

We forgot, or rather avoided to think, that what we delayed to do must be done at last, and done with more difficulty, as it was delayed longer; that while we were complaining, and they were eluding, or answering our complaints, fort was rising upon fort, and one invasion made a precedent for another.

This confidence of the *French* is exalted by some real advantages. If they possess in those countries less than we, they have more to gain, and less to hazard; if they are less numerous, they are better united.

The *French* compose one body with one head. They have all the same interest, and agree to pursue it by the same means. They are subject to a governor commission'd by an absolute monarch, and participating the authority of his master. Designs are therefore formed without debate, and executed without impediment. They have yet more martial than mercantile ambition, and seldom suffer their military schemes to be entangled with collateral projects of gain: they have no wish but for conquest, of which they justly consider riches as the consequence.

Some advantages they will always have as invaders. They make war at the hazard of their enemies: the contest being carried on in our territories we must lose more by a victory than they will suffer by a defeat. They will subsist, while they stay, upon our plantations, and perhaps destroy them when they can stay no longer. If we pursue them and carry the war into their dominions, our difficulties will encrease every step as we advance, for we shall leave plenty behind us, and find nothing in *Canada*, but lakes and forests barren and trackless, our enemies will shut themselves up in their forts, against which it is difficult to bring cannon through so rough a country, and which if they are provided with good magazines will soon starve those who besiege them.

All these are the natural effects of their government, and situation; they are accidentally more formidable as they are less happy. But the favour of the

Indians which they enjoy, with very few exceptions, among all the nations of the northern continent, we ought to consider with other thoughts; this favour we might have enjoyed, if we had been careful to deserve it. The *French* by having these savage nations on their side, are always supplied with spies, and guides, and with auxiliaries, like the *Tartars* to the *Turks* or the Hussars to the *Germans*, of no great use against troops ranged in order of battle, but very well qualified to maintain a war among woods and rivulets, where much mischief may be done by unexpected onsets, and safety be obtained by quick retreats. They can waste a colony by sudden inroads, surprise the straggling planters, frighten the inhabitants into towns, hinder the cultivation of lands, and starve those whom they are not able to conquer.

(To be continued.)

Review of Jonas Hanway, An Essay on Tea

OUR readers may perhaps remember, that we gave them a short account of this book, with a letter extracted from it in *Novem.* 1756. The author then sent us an injunction to forbear his work till a second edition should appear: this prohibition was rather too magisterial; for an author is no longer the sole master of a book which he has given to the public; yet he has been punctually obeyed; we had no desire to offend him, and if his character may be estimated by his book, he is a man whose failings may well be pardoned for his virtues.

The second edition is now sent into the world, *corrected and enlarged*, and yielded up by the author to the attacks of criticism. But he shall find in us no malignity of censure. We wish indeed, that among other corrections he had submitted his pages to the inspection of a grammarian, that the elegancies of one line might not have been disgraced by the improprieties of another; but with us to mean well is a degree of merit which over-balances much greater errors than impurity of stile.

We have already given in our collections, one of the letters, in which Mr. *Hanway* endeavours to show, that the consumption of Tea, is injurious to the interest of our country. We shall now endeavour to follow him regularly through all his observations on this modern luxury; but it can scarcely be candid, not to make a previous declaration, that he is to expect little justice from the author of this extract, a hardened and shameless tea-drinker, who has for twenty years diluted his meals with only the infusion of this fascinating plant, whose kettle has scarcely time to cool, who with Tea amuses the evening, with Tea solaces the midnights, and with Tea welcomes the morning.

He begins, by refuting a popular notion, that *Bohea* and *Green Tea* are leaves of the same shrub, gathered at different times of the year. He is of opinion, that they are produced by different shrubs. The leaves of Tea are gathered in dry weather; then dried and curled over the fire in copper pans. The *Chinese* use little green tea, imagining that it hinders digestion and excites fevers. How it should have either effect is not easily discovered, and if we consider the innumerable prejudices which prevail concerning our own plants, we shall very little regard these opinions of the *Chinese* vulgar, which experience does not confirm.

When the *Chinese* drink tea, they infuse it slightly, and extract only the more volatile parts, but though this seems to require great quantities at a time, yet the author believes, perhaps only because he has an inclination to believe it, that the *English* and *Dutch* use more than all the inhabitants of that extensive empire. The *Chinese* drink it sometimes with acids, seldom with sugar; and this practice, our author, who has no intention to find any thing right at home, recommends to his countrymen.

The history of the rise and progress of tea-drinking is truly curious. Tea was first imported from *Holland* by the earls of *Arlington* and *Ossory* in 1666: from their ladies the women of quality learned its use. Its price was then three pounds a pound, and continued the same to 1707. In 1715, we began to use green tea, and the practice of drinking it descended to the lower class of the people. In 1720, the *French* began to send it hither by a clandestine commerce. From 1717 to 1726, we imported annually seven hundred thousand pounds. From 1732 to 1742, a million and two hundred thousand pounds were every year brought to *London*; in some years afterwards three millions, and in 1755, near four millions of pounds, or two thousand tuns, in which we are not to reckon that which is surreptitiously introduced, which perhaps is nearly as much. Such quantities are indeed sufficient to alarm us; it is at least worth enquiry, to know what are the qualities of such a plant, and what the consequences of such a trade.

He then proceeds to enumerate the mischiefs of tea, and seems willing to charge upon it every mischief that he can find. He begins however, by questioning the virtues ascribed to it, and denies that the crews of the *Chinese* ships are preserved in their voyage homewards from the scurvy by tea. About this report I have made some enquiry, and though I cannot find that these crews are wholly exempt from scorbutic maladies; they seem to suffer them less than other mariners in any course of equal length. This I ascribe to the tea, not as possessing any medicinal qualities, but as tempting them to drink more water, to dilute their salt food more copiously, and perhaps to forbear punch, or other strong liquors.

He then proceeds in the pathetic strain, to tell the ladies how, by drinking tea they injure their health, and, what is yet more dear, their beauty.

'To what can we ascribe the numerous complaints which prevail? how many *sweet creatures* of your sex, languish with a *weak digestion, low spirits, lassitudes, melancholy*, and twenty disorders, which in spite of the *faculty* have yet no names, except the general one of *nervous complaints?* let them change their diet, and among other articles leave off drinking tea, it is more than probable the greatest part of them will be restored to health.

Hot water is also very hurtful to the teeth. The *Chinese* do not drink their tea so hot as we do, and yet they have bad teeth. This cannot be ascribed entirely to *sugar*, for they use very little, as already observed: but we all know that *hot* or *cold* things which *pain* the teeth, destroy them also. If we drank less tea, and used gentle *acids* for the gums and teeth, particularly *sour oranges*, though we had a less number of *French dentists*, I fancy this *essential* part of beauty would be much *better* preserved.

The women in the united provinces who *sip tea* from morning till night, are also as remarkable for *bad teeth*. They also look pallid, and many are troubled with certain feminine disorders arising from a relaxed habit. The *Portuguese* ladies, on the other hand, entertain with *sweet-meats*, and yet they have very *good teeth:* but their food in general is more of the farinaceous and vegetable kind than ours. They also *drink cold water* instead of *sipping hot*, and never taste any fermented liquors; for these reasons the use of *sugar*, does not seem to be at all pernicious to them.

Men seem to have lost their stature, and comeliness; and women their beauty. I am not *young*, but methinks there is not quite so much *beauty* in this land as there was. Your very *chambermaids* have lost their bloom, I suppose by *sipping tea*. Even the agitations of the passions at *cards* are not so great enemies to female charms. What *Shakespeare* ascribes to the concealment of love, is *in this age* more frequently occasioned by the use of *tea*.'

To raise the fright still higher, he quotes an account of a pig's tail scalded with tea, on which however he does not much insist.

Of these dreadful effects, some are perhaps imaginary, and some may have another cause. That there is less beauty in the present race of females, than in those who entered the world with us, all of us are inclined to think on whom beauty has ceased to smile; but our fathers and grand-fathers made the same complaint before us, and our posterity will still find beauties irresistibly powerful.

That the diseases commonly called nervous, tremours, fits, habitual depression, and all the maladies which proceed from laxity and debility, are more frequent than in any former time, is, I believe, true, however deplorable. But this new race of evils, will not be expelled by the prohibition of tea. This general languor is the effect of general luxury, of general idleness. If it be most to be found among tea drinkers, the reason is, that tea is one of the stated amusements of the idle and luxurious. The whole mode of life is changed, every kind of voluntary labour, every exercise that strengthened the nerves, and hardened the muscles, is fallen into disuse. The inhabitants are crowded together in populous cities, so that no occasion of life requires much motion; every one is near to all that he wants; and the rich and delicate seldom pass from one street to another, but in carriages of pleasure. Yet we eat and drink, or strive to eat and drink like the hunters and huntresses, the farmers and the housewives of the former generation, and they that pass ten hours in bed, and eight at cards, and the greater part of the other six at the table, are taught to impute to tea, all the diseases which a life unnatural in all its parts, may chance to bring upon them.

Tea, among the greater part of those who use it most, is drunk in no great quantity. As it neither exhilerates the heart, nor stimulates the palate; it is commonly an entertainment merely nominal, a pretence for assembling to prattle, for interrupting business or diversifying idleness. They who drink one cup, and who drink twenty, are equally punctual in preparing or partaking it; and indeed, there are few but discover by their indifference about it, that they are brought together not by the tea, but the tea table. Three cups make the common quantity, so slightly impregnated, that perhaps they might be tinged with the *Athenian* cicuta, and produce less effects than those letters charge upon tea.

Our author proceeds to shew yet other bad qualities of this hated leaf.

'Green tea, when made strong even by infusion, is an *emetic*, nay, I am told it is used as such in *China*, a decoction of it certainly performs this operation; yet by long use it is drank by many without such an effect. The infusion also, when it is made strong, and stands long to draw the grosser particles, will *convulse* the bowels: even in the manner *commonly* used it has this effect on some constitutions, as I have already remarked to you from my *own experience*.

'You see I confess my *weakness* without reserve, but those who are very fond of tea, if their digestion is weak, and they find themselves disordered, they generally ascribe it to any *cause* except the *true* one. I am aware that the effect just mentioned is imputed to the hot water; let it be so, and my argument is still good: but who pretends to say it is not *partly* owing to particular kinds of tea; perhaps such as partake of *copperas*, which there is cause to apprehend, is sometimes the case: if we judge from the manner in which it is said to be cured, together with its ordinary effects, there is some foundation for this opinion. Put a drop of strong tea, either *green* or *bohea*, but chiefly the former, on the blade of a knife, though it is not corrosive in the same manner as vitriol, yet there appears to be a corrosive quality in it, very different from that of fruit which stain the knife.'

He afterwards quotes *Paulli* to prove, that tea is a *desiccative, and ought not to be used after the fortieth year*. I have then long exceeded the limits of permission, but I comfort myself, that all the enemies of tea cannot be in the right. If tea be desiccative according to *Paulli*, it cannot weaken the fibres, as our author imagines; if it be emetic, it must constringe the stomach, rather than relax it.

The formidable quality of tinging the knife, it has in common with acorns, the bark, and leaves of oak, and every astringent bark or leaf, the copperas which is given to the tea, is really in the knife. Ink may be made of any ferrugineous matter and astringent vegetable, as it is generally made of galls and copperas.

From tea the writer digresses to spirituous liquors, about which he will have no controversy with the *Literary Magazine*, we shall therefore insert almost his whole letter, and add to it one testimony, that the mischiefs arising on every side from this compendious mode of drunkenness, are enormous and insupportable; equally to be found among the great and the mean; filling palaces with disquiet and distraction, harder to be born, as it cannot be mentioned; and overwhelming multitudes with incurable diseases and unpitied poverty.

'Though *tea* and *gin* have spread their baneful influence over this island, and his majesty's other dominions, yet you may be well assured, that the governors of the foundling hospital will exert their utmost skill and vigilance, to prevent the children under their care from being poisoned, or enervated by one or the other. This, however, is not the case of *workhouses:* it is well known, to the shame of those who are charged with the care of them, that *gin* has been too often permitted to enter their gates; and the debauched appetites of the people who inhabit these houses, has been urged as a reason for it.

'*Desperate* diseases require *desperate* remedies: if laws are rigidly executed against murderers in the highway, those who provide a draught of gin, which we see is *murderous*, ought not to be *countenanced*. I am now informed, that in certain hospitals, where the number of the *sick* used to be about 5600 in 14 years,

' From 1704, to 1718, they increased to } 8189
' From 1718, to 1734, still augmented to } 12710
' And from 1734, to 1749, *multiplied* to } 38147.

'What a dreadful *spectre* does this exhibit! nor must we wonder when satisfactory evidence was given before the great council of the nation, that near eight millions of gallons of distilled spirits, at the standard it is commonly reduced to for drinking, was actually consumed annually in drams! the shocking difference in the numbers of the *sick*, and we may presume of the *dead* also, was supposed to keep pace with *gin:* and the most ingenious and unprejudiced physicians ascribed it to this cause. What is to be done under these melancholy circumstances? shall we still countenance the *distillery*, for the sake of the *revenue*; out of tenderness to the *few* who will suffer by its being abolished; for fear of the madness of the people; or that foreigners will run it in upon us? there can be no *evil* so great as that we now suffer, except the making the same consumption, and paying for it to foreigners in *money*, which I hope never will be the case.

'As to the *revenue*, it certainly may be replaced by taxes upon the *necessaries* of life, even upon the *bread we eat*, or in other words, upon the *land*, which is the great source of supply to the *public*, and to *individuals*. Nor can I persuade myself, but that the people may be *weaned* from the habit of poisoning themselves. The difficulty of *smugling* a bulky *liquid*, joined to the severity which *ought* to be exercised towards smuglers, whose *illegal* commerce is of so *infernal* a nature, must, in time, produce the effect desired. Spirituous liquors being abolished, instead of having the most undisciplined and abandoned poor, we might soon boast a race of men, temperate, religious, and industrious, even to a *proverb*. We should soon see the *ponderous* burden of the *poors-rate* decrease, and the *beauty* and *strength* of the land rejuvenate. Schools, workhouses and hospitals, might then be sufficient to clear our streets of distress and misery, which never will be the case whilst the love of poison prevails, and the means of ruin, is sold in above one thousand houses in the *city* of *London*, in two thousand two hundred in *Westminster*, and one thousand nine hundred and thirty in *Holborn* and St. *Giles's*.

'But if other uses still demand *liquid fire*, I would really propose, that it should be sold only in quart bottles, sealed up with the king's seal, with a very high duty, and none sold without being mixed with a *strong emetic*.

'Many become objects of charity by their *intemperance*, and this excludes others who are such by the unavoidable accidents of life; or who cannot by any means support themselves. Hence it appears, that the introducing *new habits* of life, is the most substantial charity: and that the *regulation* of charity-schools, hospitals and workhouses, nor the augmentation of their number, can make them answer the wise ends for which they were instituted.

'The children of beggars should be also taken from them, and bred up to labour, as children of the public. Thus the *distressed* might be relieved, at a sixth part of the present expence; the idle be compelled to *work*, or *starve*; and the *mad* be sent to *Bedlam*. We should not see human nature disgraced by the aged, the maimed, the sickly, and young children, begging their bread, nor would compassion be abused by those who have reduced it to an *art* to catch the unwary. Nothing is wanting but common sense and *honesty* in the execution of *laws*.

'To prevent such abuse in the *streets*, seems more practicable than to abolish *bad habits within doors*, where *greater* numbers perish. We see in many familiar instances the fatal effects of example. The careless spending of time among *servants*, who are charged with the care of infants, is often fatal: the nurse frequently destroys the child! the poor infant being left neglected, expires whilst she is sipping her tea! this may appear to you as *rank prejudice*, or *jest*; but I am assured, from the most *indubitable* evidence, that many very extraordinary cases of this kind, have *really* happened among those whose *duty* does not permit of such kind of habits.

'It is partly from such causes, that nurses of the children of the *public* often *forget* themselves, and become *impatient* when infants cry: the next step to this, is using extraordinary means to quiet them. I have already mentioned the term *killing nurse*, as known in some workhouses: *Venice treacle*, *Poppey water*, and *Godfrey's cordial*, have been the *kind* instruments of lulling the child to his *everlasting* rest. If these *pious* women could send up an ejaculation when the child expired, all was *well*, and no questions *asked* by the *superiors*.

An ingenious friend of mine informs me, that this has been so often the case, in some workhouses, that *Venice* treacle has acquired the appellation of *the Lord have mercy upon me*, in allusion to the nurses *hackneyed* expression of *pretended* grief when infants expire! *Farewel.*'

I know not upon what observation Mr. *Hanway* founds his confidence in the governors of the *Foundling Hospital*, men of whom I have not any knowledge, but whom I intreat to consider a little the minds as well as bodies of the children. I am inclined to believe irreligion equally pernicious with gin and tea, and therefore think it not unseasonable to mention, that when a few months ago I wandered through the hospital, I found not a child that seemed to have heard of his creed or the commandments. To breed up children in this manner, is to rescue them from an early grave, that they may find employment for the gibbet; from dying in innocence, that they may perish by their crimes.

Having considered the effects of tea upon the health of the drinker, which, I think, he has aggravated in the vehemence of his zeal, and which, after soliciting them by this watery luxury, year after year, I have not yet felt; he proceeds to examine how it may be shewn to affect our interest; and first calculates the national loss by the time spent in drinking tea. I have no desire to appear captious, and shall therefore readily admit, that tea is a liquor not proper for the lower classes of the people, as it supplies no strength to labour, or relief to disease, but gratifies the taste without nourishing the body. It is a barren superfluity, to which those who can hardly procure what nature requires, cannot prudently habituate themselves. Its proper use is to amuse the idle, and relax the studious, and dilute the full meals of those who cannot use exercise, and will not use abstinence. That time is lost in this insipid entertainment, cannot be denied; many trifle away at the tea-table, those moments which would be better spent; but that any national detriment can be inferred from this waste of time, does not evidently appear, because I know not that any work remains undone for want of hands. Our manufactures seem to be limited, not by the possibility of work, but by the possibility of sale.

His next argument is more clear. He affirms, that one hundred and fifty thousand pounds in silver are paid to the *Chinese* annually, for three millions of pounds of tea, and that for two millions more brought clandestinely from the neighbouring coasts, we pay at twenty-pence a pound, one hundred sixty-six thousand six hundred and sixty-six pounds. The author justly conceives, that this computation will waken us; for, says he, 'The loss of health, the loss of time, the injury of morals, are not very sensibly felt by some, who are alarmed when you talk of the loss of money.' But he excuses the *East-India* company, as men not obliged to be political arithmeticians, or to enquire so much what the nation loses, as how themselves may grow rich. It is certain, that they who drink tea, have no right to complain of those that import it, but if Mr. *Hanway*'s computation be just, the importation and the use of it ought at once to be stopped by a penal law.

The author allows one slight argument in favour of tea, which, in my opinion, might be with far greater justice urged, both against that, and many other parts of our naval trade. 'The tea trade employs, he tells us, six ships, and five or six hundred seamen sent annually to *China*. It likewise brings in a revenue of three hundred and sixty thousand pounds, which, as a tax on luxury, may be considered as of great utility to the state.' The utility of this tax I cannot find; a tax on luxury is no better than another tax, unless it hinders luxury, which cannot be said of the impost upon tea, while it is thus used by the great and the mean, the rich and the poor. The truth is, that by the loss of one hundred and fifty thousand pounds, we procure the means of shifting three hundred and sixty thousand at best, only from one hand to another; but perhaps, sometimes into hands, by which it is not very honestly employed. Of the five or six hundred seamen sent to *China*, I am told, that sometimes half, commonly a third part perish in the voyage; so that instead of setting this navigation against the inconveniencies already alleged, we may add to them, the yearly loss of two hundred men in the prime of life, and reckon, that the trade to *China* has destroyed ten thousand men since the beginning of this century.

If tea be thus pernicious, if it impoverishes our country, if it raises temptation, and gives opportunity to illicit commerce, which I have always looked on as one of the strongest evidences of the inefficacy of our law, the weakness of our government, and the corruption of our people, let us at once resolve to prohibit it for ever.

'If the *question* was how to promote industry, most *advantageously*, in lieu of our tea-trade, supposing every branch of our commerce to be already fully supplied with men and money? if a *quarter* the sum now spent in tea, were laid out annually in plantations, in making public gardens, in paving and widening streets, in making *roads*, in rendering *rivers* navigable, erecting *palaces*, building *bridges*, or neat and convenient *houses*, where are now only *huts*; *draining* lands, or rendering those which are now *barren* of some *use*; should we not be gainers, and provide more for health, pleasure, and long life, compared with the consequences of the *tea-trade?*'

Our riches would be much better employed to these purposes, but if this project does not please, let us first resolve to save our money, and we shall afterwards very easily find ways to spend it.

Review of Soame Jenyns, A Free Inquiry

THIS is a treatise consisting of six letters upon a very difficult and important question, which I am afraid this author's endeavours will not free from the perplexity, which has intangled the speculatists of all ages, and which must always continue while *we see* but *in part*. He calls it a *Free* enquiry, and indeed his *freedom* is, I think, greater than his modesty. Though he is far from the contemptible arrogance, or the impious licentiousness of *Bolingbroke*, yet he decides too easily upon questions out of the reach of human determination, with too little consideration of mortal weakness, and with too much vivacity for the necessary caution.

In the first letter *on evil in general*, he observes, that 'it is the solution of this important question, *whence came evil*, alone, that can ascertain the moral characteristic of God, without which there is an end of all distinction between good and evil.' Yet he begins this enquiry by this declaration. 'That there is a supreme being, infinitely powerful, wise and benevolent, the great creator and preserver of all things, is a truth so clearly demonstrated, that it shall be here taken for granted.' What is this but to say, that we have already reason to grant the existence of those attributes of God, which the present enquiry is designed to prove? The present enquiry is then surely made to no purpose. The attributes to the demonstration of which the solution of this great question is necessary, have been demonstrated without any solution, or by means of the solution of some former writer.

He rejects the *Manichean* system, but imputes to it an absurdity, from which, amidst all its absurdities it seems to be free, and adopts the system of Mr. *Pope*. 'That pain is no evil, if asserted with regard to the individuals who suffer it, is downright nonsense; but if considered as it affects the universal system, is an undoubted truth, and means only that there is no more pain in it than what is necessary to the production of happiness. How many soever of these evils then force themselves into the creation, so long as the good preponderates, it is a work well worthy of infinite wisdom and benevolence; and, notwithstanding the imperfections of its parts, the whole is most undoubtedly perfect.' And in the former part of the letter, he gives the principle of his system in these words:

'Omnipotence cannot work contradictions, it can only effect all possible things. But so little are we acquainted with the whole system of nature, that we know not what are possible, and what are not: but if we may judge from that constant mixture of pain with pleasure, and inconveniency with advantage, which we must observe in every thing around us, we have reason to conclude, that to endue created beings with perfection, that is, to produce good exclusive of evil, is one of those impossibilities which even infinite power cannot accomplish.'

This is elegant and acute, but will by no means calm discontent or silence curiosity; for whether evil can be wholly separated from good or not, it is plain that they may be mixed in various degrees, and as far as human eyes can judge, the degree of evil might have been less without any impediment to good.

The second Letter *on the Evils of Imperfection*, is little more than a paraphrase of *Pope*'s epistles, or yet less than a paraphrase, a mere translation of poetry into prose. This is surely to attack difficulty with very disproportionate abilities, to cut the *Gordian* knot with very blunt instruments. When we are told of the insufficiency of former solutions, why is one of the latest, which no man can have forgotten, given us again? I am told, that this pamphlet is not the effort of hunger; What can it be then but the product of vanity? and yet how can vanity be gratified by plagiarism, or transcription? When this speculatist finds himself prompted to another performance, let him consider whether he is about to disburthen his mind or employ his fingers; and if I might venture to offer him a subject, I should wish that he would solve this question, Why he that has nothing to write, should desire to be a writer?

Yet is not this letter without some sentiments, which though not new, are of great importance, and may be read with pleasure in the thousandth repetition.

'Whatever we enjoy is purely a free gift from our Creator; but that we enjoy no more, can never sure be deemed an injury, or a just reason to question his infinite benevolence. All our happiness is owing to his goodness; but that it is no greater, is owing only to ourselves, that is, to our not having any inherent right to any happiness, or even to any existence at all. This is no more to be imputed to God, than the wants of a beggar to the person who has relieved him: that he had something was owing to his benefactor: but that he had no more, only to his own original poverty.'

Thus far he speaks what every man must approve, and what every wise man has said before him. He then gives us the system of subordination, not invented, for it was known I think to the *Arabian* metaphysicians, but adopted by *Pope*; and from him borrowed by the diligent researches of this great investigator.

'No system can possibly be formed, even in imagination, without a subordination of parts. Every animal body must have different members, subservient to each other; every picture must be composed of various colours, and of light and shade; all harmony must be formed of trebles, tenors, and basses; every beautiful and useful edifice must consist of higher and lower, more and less magnificent apartments. This is in the very essence of all created things, and therefore cannot be prevented by any means whatever, unless by not creating them at all.'

These instances are used instead of *Pope*'s *Oak* and *weeds*, or *Jupiter* and his *satellites*; but neither *Pope*, nor this writer have much contributed to solve the difficulty. Perfection or imperfection of unconscious beings has no meaning as referred to themselves; the *bass* and the *treble* are equally perfect; the mean and magnificent apartments feel no pleasure or pain from the comparison. *Pope* might ask the *weed*, why it was less than the *Oak*, but the *weed* would never ask the question for itself. The *bass* and *treble* differ only to the hearer, meanness and magnificence only to the inhabitant. There is no evil but must inhere in a conscious being, or be referred to it; that is, evil must be felt before it is evil. Yet even on this subject many questions might be offered which human understanding has not yet answered, and which the present haste of this extract will not suffer me to dilate.

He proceeds to an humble detail of *Pope*'s opinion: 'The universe is a system whose very essence consists in subordination; a scale of beings descending by insensible degrees from infinite perfection to absolute nothing: in which, tho' we may justly expect to find perfection in the whole, could we possibly comprehend it; yet would it be the highest absurdity to hope for it in all its parts, because the beauty and happiness of the whole depend altogether on the just inferiority of its parts, that is, on the comparative imperfections of the several beings of which it is composed.'

'It would have been no more an instance of God's wisdom to have created no beings but of the highest and most perfect order, than it would be of a painter's art, to cover his whole piece with one single colour the most beautiful he could compose. Had he confined himself to such, nothing could have existed but demi-gods, or archangels, and then all inferior orders must have been void and uninhabited: but as it is surely more agreeable to infinite benevolence, that all these should be filled up with beings capable of enjoying happiness themselves, and contributing to that of others, they must necessarily be filled with inferior beings, that is, with such as are less perfect, but from whose existence, notwithstanding that less perfection, more felicity upon the whole accrues to the universe, than if no such had been created. It is moreover highly probable, that there is such a connection between all ranks and orders by subordinate degrees, that they mutually support each others existence, and every one in its place is absolutely necessary towards sustaining the whole vast and magnificent fabrick.'

'Our pretences for complaint could be of this only, that we are not so high in the scale of existence as our ignorant ambition may desire: a pretence which must eternally subsist; because, were we ever so much higher, there would be still room for infinite power to exalt us; and since no link in the chain can be broke, the same reason for disquiet must remain to those who succeed to that chasm, which must be occasioned by our preferment. A man can have no reason to repine, that he is not an angel; nor a horse, that he is not a man; much less, that in their several stations they possess not the faculties of another; for this would be an insufferable misfortune.'

This doctrine of the regular subordination of beings, the scale of existence, and the chain of nature, I have often considered, but always left the Inquiry in doubt and uncertainty.

That every being not infinite, compared with infinity, must be imperfect, is evident to intuition; that whatever is imperfect must have a certain line which it cannot pass, is equally certain. But the reason which determined this limit, and for which such being was suffered to advance thus far and no further, we shall never be able to discern. Our discoverers tell us, the Creator has made beings of all orders, and that therefore one of them must be such as man. But this system seems to be established on a concession which if it be refused cannot be extorted.

Every reason which can be brought to prove, that there are beings of every possible sort, will prove that there is the greatest number possible of every sort of beings; but this with respect to man we know, if we know any thing, not to be true.

It does not appear even to the imagination, that of three orders of being, the first and the third receive any advantage from the imperfection of the second, or that indeed they may not equally exist, though the second had never been, or should cease to be, and why should that be concluded necessary, which cannot be proved even to be useful?

The scale of existence from infinity to nothing, cannot possibly have being. The highest being not infinite must be, as has been often observed, at an infinite distance below infinity. *Cheyne*, who, with the desire inherent in mathematicians to reduce every thing to mathematical images, considers all existence as a *cone*, allows that the basis is at an infinite distance from the body. And in this distance between finite and infinite, there will be room for ever for an infinite series of indefinable existence.

Between the lowest positive existence and nothing, wherever we suppose positive existence to cease, is another chasm infinitely deep; where there is room again for endless orders of subordinate nature, continued for ever and for ever, and yet infinitely superior to non-existence.

To these meditations humanity is unequal. But yet we may ask, not of our maker, but of each other, since on the one side creation, wherever it stops, must stop infinitely below infinity, and on the other infinitely above nothing, what necessity there is that it should proceed so far either way, that beings so high or so low should ever have existed. We may ask; but I believe no created wisdom can give an adequate answer.

Nor is this all. In the scale, wherever it begins or ends, are infinite vacuities. At whatever distance we suppose the next order of beings to be above man, there is room for an intermediate order of beings between them; and if for one order then for infinite orders; since every thing that admits of more or less, and consequently all the parts of that which admits them, may be infinitely divided. So that, as far as we can judge, there may be room in the vacuity between any two steps of the scale, or between any two points of the cone of being for infinite exertion of infinite power.

Thus it appears how little reason those who repose their reason upon the scale of being have to triumph over them who recur to any other expedient of solution, and what difficulties arise on every side to repress the rebellions of presumptuous decision. *Qui pauca considerat, facile pronunciat.* In our passage through the boundless ocean of disquisition we often take fogs for land, and after having long toiled to approach them find, instead of repose and harbours, new storms of objection and fluctuations of uncertainty.

We are next entertained with *Pope*'s alleviations of those evils which we are doomed to suffer.

'Poverty, or the want of riches, is generally compensated by having more hopes and fewer fears, by a greater share of health, and a more exquisite relish of the smallest enjoyments, than those who possess them are usually bless'd with. The want of taste and genius, with all the pleasures that arise from them, are commonly recompensed by a more useful kind of common sense, together with a wonderful delight, as well as success, in the busy pursuits of a scrambling world. The sufferings of the sick are greatly relieved by many trifling gratifications imperceptible to others, and sometimes almost repaid by the inconceivable transports occasioned by the return of health and vigour. Folly cannot be very grievous, because imperceptible; and I doubt not but there is some truth in that rant of a mad poet, that there is a pleasure in being mad, which none but madmen know. Ignorance, or the want of knowledge and literature, the appointed lot of all born to poverty, and the drudgeries of life, is the only opiate capable of infusing that insensibility which can enable them to endure the miseries of the one, and the fatigues of the other. It is a cordial administered by the gracious hand of providence; of which they ought never to be deprived by an ill-judged and improper education. It is the basis of all subordination, the support of society, and the privilege of individuals: and I have ever thought it a most remarkable instance of the divine wisdom, that whereas in all animals, whose individuals rise little above the rest of their species, knowledge is instinctive; in man whose individuals are so widely different, it is acquired by education; by which means the prince and the labourer, the philosopher and the peasant, are in some measure fitted for their respective situations.'

Much of these positions is perhaps true, and the whole paragraph might well pass without censure, were not objections necessary to the establishment of knowledge. *Poverty* is very gently paraphrased by *want of riches*. In that sense almost every man may in his own opinion be poor. But there is another poverty which is *want of competence*, of all that can soften the miseries of life, of all that diversify attention, or delight imagination. There is yet another poverty which is *want of necessaries*, a species of poverty which no care of the publick, no charity of particulars, can preserve many from feeling openly, and many secretly.

That hope and fear are inseparably or very frequently connected with poverty, and riches, my surveys of life have not informed me. The milder degrees of poverty are sometimes supported by hope, but the more severe often sink down in motionless despondence. Life must be seen before it can be known. This author and *Pope* perhaps never saw the miseries which they imagine thus easy to be born. The poor indeed are insensible of many little vexations which sometimes imbitter the possessions and pollute the enjoyments of the rich. They are not pained by casual incivility, or mortified by the mutilation of a compliment; but this happiness is like that of a malefactor who ceases to feel the cords that bind him when the pincers are tearing his flesh.

That want of taste for one enjoyment is supplied by the pleasures of some other, may be fairly allowed. But the compensations of sickness I have never found near to equivalence, and the transports of recovery only prove the intenseness of the pain.

With folly no man is willing to confess himself very intimately acquainted, and therefore its pains and pleasures are kept secret. But what the author says of its happiness seems applicable only to fatuity, or gross dulness, for that inferiority of understanding which makes one man without any other reason the slave, or tool, or property of another, which makes him sometimes useless, and sometimes ridiculous, is often felt with very quick sensibility. On the happiness of madmen, as the case is not very frequent, it is not necessary to raise a disquisition, but I cannot forbear to observe, that I never yet knew disorders of mind encrease felicity: every madman is either arrogant and irascible, or gloomy and suspicious, or possessed by some passion or notion destructive to his quiet. He has always discontent in his look, and malignity in his bosom. And, if we had the power of choice, he would soon repent who should resign his reason to secure his peace.

Concerning the portion of ignorance necessary to make the condition of the lower classes of mankind safe to the public and tolerable to themselves, both morals and policy exact a nicer enquiry than will be very soon or very easily made. There is undoubtedly a degree of knowledge which will direct a man to refer all to providence, and to acquiesce in the condition which omniscient goodness has determined to allot him; to consider this world as a phantom that must soon glide from before his eyes, and the distresses and vexations that encompass him, as dust scattered in his path, as a blast that chills him for a moment, and passes off for ever.

Such wisdom, arising from the comparison of a part with the whole of our existence, those that want it most cannot possibly obtain from philosophy, nor unless the method of education and the general tenour of life are changed, will very easily receive it from religion. The bulk of mankind is not likely to be very wise or very good: and I know not whether there are not many states of life, in which all knowledge less than the highest wisdom, will produce discontent and danger. I believe it may be sometimes found, that a *little learning* is to a poor man a *dangerous thing*. But such is the condition of humanity, that we easily see, or quickly feel the wrong, but cannot always distinguish the right. Whatever knowledge is superfluous, in irremediable poverty, is hurtful, but the difficulty is to determine when poverty is irremediable, and at what point superfluity begins. Gross ignorance every man has found equally dangerous with perverted knowledge. Men left wholly to their appetites and their instincts, with little sense of moral or religious obligation, and with very faint distinctions of right and wrong, can never be safely employed or confidently trusted: they can be honest only by obstinacy, and diligent only by compulsion or caprice. Some instruction, therefore, is necessary, and much perhaps may be dangerous.

Though it should be granted that those who are *born to poverty and drudgery* should not be *deprived* by an *improper education* of the *opiate* of *ignorance*; even this concession will not be of much use to direct our practice, unless it be determined who are those that are *born to poverty*. To entail irreversible poverty upon generation after generation only because the ancestor happened to be poor, is in itself cruel, if not unjust, and is wholly contrary to the maxims of a commercial nation, which always suppose and promote a rotation of property, and offer every individual a chance of mending his condition by his diligence. Those who communicate literature to the son of a poor man, consider him as one not born to poverty, but to the necessity of deriving a better fortune from himself. In this attempt, as in others, many fail, and many succeed. Those that fail will feel their misery more acutely; but since poverty is now confessed to be such a calamity as cannot be born without the opiate of insensibility, I hope the happiness of those whom education enables to escape from it, may turn the ballance against that exacerbation which the others suffer.

I am always afraid of determining on the side of envy or cruelty. The privileges of education may sometimes be improperly bestowed, but I shall always fear to with-hold them, lest I should be yielding to the suggestions of pride, while I persuade myself that I am following the maxims of policy; and under the appearance of salutary restraints, should be indulging the lust of dominion, and that malevolence which delights in seeing others depressed.

Pope's doctrine is at last exhibited in a comparison, which, like other proofs of the same kind, is better adapted to delight the fancy than convince the reason.

'Thus the universe resembles a large and well-regulated family, in which all the officers and servants, and even the domestic animals, are subservient to each other in a proper subordination: each enjoys the privileges and perquisites peculiar to his place, and at the same time contributes by that just subordination to the magnificence and happiness of the whole.'

The magnificence of a house is of use or pleasure always to the master, and sometimes to the domestics. But the magnificence of the universe adds nothing to the supreme Being; for any part of its inhabitants with which human knowledge is acquainted, an universe much less spacious or splendid would have been sufficient; and of happiness it does not appear that any is communicated from the Beings of a lower world to those of a higher.

The enquiry after the cause of *natural evil* is continued in the third letter, in which, as in the former, there is mixture of borrowed truth, and native folly, of some notions just and trite, with others uncommon and ridiculous.

His opinion of the value and importance of happiness is certainly just, and I shall insert it, not that it will give any information to any reader, but it may serve to shew how the most common notion may be swelled in sound, and diffused in bulk, till it shall perhaps astonish the author himself.

'Happiness is the only thing of real value in existence; neither riches, nor power, nor wisdom, nor learning, nor strength, nor beauty, nor virtue, nor religion, nor even life itself, being of any importance but as they contribute to is production. All these are in themselves neither good nor evil; happiness alone is their great end, and they desireable only as they tend to promote it.'

Success produces confidence. After this discovery of the value of happiness, he proceeds without any distrust of himself to tell us what has been hid from all former enquirers.

'The true solution of this important question, so long and so vainly searched for by the philosophers of all ages and all countries, I take to be at last no more than this, that these real evils proceed from the same source as those imaginary ones of imperfection before treated of, namely, from that subordination, without which no created system can subsist; all subordination implying imperfection, all imperfection evil, and all evil some kind of inconveniency or suffering: so that there must be particular inconveniencies and sufferings annexed to every particular rank of created beings by the circumstances of things, and their modes of existence.

'God indeed might have made us quite other creatures, and placed us in a world quite differently constituted; but then we had been no longer men, and whatever beings had occupied our stations in the universal system, they must have been liable to the same inconveniences.'

In all this there is nothing that can silence the enquiries of curiosity, or calm the perturbations of doubt. Whether subordination implies imperfection may be disputed. The means respecting themselves, may be as perfect as the end. The weed as a weed is no less perfect than the oak as an oak. That *imperfection implies evil, and evil suffering* is by no means evident. Imperfection may imply privative evil, or the absence of some good, but this privation produces no suffering, but by the help of knowledge. An infant at the breast is yet an imperfect man, but there is no reason for belief that he is unhappy by his immaturity, unless some positive pain be super-added.

When this author presumes to speak of the universe, I would advise him a little to distrust his own faculties, however large and comprehensive. Many words easily understood on common occasion, become uncertain and figurative when applied to the works of Omnipotence. Subordination in human affairs is well understood, but when it is attributed to the universal system, its meaning grows less certain, like the petty distinctions of locality, which are of good use upon our own globe, but have no meaning with regard to infinite space, in which nothing is *high* or *low*.

That if man, by exaltation to a higher nature were exempted from the evils which he now suffers, some other being must suffer them; that if man were not man, some other being must be man, is a position arising from his established notion of the scale of being. A notion to which *Pope* has given some importance by adopting it, and of which I have therefore endeavoured to shew the uncertainty and inconsistency. This scale of being I have demonstrated to be raised by presumptuous imagination, to rest on nothing at the bottom, to lean on nothing at the top, and to have vacuities from step to step through which any order of being may sink into nihility without any inconvenience, so far as we can judge, to the next rank above or below it. We are therefore little enlightned by a writer who tells us that any being in the state of man must suffer what man suffers, when the only question, that requires to be resolved is, Why any being is in this state?

Of poverty and labour he gives just and elegant representations, which yet do not remove the difficulty of the first and fundamental question, though supposing the present state of man necessary, they may supply some motives to content.

'Poverty is what all could not possibly have been exempted from, not only by reason of the fluctuating nature of human possessions, but because the world could not subsist without it; for had all been rich, none could have submitted to the commands of another, or the necessary drudgeries of life; thence all governments must have been dissolved, arts neglected, and lands uncultivated, and so an universal penury have overwhelmed all, instead of now and then pinching a few. Hence, by the by, appears the great excellence of charity, by which men are enabled by a particular distribution of the blessings and enjoyments of life, on proper occasions, to prevent that poverty which by a general one omnipotence itself could never have prevented: so that, by inforcing this duty, God as it were demands our assistance to promote universal happiness, and to shut out misery at every door, where it strives to intrude itself.

'Labour, indeed, God might easily have excused us from, since at his command, the earth would readily have poured forth all her treasures without our inconsiderable assistance: but if the severest labour cannot sufficiently subdue the malignity of human nature, what plots and machinations, what wars, rapine and devastation, what profligacy and licentiousness must have been the consequences of universal idleness! so that labour ought only to be looked upon as a task kindly imposed upon us by our indulgent creator, necessary to preserve our health, our safety and our innocence.'

I am afraid that *the latter end of his commonwealth forgets the beginning.* If God *could easily have excused us from labour*, I do not comprehend why *he could not possibly have exempted all from poverty.* For poverty, in its easier and more tolerable degree, is little more than necessity of labour, and, in its more severe and deplorable state, little more than inability for labour. To be poor is to work for others, or to want the succour of others without work. And the same exuberant fertility which would make work unnecessary might make poverty impossible.

Surely a man who seems not completely master of his own opinion, should have spoken more cautiously of omnipotence, nor have presumed to say what it could perform, or what it could prevent. I am in doubt whether those who stand highest in *the scale of being* speak this confidently of the dispensations of their maker.

> *For fools rush in, where angels fear to tread.*

Of our inquietudes of mind his account is still less reasonable. 'Whilst men are injured, they must be inflamed with anger; and whilst they see cruelties, they must be melted with pity; whilst they perceive danger they must be sensible of fear.' This is to give a reason for all evil, by shewing that one evil produces another. If there is danger there ought to be fear; but if fear is an evil, why should there be danger? His vindication of pain is of the same kind; pain is useful to alarm us, that we may shun greater evils, but those greater evils must be presupposed that the fitness of pain may appear.

Treating on death, he has expressed the known and true doctrine with spriteliness of fancy and neatness of diction. I shall therefore insert it. There are truths which, as they are always necessary, do not grow stale by repetition.

'Death, the last and most dreadful of all evils, is so far from being one, that it is the infallible cure for all others.

> *To die, is landing on some silent shore,*
> *Where billows never beat, nor tempests roar.*
> *Ere well we feel the friendly stroke, 'tis o'er.*
> GARTH.

'For, abstracted from the sickness and sufferings usually attending it, it is no more than the expiration of that term of life God was pleased to bestow on us, without any claim or merit on our part. But was it an evil ever so great, it could not be remedied but by one much greater, which is by living for ever; by which means our wickedness, unrestrained by the prospect of a future state, would grow so insupportable, our sufferings so intolerable by perseverance, and our pleasures so tiresome by repetition, that no being in the universe could be so compleatly miserable as a species of immortal men. We have no reason, therefore, to look upon death as an evil, or to fear it as a punishment, even without any supposition of a future life: but if we consider it as a passage to a more perfect state, or a remove only in an eternal succession of still improving states (for which we have the strongest reasons) it will then appear a new favour from the divine munificence; and a man must be as absurd to repine at dying, as a traveller would be, who proposed to himself a delightful tour through various unknown countries, to lament that he cannot take up his residence at the first dirty inn which he baits at on the road.

'The instability of human life, or the changes of its successive periods, of which we so frequently complain, are no more than the necessary progress of it to this necessary conclusion; and are so far from being evils deserving these complaints, that they are the source of our greatest pleasures as they are the source of all novelty, from which our greatest pleasures are ever derived. The continual succession of seasons in the human life, by daily presenting to us new scenes, render it agreeable, and like those of the year, afford us delights by their change, which the choicest of them could not give us by their continuance. In the spring of life, the gilding of the sun shine, the verdure of the fields, and the variegated paintings of the sky, are so exquisite in the eye of infants at their first looking abroad into a new world, as nothing perhaps afterwards can equal. The heat and vigour of the succeeding summer of youth ripens for us new pleasures, the blooming maid, the nightly revel, and the jovial chace: the serene autumn of complete manhood feasts us with the golden harvests of our worldly pursuits: nor is the hoary winter of old age destitute of its peculiar comforts and enjoyments, of which the recollection and relation of those past are perhaps none of the least; and at last death opens to us a new prospect, from whence we shall probably look back upon the diversions and occupations of this world with the same contempt we do now on our tops and hobby-horses, and with the same surprize, that they could ever so much entertain or engage us.'

I would not willingly detract from the beauty of this paragraph, and in gratitude to him who has so well inculcated such important truths, I will venture to admonish him, since the chief comfort of the old is the recollection of the past, so to employ his time and his thoughts, that when the imbecillity of age shall come upon him, he may be able to recreate its languors by the remembrance of hours spent, not in presumptuous decisions, but modest inquiries, not in dogmatical limitations of omnipotence, but in humble acquiescence and fervent adoration. Old age will shew him that much of the book now before us has no other use than to perplex the scrupulous, and to shake the weak, to encourage impious presumption, or stimulate idle curiosity.

Having thus dispatched the consideration of particular evils, he comes at last to a general reason for which *evil* may be said to be *our good*. He is of opinion that there is some inconceivable benefit in pain abstractedly considered; that pain however inflicted, or wherever felt, communicates some good to the general system of being, and that every animal is some way or other the better for the pain of every other animal. This opinion he carries so far as to suppose that there passes some principle of union through all animal life, as attraction is communicated to all corporeal nature, and that the evils suffered on this globe, may by some inconceivable means contribute to the felicity of the inhabitants of the remotest planet.

How the origin of evil is brought nearer to human conception by any *inconceiveable* means, I am not able to discover. We believed that the present system of creation was right, though we could not explain the adaptation of one part to the other, or for the whole succession of causes and consequences. Where has this enquirer added to the little knowledge that we had before? He has told us of the benefits of evil, which no man feels, and relations between distant parts of universe, which he cannot himself conceive. There was enough in this question inconceivable before, and we have little advantage from a new inconceivable solution.

I do not mean to reproach this author for not knowing what is equally hidden from learning and from ignorance. The shame is to impose words for ideas upon ourselves or others. To imagine that we are going forward when we are only turning round. To think that there is any difference between him that gives no reason, and him that gives a reason, which by his own confession cannot be conceived.

But that he may not be thought to conceive nothing but things inconceivable, he has at last thought on a way by which human sufferings may produce good effects. He imagines that as we have not only animals for food, but choose some for our diversion, the same privilege may be allowed to some beings above us, *who may deceive, torment, or destroy as for the ends only of their own pleasure or utility.* This he again finds impossible to be conceived, *but that impossibility lessons not the probability of the conjecture, which by analogy is so strongly confirmed.*

I cannot resist the temptation of contemplating this analogy, which I think he might have carried further very much to the advantage of his argument. He might have shewn that these *hunters whose game is man* have many sports analagous to our own. As we drown whelps and kittens, they amuse themselves now and then with sinking a ship, and stand round the fields of *Blenheim* or the walls of *Prague*, as we encircle a cock-pit. As we shoot a bird flying, they take a man in the midst of his business or pleasure, and knock him down with an apoplexy. Some of them, perhaps, are virtuosi, and delight in the operations of an asthma, as a human philosopher in the effects of the air pump. To swell a man with a tympany is as good sport as to blow a frog. Many a merry bout have these frolic beings at the vicissitudes of an ague, and good sport it is to see a man tumble with an epilepsy, and revive and tumble again, and all this he knows not why. As they are wiser and more powerful than we, they have more exquisite diversions, for we have no way of procuring any sport so brisk and so lasting as the paroxysms of the gout and stone which undoubtedly must make high mirth, especially if the play be a little diversified with the blunders and puzzles of the blind and deaf. We know not how far their sphere of observation may extend. Perhaps now and then a merry being may place himself in such a situation as to enjoy at once all the varieties of an epidemical disease, or amuse his leisure with the tossings and contortions of every possible pain exhibited together.

One sport the merry malice of these beings has found means of enjoying to which we have nothing equal or similar. They now and then catch a mortal proud of his parts, and flattered either by the submission of those who court his kindness, or the notice of those who suffer him to court theirs. A head thus prepared for the reception of false opinions, and the projection of vain designs, they easily fill with idle notions, till in time they make their plaything an author: their first diversion commonly begins with an Ode or an epistle, then rises perhaps to a political irony, and is at last brought to its height, by a treatise of philosophy. Then begins the poor animal to entangle himself in sophisms, and flounder in absurdity, to talk confidently of the scale of being, and to give solutions which himself confesses impossible to be understood. Sometimes, however, it happens that their pleasure is without much mischief. The author feels no pain, but while they are wondering at the extravagance of his opinion, and pointing him out to one another as a new example of human folly, he is enjoying his own applause, and that of his companions, and perhaps is elevated with the hope of standing at the head of a new sect.

Many of the books which now croud the world, may be justly suspected to be written for the sake of some invisible order of beings, for surely they are of no use to any of the corporeal inhabitants of the world. Of the productions of the last bounteous year, how many can be said to serve any purpose of use or pleasure. The only end of writing is to enable the readers better to enjoy life, or better to endure it: and how will either of those be put more in our power by him who tells us, that we are puppets, of which some creature not much wiser than ourselves manages the wires. That a set of beings unseen and unheard, are hovering about us, trying experiments upon our sensibility, putting us in agonies to see our limbs quiver, torturing us to madness, that they may laugh at our vagaries, sometimes obstructing the bile, that they may see how a man looks when he is yellow; sometimes breaking a traveller's bones to try how he will get home; sometimes wasting a man to a skeleton, and sometimes killing him fat for the greater elegance of his hide.

This is an account of natural evil which though, like the rest, not quite new is very entertaining, though I know not how much it may contribute to patience. The only reason why we should contemplate evil is, that we may bear it better, and I am afraid nothing is much more placidly endured, for the sake of making others sport.

The first pages of the fourth letter are such as incline me both to hope and wish that I shall find nothing to blame in the succeeding part. He offers a criterion of action, an account of virtue and vice, for which I have often contended, and which must be embraced by all who are willing to know why they act, or why they forbear, to give any reason of their conduct to themselves or others.

'In order to find out the true origin of moral evil, it will be necessary, in the first place, to enquire into its nature and essence; or what it is that constitutes one action evil, and another good. Various have been the opinions of various authors on this criterion of virtue; and this variety has rendered that doubtful, which must otherwise have been clear and manifest to the meanest capacity. Some indeed have denied that there is any such thing, because different ages and nations have entertained different sentiments concerning it: but this is just as reasonable as to assert, that there are neither sun, moon, nor stars, because astronomers have supported different systems of the motions and magnitudes of these celestial bodies. Some have placed it in conformity to truth, some to the fitness of things, and others to the will of God. But all this is merely superficial: they resolve us not why truth, or the fitness of things, are either eligible or obligatory, or why God should require us to act in one manner rather than another. The true reason of which can possibly be no other than this, because some actions produce happiness, and others misery: so that all moral good and evil are nothing more than the production of natural. This alone it is that makes truth preferable to falshood, this that determines the fitness of things, and this that induces God to command some actions, and forbid others. They who extol the truth, beauty, and harmony of virtue, exclusive of its consequences, deal but in pompous nonsense; and they who would persuade us, that good and evil are things indifferent, depending wholly on the will of God, do but confound the nature of things, as well as all our notions of God himself, by representing him capable of willing contradictions; that is, that we should be, and be happy, and at the same time that we should torment and destroy each other; for injuries cannot be made benefits, pain cannot be made pleasure, and consequently vice cannot be made virtue by any power whatever. It is the consequences, therefore, of all human actions that must stamp their value. So far as the general practice of any action tends to produce good, and introduce happiness into the world, so far we may pronounce it virtuous; so much evil as it occasions, such is the degree of vice it contains. I say the general practice, because we must always remember in judging by this rule, to apply it only to the general species of actions, and not to particular actions; for the infinite wisdom of God, desirous to set bounds to the destructive consequences which must otherwise have followed from the universal depravity of mankind, has so wonderfully contrived the nature of things, that our most vitious actions may sometimes accidentally and collaterally produce good. Thus, for instance, robbery may disperse useless hoards to the benefit of the public; adultery may bring heirs and good humour too into many families, where they would otherwise have been wanting; and murder free the world from tyrants and oppressors. Luxury maintains its thousands, and vanity its ten thousands. Superstition and arbitrary power contribute to the grandeur of many nations, and the liberties of others are preserved by the perpetual contentions of avarice, knavery, selfishness, and ambition: and thus the worst of vices, and the worst of men are often compelled by providence to serve the most beneficial purposes, contrary to their own malevolent tendencies and inclinations; and thus private vices become public benefits by the force only of accidental circumstances. But this impeaches not the truth of the criterion of virtue before mentioned, the only solid foundation on which any true system of ethicks can be built, the only plain, simple, and uniform rule by which we can pass any judgment on our actions; but by this we may be enabled, not only to determine which are good, and which are evil, but almost mathematically to demonstrate the proportion of virtue, or vice which belongs to each, by comparing them with the degrees of happiness or misery which they occasion. But tho' the production of happiness is the essence of virtue, it is by no means the end: the great end is the probation of mankind, or the giving them an opportunity of exalting or degrading themselves in another state by their behaviour in the present. And thus indeed it answers two most important purposes; those are, the conservation of our happiness, and the test of our obedience; for had not such a test seemed necessary to God's infinite wisdom, and productive of universal good, he would never have permitted the happiness of men, even in this life, to have depended on so precarious a tenure, as their mutual good behaviour to each other. For it is observable, that he who best knows our formation, has trusted no one thing of importance to our reason or virtue: he trusts only to our appetites for the support of the individual, and the continuance of our species; to our vanity or compassion, for our bounty to others; and to our fears, for the preservation of ourselves; often to our vices for the support of government, and sometimes to our follies for the preservation of our religion. But since some test of our obedience was necessary, nothing sure could have been commanded for that end so fit and proper, and at the same time so useful, as the practice of virtue: nothing have been so justly rewarded with happiness, as the production of happiness in conformity to the will of God. It is this conformity alone which adds merit to virtue, and constitutes the essential difference between morality and religion. Morality obliges men to live honestly and soberly, because such behaviour is most conducive to publick happiness, and consequently to their own; religion, to pursue the same course, because conformable to the will of their creator. Morality induces them to embrace virtue from prudential considerations; religion from those of gratitude and obedience. Morality therefore, entirely abstracted from religion, can have nothing meritorious in it; it being but wisdom, prudence, or good œconomy, which, like health, beauty, or riches, are rather obligations conferred upon us by God, than merits in us towards him; for tho' we may be justly punished for injuring ourselves, we can claim no reward for self-preservation; as suicide deserves punishment and infamy, but a man deserves no reward or honours for not being guilty of it. This I take to be the meaning of all those passages in our scriptures in which works are represented to have no merit without faith; that is, not without believing in historical facts, in creeds, and articles; but without being done in pursuance of our belief in God, and in obedience to his commands. And now, having mentioned scripture, I cannot omit observing, that the christian is the only religious or moral institution in the world, that ever set in a right light these two material points, the essence and the end of virtue; that ever founded the one in the production of happiness, that is, in universal benevolence, or, in their language, charity to all men; the other, in the probation of man, and his obedience to his creator. Sublime and magnificent as was the philosophy of the ancients, all their moral systems were deficient in these two important articles. They were all built on the sandy foundations of the innate beauty of virtue, or enthusiastick patriotism; and their great point in view was the contemptible reward of human glory; foundations which were by no means able to support the magnificent structures which they erected upon them; for the beauty of virtue independent of its effects, is unmeaning nonsense; patriotism which injures mankind in general for the sake of a particular country, is but a more extended selfishness, and really criminal; and all human glory but a mean and ridiculous delusion. The whole affair then of religion and morality, the subject of so many thousand volumes, is in short no more than this: The supreme being, infinitely good, as well as powerful, desirous to diffuse happiness by all possible means, has created innumerable ranks and orders of Beings, all subservient to each other by proper subordination. One of these is occupied by Man, a creature endued with such a certain degree of knowledge, reason, and free-will, as is suitable to his situation, and placed for a time on this globe as in a school of probation and education. Here he has an opportunity given him of improving or debasing his nature, in such a manner as to render himself fit for a rank of higher perfection and happiness, or to degrade himself to a state of greater imperfection and misery; necessary indeed towards carrying on the business of the universe, but very grievous and burthensome to those individuals, who, by their own misconduct, are obliged to submit to it. The test of this his behaviour, is doing good, that is, co-operating with his creator, as far as his narrow sphere of action will permit, in the production of happiness. And thus the happiness and misery of a future state will be the just reward or punishment of promoting or preventing happiness in this. So artificially by this means is the nature of all human virtue and vice contrived, that their rewards and punishments are woven as it were in their very essence; their immediate effects give us a foretaste of their future, and their fruits in the present life are the proper samples of what they must unavoidably produce in another. We have reason given us to distinguish these consequences, and regulate our conduct; and, lest that should neglect its post, Conscience also is appointed as an instinctive kind of monitor, perpetually to remind us both of our interest and our duty.'

Si sic omnia dixisset! To this account of the essence of vice and virtue, it is only necessary to add, that the consequences of human actions being sometimes uncertain and sometimes remote, it is not possible in many cases for most men, nor in all cases for any man to determine what actions will ultimately produce happiness, and therefore it was proper that *Revelation* should lay down a rule to be followed invariably in opposition to appearances, and in every change of circumstances, by which we may be certain to promote the general felicity, and be set free from the dangerous temptation of *doing evil that good may come.*

Because it may easily happen, and in effect will happen very frequently, that our own private happiness may be promoted by an act injurious to others, when yet no man can be obliged by nature to prefer ultimately the happiness of others to his own. Therefore, to the instructions of infinite wisdom it was necessary that infinite power should add penal sanctions. That every man to whom those instructions shall be imparted may know, that he can never ultimately injure himself by benefiting others, or ultimately by injuring others benefit himself; but that however the lot of the good and bad may be huddled together in the seeming confusion of our present state, the time shall undoubtedly come, when the most virtuous will be most happy.

I am sorry that the remaining part of this letter is not equal to the first. The author has indeed engaged in a disquisition in which we need not wonder if he fails, in the solution of questions on which philosophers have employed their abilities from the earliest times,

And found no end in wandering mazes lost.

He denies that man was created *perfect*, because the system requires subordination, and because the power of losing his perfection of *rendering himself wicked and miserable is the highest imperfection imaginable.* Besides the regular gradations of the scale of being required somewhere *such a creature as man with all his infirmities about him, and the total removal of those would be altering his nature, and when he became perfect he must cease to be man.*

I have already spent some considerations on the *scale of being*, of which yet I am obliged to renew the mention whenever a new argument is made to rest upon it, and I must therefore again remark, that consequences cannot have greater certainty than the postulate from which they are drawn, and that no system can be more hypothetical than this, and perhaps no hypothesis more absurd.

He again deceives himself with respect to the perfection with which *man* is held to be originally vested. *That man came perfect, that is indeed with all possible perfection, out of the hands of his creator, is a false notion, derived from the philosophers.—The universal system required subordination, and consequently comparative imperfection.* That *man was ever indued with all possible perfection,* that is with all perfection of which the idea is not contradictory or destructive of itself, is undoubtedly *false.* But it can hardly be called *a false notion,* because no man ever thought it, nor can it be derived from the *philosophers;* for without pretending to guess what philosophers he may mean, it is very safe to affirm, that no philosopher ever said it. Of those who now maintain that *man* was once perfect, who may very easily be found, let the author enquire whether *man* was ever omniscient, whether he was ever omnipotent, whether he ever had even the lower power of Archangels or Angels. Their answers will soon inform him, that the supposed perfection of *man* was not absolute, but respective, that he was perfect in a sense consistent enough with subordination, perfect not as compared with different beings, but with himself in his present degeneracy, not perfect as an angel, but perfect as man.

From this perfection, whatever it was, he thinks it necessary that man should be debarred, because pain is necessary to the good of the universe; and the pain of one order of beings extending its salutary influence to innumerable orders above and below, it was necessary that man should suffer; but because it is not suitable to justice that pain should be inflicted on innocence, it was necessary that man should be criminal.

This is given as a satisfactory account of the original of moral evil, which amounts only to this, that God created beings whose guilt he foreknew, in order that he might have proper objects of pain, because the pain of part is no man knows how or why, necessary to the felicity of the whole.

The perfection which man once had, may be so easily conceived, that without any unusual strain of imagination we can figure its revival. All the duties to God or man that we neglected we may fancy performed, all the crimes that are committed we may conceive forborn. Man will then be restored to his moral perfections, and into what head can it enter that by this change the universal system would be shaken, or the condition of any order of beings altered for the worse.

He comes in the fifth letter to political, and in the sixth to religious evils. Of political evil, if we suppose the origin of moral evil discovered the account is by no means difficult: polity being only the conduct of immoral men in public affairs. The evils of each particular kind of government are very clearly and elegantly displayed, and from their secondary causes very rationally deduced, but the first cause lies still in its antient obscurity. There is in this letter nothing new, nor any thing eminently instructive; one of his practical deductions, that *from government evils cannot be eradicated, and their excess only can be prevented*, has been always allowed; the question upon which all dissension arises; is when that excess begins, at what point men shall cease to bear, and attempt to remedy.

Another of his precepts, though not new, well deserves to be transcribed, because it cannot be too frequently impressed.

'What has here been said of their imperfections and abuses, is by no means intended as a defence of them: every wise man ought to redress them to the utmost of his power; which can be effected by one method only: that is, by a reformation of Manners: for as all political evils derive their original from moral, these can never be remov'd, until those are first amended. He, therefore, who strictly adheres to virtue and sobriety in his conduct, and inforces them by his example, does more real service to a state, than he who displaces a minister, or dethrones a tyrant; this gives but a temporary relief, but that exterminates the cause of the disease. No immoral man then can possibly be a true patriot; and all those who profess outrageous zeal for the liberty and prosperity of their country, and at the same time infringe her laws, affront her religion, and debauch her people, are but despicable quacks, by fraud or ignorance increasing the disorders they pretend to remedy.'

Of religion he has said nothing but what he has learned, or might have learned from the divines, that it is not universal, because it must be received upon conviction, and successively received by those whom conviction reached; that its evidences and sanctions are not irresistible, because it was intended to induce, not to compel, and that it is obscure, because we want faculties to comprehend it. What he means by his assertion that it wants policy I do not well understand, he does not mean to deny that a good christian will be a good governor or a good subject, and he has before justly observed, that the good man only is a patriot.

Religion, has been, he says, corrupted by the wickedness of those to whom it was communicated, and has lost part of its efficacy by its connection with temporal interest and human passion.

He justly observes, that from all this, no conclusion can be drawn against the divine original of christianity, since the objections arise not from the nature of the revelation, but of him to whom it is communicated.

All this is known, and all this is true, but why, we have not yet discovered. Our author, if I understand him right, pursues the argument thus: The religion of man produces evils, because the morality of man is imperfect; his morality is imperfect, that he may be justly a subject of punishment: he is made subject to punishment, because the pain of part is necessary to the happiness of the whole; pain is necessary to happiness no mortal can tell why or how.

Thus, after having clambered with great labour from one step of argumentation to another, instead of rising into the light of knowledge, we are devolved back into dark ignorance, and all our effort ends in belief that for the evils of life there is some good reason, and in confession, that the reason cannot be found. This is all that has been produced by the revival of *Chrysippus*'s untractableness of matter, and the *Arabian* scale of existence. A system has been raised, which is so ready to fall to pieces of itself, that no great praise can be derived from its destruction. To object is always easy, and it has been well observed by a late writer, that *the hand which cannot build a hovel, may demolish a temple.*

Of the Duty of a Journalist

It is an unpleasing consideration that Virtue cannot be inferred from Knowledge; that many can teach others those Duties which they never practise themselves; yet, tho' there may be speculative Knowledge without actual Performance, there can be no Performance without Knowledge; and the present state of many of our Papers is such that it may be doubted not only whether the Compilers know their Duty, but whether they have endeavoured or wished to know it.

A Journalist is an Historian, not indeed of the highest Class, nor of the number of those whose works bestow immortality upon others or themselves; yet, like other Historians, he distributes for a time Reputation or Infamy, regulates the opinion of the week, raises hopes and terrors, inflames or allays the violence of the people. He ought therefore to consider himself as subject at least to the first law of History, the Obligation to tell Truth. The Journalist, indeed, however honest, will frequently deceive, because he will frequently be deceived himself. He is obliged to transmit the earliest intelligence before he knows how far it may be credited; he relates transactions yet fluctuating in uncertainty; he delivers reports of which he knows not the Authors. It cannot be expected that he should know more than he is told, or that he should not sometimes be hurried down the current of a popular clamour. All that he can do is to consider attentively, and determine impartially, to admit no falsehoods by design, and to retract those which he shall have adopted by mistake.

This is not much to be required, and yet this is more than the Writers of News seem to exact from themselves. It must surely sometimes raise indignation to observe with what serenity of confidence they relate on one day, what they know not to be true, because they hope that it will please; and with what shameless tranquillity they contradict it on the next day, when they find that it will please no longer. How readily they receive any report that will disgrace our enemies, and how eagerly they accumulate praises upon a name, which caprice or accident has made a Favourite. They know, by experience, however destitute of reason, that what is desired will be credited without nice examination: they do not therefore always limit their narratives by possibility, but slaughter armies without battles, and conquer countries without invasions.

There are other violations of truth admitted only to gratify idle curiosity, which yet are mischievous in their consequences, and hateful in their contrivance. Accounts are sometimes published of robberies and murders which never were committed, men's minds are terrified with fictitious dangers, the publick indignation is raised, and the Government of our country depreciated and contemned. These Scriblers, who give false alarms, ought to be taught, by some public animadversion, that to relate crimes is to teach them, and that as most men are content to follow the herd, and to be like their neighbours, nothing contributes more to the frequency of wickedness, than the representation of it as already frequent.

There is another practice, of which the injuriousness is more apparent, and which, if the law could succour the Poor, is now punishable by law. The Advertisement of Apprentices who have left their Masters, and who are often driven away by cruelty or hunger; the minute descriptions of men whom the law has not considered as criminal, and the insinuations often published in such a manner, that, though obscure to the publick, they are well understood where they can do most mischief; and many other practices by which particular interests are injured, are to be diligently avoided by an honest Journalist, whose business is only to tell transactions of general importance, or uncontested notoriety, or by Advertisements to promote private convenience without disturbance of private quiet.

Thus far the Journalist is obliged to deviate from the common methods of his Competitors by the laws of unvariable morality. Other improvements may be expected from him as conducive to delight or information. It is common to find passages, in Papers of Intelligence, which cannot be understood: Obscure places are sometimes mentioned without any information from Geography or History. Sums of money are reckoned by coins or denominations, of which the value is not known in this country. Terms of war and navigation are inserted, which are utterly unintelligible to all who are not engaged in military or naval business. A Journalist, above most other men, ought to be acquainted with the lower orders of mankind, that he may be able to judge, what will be plain and what will be obscure; what will require a Comment, and what will be apprehended without Explanation. He is to consider himself not as writing to Students or Statesmen alone, but to Women, Shopkeepers, and Artisans, who have little time to bestow upon mental attainments, but desire, upon easy terms, to know how the world goes; who rises, and who falls; who triumphs, and who is defeated.

If the Writer of this Journal shall be able to execute his own Plan; if he shall carefully enquire after Truth, and diligently impart it; if he shall resolutely refuse to admit into his Paper whatever is injurious to private Reputation; if he shall relate transactions with greater clearness than others, and sell more instruction at a cheaper rate, he hopes that his labours will not be overlooked. This he promises to endeavour; and, if this Promise shall obtain the Favour of an early Attention, he desires that Favour to be continued only as it is deserved.

The Idler

No. 1. Saturday, 15 April 1758.

Vacui sub umbra
Lusimus.
HOR.

Those who attempt periodical Essays seem to be often stopped in the beginning, by the difficulty of finding a proper Title. Two Writers, since the time of the Spectator, have assumed his Name, without any pretensions to lawful inheritance;

an effort was once made to revive the Tatler; and the strange appellations, by which other Papers have been called, show that the Authours were distressed, like the Natives of *America*, who come to the *Europeans* to beg a Name.

It will be easily believed of the *Idler*, that if his Title had required any search, he never would have found it. Every mode of life has its conveniencies. The *Idler*, who habituates himself to be satisfied with what he can most easily obtain, not only escapes labours which are often fruitless, but sometimes succeeds better than those who despise all that is within their reach, and think every thing more valuable as it is harder to be acquired.

If similitude of manners be a motive to kindness, the *Idler* may flatter himself with universal Patronage. There is no single character under which such numbers are comprised. Every man is, or hopes to be, an *Idler*. Even those who seem to differ most from us are hastening to encrease our Fraternity; as peace is the end of war, so to be idle is the ultimate purpose of the busy.

There is perhaps no Appellation by which a Writer can better denote his Kindred to the human Species. It has been found hard to describe Man by an adequate Definition. Some Philosophers have called him a reasonable Animal, but others have considered Reason as a Quality of which many creatures partake. He has been termed likewise a laughing Animal; but it is said that some Men have never laughed. Perhaps Man may be more properly distinguished as an Idle Animal; for there is no Man who is not sometimes Idle. It is at least a Definition from which none that shall find it in this Paper can be excepted; for who can be more idle than the Reader of the *Idler*?

That the Definition may be complete, Idleness must be not only the general, but the peculiar characteristic of Man; and perhaps Man is the only Being that can properly be called Idle, that does by others what he might do himself, or sacrifices Duty or Pleasure to the Love of Ease.

Scarcely any Name can be imagined from which less envy or competition is to be dreaded. The *Idler* has no Rivals or Enemies. The Man of Business forgets him; the Man of Enterprize despises him; and though such as tread the same track of Life, fall commonly into jealousy and discord, *Idlers* are always found to associate in Peace, and he who is most famed for doing Nothing, is glad to meet another as idle as himself.

What is to be expected from this Paper, whether it will be uniform or various, learned or familiar, serious or gay, political or moral, continued or interrupted, it is hoped that no Reader will enquire. That the *Idler* has some scheme, cannot be doubted; for to form schemes is the *Idler*'s privilege. But tho' he has many projects in his head, he is now grown sparing of communication, having observed, that his hearers are apt to remember what he forgets himself; that his tardiness of execution exposes him to the encroachments of those who catch a hint and fall to work; and that very specious plans, after long contrivance and pompous displays, have subsided in weariness without a trial, and without miscarriage have been blasted by derision.

Something the *Idler's* Character may be supposed to promise. Those that are curious after diminutive History, who watch the Revolutions of Families, and the Rise and Fall of Characters either Male or Female, will hope to be gratified by this Paper; for the *Idler* is always inquisitive and seldom retentive. He that delights in Obloquy and Satire, and wishes to see Clouds gathering over any Reputation that dazzles him with its Brightness, will snatch up the *Idler's* Essays with a beating Heart. The *Idler* is naturally censorious; those who attempt nothing themselves think every thing easily performed, and consider the unsuccessful always as criminal.

I think it necessary to give notice, that I make no contract, nor incur any obligation. If those who depend on the *Idler* for intelligence and entertainment, should suffer the disappointment which commonly follows ill-placed expectations, they are to lay the blame only on themselves.

Yet Hope is not wholly to be cast away. The *Idler*, tho' sluggish, is yet alive, and may sometimes be stimulated to vigour and activity. He may descend into profoundness, or tower into sublimity; for the diligence of an *Idler* is rapid and impetuous, as ponderous bodies forced into velocity move with violence proportionate to their weight.

But these vehement exertions of intellect cannot be frequent, and he will therefore gladly receive help from any Correspondent, who shall enable him to please without his own labour. He excludes no style, he prohibits no subject; only let him that writes to the *Idler* remember, that his letters must not be long; no words are to be squandered in declarations of esteem, or confessions of inability; conscious Dulness has little right to be prolix, and Praise is not so welcome to the *Idler* as Quiet.

No. 5. Saturday, 13 May 1758.

Κάλλος,

ἀντ᾽ ἀσπίδων ἁπασῶν,

ἀντ᾽ ἐγχέων ἁπάντων

ANAC.

Our Military Operations are at last begun; our troops are marching in all the pomp of war, and a camp is marked out on the Isle of Wight; the heart of every Englishman now swells with confidence, though somewhat softened by generous compassion for the consternation and distresses of our enemies.

This formidable armament and splendid march produce different effects upon different minds, according to the boundless diversities of temper, occupation, and habits of thought.

Many a tender Maiden considers her Lover as already lost, because he cannot reach the camp but by crossing the sea; Men, of a more political understanding, are persuaded that we shall now see, in a few days, the Ambassadors of France supplicating for pity. Some are hoping for a bloody battle, because a bloody battle makes a vendible narrative; some are composing songs of victory; some planning arches of triumph; and some are mixing fireworks for the celebration of a peace.

Of all extensive and complicated objects different parts are selected by different eyes; and minds are variously affected, as they vary their attention. The care of the publick is now fixed upon our Soldiers, who are leaving their native country to wander, none can tell how long, in the pathless desarts of the *Isle of Wight*. The Tender sigh for their sufferings, and the Gay drink to their success. I, who look, or believe myself to look, with more philosophick eyes, on human affairs, must confess, that I saw the troops march with little emotion; my thoughts were fixed upon other scenes, and the tear stole into my eyes, not for those who were going away, but for those who were left behind.

We have no reason to doubt but our troops will proceed with proper caution; there are men among them who can take care of themselves. But how shall the Ladies endure without them? By what arts can they, who have long had no joy, but from the civilities of a Soldier, now amuse their hours, and solace their separation?

Of fifty thousand men, now destined to different stations, if we allow each to have been occasionally necessary only to four women, a short computation will inform us, that two hundred thousand Ladies are left to languish in distress; two hundred thousand Ladies, who must run to Sales and Auctions without an attendant; sit at the Play, without a Critick to direct their opinion; buy their Fans by their own judgment; dispose Shells by their own invention; walk in the Mall without a Gallant; go to the Gardens without a Protector; and shuffle Cards with vain impatience for want of a fourth to complete the party.

Of these Ladies, some, I hope, have lapdogs, and some monkeys, but they are unsatisfactory companions. Many useful offices are performed by men of scarlet, to which neither dog nor monkey has adequate abilities: A parrot, indeed, is as fine as a Colonel, and if he has been much used to good company, is not wholly without conversation; but a parrot, after all, is a poor little creature, and has neither sword nor shoulder-knot, can neither dance nor play at cards.

Since the soldiers must obey the call of their duty, and go to that side of the kingdom which faces *France*, I know not why the Ladies, who cannot live without them, should not follow them. The prejudices and pride of man have long presumed the sword and spindle made for different hands, and denied the other sex, to partake the grandeur of military glory. This notion may be consistently enough received in *France*, where the Salic law excludes females from the Throne; but we, who allow them to be Sovereigns, may surely suppose them capable to be soldiers.

It were to be wished that some man, whose experience and authority might enforce regard, would propose that our encampments for the present year should comprise an equal number of men and women, who should march and fight in mingled bodies. If proper Colonels were once appointed, and the drums ordered to beat for female volunteers, our regiments would soon be filled without the reproach or cruelty of an impress.

Of these Heroines, some might serve on foot, under the denomination of the *Female Buffs*, and some on horseback, with the title of *Lady Hussars*.

What objections can be made to this scheme I have endeavoured maturely to consider; and cannot find that a modern soldier has any duties, except that of obedience, which a Lady cannot perform. If the hair has lost its powder, a Lady has a puff. If a coat be spotted, a Lady has a brush. Strength is of less importance since fire-arms have been used; blows of the hand are now seldom exchanged; and what is there to be done in the charge or the retreat beyond the powers of a sprightly maiden?

Our masculine squadrons will not suppose themselves disgraced by their auxiliaries, till they have done something which women could not have done. The troops of *Braddock* never saw their enemies, and perhaps were defeated by women. If our *American* General had headed an army of girls, he might still have built a fort, and taken it. Had *Minorca* been defended by a female garrison, it might have been surrendered, as it was, without a breach; and I cannot but think, that seven thousand women might have ventured to look at *Rochfort*, sack a village, rob a vineyard, and return in safety.

No. 10. Saturday, 17 June 1758.

Credulity, or Confidence of opinion too great for the evidence from which opinion is derived, we find to be a general weakness imputed by every sect and party to all others, and indeed by every man to every other man.

Of all kinds of Credulity, the most obstinate and wonderful is that of political zealots; of men, who, being numbered, they know not how nor why, in any of the parties that divide a state, resign the use of their own eyes and ears, and resolve to believe nothing that does not favour those whom they profess to follow.

The Bigot of Philosophy is seduced by authorities which he has not always opportunities to examine, is intangled in systems by which truth and falshood are inextricably complicated, or undertakes to talk on subjects, which Nature did not form him able to comprehend.

The Cartesian, who denies that his horse feels the spur, or that the hare is afraid when the hounds approach her; the Disciple of *Malbranche*, who maintains that the man was not hurt by the bullet, which, according to vulgar apprehensions, swept away his legs; the Follower of *Berkley*, who, while he sits writing at his table, declares that he has neither table, paper, nor fingers;

have all the honour at least of being deceived by fallacies not easily detected, and may plead that they did not forsake truth, but for appearances which they were not able to distinguish from it.

But the man who engages in a party has seldom to do with any thing remote or abstruse. The present state of things is before his eyes; and, if he cannot be satisfied without retrospection, yet he seldom extends his views beyond the historical events of the last century. All the knowledge that he can want is within his attainment, and most of the arguments which he can hear are within his capacity.

Yet so it is that an *Idler* meets every hour of his life with men who have different opinions upon every thing past, present, and future; who deny the most notorious facts, contradict the most cogent truths, and persist in asserting to-day what they asserted yesterday, in defiance of evidence, and contempt of confutation.

Two of my companions, who are grown old in Idleness, are *Tom Tempest* and *Jack Sneaker*. Both of them consider themselves as neglected by their parties, and therefore intitled to credit, for why should they favour ingratitude? They are both men of integrity where no factious interest is to be promoted, and both lovers of truth, when they are not heated with political debate.

Tom Tempest is a steady friend to the House of *Stuart*. He can recount the prodigies that have appeared in the sky, and the calamities that have afflicted the nation every year from the Revolution, and is of opinion, that if the exiled family had continued to reign, there would have neither been worms in our ships nor caterpillars on our trees. He wonders that the nation was not awakened by the hard frost to a revocation of the true King, and is hourly afraid that the whole island will be lost in the sea. He believes that King *William* burned *Whitehall* that he might steal the furniture, and that *Tillotson* died an Atheist. Of Queen *Anne* he speaks with more tenderness, owns that she meant well, and can tell by whom and why she was poisoned. In the succeeding reigns all has been corruption, malice, and design. He believes that nothing ill has ever happened for these forty years by chance or error; he holds that the battle of *Dettingen* was won by mistake, and that of *Fontenoy* lost by contract; that the *Victory* was sunk by a private order; that *Cornhill* was fired by emissaries from the Council; and the arch of *Westminster-Bridge* was so contrived as to sink on purpose that the nation might be put to charge. He considers the new road to *Islington* as an encroachment on liberty, and often asserts that *broad wheels* will be the ruin of *England*.

Tom is generally vehement and noisy, but nevertheless has some secrets which he always communicates in a whisper. Many and many a time has *Tom* told me, in a corner, that our miseries were almost at an end, and that we should see, in a month, another Monarch on the Throne; the time elapses without a Revolution; *Tom* meets me again with new intelligence, the whole scheme is now settled, and we shall see great events in another month.

Jack Sneaker is a hearty adherent to the present establishment; he has known those who saw the bed into which the Pretender was conveyed in a warming-pan. He often rejoices that the nation was not enslaved by the *Irish*. He believes that King *William* never lost a battle, and that if he had lived one year longer he would have conquered *France*. He holds that *Charles* the First was a Papist. He allows there were some good men in the reign of Queen *Anne*, but the Peace of *Utrecht* brought a blast upon the nation, and has been the cause of all the evil that we have suffered to the present hour. He believes that the scheme of the *South Sea* was well intended, but that it miscarried by the influence of *France*. He considers a standing army as the bulwark of liberty, thinks us secured from corruption by septennial Parliaments, relates how we are enriched and strengthened by the Electoral Dominions, and declares that the public debt is a blessing to the nation.

Yet amidst all this prosperity, poor *Jack* is hourly disturbed by the dread of Popery. He wonders that some stricter laws are not made against Papists, and is sometimes afraid that they are busy with *French* gold among the Bishops and Judges.

He cannot believe that the Nonjurors are so quiet for nothing, they must certainly be forming some plot for the establishment of Popery; he does not think the present Oaths sufficiently binding, and wishes that some better security could be found for the succession of *Hanover*. He is zealous for the naturalization of foreign Protestants, and rejoiced at the admission of the *Jews* to the *English* privileges, because he thought a *Jew* would never be a Papist.

No. 17. Saturday, 5 August 1758.

The rainy weather which has continued the last month, is said to have given great disturbance to the inspectors of barometers. The oraculous glasses have deceived their votaries; shower has succeeded shower, though they predicted sunshine and dry skies; and by fatal confidence in these fallacious promises, many coats have lost their gloss, and many curls been moistened to flaccidity.

This is one of the distresses to which mortals subject themselves by the pride of speculation. I had no part in this learned disappointment, who am content to credit my senses, and to believe that rain will fall when the air blackens, and that the weather will be dry when the sun is bright. My caution indeed does not always preserve me from a shower. To be wet may happen to the genuine *Idler*, but to be wet in opposition to Theory, can befall only the *Idler* that pretends to be busy. Of those that spin out life in trifles, and die without a memorial, many flatter themselves with high opinions of their own importance, and imagine that they are every day adding some improvement to human life. To be idle and to be poor have always been reproaches, and therefore every man endeavours with his utmost care, to hide his poverty from others, and his *Idleness* from himself.

Among those whom I never could persuade to rank themselves with *Idlers*, and who speak with indignation of my morning sleeps and nocturnal rambles; one passes the day in catching spiders that he may count their eyes with a microscope; another erects his head, and exhibits the dust of a marigold separated from the flower with dexterity worthy of *Leeuwenhoeck* himself. Some turn the wheel of Electricity, some suspend rings to a loadstone, and find that what they did yesterday they can do again to-day. Some register the changes of the wind, and die fully convinced that the wind is changeable.

There are men yet more profound, who have heard that two colourless liquors may produce a colour by union, and that two cold bodies will grow hot if they are mingled: they mingle them, and produce the effect expected, say it is strange, and mingle them again.

The *Idlers* that sport only with inanimate nature may claim some indulgence; if they are useless they are still innocent: but there are others, whom I know not how to mention without more emotion than my love of quiet willingly admits. Among the inferiour Professors of medical knowledge, is a race of wretches, whose lives are only varied by varieties of cruelty; whose favourite amusement is to nail dogs to tables and open them alive; to try how long life may be continued in various degrees of mutilation, or with the excision or laceration of the vital parts; to examine whether burning irons are felt more acutely by the bone or tendon; and whether the more lasting agonies are produced by poison forced into the mouth or injected into the veins.

It is not without reluctance that I offend the sensibility of the tender mind with images like these. If such cruelties were not practised it were to be desired that they should not be conceived, but since they are published every day with ostentation, let me be allowed once to mention them, since I mention them with abhorrence.

Mead has invidiously remarked of *Woodward* that he gathered shells and stones, and would pass for a Philosopher. With pretensions much less reasonable, the anatomical novice tears out the living bowels of an animal, and stiles himself Physician, prepares himself by familiar cruelty for that profession which he is to exercise upon the tender and the helpless, upon feeble bodies and broken minds, and by which he has opportunities to extend his arts of torture, and continue those experiments upon infancy and age, which he has hitherto tried upon cats and dogs.

What is alleged in defence of these hateful practices, every one knows; but the truth is, that by knives, fire, and poison, knowledge is not always sought, and is very seldom attained. The experiments that have been tried, are tried again; he that burned an animal with irons yesterday, will be willing to amuse himself with burning another to-morrow. I know not, that by living dissections any discovery has been made by which a single malady is more easily cured. And if the knowledge of Physiology has been somewhat encreased, he surely buys knowledge dear, who learns the use of the lacteals at the expence of his humanity. It is time that universal resentment should arise against these horrid operations, which tend to harden the heart, extinguish those sensations which give man confidence in man, and make the Physician more dreadful than the gout or stone.

No. [22]. Saturday, 9 September 1758.

Many Naturalists are of opinion, that the Animals which we commonly consider as mute, have the power of imparting their thoughts to one another. That they can express general sensations is very certain; every Being that can utter sounds, has a different voice for pleasure and for pain. The Hound informs his fellows when he scents his game; the Hen calls her chickens to their food by her cluck, and drives them from danger by her scream.

Birds have the greatest variety of notes; they have indeed a variety, which seems almost sufficient to make a speech adequate to the purposes of a life, which is regulated by instinct, and can admit little change or improvement. To the cries of Birds, curiosity or superstition has been always attentive, many have studied the language of the feathered tribes, and some have boasted that they understood it.

The most skilful or most confident interpreters of the Silvan Dialogues have been commonly found among the Philosophers of the East, in a country where the calmness of the air, and the mildness of the seasons, allow the Student to pass a great part of the year in groves and bowers. But what may be done in one place by peculiar opportunities, may be performed in another by peculiar diligence. A Shepherd of Bohemia has, by long abode in the forests, enabled himself to understand the voice of Birds, at least he relates with great confidence a story of which the credibility may be considered by the learned.

As I was sitting, (said he) within a hollow rock, and watching my Sheep that fed in the valley, I heard two Vultures interchangeably crying on the summit of the cliff. Both voices were earnest and deliberate. My curiosity prevailed over my care of the flock; I climbed slowly and silently from crag to crag, concealed among the shrubs, till I found a cavity where I might sit and listen without suffering, or giving disturbance.

I soon perceived, that my labour would be well repaid; for an old Vulture was sitting on a naked prominence, with her young about her, whom she was instructing in the arts of a Vulture's life, and preparing, by the last Lecture, for their final dismission to the mountains and the skies.

My children, said the old Vulture, you will the less want my instructions because you have had my practice before your eyes; you have seen me snatch from the Farm the Houshold Fowl, you have seen me seize the Leveret in the Bush, and the Kid in the Pasture, you know how to fix your talons, and how to balance your flight when you are laden with your prey. But you remember the taste of more delicious food; I have often regaled you with the flesh of man. Tell us, said the young Vultures, where man may be found, and how he may be known; his flesh is surely the natural food of a Vulture. Why have you never brought a Man in your talons to the Nest? He is too bulky, said the Mother; when we find a Man, we can only tear away his flesh and leave his bones upon the ground. Since man is so big, said the young ones, how do you kill him. You are afraid of the Wolf and of the Bear, by what power are Vultures superior to Man, is Man more defenseless than a Sheep? We have not the strength of Man, returned the Mother, and I am sometimes in doubt whether we have the subtilty; and the Vultures would seldom feast upon his flesh, had not nature, that devoted him to our uses, infused into him a strange ferocity, which I have never observed in any other Being that feeds upon the Earth. Two herds of Men will often meet and shake the Earth with noise, and fill the Air with fire. When you hear noise and see fire which flashes along the ground, hasten to the place with your swiftest wing, for men are surely destroying one another; you will then find the ground smoking with blood and covered with carcasses, of which many are dismembered and mangled for the convenience of the Vulture. But when Men have killed their prey, said the Pupil, Why do they not eat it? When the Wolf has killed a Sheep he suffers not the Vulture to touch it till he has satisfied himself. Is not Man another kind of Wolf? Man, said the Mother, is the only Beast who kills that which he does not devour, and this quality makes him so much a benefactor to our species. If Men kill our prey and lay it in our way, said the young one, what need shall we have of labouring for ourselves? Because Man will, sometimes, replied the Mother, remain for a long time quiet in his den. The old Vultures will tell you when you are to watch his motions. When you see men in great numbers moving close together, like a flight of Storks, you may conclude that they are hunting, and that you will soon revel in human blood. But still, said the young one, I would gladly know the reason of this mutual slaughter. I could never kill what I could not eat. My Child, said the Mother, this is a question which I cannot answer, tho' I am reckoned the most subtile Bird of the mountain. When I was young I used frequently to visit the ayry of an old Vulture who dwelt upon the Carpathian rocks; he had made many observations; he knew the places that afforded prey round his habitation, as far in every direction as the strongest wing can fly between the rising and setting of the Summer Sun; he had fed year after year on the entrails of Men. His opinion was, That Men had only the appearance of Animal Life, being really Vegetables with a power of motion; and that as the boughs of an Oak are dashed together by the storm, that Swine may fatten upon the falling Acorns, so Men are by some unaccountable power driven one against another, till they lose their motion, that Vultures may be fed. Others think they have observed something of contrivance and policy among these mischievous Beings, and those that hover more closely round them, pretend, that there is, in every herd, one that gives directions to the rest, and seems to be more eminently delighted with a wide carnage. What it is that intitles him to such pre-eminence we know not; he is seldom the biggest or the swiftest, but he shews by his eagerness and diligence that he is, more than any of the others, a friend to Vultures.

No. 22. Saturday, 16 September 1758.

To the IDLER,

SIR,

As I was passing lately under one of the gates of this city, I was struck with horror by a rueful cry, which summoned me *to remember the poor Debtors*.

The wisdom and justice of the *English* laws are, by *Englishmen* at least, loudly celebrated; but scarcely the most zealous admirers of our Institutions can think that law wise, which when men are capable of work, obliges them to beg; or just, which exposes the liberty of one to the passions of another.

The prosperity of a people is proportionate to the number of hands and minds usefully employed. To the community sedition is a fever, corruption is a gangrene, and idleness an atrophy. Whatever body, and whatever society, wastes more than it acquires, must gradually decay; and every being that continues to be fed, and ceases to labour, takes away something from the public stock.

The confinement, therefore, of any man in the sloth and darkness of a prison, is a loss to the nation, and no gain to the Creditor. For of the multitudes who are pining in those cells of misery, a very small part is suspected of any fraudulent act by which they retain what belongs to others. The rest are imprisoned by the wantonness of pride, the malignity of revenge, or the acrimony of disappointed expectation.

If those, who thus rigorously exercise the power which the law has put into their hands, be asked, why they continue to imprison those whom they know to be unable to pay them: One will answer, that his Debtor once lived better than himself; another, that his wife looked above her neighbours, and his children went in silk cloaths to the dancing school; and another, that he pretended to be a joker and a wit. Some will reply, that if they were in debt they should meet with the same treatment; some, that they owe no more than they can pay, and need therefore give no account of their actions. Some will confess their resolution, that their Debtors shall rot in jail; and some will discover, that they hope, by cruelty, to wring the payment from their friends.

The end of all civil regulations is to secure private happiness from private malignity; to keep individuals from the power of one another; but this end is apparently neglected, when a man, irritated with loss, is allowed to be the judge of his own cause, and to assign the punishment of his own pain; when the distinction between guilt and unhappiness, between casualty and design, is intrusted to eyes blind with interest, to understandings depraved by resentment.

Since Poverty is punished among us as a crime, it ought at least to be treated with the same lenity as other crimes; the offender ought not to languish, at the will of him whom he has offended, but to be allowed some appeal to the justice of his country. There can be no reason, why any Debtor should be imprisoned, but that he may be compelled to payment; and a term should therefore be fixed, in which the Creditor should exhibit his accusation of concealed property. If such property can be discovered, let it be given to the Creditor; if the charge is not offered, or cannot be proved, let the prisoner be dismissed.

Those who made the laws, have apparently supposed, that every deficiency of payment is the crime of the Debtor. But the truth is, that the Creditor always shares the act, and often more than shares the guilt of improper trust. It seldom happens that any man imprisons another but for debts which he suffered to be contracted, in hope of advantage to himself, and for bargains in which he proportioned his profit to his own opinion of the hazard; and there is no reason, why one should punish the other, for a contract in which both concurred.

Many of the inhabitants of prisons may justly complain of harder treatment. He that once owes more than he can pay, is often obliged to bribe his Creditor to patience, by encreasing his debt. Worse and worse commodities, at a higher and higher price, are forced upon him; he is impoverished by compulsive traffick, and at last overwhelmed, in the common receptacles of misery, by debts, which, without his own consent, were accumulated on his head. To the relief of this distress, no other objection can be made, but that by an easy dissolution of debts, fraud will be left without punishment, and imprudence without awe, and that when insolvency shall be no longer punishable, credit will cease.

The motive to credit, is the hope of advantage. Commerce can never be at a stop, while one man wants what another can supply; and credit will never be denied, while it is likely to be repaid with profit. He that trusts one whom he designs to sue, is criminal by the act of trust; the cessation of such insidious traffick is to be desired, and no reason can be given why a change of the law should impair any other.

We see nation trade with nation, where no payment can be compelled. Mutual convenience produces mutual confidence, and the Merchants continue to satisfy the demands of each other, though they have nothing to dread but the loss of trade.

It is vain to continue an institution, which experience shews to be ineffectual. We have now imprisoned one generation of Debtors after another, but we do not find that their numbers lessen. We have now learned, that rashness and imprudence will not be deterred from taking credit; let us try whether fraud and avarice may be more easily restrained from giving it.

I am, Sir, &c.

No. 23. Saturday, 23 September 1758.

Life has no pleasure higher or nobler than that of Friendship. It is painful to consider, that this sublime enjoyment may be impaired or destroyed by innumerable causes, and that there is no human possession of which the duration is less certain.

Many have talked, in very exalted language, of the perpetuity of Friendship, of invincible Constancy, and unalienable Kindness; and some examples have been seen of men who have continued faithful to their earliest choice, and whose affection has predominated over changes of fortune, and contrariety of opinion.

But these instances are memorable, because they are rare. The Friendship which is to be practised or expected by common mortals, must take its rise from mutual pleasure, and must end when the power ceases of delighting each other.

Many accidents therefore may happen, by which the ardour of kindness will be abated, without criminal baseness or contemptible inconstancy on either part. To give pleasure is not always in our power; and little does he know himself, who believes that he can be always able to receive it.

Those who would gladly pass their days together may be separated by the different course of their affairs; and Friendship, like Love, is destroyed by long absence, though it may be encreased by short intermissions. What we have missed long enough to want it, we value more when it is regained; but that which has been lost till it is forgotten, will be found at last with little gladness, and with still less, if a substitute has supplied the place. A man deprived of the companion to whom he used to open his bosom, and with whom he shared the hours of leisure and merriment, feels the day at first hanging heavy on him; his difficulties oppress, and his doubts distract him; he sees time come and go without his wonted gratification, and all is sadness within and solitude about him. But this uneasiness never lasts long, necessity produces expedients, new amusements are discovered, and new conversation is admitted.

No expectation is more frequently disappointed, than that which naturally arises in the mind, from the prospect of meeting an old Friend, after long separation. We expect the attraction to be revived, and the coalition to be renewed; no man considers how much alteration time has made in himself, and very few enquire what effect it has had upon others. The first hour convinces them, that the pleasure, which they have formerly enjoyed, is for ever at an end; different scenes have made different impressions, the opinions of both are changed, and that similitude of manners and sentiment is lost, which confirmed them both in the approbation of themselves.

Friendship is often destroyed by opposition of interest, not only by the ponderous and visible interest, which the desire of wealth and greatness forms and maintains, but by a thousand secret and slight competitions, scarcely known to the mind upon which they operate. There is scarcely any man without some favourite trifle which he values above greater attainments, some desire of petty praise which he cannot patiently suffer to be frustrated. This minute ambition is sometimes crossed before it is known, and sometimes defeated by wanton petulance; but such attacks are seldom made without the loss of Friendship; for whoever has once found the vulnerable part will always be feared, and the resentment will burn on in secret of which shame hinders the discovery.

This, however, is a slow malignity, which a wise man will obviate as inconsistent with quiet, and a good man will repress as contrary to virtue; but human happiness is sometimes violated by some more sudden strokes.

A dispute begun in jest, upon a subject which a moment before was on both parts regarded with careless indifference, is continued by the desire of conquest, till vanity kindles into rage, and opposition rankles into enmity. Against this hasty mischief I know not what security can be obtained; men will be sometimes surprized into quarrels, and though they might both hasten to reconciliation, as soon as their tumult has subsided, yet two minds will seldom be found together, which can at once subdue their discontent, or immediately enjoy the sweets of peace, without remembring the wounds of the conflict.

Friendship has other enemies. Suspicion is always hardening the cautious, and Disgust repelling the delicate. Very slender differences will sometimes part those whom long reciprocation of civility or beneficence has united. *Lonelove* and *Ranger* retired into the country to enjoy the company of each other, and returned in six weeks cold and petulant; *Ranger's* pleasure was to walk in the fields, and *Lonelove's* to sit in a bower; each had complied with the other in his turn, and each was angry that compliance had been exacted.

The most fatal disease of Friendship is gradual decay, or dislike hourly encreased by causes too slender for complaint, and too numerous for removal. Those who are angry may be reconciled; those who have been injured may receive a recompence; but when the desire of pleasing and willingness to be pleased is silently diminished, the renovation of Friendship is hopeless; as, when the vital powers sink into languor, there is no longer any use of the Physician.

No. 27. Saturday, 21 October 1758.

It has been the endeavour of all those whom the world has reverenced for superior wisdom, to persuade man to be acquainted with himself, to learn his own powers and his own weakness, to observe by what evils he is most dangerously beset, and by what temptations most easily overcome.

This counsel has been often given with serious dignity, and often received with appearance of conviction; but, as very few can search deep into their own minds without meeting what they wish to hide from themselves, scarce any man persists in cultivating such disagreeable acquaintance, but draws the veil again between his eyes and his heart, leaves his passions and appetites as he found them, and advises others to look into themselves.

This is the common result of enquiry even among those that endeavour to grow wiser or better, but this endeavour is far enough from frequency; the greater part of the multitudes that swarm upon the earth, have never been disturbed by such uneasy curiosity, but deliver themselves up to business or to pleasure, plunge into the current of life, whether placid or turbulent, and pass on from one point of prospect to another, attentive rather to any thing than the state of their minds; satisfied, at an easy rate, with an opinion that they are no worse than others, that every man must mind his own interest, or that their pleasures hurt only themselves, and are therefore no proper subjects of censure.

Some, however, there are, whom the intrusion of scruples, the recollection of better notions, or the latent reprehension of good examples, will not suffer to live entirely contented with their own conduct; these are forced to pacify the mutiny of reason with fair promises, and quiet their thoughts with designs of calling all their actions to review, and planning a new scheme for the time to come.

There is nothing which we estimate so fallaciously as the force of our own resolutions, nor any fallacy which we so unwillingly and tardily detect. He that has resolved a thousand times, and a thousand times deserted his own purpose, yet suffers no abatement of his confidence, but still believes himself his own master, and able, by innate vigour of soul, to press forward to his end, through all the obstructions that inconveniences or delights can put in his way.

That this mistake should prevail for a time is very natural. When conviction is present, and temptation out of sight, we do not easily conceive how any reasonable being can deviate from his true interest. What ought to be done while it yet hangs only in speculation, is so plain and certain, that there is no place for doubt; the whole soul yields itself to the predominance of truth, and readily determines to do what, when the time of action comes, will be at last omitted.

I believe most men may review all the lives that have passed within their observation, without remembering one efficacious resolution, or being able to tell a single instance of a course of practice suddenly changed in consequence of a change of opinion, or an establishment of determination. Many indeed alter their conduct, and are not at fifty what they were at thirty, but they commonly varied imperceptibly from themselves, followed the train of external causes, and rather suffered reformation than made it.

It is not uncommon to charge the difference between promise and performance, between profession and reality, upon deep design and studied deceit; but the truth is, that there is very little hypocrisy in the world; we do not so often endeavour or wish to impose on others as on ourselves; we resolve to do right, we hope to keep our resolutions, we declare them to confirm our own hope, and fix our own inconstancy by calling witnesses of our actions; but at last habit prevails, and those whom we invited to our triumph, laugh at our defeat.

Custom is commonly too strong for the most resolute resolver though furnished for the assault with all the weapons of philosophy. "He that endeavours to free himself from an ill habit, says *Bacon*, must not change too much at a time lest he should be discouraged by difficulty; nor too little, for then he will make but slow advances." This is a precept which may be applauded in a book, but will fail in the trial, in which every change will be found too great or too little. Those who have been able to conquer habit, are like those that are fabled to have returned from the realms of *Pluto*:

> *Pauci, quos æquus amavit*
> *Jupiter, atque ardens evexit ad æthera virtus.*

They are sufficient to give hope but not security, to animate the contest but not to promise victory.

Those who are in the power of evil habits, must conquer them as they can, and conquered they must be, or neither wisdom nor happiness can be attained; but those who are not yet subject to their influence, may, by timely caution, preserve their freedom, they may effectually resolve to escape the tyrant, whom they will very vainly resolve to conquer.

No. 30. Saturday, 11 November 1758.

The desires of man encrease with his acquisitions; every step which he advances brings something within his view, which he did not see before, and which, as soon as he sees it, he begins to want. Where necessity ends curiosity begins, and no sooner are we supplied with every thing that nature can demand, than we sit down to contrive artificial appetites.

By this restlessness of mind, every populous and wealthy city is filled with innumerable employments, for which the greater part of mankind is without a name; with artificers whose labour is exerted in producing such petty conveniences, that many shops are furnished with instruments, of which the use can hardly be found without enquiry, but which he that once knows them, quickly learns to number among necessary things.

Such is the diligence, with which, in countries completely civilized, one part of mankind labours for another, that wants are supplied faster than they can be formed, and the idle and luxurious find life stagnate, for want of some desire to keep it in motion. This species of distress furnishes a new set of occupations, and multitudes are busied, from day to day, in finding the rich and the fortunate something to do.

It is very common to reproach those artists as useless, who produce only such superfluities as neither accommodate the body nor improve the mind; and of which no other effect can be imagined, than that they are the occasions of spending money, and consuming time.

But this censure will be mitigated, when it is seriously considered, that money and time are the heaviest burthens of life, and that the unhappiest of all mortals are those who have more of either than they know how to use. To set himself free from these incumbrances, one hurries to *New-market*; another travels over *Europe*; one pulls down his house and calls architects about him; another buys a seat in the country, and follows his hounds over hedges and through rivers; one makes collections of shells, and another searches the world for tulips and carnations.

He is surely a public benefactor who finds employment for those to whom it is thus difficult to find it for themselves. It is true that this is seldom done merely from generosity or compassion, almost every man seeks his own advantage in helping others, and therefore it is too common for mercenary officiousness, to consider rather what is grateful than what is right.

We all know that it is more profitable to be loved than esteemed, and ministers of pleasure will always be found, who study to make themselves necessary, and to supplant those who are practising the same arts.

One of the amusements of idleness is reading without the fatigue of close attention, and the world therefore swarms with writers whose wish is not to be studied but to be read.

No species of literary men has lately been so much multiplied as the writers of news. Not many years ago the nation was content with one Gazette; but now we have not only in the metropolis papers for every morning and every evening, but almost every large town has its weekly historian, who regularly circulates his periodical intelligence, and fills the villages of his district with conjectures on the events of war, and with debates on the true interest of *Europe*.

To write news in its perfection requires such a combination of qualities, that a man completely fitted for the task is not always to be found. In Sir *Henry Wotton's* jocular definition, *An Ambassador* is said to be *a man of virtue sent abroad to tell lies for the advantage of his country*; a News-writer is *a man without virtue, who writes lies at home for his own profit*. To these compositions is required neither genius nor knowledge, neither industry nor sprightliness, but contempt of shame, and indifference to truth are absolutely necessary. He who by a long familiarity with infamy has obtained these qualities, may confidently tell to-day what he intends to contradict to-morrow; he may affirm fearlessly what he knows that he shall be obliged to recant, and may write letters from *Amsterdam* or *Dresden* to himself.

In a time of war the nation is always of one mind, eager to hear something good of themselves and ill of the enemy. At this time the task of News-writers is easy, they have nothing to do but to tell that a battle is expected, and afterwards that a battle has been fought, in which we and our friends, whether conquering or conquered, did all, and our enemies did nothing.

Scarce any thing awakens attention like a tale of cruelty. The Writer of news never fails in the intermission of action to tell how the enemies murdered children and ravished virgins; and if the scene of action be somewhat distant, scalps half the inhabitants of a province.

Among the calamities of War may be justly numbered the diminution of the love of truth, by the falshoods which interest dictates and credulity encourages. A Peace will equally leave the Warriour and Relator of Wars destitute of employment; and I know not whether more is to be dreaded from streets filled with Soldiers accustomed to plunder, or from garrets filled with Scribblers accustomed to lie.

No. 31. Saturday, 18 November 1758.

Many moralists have remarked, that Pride has of all human vices the widest dominion, appears in the greatest multiplicity of forms, and lies hid under the greatest variety of disguises; of disguises, which, like the moon's *veil of brightness*, are both its *lustre and its shade*, and betray it to others, tho' they hide it from ourselves.

It is not my intention to degrade Pride from this pre-eminence of mischief, yet I know not whether Idleness may not maintain a very doubtful and obstinate competition.

There are some that profess Idleness in its full dignity, who call themselves the *Idle*, as *Busiris* in the play *calls himself the Proud*; who boast that they do nothing, and thank their stars that they have nothing to do; who sleep every night till they can sleep no longer, and rise only that exercise may enable them to sleep again; who prolong the reign of darkness by double curtains, and never see the sun but to *tell him how they hate his beams*; whose whole labour is to vary the postures of indulgence, and whose day differs from their night but as a couch or chair differs from a bed.

These are the true and open votaries of Idleness, for whom she weaves the garlands of poppies, and into whose cup she pours the waters of oblivion; who exist in a state of unruffled stupidity, forgetting and forgotten; who have long ceased to live, and at whose death the survivors can only say, that they have ceased to breathe.

But Idleness predominates in many lives where it is not suspected, for being a vice which terminates in itself, it may be enjoyed without injury to others, and is therefore not watched like Fraud, which endangers property, or like Pride which naturally seeks its gratifications in another's inferiority. Idleness is a silent and peaceful quality, that neither raises envy by ostentation, nor hatred by opposition; and therefore no body is busy to censure or detect it.

As Pride sometimes is hid under humility, Idleness is often covered by turbulence and hurry. He that neglects his known duty and real employment, naturally endeavours to croud his mind with something that may bar out the remembrance of his own folly, and does any thing but what he ought to do with eager diligence, that he may keep himself in his own favour.

Some are always in a state of preparation, occupied in previous measures, forming plans, accumulating materials, and providing for the main affair. These are certainly under the secret power of Idleness. Nothing is to be expected from the workman whose tools are for ever to be sought. I was once told by a great master, that no man ever excelled in painting, who was eminently curious about pencils and colours.

There are others to whom Idleness dictates another expedient, by which life may be passed unprofitably away without the tediousness of many vacant hours. The art is, to fill the day with petty business, to have always something in hand which may raise curiosity, but not solicitude, and keep the mind in a state of action, but not of labour.

This art has for many years been practised by my old friend *Sober*, with wonderful success. *Sober* is a man of strong desires and quick imagination, so exactly ballanced by the love of ease, that they can seldom stimulate him to any difficult undertaking; they have, however, so much power, that they will not suffer him to lie quite at rest, and though they do not make him sufficiently useful to others, they make him at least weary of himself.

Mr. *Sober's* chief pleasure is conversation; there is no end of his talk or his attention; to speak or to hear is equally pleasing; for he still fancies that he is teaching or learning something, and is free for the time from his own reproaches.

But there is one time at night when he must go home, that his friends may sleep; and another time in the morning, when all the world agrees to shut out interruption. These are the moments of which poor *Sober* trembles at the thought. But the misery of these tiresome intervals, he has many means of alleviating. He has persuaded himself that the manual arts are undeservedly overlooked; he has observed in many trades the effects of close thought, and just ratiocination. From speculation he proceeded to practice, and supplied himself with the tools of a carpenter, with which he mended his coal-box very successfully, and which he still continues to employ, as he finds occasion.

He has attempted at other times the crafts of the Shoe-maker, Tinman, Plumber, and Potter; in all these arts he has failed, and resolves to qualify himself for them by better information. But his daily amusement is Chemistry. He has a small furnace, which he employs in distillation, and which has long been the solace of his life. He draws oils and waters, and essences and spirits, which he knows to be of no use; sits and counts the drops as they come from his retort, and forgets that, while a drop is falling, a moment flies away.

Poor *Sober!* I have often teaz'd him with reproof, and he has often promised reformation; for no man is so much open to conviction as the *Idler*, but there is none on whom it operates so little. What will be the effect of this paper I know not; perhaps he will read it and laugh, and light the fire in his furnace; but my hope is that he will quit his trifles, and betake himself to rational and useful diligence.

No. 32. Saturday, 25 November 1758.

Among the innumerable mortifications that waylay human arrogance on every side may well be reckoned our ignorance of the most common objects and effects, a defect of which we become more sensible by every attempt to supply it. Vulgar and inactive minds confound familiarity with knowledge, and conceive themselves informed of the whole nature of things when they are shewn their form or told their use; but the Speculatist, who is not content with superficial views, harrasses himself with fruitless curiosity, and still as he enquires more perceives only that he knows less.

Sleep is a state in which a great part of every life is passed. No animal has been yet discovered, whose existence is not varied with intervals of insensibility; and some late Philosophers have extended the Empire of Sleep over the vegetable world.

Yet of this change so frequent, so great, so general, and so necessary, no searcher has yet found either the efficient or final cause; or can tell by what power the mind and body are thus chained down in irresistible stupefaction; or what benefits the animal receives from this alternate suspension of its active powers.

Whatever may be the multiplicity or contrariety of opinions upon this subject, Nature has taken sufficient care that Theory shall have little influence on Practice. The most diligent enquirer is not able long to keep his eyes open; the most eager disputant will begin about midnight to desert his argument, and once in four and twenty hours, the gay and the gloomy, the witty and the dull, the clamorous and the silent, the busy and the idle, are all overpowered by the gentle tyrant, and all lie down in the equality of Sleep.

Philosophy has often attempted to repress insolence by asserting that all conditions are levelled by Death; a position which, however it may deject the happy, will seldom afford much comfort to the wretched. It is far more pleasing to consider that Sleep is equally a leveller with Death; that the time is never at a great distance, when the balm of rest shall be effused alike upon every head, when the diversities of life shall stop their operation, and the high and the low shall lie down together.

It is somewhere recorded of *Alexander*, that in the pride of conquests, and intoxication of flattery, he declared that he only perceived himself to be a man by the necessity of Sleep. Whether he considered Sleep as necessary to his mind or body it was indeed a sufficient evidence of human infirmity; the body which required such frequency of renovation gave but faint promises of immortality; and the mind which, from time to time, sunk gladly into insensibility, had made no very near approaches to the felicity of the supreme and self-sufficient Nature.

I know not what can tend more to repress all the passions that disturb the peace of the world, than the consideration that there is no height of happiness or honour, from which man does not eagerly descend to a state of unconscious repose; that the best condition of life is such, that we contentedly quit its good to be disentangled from its evils; that in a few hours splendour fades before the eye, and praise itself deadens in the ear; the senses withdraw from their objects, and reason favours the retreat.

What then are the hopes and prospects of covetousness, ambition and rapacity? Let him that desires most have all his desires gratified, he never shall attain a state, which he can, for a day and a night, contemplate with satisfaction, or from which, if he had the power of perpetual vigilance, he would not long for periodical separations.

All envy would be extinguished if it were universally known that there are none to be envied, and surely none can be much envied who are not pleased with themselves. There is reason to suspect that the distinctions of mankind have more shew than value, when it is found that all agree to be weary alike of pleasures and of cares, that the powerful and the weak, the celebrated and obscure, join in one common wish, and implore from Nature's hand the nectar of oblivion.

Such is our desire of abstraction from ourselves, that very few are satisfied with the quantity of stupefaction which the needs of the body force upon the mind. *Alexander* himself added intemperance to sleep, and solaced with the fumes of wine the sovereignty of the world. And almost every man has some art, by which he steals his thoughts away from his present state.

It is not much of life that is spent in close attention to any important duty. Many hours of every day are suffered to fly away without any traces left upon the intellects. We suffer phantoms to rise up before us, and amuse ourselves with the dance of airy images, which after a time we dismiss for ever, and know not how we have been busied.

Many have no happier moments than those that they pass in solitude, abandoned to their own imagination, which sometimes puts sceptres in their hands or mitres on their heads, shifts the scene of pleasure with endless variety, bids all the forms of beauty sparkle before them, and gluts them with every change of visionary luxury.

It is easy in these semi-slumbers to collect all the possibilities of happiness, to alter the course of the Sun, to bring back the past, and anticipate the future, to unite all the beauties of all seasons, and all the blessings of all climates, to receive and bestow felicity, and forget that misery is the lot of man. All this is a voluntary dream, a temporary recession from the realities of life to airy fictions; and habitual subjection of reason to fancy.

Others are afraid to be alone, and amuse themselves by a perpetual succession of companions, but the difference is not great, in solitude we have our dreams to ourselves, and in company we agree to dream in concert. The end sought in both is forgetfulness of ourselves.

No. 36. Saturday, 23 December 1758.

The great differences that disturb the peace of mankind, are not about ends but means. We have all the same general desires, but how those desires shall be accomplished will for ever be disputed. The ultimate purpose of government is temporal, and that of religion is eternal happiness. Hitherto we agree; but here we must part, to try, according to the endless varieties of passion and understanding combined with one another, every possible form of Government, and every imaginable tenet of Religion.

We are told by *Cumberland*, that *Rectitude*, applied to action or contemplation, is merely metaphorical; and that as a *right* line describes the shortest passage from point to point, so a *right* action effects a good design by the fewest means; and so likewise a *right* opinion is that which connects distant truths by the shortest train of intermediate propositions.

To find the nearest way from truth to truth, or from purpose to effect, not to use more instruments where fewer will be sufficient, not to move by wheels and levers what will give way to the naked hand, is the great proof of a healthful and vigorous mind, neither feeble with helpless ignorance, nor overburdened with unwieldy knowledge.

But there are men who seem to think nothing so much the characteristick of a genius, as to do common things in an uncommon manner; like *Hudibras* to *tell the clock by Algebra*, or like the Lady in Dr. *Young's* Satires, *to drink Tea by stratagem*. To quit the beaten track only because it is known, and take a new path, however crooked or rough, because the strait was found out before.

Every man speaks and writes with intent to be understood, and it can seldom happen but he that understands himself might convey his notions to another, if, content to be understood, he did not seek to be admired; but when once he begins to contrive how his sentiments may be received, not with most ease to his reader, but with most advantage to himself, he then transfers his consideration from words to sounds, from sentences to periods, and as he grows more elegant becomes less intelligible.

It is difficult to enumerate every species of Authors whose labours counteract themselves. The man of exuberance and copiousness, who diffuses every thought thro' so many diversities of expression, that it is lost like water in a mist. The ponderous dictator of sentences, whose notions are delivered in the lump, and are, like uncoined bullion, of more weight than use. The liberal illustrator, who shews by examples and comparisons what was clearly seen when it was first proposed; and the stately son of demonstration, who proves with mathematical formality what no man has yet pretended to doubt.

There is a mode of style for which I know not that the Masters of Oratory have yet found a name, a style by which the most evident truths are so obscured that they can no longer be perceived, and the most familiar propositions so disguised that they cannot be known. Every other kind of eloquence is the dress of sense, but this is the mask, by which a true Master of his art will so effectually conceal it, that a man will as easily mistake his own positions if he meets them thus transformed, as he may pass in a masquerade his nearest acquaintance.

This style may be called the *terrifick*, for its chief intention is to terrify and amaze; it may be termed the *repulsive*, for its natural effect is to drive away the reader; or it may be distinguished, in plain *English*, by the denomination of the *bugbear style*, for it has more terror than danger, and will appear less formidable, as it is more nearly approached.

A mother tells her infant, that *two and two make four*, the child remembers the proposition, and is able to count four to all the purposes of life, till the course of his education brings him among philosophers, who fright him from his former knowledge, by telling him that four is a certain aggregate of unites; that all numbers being only the repetition of an unite, which, though not a number itself, is the parent, root, or original of all number, *four* is the denomination assigned to a certain number of such repetitions. The only danger is, lest, when he first hears these dreadful sounds, the pupil should run away; if he has but the courage to stay till the conclusion, he will find that, when speculation has done its worst, two and two still make four.

An illustrious example of this species of eloquence, may be found in *Letters concerning Mind*. The author begins by declaring, that *the sorts of things are things that now are, have been, and shall be, and the things that strictly* ARE. In this position, except the last clause, in which he uses something of the scholastick language, there is nothing but what every man has heard and imagines himself to know. But who would not believe that some wonderful novelty is presented to his intellect, when he is afterwards told, in the true *bugbear* style, that *the* Ares, *in the former sense, are things that lie between the* Have-beens *and* Shall-bes. *The* Have-beens *are things that are past; the* Shall-bes *are things that are to come; and the things that* ARE, *in the latter sense, are things that have not been, nor shall be, nor stand in the midst of such as are before them or shall be after them. The things that have been, and shall be, have respect to present, past, and future. Those likewise that now* ARE *have moreover place; that, for instance, which is here, that which is to the east, that which is to the west.*

All this, my dear reader, is very strange; but though it be strange, it is not new; survey these wonderful sentences again, and they will be found to contain nothing more than very plain truths, which till this Author arose had always been delivered in plain language.

No. 38. Saturday, 6 January 1759.

Since the publication of the letter, concerning the condition of those who are confined in Gaols by their Creditors, an enquiry is said to have been made, by which it appears that more than* twenty thousand are at this time prisoners for debt.

We often look with indifference on the successive parts of that, which, if the whole were seen together, would shake us with emotion. A Debtor is dragged to prison, pitied for a moment, and then forgotten; another follows him, and is lost alike in the caverns of oblivion; but when the whole mass of calamity rises up at once, when twenty thousand reasonable Beings are heard all groaning in unnecessary misery, not by the infirmity of nature, but the mistake or negligence of policy, who can forbear to pity and lament, to wonder and abhor.

There is here no need of declamatory vehemence; we live in an age of Commerce and Computation; let us therefore coolly enquire what is the sum of evil which the imprisonment of Debtors brings upon our country.

It seems to be the opinion of the later computists, that the inhabitants of *England* do not exceed six millions, of which twenty thousand is the three-hundredth part. What shall we say of the humanity or the wisdom of a nation, that voluntarily sacrifices one in every three hundred to lingering destruction!

The misfortunes of an individual do not extend their influence to many; yet, if we consider the effects of consanguinity and friendship, and the general reciprocation of wants and benefits, which make one man dear or necessary to another, it may reasonably be supposed, that every man languishing in prison gives trouble of some kind to two others who love or need him. By this multiplication of misery we see distress extended to the hundredth part of the whole society.

If we estimate at a shilling a day what is lost by the inaction and consumed in the support of each man thus chained down to involuntary idleness, the publick loss will rise in one year to three hundred thousand pounds; in ten years to more than a sixth part of our circulating coin.

I am afraid that those who are best acquainted with the state of our prisons, will confess that my conjecture is too near the truth, when I suppose that the corrosion of resentment, the heaviness of sorrow, the corruption of confined air, the want of exercise, and sometimes of food, the contagion of diseases from which there is no retreat, and the severity of tyrants against whom there can be no resistance, and all the complicated horrors of a prison, put an end every year to the life of one in four of those that are shut up from the common comforts of human life.

---

* This number was at that time confidently published, but the authour has since found reason to question the calculation.

Thus perish yearly five thousand men, overborne with sorrow, consumed by famine, or putrified by filth; many of them in the most vigorous and useful part of life; for the thoughtless and imprudent are commonly young, and the active and busy are seldom old.

According to the rule generally received, which supposes that one in thirty dies yearly, the race of man may be said to be renewed at the end of thirty years. Who would have believed till now, that of every *English* generation an hundred and fifty thousand perish in our gaols! That in every century, a nation eminent for science, studious of commerce, ambitious of empire, should willingly lose, in noisome dungeons, five hundred thousand of its inhabitants: A number greater than has ever been destroyed in the same time by the Pestilence and Sword!

A very late occurrence may shew us the value of the number which we thus condemn to be useless; in the re-establishment of the Trained Bands, thirty thousand are considered as a force sufficient against all exigencies: While, therefore, we detain twenty thousand in prison, we shut up in darkness and uselessness two thirds of an army which ourselves judge equal to the defence of our country.

The monastick institutions have been often blamed, as tending to retard the increase of mankind. And perhaps retirement ought rarely to be permitted, except to those whose employment is consistent with abstraction, and who, tho' solitary, will not be idle; to those whom infirmity makes useless to the commonwealth, or to those who have paid their due proportion to Society, and who, having lived for others, may be honourably dismissed to live for themselves. But whatever be the evil or the folly of these retreats, those have no right to censure them whose prisons contain greater numbers than the Monasteries of other countries. It is, surely, less foolish and less criminal to permit inaction than compel it; to comply with doubtful opinions of happiness, than condemn to certain and apparent misery; to indulge the extravagancies of erroneous piety, than to multiply and enforce temptations to wickedness.

The misery of gaols is not half their evil; they are filled with every corruption which poverty and wickedness can generate between them; with all the shameless and profligate enormities that can be produced by the impudence of ignominy, the rage of want, and the malignity of despair. In a prison the awe of the publick eye is lost, and the power of the law is spent; there are few fears, there are no blushes. The lewd inflame the lewd, the audacious harden the audacious. Every one fortifies himself as he can against his own sensibility, endeavours to practise on others the arts which are practised on himself; and gains the kindness of his associates by similitude of manners.

Thus some sink amidst their misery, and others survive only to propagate villainy. It may be hoped that our Lawgivers will at length take away from us this power of starving and depraving one another: but, if there be any reason why this inveterate evil should not be removed in our age, which true policy has enlightened beyond any former time, let those, whose writings form the opinions and the practices of their contemporaries, endeavour to transfer the reproach of such imprisonment from the Debtor to the Creditor, till universal infamy shall pursue the wretch, whose wantonness of power, or revenge of disappointment, condemns another to torture and to ruin; till he shall be hunted through the world as an enemy to man, and find in riches no shelter from contempt.

Surely, he whose Debtor has perished in prison, though he may acquit himself of deliberate murder, must at least have his mind clouded with discontent, when he considers how much another has suffered from him; when he thinks on the wife bewailing her husband, or the children begging the bread which their father would have earned. If there are any made so obdurate by avarice or cruelty, as to revolve these consequences without dread or pity, I must leave them to be awakened by some other power, for I write only to human Beings.

No. 40. Saturday, 20 January 1759.

The practice of appending to the narratives of public transactions, more minute and domestic intelligence, and filling the News-papers with advertisements, has grown up by slow degrees to its present state.

Genius is shewn only by Invention. The man who first took advantage of the general curiosity that was excited by a siege or battle, to betray the Readers of News into the knowledge of the shop where the best Puffs and Powder were to be sold, was undoubtedly a man of great sagacity, and profound skill in the nature of Man. But when he had once shewn the way, it was easy to follow him; and every man now knows a ready method of informing the Publick of all that he desires to buy or sell, whether his wares be material or intellectual; whether he makes Cloaths, or teaches the Mathematics; whether he be a Tutor that wants a Pupil, or a Pupil that wants a Tutor.

Whatever is common is despised. Advertisements are now so numerous that they are very negligently perused, and it is therefore become necessary to gain attention by magnificence of promises, and by eloquence sometimes sublime and sometimes pathetic.

Promise, large Promise, is the soul of an Advertisement. I remember a *wash-ball* that had a quality truly wonderful, it gave *an exquisite edge to the razor*. And there are now to be sold *for ready money only*, some *Duvets for bed-coverings, of down, beyond comparison superior to what is called Otter Down*, and indeed such, that its *many excellencies cannot be here set forth*. With one excellence we are made acquainted, *It is warmer than four or five blankets, and lighter than one.*

There are some, however, that know the prejudice of mankind in favour of modest sincerity. The Vender of the *Beautifying Fluid* sells a lotion that repels pimples, washes away freckles, smooths the skin, and plumps the flesh; and yet, with a generous abhorrence of ostentation, confesses, that it will not *restore the bloom of fifteen to a Lady of fifty.*

The true pathos of Advertisements must have sunk deep into the heart of every man that remembers the zeal shewn by the Seller of the Anodyne Necklace, for the ease and safety *of poor toothing infants*, and the affection with which he warned every mother, that *she would never forgive herself* if her infant should perish without a Necklace.

I cannot but remark to the celebrated Author who gave, in his notifications of the Camel and Dromedary, so many specimens of the genuine sublime, that there is now arrived another subject yet more worthy of his pen. *A famous Mohawk Indian warrior, who took* Dieskaw *the French General prisoner, dressed in the same manner with the native Indians when they go to war, with his face and body painted, with his scalping knife, Tom-ax, and all other implements of war: A sight worthy the curiosity of every true Briton!* This is a very powerful description; but a Critic of great refinement would say that it conveys rather *horror* than *terror.* An *Indian*, dressed as he goes to war, may bring company together; but if he carries the scalping knife and tom ax, there are many true Britons that will never be persuaded to see him but through a grate.

It has been remarked by the severer judges, that the salutary sorrow of tragick scenes is too soon effaced by the merriment of the Epilogue; the same inconvenience arises from the improper disposition of Advertisements. The noblest objects may be so associated as to be made ridiculous. The Camel and Dromedary themselves might have lost much of their dignity between *The true Flower of Mustard* and *The Original Daffy's Elixir*; and I could not but feel some indignation when I found this illustrious *Indian* warrior immediately succeeded by *A fresh Parcel of Dublin Butter.*

The trade of advertising is now so near to perfection, that it is not easy to propose any improvement. But as every art ought to be exercised in due subordination to the publick good, I cannot but propose it as a moral question to these masters of the publick ear, Whether they do not sometimes play too wantonly with our passions, as when the Register of Lottery Tickets invites us to his shop by an account of the prize which he sold last year; and whether the advertising Controvertists do not indulge asperity of language without any adequate provocation; as in the dispute about *Straps for Razors*, now happily subsided, and in the altercation which at present subsists concerning *Eau de Luce.*

In an Advertisement it is allowed to every man to speak well of himself, but I know not why he should assume the privilege of censuring his neighbour. He may proclaim his own virtue or skill, but ought not to exclude others from the same pretensions.

Every man that advertises his own excellence, should write with some consciousness of a character which dares to call the attention of the Publick. He should remember that his name is to stand in the same paper with those of the King of *Prussia*, and the Emperor of *Germany*, and endeavour to make himself worthy of such association.

Some regard is likewise to be paid to posterity. There are men of diligence and curiosity who treasure up the Papers of the Day merely because others neglect them, and in time they will be scarce. When these collections shall be read in another century, how will numberless contradictions be reconciled, and how shall Fame be possibly distributed among the Tailors and Boddice-makers of the present age?

Surely these things deserve consideration. It is enough for me to have hinted my desire that these abuses may be rectified; but such is the state of nature, that what all have the right of doing, many will attempt without sufficient care or due qualifications.

No. 41. Saturday, 27 January 1759.

The following Letter relates to an affliction perhaps not necessary to be imparted to the Publick, but I could not persuade myself to suppress it, because I think I know the sentiments to be sincere, and I feel no disposition to provide for this day any other entertainment.

> *At tu quisquis eris, miseri qui cruda poetæ*
> *Credideris fletu funera digna tuo,*
> *Hæc postrema tibi sit flendi causa, fluatque*
> *Lenis inoffenso vitaque morsque gradu.*

Mr. IDLER,

Notwithstanding the warnings of Philosophers, and the daily examples of losses and misfortunes which life forces upon our observation, such is the absorption of our thoughts in the business of the present day, such the resignation of our reason to empty hopes of future felicity, or such our unwillingness to foresee what we dread, that every calamity comes suddenly upon us, and not only presses us as a burthen, but crushes as a blow.

There are evils which happen out of the common course of nature, against which it is no reproach not to be provided. A flash of lightning intercepts the traveller in his way. The concussion of an earthquake heaps the ruins of cities upon their inhabitants. But other miseries time brings, though silently yet visibly forward by its even lapse, which yet approach us unseen because we turn our eyes away, and seize us unresisted because we could not arm ourselves against them, but by setting them before us.

That it is vain to shrink from what cannot be avoided, and to hide that from ourselves which must some time be found, is a truth which we all know, but which all neglect, and perhaps none more than the speculative reasoner, whose thoughts are always from home, whose eye wanders over life, whose fancy dances after meteors of happiness kindled by itself, and who examines every thing rather than his own state.

Nothing is more evident than that the decays of age must terminate in death; yet there is no man, says *Tully*, who does not believe that he may yet live another year; and there is none who does not, upon the same principle, hope another year for his parent or his friend; but the fallacy will be in time detected; the last year, the last day must come. It has come and is past. The life which made my own life pleasant is at an end, and the gates of death are shut upon my prospects.

The loss of a friend upon whom the heart was fixed, to whom every wish and endeavour tended, is a state of dreary desolation in which the mind looks abroad impatient of itself, and finds nothing but emptiness and horror. The blameless life, the artless tenderness, the pious simplicity, the modest resignation, the patient sickness, and the quiet death, are remembered only to add value to the loss, to aggravate regret for what cannot be amended, to deepen sorrow for what cannot be recalled.

These are the calamities by which Providence gradually disengages us from the love of life. Other evils fortitude may repel, or hope may mitigate; but irreparable privation leaves nothing to exercise resolution or flatter expectation. The dead cannot return, and nothing is left us here but languishment and grief.

Yet such is the course of nature, that whoever lives long must outlive those whom he loves and honours. Such is the condition of our present existence, that life must one time lose its associations, and every inhabitant of the earth must walk downward to the grave alone and unregarded, without any partner of his joy or grief, without any interested witness of his misfortunes or success.

Misfortune, indeed, he may yet feel, for where is the bottom of the misery of man? But what is success to him that has none to enjoy it. Happiness is not found in self-contemplation; it is perceived only when it is reflected from another.

We know little of the state of departed souls, because such knowledge is not necessary to a good life. Reason deserts us at the brink of the grave, and can give no further intelligence. Revelation is not wholly silent. *There is joy in the Angels of Heaven over one sinner that repenteth*; and surely this joy is not incommunicable to souls disentangled from the body, and made like Angels.

Let Hope therefore dictate, what Revelation does not confute, that the union of souls may still remain; and that we who are struggling with sin, sorrow, and infirmities, may have our part in the attention and kindness of those who have finished their course and are now receiving their reward.

These are the great occasions which force the mind to take refuge in Religion: when we have no help in ourselves, what can remain but that we look up to a higher and a greater Power; and to what hope may we not raise our eyes and hearts, when we consider that the Greatest POWER is the BEST.

Surely there is no man who, thus afflicted, does not seek succour in the *Gospel*, which has brought *Life and Immortality to light*. The Precepts of *Epicurus*, who teaches us to endure what the Laws of the Universe make necessary, may silence but not content us. The dictates of *Zeno*, who commands us to look with indifference on external things, may dispose us to conceal our sorrow, but cannot assuage it. Real alleviation of the loss of friends, and rational tranquillity in the prospect of our own dissolution, can be received only from the promises of him in whose hands are life and death, and from the assurance of another and better state, in which all tears will be wiped from the eyes, and the whole soul shall be filled with joy. Philosophy may infuse stubbornness, but Religion only can give Patience.

I am, &c.

No. 44. Saturday, 17 February 1759.

Memory is, among the faculties of the human mind, that of which we make the most frequent use, or rather that of which the agency is incessant or perpetual. Memory is the primary and fundamental power, without which there could be no other intellectual operation. Judgment and Ratiocination suppose something already known, and draw their decisions only from experience. Imagination selects ideas from the treasures of Remembrance, and produces novelty only by varied combinations. We do not even form conjectures of distant, or anticipations of future events, but by concluding what is possible from what is past.

The two offices of Memory are Collection and Distribution; by one images are accumulated, and by the other produced for use. Collection is always the employment of our first years, and Distribution commonly that of our advanced age.

To collect and reposite the various forms of things, is far the most pleasing part of mental occupation. We are naturally delighted with novelty, and there is a time when all that we see is new. When first we enter into the world, whithersoever we turn our eyes, they meet Knowledge with Pleasure at her side; every diversity of Nature pours ideas in upon the soul; neither search nor labour are necessary; we have nothing more to do than to open our eyes, and curiosity is gratified.

Much of the pleasure which the first survey of the world affords, is exhausted before we are conscious of our own felicity, or able to compare our condition with some other possible state. We have therefore few traces of the joy of our earliest discoveries; yet we all remember a time when Nature had so many untasted gratifications, that every excursion gave delight which can now be found no longer, when the noise of a torrent, the rustle of a wood, the song of birds, or the play of lambs, had power to fill the attention, and suspend all perception of the course of time.

But these easy pleasures are soon at an end; we have seen in a very little time so much, that we call out for new objects of observation, and endeavour to find variety in books and life. But study is laborious, and not always satisfactory; and Conversation has its pains as well as pleasures; we are willing to learn, but not willing to be taught; we are pained by ignorance, but pained yet more by another's knowledge.

From the vexation of pupillage men commonly set themselves free about the middle of life, by shutting up the avenues of intelligence, and resolving to rest in their present state; and they, whose ardour of enquiry continues longer, find themselves insensibly forsaken by their instructors. As every man advances in life, the proportion between those that are younger, and that are older than himself, is continually changing; and he that has lived half a century, finds few that do not require from him that information which he once expected from those that went before him.

Then it is that the magazines of memory are opened, and the stores of accumulated knowledge are displayed by vanity or benevolence, or in honest commerce of mutual interest. Every man wants others, and is therefore glad when he is wanted by them. And as few men will endure the labour of intense meditation without necessity, he that has learned enough for his profit or his honour, seldom endeavours after further acquisitions.

The pleasure of recollecting speculative notions would not be much less than that of gaining them, if they could be kept pure and unmingled with the passages of life; but such is the necessary concatenation of our thoughts, that good and evil are linked together, and no pleasure recurs but associated with pain. Every revived idea reminds us of a time when something was enjoyed that is now lost, when some hope was yet not blasted, when some purpose had yet not languished into sluggishness or indifference.

Whether it be that life has more vexations than comforts, or, what is in the event just the same, that evil makes deeper impression than good, it is certain that few can review the time past without heaviness of heart. He remembers many calamities incurred by folly, many opportunities lost by negligence. The shades of the dead rise up before him, and he laments the companions of his youth, the partners of his amusements, the assistants of his labours, whom the hand of death has snatched away.

When an offer was made to *Themistocles* of teaching him the art of Memory, he answered, that he would rather wish for the art of Forgetfulness. He felt his imagination haunted by phantoms of misery which he was unable to suppress, and would gladly have calmed his thoughts with some *oblivious antidote*. In this we all resemble one another; the hero and the sage are, like vulgar mortals, overburthened by the weight of life, all shrink from recollection, and all wish for an art of Forgetfulness.

No. 48. Saturday, 17 March 1759.

There is no kind of idleness, by which we are so easily seduced, as that which dignifies itself by the appearance of business, and by making the loiterer imagine that he has something to do which must not be neglected, keeps him in perpetual agitation, and hurries him rapidly from place to place.

He that sits still, or reposes himself upon a couch, no more deceives himself than he deceives others; he knows that he is doing nothing, and has no other solace of his insignificance than the resolution which the lazy hourly make, of changing his mode of life.

To do nothing every man is ashamed, and to do much almost every man is unwilling or afraid. Innumerable expedients have therefore been invented to produce motion without labour, and employment without solicitude. The greater part of those whom the kindness of fortune has left to their own direction, and whom want does not keep chained to the counter or the plow, play throughout life with the shadows of business, and know not at last what they have been doing.

These imitators of action are of all denominations. Some are seen at every Auction without intention to purchase; others appear punctually at the *Exchange*, though they are known there only by their faces. Some are always making parties, to visit Collections for which they have no taste, and some neglect every pleasure and every duty to hear questions in which they have no interest, debated in Parliament.

These men never appear more ridiculous, than in the distress which they imagine themselves to feel, from some accidental interruption of those empty pursuits. A Tiger newly imprisoned is indeed more formidable, but not more angry than *Jack Tulip* with-held from a Florist's feast, or *Tom Distich* hindered from seeing the first representation of a Play.

As political affairs are the highest and most extensive of temporal concerns; the mimick of a Politician is more busy and important than any other trifler. Monsieur *le Noir*, a man who, without property or importance in any corner of the earth, has, in the present confusion of the world, declared himself a steady adherent to the *French*, is made miserable by a wind that keeps back the packet-boat, and still more miserable, by every account of a *Malouin* privateer caught in his cruize; he knows well that nothing can be done or said by him which can produce any effect but that of laughter, that he can neither hasten nor retard good or evil, that his joys and sorrows have scarcely any partakers; yet such is his zeal, and such his curiosity, that he would run barefooted to *Gravesend*, for the sake of knowing first that the *English* had lost a tender, and would ride out to meet every mail from the Continent if he might be permitted to open it.

Learning is generally confessed to be desirable, and there are some who fancy themselves always busy in acquiring it. Of these ambulatory Students, one of the most busy is my friend *Tom Restless*.

Tom has long had a mind to be a man of knowledge, but he does not care to spend much time among Authors, for he is of opinion that few books deserve the labour of perusal, that they give the mind an unfashionable cast, and destroy that freedom of thought and easiness of manners indispensibly requisite to acceptance in the world. *Tom* has therefore found another way to wisdom. When he rises he goes into a Coffee-house, where he creeps so near to men whom he takes to be reasoners as to hear their discourse, and endeavours to remember something which, when it has been strained thro' *Tom's* head, is so near to nothing that what it once was cannot be discovered. This he carries round from friend to friend thro' a circle of visits, till hearing what each says upon the question he becomes able at dinner to say a little himself, and as every great genius relaxes himself among his inferiors, meets with some who wonder how so young a man can talk so wisely.

At night he has a new feast prepared for his intellects; he always runs to a disputing society, or a speaking club, where he half hears what, if he had heard the whole, he would but half understand; goes home pleased with the consciousness of a day well spent, lies down full of ideas, and rises in the morning empty as before.

No. 49. Saturday, 24 March 1759.

I supped three nights ago with my friend *Will Marvel*. His affairs obliged him lately to take a journey into *Devonshire*, from which he has just returned. He knows me to be a very patient hearer, and was glad of my company, as it gave him an opportunity of disburthening himself by a minute relation of the casualties of his expedition.

Will is not one of those who go out and return with nothing to tell. He has a story of his travels, which will strike a home-bred citizen with horror, and has in ten days suffered so often the extremes of terror and joy, that he is in doubt whether he shall ever again expose either his body or mind to such danger and fatigue.

When he left *London* the morning was bright, and a fair day was promised. But *Will* is born to struggle with difficulties. That happened to him, which has sometimes, perhaps, happened to others. Before he had gone more than ten miles it began to rain. What course was to be taken! His soul disdained to turn back. He did what the king of *Prussia* might have done, he flapped his hat, buttoned up his cape, and went forwards, fortifying his mind, by the stoical consolation, that whatever is violent will be short.

His constancy was not long tried; at the distance of about half a mile he saw an inn, which he entered wet and weary, and found civil treatment and proper refreshment. After a respite of about two hours he looked abroad, and seeing the sky clear, called for his horse and passed the first stage without any other memorable accident.

Will considered, that labour must be relieved by pleasure, and that the strength which great undertakings require must be maintained by copious nutriment; he therefore ordered himself an elegant supper, drank two bottles of claret, and passed the beginning of the night in sound sleep; but waking before light, was forewarned of the troubles of the next day, by a shower beating against his windows with such violence as to threaten the dissolution of nature. When he arose he found what he expected, that the country was under water. He joined himself, however, to a company that was travelling the same way, and came safely to the place of dinner, tho' every step of his horse dashed the mud into the air.

In the afternoon, having parted from his company, he set forward alone, and passed many collections of water of which it was impossible to guess the depth, and which he now cannot review without some censure of his own rashness; but what a man undertakes he must perform, and *Marvel* hates a coward at his heart.

Few that lie warm in their beds, think what others undergo, who have perhaps been as tenderly educated, and have as acute sensations as themselves. My friend was now to lodge the second night almost fifty miles from home, in a house which he never had seen before, among people to whom he was totally a stranger, not knowing whether the next man he should meet would prove good or bad; but seeing an inn of a good appearance, he rode resolutely into the yard, and knowing that respect is often paid in proportion as it is claimed, delivered his injunction to the hostler with spirit, and entering the house, called vigorously about him.

On the third day up rose the sun and Mr. *Marvel*. His troubles and his dangers were now such, as he wishes no other man ever to encounter. The ways were less frequented, and the country more thinly inhabited. He rode many a lonely hour thro' mire and water, and met not a single soul for two miles together with whom he could exchange a word. He cannot deny that, looking round upon the dreary region, and seeing nothing but bleak fields and naked trees, hills obscured by fogs, and flats covered with inundations, he did for some time suffer melancholy to prevail upon him, and wished himself again safe at home. One comfort he had, which was to consider, that none of his friends were in the same distress, for whom, if they had been with him, he should have suffered more than for himself; he could not forbear sometimes to consider how happily the *Idler* is settled in an easier condition, who, surrounded like him with terrors, could have done nothing but lie down and die.

Amidst these reflections he came to a town and found a dinner, which disposed him to more chearful sentiments: but the joys of life are short, and its miseries are long; he mounted and travelled fifteen miles more thro' dirt and desolation.

At last the sun set, and all the horrors of darkness came upon him. He then repented the weak indulgence by which he had gratified himself at noon with too long an interval of rest: yet he went forward along a path which he could no longer see, sometimes rushing suddenly into water, and sometimes incumbered with stiff clay, ignorant whither he was going, and uncertain whether his next step might not be the last.

In this dismal gloom of nocturnal peregrination his horse unexpectedly stood still. *Marvel* had heard many relations of the instinct of horses, and was in doubt what danger might be at hand. Sometimes he fancied that he was on the bank of a river still and deep, and sometimes that a dead body lay across the track. He sat still awhile to recollect his thoughts; and as he was about to alight and explore the darkness, out stepped a man with a lantern, and opened the turnpike. He hired a guide to the town, arrived in safety, and slept in quiet.

The rest of his journey was nothing but danger. He climbed and descended precipices on which vulgar mortals tremble to look; he passed marshes like the *Serbonian bog, where armies whole have sunk*; he forded rivers where the current roared like the *Egre* of the *Severn*; or ventured himself on bridges that trembled under him, from which he looked down on foaming whirlpools, or dreadful abysses; he wandered over houseless heaths, amidst all the rage of the Elements, with the snow driving in his face, and the tempest howling in his ears.

Such are the colours in which *Marvel* paints his adventures. He has accustomed himself to sounding words and hyperbolical images, till he has lost the power of true description. In a road through which the heaviest carriages pass without difficulty, and the post-boy every day and night goes and returns, he meets with hardships like those which are endured in *Siberian* deserts, and misses nothing of romantic danger but a giant and a dragon. When his dreadful story is told in proper terms, it is only, that the way was dirty in winter, and that he experienced the common vicissitudes of rain and sunshine.

No. 50. Saturday, 31 March 1759.

The character of Mr. *Marvel* has raised the merriment of some and the contempt of others, who do not sufficiently consider how often they hear and practise the same arts of exaggerated narration.

There is not, perhaps, among the multitudes of all conditions that swarm upon the earth, a single man who does not believe that he has something extraordinary to relate of himself; and who does not, at one time or other, summon the attention of his friends to the casualties of his adventures and the vicissitudes of his fortune; casualties and vicissitudes that happen alike in lives uniform and diversified; to the Commander of armies, and the Writer at a desk; to the Sailor who resigns himself to the wind and water, and the Farmer whose longest journey is to the market.

In the present state of the world man may pass thro' *Shakespear*'s seven stages of life, and meet nothing singular or wonderful. But such is every man's attention to himself, that what is common and unheeded when it is only seen, becomes remarkable and peculiar when we happen to feel it.

It is well enough known to be according to the usual process of Nature, that men should sicken and recover, that some designs should succeed and others miscarry, that friends should be separated and meet again, that some should be made angry by endeavours to please them, and some be pleased when no care has been used to gain their approbation; that men and women should at first come together by chance, like each other so well as to commence acquaintance, improve acquaintance into fondness, increase or extinguish fondness by marriage, and have children of different degrees of intellects and virtue, some of whom die before their parents, and others survive them.

Yet let any man tell his own story, and nothing of all this has ever befallen him according to the common order of things; something has always discriminated his case; some unusual concurrence of events has appeared which made him more happy or more miserable than other mortals; for in pleasures or calamities, however common, every one has comforts and afflictions of his own.

It is certain that without some artificial augmentations, many of the pleasures of life, and almost all its embellishments, would fall to the ground. If no man was to express more delight than he felt, those who felt most would raise little envy. If travellers were to describe the most laboured performances of art with the same coldness as they survey them, all expectations of happiness from change of place would cease. The Pictures of *Raphael* would hang without spectators, and the Gardens of *Versailles* might be inhabited by hermits. All the pleasure that is received ends in an opportunity of splendid falshood, in the power of gaining notice by the display of beauties which the eye was weary of beholding, and a history of happy moments, of which, in reality, the most happy was the last.

The ambition of superior sensibility and superior eloquence disposes the lovers of arts to receive rapture at one time, and communicate it at another; and each labours first to impose upon himself, and then to propagate the imposture.

Pain is less subject than pleasure to caprices of expression. The torments of disease, and the grief for irremediable misfortunes, sometimes are such as no words can declare, and can only be signified by groans, or sobs, or inarticulate ejulations. Man has from nature a mode of utterance peculiar to pain, but he has none peculiar to pleasure, because he never has pleasure but in such degrees as the ordinary use of language may equal or surpass.

It is nevertheless certain, that many pains as well as pleasures are heightened by rhetorical affectation, and that the picture is, for the most part, bigger than the life.

When we describe our sensations of another's sorrows, either in friendly or ceremonious condolence, the customs of the world scarcely admit of rigid veracity. Perhaps the fondest friendship would enrage oftner than comfort, were the tongue on such occasions faithfully to represent the sentiments of the heart; and I think the strictest moralists allow forms of address to be used without much regard to their literal acceptation, when either respect or tenderness requires them, because they are universally known to denote not the degree but the species of our sentiments.

But the same indulgence cannot be allowed to him who aggravates dangers incurred or sorrow endured by himself, because he darkens the prospect of futurity, and multiplies the pains of our condition by useless terror. Those who magnify their delights are less criminal deceivers, yet they raise hopes which are sure to be disappointed. It would be undoubtedly best, if we could see and hear every thing as it is, that nothing might be too anxiously dreaded, or too ardently pursued.

No. 51. Saturday, 7 April 1759.

It has been commonly remarked, that eminent men are least eminent at home, that bright characters lose much of their splendor at a nearer view, and many who fill the world with their fame, excite very little reverence among those that surround them in their domestick privacies.

To blame or to suspect is easy and natural. When the fact is evident, and the cause doubtful, some accusation is always engendered between idleness and malignity. This disparity of general and familiar esteem is therefore imputed to hidden vices, and to practices indulged in secret, but carefully covered from the publick eye.

Vice will indeed always produce contempt. The Dignity of *Alexander*, tho' nations fell prostrate before him, was certainly held in little veneration by the partakers of his midnight revels, who had seen him, in the madness of wine, murder his friend, or set fire to the *Persian* palace at the instigation of a harlot; and it is well remembered among us, that the Avarice of *Marlborough* kept him in subjection to his wife, while he was dreaded by *France* as her Conqueror, and honoured by the Emperor as his Deliverer.

But though where there is vice there must be want of reverence, it is not reciprocally true, that when there is want of reverence there is always vice. That awe which great actions or abilities impress will be inevitably diminished by acquaintance, tho' nothing either mean or criminal should be found.

Of men, as of every thing else, we must judge according to our knowledge. When we see of a Hero only his Battles, or of a Writer only his Books, we have nothing to allay our ideas of their Greatness. We consider the one only as the Guardian of his country, and the other only as the Instructor of mankind. We have neither opportunity nor motive to examine the minuter parts of their lives, or the less apparent peculiarities of their characters; we name them with habitual respect, and forget, what we still continue to know, that they are men like other mortals.

But such is the constitution of the world, that much of life must be spent in the same manner by the wise and the ignorant, the exalted and the low. Men, however distinguished by external accidents or intrinsick qualities, have all the same wants, the same pains, and, as far as the senses are consulted, the same pleasures. The petty cares and petty duties are the same in every station to every understanding, and every hour brings some occasion on which we all sink to the common level. We are all naked till we are dressed, and hungry till we are fed; and the General's Triumph, and Sage's Disputation, end, like the humble labours of the Smith or Plowman, in a dinner or in sleep.

Those notions which are to be collected by reason in opposition to the senses, will seldom stand forward in the mind, but lie treasured in the remoter repositories of memory, to be found only when they are sought. Whatever any man may have written or done, his precepts or his valour will scarcely over-ballance the unimportant uniformity which runs thro' his time. We do not easily consider him as great, whom our own eyes shew us to be little; nor labour to keep present to our thoughts the latent excellencies of him who shares with us all our weaknesses and many of our follies; who like us is delighted with slight amusements, busied with trifling employments, and disturbed by little vexations.

Great powers cannot be exerted, but when great exigencies make them necessary. Great exigencies can happen but seldom, and therefore those qualities which have a claim to the veneration of mankind, lie hid, for the most part, like subterranean treasures, over which the foot passes as on common ground, till necessity breaks open the golden cavern.

In the ancient celebrations of victory, a slave was placed on the triumphal car, by the side of the General, who reminded him by a short sentence, that he was a Man. Whatever danger there might be lest a Leader, in his passage to the Capitol, should forget the frailties of his nature, there was surely no need of such an admonition; the intoxication could not have continued long; he would have been at home but a few hours before some of his dependents would have forgot his greatness, and shewn him, that notwithstanding his laurels he was yet a man.

There are some who try to escape this domestic degradation, by labouring to appear always wise or always great; but he that strives against nature, will for ever strive in vain. To be grave of mien and slow of utterance; to look with solicitude and speak with hesitation, is attainable at will; but the shew of Wisdom is ridiculous when there is nothing to cause doubt, as that of Valour where there is nothing to be feared.

A man who has duly considered the condition of his being, will contentedly yield to the course of things: he will not pant for distinction where distinction would imply no merit, but tho' on great occasions he may wish to be greater than others, he will be satisfied in common occurrences not to be less.

No. 57. Saturday, 19 May 1759.

Prudence is of more frequent use than any other intellectual quality; it is exerted on slight occasions, and called into act by the cursory business of common life.

Whatever is universally necessary, has been granted to mankind on easy terms. Prudence, as it is always wanted, is without great difficulty obtained. It requires neither extensive view nor profound search, but forces itself, by spontaneous impulse, upon a mind neither great nor busy, neither ingrossed by vast designs nor distracted by multiplicity of attention.

Prudence operates on life in the same manner as rules on composition; it produces vigilance rather than elevation, rather prevents loss than procures advantages; and often escapes miscarriages, but seldom reaches either power or honour. It quenches that ardour of enterprize, by which every thing is done that can claim praise or admiration, and represses that generous temerity which often fails and often succeeds. Rules may obviate faults, but can never confer beauties; and Prudence keeps life safe, but does not often make it happy. The world is not amazed with prodigies of excellence, but when Wit tramples upon Rules, and Magnanimity breaks the chains of Prudence.

One of the most prudent of all that have fallen within my observation, is my old companion *Sophron*, who has passed through the world in quiet, by perpetual adherence to a few plain maxims, and wonders how contention and distress can so often happen.

The first principle of *Sophron* is to *run no hazards*. Tho' he loves money, he is of opinion, that frugality is a more certain source of riches than industry. It is to no purpose that any prospect of large profit is set before him; he believes little about futurity, and does not love to trust his money out of his sight, for nobody knows what may happen. He has a small estate which he lets at the old rent, because *it is better to have a little than nothing*; but he rigorously demands payment on the stated day, for *he that cannot pay one quarter cannot pay two.* If he is told of any improvements in Agriculture, he likes the old way, has observed that changes very seldom answer expectation, is of opinion that our forefathers knew how to till the ground as well as we; and concludes with an argument that nothing can overpower, that the expence of planting and fencing is immediate, and the advantage distant, and that *he is no wise man who will quit a certainty for an uncertainty.*

Another of *Sophron*'s rules is, *to mind no business but his own.* In the State he is of no party; but hears and speaks of publick affairs with the same coldness as of the administration of some ancient republick. If any flagrant act of Fraud or Oppression is mentioned, he hopes that *all is not true that is told*: if Misconduct or Corruption puts the nation in a flame, he hopes that *every man means well.* At Elections he leaves his dependents to their own choice, and declines to vote himself, for every Candidate is a good man, whom he is unwilling to oppose or offend.

If disputes happen among his neighbours he observes an invariable and cold neutrality. His punctuality has gained him the reputation of honesty, and his caution that of wisdom, and few would refuse to refer their claims to his award. He might have prevented many expensive law-suits, and quenched many a feud in its first smoke, but always refuses the office of Arbitration, because he must decide against one or the other.

With the affairs of other families he is always unacquainted. He sees estates bought and sold, squandered and increased, without praising the economist or censuring the spendthrift. He never courts the rising lest they should fall, nor insults the fallen lest they should rise again. His caution has the appearance of virtue, and all who do not want his help praise his benevolence; but if any man solicits his assistance, he has just sent away all his money; and when the petitioner is gone declares to his family that he is sorry for his misfortunes, has always looked upon him with particular kindness, and therefore could not lend him money, lest he should destroy their friendship by the necessity of enforcing payment.

Of domestic misfortunes he has never heard. When he is told the hundredth time of a Gentleman's daughter who has married the coachman, he lifts up his hands with astonishment, for he always thought her a very sober girl. When nuptial quarrels, after having filled the country with talk and laughter, at last end in separation, he never can conceive how it happened, for he looked upon them as a happy couple.

If his advice is asked, he never gives any particular direction, because events are uncertain, and he will bring no blame upon himself; but he takes the consulter tenderly by the hand, tells him he makes his case his own, and advises him not to act rashly, but to weigh the reasons on both sides; observes that a man may be as easily too hasty as too slow, and that as many fail by doing too much as too little; that *a wise man has two ears and one tongue*; and *that little said is soon amended*; that he could tell him this and that, but that after all every man is the best judge of his own affairs.

With this some are satisfied, and go home with great reverence of *Sophron*'s wisdom, and none are offended, because every one is left in full possession of his own opinion.

Sophron gives no characters. It is equally vain to tell him of Vice and Virtue, for he has remarked that no man likes to be censured, and that very few are delighted with the praises of another. He has a few terms which he uses to all alike. With respect to fortune, he believes every family to be in good circumstances; he never exalts any understanding by lavish praise, yet he meets with none but very sensible people. Every man is honest and hearty, and every woman is a good creature.

Thus *Sophron* creeps along, neither loved nor hated, neither favoured nor opposed; he has never attempted to grow rich for fear of growing poor, and has raised no friends for fear of making enemies.

No. 58. Saturday, 26 May 1759.

Pleasure is very seldom found where it is sought. Our brightest blazes of gladness are commonly kindled by unexpected sparks. The flowers which scatter their odours from time to time in the paths of life, grow up without culture from seeds scattered by chance.

Nothing is more hopeless than a scheme of merriment. Wits and humorists are brought together from distant quarters by preconcerted invitations; they come attended by their admirers prepared to laugh and to applaud: They gaze a-while on each other, ashamed to be silent, and afraid to speak; every man is discontented with himself, grows angry with those that give him pain, and resolves that he will contribute nothing to the merriment of such worthless company. Wine inflames the general malignity, and changes sullenness to petulance, till at last none can bear any longer the presence of the rest. They retire to vent their indignation in safer places, where they are heard with attention; their importance is restored, they recover their good humour, and gladden the night with wit and jocularity.

Merriment is always the effect of a sudden impression. The jest which is expected is already destroyed. The most active imagination will be sometimes torpid, under the frigid influence of melancholy, and sometimes occasions will be wanting to tempt the mind, however volatile, to sallies and excursions. Nothing was ever said with uncommon felicity, but by the co-operation of chance; and therefore, wit as well as valour must be content to share its honours with fortune.

All other pleasures are equally uncertain; the general remedy of uneasiness is change of place; almost every one has some journey of Pleasure in his mind, with which he flatters his expectation. He that travels in theory has no inconveniences; he has shade and sunshine at his disposal, and wherever he alights finds tables of plenty and looks of gaiety. These ideas are indulged till the day of departure arrives, the chaise is called, and the progress of happiness begins.

A few miles teach him the fallacies of imagination. The road is dusty, the air is sultry, the horses are sluggish, and the postilion brutal. He longs for the time of dinner that he may eat and rest. The inn is crouded, his orders are neglected, and nothing remains but that he devour in haste what the cook has spoiled, and drive on in quest of better entertainment. He finds at night a more commodious house, but the best is always worse than he expected.

He at last enters his native province, and resolves to feast his mind with the conversation of his old friends, and the recollection of juvenile frolicks.

He stops at the house of his friend whom he designs to overpower with pleasure by the unexpected interview. He is not known till he tells his name, and revives the memory of himself by a gradual explanation. He is then coldly received, and ceremoniously feasted. He hastes away to another whom his affairs have called to a distant place, and having seen the empty house, goes away disgusted, by a disappointment which could not be intended because it could not be foreseen. At the next house he finds every face clouded with misfortune, and is regarded with malevolence as an unreasonable intruder, who comes not to visit but to insult them.

It is seldom that we find either men or places such as we expect them. He that has pictured a prospect upon his fancy, will receive little pleasure from his eyes; he that has anticipated the conversation of a wit, will wonder to what prejudice he owes his reputation. Yet it is necessary to hope, tho' hope should always be deluded, for hope itself is happiness, and its frustrations, however frequent, are yet less dreadful than its extinction.

No. 59. Saturday, 2 June 1759.

In the common enjoyments of life, we cannot very liberally indulge the present hour, but by anticipating part of the pleasure which might have relieved the tediousness of another day; and any uncommon exertion of strength, or perseverance in labour, is succeeded by a long interval of languor and weariness. Whatever advantage we snatch beyond the certain portion allotted us by nature, is like money spent before it is due, which at the time of regular payment will be missed and regretted.

Fame, like all other things which are supposed to give or to encrease happiness, is dispensed with the same equality of distribution. He that is loudly praised will be clamorously censured; he that rises hastily into fame will be in danger of sinking suddenly into oblivion.

Of many writers who filled their age with wonder, and whose names we find celebrated in the books of their cotemporaries, the works are now no longer to be seen, or are seen only amidst the lumber of libraries which are seldom visited, where they lie only to shew the deceitfulness of hope, and the uncertainty of honour.

Of the decline of reputation many causes may be assigned. It is commonly lost because it never was deserved, and was conferred at first, not by the suffrage of criticism, but by the fondness of friendship, or servility of flattery. The great and popular are very freely applauded, but all soon grow weary of echoing to each other a name which has no other claim to notice, but that many mouths are pronouncing it at once.

But many have lost the final reward of their labours, because they were too hasty to enjoy it. They have laid hold on recent occurrences, and eminent names, and delighted their readers with allusions and remarks, in which all were interested, and to which all therefore were attentive. But the effect ceased with its cause; the time quickly came when new events drove the former from memory, when the vicissitudes of the world brought new hopes and fears, transferred the love and hatred of the public to other agents, and the writer whose works were no longer assisted by gratitude or resentment, was left to the cold regard of idle curiosity.

He that writes upon general principles, or delivers universal truths, may hope to be often read, because his work will be equally useful at all times and in every country, but he cannot expect it to be received with eagerness, or to spread with rapidity, because desire can have no particular stimulation; that which is to be loved long must be loved with reason rather than with passion. He that lays out his labours upon temporary subjects, easily finds readers, and quickly loses them; for what should make the book valued when its subject is no more.

These observations will shew the reason why the Poem of *Hudibras* is almost forgotten however embellished with sentiments and diversified with allusions, however bright with wit, and however solid with truth. The hypocrisy which it detected, and the folly which it ridiculed, have long vanished from public notice. Those who had felt the mischiefs of discord, and the tyranny of usurpation, read it with rapture, for every line brought back to memory something known, and gratified resentment, by the just censure of something hated. But the book which was once quoted by princes, and which supplied conversation to all the assemblies of the gay and witty, is now seldom mentioned, and even by those that affect to mention it, is seldom read. So vainly is wit lavished upon fugitive topics, so little can architecture secure duration when the ground is false.

No. 60. Saturday, 9 June 1759.

Criticism is a study by which men grow important and formidable at very small expence. The power of invention has been conferred by Nature upon few, and the labour of learning those sciences which may, by mere labour, be obtained, is too great to be willingly endured; but every man can exert such judgment as he has upon the works of others; and he whom Nature has made weak, and Idleness keeps ignorant, may yet support his vanity by the name of a Critick.

I hope it will give comfort to great numbers who are passing thro' the world in obscurity, when I inform them how easily distinction may be obtained. All the other powers of literature are coy and haughty, they must be long courted, and at last are not always gained; but Criticism is a goddess easy of access and forward of advance, who will meet the slow and encourage the timorous; the want of meaning she supplies with words, and the want of spirit she recompenses with malignity.

This profession has one recommendation peculiar to itself, that it gives vent to malignity without real mischief. No genius was ever blasted by the breath of Criticks. The poison which, if confined, would have burst the heart, fumes away in empty hisses, and malice is set at ease with very little danger to merit. The Critick is the only man whose triumph is without another's pain, and whose greatness does not rise upon another's ruin.

To a study at once so easy and so reputable, so malicious and so harmless, it cannot be necessary to invite my readers by a long or laboured exhortation; it is sufficient, since all would be Criticks if they could, to shew by one eminent example that all can be Criticks if they will.

Dick Minim, after the common course of puerile studies, in which he was no great proficient, was put apprentice to a Brewer, with whom he had lived two years, when his uncle died in the city, and left him a large fortune in the stocks. *Dick* had for six months before used the company of the lower players, of whom he had learned to scorn a trade, and being now at liberty to follow his genius, he resolved to be a man of wit and humour. That he might be properly initiated in his new character, he frequented the coffee-houses near the theatres, where he listened very diligently day, after day, to those who talked of language and sentiments, and unities and catastrophes, till by slow degrees he began to think that he understood something of the Stage, and hoped in time to talk himself.

But he did not trust so much to natural sagacity, as wholly to neglect the help of books. When the theatres were shut, he retired to *Richmond* with a few select writers, whose opinions he impressed upon his memory by unwearied diligence; and when he returned with other wits to the town, was able to tell, in very proper phrases, that the chief business of art is to copy nature; that a perfect writer is not to be expected, because genius decays as judgment increases; that the great art is the art of blotting, and that according to the rule of *Horace* every piece should be kept nine years.

Of the great Authors he now began to display the Characters, laying down as an universal position that all had beauties and defects. His opinion was, that *Shakespear*, committing himself wholly to the impulse of Nature, wanted that correctness which learning would have given him; and that *Johnson*, trusting to learning, did not sufficiently cast his eye on Nature. He blamed the *Stanza* of *Spenser*, and could not bear the *Hexameters* of *Sidney*. *Denham* and *Waller* he held the first reformers of *English* Numbers, and thought that if *Waller* could have obtained the strength of *Denham*, or *Denham* the sweetness of *Waller*, there had been nothing wanting to complete a Poet. He often expressed his commiseration of *Dryden*'s poverty, and his indignation at the age which suffered him to write for bread; he repeated with rapture the first lines of *All for Love*, but wondered at the corruption of taste which could bear any thing so unnatural as rhyming Tragedies. In *Otway* he found uncommon powers of moving the passions, but was disgusted by his general negligence, and blamed him for making a Conspirator his Hero; and never concluded his disquisition, without remarking how happily the sound of the clock is made to alarm the audience. *Southern* would have been his favourite, but that he mixes comick with tragick scenes, intercepts the natural course of the passions, and fills the mind with a wild confusion of mirth and melancholy. The versification of *Rowe* he thought too melodious for the stage, and too little varied in different passions. He made it the great fault of *Congreve*, that all his persons were wits, and that he always wrote with more art than nature. He considered *Cato* rather as a poem than a play, and allowed *Addison* to be the complete master of Allegory and grave humour, but paid no great deference to him as a Critick. He thought the chief merit of *Prior* was in his easy tales and lighter poems, tho' he allowed that his *Solomon* had many noble sentiments elegantly expressed. In *Swift* he discovered an inimitable vein of irony, and an easiness which all would hope and few would attain. *Pope* he was inclined to degrade from a Poet to a Versifier, and thought his Numbers rather luscious than sweet. He often lamented the neglect of *Phædra and Hippolitus*, and wished to see the stage under better regulations.

These assertions passed commonly uncontradicted; and if now and then an opponent started up, he was quickly repressed by the suffrages of the company, and *Minim* went away from every dispute with elation of heart and increase of confidence.

He now grew conscious of his abilities, and began to talk of the present state of dramatick Poetry; wondered what was become of the comick genius which supplied our ancestors with wit and pleasantry, and why no writer could be found that durst now venture beyond a Farce. He saw no reason for thinking that the vein of humour was exhausted, since we live in a country where liberty suffers every character to spread itself to its utmost bulk, and which therefore produces more originals than all the rest of the world together. Of Tragedy he concluded business to be the soul, and yet often hinted that love predominates too much upon the modern stage.

He was now an acknowledged Critick, and had his own seat in the coffee-house, and headed a party in the pit. *Minim* has more vanity than ill-nature, and seldom desires to do much mischief; he will perhaps murmur a little in the ear of him that sits next him, but endeavours to influence the audience to favour, by clapping when an actor exclaims *ye Gods*, or laments the misery of his country.

By degrees he was admitted to Rehearsals, and many of his friends are of opinion, that our present Poets are indebted to him for their happiest thoughts; by his contrivance the bell was rung twice in *Barbarossa*, and by his persuasion the author of *Cleone* concluded his Play without a couplet; for what can be more absurd, said *Minim*, than that part of a play should be rhymed, and part written in blank verse? and by what acquisition of faculties is the Speaker who never could find rhymes before, enabled to rhyme at the conclusion of an Act!

He is the great investigator of hidden beauties, and is particularly delighted when he finds *the Sound an Echo to the Sense*. He has read all our Poets with particular attention to this delicacy of Versification, and wonders at the supineness with which their Works have been hitherto perused, so that no man has found the sound of a Drum in this distich,

> When Pulpit, Drum ecclesiastic,
> Was beat with fist instead of a stick;

and that the wonderful lines upon Honour and a Bubble have hitherto passed without notice.

> Honour is like the glassy Bubble,
> Which costs Philosophers such trouble,
> Where one part crack'd, the whole does fly,
> And Wits are crack'd to find out why.

In these Verses, says *Minim*, we have two striking accommodations of the Sound to the Sense. It is impossible to utter the two lines emphatically without an act like that which they describe; *Bubble* and *Trouble* causing a momentary inflation of the Cheeks by the retention of the breath, which is afterwards forcibly emitted, as in the practice of *blowing bubbles*. But the greatest excellence is in the third line, which is *crack'd* in the middle to express a crack, and then shivers into monosyllables. Yet has this diamond lain neglected with common stones, and among the innumerable admirers of *Hudibras* the observation of this superlative passage has been reserved for the sagacity of *Minim*.

No. 61. Saturday, 16 June 1759.

Mr. *Minim* had now advanced himself to the zenith of critical reputation; when he was in the Pit, every eye in the Boxes was fixed upon him, when he entered his Coffee-house, he was surrounded by circles of candidates, who passed their noviciate of literature under his tuition; his opinion was asked by all who had no opinion of their own, and yet loved to debate and decide; and no composition was supposed to pass in safety to posterity, till it had been secured by *Minim*'s approbation.

Minim professes great admiration of the wisdom and munificence by which the Academies of the Continent were raised, and often wishes for some standard of taste, for some tribunal, to which merit may appeal from caprice, prejudice, and malignity. He has formed a plan for an Academy of Criticism, where every work of Imagination may be read before it is printed, and which shall authoritatively direct the Theatres what pieces to receive or reject, to exclude or to revive.

Such an institution would, in *Dick*'s opinion, spread the fame of *English* literature over *Europe*, and make *London* the metropolis of elegance and politeness, the place to which the learned and ingenious of all countries would repair for instruction and improvement, and where nothing would any longer be applauded or endured that was not conformed to the nicest rules, and finished with the highest elegance.

Till some happy conjunction of the planets shall dispose our Princes or Ministers to make themselves immortal by such an Academy, *Minim* contents himself to preside four nights in a week in a Critical Society selected by himself, where he is heard without contradiction, and whence his judgment is disseminated through the great vulgar and the small.

When he is placed in the chair of Criticism, he declares loudly for the noble simplicity of our ancestors, in opposition to the petty refinements, and ornamental luxuriance. Sometimes he is sunk in despair, and perceives false delicacy daily gaining ground, and sometimes brightens his countenance with a gleam of hope, and predicts the revival of the true sublime. He then fulminates his loudest censures against the monkish barbarity of rhyme; wonders how beings that pretend to reason can be pleased with one line always ending like another; tells how unjustly and unnaturally sense is sacrificed to sound; how often the best thoughts are mangled by the necessity of confining or extending them to the dimensions of a couplet; and rejoices that genius has, in our days, shaken off the shackles which had encumbered it so long. Yet he allows that rhyme may sometimes be borne, if the lines be often broken, and the pauses judiciously diversified.

From Blank Verse he makes an easy transition to *Milton*, whom he produces as an example of the slow advance of lasting reputation. *Milton* is the only writer whose books *Minim* can read for ever without weariness. What cause it is that exempts this pleasure from satiety he has long and diligently enquired, and believes it to consist in the perpetual variation of the numbers, by which the ear is gratified and the attention awakened. The lines that are commonly thought rugged and unmusical, he conceives to have been written to temper the melodious luxury of the rest, or to express things by a proper cadence: for he scarcely finds a verse that has not this favourite beauty; he declares that he could shiver in a hot-house when he reads that

> the ground
> Burns frore, and cold performs th' effect of fire.

And that when *Milton* bewails his blindness, the verse

> So thick a drop serene has quench'd these orbs,

has, he knows not how, something that strikes him with an obscure sensation like that which he fancies would be felt from the sound of Darkness.

Minim is not so confident of his rules of Judgment as not very eagerly to catch new light from the name of the author. He is commonly so prudent as to spare those whom he cannot resist, unless, as will sometimes happen, he finds the publick combined against them. But a fresh pretender to fame he is strongly inclined to censure, 'till his own honour requires that he commend him. 'Till he knows the success of a composition, he intrenches himself in general terms; there are some new thoughts and beautiful passages, but there is likewise much which he would have advised the author to expunge. He has several favourite epithets, of which he has never settled the meaning, but which are very commodiously applied to books which he has not read, or cannot understand. One is *manly*, another is *dry*, another *stiff*, and another *flimzy*; sometimes he discovers delicacy of style, and sometimes meets with *strange expressions*.

He is never so great, or so happy, as when a youth of promising parts is brought to receive his directions for the prosecution of his studies. He then puts on a very serious air; he advises the pupil to read none but the best Authors, and, when he finds one congenial to his own mind, to study his beauties, but avoid his faults, and, when he sits down to write, to consider how his favourite Author would think at the present time on the present occasion. He exhorts him to catch those moments when he finds his thoughts expanded and his genius exalted, but to take care lest imagination hurry him beyond the bounds of Nature. He holds Diligence the mother of Success, yet enjoins him, with great earnestness, not to read more than he can digest, and not to confuse his mind by pursuing studies of contrary tendencies. He tells him, that every man has his genius, and that *Cicero* could never be a Poet. The boy retires illuminated, resolves to follow his genius, and to think how *Milton* would have thought; and *Minim* feasts upon his own beneficence till another day brings another Pupil.

No. 65. Saturday, 14 July 1759.

The Sequel of *Clarendon*'s History,* at last happily published, is an accession to *English* Literature equally agreeable to the admirers of elegance and the lovers of truth; many doubtful facts may now be ascertained, and many questions, after long debate, may be determined by decisive authority. He that records transactions in which himself was engaged, has not only an opportunity of knowing innumerable particulars which escape spectators, but has his natural powers exalted by that ardour which always rises at the

---

* It would be proper to reposite, in some publick Place, the Manuscript of *Clarendon*, which has not escaped all suspicion of unfaithful publication.

remembrance of our own importance, and by which every man is enabled to relate his own actions better than another's.

The difficulties thro' which this Work has struggled into light, and the delays with which our hopes have been long mocked, naturally lead the mind to the consideration of the common fate of posthumous compositions.

He who sees himself surrounded by admirers, and whose vanity is hourly feasted with all the luxuries of studied praise, is easily persuaded that his influence will be extended beyond his life; that they who cringe in his presence will reverence his memory, and that those who are proud to be numbered among his friends, will endeavour to vindicate his choice by zeal for his reputation.

With hopes like these, to the Executors of *Swift* was committed the History of the last years of Queen *Anne*, and to those of *Pope* the Works which remained unprinted in his closet. The performances of *Pope* were burnt by those whom he had perhaps selected from all mankind as most likely to publish them; and the History had likewise perished, had not a straggling transcript fallen into busy hands.

The Papers left in the closet of *Peiresc* supplied his heirs with a whole winter's fuel, and many of the labours of the learned Bishop *Lloyd* were consumed in the kitchen of his descendants.

Some Works, indeed, have escaped total destruction, but yet have had reason to lament the fate of Orphans exposed to the frauds of unfaithful Guardians. How *Hale* would have borne the mutilations which his *Pleas of the Crown* have suffered from the Editor, they who know his character will easily conceive.

The original Copy of *Burnet*'s History, tho' promised to some publick Library, has been never given; and who then can prove the fidelity of the publication, when the authenticity of *Clarendon*'s History, tho' printed with the sanction of one of the first Universities of the World, had not an unexpected manuscript been happily discovered, would, with the help of factious credulity, have been brought into question by the two lowest of all human beings, a Scribbler for a Party, and a Commissioner of Excise?

Vanity is often no less mischievous than negligence or dishonesty. He that possesses a valuable Manuscript, hopes to raise its esteem by concealment, and delights in the distinction which he imagines himself to obtain by keeping the key of a treasure which he neither uses nor imparts. From him it falls to some other owner, less vain but more negligent, who considers it as useless lumber, and rids himself of the incumbrance.

Yet there are some works which the Authors must consign unpublished to posterity, however uncertain be the event, however hopeless be the trust. He that writes the history of his own times, if he adheres steadily to truth, will write that which his own times will not easily endure. He must be content to reposite his book till all private passions shall cease, and love and hatred give way to curiosity.

But many leave the labour of half their life to their executors and to chance, because they will not send them abroad unfinished, and are unable to finish them, having prescribed to themselves such a degree of exactness as human diligence scarcely can attain. *Lloyd*, says *Burnet*, *did not lay out his learning with the same diligence as he laid it in.* He was always hesitating and enquiring, raising objections and removing them, and waiting for clearer light and fuller discovery. *Baker*, after many years past in Biography, left his manuscripts to be buried in a library, because that was imperfect which could never be perfected.

Of these learned men let those who aspire to the same praise, imitate the diligence and avoid the scrupulosity. Let it be always remembered that life is short, that knowledge is endless, and that many doubts deserve not to be cleared. Let those whom nature and study have qualified to teach mankind, tell us what they have learned while they are yet able to tell it, and trust their reputation only to themselves.

No. 66. Saturday, 21 July 1759.

No complaint is more frequently repeated among the learned, than that of the waste made by time among the labours of Antiquity. Of those who once filled the civilized world with their renown nothing is now left but their names, which are left only to raise desires that never can be satisfied, and sorrow which never can be comforted.

Had all the writings of the ancients been faithfully delivered down from age to age, had the *Alexandrian* library been spared, and the *Palatine* repositories remained unimpaired, how much might we have known of which we are now doomed to be ignorant; how many laborious enquiries, and dark conjectures, how many collations of broken hints and mutilated passages might have been spared. We should have known the Successions of Princes, the Revolutions of Empire, the Actions of the Great, and Opinions of the Wise, the Laws and Constitutions of every State, and the Arts by which public Grandeur and Happiness are acquired and preserved. We should have traced the progress of Life, seen Colonies from distant regions take possession of *European* deserts, and troops of Savages settled into Communities by the desire of keeping what they had acquired; we should have traced the gradations of civility, and travelled upward to the original of things by the light of History, till in remoter times it had glimmered in fable, and at last sunk into darkness.

If the works of imagination had been less diminished, it is likely that all future times might have been supplied with inexhaustible amusement by the fictions of Antiquity. The Tragedies of *Sophocles* and *Euripides* would have shewn all the stronger passions in all their diversities, and the Comedies of *Menander* would have furnished all the maxims of domestic life. Nothing would have been necessary to moral wisdom but to have studied these great

Masters, whose knowledge would have guided doubt, and whose authority would have silenced cavils.

Such are the thoughts that rise in every Student, when his curiosity is eluded, and his searches are frustrated; yet it may perhaps be doubted, whether our complaints are not sometimes inconsiderate, and whether we do not imagine more evil than we feel. Of the Ancients, enough remains to excite our emulation, and direct our endeavours. Many of the works which time has left us, we know to have been those that were most esteemed, and which Antiquity itself considered as Models; so that having the Originals, we may without much regret lose the imitations. The obscurity which the want of contemporary writers often produces, only darkens single passages, and those commonly of slight importance. The general tendency of every piece may be known, and tho' that diligence deserves praise which leaves nothing unexamined, yet its miscarriages are not much to be lamented; for the most useful truths are always universal, and unconnected with accidents and customs.

Such is the general conspiracy of human nature against contemporary merit, that if we had inherited from Antiquity enough to afford employment for the laborious, and amusement for the idle, I know not what room would have been left for modern genius or modern industry; almost every subject would have been preoccupied, and every style would have been fixed by a precedent from which few would have ventured to depart. Every writer would have had a rival, whose superiority was already acknowledged, and to whose fame his work would, even before it was seen, be marked out for a sacrifice.

We see how little the united experience of mankind have been able to add to the heroic characters displayed by *Homer*, and how few incidents the fertile imagination of modern *Italy* has yet produced, which may not be found in the *Iliad* and *Odyssey*. It is likely, that if all the works of the *Athenian* Philosophers had been extant, *Malbranche* and *Locke* would have been condemned to be silent readers of the ancient Metaphysicians; and it is apparent, that if the old writers had all remained, the *Idler* could not have written a disquisition on the loss.

No. 72. Saturday, 1 September 1759.

Men complain of nothing more frequently than of deficient Memory; and indeed, every one finds that many of the ideas which he desired to retain have slipped irretrievably away; that the acquisitions of the mind are sometimes equally fugitive with the gifts of fortune; and that a short intermission of attention more certainly lessens knowledge than impairs an estate.

To assist this weakness of our nature many methods have been proposed, all of which may be justly suspected of being ineffectual; for no art of memory, however its effects have been boasted or admired, has been ever adopted into general use, nor have those who possessed it, appeared to excel others in readiness of recollection or multiplicity of attainments.

There is another art of which all have felt the want, tho' *Themistocles* only confessed it. We suffer equal pain from the pertinacious adhesion of unwelcome images, as from the evanescence of those which are pleasing and useful; and it may be doubted whether we should be more benefited by the art of Memory or the art of Forgetfulness.

Forgetfulness is necessary to Remembrance. Ideas are retained by renovation of that impression which time is always wearing away, and which new images are striving to obliterate. If useless thoughts could be expelled from the mind, all the valuable parts of our knowledge would more frequently recur, and every recurrence would reinstate them in their former place.

It is impossible to consider, without some regret, how much might have been learned, or how much might have been invented by a rational and vigorous application of time, uselessly or painfully passed in the revocation of events, which have left neither good nor evil behind them, in grief for misfortunes either repaired or irreparable, in resentment of injuries known only to ourselves, of which death has put the authors beyond our power.

Philosophy has accumulated precept upon precept, to warn us against the anticipation of future calamities. All useless misery is certainly folly, and he that feels evils before they come may be deservedly censured; yet surely to dread the future is more reasonable than to lament the past. The business of life is to go forwards; he who sees evil in prospect meets it in his way, but he who catches it by retrospection turns back to find it. That which is feared may sometimes be avoided, but that which is regretted to-day may be regretted again to-morrow.

Regret is indeed useful and virtuous, and not only allowable but necessary, when it tends to the amendment of life, or to admonition of error which we may be again in danger of committing. But a very small part of the moments spent in meditation on the past, produce any reasonable caution or salutary sorrow. Most of the mortifications that we have suffered, arose from the concurrence of local and temporary circumstances, which can never meet again; and most of our disappointments have succeeded those expectations, which life allows not to be formed a second time.

It would add much to human happiness, if an art could be taught of forgetting all of which the remembrance is at once useless and afflictive, if that pain which never can end in pleasure could be driven totally away, that the mind might perform its functions without incumbrance, and the past might no longer encroach upon the present.

Little can be done well to which the whole mind is not applied; the business of every day calls for the day to which it is assigned, and he will have no leisure to regret yesterday's vexations who resolves not to have a new subject of regret tomorrow.

But to forget or to remember at pleasure, are equally beyond the power of man. Yet as memory may be assisted by method, and the decays of knowledge repaired by stated times of recollection, so the power of forgetting is capable of improvement. Reason will, by a resolute contest, prevail over imagination, and the power may be obtained of transferring the attention as judgment shall direct.

The incursions of troublesome thoughts are often violent and importunate; and it is not easy to a mind accustomed to their inroads to expel them immediately by putting better images into motion; but this enemy of quiet is above all others weakened by every defeat; the reflection which has been once overpowered and ejected, seldom returns with any formidable vehemence.

Employment is the great instrument of intellectual dominion. The mind cannot retire from its enemy into total vacancy, or turn aside from one object but by passing to another. The gloomy and the resentful are always found among those who have nothing to do, or who do nothing. We must be busy about good or evil, and he to whom the present offers nothing will often be looking backward on the past.

No. 81. Saturday, 3 November 1759.

As the *English* army was passing towards *Quebec* along a soft savanna between a mountain and a lake, one of the petty Chiefs of the inland regions stood upon a rock surrounded by his clan, and from behind the shelter of the bushes contemplated the art and regularity of *European* war. It was evening, the tents were pitched, he observed the security with which the troops rested in the night, and the order with which the march was renewed in the morning. He continued to pursue them with his eye till they could be seen no longer, and then stood for some time silent and pensive.

Then turning to his followers, "My children (said he) I have often heard from men hoary with long life, that there was a time when our ancestors were absolute lords of the woods, the meadows, and the lakes, wherever the eye can reach or the foot can pass. They fished and hunted, feasted and danced, and when they were weary lay down under the first thicket, without danger and without fear. They changed their habitations as the seasons required, convenience prompted, or curiosity allured them, and sometimes gathered the fruits of the mountain, and sometimes sported in canoes along the coast.

"Many years and ages are supposed to have been thus passed in plenty and security; when at last, a new race of men entered our country from the great Ocean. They inclosed themselves in habitations of stone, which our ancestors could neither enter by violence, nor destroy by fire. They issued from those fastnesses, sometimes covered like the armadillo with shells, from which the lance rebounded on the striker, and sometimes carried by mighty beasts which had never been seen in our vales or forests, of such strength and swiftness, that flight and opposition were vain alike. Those invaders ranged over the continent, slaughtering in their rage those that resisted, and those that submitted, in their mirth. Of those that remained, some were buried in caverns, and condemned to dig metals for their masters; some were employed in tilling the ground, of which foreign tyrants devour the produce; and when the sword and the mines have destroyed the natives, they supply their place by human beings of another colour, brought from some distant country to perish here under toil and torture.

"Some there are who boast their humanity, and content themselves to seize our chaces and fisheries, who drive us from every track of ground where fertility and pleasantness invite them to settle, and make no war upon us except when we intrude upon our own lands.

"Others pretend to have purchased a right of residence and tyranny; but surely the insolence of such bargains is more offensive than the avowed and open dominion of force. What reward can induce the possessor of a country to admit a stranger more powerful than himself? Fraud or terror must operate in such contracts; either they promised protection which they never have afforded, or instruction which they never imparted. We hoped to be secured by their favour from some other evil, or to learn the arts of *Europe*, by which we might be able to secure ourselves. Their power they have never exerted in our defence, and their arts they have studiously concealed from us. Their treaties are only to deceive, and their traffick only to defraud us. They have a written Law among them, of which they boast as derived from him who made the Earth and Sea, and by which they profess to believe that man will be made happy when life shall forsake him. Why is not this Law communicated to us? It is concealed because it is violated. For how can they preach it to an *Indian* nation, when I am told that one of its first precepts forbids them to do to others what they would not that others should do to them.

"But the time perhaps is now approaching when the pride of usurpation shall be crushed, and the cruelties of invasion shall be revenged. The Sons of Rapacity have now drawn their swords upon each other, and referred their claims to the decision of war; let us look unconcerned upon the slaughter, and remember that the death of every *European* delivers the country from a tyrant and a robber; for what is the claim of either nation, but the claim of the vultur to the leveret, of the tiger to the faun? Let them then continue to dispute their title to regions which they cannot people, to purchase by danger and blood the empty dignity of dominion over mountains which they will never climb, and rivers which they will never pass. Let us endeavour, in the mean time, to learn their discipline, and to forge their weapons; and when they shall be weakened with mutual slaughter, let us rush down upon them, force their remains to take shelter in their ships, and reign once more in our native country."

No. 84. Saturday, 24 November 1759.

Biography is, of the various kinds of narrative writing, that which is most eagerly read, and most easily applied to the purposes of life.

In Romances, when the wild field of Possibility lies open to invention, the incidents may easily be made more numerous, the vicissitudes more sudden, and the events more wonderful; but from the time of life when Fancy begins to be over-ruled by Reason and corrected by Experience, the most artful tale raises little curiosity when it is known to be false; tho' it may, perhaps, be sometimes read as a model of a neat or elegant stile, not for the sake of knowing what it contains, but how it is written; or those that are weary of themselves, may have recourse to it as a pleasing dream, of which, when they awake, they voluntarily dismiss the images from their minds.

The examples and events of History press, indeed, upon the mind with the weight of truth; but when they are reposited in the memory, they are oftener employed for shew than use, and rather diversify conversation than regulate life. Few are engaged in such scenes as give them opportunities of growing wiser by the downfal of Statesmen or the defeat of Generals. The stratagems of War, and the intrigues of Courts, are read by far the greater part of mankind with the same indifference as the adventures of fabled Heroes, or the revolutions of a Fairy Region. Between falsehood and useless truth there is little difference. As gold which he cannot spend will make no man rich, so knowledge which he cannot apply will make no man wise.

The mischievous consequences of vice and folly, of irregular desires and predominant passions, are best discovered by those relations which are levelled with the general surface of life, which tell not how any man became great, but how he was made happy; not how he lost the favour of his Prince, but how he became discontented with himself.

Those relations are therefore commonly of most value in which the writer tells his own story. He that recounts the life of another, commonly dwells most upon conspicuous events, lessens the familiarity of his tale to increase its dignity, shews his favourite at a distance decorated and magnified like the ancient actors in their tragick dress, and endeavours to hide the man that he may produce a hero.

But if it be true which was said by a *French* Prince, *That no man was a Hero to the servants of his chamber*, it is equally true that every man is yet less a Hero to himself. He that is most elevated above the croud by the importance of his employments or the reputation of his genius, feels himself affected by fame or business but as they influence his domestick life. The high and low, as they have the same faculties and the same senses, have no less similitude in their pains and pleasures. The sensations are the same in all, tho' produced by very different occasions. The Prince feels the same pain when an invader seizes a province, as the Farmer when a thief drives away his cow. Men thus equal in themselves will appear equal in honest and impartial Biography; and those whom Fortune or Nature place at the greatest distance may afford instruction to each other.

The writer of his own life has at least the first qualification of an Historian, the knowledge of the truth; and though it may be plausibly objected that his temptations to disguise it are equal to his opportunities of knowing it, yet I cannot but think that impartiality may be expected with equal confidence from him that relates the passages of his own life, as from him that delivers the transactions of another.

Certainty of knowledge not only excludes mistake but fortifies veracity. What we collect by conjecture, and by conjecture only can one man judge of another's motives or sentiments, is easily modified by fancy or by desire; as objects imperfectly discerned, take forms from the hope or fear of the beholder. But that which is fully known cannot be falsified but with reluctance of understanding, and alarm of conscience; of Understanding, the lover of Truth; of Conscience, the sentinel of Virtue.

He that writes the Life of another is either his friend or his enemy, and wishes either to exalt his praise or aggravate his infamy; many temptations to falsehood will occur in the disguise of passions, too specious to fear much resistance. Love of Virtue will animate Panegyrick, and hatred of Wickedness imbitter Censure. The Zeal of Gratitude, the Ardour of Patriotism, Fondness for an Opinion, or Fidelity to a Party, may easily overpower the vigilance of a mind habitually well disposed, and prevail over unassisted and unfriended Veracity.

But he that speaks of himself has no motive to Falshood or Partiality except Self-love, by which all have so often been betrayed, that all are on the watch against its artifices. He that writes an Apology for a single Action, to confute an Accusation, or recommend himself to Favour, is indeed always to be suspected of favouring his own cause; but he that sits down calmly and voluntarily to review his Life for the admonition of Posterity, or to amuse himself, and leaves this account unpublished, may be commonly presumed to tell Truth, since Falshood cannot appease his own Mind, and Fame will not be heard beneath the Tomb.

No. 88. Saturday, 22 December 1759.

When the Philosophers of the last Age were first congregated into the Royal Society, great expectations were raised of the sudden progress of useful Arts; the time was supposed to be near when Engines should turn by a perpetual Motion, and Health be secured by the universal Medicine; when Learning should be facilitated by a real Character, and Commerce extended by ships which could reach their Ports in defiance of the Tempest.

But Improvement is naturally slow. The Society met and parted without any visible diminution of the miseries of life. The Gout and Stone were still painful, the Ground that was not plowed brought no Harvest, and neither Oranges nor Grapes would grow upon the Hawthorn. At last, those who were disappointed began to be angry; those likewise who hated innovation were glad to gain an opportunity of ridiculing men who had depreciated, perhaps with too much arrogance, the Knowledge of Antiquity. And it appears from some of their earliest Apologies, that the Philosophers felt with great sensibility the unwelcome importunities of those who were daily asking, "What have ye done?"

The truth is, that little had been done compared with what Fame had been suffered to promise; and the question could only be answered by general apologies and by new hopes, which, when they were frustrated, gave a new occasion to the same vexatious enquiry.

This fatal question has disturbed the quiet of many other minds. He that in the latter part of his life too strictly enquires what he has done, can very seldom receive from his own heart such an account as will give him satisfaction.

We do not indeed so often disappoint others as ourselves. We not only think more highly than others of our own abilities, but allow ourselves to form hopes which we never communicate, and please our thoughts with employments which none ever will allot us, and with elevations to which we are never expected to rise; and when our days and years have passed away in common business or common amusements, and we find at last that we have suffered our purposes to sleep till the time of action is past, we are reproached only by our own reflections; neither our friends nor our enemies wonder that we live and die like the rest of mankind, that we live without notice and die without memorial; they know not what task we had proposed, and therefore cannot discern whether it is finished.

He that compares what he has done with what he has left undone, will feel the effect which must always follow the comparison of imagination with reality; he will look with contempt on his own unimportance, and wonder to what purpose he came into the world; he will repine that he shall leave behind him no evidence of his having been, that he has added nothing to the system of life, but has glided from Youth to Age among the crowd, without any effort for distinction.

Man is seldom willing to let fall the opinion of his own dignity, or to believe that he does little only because every individual is a very little being. He is better content to want Diligence than Power, and sooner confesses the Depravity of his Will than the Imbecillity of his Nature.

From this mistaken notion of human Greatness it proceeds, that many who pretend to have made great Advances in Wisdom so loudly declare that they despise themselves. If I had ever found any of the Self-contemners much irritated or pained by the consciousness of their meanness, I should have given them consolation by observing, that a little more than nothing is as much as can be expected from a being who with respect to the multitudes about him is himself little more than nothing. Every man is obliged by the supreme Master of the Universe to improve all the opportunities of Good which are afforded him, and to keep in continual activity such Abilities as are bestowed upon him. But he has no reason to repine though his Abilities are small and his Opportunities few. He that has improved the Virtue or advanced the Happiness of one Fellow-creature, he that has ascertained a single moral Proposition, or added one useful Experiment to natural Knowledge, may be contented with his own Performance, and, with respect to mortals like himself, may demand, like *Augustus*, to be dismissed at his departure with Applause.

No. 94. Saturday, 2 February 1760.

It is common to find young men ardent and diligent in the pursuit of knowledge, but the progress of life very often produces laxity and indifference; and not only those who are at liberty to chuse their business and amusements, but those likewise whose professions engage them in literary enquiries pass the latter part of their time without improvement, and spend the day rather in any other entertainment than that which they might find among their books.

This abatement of the vigour of curiosity is sometimes imputed to the insufficiency of Learning. Men are supposed to remit their labours, because they find their labours to have been vain; and to search no longer after Truth and Wisdom, because they at last despair of finding them.

But this reason is for the most part very falsely assigned. Of Learning, as of Virtue, it may be affirmed, that it is at once honoured and neglected. Whoever forsakes it will for ever look after it with longing, lament the loss which he does not endeavour to repair, and desire the good which he wants resolution to seize and keep. The Idler never applauds his own Idleness, nor does any man repent of the diligence of his youth.

So many hindrances may obstruct the acquisition of Knowledge, that there is little reason for wondering that it is in a few hands. To the greater part of mankind the duties of life are inconsistent with much study, and the hours which they would spend upon letters must be stolen from their occupations and their families. Many suffer themselves to be lured by more spritely and luxurious pleasures from the shades of Contemplation, where they find seldom more than a calm delight, such as, though greater than all others, if its certainty and its duration be reckoned with its power of gratification, is yet easily quitted for some extemporary joy, which the present moment offers, and another perhaps will put out of reach.

It is the great excellence of Learning that it borrows very little from time or place; it is not confined to season or to climate, to cities or to the country, but may be cultivated and enjoyed where no other pleasure can be obtained. But this quality, which constitutes much of its value, is one occasion of neglect; what may be done at all times with equal propriety, is deferred from day to day, till the mind is gradually reconciled to the omission, and the attention is turned to other objects. Thus habitual idleness gains too much power to be conquered, and the soul shrinks from the idea of intellectual labour and intenseness of meditation.

That those who profess to advance Learning sometimes obstruct it, cannot be denied; the continual multiplication of books not only distracts choice but disappoints enquiry. To him that has moderately stored his mind with images, few writers afford any novelty; or what little they have to add to the common stock of Learning is so buried in the mass of general notions, that, like silver mingled with the oar of lead, it is too little to pay for the labour of separation; and he that has often been deceived by the promise of a title, at last grows weary of examining, and is tempted to consider all as equally fallacious.

There are indeed some repetitions always lawful, because they never deceive. He that writes the History of past times, undertakes only to decorate known facts by new beauties of method or of style, or at most to illustrate them by his own reflections. The Author of a system, whether moral or physical, is obliged to nothing beyond care of selection and regularity of disposition. But there are others who claim the name of Authors merely to disgrace it, and fill the world with volumes only to bury letters in their own rubbish. The Traveller who tells, in a pompous Folio, that he saw the *Pantheon* at *Rome*, and the *Medicean Venus* at *Florence*; the Natural Historian who, describing the productions of a narrow Island, recounts all that it has in common with every other part of the world; the Collector of Antiquities, that accounts every thing a curiosity which the Ruins of *Herculaneum* happen to emit, though an instrument already shewn in a thousand repositories, or a cup common to the ancients, the moderns, and all mankind, may be justly censured as the Persecutors of Students, and the Thieves of that Time which never can be restored.

No. 100. Saturday, 15 March 1760.

To the IDLER.

SIR,

The uncertainty and defects of Language have produced very frequent complaints among the Learned; yet there still remain many words among us undefined, which are very necessary to be rightly understood, and which produce very mischievous mistakes when they are erroneously interpreted.

I lived in a state of celibacy beyond the usual time. In the hurry first of pleasure and afterwards of business, I felt no want of a domestick companion; but becoming weary of labour I soon grew more weary of idleness, and thought it reasonable to follow the custom of life, and to seek some solace of my cares in female tenderness, and some amusement of my leisure in female chearfulness.

The choice which has been long delayed is commonly made at last with great caution. My resolution was to keep my passions neutral, and to marry only in compliance with my reason. I drew upon a page of my pocket book a scheme of all female virtues and vices, with the vices which border upon every virtue, and the virtues which are allied to every vice. I considered that wit was sarcastick, and magnanimity imperious; that avarice was economical, and ignorance obsequious; and having estimated the good and evil of every quality, employed my own diligence and that of my friends to find the lady in whom nature and reason had reached that happy mediocrity which is equally remote from exuberance and deficience.

Every woman had her admirers and her censurers, and the expectations which one raised were by another quickly depressed: yet there was one in whose favour almost all suffrages concurred. Miss *Gentle* was universally allowed to be a good sort of woman. Her fortune was not large, but so prudently managed, that she wore finer cloaths and saw more company than many who were known to be twice as rich. Miss *Gentle*'s visits were every where welcome, and whatever family she favoured with her company, she always left behind her such a degree of kindness as recommended her to others; every day extended her acquaintance, and all who knew her declared that they never met with a better sort of woman.

To Miss *Gentle* I made my addresses, and was received with great equality of temper. She did not in the days of courtship assume the privilege of imposing rigorous commands, or resenting slight offences. If I forgot any of her injunctions I was gently reminded, if I missed the minute of appointment I was easily forgiven. I foresaw nothing in marriage but a halcyon calm, and longed for the happiness which was to be found in the inseparable society of a good sort of woman.

The jointure was soon settled by the intervention of friends, and the day came in which Miss *Gentle* was made mine for ever. The first month was passed easily enough in receiving and repaying the civilities of our friends. The bride practised with great exactness all the niceties of ceremony, and distributed her notice in the most punctilious proportions to the friends who surrounded us with their happy auguries.

But the time soon came when we were left to ourselves, and were to receive our pleasures from each other, and I then began to perceive that I was not formed to be much delighted by a good sort of woman. Her great principle is, that the orders of a family must not be broken. Every hour of the day has its employment inviolably appropriated, nor will any importunity persuade her to walk in the garden, at the time which she has devoted to her needlework, or to sit up stairs in that part of the forenoon, which she has accustomed herself to spend in the back parlour. She allows herself to sit half an hour after breakfast, and an hour after dinner; while I am talking or reading to her, she keeps her eye upon her watch, and when the minute of departure comes, will leave an argument unfinished, or the intrigue of a play unravelled. She once called me to supper when I was watching an eclipse, and summoned me at another time to bed when I was going to give directions at a fire.

Her conversation is so habitually cautious, that she never talks to me but in general terms, as to one whom it is dangerous to trust. For discriminations of character she has no names; all whom she mentions are honest men and agreeable women. She smiles not by sensation but by practice. Her laughter is never excited but by a joke, and her notion of a joke is not very delicate. The repetition of a good joke does not weaken its effect; if she has laughed once, she will laugh again.

She is an enemy to nothing but ill nature and pride, but she has frequent reason to lament that they are so frequent in the world. All who are not equally pleased with the good and bad, with the elegant and gross, with the witty and the dull, all who distinguish excellence from defect she considers as ill-natured; and she condemns as proud all who repress impertinence or quell presumption, or expect respect from any other eminence than that of fortune, to which she is always willing to pay homage.

There are none whom she openly hates; for if once she suffers, or believes herself to suffer, any contempt or insult, she never dismisses it from her mind but takes all opportunities to tell how easily she can forgive. There are none whom she loves much better than others; for when any of her acquaintance decline in the opinion of the world she always finds it inconvenient to visit them; her affection continues unaltered but it is impossible to be intimate with the whole town.

She daily exercises her benevolence by pitying every misfortune that happens to every family within her circle of notice; she is in hourly terrors lest one should catch cold in the rain, and another be frighted by the high wind. Her charity she shews by lamenting that so many poor wretches should languish in the streets, and by wondering what the great can think on that they do so little good with such large estates.

Her house is elegant and her table dainty though she has little taste of elegance, and is wholly free from vicious luxury; but she comforts herself that nobody can say that her house is dirty, or that her dishes are not well drest.

This, Mr. *Idler*, I have found by long experience to be the character of a good sort of woman, which I have sent you for the information of those by whom *a good sort of woman* and *a good woman* may happen to be used as equivalent terms, and who may suffer by the mistake like

Your humble servant,
TIM WARNER.

No. 103. Saturday, 5 April 1760.

Respicere ad longæ jussit spatia ultima vitæ.
JUV.

Much of the Pain and Pleasure of mankind arises from the conjectures which every one makes of the thoughts of others; we all enjoy praise which we do not hear, and resent contempt which we do not see. The *Idler* may therefore be forgiven, if he suffers his Imagination to represent to him what his readers will say or think when they are informed that they have now his last paper in their hands.

Value is more frequently raised by scarcity than by use. That which lay neglected when it was common, rises in estimation as its quantity becomes less. We seldom learn the true want of what we have till it is discovered that we can have no more.

This essay will, perhaps, be read with care even by those who have not yet attended to any other; and he that finds this late attention recompensed, will not forbear to wish that he had bestowed it sooner.

Though the *Idler* and his readers have contracted no close friendship they are perhaps both unwilling to part. There are few things not purely evil, of which we can say, without some emotion of uneasiness, *this is the last.* Those who never could agree together, shed tears when mutual discontent has determined them to final separation; of a place which has been frequently visited, tho' without pleasure, the last look is taken with heaviness of heart; and the *Idler*, with all his chilness of tranquillity, is not wholly unaffected by the thought that his last essay is now before him.

This secret horrour of the last is inseparable from a thinking being whose life is limited, and to whom death is dreadful. We always make a secret comparison between a part and the whole; the termination of any period of life reminds us that life itself has likewise its termination; when we have done any thing for the last time, we involuntarily reflect that a part of the days allotted us is past, and that as more is past there is less remaining.

It is very happily and kindly provided, that in every life there are certain pauses and interruptions, which force consideration upon the careless, and seriousness upon the light; points of time where one course of action ends and another begins; and by vicissitude of fortune, or alteration of employment, by change of place, or loss of friendship, we are forced to say of something, *this is the last.*

An even and unvaried tenour of life always hides from our apprehension the approach of its end. Succession is not perceived but by variation; he that lives to-day as he lived yesterday, and expects that, as the present day is, such will be the morrow, easily conceives time as running in a circle and returning to itself. The uncertainty of our duration is impressed commonly by dissimilitude of condition; it is only by finding life changeable that we are reminded of its shortness.

This conviction, however forcible at every new impression, is every moment fading from the mind; and partly by the inevitable incursion of new images, and partly by voluntary exclusion of unwelcome thoughts, we are again exposed to the universal fallacy; and we must do another thing for the last time, before we consider that the time is nigh when we shall do no more.

As the last *Idler* is published in that solemn week which the Christian world has always set apart for the examination of the conscience, the review of life, the extinction of earthly desires and the renovation of holy purposes, I hope that my readers are already disposed to view every incident with seriousness, and improve it by meditation; and that when they see this series of trifles brought to a conclusion, they will consider that by outliving the *Idler*, they have past weeks, months, and years which are now no longer in their power; that an end must in time be put to every thing great as to every thing little; that to life must come its last hour, and to this system of being its last day, the hour at which probation ceases, and repentance will be vain; the day in which every work of the hand, and imagination of the heart shall be brought to judgment, and an everlasting futurity shall be determined by the past.

Letter to Sarah Johnson

SATURDAY 20 JANUARY 1759

Dear honoured Mother,   Jan. 20, 1759
Neither your condition nor your character make it fit for me to say much. You have been the best mother, and I believe the best woman in the world. I thank you for your indulgence to me, and beg forgiveness of all that I have done ill, and all that I have omitted to do well. God grant you his Holy Spirit, and receive you to everlasting happiness, for Jesus Christ's sake. Amen. Lord Jesus receive your spirit. Amen. I am, dear, dear Mother, your dutiful Son,

SAM. JOHNSON

Letter to William Strahan

SATURDAY 20 JANUARY 1759

Sir: Jan. 20, 1759
When I was with you last night I told you of a thing which I was preparing for the press. The title will be The choice of Life or The History of——Prince of Abissinia.

It will make about two volumes like little Pompadour that is about one middling volume. The bargain which I made with Mr. Johnston was seventy five pounds (or guineas) a volume, and twenty five pounds for the second Edition. I will sell this either at that price or for sixty, the first edition of which he shall himself fix the number, and the property then to revert to me, or for forty pounds, and share the profit that is retain half the copy. I shall have occasion for thirty pounds on Monday night when I shall deliver the book which I must entreat you upon such delivery to procure me. I would have it offered to Mr. Johnston, but have no doubt of selling it, on some of the terms mentioned.

I will not print my name but expect it to be known. I am, Dear sir, your most humble servant,

SAM. JOHNSON

Get me the money if you can.

Letter to Lucy Porter
TUESDAY 23 JANUARY 1759

Jan. 23, 1759

You will conceive my sorrow for the loss of my mother, of the best mother. If she were to live again, surely I should behave better to her. But she is happy, and what is past is nothing to her; and for me, since I cannot repair my faults to her, I hope repentance will efface them. I return you and all those that have been good to her my sincerest thanks, and pray God to repay you all with infinite advantage. Write to me, and comfort me, dear child. I shall be glad likewise, if Kitty will write to me. I shall send a bill of twenty pounds in a few days, which I thought to have brought to my mother; but God suffered it not. I have not power or composure to say much more. God bless you, and bless us all. I am, dear Miss, Your affectionate humble Servant,

SAM. JOHNSON

Diary entry and prayer
TUESDAY 23 JANUARY 1759

Jan. 23.

The day on which my dear Mother was buried. Repeated on my fast, with the addition.

Almighty God, merciful Father, in whose hands are life and death, sanctify unto me the sorrow which I now feel. Forgive me whatever I have done unkindly to my mother, and whatever I have omitted to do kindly. Make me to remember her good precepts and good example, and to reform my life according to thy holy word, that I may lose no more opportunities of good. I am sorrowful, O Lord; let not my sorrow be without fruit. Let it be followed by holy resolutions, and lasting amendment, that when I shall die like my mother, I may be received to everlasting life.

I commend, O Lord, so far as it may be lawful, into thy hands, the soul of my departed mother, beseeching Thee to grant her whatever is most beneficial to her in her present state.

O Lord, grant me thy Holy Spirit, and have mercy upon me for Jesus Christ's sake. Amen.

And, O Lord, grant unto me that am now about to return to the common comforts and business of the world, such moderation in all enjoyments, such diligence in honest labour, and such purity of mind, that, amidst the changes, miseries, or pleasures of life, I may keep my mind fixed upon Thee, and improve every day in grace, till I shall be received into thy kingdom of eternal happiness.

I returned thanks for my mother's good example, and implored pardon for neglecting it.

I returned thanks for the alleviation of my sorrow.

The dream of my brother I shall remember.

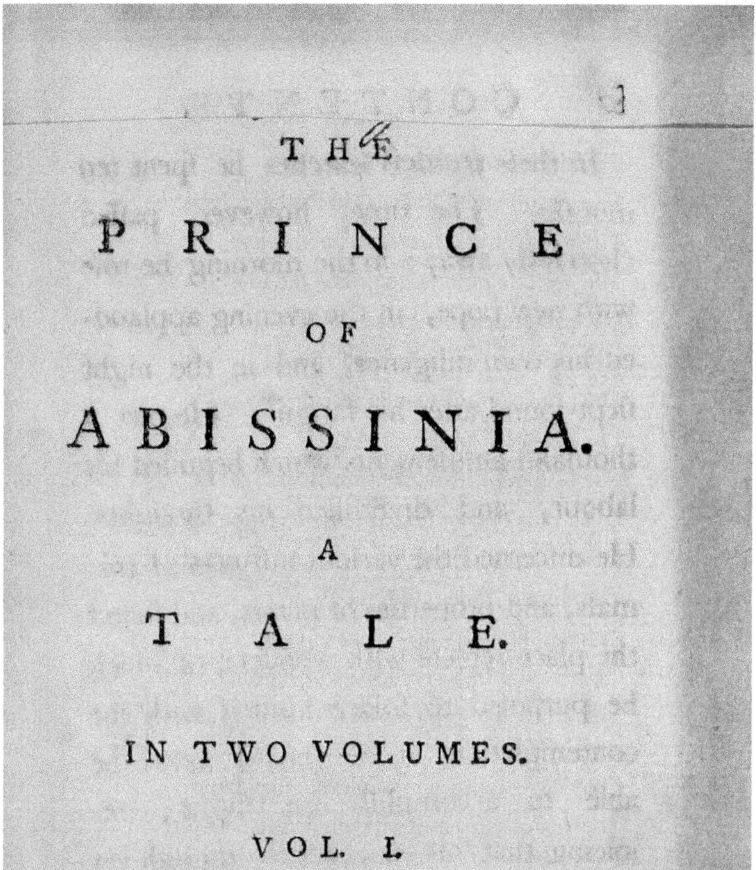

THE

PRINCE

OF

ABISSINIA.

A

TALE.

IN TWO VOLUMES.

VOL. I.

LONDON:

Printed for R. and J. DODSLEY, in Pall-Mall;
and W. JOHNSTON, in Ludgate-Street.
MDCCLIX.

FIGURE 7 *The Prince of Abissinia [Rasselas]* (1759), title page (Bodl. Vet. A5 f. 2417). Courtesy of the Bodleian Library, University of Oxford.

Rasselas

Contents

CHAP. I

Description of a palace in a valley

YE who listen with credulity to the whispers of fancy, and pursue with eagerness the phantoms of hope; who expect that age will perform the promises of youth, and that the deficiencies of the present day will be supplied by the morrow; attend to the history of Rasselas prince of Abissinia.

Rasselas was the fourth son of the mighty emperour, in whose dominions the Father of waters begins his course; whose bounty pours down the streams of plenty, and scatters over half the world the harvests of Egypt.

According to the custom which has descended from age to age among the monarchs of the torrid zone, Rasselas was confined in a private palace, with the other sons and daughters of Abissinian royalty, till the order of succession should call him to the throne.

The place, which the wisdom or policy of antiquity had destined for the residence of the Abissinian princes, was a spacious valley in the kingdom of Amhara, surrounded on every side by mountains, of which the summits over-hang the middle part. The only passage, by which it could be entered, was a cavern that passed under a rock, of which it has long been disputed whether it was the work of nature or of human industry. The outlet of the cavern was concealed by a thick wood, and the mouth which opened into the valley was closed with gates of iron, forged by the artificers of ancient days, so massy that no man could, without the help of engines, open or shut them.

From the mountains on every side, rivulets descended that filled all the valley with verdure and fertility, and formed a lake in the middle inhabited by fish of every species, and frequented by every fowl whom nature has taught to dip the wing in water. This lake discharged its superfluities by a stream which entered a dark cleft of the mountain on the northern side, and fell with dreadful noise from precipice to precipice till it was heard no more.

The sides of the mountains were covered with trees, the banks of the brooks were diversified with flowers; every blast shook spices from the rocks, and every month dropped fruits upon the ground. All animals that bite the grass, or brouse the shrub, whether wild or tame, wandered in this extensive circuit, secured from beasts of prey by the mountains which confined them. On one part were flocks and herds feeding in the pastures, on another all the beasts of chase frisking in the lawns; the sprightly kid was bounding on the rocks, the subtle monkey frolicking in the trees, and the solemn elephant reposing in the shade. All the diversities of the world were brought together, the blessings of nature were collected, and its evils extracted and excluded.

The valley, wide and fruitful, supplied its inhabitants with the necessaries of life, and all delights and superfluities were added at the annual visit which the emperour paid his children, when the iron gate was opened to the sound of musick; and during eight days every one that resided in the valley was required to propose whatever might contribute to make seclusion pleasant, to fill up the vacancies of attention, and lessen the tediousness of time. Every desire was immediately granted. All the artificers of pleasure were called to gladden the festivity; the musicians exerted the power of harmony, and the dancers shewed their activity before the princes, in hope that they should pass their lives in this blissful captivity to which these only were admitted whose performance was thought able to add novelty to luxury. Such was the appear-ance of security and delight which this retirement afforded, that they to whom it was new always desired that it might be perpetual; and as those, on whom the iron gate had once closed, were never suffered to return, the effect of longer experience could not be known. Thus every year produced new schemes of delight, and new competitors for imprisonment.

The palace stood on an eminence raised about thirty paces above the surface of the lake. It was divided into many squares or courts, built with greater or less magnificence according to the rank of those for whom they were designed. The roofs were turned into arches of massy stone joined with a cement that grew harder by time, and the building stood from century to century, deriding the solstitial rains and equinoctial hurricanes, without need of reparation.

This house, which was so large as to be fully known to none but some ancient officers who successively inherited the secrets of the place, was built as if suspicion herself had dictated the plan. To every room there was an open and secret passage, every square had a communication with the rest, either from the upper stories by private galleries, or by subterranean passages from the lower apartments. Many of the columns had unsuspected cavities, in which a long race of monarchs had reposited their treasures. They then closed up the opening with marble, which was never to be removed but in the utmost exigencies of the kingdom; and recorded their accumulations in a book which was itself concealed in a tower not entered but by the emperour, attended by the prince who stood next in succession.

CHAP. II

The discontent of Rasselas in the happy valley

HERE the sons and daughters of Abissinia lived only to know the soft vicissitudes of pleasure and repose, attended by all that were skilful to delight, and gratified with whatever the senses can enjoy. They wandered in gardens of fragrance, and slept in the fortresses of security. Every art was practised to make them pleased with their own condition. The sages who instructed them, told them of nothing but the miseries of publick life, and described all beyond the mountains as regions of calamity, where discord was always raging, and where man preyed upon man.

To heighten their opinion of their own felicity, they were daily entertained with songs, the subject of which was the *happy valley*. Their appetites were excited by frequent enumerations of different enjoyments, and revelry and merriment was the business of every hour from the dawn of morning to the close of even.

These methods were generally successful; few of the Princes had ever wished to enlarge their bounds, but passed their lives in full conviction that they had all within their reach that art or nature could bestow, and pitied those whom fate had excluded from this seat of tranquility, as the sport of chance, and the slaves of misery.

Thus they rose in the morning, and lay down at night, pleased with each other and with themselves, all but Rasselas, who, in the twenty-sixth year of his age, began to withdraw himself from their pastimes and assemblies, and to delight in solitary walks and silent meditation. He often sat before tables covered with luxury, and forgot to taste the dainties that were placed before him:

he rose abruptly in the midst of the song, and hastily retired beyond the sound of musick. His attendants observed the change and endeavoured to renew his love of pleasure: he neglected their officiousness, repulsed their invitations, and spent day after day on the banks of rivulets sheltered with trees, where he sometimes listened to the birds in the branches, sometimes observed the fish playing in the stream, and anon cast his eyes upon the pastures and mountains filled with animals, of which some were biting the herbage, and some sleeping among the bushes.

This singularity of his humour made him much observed. One of the Sages, in whose conversation he had formerly delighted, followed him secretly, in hope of discovering the cause of his disquiet. Rasselas, who knew not that any one was near him, having for some time fixed his eyes upon the goats that were brousing among the rocks, began to compare their condition with his own.

'What,' said he, 'makes the difference between man and all the rest of the animal creation? Every beast that strays beside me has the same corporal necessities with myself; he is hungry and crops the grass, he is thirsty and drinks the stream, his thirst and hunger are appeased, he is satisfied and sleeps; he rises again and is hungry, he is again fed and is at rest. I am hungry and thirsty like him, but when thirst and hunger cease I am not at rest; I am, like him, pained with want, but am not, like him, satisfied with fulness. The intermediate hours are tedious and gloomy; I long again to be hungry that I may again quicken my attention. The birds peck the berries or the corn, and fly away to the groves where they sit in seeming happiness on the branches, and waste their lives in tuning one unvaried series of sounds. I likewise can call the lutanist and the singer, but the sounds that pleased me yesterday weary me to day, and will grow yet more wearisome to morrow. I can discover within me no power of perception which is not glutted with its proper pleasure, yet I do not feel myself delighted. Man has surely some latent sense for which this place affords no gratification, or he has some desires distinct from sense which must be satisfied before he can be happy.'

After this he lifted up his head, and seeing the moon rising, walked towards the palace. As he passed through the fields, and saw the animals around him, 'Ye, said he, are happy, and need not envy me that walk thus among you, burthened with myself; nor do I, ye gentle beings, envy your felicity; for it is not the felicity of man. I have many distresses from which ye are free; I fear pain when I do not feel it; I sometimes shrink at evils recollected, and sometimes start at evils anticipated: surely the equity of providence has ballanced peculiar sufferings with peculiar enjoyments.'

With observations like these the prince amused himself as he returned, uttering them with a plaintive voice, yet with a look that discovered him to feel some complacence in his own perspicacity, and to receive some solace of the miseries of life, from consciousness of the delicacy with which he felt, and the eloquence with which he bewailed them. He mingled cheerfully in the diversions of the evening, and all rejoiced to find that his heart was lightened.

CHAP. III

The wants of him that wants nothing

ON the next day his old instructor, imagining that he had now made himself acquainted with his disease of mind, was in hope of curing it by counsel, and officiously sought an opportunity of conference, which the prince, having long considered him as one whose intellects were exhausted, was not very willing to afford: 'Why, said he, does this man thus intrude upon me; shall I be never suffered to forget those lectures which pleased only while they were new, and to become new again must be forgotten?' He then walked into the wood, and composed himself to his usual meditations; when, before his thoughts had taken any settled form, he perceived his persuer at his side, and was at first prompted by his impatience to go hastily away; but, being unwilling to offend a man whom he had once reverenced and still loved, he invited him to sit down with him on the bank.

The old man, thus encouraged, began to lament the change which had been lately observed in the prince, and to enquire why he so often retired from the pleasures of the palace, to loneliness and silence. 'I fly from pleasure, said the prince, because pleasure has ceased to please; I am lonely because I am miserable, and am unwilling to cloud with my presence the happiness of others.' 'You, Sir, said the sage, are the first who has complained of misery in the *happy valley*. I hope to convince you that your complaints have no real cause. You are here in full possession of all that the emperour of Abissinia can bestow; here is neither labour to be endured nor danger to be dreaded, yet here is all that labour or danger can procure or purchase. Look round and tell me which of your wants is without supply: if you want nothing, how are you unhappy?'

'That I want nothing, said the prince, or that I know not what I want, is the cause of my complaint; if I had any known want, I should have a certain wish; that wish would excite endeavour, and I should not then repine to see the sun move so slowly towards the western mountain, or lament when the day breaks and sleep will no longer hide me from myself. When I see the kids and the lambs chasing one another, I fancy that I should be happy if I had something to persue. But, possessing all that I can want, I find one day and one hour exactly like another, except that the latter is still more tedious than the former. Let your experience inform me how the day may now seem as short as in my childhood, while nature was yet fresh, and every moment shewed me what I never had observed before. I have already enjoyed too much; give me something to desire.'

The old man was surprized at this new species of affliction, and knew not what to reply, yet was unwilling to be silent. 'Sir, said he, if you had seen the miseries of the world, you would know how to value your present state.' 'Now, said the prince, you have given me something to desire; I shall long to see the miseries of the world, since the sight of them is necessary to happiness.'

CHAP. IV

The prince continues to grieve and muse

AT this time the sound of musick proclaimed the hour of repast, and the conversation was concluded. The old man went away sufficiently discontented to find that his reasonings had produced the only conclusion which they were intended to prevent. But in the decline of life shame and grief are of short duration; whether it be that we bear easily what we have born long, or that, finding ourselves in age less regarded, we less regard others; or, that we look with slight regard upon afflictions, to which we know that the hand of death is about to put an end.

The prince, whose views were extended to a wider space, could not speedily quiet his emotions. He had been before terrified at the length of life which nature promised him, because he considered that in a long time much must be endured; he now rejoiced in his youth, because in many years much might be done.

This first beam of hope, that had been ever darted into his mind, rekindled youth in his cheeks, and doubled the lustre of his eyes. He was fired with the desire of doing something, though he knew not yet with distinctness, either end or means.

He was now no longer gloomy and unsocial; but, considering himself as master of a secret stock of happiness, which he could enjoy only by concealing it, he affected to be busy in all schemes of diversion, and endeavoured to make others pleased with the state of which he himself was weary. But pleasures never can be so multiplied or continued, as not to leave much of life unemployed; there were many hours, both of the night and day, which he could spend without suspicion in solitary thought. The load of life was much lightened: he went eagerly into the assemblies, because he supposed the frequency of his presence necessary to the success of his purposes; he retired gladly to privacy, because he had now a subject of thought.

His chief amusement was to picture to himself that world which he had never seen; to place himself in various conditions; to be entangled in imaginary difficulties, and to be engaged in wild adventures: but his benevolence always terminated his projects in the relief of distress, the detection of fraud, the defeat of oppression, and the diffusion of happiness.

Thus passed twenty months of the life of Rasselas. He busied himself so intensely in visionary bustle, that he forgot his real solitude; and, amidst hourly preparations for the various incidents of human affairs, neglected to consider by what means he should mingle with mankind.

One day, as he was sitting on a bank, he feigned to himself an orphan virgin robbed of her little portion by a treacherous lover, and crying after him for restitution and redress. So strongly was the image impressed upon his mind, that he started up in the maid's defence, and run forward to seize the plunderer with all the eagerness of real persuit. Fear naturally quickens the flight of guilt. Rasselas could not catch the fugitive with his utmost efforts; but, resolving to weary, by perseverance, him whom he could not surpass in speed, he pressed on till the foot of the mountain stopped his course. Here he recollected himself, and smiled at his own useless impetuosity. Then raising his eyes to the mountain, 'This, said he, is the fatal obstacle that hinders at once the enjoyment of pleasure, and the exercise of virtue. How long is it that my hopes and wishes have flown beyond this boundary of my life, which yet I never have attempted to surmount!'

Struck with this reflection, he sat down to muse, and remembered, that since he first resolved to escape from his confinement, the sun had passed twice over him in his annual course. He now felt a degree of regret with which he had never been before acquainted. He considered how much might have been done in the time which had passed, and left nothing real behind it. He compared twenty months with the life of man. 'In life, said he, is not to be counted the ignorance of infancy, or imbecility of age. We are long before we are able to think, and we soon cease from the power of acting. The true period of human existence may be reasonably estimated as forty years, of which I have mused away the four and twentieth part. What I have lost was certain, for I have certainly possessed it; but of twenty months to come who can assure me?'

The consciousness of his own folly pierced him deeply, and he was long before he could be reconciled to himself 'The rest of my time, said he, has been lost by the crime or folly of my ancestors, and the absurd institutions of my country; I remember it with disgust, yet without remorse: but the months that have passed since new light darted into my soul, since I formed a scheme of reasonable felicity, have been squandered by my own fault. I have lost that which can never be restored: I have seen the sun rise and set for twenty months, an idle gazer on the light of heaven: In this time the birds have left the nest of their mother, and committed themselves to the woods and to the skies: the kid has forsaken the teat, and learned by degrees to climb the rocks in quest of independant sustenance. I only have made no advances, but am still helpless and ignorant. The moon by more than twenty changes, admonished me of the flux of life; the stream that rolled before my feet upbraided my inactivity. I sat feasting on intellectual luxury, regardless alike of the examples of the earth, and the instructions of the planets. Twenty months are past, who shall restore them!'

These sorrowful meditations fastened upon his mind; he past four months in resolving to lose no more time in idle resolves, and was awakened to more vigorous exertion by hearing a maid, who had broken a porcelain cup, remark, that what cannot be repaired is not to be regretted.

This was obvious; and Rasselas reproached himself that he had not discovered it, having not known, or not considered, how many useful hints are obtained by chance, and how often the mind, hurried by her own ardour to distant views, neglects the truths that lie open before her. He, for a few hours, regretted his regret, and from that time bent his whole mind upon the means of escaping from the valley of happiness.

CHAP. V

The prince meditates his escape

HE now found that it would be very difficult to effect that which it was very easy to suppose effected. When he looked round about him, he saw himself confined by the bars of nature which had never yet been broken, and by the gate, through which none that once had passed it were ever able to return. He was now impatient as an eagle in a grate. He passed week after week in clambering the mountains, to see if there was any aperture which the bushes might conceal, but found all the summits inaccessible by their prominence. The iron gate he despaired to open; for it was not only secured with all the power of art, but was always watched by successive sentinels, and was by its position exposed to the perpetual observation of all the inhabitants.

He then examined the cavern through which the waters of the lake were discharged; and, looking down at a time when the sun shone strongly upon its mouth, he discovered it to be full of broken rocks, which, though they permitted the stream to flow through many narrow passages, would stop any body of solid bulk. He returned discouraged and dejected; but, having now known the blessing of hope, resolved never to despair.

In these fruitless searches he spent ten months. The time, however, passed chearfully away: in the morning he rose with new hope, in the evening applauded his own diligence, and in the night slept sound after his fatigue. He met a thousand amusements which beguiled his labour, and diversified his thoughts. He discerned the various instincts of animals, and properties of plants, and found the place replete with wonders, of which he purposed to solace himself with the contemplation, if he should never be able to accomplish his flight; rejoicing that his endeavours, though yet unsucessful, had supplied him with a source of inexhaustible enquiry.

But his original curiosity was not yet abated; he resolved to obtain some knowledge of the ways of men. His wish still continued, but his hope grew less. He ceased to survey any longer the walls of his prison, and spared to search by new toils for interstices which he knew could not be found, yet determined to keep his design always in view, and lay hold on any expedient that time should offer.

CHAP. VI

A dissertation on the art of flying

AMONG the artists that had been allured into the happy valley, to labour for the accommodation and pleasure of its inhabitants, was a man eminent for his knowledge of the mechanick powers, who had contrived many engines both of use and recreation. By a wheel, which the stream turned, he forced the water into a tower, whence it was distributed to all the apartments of the palace. He erected a pavillion in the garden, around which he kept the air always cool by artificial showers. One of the groves, appropriated to the ladies, was ventilated by fans, to which the rivulet that run through it gave a constant motion; and instruments of soft musick were placed at proper distances, of which some played by the impulse of the wind, and some by the power of the stream.

This artist was sometimes visited by Rasselas, who was pleased with every kind of knowledge, imagining that the time would come when all his acquisitions should be of use to him in the open world. He came one day to amuse himself in his usual manner, and found the master busy in building a sailing chariot: he saw that the design was practicable upon a level surface, and with expressions of great esteem solicited its completion. The workman was pleased to find himself so much regarded by the prince, and resolved to gain yet higher honours. 'Sir, said he, you have seen but a small part of what the mechanick sciences can perform. I have been long of opinion, that, instead of the tardy conveyance of ships and chariots, man might use the swifter migration of wings; that the fields of air are open to knowledge, and that only ignorance and idleness need crawl upon the ground.'

This hint rekindled the prince's desire of passing the mountains; having seen what the mechanist had already performed, he was willing to fancy that he could do more; yet resolved to enquire further before he suffered hope to afflict him by disappointment. 'I am afraid, said he to the artist, that your imagination prevails over your skill, and that you now tell me rather what you wish than what you know. Every animal has his element assigned him; the birds have the air, and man and beasts the earth.' 'So, replied the mechanist, fishes have the water, in which yet beasts can swim by nature, and men by art. He that can swim needs not despair to fly: to swim is to fly in a grosser fluid, and to fly is to swim in a subtler. We are only to proportion our power of resistance to the different density of the matter through which we are to pass. You will be necessarily upborn by the air, if you can renew any impulse upon it, faster than the air can recede from the pressure.'

'But the exercise of swimming, said the prince, is very laborious; the strongest limbs are soon wearied; I am afraid the act of flying will be yet more violent, and wings will be of no great use, unless we can fly further than we can swim.'

'The labour of rising from the ground, said the artist, will be great, as we see it in the heavier domestick fowls; but, as we mount higher, the earth's attraction, and the body's gravity, will be gradually diminished, till we shall arrive at a region where the man will float in the air without any tendency to fall: no care will then be necessary, but to move forwards, which the gentlest impulse will effect. You, Sir, whose curiosity is so extensive, will easily conceive with what pleasure a philosopher, furnished with wings, and hovering in the sky, would see the earth, and all its inhabitants, rolling beneath him, and presenting to him successively, by its diurnal motion, all the countries within the same parallel. How must it amuse the pendent spectator to see the moving scene of land and ocean, cities and desarts! To survey with equal security the marts of trade, and the fields of battle; mountains infested by barbarians, and fruitful regions gladdened by plenty, and lulled by peace! How easily shall we then trace the Nile through all his passage; pass over to distant regions, and examine the face of nature from one extremity of the earth to the other!'

'All this, said the prince, is much to be desired, but I am afraid that no man will be able to breathe in these regions of speculation and tranquility. I have been told, that respiration is difficult upon lofty mountains, yet from these precipices, though so high as to produce great tenuity of the air, it is very easy to fall: therefore I suspect, that from any height, where life can be supported, there may be danger of too quick descent.'

'Nothing, replied the artist, will ever be attempted, if all possible objections must be first overcome. If you will favour my project I will try the first flight at my own hazard. I have considered the structure of all volant animals, and find the folding continuity of the bat's wings most easily accommodated to the human form. Upon this model I shall begin my task to morrow, and in a year expect to tower into the air beyond the malice or persuit of man. But I will work only on this condition, that the art shall not be divulged, and that you shall not require me to make wings for any but ourselves.'

'Why, said Rasselas, should you envy others so great an advantage? All skill ought to be exerted for universal good; every man has owed much to others, and ought to repay the kindness that he has received.'

'If men were all virtuous, returned the artist, I should with great alacrity teach them all to fly. But what would be the security of the good, if the bad could at pleasure invade them from the sky? Against an army sailing through the cloud neither walls, nor mountains, nor seas, could afford any security. A flight of northern savages might hover in the wind, and light at once with irresistible violence upon the capital of a fruitful region that was rolling under them. Even this valley, the retreat of princes, the abode of happiness, might be violated by the sudden descent of some of the naked nations that swarm on the coast of the southern sea.'

The prince promised secrecy, and waited for the performance, not wholly hopeless of success. He visited the work from time to time, observed its progress, and remarked many ingenious contrivances to facilitate motion, and unite levity with strength. The artist was every day more certain that he should leave vultures and eagles behind him, and the contagion of his confidence seized upon the prince.

In a year the wings were finished, and, on a morning appointed, the maker appeared furnished for flight on a little promontory: he waved his pinions a while to gather air, then leaped from his stand, and in an instant dropped into the lake. His wings, which were of no use in the air, sustained him in the water, and the prince drew him to land, half dead with terrour and vexation.

CHAP. VII

The prince finds a man of learning

THE prince was not much afflicted by this disaster, having suffered himself to hope for a happier event, only because he had no other means of escape in view. He still persisted in his design to leave the happy valley by the first opportunity.

His imagination was now at a stand; he had no prospect of entering into the world; and, notwithstanding all his endeavours to support himself, discontent by degrees preyed upon him, and he began again to lose his thoughts in sadness, when the rainy season, which in these countries is periodical, made it inconvenient to wander in the woods.

The rain continued longer and with more violence than had been ever known: the clouds broke on the surrounding mountains, and the torrents streamed into the plain on every side, till the cavern was too narrow to discharge the water. The lake overflowed its banks, and all the level of the valley was covered with the inundation. The eminence, on which the palace was built, and some other spots of rising ground, were all that the eye could now discover. The herds and flocks left the pastures, and both the wild beasts and the tame retreated to the mountains.

This inundation confined all the princes to domestick amusements, and the attention of Rasselas was particularly seized by a poem, which Imlac rehearsed upon the various conditions of humanity. He commanded the poet to attend him in his apartment, and recite his verses a second time; then entering into familiar talk, he thought himself happy in having found a man who knew the world so well, and could so skilfully paint the scenes of life. He asked a thousand questions about things, to which, though common to all other mortals, his confinement from childhood had kept him a stranger. The poet pitied his ignorance, and loved his curiosity, and entertained him from day to day with novelty and instruction, so that the prince regretted the necessity of sleep, and longed till the morning should renew his pleasure.

As they were sitting together, the prince commanded Imlac to relate his history, and to tell by what accident he was forced, or by what motive induced, to close his life in the happy valley. As he was going to begin his narrative, Rasselas was called to a concert, and obliged to restrain his curiosity till the evening.

CHAP. VIII

The history of Imlac

THE close of the day is, in the regions of the torrid zone, the only season of diversion and entertainment, and it was therefore midnight before the musick ceased, and the princesses retired. Rasselas then called for his companion and required him to begin the story of his life.

'Sir, said Imlac, my history will not be long: the life that is devoted to knowledge passes silently away, and is very little diversified by events. To talk in publick, to think in solitude, to read and to hear, to inquire, and answer inquiries, is the business of a scholar. He wanders about the world without pomp or terrour, and is neither known nor valued but by men like himself.

'I was born in the kingdom of Goiama, at no great distance from the fountain of the Nile. My father was a wealthy merchant, who traded between the inland countries of Africk and the ports of the red sea. He was honest, frugal and diligent, but of mean sentiments, and narrow comprehension: he desired only to be rich, and to conceal his riches, lest he should be spoiled by the governours of the province.'

'Surely, said the prince, my father must be negligent of his charge, if any man in his dominions dares take that which belongs to another. Does he not know that kings are accountable for injustice permitted as well as done? If I were emperour, not the meanest of my subjects should be oppressed with impunity. My blood boils when I am told that a merchant durst not enjoy his honest gains for fear of losing them by the rapacity of power. Name the governour who robbed the people, that I may declare his crimes to the emperour.'

'Sir, said Imlac, your ardour is the natural effect of virtue animated by youth: the time will come when you will acquit your father, and perhaps hear with less impatience of the governour. Oppression is, in the Abissinian dominions, neither frequent nor tolerated; but no form of government has been yet discovered, by which cruelty can be wholly prevented. Subordination supposes power on one part and subjection on the other; and if power be in the hands of men, it will sometimes be abused. The vigilance of the supreme magistrate may do much, but much will still remain undone. He can never know all the crimes that are committed, and can seldom punish all that he knows.'

'This, said the prince, I do not understand, but I had rather hear thee than dispute. Continue thy narration.'

'My father, proceeded Imlac, originally intended that I should have no other education, than such as might qualify me for commerce; and discovering in me great strength of memory, and quickness of apprehension, often declared his hope that I should be some time the richest man in Abissinia.'

'Why, said the prince, did thy father desire the increase of his wealth, when it was already greater than he durst discover or enjoy? I am unwilling to doubt thy veracity, yet inconsistencies cannot both be true.'

'Inconsistencies, answered Imlac, cannot both be right, but, imputed to man, they may both be true. Yet diversity is not inconsistency. My father might expect a time of greater security. However, some desire is necessary to keep life in motion, and he, whose real wants are supplied, must admit those of fancy.'

'This, said the prince, I can in some measure conceive. I repent that I interrupted thee.'

'With this hope, proceeded Imlac, he sent me to school; but when I had once found the delight of knowledge, and felt the pleasure of intelligence and the pride of invention, I began silently to despise riches, and determined to disappoint the purpose of my father, whose grossness of conception raised my pity. I was twenty years old before his tenderness would expose me to the fatigue of travel, in which time I had been instructed, by successive masters, in all the literature of my native country. As every hour taught me something new, I lived in a continual course of gratifications; but, as I advanced towards manhood, I lost much of the reverence with which I had been used to look on my instructors; because, when the lesson was ended, I did not find them wiser or better than common men.

'At length my father resolved to initiate me in commerce, and, opening one of his subterranean treasuries, counted out ten thousand pieces of gold. This, young man, said he, is the stock with which you must negociate. I began with less than the fifth part, and you see how diligence and parsimony have increased it. This is your own to waste or to improve. If you squander it by negligence or caprice, you must wait for my death before you will be rich: if, in four years, you double your stock, we will thenceforward let subordination cease, and live together as friends and partners; for he shall always be equal with me, who is equally skilled in the art of growing rich.

'We laid our money upon camels, concealed in bales of cheap goods, and travelled to the shore of the red sea. When I cast my eye on the expanse of waters my heart bounded like that of a prisoner escaped. I felt an unextinguishable curiosity kindle in my mind, and resolved to snatch this opportunity of seeing the manners of other nations, and of learning sciences unknown in Abissinia.

'I remembered that my father had obliged me to the improvement of my stock, not by a promise which I ought not to violate, but by a penalty which I was at liberty to incur; and therefore determined to gratify my predominant desire, and by drinking at the fountains of knowledge, to quench the thirst of curiosity.

'As I was supposed to trade without connexion with my father, it was easy for me to become acquainted with the master of a ship, and procure a passage to some other country. I had no motives of choice to regulate my voyage; it was sufficient for me that, wherever I wandered, I should see a country which I had not seen before. I therefore entered a ship bound for Surat, having left a letter for my father declaring my intention.

CHAP. IX

The history of Imlac continued

'WHEN I first entered upon the world of waters, and lost sight of land, I looked round about me with pleasing terrour, and thinking my soul enlarged by the boundless prospect, imagined that I could gaze round for ever without satiety; but, in a short time, I grew weary of looking on barren uniformity, where I could only see again what I had already seen. I then descended into the ship, and doubted for a while whether all my future pleasures would not end like this in disgust and disappointment. Yet, surely, said I, the ocean and the land are very different; the only variety of water is rest and motion, but the earth has mountains and vallies, desarts and cities: it is inhabited by men of different customs and contrary opinions; and I may hope to find variety in life, though I should miss it in nature.

'With this thought I quieted my mind; and amused myself during the voyage, sometimes by learning from the sailors the art of navigation, which I have never practised, and sometimes by forming schemes for my conduct in different situations, in not one of which I have been ever placed.

'I was almost weary of my naval amusements when we landed safely at Surat. I secured my money, and purchasing some commodities for show, joined myself to a caravan that was passing into the inland country. My companions, for some reason or other, conjecturing that I was rich, and, by my inquiries and admiration, finding that I was ignorant, considered me as a novice whom they had a right to cheat, and who was to learn at the usual expence the art of fraud. They exposed me to the theft of servants, and the exaction of officers, and saw me plundered upon false pretences, without any advantage to themselves, but that of rejoicing in the superiority of their own knowledge.'

'Stop a moment, said the prince. Is there such depravity in man, as that he should injure another without benefit to himself? I can easily conceive that all are pleased with superiority; but your ignorance was merely accidental, which, being neither your crime nor your folly, could afford them no reason to applaud themselves; and the knowledge which they had, and which you wanted, they might as effectually have shown by warning, as betraying you.'

'Pride, said Imlac, is seldom delicate, it will please itself with very mean advantages; and envy feels not its own happiness, but when it may be compared with the misery of others. They were my enemies because they grieved to think me rich, and my oppressors because they delighted to find me weak.'

'Proceed, said the prince: I doubt not of the facts which you relate, but imagine that you impute them to mistaken motives.'

'In this company, said Imlac, I arrived at Agra, the capital of Indostan, the city in which the great Mogul commonly resides. I applied myself to the language of the country, and in a few months was able to converse with the learned men; some of whom I found morose and reserved, and others easy and communicative; some were unwilling to teach another what they had with difficulty learned themselves; and some shewed that the end of their studies was to gain the dignity of instructing.

'To the tutor of the young princes I recommended myself so much, that I was presented to the emperour as a man of uncommon knowledge. The emperour asked me many questions concerning my country and my travels; and though I cannot now recollect any thing that he uttered above the power of a common man, he dismissed me astonished at his wisdom, and enamoured of his goodness.

'My credit was now so high, that the merchants, with whom I had travelled, applied to me for recommendations to the ladies of the court. I was surprised at their confidence of solicitation, and gently reproached them with their practices on the road. They heard me with cold indifference, and shewed no tokens of shame or sorrow.

'They then urged their request with the offer of a bribe; but what I would not do for kindness I would not do for money; and refused them, not because they had injured me, but because I would not enable them to injure others; for I knew they would have made use of my credit to cheat those who should buy their wares.

'Having resided at Agra till there was no more to be learned, I travelled into Persia, where I saw many remains of ancient magnificence, and observed many new accommodations of life. The Persians are a nation eminently social, and their assemblies afforded me daily opportunities of remarking characters and manners, and of tracing human nature through all its variations.

'From Persia I passed into Arabia, where I saw a nation at once pastoral and warlike; who live without any settled habitation; whose only wealth is their flocks and herds; and who have yet carried on, through all ages, an hereditary war with all mankind, though they neither covet nor envy their possessions.

CHAP. X

Imlac's history continued. A dissertation upon poetry

'WHEREVER I went, I found that poetry was considered as the highest learning, and regarded with a veneration somewhat approaching to that which man would pay to the Angelick Nature. And it yet fills me with wonder, that, in almost all countries, the most ancient poets are considered as the best: whether it be that every other kind of knowledge is an acquisition gradually attained, and poetry is a gift conferred at once; or that the first poetry of every nation surprised them as a novelty, and retained the credit by consent which it received by accident at first: or whether, as the province of poetry is to describe Nature and passion, which are always the same, the first writers took possession of the most striking objects for description, and the most probable occurrences for fiction, and left nothing to those that followed them, but transcription of the same events, and new combinations of the same images. Whatever be the reason, it is commonly observed that the early writers are in possession of nature, and their followers of art: that the first excel in strength and invention, and the latter in elegance and refinement.

'I was desirous to add my name to this illustrious fraternity. I read all the poets of Persia and Arabia, and was able to repeat by memory the volumes that are suspended in the mosque of Mecca. But I soon found that no man was ever great by imitation. My desire of excellence impelled me to transfer my attention to nature and to life. Nature was to be my subject, and men to be my auditors: I could never describe what I had not seen: I could not hope to move those with delight or terrour, whose interests and opinions I did not understand.

'Being now resolved to be a poet, I saw every thing with a new purpose; my sphere of attention was suddenly magnified: no kind of knowledge was to be overlooked. I ranged mountains and deserts for images and resemblances, and pictured upon my mind every tree of the forest and flower of the valley. I observed with equal care the crags of the rock and the pinnacles of the palace. Sometimes I wandered along the mazes of the rivulet, and sometimes watched the changes of the summer clouds. To a poet nothing can be useless. Whatever is beautiful, and whatever is dreadful, must be familiar to his imagination: he must be conversant with all that is awfully vast or elegantly little. The plants of the garden, the animals of the wood, the minerals of the earth, and meteors of the sky, must all concur to store his mind with inexhaustible variety: for every idea is useful for the inforcement or decoration of moral or religious truth; and he, who knows most, will have most power of diversifying his scenes, and of gratifying his reader with remote allusions and unexpected instruction.

'All the appearances of nature I was therefore careful to study, and every country which I have surveyed has contributed something to my poetical powers.'

'In so wide a survey, said the prince, you must surely have left much unobserved. I have lived, till now, within the circuit of these mountains, and yet cannot walk abroad without the sight of something which I had never beheld before, or never heeded.'

'The business of a poet, said Imlac, is to examine, not the individual, but the species; to remark general properties and large appearances: he does not number the streaks of the tulip, or describe the different shades in the verdure of the forest. He is to exhibit in his portraits of nature such prominent and striking features, as recal the original to every mind; and must neglect the minuter discriminations, which one may have remarked, and another have neglected, for those characteristicks which are alike obvious to vigilance and carelessness.

'But the knowledge of nature is only half the task of a poet; he must be acquainted likewise with all the modes of life. His character requires that he estimate the happiness and misery of every condition; observe the power of all the passions in all their combinations, and trace the changes of the human mind as they are modified by various institutions and accidental influences of climate or custom, from the spriteliness of infancy to the despondence of decrepitude. He must divest himself of the prejudices of his age or country; he must consider right and wrong in their abstracted and invariable state; he must disregard present laws and opinions, and rise to general and transcendental truths, which will always be the same: he must therefore content himself with the slow progress of his name; contemn the applause of his own time, and commit his claims to the justice of posterity. He must write as the interpreter of nature, and the legislator of mankind, and consider himself as presiding over the thoughts and manners of future generations; as a being superiour to time and place.

'His labour is not yet at an end: he must know many languages and many sciences; and, that his stile may be worthy of his thoughts, must, by incessant practice, familiarize to himself every delicacy of speech and grace of harmony.'

CHAP. XI

Imlac's narrative continued. A hint on pilgrimage

IMLAC now felt the enthusiastic fit, and was proceeding to aggrandize his own profession, when the prince cried out, 'Enough! Thou hast convinced me, that no human being can ever be a poet. Proceed with thy narration.'

'To be a poet, said Imlac, is indeed very difficult.' 'So difficult, returned the prince, that I will at present hear no more of his labours. Tell me whither you went when you had seen Persia.'

'From Persia, said the poet, I travelled through Syria, and for three years resided in Palestine, where I conversed with great numbers of the northern and western nations of Europe; the nations which are now in possession of all power and knowledge; whose armies are irresistible, and whose fleets command the remotest parts of the globe. When I compared these men with the natives of our own kingdom, and those that surround us, they appeared almost another order of beings. In their countries it is difficult to wish for any thing that may not be obtained: a thousand arts, of which we never heard, are continually labouring for their convenience and pleasure; and whatever their own climate has denied them is supplied by their commerce.'

'By what means, said the prince, are the Europeans thus powerful? or why, since they can so easily visit Asia and Africa for trade or conquest, cannot the Asiaticks and Africans invade their coasts, plant colonies in their ports, and give laws to their natural princes? The same wind that carries them back would bring us thither.'

'They are more powerful, Sir, than we, answered Imlac, because they are wiser; knowledge will always predominate over ignorance, as man governs the other animals. But why their knowledge is more than ours, I know not what reason can be given, but the unsearchable will of the Supreme Being.'

'When, said the prince with a sigh, shall I be able to visit Palestine, and mingle with this mighty confluence of nations? Till that happy moment shall arrive, let me fill up the time with such representations as thou canst give me. I am not ignorant of the motive that assembles such numbers in that place, and cannot but consider it as the center of wisdom and piety, to which the best and wisest men of every land must be continually resorting.'

'There are some nations, said Imlac, that send few visitants to Palestine; for many numerous and learned sects in Europe, concur to censure pilgrimage as superstitious, or deride it as ridiculous.'

'You know, said the prince, how little my life has made me acquainted with diversity of opinions: it will be too long to hear the arguments on both sides; you, that have considered them, tell me the result.'

'Pilgrimage, said Imlac, like many other acts of piety, may be reasonable or superstitious, according to the principles upon which it is performed. Long journies in search of truth are not commanded. Truth, such as is necessary to the regulation of life, is always found where it is honestly sought. Change of place is no natural cause of the increase of piety, for it inevitably produces dissipation of mind. Yet, since men go every day to view the fields where great actions have been performed, and return with stronger impressions of the event, curiosity of the same kind may naturally dispose us to view that country whence our religion had its beginning; and I believe no man surveys those awful scenes without some confirmation of holy resolutions. That the Supreme Being may be more easily propitiated in one place than in another, is the dream of idle superstition; but that some places may operate upon our own minds in an uncommon manner, is an opinion which hourly experience will justify. He who supposes that his vices may be more successfully combated in

Palestine, will, perhaps, find himself mistaken, yet he may go thither without folly: he who thinks they will be more freely pardoned, dishonours at once his reason and religion.'

'These, said the prince, are European distinctions. I will consider them another time. What have you found to be the effect of knowledge? Are those nations happier than we?'

'There is so much infelicity, said the poet, in the world, that scarce any man has leisure from his own distresses to estimate the comparative happiness of others. Knowledge is certainly one of the means of pleasure, as is confessed by the natural desire which every mind feels of increasing its ideas. Ignorance is mere privation, by which nothing can be produced: it is a vacuity in which the soul sits motionless and torpid for want of attraction; and, without knowing why, we always rejoice when we learn, and grieve when we forget. I am therefore inclined to conclude, that, if nothing counteracts the natural consequence of learning, we grow more happy as our minds take a wider range.

'In enumerating the particular comforts of life we shall find many advantages on the side of the Europeans. They cure wounds and diseases with which we languish and perish. We suffer inclemencies of weather which they can obviate. They have engines for the despatch of many laborious works, which we must perform by manual industry. There is such communication between distant places, that one friend can hardly be said to be absent from another. Their policy removes all publick inconveniencies: they have roads cut through their mountains, and bridges laid upon their rivers. And, if we descend to the privacies of life, their habitations are more commodious, and their possessions are more secure.'

'They are surely happy, said the prince, who have all these conveniencies, of which I envy none so much as the facility with which separated friends interchange their thoughts.'

'The Europeans, answered Imlac, are less unhappy than we, but they are not happy. Human life is every where a state in which much is to be endured, and little to be enjoyed.'

CHAP. XII

The story of Imlac continued

'I AM not yet willing, said the prince, to suppose that happiness is so parsimoniously distributed to mortals; nor can believe but that, if I had the choice of life, I should be able to fill every day with pleasure. I would injure no man, and should provoke no resentment: I would relieve every distress, and should enjoy the benedictions of gratitude. I would choose my friends among the wise, and my wife among the virtuous; and therefore should be in no danger from treachery, or unkindness. My children should, by my care, be learned and pious, and would repay to my age what their childhood had received. What would dare to molest him who might call on every side to thousands enriched by his bounty, or assisted by his power? And why should not life glide quietly away in the soft reciprocation of protection and reverence? All this may be done without the help of European refinements, which appear by their effects to be rather specious than useful. Let us leave them and persue our journey.'

'From Palestine, said Imlac, I passed through many regions of Asia; in the more civilized kingdoms as a trader, and among the Barbarians of the mountains as a pilgrim. At last I began to long for my native country, that I might repose after my travels, and fatigues, in the places where I had spent my earliest years, and gladden my old companions with the recital of my adventures. Often did I figure to myself those, with whom I had sported away the gay hours of dawning life, sitting round me in its evening, wondering at my tales, and listening to my counsels.

'When this thought had taken possession of my mind, I considered every moment as wasted which did not bring me nearer to Abissinia. I hastened into Egypt, and, notwithstanding my impatience, was detained ten months in the contemplation of its ancient magnificence, and in enquiries after the remains of its ancient learning. I found in Cairo a mixture of all nations; some brought thither by the love of knowledge, some by the hope of gain, and many by the desire of living after their own manner without observation, and of lying hid in the obscurity of multitudes: for, in a city, populous as Cairo, it is possible to obtain at the same time the gratifications of society, and the secrecy of solitude.

'From Cairo I travelled to Suez, and embarked on the Red sea, passing along the coast till I arrived at the port from which I had departed twenty years before. Here I joined myself to a caravan and re-entered my native country.

'I now expected the caresses of my kinsmen, and the congratulations of my friends, and was not without hope that my father, whatever value he had set upon riches, would own with gladness and pride a son who was able to add to the felicity and honour of the nation. But I was soon convinced that my thoughts were vain. My father had been dead fourteen years, having divided his wealth among my brothers, who were removed to some other provinces. Of my companions the greater part was in the grave, of the rest some could with difficulty remember me, and some considered me as one corrupted by foreign manners.

'A man used to vicissitudes is not easily dejected. I forgot, after a time, my disappointment, and endeavoured to recommend myself to the nobles of the kingdom: they admitted me to their tables, heard my story, and dismissed me. I opened a school, and was prohibited to teach. I then resolved to sit down in the quiet of domestick life, and addressed a lady that was fond of my conversation, but rejected my suit, because my father was a merchant.

'Wearied at last with solicitation and repulses, I resolved to hide myself for ever from the world, and depend no longer on the opinion or caprice of others. I waited for the time when the gate of the *happy valley* should open, that I might bid farewell to hope and fear: the day came; my performance was distinguished with favour, and I resigned myself with joy to perpetual confinement.'

'Hast thou here found happiness at last? said Rasselas. Tell me without reserve; art thou content with thy condition? or, dost thou wish to be again wandering and inquiring? All the inhabitants of this valley celebrate their lot, and, at the annual visit of the emperour, invite others to partake of their felicity.'

'Great prince, said Imlac, I shall speak the truth: I know not one of all your attendants who does not lament the hour when he entered this retreat. I am less unhappy than the rest, because I have a mind replete with images, which I can vary and combine at pleasure. I can amuse my solitude by the renovation of the knowledge which begins to fade from my memory, and by recollection of the accidents of my past life. Yet all this ends in the sorrowful consideration, that my acquirements are now useless, and that none of my pleasures can be again enjoyed. The rest, whose minds have no impression but of the present moment, are either corroded by malignant passions, or sit stupid in the gloom of perpetual vacancy.'

'What passions can infest those, said the prince, who have no rivals? We are in a place where impotence precludes malice, and where all envy is repressed by community of enjoyments.'

'There may be community, said Imlac, of material possessions, but there can never be community of love or of esteem. It must happen that one will please more than another; he that knows himself despised will always be envious; and still more envious and malevolent, if he is condemned to live in the presence of those who despise him. The invitations, by which they allure others to a state which they feel to be wretched, proceed from the natural malignity of hopeless misery. They are weary of themselves, and of each other, and expect to find relief in new companions. They envy the liberty which their folly has forfeited, and would gladly see all mankind imprisoned like themselves.

'From this crime, however, I am wholly free. No man can say that he is wretched by my persuasion. I look with pity on the crowds who are annually soliciting admission to captivity, and wish that it were lawful for me to warn them of their danger.'

'My dear Imlac, said the prince, I will open to thee my whole heart. I have long meditated an escape from the happy valley. I have examined the mountains on every side, but find myself insuperably barred: teach me the way to break my prison; thou shalt be the companion of my flight, the guide of my rambles, the partner of my fortune, and my sole director in the *choice of life*.'

'Sir, answered the poet, your escape will be difficult, and, perhaps, you may soon repent your curiosity. The world, which you figure to yourself smooth and quiet as the lake in the valley, you will find a sea foaming with tempests, and boiling with whirlpools: you will be sometimes overwhelmed by the waves of violence, and sometimes dashed against the rocks of treachery. Amidst wrongs and frauds, competitions and anxieties, you will wish a thousand times for these seats of quiet, and willingly quit hope to be free from fear.'

'Do not seek to deter me from my purpose, said the prince: I am impatient to see what thou hast seen; and, since thou art thyself weary of the valley, it is evident, that thy former state was better than this. Whatever be the consequence of my experiment, I am resolved to judge with my own eyes of the various conditions of men, and then to make deliberately my *choice of life*.'

'I am afraid, said Imlac, you are hindered by stronger restraints than my persuasions; yet, if your determination is fixed, I do not counsel you to despair. Few things are impossible to diligence and skill.'

CHAP. XIII

Rasselas discovers the means of escape

The prince now dismissed his favourite to rest, but the narrative of wonders and novelties filled his mind with perturbation. He revolved all that he had heard, and prepared innumerable questions for the morning.

Much of his uneasiness was now removed. He had a friend to whom he could impart his thoughts, and whose experience could assist him in his designs. His heart was no longer condemned to swell with silent vexation. He thought that even the *happy valley* might be endured with such a companion, and that, if they could range the world together, he should have nothing further to desire.

In a few days the water was discharged, and the ground dried. The prince and Imlac then walked out together to converse without the notice of the rest. The prince, whose thoughts were always on the wing, as he passed by the gate, said, with a countenance of sorrow, 'Why art thou so strong, and why is man so weak?'

'Man is not weak, answered his companion; knowledge is more than equivalent to force. The master of mechanicks laughs at strength. I can burst the gate, but cannot do it secretly. Some other expedient must be tried.'

As they were walking on the side of the mountain, they observed that the conies, which the rain had driven from their burrows, had taken shelter among the bushes, and formed holes behind them, tending upwards in an oblique line. 'It has been the opinion of antiquity, said Imlac, that human reason borrowed many arts from the instinct of animals; let us, therefore, not think ourselves degraded by learning from the coney. We may escape by piercing the mountain in the same direction. We will begin where the summit hangs over the middle part, and labour upward till we shall issue out beyond the prominence.'

The eyes of the prince, when he heard this proposal, sparkled with joy. The execution was easy, and the success certain.

No time was now lost. They hastened early in the morning to chuse a place proper for their mine. They clambered with great fatigue among crags and brambles, and returned without having discovered any part that favoured their design. The second and the third day were spent in the same manner, and with the same frustration. But, on the fourth, they found a small cavern, concealed by a thicket, where they resolved to make their experiment.

Imlac procured instruments proper to hew stone and remove earth and they fell to their work on the next day with more eagerness than vigour. They were presently exhausted by their efforts, and sat down to pant upon the grass. The prince, for the moment, appeared to be discouraged. 'Sir, said his companion, practice will enable us to continue our labour for a longer time; mark, however, how far we have advanced, and you will find that our toil will some time have an end. Great works are performed, not by strength but perseverance: yonder palace was raised by single stones, yet you see its height and spaciousness. He that shall walk with vigour three hours a day will pass in seven years a space equal to the circumference of the globe.'

They returned to their work day after day, and, in a short time, found a fissure in the rock, which enabled them to pass far with very little obstruction. This Rasselas considered as a good omen. 'Do not disturb your mind, said Imlac, with other hopes or fears than reason may suggest: if you are pleased with prognosticks of good, you will be terrified likewise with tokens of evil, and your whole life will be a prey to superstition. Whatever facilitates our work is more than an omen, it is a cause of success. This is one of those pleasing surprises which often happen to active resolution. Many things difficult to design prove easy to performance.'

CHAP. XIV

Rasselas and Imlac receive an unexpected visit

They had now wrought their way to the middle, and solaced their toil with the approach of liberty, when the prince, coming down to refresh himself with air, found his sister Nekayah standing before the mouth of the cavity. He started and stood confused, afraid to tell his design, and yet hopeless to conceal it. A few moments determined him to repose on her fidelity, and secure her secrecy by a declaration without reserve.

'Do not imagine, said the princess, that I came hither as a spy: I had long observed from my window, that you and Imlac directed your walk every day towards the same point, but I did not suppose you had any better reason for the preference than a cooler shade, or more fragrant bank; nor followed you with any other design than to partake of your conversation. Since then not suspicion but fondness has detected you, let me not lose the advantage of my discovery. I am equally weary of confinement with yourself, and not less desirous of knowing what is done or suffered in the world. Permit me to fly with you from this tasteless tranquility, which will yet grow more loathsome when you have left me. You may deny me to accompany you, but cannot hinder me from following.'

The prince, who loved Nekayah above his other sisters, had lost an opportunity of shewing his confidence by a voluntary communication. It was therefore agreed that she should leave the valley with them; and that, in the mean time, she should watch, lest any other straggler should, by chance or curiosity, follow them to the mountain.

At length their labour was at an end; they saw light beyond the prominence, and, issuing to the top of the mountain, beheld the Nile, yet a narrow current, wandering beneath them.

The prince looked round with rapture, anticipated all the pleasures of travel, and in thought was already transported beyond his father's dominions. Imlac, though very joyful at his escape, had less expectation of pleasure in the world, which he had before tried, and of which he had been weary.

Rasselas was so much delighted with a wider horizon, that he could not soon be persuaded to return into the valley. He informed his sister that the way was open, and that nothing now remained but to prepare for their departure.

CHAP. XV

The prince and princess leave the valley, and see many wonders

THE prince and princess had jewels sufficient to make them rich whenever they came into a place of commerce, which, by Imlac's direction, they hid in their cloaths, and, on the night of the next full moon, all left the valley. The princess was followed only by a single favourite, who did not know whither she was going. They clambered through the cavity, and began to go down on the other side. The princess and her maid turned their eyes towards every part, and, seeing nothing to bound their prospect, considered themselves as in danger of being lost in a dreary vacuity. They stopped and trembled. 'I am almost afraid, said the princess, to begin a journey of which I cannot perceive an end, and to venture into this immense plain where I may be approached on every side by men whom I never saw.' The prince felt nearly the same emotions, though he thought it more manly to conceal them.

Imlac smiled at their terrors, and encouraged them to proceed; but the princess continued irresolute till she had been imperceptibly drawn forward too far to return.

In the morning they found some shepherds in the field, who set milk and fruits before them. The princess wondered that she did not see a palace ready for her reception, and a table spread with delicacies; but, being faint and hungry, she drank the milk and eat the fruits, and thought them of a higher flavour than the products of the valley.

They travelled forward by easy journeys, being all unaccustomed to toil or difficulty, and knowing, that though they might be missed, they could not be persued. In a few days they came into a more populous region, where Imlac was diverted with the admiration which his companions expressed at the diversity of manners, stations and employments.

Their dress was such as might not bring upon them the suspicion of having any thing to conceal, yet the prince, wherever he came, expected to be obeyed, and the princess was frighted, because those that came into her presence did not prostrate themselves before her. Imlac was forced to observe them with great vigilance, lest they should betray their rank by their unusual behaviour, and detained them several weeks in the first village to accustom them to the sight of common mortals.

By degrees the royal wanderers were taught to understand that they had for a time laid aside their dignity, and were to expect only such regard as liberality and courtesy could procure. And Imlac, having, by many admonitions, prepared them to endure the tumults of a port, and the ruggedness of the commercial race, brought them down to the seacoast.

The prince and his sister, to whom every thing was new, were gratified equally at all places, and therefore remained for some months at the port without any inclination to pass further. Imlac was content with their stay, because he did not think it safe to expose them, unpractised in the world, to the hazards of a foreign country.

At last he began to fear lest they should be discovered, and proposed to fix a day for their departure. They had no pretensions to judge for themselves, and referred the whole scheme to his direction. He therefore took passage in a ship to Suez; and, when the time came, with great difficulty prevailed on the princess to enter the vessel. They had a quick and prosperous voyage, and from Suez travelled by land to Cairo.

CHAP. XVI

They enter Cairo, and find every man happy

As they approached the city, which filled the strangers with astonishment, 'This, said Imlac to the prince, is the place where travellers and merchants assemble from all the corners of the earth. You will here find men of every character, and every occupation. Commerce is here honourable: I will act as a merchant, and you shall live as strangers, who have no other end of travel than curiosity; it will soon be observed that we are rich; our reputation will procure us access to all whom we shall desire to know; you will see all the conditions of humanity, and enable yourself at leisure to make your *choice of life.*'

They now entered the town, stunned by the noise, and offended by the crowds. Instruction had not yet so prevailed over habit but that they wondered to see themselves pass undistinguished along the street, and met by the lowest of the people without reverence or notice. The princess could not at first bear the thought of being levelled with the vulgar, and, for some days, continued in her chamber, where she was served by her favourite Pekuah as in the palace of the valley.

Imlac, who understood traffick, sold part of the jewels the next day, and hired a house, which he adorned with such magnificence, that he was immediately considered as a merchant of great wealth. His politeness attracted many acquaintance, and his generosity made him courted by many dependants. His table was crowded by men of every nation, who all admired his knowledge, and solicited his favour. His companions, not being able to mix in the conversation, could make no discovery of their ignorance or surprise, and were gradually initiated in the world as they gained knowledge of the language.

The prince had, by frequent lectures, been taught the use and nature of money; but the ladies could not, for a long time, comprehend what the merchants did with small pieces of gold and silver, or why things of so little use should be received as equivalent to the necessaries of life.

They studied the language two years, while Imlac was preparing to set before them the various ranks and conditions of mankind. He grew acquainted with all who had any thing uncommon in their fortune or conduct. He frequented the voluptuous and the frugal, the idle and the busy, the merchants and the men of learning.

The prince, being now able to converse with fluency, and having learned the caution necessary to be observed in his intercourse with strangers, began to accompany Imlac to places of resort, and to enter into all assemblies, that he might make his *choice of life*.

For some time he thought choice needless, because all appeared to him equally happy. Wherever he went he met gayety and kindness, and heard the song of joy, or the laugh of carelessness. He began to believe that the world overflowed with universal plenty, and that nothing was withheld either from want or merit; that every hand showered liberality, and every heart melted with benevolence: 'and who then, says he, will be suffered to be wretched?'

Imlac permitted the pleasing delusion, and was unwilling to crush the hope of inexperience; till one day, having sat a while silent, 'I know not, said the prince, what can be the reason that I am more unhappy than any of our friends. I see them perpetually and unalterably chearful, but feel my own mind restless and uneasy. I am unsatisfied with those pleasures which I seem most to court; I live in the crowds of jollity, not so much to enjoy company as to shun myself, and am only loud and merry to conceal my sadness.'

'Every man, said Imlac, may, by examining his own mind, guess what passes in the minds of others: when you feel that your own gaiety is counterfeit, it may justly lead you to suspect that of your companions not to be sincere. Envy is commonly reciprocal. We are long before we are convinced that happiness is never to be found, and each believes it possessed by others, to keep alive the hope of obtaining it for himself. In the assembly, where you passed the last night, there appeared such spriteliness of air, and volatility of fancy as might have suited beings of an higher order, formed to inhabit serener regions inaccessible to care or sorrow: yet believe me, prince, there was not one who did not dread the moment when solitude should deliver him to the tyranny of reflection.'

'This, said the prince, may be true of others, since it is true of me; yet, whatever be the general infelicity of man, one condition is more happy than another, and wisdom surely directs us to take the least evil in the *choice of life.*'

'The causes of good and evil, answered Imlac, are so various and uncertain, so often entangled with each other, so diversified by various relations, and so much subject to accidents which cannot be foreseen, that he who would fix his condition upon incontestable reasons of preference, must live and die inquiring and deliberating.'

'But surely, said Rasselas, the wise men, to whom we listen with reverence and wonder, chose that mode of life for themselves which they thought most likely to make them happy.'

'Very few, said the poet, live by choice. Every man is placed in his present condition by causes which acted without his foresight, and with which he did not always willingly cooperate; and therefore you will rarely meet one who does not think the lot of his neighbour better than his own.'

'I am pleased to think, said the prince, that my birth has given me at least one advantage over others, by enabling me to determine for myself. I have here the world before me; I will review it at leisure: surely happiness is somewhere to be found.'

CHAP. XVII

The prince associates with young men of spirit and gaiety

RASSELAS rose next day, and resolved to begin his experiments upon life. 'Youth, cried he, is the time of gladness: I will join myself to the young men, whose only business is to gratify their desires, and whose time is all spent in a succession of enjoyments.'

To such societies he was readily admitted, but a few days brought him back weary and disgusted. Their mirth was without images, their laughter without motive; their pleasures were gross and sensual, in which the mind had no part; their conduct was at once wild and mean; they laughed at order and at law, but the frown of power dejected, and the eye of wisdom abashed them.

The prince soon concluded, that he should never be happy in a course of life of which he was ashamed. He thought it unsuitable to a reasonable being to act without a plan, and to be sad or chearful only by chance. 'Happiness, said he, must be something solid and permanent, without fear and without uncertainty.

But his young companions had gained so much of his regard by their frankness and courtesy, that he could not leave them without warning and remonstrance. 'My friends, said he, I have seriously considered our manners and our prospects, and find that we have mistaken our own interest. The first years of man must make provision for the last. He that never thinks never can be wise. Perpetual levity must end in ignorance; and intemperance, though it may fire the spirits for an hour, will make life short or miserable. Let us consider that youth is of no long duration, and that in maturer age, when the enchantments of fancy shall cease, and phantoms of delight dance no more about us, we shall have no comforts but the esteem of wise men, and the means of doing good. Let us, therefore, stop, while to stop is in our power: let us live as men who are sometime to grow old, and to whom it will be the most dreadful of all evils not to count their past years but by follies, and to be reminded of their former luxuriance of health only by the maladies which riot has produced.' They stared a while in silence one upon another, and, at last, drove him away by a general chorus of continued laughter.

The consciousness that his sentiments were just, and his intentions kind, was scarcely sufficient to support him against the horrour of derision. But he recovered his tranquility, and persued his search.

CHAP. XVIII

The prince finds a wise and happy man

As he was one day walking in the street, he saw a spacious building which all were, by the open doors, invited to enter: he followed the stream of people, and found it a hall or school of declamation, in which professors read lectures to their auditory. He fixed his eye upon a sage raised above the rest, who discoursed with great energy on the government of the passions. His look was venerable, his action graceful, his pronunciation clear, and his diction elegant. He shewed, with great strength of sentiment, and variety of illustration, that human nature is degraded and debased, when the lower faculties predominate over the higher; that when fancy, the parent of passion, usurps the dominion of the mind, nothing ensues but the natural effect of unlawful government, perturbation and confusion; that she betrays the fortresses of the intellect to rebels, and excites her children to sedition against reason their lawful sovereign. He compared reason to the sun, of which the light is constant, uniform, and lasting; and fancy to a meteor, of bright but transitory lustre, irregular in its motion, and delusive in its direction.

He then communicated the various precepts given from time to time for the conquest of passion, and displayed the happiness of those who had obtained the important victory, after which man is no longer the slave of fear, nor the fool of hope; is no more emaciated by envy, inflamed by anger, emasculated by tenderness, or depressed by grief; but walks on calmly through the tumults or the privacies of life, as the sun persues alike his course through the calm or the stormy sky.

He enumerated many examples of heroes immovable by pain or pleasure, who looked with indifference on those modes or accidents to which the vulgar give the names of good and evil. He exhorted his hearers to lay aside their prejudices, and arm themselves against the shafts of malice or misfortune, by invulnerable patience; concluding, that this state only was happiness, and that this happiness was in every one's power.

Rasselas listened to him with the veneration due to the instructions of a superior being, and, waiting for him at the door, humbly implored the liberty of visiting so great a master of true wisdom. The lecturer hesitated a moment, when Rasselas put a purse of gold into his hand, which he received with a mixture of joy and wonder.

'I have found, said the prince, at his return to Imlac, a man who can teach all that is necessary to be known, who, from the unshaken throne of rational fortitude, looks down on the scenes of life changing beneath him. He speaks, and attention watches his lips. He reasons, and conviction closes his periods. This man shall be my future guide: I will learn his doctrines, and imitate his life.'

'Be not too hasty, said Imlac, to trust, or to admire, the teachers of morality: they discourse like angels, but they live like men.'

Rasselas, who could not conceive how any man could reason so forcibly without feeling the cogency of his own arguments, paid his visit in a few days, and was denied admission. He had now learned the power of money, and made his way by a piece of gold to the inner apartment, where he found the philosopher in a room half darkened, with his eyes misty, and his face pale. 'Sir, said he, you are come at a time when all human friendship is useless; what I suffer cannot be remedied, what I have lost cannot be supplied. My daughter, my only daughter, from whose tenderness I expected all the comforts of my age, died last night of a fever. My views, my purposes, my hopes are at an end: I am now a lonely being disunited from society.'

'Sir, said the prince, mortality is an event by which a wise man can never be surprised: we know that death is always near, and it should therefore always be expected.' 'Young man, answered the philosopher, you speak like one that has never felt the pangs of separation.' 'Have you then forgot the precepts, said Rasselas, which you so powerfully enforced? Has wisdom no strength to arm the heart against calamity? Consider, that external things are naturally variable, but truth and reason are always the same.' 'What comfort, said the mourner, can truth and reason afford me? of what effect are they now, but to tell me, that my daughter will not be restored?'

The prince, whose humanity would not suffer him to insult misery with reproof, went away convinced of the emptiness of rhetorical sound, and the inefficacy of polished periods and studied sentences.

CHAP. XIX

A glimpse of pastoral life

HE was still eager upon the same enquiry; and, having heard of a hermit, that lived near the lowest cataract of the Nile, and filled the whole country with the fame of his sanctity, resolved to visit his retreat, and enquire whether that felicity, which publick life could not afford, was to be found in solitude; and whether a man, whose age and virtue made him venerable, could teach any peculiar art of shunning evils, or enduring them.

Imlac and the princess agreed to accompany him, and, after the necessary preparations, they began their journey. Their way lay through fields, where shepherds tended their flocks, and the lambs were playing upon the pasture. 'This, said the poet, is the life which has been often celebrated for its innocence and quiet: let us pass the heat of the day among the shepherds tents, and know whether all our searches are not to terminate in pastoral simplicity.'

The proposal pleased them, and they induced the shepherds, by small presents and familiar questions, to tell their opinion of their own state: they were so rude and ignorant, so little able to compare the good with the evil of the occupation, and so indistinct in their narratives and descriptions, that very little could be learned from them. But it was evident that their hearts were cankered with discontent; that they considered themselves as condemned to labour for the luxury of the rich, and looked up with stupid malevolence toward those that were placed above them.

The princess pronounced with vehemence, that she would never suffer these envious savages to be her companions, and that she should not soon be desirous of seeing any more specimens of rustick happiness; but could not believe that all the accounts of primeval pleasures were fabulous, and was yet in doubt whether life had any thing that could be justly preferred to the placid gratifications of fields and woods. She hoped that the time would come, when with a few virtuous and elegant companions, she should gather flowers planted by her own hand, fondle the lambs of her own ewe, and listen, without care, among brooks and breezes, to one of her maidens reading in the shade.

CHAP. XX

The dangers of prosperity

ON the next day they continued their journey, till the heat compelled them to look round for shelter. At a small distance they saw a thick wood, which they no sooner entered than they perceived that they were approaching the habitations of men. The shrubs were diligently cut away to open walks where the shades were darkest; the boughs of opposite trees were artificially interwoven; seats of flowery turf were raised in vacant spaces, and a rivulet, that wantoned along the side of a winding path, had its banks sometimes opened into small basons, and its stream sometimes obstructed by little mounds of stone heaped together to increase its murmurs.

They passed slowly through the wood, delighted with such unexpected accommodations, and entertained each other with conjecturing what, or who, he could be, that, in those rude and unfrequented regions, had leisure and art for such harmless luxury.

As they advanced, they heard the sound of musick, and saw youths and virgins dancing in the grove; and, going still further, beheld a stately palace built upon a hill surrounded with woods. The laws of eastern hospitality allowed them to enter, and the master welcomed them like a man liberal and wealthy.

He was skilful enough in appearances soon to discern that they were no common guests, and spread his table with magnificence. The eloquence of Imlac caught his attention, and the lofty courtesy of the princess excited his respect. When they offered to depart he entreated their stay, and was the next day still more unwilling to dismiss them than before. They were easily persuaded to stop, and civility grew up in time to freedom and confidence.

The prince now saw all the domesticks cheerful, and all the face of nature smiling round the place, and could not forbear to hope that he should find here what he was seeking; but when he was congratulating the master upon his possessions, he answered with a sigh, 'My condition has indeed the appearance of happiness, but appearances are delusive. My prosperity puts my life in danger; the Bassa of Egypt is my enemy, incensed only by my wealth and popularity. I have been hitherto protected against him by the princes of the country; but, as the favour of the great is uncertain, I know not how soon my defenders may be persuaded to share the plunder with the Bassa. I have sent my treasures into a distant country, and, upon the first alarm, am prepared to follow them. Then will my enemies riot in my mansion, and enjoy the gardens which I have planted.'

They all joined in lamenting his danger, and deprecating his exile; and the princess was so much disturbed with the tumult of grief and indignation, that she retired to her apartment. They continued with their kind inviter a few days longer, and then went forward to find the hermit.

CHAP. XXI

The happiness of solitude. The hermit's history

THEY came on the third day, by the direction of the peasants, to the Hermit's cell: it was a cavern in the side of the mountain, over-shadowed with palm-trees; at such a distance from the cataract, that nothing more was heard than a gentle uniform murmur, such as composed the mind to pensive meditation, especially when it was assisted by the wind whistling among the branches. The first rude essay of nature had been so much improved by human labour, that the cave contained several apartments, appropriated to different uses, and often afforded lodging to travellers, whom darkness or tempests happened to overtake.

The Hermit sat on a bench at the door, to enjoy the coolness of the evening. On one side lay a book with pens and papers, on the other mechanical instruments of various kinds. As they approached him unregarded, the princess observed that he had not the countenance of a man that had found, or could teach, the way to happiness.

They saluted him with great respect, which he repaid like a man not unaccustomed to the forms of courts, 'My children, said he, if you have lost your way, you shall be willingly supplied with such conveniences for the night as this cavern will afford. I have all that nature requires, and you will not expect delicacies in a Hermit's cell.'

They thanked him, and entering, were pleased with the neatness and regularity of the place. The Hermit set flesh and wine before them, though he fed only upon fruits and water. His discourse was chearful without levity, and pious without enthusiasm. He soon gained the esteem of his guests, and the princess repented of her hasty censure.

At last Imlac began thus: 'I do not now wonder that your reputation is so far extended; we have heard at Cairo of your wisdom, and came hither to implore your direction for this young man and maiden in the *choice of life*.'

'To him that lives well, answered the hermit, every form of life is good; nor can I give any other rule for choice, than to remove from all apparent evil.'

'He will remove most certainly from evil, said the prince, who shall devote himself to that solitude which you have recommended by your example.'

'I have indeed lived fifteen years in solitude, said the hermit, but have no desire that my example should gain any imitators. In my youth I professed arms, and was raised by degrees to the highest military rank. I have traversed wide countries at the head of my troops, and seen many battles and sieges. At last, being disgusted by the preferent of a younger officer, and feeling that my vigour was beginning to decay, I resolved to close my life in peace, having found the world full of snares, discord, and misery. I had once escaped from the persuit of the enemy by the shelter of this cavern, and therefore chose it for my final residence. I employed artificers to form it into chambers, and stored it with all that I was likely to want.

'For some time after my retreat, I rejoiced like a tempest-beaten sailor at his entrance into the harbour, being delighted with the sudden change of the noise and hurry of war, to stillness and repose. When the pleasure of novelty went away, I employed my hours in examining the plants which grow in the valley, and the minerals which I collected from the rocks. But that enquiry is now grown tasteless and irksome. I have been for some time unsettled and distracted: my mind is disturbed with a thousand perplexities of doubt, and vanities of imagination, which hourly prevail upon me, because I have no opportunities of relaxation or diversion. I am sometimes ashamed to think that I could not secure myself from vice, but by retiring from the exercise of virtue, and begin to suspect that I was rather impelled by resentment, than led by devotion, into solitude. My fancy riots in scenes of folly, and I lament that I have lost so much, and have gained so little. In solitude, if I escape the example of bad men, I want likewise the counsel and conversation of the good. I have been long comparing the evils with the advantages of society, and resolve to return into the world tomorrow. The life of a solitary man will be certainly miserable, but not certainly devout.'

They heard his resolution with surprise, but, after a short pause, offered to conduct him to Cairo. He dug up a considerable treasure which he had hid among the rocks, and accompanied them to the city, on which, as he approached it, he gazed with rapture.

CHAP. XXII

The happiness of a life led according to nature

RASSELAS went often to an assembly of learned men, who met at stated times to unbend their minds, and compare their opinions. Their manners were somewhat coarse, but their conversation was instructive, and their disputations acute, though sometimes too violent, and often continued till neither controvertist remembered upon what question they began. Some faults were almost general among them: every one was desirous to dictate to the rest, and every one was pleased to hear the genius or knowledge of another depreciated.

In this assembly Rasselas was relating his interview with the hermit, and the wonder with which he heard him censure a course of life which he had so deliberately chosen, and so laudably followed. The sentiments of the hearers were various. Some were of opinion, that the folly of his choice had been justly punished by condemnation to perpetual perseverance. One of the youngest among them, with great vehemence, pronounced him an hypocrite. Some talked of the right of society to the labour of individuals, and considered retirement as a desertion of duty. Others readily allowed, that there was a time when the claims of the publick were satisfied, and when a man might properly sequester himself, to review his life, and purify his heart.

One, who appeared more affected with the narrative than the rest, thought it likely, that the hermit would, in a few years, go back to his retreat, and, perhaps, if shame did not restrain, or death intercept him, return once more from his retreat into the world: 'For the hope of happiness, said he, is so strongly impressed, that the longest experience is not able to efface it. Of the present state, whatever it be, we feel, and are forced to confess, the misery, yet, when the same state is again at a distance, imagination paints it as desirable. But the time will surely come, when desire will be no longer our torment, and no man shall be wretched but by his own fault.'

'This, said a philosopher, who had heard him with tokens of great impatience, is the present condition of a wise man. The time is already come, when none are wretched but by their own fault. Nothing is more idle, than to inquire after happiness, which nature has kindly placed within our reach. The way to be happy is to live according to nature, in obedience to that universal and unalterable law with which every heart is originally impressed; which is not written on it by precept, but engraven by destiny, not instilled by education but infused at our nativity. He that lives according to nature will suffer nothing from the delusions of hope, or importunities of desire: he will receive and reject with equability of temper; and act or suffer as the reason of things shall alternately prescribe. Other men may amuse themselves with subtle definitions, or intricate raciocination. Let them learn to be wise by easier means: let them observe the hind of the forest, and the linnet of the grove: let them consider the life of animals, whose motions are regulated by instinct; they obey their guide and are happy. Let us therefore, at length, cease to dispute, and learn to live; throw away the incumbrance of precepts, which they who utter them with so much pride and pomp do not understand, and carry with us this simple and intelligible maxim, That deviation from nature is deviation from happiness.'

When he had spoken, he looked round him with a placid air, and enjoyed the consciousness of his own beneficence. 'Sir, said the prince, with great modesty, as I, like all the rest of mankind, am desirous of felicity, my closest attention has been fixed upon your discourse: I doubt not the truth of a position which a man so learned has so confidently advanced. Let me only know what it is to live according to nature.'

'When I find young men so humble and so docile, said the philosopher, I can deny them no information which my studies have enabled me to afford. To live according to nature, is to act always with due regard to the fitness arising from the relations and qualities of causes and effects; to concur with the great and unchangeable scheme of universal felicity; to co-operate with the general disposition and tendency of the present system of things.'

The prince soon found that this was one of the sages whom he should understand less as he heard him longer. He therefore bowed and was silent, and the philosopher, supposing him satisfied, and the rest vanquished, rose up and departed with the air of a man that had co-operated with the present system.

CHAP. XXIII

The prince and his sister divide between them the work of observation

RASSELAS returned home full of reflexions, doubtful how to direct his future steps. Of the way to happiness he found the learned and simple equally ignorant; but, as he was yet young, he flattered himself that he had time remaining for more experiments, and further enquiries. He communicated to Imlac his observations and his doubts, but was answered by him with new doubts, and remarks that gave him no comfort. He therefore discoursed more frequently and freely with his sister, who had yet the same hope with himself, and always assisted him to give some reason why, though he had been hitherto frustrated, he might succeed at last.

'We have hitherto, said she, known but little of the world: we have never yet been either great or mean. In our own country, though we had royalty, we had no power, and in this we have not yet seen the private recesses of domestick peace. Imlac favours not our search, lest we should in time find him mistaken. We will divide the task between us: you shall try what is to be found in the splendour of courts, and I will range the shades of humbler life. Perhaps command and authority may be the supreme blessings, as they afford most opportunities of doing good: or, perhaps, what this world can give may be found in the modest habitations of middle fortune; too low for great designs, and too high for penury and distress.'

CHAP. XXIV

The prince examines the happiness of high stations

RASSELAS applauded the design, and appeared next day with a splendid retinue at the court of the Bassa. He was soon distinguished for his magnificence, and admitted, as a prince whose curiosity had brought him from distant countries, to an intimacy with the great officers, and frequent conversation with the Bassa himself.

He was at first inclined to believe, that the man must be pleased with his own condition, whom all approached with reverence, and heard with obedience, and who had the power to extend his edicts to a whole kingdom. 'There can be no pleasure, said he, equal to that of feeling at once the joy of thousands all made happy by wise administration. Yet, since, by the law of subordination, this sublime delight can be in one nation but the lot of one, it is surely reasonable to think that there is some satisfaction more popular and accessible, and that millions can hardly be subjected to the will of a single man, only to fill his particular breast with incommunicable content.'

These thoughts were often in his mind, and he found no solution of the difficulty. But as presents and civilities gained him more familiarity, he found that almost every man who stood high in employment hated all the rest, and was hated by them, and that their lives were a continual succession of plots and detections, stratagems and escapes, faction and treachery. Many of those, who surrounded the Bassa, were sent only to watch and report his conduct; every tongue was muttering censure and every eye was searching for a fault.

At last the letters of revocation arrived, the Bassa was carried in chains to Constantinople, and his name was mentioned no more.

'What are we now to think of the prerogatives of power, said Rasselas to his sister; is it without any efficacy to good? or, is the subordinate degree only dangerous, and the supreme safe and glorious? Is the Sultan the only happy man in his dominions? or, is the Sultan himself subject to the torments of suspicion, and the dread of enemies?'

In a short time the second Bassa was deposed. The Sultan, that had advanced him, was murdered by the Janisaries, and his successor had other views and different favourites.

CHAP. XXV

The princess persues her enquiry with more diligence than success

THE princess, in the mean time, insinuated herself into many families; for there are few doors, through which liberality, joined with good humour, cannot find its way. The daughters of many houses were airy and chearful, but Nekayah had been too long accustomed to the conversation of Imlac and her brother to be much pleased with childish levity and prattle which had no meaning. She found their thoughts narrow, their wishes low, and their merriment often artificial. Their pleasures, poor as they were, could not be preserved pure, but were embittered by petty competitions and worthless emulation. They were always jealous of the beauty of each other; of a quality to which solicitude can add nothing, and from which detraction can take nothing away. Many were in love with triflers like themselves, and many fancied that they were in love when in truth they were only idle. Their affection was seldom fixed on sense or virtue, and therefore seldom ended but in vexation. Their grief, however, like their joy, was transient; every thing floated in their mind unconnected with the past or future, so that one desire easily gave way to another, as a second stone cast into the water effaces and confounds the circles of the first.

With these girls she played as with inoffensive animals, and found them proud of her countenance, and weary of her company.

But her purpose was to examine more deeply, and her affability easily persuaded the hearts that were swelling with sorrow to discharge their secrets in her ear: and those whom hope flattered, or prosperity delighted, often courted her to partake their pleasures.

The princess and her brother commonly met in the evening in a private summer-house on the bank of the Nile, and related to each other the occurrences of the day. As they were sitting together, the princess cast her eyes upon the river that flowed before her. 'Answer, said she, great father of waters, thou that rollest thy floods through eighty nations, to the invocations of the daughter of thy native king. Tell me if thou waterest, through all thy course, a single habitation from which thou dost not hear the murmurs of complaint?'

'You are then, said Rasselas, not more successful in private houses than I have been in courts.' 'I have, since the last partition of our provinces, said the princess, enabled myself to enter familiarly into many families, where there was the fairest show of prosperity and peace, and know not one house that is not haunted by some fury that destroys its quiet.

'I did not seek ease among the poor, because I concluded that there it could not be found. But I saw many poor whom I had supposed to live in affluence. Poverty has, in large cities, very different appearances: it is often concealed in splendour, and often in extravagance. It is the care of a very great part of mankind to conceal their indigence from the rest: they support themselves by temporary expedients, and every day is lost in contriving for the morrow.

'This, however, was an evil, which, though frequent, I saw with less pain, because I could relieve it. Yet some have refused my bounties; more offended with my quickness to detect their wants, than pleased with my readiness to succour them: and others, whose exigencies compelled them to admit my kindness, have never been able to forgive their benefactress. Many, however, have been sincerely grateful without the ostentation of gratitude, or the hope of other favours.'

CHAP. XXVI

The princess continues her remarks upon private life

NEKAYAH perceiving her brother's attention fixed, proceeded in her narrative. 'In families, where there is or is not poverty, there is commonly discord: if a kingdom be, as Imlac tells us, a great family, a family likewise is a little kingdom, torn with factions and exposed to revolutions. An unpractised observer expects the love of parents and children to be constant and equal; but this kindness seldom continues beyond the years of infancy: in a short time the children become rivals to their parents. Benefits are allayed by reproaches, and gratitude debased by envy.

'Parents and children seldom act in concert: each child endeavours to appropriate the esteem or fondness of the parents, and the parents, with yet less temptation, betray each other to their children; thus some place their confidence in the father, and some in the mother, and, by degrees, the house is filled with artifices and feuds.

'The opinions of children and parents, of the young and the old, are naturally opposite, by the contrary effects of hope and despondence, of expectation and experience, without crime or folly on either side. The colours of life in youth and age appear different, as the face of nature in spring and winter. And how can children credit the assertions of parents, which their own eyes show them to be false?

'Few parents act in such a manner as much to enforce their maxims by the credit of their lives. The old man trusts wholly to slow contrivance and gradual progression: the youth expects to force his way by genius, vigour, and precipitance. The old man pays regard to riches, and the youth reverences virtue. The old man deifies prudence: the youth commits himself to magnanimity and chance. The young man, who intends no ill, believes that none is intended, and therefore acts with openness and candour: but his father, having suffered the injuries of fraud, is impelled to suspect, and too often allured to practice it. Age looks with anger on the temerity of youth, and youth with contempt on the scrupulosity of age. Thus parents and children, for the greatest part, live on to love less and less: and, if those whom nature has thus closely united are the torments of each other, where shall we look for tenderness and consolation?'

'Surely, said the prince, you must have been unfortunate in your choice of acquaintance: I am unwilling to believe, that the most tender of all relations is thus impeded in its effects by natural necessity.'

'Domestick discord, answered she, is not inevitably and fatally necessary; but yet is not easily avoided. We seldom see that a whole family is virtuous: the good and evil cannot well agree; and the evil can yet less agree with one another: even the virtuous fall sometimes to variance, when their virtues are of different kinds and tending to extremes. In general, those parents have most reverence who most deserve it: for he that lives well cannot be despised.

'Many other evils infest private life. Some are the slaves of servants whom they have trusted with their affairs. Some are kept in continual anxiety to the caprice of rich relations, whom they cannot please, and dare not offend. Some husbands are imperious, and some wives perverse: and, as it is always more easy to do evil than good, though the wisdom or virtue of one can very rarely make many happy, the folly or vice of one may often make many miserable.'

'If such be the general effect of marriage, said the prince, I shall, for the future, think it dangerous to connect my interest with that of another, lest I should be unhappy by my partner's fault.'

'I have met, said the princess, with many who live single for that reason; but I never found that their prudence ought to raise envy. They dream away their time without friendship, without fondness, and are driven to rid themselves of the day, for which they have no use, by childish amusements, or vicious delights. They act as beings under the constant sense of some known inferiority, that fills their minds with rancour, and their tongues with censure. They are peevish at home, and malevolent abroad; and, as the outlaws of human nature, make it their business and their pleasure to disturb that society which debars them from its privileges. To live without feeling or exciting sympathy, to be fortunate without adding to the felicity of others, or afflicted without tasting the balm of pity, is a state more gloomy than solitude: it is not retreat but exclusion from mankind. Marriage has many pains, but celibacy has no pleasures.'

'What then is to be done? said Rasselas; the more we enquire, the less we can resolve. Surely he is most likely to please himself that has no other inclination to regard.'

CHAP. XXVII

Disquisition upon greatness

THE conversation had a short pause. The prince having considered his sister's observations, told her, that she had surveyed life with prejudice, and supposed misery where she did not find it. 'Your narrative, says he, throws yet a darker gloom upon the prospects of futurity: the predictions of Imlac were but faint sketches of the evils painted by Nekayah. I have been lately convinced that quiet is not the daughter of grandeur, or of power: that her presence is not to be bought by wealth, nor enforced by conquest. It is evident, that as any man acts in a wider compass, he must be more exposed to opposition from enmity or miscarriage from chance; whoever has many to please or to govern, must use the ministry of many agents, some of whom will be wicked, and some ignorant; by some he will be misled, and by others betrayed. If he gratifies one he will offend another: those that are not favoured will think themselves injured; and, since favours can be conferred but upon few, the greater number will be always discontented.'

'The discontent, said the princess, which is thus unreasonable, I hope that I shall always have spirit to despise, and you, power to repress.'

'Discontent, answered Rasselas, will not always be without reason under the most just or vigilant administration of publick affairs. None however attentive, can always discover that merit which indigence or faction may happen to obscure; and none, however powerful, can always reward it. Yet, he that sees inferiour desert advanced above him, will naturally impute that preference to partiality or caprice; and, indeed, it can scarcely be hoped that any man, however magnanimous by nature, or exalted by condition, will be able to persist for ever in fixed and inexorable justice of distribution: he will sometimes indulge his own affections, and sometimes those of his favourites; he will permit some to please him who can never serve him; he will discover in those whom he loves qualities which in reality they do not possess; and to those, from whom he receives pleasure, he will in his turn endeavour to give it. Thus will recommendations sometimes prevail which were purchased by money, or by the more destructive bribery of flattery and servility.'

'He that has much to do will do something wrong, and of that wrong must suffer the consequences; and, if it were possible that he should always act rightly, yet when such numbers are to judge of his conduct, the bad will censure and obstruct him by malevolence, and the good sometimes by mistake.

'The highest stations cannot therefore hope to be the abodes of happiness, which I would willingly believe to have fled from thrones and palaces to seats of humble privacy and placid obscurity. For what can hinder the satisfaction, or intercept the expectations, of him whose abilities are adequate to his employments, who sees with his own eyes the whole circuit of his influence, who chooses by his own knowledge all whom he trusts, and whom none are tempted to deceive by hope or fear? Surely he has nothing to do but to love and to be loved, to be virtuous and to be happy.'

'Whether perfect happiness would be procured by perfect goodness, said Nekayah, this world will never afford an opportunity of deciding. But this, at least, may be maintained, that we do not always find visible happiness in proportion to visible virtue. All natural and almost all political evils, are incident alike to the bad and good: they are confounded in the misery of a famine, and not much distinguished in the fury of a faction; they sink together in a tempest, and are driven together from their country by invaders. All that virtue can afford is quietness of conscience, a steady prospect of a happier state; this may enable us to endure calamity with patience; but remember that patience must suppose pain.'

CHAP. XXVIII

Rasselas and Nekayah continue their conversation

'DEAR princess, said Rasselas, you fall into the common errours of exaggeratory declamation, by producing, in a familiar disquisition, examples of national calamities, and scenes of extensive misery, which are found in books rather than in the world, and which, as they are horrid, are ordained to be rare. Let us not imagine evils which we do not feel, nor injure life by misrepresentations. I cannot bear that querulous eloquence which threatens every city with a siege like that of Jerusalem, that makes famine attend on every flight of locusts, and suspends pestilence on the wing of every blast that issues from the south.

'On necessary and inevitable evils, which overwhelm kingdoms at once, all disputation is vain: when they happen they must be endured. But it is evident, that these bursts of universal distress are more dreaded than felt: thousands and ten thousands flourish in youth, and wither in age, without the knowledge of any other than domestick evils, and share the same pleasures and vexations whether their kings are mild or cruel, whether the armies of their country persue their enemies, or retreat before them. While courts are disturbed with intestine competitions, and ambassadours are negotiating in foreign countries, the smith still plies his anvil, and the husbandman drives his plow forward; the necessaries of life are required and obtained, and the successive business of the seasons continues to make its wonted revolutions.

'Let us cease to consider what, perhaps, may never happen, and what, when it shall happen, will laugh at human speculation. We will not endeavour to modify the motions of the elements, or to fix the destiny of kingdoms. It is our business to consider what beings like us may perform; each labouring for his own happiness, by promoting within his circle, however narrow, the happiness of others.

'Marriage is evidently the dictate of nature; men and women were made to be companions of each other, and therefore I cannot be persuaded but that marriage is one of the means of happiness.'

'I know not, said the princess, whether marriage be more than one of the innumerable modes of human misery. When I see and reckon the various forms of connubial infelicity, the unexpected causes of lasting discord, the diversities of temper, the oppositions of opinion, the rude collisions of contrary desire where both are urged by violent impulses, the obstinate contests of disagreeing virtues, where both are supported by consciousness of good intention, I am sometimes disposed to think with the severer casuists of most nations, that marriage is rather permitted than approved, and that none, but by the instigation of a passion too much indulged, entangle themselves with indissoluble compacts.'

'You seem to forget, replied Rasselas, that you have, even now, represented celibacy as less happy than marriage. Both conditions may be bad, but they cannot both be worst. Thus it happens when wrong opinions are entertained, that they mutually destroy each other, and leave the mind open to truth.'

'I did not expect, answered the princess, to hear that imputed to falshood which is the consequence only of frailty. To the mind, as to the eye, it is difficult to compare with exactness objects vast in their extent, and various in their parts. Where we see or conceive the whole at once we readily note the discriminations and decide the preference: but of two systems, of which neither can be surveyed by any human being in its full compass of magnitude and multiplicity of complication, where is the wonder, that judging of the whole by parts, I am alternately affected by one and the other as either presses on my memory or fancy? We differ from ourselves just as we differ from each other, when we see only part of the question, as in the multifarious relations of politicks and morality: but when we perceive the whole at once, as in numerical computations, all agree in one judgment, and none ever varies his opinion.'

"Let us not add, said the prince, to the other evils of life, the bitterness of controversy, nor endeavour to vie with each other in subtilties of argument. We are employed in a search, of which both are equally to enjoy the success, or suffer by the miscarriage. It is therefore fit that we assist each other. You surely conclude too hastily from the infelicity of marriage against its institution; will not the misery of life prove equally that life cannot be the gift of heaven? The world must be peopled by marriage, or peopled without it.'

'How the world is to be peopled, returned Nekayah, is not my care, and needs not be yours. I see no danger that the present generation should omit to leave successors behind them: we are not now enquiring for the world, but for ourselves.'

CHAP. XXIX

The debate on marriage continued

'THE good of the whole, says Rasselas, is the same with the good of all its parts. If marriage be best for mankind it must be evidently best for individuals, or a permanent and necessary duty must be the cause of evil, and some must be inevitably sacrificed to the convenience of others. In the estimate which you have made of the two states, it appears that the incommodities of a single life are, in a great measure, necessary and certain, but those of the conjugal state accidental and avoidable.

'I cannot forbear to flatter myself that prudence and benevolence will make marriage happy. The general folly of mankind is the cause of general complaint. What can be expected but disappointment and repentance from a choice made in the immaturity of youth, in the ardour of desire, without judgment, without foresight, without an enquiry after conformity of opinions, similarity of manners, rectitude of judgment, or purity of sentiment.

'Such is the common process of marriage. A youth and maiden meeting by chance, or brought together by artifice, exchange glances, reciprocate civilities, go home, and dream of one another. Having little to divert attention, or diversify thought, they find themselves uneasy when they are apart, and therefore conclude that they shall be happy together. They marry, and discover what nothing but voluntary blindness had before concealed; they wear out life in altercations, and charge nature with cruelty.

'From those early marriages proceeds likewise the rivalry of parents and children: the son is eager to enjoy the world before the father is willing to forsake it, and there is hardly room at once for two generations. The daughter begins to bloom before the mother can be content to fade, and neither can forbear to wish for the absence of the other.

'Surely all these evils may be avoided by that deliberation and delay which prudence prescribes to irrevocable choice. In the variety and jollity of youthful pleasures life may be well enough supported without the help of a partner. Longer time will increase experience, and wider views will allow better opportunities of enquiry and selection: one advantage, at least, will be certain; the parents will be visibly older than their children.'

'What reason cannot collect, said Nekayah, and what experiment has not yet taught, can be known only from the report of others. I have been told that late marriages are not eminently happy. This is a question too important to be neglected, and I have often proposed it to those, whose accuracy of remark, and comprehensiveness of knowledge, made their suffrages worthy of regard. They have generally determined, that it is dangerous for a man and woman to suspend their fate upon each other, at a time when opinions are fixed, and habits are established; when friendships have been contracted on both sides, when life has been planned into method, and the mind has long enjoyed the contemplation of its own prospects.

'It is scarcely possible that two travelling through the world under the conduct of chance, should have been both directed to the same path, and it will not often happen that either will quit the track which custom has made pleasing. When the desultory levity of youth has settled into regularity, it is soon succeeded by pride ashamed to yield, or obstinacy delighting to contend. And even though mutual esteem produces mutual desire to please, time itself, as it modifies unchangeably the external mien, determines likewise the direction of the passions, and gives an inflexible rigidity to the manners. Long customs are not easily broken: he that attempts to change the course of his own life, very often labours in vain; and how shall we do that for others which we are seldom able to do for ourselves?'

'But surely, interposed the prince, you suppose the chief motive of choice forgotten or neglected. Whenever I shall seek a wife, it shall be my first question, whether she be willing to be led by reason?'

'Thus it is, said Nekayah, that philosophers are deceived. There are a thousand familiar disputes which reason never can decide; questions that elude investigation, and make logick ridiculous; cases where something must be done, and where little can be said. Consider the state of mankind, and enquire how few can be supposed to act upon any occasions, whether small or great, with all the reasons of action present to their minds. Wretched would be the pair above all names of wretchedness, who should be doomed to adjust by reason every morning all the minute detail of a domestick day.

'Those who marry at an advanced age, will probably escape the encroachments of their children; but, in diminution of this advantage, they will be likely to leave them, ignorant and helpless, to a guardian's mercy: or, if that should not happen, they must at least go out of the world before they see those whom they love best either wise or great.

'From their children, if they have less to fear, they have less also to hope, and they lose, without equivalent the joys of early love, and the convenience of uniting with manners pliant, and minds susceptible of new impressions, which might wear away their dissimilitudes by long cohabitation, as soft bodies, by continual attrition, conform their surfaces to each other.

'I believe it will be found that those who marry late are best pleased with their children, and those who marry early with their partners.'

'The union of these two affections, said Rasselas, would produce all that could be wished. Perhaps there is a time when marriage might unite them, a time neither too early for the father, nor too late for the husband.'

'Every hour, answered the princess, confirms my prejudice in favour of the position so often uttered by the mouth of Imlac, "That nature sets her gifts on the right hand and on the left." Those conditions, which flatter hope and attract desire, are so constituted, that, as we approach one, we recede from another. There are goods so opposed that we cannot seize both, but, by too much prudence, may pass between them at too great a distance to reach either. This is often the fate of long consideration; he does nothing who endeavours to do more than is allowed to humanity. Flatter not yourself with contrarieties of pleasure. Of the blessings set before you make your choice, and be content. No man can taste the fruits of autumn while he is delighting his scent with the flowers of the spring: no man can, at the same time, fill his cup from the source and from the mouth of the Nile.'

CHAP. XXX

Imlac enters, and changes the conversation

HERE Imlac entered, and interrupted them. 'Imlac, said Rasselas, I have been taking from the princess the dismal history of private life, and am almost discouraged from further search.'

'It seems to me, said Imlac, that while you are making the choice of life, you neglect to live. You wander about a single city, which, however large and diversified, can now afford few novelties, and forget that you are in a country, famous among the earliest monarchies for the power and wisdom of its inhabitants; a country where the sciences first dawned that illuminate the world, and beyond which the arts cannot be traced of civil society or domestick life.

'The old Egyptians have left behind them monuments of industry and power before which all European magnificence is confessed to fade away. The ruins of their architecture are the schools of modern builders, and from the wonders which time has spared we may conjecture, though uncertainly, what it has destroyed.'

'My curiosity, said Rasselas, does not very strongly lead me to survey piles of stone, or mounds of earth; my business is with man. I came hither not to measure fragments of temples, or trace choaked aqueducts, but to look upon the various scenes of the present world.'

'The things that are now before us, said the princess, require attention, and deserve it. What have I to do with the heroes or the monuments of ancient times? with times which never can return, and heroes, whose form of life was different from all that the present condition of mankind requires or allows.'

'To know any thing, returned the poet, we must know its effects; to see men we must see their works, that we may learn what reason has dictated, or passion has incited, and find what are the most powerful motives of action. To judge rightly of the present we must oppose it to the past; for all judgment is comparative, and of the future nothing can be known. The truth is, that no mind is much employed upon the present: recollection and anticipation fill up almost all our moments. Our passions are joy and grief, love and hatred, hope and fear. Of joy and grief the past is the object, and the future of hope and fear; even love and hatred respect the past, for the cause must have been before the effect.

'The present state of things is the consequence of the former, and it is natural to inquire what were the sources of the good that we enjoy, or of the evil that we suffer. If we act only for ourselves, to neglect the study of history is not prudent: if we are entrusted with the care of others, it is not just. Ignorance, when it is voluntary, is criminal; and he may properly be charged with evil who refused to learn how he might prevent it.

'There is no part of history so generally useful as that which relates the progress of the human mind, the gradual improvement of reason, the successive advances of science, the vicissitudes of learning and ignorance, which are the light and darkness of thinking beings, the extinction and resuscitation of arts, and all the revolutions of the intellectual world. If accounts of battles and invasions are peculiarly the business of princes, the useful or elegant arts are not to be neglected; those who have kingdoms to govern, have understandings to cultivate.

'Example is always more efficacious than precept. A soldier is formed in war, and a painter must copy pictures. In this, contemplative life has the advantage: great actions are seldom seen, but the labours of art are always at hand for those who desire to know what art has been able to perform.

'When the eye or the imagination is struck with any uncommon work the next transition of an active mind is to the means by which it was performed. Here begins the true use of such contemplation; we enlarge our comprehension by new ideas, and perhaps recover some art lost to mankind, or learn what is less perfectly known in our own country. At least we compare our own with former times, and either rejoice at our improvements, or, what is the first motion towards good, discover our defects.'

'I am willing, said the prince, to see all that can deserve my search.' 'And I, said the princess, shall rejoice to learn something of the manners of antiquity.'

'The most pompous monument of Egyptian greatness, and one of the most bulky works of manual industry, said Imlac, are the pyramids; fabricks raised before the time of history, and of which the earliest narratives afford us only uncertain traditions. Of these the greatest is still standing, very little injured by time.'

'Let us visit them to morrow, said Nekayah. I have often heard of the pyramids, and shall not rest, till I have seen them within and without with my own eyes.'

CHAP. XXXI

They visit the pyramids

THE resolution being thus taken, they set out the next day. They laid tents upon their camels, being resolved to stay among the pyramids till their curiosity was fully satisfied. They travelled gently, turned aside to every thing remarkable, stopped from time to time and conversed with the inhabitants, and observed the various appearances of towns ruined and inhabited, of wild and cultivated nature.

When they came to the Great Pyramid they were astonished at the extent of the base, and the height of the top. Imlac explained to them the principles upon which the pyramidal form was chosen for a fabrick intended to co-extend its duration with that of the world: he showed that its gradual diminution gave it such stability, as defeated all the common attacks of the elements, and could scarcely be overthrown by earthquakes themselves, the least resistible of natural violence. A concussion that should shatter the pyramid would threaten the dissolution of the continent.

They measured all its dimensions, and pitched their tents at its foot. Next day they prepared to enter its interiour apartments, and having hired the common guides climbed up to the first passage, when the favourite of the princess, looking into the cavity, stepped back and trembled. 'Pekuah, said the princess, of what art thou afraid?' 'Of the narrow entrance, answered the lady, and of the dreadful gloom. I dare not enter a place which must surely be inhabited by unquiet souls. The original possessors of these dreadful vaults will start up before us, and, perhaps, shut us in for ever.' She spoke, and threw her arms round the neck of her mistress.

'If all your fear be of apparitions, said the prince, I will promise you safety: there is no danger from the dead; he that is once buried will be seen no more.'

'That the dead are seen no more, said Imlac, I will not undertake to maintain against the concurrent and unvaried testimony of all ages, and of all nations. There is no people, rude or learned, among whom apparitions of the dead are not related and believed. This opinion, which, perhaps, prevails as far as human nature is diffused, could become universal only by its truth: those, that never heard of one another, would not have agreed in a tale which nothing but experience can make credible. That it is doubted by single cavillers can very little weaken the general evidence, and some who deny it with their tongues confess it by their fears.

'Yet I do not mean to add new terrours to those which have already seized upon Pekuah. There can be no reason why spectres should haunt the pyramid more than other places, or why they should have power or will to hurt innocence and purity. Our entrance is no violation of their privileges; we can take nothing from them, how then can we offend them?'

'My dear Pekuah, said the princess, I will always go before you, and Imlac shall follow you. Remember that you are the companion of the princess of Abissinia.'

'If the princess is pleased that her servant should die, returned the lady, let her command some death less dreadful than enclosure in this horrid cavern. You know I dare not disobey you: I must go if you command me; but, if I once enter, I never shall come back.'

The princess saw that her fear was too strong for expostulation or reproof, and embracing her, told her that she should stay in the tent till their return. Pekuah was yet not satisfied, but entreated the princess not to persue so dreadful a purpose, as that of entering the recesses of the pyramid. 'Though I cannot teach courage, said Nekayah, I must not learn cowardise; nor leave at last undone what I came hither only to do.'

CHAP. XXXII

They enter the pyramid

PEKUAH descended to the tents and the rest entered the pyramid: they passed through the galleries, surveyed the vaults of marble, and examined the chest in which the body of the founder is supposed to have been reposited. They then sat down in one of the most spacious chambers to rest a while before they attempted to return.

'We have now, said Imlac, gratified our minds with an exact view of the greatest work of man, except the wall of China.'

'Of the wall it is very easy to assign the motives. It secured a wealthy and timorous nation from the incursions of Barbarians, whose unskilfulness in arts made it easier for them to supply their wants by rapine than by industry, and who from time to time poured in upon the habitations of peaceful commerce, as vultures descend upon domestick fowl. Their celerity and fierceness made the wall necessary, and their ignorance made it efficacious.

'But for the pyramids no reason has ever been given adequate to the cost and labour of the work. The narrowness of the chambers proves that it could afford no retreat from enemies, and treasures might have been reposited at far less expence with equal security. It seems to have been erected only in compliance with that hunger of imagination which preys incessantly upon life, and must be always appeased by some employment. Those who have already all that they can enjoy, must enlarge their desires. He that has built for use, till use is supplied, must begin to build for vanity, and extend his plan to the utmost power of human performance, that he may not be soon reduced to form another wish.

'I consider this mighty structure as a monument of the insufficiency of human enjoyments. A king, whose power is unlimited, and whose treasures surmount all real and imaginary wants, is compelled to solace, by the erection of a pyramid, the satiety of dominion and tastelessness of pleasures, and to amuse the tediousness of declining life, by seeing thousands labouring without end, and one stone, for no purpose, laid upon another. Whoever thou art, that, not content with a moderate condition, imaginest happiness in royal magnificence, and dreamest that command or riches can feed the appetite of novelty with perpetual gratifications, survey the pyramids, and confess thy folly!'

CHAP. XXXIII

The princess meets with an unexpected misfortune

THEY rose up, and returned through the cavity at which they had entered, and the princess prepared for her favourite a long narrative of dark labyrinths, and costly rooms, and of the different impressions which the varieties of the way had made upon her. But, when they came to their train, they found every one silent and dejected: the men discovered shame and fear in their countenances, and the women were weeping in the tents.

What had happened they did not try to conjecture, but immediately enquired. 'You had scarcely entered into the pyramid, said one of the attendants, when a troop of Arabs rushed upon us: we were too few to resist them, and too slow to escape. They were about to search the tents, set us on our camels, and drive us along before them, when the approach of some Turkish horsemen put them to flight; but they seized the lady Pekuah with her two maids, and carried them away: the Turks are now persuing them by our instigation, but I fear they will not be able to overtake them.' The princess was overpowered with surprise and grief. Rasselas, in the first heat of his resentment, ordered his servants to follow him, and prepared to persue the robbers with his sabre in his hand. 'Sir, said Imlac, what can you hope from violence or valour? the Arabs are mounted on horses trained to battle and retreat; we have only beasts of burden. By leaving our present station we may lose the princess, but cannot hope to regain Pekuah.'

In a short time the Turks returned, having not been able to reach the enemy. The princess burst out into new lamentations, and Rasselas could scarcely forbear to reproach them with cowardice; but Imlac was of opinion, that the escape of the Arabs was no addition to their misfortune, for, perhaps, they would have killed their captives rather than have resigned them.

CHAP. XXXIV

They return to Cairo without Pekuah

THERE was nothing to be hoped from longer stay. They returned to Cairo repenting of their curiosity, censuring the negligence of the government, lamenting their own rashness which had neglected to procure a guard, imagining many expedients by which the loss of Pekuah might have been prevented, and resolving to do something for her recovery, though none could find any thing proper to be done.

Nekayah retired to her chamber, where her women attempted to comfort her, by telling her that all had their troubles, and that lady Pekuah had enjoyed much happiness in the world for a long time, and might reasonably expect a change of fortune. They hoped that some good would befal her wheresoever she was, and that their mistress would find another friend who might supply her place.

The princess made them no answer, and they continued the form of condolence, not much grieved in their hearts that the favourite was lost.

Next day the prince presented to the Bassa a memorial of the wrong which he had suffered, and a petition for redress. The Bassa threatened to punish the robbers, but did not attempt to catch them, nor, indeed, could any account or description be given by which he might direct the persuit.

It soon appeared that nothing would be done by authority. Governors, being accustomed to hear of more crimes than they can punish, and more wrongs than they can redress, set themselves at ease by indiscriminate negligence, and presently forget the request when they lose sight of the petitioner.

Imlac then endeavoured to gain some intelligence by private agents. He found many who pretended to an exact knowledge of all the haunts of the Arabs, and to regular correspondence with their chiefs, and who readily undertook the recovery of Pekuah. Of these, some were furnished with money for their journey, and came back no more; some were liberally paid for accounts which a few days discovered to be false. But the princess would not suffer any means, however improbable, to be left untried. While she was doing something she kept her hope alive. As one expedient failed, another was suggested; when one messenger returned unsuccessful, another was despatched to a different quarter.

Two months had now passed, and of Pekuah nothing had been heard; the hopes which they had endeavoured to raise in each other grew more languid, and the princess, when she saw nothing more to be tried, sunk down inconsolable in hopeless dejection. A thousand times she reproached herself with the easy compliance by which she permitted her favourite to stay behind her. 'Had not my fondness, said she, lessened my authority, Pekuah had not dared to talk of her terrours. She ought to have feared me more than spectres. A severe look would have overpowered her; a peremptory command would have compelled obedience. Why did foolish indulgence prevail upon me? Why did I not speak and refuse to hear?'

'Great princess, said Imlac, do not reproach yourself for your virtue, or consider that as blameable by which evil has accidentally been caused. Your tenderness for the timidity of Pekuah was generous and kind. When we act according to our duty, we commit the event to him by whose laws our actions are governed, and who will suffer none to be finally punished for obedience. When, in prospect of some good, whether natural or moral, we break the rules prescribed us, we withdraw from the direction of superiour wisdom, and take all consequences upon ourselves. Man cannot so far know the connexion of causes and events, as that he may venture to do wrong in order to do right. When we persue our end by lawful means, we may always console our miscarriage by the hope of future recompense. When we consult only our own policy, and attempt to find a nearer way to good, by overleaping the settled boundaries of right and wrong, we cannot be happy even by success, because we cannot escape the consciousness of our fault; but, if we miscarry, the disappointment is irremediably embittered. How comfortless is the sorrow of him, who feels at once the pangs of guilt, and the vexation of calamity which guilt has brought upon him?

'Consider, princess, what would have been your condition, if the lady Pekuah had entreated to accompany you, and, being compelled to stay in the tents, had been carried away; or how would you have born the thought, if you had forced her into the pyramid, and she had died before you in agonies of terrour.'

'Had either happened, said Nekayah, I could not have endured life till now: I should have been tortured to madness by the remembrance of such cruelty, or must have pined away in abhorrence of myself.'

'This at least, said Imlac, is the present reward of virtuous conduct, that no unlucky consequence can oblige us to repent it.'

CHAP. XXXV

The princess languishes for want of Pekuah

NEKAYAH, being thus reconciled to herself, found that no evil is insupportable but that which is accompanied with consciousness of wrong. She was, from that time, delivered from the violence of tempestuous sorrow, and sunk into silent pensiveness and gloomy tranquillity. She sat from morning to evening recollecting all that had been done or said by her Pekuah, treasured up with care every trifle on which Pekuah had set an accidental value, and which might recal to mind any little incident or careless conversation. The sentiments of her, whom she now expected to see no more, were treasured in her memory as rules of life, and she deliberated to no other end than to conjecture on any occasion what would have been the opinion and counsel of Pekuah.

The women, by whom she was attended, knew nothing of her real condition, and therefore she could not talk to them but with caution and reserve. She began to remit her curiosity, having no great care to collect notions which she had no convenience of uttering. Rasselas endeavoured first to comfort and afterwards to divert her; he hired musicians, to whom she seemed to listen, but did not hear them, and procured masters to instruct her in various arts, whose lectures, when they visited her again, were again to be repeated. She had lost her taste of pleasure and her ambition of excellence. And her mind, though forced into short excursions, always recurred to the image of her friend.

Imlac was every morning earnestly enjoined to renew his enquiries, and was asked every night whether he had yet heard of Pekuah, till not being able to return the princess the answer that she desired, he was less and less willing to come into her presence. She observed his backwardness, and commanded him to attend her. 'You are not, said she, to confound impatience with resentment, or to suppose that I charge you with negligence, because I repine at your unsuccessfulness. I do not much wonder at your absence; I know that the unhappy are never pleasing, and that all naturally avoid the contagion of misery. To hear complaints is wearisome alike to the wretched and the happy; for who would cloud by adventitious grief the short gleams of gaiety which life allows us? or who, that is struggling under his own evils, will add to them the miseries of another?

'The time is at hand, when none shall be disturbed any longer by the sighs of Nekayah: my search after happiness is now at an end. I am resolved to retire from the world with all its flatteries and deceits, and will hide myself in solitude, without any other care than to compose my thoughts, and regulate my hours by a constant succession of innocent occupations, till, with a mind purified from all earthly desires, I shall enter into that state, to which all are hastening, and in which I hope again to enjoy the friendship of Pekuah.'

'Do not entangle your mind, said Imlac, by irrevocable determinations, nor increase the burthen of life by a voluntary accumulation of misery: the weariness of retirement will continue or increase when the loss of Pekuah is forgotten. That you have been deprived of one pleasure is no very good reason for rejection of the rest.'

'Since Pekuah was taken from me, said the princess, I have no pleasure to reject or to retain. She that has no one to love or trust has little to hope. She wants the radical principle of happiness. We may, perhaps, allow that what satisfaction this world can afford, must arise from the conjunction of wealth, knowledge and goodness: wealth is nothing but as it is bestowed, and knowledge nothing but as it is communicated: they must therefore be imparted to others, and to whom could I now delight to impart them? Goodness affords the only comfort which can be enjoyed without a partner, and goodness may be practised in retirement.'

'How far solitude may admit goodness, or advance it, I shall not, replied Imlac, dispute at present. Remember the confession of the pious hermit. You will wish to return into the world, when the image of your companion has left your thoughts.' 'That time, said Nekayah, will never come. The generous frankness, the modest obsequiousness, and the faithful secrecy of my dear Pekuah, will always be more missed, as I shall live longer to see vice and folly.'

'The state of a mind oppressed with a sudden calamity, said Imlac, is like that of the fabulous inhabitants of the new created earth, who, when the first night came upon them, supposed that day never would return. When the clouds of sorrow gather over us, we see nothing beyond them, nor can imagine how they will be dispelled: yet a new day succeeded to the night, and sorrow is never long without a dawn of ease. But they who restrain themselves from receiving comfort, do as the savages would have done, had they put out their eyes when it was dark. Our minds, like our bodies, are in continual flux; something is hourly lost, and something acquired. To lose much at once is inconvenient to either, but while the vital powers remain uninjured, nature will find the means of reparation. Distance has the same effect on the mind as on the eye, and while we glide along the stream of time, whatever we leave behind us is always lessening, and that which we approach increasing in magnitude. Do not suffer life to stagnate; it will grow muddy for want of motion: commit yourself again to the current of the world; Pekuah will vanish by degrees; you will meet in your way some other favourite, or learn to diffuse yourself in general conversation.'

'At least, said the prince, do not despair before all remedies have been tried: the enquiry after the unfortunate lady is still continued, and shall be carried on with yet greater diligence, on condition that you will promise to wait a year for the event, without any unalterable resolution.'

Nekayah thought this a reasonable demand, and made the promise to her brother, who had been advised by Imlac to require it. Imlac had, indeed, no great hope of regaining Pekuah, but he supposed, that if he could secure the interval of a year, the princess would be then in no danger of a cloister.

CHAP. XXXVI

Pekuah is still remembered. The progress of sorrow

NEKAYAH, seeing that nothing was omitted for the recovery of her favourite, and having, by her promise, set her intention of retirement at a distance, began imperceptibly to return to common cares and common pleasures. She rejoiced without her own consent at the suspension of her sorrows, and sometimes caught herself with indignation in the act of turning away her mind from the remembrance of her, whom yet she resolved never to forget.

She then appointed a certain hour of the day for meditation on the merits and fondness of Pekuah, and for some weeks retired constantly at the time fixed, and returned with her eyes swollen and her countenance clouded. By degrees she grew less scrupulous, and suffered any important and pressing avocation to delay the tribute of daily tears. She then yielded to less occasions; sometimes forgot what she was indeed afraid to remember, and, at last, wholly released herself from the duty of periodical affliction.

Her real love of Pekuah was yet not diminished. A thousand occurrences brought her back to memory, and a thousand wants, which nothing but the confidence of friendship can supply, made her frequently regretted. She, therefore, solicited Imlac never to desist from enquiry, and to leave no art of intelligence untried, that, at least, she might have the comfort of knowing that she did not suffer by negligence or sluggishness. 'Yet what, said she, is to be expected from our persuit of happiness, when we find the state of life to be such, that happiness itself is the cause of misery? Why should we endeavour to attain that, of which the possession cannot be secured? I shall henceforward fear to yield my heart to excellence, however bright, or to fondness, however tender, lest I should lose again what I have lost in Pekuah.'

CHAP. XXXVII

The Princess hears news of Pekuah

In seven months, one of the messengers, who had been sent away upon the day when the promise was drawn from the princess, returned, after many unsuccessful rambles, from the borders of Nubia, with an account that Pekuah was in the hands of an Arab chief, who possessed a castle or fortress on the extremity of Egypt. The Arab, whose revenue was plunder, was willing to restore her, with her two attendants, for two hundred ounces of gold.

The price was no subject of debate. The princess was in extasies when she heard that her favourite was alive, and might so cheaply be ransomed. She could not think of delaying for a moment Pekuah's happiness or her own, but entreated her brother to send back the messenger with the sum required. Imlac, being consulted, was not very confident of the veracity of the relator, and was still more doubtful of the Arab's faith, who might, if he were too liberally trusted, detain at once the money and the captives. He thought it dangerous to put themselves in the power of the Arab, by going into his district, and could not expect that the Rover would so much expose himself as to come into the lower country, where he might be seized by the forces of the Bassa.

It is difficult to negotiate where neither will trust. But Imlac, after some deliberation, directed the messenger to propose that Pekuah should be conducted by ten horsemen to the monastery of St. Anthony, which is situated in the deserts of Upper-Egypt, where she should be met by the same number, and her ransome should be paid.

That no time might be lost, as they expected that the proposal would not be refused, they immediately began their journey to the monastery; and, when they arrived, Imlac went forward with the former messenger to the Arab's fortress. Rasselas was desirous to go with them, but neither his sister nor Imlac would consent. The Arab, according to the custom of his nation, observed the laws of hospitality with great exactness to those who put themselves into his power, and, in a few days, brought Pekuah with her maids, by easy journeys, to their place appointed, where receiving the stipulated price, he restored her with great respect to liberty and her friends, and undertook to conduct them back towards Cairo beyond all danger of robbery or violence.

The princess and her favourite embraced each other with transport too violent to be expressed, and went out together to pour the tears of tenderness in secret, and exchange professions of kindness and gratitude. After a few hours they returned into the refectory of the convent, where, in the presence of the prior and his brethren, the prince required of Pekuah the history of her adventures.

CHAP. XXXVIII

The adventures of the lady Pekuah

'At what time, and in what manner, I was forced away, said Pekuah, your servants have told you. The suddenness of the event struck me with surprise, and I was at first rather stupified than agitated with any passion of either fear or sorrow. My confusion was encreased by the speed and tumult of our flight while we were followed by the Turks, who, as it seemed, soon despaired to overtake us, or were afraid of those whom they made a shew of menacing.

'When the Arabs saw themselves out of danger they slackened their course, and, as I was less harassed by external violence, I began to feel more uneasiness in my mind. After some time we stopped near a spring shaded with trees in a pleasant meadow, where we were set upon the ground, and offered such refreshments as our masters were partaking. I was suffered to sit with my maids apart from the rest, and none attempted to comfort or insult us. Here I first began to feel the full weight of my misery. The girls sat weeping in silence, and from time to time looked on me for succour. I knew not to what condition we were doomed, nor could conjecture where would be the place of our captivity, or whence to draw any hope of deliverance. I was in the hands of robbers and savages, and had no reason to suppose that their pity was more than their justice, or that they would forbear the gratification of any ardour of desire, or caprice of cruelty. I, however, kissed my maids, and endeavoured to pacify them by remarking, that we were yet treated with decency, and that, since we were now carried beyond persuit, there was no danger of violence to our lives.

'When we were to be set again on horseback, my maids clung round me, and refused to be parted, but I commanded them not to irritate those who had us in their power. We travelled the remaining part of the day through an unfrequented and pathless country, and came by moonlight to the side of a hill, where the rest of the troop was stationed. Their tents were pitched, and their fires kindled, and our chief was welcomed as a man much beloved by his dependants.

'We were received into a large tent, where we found women who had attended their husbands in the expedition. They set before us the supper which they had provided, and I eat it rather to encourage my maids than to comply with any appetite of my own. When the meat was taken away they spread the carpets for repose. I was weary, and hoped to find in sleep that remission of distress which nature seldom denies. Ordering myself therefore to be undrest, I observed that the women looked very earnestly upon me, not expecting, I suppose, to see me so submissively attended. When my upper vest was taken off, they were apparently struck with the splendour of my cloaths, and one of them timorously laid her hand upon the embroidery. She then went out, and, in a short time, came back with another woman, who seemed to be of higher rank, and greater authority. She did, at her entrance, the usual act of reverence, and, taking me by the hand, placed me in a smaller tent, spread with finer carpets, where I spent the night quietly with my maids.

'In the morning, as I was sitting on the grass, the chief of the troop came towards me. I rose up to receive him, and he bowed with great respect. 'Illustrious lady, said he, my fortune is better than I had presumed to hope; I am told by my women, that I have a princess in my camp.' Sir, answered I, your women have deceived themselves and you; I am not a princess, but an unhappy stranger who intended soon to have left this country, in which I am now to be imprisoned for ever. 'Whoever, or whencesoever, you are, returned the Arab, your dress, and that of your servants, show your rank to be high, and your wealth to be great. Why should you, who can so easily procure your ransome, think yourself in danger of perpetual captivity? The purpose of my incursions is to encrease my riches, or more properly to gather tribute. The sons of Ishmael are the natural and hereditary lords of this part of the continent, which is usurped by late invaders, and lowborn tyrants, from whom we are compelled to take by the sword what is denied to justice. The violence of war admits no distinction; the lance that is lifted at guilt and power will sometimes fall on innocence and gentleness.'

'How little, said I, did I expect that yesterday it should have fallen upon me.'

'Misfortunes, answered the Arab, should always be expected. If the eye of hostility could learn reverence or pity, excellence like yours had been exempt from injury. But the angels of affliction spread their toils alike for the virtuous and the wicked, for the mighty and the mean. Do not be disconsolate; I am not one of the lawless and cruel rovers of the desart; I know the rules of civil life: I will fix your ransome, give a passport to your messenger, and perform my stipulation with nice punctuality.'

'You will easily believe that I was pleased with his courtesy; and finding that his predominant passion was desire of money, I began now to think my danger less, for I knew that no sum would be thought too great for the release of Pekuah. I told him that he should have no reason to charge me with ingratitude, if I was used with kindness, and that any ransome, which could be expected for a maid of common rank, would be paid, but that he must not persist to rate me as a princess. He said, he would consider what he should demand, and then, smiling, bowed and retired.

'Soon after the women came about me, each contending to be more officious than the other, and my maids themselves were served with reverence. We travelled onward by short journeys. On the fourth day the chief told me, that my ransome must be two hundred ounces of gold, which I not only promised him, but told him, that I would add fifty more, if I and my maids were honourably treated.

'I never knew the power of gold before. From that time I was the leader of the troop. The march of every day was longer or shorter as I commanded, and the tents were pitched where I chose to rest. We now had camels and other conveniencies for travel, my own women were always at my side, and I amused myself with observing the manners of the vagrant nations, and with viewing remains of ancient edifices with which these deserted countries appear to have been, in some distant age, lavishly embellished.

'The chief of the band was a man far from illiterate: he was able to travel by the stars or the compass, and had marked in his erratick expeditions such places as are most worthy the notice of a passenger. He observed to me, that buildings are always best preserved in places little frequented, and difficult of access: for, when once a country declines from its primitive splendour, the more inhabitants are left, the quicker ruin will be made. Walls supply stones more easily than quarries, and palaces and temples will be demolished to make stables of granate, and cottages of porphyry.

CHAP. XXXIX

The adventures of Pekuah continued

'WE wandered about in this manner for some weeks, whether, as our chief pretended, for my gratification, or, as I rather suspected, for some convenience of his own. I endeavoured to appear contented where sullenness and resentment would have been of no use, and that endeavour conduced much to the calmness of my mind; but my heart was always with Nekayah, and the troubles of the night much overbalanced the amusements of the day. My women, who threw all their cares upon their mistress, set their minds at ease from the time when they saw me treated with respect, and gave themselves up to the incidental alleviations of our fatigue without solicitude or sorrow. I was pleased with their pleasure, and animated with their confidence. My condition had lost much of its terrour, since I found that the Arab ranged the country merely to get riches. Avarice is an uniform and tractable vice: other intellectual distempers are different in different constitutions of mind; that which sooths the pride of one will offend the pride of another; but to the favour of the covetous there is a ready way, bring money and nothing is denied.

'At last we came to the dwelling of our chief, a strong and spacious house built with stone in an island of the Nile, which lies, as I was told, under the tropick. 'Lady, said the Arab, you shall rest after your journey a few weeks in this place, where you are to consider yourself as sovereign. My occupation is war: I have therefore chosen this obscure residence, from which I can issue unexpected, and to which I can retire unpersued. You may now repose in security: here are few pleasures, but here is no danger.' He then led me into the inner apartments, and seating me on the richest couch, bowed to the ground. His women, who considered me as a rival, looked on me with malignity; but being soon informed that I was a great lady detained only for my ransome, they began to vie with each other in obsequiousness and reverence.

'Being again comforted with new assurances of speedy liberty, I was for some days diverted from impatience by the novelty of the place. The turrets overlooked the country to a great distance, and afforded a view of many windings of the stream. In the day I wandered from one place to another as the course of the sun varied the splendour of the prospect, and saw many things which I had never seen before. The crocodiles and river-horses are common in this unpeopled region, and I often looked upon them with terrour, though I knew that they could not hurt me. For some time I expected to see mermaids and tritons, which, as Imlac has told me, the European travellers have stationed in the Nile, but no such beings ever appeared, and the Arab, when I enquired after them, laughed at my credulity.

'At night the Arab always attended me to a tower set apart for celestial observations, where he endeavoured to teach me the names and courses of the stars. I had no great inclination to this study, but an appearance of attention was necessary to please my instructor, who valued himself for his skill, and, in a little while, I found some employment requisite to beguile the tediousness of time, which was to be passed always amidst the same objects. I was weary of looking in the morning on things from which I had turned away weary in the evening: I therefore was at last willing to observe the stars rather than do nothing, but could not always compose my thoughts, and was very often thinking on Nekayah when others imagined me contemplating the sky. Soon after the Arab went upon another expedition, and then my only pleasure was to talk with my maids about the accident by which we were carried away, and the happiness that we should all enjoy at the end of our captivity.'

'There were women in your Arab's fortress, said the princess, why did you not make them your companions, enjoy their conversation, and partake their diversions? In a place where they found business or amusement, why should you alone sit corroded with idle melancholy? or why should not you bear for a few months that condition to which they were condemned for life?'

'The diversions of the women, answered Pekuah, were only childish play, by which the mind accustomed to stronger operations could not be kept busy. I could do all which they delighted in doing by powers merely sensitive, while my intellectual faculties were flown to Cairo. They ran from room to room as a bird hops from wire to wire in his cage. They danced for the sake of motion, as lambs frisk in a meadow. One sometimes pretended to be hurt that the rest might be alarmed, or hid herself that another might seek her. Part of their time passed in watching the progress of light bodies that floated on the river, and part in marking the various forms into which clouds broke in the sky.

'Their business was only needlework, in which I and my maids sometimes helped them; but you know that the mind will easily straggle from the fingers, nor will you suspect that captivity and absence from Nekayah could receive solace from silken flowers.

'Nor was much satisfaction to be hoped from their conversation: for of what could they be expected to talk? They had seen nothing; for they had lived from early youth in that narrow spot: of what they had not seen they could have no knowledge, for they could not read. They had no ideas but of the few things that were within their view, and had hardly names for any thing but their cloaths and their food. As I bore a superior character, I was often called to terminate their quarrels, which I decided as equitably as I could. If it could have amused me to hear the complaints of each against the rest, I might have been often detained by long stories, but the motives of their animosity were so small that I could not listen without intercepting the tale.'

'How, said Rasselas, can the Arab, whom you represented as a man of more than common accomplishments, take any pleasure in his seraglio, when it is filled only with women like these. Are they exquisitely beautiful?'

'They do not, said Pekuah, want that unaffecting and ignoble beauty which may subsist without spriteliness or sublimity, without energy of thought or dignity of virtue. But to a man like the Arab such beauty was only a flower casually plucked and carelessly thrown away. Whatever pleasures he might find among them, they were not those of friendship or society. When they were playing about him he looked on them with inattentive superiority: when they vied for his regard he sometimes turned away disgusted. As they had no knowledge, their talk could take nothing from the tediousness of life: as they had no choice, their fondness, or appearance of fondness, excited in him neither pride nor gratitude; he was not exalted in his own esteem by the smiles of a woman who saw no other man, nor was much obliged by that regard, of which he could never know the sincerity, and which he might often perceive to be exerted not so much to delight him as to pain a rival. That which he gave, and they received, as love, was only a careless distribution of superfluous time, such love as man can bestow upon that which he despises, such as has neither hope nor fear, neither joy nor sorrow.

'You have reason lady to think yourself happy, said Imlac, that you have been thus easily dismissed. How could a mind, hungry for knowledge, be willing, in an intellectual famine, to lose such a banquet as Pekuah's conversation?'

'I am inclined to believe, answered Pekuah, that he was for some time in suspense; notwithstanding his promise, whenever I proposed to dispatch a messenger to Cairo, he found some excuse for delay. While I was detained in his house he made many incursions into the neighbouring countries, and, perhaps, he would have refused to discharge me, had his plunder been equal to his wishes. He returned always courteous, related his adventures, delighted to hear my observations, and endeavoured to advance my acquaintance with the stars. When I importuned him to send away my letters, he soothed me with professions of honour and sincerity; and, when I could be no longer decently denied, put his troop again in motion, and left me to govern in his absence. I was much afflicted by this studied procrastination, and was sometimes afraid that I should be forgotten; that you would leave Cairo, and I must end my days in an island of the Nile.

'I grew at last hopeless and dejected, and cared so little to entertain him, that he for a while more frequently talked with my maids. That he should fall in love with them, or with me, might have been equally fatal, and I was not much pleased with the growing friendship. My anxiety was not long; for, as I recovered some degree of chearfulness, he returned to me, and I could not forbear to despise my former uneasiness.

'He still delayed to send for my ransome, and would, perhaps, never have determined, had not your agent found his way to him. The gold, which he would not fetch, he could not reject when it was offered. He hastened to prepare for our journey hither, like a man delivered from the pain of an intestine conflict. I took leave of my companions in the house, who dismissed me with cold indifference.'

Nekayah, having heard her favourite's relation, rose and embraced her, and Rasselas gave her an hundred ounces of gold, which she presented to the Arab for the fifty that were promised.

CHAP. XL

The history of a man of learning

THEY returned to Cairo, and were so well pleased at finding themselves together, that none of them went much abroad. The prince began to love learning, and one day declared to Imlac, that he intended to devote himself to science, and pass the rest of his days in literary solitude.

'Before you make your final choice, answered Imlac, you ought to examine its hazards, and converse with some of those who are grown old in the company of themselves. I have just left the observatory of one of the most learned astronomers in the world, who has spent forty years in unwearied attention to the motions and appearances of the celestial bodies, and has drawn out his soul in endless calculations. He admits a few friends once a month to hear his deductions and enjoy his discoveries. I was introduced as a man of knowledge worthy of his notice. Men of various ideas and fluent conversation are commonly welcome to those whose thoughts have been long fixed upon a single point, and who find the images of other things stealing away. I delighted him with my remarks, he smiled at the narrative of my travels, and was glad to forget the constellations, and descend for a moment into the lower world.

'On the next day of vacation I renewed my visit, and was so fortunate as to please him again. He relaxed from that time the severity of his rule, and permitted me to enter at my own choice. I found him always busy, and always glad to be relieved. As each knew much which the other was desirous of learning, we exchanged our notions with great delight. I perceived that I had every day more of his confidence, and always found new cause of admiration in the profundity of his mind. His comprehension is vast, his memory capacious and retentive, his discourse is methodical, and his expression clear.

'His integrity and benevolence are equal to his learning. His deepest researches and most favourite studies are willingly interrupted for any opportunity of doing good by his counsel or his riches. To his closest retreat at his most busy moments, all are admitted that want his assistance: 'For though I exclude idleness and pleasure, I will never, says he, bar my doors against charity. To man is permitted the contemplation of the skies, but the practice of virtue is commanded.

'Surely, said the princess, this man is happy.'

'I visited him, said Imlac, with more and more frequency and was every time more enamoured of his conversation: he was sublime without haughtiness, courteous without formality, and communicative without ostentation. I was at first, great princess, of your opinion, thought him the happiest of mankind, and often congratulated him on the blessing that he enjoyed. He seemed to hear nothing with indifference but the praises of his condition, to which he always returned a general answer, and diverted the conversation to some other topick.

'Amidst this willingness to be pleased, and labour to please, I had quickly reason to imagine that some painful sentiment pressed upon his mind. He often looked up earnestly towards the sun, and let his voice fall in the midst of his discourse. He would sometimes, when we were alone, gaze upon me in silence with the air of a man who longed to speak what he was yet resolved to suppress. He would often send for me with vehement injunctions of haste, though, when I came to him, he had nothing extraordinary to say. And sometimes, when I was leaving him, would call me back, pause a few moments and then dismiss me.

CHAP. XLI

The astronomer discovers the cause of his uneasiness

'AT last the time came when the secret burst his reserve. We were sitting together last night in the turret of his house, watching the emersion of a satellite of Jupiter. A sudden tempest clouded the sky, and disappointed our observation. We sat a while silent in the dark, and then he addressed himself to me in these words: 'Imlac, I have long considered thy friendship as the greatest blessing of my life. Integrity without knowledge is weak and useless, and knowledge without integrity is dangerous and dreadful. I have found in thee all the qualities requisite for trust, benevolence, experience, and fortitude. I have long discharged an office which I must soon quit at the call of nature, and shall rejoice in the hour of imbecility and pain to devolve it upon thee.'

'I thought myself honoured by this testimony, and protested that whatever could conduce to his happiness would add likewise to mine.'

'Hear, Imlac, what thou wilt not without difficulty credit. I have possessed for five years the regulation of weather, and the distribution of the seasons: the sun has listened to my dictates, and passed from tropick to tropick by my direction; the clouds, at my call, have poured their waters, and the Nile has overflowed at my command; I have restrained the rage of the dog-star, and mitigated the fervours of the crab. The winds alone, of all the elemental powers, have hitherto refused my authority, and multitudes have perished by equinoctial tempests which I found myself unable to prohibit or restrain. I have administered this great office with exact justice, and made to the different nations of the earth an impartial dividend of rain and sunshine. What must have been the misery of half the globe, if I had limited the clouds to particular regions, or confined the sun to either side of the equator?'

CHAP. XLII

The opinion of the astronomer is explained and justified

'I SUPPOSE he discovered in me, through the obscurity of the room, some tokens of amazement and doubt, for, after a short pause, he proceeded thus:

'Not to be easily credited will neither surprise nor offend me; for I am, probably, the first of human beings to whom this trust has been imparted. Nor do I know whether to deem this distinction as reward or punishment;

since I have possessed it I have been far less happy than before, and nothing but the consciousness of good intention could have enabled me to support the weariness of unremitted vigilance.'

'How long, Sir, said I, has this great office been in your hands?'

'About ten years ago, said he, my daily observations of the changes of the sky led me to consider, whether, if I had the power of the seasons, I could confer greater plenty upon the inhabitants of the earth. This contemplation fastened on my mind, and I sat days and nights in imaginary dominion, pouring upon this country and that the showers of fertility, and seconding every fall of rain with a due proportion of sunshine. I had yet only the will to do good, and did not imagine that I should ever have the power.

'One day as I was looking on the fields withering with heat, I felt in my mind a sudden wish that I could send rain on the southern mountains, and raise the Nile to an inundation. In the hurry of my imagination I commanded rain to fall, and, by comparing the time of my command, with that of the inundation, I found that the clouds had listned to my lips.'

'Might not some other cause, said I, produce this concurrence? the Nile does not always rise on the same day.'

'Do not believe, said he with impatience, that such objections could escape me: I reasoned long against my own conviction, and laboured against truth with the utmost obstinacy. I sometimes suspected myself of madness, and should not have dared to impart this secret but to a man like you, capable of distinguishing the wonderful from the impossible, and the incredible from the false.'

'Why, Sir, said I, do you call that incredible, which you know, or think you know, to be true?'

'Because, said he, I cannot prove it by any external evidence; and I know too well the laws of demonstration to think that my conviction ought to influence another, who cannot, like me, be conscious of its force. I, therefore, shall not attempt to gain credit by disputation. It is sufficient that I feel this power, that I have long possessed, and every day exerted it. But the life of man is short, the infirmities of age increase upon me, and the time will soon come when the regulator of the year must mingle with the dust. The care of appointing a successor has long disturbed me; the night and the day have been spent in comparisons of all the characters which have come to my knowledge, and I have yet found none so worthy as thyself.'

CHAP. XLIII

The astronomer leaves Imlac his directions

'Hear therefore, what I shall impart, with attention, such as the welfare of a world requires. If the task of a king be considered as difficult, who has the care only of a few millions, to whom he cannot do much good or harm, what must be the anxiety of him, on whom depend the action of the elements, and the great gifts of light and heat!—Hear me therefore with attention.

'I have diligently considered the position of the earth and sun, and formed innumerable schemes in which I changed their situation. I have sometimes turned aside the axis of the earth, and sometimes varied the ecliptick of the sun: but I have found it impossible to make a disposition by which the world may be advantaged; what one region gains, another loses by any imaginable alteration, even without considering the distant parts of the solar system with which we are unacquainted. Do not, therefore, in thy administration of the year, indulge thy pride by innovation; do not please thyself with thinking that thou canst make thyself renowned to all future ages, by disordering the seasons. The memory of mischief is no desirable fame. Much less will it become thee to let kindness or interest prevail. Never rob other countries of rain to pour it on thine own. For us the Nile is sufficient.

'I promised that when I possessed the power, I would use it with inflexible integrity, and he dismissed me, pressing my hand. My heart, said he, will be now at rest, and my benevolence will no more destroy my quiet: I have found a man of wisdom and virtue, to whom I can chearfully bequeath the inheritance of the sun.'

The prince heard this narration with very serious regard, but the princess smiled, and Pekuah convulsed herself with laughter. 'Ladies, said Imlac, to mock the heaviest of human afflictions is neither charitable nor wise. Few can attain this man's knowledge, and few practise his virtues; but all may suffer his calamity. Of the uncertainties of our present state, the most dreadful and alarming is the uncertain continuance of reason.'

The princess was recollected, and the favourite was abashed. Rasselas, more deeply affected, enquired of Imlac, whether he thought such maladies of the mind frequent, and how they were contracted.

CHAP. XLIV

The dangerous prevalence of imagination

'Disorders of intellect, answered Imlac, happen much more often than superficial observers will easily believe. Perhaps, if we speak with rigorous exactness, no human mind is in its right state. There is no man whose imagination does not sometimes predominate over his reason, who can regulate his attention wholly by his will, and whose ideas will come and go at his command. No man will be found in whose mind airy notions do not sometimes tyrannise, and force him to hope or fear beyond the limits of sober probability. All power of fancy over reason is a degree of insanity; but while this power is such as we can controul and repress, it is not visible to others, nor considered as any depravation of the mental faculties: it is not pronounced madness but when it comes ungovernable, and apparently influences speech or action.

'To indulge the power of fiction, and send imagination out upon the wing, is often the sport of those who delight too much in silent speculation. When we are alone we are not always busy; the labour of excogitation is too violent to last long; the ardour of enquiry will sometimes give way to idleness or satiety. He who has nothing external that can divert him, must find pleasure in his own thoughts, and must conceive himself what he is not; for who is pleased with what he is? He then expatiates in boundless futurity, and culls from all imaginable conditions that which for the present moment he should most desire, amuses his desires with impossible enjoyments, and confers upon his pride unattainable dominion. The mind dances from scene to scene, unites all pleasures in all combinations, and riots in delights which nature and fortune, with all their bounty, cannot bestow.

'In time some particular train of ideas fixes the attention, all other intellectual gratifications are rejected, the mind, in weariness or leisure, recurs constantly to the favourite conception, and feasts on the luscious falsehood whenever she is offended with the bitterness of truth. By degrees the reign of fancy is confirmed; she grows first imperious, and in time despotick. Then fictions begin to operate as realities, false opinions fasten upon the mind, and life passes in dreams of rapture or of anguish.

'This, Sir, is one of the dangers of solitude, which the hermit has confessed not always to promote goodness, and the astronomer's misery has proved to be not always propitious to wisdom.'

'I will no more, said the favourite, imagine myself the queen of Abissinia. I have often spent the hours, which the princess gave to my own disposal, in adjusting ceremonies and regulating the court; I have repressed the pride of the powerful, and granted the petitions of the poor; I have built new palaces in more happy situations, planted groves upon the tops of mountains, and have exulted in the beneficence of royalty, till, when the princess entered, I had almost forgotten to bow down before her.'

'And I, said the princess, will not allow myself any more to play the shepherdess in my waking dreams. I have often soothed my thoughts with the quiet and innocence of pastoral employments, till I have in my chamber heard the winds whistle, and the sheep bleat; sometimes freed the lamb entangled in the thicket, and sometimes with my crook encountered the wolf. I have a dress like that of the village maids, which I put on to help my imagination, and a pipe on which I play softly, and suppose myself followed by my flocks.'

'I will confess, said the prince, an indulgence of fantastick delight more dangerous than yours. I have frequently endeavoured to image the possibility of a perfect government, by which all wrong should be restrained, all vice reformed, and all the subjects preserved in tranquility and innocence. This thought produced innumerable schemes of reformation, and dictated many useful regulations and salutary edicts. This has been the sport and sometimes the labour of my solitude; and I start, when I think with how little anguish I once supposed the death of my father and my brothers.'

'Such, says Imlac, are the effects of visionary schemes: when we first form them we know them to be absurd, but familiarise them by degrees, and in time lose sight of their folly.'

CHAP. XLV

They discourse with an old man

THE evening was now far past, and they rose to return home. As they walked along the bank of the Nile, delighted with the beams of the moon quivering on the water, they saw at a small distance an old man, whom the prince had often heard in the assembly of the sages. 'Yonder, said he, is one whose years have calmed his passions, but not clouded his reason: let us close the disquisitions of the night, by enquiring what are his sentiments of his own state, that we may know whether youth alone is to struggle with vexation, and whether any better hope remains for the latter part of life.'

Here the sage approached and saluted them. They invited him to join their walk, and prattled a while as acquaintance that had unexpectedly met one another. The old man was chearful and talkative, and the way seemed short in his company. He was pleased to find himself not disregarded, accompanied them to their house, and, at the prince's request, entered with them. They placed him in the seat of honour, and set wine and conserves before him.

'Sir, said the princess, an evening walk must give to a man of learning, like you, pleasures which ignorance and youth can hardly conceive. You know the qualities and the causes of all that you behold, the laws by which the river flows, the periods in which the planets perform their revolutions. Every thing must supply you with contemplation, and renew the consciousness of your own dignity.'

'Lady, answered he, let the gay and the vigorous expect pleasure in their excursions, it is enough that age can obtain ease. To me the world has lost its novelty: I look round, and see what I remember to have seen in happier days. I rest against a tree, and consider, that in the same shade I once disputed upon the annual overflow of the Nile with a friend who is now silent in the grave. I cast my eyes upwards, fix them on the changing moon, and think with pain on the vicissitudes of life. I have ceased to take much delight in physical truth; for what have I to do with those things which I am soon to leave?'

'You may at least recreate yourself, said Imlac, with the recollection of an honourable and useful life, and enjoy the praise which all agree to give you.'

'Praise, said the sage, with a sigh, is to an old man an empty sound. I have neither mother to be delighted with the reputation of her son, nor wife to partake the honours of her husband. I have outlived my friends and my rivals. Nothing is now of much importance; for I cannot extend my interest beyond myself. Youth is delighted with applause, because it is considered as the earnest of some future good, and because the prospect of life is far extended: but to me, who am now declining to decrepitude, there is little to be feared from the malevolence of men, and yet less to be hoped from their affection or esteem. Something they may yet take away, but they can give me nothing. Riches would now be useless, and high employment would be pain. My retrospect of life recalls to my view many opportunities of good neglected, much time squandered upon trifles, and more lost in idleness and vacancy. I leave many great designs unattempted, and many great attempts unfinished. My mind is burthened with no heavy crime, and therefore I compose myself to tranquility; endeavour to abstract my thoughts from hopes and cares, which, though reason knows them to be vain, still try to keep their old possession of the heart; expect, with serene humility, that hour which nature cannot long delay; and hope to possess in a better state that happiness which here I could not find, and that virtue which here I have not attained.'

He rose and went away, leaving his audience not much elated with the hope of long life. The prince consoled himself with remarking, that it was not reasonable to be disappointed by this account; for age had never been considered as the season of felicity, and, if it was possible to be easy in decline and weakness, it was likely that the days of vigour and alacrity might be happy: that the moon of life might be bright, if the evening could be calm.

The princess suspected that age was querulous and malignant, and delighted to repress the expectations of those who had newly entered the world. She had seen the possessors of estates look with envy on their heirs, and known many who enjoy pleasure no longer than they can confine it to themselves.

Pekuah conjectured, that the man was older than he appeared, and was willing to impute his complaints to delirious dejection; or else supposed that he had been unfortunate, and was therefore discontented: 'For nothing, said she, is more common than to call our own condition, the condition of life.'

Imlac, who had no desire to see them depressed, smiled at the comforts which they could so readily procure to themselves, and remembered, that at the same age, he was equally confident of unmingled prosperity, and equally fertile of consolatory expedients. He forbore to force upon them unwelcome knowledge, which time itself would too soon impress. The princess and her lady retired; the madness of the astronomer hung upon their minds, and they desired Imlac to enter upon his office, and delay next morning the rising of the sun.

CHAP. XLVI

The princess and Pekuah visit the astronomer

THE princess and Pekuah having talked in private of Imlac's astronomer, thought his character at once so amiable and so strange, that they could not be satisfied without a nearer knowledge, and Imlac was requested to find the means of bringing them together.

This was somewhat difficult; the philosopher had never received any visits from women, though he lived in a city that had in it many Europeans who followed the manners of their own countries, and many from other parts of the world that lived there with European liberty. The ladies would not be refused, and several schemes were proposed for the accomplishment of their design. It was proposed to introduce them as strangers in distress, to whom the sage was always accessible; but, after some deliberation, it appeared, that by this artifice, no acquaintance could be formed, for their conversation would be short, and they could not decently importune him often. 'This, said Rasselas, is true; but I have yet a stronger objection against the misrepresentation of your state. I have always considered it as treason against the great republick of human nature, to make any man's virtues the means of deceiving him, whether on great or little occasions. All imposture weakens confidence and chills benevolence. When the sage finds that you are not what you seemed, he will feel the resentment natural to a man who, conscious of great abilities, discovers that he has been tricked by understandings meaner than his own, and, perhaps, the distrust, which he can never afterwards wholly lay aside, may stop the voice of counsel, and close the hand of charity; and where will you find the power of restoring his benefactions to mankind, or his peace to himself?'

To this no reply was attempted, and Imlac began to hope that their curiosity would subside; but, next day, Pekuah told him, she had now found an honest pretence for a visit to the astronomer, for she would solicit permission to continue under him the studies in which she had been initiated by the Arab, and the princess might go with her either as a fellow-student, or because a woman could not decently come alone. 'I am afraid, said Imlac, that he will be soon weary of your company: men advanced far in knowledge do not love to repeat the elements of their art, and I am not certain that even of the elements, as he will deliver them connected with inferences, and mingled with reflections, you are a very capable auditress.' 'That, said Pekuah, must be my care: I ask of you only to take me thither. My knowledge is, perhaps, more than you imagine it, and by concurring always with his opinions I shall make him think it greater than it is.'

The astronomer, in pursuance of this resolution, was told, that a foreign lady, travelling in search of knowledge, had heard of his reputation, and was desirous to become his scholar. The uncommonness of the proposal raised at once his surprize and curiosity, and when, after a short deliberation, he consented to admit her, he could not stay without impatience till the next day.

The ladies dressed themselves magnificently, and were attended by Imlac to the astronomer, who was pleased to see himself approached with respect by persons of so splendid an appearance. In the exchange of the first civilities he was timorous and bashful; but when the talk became regular, he recollected his powers, and justified the character which Imlac had given. Enquiring of Pekuah what could have turned her inclination towards astronomy, he received from her a history of her adventure at the pyramid, and of the time passed in the Arab's island. She told her tale with ease and elegance, and her conversation took possession of his heart. The discourse was then turned to astronomy: Pekuah displayed what she knew: he looked upon her as a prodigy of genius, and intreated her not to desist from a study which she had so happily begun.

They came again and again, and were every time more welcome than before. The sage endeavoured to amuse them, that they might prolong their visits, for he found his thoughts grow brighter in their company; the clouds of solicitude vanished by degrees, as he forced himself to entertain them, and he grieved when he was left at their departure to his old employment of regulating the seasons.

The princess and her favourite had now watched his lips for several months, and could not catch a single word from which they could judge whether he continued, or not, in the opinion of his preternatural commission. They often contrived to bring him to an open declaration, but he easily eluded all their attacks, and on which side soever they pressed him escaped from them to some other topick.

As their familiarity increased they invited him often to the house of Imlac, where they distinguished him by extraordinary respect. He began gradually to delight in sublunary pleasures. He came early and departed late; laboured to recommend himself by assiduity and compliance; excited their curiosity after new arts, that they might still want his assistance; and when they made any excursion of pleasure or enquiry, entreated to attend them.

By long experience of his integrity and wisdom, the prince and his sister were convinced that he might be trusted without danger; and lest he should draw any false hopes from the civilities which he received, discovered to him their condition with the motives of their journey, and required his opinion on the choice of life.

'Of the various conditions which the world spreads before you, which you shall prefer, said the sage, I am not able to instruct you. I can only tell that I have chosen wrong. I have passed my time in study without experience; in the attainment of sciences which can, for the most part, be but remotely useful to mankind. I have purchased knowledge at the expence of all the common comforts of life: I have missed the endearing elegance of female friendship, and the happy commerce of domestick tenderness. If I have obtained any pre-rogatives above other students, they have been accompanied with fear, dis-quiet, and scrupulosity; but even of these prerogatives, whatever they were, I have, since my thoughts have been diversified by more intercourse with the world, begun to question the reality. When I have been for a few days lost in pleasing dissipation, I am always tempted to think that my enquiries have ended in errour, and that I have suffered much, and suffered it in vain.'

Imlac was delighted to find that the sage's understanding was breaking through its mists, and resolved to detain him from the planets till he should forget his task of ruling them, and reason should recover its original influence.

From this time the astronomer was received into familiar friendship, and partook of all their projects and pleasures: his respect kept him attentive, and the activity of Rasselas did not leave much time unengaged. Something was always to be done; the day was spent in making observations which furnished talk for the evening, and the evening was closed with a scheme for the morrow.

The sage confessed to Imlac, that since he had mingled in the gay tumults of life, and divided his hours by a succession of amusements, he found the conviction of his authority over the skies fade gradually from his mind, and began to trust less to an opinion which he never could prove to others, and which he now found subject to variation from causes in which reason had no part. 'If I am accidentally left alone for a few hours, said he, my inveterate persuasion rushes upon my soul, and my thoughts are chained down by some irresistible violence, but they are soon disentangled by the prince's conversation, and instantaneously released at the entrance of Pekuah. I am like a man habit-ually afraid of spectres, who is set at ease by a lamp, and wonders at the dread which harrassed him in the dark, yet, if his lamp be extinguished, feels again the terrours which he knows that when it is light he shall feel no more. But I am sometimes afraid lest I indulge my quiet by criminal negligence, and vol-untarily forget the great charge with which I am intrusted. If I favour myself in a known errour, or am determined by my own ease in a doubtful question of this importance, how dreadful is my crime!'

'No disease of the imagination, answered Imlac, is so difficult of cure, as that which is complicated with the dread of guilt: fancy and conscience then act interchangeably upon us, and so often shift their places, that the illusions of one are not distinguished from the dictates of the other. If fancy presents images not moral or religious, the mind drives them away when they give it pain, but when melancholick notions take the form of duty, they lay hold on the faculties without opposition, because we are afraid to exclude or banish them. For this reason the superstitious are often melancholy, and the melancholy almost always superstitious.

'But do not let the suggestions of timidity overpower your better reason: the danger of neglect can be but as the probability of the obligation, which when you consider it with freedom, you find very little, and that little growing every day less. Open your heart to the influence of the light which, from time to time, breaks in upon you: when scruples importune you, which you in your lucid moments know to be vain, do not stand to parley but fly to business or to Pekuah, and keep this thought always prevalent, that you are only one atom of the mass of humanity, and have neither such virtue nor vice, as that you should be singled out for supernatural favours or afflictions.'

CHAP. XLVII

The prince enters and brings a new topick

'ALL this, said the astronomer, I have often thought, but my reason has been so long subjugated by an uncontrolable and overwhelming idea, that it durst not confide in its own decisions. I now see how fatally I betrayed my quiet, by suffering chimeras to prey upon me in secret; but melancholy shrinks from communication, and I never found a man before, to whom I could impart my troubles, though I had been certain of relief. I rejoice to find my own sentiments confirmed by yours, who are not easily deceived, and can have no motive or purpose to deceive. I hope that time and variety will dissipate the gloom that has so long surrounded me, and the latter part of my days will be spent in peace.'

'Your learning and virtue, said Imlac, may justly give you hopes.'

Rasselas then entered with the princess and Pekuah, and enquired whether they had contrived any new diversion for the next day. 'Such, said Nekayah, is the state of life, that none are happy but by the anticipation of change: the change itself is nothing; when we have made it, the next wish is to change again. The world is not yet exhausted; let me see something to morrow which I never saw before.'

'Variety, said Rasselas, is so necessary to content, that even the happy valley disgusted me by the recurrence of its luxuries; yet I could not forbear to reproach myself with impatience, when I saw the monks of St. Anthony support without complaint, a life, not of uniform delight, but uniform hardship.'

'Those men, answered Imlac, are less wretched in their silent convent than the Abissinian princes in their prison of pleasure. Whatever is done by the monks is incited by an adequate and reasonable motive. Their labour supplies them with necessaries; it therefore cannot be omitted, and is certainly rewarded. Their devotion prepares them for another state, and reminds them of its approach, while it fits them for it. Their time is regularly distributed; one duty succeeds another, so that they are not left open to the distraction of unguided choice, nor lost in the shades of listless inactivity. There is a certain task to be performed at an appropriated hour; and their toils are cheerful, because they consider them as acts of piety, by which they are always advancing towards endless felicity.'

'Do you think, said Nekayah, that the monastick rule is a more holy and less imperfect state than any other? May not he equally hope for future happiness who converses openly with mankind, who succours the distressed by his charity, instructs the ignorant by his learning, and contributes by his industry to the general system of life; even though he should omit some of the mortifications which are practised in the cloister, and allow himself such harmless delights as his condition may place within his reach?'

'This, said Imlac, is a question which has long divided the wise, and perplexed the good. I am afraid to decide on either part. He that lives well in the world is better than he that lives well in a monastery. But, perhaps, every one is not able to stem the temptations of publick life; and, if he cannot conquer, he may properly retreat. Some have little power to do good, and have likewise little strength to resist evil. Many weary of their conflicts with adversity, and are willing to eject those passions which have long busied them in vain. And many are dismissed by age and diseases from the more laborious duties of society. In monasteries the weak and timorous may be happily sheltered, the weary may repose, and the penitent may meditate. Those retreats of prayer and contemplation have something so congenial to the mind of man that, perhaps, there is scarcely one that does not purpose to close his life in pious abstraction with a few associates serious as himself.'

'Such, said Pekuah, has often been my wish, and I have heard the princess declare, that she should not willingly die in a croud.'

'The liberty of using harmless pleasures, proceeded Imlac, will not be disputed; but it is still to be examined what pleasures are harmless. The evil of any pleasure that Nekayah can image is not in the act itself, but in its consequences. Pleasure, in itself harmless, may become mischievous, by endearing to us a state which we know to be transient and probatory, and withdrawing our thoughts from that, of which every hour brings us nearer to the beginning, and of which no length of time will bring us to the end. Mortification is not virtuous in itself, nor has any other use, but that it disengages us from the allurements of sense. In the state of future perfection, to which we all aspire, there will be pleasure without danger, and security without restraint.'

The princess was silent, and Rasselas, turning to the astronomer, asked him, whether he could not delay her retreat, by shewing her something which she had not seen before.

'Your curiosity, said the sage, has been so general, and your pursuit of knowledge so vigorous, that novelties are not now very easily to be found: but what you can no longer procure from the living may be given by the dead. Among the wonders of this country are the catacombs, or the ancient repositories, in which the bodies of the earliest generations were lodged, and where, by the virtue of the gums which embalmed them, they yet remain without corruption.'

'I know not, said Rasselas, what pleasure the sight of the catacombs can afford; but, since nothing else is offered, I am resolved to view them, and shall place this with many other things which I have done, because I would do something.'

They hired a guard of horsemen, and the next day visited the catacombs. When they were about to descend into the sepulchral caves, 'Pekuah, said the princess, we are now again invading the habitations of the dead; I know that you will stay behind; let me find you safe when I return.' 'No, I will not be left, answered Pekuah; I will go down between you and the prince.'

They then all descended, and roved with wonder through the labyrinth of subterraneous passages, where the bodies were laid in rows on either side.

CHAP. XLVIII

Imlac discourses on the nature of the soul

'WHAT reason, said the prince, can be given, why the Egyptians should thus expensively preserve those carcasses which some nations consume with fire, others lay to mingle with the earth, and all agree to remove from their sight, as soon as decent rites can be performed?'

'The original of ancient customs, said Imlac, is commonly unknown; for the practice often continues when the cause has ceased; and concerning superstitious ceremonies it is vain to conjecture; for what reason did not dictate reason cannot explain. I have long believed that the practice of embalming arose only from tenderness to the remains of relations or friends, and to this opinion I am more inclined, because it seems impossible that this care should have been general: had all the dead been embalmed, their repositories must in time have been more spacious than the dwellings of the living. I suppose only the rich or honourable were secured from corruption, and the rest left to the course of nature.

'But it is commonly supposed that the Egyptians believed the soul to live as long as the body continued undissolved and therefore tried this method of eluding death.'

'Could the wise Egyptians, said Nekayah, think so grossly of the soul? If the soul could once survive its separation, what could it afterwards receive or suffer from the body?'

'The Egyptians would doubtless think erroneously, said the astronomer, in the darkness of heathenism, and the first dawn of philosophy. The nature of the soul is still disputed amidst all our opportunities of clearer knowledge: some yet say that it may be material, who, nevertheless, believe it to be immortal.'

'Some, answered Imlac, have indeed said that the soul is material, but I can scarcely believe that any man has thought it, who knew how to think; for all the conclusions of reason enforce the immateriality of mind, and all the notices of sense and investigations of science concur to prove the unconsciousness of matter.

'It was never supposed that cogitation is inherent in matter, or that every particle is a thinking being. Yet, if any part of matter be devoid of thought, what part can we suppose to think? Matter can differ from matter only in form, density, bulk, motion, and direction of motion: to which of these, however varied or combined, can consciousness be annexed? To be round or square, to be solid or fluid, to be great or little, to be moved slowly or swiftly one way or another, are modes of material existence, all equally alien from the nature of cogitation. If matter be once without thought, it can only be made to think by some new modification, but all the modifications which it can admit are equally unconnected with cogitative powers.'

'But the materialists, said the astronomer, urge that matter may have qualities with which we are unacquainted.'

'He who will determine, returned Imlac, against that which he knows, because there may be something which he knows not; he that can set hypothetical possibility against acknowledged certainty, is not to be admitted among reasonable beings. All that we know of matter is, that matter is inert, senseless and lifeless; and if this conviction cannot be opposed but by referring us to something that we know not, we have all the evidence that human intellect can admit. If that which is known may be over-ruled by that which is unknown, no being, not omniscient, can arrive at certainty.'

'Yet let us not, said the astronomer, too arrogantly limit the Creator's power.'

'It is no limitation of omnipotence, replied the poet, to suppose that one thing is not consistent with another, that the same proposition cannot be at once true and false, that the same number cannot be even and odd, that cogitation cannot be conferred on that which is created incapable of cogitation.'

'I know not, said Nekayah, any great use of this question. Does that immateriality, which, in my opinion, you have sufficiently proved, necessarily include eternal duration?'

'Of immateriality, said Imlac, our ideas are negative, and therefore obscure. Immateriality seems to imply a natural power of perpetual duration as a consequence of exemption from all causes of decay: whatever perishes, is destroyed by the solution of its contexture, and separation of its parts; nor can we conceive how that which has no parts, and therefore admits no solution, can be naturally corrupted or impaired.'

'I know not, said Rasselas, how to conceive any thing without extension: what is extended must have parts, and you allow, that whatever has parts may be destroyed.'

'Consider your own conceptions, replied Imlac, and the difficulty will be less. You will find substance without extension. An ideal form is no less real than material bulk: yet an ideal form has no extension. It is no less certain, when you think on a pyramid, that your mind possesses the idea of a pyramid, than that the pyramid itself is standing. What space does the idea of a pyramid occupy more than the idea of a grain of corn? or how can either idea suffer laceration? As is the effect such is the cause; as thought is, such is the power that thinks; a power impassive and indiscerptible.'

'But the Being, said Nekayah, whom I fear to name, the Being which made the soul, can destroy it.'

'He, surely, can destroy it, answered Imlac, since, however unperishable, it receives from a superiour nature its power of duration. That it will not perish by any inherent cause of decay, or principle of corruption, may be shown by philosophy; but philosophy can tell no more. That it will not be annihilated by him that made it, we must humbly learn from higher authority.'

The whole assembly stood a while silent and collected. 'Let us return, said Rasselas, from this scene of mortality. How gloomy would be these mansions of the dead to him who did not know that he shall never die; that what now acts shall continue its agency, and what now thinks shall think on for ever. Those that lie here stretched before us, the wise and the powerful of antient times, warn us to remember the shortness of our present state; they were, perhaps, snatched away while they were busy, like us, in the choice of life.'

'To me, said the princess, the choice of life is become less important; I hope hereafter to think only on the choice of eternity.'

They then hastened out of the caverns, and, under the protection of their guard, returned to Cairo.

CHAP. XLIX

The conclusion, in which nothing is concluded

IT was now the time of the inundation of the Nile: a few days after their visit to the catacombs, the river began to rise.

They were confined to their house. The whole region being under water gave them no invitation to any excursions, and, being well supplied with materials for talk, they diverted themselves with comparisons of the different forms of life which they had observed, and with various schemes of happiness which each of them had formed.

Pekuah was never so much charmed with any place as the convent of St. Anthony, where the Arab restored her to the princess, and wished only to fill it with pious maidens, and to be made prioress of the order: she was weary of expectation and disgust, and would gladly be fixed in some unvariable state.

The princess thought, that of all sublunary things, knowledge was the best: She desired first to learn all sciences, and then purposed to found a college of learned women, in which she would preside, that, by conversing with the old, and educating the young, she might divide her time between the acquisition and communication of wisdom, and raise up for the next age models of prudence, and patterns of piety.

The prince desired a little kingdom, in which he might administer justice in his own person, and see all the parts of government with his own eyes; but he could never fix the limits of his dominion, and was always adding to the number of his subjects.

Imlac and the astronomer were contented to be driven along the stream of life without directing their course to any particular port.

Of these wishes that they had formed they well knew that none could be obtained. They deliberated a while what was to be done, and resolved, when the inundation should cease, to return to Abissinia.

The Bravery of the English Common Soldiers

By those who have compared the military genius of the English with that of the French nation, it is remarked, that *the French officers will always lead, if the soldiers will follow*; and that *the English soldiers will always follow, if their officers will lead.*

In all pointed sentences some degree of accuracy must be sacrificed to conciseness; and, in this comparison, our officers seem to lose what our soldiers gain. I know not any reason for supposing that the English officers are less willing than the French to lead; but it is, I think, universally allowed that the English soldiers are more willing to follow. Our nation may boast, beyond any other people in the world, of a kind of epidemic bravery, diffused equally through all its ranks. We can shew a peasantry of heroes, and fill our armies with clowns, whose courage may vie with that of their general.

There may be some pleasure in tracing the causes of this plebeian magnanimity. The qualities which commonly make an army formidable, are long habits of regularity, great exactness of discipline, and great confidence in the commander. Regularity may in time, produce a kind of mechanical obedience to signals and commands, like that which the perverse Cartesians impute to animals: discipline may impress such an awe upon the mind, that any danger shall be less dreaded than the danger of punishment; and confidence in the wisdom or fortune of the general, may induce the soldiers to follow him blindly to the most dangerous enterprize.

What may be done by discipline and regularity, may be seen in the troops of the Russian Empress, and Prussian Monarch. We find that they may be broken without confusion, and repulsed without flight.

But the English troops have none of these requisites, in any eminent degree. Regularity is by no means part of their character: they are rarely exercised, and therefore shew very little dexterity in their evolutions as bodies of men, or in the manual use of their weapons as individuals: they neither are thought by others, nor by themselves, more active or exact than their enemies, and therefore derive none of their courage from such imaginary superiority.

The manner in which they are dispersed in quarters over the country during times of peace, naturally produces laxity of discipline: they are very little in sight of their officers; and, when they are not engaged in the slight duty of the guard, are suffered to live every man his own way.

The equality of English privileges, the impartiality of our laws, the freedom of our tenures, and the prosperity of our trade, dispose us very little to reverence of superiors. It is not to any great esteem of the officers that the English soldier is indebted for his spirit in the hour of battle: for perhaps it does not often happen that he thinks much better of his leader than of himself. The French Count, who has lately published the *Art of War*, remarks how much soldiers are animated, when they see all their dangers shared by those who were born to be their masters, and whom they consider as beings of a different rank. The Englishman despises such motives of courage: he was born without a master; and looks not on any man, however dignified by lace or titles, as deriving from Nature any claims to his respect, or inheriting any qualities superior to his own.

There are some, perhaps, who would imagine that every Englishman fights better than the subjects of absolute governments, because he has more to defend. But what has the English more than the French soldier? Property they are both commonly without. Liberty is, to the lowest rank of every nation, little more than the choice of working or starving; and this choice is, I suppose, equally allowed in every country. The English soldier seldom has his head very full of the constitution; nor has there been, for more than a century, any war that put the property or liberty of a single Englishman in danger.

Whence then is the courage of the English vulgar? It proceeds, in my opinion, from that dissolution of dependance which obliges every man to regard his own character. While every man is fed by his own hands, he has no need of any servile arts: he may always have wages for his labour; and is no less necessary to his employer, than his employer is to him. While he looks for no protection from others, he is naturally roused to be his own protector; and having nothing to abate his esteem of himself, he consequently aspires to the esteem of others. Thus every man that crowds our streets is a man of honour, disdainful of obligation, impatient of reproach, and desirous of extending his reputation among those of his own rank; and as courage is in most frequent use, the fame of courage is most eagerly pursued. From this neglect of subordination I do not deny that some inconveniencies may from time to time proceed: the power of the law does not always sufficiently supply the want of reverence, or maintain the proper distinction between different ranks: but good and evil will grow up in this world together; and they who complain, in peace, of the insolence of the populace, must remember that their insolence in peace is bravery in war.

Review of William Tytler, Mary Queen of Scots

WE live in an age in which there is much talk of independance, of private judgment, of liberty of thought, and liberty of press. Our clamorous praises of liberty sufficiently prove that we enjoy it; and if by liberty nothing else be meant, than security from the persecutions of power, it is so fully possessed by us that little more is to be desired, except that one should talk of it less, and use it better.

But a social being can scarcely rise to complete independance; he that has any wants, which others can supply, must study the gratification of them whose assistance he expects; this is equally true, whether his wants be wants of nature or of vanity. The writers of the present time are not always candidates for preferment, nor often the hirelings of a patron. They profess to serve no interest, and speak with loud contempt of sycophants and slaves.

There is, however, a power from whose influence neither they nor their predecessors have ever been free. Those who have set greatness at defiance have yet been the slaves of fashion. When an opinion has once become popular, very few are willing to oppose it. Idleness is more willing to credit than enquire; cowardice is afraid of controversy, and vanity of answer; and he that writes merely for sale is tempted to court purchasers by flattering the prejudices of the publick.

It has now been fashionable for near half a century to defame and vilify the house of *Stuart*, and to exalt and magnify the reign of *Elizabeth*. The *Stuarts* have found few apologists, for the dead cannot pay for praise; and who will, without reward, oppose the tide of popularity? Yet there remains still among us, not wholly extinguished, a zeal for truth, a desire of establishing right, in opposition to fashion. The author, whose work is now before us, has attempted a vindication of *Mary* of *Scotland*, whose name has for some years been generally resigned to infamy, and who has been considered as the murderer of her husband, and condemned by her own letters.

Of these letters, the author of this vindication confesses the importance to be such, that *if they be genuine the Queen was guilty, and if they be spurious she was innocent.* He has therefore undertaken to prove them spurious, and divided his treatise into six parts.

In the *first* is contained the history of the letters from their discovery by the earl of *Morton*, their being produced against Q. *Mary*, and their several apparances in *England* before Q. *Elizabeth* and her commissioners, untill they were finally delivered back again to the earl of *Morton*.

The *second* contains a short abstract of Mr *Goodall*'s arguments for proving the letters to be spurious and forged; and of Dr *Robertson* and Mr *Hume*'s objections by way of answer to Mr *Goodall*, with critical observations on these authors.

The *third* contains an examination of the arguments of Dr *Robertson* and Mr *Hume*, in support of the authenticity of the letters.

The *fourth* contains an examination of the confession of *Nicholas Hubert*, commonly called *French Paris*, with observations shewing the same to be a forgery.

The *fifth* contains a short recapitulation or summary of the arguments on both sides of the question. And,

The *last* is an historical collection of the direct or positive evidence still on record, tending to show what part the earls of *Murray*, and *Morton*, and secretary *Lethington* had in the murder of the lord *Darnley*.

The author apologises for the length of this book, by observing, that it necessarily comprises a great number of particulars, which could not easily be contracted: the same plea may be made for the imperfection of our extract, which will naturally fall below the force of the book, because we can only select parts of that evidence, which owes its strength to its concatenation, and which will be weakened whenever it is disjoined.

The account of the seizure of these controverted letters is thus given by the queen's enemies.

'That in the castell of *Edinburgh* thair was left be the Erle of *Bochwell*, before his fleeing away, and was send for be ane *George Dalgleish*, his servand, who was taken be the Erle of *Mortoun*, ane small gylt coffer, not fully ane fute lang, garnisht in sindrie places, with the *Roman* letter F. under ane king's crowne; wharin were certain letteris and writings weel knawin, and be aithis to be affirmit to have been written with the Quene of *Scottis* awn hand to the Erle.'

The papers in the box were said to be eight letters in *French*, some love sonnets in *French* also, and a promise of marriage by the Queen to *Bothwell*.

To the reality or these letters our author makes some considerable objections, from the nature of things, but as such arguments do not always convince we will pass to the evidence of facts.

On *June* 15, 1567, the queen delivered herself to *Morton*, and his party, who imprisoned her.

June 20, 1967, *Dalgleish* was seized, and six days after was examined by *Morton*; his examination is still extant, and there is no mention of this fatal box.

Dec. 4, 1567, *Murray*'s secret council published an act, in which is the first mention of these letters, & in which they are said to be *written and subscrivit with her awin hand*. Ten days after *Murray*'s first parliament met, and passed an act, in which they mention *previe letters written halelie* [wholly] *with her awin hand*. The difference between *written and subscribed*, and *wholly written*, gives the author just reason to suspect, first, a forgery, and then a variation of the forgery. It is indeed very remarkable, that the first account asserts more than the second, though the second contains all the truth, for the letters, whether *written* by the queen or not were not *subscribed*. Had the second account differed from the first only by something added, the first might have contained truth, though not all the truth, but as the second corrects the first by diminution, the first cannot be cleared from falshood.

In *October* 1568, these letters were shewn at *York* to *Elizabeth*'s commissioners, by the agents of *Murray*, but not in their publick character as commissioners, but by way of private information, and were not therefore exposed to *Mary*'s commissioners. *Mary*, however, hearing that some letters were intended to be produced against her, directed her commissioners to require them for her inspection, and, in the mean time, to declare them *false and feigned, forged and invented*, observing that there were many that could counterfeit her hand.

To counterfeit a name is easy, to counterfeit a hand through eight letters very difficult. But it does not appear that the letters were ever shewn to those who would desire to detect them, and to the *English* commissioners a rude and remote imitation might be sufficient, since they were not shewn as judicial proofs; and why they were not shewn as proofs no other reason can be given than they must have then been examined and that examination would have detected the forgery.

These letters, thus timorously and suspiciously communicated, were all the evidence against *Mary*; for the servants of *Bothwell*, executed for the murder of the king, acquitted the Queen at the hour of death. These letters were so necessary to *Murray*, that he alledges them as the reason of the queen's imprisonment, tho' he imprisoned her on the 16th, and pretended not to have intercepted the letters before the 20th of *June*.

Of these letters, on which the fate of princes and kingdoms was suspended, the authority should have been put out of doubt, yet that such letters were ever found, there is no witness but *Morton*, who accused the queen, and *Crawfurd*, a dependant on *Lennox*, another of her accusers. *Dalgleish*, the bearer, was hanged without any interrogatories concerning them, & *Hulet*, mentioned in them, tho' then in prison, was never called to authenticate them, nor was his confession produced against *Mary* till death had left him no power to disown it.

Elizabeth, indeed, was easily satisfied, she declared herself ready to receive the proofs against *Mary*, and absolutely refused *Mary* the liberty of confronting her accusers, and making her defence. Before such a judge a very little proof would be sufficient. She gave the accusers of *Mary* leave to go to *Scotland*, and the box and letters were seen no more. They have been since lost, and the discovery, which comparison of writing might have made, is now no longer possible. *Hume* has, however, endeavoured to palliate the conduct of *Elizabeth*, but *his account*, says our author, *is contradicted almost in every sentence by the records, which, it appears, he has himself perused.*

In the next part, the authenticity of the letters is examined, and it seems to be proved beyond contradiction, that the *French* letters, supposed to have been written by *Mary*, are translated from the *Scotch* copy, and, if originals, which it was so much the interest of such numbers to preserve, are wanting, it is much more likely that they never existed, than that they have been lost.

The arguments, used by Dr *Robertson*, to prove the genuineness of the letters are next examined. *Robertson* makes use principally of what he calls the *internal evidence*, which, amounting at most to conjecture, is opposed by conjecture equally probable.

In examining the confession of *Nicholas Hubert*, or *French Paris*, this new apologist of *Mary* seems to gain ground upon her accuser. *Paris* is mentioned in the letters, as the bearer of them to *Bothwell*; when the rest of *Bothwell's* servants were executed, clearing the queen in the last moment, *Paris*, instead of suffering his trial with the rest at *Edinburgh*, was conveyed to St *Andrews*, where *Murray* was absolute, put into a dungeon of *Murray's* citadel, and two years after condemned by *Murray* himself nobody knew how. Several months after his death, a confession in his name, without the regular testifications, was sent to *Cecil*, at what exact time nobody can tell.

Of this confession, *Lesly*, bishop of *Ross*, openly denied the genuineness, in a book printed at *London*, and suppressed by *Elizabeth*; and another historian of that time declares that *Paris* died without any confession; and the confession itself was never shewn to *Mary*, or to *Mary's* commissioners. The author makes this reflection:

'From the violent presumptions that arise from their carrying this poor ignorant stranger from *Edinburgh*, the ordinary seat of justice; their keeping him hid from all the world, in a remote dungeon, and not producing him with their other evidences, so as he might have been publickly questioned; the positive and direct testimony of the author of *Crawford's* manuscript, then living, and on the spot at the time; with the public affirmation of the bishop of *Ross* at the time of *Paris's* death, that he had vindicated the queen with his dying breath; the behaviour of *Murray*, *Morton*, *Buchanan*, and even of *Hay*, the attester of this pretended confession, on that occasion; their close and reserved silence at the time when they must have had this confession of *Paris* in their pocket; and their publishing every other circumstance that could tend to blacken the queen, and yet omitting this confession, the only direct evidence of her supposed guilt; all this duly and dispassionately considered, I think, one may safely conclude, that it was judged not fit to expose so soon to light this piece of evidence against the queen; which a cloud of witnesses, living, and present at *Paris's* execution, would surely have given clear testimony against, as a notorious imposture.'

Mr *Hume*, indeed, observes, 'It is in vain at present to seek for improbabilities in *Nicholas Hubert*'s dying confession, and to magnify the smallest difficulties into a contradiction. It was certainly a *regular judicial* paper, given in regularly and judicially, and ought to have been canvassed at the time, if the persons, whom it concerned, had been assured of their innocence.'—To which our author makes a reply, which cannot be shortened without weakening it:

'Upon what does this author ground his sentence? Upon two very plain reasons, *first*, That the confession was a judicial one, that is, taken in presence, or by authority of a judge. And *secondly*, That it was regularly and judicially given in; that must be understood during the time of the conferences before queen *Elizabeth* and her council, in presence of *Mary*'s commissioners; at which time she ought to have canvassed it, says our author, if she knew her innocence.

That it was not a judicial confession, is evident: The paper itself does not bear any such mark; nor does it mention that it was taken in presence of any person, or by any authority whatsoever; and, by comparing it with the judicial examinations of *Dalgleish*, *Hay*, and *Hepburn*, in page 146, it is apparent, that it is destitute of every formality requisite in a judicial evidence. In what dark corner, then, this strange production was generated, our author may endeavour to find out, if he can.

As to his second assertion, that it was regularly and judicially given in, and therefore ought to have been canvassed by *Mary* during the conferences. We have already seen that this likewise is not fact: The conferences broke up in *February* 1569: *Nicholas Hubert* was not hanged till *August* thereafter, and his dying confession, as Mr *Hume* calls it, is only dated the 10th of that month. How then can this gentleman gravely tell us that this confession was judicially given in, and ought to have been at that very time canvassed by queen *Mary* and her commissioners? Such positive assertions, apparently contrary to fact, are unworthy the character of an historian, and may very justly render his decision, with respect to evidences of a higher nature, very dubious. In answer then to Mr *Hume*: As the queen's accusers did not chuse to produce this material witness, *Paris*, whom they had alive, and in their hands, nor any declaration or confession from him at the critical and proper time for having it canvassed by the queen, I apprehend our author's conclusion may fairly be used against himself; that it is in vain at present to support the improbabilities and absurdities in a confession, taken in a clandestine way, no body knows how; and produced after *Paris*'s death, by no body knows whom; and from every appearance destitute of every formality requisite and common to such sort of evidence: For these reasons, I am under no sort of hesitation to give sentence against *Nicholas Hubert*'s confession, as a gross imposture and forgery.

The state of the evidence relating to the letters is this:

Morton affirms that they were taken in the hands of *Dalgleish*. The examination of *Dalgleish* is still extant, and he appears never to have been once interrogated concerning the letters.

Morton and *Murray* affirm that they were written by the queen's hand; they were carefully concealed from *Mary* and her commissioners, and were never collated by one man, who could desire to disprove them.

Several of the incidents mentioned in the letters are confirmed by the oath of *Crawfurd*, one of *Lennox*'s defendants, and some of the incidents are so minute as that they could scarcely be thought on by a forger. *Crawfurd*'s testimony is not without suspicion. Whoever practices forgery endeavours to make truth the vehicle of falshood. Of a prince's life very minute incidents are known, and if any are too slight to be remarked, they may be safely feigned, for they are likewise too slight to be contradicted. But there are still more reasons for doubting the genuineness of these letters. They had no date of time or place, no seal, no direction, no superscription.

The only evidences that could prove their authenticity were *Dalgleish*, and *Paris*, of which *Dalgleish*, at his tryal, was never questioned about them, *Paris* was never publickly tried, tho' he was kept alive thro' the time of the conference.

The servants of *Bothwell*, who were put to death for the king's murder, cleared *Mary* with their last words.

The letters were first declared to be subscribed, and were then produced without subscription.

They were shewn during the conferences at *York* privately to the *English* commissioners, but were concealed from the commissioners of *Mary*.

Mary always sollicited the perusal of these letters, and was always denied it.

She demanded to be heard in person by *Elizabeth*, before the nobles of *England*, and the ambassadors of other princes, and was refused.

When *Mary* persisted in demanding copies of the letters, her commissioners were dismissed with their box to *Scotland*, and the letters were seen no more.

The *French* letters, which for almost two centuries have been considered as originals, by the enemies of *Mary*'s memory, are now discovered to be forgeries, and acknowledged to be translations, and perhaps *French* translations of a *Latin* translation. And the modern accusers of *Mary* are forced to infer from these letters, which now exist, that other letters existed formerly, which have been lost in spite of curiosity, malice, and interest.

The rest of this treatise is employed in an endeavour to prove that *Mary*'s accusers were the murderer's of *Darnley*; thro' this enquiry it is not necessary to follow him, only let it be observed, that, if these letters were forged by them, they may easily be thought capable of other crimes. That the letters were forged is now made so probable, that perhaps they will never more be cited as testimonies.

THE GREAT CHAM OF
LITERATURE

Letter to Giuseppe Baretti

WEDNESDAY 10 JUNE 1761

London, June 10, 1761

You reproach me very often with parsimony of writing: but you may discover by the extent of my paper, that I design to recompense rarity by length. A short letter to a distant friend is, in my opinion, an insult like that of a slight bow or cursory salutation;—a proof of unwillingness to do much, even where there is a necessity of doing something. Yet it must be remembered, that he who continues the same course of life in the same place, will have little to tell. One week and one year are very like another. The silent changes made by time are not always perceived; and if they are not perceived, cannot be recounted. I have risen and lain down, talked and mused, while you have roved over a considerable part of Europe: yet I have not envied my Baretti any of his pleasures, though perhaps I have envied others his company; and I am glad to have other nations made acquainted with the character of the English, by a traveller who has so nicely inspected our manners, and so successfully studied our literature. I received your kind letter from Falmouth, in which you gave me notice of your departure for Lisbon; and another from Lisbon, in which you told me, that you were to leave Portugal in a few days. To either of these how could any answer be returned? I have had a third from Turin, complaining that I have not answered the former. Your English stile still continues in its purity and vigour. With vigour your genius will supply it; but its purity must be continued by close attention. To use two languages familiarly, and without contaminating one by the other, is very difficult; and to use more than two, is hardly to be hoped. The praises which some have received for their multiplicity of languages, may be sufficient to excite industry, but can hardly generate confidence.

I know not whether I can heartily rejoice at the kind reception which you have found, or at the popularity to which you are exalted. I am willing that your merit should be distinguished; but cannot wish that your affections may be gained. I would have you happy wherever you are: yet I would have you wish to return to England. If ever you visit us again, you will find the kindness of your friends undiminished. To tell you how many enquiries are made after you would be tedious, or if not tedious, would be vain; because you may be told in a very few words, that all who knew you, wish you well; and all that you embraced at your departure, will caress you at your return: therefore do not let Italian academicians nor Italian ladies drive us from your thoughts. You may find among us what you will leave behind, soft smiles and easy sonnets. Yet I shall not wonder if all our invitations should be rejected: for there is a pleasure in being considerable at home, which is not easily resisted.

By conducting Mr. Southwell to Venice, you fulfilled, I know, the original contract: yet I would wish you not wholly to lose him from your notice, but to recommend him to such acquaintance as may best secure him from suffering by his own follies, and to take such general care both of his safety and his interest as may come within your power. His relations will thank you for any such gratuitous attention: at least they will not blame you for any evil that may happen, whether they thank you or not for any good.

You know that we have a new King and a new Parliament. Of the new Parliament Fitzherbert is a member. We were so weary of our old King, that we are much pleased with his successor; of whom we are so much inclined to hope great things, that most of us begin already to believe them. The young man is hitherto blameless; but it would be unreasonable to expect much from the immaturity of juvenile years, and the ignorance of princely education. He has been long in the hands of the Scots, and has already favoured them more than the English will contentedly endure. But perhaps he scarcely knows whom he has distinguished, or whom he has disgusted.

The Artists have instituted a yearly exhibition of pictures and statues, in imitation, as I am told, of foreign Academies. This year was the second exhibition. They please themselves much with the multitude of spectators, and imagine that the English school will rise in reputation. Reynolds is without a rival, and continues to add thousands to thousands, which he deserves, among other excellencies, by retaining his kindness for Baretti. This exhibition has filled the heads of the Artists and lovers of art. Surely life, if it be not long, is tedious, since we are forced to call in the assistance of so many trifles to rid us of our time, of that time which never can return.

I know my Baretti will not be satisfied with a letter in which I give him no account of myself: yet what account shall I give him? I have not, since the day of our separation, suffered or done any thing considerable. The only change in my way of life is, that I have frequented the theatre more than in former seasons. But I have gone thither only to escape from myself. We have had many new farces, and the comedy called The Jealous Wife, which, though not written with much genius, was yet so well adapted to the stage, and so well exhibited by the actors, that it was crowded for near twenty nights. I am digressing from myself to the play-house; but a barren plan must be filled with episodes. Of myself I have nothing to say, but that I have hitherto lived without the concurrence of my own judgment; yet I continue to flatter myself, that, when you return, you will find me mended. I do not wonder that, where the monastick life is permitted, every order finds votaries, and every monastery inhabitants. Men will submit to any rule, by which they may be exempted from the tyranny of caprice and of chance. They are glad to supply by external authority their own want of constancy and resolution, and court the government of others, when long experience has convinced them of their own inability to govern themselves. If I were to visit Italy, my curiosity would be more attracted by convents than by palaces; though I am afraid that I should find expectation in both places equally disappointed, and life in both places supported with impatience, and quitted with reluctance. That it must be so soon quitted, is a powerful remedy against impatience; but what shall free us from reluctance? Those who have endeavoured to teach us to die well, have taught few to die willingly; yet I cannot but hope that a good life might end at last in a contented death.

You see to what a train of thought I am drawn by the mention of myself. Let me now turn my attention upon you. I hope you take care to keep an exact journal, and to register all occurrences and observations; for your friends here expect such a book of travels as has not been often seen. You have given us good specimens in your letters from Lisbon. I wish you had staid longer in Spain, for no country is less known to the rest of Europe; but the quickness of your discernment must make amends for the celerity of your motions. He that knows which way to direct his view, sees much in a little time.

Write to me very often, and I will not neglect to write to you; and I may perhaps in time get something to write: at least, you will know by my letters, whatever else they may have or want, that I continue to be, Your most affectionate friend,

SAM. JOHNSON

Letter to James Boswell

THURSDAY 8 DECEMBER 1763

Dear Sir   London, Dec. 8, 1763

You are not to think yourself forgotten or criminally neglected that you have had yet no letter from me—I love to see my friends to hear from them to talk to them and to talk of them, but it is not without a considerable effort of resolution that I prevail upon myself to write. I would not however gratify my own indolence by the omission of any important duty or any office of real kindness.

To tell you that I am or am not well, that I have or have not been in the country, that I drank your health in the Room in which we sat last together and that your acquaintance continue to speak of you with their former kindness topicks with which those letters are commonly filled which are written only for the sake of writing I seldom shall think worth communication but if I can have it in my power to calm any harrassing disquiet to excite any virtuous desire to rectify any important opinion or fortify any generous resolution you need not doubt but I shall at least wish to prefer the pleasure of gratifying a friend much less esteemed than yourself before the gloomy calm of idle Vacancy. Whether I shall easily arrive at an exact punctuality of correspondance I cannot tell. I shall at present expect that you will receive this in return for two which I have had from you. The first indeed gave me an account so hopeless of the state of your mind that it hardly admitted or deserved an answer; by the second I was much better pleased and the pleasure will still be increased by such a narrative of the progress of your studys as may evince the continuence of an equal and rational application of your mind to some usefull enquiry.

You will perhaps wish to ask what Study I would recommend. I shall not speak of Theology because it ought not to be considered as a question whether you shall endevour to know the will of God.

I shall therefore consider only such Studies as we are at liberty to pursue or to neglect, and of these I know not how you will make a better choice than by studying the civil Law as your father advises and the Ancient languages as you had determined for yourself; at least resolve while you remain in any setled residence to spend a certain number of hours every day amongst your Books. The dissipation of thought of which you complain is nothing more than the Vacillation of a mind suspended between different motives and changing its direction as any motive gains or loses Strength. If you can but kindle in your mind any strong desire, if you can but keep predominant any Wish for some particular excellence or attainment the Gusts of imagination will break away without any effect upon your conduct and commonly without any traces left upon the Memory.

There lurks perhaps in every human heart a desire of distinction which inclines every Man first to hope and then to believe that Nature has given him something peculiar to himself. This vanity makes one mind nurse aversions and another actuate desires till they rise by art much above their original state of power and as affectation in time improves to habit, they at last tyrannise over him who at first encouraged them only for Show. Every desire is a Viper in the Bosom who while he was chill was harmless but when warmth gave him strength exerted it in poison. You know a gentleman who when first he set his foot into the gay World as he prepared himself to whirl in the Vortex of pleasure imagined a total indifference and universal negligence to be the most agreable concomitants of Youth and the strongest indication of any airy temper and a quick apprehension. Vacant to every object and sensible of every impulse he thought that all appearance of diligence would deduct something from the reputation of Genius and hoped that he should appear to attain amidst all the ease of carelessness and all the tumult of diversion that knowledge and those accomplishments which Mortals of the common fabrick obtain only by mute abstraction and solitary drudgery. He tried this scheme of life awhile was made weary of it by his sence and his Virtue; he then wished to return to his Studies and finding long habits of idleness and pleasure harder to be cured than he expected still willing to retain his claim to some extraordinary pre-rogitives resolved the common consequences of irregularity into an unalter-able decree of destiny and concluded that Nature had originally formed him incapable of rational employment.

Let all such fancys illusive and destructive be banished henceforward from your thoughts forever. Resolve and keep your resolution. Chuse and pursue your choice. If you spend this day in Study you will find yourself still more able to study tomorrow. Not that you are to expect that you shall at once obtain a compleat Victory. Depravity is not very easily overcome. Resolution will some-times relax and diligence will sometimes be interrupted. But let no accidental surprize or deviation whether short or long dispose you to despondency. Consider these failings as incident to all Mankind, begin again where you left off and endevour to avoid the Seducements that prevailed over you before.

This my Dear Boswell is advice which perhaps has been often given you, and given you without effect, but this advice if you will not take from others you must take from your own reflections, if you purpose to do the dutys of the station to which the Bounty of providence has called you.

Let me have a long letter from you as soon as you can. I hope you continue your journal and enrich it with many observations upon the country in which you reside. It will be a favour if you can get me any books in the Frisick Language and can enquire how the poor are maintained in the Seven Provinces. I am, Dear Sir, your most affectionate servant,

SAM. JOHNSON

Diary entry

SATURDAY 21 APRIL 1764

April 21, 1764, 3 in the morning.

MY indolence, since my last reception of the Sacrament, has sunk into grosser sluggishness, and my dissipation spread into wilder negligence. My thoughts have been clouded with sensuality; and, except that from the beginning of this year I have in some measure forborn excess of strong drink, my appetites have predominated over my reason. A kind of strange oblivion has overspread me, so that I know not what has become of the last year; and perceive that incidents and intelligence pass over me without leaving any impression.

This is not the life to which heaven is promised. I purpose to approach the altar again to-morrow. Grant, O Lord, that I may receive the Sacrament with such resolutions of a better life as may by thy grace be effectual, for the sake of Jesus Christ. Amen.

April 21. I read the whole Gospel of St. JOHN. Then sat up till the 22d.

> My purpose is from this time,
> To reject or expel sensual images, and idle thoughts.
> To provide some useful amusement for leisure time.
> To avoid idleness.
> To rise early.
> To study a proper portion of every day.
> To worship God diligently.
> To read the Scriptures.
> To let no week pass without reading some part.
> To write down my observations.   10
> I will renew my resolutions made at Tetty's death.

I perceive an insensibility and heaviness upon me. I am less than commonly oppressed with the sense of sin, and less affected with the shame of idleness. Yet I will not despair. I will pray to God for resolution, and will endeavour to strengthen my faith in Christ, by commemorating his death.

I prayed for Tett.

A Reply to Impromptu Verses by Baretti

> At sight of sparkling Bowls or beauteous Dames
> When fondness melts me, or when wine inflames,
> I too can feel the rapture fierce and strong
> I too can pour the extemporary song;
> But though the number for a moment please,
> Though musick thrills, or sudden sallies seize,
> Yet lay the Sonnet for an hour aside,
> Its charms are fled and all its power destroy'd:
> What soon is perfect, soon alike is past;
> That slowly grows which must for ever last.   10

The Plays of Shakespeare
Preface

THAT praises are without reason lavished on the dead, and that the honours due only to excellence are paid to antiquity, is a complaint likely to be always continued by those, who, being able to add nothing to truth, hope for eminence from the heresies of paradox; or those, who, being forced by disappointment

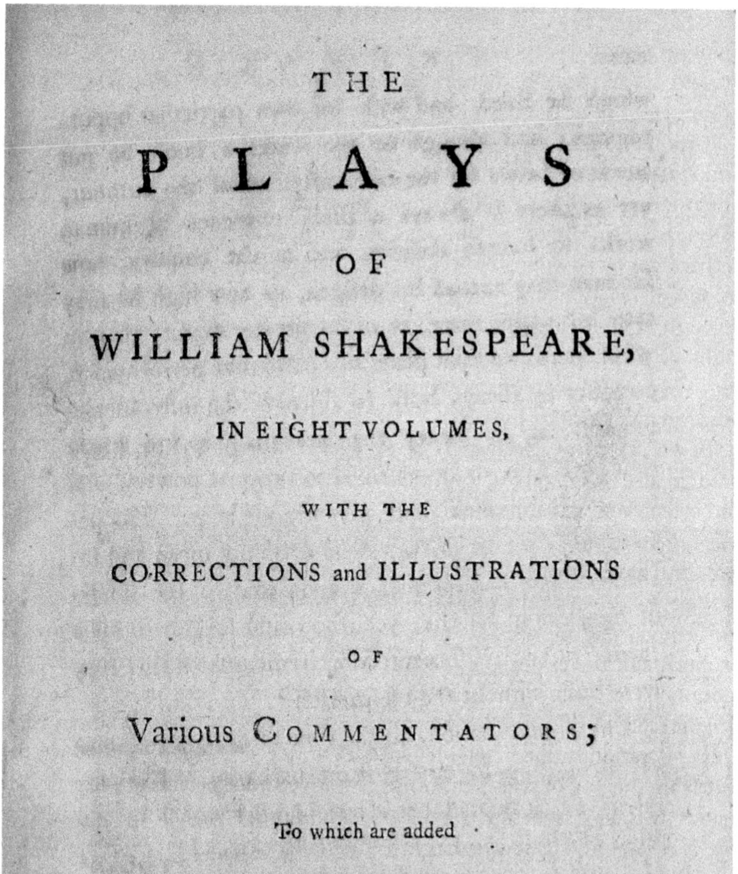

THE

P L A Y S

OF

WILLIAM SHAKESPEARE,

IN EIGHT VOLUMES,

WITH THE

CORRECTIONS and ILLUSTRATIONS

O F

Various COMMENTATORS;

To which are added

NOTES by SAM. JOHNSON.

L O N D O N:

Printed for J. and R. TONSON, H. WOODFALL, J. RIVINGTON,
R. BALDWIN, L. HAWES, CLARK and COLLINS, T. LONGMAN,
W. JOHNSTON, T. CASLON, C. CORBET, T. LOWNDS,
and the Executors of B. DODD.
M,DCC,LXV.

FIGURE 8 *The Plays of William Shakespeare* (1765), title page (Bodl. M. adds. 50 e. 1). Courtesy of the Bodleian Library, University of Oxford.

upon consolatory expedients, are willing to hope from posterity what the present age refuses, and flatter themselves that the regard which is yet denied by envy, will be at last bestowed by time.

Antiquity, like every other quality that attracts the notice of mankind, has undoubtedly votaries that reverence it, not from reason, but from prejudice. Some seem to admire indiscriminately whatever has been long preserved, without considering that time has sometimes co-operated with chance; all perhaps are more willing to honour past than present excellence; and the mind contemplates genius through the shades of age, as the eye surveys the sun through artificial opacity. The great contention of criticism is to find the faults of the moderns, and the beauties of the ancients. While an authour is yet living we estimate his powers by his worst performance, and when he is dead we rate them by his best.

To works, however, of which the excellence is not absolute and definite, but gradual and comparative; to works not raised upon principles demonstrative and scientifick, but appealing wholly to observation and experience, no other test can be applied than length of duration and continuance of esteem. What mankind have long possessed they have often examined and compared, and if they persist to value the possession, it is because frequent comparisons have confirmed opinion in its favour. As among the works of nature no man can properly call a river deep or a mountain high, without the knowledge of many mountains and many rivers; so in the productions of genius, nothing can be stiled excellent till it has been compared with other works of the same kind. Demonstration immediately displays its power, and has nothing to hope or fear from the flux of years; but works tentative and experimental must be estimated by their proportion to the general and collective ability of man, as it is discovered in a long succession of endeavours. Of the first building that was raised, it might be with certainty determined that it was round or square, but whether it was spacious or lofty must have been referred to time. The Pythagorean scale of numbers was at once discovered to be perfect; but the poems of *Homer* we yet know not to transcend the common limits of human intelligence, but by remarking, that nation after nation, and century after century, has been able to do little more than transpose his incidents, new name his characters, and paraphrase his sentiments.

The reverence due to writings that have long subsisted arises therefore not from any credulous confidence in the superior wisdom of past ages, or gloomy persuasion of the degeneracy of mankind, but is the consequence of acknowledged and indubitable positions, that what has been longest known has been most considered, and what is most considered is best understood.

The Poet, of whose works I have undertaken the revision, may now begin to assume the dignity of an ancient, and claim the privilege of established fame and prescriptive veneration. He has long outlived his century, the term commonly fixed as the test of literary merit. Whatever advantages he might once derive from personal allusions, local customs, or temporary opinions, have for many years been lost; and every topick of merriment or motive of sorrow, which the modes of artificial life afforded him, now only obscure the scenes which they once illuminated. The effects of favour and competition are at an end; the tradition of his friendships and his enmities has perished; his works support no opinion with arguments, nor supply any faction with invectives; they can neither indulge vanity nor gratify malignity, but are read without any other reason than the desire of pleasure, and are therefore praised only as pleasure is obtained; yet, thus unassisted by interest or passion, they have past through variations of taste and changes of manners, and, as they devolved from one generation to another, have received new honours at every transmission.

But because human judgment, though it be gradually gaining upon certainty, never becomes infallible; and approbation, though long continued, may yet be only the approbation of prejudice or fashion; it is proper to inquire, by what peculiarities of excellence *Shakespeare* has gained and kept the favour of his countrymen.

Nothing can please many, and please long, but just representations of general nature. Particular manners can be known to few, and therefore few only can judge how nearly they are copied. The irregular combinations of fanciful invention may delight a-while, by that novelty of which the common satiety of life sends us all in quest; but the pleasures of sudden wonder are soon exhausted, and the mind can only repose on the stability of truth.

Shakespeare is above all writers, at least above all modern writers, the poet of nature; the poet that holds up to his readers a faithful mirrour of manners and of life. His characters are not modified by the customs of particular places, unpractised by the rest of the world; by the peculiarities of studies or professions, which can operate but upon small numbers; or by the accidents of transient fashions or temporary opinions: they are the genuine progeny of common humanity, such as the world will always supply, and observation will always find. His persons act and speak by the influence of those general passions and principles by which all minds are agitated, and the whole system of life is continued in motion. In the writings of other poets a character is too often an individual; in those of *Shakespeare* it is commonly a species.

It is from this wide extension of design that so much instruction is derived. It is this which fills the plays of *Shakespeare* with practical axioms and domestick wisdom. It was said of *Euripides*, that every verse was a precept; and it may be said of *Shakespeare*, that from his works may be collected a system of civil and œconomical prudence. Yet his real power is not shown in the splendour of particular passages, but by the progress of his fable, and, the tenour of his dialogue; and he that tries to recommend him by select quotations, will succeed like the pedant in *Hierocles*, who, when he offered his house to sale, carried a brick in his pocket as a specimen.

It will not easily be imagined how much *Shakespeare* excells in accommodating his sentiments to real life, but by comparing him with other authours. It was observed of the ancient schools of declamation, that the more diligently they were frequented, the more was the student disqualified for the world, because he found nothing there which he should ever meet in any other place. The same remark may be applied to every stage but that of *Shakespeare*. The theatre, when it is under any other direction, is peopled by such characters as were never seen, conversing in a language which was never heard, upon topicks which will never arise in the commerce of mankind. But the dialogue of this authour is often so evidently determined by the incident which produces it, and is pursued with so much ease and simplicity, that it seems scarcely to claim the merit of fiction, but to have been gleaned by diligent selection out of common conversation, and common occurrences.

Upon every other stage the universal agent is love, by whose power all good and evil is distributed, and every action quickened or retarded. To bring a lover, a lady and a rival into the fable; to entangle them in contradictory obligations, perplex them with oppositions of interest, and harrass them with violence of desires inconsistent with each other; to make them meet in rapture and part in agony; to fill their mouths with hyperbolical joy and outrageous sorrow; to distress them as nothing human ever was distressed; to deliver them as nothing human ever was delivered, is the business of a modern dramatist. For this probability is violated, life is misrepresented, and language is depraved. But love is only one of many passions, and as it has no great influence upon the sum of life, it has little operation in the dramas of a poet, who caught his ideas from the living world, and exhibited only what he saw before him. He knew, that any other passion, as it was regular or exorbitant, was a cause of happiness or calamity.

Characters thus ample and general were not easily discriminated and preserved, yet perhaps no poet ever kept his personages more distinct from each other. I will not say with *Pope*, that every speech may be assigned to the proper speaker, because many speeches there are which have nothing characteristical; but, perhaps, though some may be equally adapted to every person, it will be difficult to find, any that can be properly transferred from the present possessor to another claimant. The choice is right, when there is reason for choice.

Other dramatists can only gain attention by hyperbolical or aggravated characters, by fabulous and unexampled excellence or depravity, as the writers of barbarous romances invigorated the reader by a giant and a dwarf; and he that should form his expectations of human affairs from the play, or from the tale, would be equally deceived. *Shakespeare* has no heroes; his scenes are occupied only by men, who act and speak as the reader thinks that he should himself have spoken or acted on the same occasion: Even where the agency is supernatural the dialogue is level with life. Other writers disguise the most natural passions and most frequent incidents; so that he who contemplates them in the book will not know them in the world: *Shakespeare* approximates the remote, and familiarizes the wonderful; the event which he represents will not happen, but if it were possible, its effects would be probably such as he has assigned; and it may be said, that he has not only shewn human nature as it acts in real exigences, but as it would be found in trials, to which it cannot be exposed.

This therefore is the praise of *Shakespeare*, that his drama is the mirrour of life; that he who has mazed his imagination, in following the phantoms which other writers raise up before him, may here be cured of his delirious extasies, by reading human sentiments in human language; by scenes from which a hermit may estimate the transactions of the world, and a confessor predict the progress of the passions.

His adherence to general nature has exposed him to the censure of criticks, who form their judgments upon narrower principles. *Dennis* and *Rhymer* think his *Romans* not sufficiently Roman; and *Voltaire* censures his kings as not completely royal. *Dennis* is offended, that *Menenius*, a senator of *Rome*, should play the buffoon; and *Voltaire* perhaps thinks decency violated when the *Danish* Usurper is represented as a drunkard. But *Shakespeare* always makes nature predominate over accident; and if he preserves the essential character, is not very careful of distinctions superinduced and adventitious. His story requires Romans or kings, but he thinks only on men. He knew that *Rome*, like every other city, had men of all dispositions; and wanting a buffoon, he went into the senate-house for that which the senate-house would certainly have afforded him. He was inclined to shew an usurper and a murderer not only odious but despicable, he therefore added drunkenness to his other qualities, knowing that kings love wine like other men, and that wine exerts its natural power upon kings. These are the petty cavils of petty minds; a poet overlooks the casual distinction of country and condition, as a painter, satisfied with the figure, neglects the drapery.

The censure which he has incurred by mixing comick and tragick scenes, as it extends to all his works, deserves more consideration. Let the fact be first stated, and then examined.

Shakespeare's plays are not in the rigorous or critical sense either tragedies or comedies, but compositions of a distinct kind; exhibiting the real state of sublunary nature, which partakes of good and evil, joy and sorrow, mingled with endless variety of proportion and innumerable modes of combination; and expressing the course of the world, in which the loss of one is the gain of another; in which, at the same time, the reveller is hasting to his wine, and the mourner burying his friend; in which the malignity of one is sometimes defeated by the frolick of another; and many mischiefs and many benefits are done and hindered without design.

Out of this chaos of mingled purposes and casualties the ancient poets, according to the laws which custom had prescribed, selected some the crimes of men, and some their absurdities; some the momentous vicissitudes of life, and some the lighter occurrences; some the terrours of distress, and some the gayeties of prosperity. Thus rose the two modes of imitation, known by the names of *tragedy* and *comedy*, compositions intended to promote different ends by contrary means, and considered as so little allied, that I do not recollect among the *Greeks* or *Romans* a single writer who attempted both.

Shakespeare has united the powers of exciting laughter and sorrow not only in one mind but in one composition. Almost all his plays are divided between serious and ludicrous characters, and, in the successive evolutions of the design, sometimes produce seriousness and sorrow, and sometimes levity and laughter.

That this is a practice contrary to the rules of criticism will be readily allowed; but there is always an appeal open from criticism to nature. The end of writing is to instruct; the end of poetry is to instruct by pleasing. That the mingled drama may convey all the instruction of tragedy or comedy cannot be denied, because it includes both in its alterations of exhibition, and approaches nearer than either to the appearance of life, by shewing how great machinations and slender designs may promote or obviate one another, and the high and the low co-operate in the general system by unavoidable concatenation.

It is objected, that by this change of scenes the passions are interrupted in their progression, and that the principal event, being not advanced by a due gradation of preparatory incidents, wants at last the power to move, which constitutes the perfection of dramatick poetry. This reasoning is so specious, that it is received as true even by those who in daily experience feel it to be false. The interchanges of mingled scenes seldom fail to produce the intended vicissitudes of passion. Fiction cannot move so much, but that the attention may be easily transferred; and though it must be allowed that pleasing melancholy be sometimes interrupted by unwelcome levity, yet let it be considered likewise, that melancholy is often not pleasing, and that the disturbance of one man may be the relief of another; that different auditors have different habitudes; and that, upon the whole, all pleasure consists in variety.

The players, who in their edition divided our authour's works into comedies, histories, and tragedies, seem not to have distinguished the three kinds, by any very exact or definite ideas.

An action which ended happily to the principal persons, however serious or distressful through its intermediate incidents, in their opinion constituted a comedy. This idea of a comedy continued long amongst us, and plays were written, which, by changing the catastrophe, were tragedies to-day and comedies to-morrow.

Tragedy was not in those times a poem of more general dignity or elevation than comedy; it required only a calamitous conclusion, with which the common criticism of that age was satisfied, whatever lighter pleasure it afforded in its progress.

History was a series of actions, with no other than chronological succession, independent of each other, and without any tendency to introduce or regulate the conclusion. It is not always very nicely distinguished from tragedy.

There is not much nearer approach to unity of action in the tragedy of *Antony and Cleopatra*, than in the history of *Richard the Second*. But a history might be continued through many plays; as it had no plan, it had no limits.

Through all these denominations of the drama, *Shakespeare*'s mode of composition is the same; an interchange of seriousness and merriment, by which the mind is softened at one time, and exhilarated at another. But whatever be his purpose, whether to gladden or depress, or to conduct the story, without vehemence or emotion, through tracts of easy and familiar dialogue, he never fails to attain his purpose; as he commands us, we laugh or mourn, or sit silent with quiet expectation, in tranquillity without indifference.

When *Shakespeare*'s plan is understood, most of the criticisms of *Rhymer* and *Voltaire* vanish away. The play of *Hamlet* is opened, without impropriety, by two sentinels; *Iago* bellows at *Brabantio*'s window, without injury to the scheme of the play, though in terms which a modern audience would not easily endure; the character of *Polonius* is seasonable and useful; and the Grave-diggers themselves may be heard with applause.

Shakespeare engaged in dramatick poetry with the world open before him; the rules of the ancients were yet known to few; the publick judgment was unformed; he had no example of such fame as might force him upon imitation, nor criticks of such authority as might restrain his extravagance: He therefore indulged his natural disposition, and his disposition, as *Rhymer* has remarked, led him to comedy. In tragedy he often writes with great appearance of toil and study, what is written at last with little felicity; but in his comick scenes, he seems to produce without labour, what no labour can improve. In tragedy he is always struggling after some occasion to be comick, but in comedy he seems to repose, or to luxuriate, as in a mode of thinking congenial to his nature. In his tragick scenes there is always something wanting, but his comedy often surpasses expectation or desire. His comedy pleases by the thoughts and the language, and his tragedy for the greater part by incident and action. His tragedy seems to be skill, his comedy to be instinct.

The force of his comick scenes has suffered little diminution from the changes made by a century and a half, in manners or in words. As his personages act upon principles arising from genuine passion, very little modified by particular forms, their pleasures and vexations are communicable to all times and to all places; they are natural, and therefore durable; the adventitious peculiarities of personal habits, are only superficial dies, bright and pleasing for a little while, yet soon fading to a dim tinct, without any remains of former lustre; but the discriminations of true passion are the colours of nature; they pervade the whole mass, and can only perish with the body that exhibits them. The accidental compositions of heterogeneous modes are dissolved by the chance which combined them; but the uniform simplicity of primitive qualities neither admits increase, nor suffers decay. The sand heaped by one flood is scattered by another, but the rock always continues in its place. The stream of time, which is continually washing the dissoluble fabricks of other poets, passes without injury by the adamant of *Shakespeare*.

If there be, what I believe there is, in every nation, a stile which never becomes obsolete, a certain mode of phraseology so consonant and congenial to the analogy and principles of its respective language as to remain settled and unaltered; this stile is probably to be sought in the common intercourse of life, among those who speak only to be understood, without ambition of elegance. The polite are always catching modish innovations, and the learned depart from established forms of speech, in hope of finding or making better; those who wish for distinction forsake the vulgar, when the vulgar is right; but there is a conversation above grossness and below refinement, where propriety resides, and where this poet seems to have gathered his comick dialogue. He is therefore more agreeable to the ears of the present age than any other authour equally remote, and among his other excellencies deserves to be studied as one of the original masters of our language.

These observations are to be considered not as unexceptionably constant, but as containing general and predominant truth. *Shakespeare*'s familiar dialogue is affirmed to be smooth and clear, yet not wholly without ruggedness or difficulty; as a country may be eminently fruitful, though it has spots unfit for cultivation: His characters are praised as natural, though their sentiments are sometimes forced, and their actions improbable; as the earth upon the whole is spherical, though its surface is varied with protuberances and cavities.

Shakespeare with his excellencies has likewise faults, and faults sufficient to obscure and overwhelm any other merit. I shall shew them in the proportion in which they appear to me, without envious malignity or superstitious veneration. No question can be more innocently discussed than a dead poet's pretensions to renown; and little regard is due to that bigotry which sets candour higher than truth.

His first defect is that to which may be imputed most of the evil in books or in men. He sacrifices virtue to convenience, and is so much more careful to please than to instruct, that he seems to write without any moral purpose. From his writings indeed a system of social duty may be selected, for he that thinks reasonably must think morally; but his precepts and axioms drop casually from him; he makes no just distribution of good or evil, nor is always careful to shew in the virtuous a disapprobation of the wicked; he carries his persons indifferently through right and wrong, and at the close dismisses them without further care, and leaves their examples to operate by chance. This fault the barbarity of his age cannot extenuate; for it is always a writer's duty to make the world better, and justice is a virtue independant on time or place.

The plots are often so loosely formed, that a very slight consideration may improve them, and so carelessly pursued, that he seems not always fully to comprehend his own design. He omits opportunities of instructing or delighting which the train of his story seems to force upon him, and apparently rejects those exhibitions which would be more affecting, for the sake of those which are more easy.

It may be observed, that in many of his plays the latter part is evidently neglected. When he found himself near the end of his work, and, in view of his reward, he shortened the labour, to snatch the profit. He therefore remits his efforts where he should most vigorously exert them, and his catastrophe is improbably produced or imperfectly represented.

He had no regard to distinction of time or place, but gives to one age or nation, without scruple, the customs, institutions, and opinions of another, at the expence not only of likelihood, but of possibility. These faults *Pope* has endeavoured, with more zeal than judgment, to transfer to his imagined inter-polators. We need not wonder to find *Hector* quoting *Aristotle*, when we see the loves of *Theseus* and *Hippolyta* combined with the *Gothick* mythology of fair-ies. *Shakespeare*, indeed, was not the only violator of chronology, for in the same age *Sidney*, who wanted not the advantages of learning, has, in his *Arcadia*, confounded the pastoral with the feudal times, the days of innocence, quiet and security, with those of turbulence, violence and adventure.

In his comick scenes he is seldom very successful, when he engages his characters in reciprocations of smartness and contest of sarcasm; their jests are commonly gross, and their pleasantry licentious; neither his gentlemen nor his ladies have much delicacy, nor are sufficiently distinguished from his clowns by any appearance of refined manners. Whether he represented the real con-versation of his time is not easy to determine; the reign of *Elizabeth* is com-monly supposed to have been a time of stateliness, formality and reserve, yet perhaps the relaxations of that severity were not very elegant. There must, however, have been always some modes of gayety preferable to others, and a writer ought to chuse the best.

In tragedy his performance seems constantly to be worse, as his labour is more. The effusions of passion which exigence forces out are for the most part striking and energetick; but whenever he solicits his invention, or strains his faculties, the offspring of his throes is tumour, meanness, tediousness, and obscurity.

In narration he affects a disproportionate pomp of diction and a wearisome train of circumlocution, and tells the incident imperfectly in many words, which might have been more plainly delivered in few. Narration in dramatick poetry is naturally tedious, as it is unanimated and inactive, and obstructs the progress of the action; it should therefore always be rapid, and enlivened by frequent interruption. *Shakespeare* found it an encumbrance, and instead of lightening it by brevity, endeavoured to recommend it by dignity and splendour.

His declamations or set speeches are commonly cold and weak, for his power was the power of nature; when he endeavoured, like other tragick writers, to catch opportunities of amplification, and instead of inquiring what the occasion demanded, to show how much his stores of knowledge could supply, he seldom escapes without the pity or resentment of his reader.

It is incident to him to be now and then entangled with an unwieldy sentiment, which he cannot well express, and will not reject; he struggles with it a while, and if it continues stubborn, comprises it in words such as occur, and leaves it to be disentangled and evolved by those who have more leisure to bestow upon it.

Not that always where the language is intricate the thought is subtle, or the image always great where the line is bulky; the equality of words to things is very often neglected, and trivial sentiments and vulgar ideas disappoint the attention, to which they are recommended by sonorous epithets and swelling figures.

But the admirers of this great poet have never less reason to indulge their hopes of supreme excellence, than when he seems fully resolved to sink them in dejection, and mollify them with tender emotions by the fall of greatness, the danger of innocence, or the crosses of love. He is not long soft and pathetick without some idle conceit, or contemptible equivocation. He no sooner begins to move, than he counteracts himself; and terrour and pity, as they are rising in the mind, are checked and blasted by sudden frigidity.

A quibble is to *Shakespeare*, what luminous vapours are to the traveller; he follows it at all adventures, it is sure to lead him out of his way, and sure to engulf him in the mire. It has some malignant power over his mind, and its fascinations are irresistible. Whatever be the dignity or profundity of his disquisition, whether he be enlarging knowledge or exalting affection, whether he be amusing attention with incidents, or enchaining it in suspense, let but a quibble spring up before him, and he leaves his work unfinished. A quibble is the golden apple for which he will always turn aside from his career, or stoop from his elevation. A quibble poor and barren as it is, gave him such delight, that he was content to purchase it, by the sacrifice of reason, propriety and truth. A quibble was to him the fatal *Cleopatra* for which he lost the world, and was content to lose it.

It will be thought strange, that, in enumerating the defects of this writer, I have not yet mentioned his neglect of the unities; his violation of those laws which have been instituted and established by the joint authority of poets and of criticks.

For his other deviations from the art of writing, I resign him to critical justice, without making any other demand in his favour, than that which must be indulged to all human excellence; that his virtues be rated with his failings: But, from the censure which this irregularity may bring upon him, I shall, with due reverence to that learning which I must oppose, adventure to try how I can defend him.

His histories, being neither tragedies nor comedies, are not subject to any of their laws; nothing more is necessary to all the praise which they expect, than that the changes of action be so prepared as to be understood, that the incidents be various and affecting, and the characters consistent, natural and distinct. No other unity is intended, and therefore none is to be sought.

In his other works he has well enough preserved the unity of action. He has not, indeed, an intrigue regularly perplexed and regularly unravelled; he does not endeavour to hide his design only to discover it, for this is seldom the order of real events, and *Shakespeare* is the poet of nature: But his plan has commonly what *Aristotle* requires, a beginning, a middle, and an end; one event is concatenated with another, and the conclusion follows by easy consequence. There are perhaps some incidents that might be spared, as in other poets there is much talk that only fills up time upon the stage; but the general system makes gradual advances, and the end of the play is the end of expectation.

To the unities of time and place he has shewn no regard, and perhaps a nearer view of the principles on which they stand will diminish their value, and withdraw from them the veneration which, from the time of *Corneille*, they have very generally received by discovering that they have given more trouble to the poet, than pleasure to the auditor.

The necessity of observing the unities of time and place arises from the supposed necessity of making the drama credible. The criticks hold it impossible, that an action of months or years can be possibly believed to pass in three hours; or that the spectator can suppose himself to sit in the theatre, while ambassadors go and return between distant kings, while armies are levied and towns besieged, while an exile wanders and returns, or till he whom they saw courting his mistress, shall lament the untimely fall of his son. The mind revolts from evident falsehood, and fiction loses its force when it departs from the resemblance of reality.

From the narrow limitation of time necessarily arises the contraction of place. The spectator, who knows that he saw the first act at *Alexandria*, cannot suppose that he sees the next at *Rome*, at a distance to which not the dragons of *Medea* could, in so short a time, have transported him; he knows with certainty that he has not changed his place; and he knows that place cannot change itself; that what was a house cannot become a plain; that what was *Thebes* can never be *Persepolis*.

Such is the triumphant language with which a critick exults over the misery of an irregular poet, and exults commonly without resistance or reply. It is time therefore to tell him, by the authority of *Shakespeare*, that he assumes, as an unquestionable principle, a position, which, while his breath is forming it into words, his understanding pronounces to be false. It is false, that any representation is mistaken for reality; that any dramatick fable in its materiality was ever credible, or, for a single moment, was ever credited.

The objection arising from the impossibility of passing the first hour at *Alexandria*, and the next at *Rome*, supposes, that when the play opens the spectator really imagines himself at *Alexandria*, and believes that his walk to the theatre has been a voyage to *Egypt*, and that he lives in the days of *Antony* and *Cleopatra*. Surely he that imagines this, may imagine more. He that can take the stage at one time for the palace of the *Ptolemies*, may take it in half an hour for the promontory of *Actium*. Delusion, if delusion be admitted, has no certain limitation; if the spectator can be once persuaded, that his old acquaintance are *Alexander* and *Cæsar*, that a room illuminated with candles is the plain of *Pharsalia*, or the bank of *Granicus*, he is in a state of elevation above the reach of reason, or of truth, and from the heights of empyrean poetry, may despise the circumscriptions of terrestrial nature. There is no reason why a mind thus wandering in extasy should count the clock, or why an hour should not be a century in that calenture of the brains that can make the stage a field.

The truth is, that the spectators are always in their senses, and know, from the first act to the last, that the stage is only a stage, and that the players are only players. They come to hear a certain number of lines recited with just gesture and elegant modulation. The lines relate to some action, and an action must be in some place; but the different actions that compleat a story may be in places very remote from each other; and where is the absurdity of allowing that space to represent first *Athens*, and then *Sicily*, which was always known to be neither *Sicily* nor *Athens*, but a modern theatre.

By supposition, as place is introduced, time may be extended; the time required by the fable elapses for the most part between the acts; for, of so much of the action as is represented, the real and poetical duration is the same. If, in the first act, preparations for war against *Mithridates* are represented to be made in *Rome*, the event of the war may, without absurdity, be represented, in the catastrophe, as happening in *Pontus*; we know that there is neither war, nor preparation for war; we know that we are neither in *Rome* nor *Pontus*; that neither *Mithridates* nor *Lucullus* are before us. The drama exhibits successive imitations of successive actions, and why may not the second imitation represent an action that happened years after the first; if it be so connected with it, that nothing but time can be supposed to intervene. Time is, of all modes of existence, most obsequious to the imagination; a lapse of years is as easily conceived as a passage of hours. In contemplation we easily contract the time of real actions, and therefore willingly permit it to be contracted when we only see their imitation.

It will be asked, how the drama moves, if it is not credited. It is credited with all the credit due to a drama. It is credited, whenever it moves, as a just picture of a real original; as representing to the auditor what he would himself feel, if he were to do or suffer what is there feigned to be suffered or to be done. The reflection that strikes the heart is not, that the evils before us are real evils, but that they are evils to which we ourselves may be exposed. If there be any fallacy, it is not that we fancy the players, but that we fancy ourselves unhappy for a moment; but we rather lament the possibility than suppose the presence of misery, as a mother weeps over her babe, when she remembers that death may take it from her. The delight of tragedy proceeds from our consciousness of fiction; if we thought murders and treasons real, they would please no more.

Imitations produce pain or pleasure, not because they are mistaken for realities, but because they bring realities to mind. When the imagination is recreated by a painted landscape, the trees are not supposed capable to give us shade, or the fountains coolness; but we consider, how we should be pleased with such fountains playing beside us, and such woods waving over us. We are agitated in reading the history of *Henry* the Fifth, yet no man takes his book for the field of *Agencourt*. A dramatick exhibition is a book recited with concomitants that encrease or diminish its effect. Familiar comedy is often more powerful on the theatre, than in the page; imperial tragedy is always less. The humour of *Petruchio* may be heightened by grimace; but what voice or what gesture can hope to add dignity or force to the soliloquy of *Cato*.

A play read, affects the mind like a play acted. It is therefore evident, that the action is not supposed to be real, and it follows that between the acts a longer or shorter time may be allowed to pass, and that no more account of space or duration is to be taken by the auditor of a drama, than by the reader of a narrative, before whom may pass in an hour the life of a hero, or the revolutions of an empire.

Whether *Shakespeare* knew the unities, and rejected them by design, or deviated from them by happy ignorance, it is, I think, impossible to decide, and useless to inquire. We may reasonably suppose, that, when he rose to notice, he did not want the counsels and admonitions of scholars and criticks, and that he at last deliberately persisted in a practice, which he might have begun by chance. As nothing is essential to the fable, but unity of action, and as the unities of time and place arise evidently from false assumptions, and, by circumscribing the extent of the drama, lessen its variety, I cannot think it much to be lamented, that they were not known by him, or not observed: Nor, if such another poet could arise, should I very vehemently reproach him, that his first act passed at *Venice*, and his next in *Cyprus*. Such violations of rules merely positive, become the comprehensive genius of *Shakespeare*, and such censures are suitable to the minute and slender criticism of *Voltaire:*

> *Non usque adeo permiscuit imis*
> *Longus summa dies, ut non, si voce Metelli*
> *Serventur leges, malint a Cæsare tolli.*

Yet when I speak thus slightly of dramatick rules, I cannot but recollect how much wit and learning may be produced against me; before such authorities I am afraid to stand, not that I think the present question one of those that are to be decided by mere authority, but because it is to be suspected, that these precepts have not been so easily received but for better reasons than I have yet been able to find. The result of my enquiries, in which it would be ludicrous to boast of impartiality, is, that the unities of time and place are not essential to a just drama, that though they may sometimes conduce to pleasure, they are always to be sacrificed to the nobler beauties of variety and instruction; and that a play, written with nice observation of critical rules, is to be contemplated as an elaborate curiosity, as the product of superfluous and ostentatious art, by which is shewn, rather what is possible, than what is necessary.

He that, without diminution of any other excellence, shall preserve all the unities unbroken, deserves the like applause with the architect, who shall display all the orders of architecture in a citadel, without any deduction from its strength; but the principal beauty of a citadel is to exclude the enemy; and the greatest graces of a play, are to copy nature and instruct life.

Perhaps, what I have here not dogmatically but deliberately written, may recal the principles of the drama to a new examination. I am almost frighted at my own temerity; and when I estimate the fame and the strength of those that maintain the contrary opinion, am ready to sink down in reverential silence; as *Æneas* withdrew from the defence of *Troy*, when he saw *Neptune* shaking the wall, and *Juno* heading the besiegers.

Those whom my arguments cannot persuade to give their approbation to the judgment of *Shakespeare*, will easily, if they consider the condition of his life, make some allowance for his ignorance.

Every man's performances, to be rightly estimated, must be compared with the state of the age in which he lived, and with his own particular opportunities; and though to the reader a book be not worse or better for the circumstances of the authour, yet as there is always a silent reference of human works to human abilities, and as the enquiry, how far man may extend his designs, or how high he may rate his native force, is of far greater dignity than in what rank we shall place any particular performance, curiosity is always busy to discover the instruments, as well as to survey the workmanship, to know how much is to be ascribed to original powers, and how much to casual and adventitious help. The palaces of *Peru* or *Mexico* were certainly mean and incommodious habitations, if compared to the houses of *European* monarchs; yet who could forbear to view them with astonishment, who remembered that they were built without the use of iron?

The *English* nation, in the time of *Shakespeare*, was yet struggling to emerge from barbarity. The philology of *Italy* had been transplanted hither in the reign of *Henry* the Eighth; and the learned languages had been successfully cultivated by *Lilly*, *Linacer*, and *More*; by *Pole*, *Cheke*, and *Gardiner*; and afterwards by *Smith*, *Clerk*, *Haddon*, and *Ascham*. Greek was now taught to boys in the principal schools; and those who united elegance with learning, read, with great diligence, the *Italian* and *Spanish* poets. But literature was yet confined to professed scholars, or to men and women of high rank. The publick was gross and dark; and to be able to read and write, was an accomplishment still valued for its rarity.

Nations, like individuals, have their infancy. A people newly awakened to literary curiosity, being yet unacquainted with the true state of things, knows not how to judge of that which is proposed as its resemblance. Whatever is remote from common appearances is always welcome to vulgar, as to childish credulity; and of a country unenlightened by learning, the whole people is the vulgar. The study of those who then aspired to plebeian learning was laid out upon adventures, giants, dragons, and enchantments. *The Death of Arthur* was the favourite volume.

The mind, which has feasted on the luxurious wonders of fiction, has no taste of the insipidity of truth. A play which imitated only the common occurrences of the world, would, upon the admirers of *Palmerin* and *Guy* of *Warwick*, have made little impression; he that wrote for such an audience was under the necessity of looking round for strange events and fabulous transactions, and that incredibility, by which maturer knowledge is offended, was the chief recommendation of writings, to unskilful curiosity.

Our authour's plots are generally borrowed from novels, and it is reasonable to suppose, that he chose the most popular, such as were read by many, and related by more; for his audience could not have followed him through the intricacies of the drama, had they not held the thread of the story in their hands.

The stories, which we now find only in remoter authours, were in his time accessible and familiar. The fable of *As you like it*, which is supposed to be copied from *Chaucer*'s Gamelyn, was a little pamphlet of those times; and old Mr. *Cibber* remembered the tale of *Hamlet* in plain *English* prose, which the criticks have now to seek in *Saxo Grammaticus*.

His *English* histories he took from *English* chronicles and *English* ballads; and as the ancient writers were made known to his countrymen by versions, they supplied him with new subjects; he dilated some of *Plutarch*'s lives into plays, when they had been translated by *North*.

His plots, whether historical or fabulous, are always crouded with incidents, by which the attention of a rude people was more easily caught than by sentiment or argumentation; and such is the power of the marvellous even over those who despise it, that every man finds his mind more strongly seized by the tragedies of *Shakespeare* than of any other writer; others please us by particular speeches, but he always makes us anxious for the event, and has perhaps excelled all but *Homer* in securing the first purpose of a writer, by exciting restless and unquenchable curiosity, and compelling him that reads his work to read it through.

The shows and bustle with which his plays abound have the same original. As knowledge advances, pleasure passes from the eye to the ear, but returns, as it declines, from the ear to the eye. Those to whom our authour's labours were exhibited had more skill in pomps or processions than in poetical language, and perhaps wanted some visible and discriminated events, as comments on the dialogue. He knew how he should most please; and whether his practice is more agreeable to nature, or whether his example has prejudiced the nation, we still find that on our stage something must be done as well as said, and inactive declamation is very coldly heard, however musical or elegant, passionate or sublime.

Voltaire expresses his wonder, that our authour's extravagancies are endured by a nation, which has seen the tragedy of *Cato*. Let him be answered, that *Addison* speaks the language of poets, and *Shakespeare*, of men. We find in *Cato* innumerable beauties which enamour us of its authour, but we see nothing that acquaints us with human sentiments or human actions; we place it with the fairest and the noblest progeny which judgment propagates by conjunction with learning, but *Othello* is the vigorous and vivacious offspring of observation impregnated by genius. *Cato* affords a splendid exhibition of artificial and fictitious manners, and delivers just and noble sentiments, in diction easy, elevated and harmonious, but its hopes and fears communicate no vibration to the heart; the composition refers us only to the writer; we pronounce the name of *Cato*, but we think on *Addison*.

The work of a correct and regular writer is a garden accurately formed and diligently planted, varied with shades, and scented with flowers; the composition of *Shakespeare* is a forest, in which oaks extend their branches, and pines tower in the air, interspersed sometimes with weeds and brambles, and sometimes giving shelter to myrtles and to roses; filling the eye with awful pomp, and gratifying the mind with endless diversity. Other poets display cabinets of precious rarities, minutely finished, wrought into shape, and polished unto brightness. *Shakespeare* opens a mine which contains gold and diamonds in unexhaustible plenty, though clouded by incrustations, debased by impurities, and mingled with a mass of meaner minerals.

It has been much disputed, whether *Shakespeare* owed his excellence to his own native force, or whether he had the common helps of scholastick education, the precepts of critical science, and the examples of ancient authours.

There has always prevailed a tradition, that *Shakespeare* wanted learning, that he had no regular education, nor much skill in the dead languages. *Johnson*, his friend, affirms, that *he had small Latin, and no Greek*; who, besides that he had no imaginable temptation to falsehood, wrote at a time when the character and acquisitions of *Shakespeare* were known to multitudes. His evidence ought therefore to decide the controversy, unless some testimony of equal force could be opposed.

Some have imagined, that they have discovered deep learning in many imitations of old writers; but the examples which I have known urged, were drawn from books translated in his time; or were such easy coincidencies of thought, as will happen to all who consider the same subjects; or such remarks on life or axioms of morality as float in conversation, and are transmitted through the world in proverbial sentences.

I have found it remarked, that, in this important sentence, *Go before, I'll follow*, we read a translation of, *I prae, sequar.* I have been told, that when *Caliban*, after a pleasing dream, says, *I cry'd to sleep again*, the authour imitates *Anacreon*, who had, like every other man, the same wish on the same occasion.

There are a few passages which may pass for imitations, but so few, that the exception only confirms the rule; he obtained them from accidental quotations, or by oral communication, and as he used what he had, would have used more if he had obtained it.

The *Comedy of Errors* is confessedly taken from the *Menæchmi* of *Plautus*; from the only play of *Plautus* which was then in *English*. What can be more probable, than that he who copied that, would have copied more; but that those which were not translated were inaccessible?

Whether he knew the modern languages is uncertain. That his plays have some *French* scenes proves but little; he might easily procure them to be written, and probably, even though he had known the language in the common degree, he could not have written it without assistance. In the story of *Romeo* and *Juliet* he is observed to have followed the *English* translation, where it deviates from the *Italian*; but this on the other part proves nothing against his knowledge of the original. He was to copy, not what he knew himself, but what was known to his audience.

It is most likely that he had learned *Latin* sufficiently to make him acquainted with construction, but that he never advanced to an easy perusal of the *Roman* authours. Concerning his skill in modern languages, I can find no sufficient ground of determination; but as no imitations of *French* or *Italian* authours have been discovered, though the *Italian* poetry was then high in esteem, I am inclined to believe, that he read little more than *English*, and chose for his fables only such tales as he found translated.

That much knowledge is scattered over his works is very justly observed by *Pope*, but it is often such knowledge as books did not supply. He that will understand *Shakespeare*, must not be content to study him in the closet, he must look for his meaning sometimes among the sports of the field, and sometimes among the manufactures of the shop.

There is however proof enough that he was a very diligent reader, nor was our language then so indigent of books, but that he might very liberally indulge his curiosity without excursion into foreign literature. Many of the *Roman* authours were translated, and some of the *Greek*; the reformation had filled the kingdom with theological learning; most of the topicks of human disquisition had found *English* writers; and poetry had been cultivated, not only with diligence, but success. This was a stock of knowledge sufficient for a mind so capable of appropriating and improving it.

But the greater part of his excellence was the product of his own genius. He found the *English* stage in a state of the utmost rudeness; no essays either in tragedy or comedy had appeared, from which it could be discovered to what degree of delight either one or other might be carried. Neither character nor dialogue were yet understood. *Shakespeare* may be truly said to have introduced them both amongst us, and in some of his happier scenes to have carried them both to the utmost height.

By what gradations of improvement he proceeded, is not easily known; for the chronology of his works is yet unsettled. *Rowe* is of opinion, that *perhaps we are not to look for his beginning, like those of other writers, in his least perfect works; art had so little, and nature so large a share in what he did, that for ought I know,* says he, *the performances of his youth, as they were the most vigorous, were the best.* But the power of nature is only the power of using to any certain purpose the materials which diligence procures, or opportunity supplies. Nature gives no man knowledge, and when images are collected by study and experience, can only assist in combining or applying them. *Shakespeare,* however favoured by nature, could impart only what he had learned; and as he must increase his ideas, like other mortals, by gradual acquisition, he, like them, grew wiser as he grew older, could display life better, as he knew it more, and instruct with more efficacy, as he was himself more amply instructed.

There is a vigilance of observation and accuracy of distinction which books and precepts cannot confer; from this almost all original and native excellence proceeds. *Shakespeare* must have looked upon mankind with perspicacity, in the highest degree curious and attentive. Other writers borrow their characters from preceding writers, and diversify them only by the accidental appendages of present manners; the dress is a little varied, but the body is the same. Our authour had both matter and form to provide; for except the characters of *Chaucer*, to whom I think he is not much indebted, there were no writers in *English*, and perhaps not many in other modern languages, which shewed life in its native colours.

The contest about the original benevolence or malignity of man had not yet commenced. Speculation had not yet attempted to analyse the mind, to trace the passions to their sources, to unfold the seminal principles of vice and virtue, or sound the depths of the heart for the motives of action. All those enquiries, which from that time that human nature became the fashionable study, have been made sometimes with nice discernment, but often with idle subtilty, were yet unattempted. The tales, with which the infancy of learning was satisfied, exhibited only the superficial appearances of action, related the events but omitted the causes, and were formed for such as delighted in wonders rather than in truth. Mankind was not then to be studied in the closet; he that would know the world, was under the necessity of gleaning his own remarks, by mingling as he could in its business and amusements.

Boyle congratulated himself upon his high birth, because it favoured his curiosity, by facilitating his access. *Shakespeare* had no such advantage; he came to *London* a needy adventurer, and lived for a time by very mean employments. Many works of genius and learning have been performed in states of life, that appear very little favourable to thought or to enquiry; so many, that he who considers them is inclined to think that he sees enterprise and perseverance predominating over all external agency, and bidding help and hindrance vanish before them. The genius of *Shakespeare* was not to be depressed by the weight of poverty, nor limited by the narrow conversation to which men in want are inevitably condemned; the incumbrances of his fortune were shaken from his mind, *as dewdrops from a lion's mane.*

Though he had so many difficulties to encounter, and so little assistance to surmount them, he has been able to obtain an exact knowledge of many modes of life, and many casts of native dispositions; to vary them with great multiplicity; to mark them by nice distinctions; and to shew them in full view by proper combinations. In this part of his performances he had none to imitate, but has himself been imitated by all succeeding writers; and it may be doubted, whether from all his successors more maxims of theoretical knowledge, or more rules of practical prudence, can be collected, than he alone has given to his country.

Nor was his attention confined to the actions of men; he was an exact surveyor of the inanimate world; his descriptions have always some peculiarities, gathered by contemplating things as they really exist. It may be observed, that the oldest poets of many nations preserve their reputation, and that the following generations of wit, after a short celebrity, sink into oblivion. The first, whoever they be, must take their sentiments and descriptions immediately from knowledge; the resemblance is therefore just, their descriptions are verified by every eye, and their sentiments acknowledged by every breast. Those whom their fame invites to the same studies, copy partly them, and partly nature, till the books of one age gain such authority, as to stand in the place of nature to another, and imitation, always deviating a little, becomes at last capricious and casual. *Shakespeare,* whether life or nature be his subject, shews plainly, that he has seen with his own eyes; he gives the image which he receives, not weakened or distorted by the intervention of any other mind; the ignorant feel his representations to be just, and the learned see that they are compleat.

Perhaps it would not be easy to find any authour, except *Homer,* who invented so much as *Shakespeare,* who so much advanced the studies which he cultivated, or effused so much novelty upon his age or country. The form, the characters, the language, and the shows of the *English* drama are his. *He seems,* says *Dennis, to have been the very original of our* English *tragical harmony, that is, the harmony of blank verse, diversified often by dissyllable and trissyllable terminations. For the diversity distinguishes it from heroick harmony, and by bringing it nearer to common use makes it more proper to gain attention, and more fit for*

action and dialogue. Such verse we make when we are writing prose; we make such
verse in common conversation.

I know not whether this praise is rigorously just. The dissyllable termination,
which the critick rightly appropriates to the drama, is to be found, though,
I think, not in *Gorboduc* which is confessedly before our authour; yet in
Hieronnymo, of which the date is not certain, but which there is reason to believe
at least as old as his earliest plays. This however is certain, that he is the first who
taught either tragedy or comedy to please, there being no theatrical piece of any
older writer, of which the name is known, except to antiquaries and collectors of
books, which are sought because they are scarce, and would not have been
scarce, had they been much esteemed.

To him we must ascribe the praise, unless *Spenser* may divide it with him, of
having first discovered to how much smoothness and harmony the *English* language could be softened. He has speeches, perhaps sometimes scenes, which
have all the delicacy of *Rowe*, without his effeminacy. He endeavours indeed
commonly to strike by the force and vigour of his dialogue, but he never exe-
cutes his purpose better, than when he tries to sooth by softness.

Yet it must be at last confessed, that as we owe every thing to him, he owes
something to us; that, if much of his praise is paid by perception and judgement, much is likewise given by custom and veneration. We fix our eyes upon
his graces, and turn them from his deformities, and endure in him what we
should in another loath or despise. If we endured without praising, respect
for the father of our drama might excuse us; but I have seen, in the book of
some modern critick, a collection of anomalies which shew that he has corrupted language by every mode of depravation, but which his admirer has
accumulated as a monument of honour.

He has scenes of undoubted and perpetual excellence, but perhaps not
one play, which, if it were now exhibited as the work of a contemporary
writer, would be heard to the conclusion. I am indeed far from thinking, that
his works were wrought to his own ideas of perfection; when they were such
as would satisfy the audience, they satisfied the writer. It is seldom that
authours, though more studious of fame than *Shakespeare*, rise much above
the standard of their own age; to add a little to what is best will always be sufficient for present praise, and those who find themselves exalted into fame,
are willing to credit their encomiasts, and to spare the labour of contending
with themselves.

It does not appear, that *Shakespeare* thought his works worthy of posterity,
that he levied any ideal tribute upon future times, or had any further prospect, than of present popularity and present profit. When his plays had been
acted, his hope was at an end; he solicited no addition of honour from the
reader. He therefore made no scruple to repeat the same jests in many dialogues, or to entangle different plots by the same knot of perplexity, which
may be at least forgiven him, by those who recollect, that of *Congreve*'s four

comedies, two are concluded by a marriage in a mask, by a deception, which perhaps never happened, and which, whether likely or not, he did not invent.

So careless was this great poet of future fame, that, though he retired to ease and plenty, while he was yet little *declined into the vale of years*, before he could be disgusted with fatigue, or disabled by infirmity, he made no collection of his works, nor desired to rescue those that had been already published from the depravations that obscured them, or secure to the rest a better destiny, by giving them to the world in their genuine state.

Of the plays which bear the name of *Shakespeare* in the late editions, the greater part were not published till about seven years after his death, and the few which appeared in his life are apparently thrust into the world without the care of the authour, and therefore probably without his knowledge.

Of all the publishers, clandestine or professed, their negligence and unskilfulness has by the late revisers been sufficiently shown. The faults of all are indeed numerous and gross, and have not only corrupted many passages perhaps beyond recovery, but have brought others into suspicion, which are only obscured by obsolete phraseology, or by the writer's unskilfulness and affectation. To alter is more easy than to explain, and temerity is a more common quality than diligence. Those who saw that they must employ conjecture to a certain degree, were willing to indulge it a little further. Had the authour published his own works, we should have sat quietly down to disentangle his intricacies, and clear his obscurities; but now we tear what we cannot loose, and eject what we happen not to understand.

The faults are more than could have happened without the concurrence of many causes. The stile of *Shakespeare* was in itself ungrammatical, perplexed and obscure; his works were transcribed for the players by those who may be supposed to have seldom understood them; they were transmitted by copiers equally unskilful, who still multiplied errours; they were perhaps sometimes mutilated by the actors, for the sake of shortening the speeches; and were at last printed without correction of the press.

In this state they remained, not as Dr. *Warburton* supposes, because they were unregarded, but because the editor's art was not yet applied to modern languages, and our ancestors were accustomed to so much negligence of *English* printers, that they could very patiently endure it. At last an edition was undertaken by *Rowe*; not because a poet was to be published by a poet, for *Rowe* seems to have thought very little on correction or explanation, but that our authour's works might appear like those of his fraternity, with the appendages of a life and recommendatory preface. *Rowe* has been clamorously blamed for not performing what he did not undertake, and it is time that justice be done him, by confessing, that though he seems to have had no thought of corruption beyond the printer's errours, yet he has made many emendations, if they were not made before, which his successors have received without acknowledgment, and which, if they had produced them, would have filled pages and pages with censures of the stupidity by which the faults were committed, with displays of the absurdities which they involved, with ostentatious expositions of the new reading, and self congratulations on the happiness of discovering it.

Of *Rowe*, as of all the editors, I have preserved the preface, and have likewise retained the authour's life, though not written with much elegance or spirit; it relates however what is now to be known, and therefore deserves to pass through all succeeding publications.

The nation had been for many years content enough with Mr. *Rowe's* performance, when Mr. *Pope* made them acquainted with the true state of *Shakespear's* text, shewed that it was extremely corrupt, and gave reason to hope that there were means of reforming it. He collated the old copies, which none had thought to examine before, and restored many lines to their integrity; but, by a very compendious criticism, he rejected whatever he disliked, and thought more of amputation than of cure.

I know not why he is commended by Dr. *Warburton* for distinguishing the genuine from the spurious plays. In this choice he exerted no judgement of his own; the plays which he received, were given by *Hemings* and *Condel*, the first editors; and those which he rejected, though, according to the licentiousness of the press in those times, they were printed during *Shakespear's* life, with his name, had been omitted by his friends, and were never added to his works before the edition of 1664, from which they were copied by the later printers.

This was a work which *Pope* seems to have thought unworthy of his abilities, being not able to suppress his contempt of *the dull duty of an editor*. He understood but half his undertaking. The duty of a collator is indeed dull, yet, like other tedious tasks, is very necessary; but an emendatory critick would ill discharge his duty, without qualities very different from dulness. In perusing a corrupted piece, he must have before him all possibilities of meaning, with all possibilities of expression. Such must be his comprehension of thought, and such his copiousness of language. Out of many readings possible, he must be able to select that which best suits with the state, opinions, and modes of language prevailing in every age, and with his authour's particular cast of thought, and turn of expression. Such must be his knowledge, and such his taste. Conjectural criticism demands more than humanity possesses, and he that exercises it with most praise has very frequent need of indulgence. Let us now be told no more of the dull duty of an editor.

Confidence is the common consequence of success. They whose excellence of any kind has been loudly celebrated, are ready to conclude, that their powers are universal. *Pope's* edition fell below his own expectations, and he was so much offended, when he was found to have left any thing for others to do, that he past the latter part of his life in a state of hostility with verbal criticism.

I have retained all his notes, that no fragment of so great a writer may be lost; his preface, valuable alike for elegance of composition and justness of remark, and containing a general criticism on his authour, so extensive that little can be added, and so exact, that little can be disputed, every editor has an interest to suppress, but that every reader would demand its insertion.

Pope was succeeded by *Theobald*, a man of narrow comprehension and small acquisitions, with no native and intrinsick splendour of genius, with little of the artificial light of learning, but zealous for minute accuracy, and not negligent in pursuing it. He collated the ancient copies, and rectified many errors. A man so anxiously scrupulous might have been expected to do more, but what little he did was commonly right.

In his reports of copies and editions he is not to be trusted, without examination. He speaks sometimes indefinitely of copies, when he has only one. In his enumeration of editions, he mentions the two first folios as of high, and the third folio as of middle authority; but the truth is, that the first is equivalent to all others, and that the rest only deviate from it by the printer's negligence. Whoever has any of the folios has all, excepting those diversities which mere reiteration of editions will produce. I collated them all at the beginning, but afterwards used only the first.

Of his notes I have generally retained those which he retained himself in his second edition, except when they were confuted by subsequent annotators, or were too minute to merit preservation. I have sometimes adopted his restoration of a comma, without inserting the panegyrick in which he celebrated himself for his atchievement. The exuberant excrescence of diction I have often lopped, his triumphant exultations over *Pope* and *Rowe* I have sometimes suppressed, and his contemptible ostentation I have frequently concealed; but I have in some places shewn him, as he would have shewn himself, for the reader's diversion, that the inflated emptiness of some notes may justify or excuse the contraction of the rest.

Theobald, thus weak and ignorant, thus mean and faithless, thus petulant and ostentatious, by the good luck of having *Pope* for his enemy, has escaped, and escaped alone, with reputation, from this undertaking. So willingly does the world support those who solicite favour, against those who command reverence; and so easily is he praised, whom no man can envy.

Our authour fell then into the hands of Sir *Thomas Hanmer*, the *Oxford* editor, a man, in my opinion, eminently qualified by nature for such studies. He had, what is the first requisite to emendatory criticism, that intuition by which the poet's intention is immediately discovered, and that dexterity of intellect which dispatches its work by the easiest means. He had undoubtedly read much; his acquaintance with customs, opinions, and traditions, seems to have been large; and he is often learned without shew. He seldom passes what he does not understand, without an attempt to find or to make a meaning, and sometimes hastily makes what a little more attention would have found. He is solicitous to reduce to grammar, what he could not be sure that his authour intended to be grammatical. *Shakespeare* regarded more the series of ideas, than of words; and his language, not being designed for the reader's desk, was all that he desired it to be, if it conveyed his meaning to the audience.

Hanmer's care of the metre has been too violently censured. He found the measures reformed in so many passages, by the silent labours of some editors, with the silent acquiescence of the rest, that he thought himself allowed to extend a little further the license, which had already been carried so far without reprehension; and of his corrections in general, it must be confessed, that they are often just, and made commonly with the least possible violation of the text.

But, by inserting his emendations, whether invented or borrowed, into the page, without any notice of varying copies, he has appropriated the labour of his predecessors, and made his own edition of little authority. His confidence indeed, both in himself and others, was too great; he supposes all to be right that was done by *Pope* and *Theobald*; he seems not to suspect a critick of fallibility, and it was but reasonable that he should claim what he so liberally granted.

As he never writes without careful enquiry and diligent consideration, I have received all his notes, and believe that every reader will wish for more.

Of the last editor it is more difficult to speak. Respect is due to high place, tenderness to living reputation, and veneration to genius and learning; but he cannot be justly offended at that liberty of which he has himself so frequently given an example, nor very solicitous what is thought of notes, which he ought never to have considered as part of his serious employments, and which, I suppose, since the ardour of composition is remitted, he no longer numbers among his happy effusions.

The original and predominant errour of his commentary, is acquiescence in his first thoughts; that precipitation which is produced by consciousness of quick discernment; and that confidence which presumes to do, by surveying the surface, what labour only can perform, by penetrating the bottom. His notes exhibit sometimes perverse interpretations, and sometimes improbable conjectures; he at one time gives the authour more profundity of meaning than the sentence admits; and at another discovers absurdities, where the sense is plain to every other reader. But his emendations are likewise often happy and just; and his interpretation of obscure passages learned and sagacious.

Of his notes, I have commonly rejected those, against which the general voice of the publick has exclaimed, or which their own incongruity immediately condemns, and which, I suppose, the authour himself would desire to be forgotten. Of the rest, to part I have given the highest approbation, by inserting the offered reading in the text; part I have left to the judgment of the reader, as doubtful, though specious; and part I have censured without reserve, but I am sure without bitterness of malice, and, I hope, without wantonness of insult.

It is no pleasure to me, in revising my volumes, to observe how much paper is wasted in confutation. Whoever considers the revolutions of learning, and the various questions of greater or less importance, upon which wit and reason have exercised their powers, must lament the unsuccessfulness of enquiry, and the slow advances of truth, when he reflects, that great part of the labour of every writer is only the destruction of those that went before him. The first care of the builder of a new system, is to demolish the fabricks which are standing. The chief desire of him that comments an authour, is to shew how much other commentators have corrupted and obscured him. The opinions prevalent in one age, as truths above the reach of controversy, are confuted and rejected in another, and rise again to reception in remoter times. Thus the human mind is kept in motion without progress. Thus sometimes truth and errour, and sometimes contrarieties of errour, take each others place by reciprocal invasion. The tide of seeming knowledge which is poured over one generation, retires and leaves another naked and barren; the sudden meteors of intelligence which for a while appear to shoot their beams into the regions of obscurity, on a sudden withdraw their lustre, and leave mortals again to grope their way.

These elevations and depressions of renown, and the contradictions to which all improvers of knowledge must for ever be exposed, since they are not escaped by the highest and brightest of mankind, may surely be endured with patience by criticks and annotators, who can rank themselves but as the satellites of their authours. How canst thou beg for life, says *Achilles* to his captive, when thou knowest that thou art now to suffer only what must another day be suffered by *Achilles?*

Dr. *Warburton* had a name sufficient to confer celebrity on those who could exalt themselves into antagonists, and his notes have raised a clamour too loud to be distinct. His chief assailants are the authours of *the Canons of criticism* and of the *Review of* Shakespeare's *text*; of whom one ridicules his errours with airy petulance, suitable enough to the levity of the controversy; the other attacks them with gloomy malignity, as if he were dragging to justice an assassin or incendiary. The one stings like a fly, sucks a little blood, takes a gay flutter, and returns for more; the other bites like a viper, and would be glad to leave inflammations and gangrene behind him. When I think on one, with his confederates, I remember the danger of *Coriolanus*, who was afraid that *girls with spits, and boys with stones, should slay him in puny battle*; when the other crosses my imagination, I remember the prodigy in *Macbeth,*

> *An eagle tow'ring in his pride of place,*
> *Was by a mousing owl hawk'd at and kill'd.*

Let me however do them justice. One is a wit, and one a scholar. They have both shewn acuteness sufficient in the discovery of faults, and have both advanced some probable interpretations of obscure passages; but when they aspire to conjecture and emendation, it appears how falsely we all estimate our own abilities, and the little which they have been able to perform might have taught them more candour to the endeavours of others.

Before Dr. *Warburton*'s edition, *Critical observations on* Shakespeare had been published by Mr. *Upton*, a man skilled in languages, and acquainted with books, but who seems to have had no great vigour of genius or nicety of taste. Many of his explanations are curious and useful, but he likewise, though he professed to oppose the licentious confidence of editors, and adhere to the old copies, is unable to restrain the rage of emendation, though his ardour is ill seconded by his skill. Every cold empirick, when his heart is expanded by a successful experiment, swells into a theorist, and the laborious collator at some unlucky moment frolicks in conjecture.

Critical, historical and explanatory notes have been likewise published upon *Shakespeare* by Dr. *Grey*, whose diligent perusal of the old *English* writers has enabled him to make some useful observations. What he undertook he has well enough performed, but as he neither attempts judicial nor emendatory criticism, he employs rather his memory than his sagacity. It were to be wished that all would endeavour to imitate his modesty who have not been able to surpass his knowledge.

I can say with great sincerity of all my predecessors, what I hope will hereafter be said of me, that not one has left *Shakespeare* without improvement, nor is there one to whom I have not been indebted for assistance and information. Whatever I have taken from them it was my intention to refer to its original authour, and it is certain, that what I have not given to another, I believed when I wrote it to be my own. In some perhaps I have been anticipated; but if I am ever found to encroach upon the remarks of any other commentator, I am willing that the honour, be it more or less, should be transferred to the first claimant, for his right, and his alone, stands above dispute; the second can prove his pretensions only to himself, nor can himself always distinguish invention, with sufficient certainty, from recollection.

They have all been treated by me with candour, which they have not been careful of observing to one another. It is not easy to discover from what cause the acrimony of a scholiast can naturally proceed. The subjects to be discussed by him are of very small importance; they involve neither property nor liberty; nor favour the interest of sect or party. The various readings of copies, and different interpretations of a passage, seem to be questions that might exercise the wit, without engaging the passions. But, whether it be, that *small things make mean men proud*, and vanity catches small occasions; or that all contrariety of opinion, even in those that can defend it no longer, makes proud men angry; there is often found in commentaries a spontaneous strain of invective and contempt, more eager and venomous than is vented by the most furious controvertist in politicks against those whom he is hired to defame.

Perhaps the lightness of the matter may conduce to the vehemence of the agency; when the truth to be investigated is so near to inexistence, as to escape attention, its bulk is to be enlarged by rage and exclamation: That to which all would be indifferent in its original state, may attract notice when the fate of a name is appended to it. A commentator has indeed great temptations to supply by turbulence what he wants of dignity, to beat his little gold to a spacious surface, to work that to foam which no art or diligence can exalt to spirit.

The notes which I have borrowed or written are either illustrative, by which difficulties are explained; or judicial, by which faults and beauties are remarked; or emendatory, by which depravations are corrected.

The explanations transcribed from others, if I do not subjoin any other interpretation, I suppose commonly to be right, at least I intend by acquiescence to confess, that I have nothing better to propose.

After the labours of all the editors, I found many passages which appeared to me likely to obstruct the greater number of readers, and thought it my duty to facilitate their passage. It is impossible for an expositor not to write too little for some, and too much for others. He can only judge what is necessary by his own experience; and how long soever he may deliberate, will at last explain many lines which the learned will think impossible to be mistaken, and omit many for which the ignorant will want his help. These are censures merely relative, and must be quietly endured. I have endeavoured to be neither superfluously copious, nor scrupulously reserved, and hope that I have made my authour's meaning accessible to many who before were frighted from perusing him, and contributed something to the publick, by diffusing innocent and rational pleasure.

The compleat explanation of an authour not systematick and consequential, but desultory and vagrant, abounding in casual allusions and light hints, is not to be expected from any single scholiast. All personal reflections, when names are suppressed, must be in a few years irrecoverably obliterated; and customs, too minute to attract the notice of law, such as modes of dress, formalities of conversation, rules of visits, disposition of furniture, and practices of ceremony, which naturally find places in familiar dialogue, are so fugitive and unsubstantial, that they are not easily retained or recovered. What can be known, will be collected by chance, from the recesses of obscure and obsolete papers, perused commonly with some other view. Of this knowledge every man has some, and none has much; but when an authour has engaged the publick attention, those who can add any thing to his illustration, communicate their discoveries, and time produces what had eluded diligence.

To time I have been obliged to resign many passages, which, though I did not understand them, will perhaps hereafter be explained, having, I hope, illustrated some, which others have neglected or mistaken, sometimes by short remarks, or marginal directions, such as every editor has added at his will, and often by comments more laborious than the matter will seem to deserve; but that which is most difficult is not always most important, and to an editor nothing is a trifle by which his authour is obscured.

The poetical beauties or defects I have not been very diligent to observe. Some plays have more, and some fewer judicial observations, not in proportion to their difference of merit, but because I gave this part of my design to chance and to caprice. The reader, I believe, is seldom pleased to find his opinion anticipated; it is natural to delight more in what we find or make, than in what we receive. Judgement, like other faculties, is improved by practice, and its advancement is hindered by submission to dictatorial decisions, as the memory grows torpid by the use of a table book. Some initiation is however necessary; of all skill, part is infused by precept, and part is obtained by habit; I have therefore shewn so much as may enable the candidate of criticism to discover the rest.

To the end of most plays, I have added short strictures, containing a general censure of faults, or praise of excellence; in which I know not how much I have concurred with the current opinion; but I have not, by any affectation of singularity, deviated from it. Nothing is minutely and particularly examined, and therefore it is to be supposed, that in the plays which are condemned there is much to be praised, and in these which are praised much to be condemned.

The part of criticism in which the whole succession of editors has laboured with the greatest diligence, which has occasioned the most arrogant ostentation, and excited the keenest acrimony, is the emendation of corrupted passages, to which the publick attention having been first drawn by the violence of the contention between *Pope* and *Theobald*, has been continued by the persecution, which, with a kind of conspiracy, has been since raised against all the publishers of *Shakespeare*.

That many passages have passed in a state of depravation through all the editions is indubitably certain; of these the restoration is only to be attempted by collation of copies or sagacity of conjecture. The collator's province is safe and easy, the conjecturer's perilous and difficult. Yet as the greater part of the plays are extant only in one copy, the peril must not be avoided, nor the difficulty refused.

Of the readings which this emulation of amendment has hitherto produced, some from the labours of every publisher I have advanced into the text; those are to be considered as in my opinion sufficiently supported; some I have rejected without mention, as evidently erroneous; some I have left in the notes without censure or approbation, as resting in equipoise between objection and defence; and some, which seemed specious but not right, I have inserted with a subsequent animadversion.

Having classed the observations of others, I was at last to try what I could substitute for their mistakes, and how I could supply their omissions. I collated such copies as I could procure, and wished for more, but have not found the collectors of these rarities very communicative. Of the editions which chance or kindness put into my hands I have given an enumeration, that I may not be blamed for neglecting what I had not the power to do.

By examining the old copies, I soon found that the later publishers, with all their boasts of diligence, suffered many passages to stand unauthorised, and contented themselves with *Rowe*'s regulation of the text, even where they knew it to be arbitrary, and with a little consideration might have found it to be wrong. Some of these alterations are only the ejection of a word for one that appeared to him more elegant or more intelligible. These corruptions I have often silently rectified; for the history of our language, and the true force of our words, can only be preserved, by keeping the text of authours free from adulteration. Others, and those very frequent, smoothed the cadence, or regulated the measure; on these I have not exercised the same rigour; if only a word was transposed, or a particle inserted or omitted, I have sometimes suffered the line to stand; for the inconstancy of the copies is such, as that some liberties may be easily permitted. But this practice I have not suffered to proceed far, having restored the primitive diction wherever it could for any reason be preferred.

The emendations, which comparison of copies supplied, I have inserted in the text; sometimes where the improvement was slight, without notice, and sometimes with an account of the reasons of the change.

Conjecture, though it be sometimes unavoidable, I have not wantonly nor licentiously indulged. It has been my settled principle, that the reading of the ancient books is probably true, and therefore is not to be disturbed for the sake of elegance, perspicuity, or mere improvement of the sense. For though much credit is not due to the fidelity, nor any to the judgement of the first publishers, yet they who had the copy before their eyes were more likely to read it right, than we who only read it by imagination. But it is evident that they have often made strange mistakes by ignorance or negligence, and that therefore something may be properly attempted by criticism, keeping the middle way between presumption and timidity.

Such criticism I have attempted to practise, and where any passage appeared inextricably perplexed, have endeavoured to discover how it may be recalled to sense, with least violence. But my first labour is, always to turn the old text on every side, and try if there be any interstice, through which light can find its way; nor would *Huetius* himself condemn me, as refusing the trouble of research, for the ambition of alteration. In this modest industry I have not been unsuccessful. I have rescued many lines from the violations of temerity, and secured many scenes from the inroads of correction. I have adopted the *Roman* sentiment, that it is more honourable to save a citizen, than to kill an enemy, and have been more careful to protect than to attack.

I have preserved the common distribution of the plays into acts, though I believe it to be in almost all the plays void of authority. Some of those which are divided in the later editions have no division in the first folio, and some that are divided in the folio have no division in the preceding copies. The settled mode of the theatre requires four intervals in the play, but few, if any, of our authour's compositions can be properly distributed in that manner. An act is so much of the drama as passes without intervention of time or change of place. A pause makes a new act. In every real, and therefore in every imitative action, the intervals may be more or fewer, the restriction of five acts being accidental and arbitrary. This *Shakespeare* knew, and this he practised; his plays were written, and at first printed in one unbroken continuity, and ought now to be exhibited with short pauses, interposed as often as the scene is changed, or any considerable time is required to pass. This method would at once quell a thousand absurdities.

In restoring the authour's works to their integrity, I have considered the punctuation as wholly in my power; for what could be their care of colons and commas, who corrupted words and sentences. Whatever could be done by adjusting points is therefore silently performed, in some plays with much diligence, in others with less; it is hard to keep a busy eye steadily fixed upon evanescent atoms, or a discursive mind upon evanescent truth.

The same liberty has been taken with a few particles, or other words of slight effect. I have sometimes inserted or omitted them without notice. I have done that sometimes, which the other editors have done always, and which indeed the state of the text may sufficiently justify.

The greater part of readers, instead of blaming us for passing trifles, will wonder that on mere trifles so much labour is expended, with such importance of debate, and such solemnity of diction. To these I answer with confidence, that they are judging of an art which they do not understand; yet cannot much reproach them with their ignorance, nor promise that they would become in general, by learning criticism, more useful, happier or wiser.

As I practised conjecture more, I learned to trust it less; and after I had printed a few plays, resolved to insert none of my own readings in the text. Upon this caution I now congratulate myself, for every day encreases my doubt of my emendations.

Since I have confined my imagination to the margin, it must not be considered as very reprehensible, if I have suffered it to play some freaks in its own dominion. There is no danger in conjecture, if it be proposed as conjecture; and while the text remains uninjured, those changes may be safely offered, which are not considered even by him that offers them as necessary or safe.

If my readings are of little value, they have not been ostentatiously displayed or importunately obtruded. I could have written longer notes, for the art of writing notes is not of difficult attainment. The work is performed, first by railing at the stupidity, negligence, ignorance, and asinine tastelessness of the former editors, and shewing, from all that goes before and all that follows, the inelegance and absurdity of the old reading; then by proposing something, which to superficial readers would seem specious, but which the editor rejects with indignation; then by producing the true reading, with a long paraphrase, and concluding with loud acclamations on the discovery, and a sober wish for the advancement and prosperity of genuine criticism.

All this may be done, and perhaps done sometimes without impropriety. But I have always suspected that the reading is right, which requires many words to prove it wrong; and the emendation wrong, that cannot without so much labour appear to be right. The justness of a happy restoration strikes at once, and the moral precept may be well applied to criticism, *quod dubitas ne feceris.*

To dread the shore which he sees spread with wrecks, is natural to the sailor. I had before my eye, so many critical adventures ended in miscarriage, that caution was forced upon me. I encountered in every page Wit struggling with its own sophistry, and Learning confused by the multiplicity of its views. I was forced to censure those whom I admired, and could not but reflect, while I was dispossessing their emendations, how soon the same fate might happen to my own, and how many of the readings which I have corrected may be by some other editor defended and established.

> *Criticks, I saw, that other's names efface,*
> *And fix their own, with labour, in the place;*
> *Their own, like others, soon their place resign'd,*
> *Or disappear'd, and left the first behind.*
>
> POPE.

That a conjectural critick should often be mistaken, cannot be wonderful, either to others or himself, if it be considered, that in his art there is no system, no principal and axiomatical truth that regulates subordinate positions. His chance of errour is renewed at every attempt; an oblique view of the passage, a slight misapprehension of a phrase, a casual inattention to the parts connected, is sufficient to make him not only fail, but fail ridiculously; and when he succeeds best, he produces perhaps but one reading of many probable, and he that suggests another will always be able to dispute his claims.

It is an unhappy state, in which danger is hid under pleasure. The allurements of emendation are scarcely resistible. Conjecture has all the joy and all the pride of invention, and he that has once started a happy change, is too much delighted to consider what objections may rise against it.

Yet conjectural criticism has been of great use in the learned world; nor is it my intention to depreciate a study, that has exercised so many mighty minds, from the revival of learning to our own age, from the Bishop of *Aleria* to English *Bentley.* The criticks on ancient authours have, in the exercise of their sagacity, many assistances, which the editor of *Shakespeare* is condemned to want. They are employed upon grammatical and settled languages, whose construction contributes so much to perspicuity, that *Homer* has fewer passages unintelligible than *Chaucer.* The words have not only a known regimen, but invariable quantities, which direct and confine the choice. There are commonly more manuscripts than one; and they do not often conspire in the same mistakes. Yet *Scaliger* could confess to *Salmasius* how little satisfaction his emendations gave him. *Illudunt nolis conjecturæ nostræ, quarum nos pudet, posteaquam in meliores codices incidimus.* And *Lipsius* could complain, that criticks were making faults, by trying to remove them, *Ut olim vitiis, ita nunc remediis laboratur.* And indeed, where mere conjecture is to be used, the emendations of *Scaliger* and *Lipsius*, notwithstanding their wonderful sagacity and erudition, are often vague and disputable, like mine or *Theobald*'s.

Perhaps I may not be more censured for doing wrong, than for doing little; for raising in the publick expectations, which at last I have not answered. The expectation of ignorance is indefinite, and that of knowledge is often tyrannical. It is hard to satisfy those who know not what to demand, or those who demand by design what they think impossible to be done. I have indeed disappointed no opinion more than my own; yet I have endeavoured to perform my task with no slight solicitude. Not a single passage in the whole work has appeared to me corrupt, which I have not attempted to restore; or obscure, which I have not endeavoured to illustrate. In many I have failed like others; and from many, after all my efforts, I have retreated, and confessed the repulse. I have not passed over, with affected superiority, what is equally difficult to the reader and to myself, but where I could not instruct him, have owned my ignorance. I might easily have accumulated a mass of seeming learning upon easy scenes; but it ought not to be imputed to negligence, that, where nothing was necessary, nothing has been done, or that, where others have said enough, I have said no more.

Notes are often necessary, but they are necessary evils. Let him, that is yet unacquainted with the powers of *Shakespeare*, and who desires to feel the highest pleasure that the drama can give, read every play from the first scene to the last, with utter negligence of all his commentators. When his fancy is once on the wing, let it not stoop at correction or explanation. When his attention is strongly engaged, let it disdain alike to turn aside to the name of *Theobald* and *Pope*. Let him read on through brightness and obscurity, through integrity and corruption; let him preserve his comprehension of the dialogue and his interest in the fable. And when the pleasures of novelty have ceased, let him attempt exactness; and read the commentators.

Particular passages are cleared by notes, but the general effect of the work is weakened. The mind is refrigerated by interruption; the thoughts are diverted from the principal subject; the reader is weary, he suspects not why; and at last throws away the book, which he has too diligently studied.

Parts are not to be examined till the whole has been surveyed; there is a kind of intellectual remoteness necessary for the comprehension of any great work in its full design and its true proportions; a close approach shews the smaller niceties, but the beauty of the whole is discerned no longer.

It is not very grateful to consider how little the succession of editors has added to this authour's power of pleasing. He was read, admired, studied, and imitated, while he was yet deformed with all the improprieties which ignorance and neglect could accumulate upon him; while the reading was yet not rectified, nor his allusions understood; yet then did *Dryden* pronounce "that *Shakespeare* was the man, who, of all modern and perhaps ancient poets, had the largest and most comprehensive soul. All the images of nature were still present to him, and he drew them not laboriously, but luckily: When he describes any thing, you more than see it, you feel it too. Those who accuse him to have wanted learning, give him the greater commendation: he was naturally learned: he needed not the spectacles of books to read nature; he looked inwards, and found her there. I cannot say he is every where alike; were he so, I should do him injury to compare him with the greatest of mankind. He is many times flat and insipid; his comick wit degenerating into clenches, his serious swelling into bombast. But he is always great, when some great occasion is presented to him: No man can say, he ever had a fit subject for his wit, and did not then raise himself as high above the rest of poets,

> *Quantum lenta solent inter viburne cupressi."*

It is to be lamented, that such a writer should want a commentary; that his language should become obsolete, or his sentiments obscure. But it is vain to carry wishes beyond the condition of human things; that which must happen to all, has happened to *Shakespeare*, by accident and time; and more than has been suffered by any other writer since the use of types, has been suffered by him through his own negligence of fame, or perhaps by that superiority of mind, which despised its own performances, when it compared them with its powers, and judged those works unworthy to be preserved, which the criticks of following ages were to contend for the fame of restoring and explaining.

Among these candidates of inferiour fame, I am now to stand the judgment of the publick; and wish that I could confidently produce my commentary as equal to the encouragement which I have had the honour of receiving. Every work of this kind is by its nature deficient, and I should feel little solicitude about the sentence, were it to be pronounced only by the skilful and the learned.

Diary entry

WEDNESDAY I JANUARY 1766

Jan. 1, after 2 in the morning.

Almighty and most merciful Father; I again appear in thy presence the wretched mispender of another year, which thy mercy has allowed me. O Lord, let me not sink into total depravity, look down upon me, and rescue me at last from the captivity of sin. Impart to me good resolutions, and give me strength and perseverance to perform them. Take not from me thy Holy Spirit, but grant that I may redeem the time lost, and that by temperance and diligence, by sincere repentance and faithful obedience, I may finally obtain everlasting happiness for the sake of Jesus Christ our Lord. Amen.

The Fountains: A Fairy Tale

Felix qui potuit boni
Fontem visere lucidum.
BOETHIUS.

As FLORETTA was wandering in a meadow at the foot of Plinlimmon, she heard a little bird cry in such a note as she had never observed before, and looking round her, saw a lovely Goldfinch entangled by a lime-twig, and a Hawk hovering over him, as at the point of seizing him in his talons.

FLORETTA longed to rescue the little bird, but was afraid to encounter the Hawk, who looked fiercely upon her without any apparent dread of her approach, and as she advanced seemed to increase in bulk, and clapped his wings in token of defiance. FLORETTA stood deliberating a few moments, but seeing her mother at no great distance, took courage, and snatched the twig with the little bird upon it. When she had disengaged him she put him in her bosom, and the Hawk flew away.

FLORETTA shewing her bird to her mother, told her from what danger she had rescued him; her mother, after admiring his beauty, said, that he would be a very proper inhabitant of the little gilded cage, which had hung empty since the Starling died for want of water, and that he should be placed at the chamber window, for it would be wonderfully pleasant to hear him in the morning.

FLORETTA, with tears in her eyes, replied, that he had better have been devoured by the Hawk than die for want of water, and that she would not save him from a less evil to put him in danger of a greater: She therefore took him into her hand, cleaned his feathers from the bird-lime, looked upon him with great tenderness, and, having put his bill to her lips, dismissed him into the air.

HE flew in circles round her as she went home, and perching on a tree before the door, delighted them a while with such sweetness of song, that her mother reproved her for not putting him in the cage. FLORETTA endeavoured to look grave, but silently approved her own act, and wished her mother more generosity. Her mother guessed her thoughts, and told her, that when she was older she would be wiser.

FLORETTA however did not repent, but hoped to hear her little bird the next morning singing at liberty. She waked early and listened, but no Goldfinch could she hear. She rose, and walking again in the same meadow, went to view the bush where she had seen the lime-twig the day before.

WHEN she entered the thicket, and was near the place for which she was looking, from behind a blossoming hawthorn advanced a female form of very low stature, but of elegant proportion and majestick air, arrayed in all the colours of the meadow, and sparkling as she moved like a dew-drop in the sun.

FLORETTA was too much disordered to speak or fly, and stood motionless between fear and pleasure, when the little lady took her by the hand.

I am, said she, one of that order of beings which some call Fairies, and some Piskies: We have always been known to inhabit the crags and caverns of Plinlimmon. The maids and shepherds when they wander by moonlight have often heard our musick, and sometimes seen our dances.

I am the chief of the Fairies of this region, and am known among them by the name of Lady LILINET of the Blue Rock. As I lived always in my own mountain, I had very little knowledge of human manners, and thought better of mankind than other Fairies found them to deserve; I therefore often opposed the mischievous practices of my sisters without always enquiring whether they were just. I extinguished the light that was kindled to lead a traveller into a marsh, and found afterwards that he was hasting to corrupt a virgin: I dissipated a mist which assumed the form of a town, and was raised to decoy a monopolizer of corn from his way to the next market: I removed a thorn, artfully planted to prick the foot of a churl, that was going to hinder the Poor from following his reapers; and defeated so many schemes of obstruction and punishment, that I was cited before the Queen as one who favoured wickedness and opposed the execution of fairy justice.

HAVING never been accustomed to suffer control, and thinking myself disgraced by the necessity of defence, I so much irritated the Queen by my sullenness and petulance, that in her anger she transformed me into a Goldfinch. *In this form*, says she, *I doom thee to remain till some human being shall show thee kindness without any prospect of interest.*

I flew out of her presence not much dejected; for I did not doubt but every reasonable being must love that which having never offended, could not be hated, and, having no power to hurt, could not be feared.

I therefore fluttered about the villages, and endeavoured to force myself into notice.

HAVING heard that nature was least corrupted among those who had no acquaintance with elegance and splendor, I employed myself for five years in hopping before the doors of cottages, and often sat singing on the thatched roof; my motions were seldom seen nor my notes heard, no kindness was ever excited, and all the reward of my officiousness was to be aimed at with a stone when I stood within a throw.

THE stones never hurt me, for I had still the power of a Fairy.

I then betook myself to spacious and magnificent habitations, and sung in bowers by the walks or on the banks of fountains.

IN these places where novelty was recommended by satiety, and curiosity excited by leisure, my form and my voice were soon distinguished, and I was known by the name of the pretty Goldfinch; the inhabitants would walk out to listen to my musick, and at last it was their practice to court my visits by scattering meat in my common haunts.

THIS was repeated till I went about pecking in full security, and expected to regain my original form, when I observed two of my most liberal benefactors silently advancing with a net behind me. I flew off, and fluttering beside them pricked the leg of each, and left them halting and groaning with the cramp.

I then went to another house, where for two springs and summers I entertained a splendid family with such melody as they had never heard in the woods before. The winter that followed the second summer was remarkably cold, and many little birds perished in the field. I laid myself in the way of one of the ladies as benumbed with cold and faint with hunger; she picked me up with great joy, telling her companions that she had found the Goldfinch that sung so finely all summer in the myrtle hedge, that she would lay him where he should die, for she could not bear to kill him, and would then pick his fine feathers very carefully, and stick them in her muff.

FINDING that her fondness and her gratitude could give way to so slight an interest, I chilled her fingers that she could not hold me, then flew at her face, and with my beak gave her nose four pecks that left four black spots indelible behind them, and broke a match by which she would have obtained the finest equipage in the county.

AT length the Queen repented of her sentence, and being unable to revoke it, assisted me to try experiments upon man, to excite his tenderness, and attract his regard.

WE made many attempts in which we were always disappointed. At last she placed me in your way held by a lime-twig, and herself in the shape of a Hawk made the shew of devouring me. You, my dear, have rescued me from the seeming danger without desiring to detain me in captivity, or seeking any other recompence than the pleasure of benefiting a feeling creature.

THE Queen is so much pleased with your kindness, that I am come, by her permission, to reward you with a greater favour than ever Fairy bestowed before.

THE former gifts of Fairies, though bounties in design, have proved commonly mischiefs in the event. We have granted mortals to wish according to their own discretion, and their discretion being small, and their wishes irreversible, they have rashly petitioned for their own destruction. But you, my dearest FLORETTA, shall have, what none have ever before obtained from us, the power of indulging your wish, and the liberty of retracting it. Be bold and follow me.

FLORETTA was easily persuaded to accompany the Fairy, who led her through a labyrinth of craggs and shrubs, to a cavern covered by a thicket on the side of the mountain.

THIS cavern, said she, is the court of LILINET your friend; in this place you shall find a certain remedy for all real evils. LILINET then went before her through a long subterraneous passage, where she saw many beautiful Fairies, who came to gaze at the stranger, but who, from reverence to their mistress, gave her no disturbance. She heard from remote corners of the gloomy cavern the roar of winds and the fall of waters, and more than once entreated to return; but LILINET assuring her that she was safe, persuaded her to proceed till they came to an arch, into which the light found its way through a fissure of the rock.

THERE LILINET seated herself and her guest upon a bench of agate, and pointing to two Fountains that bubbled before them, said, Now attend, my dear FLORETTA, and enjoy the gratitude of a Fairy. Observe the two Fountains that spring up in the middle of the vault, one into a bason of alabaster, and the other into a bason of dark flint. The one is called the Spring of Joy, the other of Sorrow; they rise from distant veins in the rock, and burst out in two places, but after a short course unite their streams, and run ever after in one mingled current.

BY drinking of these fountains, which, though shut up from all other human beings, shall be always accessible to you, it will be in your power to regulate your future life.

WHEN you are drinking the water of joy from the alabaster fountain, you may form your wish, and it shall be granted. As you raise your wish higher, the water will be sweeter and sweeter to the taste; but beware that you are not tempted by its increasing sweetness to repeat your draughts, for the ill effects of your wish can only be removed by drinking the spring of sorrow from the bason of flint, which will be bitter in the same proportion as the water of joy was sweet. Now, my FLORETTA, make the experiment, and give me the first proof of moderate desires. Take the golden cup that stands on the margin of the spring of joy, form your wish and drink.

FLORETTA wanted no time to deliberate on the subject of her wish; her first desire was the increase of her beauty. She had some disproportion of features. She took the cup and wished to be agreeable; the water was sweet, and she drank copiously; and in the fountain, which was clearer than crystal, she saw that her face was completely regular.

SHE then filled the cup again, and wished for a rosy bloom upon her cheeks: the water was sweeter than before, and the colour of her cheeks was heightened.

SHE next wished for a sparkling eye: The water grew yet more pleasant, and her glances were like the beams of the sun.

SHE could not yet stop; she drank again, desired to be made a perfect beauty, and a perfect beauty she became.

SHE had now whatever her heart could wish; and making an humble reverence to LILINET, requested to be restored to her own habitation. They went back, and the Fairies in the way wondered at the change of FLORETTA's form. She came home delighted to her mother, who, on seeing the improvement, was yet more delighted than herself.

HER mother from that time pushed her forward into publick view: FLORETTA was at all the resorts of idleness and assemblies of pleasure; she was fatigued with balls, she was cloyed with treats, she was exhausted by the necessity of returning compliments. This life delighted her awhile, but custom soon destroyed its pleasure. She found that the men who courted her today resigned her on the morrow to other flatterers, and that the women attacked her reputation by whispers and calumnies, till without knowing how she had offended, she was shunned as infamous.

SHE knew that her reputation was destroyed by the envy of her beauty, and resolved to degrade herself from the dangerous pre-eminence. She went to the bush where she rescued the bird, and called for LADY LILINET. Immediately LILINET appeared, and discovered by FLORETTA's dejected look that she had drank too much from the alabaster fountain.

FOLLOW me, she cried, my FLORETTA, and be wiser for the future.

THEY went to the fountains, and FLORETTA began to taste the waters of sorrow, which were so bitter that she withdrew more than once the cup from her mouth: At last she resolutely drank away the perfection of beauty, the sparkling eye and rosy bloom, and left herself only agreeable.

SHE lived for some time with great content; but content is seldom lasting. She had a desire in a short time again to taste the waters of joy: she called for the conduct of LILINET, and was led to the alabaster fountain, where she drank, and wished for a faithful Lover.

AFTER her return she was soon addressed by a young man, whom she thought worthy of her affection. He courted, and flattered, and promised; till at last she yielded up her heart. He then applied to her parents; and, finding her fortune less than he expected, contrived a quarrel and deserted her.

EXASPERATED by her disappointment, she went in quest of LILINET, and expostulated with her for the deceit which she had practised. LILINET asked her with a smile, for what she had been wishing; and being told, made her this reply. You are not, my dear, to wonder or complain: You may wish for yourself, but your wishes can have no effect upon another. You may become lovely by the efficacy of the fountain, but that you shall be loved is by no means a certain consequence; for you cannot confer upon another either discernment or fidelity: That happiness which you must derive from others, it is not in my power to regulate or bestow.

FLORETTA was for some time so dejected by this limitation of the fountain's power, that she thought it unworthy of another visit; but being on some occasion thwarted by her mother's authority, she went to LILINET, and drank at the alabaster fountain for a spirit to do her own way.

LILINET saw that she drank immoderately, and admonished her of her danger; but *spirit* and *her own way* gave such sweetness to the water, that she could not prevail upon herself to forbear, till LILINET in pure compassion snatched the cup out of her hand.

WHEN she came home every thought was contempt, and every action was rebellion: She had drunk into herself a spirit to resist, but could not give her mother a disposition to yield; the old lady asserted her right to govern; and, though she was often foiled by the impetuosity of her daughter, she supplied by pertinacy what she wanted in violence; so that the house was in continual tumult by the pranks of the daughter and opposition of the mother.

IN time, FLORETTA was convinced that spirit had only made her a capricious termagant, and that her own ways ended in errour, perplexity and disgrace; she perceived that the vehemence of mind, which to a man may sometimes procure awe and obedience, produce to a woman nothing but detestation; she therefore went back, and by a large draught from the flinty fountain, though the water was very bitter, replaced herself under her mother's care, and quitted her spirit, and her own way.

FLORETTA's fortune was moderate, and her desires were not larger, till her mother took her to spend a summer at one of the places which wealth and idleness frequent, under pretence of drinking the waters. She was now no longer a perfect beauty, and therefore conversation in her presence took its course as in other company, opinions were freely told, and observations made without reserve. Here FLORETTA first learned the importance of money. When she saw a woman of mean air and empty talk draw the attention of the place, she always discovered upon enquiry that she had so many thousands to her fortune.

SHE soon perceived that where these golden goddesses appeared, neither birth, nor elegance, nor civility had any power of attraction, that every art of entertainment was devoted to them, and that the great and the wise courted their regard.

THE desire after wealth was raised yet higher by her mother, who was always telling her how much neglect she suffered for want of fortune, and what distinctions if she had but a fortune her good qualities would obtain. Her narrative of the day was always, that FLORETTA walked in the morning, but was not spoken to because she had a small fortune, and that FLORETTA danced at the ball better than any of them, but nobody minded her for want of a fortune.

THIS want, in which all other wants appeared to be included, FLORETTA was resolved to endure no longer, and came home flattering her imagination in secret with the riches which she was now about to obtain.

ON the day after her return she walked out alone to meet lady LILINET, and went with her to the fountain: Riches did not taste so sweet as either beauty or spirit, and therefore she was not immoderate in her draught.

WHEN they returned from the cavern, LILINET gave her wand to a Fairy that attended her, with an order to conduct FLORETTA to the Black Rock.

THE way was not long, and they soon came to the mouth of a mine in which there was a hidden treasure, guarded by an earthy Fairy deformed and shaggy, who opposed the entrance of FLORETTA till he recognized the wand of the Lady of the Mountain. Here FLORETTA saw vast heaps of gold and silver and gems, gathered and reposited in former ages, and entrusted to the guard of the Fairies of the earth. The little Fairy delivered the orders of her mistress, and the surly sentinel promised to obey them.

FLORETTA, wearied with her walk, and pleased with her success, went home to rest, and when she waked in the morning, first opened her eyes upon a cabinet of jewels, and looking into her drawers and boxes, found them filled with gold.

FLORETTA was now as fine as the finest. She was the first to adopt any expensive fashion, to subscribe to any pompous entertainment, to encourage any foreign artist, or engage in any frolick of which the cost was to make the pleasure.

SHE was on a sudden the favourite of every place. Report made her wealth thrice greater than it really was, and wherever she came, all was attention, reverence and obedience. The ladies who had formerly slighted her, or by whom she had been formerly caressed, gratified her pride by open flattery and private murmurs. She sometimes over-heard them railing at upstarts, and wondering whence some people came, or how their expences were supplied. This incited her to heighten the splendour of her dress, to increase the number of her retinue, and to make such propositions of costly schemes, that her rivals were forced to desist from contest.

BUT she now began to find that the tricks which can be played with money will seldom bear to be repeated, that admiration is a short-lived passion, and that the pleasure of expence is gone when wonder and envy are no more excited. She found that respect was an empty form, and that all those who crouded round her were drawn to her by vanity or interest.

IT was however pleasant to be able on any terms to elevate and to mortify, to raise hopes and fears; and she would still have continued to be rich, had not the ambition of her mother contrived to marry her to a Lord, whom she despised as ignorant, and abhorred as profligate. Her mother persisted in her importunity; and FLORETTA having now lost the spirit of resistance, had no other refuge than to divest herself of her fairy fortune.

SHE implored the assistance of LILINET, who praised her resolution. She drank chearfully from the flinty fountain, and found the waters not extremely bitter. When she returned she went to bed, and in the morning perceived that all her riches had been conveyed away she knew not how, except a few ornamental jewels, which LILINET had ordered to be carried back as a reward for her dignity of mind.

SHE was now almost weary of visiting the fountain, and solaced herself with such amusements as every day happened to produce: At last there arose in her imagination a strong desire to become a Wit.

THE pleasures with which this new character appeared to teem were so numerous and so great, that she was impatient to enjoy them; and rising before the sun, hastened to the place where she knew that her fairy patroness was always to be found. LILINET was willing to conduct her, but could now scarcely restrain her from leading the way but by telling her, that if she went first the Fairies of the cavern would refuse her passage.

THEY came in time to the fountain, and FLORETTA took the golden cup into her hand; she filled it and drank, and again she filled it, for wit was sweeter than riches, spirit, or beauty.

As she returned she felt new successions of imagery rise in her mind, and whatever her memory offered to her imagination, assumed a new form, and connected itself with things to which it seemed before to have no relation. All the appearances about her were changed, but the novelties exhibited were commonly defects. She now saw that almost every thing was wrong, without often seeing how it could be better; and frequently imputed to the imperfection of art these failures which were caused by the limitation of nature.

WHEREVER she went, she breathed nothing but censure and reformation. If she visited her friends, she quarrelled with the situation of their houses, the disposition of their gardens, the direction of their walks, and the termination of their views. It was vain to shew her fine furniture, for she was always ready to tell how it might be finer, or to conduct her through spacious apartments, for her thoughts were full of nobler fabricks, of airy palaces and hesperian gardens. She admired nothing and praised but little.

HER conversation was generally thought uncivil. If she received flatteries, she seldom repaid them; for she set no value upon vulgar praise. She could not hear a long story without hurrying the speaker on to the conclusion; and obstructed the mirth of her companions, for she rarely took notice of a good jest, and never laughed except when she was delighted.

THIS behaviour made her unwelcome wherever she went; nor did her speculation upon human manners much contribute to forward her reception. She now saw the disproportions between language and sentiment, between passion and exclamation; she discovered the defects of every action, and the uncertainty of every conclusion; she knew the malignity of friendship, the avarice of liberality, the anxiety of content, and the cowardice of temerity.

To see all this was pleasant, but the greatest of all pleasures was to shew it. To laugh was something, but it was much more to make others laugh. As every deformity of character made a strong impression upon her, she could not always forbear to transmit it to others; as she hated false appearances she thought it her duty to detect them, till, between wantonness and virtue, scarce any that she knew escaped without some wounds by the shafts of ridicule; not that her merriment was always the consequence of total contempt, for she often honoured virtue where she laughed at affectation.

FOR these practices, and who can wonder, the cry was raised against her from every quarter, and to hunt her down was generally determined. Every eye was watching for a fault, and every tongue was busy to supply its share of defamation. With the most unpolluted purity of mind, she was censured as too free of favours, because she was not afraid to talk with men: With generous sensibility of every human excellence, she was thought cold or envious, because she would not scatter praise with undistinguishing profusion: With tenderness that agonized at real misery, she was charged with delight in the pain of others, when she would not condole with those whom she knew to counterfeit affliction. She derided false appearances of kindness and of pity, and was therefore avoided as an enemy to society. As she seldom commended or censured but with some limitations and exceptions, the world condemned her as indifferent to the good and bad; and because she was often doubtful where others were confident, she was charged with laxity of principles, while her days were distracted and her rest broken by niceties of honour and scruples of morality.

REPORT had now made her so formidable that all flattered and all shunned her. If a Lover gave a ball to his mistress and her friends, it was stipulated that FLORETTA should not be invited. If she entered a publick room the ladies courtsied, and shrunk away, for there was no such thing as speaking, but FLORETTA would find something to criticise. If a girl was more spritely than her Aunt, she was threatened that in a little time she would be like FLORETTA. Visits were very diligently paid when FLORETTA was known not to be at home; and no mother trusted her daughter to herself without a caution, if she should meet FLORETTA to leave the company as soon as she could.

WITH all this FLORETTA made sport at first, but in time grew weary of general hostility. She would have been content with a few friends, but no friendship was durable; it was the fashion to desert her, and with the fashion what fidelity will contend? She could have easily amused herself in solitude, but that she thought it mean to quit the field to treachery and folly.

PERSECUTION at length tired her constancy, and she implored LILINET to rid her of her wit: LILINET complied and walked up the mountain, but was often forced to stop and wait for her follower. When they came to the flinty fountain, FLORETTA filled a small cup and slowly brought it to her lips, but the water was insupportably bitter. She just tasted it, and dashed it to the ground, diluted the bitterness at the fountain of alabaster, and resolved to keep her wit with all its consequences.

BEING now a wit for life, she surveyed the various conditions of mankind with such superiority of sentiment, that she found few distinctions to be envied or desired, and therefore did not very soon make another visit to the fountain. At length being alarmed by sickness, she resolved to drink length of life from the golden cup. She returned elated and secure, for though the longevity acquired was indeterminate, she considered death as far distant, and therefore suffered it not to intrude upon her pleasures.

BUT length of life included not perpetual health. She felt herself continually decaying, and saw the world fading about her. The delights of her early days would delight no longer, and however widely she extended her view, no new pleasure could be found; her friends, her enemies, her admirers, her rivals dropped one by one into the grave, and with those who succeeded them she had neither community of joys nor strife of competition.

BY this time she began to doubt whether old age were not dangerous to virtue; whether pain would not produce peevishness, and peevishness impair benevolence. She thought that the spectacle of life might be too long continued, and the vices which were often seen might raise less abhorrence; that resolution might be sapped by time, and let that virtue sink, which in its firmest state it had not without difficulty supported; and that it was vain to delay the hour which must come at last, and might come at a time of less preparation and greater imbecillity.

THESE thoughts led her to LILINET, whom she accompanied to the flinty fountain; where, after a short combat with herself, she drank the bitter water. They walked back to the favourite bush pensive and silent; And now, said she, accept my thanks for the last benefit that FLORETTA can receive. Lady LILINET dropped a tear, impressed upon her lips the final kiss, and resigned her, as she resigned herself, to the course of Nature.

Letter to James Boswell

SATURDAY 9 SEPTEMBER 1769

Dear Sir: Brighthelmston, Septr. 9, 1769

Why do you charge me with unkindness? I have omitted nothing that could do you good or give you pleasure unless it be that I have forborn to tell you my opinion of your Account of Corsica. I believe my opinion if you think well of my judgement might have given you pleasure but when it is considered how much vanity is excited by praise I am not sure that it would have done you good. Your History is like other histories but your journal is in a very high degree curious and deligh[t]ful. There is between the history and the journal that difference which there will always be found between notions borrowed from without, and notions generated within. Your history was copied from books. Your journal rose out of your own experience and observation. You express images which operated strongly upon yourself and you have impressed them with great force upon your readers. I know not

THE

FALSE ALARM.

LONDON:

Printed for T. CADELL in the Strand.

MDCCLXX.

FIGURE 9 *The False Alarm*, title page (Bodl. G. Pamph. 1933 [4]). Courtesy of the Bodleian Library, University of Oxford.

whether I could name any narrative by which curiosity is better excited or better gratified.

I am glad that you are going to be married and as I wish you well in things of less importance wish you well with proportionate ardour in this crisis of your life. What I can contribute to your happiness I should be very unwilling to withhold for I have always loved and valued you and shall love you and value you still more as you become more regular and useful effects which a happy Marriage will hardly fail to produce.

I do not find that I am likely to come back very soon from this place. I shall perhaps stay a fortnight longer and a fortnight is a long time to a lover absent from his Mistress. Would a fortnight ever have an end? I am, Dear Sir, your most affectionate, humble servant,

SAM. JOHNSON

The False Alarm

ONE of the chief advantages derived by the present generation from the improvement and diffusion of Philosophy, is deliverance from unnecessary terrours, and exemption from false alarms. The unusual appearances, whether regular or accidental, which once spread consternation over ages of ignorance, are now the recreations of inquisitive security. The sun is no more lamented when it is eclipsed, than when it sets; and meteors play their coruscations without prognostick or prediction.

THE advancement of political knowledge may be expected to produce in time the like effects. Causeless discontent and seditious violence will grow less frequent, and less formidable, as the science of Government is better ascertained by a diligent study of the theory of Man.

IT is not indeed to be expected, that physical and political truth should meet with equal acceptance, or gain ground upon the world with equal facility. The notions of the naturalist find mankind in a state of neutrality, or at worst have nothing to encounter but prejudice and vanity; prejudice without malignity, and vanity without interest. But the politician's improvements are opposed by every passion that can exclude conviction or suppress it; by ambition, by avarice, by hope, and by terrour, by public faction, and private animosity.

IT is evident, whatever be the cause, that this nation, with all its renown for speculation and for learning, have yet made little proficiency in civil wisdom. We are still so much unacquainted with our own state, and so unskilful in the pursuit of happiness, that we shudder without danger, and complain without grievances, and suffer our quiet to be disturbed, and our commerce to be interrupted, by an opposition to the government, raised only by interest, and supported only by clamour, which yet has so far prevailed upon ignorance and timidity, that many favour it as reasonable, and many dread it as powerful.

WHAT is urged by those who have been so industrious to spread suspicion, and incite fury from one end of the kingdom to the other, may be known by perusing the papers which have been at once presented as petitions to the King, and exhibited in print as remonstrances to the people. It may therefore not be improper to lay before the public the reflections of a man who cannot favour the opposition, for he thinks it wicked, and cannot fear it, for he thinks it weak.

THE grievance which has produced all this tempest of outrage, the oppression in which all other oppressions are included, the invasion which has left us no property, the alarm that suffers no patriot to sleep in quiet, is comprised in a vote of the House of Commons, by which the freeholders of Middlesex are deprived of a Briton's birth-right, representation in parliament.

THEY have indeed received the usual writ of election, but that writ, alas! was malicious mockery; they were insulted with the form, but denied the reality, for there was one man excepted from their choice.

Non de vi, neque cæde, nec veneno,
Sed lis est mihi de tribus capellis.

THE character of the man thus fatally excepted, I have no purpose to delineate. Lampoon itself would disdain to speak ill of him of whom no man speaks well. It is sufficient that he is expelled the House of Commons, and confined in jail as being legally convicted of sedition and impiety.

THAT this man cannot be appointed one of the guardians and counsellors of the church and state, is a grievance not to be endured. Every lover of liberty stands doubtful of the fate of posterity, because the chief county in England cannot take its representative from a jail.

WHENCE Middlesex should obtain the right of being denominated the chief county, cannot easily be discovered; it is indeed the county where the chief city happens to stand, but how that city treated the favourite of Middlesex, is not yet forgotten. The county, as distinguished from the city, has no claim to particular consideration.

THAT a man was in jail for sedition and impiety, would, I believe, have been within memory a sufficient reason why he should not come out of jail a legislator. This reason, notwithstanding the mutability of fashion, happens still to operate on the House of Commons. Their notions, however strange, may be justified by a common observation, that few are mended by imprisonment, and that he whose crimes have made confinement necessary, seldom makes any other use of his enlargement, than to do with greater cunning what he did before with less.

BUT the people have been told with great confidence, that the House cannot control the right of constituting representatives; that he who can persuade lawful electors to chuse him, whatever be his character, is lawfully chosen, and has a claim to a seat in Parliament, from which no human authority can depose him.

HERE, however, the patrons of opposition are in some perplexity. They are forced to confess, that by a train of precedents sufficient to establish a custom of Parliament, the House of Commons has jurisdiction over its own members; that the whole has power over individuals; and that this power has been exercised sometimes in imprisonment, and often in expulsion.

THAT such power should reside in the House of Commons in some cases, is inevitably necessary, since it is required by every polity, that where there is a possibility of offence, there should be a possibility of punishment. A member of the House cannot be cited for his conduct in Parliament before any other court; and therefore, if the House cannot punish him, he may attack with impunity the rights of the people, and the title of the King.

THIS exemption from the authority of other courts was, I think, first established in favour of the five members in the long parliament. It is not to be considered as an usurpation, for it is implied in the principles of government. If legislative powers are not co-ordinate, they cease in part to be legislative; and if they be co-ordinate, they are unaccountable; for to whom must that power account, which has no superiour?

THE House of Commons is indeed dissoluble by the King, as the nation has of late been very clamorously told; but while it subsists it is co-ordinate with the other powers, and this co-ordination ceases only when the House by dissolution ceases to subsist.

As the particular representatives of the people, are in their public character above the controul of the courts of law, they must be subject to the jurisdiction of the House, and as the House, in the exercise of its authority, can be neither directed nor restrained, its own resolutions must be its laws, at least, if there is no antecedent decision of the whole legislature.

THIS privilege, not confirmed by any written law or positive compact, but by the resistless power of political necessity, they have exercised, probably from their first institution, but certainly, as their records inform us, from the 23d of Elizabeth, when they expelled a member for derogating from their privileges.

IT may perhaps be doubted, whether it was originally necessary, that this right of control and punishment, should extend beyond offences in the exercise of parliamentary duty, since all other crimes are cognizable by other courts. But they, who are the only judges of their own rights, have exerted the power of expulsion on other occasions, and when wickedness arrived at a certain magnitude, have considered an offence against society as an offence against the House.

THEY have therefore divested notorious delinquents of their legislative character, and delivered them up to shame or punishment, naked and unprotected, that they might not contaminate the dignity of Parliament.

IT is allowed that a man attainted of felony, is not eligible in Parliament. They probably judged, that not being bound to the forms of law, they might treat these as felons, whose crimes were in their opinion equivalent to felony; and that as a known felon could not be chosen, a man so like a felon, that he could not easily be distinguished, ought to be expelled.

THE first laws had no law to enforce them, the first authority was constituted by itself. The power exercised by the House of Commons is of this kind, a power rooted in the principles of government, and branched out by occasional practice; a power which necessity made just, and precedents have made legal.

IT will occur that authority thus uncontrolable may, in times of heat and contest, be oppressively and injuriously exerted, and that he who suffers injustice, is without redress, however innocent, however miserable.

THE position is true but the argument is useless. The Commons must be controlled, or be exempt from control. If they are exempt they may do injury which cannot be redressed, if they are controlled they are no longer legislative.

IF the possibility of abuse be an argument against authority, no authority ever can be established; if the actual abuse destroys its legality, there is no legal government now in the world.

THIS power, which the Commons have so long exercised, they ventured to use once more against Mr. Wilkes, and on the 3d of February, 1769, expelled him the House, *for having printed and published a seditious libel, and three obscene and impious libels.*

IF these imputations were just, the expulsion was surely seasonable, and that they were just, the House had reason to determine, as he had confessed himself, at the bar, the author of the libel which they term seditious, and was convicted in the King's Bench of both the publications.

BUT the Freeholders of Middlesex were of another opinion. They either thought him innocent, or were not offended by his guilt. When a writ was issued for the election of a knight for Middlesex, in the room of John Wilkes, Esq; expelled the House, his friends on the sixteenth of February chose him again.

ON the 17th, it was resolved, *that* John Wilkes, Esq; *having been in this Session of Parliament expelled the House, was, and is, incapable of being elected a member to serve in this present Parliament.*

As there was no other candidate, it was resolved, at the same time, that the election of the sixteenth was a void election.

THE Freeholders still continued to think that no other man was fit to represent them, and on the sixteenth of March elected him once more. Their resolution was now so well known, that no opponent ventured to appear.

THE Commons began to find, that power without materials for operation can produce no effect. They might make the election void for ever, but if no other candidate could be found, their determination could only be negative. They, however, made void the last election, and ordered a new writ.

ON the thirteenth of April was a new election, at which Mr. Lutterel, and others, offered themselves candidates. Every method of intimidation was used, and some acts of violence were done to hinder Mr. Lutterel from appearing. He was not deterred, and the poll was taken, which exhibited for

Mr. Wilkes, — 1143

Mr. Lutterel, — 296

The sheriff returned Mr. Wilkes, but the House, on April the fifteenth, determined that Mr. Lutterel was lawfully elected.

FROM this day begun the clamour, which has continued till now. Those who had undertaken to oppose the ministry, having no grievance of greater magnitude, endeavoured to swell this decision into bulk, and distort it into deformity, and then held it out to terrify the nation.

EVERY artifice of sedition has been since practised to awaken discontent and inflame indignation. The papers of every day have been filled with the exhortations and menaces of faction. The madness has spread through all ranks and through both sexes; women and children have clamoured for Mr. Wilkes, honest simplicity has been cheated into fury, and only the wise have escaped infection.

THE greater part may justly be suspected of not believing their own position, and with them it is not necessary to dispute. They cannot be convinced, who are convinced already, and it is well known that they will not be ashamed.

THE decision, however, by which the smaller number of votes was preferred to the greater, has perplexed the minds of some, whose opinions it were indecent to despise, and who by their integrity will deserve to have their doubts appeased.

EVERY diffuse and complicated question may be examined by different methods, upon different principles, and that truth, which is easily found by one investigator, may be missed by another, equally honest and equally diligent.

THOSE who enquire whether a smaller number of legal votes, can elect a representative in opposition to a greater, must receive from every tongue the same answer.

THE question, therefore, must be, whether a smaller number of legal votes, shall not prevail against a greater number of votes not legal. It must be considered, that those votes only are legal which are legally given, and that those only are legally given, which are given for a legal candidate.

IT remains then to be discussed, whether a man expelled, can be so disqualified by a vote of the House, as that he shall be no longer eligible by lawful electors.

HERE we must again recur, not to positive institutions, but to the unwritten law of social nature, to the great and pregnant principle of political necessity.

All government supposes subjects, all authority implies obedience. To suppose in one the right to command what another has the right to refuse is absurd and contradictory. A state so constituted must rest for ever in motionless equipoise, with equal attractions of contrary tendency, with equal weights of power balancing each other.

LAWS which cannot be enforced, can neither prevent nor rectify disorders. A sentence which cannot be executed can have no power to warn or to reform. If the Commons have only the power of dismissing for a few days the man whom his constituents can immediately send back, if they can expel but cannot exclude, they have nothing more than nominal authority, to which perhaps obedience never may be paid.

THE representatives of our ancestors had an opinion very different: they fined and imprisoned their members; on great provocation they disabled them for ever, and this power of pronouncing perpetual disability is maintained by Selden himself.

THESE claims seem to have been made and allowed, when the constitution of our government had not yet been sufficiently studied. Such powers are not legal, because they are not necessary; and of that power which only necessity justifies, no more is to be admitted than necessity obtrudes.

THE Commons cannot make laws, they can only pass resolutions, which, like all resolutions, are of force only to those that make them, and to those only while they are willing to observe them.

THE vote of the House of Commons has therefore only so far the force of a law, as that force is necessary to preserve the vote from losing its efficacy, it must begin by operating upon themselves, and extends its influence to others, only by consequences arising from the first intention. He that starts game on his own manor, may pursue it into another.

THEY can properly make laws only for themselves: a member, while he keeps his seat, is subject to these laws; but when he is expelled, the jurisdiction ceases, for he is now no longer in their dominion.

THE disability, which a vote can super-induce to expulsion, is no more than was included in expulsion itself; it is only a declaration of the House, that they will permit no longer him whom they thus censure to sit in Parliament; a declaration made by that right which they necessarily possess, of regulating their own House, and of inflicting punishment on their own delinquents.

THEY have therefore no other way to enforce the sentence of incapacity, than that of adhering to it. They cannot otherwise punish the candidate so disqualified for offering himself, nor the electors for accepting him. But if he has any competitor, that competitor must prevail, and if he has none, his election will be void; for the right of the House to reject, annihilates with regard to the man so rejected, the right of electing.

IT has been urged, that the power of the House terminates with their session; since a prisoner committed by the Speaker's warrant cannot be detained during the recess. Their power indeed ceases with the session, so far as it operates by the agency of others, because, when they do not sit, they can employ no agent, having no longer any legal existence. But the power which operates on themselves revives at their meeting, when the subject of that power still subsists. They can in the next session refuse to readmit him, whom in the former session they expelled.

THAT expulsion inferred exclusion, in the present case, must be, I think, easily admitted. The expulsion and the writ issued for a new election were in the same session, and since the House is by the rule of Parliament bound for the session by a vote once passed, the expelled member cannot be admitted. He that cannot be admitted, cannot be elected, and the votes given to a man ineligible being given in vain, the highest number for an eligible candidate becomes a majority.

To these conclusions, as to most moral, and to all political positions, many objections may be made. The perpetual subject of political disquisition is not absolute, but comparative good. Of two systems of government, or two laws relating to the same subject, neither will ever be such as theoretical nicety would desire, and therefore neither can easily force its way against prejudice and obstinacy; each will have its excellencies and defects, and every man, with a little help from pride, may think his own the best.

IT seems to be the opinion of many, that expulsion is only a dismission of the representative to his constituents, with such a testimony against him as his sentence may comprise; and that if his constituents, notwithstanding the censure of the House, thinking his case hard, his fault trifling, or his excellencies such as overbalance it, should again choose him as still worthy of their trust, the House cannot refuse him, for his punishment has purged his fault, and the right of electors must not be violated.

THIS is plausible but not cogent. It is a scheme of representation, which would make a specious appearance in a political romance, but cannot be brought into practice among us, who see every day the towering head of speculation bow down unwillingly to grovelling experience.

GOVERNMENTS formed by chance, and gradually improved by such expedients, as the successive discovery of their defects happened to suggest, are never to be tried by a regular theory. They are fabricks of dissimilar materials, raised by different architects, upon different plans. We must be content with them as they are; should we attempt to mend their disproportions, we might easily demolish, and difficultly rebuild them.

LAWS are now made, and customs are established; these are our rules, and by them we must be guided.

IT is uncontrovertibly certain, that the Commons never intended to leave electors the liberty of returning them an expelled member, for they always require one to be chosen in the room of him that is expelled, and I see not with what propriety a man can be rechosen in his own room.

EXPULSION, if this were its whole effect, might very often be desireable. Sedition, or obscenity, might be no greater crimes in the opinion of other electors, than in that of the freeholders of Middlesex; and many a wretch, whom his colleagues should expel, might come back persecuted into fame, and provoke with harder front a second expulsion.

MANY of the representatives of the people, can hardly be said to have been chosen at all. Some by inheriting a borough inherit a seat; and some sit by the favour of others, whom perhaps they may gratify by the act which provoked the expulsion. Some are safe by their popularity, and some by their alliances. None would dread expulsion, if this doctrine were received, but those who bought their elections, and who would be obliged to buy them again at a higher price.

BUT as uncertainties are to be determined by things certain, and customs to be explained, where it is possible, by written law, the patriots have triumphed with a quotation from an act of the 4th and 5th Anne, which permits those to be rechosen, whose seats are vacated by the acceptance of a place of profit. This they wisely consider as an expulsion, and from the permission, in this case, of a re-election, infer that every other expulsion, leaves the delinquent entitled to the same indulgence. This is the paragraph.

"IF any person, *being chosen a member* of the House of Commons, shall accept of any office from the crown, *during such time as he shall continue a member*, his election shall be, and is hereby declared to be void, and a new writ shall issue for a new election, as if such person so accepting was naturally dead. *Nevertheless such person shall be capable of being again elected*, as if his place had not become void as aforesaid."

How this favours the doctrine of readmission by a second choice, I am not able to discover. The statute of 30 Ch. II. had enacted, That *he who should sit in the House of Commons, without taking the oaths and subscribing the test, should be disabled to sit in the House during that Parliament, and a writ should issue for the election of a new member, in place of the member so disabled, as if such member had naturally died.*

THIS last clause is apparently copied in the act of Anne, but with the common fate of imitators. In the act of Charles, the political death continued during the Parliament, in that of Anne it was hardly worth the while to kill the man whom the next breath was to revive. It is, however, apparent, that in the opinion of the Parliament, the dead-doing lines would have kept him motionless, if he had not been recovered by a kind reception. A seat vacated, could not be regained without express permission of the same statute.

THE right of being chosen again to a seat thus vacated, is not enjoyed by any general right, but required a special clause, and solicitous provision.

BUT what resemblance can imagination conceive between one man vacating his seat, by a mark of favour from the crown, and another driven from it for sedition and obscenity. The acceptance of a place contaminates no character;

the crown that gives it, intends to give with it always dignity, sometimes authority. The commons, it is well known, think not worse of themselves or others for their offices of profit; yet profit, implies temptation, and may expose a representative to the suspicion of his constituents; though if they still think him worthy of their confidence, they may again elect him.

SUCH is the consequence. When a man is dismissed by law to his constituents, with new trust and new dignity, they may, if they think him incorruptible, restore him to his seat; what can follow, therefore, but that when the House drives out a varlet with public infamy, he goes away with the like permission to return.

IF infatuation be, as the proverb tells us, the forerunner of destruction, how near must be the ruin of a nation that can be incited against it's governors, by sophistry like this. I may be excused if I catch the panick, and join my groans at this alarming crisis, with the general lamentation of weeping patriots.

ANOTHER objection is, that the Commons, by pronouncing the sentence of disqualification, make a law, and take upon themselves, the power of the whole legislature. Many quotations are then produced to prove that the House of Commons can make no laws.

THREE acts have been cited, disabling members for different terms on different occasions, and it is profoundly remarked, that if the Commons could by their own power have made a disqualification, their jealousy of their privileges, would never have admitted the concurrent sanction of the other powers.

I MUST forever remind these puny controvertists, that those acts are laws of permanent obligation: that two of them are now in force, and that the other expired only when it had fulfilled its end. Such laws the Commons cannot make; they could, perhaps, have determined for themselves, they would expel all who should not take the test, but they could leave no authority behind them, that should oblige the next Parliament to expel them. They could refuse the South Sea directors, but they could not entail the refusal. They can disqualify by vote, but not by law; they cannot know that the sentence of disqualification pronounced to day may not become void to-morrow, by the dissolution of their own House. Yet while the same parliament sits, the disqualification continues unless the vote be rescinded, and while it so continues, makes the votes, which freeholders may give to the interdicted candidate, useless and dead, since there cannot exist, with respect to the same subject at the same time, an absolute power to chuse and an absolute power to reject.

IN 1614, the attorney-general was voted incapable of a seat in the House of Commons, and the nation is triumphantly told, that though the vote never was revoked, the attorney-general is now a member. He certainly may now be a member without revocation of the vote. A law is of perpetual obligation, but a vote is nothing when the voters are gone. A law is a compact reciprocally made by the legislative powers, and therefore not to be abrogated but by all the parties. A vote is simply a resolution, which binds only him that is willing to be bound.

I HAVE thus punctiliously and minutely persued this disquisition, because I suspect that these reasoners, whose business is to deceive others, have sometimes deceived themselves, and I am willing to free them from their embarrassment, though I do not expect much gratitude for my kindness.

OTHER objections are yet remaining, for of political objections there cannot easily be an end. It has been observed, that vice is no proper cause of expulsion, for if the worst man in the House were always to be expelled, in time none would be left. But no man is expelled for being worst, he is expelled for being enormously bad; his conduct is compared, not with that of others, but with the rule of action.

THE punishment of expulsion being in its own nature uncertain, may be too great or too little for the fault.

THIS must be the case of many punishments. Forfeiture of chattels is nothing to him that has no possessions. Exile itself may be accidentally a good; and indeed any punishment less than death is very different to different men.

BUT if this precedent be admitted and established, no man can hereafter be sure that he shall be represented by him whom he would choose. One half of the House may meet early in the morning, and snatch an opportunity to expel the other, and the greater part of the nation may by this stratagem be without its lawful representatives.

He that sees all this, sees very far. But I can tell him of greater evils yet behind. There is one possibility of wickedness, which, at this alarming crisis, has not yet been mentioned. Every one knows the malice, the subtilty, the industry, the vigilance, and the greediness of the Scots. The Scotch members are about the number sufficient to make a House. I propose it to the consideration of the Supporters of the Bill of Rights, whether there is not reason to suspect, that these hungry intruders from the North, are now contriving to expel all the English. We may then curse the hour in which it was determined, that expulsion and exclusion are the same. For who can guess what may be done when the Scots have the whole House to themselves?

THUS agreeable to custom and reason, thus consistent with the practice of former times, and thus consequential to the original principles of government, is that decision by which so much violence of discontent has been excited, which has been so dolorously bewailed, and so outrageously resented.

LET us however not be seduced to put too much confidence in justice or in truth, they have often been found inactive in their own defence, and give more confidence than help to their friends and their advocates. It may perhaps be prudent to make one momentary concession to falsehood, by supposing the vote in Mr. Lutterel's favour to be wrong.

ALL wrong ought to be rectified. If Mr. Wilkes is deprived of a lawful seat, both he and his electors have reason to complain; but it will not be easily found, why, among the innumerable wrongs of which a great part of mankind are hourly complaining, the whole care of the public should be transferred to Mr. Wilkes and the freeholders of Middlesex, who might all sink into non-existence, without any other effect, than that there would be room made for a new rabble, and a new retailer of sedition and obscenity. The cause of our country would suffer little; the rabble, whencesoever they come, will be always patriots, and always Supporters of the Bill of Rights.

THE House of Commons decides the disputes arising from elections. Was it ever supposed, that in all cases their decisions were right? Every man whose lawful election is defeated, is equally wronged with Mr. Wilkes, and his constituents feel their disappointment with no less anguish than the freeholders of Middlesex. These decisions have often been apparently partial, and sometimes tyrannically oppressive. A majority has been given to a favourite candidate, by expunging votes which had always been allowed, and which therefore had the authority by which all votes are given, that of custom uninterrupted. When the Commons determine who shall be constituents, they may, with some propriety, be said to make law, because those determinations have hitherto, for the sake of quiet, been adopted by succeeding Parliaments. A vote therefore of the House, when it operates as a law, is to individuals a law only temporary, but to communities perpetual.

YET though all this has been done, and though at every new Parliament much of this is expected to be done again, it has never produced in any former time such an *alarming crisis*. We have found by experience, that though a squire has given ale and venison in vain, and a borough has been compelled to see its dearest interest in the hands of him whom it did not trust, yet the general state of the nation has continued the same. The sun has risen, and the corn has grown, and whatever talk has been of the danger of property, yet he that ploughed the field commonly reaped it, and he that built a house was master of the door: the vexation excited by injustice suffered, or supposed to be suffered, by any private man, or single community, was local and temporary, it neither spread far, nor lasted long.

THE nation looked on with little care, because there did not seem to be much danger. The consequence of small irregularities was not felt, and we had not yet learned to be terrified by very distant enemies.

BUT quiet and security are now at an end. Our vigilance is quickened, and our comprehension is enlarged. We not only see events in their causes, but before their causes; we hear the thunder while the sky is clear, and see the mine sprung before it is dug. Political wisdom has, by the force of English genius, been improved at last to political intuition.

BUT it cannot, I am afraid, be said, that as we are grown wise, we are made happy. It is said of those who have the wonderful power called second sight, that they seldom see any thing but evil: political second sight has the same effect; we hear of nothing but of an alarming crisis of violated rights, and expiring liberties. The morning rises upon new wrongs, and the dreamer passes the night in imaginary shackles.

The sphere of anxiety is now enlarged; he that hitherto cared only for himself, now cares for the public; for he has learned that the happiness of individuals is comprised in the prosperity of the whole, and that his county never suffers but he suffers with it, however it happens that he feels no pain.

FIRED with this fever of epidemic patriotism; the taylor slips his thimble, the drapier drops his yard, and the blacksmith lays down his hammer; they meet at an honest alehouse, consider the state of the nation, read or hear the last petition, lament the miseries of the time, are alarmed at the dreadful crisis, and subscribe to the support of the Bill of Rights.

IT sometimes indeed happens, that an intruder of more benevolence than prudence attempts to disperse their cloud of dejection, and ease their hearts by seasonable consolation. He tells them, that though the government cannot be too diligently watched, it may be too hastily accused; and that, though private judgment is every man's right, yet we cannot judge of what we do not know. That we feel at present no evils which government can alleviate, and that the publick business is committed to men who have as much right to confidence as their adversaries. That the freeholders of Middlesex, if they could not choose Mr. Wilkes, might have chosen any other man, and that *he trusts we have within the realm five hundred as good as he*: that if this which has happened to Middlesex had happened to every other county, that one man should be made incapable of being elected, it could produce no great change in the Parliament, nor much contract the power of election; that what has been done is probably right, and that if it be wrong it is of little consequence, since a like case cannot easily occur; that expulsions are very rare, and if they should, by unbounded insolence of faction, become more frequent, the electors may easily provide a second choice.

ALL this he may say, but not half of this will be heard; his opponents will stun him and themselves with a confused sound of places, venality and corruption, oppression and invasion, slavery and ruin.

OUTCRIES like these, uttered by malignity, and ecchoed by folly; general accusations of indeterminate wickedness, and obscure hints of impossible designs, dispersed among those that do not know their meaning, by those that know them to be false, have disposed part of the nation, though but a small part, to pester the court with ridiculous petitions.

THE progress of a petition is well known. An ejected placeman goes down to his county or his borough, tells his friends of his inability to serve them, and his constituents of the corruption of the government. His friends readily understand that he who can get nothing, will have nothing to give. They agree to proclaim a meeting, meat and drink are plentifully provided, a crowd is easily brought together, and those who think that they know the reason of their meeting, undertake to tell those who know it not. Ale and clamour unite their powers, the crowd, condensed and heated, begins to ferment with the leven of sedition. All see a thousand evils, though they cannot show them, and grow impatient for a remedy, though they know not what.

A SPEECH is then made by the Cicero of the day, he says much, and suppresses more, and credit is equally given to what he tells, and what he conceals. The petition is read and universally approved. Those who are sober enough to write add their names, and the rest would sign it if they could.

EVERY man goes home and tells his neighbour of the glories of the day; how he was consulted and what he advised; how he was invited into the great room, where his lordship called him by his name; how he was caressed by Sir Francis, Sir Joseph, or Sir George; how he eat turtle and venison, and drank unanimity to the three brothers.

THE poor loiterer, whose shop had confined him, or whose wife had locked him up, hears the tale of luxury with envy, and at last enquires what was their petition. Of the petition nothing is remembered by the narrator, but that it spoke much of fears and apprehensions, and something very alarming, and that he is sure it is against the government; the other is convinced that it must be right, and wishes he had been there, for he loves wine and venison, and is resolved as long as he lives to be against the government.

THE petition is then handed from town to town, and from house to house, and wherever it comes the inhabitants flock together, that they may see that which must be sent to the King. Names are easily collected. One man signs because he hates the papists; another because he has vowed destruction to the turnpikes; one because it will vex the parson; another because he owes his landlord nothing; one because he is rich; another because he is poor; one to shew that he is not afraid, and another to shew that he can write.

THE passage, however, is not always smooth. Those who collect contributions to sedition, sometimes apply to a man of higher rank and more enlightened mind, who instead of lending them his name, calmly reproves them for being seducers of the people.

YOU who are here, says he, complaining of venality, are yourselves the agents of those, who having estimated themselves at too high a price, are only angry that they are not bought. You are appealing from the parliament to the rabble, and inviting those, who scarcely, in the most common affairs, distinguish right from wrong, to judge of a question complicated with law written and unwritten, with the general principles of government, and the particular customs of the House of Commons; you are shewing them a grievance, so distant that they cannot see it, and so light that they cannot feel it; for how, but by unnecessary intelligence and artificial provocation, should the farmers and shopkeepers of Yorkshire and Cumberland know or care how Middlesex is represented. Instead of wandering thus round the county to exasperate the rage of party, and darken the suspicions of ignorance, it is the duty of men like you, who have leisure for enquiry, to lead back the people to their honest labour; to tell them, that submission is the duty of the ignorant, and content the virtue of the poor; that they have no skill in the art of government, not any interest in the dissentions of the great; and when you meet with any, as some there are, whose understandings are capable of conviction, it will become you to allay this foaming ebullition, by shewing them that they have as much happiness as the condition of life will easily receive, and that a government, of which an erroneous or unjust representation of Middlesex is the greatest crime that interest can discover, or malice can upbraid, is a government approaching nearer to perfection, than any that experience has known, or history related.

THE drudges of sedition wish to change their ground, they hear him with sullen silence, feel conviction without repentance, and are confounded but not abashed; they go forward to another door, and find a kinder reception from a man enraged against the government, because he has just been paying the tax upon his windows.

THAT a petition for a dissolution of the Parliament will at all times have its favourers, may be easily imagined. The people indeed do not expect that one House of Commons will be much honester or much wiser than another; they do not suppose that the taxes will be lightened; or though they have been so often taught to hope it, that soap and candles will be cheaper; they expect no redress of grievances, for of no grievances but taxes do they complain; they wish not the extension of liberty, for they do not feel any restraint; about the security of privilege or property they are totally careless, for they see no property invaded, nor know, till they are told, that any privilege has suffered violation.

LEAST of all do they expect, that any future Parliament will lessen its own powers, or communicate to the people that authority which it has once obtained.

YET a new Parliament is sufficiently desirable. The year of election is a year of jollity; and what is still more delightful, a year of equality. The glutton now eats the delicacies for which he longed when he could not purchase them, and the drunkard has the pleasure of wine without the cost. The drone lives a while without work, and the shopkeeper, in the flow of money, raises his price. The mechanic that trembled at the presence of Sir Joseph, now bids him come again for an answer; and the poacher, whose gun has been seized, now finds an opportunity to reclaim it. Even the honest man is not displeased to see himself important, and willingly resumes in two years that power which he had resigned for seven. Few love their friends so well as not to desire superiority by unexpensive benefaction.

YET, notwithstanding all these motives to compliance, the promoters of petitions have not been successful. Few could be persuaded to lament evils which they did not suffer, or to solicit for redress which they do not want. The petition has been, in some places, rejected; and perhaps in all but one, signed only by the meanest and grossest of the people.

SINCE this expedient now invented or revived to distress the government, and equally practicable at all times by all who shall be excluded from power and from profit, has produced so little effect, let us consider the opposition as no longer formidable. The great engine has recoiled upon them. They thought that *the terms* they *sent were terms of weight*, which would have *amazed all and stumbled many*; but the consternation is now over, and their foes *stand upright*, as before.

WITH great propriety and dignity the king has, in his speech, neglected or forgotten them. He might easily know, that what was presented as the sense of the people, is the sense only of the profligate and dissolute; and that whatever Parliament should be convened, the same petitioners would be ready, for the same reason, to request its dissolution.

As we once had a rebellion of the clowns, we have now an opposition of the pedlars. The quiet of the nation has been for years disturbed by a faction, against which all factions ought to conspire; for its original principle is the desire of levelling; it is only animated under the name of zeal, by the natural malignity of the mean against the great.

WHEN in the confusion which the English invasions produced in France, the vilains, imagining that they had found the golden hour of emancipation, took arms in their hands, the knights of both nations considered the cause as common, and, suspending the general hostility, united to chastise them.

THE whole conduct of this despicable faction is distinguished by plebeian grossness, and savage indecency. To misrepresent the actions and the principles of their enemies is common to all parties; but the insolence of invective, and brutality of reproach, which have lately prevailed, are peculiar to this.

AN infallible characteristic of meanness is cruelty. This is the only faction that has shouted at the condemnation of a criminal, and that, when his innocence procured his pardon, has clamoured for his blood.

ALL other parties, however enraged at each other, have agreed to treat the throne with decency; but these low-born railers have attacked not only the authority, but the character of their Sovereign, and have endeavoured, surely without effect, to alienate the affections of the people from the only king, who, for almost a century, has much appeared to desire, or much endeavoured to deserve them. They have insulted him with rudeness and with menaces, which were never excited by the gloomy sullenness of William, even when half the nation denied him their allegiance; nor by the dangerous bigotry of James, unless when he was finally driven from his palace, and with which scarcely the open hostilities of rebellion ventured to vilify the unhappy Charles, even in the remarks on the cabinet of Naseby.

IT is surely not unreasonable to hope, that the nation will consult its dignity, if not its safety, and disdain to be protected or enslaved by the declaimers or the plotters of a city-tavern. Had Rome fallen by the Catilinarian conspiracy, she might have consoled her fate by the greatness of her destroyers; but what would have alleviated the disgrace of England, had her government been changed by Tiler or by Ket.

ONE part of the nation has never before contended with the other, but for some weighty and apparent interest. If the means were violent, the end was great. The civil war was fought for what each army called and believed the best religion, and the best government. The struggle in the reign of Anne, was to exclude or restore an exiled king. We are now disputing, with almost equal animosity, whether Middlesex shall be represented or not by a criminal from a jail.

THE only comfort left in such degeneracy is, that a lower state can be no longer possible.

IN this contemptuous censure, I mean not to include every single man. In all lead, says the chemist, there is silver; and in all copper there is gold. But mingled masses are justly denominated by the greater quantity, and when the precious particles are not worth extraction, a faction and a pig must be melted down together to the forms and offices that chance allots them.

Fiunt urceoli, pelves, sartago, patellæ.

A FEW weeks will now shew whether the Government can be shaken by empty noise, and whether the faction which depends upon its influence, has not deceived alike the public and itself. That it should have continued till now, is sufficiently shameful. None can indeed wonder that it has been supported by the sectaries, the constant fomenters of sedition, and never-failing confederates of the rabble, of whose religion little now remains but hatred of establishments, and who are angry to find separation now only tolerated, which was once rewarded; but every honest man must lament, that it has been regarded with frigid neutrality by the Tories, who, being long accustomed to signalize their principles by opposition to the court, do not yet consider that they have at last a king who knows not the name of party, and who wishes to be the common father of all his people.

As a man inebriated only by vapours, soon recovers in the open air; a nation discontented to madness, without any adequate cause, will return to its wits and its allegiance when a little pause has cooled it to reflexion. Nothing, therefore, is necessary, at this alarming crisis, but to consider the alarm as false. To make concessions is to encourage encroachment. Let the court despise the faction, and the disappointed people will soon deride it.

FINIS.

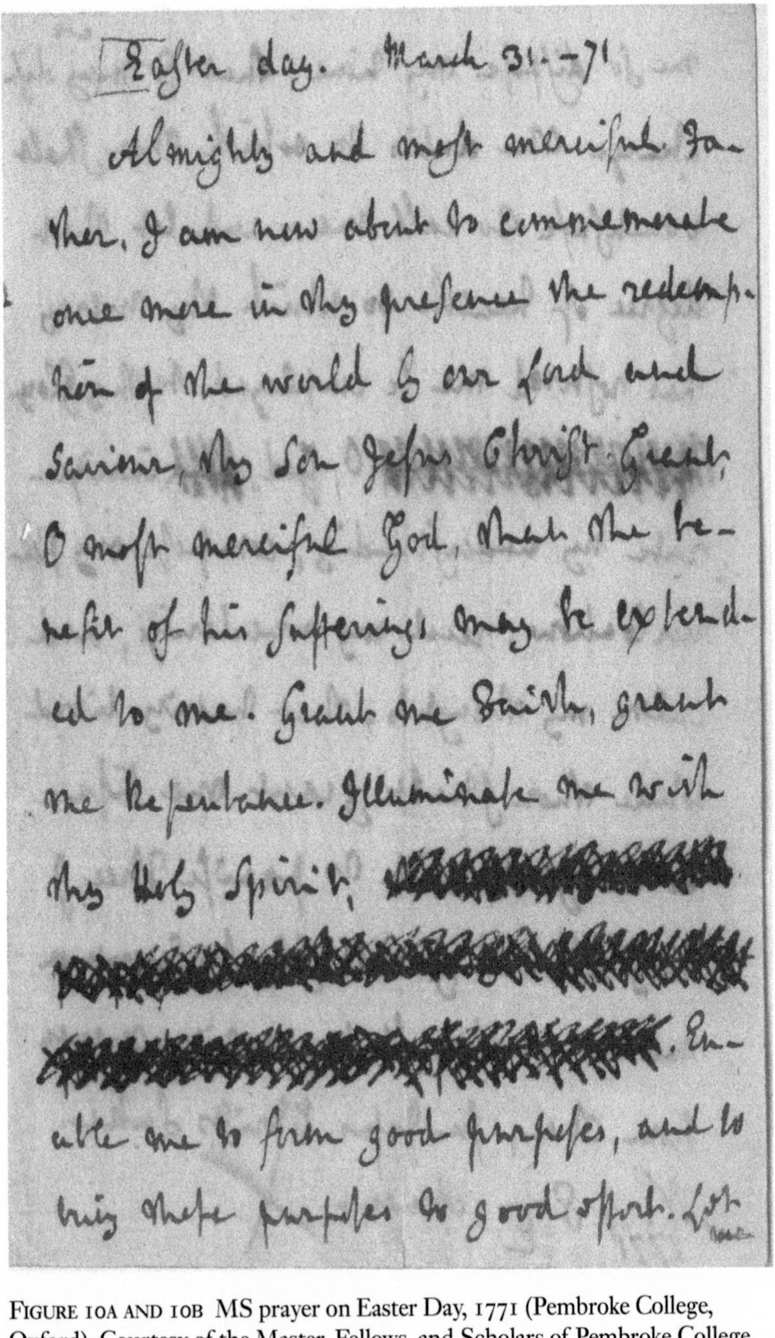

Easter day. March 31. –71

Almighty and most merciful Father, I am now about to commemorate once more in thy presence the redemption of the world by our Lord and Saviour, thy son Jesus Christ. Grant, O most merciful God, that the benefit of his sufferings may be extended to me. Grant me faith, grant me Repentance. Illuminate me with thy Holy Spirit.

~~[struck through]~~
~~[struck through]~~
~~[struck through]~~

Enable me to form good purposes, and to bring these purposes to good effect. Let

FIGURE 10A AND 10B MS prayer on Easter Day, 1771 (Pembroke College, Oxford). Courtesy of the Master, Fellows, and Scholars of Pembroke College, Oxford.

me so dispose my time, that I may discharge the duties to which thou shalt vouchsafe to call me; and let that degree of health to which thy mercy has restored me be employed to thy Glory. ~~xxxxxxxxxxxxxxxx~~ O God, ~~xxx~~ invigorate my understanding, compose my perturbations, recal my wanderings, and calm my thoughts, that having lived while thou shalt grant me life, to do good and to praise Thee, I may when thou shalt summon me to another state, receive mercy from thee, for Jesus Christs sake. Amen.

N. S. E.
1771

Prayer on Easter Day

SUNDAY 31 MARCH 1771

March 31.

ALmighty and most merciful Father, I am now about to commemorate once more, in thy presence, the redemption of the world by our Lord and Saviour thy Son Jesus Christ. Grant, O most merciful God, that the benefit of his sufferings may be extended to me. Grant me faith, grant me repentance. Illuminate me with thy Holy Spirit, enable me to form good purposes, and to bring these purposes to good effect. Let me so dispose my time, that I may discharge the duties to which Thou shalt vouchsafe to call me; and let that degree of health, to which thy mercy has restored me, be employed to thy glory. O God, invigorate my understanding, compose my perturbations, recal my wanderings, and calm my thoughts; that having lived while Thou shalt grant me life, to do good and to praise Thee, I may, when thy call shall summon me to another state, receive mercy from Thee, for Jesus Christ's sake. Amen.

Parodies of Bishop Percy's Hermit of Warkworth

I

I put my hat upon my head
    And walk'd into the Strand,
And there I met another man
    Who's hat was in his hand.

2

The tender infant, meek and mild,
    Fell down upon the stone;
The nurse took up the squealing child,
    But still the child squeal'd on.

3

I therefore pray thee, Renny dear,
    That thou wilt give to me,
With cream and sugar soften'd well,
    Another dish of tea.

Nor fear that I, my gentle maid,
  Shall long detain the cup,
When once unto the bottom I
  Have drank the liquor up.

Yet hear, alas! this mournful truth,
  Nor hear it with a frown; –   10
Thou canst not make the tea so fast
  As I can gulp it down.

Γνωθι σεαυτον

(POST LEXICON ANGLICANUM AUCTUM ET EMENDATUM)

Lexicon ad finem longo luctamine tandem
Scaliger ut duxit, tenuis pertæsus opellæ
Vile indignatus Studium, nugasque molestas
Ingemit exosus, scribendaque lexica mandat
Damnatis pœnam pro pœnis omnibus unam.
  Ille quidem recte, sublimis, doctus, et acer,
Quem decuit majora sequi, majoribus aptum,
Qui veterum modo facta ducum, modo carmina vatum,
Gesserat et quicquid Virtus, Sapientia quicquid
Dixerat, imperiique vices, cœlique meatus,   10
Ingentemque animo seclorum volverat orbem.
  Fallimur exemplis; temere sibi turba scholarum
Ima tuas credit permitti, Scaliger, iras.
Quisque suum nôrit modulum; tibi, prime virorum
Ut studiis sperem, aut ausim par esse querelis
Non mihi sorte datum, lenti seu sanguinis obsint
Frigora, seu nimium longo jacuisse veterno,
Sive mihi mentem dederit Natura minorem.
  Te sterili functum cura, vocumque salebris
Tuto eluctatum spatiis Sapientia dia   20
Excipit ætheris, Ars omnis plaudit amica
Linguarumque omni terra discordia concors
Multiplici reducem circumsonat ore magistrum.
  Me, pensi immunis cum jam mihi reddor, inertis
Desidiæ sors dura manet, graviorque labore
Tristis et atra quies, et tardæ tædia vitæ
Nascuntur curis curæ, vexatque dolorum

Importuna cohors, vacuæ mala somnia mentis.
Nunc clamosa juvant nocturnæ gaudia mensæ
Nunc loca sola placent, frustra te, Somne, recumbens   30
Alme voco, impatiens noctis metuensque diei.
Omnia percurro trepidus, circum omnia lustro
Si qua usquam pateat melioris semita vitæ,
Nec quid agam invenio; meditatus grandia cogor
Notior ipse mihi fieri, incultumque fateri
Pectus, et ingenium vano se robore jactans.
Ingenium, nisi materiem Doctrina ministret,
Cessat inops rerum, ut torpet, si marmoris absit
Copia Phidiaci fœcunda potentia cœli.
Quicquid agam, quocunque ferar, conatibus obstat   40
Res angusta domi, et macræ penuria mentis.
    Non Rationis opes Animus nunc parta recensens
Conspicit aggestas, et se miratur in illis
Nec sibi de gaza, præsens quod postulet usus
Summus adesse jubet celsa dominator ab arce
Non operum serie, seriem dum computat ævi,
Præteritis fruitur, lætos aut sumit honores
Ipse sui judex, actæ bene munera vitæ
Sed sua regna videns, loca nocte silentia late
Horret, ubi vanæ species, umbræque fugaces,   50
Et rerum volitant raræ per inane figuræ.
    Quid faciam? tenebrisne pigram damnare senectam
Restat? an accingar studiis gravioribus audax?
Aut, hoc si nimium est, tandem nova lexica poscam?

Letter to James Boswell

WEDNESDAY 24 FEBRUARY 1773

Dear Sir,   London, Feb. 24, 1773

I have read your kind letter much more than the elegant Pindar which it
accompanied. I am always glad to find myself not forgotten, and to be forgotten by you would give me great uneasiness. My northern friends have never
been unkind to me: I have from you, dear Sir, testimonies of affection, which
I have not often been able to excite; and Dr. Beattie rates the testimony which
I was desirous of paying to his merit, much higher than I should have thought
it reasonable to expect.

I have heard of your masquerade. What says your Synod to such innovations? I am not studiously scrupulous, nor do I think a masquerade either evil in itself, or very likely to be the occasion of evil; yet as the world thinks it a very licentious relaxation of manners, I would not have been one of the *first* masquers in a country where no masquerade had ever been before.

A new edition of my great Dictionary is printed, from a copy which I was persuaded to revise; but having made no preparation, I was able to do very little. Some superfluities I have expunged, and some faults I have corrected, and here and there have scattered a remark; but the main fabrick of the work remains as it was. I had looked very little into it since I wrote it, and, I think, I found it full as often better, as worse, than I expected.

Baretti and Davies have had a furious quarrel; a quarrel, I think, irreconcileable. Dr. Goldsmith has a new comedy, which is expected in the spring. No name is yet given it. The chief diversion arises from a stratagem by which a lover is made to mistake his future father-in-law's house for an inn. This, you see, borders upon farce. The dialogue is quick and gay, and the incidents are so prepared as not to seem improbable.

I am sorry that you lost your cause of Intromission, because I yet think the arguments on your side unanswerable. But you seem, I think, to say that you gained reputation even by your defeat; and reputation you will daily gain, if you keep Lord Auchinleck's precept in your mind, and endeavour to consolidate in your mind a firm and regular system of law, instead of picking up occasional fragments.

My health seems in general to improve; but I have been troubled for many weeks with a vexatious catarrh, which is sometimes sufficiently distressful. I have not found any great effects from bleeding and physick; and am afraid, that I must expect help from brighter days and softer air.

Write to me now and then; and whenever any good befalls you, make haste to let me know it, for no one will rejoice at it more than, dear Sir, Your most humble servant,

SAM. JOHNSON

You continue to stand very high in the favour of Mrs. Thrale.

Diary entry

THURSDAY 22 JULY 1773

July 22, —73.

THIS day I found this book, with the resolutions; some of which I had forgotten, but remembered my design of reading the Pentateuch and Gospels, though I have not persued it.

Of the time past since these resolutions were made, I can give no very laudable account. Between Easter and Whitsuntide, having always considered that time as propitious to study, I attempted to learn the Low Dutch language; my application was very slight, and my memory very fallacious, though whether more than in my earlier years, I am not very certain. My progress was interrupted by a fever, which, by the imprudent use of a small print, left an inflammation in my useful eye, which was not removed but by two copious bleedings, and the daily use of catharticks for a long time. The effect yet remains.

My memory has been for a long time very much confused. Names, and persons, and events, slide away strangely from me. But I grow easier.

The other day, looking over old papers, I perceived a resolution to rise early always occurring. I think I was ashamed, or grieved, to find how long and how often I had resolved, what yet, except for about one half year, I have never done. My nights are now such as give me no quiet rest; whether I have not lived resolving till the possibility of performance is past, I know not. God help me, I will yet try.

Diary entries

MONDAY 25 AND TUESDAY 26 JULY 1774

25. We saw Hakeston, the seat of Sir Rowland Hill, and were conducted by Miss Hill over a large tract of rocks and woods, a region abounding with striking scenes and terrifick grandeur. We were always on the brink of a precipice, or at the foot of a lofty rock, but the steeps were seldom naked; in many places Oaks of uncommon magnitude shot up from the crannies of stone, and where there were not tall trees, there were underwoods and bushes. Round the rocks is a narrow path, cut upon the stone which is very frequently hewn into steps, but art has proceeded no further than [to] make the succession of wonders safely accessible. The whole circuit is somewhat laborious, it is terminated by a grotto cut in the rock to a great extent with many windings and supported by pillars, not hewn into regularity, but such as imitate the sports of nature, by asperi[ties] and protuberances. The place is without any dampness, and would afford a habitation not uncomfortable. There were from space to space seats in the rock. Though it wants water it excells Dovedale, by the extent of its prospects, the awfulness of its shades, the horrors of its precipices, the verdure of its hollows and the loftiness of its rocks. The Ideas which it forces upon the mind, are the sublime, the dreadful, and the vast. Above, is inaccessible altitude, below, is horrible profundity. But it excells the Garden of Ilam only in extent. Ilam has grandeur tempered with softness. The walker congratulates his own arrival at the place, and is grieved to think that he

must ever leave it. As he looks up to the rocks his thoughts are elevated; as he turns his eyes on the vallies, he is composed and soothed. He that mounts the precipices at Hawkeston, wonders how he came hither, and doubts how he shall return. His walk is an adventure and his departure an escape. He has not the tranquillity, but the horrour of solitude, a kind of turbulent pleasure between fright and admiration. Ilam is the fit abode of pastoral virtue, and might properly diffuse its shades over nymphs and swains. Hawkeston can have no fitter inhabitants than Giants of mighty bone, and bold emprise, men of lawless courage and heroic violence. Hawkestone should be described by Milton and Ilam by Parnel.

Miss Hill showed the whole succession of wonders with great civility.

The House was magnificent compared with the rank of the owner.

26. We left Cumbermere, where we have been treated with great civility. Sir L. is gross, the Lady weak and ignorant. The House is spacious but not magnificent, built at different times with different materials, part is of timber, part of stone or brick, plaistered and painted to look like timber. It is the best house that I ever saw of that kind. The Meer or lake is large with a small island, on which there is a summer house shaded with great trees. Some were hollow and have seats in their trunks.

In the afternoon we came to West Chester (my father went to the fair when I had the small pox). We walked round the walls which are compleat, and contain one Mile, three quarters, and one hundred and one yards; within them are many gardens. They are very high, and two may walk very commodiously side by side. On the inside is a rail; there are towers from space to space, not very frequent, and I think, not all compleat.

The Patriot

> They bawl for Freedom in their senseless mood,
> Yet still revolt when Truth would set them free,
> License they mean, when they cry Liberty,
> For who loves that must first be wise and good.
>
> Milton.

To improve the golden moment of opportunity, and catch the good that is within our reach, is the great art of life. Many wants are suffered, which might once have been supplied; and much time is lost in regretting the time which had been lost before.

At the end of every seven years comes the Saturnalian season, when the freemen of Great Britain may please themselves with the choice of their representatives. This happy day has now arrived, somewhat sooner than it could be claimed.

To select and depute those, by whom laws are to be made, and taxes to be granted, is a high dignity and an important trust: and it is the business of every elector to consider, how this dignity may be well sustained, and this trust faithfully discharged.

It ought to be deeply impressed on the minds of all who have voices in this national deliberation, that no man can deserve a seat in parliament who is not a PATRIOT. No other man will protect our rights, no other man can merit our confidence.

A *Patriot* is he whose public conduct is regulated by one single motive, the love of his country; who, as an agent in parliament, has for himself neither hope nor fear, neither kindness nor resentment, but refers every thing to the common interest.

That of five hundred men, such as this degenerate age affords, a majority can be found thus virtuously abstracted, who will affirm? Yet there is no good in despondence: vigilance and activity often effect more than was expected. Let us take a Patriot where we can meet him; and that we may not flatter ourselves by false appearances, distinguish those marks which are certain, from those which may deceive: for a man may have the external appearance of a Patriot, without the constituent qualities; as false coins have often lustre, tho' they want weight.

Some claim a place in the list of Patriots by an acrimonious and unremitting opposition to the Court.

This mark is by no means infallible. Patriotism is not necessarily included in rebellion. A man may hate his King, yet not love his Country. He that has been refused a reasonable or unreasonable request, who thinks his merit underrated, and sees his influence declining, begins soon to talk of natural equality, the absurdity of *many, made for one*, the original compact, the foundation of authority, and the majesty of the people. As his political melancholy increases, he tells, and perhaps dreams of the advances of the prerogative, and the dangers of arbitrary power; yet his design in all his declamation is not to benefit his country, but to gratify his malice.

These, however, are the most honest of the opponents of government; their patriotism is a species of disease; and they feel some part of what they express. But the greater, far the greater number of those who rave and rail, and enquire and accuse, neither suspect, nor fear, nor care for the public; but hope to force their way to riches by virulence and invective, and are vehement and clamorous, only that they may be sooner hired to be silent.

A man sometimes starts up a Patriot, only by disseminating discontent and propagating reports of secret influence, of dangerous counsels, of violated rights and encroaching usurpation.

This practice is no certain note of Patriotism. To instigate the populace with rage beyond the provocation, is to suspend public happiness, not to destroy it. He is no lover of his country, that unnecessarily disturbs its peace. Few errors, and few faults of government can justify an appeal to the rabble; who ought not to judge of what they cannot understand, and whose opinions are not propagated by reason, but caught by contagion.

The fallaciousness of this note of patriotism is particularly apparent, when the clamour continues after the evil is past. They who are now filling our ears with Mr. Wilkes, and the Freeholders of Middlesex, lament a grievance, which is now at an end. Mr. Wilkes may be chosen, if any will choose him, and the precedent of his exclusion makes not any honest, or any decent man, think himself in danger.

It may be doubted whether the name of a Patriot can be fairly given as the reward of secret satire, or open outrage. To fill the newspapers with sly hints of corruption and intrigue, to circulate the Middlesex Journal and London Pacquet, may indeed be zeal; but it may likewise be interest and malice. To offer a petition, not expected to be granted; to insult a King with a rude remonstrance, only because there is no punishment for legal insolence, is not courage, for there is no danger; nor patriotism, for it tends to the subversion of order, and lets wickedness loose upon the land, by destroying the reverence due to sovereign authority.

It is the quality of Patriotism to be jealous and watchful, to observe all secret machinations, and to see public dangers at a distance. The true *Lover of his country* is ready to communicate his fears and to sound the alarm, whenever he perceives the approach of mischief. But he sounds no alarm, when there is no enemy: he never terrifies his countrymen, till he is terrified himself. The patriotism therefore may be justly doubted of him, who professes to be disturbed by incredibilities; who tells, that the last peace was obtained by bribing the Princess of Wales; that the King is grasping at arbitrary power; and that because the French in the new conquests enjoy their own laws, there is a design at court of abolishing in England the trial by juries.

Still less does the true Patriot circulate opinions, which he knows to be false. No man, who loves his country, fills the nation with clamorous complaints, that the Protestant religion is in danger, because *Popery is established in the extensive province of Quebec*, a falsehood so open and shameless, that it can need no confutation among those, who know, that of which it is almost impossible for the most unenlightened zealot to be ignorant,

That Quebec is on the other side of the Atlantic, at too great a distance, to do much good or harm to the European world:

That the inhabitants, being French, were always Papists, who are certainly more dangerous, as enemies than as subjects:

That though the province be wide, the people are few, probably not so many as may be found in one of the larger English counties:

That persecution is not more virtuous in a Protestant than a Papist; and that while we blame Lewis the Fourteenth, for his dragoons and his gallies, we ought, when power comes into our hands, to use it with greater equity:

That when Canada with its inhabitants was yielded, the free enjoyment of their religion was stipulated; a condition, of which King William, who was no propagator of Popery, gave an example nearer home, at the surrender of Limeric:

That in an age, where every mouth is open for *liberty of conscience*, it is equitable to shew some regard to the conscience of a Papist, who may be supposed, like other men, to think himself safest in his own religion; and that those at least, who enjoy a toleration, ought not to deny it to our new subjects.

If liberty of conscience be a natural right, we have no power to with-hold it; if it be an indulgence, it may be allowed to Papists, while it is not denied to other sects.

A Patriot is necessarily and invariably a lover of the people. But even this mark may sometimes deceive us.

The people is a very heterogeneous and confused mass of the wealthy and the poor, the wise and the foolish, the good and the bad. Before we confer on a man, who caresses the people, the title of Patriot, we must examine to what part of the people he directs his notice. It is proverbially said, that he who dissembles his own character, may be known by that of his companions. If the candidate of Patriotism endeavours to infuse right opinions into the higher ranks, and by their influence to regulate the lower; if he consorts chiefly with the wise, the temperate, the regular and the virtuous; his love of the people may be urged in his favour. But if his first or principal application be to the indigent, who are always inflammable; to the weak, who are naturally suspicious; to the ignorant, who are easily misled, and to the profligate, who have no hope, but from mischief and confusion; his love of the people proves little in his favour. No man can reasonably be thought a lover of his country, for roasting an ox, or burning a boot, or attending the meeting at Mile-end, or registering his name in the Lumber-troop. He may, among the drunkards, be a *hearty fellow*, and among sober handicraftsmen, a *free spoken gentleman*; but he must have some better distinction, before he is a *Patriot*.

A Patriot is always ready to countenance the just claims, and animate the reasonable hopes of the people; he reminds them frequently of their rights, and stimulates them to resent encroachments, and to multiply securities.

But all this may be done in appearance, without real patriotism. He that raises false hopes to serve a present purpose, only makes a way for disappointment and discontent. He who promises to endeavour, what he knows his endeavours unable to effect, means only to delude his followers by an empty clamour of ineffectual zeal.

A true Patriot is no lavish promiser: he undertakes not to shorten parliaments; to repeal laws; or to change the mode of representation, transmitted by our ancestors: he knows, that futurity is not in his power, and that all times are not alike favourable to change.

Much less does he make a vague and indefinite promise of obeying the mandates of his constituents. He knows the prejudices of faction, and the inconstancy of the multitude. He would first enquire, how the opinion of his constituents shall be taken. Popular instructions are commonly the work, not of the wise and steady, but the violent and rash; and meetings held for directing representatives are seldom attended, but by the idle and the dissolute; and he is not without suspicion, that of his constituents, as of other numbers of men, the smaller part may often be the wiser.

He considers himself as deputed to promote the public good, and to preserve his constituents, with the rest of his countrymen, not only from being hurt by others, but from hurting themselves.

The common marks of patriotism having been examined, and shewn to be such as artifice may counterfeit, or folly misapply, it cannot be improper to consider, whether there are not some characteristical modes of speaking or acting, which may prove a man to be NOT A PATRIOT.

In this enquiry, perhaps clearer evidence may be discovered, and firmer persuasion attained: for it is commonly easier to know what is wrong than what is right; to find what we should avoid, than what we should pursue.

As war is one of the heaviest of national evils, a calamity, in which every species of misery is involved; as it sets the general safety to hazard, suspends commerce, and desolates the country; as it exposes great numbers to hardships, dangers, captivity and death; no man, who desires the public prosperity, will inflame national resentment by aggravating minute injuries, or enforcing disputable rights of little importance.

It may therefore be safely pronounced, that those men are no Patriots, who when the national honour was vindicated in the sight of Europe, and the Spaniards having invaded what they called their own, had shrunk to a disavowal of their attempt and a cession of their claim, would still have instigated us to a war for a bleak and barren spot in the Magellanic ocean, of which no use could be made, unless it were a place of exile for the hypocrites of patriotism.

Yet let it not be forgotten, that by the howling violence of patriotic rage, the nation was for a time exasperated to such madness, that for a barren rock under a stormy sky, we might have now been fighting and dying, had not our competitors been wiser than ourselves; and those who are now courting the favour of the people by noisy professions of public spirit, would, while they were counting the profits of their artifice, have enjoyed the patriotic pleasure of hearing sometimes, that thousands had been slaughtered in a battle, and sometimes that a navy had been dispeopled by poisoned air and corrupted food.

He that wishes to see his country robbed of its rights, cannot be a Patriot.

That man therefore is no Patriot, who justifies the ridiculous claims of American usurpation; who endeavours to deprive the nation of its natural and lawful authority over its own colonies: those colonies, which were settled under English protection; were constituted by an English charter; and have been defended by English arms.

To suppose, that by sending out a colony, the nation established an independent power; that when, by indulgence and favour, emigrants are become rich, they shall not contribute to their own defence, but at their own pleasure; and that they shall not be included, like millions of their fellow subjects, in the general system of representation; involves such an accumulation of absurdity, as nothing but the shew of patriotism could palliate.

He that accepts protection, stipulates obedience. We have always protected the Americans; we may therefore subject them to government.

The less is included in the greater. That power which can take away life, may seize upon property. The parliament may enact for America a law of capital punishment; it may therefore establish a mode and proportion of taxation.

But there are some who lament the state of the poor Bostonians, because they cannot all be supposed to have committed acts of rebellion; yet all are involved in the penalty imposed. This, they say, is to violate the just rule of justice, by condemning the innocent to suffer with the guilty.

This deserves some notice, as it seems dictated by justice and humanity, however, it may raise contempt, by the ignorance which it betrays of the state of man, and the system of things. That the innocent should be confounded with the guilty, is undoubtedly an evil; but it is an evil which no care or caution can prevent. National crimes require national punishments, of which many must necessarily have their part, who have not incurred them by personal guilt. If rebels should fortify a town, the cannon of lawful authority will endanger equally the harmless burghers and the criminal garrison.

In some cases, those suffer most who are least intended to be hurt. If the French in the late war had taken an English city, and permitted the natives to keep their dwellings, how could it have been recovered, but by the slaughter of our friends? A bomb might as well destroy an Englishman as a Frenchman; and by famine we know that the inhabitants would be the first that should perish.

This infliction of promiscuous evil may therefore be lamented, but cannot be blamed. The power of lawful government must be maintained; and the miseries which rebellion produces, can be charged only on the rebels.

That man likewise is *not a Patriot*, who denies his governours their due praise, and who conceals from the people the benefits which they receive. Those therefore can lay no claim to this illustrious appellation, who impute want of public spirit to the late parliament; an assembly of men, whom, notwithstanding some fluctuation of counsel, and some weakness of agency, the nation must always remember with gratitude, since it is indebted to them for a very ample concession in the resignation of protections, and a wise and honest attempt to improve the constitution, in the new judicature instituted for the trial of elections.

The right of protection, which might be necessary when it was first claimed, and was very consistent with that liberality of immunities in which the feudal constitution delighted, was by its nature liable to abuse, and had in reality been sometimes misapplied, to the evasion of the law, and the defeat of justice. The evil was perhaps not adequate to the clamour; nor is it very certain, that the possible good of this privilege was not more than equal to the possible evil. It is however plain, that whether they gave any thing or not to the public, they at least lost something from themselves. They divested their dignity of a very splendid distinction, and shewed that they were more willing than their predecessors to stand on a level with their fellow-subjects.

The new mode of trying elections, if it be found effectual, will diffuse its consequences further than seems yet to be foreseen. It is, I believe, generally considered as advantageous only to those who claim seats in parliament; but, if to chuse representatives be one of the most valuable rights of Englishmen, every voter must consider that law as adding to his happiness, which makes his suffrage efficacious; since it was vain to chuse, while the election could be controled by any other power.

With what imperious contempt of ancient rights, and what audaciousness of arbitrary authority, former parliaments have judged the disputes about elections, it is not necessary to relate. The claim of a candidate, and the right of electors are said scarcely to have been, even in appearance, referred to conscience; but to have been decided by party, by passion, by prejudice, or by frolick. To have friends in the borough was of little use to him, who wanted friends in the house; a pretence was easily found to evade a majority, and the seat was at last his, that was chosen not by his electors but his judges.

Thus the nation was insulted with a mock election, and the parliament was filled with spurious representatives; one of the most important claims, that of a right to sit in the supreme council of the kingdom, was debated in jest, and no man could be confident of success from the justice of his cause.

A disputed election is now tried with the same scrupulousness and solemnity, as any other title. The candidate, that has deserved well of his neighbours, may now be certain of enjoying the effect of their approbation; and the elector, who has voted honestly for known merit, may be certain that he has not voted in vain.

Such was the parliament, which some of those, who are now aspiring to sit in another, have taught the rabble to consider as an unlawful convention of men, worthless, venal, and prostitute, slaves of the court, and tyrants of the people.

That the next House of Commons may act upon the principles of the last, with more constancy and higher spirit, must be the wish of all, who wish well to the public; and it is surely not too much to expect, that the nation will recover from its delusion, and unite in a general abhorrence of those, who by deceiving the credulous with fictitious mischiefs, overbearing the weak by audacity of falsehood, by appealing to the judgment of ignorance, and flattering the vanity of meanness, by slandering honesty and insulting dignity, have gathered round them whatever the kingdom can supply of base, and gross, and profligate; and *raised by merit to this bad eminence*, arrogate to themselves the name of PATRIOTS.

FINIS.

A Journey to the Western Islands of Scotland

I HAD desired to visit the *Hebrides*, or Western Islands of Scotland, so long, that I scarcely remember how the wish was originally excited; and was in the Autumn of the year 1773 induced to undertake the journey, by finding in Mr. Boswell a companion, whose acuteness would help my inquiry, and whose gaiety of conversation and civility of manners are sufficient to counteract the inconveniencies of travel, in countries less hospitable than we have passed.

On the eighteenth of August we left Edinburgh, a city too well known to admit description, and directed our course northward, along the eastern coast of Scotland, accompanied the first day by another gentleman, who could stay with us only long enough to shew us how much we lost at separation.

As we crossed the *Frith* of *Forth*, our curiosity was attracted by *Inch Keith*, a small island, which neither of my companions had ever visited, though, lying within their view, it had all their lives solicited their notice. Here, by climbing with some difficulty over shattered crags, we made the first experiment of unfrequented coasts. Inch Keith is nothing more than a rock covered with a thin layer of earth, not wholly bare of grass, and very fertile of thistles. A small herd of cows grazes annually upon it in the summer. It seems never to have afforded to man or beast a permanent habitation.

We found only the ruins of a small fort, not so injured by time but that it might be easily restored to its former state. It seems never to have been intended as a place of strength, nor was built to endure a siege, but merely to afford cover to a few soldiers, who perhaps had the charge of a battery, or were stationed to give signals of approaching danger. There is therefore no provision of water within the walls, though the spring is so near, that it might have been easily enclosed. One of the stones had this inscription: "Maria Reg. 1564." It has probably been neglected from the time that the whole island had the same king.

We left this little island with our thoughts employed awhile on the different appearance that it would have made, if it had been placed at the same distance from London, with the same facility of approach; with what emulation of price a few rocky acres would have been purchased, and with what expensive industry they would have been cultivated and adorned.

When we landed, we found our chaise ready, and passed through *Kinghorn*, *Kirkaldy*, and *Cowpar*, places not unlike the small or straggling market-towns in those parts of England where commerce and manufactures have not yet produced opulence.

Though we were yet in the most populous part of Scotland, and at so small a distance from the capital, we met few passengers.

The roads are neither rough nor dirty; and it affords a southern stranger a new kind of pleasure to travel so commodiously without the interruption of toll-gates. Where the bottom is rocky, as it seems commonly to be in Scotland, a smooth way is made indeed with great labour, but it never wants repairs; and in those parts where adventitious materials are necessary, the ground once consolidated is rarely broken; for the inland commerce is not great, nor are heavy commodities often transported otherwise than by water. The carriages in common use are small carts, drawn each by one little horse; and a man seems to derive some degree of dignity and importance from the reputation of possessing a two-horse cart.

ST. ANDREWS.

At an hour somewhat late we came to St. Andrews, a city once archiepiscopal; where that university still subsists in which philosophy was formerly taught by Buchanan, whose name has as fair a claim to immortality as can be conferred by modern latinity, and perhaps a fairer than the instability of vernacular languages admits.

We found, that by the interposition of some invisible friend, lodgings had been provided for us at the house of one of the professors, whose easy civility quickly made us forget that we were strangers; and in the whole time of our stay we were gratified by every mode of kindness, and entertained with all the elegance of lettered hospitality.

In the morning we rose to perambulate a city, which only history shews to have once flourished, and surveyed the ruins of ancient magnificence, of which even the ruins cannot long be visible, unless some care be taken to preserve them; and where is the pleasure of preserving such mournful memorials? They have been till very lately so much neglected, that every man carried away the stones who fancied that he wanted them.

The cathedral, of which the foundations may be still traced, and a small part of the wall is standing, appears to have been a spacious and majestick building, not unsuitable to the primacy of the kingdom. Of the architecture, the poor remains can hardly exhibit, even to an artist, a sufficient specimen. It was demolished, as is well known, in the tumult and violence of Knox's reformation.

Not far from the cathedral, on the margin of the water, stands a fragment of the castle, in which the archbishop anciently resided. It was never very large, and was built with more attention to security than pleasure. Cardinal Beatoun is said to have had workmen employed in improving its fortifications at the time when he was murdered by the ruffians of reformation, in the manner of which Knox has given what he himself calls a merry narrative.

The change of religion in Scotland, eager and vehement as it was, raised an epidemical enthusiasm, compounded of sullen scrupulousness and warlike ferocity, which, in a people whom idleness resigned to their own thoughts, and who, conversing only with each other, suffered no dilution of their zeal from the gradual influx of new opinions, was long transmitted in its full strength from the old to the young, but by trade and intercourse with England, is now visibly abating, and giving way too fast to their laxity of practice and indifference of opinion, in which men, not sufficiently instructed to find the middle point, too easily shelter themselves from rigour and constraint.

The city of St. Andrews, when it had lost its archiepiscopal preeminence, gradually decayed: One of its streets is now lost; and in those that remain, there is the silence and solitude of inactive indigence and gloomy depopulation.

The university, within a few years, consisted of three colleges, but is now reduced to two; the college of St. Leonard being lately dissolved by the sale of its buildings and the appropriation of its revenues to the professors of the two others. The chapel of the alienated college is yet standing, a fabrick not inelegant of external structure; but I was always, by some civil excuse, hindred from entering it. A decent attempt, as I was since told, has been made to convert it into a kind of greenhouse, by planting its area with shrubs. This new method of gardening is unsuccessful; the plants do not hitherto prosper. To what use it will next be put I have no pleasure in conjecturing. It is something that its present state is at least not ostentatiously displayed. Where there is yet shame, there may in time be virtue.

The dissolution of St. Leonard's college was doubtless necessary; but of that necessity there is reason to complain. It is surely not without just reproach, that a nation, of which the commerce is hourly extending, and the wealth encreasing, denies any participation of its prosperity to its literary societies; and while its merchants or its nobles are raising palaces, suffers its universities to moulder into dust.

Of the two colleges yet standing, one is by the institution of its founder appropriated to Divinity. It is said to be capable of containing fifty students; but more than one must occupy a chamber. The library, which is of late erection, is not very spacious, but elegant and luminous.

The doctor, by whom it was shewn, hoped to irritate or subdue my English vanity by telling me, that we had no such repository of books in England.

Saint Andrews seems to be a place eminently adapted to study and education, being situated in a populous, yet a cheap country, and exposing the minds and manners of young men neither to the levity and dissoluteness of a capital city, nor to the gross luxury of a town of commerce, places naturally unpropitious to learning; in one the desire of knowledge easily gives way to the love of pleasure, and in the other, is in danger of yielding to the love of money.

The students however are represented as at this time not exceeding a hundred. Perhaps it may be some obstruction to their increase that there is no episcopal chapel in the place. I saw no reason for imputing their paucity to the present professors; nor can the expence of an academical education be very reasonably objected. A student of the highest class may keep his annual session, or as the English call it, his term, which lasts seven months, for about fifteen pounds, and one of lower rank for less than ten; in which board, lodging, and instruction are all included.

The chief magistrate resident in the university, answering to our vice-chancellor, and to the *rector magnificus* on the continent, had commonly the title of Lord Rector; but being addressed only as *Mr. Rector* in an inaugur-atory speech by the present chancellor, he has fallen from his former dignity of style. Lordship was very liberally annexed by our ancestors to any station or character of dignity: They said, the *Lord General*, and *Lord Ambassador;* so we still say, *my Lord*, to the judge upon the circuit, and yet retain in our Liturgy *the Lords of the Council.*

In walking among the ruins of religious buildings, we came to two vaults over which had formerly stood the house of the subprior. One of the vaults was inhabited by an old woman, who claimed the right of abode there, as the widow of a man whose ancestors had possessed the same gloomy mansion for no less than four generations. The right, however it began, was considered as established by legal prescription, and the old woman lives undisturbed. She thinks however that she has a claim to something more than sufferance; for as her husband's name was Bruce, she is allied to royalty, and told Mr. Boswell that when there were persons of quality in the place, she was distinguished by some notice; that indeed she is now neglected, but she spins a thread, has the company of her cat, and is troublesome to nobody.

Having now seen whatever this ancient city offered to our curiosity, we left it with good wishes, having reason to be highly pleased with the attention that was paid us. But whoever surveys the world must see many things that give him pain. The kindness of the professors did not contribute to abate the uneasy remembrance of an university declining, a college alienated, and a church pro-faned and hastening to the ground.

St. Andrews indeed has formerly suffered more atrocious ravages and more extensive destruction, but recent evils affect with greater force. We were rec-onciled to the sight of archiepiscopal ruins. The distance of a calamity from the present time seems to preclude the mind from contact or sympathy. Events long past are barely known; they are not considered. We read with as little emotion the violence of Knox and his followers, as the irruptions of Alaric and the Goths. Had the university been destroyed two centuries ago, we should not have regretted it; but to see it pining in decay and struggling for life, fills the mind with mournful images and ineffectual wishes.

ABERBROTHIC.

As we knew sorrow and wishes to be vain, it was now our business to mind our way. The roads of Scotland afford little diversion to the traveller, who seldom sees himself either encountered or overtaken, and who has nothing to contem-plate but grounds that have no visible boundaries, or are separated by walls of loose stone. From the bank of the Tweed to St. Andrews I had never seen a single tree, which I did not believe to have grown up far within the present century. Now and then about a gentleman's house stands a small plantation, which in Scotch is called a *policy*, but of these there are few, and those few all very young. The variety of sun and shade is here utterly unknown. There is no tree for either shelter or timber. The oak and the thorn is equally a stranger, and the whole country is extended in uniform nakedness, except that in the road between *Kirkaldy* and *Cowpar*, I passed for a few yards between two hedges. A tree might be a show in Scotland as a horse in Venice. At St. Andrews Mr. Boswell found only one, and recommended it to my notice; I told him that it was rough and low, or looked as if I thought so. This, said he, is nothing to another a few miles off. I was still less delighted to hear that another tree was not to be seen nearer. Nay, said a gentleman that stood by, I know but of this and that tree in the county.

The Lowlands of Scotland had once undoubtedly an equal portion of woods with other countries. Forests are every where gradually diminished, as architecture and cultivation prevail by the increase of people and the introduction of arts. But I believe few regions have been denuded like this, where many centuries must have passed in waste without the least thought of future supply. Davies observes in his account of Ireland, that no Irishman had ever planted an orchard. For that negligence some excuse might be drawn from an unsettled state of life, and the instability of property; but in Scotland possession has long been secure, and inheritance regular, yet it may be doubted whether before the Union any man between Edinburgh and England had ever set a tree.

Of this improvidence no other account can be given than that it probably began in times of tumult, and continued because it had begun. Established custom is not easily broken, till some great event shakes the whole system of things, and life seems to recommence upon new principles. That before the Union the Scots had little trade and little money, is no valid apology; for plantation is the least expensive of all methods of improvement. To drop a seed into the ground can cost nothing, and the trouble is not great of protecting the young plant, till it is out of danger; though it must be allowed to have some difficulty in places like these, where they have neither wood for palisades, nor thorns for hedges.

Our way was over the Firth of Tay, where, though the water was not wide, we paid four shillings for ferrying the chaise. In Scotland the necessaries of life are easily procured, but superfluities and elegancies are of the same price at least as in England, and therefore may be considered as much dearer.

We stopped a while at Dundee, where I remember nothing remarkable, and mounting our chaise again, came about the close of the day to Aberbrothick.

The monastery of Aberbrothick is of great renown in the history of Scotland. Its ruins afford ample testimony of its ancient magnificence: Its extent might, I suppose, easily be found by following the walls among the grass and weeds, and its height is known by some parts yet standing. The arch of one of the gates is entire, and of another only so far dilapidated as to diversify the appearance.

A square apartment of great loftiness is yet standing; its use I could not conjecture, as its elevation was very disproportionate to its area. Two corner towers, particularly attracted our attention. Mr. Boswell, whose inquisitiveness is seconded by great activity, scrambled in at a high window, but found the stairs within broken, and could not reach the top. Of the other tower we were told that the inhabitants sometimes climbed it, but we did not immediately discern the entrance, and as the night was gathering upon us, thought proper to desist. Men skilled in architecture might do what we did not attempt: They might probably form an exact ground-plot of this venerable edifice. They may from some parts yet standing conjecture its general form, and perhaps by comparing it with other buildings of the same kind and the same age, attain an idea very near to truth. I should scarcely have regretted my journey, had it afforded nothing more than the sight of Aberbrothick.

ABERDEEN.

We came somewhat late to Aberdeen, and found the inn so full, that we had some difficulty in obtaining admission, till Mr. Boswell made himself known: His name overpowered all objection, and we found a very good house and civil treatment.

I received the next day a very kind letter from Sir Alexander Gordon, whom I had formerly known in London, and after a cessation of all intercourse for near twenty years met here professor of physic in the King's College. Such unexpected renewals of acquaintance may be numbered among the most pleasing incidents of life.

The knowledge of one professor soon procured me the notice of the rest, and I did not want any token of regard, being conducted wherever there was any thing which I desired to see, and entertained at once with the novelty of the place, and the kindness of communication.

To write of the cities of our own island with the solemnity of geographical description, as if we had been cast upon a newly discovered coast, has the appearance of very frivolous ostentation; yet as Scotland is little known to the greater part of those who may read these observations, it is not superfluous to relate, that under the name of Aberdeen are comprised two towns standing about a mile distant from each other, but governed, I think, by the same magistrates.

Old Aberdeen is the ancient episcopal city, in which are still to be seen the remains of the cathedral. It has the appearance of a town in decay, having been situated in times when commerce was yet unstudied, with very little attention to the commodities of the harbour.

New Aberdeen has all the bustle of prosperous trade, and all the shew of increasing opulence. It is built by the waterside. The houses are large and lofty, and the streets spacious and clean. They build almost wholly with the granite used in the new pavement of the streets of London, which is well known not to want hardness, yet they shape it easily. It is beautiful and must be very lasting.

What particular parts of commerce are chiefly exercised by the merchants of Aberdeen, I have not inquired. The manufacture which forces itself upon a stranger's eye is that of knit-stockings, on which the women of the lower class are visibly employed.

In each of these towns there is a college, or in stricter language, an university; for in both there are professors of the same parts of learning, and the colleges hold their sessions and confer degrees separately, with total independence of one on the other.

In old Aberdeen stands the King's College, of which the first president was *Hector Boece*, or *Boethius*, who may be justly reverenced as one of the revivers of elegant learning. When he studied at Paris, he was acquainted with *Erasmus*, who afterwards gave him a public testimony of his esteem, by inscribing to him a catalogue of his works. The stile of Boethius, though, perhaps, not always rigorously pure, is formed with great diligence upon ancient models, and wholly uninfected with monastic barbarity. His history is written with elegance and vigour, but his fabulousness and credulity are justly blamed. His fabulousness, if he was the author of the fictions, is a fault for which no apology can be made; but his credulity may be excused in an age, when all men were credulous. Learning was then rising on the world; but ages so long accustomed to darkness, were too much dazzled with its light to see any thing distinctly. The first race of scholars, in the fifteenth century, and some time after, were, for the most part, learning to speak, rather than to think, and were therefore more studious of elegance than of truth. The contemporaries of Boethius thought it sufficient to know what the ancients had delivered. The examination of tenets and of facts was reserved for another generation.

Boethius, as president of the university, enjoyed a revenue of forty Scottish marks, about two pounds four shillings and sixpence of sterling money. In the present age of trade and taxes, it is difficult even for the imagination so to raise the value of money, or so to diminish the demands of life, as to suppose four and forty shillings a year, an honourable stipend; yet it was probably equal, not only to the needs, but to the rank of Boethius. The wealth of England was undoubtedly to that of Scotland more than five to one, and it is known that Henry the eighth, among whose faults avarice was never reckoned, granted to Roger Ascham, as a reward of his learning, a pension of ten pounds a year.

The other, called the Marischal College, is in the new town. The hall is large and well lighted. One of its ornaments is the picture of Arthur Johnston, who was principal of the college, and who holds among the Latin poets of Scotland the next place to the elegant Buchanan.

In the library I was shewn some curiosities; a Hebrew manuscript of exquisite penmanship, and a Latin translation of Aristotle's Politicks by *Leonardus Aretinus*, written in the Roman character with nicety and beauty, which, as the art of printing has made them no longer necessary, are not now to be found. This was one of the latest performances of the transcribers, for Aretinus died but about twenty years before typography was invented. This version has been printed, and may be found in libraries, but is little read; for the same books have been since translated both by *Victorius* and *Lambinus*, who lived in an age more cultivated, but perhaps owed in part to *Aretinus* that they were able to excel him. Much is due to those who first broke the way to knowledge, and left only to their successors the task of smoothing it.

In both these colleges the methods of instruction are nearly the same; the lectures differing only by the accidental difference of diligence, or ability in the professors. The students wear scarlet gowns and the professors black, which is, I believe, the academical dress in all the *Scottish* universities, except that of Edinburgh, where the scholars are not distinguished by any particular habit. In the King's College there is kept a public table, but the scholars of the Marischal College are boarded in the town. The expence of living is here, according to the information that I could obtain, somewhat more than at St. Andrews.

The course of education is extended to four years, at the end of which those who take a degree, who are not many, become masters of arts, and whoever is a master may, if he pleases, immediately commence doctor. The title of doctor, however, was for a considerable time bestowed only on physicians. The advocates are examined and approved by their own body; the ministers were not ambitious of titles, or were afraid of being censured for ambition; and the doctorate in every faculty was commonly given or sold into other countries. The ministers are now reconciled to distinction, and as it must always happen that some will excel others, have thought graduation a proper testimony of uncommon abilities or acquisitions.

The indiscriminate collation of degrees has justly taken away that respect which they originally claimed as stamps, by which the literary value of men so distinguished was authoritatively denoted. That academical honours, or any others should be conferred with exact proportion to merit, is more than human judgment or human integrity have given reason to expect. Perhaps degrees in universities cannot be better adjusted by any general rule than by the length of time passed in the public profession of learning. An English or Irish doctorate cannot be obtained by a very young man, and it is reasonable to suppose, what is likewise by experience commonly found true, that he who is by age qualified to be a doctor, has in so much time gained learning sufficient not to disgrace the title, or wit sufficient not to desire it.

The Scotch universities hold but one term or session in the year. That of St. Andrews continues eight months, that of Aberdeen only five, from the first of November to the first of April.

In Aberdeen there is an English chapel, in which the congregation was numerous and splendid. The form of public worship used by the church of England is in Scotland legally practised in licensed chapels served by clergymen of English

or Irish ordination, and by tacit connivance quietly permitted in separate congregations supplied with ministers by the successors of the bishops who were
deprived at the Revolution.

We came to Aberdeen on Saturday August 21. On Monday we were invited
into the town-hall, where I had the freedom of the city given me by the Lord
Provost. The honour conferred had all the decorations that politeness could
add, and what I am afraid I should not have had to say of any city south of the
Tweed, I found no petty officer bowing for a fee.

The parchment containing the record of admission is, with the seal appending, fastened to a riband and worn for one day by the new citizen in his hat.

By a lady who saw us at the chapel, the Earl of Errol was informed of our
arrival, and we had the honour of an invitation to his seat, called Slanes Castle,
as I am told, improperly, from the castle of that name, which once stood at a
place not far distant.

The road beyond Aberdeen grew more stony, and continued equally naked of
all vegetable decoration. We travelled over a tract of ground near the sea, which,
not long ago, suffered a very uncommon, and unexpected calamity. The sand of
the shore was raised by a tempest in such quantities, and carried to such a distance, that an estate was overwhelmed and lost. Such and so hopeless was the
barrenness superinduced, that the owner, when he was required to pay the usual
tax, desired rather to resign the ground.

ELGIN.

Finding nothing to detain us at Bamff, we set out in the morning, and having
breakfasted at Cullen, about noon came to *Elgin*, where in the inn, that we supposed the best, a dinner was set before us, which we could not eat. This was the
first time, and except one, the last, that I found any reason to complain of a
Scotish table; and such disappointments, I suppose, must be expected in every
country, where there is no great frequency of travellers.

The ruins of the cathedral of Elgin afforded us another proof of the waste
of reformation. There is enough yet remaining to shew, that it was once magnificent. Its whole plot is easily traced. On the north side of the choir, the
chapterhouse, which is roofed with an arch of stone, remains entire; and on
the south side, another mass of building, which we could not enter, is preserved by the care of the family of Gordon; but the body of the church is a
mass of fragments.

A paper was here put into our hands, which deduced from sufficient authorities the history of this venerable ruin. The church of Elgin had, in the intestine tumults of the barbarous ages, been laid waste by the irruption of a
highland chief, whom the bishop had offended; but it was gradually restored to
the state, of which the traces may be now discerned, and was at last not destroyed by the tumultuous violence of Knox, but more shamefully suffered to

dilapidate by deliberate robbery and frigid indifference. There is still extant, in the books of the council, an order, of which I cannot remember the date, but which was doubtless issued after the Reformation, directing that the lead, which covers the two cathedrals of Elgin and Aberdeen, shall be taken away, and converted into money for the support of the army. A Scotch army was in those times very cheaply kept; yet the lead of two churches must have born so small a proportion to any military expence, that it is hard not to believe the reason alleged to be merely popular, and the money intended for some private purse. The order however was obeyed; the two churches were stripped, and the lead was shipped to be sold in Holland. I hope every reader will rejoice that this cargo of sacrilege was lost at sea.

Let us not however make too much haste to despise our neighbours. Our own cathedrals are mouldering by unregarded dilapidation. It seems to be part of the despicable philosophy of the time to despise monuments of sacred magnificence, and we are in danger of doing that deliberately, which the Scots did not do but in the unsettled state of an imperfect constitution.

Those who had once uncovered the cathedrals never wished to cover them again; and being thus made useless, they were first neglected, and perhaps, as the stone was wanted, afterwards demolished.

Elgin seems a place of little trade, and thinly inhabited. The episcopal cities of Scotland, I believe, generally fell with their churches, though some of them have since recovered by a situation convenient for commerce. Thus *Glasgow*, though it has no longer an archbishop, has risen beyond its original state by the opulence of its traders; and *Aberdeen*, though its ancient stock had decayed, flourishes by a new shoot in another place.

In the chief street of Elgin, the houses jut over the lowest story, like the old buildings of timber in London, but with greater prominence; so that there is sometimes a walk for a considerable length under a cloister, or portico, which is now indeed frequently broken, because the new houses have another form, but seems to have been uniformly continued in the old city.

INVERNESS.

Inverness was the last place which had a regular communication by high roads with the southern counties. All the ways beyond it have, I believe, been made by the soldiers in this century. At *Inverness* therefore *Cromwell*, when he subdued *Scotland*, stationed a garrison, as at the boundary of the Highlands. The soldiers seem to have incorporated afterwards with the inhabitants, and to have peopled the place with an English race; for the language of this town has been long considered as peculiarly elegant.

Here is a castle, called the castle of Macbeth, the walls of which are yet standing. It was no very capacious edifice, but stands upon a rock so high and steep, that I think it was once not accessible, but by the help of ladders, or a bridge.

Over against it, on another hill, was a fort built by *Cromwell*, now totally demolished; for no faction of Scotland loved the name of *Cromwell*, or had any desire to continue his memory.

Yet what the Romans did to other nations, was in a great degree done by Cromwell to the Scots; he civilized them by conquest, and introduced by useful violence the arts of peace. I was told at *Aberdeen* that the people learned from Cromwell's soldiers to make shoes and to plant kail.

How they lived without kail, it is not easy to guess: They cultivate hardly any other plant for common tables, and when they had not kail they probably had nothing. The numbers that go barefoot are still sufficient to shew that shoes may be spared: They are not yet considered as necessaries of life; for tall boys, not otherwise meanly dressed, run without them in the streets and in the islands; the sons of gentlemen pass several of their first years with naked feet.

I know not whether it be not peculiar to the Scots to have attained the liberal, without the manual arts, to have excelled in ornamental knowledge, and to have wanted not only the elegancies, but the conveniencies of common life. Literature soon after its revival found its way to *Scotland*, and from the middle of the sixteenth century, almost to the middle of the seventeenth, the politer studies were very diligently pursued. The Latin poetry of *Deliciae Poetarum Scotorum* would have done honour to any nation, at least till the publication of *May's Supplement* the English had very little to oppose.

Yet men thus ingenious and inquisitive were content to live in total ignorance of the trades by which human wants are supplied, and to supply them by the grossest means. Till the Union made them acquainted with English manners, the culture of their lands was unskilful, and their domestick life unformed; their tables were coarse as the feasts of Eskimeaux, and their houses filthy as the cottages of Hottentots.

Since they have known that their condition was capable of improvement, their progress in useful knowledge has been rapid and uniform. What remains to be done they will quickly do, and then wonder, like me, why that which was so necessary and so easy was so long delayed. But they must be for ever content to owe to the English that elegance and culture, which, if they had been vigilant and active, perhaps the English might have owed to them.

Here the appearance of life began to alter. I had seen a few women with plaids at *Aberdeen*; but at *Inverness* the Highland manners are common. There is I think a kirk, in which only the Erse language is used. There is likewise an English chapel, but meanly built, where on Sunday we saw a very decent congregation.

We were now to bid farewel to the luxury of travelling, and to enter a country upon which perhaps no wheel has ever rolled. We could indeed have used our post-chaise one day longer, along the military road to Fort *Augustus*, but we could have hired no horses beyond Inverness, and we were not so sparing of ourselves, as to lead them, merely that we might have one day longer the indulgence of a carriage.

At Inverness therefore we procured three horses for ourselves and a servant, and one more for our baggage, which was no very heavy load. We found in the course of our journey the convenience of having disencumbered ourselves, by laying aside whatever we could spare; for it is not to be imagined without experience, how in climbing crags, and treading bogs, and winding through narrow and obstructed passages, a little bulk will hinder, and a little weight will burthen; or how often a man that has pleased himself at home with his own resolution, will, in the hour of darkness and fatigue, be content to leave behind him every thing but himself.

LOUGH NESS.

We took two Highlanders to run beside us, partly to shew us the way, and partly to take back from the seaside the horses, of which they were the owners. One of them was a man of great liveliness and activity, of whom his companion said, that he would tire any horse in Inverness. Both of them were civil and ready-handed. Civility seems part of the national character of Highlanders. Every chieftain is a monarch, and politeness, the natural product of royal government, is diffused from the laird through the whole clan. But they are not commonly dexterous: their narrowness of life confines them to a few operations, and they are accustomed to endure little wants more than to remove them

We mounted our steeds on the thirtieth of August, and directed our guides to conduct us to Fort Augustus. It is built at the head of Lough Ness, of which *Inverness* stands at the outlet. The way between them has been cut by the soldiers, and the greater part of it runs along a rock, levelled with great labour and exactness, near the waterside.

Most of this day's journey was very pleasant. The day, though bright, was not hot; and the appearance of the country, if I had not seen the Peak, would have been wholly new. We went upon a surface so hard and level, that we had little care to hold the bridle, and were therefore at full leisure for contemplation. On the left were high and steep rocks shaded with birch, the hardy native of the North, and covered with fern or heath. On the right the limpid waters of *Lough Ness* were beating their bank, and waving their surface by a gentle agitation. Beyond them were rocks sometimes covered with verdure, and sometimes towering in horrid nakedness. Now and then we espied a little cornfield, which served to impress more strongly the general barrenness.

Lough Ness is about twenty-four miles long, and from one mile to two miles broad. It is remarkable that *Boethius*, in his description of Scotland, gives it twelve miles of breadth. When historians or geographers exhibit false accounts of places far distant, they may be forgiven, because they can tell but what they are told; and that their accounts exceed the truth may be justly supposed, because most men exaggerate to others, if not to themselves: but *Boethius* lived at no great distance; if he never saw the lake, he must have been very incurious, and if he had seen it, his veracity yielded to very slight temptations.

Lough Ness, though not twelve miles broad, is a very remarkable diffusion of water without islands. It fills a large hollow between two ridges of high rocks, being supplied partly by the torrents which fall into it on either side, and partly, as is supposed, by springs at the bottom. Its water is remarkably clear and pleasant, and is imagined by the natives to be medicinal. We were told, that it is in some places a hundred and forty fathoms deep, a profundity scarcely credible, and which probably those that relate it have never sounded. Its fish are salmon, trout, and pike.

It was said at fort *Augustus*, that *Lough Ness* is open in the hardest winters, though a lake not far from it is covered with ice. In discussing these exceptions from the course of nature, the first question is, whether the fact be justly stated. That which is strange is delightful, and a pleasing error is not willingly detected. Accuracy of narration is not very common, and there are few so rigidly philosophical, as not to represent as perpetual, what is only frequent, or as constant, what is really casual. If it be true that *Lough Ness* never freezes, it is either sheltered by its high banks from the cold blasts, and exposed only to those winds which have more power to agitate than congeal; or it is kept in perpetual motion by the rush of streams from the rocks that inclose it. Its profundity though it should be such as is represented can have little part in this exemption; for though deep wells are not frozen, because their water is secluded from the external air, yet where a wide surface is exposed to the full influence of a freezing atmosphere, I know not why the depth should keep it open. Natural philosophy is now one of the favourite studies of the Scottish nation, and *Lough Ness* well deserves to be diligently examined.

The road on which we travelled, and which was itself a source of entertainment, is made along the rock, in the direction of the lough, sometimes by breaking off protuberances, and sometimes by cutting the great mass of stone to a considerable depth. The fragments are piled in a loose wall on either side, with apertures left at very short spaces, to give a passage to the wintry currents. Part of it is bordered with low trees, from which our guides gathered nuts, and would have had the appearance of an English lane, except that an English lane is almost always dirty. It has been made with great labour, but has this advantage, that it cannot, without equal labour, be broken up.

Within our sight there were goats feeding or playing. The mountains have red deer, but they came not within view; and if what is said of their vigilance and subtlety be true, they have some claim to that palm of wisdom, which the eastern philosopher, whom Alexander interrogated, gave to those beasts which live furthest from men.

Near the way, by the waterside, we espied a cottage. This was the first Highland Hut that I had seen; and as our business was with life and manners, we were willing to visit it. To enter a habitation without leave, seems to be not considered here as rudeness or intrusion. The old laws of hospitality still give this licence to a stranger.

A hut is constructed with loose stones, ranged for the most part with some tendency to circularity. It must be placed where the wind cannot act upon it with violence, because it has no cement; and where the water will run easily away, because it has no floor but the naked ground. The wall, which is commonly about six feet high, declines from the perpendicular a little inward. Such rafters as can be procured are then raised for a roof, and covered with heath, which makes a strong and warm thatch, kept from flying off by ropes of twisted heath, of which the ends, reaching from the center of the thatch to the top of the wall, are held firm by the weight of a large stone. No light is admitted but at the entrance, and through a hole in the thatch, which gives vent to the smoke. This hole is not directly over the fire, lest the rain should extinguish it; and the smoke therefore naturally fills the place before it escapes. Such is the general structure of the houses in which one of the nations of this opulent and powerful island has been hitherto content to live. Huts however are not more uniform than palaces; and this which we were inspecting was very far from one of the meanest, for it was divided into several apartments; and its inhabitants possessed such property as a pastoral poet might exalt into riches.

When we entered, we found an old woman boiling goats-flesh in a kettle. She spoke little English, but we had interpreters at hand; and she was willing enough to display her whole system of economy. She has five children, of which none are yet gone from her. The eldest, a boy of thirteen, and her husband, who is eighty years old, were at work in the wood. Her two next sons were gone to *Inverness* to buy *meal*, by which oatmeal is always meant. Meal she considered as expensive food, and told us, that in Spring, when the goats gave milk, the children could live without it. She is mistress of sixty goats, and I saw many kids in an enclosure at the end of her house. She had also some poultry. By the lake we saw a potatoe-garden, and a small spot of ground on which stood four shucks, containing each twelve sheaves of barley. She has all this from the labour of their own hands, and for what is necessary to be bought, her kids and her chickens are sent to market.

With the true pastoral hospitality, she asked us to sit down and drink whisky. She is religious, and though the kirk is four miles off, probably eight English miles, she goes thither every Sunday. We gave her a shilling, and she begged snuff; for snuff is the luxury of a Highland cottage.

Soon afterwards we came to the *General's Hut*, so called because it was the temporary abode of Wade, while he superintended the works upon the road. It is now a house of entertainment for passengers, and we found it not ill stocked with provisions.

ANOCH.

Early in the afternoon we came to Anoch, a village in *Glenmorrison* of three huts, one of which is distinguished by a chimney. Here we were to dine and lodge, and were conducted through the first room, that had the chimney, into another lighted by a small glass window. The landlord attended us with great civility, and told us what he could give us to eat and drink. I found some books on a shelf, among which were a volume or more of Prideaux's Connection.

This I mentioned as something unexpected, and perceived that I did not please him. I praised the propriety of his language, and was answered that I need not wonder, for he had learned it by grammar.

By subsequent opportunities of observation, I found that my host's diction had nothing peculiar. Those Highlanders that can speak English, commonly speak it well, with few of the words, and little of the tone by which a Scotchman is distinguished. Their language seems to have been learned in the army or the navy, or by some communication with those who could give them good examples of accent and pronunciation. By their Lowland neighbours they would not willingly be taught; for they have long considered them as a mean and degenerate race. These prejudices are wearing fast away; but so much of them still remains, that when I asked a very learned minister in the islands, which they considered as their most savage clans: "*Those*, said he, *that live next the Lowlands.*"

As we came hither early in the day, we had time sufficient to survey the place. The house was built like other huts of loose stones, but the part in which we dined and slept was lined with turf and wattled with twigs, which kept the earth from falling. Near it was a garden of turnips and a field of potatoes. It stands in a glen, or valley, pleasantly watered by a winding river. But this country, however it may delight the gazer or amuse the naturalist, is of no great advantage to its owners. Our landlord told us of a gentleman, who possesses lands, eighteen Scotch miles in length, and three in breadth; a space containing at least a hundred square English miles. He has raised his rents, to the danger of depopulating his farms, and he fells his timber, and by exerting every art of augmentation, has obtained an yearly revenue of four hundred pounds, which for a hundred square miles is three half-pence an acre.

Some time after dinner we were surprised by the entrance of a young woman, not inelegant either in mien or dress, who asked us whether we would have tea. We found that she was the daughter of our host, and desired her to make it. Her conversation, like her appearance, was gentle and pleasing. We knew that the girls of the Highlands are all gentlewomen, and treated her with great respect, which she received as customary and due, and was neither elated by it, nor confused, but repaid my civilities without embarrassment, and told me how much I honoured her country by coming to survey it.

She had been at *Inverness* to gain the common female qualifications, and had, like her father, the English pronunciation. I presented her with a book, which I happened to have about me, and should not be pleased to think that she forgets me.

In the evening the soldiers, whom we had passed on the road, came to spend at our inn the little money that we had given them. They had the true military impatience of coin in their pockets, and had marched at least six miles to find the first place where liquor could be bought. Having never been before in a place so wild and unfrequented, I was glad of their arrival, because I knew that we had made them friends, and to gain still more of their good will, we went to them, where they were carousing in the barn, and added something to our former gift. All that we gave was not much, but it detained them in the barn, either merry or quarrelling, the whole night, and in the morning they went back to their work, with great indignation at the bad qualities of whisky.

We had gained so much the favour of our host, that, when we left his house in the morning, he walked by us a great way, and entertained us with conversation both on his own condition, and that of the country. His life seemed to be merely pastoral, except that he differed from some of the ancient Nomades in having a settled dwelling. His wealth consists of one hundred sheep, as many goats, twelve milk-cows, and twenty-eight beeves ready for the drovers.

From him we first heard of the general dissatisfaction, which is now driving the Highlanders into the other hemisphere; and when I asked him whether they would stay at home, if they were well treated, he answered with indignation, that no man willingly left his native country. Of the farm, which he himself occupied, the rent had, in twenty-five years, been advanced from five to twenty pounds, which he found himself so little able to pay, that he would be glad to try his fortune in some other place. Yet he owned the reasonableness of raising the Highland rents in a certain degree, and declared himself willing to pay ten pounds for the ground which he had formerly had for five.

Our host having amused us for a time, resigned us to our guides. The journey of this day was long, not that the distance was great, but that the way was difficult. We were now in the bosom of the Highlands, with full leisure to contemplate the appearance and properties of mountainous regions, such as have been, in many countries, the last shelters of national distress, and are every where the scenes of adventures, stratagems, surprises and escapes.

Mountainous countries are not passed but with difficulty, not merely from the labour of climbing; for to climb is not always necessary: but because that which is not mountain is commonly bog, through which the way must be picked with caution. Where there are hills, there is much rain, and the torrents pouring down into the intermediate spaces, seldom find so ready an outlet, as not to stagnate, till they have broken the texture of the ground.

Of the hills, which our journey offered to the view on either side, we did not take the height, not did we see any that astonished us with their loftiness.

Towards the summit of one, there was a white spot, which I should have called a naked rock, but the guides, who had better eyes, and were acquainted with the phænomena of the country, declared it to be snow. It had already lasted to the end of August, and was likely to maintain its contest with the sun, till it should be reinforced by winter.

The height of mountains philosophically considered is properly computed from the surface of the next sea; but as it affects the eye or imagination of the passenger, as it makes either a spectacle or an obstruction, it must be reckoned from the place where the rise begins to make a considerable angle with the plain. In extensive continents the land may, by gradual elevation, attain great height, without any other appearance than that of a plane gently inclined, and if a hill placed upon such raised ground be described, as having its altitude equal to the whole space above the sea, the representation will be fallacious.

These mountains may be properly enough measured from the inland base; for it is not much above the sea. As we advanced at evening towards the western coast, I did not observe the declivity to be greater than is necessary for the discharge of the inland waters.

We passed many rivers and rivulets, which commonly ran with a clear shallow stream over a hard pebbly bottom. These channels, which seem so much wider than the water that they convey would naturally require, are formed by the violence of wintry floods, produced by the accumulation of innumerable streams that fall in rainy weather from the hills, and bursting away with resistless impetuosity, make themselves a passage proportionate to their mass.

Such capricious and temporary waters cannot be expected to produce many fish. The rapidity of the wintry deluge sweeps them away, and the scantiness of the summer stream would hardly sustain them above the ground. This is the reason why in fording the northern rivers, no fishes are seen, as in England, wandering in the water.

Of the hills many may be called with Homer's Ida *abundant in springs*, but few can deserve the epithet which he bestows upon Pelion by *waving their leaves*. They exhibit very little variety; being almost wholly covered with dark heath, and even that seems to be checked in its growth. What is not heath is nakedness, a little diversified by now and then a stream rushing down the steep. An eye accustomed to flowery pastures and waving harvests is astonished and repelled by this wide extent of hopeless sterility. The appearance is that of matter incapable of form or usefulness, dismissed by nature from her care and disinherited of her favours, left in its original elemental state, or quickened only with one sullen power of useless vegetation.

It will very readily occur, that this uniformity of barrenness can afford very little amusement to the traveller; that it is easy to sit at home and conceive rocks and heath, and waterfalls; and that these journeys are useless labours, which neither impregnate the imagination, nor enlarge the understanding. It is true that of far the greater part of things, we must content ourselves with

such knowledge as description may exhibit, or analogy supply; but it is true likewise, that these ideas are always incomplete, and that at least, till we have compared them with realities, we do not know them to be just. As we see more, we
become possessed of more certainties, and consequently gain more principles
of reasoning, and found a wider basis of analogy.

Regions mountainous and wild, thinly inhabited, and little cultivated,
make a great part of the earth, and he that has never seen them, must live
unacquainted with much of the face of nature, and with one of the great
scenes of human existence.

As the day advanced towards noon, we entered a narrow valley not very
flowery, but sufficiently verdant. Our guides told us, that the horses could not
travel all day without rest or meat, and intreated us to stop here, because no
grass would be found in any other place. The request was reasonable and the
argument cogent. We therefore willingly dismounted and diverted ourselves
as the place gave us opportunity.

I sat down on a bank, such as a writer of Romance might have delighted to
feign. I had indeed no trees to whisper over my head, but a clear rivulet streamed
at my feet. The day was calm, the air soft, and all was rudeness, silence, and
solitude. Before me, and on either side, were high hills, which by hindering
the eye from ranging, forced the mind to find entertainment for itself. Whether
I spent the hour well I know not; for here I first conceived the thought of this
narration.

We were in this place at ease and by choice, and had no evils to suffer or to
fear; yet the imaginations excited by the view of an unknown and untravelled
wilderness are not such as arise in the artificial solitude of parks and gardens,
a flattering notion of self-sufficiency, a placid indulgence of voluntary delusions, a secure expansion of the fancy, or a cool concentration of the mental
powers. The phantoms which haunt a desert are want, and misery, and danger;
the evils of dereliction rush upon the thoughts; man is made unwillingly
acquainted with his own weakness, and meditation shews him only how little
he can sustain, and how little he can perform. There were no traces of inhabitants, except perhaps a rude pile of clods called a summer hut, in which a
herdsman had rested in the favourable seasons. Whoever had been in the place
where I then sat, unprovided with provisions and ignorant of the country,
might, at least before the roads were made, have wandered among the rocks,
till he had perished with hardship, before he could have found either food or
shelter. Yet what are these hillocks to the ridges of Taurus, or these spots of
wildness to the desarts of America?

It was not long before we were invited to mount, and continued our journey along the side of a lough, kept full by many streams, which with more or
less rapidity and noise, crossed the road from the hills on the other hand.
These currents, in their diminished state, after several dry months, afford,
to one who has always lived in level countries, an unusual and delightful

spectacle; but in the rainy season, such as every winter may be expected to bring, must precipitate an impetuous and tremendous flood. I suppose the way by which we went, is at that time impassable.

THE HIGHLANDS.

As we continued our journey, we were at leisure to extend our speculations, and to investigate the reason of those peculiarities by which such rugged regions as these before us are generally distinguished.

Mountainous countries commonly contain the original, at least the oldest race of inhabitants, for they are not easily conquered, because they must be entered by narrow ways, exposed to every power of mischief from those that occupy the heights; and every new ridge is a new fortress, where the defendants have again the same advantages. If the assailants either force the strait, or storm the summit, they gain only so much ground; their enemies are fled to take possession of the next rock, and the pursuers stand at gaze, knowing neither where the ways of escape wind among the steeps, nor where the bog has firmness to sustain them: besides that, mountaineers have an agility in climbing and descending distinct from strength or courage, and attainable only by use.

If the war be not soon concluded, the invaders are dislodged by hunger; for in those anxious and toilsome marches, provisions cannot easily be carried, and are never to be found. The wealth of mountains is cattle, which, while the men stand in the passes, the women drive away. Such lands at last cannot repay the expence of conquest, and therefore perhaps have not been so often invaded by the mere ambition of dominion; as by resentment of robberies and insults, or the desire of enjoying in security the more fruitful provinces.

As mountains are long before they are conquered, they are likewise long before they are civilized. Men are softened by intercourse mutually profitable, and instructed by comparing their own notions with those of others. Thus Cæsar found the maritime parts of Britain made less barbarous by their commerce with the Gauls. Into a barren and rough tract no stranger is brought either by the hope of gain or of pleasure. The inhabitants having neither commodities for sale, nor money for purchase, seldom visit more polished places, or if they do visit them, seldom return.

It sometimes happens that by conquest, intermixture, or gradual refinement, the cultivated parts of a country change their language. The mountaineers then become a distinct nation, cut off by dissimilitude of speech from conversation with their neighbours. Thus in Biscay, the original Cantabrian, and in Dalecarlia, the old Swedish still subsists. Thus Wales and the Highlands speak the tongue of the first inhabitants of Britain, while the other parts have received first the Saxon, and in some degree afterwards the French, and then formed a third language between them.

That the primitive manners are continued where the primitive language is spoken, no nation will desire me to suppose, for the manners of mountaineers are commonly savage, but they are rather produced by their situation than derived from their ancestors.

Such seems to be the disposition of man, that whatever makes a distinction produces rivalry. England, before other causes of enmity were found, was disturbed for some centuries by the contests of the northern and southern counties; so that at Oxford, the peace of study could for a long time be preserved only by chusing annually one of the Proctors from each side of the Trent. A tract intersected by many ridges of mountains, naturally divides its inhabitants into petty nations, which are made by a thousand causes enemies to each other. Each will exalt its own chiefs, each will boast the valour of its men, or the beauty of its women, and every claim of superiority irritates competition; injuries will sometimes be done, and be more injuriously defended; retaliation will sometimes be attempted, and the debt exacted with too much interest.

In the Highlands it was a law, that if a robber was sheltered from justice, any man of the same clan might be taken in his place. This was a kind of irregular justice, which, though necessary in savage times, could hardly fail to end in a feud, and a feud once kindled among an idle people with no variety of pursuits to divert their thoughts, burnt on for ages either sullenly glowing in secret mischief, or openly blazing into publick violence. Of the effects of this violent judicature, there are not wanting memorials. The cave is now to be seen to which one of the Campbells, who had injured the Macdonalds, retired with a body of his own clan. The Macdonalds required the offender, and being refused, made a fire at the mouth of the cave, by which he and his adherents were suffocated together.

Mountaineers are warlike, because by their feuds and competitions they consider themselves as surrounded with enemies, and are always prepared to repel incursions, or to make them. Like the Greeks in their unpolished state, described by Thucydides, the Highlanders, till lately, went always armed, and carried their weapons to visits, and to church.

Mountaineers are thievish, because they are poor, and having neither manufactures nor commerce, can grow richer only by robbery. They regularly plunder their neighbours, for their neighbours are commonly their enemies; and having lost that reverence for property, by which the order of civil life is preserved, soon consider all as enemies, whom they do not reckon as friends, and think themselves licensed to invade whatever they are not obliged to protect.

By a strict administration of the laws, since the laws have been introduced into the Highlands, this disposition to thievery is very much represt. Thirty years ago no herd had ever been conducted through the mountains, without paying tribute in the night, to some of the clans; but cattle are now driven, and passengers travel without danger, fear, or molestation.

Among a warlike people, the quality of highest esteem is personal courage, and with the ostentatious display of courage are closely connected promptitude of offence and quickness of resentment. The Highlanders, before they were disarmed, were so addicted to quarrels, that the boys used to follow any publick procession or ceremony, however festive, or however solemn, in expectation of the battle, which was sure to happen before the company dispersed.

Mountainous regions are sometimes so remote from the seat of government, and so difficult of access, that they are very little under the influence of the sovereign, or within the reach of national justice. Law is nothing without power; and the sentence of a distant court could not be easily executed, nor perhaps very safely promulgated, among men ignorantly proud and habitually violent, unconnected with the general system, and accustomed to reverence only their own lords. It has therefore been necessary to erect many particular jurisdictions, and commit the punishment of crimes, and the decision of right to the proprietors of the country who could enforce their own decrees. It immediately appears that such judges will be often ignorant, and often partial; but in the immaturity of political establishments no better expedient could be found. As government advances towards perfection, provincial judicature is perhaps in every empire gradually abolished.

Those who had thus the dispensation of law, were by consequence themselves lawless. Their vassals had no shelter from outrages and oppressions; but were condemned to endure, without resistance, the caprices of wantonness, and the rage of cruelty.

In the Highlands, some great lords had an hereditary jurisdiction over counties; and some chieftains over their own lands; till the final conquest of the Highlands afforded an opportunity of crushing all the local courts, and of extending the general benefits of equal law to the low and the high, in the deepest recesses and obscurest corners.

While the chiefs had this resemblance of royalty, they had little inclination to appeal, on any question, to superior judicatures. A claim of lands between two powerful lairds was decided like a contest for dominion between sovereign powers. They drew their forces into the field, and right attended on the strongest. This was, in ruder times, the common practice, which the kings of Scotland could seldom control.

Even so lately as in the last years of King William, a battle was fought at *Mull Roy*, on a plain a few miles to the south of *Inverness*, between the clans of *Mackintosh* and *Macdonald* of *Keppoch*. *Col Macdonald*, the head of a small clan, refused to pay the dues demanded from him by *Mackintosh*, as his superior lord. They disdained the interposition of judges and laws, and calling each his followers to maintain the dignity of the clan, fought a formal battle, in which several considerable men fell on the side of *Mackintosh*, without a complete victory to either. This is said to have been the last open war made between the clans by their own authority.

The Highland lords made treaties, and formed alliances, of which some traces may still be found, and some consequences still remain as lasting evidences of petty regality. The terms of one of these confederacies were, that each should support the other in the right, or in the wrong, except against the king.

The inhabitants of mountains form distinct races, and are careful to preserve their genealogies. Men in a small district necessarily mingle blood by intermarriages, and combine at last into one family, with a common interest in the honour and disgrace of every individual. Then begins that union of affections, and cooperation of endeavours, that constitute a clan. They who consider themselves as ennobled by their family, will think highly of their progenitors, and they who through successive generations live always together in the same place, will preserve local stories and hereditary prejudices. Thus every Highlander can talk of his ancestors, and recount the outrages which they suffered from the wicked inhabitants of the next valley.

Such are the effects of habitation among mountains, and such were the qualities of the Highlanders, while their rocks secluded them from the rest of mankind, and kept them an unaltered and discriminated race. They are now losing their distinction, and hastening to mingle with the general community.

GLENELG.

We left *Auknasheals* and the *Macraes* in the afternoon, and in the evening came to *Ratiken*, a high hill on which a road is cut, but so steep and narrow, that it is very difficult. There is now a design of making another way round the bottom. Upon one of the precipices, my horse, weary with the steepness of the rise, staggered a little, and I called in haste to the Highlander to hold him. This was the only moment of my journey, in which I thought myself endangered.

Having surmounted the hill at last, we were told that at *Glenelg*, on the seaside, we should come to the house of lime and slate and glass. This image of magnificence raised our expectation. At last we came to our inn weary and peevish, and began to inquire for meat and beds.

Of the provisions the negative catalogue was very copious. Here was no meat, no milk, no bread, no eggs, no wine. We did not express much satisfaction. Here however we were to stay. Whisky we might have, and I believe at last they caught a fowl and killed it. We had some bread, and with that we prepared ourselves to be contented, when we had a very eminent proof of Highland hospitality. Along some miles of the way, in the evening, a gentleman's servant had kept us company on foot with very little notice on our part. He left us near *Glenelg*, and we thought on him no more till he came to us again, in about two hours, with a present from his master of rum and sugar. The man had mentioned his company, and the gentleman, whose name, I think, is *Gordon*, well knowing the penury of the place, had this attention to two men, whose names perhaps he had not heard, by whom his kindness was not likely to be ever repaid, and who could be recommended to him only by their necessities.

We were now to examine our lodging. Out of one of the beds, on which we were to repose, started up, at our entrance, a man black as a Cyclops from the forge. Other circumstances of no elegant recital concurred to disgust us. We had been frighted by a lady at Edinburgh, with discouraging representations of Highland lodgings. Sleep, however, was necessary. Our Highlanders had at last found some hay, with which the inn could not supply them. I directed them to bring a bundle into the room, and slept upon it in my riding coat. Mr. Boswell being more delicate, laid himself sheets with hay over and under him, and lay in linen like a gentleman.

SKY. ARMIDEL.

In the morning, September the second, we found ourselves on the edge of the sea. Having procured a boat, we dismissed our Highlanders, whom I would recommend to the service of any future travellers, and were ferried over to the Isle of Sky. We landed at *Armidel*, where we were met on the sands by Sir Alexander Macdonald, who was at that time there with his lady, preparing to leave the island and reside at Edinburgh.

Armidel is a neat house, built where the *Macdonalds* had once a seat, which was burnt in the commotions that followed the Revolution. The walled orchard, which belonged to the former house, still remains. It is well shaded by tall ash trees, of a species, as Mr. Janes the fossilist informed me, uncommonly valuable. This plantation is very properly mentioned by Dr. *Campbell*, in his new account of the state of *Britain*, and deserves attention; because it proves that the present nakedness of the *Hebrides* is not wholly the fault of Nature.

As we sat at Sir Alexander's table, we were entertained, according to the ancient usage of the North, with the melody of the bagpipe. Every thing in those countries has its history. As the bagpiper was playing, an elderly Gentleman informed us, that in some remote time, the *Macdonalds* of Glengary having been injured, or offended by the inhabitants of *Culloden*, and resolving to have justice or vengeance, came to *Culloden* on a Sunday, where finding their enemies at worship, they shut them up in the church, which they set on fire; and this, said he, is the tune that the piper played while they were burning.

Narrations like this, however uncertain, deserve the notice of a traveller, because they are the only records of a nation that has no historians, and afford the most genuine representation of the life and character of the ancient Highlanders.

Under the denomination of *Highlander* are comprehended in Scotland all that now speak the Erse language, or retain the primitive manners, whether they live among the mountains or in the islands; and in that sense I use the name, when there is not some apparent reason for making a distinction.

In *Sky* I first observed the use of Brogues, a kind of artless shoes, stitched with thongs so loosely, that though they defend the foot from stones, they do not exclude water. Brogues were formerly made of raw hides, with the hair inwards, and such are perhaps still used in rude and remote parts; but they are said not to last above two days. Where life is somewhat improved, they are now made of leather tanned with oak bark, as in other places, or with the bark of birch, or roots of tormentil, a substance recommended in defect of bark, about forty years ago, to the Irish tanners, by one to whom the parliament of that kingdom voted a reward. The leather of *Sky* is not completely penetrated by vegetable matter, and therefore cannot be very durable.

My inquiries about brogues, gave me an early specimen of Highland information. One day I was told, that to make brogues was a domestick art, which every man practised for himself, and that a pair of brogues was the work of an hour. I supposed that the husband made brogues as the wife made an apron, till next day it was told me, that a brogue-maker was a trade, and that a pair would cost half a crown. It will easily occur that these representations may both be true, and that, in some places, men may buy them, and in others, make them for themselves; but I had both the accounts in the same house within two days.

Many of my subsequent inquiries upon more interesting topicks ended in the like uncertainty. He that travels in the Highlands may easily saturate his soul with intelligence, if he will acquiesce in the first account. The Highlander gives to every question an answer so prompt and peremptory, that skepticism itself is dared into silence, and the mind sinks before the bold reporter in unresisting credulity; but, if a second question be ventured, it breaks the enchantment; for it is immediately discovered, that what was told so confidently was told at hazard, and that such fearlessness of assertion was either the sport of negligence, or the refuge of ignorance.

If individuals are thus at variance with themselves, it can be no wonder that the accounts of different men are contradictory. The traditions of an ignorant and savage people have been for ages negligently heard, and unskilfully related. Distant events must have been mingled together, and the actions of one man given to another. These, however, are deficiencies in story, for which no man is now to be censured. It were enough, if what there is yet opportunity of examining were accurately inspected, and justly represented; but such is the laxity of Highland conversation, that the inquirer is kept in continual suspense, and by a kind of intellectual retrogradation, knows less as he hears more.

In the islands the plaid is rarely worn. The law by which the Highlanders have been obliged to change the form of their dress, has, in all the places that we have visited, been universally obeyed. I have seen only one gentleman completely clothed in the ancient habit, and by him it was worn only occasionally and wantonly. The common people do not think themselves under any legal necessity of having coats; for they say that the law against plaids was made by Lord Hardwicke, and was in force only for his life: but the same poverty that made it then difficult for them to change their clothing, hinders them now from changing it again.

The fillibeg, or lower garment, is still very common, and the bonnet almost universal; but their attire is such as produces, in a sufficient degree, the effect intended by the law, of abolishing the dissimilitude of appearance between the Highlanders and the other inhabitants of Britain; and, if dress be supposed to have much influence, facilitates their coalition with their fellow-subjects.

What we have long used we naturally like, and therefore the Highlanders were unwilling to lay aside their plaid, which yet to an unprejudiced spectator must appear an incommodious and cumbersome dress; for hanging loose upon the body, it must flutter in a quick motion, or require one of the hands to keep it close. The Romans always laid aside the gown when they had any thing to do. It was a dress so unsuitable to war, that the same word which signified a gown signified peace. The chief use of a plaid seems to be this, that they could commodiously wrap themselves in it, when they were obliged to sleep without a better cover.

In our passage from *Scotland* to *Sky*, we were wet for the first time with a shower. This was the beginning of the Highland winter, after which we were told that a succession of three dry days was not to be expected for many months. The winter of the *Hebrides* consists of little more than rain and wind. As they are surrounded by an ocean never frozen, the blasts that come to them over the water are too much softened to have the power of congelation. The salt loughs, or inlets of the sea, which shoot very far into the island, never have any ice upon them, and the pools of fresh water will never bear the walker. The snow that sometimes falls, is soon dissolved by the air, or the rain.

This is not the description of a cruel climate, yet the dark months are here a time of great distress; because the summer can do little more than feed itself, and winter comes with its cold and its scarcity upon families very slenderly provided.

CORIATACHAN IN SKY.

The third or fourth day after our arrival at *Armidel*, brought us an invitation to the isle of *Raasay*, which lies east of *Sky*. It is incredible how soon the account of any event is propagated in these narrow countries by the love of talk, which much leisure produces, and the relief given to the mind in the penury of insular conversation by a new topick. The arrival of strangers at a place so rarely visited, excites rumour, and quickens curiosity. I know not whether we touched at any corner, where Fame had not already prepared us a reception.

To gain a commodious passage to *Raasay*, it was necessary to pass over a large part of *Sky*. We were furnished therefore with horses and a guide. In the islands there are no roads, nor any marks by which a stranger may find his way. The horseman has always at his side a native of the place, who, by pursuing game, or tending cattle, or being often employed in messages or conduct, has learned where the ridge of the hill has breadth sufficient to allow a horse and his rider a passage, and where the moss or bog is hard enough to bear them. The bogs are avoided as toilsome at least, if not unsafe, and therefore the journey is made generally from precipice to precipice; from which if the eye ventures to look down, it sees below a gloomy cavity, whence the rush of water is sometimes heard.

But there seems to be in all this more alarm than danger. The Highlander walks carefully before, and the horse, accustomed to the ground, follows him with little deviation. Sometimes the hill is too steep for the horseman to keep his seat, and sometimes the moss is too tremulous to bear the double weight of horse and man. The rider then dismounts, and all shift as they can.

Journies made in this manner are rather tedious than long. A very few miles require several hours. From *Armidel* we came at night to *Coriatachan*, a house very pleasantly situated between two brooks, with one of the highest hills of the island behind it. It is the residence of Mr. *Mackinnon*, by whom we were treated with very liberal hospitality, among a more numerous and elegant company than it could have been supposed easy to collect.

The hill behind the house we did not climb. The weather was rough, and the height and steepness discouraged us. We were told that there is a cairne upon it. A cairne is a heap of stones thrown upon the grave of one eminent for dignity of birth, or splendour of atchievements. It is said that by digging, an urn is always found under these cairnes: they must therefore have been thus piled by a people whose custom was to burn the dead. To pile stones is, I believe, a northern custom, and to burn the body was the Roman practice; nor do I know when it was that these two acts of sepulture were united.

The weather was next day too violent for the continuation of our journey; but we had no reason to complain of the interruption. We saw in every place, what we chiefly desired to know, the manners of the people. We had company, and, if we had chosen retirement, we might have had books.

I never was in any house of the Islands, where I did not find books in more languages than one, if I staid long enough to want them, except one from which the family was removed. Literature is not neglected by the higher rank of the Hebridians.

It need not, I suppose, be mentioned, that in countries so little frequented as the Islands, there are no houses where travellers are entertained for money. He that wanders about these wilds, either procures recommendations to those whose habitations lie near his way, or, when night and weariness come upon him, takes the chance of general hospitality. If he finds only a cottage, he can expect little more than shelter; for the cottagers have little more for them-selves: but if his good fortune brings him to the residence of a gentleman, he will be glad of a storm to prolong his stay. There is, however, one inn by the seaside at Sconsor, in Sky, where the post-office is kept.

At the tables where a stranger is received, neither plenty nor delicacy is wanting. A tract of land so thinly inhabited, must have much wildfdowl; and I scarcely remember to have seen a dinner without them. The moorgame is every where to be had. That the sea abounds with fish, needs not be told, for it supplies a great part of Europe. The Isle of *Sky* has stags and roebucks, but no hares. They sell very numerous droves of oxen yearly to England, and therefore cannot be supposed to want beef at home. Sheep and goats are in great numbers, and they have the common domestick fowls.

But as here is nothing to be bought, every family must kill its own meat, and roast part of it somewhat sooner than Apicius would prescribe. Every kind of flesh is undoubtedly excelled by the variety and emulation of English markets; but that which is not best may be yet very far from bad, and he that shall complain of his fare in the *Hebrides*, has improved his delicacy more than his manhood.

Their fowls are not like those plumped for sale by the poulterers of London, but they are as good as other places commonly afford, except that the geese, by feeding in the sea, have universally a fishy rankness.

These geese seem to be of a middle race, between the wild and domestick kinds. They are so tame as to own a home, and so wild as sometimes to fly quite away.

Their native bread is made of oats, or barley. Of oatmeal they spread very thin cakes, coarse and hard, to which unaccustomed palates are not easily rec-onciled, the barley cakes are thicker and softer; I began to eat them without unwillingness; the blackness of their colour raises some dislike, but the taste is not disagreeable. In most houses there is wheat flower, with which we were sure to be treated, if we staid long enough to have it kneaded and baked. As neither yeast nor leaven are used among them, their bread of every kind is unfermented. They make only cakes, and never mould a loaf.

A man of the Hebrides, for of the women's diet I can give no account, as soon as he appears in the morning, swallows a glass of whisky; yet they are not a drunken race, at least I never was present at much intemperance; but no man is so abstemious as to refuse the morning dram, which they call a *skalk*.

The word *whisky* signifies water, and is applied by way of eminence to *strong water*, or distilled liquor. The spirit drunk in the North is drawn from barley. I never tasted it, except once for experiment at the inn in *Inverary*, when I thought it preferable to any *English* malt brandy. It was strong, but not pungent, and was free from the empyreumatick taste or smell. What was the process I had no opportunity of inquiring, nor do I wish to improve the art of making poison pleasant.

Not long after the dram, may be expected the breakfast, a meal in which the Scots, whether of the lowlands or mountains, must be confessed to excel us. The tea and coffee are accompanied not only with butter, but with honey, conserves, and marmalades. If an epicure could remove by a wish, in quest of sensual gratifications, wherever he had supped he would breakfast in Scotland.

In the islands however, they do what I found it not very easy to endure. They pollute the tea-table by plates piled with large slices of cheshire cheese, which mingles its less grateful odours with the fragrance of the tea.

Where many questions are to be asked, some will be omitted. I forgot to inquire how they were supplied with so much exotic luxury. Perhaps the French may bring them wine for wool, and the Dutch give them tea and coffee at the fishing season, in exchange for fresh provision. Their trade is unconstrained; they pay no customs; for there is no officer to demand them, whatever therefore is made dear only by impost, is obtained here at an easy rate.

A dinner in the Western Islands differs very little from a dinner in *England*, except that in the place of tarts, there are always set different preparations of milk. This part of their diet will admit some improvement. Though they have milk, and eggs, and sugar, few of them know how to compound them in a custard. Their gardens afford them no great variety, but they have always some vegetables on the table. Potatoes at least are never wanting, which, though they have not known them long, are now one of the principal parts of their food. They are not of the mealy, but the viscous kind.

Their more elaborate cookery, or made dishes, an Englishman at the first taste is not likely to approve, but the culinary compositions of every country are often such as become grateful to other nations only by degrees; though I have read a French author, who, in the elation of his heart, says, that French cookery pleases all foreigners, but foreign cookery never satisfies a Frenchman.

Their suppers are, like their dinners, various and plentiful. The table is always covered with elegant linen. Their plates for common use are often of that kind of manufacture which is called cream coloured, or queen's ware. They use silver on all occasions where it is common in *England*, nor did I ever find the spoon of horn, but in one house.

The knives are not often either very bright, or very sharp. They are indeed instruments of which the Highlanders have not been long acquainted with the general use. They were not regularly laid on the table, before the prohibition of arms, and the change of dress. Thirty years ago the Highlander wore his knife as a companion to his dirk or dagger, and when the company sat down to meat, the men who had knives, cut the flesh into small pieces for the women, who with their fingers conveyed it to their mouths.

There was perhaps never any change of national manners so quick, so great, and so general, as that which has operated in the Highlands, by the last conquest, and the subsequent laws. We came thither too late to see what we expected, a people of peculiar appearance, and a system of antiquated life.

The clans retain little now of their original character, their ferocity of temper is softened, their military ardour is extinguished, their dignity of independence is depressed, their contempt of government subdued, and their reverence for their chiefs abated. Of what they had before the late conquest of their country, there remain only their language and their poverty. Their language is attacked on every side. Schools are erected, in which *English* only is taught, and there were lately some who thought it reasonable to refuse them a version of the holy scriptures, that they might have no monument of their mother-tongue.

That their poverty is gradually abated, cannot be mentioned among the unpleasing consequences of subjection. They are now acquainted with money, and the possibility of gain will by degrees make them industrious. Such is the effect of the late regulations, that a longer journey than to the Highlands must be taken by him whose curiosity pants for savage virtues and barbarous grandeur.

RAASAY.

At the first intermission of the stormy weather we were informed, that the boat, which was to convey us to *Raasay*, attended us on the coast. We had from this time our intelligence facilitated, and our conversation enlarged, by the company of Mr. Macqueen, minister of a parish in *Sky*, whose knowledge and politeness give him a title equally to kindness and respect, and who, from this time, never forsook us till we were preparing to leave Sky, and the adjacent places.

The boat was under the direction of Mr. *Malcolm Macleod*, a gentleman of *Raasay*. The water was calm, and the rowers were vigorous; so that our passage was quick and pleasant. When we came near the island, we saw the laird's house, a neat modern fabrick, and found Mr. *Macleod*, the proprietor of the Island, with many gentlemen, expecting us on the beach. We had, as at all other places, some difficulty in landing. The craggs were irregularly broken, and a false step would have been very mischievous.

It seemed that the rocks might, with no great labour, have been hewn almost into a regular flight of steps; and as there are no other landing places, I considered this rugged ascent as the consequence of a form of life inured to hardships, and therefore not studious of nice accommodations. But I know not whether, for many ages, it was not considered as a part of military policy, to keep the country not easily accessible. The rocks are natural fortifications, and an enemy climbing with difficulty, was easily destroyed by those who stood high above him.

Our reception exceeded our expectations. We found nothing but civility, elegance, and plenty. After the usual refreshments, and the usual conversation, the evening came upon us. The carpet was then rolled off the floor; the musician was called, and the whole company was invited to dance, nor did ever fairies trip with greater alacrity. The general air of festivity, which predominated in this place, so far remote from all those regions which the mind has been used to contemplate as the mansions of pleasure, struck the imagination with a delightful surprise, analogous to that which is felt at an unexpected emersion from darkness into light.

When it was time to sup, the dance ceased, and six and thirty persons sat down to two tables in the same room. After supper the ladies sung *Erse* songs, to which I listened as an *English* audience to an *Italian* opera, delighted with the sound of words which I did not understand.

I inquired the subjects of the songs, and was told of one, that it was a love song, and of another, that it was a farewell composed by one of the Islanders that was going, in this epidemical fury of emigration, to seek his fortune in *America*. What sentiments would rise, on such an occasion, in the heart of one who had not been taught to lament by precedent, I should gladly have known; but the lady, by whom I sat, thought herself not equal to the work of translating.

Mr. *Macleod* is the proprietor of the islands of *Raasay, Rona,* and *Fladda,* and possesses an extensive district in *Sky.* The estate has not, during four hundred years, gained or lost a single acre. He acknowledges *Macleod* of Dunvegan as his chief, though his ancestors have formerly disputed the preeminence.

One of the old Highland alliances has continued for two hundred years, and is still subsisting between *Macleod* of *Raasay* and *Macdonald* of *Sky,* in consequence of which, the survivor always inherits the arms of the deceased; a natural memorial of military friendship. At the death of the late Sir *James Macdonald,* his sword was delivered to the present laird of *Raasay.*

The family of *Raasay* consists of the laird, the lady, three sons and ten daughters. For the sons there is a tutor in the house, and the lady is said to be very skilful and diligent in the education of her girls. More gentleness of manners, or a more pleasing appearance of domestick society, is not found in the most polished countries.

Raasay is the only inhabited island in Mr. *Macleod's* possession. *Rona* and *Fladda* afford only pasture for cattle, of which one hundred and sixty winter in *Rona,* under the superintendence of a solitary herdsman.

The length of *Raasay* is, by computation, fifteen miles, and the breadth two. These countries have never been measured, and the computation by miles is negligent and arbitrary. We observed in travelling, that the nominal and real distance of places had very little relation to each other. *Raasay* probably contains near a hundred square miles. It affords not much ground, notwithstanding its extent, either for tillage, or pasture; for it is rough, rocky, and barren. The cattle often perish by falling from the precipices. It is like the other islands, I think, generally naked of shade, but it is naked by neglect; for the laird has an orchard, and very large forest trees grow about his house. Like other hilly countries it has many rivulets. One of the brooks turns a cornmill, and at least one produces trouts.

In the streams or fresh lakes of the Islands, I have never heard of any other fish than trouts and eels. The trouts, which I have seen, are not large; the colour of their flesh is tinged as in *England*. Of their eels I can give no account, having never tasted them; for I believe they are not considered as wholesome food.

It is not very easy to fix the principles upon which mankind have agreed to eat some animals, and reject others; and as the principle is not evident, it is not uniform. That which is selected as delicate in one country, is by its neighbours abhorred as loathsome. The Neapolitans lately refused to eat potatoes in a famine. An Englishman is not easily persuaded to dine on snails with an Italian, on frogs with a Frenchman, or on horseflesh with a Tartar. The vulgar inhabitants of *Sky*, I know not whether of the other islands, have not only eels, but pork and bacon in abhorrence, and accordingly I never saw a hog in the *Hebrides*, except one at *Dunvegan*.

Raasay has wildfowl in abundance, but neither deer, hares, nor rabbits. Why it has them not, might be asked, but that of such questions there is no end. Why does any nation want what it might have? Why are not spices transplanted to *America?* Why does tea continue to be brought from China? Life improves but by slow degrees, and much in every place is yet to do. Attempts have been made to raise roebucks in *Raasay*, but without effect. The young ones it is extremely difficult to rear, and the old can very seldom be taken alive.

Hares and rabbits might be more easily obtained. That they have few or none of either in *Sky*, they impute to the ravage of the foxes, and have therefore set, for some years past, a price upon their heads, which, as the number was diminished, has been gradually raised, from three shillings and sixpence to a guinea, a sum so great in this part of the world, that, in a short time, *Sky* may be as free from foxes, as *England* from wolves. The fund for these rewards is a tax of sixpence in the pound, imposed by the farmers on themselves, and said to be paid with great willingness.

The beasts of prey in the Islands are foxes, otters, and weasels. The foxes are bigger than those of *England*; but the otters exceed ours in a far greater proportion. I saw one at *Armidel*, of a size much beyond that which I supposed them ever to attain; and Mr. *Maclean*, the heir of *Col*, a man of middle stature, informed me that he once shot an otter, of which the tail reached the ground, when he held up the head to a level with his own. I expected the otter to have a foot particularly formed for the act of swimming; but upon examination, I did not find it differing much from that of a spaniel. As he preys in the sea, he does little visible mischief, and is killed only for his fur. White otters are sometimes seen.

In *Raasay* they might have hares and rabbits, for they have no foxes. Some depredations, such as were never made before, have caused a suspicion that a fox has been lately landed in the Island by spite or wantonness. This imaginary stranger has never yet been seen, and therefore, perhaps, the mischief was done by some other animal. It is not likely that a creature so ungentle, whose head could have been sold in *Sky* for a guinea, should be kept alive only to gratify the malice of sending him to prey upon a neighbour: and the passage from *Sky* is wider than a fox would venture to swim, unless he were chased by dogs into the sea, and perhaps than his strength would enable him to cross. How beasts of prey came into any islands is not easy to guess. In cold countries they take advantage of hard winters, and travel over the ice: but this is a very scanty solution; for they are found where they have no discoverable means of coming.

The corn of this island is but little. I saw the harvest of a small field. The women reaped the corn, and the men bound up the sheaves. The strokes of the sickle were timed by the modulation of the harvest song, in which all their voices were united. They accompany in the Highlands every action, which can be done in equal time, with an appropriated strain, which has, they say, not much meaning; but its effects are regularity and cheerfulness. The ancient proceleusmatick song, by which the rowers of gallies were animated, may be supposed to have been of this kind. There is now an *oar-song* used by the *Hebridians*.

The ground of *Raasay* seems fitter for cattle than for corn, and of black cattle I suppose the number is very great. The Laird himself keeps a herd of four hundred, one hundred of which are annually sold. Of an extensive domain, which he holds in his own hands, he considers the sale of cattle as repaying him the rent, and supports the plenty of a very liberal table with the remaining product.

Raasay is supposed to have been very long inhabited. On one side of it they show caves, into which the rude nations of the first ages retreated from the weather. These dreary vaults might have had other uses. There is still a cavity near the house called the *oarcave*, in which the seamen, after one of those piratical expeditions, which in rougher times were very frequent, used, as tradition tells, to hide their oars. This hollow was near the sea, that nothing so necessary might be far to be fetched; and it was secret, that enemies, if they landed, could find nothing. Yet it is not very evident of what use it was to hide their oars from those, who, if they were masters of the coast, could take away their boats.

A proof much stronger of the distance at which the first possessors of this island lived from the present time, is afforded by the stone heads of arrows which are very frequently picked up. The people call them *Elf-bolts*, and believe that the fairies shoot them at the cattle. They nearly resemble those which Mr. *Banks* has lately brought from the savage countries in the Pacifick Ocean, and must have been made by a nation to which the use of metals was unknown.

The number of this little community has never been counted by its ruler, nor have I obtained any positive account, consistent with the result of political computation. Not many years ago, the late Laird led out one hundred men upon a military expedition. The sixth part of a people is supposed capable of bearing arms: *Raasay* had therefore six hundred inhabitants. But because it is not likely, that every man able to serve in the field would follow the summons, or that the chief would leave his lands totally defenceless, or take away all the hands qualified for labour, let it be supposed, that half as many might be permitted to stay at home. The whole number will then be nine hundred, or nine to a square mile; a degree of populousness greater than those tracts of desolation can often show. They are content with their country, and faithful to their chiefs, and yet uninfected with the fever of migration.

Near the house, at *Raasay*, is a chapel unroofed and ruinous, which has long been used only as a place of burial. About the churches, in the Islands, are small squares inclosed with stone, which belong to particular families, as repositories for the dead. At *Raasay* there is one, I think, for the proprietor, and one for some collateral house.

It is told by *Martin*, that at the death of the Lady of the Island, it has been here the custom to erect a cross. This we found not to be true. The stones that stand about the chapel at a small distance, some of which perhaps have crosses cut upon them, are believed to have been not funeral monuments, but the ancient boundaries of the sanctuary or consecrated ground.

Martin was a man not illiterate: he was an inhabitant of *Sky*, and therefore was within reach of intelligence, and with no great difficulty might have visited the places which he undertakes to describe; yet with all his opportunities, he has often suffered himself to be deceived. He lived in the last century, when the chiefs of the clans had lost little of their original influence. The mountains were yet unpenetrated, no inlet was opened to foreign novelties, and the feudal institutions operated upon life with their full force. He might therefore have displayed a series of subordination and a form of government, which, in more luminous and improved regions, have been long forgotten, and have delighted his readers with many uncouth customs that are now disused, and wild opinions that prevail no longer. But he probably had not knowledge of the world sufficient to qualify him for judging what would deserve or gain the attention of mankind. The mode of life which was familiar to himself, he did not suppose unknown to others, nor imagined that he could give pleasure by telling that of which it was, in his little country, impossible to be ignorant.

What he has neglected cannot now be performed. In nations, where there is hardly the use of letters, what is once out of sight is lost for ever. They think but little, and of their few thoughts, none are wasted on the past, in which they are neither interested by fear nor hope. Their only registers are stated observances and practical representations. For this reason an age of ignorance is an age of ceremony. Pageants, and processions, and commemorations, gradually shrink away, as better methods come into use of recording events, and preserving rights.

It is not only in *Raasay* that the chapel is unroofed and useless; through the few islands which we visited, we neither saw nor heard of any house of prayer, except in *Sky*, that was not in ruins. The malignant influence of *Calvinism* has blasted ceremony and decency together; and if the remembrance of papal superstition is obliterated, the monuments of papal piety are likewise effaced.

It has been, for many years, popular to talk of the lazy devotion of the Romish clergy; over the sleepy laziness of men that erected churches, we may indulge our superiority with a new triumph, by comparing it with the fervid activity of those who suffer them to fall.

Of the destruction of churches, the decay of religion must in time be the consequence; for while the publick acts of the ministry are now performed in houses, a very small number can be present; and as the greater part of the Islanders make no use of books, all must necessarily live in total ignorance who want the opportunity of vocal instruction.

From these remains of ancient sanctity, which are every where to be found, it has been conjectured, that, for the last two centuries, the inhabitants of the Islands have decreased in number. This argument, which supposes that the churches have been suffered to fall, only because they were no longer necessary, would have some force, if the houses of worship still remaining were sufficient for the people. But since they have now no churches at all, these venerable fragments do not prove the people of former times to have been more numerous, but to have been more devout. If the inhabitants were doubled with their present principles, it appears not that any provision for publick worship would be made. Where the religion of a country enforces consecrated buildings, the number of those buildings may be supposed to afford some indication, however uncertain, of the populousness of the place; but where by a change of manners a nation is contented to live without them, their decay implies no diminution of inhabitants.

Some of these dilapidations are said to be found in islands now uninhabited; but I doubt whether we can thence infer that they were ever peopled. The religion of the middle age, is well known to have placed too much hope in lonely austerities. Voluntary solitude was the great act of propitiation, by which crimes were effaced, and conscience was appeased; it is therefore not unlikely, that oratories were often built in places where retirement was sure to have no disturbance.

Raasay has little that can detain a traveller, except the Laird and his family; but their power wants no auxiliaries. Such a seat of hospitality, amidst the winds and waters, fills the imagination with a delightful contrariety of images. Without is the rough ocean and the rocky land, the beating billows and the howling storm: within is plenty and elegance, beauty and gaiety, the song and the dance. In *Raasay*, if I could have found an Ulysses, I had fancied a *Phœacia*.

OSTIG IN SKY.

At *Ostig*, of which Mr. *Macpherson* is minister, we were entertained for some days, then removed to *Armidel*, where we finished our observations on the island of Sky.

As this Island lies in the fifty-seventh degree, the air cannot be supposed to have much warmth. The long continuance of the sun above the horizon, does indeed sometimes produce great heat in northern latitudes; but this can only happen in sheltered places, where the atmosphere is to a certain degree stagnant, and the same mass of air continues to receive for many hours the rays of the sun, and the vapours of the earth. *Sky* lies open on the west and north to a vast extent of ocean, and is cooled in the summer by perpetual ventilation, but by the same blasts is kept warm in winter. Their weather is not pleasing. Half the year is deluged with rain. From the autumnal to the vernal equinox, a dry day is hardly known, except when the showers are suspended by a tempest. Under such skies can be expected no great exuberance of vegetation. Their winter overtakes their summer, and their harvest lies upon the ground drenched with rain. The autumn struggles hard to produce some of our early fruits. I gathered gooseberries in September; but they were small, and the husk was thick.

Their winter is seldom such as puts a full stop to the growth of plants, or reduces the cattle to live wholly on the surplusage of the summer. In the year Seventy-one they had a severe season, remembered by the name of the Black Spring, from which the island has not yet recovered. The snow lay long upon the ground, a calamity hardly known before. Part of their cattle died for want, part were unseasonably sold to buy sustenance for the owners; and, what I have not read or heard of before, the kine that survived were so emaciated and dispirited, that they did not require the male at the usual time. Many of the roebucks perished.

The soil, as in other countries, has its diversities. In some parts there is only a thin layer of earth spread upon a rock, which bears nothing but short brown heath, and perhaps is not generally capable of any better product. There are many bogs or mosses of greater or less extent, where the soil cannot be supposed to want depth, though it is too wet for the plow. But we did not observe in these any aquatick plants. The vallies and the mountains are alike darkened with heath. Some grass, however, grows here and there, and some happier spots of earth are capable of tillage.

Their agriculture is laborious, and perhaps rather feeble than unskilful. Their chief manure is sea-weed, which, when they lay it to rot upon the field, gives them a better crop than those of the Highlands. They heap sea shells upon the dunghill, which in time moulder into a fertilising substance. When they find a vein of earth where they cannot use it, they dig it up, and add it to the mould of a more commodious place.

Their corn grounds often lie in such intricacies among the craggs, that there is no room for the action of a team and plow. The soil is then turned up by manual labour, with an instrument called a crooked spade, of a form and weight which to me appeared very incommodious, and would perhaps be soon improved in a country where workmen could be easily found and easily paid. It has a narrow blade of iron fixed to a long and heavy piece of wood, which must have, about a foot and a half above the iron, a knee or flexure with the angle downwards, when the farmer encounters a stone which is the great impediment of his operations, he drives the blade under it, and bringing the knee or angle to the ground, has in the long handle a very forcible lever.

According to the different mode of tillage, farms are distinguished into *long land* and *short land*. Long land is that which affords room for a plow, and short land is turned up by the spade.

The grain which they commit to the furrows thus tediously formed, is either oats or barley. They do not sow barley without very copious manure, and then they expect from it ten for one, an increase equal to that of better countries; but the culture is so operose that they content themselves commonly with oats; and who can relate without compassion, that after all their diligence they are to expect only a triple increase? It is in vain to hope for plenty, when a third part of the harvest must be reserved for seed.

When their grain is arrived at the state which they must consider as ripeness, they do not cut, but pull the barley: to the oats they apply the sickle. Wheel carriages they have none, but make a frame of timber, which is drawn by one horse with the two points behind pressing on the ground. On this they sometimes drag home their sheaves, but often convey them home in a kind of open panier, or frame of sticks upon the horse's back.

Of that which is obtained with so much difficulty, nothing surely ought to be wasted; yet their method of clearing their oats from the husk is by parching them in the straw. Thus with the genuine improvidence of savages, they destroy that fodder for want of which their cattle may perish. From this practice they have two petty conveniencies. They dry the grain so that it is easily reduced to meal, and they escape the theft of the thresher. The taste contracted from the fire by the oats, as by every other scorched substance, use must long ago have made grateful. The oats that are not parched must be dried in a kiln.

The barns of *Sky* I never saw. That which *Macleod* of *Raasay* had erected near his house was so contrived, because the harvest is seldom brought home dry, as by perpetual perflation to prevent the mow from heating.

Of their gardens I can judge only from their tables. I did not observe that the common greens were wanting, and suppose, that by choosing an advantageous exposition, they can raise all the more hardy esculent plants. Of vegetable fragrance or beauty they are not yet studious. Few vows are made to Flora in the *Hebrides*.

They gather a little hay, but the grass is mown late; and is so often almost dry and again very wet, before it is housed, that it becomes a collection of withered stalks without taste or fragrance; it must be eaten by cattle that have nothing else, but by most English farmers would be thrown away.

In the Islands I have not heard that any subterraneous treasures have been discovered, though where there are mountains, there are commonly minerals.

One of the rocks in *Col* has a black vein, imagined to consist of the ore of lead; but it was never yet opened or essayed. In *Sky* a black mass was accidentally picked up, and brought into the house of the owner of the land, who found himself strongly inclined to think it a coal, but unhappily it did not burn in the chimney. Common ores would be here of no great value; for what requires to be separated by fire, must, if it were found, be carried away in its mineral state, here being no fewel for the smelting-house or forge. Perhaps by diligent search in this world of stone, some valuable species of marble might be discovered. But neither philosophical curiosity, nor commercial industry, have yet fixed their abode here, where the importunity of immediate want supplied but for the day, and craving on the morrow, has left little room for excursive knowledge or the pleasing fancies of distant profit.

They have lately found a manufacture considerably lucrative. Their rocks abound with kelp, a sea-plant, of which the ashes are melted into glass. They burn kelp in great quantities, and then send it away in ships, which come regularly to purchase them. This new source of riches has raised the rents of many maritime farms; but the tenants pay, like all other tenants, the additional rent with great unwillingness; because they consider the profits of the kelp as the mere product of personal labour, to which the landlord contributes nothing. However, as any man may be said to give, what he gives the power of gaining, he has certainly as much right to profit from the price of kelp as of any thing else found or raised upon his ground.

This new trade has excited a long and eager litigation between *Macdonald* and *Macleod*, for a ledge of rocks, which, till the value of kelp was known, neither of them desired the reputation of possessing.

The cattle of *Sky* are not so small as is commonly believed. Since they have sent their beeves in great numbers to southern marts, they have probably taken more care of their breed. At stated times the annual growth of cattle is driven to a fair, by a general drover, and with the money, which he returns to the farmer, the rents are paid.

The price regularly expected, is from two to three pounds a head: there was once one sold for five pounds. They go from the Islands very lean, and are not offered to the butcher, till they have been long fatted in *English* pastures.

Of their black cattle, some are without horns, called by the Scots *humble* cows, as we call a bee an *humble* bee, that wants a sting. Whether this difference be specifick, or accidental, though we inquired with great diligence, we could not be informed. We are not very sure that the bull is ever without horns, though we have been told, that such bulls there are. What is produced by putting a horned and unhorned male and female together, no man has ever tried, that thought the result worthy of observation.

Their horses are, like their cows, of a moderate size. I had no difficulty to mount myself commodiously by the favour of the gentlemen. I heard of very little cows in *Barra*, and very little horses in *Rum*, where perhaps no care is taken to prevent that diminution of size, which must always happen, where the greater and the less copulate promiscuously, and the young animal is restrained from growth by penury of sustenance.

The goat is the general inhabitant of the earth, complying with every difference of climate, and of soil. The goats of the *Hebrides* are like others: nor did I hear any thing of their sheep, to be particularly remarked.

In the penury of these malignant regions nothing is left that can be converted to food. The goats and the sheep are milked like the cows. A single meal of a goat is a quart, and of a sheep a pint. Such at least was the account, which I could extract from those of whom I am not sure that they ever had inquired.

The milk of goats is much thinner than that of cows, and that of sheep is much thicker. Sheeps milk is never eaten before it is boiled: as it is thick, it must be very liberal of curd, and the people of St. *Kilda* form it into small cheeses.

The stags of the mountains are less than those of our parks, or forests, perhaps not bigger than our fallow deer. Their flesh has no rankness, nor is inferiour in flavour to our common venison. The roebuck I neither saw nor tasted. These are not countries for a regular chase. The deer are not driven with horns and hounds. A sportsman, with his gun in his hand, watches the animal, and when he has wounded him, traces him by the blood.

They have a race of brinded greyhounds, larger and stronger than those with which we course hares, and these are the only dogs used by them for the chase.

Man is by the use of firearms made so much an overmatch for other animals, that in all countries, where they are in use, the wild part of the creation sensibly diminishes. There will probably not be long, either stags or roebucks in the Islands. All the beasts of chase would have been lost long ago in countries well inhabited, had they not been preserved by laws for the pleasure of the rich.

There are in *Sky* neither rats nor mice, but the weasel is so frequent, that he is heard in houses rattling behind chests or beds, as rats in *England*. They probably owe to his predominance that they have no other vermin; for since the great rat took possession of this part of the world, scarce a ship can touch any port, but some of his race are left behind. They have within these few years begun to infest the isle of *Col*, where being left by some trading vessel, they have increased for want of weasels to oppose them.

The inhabitants of *Sky*, and of the other Islands, which I have seen, are commonly of the middle stature, with fewer among them very tall or very short, than are seen in *England*, or perhaps, as their numbers are small, the chances of any deviation from the common measure are necessarily few. The tallest men that I saw are among those of higher rank. In regions of barrenness and scarcity, the human race is hindered in its growth by the same causes as other animals.

The ladies have as much beauty here as in other places, but bloom and softness are not to be expected among the lower classes, whose faces are exposed to the rudeness of the climate, and whose features are sometimes contracted by want, and sometimes hardened by the blasts. Supreme beauty is seldom found in cottages or work-shops, even where no real hardships are suffered. To expand the human face to its full perfection, it seems necessary that the mind should cooperate by placidness of content, or consciousness of superiority.

Their strength is proportionate to their size, but they are accustomed to run upon rough ground, and therefore can with great agility skip over the bog, or clamber the mountain. For a campaign in the wastes of *America*, soldiers better qualified could not have been found. Having little work to do, they are not willing, nor perhaps able to endure a long continuance of manual labour, and are therefore considered as habitually idle.

Having never been supplied with those accommodations, which life extensively diversified with trades affords, they supply their wants by very insufficient shifts, and endure many inconveniences, which a little attention would easily relieve. I have seen a horse carrying home the harvest on a crate. Under his tail was a stick for a crupper, held at the two ends by twists of straw. Hemp will grow in their islands, and therefore ropes may be had. If they wanted hemp, they might make better cordage of rushes, or perhaps of nettles, than of straw.

Their method of life neither secures them perpetual health, nor exposes them to any particular diseases. There are physicians in the Islands, who, I believe, all practise chirurgery, and all compound their own medicines.

It is generally supposed, that life is longer in places where there are few opportunities of luxury; but I found no instance here of extraordinary longevity. A cottager grows old over his oaten cakes, like a citizen at a turtle feast. He is indeed seldom incommoded by corpulence. Poverty preserves him from sinking under the burden of himself, but he escapes no other injury of time. Instances of long life are often related, which those who hear them are more willing to credit than examine. To be told that any man has attained a hundred years, gives hope and comfort to him who stands trembling on the brink of his own climacterick.

Length of life is distributed impartially to very different modes of life in very different climates; and the mountains have no greater examples of age and health than the lowlands, where I was introduced to two ladies of high quality; one of whom, in her ninety-fourth year, presided at her table with the full exercise of all her powers; and the other has attained her eighty-fourth, without any diminution of her vivacity, and with little reason to accuse time of depredations of her beauty.

In the Islands, as in most other places, the inhabitants are of different rank, and one does not encroach here upon another. Where there is no commerce nor manufacture, he that is born poor can scarcely become rich; and if none are able to buy estates, he that is born to land cannot annihilate his family by selling it. This was once the state of these countries. Perhaps there is no example, till within a century and half, of any family whose estate was alienated otherwise than by violence or forfeiture. Since money has been brought amongst them, they have found, like others, the art of spending more than they receive; and I saw with grief the chief of a very ancient clan, whose Island was condemned by law to be sold for the satisfaction of his creditors.

The name of highest dignity is Laird, of which there are in the extensive Isle of Sky only three, *Macdonald, Macleod*, and *Mackinnon*. The Laird is the original owner of the land, whose natural power must be very great, where no man lives but by agriculture; and where the produce of the land is not conveyed through the labyrinths of traffick, but passes directly from the hand that gathers it to the mouth that eats it. The Laird has all those in his power that live upon his farms. Kings can, for the most part, only exalt or degrade. The Laird at pleasure can feed or starve, can give bread, or withold it. This inherent power was yet strengthened by the kindness of consanguinity, and the reverence of patriarchal authority. The Laird was the father of the Clan, and his tenants commonly bore his name. And to these principles of original command was added, for many ages, an exclusive right of legal jurisdiction.

This multifarious, and extensive obligation operated with force scarcely credible. Every duty, moral or political, was absorbed in affection and adherence to the Chief. Not many years have passed since the clans knew no law but the Laird's will. He told them to whom they should be friends or enemies, what King they should obey, and what religion they should profess.

When the Scots first rose in arms against the succession of the house of *Hanover, Lovat*, the Chief of the Frasers, was in exile for a rape. The Frasers were very numerous, and very zealous against the government. A pardon was sent to *Lovat*. He came to the *English* camp, and the clan immediately deserted to him.

Next in dignity to the Laird is the Tacksman; a large taker or lease-holder of land, of which he keeps part, as a domain, in his own hand, and lets part to under tenants. The Tacksman is necessarily a man capable of securing to the Laird the whole rent, and is commonly a collateral relation. These *tacks*, or subordinate possessions, were long considered as hereditary, and the occupant was distinguished by the name of the place at which he resided. He held a middle station, by which the highest and the lowest orders were connected. He paid rent and reverence to the Laird, and received them from the tenants. This tenure still subsists, with its original operation, but not with the primitive stability. Since the islanders, no longer content to live, have learned the desire of growing rich, an ancient dependent is in danger of giving way to a higher bidder, at the expence of domestick dignity and hereditary power. The stranger, whose money buys him preference, considers himself as paying for all that he has, and is indifferent about the Laird's honour or safety. The commodiousness of money is indeed great; but there are some advantages which money cannot buy, and which therefore no wise man will by the love of money be tempted to forego.

I have found in the hither parts of *Scotland*, men not defective in judgment or general experience, who consider the Tacksman as a useless burden of the ground, as a drone who lives upon the product of an estate, without the right of property, or the merit of labour, and who impoverishes at once the landlord and the tenant. The land, say they, is let to the Tacksman at sixpence an acre, and by him to the tenant at ten-pence. Let the owner be the immediate landlord to all the tenants; if he sets the ground at eight-pence, he will increase his revenue by a fourth part, and the tenant's burthen will be diminished by a fifth.

Those who pursue this train of reasoning, seem not sufficiently to inquire whither it will lead them, nor to know that it will equally shew the propriety of suppressing all wholesale trade, of shutting up the shops of every man who sells what he does not make, and of extruding all whose agency and profit intervene between the manufacturer and the consumer. They may, by stretching their understandings a little wider, comprehend, that all those who by undertaking large quantities of manufacture, and affording employment to many labourers, make themselves considered as benefactors to the publick, have only been robbing their workmen with one hand, and their customers with the other. If Crowley had sold only what he could make, and all his smiths had wrought their own iron with their own hammers, he would have lived on less, and they would have sold their work for more. The salaries of superintendents and clerks would have been partly saved, and partly shared, and nails been sometimes cheaper by a farthing in a hundred. But then if the smith could not have found an immediate purchaser, he must have deserted his anvil; if there had by accident at any time been more sellers than buyers, the workmen must have reduced their profit to nothing, by underselling one another; and as no great stock could have been in any hand, no sudden demand of large quantities could have been answered, and the builder must have stood still till the nailer could supply him.

According to these schemes, universal plenty is to begin and end in universal misery. Hope and emulation will be utterly extinguished; and as all must obey the call of immediate necessity, nothing that requires extensive views, or provides for distant consequences, will ever be performed.

To the southern inhabitants of Scotland, the state of the mountains and the islands is equally unknown with that of *Borneo* or *Sumatra*. Of both they have only heard a little, and guess the rest. They are strangers to the language and the manners, to the advantages and wants of the people, whose life they would model, and whose evils they would remedy.

Nothing is less difficult than to procure one convenience by the forfeiture of another. A soldier may expedite his march by throwing away his arms. To banish the Tacksman is easy, to make a country plentiful by diminishing the people, is an expeditious mode of husbandry; but that abundance, which there is nobody to enjoy, contributes little to human happiness.

As the mind must govern the hands, so in every society the man of intelligence must direct the man of labour. If the Tacksmen be taken away, the Hebrides must in their present state be given up to grossness and ignorance; the tenant, for want of instruction, will be unskilful, and for want of admonition will be negligent. The Laird in these wide estates, which often consist of islands remote from one another, cannot extent his personal influence to all his tenants; and the steward having no dignity annexed to his character, can have little authority among men taught to pay reverence only to birth, and who regard the Tacksman as their hereditary superior; nor can the steward have equal zeal for the prosperity of an estate profitable only to the Laird, with the Tacksman, who has the Laird's income involved in his own.

The only gentlemen in the Islands are the Lairds, the Tacksmen, and the Ministers, who frequently improve their livings by becoming farmers. If the Tacksmen be banished, who will be left to impart knowledge, or impress civility? The Laird must always be at a distance from the greater part of his lands; and if he resides at all upon them, must drag his days in solitude, having no longer either a friend or a companion; he will therefore depart to some more comfortable residence, and leave the tenants to the wisdom and mercy of a factor.

Of tenants there are different orders, as they have greater or less stock. Land is sometimes leased to a small fellowship, who live in a cluster of huts, called a Tenants Town, and are bound jointly and separately for the payment of their rent. These, I believe, employ in the care of their cattle, and the labour of tillage, a kind of tenants yet lower; who having a hut, with grass for a certain number of cows and sheep, pay their rent by a stipulated quantity of labour.

The condition of domestick servants, or the price of occasional labour, I do not know with certainty. I was told that the maids have sheep, and are allowed to spin for their own clothing; perhaps they have no pecuniary wages, or none but in very wealthy families. The state of life, which has hitherto been purely pastoral, begins now to be a little variegated with commerce; but novelties enter by degrees, and till one mode has fully prevailed over the other, no settled notion can be formed.

Such is the system of insular subordination, which, having little variety, cannot afford much delight in the view, nor long detain the mind in contemplation. The inhabitants were for a long time perhaps not unhappy; but their content was a muddy mixture of pride and ignorance, an indifference for pleasures which they did not know, a blind veneration for their chiefs, and a strong conviction of their own importance.

Their pride has been crushed by the heavy hand of a vindictive conqueror, whose severities have been followed by laws, which, though they cannot be called cruel, have produced much discontent, because they operate upon the surface of life, and make every eye bear witness to subjection. To be compelled to a new dress has always been found painful.

Their Chiefs being now deprived of their jurisdiction, have already lost much of their influence; and as they gradually degenerate from patriarchal rulers to rapacious landlords, they will divest themselves of the little that remains.

That dignity which they derived from an opinion of their military importance, the law, which disarmed them, has abated. An old gentleman, delighting himself with the recollection of better days, related, that forty years ago, a Chieftain walked out attended by ten or twelve followers, with their arms rattling. That animating rattle has now ceased. The Chief has lost his formidable retinue; and the Highlander walks his heath unarmed and defenceless, with the peaceable submission of a French peasant or English cottager.

Their ignorance grows every day less, but their knowledge is yet of little other use than to shew them their wants. They are now in the period of education, and feel the uneasiness of discipline, without yet perceiving the benefit of instruction.

The last law, by which the Highlanders are deprived of their arms, has operated with efficacy beyond expectation. Of former statutes made with the same design, the execution had been feeble, and the effect inconsiderable. Concealment was undoubtedly practised, and perhaps often with connivance. There was tenderness, or partiality, on one side, and obstinacy on the other. But the law, which followed the victory of Culloden, found the whole nation dejected and intimidated; informations were given without danger, and without fear, and the arms were collected with such rigour, that every house was despoiled of its defence.

To disarm part of the Highlands, could give no reasonable occasion of complaint. Every government must be allowed the power of taking away the weapon that is lifted against it. But the loyal clans murmured, with some appearance of justice, that after having defended the King, they were forbidden for the future to defend themselves; and that the sword should be forfeited, which had been legally employed. Their case is undoubtedly hard, but in political regulations, good cannot be complete, it can only be predominant.

Whether by disarming a people thus broken into several tribes, and thus remote from the seat of power, more good than evil has been produced, may deserve inquiry. The supreme power in every community has the right of debarring every individual, and every subordinate society from self-defence, only because the supreme power is able to defend them; and therefore where the governor cannot act, he must trust the subject to act for himself. These Islands might be wasted with fire and sword before their sovereign would know their distress. A gang of robbers, such as has been lately found confederating themselves in the Highlands, might lay a wide region under contribution. The crew of a petty privateer might land on the largest and most wealthy of the Islands, and riot without control in cruelty and waste. It was observed by one of the Chiefs of Sky, that fifty armed men might, without resistance, ravage the country. Laws that place the subjects in such a state, contravene the first principles of the compact of authority: they exact obedience, and yield no protection.

It affords a generous and manly pleasure to conceive a little nation gathering its fruits and tending its herds with fearless confidence, though it lies open on every side to invasion, where, in contempt of walls and trenches, every man sleeps securely with his sword beside him; where all on the first approach of hostility come together at the call to battle, as at a summons to a festal show; and committing their cattle to the care of those whom age or nature has disabled, engage the enemy with that competition for hazard and for glory, which operates in men that fight under the eye of those, whose dislike or kindness they have always considered as the greatest evil or the greatest good.

This was, in the beginning of the present century, the state of the Highlands. Every man was a soldier, who partook of national confidence, and interested himself in national honour. To lose this spirit, is to lose what no small advantage will compensate.

It may likewise deserve to be inquired, whether a great nation ought to be totally commercial? whether amidst the uncertainty of human affairs, too much attention to one mode of happiness may not endanger others? whether the pride of riches must not sometimes have recourse to the protection of courage? and whether, if it be necessary to preserve in some part of the empire the military spirit, it can subsist more commodiously in any place, than in remote and unprofitable provinces, where it can commonly do little harm, and whence it may be called forth at any sudden exigence?

It must however be confessed, that a man, who places honour only in successful violence, is a very troublesome and pernicious animal in time of peace; and that the martial character cannot prevail in a whole people, but by the diminution of all other virtues. He that is accustomed to resolve all right into conquest, will have very little tenderness or equity. All the friendship in such a life can be only a confederacy of invasion, or alliance of defence. The strong must flourish by force, and the weak subsist by stratagem.

Till the Highlanders lost their ferocity, with their arms, they suffered from each other all that malignity could dictate, or precipitance could act. Every provocation was revenged with blood, and no man that ventured into a numerous company, by whatever occasion brought together, was sure of returning without a wound. If they are now exposed to foreign hostilities, they may talk of the danger, but can seldom feel it. If they are no longer martial, they are no longer quarrelsome. Misery is caused for the most part, not by a heavy crush of disaster, but by the corrosion of less visible evils, which canker enjoyment, and undermine security. The visit of an invader is necessarily rare, but domestick animosities allow no cessation.

The abolition of the local jurisdictions, which had for so many ages been exercised by the chiefs, has likewise its evil and its good. The feudal constitution naturally diffused itself into long ramifications of subordinate authority. To this general temper of the government was added the peculiar form of the country, broken by mountains into many subdivisions scarcely accessible but to the natives, and guarded by passes, or perplexed with intricacies, through which national justice could not find its way.

The power of deciding controversies, and of punishing offences, as some such power there must always be, was intrusted to the Lairds of the country, to those whom the people considered as their natural judges. It cannot be supposed that a rugged proprietor of the rocks, unprincipled and unenlightened, was a nice resolver of entangled claims, or very exact in proportioning punishment to offences. But the more he indulged his own will, the more he held his vassals in dependance. Prudence and innocence, without the favour of the Chief, conferred no security; and crimes involved no danger, when the judge was resolute to acquit.

When the chiefs were men of knowledge and virtue, the convenience of a domestick judicature was great. No long journies were necessary, nor artificial delays could be practised; the character, the alliances, and interests of the litigants were known to the court, and all false pretences were easily detected. The sentence, when it was past, could not be evaded; the power of the Laird superseded formalities, and justice could not be defeated by interest or stratagem.

I doubt not but that since the regular judges have made their circuits through the whole country, right has been every where more wisely, and more equally distributed; the complaint is, that litigation is grown troublesome, and that the magistrates are too few, and therefore often too remote for general convenience.

Many of the smaller Islands have no legal officer within them. I once asked, If a crime should be committed, by what authority the offender could be seized? and was told, that the Laird would exert his right; a right which he must now usurp, but which surely necessity must vindicate, and which is therefore yet exercised in lower degrees, by some of the proprietors, when legal processes cannot be obtained.

In all greater questions, however, there is now happily an end to all fear or hope from malice or from favour. The roads are secure in those places through which, forty years ago, no traveller could pass without a convoy. All trials of right by the sword are forgotten, and the mean are in as little danger from the powerful as in other places. No scheme of policy has, in any country, yet brought the rich and poor on equal terms into courts of judicature. Perhaps experience, improving on experience, may in time effect it.

Those who have long enjoyed dignity and power, ought not to lose it without some equivalent. There was paid to the Chiefs by the publick, in exchange for their privileges, perhaps a sum greater than most of them had ever possessed, which excited a thirst for riches, of which it shewed them the use. When the power of birth and station ceases, no hope remains but from the prevalence of money. Power and wealth supply the place of each other. Power confers the ability of gratifying our desire without the consent of others. Wealth enables us to obtain the consent of others to our gratification. Power, simply considered, whatever it confers on one, must take from another. Wealth enables its owner to give to others by taking only from himself. Power pleases the violent and proud: wealth delights the placid and the timorous. Youth therefore flies at power, and age grovels after riches.

The Chiefs, divested of their prerogatives, necessarily turned their thoughts to the improvement of their revenues, and expect more rent, as they have less homage. The tenant, who is far from perceiving that his condition is made better in the same proportion, as that of his landlord is made worse, does not immediately see why his industry is to be taxed more heavily than before. He refuses to pay the demand, and is ejected; the ground is then let to a stranger, who perhaps brings a larger stock, but who, taking the land at its full price, treats with the Laird upon equal terms, and considers him not as a Chief, but as a trafficker in land. Thus the estate perhaps is improved, but the clan is broken.

It seems to be the general opinion, that the rents have been raised with too much eagerness. Some regard must be paid to prejudice. Those who have hitherto paid but little, will not suddenly be persuaded to pay much, though they can afford it. As ground is gradually improved, and the value of money decreases, the rent may be raised without any diminution of the farmer's profits: yet it is necessary in these countries, where the ejection of a tenant is a greater evil, than in more populous places, to consider not merely what the land will produce, but with what ability the inhabitant can cultivate it. A certain stock can allow but a certain payment; for if the land be doubled, and the stock remains the same, the tenant becomes no richer. The proprietors of the Highlands might perhaps often increase their income, by subdividing the farms, and allotting to every occupier only so many acres as he can profitably employ, but that they want people.

There seems now, whatever be the cause, to be through a great part of the Highlands a general discontent. That adherence, which was lately professed by every man to the chief of his name, has now little prevalence; and he that cannot live as he desires at home, listens to the tale of fortunate islands, and happy regions, where every man may have land of his own, and eat the product of his labour without a superior.

Those who have obtained grants of American lands, have, as is well known, invited settlers from all quarters of the globe; and among other places, where oppression might produce a wish for new habitations, their emissaries would not fail to try their persuasions in the Isles of Scotland, where at the time when the clans were newly disunited from their Chiefs, and exasperated by unprecedented exactions, it is no wonder that they prevailed.

Whether the mischiefs of emigration were immediately perceived, may be justly questioned. They who went first, were probably such as could best be spared; but the accounts sent by the earliest adventurers, whether true or false, inclined many to follow them; and whole neighbourhoods formed parties for removal; so that departure from their native country is no longer exile. He that goes thus accompanied, carries with him all that makes life pleasant. He sits down in a better climate, surrounded by his kindred and his friends: they carry with them their language, their opinions, their popular songs, and hereditary merriment: they change nothing but the place of their abode; and of that change they perceive the benefit.

This is the real effect of emigration, if those that go away together settle on the same spot, and preserve their ancient union. But some relate that these adventurous visitants of unknown regions, after a voyage passed in dreams of plenty and felicity, are dispersed at last upon a Sylvan wilderness, where their first years must be spent in toil, to clear the ground which is afterwards to be tilled, and that the whole effect of their undertaking is only more fatigue and equal scarcity.

Both accounts may be suspected. Those who are gone will endeavour by every art to draw others after them; for as their numbers are greater, they will provide better for themselves. When *Nova Scotia* was first peopled, I remember a letter, published under the character of a New Planter, who related how much the climate put him in mind of Italy. Such intelligence the *Hebridians* probably receive from their transmarine correspondents. But with equal temptations of interest, and perhaps with no greater niceness of veracity, the owners of the Islands spread stories of American hardships to keep their people content at home.

Some method to stop this epidemick desire of wandering, which spreads its contagion from valley to valley, deserves to be sought with great diligence. In more fruitful countries, the removal of one only makes room for the succession of another: but in the *Hebrides*, the loss of an inhabitant leaves a lasting vacuity; for nobody born in any other parts of the world will choose this country for his residence; and an Island once depopulated will remain a desert, as long as the present facility of travel gives every one, who is discontented and unsettled, the choice of his abode.

Let it be inquired, whether the first intention of those who are fluttering on the wing, and collecting a flock that they may take their flight, be to attain good, or to avoid evil. If they are dissatisfied with that part of the globe, which their birth has allotted them, and resolve not to live without the pleasures of happier climates; if they long for bright suns, and calm skies, and flowery fields, and fragrant gardens, I know not by what eloquence they can be persuaded, or by what offers they can be hired to stay.

But if they are driven from their native country by positive evils, and disgusted by ill-treatment, real or imaginary, it were fit to remove their grievances, and quiet their resentment; since, if they have been hitherto undutiful subjects, they will not much mend their principles by American conversation.

To allure them into the army, it was thought proper to indulge them in the continuance of their national dress. If this concession could have any effect, it might easily be made. That dissimilitude of appearance, which was supposed to keep them distinct from the rest of the nation, might disincline them from coalescing with the *Pensylvanians*, or people of *Connecticut*. If the restitution of their arms will reconcile them to their country, let them have again those weapons, which will not be more mischievous at home than in the Colonies. That they may not fly from the increase of rent, I know not whether the general good does not require that the landlords be, for a time, restrained in their demands, and kept quiet by pensions proportionate to their loss.

To hinder insurrection, by driving away the people, and to govern peaceably, by having no subjects, is an expedient that argues no great profundity of politicks. To soften the obdurate, to convince the mistaken, to mollify the resentful, are worthy of a statesman; but it affords a legislator little self-applause to consider, that where there was formerly an insurrection, there is now a wilderness.

It has been a question often agitated without solution, why those northern regions are now so thinly peopled, which formerly overwhelmed with their armies the Roman empire. The question supposes what I believe is not true, that they had once more inhabitants than they could maintain, and overflowed only because they were full.

This is to estimate the manners of all countries and ages by our own. Migration, while the state of life was unsettled, and there was little communication of intelligence between distant places, was among the wilder nations of Europe, capricious and casual. An adventurous projector heard of a fertile coast unoccupied, and led out a colony; a chief of renown for bravery, called the young men together, and led them out to try what fortune would present. When Cæsar was in *Gaul*, he found the Helvetians preparing to go they knew not whither, and put a stop to their motions. They settled again in their own country, where they were so far from wanting room, that they had accumulated three years provision for their march.

The religion of the North was military; if they could not find enemies, it was their duty to make them: they travelled in quest of danger, and willingly took the chance of Empire or Death. If their troops were numerous, the countries from which they were collected are of vast extent, and without much exuberance of people great armies may be raised where every man is a soldier. But their true numbers were never known. Those who were conquered by them are their historians, and shame may have excited them to say, that they were overwhelmed with multitudes. To count is a modern practice, the ancient method was to guess; and when numbers are guessed they are always magnified.

Thus England has for several years been filled with the atchievements of seventy thousand Highlanders employed in *America*. I have heard from an English officer, not much inclined to favour them, that their behaviour deserved a very high degree of military praise; but their number has been much exaggerated. One of the ministers told me, that seventy thousand men could not have been found in all the Highlands, and that more than twelve thousand never took the field. Those that went to the American war, went to destruction. Of the old Highland regiment, consisting of twelve hundred, only seventy-six survived to see their country again.

The Gothick swarms have at least been multiplied with equal liberality. That they bore no great proportion to the inhabitants, in whose countries they settled, is plain from the paucity of northern words now found in the provincial languages. Their country was not deserted for want of room, because it was covered with forests of vast extent; and the first effect of plenitude of inhabitants is the destruction of wood. As the Europeans spread over *America*, the lands are gradually laid naked.

I would not be understood to say, that necessity had never any part in their expeditions. A nation, whose agriculture is scanty or unskilful, may be driven out by famine. A nation of hunters may have exhausted their game. I only affirm that the northern regions were not, when their irruptions subdued the Romans, overpeopled with regard to their real extent of territory, and power of fertility. In a country fully inhabited, however afterward laid waste, evident marks will remain of its former populousness. But of *Scandinavia* and *Germany*, nothing is known but that as we trace their state upwards into antiquity, their woods were greater, and their cultivated ground was less.

That causes very different from want of room may produce a general disposition to seek another country is apparent from the present conduct of the Highlanders, who are in some places ready to threaten a total secession. The numbers which have already gone, though like other numbers they may be magnified, are very great, and such as if they had gone together and agreed upon any certain settlement, might have founded an independent government in the depths of the western continent. Nor are they only the lowest and most indigent; many men of considerable wealth have taken with them their train of labourers and dependants; and if they continue the feudal scheme of polity, may establish new clans in the other hemisphere.

That the immediate motives of their desertion must be imputed to their landlords, may be reasonably concluded, because some Lairds of more prudence and less rapacity have kept their vassals undiminished. From *Raasa* only one man had been seduced, and at *Col* there was no wish to go away.

The traveller who comes hither from more opulent countries, to speculate upon the remains of pastoral life, will not much wonder that a common

Highlander has no strong adherence to his native soil; for of animal enjoyments, or of physical good, he leaves nothing that he may not find again wheresoever he may be thrown.

The habitations of men in the *Hebrides* may be distinguished into huts and houses. By a *house*, I mean a building with one story over another; by a *hut*, a dwelling with only one floor. The Laird, who formerly lived in a castle, now lives in a house; sometimes sufficiently neat, but seldom very spacious or splendid. The Tacksmen and the Ministers have commonly houses. Wherever there is a house, the stranger finds a welcome, and to the other evils of exterminating Tacksmen may be added the unavoidable cessation of hospitality, or the devolution of too heavy a burden on the Ministers.

Of the houses little can be said. They are small, and by the necessity of accumulating stores, where there are so few opportunities of purchase, the rooms are very heterogeneously filled. With want of cleanliness it were ingratitude to reproach them. The servants having been bred upon the naked earth, think every floor clean, and the quick succession of guests, perhaps not always over-elegant, does not allow much time for adjusting their apartments.

Huts are of many gradations; from murky dens, to commodious dwellings.

The wall of a common hut is always built without mortar, by a skilful adaptation of loose stones. Sometimes perhaps a double wall of stones is raised, and the intermediate space filled with earth. The air is thus completely excluded. Some walls are, I think, formed of turfs, held together by a wattle, or texture of twigs. Of the meanest huts, the first room is lighted by the entrance, and the second by the smoke-hole. The fire is usually made in the middle. But there are huts, or dwellings, of only one story, inhabited by gentlemen, which have walls cemented with mortar, glass windows, and boarded floors. Of these all have chimneys, and some chimneys have grates.

The house and the furniture are not always nicely suited. We were driven once, by missing a passage, to the hut of a gentleman, where, after a very liberal supper, when I was conducted to my chamber, I found an elegant bed of Indian cotton, spread with fine sheets. The accommodation was flattering; I undressed myself, and felt my feet in the mire. The bed stood upon the bare earth, which a long course of rain had softened to a puddle.

In pastoral countries the condition of the lowest rank of people is sufficiently wretched. Among manufacturers, men that have no property may have art and industry, which make them necessary, and therefore valuable. But where flocks and corn are the only wealth, there are always more hands than work, and of that work there is little in which skill and dexterity can be much distinguished. He therefore who is born poor never can be rich. The son merely occupies the place of the father, and life knows nothing of progression or advancement.

The petty tenants, and labouring peasants, live in miserable cabins, which afford them little more than shelter from the storms. The Boor of *Norway* is said to make all his own utensils. In the *Hebrides*, whatever might be their ingenuity, the want of wood leaves them no materials. They are probably content with such accommodations as stones of different forms and sizes can afford them.

Their food is not better than their lodging. They seldom taste the flesh of land animals; for here are no markets. What each man eats is from his own stock. The great effect of money is to break property into small parts. In towns, he that has a shilling may have a piece of meat; but where there is no commerce, no man can eat mutton but by killing a sheep.

Fish in fair weather they need not want; but, I believe, man never lives long on fish, but by constraint; he will rather feed upon roots and berries.

The only fewel of the Islands is peat. Their wood is all consumed, and coal they have not yet found. Peat is dug out of the marshes, from the depth of one foot to that of six. That is accounted the best which is nearest the surface. It appears to be a mass of black earth held together by vegetable fibres. I know not whether the earth be bituminous, or whether the fibres be not the only combustible part; which, by heating the interposed earth red hot, make a burning mass. The heat is not very strong nor lasting. The ashes are yellowish, and in a large quantity. When they dig peat, they cut it into square pieces, and pile it up to dry beside the house. In some places it has an offensive smell. It is like wood charked for the smith. The common method of making peat fires, is by heaping it on the hearth; but it burns well in grates, and in the best houses is so used.

The common opinion is, that peat grows again where it has been cut; which, as it seems to be chiefly a vegetable substance, is not unlikely to be true, whether known or not to those who relate it.

There are water mills in *Sky* and *Raasa*; but where they are too far distant, the housewives grind their oats with a quern, or handmill, which consists of two stones, about a foot and a half in diameter, the lower is a little convex, to which the concavity of the upper must be fitted. In the middle of the upper stone is a round hole, and on one side is a long handle. The grinder sheds the corn gradually into the hole with one hand, and works the handle round with the other. The corn slides down the convexity of the lower stone, and by the motion of the upper is ground in its passage. These stones are found in *Lochaber*.

The Islands afford few pleasures, except to the hardy sportsman, who can tread the moor and climb the mountain. The distance of one family from another, in a country where travelling has so much difficulty, makes frequent intercourse impracticable. Visits last several days, and are commonly paid by water; yet I never saw a boat furnished with benches, or made commodious by any addition to the first fabrick. Conveniencies are not missed where they never were enjoyed.

The solace which the bagpipe can give, they have long enjoyed; but among other changes, which the last Revolution introduced, the use of the bagpipe begins to be forgotten. Some of the chief families still entertain a piper, whose office was anciently hereditary. *Macrimmon* was piper to *Macleod*, and *Rankin* to *Maclean* of *Col*.

The tunes of the bagpipe are traditional. There has been in *Sky*, beyond all time of memory, a college of pipers, under the direction of *Macrimmon*, which is not quite extinct. There was another in *Mull*, superintended by *Rankin*, which expired about sixteen years ago. To these colleges, while the pipe retained its honour, the students of musick repaired for education. I have had my dinner exhilarated by the bagpipe, at *Armidale*, at *Dunvegan*, and in *Col*.

The general conversation of the Islanders has nothing particular. I did not meet with the inquisitiveness of which I have read, and suspect the judgment to have been rashly made. A stranger of curiosity comes into a place where a stranger is seldom seen: he importunes the people with questions, of which they cannot guess the motive, and gazes with surprise on things which they, having had them always before their eyes, do not suspect of any thing wonderful. He appears to them like some being of another world, and then thinks it peculiar that they take their turn to inquire whence he comes, and whither he is going.

The Islands were long unfurnished with instruction for youth, and none but the sons of gentlemen could have any literature. There are now parochial schools, to which the lord of every manor pays a certain stipend. Here the children are taught to read; but by the rule of their institution, they teach only *English*, so that the natives read a language which they may never use or understand. If a parish, which often happens, contains several Islands, the school being but in one, cannot assist the rest. This is the state of *Col*, which, however, is more enlightened than some other places; for the deficiency is supplied by a young gentleman, who, for his own improvement, travels every year on foot over the Highlands to the session at Aberdeen; and at his return, during the vacation, teaches to read and write in his native Island.

In *Sky* there are two grammar schools, where boarders are taken to be regularly educated. The price of board is from three pounds, to four pounds ten shillings a year, and that of instruction is half a crown a quarter. But the scholars are birds of passage, who live at school only in the summer; for in winter provisions cannot be made for any considerable number in one place. This periodical dispersion impresses strongly the scarcity of these countries.

Having heard of no boarding-school for ladies nearer than *Inverness*, I suppose their education is generally domestick. The elder daughters of the higher families are sent into the world, and may contribute by their acquisitions to the improvement of the rest.

Women must here study to be either pleasing or useful. Their deficiencies are seldom supplied by very liberal fortunes. A hundred pounds is a portion beyond the hope of any but the Laird's daughter. They do not indeed often give money with their daughters; the question is, How many cows a young lady will bring her husband. A rich maiden has from ten to forty; but two cows are a decent fortune for one who pretends to no distinction.

The religion of the Islands is that of the Kirk of *Scotland*. The gentlemen with whom I conversed are all inclined to the *English* liturgy; but they are obliged to maintain the established Minister, and the country is too poor to afford payment to another, who must live wholly on the contribution of his audience.

They therefore all attend the worship of the Kirk, as often as a visit from their Minister, or the practicability of travelling gives them opportunity; nor have they any reason to complain of insufficient pastors; for I saw not one in the Islands, whom I had reason to think either deficient in learning, or irregular in life; but found several with whom I could not converse without wishing, as my respect increased, that they had not been Presbyterians.

The ancient rigour of puritanism is now very much relaxed, though all are not yet equally enlightened. I sometimes met with prejudices sufficiently malignant, but they were prejudices of ignorance. The Ministers in the Islands had attained such knowledge as may justly be admired in men, who have no motive to study, but generous curiosity, or, what is still better, desire of usefulness; with such politeness as so narrow a circle of converse could not have supplied, but to minds naturally disposed to elegance.

Reason and truth will prevail at last. The most learned of the Scottish Doctors would now gladly admit a form of prayer, if the people would endure it. The zeal or rage of congregations has its different degrees. In some parishes the Lord's Prayer is suffered: in others it is still rejected as a form; and he that should make it part of his supplication would be suspected of heretical pravity.

The principle upon which extemporary prayer was originally introduced, is no longer admitted. The Minister formerly, in the effusion of his prayer, expected immediate, and perhaps perceptible inspiration, and therefore thought it his duty not to think before what he should say. It is now universally confessed, that men pray as they speak on other occasions, according to the general measure of their abilities and attainments. Whatever each may think of a form prescribed by another, he cannot but believe that he can himself compose by study and meditation a better prayer than will rise in his mind at a sudden call; and if he has any hope of supernatural help, why may he not as well receive it when he writes as when he speaks.

In the variety of mental powers, some must perform extemporary prayer with much imperfection; and in the eagerness and rashness of contradictory opinions, if publick liturgy be left to the private judgment of every Minister, the congregation may often be offended or misled.

There is in Scotland, as among ourselves, a restless suspicion of popish machinations, and a clamour of numerous converts to the Romish religion. The report is, I believe, in both parts of the Island equally false. The Romish religion is professed only in *Egg* and *Canna*, two small islands, into which the Reformation never made its way. If any missionaries are busy in the Highlands, their zeal entitles them to respect, even from those who cannot think favourably of their doctrine.

The political tenets of the Islanders I was not curious to investigate, and they were not eager to obtrude. Their conversation is decent and inoffensive. They disdain to drink for their principles, and there is no disaffection at their tables. I never heard a health offered by a Highlander that might not have circulated with propriety within the precincts of the King's palace.

Legal government has yet something of novelty to which they cannot perfectly conform. The ancient spirit, that appealed only to the sword, is yet among them. The tenant of *Scalpa*, an island belonging to Macdonald, took no care to bring his rent; when the landlord talked of exacting payment, he declared his resolution to keep his ground, and drive all intruders from the Island, and continued to feed his cattle as on his own land, till it became necessary for the Sheriff to dislodge him by violence.

The various kinds of superstition which prevailed here, as in all other regions of ignorance, are by the diligence of the Ministers almost extirpated.

Of *Browny*, mentioned by Martin, nothing has been heard for many years. *Browny* was a sturdy Fairy; who, if he was fed, and kindly treated, would, as they said, do a great deal of work. They now pay him no wages, and are content to labour for themselves.

In *Troda*, within these three-and-thirty years, milk was put every Saturday for *Greogach*, or *the Old Man with the Long Beard*. Whether *Greogach* was courted as kind, or dreaded as terrible, whether they meant, by giving him the milk, to obtain good, or avert evil, I was not informed. The Minister is now living by whom the practice was abolished.

They have still among them a great number of charms for the cure of different diseases; they are all invocations, perhaps transmitted to them from the times of popery, which increasing knowledge will bring into disuse.

They have opinions, which cannot be ranked with superstition because they regard only natural effects. They expect better crops of grain, by sowing their seed in the moon's increase. The moon has great influence in vulgar philosophy. In my memory it was a precept annually given in one of the *English* Almanacks, *to kill hogs when the moon was increasing, and the bacon would prove the better in boiling*.

We should have had little claim to the praise of curiosity, if we had not endeavoured with particular attention to examine the question of the *Second Sight*. Of an opinion received for centuries by a whole nation, and supposed to be confirmed through its whole descent, by a series of successive facts, it is desirable that the truth should be established, or the fallacy detected.

The *Second Sight* is an impression made either by the mind upon the eye, or by the eye upon the mind, by which things distant or future are perceived, and seen as if they were present. A man on a journey far from home falls from his horse, another, who is perhaps at work about the house, sees him bleeding on the ground, commonly with a landscape of the place where the accident befalls him. Another seer, driving home his cattle, or wandering in idleness, or musing in the sunshine, is suddenly surprised by the appearance of a bridal ceremony, or funeral procession, and counts the mourners or attendants, of whom, if he knows them, he relates the names, if he knows them not, he can describe the dresses. Things distant are seen at the instant when they happen. Of things future I know not that there is any rule for determining the time between the Sight and the event.

This receptive faculty, for power it cannot be called, is neither voluntary nor constant. The appearances have no dependence upon choice: they cannot be summoned, detained, or recalled. The impression is sudden, and the effect often painful.

By the term *Second Sight*, seems to be meant a mode of seeing, superadded to that which Nature generally bestows. In the *Earse* it is called *Taisch*; which signifies likewise a spectre, or a vision. I know not, nor is it likely that the Highlanders ever examined, whether by *Taisch*, used for *Second Sight*, they mean the power of seeing, or the thing seen.

I do not find it to be true, as it is reported, that to the *Second Sight* nothing is presented but phantoms of evil. Good seems to have the same proportion in those visionary scenes, as it obtains in real life: almost all remarkable events have evil for their basis; and are either miseries incurred, or miseries escaped. Our sense is so much stronger of what we suffer, than of what we enjoy, that the ideas of pain predominate in almost every mind. What is recollection but a revival of vexations, or history but a record of wars, treasons, and calamities? Death, which is considered as the greatest evil, happens to all. The greatest good, be it what it will, is the lot but of a part.

That they should often see death is to be expected; because death is an event frequent and important. But they see likewise more pleasing incidents. A gentleman told me, that when he had once gone far from his own Island, one of his labouring servants predicted his return, and described the livery of his attendant, which he had never worn at home; and which had been, without any previous design, occasionally given him.

Our desire of information was keen, and our inquiry frequent. Mr. Boswell's frankness and gaiety made every body communicative; and we heard many tales of these airy shows, with more or less evidence and distinctness.

It is the common talk of the Lowland *Scots*, that the notion of the *Second Sight* is wearing away with other superstitions; and that its reality is no longer supposed, but by the grossest people. How far its prevalence ever extended, or what ground it has lost, I know not. The Islanders of all degrees, whether of rank or understanding, universally admit it, except the Ministers, who universally deny it, and are suspected to deny it, in consequence of a system, against conviction. One of them honestly told me, that he came to *Sky* with a resolution not to believe it.

Strong reasons for incredulity will readily occur. This faculty of seeing things out of sight is local, and commonly useless. It is a breach of the common order of things, without any visible reason or perceptible benefit. It is ascribed only to people very little enlightened; and among them, for the most part, to the mean and the ignorant.

To the confidence of these objections it may be replied, that by presuming to determine what is fit, and what is beneficial, they presuppose more knowledge of the universal system than man has attained; and therefore depend upon principles too complicated and extensive for our comprehension; and there can be no security in the consequence, when the premises are not understood; that the *Second Sight* is only wonderful because it is rare, for, considered in itself, it involves no more difficulty than dreams, or perhaps than the regular exercise of the cogitative faculty; that a general opinion of communicative impulses, or visionary representations, has prevailed in all ages and all nations; that particular instances have been given, with such evidence, as neither *Bacon* nor *Boyle* has been able to resist; that sudden impressions, which the event has verified, have been felt by more than own or publish them; that the *Second Sight* of the *Hebrides* implies only the local frequency of a power, which is nowhere totally unknown; and that where we are unable to decide by antecedent reason, we must be content to yield to the force of testimony.

By pretension to *Second Sight*, no profit was ever sought or gained. It is an involuntary affection, in which neither hope nor fear are known to have any part. Those who profess to feel it, do not boast of it as a privilege, nor are considered by others as advantageously distinguished. They have no temptation to feign; and their hearers have no motive to encourage the imposture.

To talk with any of these seers is not easy. There is one living in *Sky*, with whom we would have gladly conversed; but he was very gross and ignorant, and knew no *English*. The proportion in these countries of the poor to the rich is such, that if we suppose the quality to be accidental, it can very rarely happen to a man of education; and yet on such men it has sometimes fallen. There is now a Second Sighted gentleman in the Highlands, who complains of the terrors to which he is exposed.

The foresight of the Seers is not always prescience: they are impressed with images, of which the event only shews them the meaning. They tell what they have seen to others, who are at that time not more knowing than themselves, but may become at last very adequate witnesses, by comparing the narrative with its verification.

To collect sufficient testimonies for the satisfaction of the publick, or of ourselves, would have required more time than we could bestow. There is, against it, the seeming analogy of things confusedly seen, and little understood; and for it, the indistinct cry of national persuasion, which may be perhaps resolved at last into prejudice and tradition. I never could advance my curiosity to conviction; but came away at last only willing to believe.

As there subsists no longer in the Islands much of that peculiar and discriminative form of life, of which the idea had delighted our imagination, we were willing to listen to such accounts of past times as would be given us. But we soon found what memorials were to be expected from an illiterate people, whose whole time is a series of distress; where every morning is labouring with expedients for the evening; and where all mental pains or pleasure arose from the dread of winter, the expectation of spring, the caprices of their Chiefs, and the motions of the neighbouring clans; where there was neither shame from ignorance, nor pride in knowledge; neither curiosity to inquire, nor vanity to communicate.

The Chiefs indeed were exempt from urgent penury, and daily difficulties; and in their houses were preserved what accounts remained of past ages. But the Chiefs were sometimes ignorant and careless, and sometimes kept busy by turbulence and contention; and one generation of ignorance effaces the whole series of unwritten history. Books are faithful repositories, which may be a while neglected or forgotten; but when they are opened again, will again impart their instruction: memory, once interrupted, is not to be recalled. Written learning is a fixed luminary, which, after the cloud that had hidden it has past away, is again bright in its proper station. Tradition is but a meteor, which, if once it falls, cannot be rekindled.

It seems to be universally supposed, that much of the local history was preserved by the Bards, of whom one is said to have been retained by every great family. After these Bards were some of my first inquiries; and I received such answers as, for a while, made me please myself with my increase of knowledge; for I had not then learned how to estimate the narration of a Highlander.

They said that a great family had a *Bard* and a *Senachi*, who were the poet and historian of the house; and an old gentleman told me that he remembered one of each. Here was a dawn of intelligence. Of men that had lived within memory, some certain knowledge might be attained. Though the office had ceased, its effects might continue; the poems might be found, though there was no poet.

Another conversation indeed informed me, that the same man was both Bard and Senachi. This variation discouraged me; but as the practice might be different in different times, or at the same time in different families, there was yet no reason for supposing that I must necessarily sit down in total ignorance.

Soon after I was told by a gentleman, who is generally acknowledged the greatest master of *Hebridian* antiquities, that there had indeed once been both Bards and Senachies; and that *Senachi* signified *the man of talk*, or of conversation; but that neither Bard nor Senachi had existed for some centuries. I have no reason to suppose it exactly known at what time the custom ceased, nor did it probably cease in all houses at once. But whenever the practice of recitation was disused, the works, whether poetical or historical, perished with the authors; for in those times nothing had been written in the *Earse* language.

Whether the *Man of talk* was a historian, whose office was to tell truth, or a storyteller, like those which were in the last century, and perhaps are now among the Irish, whose trade was only to amuse, it now would be vain to inquire.

Most of the domestick offices were, I believe, hereditary; and probably the laureat of a clan was always the son of the last laureat. The history of the race could no otherwise be communicated, or retained; but what genius could be expected in a poet by inheritance?

The nation was wholly illiterate. Neither bards nor Senachies could write or read; but if they were ignorant, there was no danger of detection; they were believed by those whose vanity they flattered.

The recital of genealogies, which has been considered as very efficacious to the preservation of a true series of ancestry, was anciently made, when the heir of the family came to manly age. This practice has never subsisted within time of memory, nor was much credit due to such rehearsers, who might obtrude fictitious pedigrees, either to please their masters, or to hide the deficiency of their own memories.

Where the Chiefs of the Highlands have found the histories of their descent is difficult to tell; for no *Earse* genealogy was ever written. In general this only is evident, that the principal house of a clan must be very ancient, and that those must have lived long in a place, of whom it is not known when they came thither.

Thus hopeless are all attempts to find any traces of Highland learning. Nor are their primitive customs and ancient manner of life otherwise than very faintly and uncertainly remembered by the present race.

The peculiarities which strike the native of a commercial country, proceeded in a great measure from the want of money. To the servants and dependents that were not domesticks, and if an estimate be made from the capacity of any of their old houses which I have seen, their domesticks could have been but few, were appropriated certain portions of land for their support. *Macdonald* has a piece of ground yet, called the Bards or Senachies field. When a beef was killed for the house, particular parts were claimed as fees by the several officers, or workmen. What was the right of each I have not learned. The head belonged to the smith, and the udder of a cow to the piper: the weaver had likewise his particular part; and so many pieces followed these prescriptive claims, that the Laird's was at last but little.

The payment of rent in kind has been so long disused in England, that it is totally forgotten. It was practised very lately in the *Hebrides*, and probably still continues, not only in St. *Kilda*, where money is not yet known, but in others of the smaller and remoter Islands. It were perhaps to be desired, that no change in this particular should have been made. When the Laird could only eat the produce of his lands, he was under the necessity of residing upon them; and when the tenant could not convert his stock into more portable riches, he could never be tempted away from his farm, from the only place where he could be wealthy. Money confounds subordination, by overpowering the distinctions of rank and birth, and weakens authority by supplying power of resistance, or expedients for escape. The feudal system is formed for a nation employed in agriculture, and has never long kept its hold where gold and silver have become common.

Their arms were anciently the *Glaymore*, or great two-handed sword, and afterwards the two-edged sword and target, or buckler, which was sustained on the left arm. In the midst of the target, which was made of wood, covered with leather, and studded with nails, a slender lance, about two feet long, was sometimes fixed; it was heavy and cumberous, and accordingly has for some time past been gradually laid aside. Very few targets were at Culloden. The dirk, or broad dagger, I am afraid, was of more use in private quarrels than in battles. The Lochaber-ax is only a slight alteration of the old *English* bill.

After all that has been said of the force and terrour of the Highland sword, I could not find that the art of defence was any part of common education. The gentlemen were perhaps sometimes skilful gladiators, but the common men had no other powers than those of violence and courage. Yet it is well known, that the onset of the Highlanders was very formidable. As an army cannot consist of philosophers, a panick is easily excited by any unwonted mode of annoyance. New dangers are naturally magnified; and men accustomed only to exchange bullets at a distance, and rather to hear their enemies than see them, are discouraged and amazed when they find themselves encountered hand to hand, and catch the gleam of steel flashing in their faces.

The Highland weapons gave opportunity for many exertions of personal courage, and sometimes for single combats in the field; like those which occur so frequently in fabulous wars. At Falkirk, a gentleman now living, was, I suppose after the retreat of the King's troops, engaged at a distance from the rest with an Irish dragoon. They were both skilful swordsmen, and the contest was not easily decided: the dragoon at last had the advantage, and the Highlander called for quarter; but quarter was refused him, and the fight continued till he was reduced to defend himself upon his knee. At that instant one of the Macleods came to his rescue; who, as it is said, offered quarter to the dragoon, but he thought himself obliged to reject what he had before refused, and, as battle gives little time to deliberate, was immediately killed.

Funerals were formerly solemnized by calling multitudes together, and entertaining them at great expence. This emulation of useless cost has been for some time discouraged, and at last in the Isle of *Sky* is almost suppressed.

Of the Earse language, as I understand nothing, I cannot say more than I have been told. It is the rude speech of a barbarous people, who had few thoughts to express, and were content, as they conceived grossly, to be grossly understood. After what has been lately talked of Highland Bards, and Highland genius, many will startle when they are told, that the *Earse* never was a written language; that there is not in the world an Earse manuscript a hundred years old; and that the sounds of the Highlanders were never expressed by letters, till some little books of piety were translated, and a metrical version of the Psalms was made by the Synod of *Argyle*. Whoever therefore now writes in this language, spells according to his own perception of the sound, and his own idea of the power of the letters. The *Welsh* and the *Irish* are cultivated tongues. The Welsh, two hundred years ago, insulted their *English* neighbours for the instability of their Orthography; while the *Earse* merely floated in the breath of the people, and could therefore receive little improvement.

When a language begins to teem with books, it is tending to refinement; as those who undertake to teach others must have undergone some labour in improving themselves, they set a proportionate value on their own thoughts, and wish to enforce them by efficacious expressions; speech becomes embodied and permanent; different modes and phrases are compared, and the best obtains an establishment. By degrees one age improves upon another. Exactness is first obtained, and afterwards elegance. But diction, merely vocal, is always in its childhood. As no man leaves his eloquence behind him, the new generations have all to learn. There may possibly be books without a polished language, but there can be no polished language without books.

That the Bards could not read more than the rest of their countrymen, it is reasonable to suppose; because, if they had read, they could probably have written; and how high their compositions may reasonably be rated, an inquirer may best judge by considering what stores of imagery, what principles of ratiocination, what comprehension of knowledge, and what delicacy of elocution he has known any man attain who cannot read. The state of the Bards was yet more hopeless. He that cannot read, may now converse with those that can; but the Bard was a barbarian among barbarians, who, knowing nothing himself, lived with others that knew no more.

There has lately been in the Islands one of these illiterate poets, who hearing the Bible read at church, is said to have turned the sacred history into verse. I heard part of a dialogue, composed by him, translated by a young lady in *Mull*, and thought it had more meaning than I expected from a man totally uneducated; but he had some opportunities of knowledge; he lived among a learned people. After all that has been done for the instruction of the Highlanders, the antipathy between their language and literature still continues; and no man that has learned only *Earse* is, at this time, able to read.

The *Earse* has many dialects, and the words used in some Islands are not always known in others. In literate nations, though the pronunciation, and sometimes the words of common speech may differ, as now in *England*, compared with the South of *Scotland*, yet there is a written diction, which pervades all dialects, and is understood in every province. But where the whole language is colloquial, he that has only one part, never gets the rest, as he cannot get it but by change of residence.

In an unwritten speech, nothing that is not very short is transmitted from one generation to another. Few have opportunities of hearing a long composition often enough to learn it, or have inclination to repeat it so often as is necessary to retain it; and what is once forgotten is lost for ever. I believe there cannot be recovered, in the whole *Earse* language, five hundred lines of which there is any evidence to prove them a hundred years old. Yet I hear that the father of Ossian boasts of two chests more of ancient poetry, which he suppresses, because they are too good for the *English*.

He that goes into the Highlands with a mind naturally acquiescent, and a credulity eager for wonders, may come back with an opinion very different from mine; for the inhabitants knowing the ignorance of all strangers in their language and antiquities, perhaps are not very scrupulous adherents to truth; yet I do not say that they deliberately speak studied falsehood, or have a settled purpose to deceive. They have inquired and considered little, and do not always feel their own ignorance. They are not much accustomed to be interrogated by others; and seem never to have thought upon interrogating themselves; so that if they do not know what they tell to be true, they likewise do not distinctly perceive it to be false.

Mr. Boswell was very diligent in his inquiries; and the result of his investigations was, that the answer to the second question was commonly such as nullified the answer to the first.

We were a while told, that they had an old translation of the scriptures; and told it till it would appear obstinacy to inquire again. Yet by continued accumulation of questions we found, that the translation meant, if any meaning there were, was nothing else than the *Irish* Bible.

We heard of manuscripts that were, or that had been in the hands of somebody's father, or grandfather; but at last we had no reason to believe they were other than Irish. Martin mentions Irish, but never any Earse manuscripts, to be found in the Islands in his time.

I suppose my opinion of the poems of Ossian is already discovered. I believe they never existed in any other form than that which we have seen. The editor, or author, never could shew the original; nor can it be shewn by any other; to revenge reasonable incredulity, by refusing evidence, is a degree of insolence, with which the world is not yet acquainted; and stubborn audacity is the last refuge of guilt. It would be easy to shew it if he had it; but whence could it be had? It is too long to be remembered, and the language formerly had nothing written. He has doubtless inserted names that circulate in popular stories, and may have translated some wandering ballads, if any can be found; and the names, and some of the images being recollected, make an inaccurate auditor imagine, by the help of Caledonian bigotry, that he has formerly heard the whole.

I asked a very learned Minister in Sky, who had used all arts to make me believe the genuineness of the book, whether at last he believed it himself? but he would not answer. He wished me to be deceived, for the honour of his country; but would not directly and formally deceive me. Yet has this man's testimony been publickly produced, as of one that held Fingal to be the work of Ossian.

It is said, that some men of integrity profess to have heard parts of it, but they all heard them when they were boys; and it was never said that any of them could recite six lines. They remember names, and perhaps some proverbial sentiments; and, having no distinct ideas, coin a resemblance without an original. The persuasion of the Scots, however, is far from universal; and in a question so capable of proof, why should doubt be suffered to continue? The editor has been heard to say, that part of the poem was received by him, in the Saxon character. He has then found, by some peculiar fortune, an unwritten language, written in a character which the natives probably never beheld.

I have yet supposed no imposture but in the publisher, yet I am far from certainty, that some translations have not been lately made, that may now be obtruded as parts of the original work. Credulity on one part is a strong temptation to deceit on the other, especially to deceit of which no personal injury is the consequence, and which flatters the author with his own ingenuity. The Scots have something to plead for their easy reception of an improbable fiction: they are seduced by their fondness for their supposed ancestors. A Scotchman must be a very sturdy moralist, who does not love *Scotland* better than truth: he will always love it better than inquiry; and if falsehood flatters his vanity, will not be very diligent to detect it. Neither ought the *English* to be much influenced by *Scotch* authority; for of the past and present state of the whole *Earse* nation, the Lowlanders are at least as ignorant as ourselves. To be ignorant is painful; but it is dangerous to quiet our uneasiness by the delusive opiate of hasty persuasion.

But this is the age in which those who could not read, have been supposed to write; in which the giants of antiquated romance have been exhibited as realities. If we know little of the ancient Highlanders, let us not fill the vacuity with *Ossian*. If we have not searched the *Magellanick* regions, let us however forbear to people them with *Patagons*.

Having waited some days at *Armidel*, we were flattered at last with a wind that promised to convey us to *Mull*. We went on board a boat that was taking in kelp, and left the Isle of *Sky* behind us. We were doomed to experience, like others, the danger of trusting to the wind, which blew against us, in a short time, with such violence, that we, being no seasoned sailors, were willing to call it a tempest. I was seasick and lay down. Mr. *Boswell* kept the deck. The master knew not well whither to go; and our difficulties might perhaps have filled a very pathetick page, had not Mr. *Maclean* of *Col*, who, with every other qualification which insular life requires, is a very active and skilful mariner, piloted us safe into his own harbour.

INCH KENNETH.

In the morning we went again into the boat, and were landed on *Inch Kenneth*, an Island about a mile long, and perhaps half a mile broad, remarkable for pleasantness and fertility. It is verdant and grassy, and fit both for pasture and tillage; but it has no trees. Its only inhabitants were Sir *Allan Maclean*, and two young ladies, his daughters, with their servants.

Romance does not often exhibit a scene that strikes the imagination more than this little desert in these depths of Western obscurity, occupied not by a gross herdsman, or amphibious fisherman, but by a gentleman and two ladies, of high birth, polished manners, and elegant conversation, who, in a habitation raised not very far above the ground, but furnished with unexpected neatness and convenience, practised all the kindness of hospitality, and refinement of courtesy.

Sir *Allan* is the Chieftain of the great clan of *Maclean*, which is said to claim the second place among the Highland families, yielding only to *Macdonald*. Though by the misconduct of his ancestors, most of the extensive territory, which would have descended to him, has been alienated, he still retains much of the dignity and authority of his birth. When soldiers were lately wanting for the *American* war, application was made to Sir *Allan*, and he nominated a hundred men for the service, who obeyed the summons, and bore arms under his command.

He had then, for some time, resided with the young ladies in *Inch Kenneth*, where he lives not only with plenty, but with elegance, having conveyed to his cottage a collection of books, and what else is necessary to make his hours pleasant.

When we landed, we were met by Sir *Allan* and the Ladies, accompanied by Miss *Macquarry*, who had passed some time with them, and now returned to *Ulva* with her father.

We all walked together to the mansion, where we found one cottage for Sir *Allan*, and I think two more for the domesticks and the offices. We entered, and wanted little that palaces afford. Our room was neatly floored, and well lighted; and our dinner, which was dressed in one of the other huts, was plentiful and delicate.

In the afternoon Sir *Allan* reminded us, that the day was Sunday, which he never suffered to pass without some religious distinction, and invited us to partake in his acts of domestick worship; which I hope neither Mr. *Boswell* nor myself will be suspected of a disposition to refuse. The elder of the Ladies read the *English* service.

Inch Kenneth was once a seminary of ecclesiasticks, subordinate, I suppose, to *Icolmkill*. Sir *Allan* had a mind to trace the foundations of the college, but neither I nor Mr. *Boswell*, who *bends* a keener *eye on vacancy*, were able to perceive them.

Our attention, however, was sufficiently engaged by a venerable chapel, which stands yet entire, except that the roof is gone. It is about sixty feet in length, and thirty in breadth. On one side of the altar is a bas relief of the blessed Virgin, and by it lies a little bell; which, though cracked, and without a clapper, has remained there for ages, guarded only by the venerableness of the place. The ground round the chapel is covered with grave-stones of Chiefs and ladies; and still continues to be a place of sepulture.

Inch Kenneth is a proper prelude to *Icolmkill*. It was not without some mournful emotion that we contemplated the ruins of religious structures, and the monuments of the dead.

On the next day we took a more distinct view of the place, and went with the boat to see oysters in the bed, out of which the boatmen forced up as many as were wanted. Even *Inch Kenneth* has a subordinate Island, named *Sandiland*, I suppose, in contempt, where we landed, and found a rock, with a surface of perhaps four acres, of which one is naked stone, another spread with sand and shells, some of which I picked up for their glossy beauty, and two covered with a little earth and grass, on which Sir *Allan* has a few sheep. I doubt not but when there was a college at *Inch Kenneth*, there was a hermitage upon *Sandiland*.

Having wandered over those extensive plains, we committed ourselves again to the winds and waters; and after a voyage of about ten minutes, in which we met with nothing very observable, were again safe upon dry ground.

We told Sir *Allan* our desire of visiting *Icolmkill*, and entreated him to give us his protection, and his company. He thought proper to hesitate a little, but the Ladies hinted, that as they knew he would not finally refuse, he would do better if he preserved the grace of ready compliance. He took their advice, and promised to carry us on the morrow in his boat.

We passed the remaining part of the day in such amusements as were in our power. Sir *Allan* related the *American* campaign, and at evening one of the Ladies played on her harpsichord, while *Col* and Mr. *Boswell* danced a *Scottish* reel with the other.

We could have been easily persuaded to a longer stay upon *Inch Kenneth*, but life will not be all passed in delight. The session at *Edinburgh* was approaching, from which Mr. *Boswell* could not be absent.

In the morning our boat was ready: it was high and strong. Sir *Allan* victualled it for the day, and provided able rowers. We now parted from the young Laird of *Col*, who had treated us with so much kindness, and concluded his favours by consigning us to Sir *Allan*. Here we had the last embrace of this amiable man, who, while these pages were preparing to attest his virtues, perished in the passage between *Ulva* and *Inch Kenneth*.

Sir *Allan*, to whom the whole region was well known, told us of a very remarkable cave, to which he would show us the way. We had been disappointed already by one cave, and were not much elevated by the expectation of another.

It was yet better to see it, and we stopped at some rocks on the coast of *Mull*. The mouth is fortified by vast fragments of stone, over which we made our way, neither very nimbly, nor very securely. The place, however, well repaid our trouble. The bottom, as far as the flood rushes in, was encumbered with large pebbles, but as we advanced was spread over with smooth sand. The breadth is about forty-five feet: the roof rises in an arch, almost regular, to a height which we could not measure; but I think it about thirty feet.

This part of our curiosity was nearly frustrated; for though we went to see a cave, and knew that caves are dark, we forgot to carry tapers, and did not discover our omission till we were wakened by our wants. Sir *Allan* then sent one of the boatmen into the country, who soon returned with one little candle. We were thus enabled to go forward, but could not venture far. Having passed inward from the sea to a great depth, we found on the right hand a narrow passage, perhaps not more than six feet wide, obstructed by great stones, over which we climbed and came into a second cave, in breadth twenty-five feet. The air in this apartment was very warm, but not oppressive, nor loaded with vapours. Our light showed no tokens of a feculent or corrupted atmosphere. Here was a square stone, called, as we are told, *Fingal's Table*.

If we had been provided with torches, we should have proceeded in our search, though we had already gone as far as any former adventurer, except some who are reported never to have returned; and, measuring our way back, we found it more than a hundred and sixty yards, the eleventh part of a mile.

Our measures were not critically exact, having been made with a walking pole, such as it is convenient to carry in these rocky countries, of which I guessed the length by standing against it. In this there could be no great errour, nor do I much doubt but the Highlander, whom we employed, reported the number right. More nicety however is better, and no man should travel unprovided with instruments for taking heights and distances.

There is yet another cause of errour not always easily surmounted, though more dangerous to the veracity of itinerary narratives, than imperfect mensuration. An observer deeply impressed by any remarkable spectacle, does not suppose, that the traces will soon vanish from his mind, and having commonly no great convenience for writing, defers the description to a time of more leisure, and better accommodation.

He who has not made the experiment, or who is not accustomed to require rigorous accuracy from himself, will scarcely believe how much a few hours take from certainty of knowledge, and distinctness of imagery; how the succession of objects will be broken, how separate parts will be confused, and how many particular features and discriminations will be compressed and conglobated into one gross and general idea.

To this dilatory notation must be imputed the false relations of travellers, where there is no imaginable motive to deceive. They trusted to memory, what cannot be trusted safely but to the eye, and told by guess what a few hours before they had known with certainty. Thus it was that *Wheeler* and *Spon* described with irreconcilable contrariety things which they surveyed together, and which both undoubtedly designed to show as they saw them.

When we had satisfied our curiosity in the cave, so far as our penury of light permitted us, we clambered again to our boat, and proceeded along the coast of *Mull* to a headland, called *Atun*, remarkable for the columnar form of the rocks, which rise in a series of pilasters, with a degree of regularity, which Sir *Allan* thinks not less worthy of curiosity than the shore of *Staffa*.

Not long after we came to another range of black rocks, which had the appearance of broken pilasters, set one behind another to a great depth. This place was chosen by Sir *Allan* for our dinner. We were easily accommodated with seats, for the stones were of all heights, and refreshed ourselves and our boatmen, who could have no other rest till we were at *Icolmkill*.

The evening was now approaching, and we were yet at a considerable distance from the end of our expedition. We could therefore stop no more to make remarks in the way, but set forward with some degree of eagerness. The day soon failed us, and the moon presented a very solemn and pleasing scene. The sky was clear, so that the eye commanded a wide circle: the sea was neither still nor turbulent: the wind neither silent nor loud. We were never far from one coast or another, on which, if the weather had become violent, we could have found shelter, and therefore contemplated at ease the region through which we glided in the tranquillity of the night, and saw now a rock and now an island grow gradually conspicuous and gradually obscure. I committed the fault which I have just been censuring, in neglecting, as we passed, to note the series of this placid navigation.

We were very near an Island, called *Nun's Island*, perhaps from an ancient convent. Here is said to have been dug the stone that was used in the buildings of *Icolmkill*. Whether it is now inhabited we could not stay to inquire.

At last we came to *Icolmkill*, but found no convenience for landing. Our boat could not be forced very near the dry ground, and our Highlanders carried us over the water.

We were now treading that illustrious Island, which was once the luminary of the *Caledonian* regions, whence savage clans and roving barbarians derived the benefits of knowledge, and the blessings of religion. To abstract the mind from all local emotion would be impossible, if it were endeavoured, and would be foolish, if it were possible. Whatever withdraws us from the power of our senses; whatever makes the past, the distant, or the future predominate over the present, advances us in the dignity of thinking beings. Far from me and from my friends, be such frigid philosophy as may conduct us indifferent and unmoved over any ground which has been dignified by wisdom, bravery, or virtue. That man is little to be envied, whose patriotism would not gain force upon the plain of *Marathon*, or whose piety would not grow warmer among the ruins of *Iona!*

We came too late to visit monuments: some care was necessary for ourselves. Whatever was in the Island, Sir *Allan* could command, for the inhabitants were *Macleans*; but having little they could not give us much. He went to the headman of the Island, whom Fame, but Fame delights in amplifying, represents as worth no less than fifty pounds. He was perhaps proud enough of his guests, but ill prepared for our entertainment; however, he soon produced more provision than men not luxurious require. Our lodging was next to be provided. We found a barn well stocked with hay, and made our beds as soft as we could.

In the morning we rose and surveyed the place. The churches of the two convents are both standing, though unroofed. They were built of unhewn stone, but solid, and not inelegant. I brought away rude measures of the buildings, such as I cannot much trust myself, inaccurately taken, and obscurely noted. Mr. *Pennant*'s delineations, which are doubtless exact, have made my unskilful description less necessary.

The episcopal church consists of two parts, separated by the belfry, and built at different times. The original church had, like others, the altar at one end, and tower at the other; but as it grew too small, another building of equal dimension was added, and the tower then was necessarily in the middle.

That these edifices are of different ages seems evident. The arch of the first church is *Roman*, being part of a circle; that of the additional building is pointed, and therefore *Gothick*, or *Saracenical*; the tower is firm, and wants only to be floored and covered.

Of the chambers or cells belonging to the monks, there are some walls remaining, but nothing approaching to a complete apartment.

The bottom of the church is so incumbered with mud and rubbish, that we could make no discoveries of curious inscriptions, and what there are have been already published. The place is said to be known where the black stones lie concealed, on which the old Highland Chiefs, when they made contracts and alliances, used to take the oath, which was considered as more sacred than any other obligation, and which could not be violated without the blackest infamy. In those days of violence and rapine, it was of great importance to impress upon savage minds the sanctity of an oath, by some particular and extraordinary circumstances. They would not have recourse to the black stones, upon small or common occasions, and when they had established their faith by this tremendous sanction, inconstancy and treachery were no longer feared.

The chapel of the nunnery is now used by the inhabitants as a kind of general cow-house, and the bottom is consequently too miry for examination.

Some of the stones which covered the later abbesses have inscriptions, which might yet be read, if the chapel were cleansed. The roof of this, as of all the other buildings, is totally destroyed, not only because timber quickly decays when it is neglected, but because in an island utterly destitute of wood, it was wanted for use, and was consequently the first plunder of needy rapacity.

The chancel of the nuns' chapel is covered with an arch of stone, to which time has done no injury; and a small apartment communicating with the choir, on the north side, like the chapterhouse in cathedrals, roofed with stone in the same manner, is likewise entire.

In one of the churches was a marble altar, which the superstition of the inhabitants has destroyed. Their opinion was, that a fragment of this stone was a defence against shipwrecks, fire, and miscarriages. In one corner of the church the bason for holy water is yet unbroken.

The cemetery of the nunnery was, till very lately, regarded with such reverence, that only women were buried in it. These reliques of veneration always produce some mournful pleasure. I could have forgiven a great injury more easily than the violation of this imaginary sanctity.

South of the chapel stand the walls of a large room, which was probably the hall, or refectory of the nunnery. This apartment is capable of repair. Of the rest of the convent there are only fragments.

Besides the two principal churches, there are, I think, five chapels yet standing, and three more remembered. There are also crosses, of which two bear the names of St. *John* and St. *Matthew*.

A large space of ground about these consecrated edifices is covered with grave-stones, few of which have any inscription. He that surveys it, attended by an insular antiquary, may be told where the Kings of many nations are buried, and if he loves to sooth his imagination with the thoughts that naturally rise in places where the great and powerful lie mingled with the dust, let him listen in submissive silence; for if he asks any questions, his delight is at an end.

Iona has long enjoyed, without any very credible attestation, the honour of being reputed the cemetery of the *Scottish* Kings. It is not unlikely, that, when the opinion of local sanctity was prevalent, the Chieftains of the Isles, and perhaps some of the *Norwegian* or *Irish* princes were reposited in this venerable enclosure. But by whom the subterraneous vaults are peopled is now utterly unknown. The graves are very numerous, and some of them undoubtedly contain the remains of men, who did not expect to be so soon forgotten.

Not far from this awful ground, may be traced the garden of the monastery: the fishponds are yet discernible, and the aqueduct, which supplied them, is still in use.

There remains a broken building, which is called the Bishop's house, I know not by what authority. It was once the residence of some man above the common rank, for it has two stories and a chimney. We were shewn a chimney at the other end, which was only a nich, without perforation, but so much does antiquarian credulity, or patriotick vanity prevail, that it was not much more safe to trust the eye of our instructor than the memory.

There is in the Island one house more, and only one, that has a chimney: we entered it, and found it neither wanting repair nor inhabitants; but to the farmers, who now possess it, the chimney is of no great value; for their fire was made on the floor, in the middle of the room, and notwithstanding the dignity of their mansion, they rejoiced, like their neighbours, in the comforts of smoke.

It is observed, that ecclesiastical colleges are always in the most pleasant and fruitful places. While the world allowed the monks their choice, it is surely no dishonour that they chose well. This Island is remarkably fruitful. The village near the churches is said to contain seventy families, which, at five in a family, is more than a hundred inhabitants to a mile. There are perhaps other villages; yet both corn and cattle are annually exported.

But the fruitfulness of *Iona* is now its whole prosperity. The inhabitants are remarkably gross, and remarkably neglected: I know not if they are visited by any Minister. The Island, which was once the metropolis of learning and piety, has now no school for education, nor temple for worship, only two inhabitants that can speak *English*, and not one that can write or read.

The people are of the clan of *Maclean*; and though Sir *Allan* had not been in the place for many years, he was received with all the reverence due to their Chieftain. One of them being sharply reprehended by him, for not sending him some rum, declared after his departure, in Mr. *Boswell's* presence, that he had no design of disappointing him, *for*, said he, *I would cut my bones for him; and if he had sent his dog for it, he should have had it.*

When we were to depart, our boat was left by the ebb at a great distance from the water, but no sooner did we wish it afloat, than the islanders gathered round it, and, by the union of many hands, pushed it down the beach; every man who could contribute his help seemed to think himself happy in the opportunity of being, for a moment, useful to his Chief.

We now left those illustrious ruins, by which Mr. *Boswell* was much affected, nor would I willingly be thought to have looked upon them without some emotion. Perhaps, in the revolutions of the world, *Iona* may be sometime again the instructress of the Western Regions.

It was no long voyage to *Mull*, where, under Sir *Allan's* protection, we landed in the evening, and were entertained for the night by Mr. *Maclean*, a Minister that lives upon the coast, whose elegance of conversation, and strength of judgement, would make him conspicuous in places of greater celebrity. Next day we dined with Dr. *Maclean*, another physician, and then travelled on to the house of a very powerful Laird, *Maclean* of *Lochbuy*; for in this country every man's name is *Maclean*.

Where races are thus numerous, and thus combined, none but the Chief of a clan is addressed by his name. The Laird of *Dunvegan* is called *Macleod*, but other gentlemen of the same family are denominated by the places where they reside, as *Raasa*, or *Talisker*. The distinction of the meaner people is made by their Christian names. In consequence of this practice, the late Laird of *Macfarlane*, an eminent genealogist, considered himself as disrespectfully treated, if the common addition was applied to him. Mr. *Macfarlane*, said he, may with equal propriety be said to many; but I, and I only, am *Macfarlane*.

Our afternoon journey was through a country of such gloomy desolation, that Mr. *Boswell* thought no part of the Highlands equally terrifick, yet we came without any difficulty, at evening, to *Lochbuy*, where we found a true Highland Laird, rough and haughty, and tenacious of his dignity; who, hearing my name, inquired whether I was of the *Johnstons* of *Glencoe*, or of *Ardnamurchan*.

Lochbuy has, like the other insular Chieftains, quitted the castle that sheltered his ancestors, and lives near it, in a mansion not very spacious or splendid. I have seen no houses in the Islands much to be envied for convenience or magnificence, yet they bear testimony to the progress of arts and civility, as they shew that rapine and surprise are no longer dreaded, and are much more commodious than the ancient fortresses.

The castles of the *Hebrides*, many of which are standing, and many ruined, were always built upon points of land, on the margin of the sea. For the choice of this situation there must have been some general reason, which the change of manners has left in obscurity. They were of no use in the days of piracy, as defences of the coast; for it was equally accessible in other places. Had they been seamarks or light-houses, they would have been of more use to the invader than the natives, who could want no such directions on their own waters: for a watchtower, a cottage on a hill would have been better, as it would have commended a wider view.

If they be considered merely as places of retreat, the situation seems not well chosen; for the Laird of an Island is safest from foreign enemies in the center: on the coast he might be more suddenly surprised than in the inland parts; and the invaders, if their enterprise miscarried, might more easily retreat. Some convenience, however, whatever it was, their position on the shore afforded; for uniformity of practice seldom continues long without good reason.

A castle in the Islands is only a single tower of three or four stories, of which the walls are sometimes eight or nine feet thick, with narrow windows, and close winding stairs of stone. The top rises in a cone, or pyramid of stone, encompassed by battlements. The intermediate floors are sometimes frames of timber, as in common houses, and sometimes arches of stone, or alternately stone and timber; so that there was very little danger from fire. In the center of every floor, from top to bottom, is the chief room, of no great extent, round which there are narrow cavities, or recesses, formed by small vacuities, or by a double wall. I know not whether there be ever more than one fire-place.

They had not capacity to contain many people, or much provision; but their enemies could seldom stay to blockade them; for if they failed in the first attack, their next care was to escape.

The walls were always too strong to be shaken by such desultory hostilities; the windows were too narrow to be entered, and the battlements too high to be scaled. The only danger was at the gates, over which the wall was built with a square cavity, not unlike a chimney, continued to the top. Through this hollow the defendants let fall stones upon those who attempted to break the gate, and poured down water, perhaps scalding water, if the attack was made with fire. The castle of *Lochbuy* was secured by double doors, of which the outer was an iron grate.

In every castle is a well and a dungeon. The use of the well is evident. The dungeon is a deep subterraneous cavity, walled on the sides, and arched on the top, into which the descent is through a narrow door, by a ladder or a rope, so that it seems impossible to escape, when the rope or ladder is drawn up. The dungeon was, I suppose, in war, a prison for such captives as were treated with severity, and, in peace, for such delinquents as had committed crimes within the Laird's jurisdiction; for the mansions of many Lairds were, till the late privation of their privileges, the halls of justice to their own tenants.

As these fortifications were the productions of mere necessity, they are built only for safety, with little regard to convenience, and with none to elegance or pleasure. It was sufficient for a Laird of the *Hebrides*, if he had a strong house, in which he could hide his wife and children from the next clan. That they are not large nor splendid is no wonder. It is not easy to find how they were raised, such as they are, by men who had no money, in countries where the labourers and artificers could scarcely be fed. The buildings in different parts of the Islands shew their degrees of wealth and power. I believe that for all the castles which I have seen beyond the *Tweed*, the ruins yet remaining of some one of those which the *English* built in *Wales*, would supply materials.

These castles afford another evidence that the fictions of romantick chivalry had for their basis the real manners of the feudal times, when every Lord of a seignory lived in his hold lawless and unaccountable, with all the licentiousness and insolence of uncontested superiority and unprincipled power. The traveller, whoever he might be, coming to the fortified habitation of a Chieftain, would, probably, have been interrogated from the battlements, admitted with caution at the gate, introduced to a petty Monarch, fierce with habitual hostility, and vigilant with ignorant suspicion; who, according to his general temper, or accidental humour, would have seated a stranger as his guest at the table, or as a spy confined him in the dungeon.

Lochbuy means the *Yellow Lake*, which is the name given to an inlet of the sea, upon which the castle of Mr. *Maclean* stands. The reason of the appellation we did not learn.

We were now to leave the *Hebrides*, where we had spent some weeks with sufficient amusement, and where we had amplified our thoughts with new scenes of nature, and new modes of life. More time would have given us a more distinct view, but it was necessary that Mr. *Boswell* should return before the courts of justice were opened; and it was not proper to live too long upon hospitality, however liberally imparted.

Of these Islands it must be confessed, that they have not many allurements, but to the mere lover of naked nature. The inhabitants are thin, provisions are scarce, and desolation and penury give little pleasure.

The people collectively considered are not few, though their numbers are small in proportion to the space which they occupy. *Mull* is said to contain six thousand, and *Sky* fifteen thousand. Of the computation respecting *Mull*, I can give no account; but when I doubted the truth of the numbers attributed to *Sky*, one of the Ministers exhibited such facts as conquered my incredulity.

Of the proportion, which the product of any region bears to the people, an estimate is commonly made according to the pecuniary price of the necessaries of life; a principle of judgment which is never certain, because it supposes what is far from truth, that the value of money is always the same, and so measures an unknown quantity by an uncertain standard. It is competent enough when the markets of the same country, at different times, and those times not too distant, are to be compared; but of very little use for the purpose of making one nation acquainted with the state of another. Provisions, though plentiful, are sold in places of great pecuniary opulence for nominal prices, to which, however scarce, where gold and silver are yet scarcer, they can never be raised.

In the *Western Islands* there is so little internal commerce, that hardly any thing has a known or settled rate. The price of things brought in, or carried out, is to be considered as that of a foreign market; and even this there is some difficulty in discovering, because their denominations of quantity are different from ours; and when there is ignorance on both sides, no appeal can be made to a common measure.

This, however, is not the only impediment. The *Scots*, with a vigilance of jealousy which never goes to sleep, always suspect that an *Englishman* despises them for their poverty, and to convince him that they are not less rich than their neighbours, are sure to tell him a price higher than the true. When *Lesley*, two hundred years ago, related so punctiliously, that a hundred hen eggs, new laid, were sold in the Islands for a peny, he supposed that no inference could possibly follow, but that eggs were in great abundance. Posterity has since grown wiser; and having learned, that nominal and real value may differ, they now tell no such stories, lest the foreigner should happen to collect, not that eggs are many, but that pence are few.

Money and wealth have by the use of commercial language been so long confounded, that they are commonly supposed to be the same; and this prejudice has spread so widely in *Scotland*, that I know not whether I found man or woman, whom I interrogated concerning payments of money, that could surmount the illiberal desire of deceiving me, by representing every thing as dearer than it is.

From *Lochbuy* we rode a very few miles to the side of *Mull*, which faces *Scotland*, where, having taken leave of our kind protector, Sir *Allan*, we embarked in a boat, in which the seat provided for our accommodation was a heap of rough brushwood; and on the twenty-second of *October* reposed at a tolerable inn on the main land.

On the next day we began our journey southwards. The weather was tempestuous. For half the day the ground was rough, and our horses were still small. Had they required much restraint, we might have been reduced to difficulties; for I think we had amongst us but one bridle. We fed the poor animals liberally, and they performed their journey well. In the latter part of the day, we came to a firm and smooth road, made by the soldiers, on which we travelled with great security, busied with contemplating the scene about us. The night came on while we had yet a great part of the way to go, though not so dark, but that we could discern the cataracts which poured down the hills, on one side, and fell into one general channel that ran with great violence on the other. The wind was loud, the rain was heavy, and the whistling of the blast, the fall of the shower, the rush of the cataracts, and the roar of the torrent, made a nobler chorus of the rough musick of nature than it had ever been my chance to hear before. The streams, which ran cross the way from the hills to the main current, were so frequent, that after a while I began to count them; and, in ten miles, reckoned fifty-five, probably missing some, and having let some pass before they forced themselves upon my notice. At last we came to *Inverary*, where we found an inn, not only commodious, but magnificent.

The difficulties of peregrination were now at an end. Mr. *Boswell* had the honour of being known to the Duke of *Argyle*, by whom we were very kindly entertained at his splendid seat, and supplied with conveniences for surveying his spacious park and rising forests.

After two days stay at *Inverary* we proceeded *Southward* over *Glencroe*, a black and dreary region, now made easily passable by a military road, which rises from either end of the glen by an acclivity not dangerously steep, but sufficiently laborious. In the middle, at the top of the hill, is a seat with this inscription, *Rest, and be thankful*. Stones were placed to mark the distances, which the inhabitants have taken away, resolved, they said, *to have no new miles*.

In this rainy season the hills streamed with waterfalls, which, crossing the way, formed currents on the other side, that ran in contrary directions as they fell to the north or south of the summit. Being, by the favour of the Duke, well mounted, I went up and down the hill with great convenience.

From *Glencroe* we passed through a pleasant country to the banks of *Loch Lomond*, and were received at the house of Sir *James Colquhoun*, who is owner of almost all the thirty islands of the Loch, which we went in a boat next morning to survey. The heaviness of the rain shortened our voyage, but we landed on one island planted with yew, and stocked with deer, and on another containing perhaps not more than half an acre, remarkable for the ruins of an old castle, on which the osprey builds her annual nest. Had *Loch Lomond* been in a happier climate, it would have been the boast of wealth and vanity to own one of the little spots which it incloses, and to have employed upon it all the arts of embellishment. But as it is, the islets, which court the gazer at a distance, disgust him at his approach, when he finds, instead of soft lawns and shady thickets, nothing more than uncultivated ruggedness.

Where the Loch discharges itself into a river, called the *Leven*, we passed a night with Mr. *Smollet*, a relation of Doctor *Smollet*, to whose memory he has raised an obelisk on the bank near the house in which he was born. The civility and respect which we found at every place, it is ungrateful to omit, and tedious to repeat. Here we were met by a post-chaise, that conveyed us to *Glasgow*.

To describe a city so much frequented as *Glasgow*, is unnecessary. The prosperity of its commerce appears by the greatness of many private houses, and a general appearance of wealth. It is the only episcopal city whose cathedral was left standing in the rage of Reformation. It is now divided into many separate places of worship, which, taken all together, compose a great pile, that had been some centuries in building, but was never finished; for the change of religion intercepted its progress, before the cross isle was added, which seems essential to a *Gothick* cathedral.

The college has not had a sufficient share of the increasing magnificence of the place. The session was begun; for it commences on the tenth of *October*, and continues to the tenth of *June*, but the students appeared not numerous, being, I suppose, not yet returned from their several homes. The division of the academical year into one session, and one recess, seems to me better accommodated to the present state of life, than that variegation of time by terms and vacations derived from distant centuries, in which it was probably convenient, and still continued in the *English* universities. So many solid months as the *Scotch* scheme of education joins together, allow and encourage a plan for each part of the year; but with us, he that has settled himself to study in the college is soon tempted into the country, and he that has adjusted his life in the country, is summoned back to his college.

Yet when I have allowed to the universities of *Scotland* a more rational distribution of time, I have given them, so far as my inquiries have informed me, all that they can claim. The students, for the most part, go thither boys, and depart before they are men; they carry with them little fundamental knowledge, and therefore the superstructure cannot be lofty. The grammar schools are not generally well supplied; for the character of a schoolmaster being there less honourable than in *England*, is seldom accepted by men who are capable to adorn it, and where the school has been deficient, the college can effect little.

Men bred in the universities of *Scotland* cannot be expected to be often decorated with the splendours of ornamental erudition, but they obtain a mediocrity of knowledge, between learning and ignorance, not inadequate to the purposes of common life, which is, I believe, very widely diffused among them, and which countenanced in general by a national combination so invidious, that their friends cannot defend it, and actuated in particulars by a spirit of enterprise, so vigorous, that their enemies are constrained to praise it, enables them to find, or to make their way to employment, riches, and distinction.

From *Glasgow* we directed our course to *Auchinleck*, an estate devolved, through a long series of ancestors, to Mr. *Boswell*'s father, the present possessor. In our way we found several places remarkable enough in themselves, but already described by those who viewed them at more leisure, or with much more skill; and stopped two days at Mr. *Campbell*'s, a gentleman married to Mrs. *Boswell*'s sister.

Auchinleck, which signifies a *stony field*, seems not now to have any particular claim to its denomination. It is a district generally level, and sufficiently fertile, but like all the *Western* side of *Scotland*, incommoded by very frequent rain. It was, with the rest of the country, generally naked, till the present possessor finding, by the growth of some stately trees near his old castle, that the ground was favourable enough to timber, adorned it very diligently with annual plantations.

Lord *Auchinleck*, who is one of the Judges of *Scotland*, and therefore not wholly at leisure for domestick business or pleasure, has yet found time to make improvements in his patrimony. He has built a house of hewn stone, very stately, and durable, and has advanced the value of his lands with great tenderness to his tenants.

I was, however, less delighted with the elegance of the modern mansion, than with the sullen dignity of the old castle. I clambered with Mr. *Boswell* among the ruins, which afford striking images of ancient life. It is, like other castles, built upon a point of rock, and was, I believe, anciently surrounded with a moat. There is another rock near it, to which the drawbridge, when it was let down, is said to have reached. Here, in the ages of tumult and rapine, the Laird was surprised and killed by the neighbouring Chief, who perhaps might have extinguished the family, had he not in a few days been seized and hanged, together with his sons, by *Douglas*, who came with his forces to the relief of *Auchinleck*.

At no great distance from the house runs a pleasing brook, by a red rock, out of which has been hewn a very agreeable and commodious summerhouse, at less expence, as Lord *Auchinleck* told me, than would have been required to build a room of the same dimensions. The rock seems to have no more dampness than any other wall. Such opportunities of variety it is judicious not to neglect.

We now returned to *Edinburgh*, where I passed some days with men of learning, whose names want no advancement from my commemoration, or with women of elegance, which perhaps disclaims a pedant's praise.

The conversation of the *Scots* grows every day less unpleasing to the *English*; their peculiarities wear fast away; their dialect is likely to become in half a century provincial and rustick, even to themselves. The great, the learned, the ambitious, and the vain, all cultivate the *English* phrase, and the *English* pronunciation, and in splendid companies *Scotch* is not much heard, except now and then from an old Lady.

There is one subject of philosophical curiosity to be found in *Edinburgh*, which no other city has to shew; a college of the deaf and dumb, who are taught to speak, to read, to write, and to practice arithmetick, by a gentleman, whose name is *Braidwood*. The number which attends him is, I think, about twelve, which he brings together into a little school, and instructs according to their several degrees of proficiency.

I do not mean to mention the instruction of the deaf as new. Having been first practised upon the son of a constable of *Spain*, it was afterwards cultivated with much emulation in *England*, by *Wallis* and *Holder*, and was lately professed by Mr. *Baker*, who once flattered me with hopes of seeing his method published. How far any former teachers have succeeded, it is not easy to know; the improvement of Mr. *Braidwood*'s pupils is wonderful. They not only speak, write, and understand what is written, but if he that speaks looks towards them, and modifies his organs by distinct and full utterance, they know so well what is spoken, that it is an expression scarcely figurative to say, they hear with the eye. That any have attained to the power mentioned by *Burnet*, of feeling sounds, by laying a hand on the speaker's mouth, I know not; but I have seen so much, that I can believe more; a single word, or a short sentence, I think, may possibly be so distinguished.

It will readily be supposed by those that consider this subject, that Mr. *Braidwood*'s scholars spell accurately. Orthography is vitiated among such as learn first to speak, and then to write, by imperfect notions of the relation between letters and vocal utterance; but to those students every character is of equal importance; for letters are to them not symbols of names, but of things; when they write they do not represent a sound, but delineate a form.

This school I visited, and found some of the scholars waiting for their master, whom they are said to receive at his entrance with smiling countenances and sparkling eyes, delighted with the hope of new ideas. One of the young Ladies had her slate before her, on which I wrote a question consisting of three figures, to be multiplied by two figures. She looked upon it, and quivering her fingers in a manner which I thought very pretty, but of which I know not whether it was art or play, multiplied the sum regularly in two lines, observing the decimal place; but did not add the two lines together, probably disdaining so easy an operation. I pointed at the place where the sum total should stand, and she noted it with such expedition as seemed to shew that she had it only to write.

It was pleasing to see one of the most desperate of human calamities capable of so much help: whatever enlarges hope, will exalt courage; after having seen the deaf taught arithmetick, who would be afraid to cultivate the *Hebrides?*

Such are the things which this journey has given me an opportunity of seeing, and such are the reflections which that sight has raised. Having passed my time almost wholly in cities, I may have been surprised by modes of life and appearances of nature, that are familiar to men of wider survey and more varied conversation. Novelty and ignorance must always be reciprocal, and I cannot but be conscious that my thoughts on national manners, are the thoughts of one who has seen but little.

FINIS.

Letter to James Macpherson

FRIDAY 20 JANUARY 1775

Jan. 20, 1775

Mr. James Macpherson—I received your foolish and impudent note. Whatever insult is offered me I will do my best to repel, and what I cannot do for myself the law will do for me. I will not desist from detecting what I think a cheat, from any fear of the menaces of a Ruffian.

You want me to retract. What shall I retract? I thought your book an imposture from the beginning, I think it upon yet surer reasons an imposture still. For this opinion I give the publick my reasons which I here dare you to refute.

But however I may despise you, I reverence truth and if you can prove the genuineness of the work I will confess it. Your rage I defy, your abilities since your Homer are not so formidable, and what I have heard of your morals disposes me to pay regard not to what you shall say, but to what you can prove.

You may print this if you will.

SAM. JOHNSON

Taxation No Tyranny

In all the parts of human knowledge, whether terminating in science merely speculative, or operating upon life private or civil, are admitted some fundamental principles, or common axioms, which being generally received are little doubted, and being little doubted have been rarely proved.

Of these gratuitous and acknowledged truths it is often the fate to become less evident by endeavours to explain them, however necessary such endeavours may be made by the misapprehensions of absurdity, or the sophistries of interest. It is difficult to prove the principles of science, because notions cannot always be found more intelligible than those which are questioned. It is difficult to prove the principles of practice, because they have for the most part not been discovered by investigation, but obtruded by experience, and the demonstrator will find, after an operose deduction, that he has been trying to make that seen which can be only felt.

Of this kind is the position, that *the supreme power of every community has the right of requiring from all its subjects such contributions as are necessary to the public safety or public prosperity*, which was considered by all mankind as comprising the primary and essential condition of all political society, till it became disputed by those zealots of anarchy, who have denied to the parliament of Britain the right of taxing the American colonies.

In favour of this exemption of the Americans from the authority of their lawful sovereign, and the dominion of their mother-country, very loud clamours have been raised, and many wild assertions advanced, which by such as borrow their opinions from the reigning fashion have been admitted as arguments; and what is strange, though their tendency is to lessen English honour, and English power, have been heard by English-men with a wish to find them true. Passion has in its first violence controlled interest, as the eddy for a while runs against the stream.

To be prejudiced is always to be weak; yet there are prejudices so near to laudable, that they have been often praised, and are always pardoned. To love their country has been considered as virtue in men, whose love could not be otherwise than blind, because their preference was made without a comparison; but it never has been my fortune to find, either in ancient or modern writers, any honourable mention of those, who have with equal blindness hated their country.

These antipatriotic prejudices are the abortions of Folly impregnated by Faction, which being produced against the standing order of Nature, have not strength sufficient for long life. They are born only to scream and perish, and leave those to contempt or detestation, whose kindness was employed to nurse them into mischief.

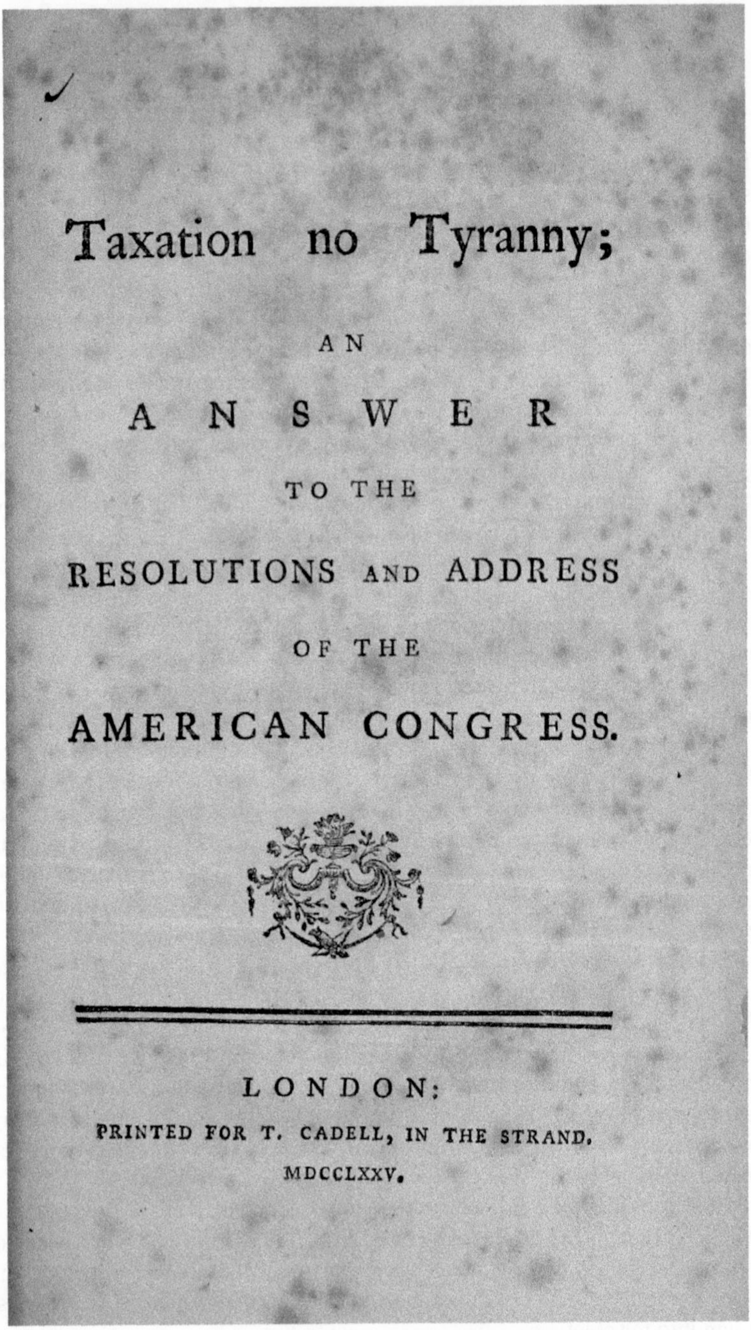

Taxation no Tyranny;

AN

ANSWER

TO THE

RESOLUTIONS AND ADDRESS

OF THE

AMERICAN CONGRESS.

LONDON:

PRINTED FOR T. CADELL, IN THE STRAND.

MDCCLXXV.

FIGURE 11 *Taxation no Tyranny* (1775), title page (Bodl. 8° Y 92 [7] Jur.).
Courtesy of the Bodleian Library, University of Oxford.

To perplex the opinion of the Publick many artifices have been used, which, as usually happens when falsehood is to be maintained by fraud, lose their force by counteracting one another.

THE nation is sometimes to be mollified by a tender tale of men, who fled from tyranny to rocks and desarts, and is persuaded to lose all claims of justice, and all sense of dignity, in compassion for a harmless people, who having worked hard for bread in a wild country, and obtained by the slow progression of manual industry the accommodations of life, are now invaded by unprecedented oppression, and plundered of their properties by the harpies of taxation.

WE are told how their industry is obstructed by unnatural restraints, and their trade confined by rigorous prohibitions; how they are forbidden to enjoy the products of their own soil, to manufacture the materials which Nature spreads before them, or to carry their own goods to the nearest market: and surely the generosity of English virtue will never heap new weight upon those that are already overladen, will never delight in that dominion, which cannot be exercised but by cruelty and outrage.

BUT while we are melting in silent sorrow, and in the transports of delicious pity, dropping both the sword and balance from our hands, another friend of the Americans thinks it better to awaken another passion, and tries to alarm our interest, or excite our veneration, by accounts of their greatness and their opulence, of the fertility of their land, and the splendour of their towns. We then begin to consider the question with more evenness of mind, are ready to conclude that those restrictions are not very oppressive which have been found consistent with this speedy growth of prosperity, and begin to think it reasonable that they, who thus flourish under the protection of our government, should contribute something towards its expence.

BUT we are then told that the Americans, however wealthy, cannot be taxed; that they are the descendants of men who left all for liberty, and that they have constantly preserved the principles and stubbornness of their progenitors; that they are too obstinate for persuasion, and too powerful for constraint; that they will laugh at argument, and defeat violence; that the continent of North America contains three millions, not of men merely, but of Whigs, of Whigs fierce for liberty, and disdainful of dominion; that they multiply with the fecundity of their own rattle-snakes, so that every quarter of a century doubles their numbers.

MEN accustomed to think themselves masters do not love to be threatened. This talk is, I hope, commonly thrown away, or raises passions different from those which it intended to excite. Instead of terrifying the English hearer to tame acquiescence, it disposes him to hasten the experiment of bending obstinacy before it is become yet more obdurate, and convinces him that it is necessary to attack a nation thus prolific while we may yet hope to prevail.

When he is told through what extent of territory we must travel to subdue them, he recollects how far, a few years ago, we travelled in their defence. When it is urged that they will shoot up like the Hydra, he naturally considers how the Hydra was destroyed.

NOTHING dejects a trader like the interruption of his profits. A commercial people, however magnanimous, shrinks at the thought of declining traffick, and an unfavourable balance. The effect of this terrour has been tried. We have been stunned with the importance of our American commerce, and heard of merchants with warehouses that are never to be emptied, and of manufacturers starving for want of work.

THAT our commerce with America is profitable, however less than ostentatious or deceitful estimates have made it, and that it is our interest to preserve it, has never been denied; but surely it will most effectually be preserved, by being kept always in our own power. Concessions may promote it for a moment, but superiority only can ensure its continuance. There will always be a part, and always a very large part of every community that have no care but for themselves, and whose care for themselves reaches little farther than impatience of immediate pain, and eagerness for the nearest good. The blind are said to feel with peculiar nicety. They who look but little into futurity, have perhaps the quickest sensation of the present. A merchant's desire is not of glory, but of gain; not of publick wealth, but of private emolument; he is therefore rarely to be consulted about war and peace, or any designs of wide extent and distant consequence.

Yet this, like other general characters, will sometimes fail. The traders of *Birmingham* have rescued themselves from all imputation of narrow selfishness by a manly recommendation to Parliament of the rights and dignity of their native country.

To these men I do not intend to ascribe an absurd and enthusiastick contempt of interest, but to give them the rational and just praise of distinguishing real from seeming good, of being able to see through the cloud of interposing difficulties, to the lasting and solid happiness of victory and settlement.

LEST all these topicks of persuasion should fail, the great actor of patriotism has tried another, in which terrour and pity are happily combined, not without a proper superaddition of that admiration which later ages have brought into the drama. The heroes of Boston, he tells us, if the Stamp Act had not been repealed, would have left their town, their port, and their trade, have resigned the splendour of opulence, and quitted the delights of neighbourhood, to disperse themselves over the country, where they would till the ground, and fish in the rivers, and range the mountains, AND BE FREE.

THESE surely are brave words. If the mere sound of freedom can operate thus powerfully, let no man hereafter doubt the story of the Pied Piper. *The removal of the people of Boston into the country* seems even to the Congress not only *difficult in its execution*, but *important in its consequences.* The difficulty of execution is best known to the Bostonians themselves; the consequence, alas! will only be, that they will leave good houses to wiser men.

YET before they quit the comforts of a warm home for the sounding something which they think better, he cannot be thought their enemy who advises them to consider well whether they shall find it. By turning fishermen or hunters, woodmen or shepherds, they may become wild, but it is not so easy to conceive them free; for who can be more a slave than he that is driven by force from the comforts of life, is compelled to leave his house to a casual comer, and whatever he does, or wherever he wanders, finds every moment some new testimony of his own subjection? If the choice of evil is freedom, the felon in the gallies has his option of labour or of stripes. The Bostonian may quit his house to starve in the fields; his dog may refuse to set, and smart under the lash, and they may then congratulate each other upon the smiles of liberty, *profuse with bliss, and pregnant with delight.*

To treat such designs as serious, would be to think too contemptuously of Bostonian understandings. The artifice indeed is not new: the blusterer who threatened in vain to destroy his opponent, has sometimes obtained his end, by making it believed that he would hang himself.

BUT terrours and pity are not the only means by which the taxation of the Americans is opposed. There are those who profess to use them only as auxiliaries to reason and justice, who tell us that to tax the colonies is usurpation and oppression, an invasion of natural and legal rights, and a violation of those principles which support the constitution of English government.

THIS question is of great importance. That the Americans are able to bear taxation is indubitable; that their refusal may be over-ruled is highly probable: but power is no sufficient evidence of truth. Let us examine our own claim, and the objections of the recusants, with caution proportioned to the event of the decision, which must convict one part of robbery, or the other of rebellion.

A tax is a payment exacted by authority from part of the community for the benefit of the whole. From whom, and in what proportion such payment shall be required, and to what uses it shall be applied, those only are to judge to whom government is intrusted. In the British dominion taxes are apportioned, levied, and appropriated by the states assembled in parliament.

OF every empire all the subordinate communities are liable to taxation, because they all share the benefits of government, and therefore ought all to furnish their proportion of the expence.

THIS the Americans have never openly denied. That it is their duty to pay the cost of their own safety they seem to admit; nor do they refuse their contribution to the exigencies, whatever they may be, of the British empire; but they make this participation of the public burden a duty of very uncertain extent, and imperfect obligation, a duty temporary, occasional and elective, of which they reserve to themselves the right of settling the degree, the time, and the duration, of judging when it may be required, and when it has been performed.

THEY allow to the supreme power nothing more than the liberty of notifying to them its demands or its necessities. Of this notification they profess to think for themselves, how far it shall influence their counsels, and of the necessities alleged, how far they shall endeavour to relieve them. They assume the exclusive power of settling not only the mode, but the quantity of this payment. They are ready to co-operate with all the other dominions of the King; but they will co-operate by no means which they do not like, and at no greater charge than they are willing to bear.

This claim, wild as it may seem, this claim, which supposes dominion without authority, and subjects without subordination, has found among the libertines of policy many clamorous and hardy vindicators. The laws of Nature, the rights of humanity, the faith of charters, the danger of liberty, the encroachments of usurpation, have been thundered in our ears, sometimes by interested faction, and sometimes by honest stupidity.

IT is said by Fontenelle, that if twenty philosophers shall resolutely deny that the presence of the sun makes the day, he will not despair but whole nations may adopt the opinion. So many political dogmatists have denied to the Mother Country the power of taxing the Colonies, and have enforced their denial with so much violence of outcry, that their sect is already very numerous, and the publick voice suspends its decision.

IN moral and political questions the contest between interest and justice has been often tedious and often fierce, but perhaps it never happened before that justice found much opposition with interest on her side.

FOR the satisfaction of this inquiry, it is necessary to consider how a Colony is constituted, what are the terms of migration as dictated by Nature, or settled by compact, and what social or political rights the man loses, or acquires, that leaves his country to establish himself in a distant plantation.

OF two modes of migration the history of mankind informs us, and so far as I can yet discover, of two only.

IN countries where life was yet unadjusted, and policy unformed, it sometimes happened that by the dissensions of heads of families, by the ambition of daring adventurers, by some accidental pressure of distress, or by the mere discontent of idleness, one part of the community broke off from the rest, and numbers, greater or smaller, forsook their habitations, put themselves under the command of some favourite of fortune, and with or without the consent of their countrymen or governors, went out to see what better regions they could occupy, and in what place, by conquest or by treaty, they could gain a habitation.

SONS of enterprise like these, who committed to their own swords their hopes and their lives, when they left their country, became another nation, with designs, and prospects, and interests, of their own. They looked back no more to their former home; they expected no help from those whom they had left behind: if they conquered, they conquered for themselves; if they were destroyed, they were not by any other power either lamented or revenged.

OF this kind seem to have been all the migrations of the old world, whether historical or fabulous, and of this kind were the eruptions of those nations which from the North invaded the Roman empire, and filled Europe with new sovereignties.

BUT when, by the gradual admission of wiser laws and gentler manners, society became more compacted and better regulated, it was found that the power of every people consisted in union, produced by one common interest, and operating in joint efforts and consistent counsels.

FROM this time Independence perceptibly wasted away. No part of the nation was permitted to act for itself. All now had the same enemies and the same friends; the Government protected individuals, and individuals were required to refer their designs to the prosperity of the Government.

BY this principle it is, that states are formed and consolidated. Every man is taught to consider his own happiness as combined with the publick prosperity, and to think himself great and powerful, in proportion to the greatness and power of his Governors.

HAD the Western continent been discovered between the fourth and tenth century, when all the Northern world was in motion; and had navigation been at that time sufficiently advanced to make so long a passage easily practicable, there is little reason for doubting but the intumescence of nations would have found its vent, like all other expansive violence, where there was least resistance; and that Huns and Vandals, instead of fighting their way to the South of Europe, would have gone by thousands and by myriads under their several chiefs to take possession of regions smiling with pleasure and waving with fertility, from which the naked inhabitants were unable to repel them.

EVERY expedition would in those days of laxity have produced a distinct and independent state. The Scandinavian heroes might have divided the country among them, and have spread the feudal subdivision of regality from Hudson's Bay to the Pacifick Ocean.

BUT Columbus came five or fix hundred years too late for the candidates of sovereignty. When he formed his project of discovery, the fluctuations of military turbulence had subsided, and Europe began to regain a settled form, by established government and regular subordination. No man could any longer erect himself into a chieftain, and lead out his fellow-subjects by his own authority to plunder or to war. He that committed any act of hostility by land or sea, without the commission of some acknowledged sovereign, was considered by all mankind as a robber or a pirate, names which were now of little credit, and of which therefore no man was ambitious.

COLUMBUS in a remoter time would have found his way to some discontented Lord, or some younger brother of a petty Sovereign, who would have taken fire at his proposal, and have quickly kindled with equal heat a troop of followers; they would have built ships, or have seized them, and have wandered with him at all adventures as far as they could keep hope in their company. But the age being now past of vagrant excursion and fortuitous hostility, he was under the necessity of travelling from court to court, scorned and repulsed as a wild projector, an idle promiser of kingdoms in the clouds: nor has any part of the world yet had reason to rejoice that he found at last reception and employment.

IN the same year, in a year hitherto disastrous to mankind, by the Portuguese was discovered the passage of the Indies, and by the Spaniards the coast of America. The nations of Europe were fired with boundless expectation, and the discoverers pursuing their enterprise, made conquests in both hemispheres of wide extent. But the adventurers were contented with plunder; though they took gold and silver to themselves, they seized islands and kingdoms in the name of their Sovereigns. When a new region was gained, a governour was appointed by that power which had given the commission to the conqueror; nor have I met with any European but Stukeley of London, that formed a design of exalting himself in the newly found countries to independent dominion.

To secure a conquest, it was always necessary to plant a colony, and territories thus occupied and settled were rightly considered as mere extensions or processes of empire; as ramifications through which the circulation of one publick interest communicated with the original source of dominion, and which were kept flourishing and spreading by the radical vigour of the Mother-country.

The Colonies of England differ no otherwise from those of other nations, than as the English constitution differs from theirs. All Government is ultimately and essentially absolute, but subordinate societies may have more immunities, or individuals greater liberty, as the operations of Government are differently concluded. An Englishman in the common course of life and action feels no restraint. An English Colony has very liberal powers of regulating its own manners and adjusting its own affairs. But an English individual may by the supreme authority be deprived of liberty, and a Colony divested of its powers, for reasons of which that authority is the only judge.

IN sovereignty there are no gradations. There may be limited royalty, there may be limited consulship; but there can be no limited government. There must in every society be some power or other from which there is no appeal, which admits no restrictions, which pervades the whole mass of the community, regulates and adjusts all subordination, enacts laws or repeals them, erects or annuls judicatures, extends or contracts privileges, exempt itself from question or control, and bounded only by physical necessity.

By this power, wherever it subsists, all legislation and jurisdiction is animated and maintained. From this all legal rights are emanations, which, whether equitably or not, may be legally recalled. It is not infallible, for it may do wrong; but it is irresistible, for it can be resisted only by rebellion, by an act which makes it questionable what shall be thenceforward the supreme power.

An English Colony is a number of persons, to whom the King grants a Charter permitting them to settle in some distant country, and enabling them to constitute a Corporation, enjoying such powers as the Charter grants, to be administered in such forms as the Charter prescribes. As a Corporation they make laws for themselves, but as a Corporation subsisting by a grant from higher authority, to the controll of that authority they continue subject.

As men are placed at a greater distance from the Supreme Council of the kingdom, they must be entrusted with ampler liberty of regulating their conduct by their own wisdom. As they are more secluded from easy recourse to national judicature, they must be more extensively commissioned to pass judgment on each other.

FOR this reason our more important and opulent Colonies see the appearance and feel the effect of a regular Legislature, which in some places has acted so long with unquestioned authority, that it has been forgotten whence that authority was originally derived.

To their Charters the Colonies owe, like other corporations, their political existence. The solemnities of legislation, the administration of justice, the security of property, are all bestowed upon them by the royal grant. Without their Charter there would be no power among them, by which any law could be made, or duties enjoined, any debt recovered, or criminal punished.

A Charter is a grant of certain powers or privileges given to a part of the community for the advantage of the whole, and is therefore liable by its nature to change or to revocation. Every act of Government aims at publick good. A Charter, which experience has shewn to be detrimental to the nation, is to be repealed; because general prosperity must always be preferred to particular interest. If a Charter be used to evil purposes, it is forfeited, as the weapon is taken away which is injuriously employed.

THE Charter therefore by which provincial governments are constituted, may be always legally, and where it is either inconvenient in its nature, or misapplied in its use, may be equitably repealed, and by such repeal the whole fabrick of subordination is immediately destroyed, the constitution sunk at once into a chaos: the society is dissolved into a tumult of individuals, without authority to command, or obligation to obey; without any punishment of wrongs but by personal resentment, or any protection of right but by the hand of the possessor.

A Colony is to the Mother-country as a member to the body, deriving its action and its strength from the general principle of vitality; receiving from the body, and communicating to it, all the benefits and evils of health and disease; liable in dangerous maladies to sharp applications, of which the body however must partake the pain; and exposed, if incurably tainted, to amputation, by which the body likewise will be mutilated.

THE Mother-country always considers the Colonies thus connected, as parts of itself; the prosperity or unhappiness of either is the prosperity or unhappiness of both; not perhaps of both in the same degree, for the body may subsist, though less commodiously, without a limb, but the limb must perish if it be parted from the body.

OUR Colonies therefore, however distant, have been hitherto treated as constituent parts of the British Empire. The inhabitants incorporated by English Charters, are intitled to all the rights of Englishmen. They are governed by English laws, entitled to English dignities, regulated by English counsels, and protected by English arms; and it seems to follow by consequence not easily avoided, that they are subject to English government, and chargeable by English taxation.

To him that considers the nature, the original, the progress, and the constitution of the Colonies, who remembers that the first discoverers had commissions from the crown, that the first settlers owe to a charter their civil forms and regular magistracy, and that all personal immunities and personal securities, by which the condition of the subject has been from time to time improved, have been exended to the Colonists, it will not be doubted but the Parliament of England has a right to bind them by statutes, and *to bind them in all cases whatsoever*, and has therefore a legal and constitutional power of laying upon them any tax or impost, whether external or internal, upon the product of land, or the manufactures of industry, in the exigencies of war, or in the time of profound peace, for the defence of America, *for the purpose of raising a revenue*, or for any other end beneficial to the Empire.

THERE are some, and those not inconsiderable for number, nor contemptible for knowledge, who except the power of taxation from the general dominion of Parliament, and hold that whatever degrees of obedience may be exacted, or whatever authority may be exercised in other acts of Government, there is still reverence to be paid to money, and that legislation passes its limits when it violates the purse.

OF this exception, which by a head not fully impregnated with politicks is not easily comprehended, it is alleged as an unanswerable reason, that the Colonies send no representatives to the House of Commons.

IT is, say the American advocates, the natural distinction of a freeman, and the legal privilege of an Englishman, that he is able to call his possessions his own, that he can sit secure in the enjoyment of inheritance or acquisition, that his house is fortified by the law, and that nothing can be taken from him but by his own consent. This consent is given for every man by his representative in parliament. The Americans unrepresented cannot consent to English taxations, as a corporation, and they will not consent as individuals.

OF this argument, it has been observed by more than one, that its force extends equally to all other laws, that a freeman is not to be exposed to punishment, or be called to any onerous service but by his own consent. The congress has extracted a position from the fanciful *Montesquieu*, that *in a free state every man being a free agent ought to be concerned in his own government.* Whatever is true of taxation is true of every other law, that he who is bound by it, without his consent, is not free, for he is not concerned in his own government.

HE that denies the English Parliament the right of taxation, denies it likewise the right of making any other laws civil or criminal, yet this power over the Colonies was never yet disputed by themselves. They have always admitted statutes for the punishment of offences, and for the redress or prevention of inconveniencies; and the reception of any law draws after it by a chain which cannot be broken, the unwelcome necessity of submitting to taxation.

THAT a free man is governed by himself, or by laws to which he has consented, is a position of mighty sound; but every man that utters it, with whatever confidence, and every man that hears it, with whatever acquiescence, if consent be supposed to imply the power of refusal, feels it to be false. We virtually and implicitly allow the institutions of any Government of which we enjoy the benefit, and solicit the protection. In wide extended dominions, though power has been diffused with the most even hand, yet a very small part of the people are either primarily or secondarily consulted in Legislation. The business of the Publick must be done by delegation. The choice of delegates is made by a select number, and those who are not electors stand idle and helpless spectators of the commonweal, *wholly unconcerned with the government of themselves.*

OF Electors the hap is but little better. They are often far from unanimity in their choice, and where the numbers approach to equality, almost half must be governed not only without, but against their choice.

HOW any man can have consented to institutions established in distant ages, it will be difficult to explain. In the most favourite residence of liberty, the consent of individuals is merely passive, a tacit admission in every community of the terms which that community grants and requires. As all are born the subjects of some state or other, we may be said to have been all born consenting to some system of Government. Other consent than this, the condition of civil life does not allow. It is the unmeaning clamour of the pedants of policy, the delirious dream of republican fanaticism.

BUT hear, ye sons and daughters of liberty, the sounds which the winds are wafting from the Western Continent. The Americans are telling one another, what, if we may judge from their noisy triumph, they have but lately discovered, and what yet is a very important truth. *That they are entitled to Life, Liberty, and Property, and that they have never ceded to any sovereign power whatever a right to dispose of either without their consent.*

WHILE this resolution stands alone, the Americans are free from singularity of opinion; their wit has not yet betrayed them to heresy. While they speak as the naked sons of Nature, they claim but what is claimed by other men, and have withheld nothing but what all withhold. They are here upon firm ground, behind entrenchments which never can be forced.

HUMANITY is very uniform. The Americans have this resemblance to Europeans, that they do not always know when they are well. They soon quit the fortress that could neither have been mined by sophistry, nor battered by declamation. Their next resolution declares, that *their ancestors, who first settled the Colonies, were, at the time of their emigration from the Mother-country, entitled to all the rights, liberties, and immunities of free and natural-born subjects within the realm of England.*

THIS likewise is true; but when this is granted, their boast of original rights is at an end; they are no longer in a State of Nature. These lords of themselves, these kings of *Me*, these demigods of independence, sink down to Colonists, governed by a Charter. If their ancestors were subjects, they acknowledged a Sovereign; if they had a right to English privileges, they were accountable to English laws, and what must grieve the Lover of Liberty to discover, had ceded to the King and Parliament, whether the right or not, at least the power, of disposing, *without their consent, of their lives, liberties, and properties.* It therefore is required of them to prove, that the Parliament ever ceded to them a dispensation from that obedience, which they owe as natural-born subjects, or any degree of independence or immunity not enjoyed by other Englishmen.

THEY say, That by such emigration they by no means forfeited, surrendered, or lost any of those rights; but that *they were, and their descendents now are, entitled to the exercise and enjoyment of all such of them as their local and other circumstances enable them to exercise and enjoy.*

THAT they who form a settlement by a lawful Charter, having committed no crime, forfeit no privileges, will be readily confessed; but what they do not forfeit by any judicial sentence, they may lose by natural effects. As man can be but in one place at once, he cannot have the advantages of multiplied residence. He that will enjoy the brightness of sunshine, must quit the coolness of the shade. He who goes voluntarily to America, cannot complain of losing what he leaves in Europe. He perhaps had a right to vote for a knight or burgess: by crossing the Atlantick he has not nullified his right; for he has made its exertion no longer possible. By his own choice he has left a country where he had a vote and little property, for another, where he has great property, but no vote. But as this preference was deliberate and unconstrained, he is still *concerned in the government of himself;* he has reduced himself from a voter to one of the innumerable multitude that have no vote. He has truly *ceded his right*, but he still is governed by his own consent; because he has consented to throw his atom of interest into the general mass of the community. Of the consequences of his own act he has no cause to complain; he has chosen, or intended to chuse, the greater good; he is represented, as himself desired, in the general representation.

BUT the privileges of an American scorn the limits of place; they are part of himself, and cannot be lost by departure from his country; they float in the air, or glide under the ocean.

DORIS amara suam non intermisceat undam.

A Planter, wherever he settles, is not only a freeman, but a legislator, *ubi imperator, ibi Roma. As the English Colonists are not represented in the British Parliament, they are entitled to a free and exclusive power of legislation in their several legislatures, in all cases of Taxation and internal polity, subject only to the negative of the Sovereign, in such manner as has been heretofore used and accustomed. We cheerfully consent to the operation of such acts of the British Parliament as are* bona fide *restrained to the regulation of our external commerce—excluding every idea of Taxation, internal or external, for raising a revenue on the subjects of America without their consent.*

THEIR reason for this claim is, *that the foundation of English Liberty, and of all Government, is a right in the People to participate in their Legislative Council.*

THEY inherit, they say, *from their ancestors, the right which their ancestors professed, of enjoying all the privileges of Englishmen.* That they inherit the right of their ancestors is allowed; but they can inherit no more. Their ancestors left a country where the representatives of the people were elected by men particularly qualified, and where those who wanted qualifications, or who did not use them, were bound by the decisions of men whom they had not deputed.

THE colonists are the descendants of men, who either had no votes in elections, or who voluntarily resigned them for something, in their opinion, of more estimation: they have therefore exactly what their ancestors left them, not a vote in making laws, or in constituting legislators, but the happiness of being protected by law, and the duty of obeying it.

WHAT their ancestors did not carry with them, neither they nor their descendants have since acquired. They have not, by abandoning their part in one legislature, obtained the power of constituting another, exclusive and independent, any more than the multitudes, who are now debarred from voting, have a right to erect a separate Parliament for themselves.

MEN are wrong for want of sense, but they are wrong by halves for want of spirit. Since the Americans have discovered that they can make a Parliament, whence comes it that they do not think themselves equally empowered to make a King? If they are subjects, whose government is constituted by a charter, they can form no body of independent legislature. If their rights are inherent and underived, they may by their own suffrages encircle with a diadem the brows of Mr. Cushing.

IT is farther declared by the Congress of Philadelphia, *that his majesty's Colonies are entitled to all the privileges and immunities granted and confirmed to them by Royal Charters, or secured to them by their several codes of provincial laws.*

THE first clause of this resolution is easily understood, and will be readily admitted. To all the privileges which a Charter can convey, they are by a Royal Charter evidently entitled. The second clause is of greater difficulty; for how can a provincial law secure privileges or immunities to a province? Provincial laws may grant to certain individuals of the province the enjoyment of gainful, or an immunity from onerous offices; they may operate upon the people to whom they relate; but no province can confer provincial privileges on itself. They may have a right to all which the King has given them; but it is a conceit of the other hemisphere, that men have a right to all which they have given to themselves.

A corporation is considered in law as an individual, and can no more extend its own immunities, than a man can by his own choice assume dignities or titles.

THE Legislature of a Colony, let not the comparison be too much disdained, is only the vestry of a larger parish, which may lay a cess on the inhabitants, and enforce the payment; but can extend no influence beyond its own district, must modify its particular regulations by the general law, and whatever may be its internal expences, is still liable to Taxes laid by superior authority.

THE Charters given to different provinces are different, and no general right can be extracted from them. The Charter of Pensylvania, where this Congress of anarchy has been impudently held contains a clause admitting in express terms Taxation by the Parliament. If in the other Charters no such reserve is made, it must have been omitted as not necessary, because it is implied in the nature of subordinate government. They who are subject to laws, are liable to Taxes. If any such immunity had been granted, it is still revocable by the Legislature, and ought to be revoked as contrary to the publick good, which is in every Charter ultimately intended.

SUPPOSE it true that any such exemption is contained in the Charter of Maryland, it can be pleaded only by the Marylanders. It is of no use for any other province, and with regard even to them, must have been considered as one of the grants in which the King has been deceived, and annulled as mischievous to the Publick, by sacrificing to one little settlement the general interest of the Empire; as infringing the system of dominion, and violating the compact of Government. But Dr. Tucker has shewn that even this Charter promises no exemption from Parliamentary Taxes.

IN the controversy agitated about the beginning of this century, whether the English laws could bind Ireland, Davenant, who defended against Molyneux the claims of England, considered it as necessary to prove nothing more, than that the present Irish might be deemed a Colony.

THE necessary connexion of representatives with Taxes, seems to have sunk deep into many of those minds, that admit sounds without their meaning.

OUR nation is represented in Parliament by an assembly as numerous as can well consist with order and dispatch, chosen by persons so differently qualified in different places, that the mode of choice seems to be, for the most part, formed by chance, and settled by custom. Of individuals far the greater part have no vote, and of the voters few have any personal knowledge of him to whom they entrust their liberty and fortune.

YET this representation has the whole effect expected or desired; that of spreading so wide the care of general interest, and the participation of publick counsels, that the interest or corruption of particular men can seldom operate with much injury to the Publick.

FOR this reason many populous and opulent towns neither enjoy nor desire particular representatives: they are included in the general scheme of publick administration, and cannot suffer but with the rest of the Empire.

IT is urged that the Americans have not the same security, and that a British Legislature may wanton with their property; yet if it be true, that their wealth is our wealth, and that their ruin will be our ruin, the Parliament has the same interest in attending to them, as to any other part of the nation. The reason why we place any confidence in our representatives is, that they must share in the good or evil which their counsels shall produce. Their share is indeed commonly consequential and remote; but it is not often possible that any immediate advantage can be extended to such numbers as may prevail against it. We are therefore as secure against intentional depravations of Government as human wisdom can make us, and upon this security the Americans may venture to repose.

IT is said by the *Old Member* who has written an *Appeal* against the Tax, that as *the produce of American labour is spent in British manufactures, the balance of trade is greatly against them; whatever you take directly in Taxes, is in effect taken from your own commerce. If the minister seizes the money with which the American should pay his debts and come to market, the merchant cannot expect him as a customer, nor can the debts already contracted be paid.—Suppose we obtain from America a million instead of one hundred thousand pounds, it would be supplying our present exigence by the future ruin of our commerce.*

ALL this is true; but the *old Member* seems not to perceive, that if his brethren of the Legislature know this as well as himself, the Americans are in no danger of oppression, since by men commonly provident they must be so taxed, as that we may not lose one way what we gain another.

THE same *old Member* has discovered, that the judges formerly thought it illegal to tax Ireland, and declares that no cases can be more alike than those of Ireland and America; yet the judges whom he quotes have mentioned a difference. Ireland, they say, *hath a Parliament of its own*. When any Colony has an independent Parliament, acknowledged by the Parliament of Britain, the cases will differ less. Yet by the 6 Geo. I. chap. 5. the Acts of the British Parliament bind Ireland.

IT is urged that when Wales, Durham, and Chester were divested of their particular privileges or ancient government, and reduced to the state of English counties, they had representatives assigned them.

To those from whom something had been taken, something in return might properly be given. To the Americans their Charters are left as they were, except that of which their sedition has deprived them. If they were to be represented in Parliament, something would be granted, though nothing is withdrawn.

THE inhabitants of Chester, Durham, and Wales, were invited to exchange their peculiar institutions for the power of voting, which they wanted before. The Americans have voluntarily resigned the power of voting to live in distant and separate governments, and what they have voluntarily quitted, they have no right to claim.

IT must always be remembered that they are represented by the same virtual representation as the greater part of Englishmen; and that if by change of place they have less share in the Legislature than is proportioned to their opulence, they by their removal gained that opulence, and had originally and have now their choice of a vote at home, or riches at a distance.

WE are told, what appears to the *old Member* and to others a position that must drive us into inextricable absurdity, that we have either no right, or the sole right of taxing the Colonies. The meaning is, that if we can tax them, they cannot tax themselves; and that if they can tax themselves, we cannot tax them. We answer with very little hesitation, that for the general use of the Empire we have the sole right of taxing them. If they have contributed any thing in their own assemblies, what they contributed was not paid, but given; it was not a tax or tribute, but a present. Yet they have the natural and legal power of levying money on themselves for provincial purposes, of providing for their own expence, at their own discretion. Let not this be thought new or strange; it is the state of every parish in the kingdom.

THE friends of the Americans are of different opinions. Some think that being unrepresented they ought to tax themselves, and others that they ought to have representatives in the British Parliament.

IF they are to tax themselves, what power is to remain in the supreme Legislature? That they must settle their own mode of levying their money is supposed. May the British Parliament tell them how much they shall contribute? If the sum may be prescribed, they will return few thanks for the power of raising it; if they are at liberty to grant or to deny, they are no longer subjects.

IF they are to be represented, what number of these western orators are to be admitted. This I suppose the parliament must settle; yet if men have a natural and unalienable right to be represented, who shall determine the number of their delegates? Let us however suppose them to send twenty-three, half as many as the kingdom of Scotland, what will this representation avail them? To pay taxes will be still a grievance. The love of money will not be lessened, nor the power of getting it increased.

WHITHER will this necessity of representation drive us? Is every petty settlement to be out of the reach of government, till it has sent a senator to Parliament; or may two or a greater number be forced to unite in a single deputation? What at last is the difference, between him that is taxed by compulsion without representation, and him that is represented by compulsion in order to be taxed?

FOR many reigns the House of Commons was in a state of fluctuation: new burgesses were added from time to time, without any reason now to be discovered; but the number has been fixed for more than a century and a half, and the king's power of increasing it has been questioned. It will hardly be thought fit to new model the constitution in favour of the planters, who, as they grow rich, may buy estates in England, and without any innovation, effectually represent their native colonies.

THE friends of the Americans indeed ask for them what they do not ask for themselves. This inestimable right of representation they have never solicited. They mean not to exchange solid money for such airy honour. They say, and say willingly, that they cannot conveniently be represented; because their inference is, that they cannot be taxed. They are too remote to share the general government, and therefore claim the privilege of governing themselves.

OF the principles contained in the resolutions of the Congress, however wild, indefinite, and obscure, such has been the influence upon American understanding, that from New-England to South-Carolina there is formed a general combination of all the Provinces against their Mother-country. The madness of independence has spread from Colony to Colony, till order is lost and government despised, and all is filled with misrule, uproar, violence, and confusion. To be quiet is disaffection, to be loyal is treason.

THE Congress of Philadelphia, an assembly convened by its own authority, and as a seditious conventicle punishable by law, has promulgated a declaration, in compliance with which the communication between Britain and the greatest part of North America is now suspended. They ceased to admit the importation of English goods in December 1774, and determine to permit the exportation of their own no longer than to November 1775.

THIS might seem enough, but they have done more. They have declared, that they shall treat all as enemies who do not concur with them in disaffection and perverseness, and that they will trade with none that shall trade with Britain.

THEY threaten to stigmatize in their Gazette those who shall consume the products or merchandise of their Mother-country, and are now searching suspected houses for prohibited goods.

THESE hostile declarations they profess themselves ready to maintain by force. They have armed the militia of their provinces and seized the publick stores of ammunition. They are therefore no longer subjects, since they refuse the laws of their Sovereign, and in defence of that refusal are making open preparations for war.

BEING now in their own opinion free states, they are not only raising armies, but forming alliances, not only hastening to rebel themselves, but seducing their neighbours to rebellion. They have published an address to the inhabitants of Quebec, in which discontent and resistance are openly incited, and with very respectful mention of *the sagacity of Frenchmen*, invite them to send deputies to the Congress of Philadelphia, to that seat of Virtue and Veracity, whence the people of England are told, that to establish popery, *a religion fraught with sanguinary and impious tenets*, even in Quebec, a country of which the inhabitants are papists, is so contrary to the constitution, that it cannot be lawfully done by the legislature itself, where it is made one of the articles of their association, to deprive the conquered French of their religious establishment; and whence the French of Quebec are, at the same time, flattered into sedition, by professions of expecting *from the liberality of sentiment, distinguishing* their *nation*, that *difference of religion will not prejudice them against a hearty amity*, because *the transcendent nature of freedom elevates all who unite in the cause above such low-minded infirmities*.

QUEBEC, however, is at a great distance. They have aimed a stroke from which they may hope for greater and more speedy mischief. They have tried to infect the people of England with the contagion of disloyalty. Their credit is happily not such as gives them influence proportionate to their malice. When they talk of their pretended immunities *guarrantied by the plighted faith of Government, and the most solemn compacts with English Sovereigns*, we think ourselves at liberty to inquire when the faith was plighted and the compact made; and when we can only find that King James and King Charles the First promised the settlers in Massachuset's Bay, now famous by the appellation of Bostonians, exemption from taxes for seven years, we infer with Mr. Mauduit, that by this *solemn compact*, they were, after the expiration of the stipulated term, liable to taxation.

WHEN they apply to our compassion, by telling us, that they are to be carried from their own country to be tried for certain offences, we are not so ready to pity them, as to advise them not to offend. While they are innocent they are safe.

WHEN they tell of laws made expressly for their punishment, we answer, that tumults and sedition were always punishable, and that the new law prescribes only the mode of execution.

WHEN it is said that the whole town of Boston is distressed for a misdemeanour of a few, we wonder at their shamelessness; for we know that the town of Boston, and all the associated provinces, are now in rebellion to defend or justify the criminals.

IF frauds in the imposts of Boston are tried by commission without a jury, they are tried here in the same mode; and why should the Bostonians expect from us more tenderness for them than for ourselves?

IF they are condemned unheard, it is because there is no need of a trial. The crime is manifest and notorious. All trial is the investigation of something doubtful. An Italian philosopher observes, that no man desires to hear what he has already seen.

IF their assemblies have been suddenly dissolved, what was the reason? Their deliberations were indecent, and their intentions seditious. The power of dissolution is granted and reserved for such times of turbulence. Their best friends have been lately soliciting the King to dissolve his Parliament, to do what they so loudly complain of suffering.

THAT the same vengeance involves the innocent and guilty is an evil to be lamented, but human caution cannot prevent it, nor human power always redress it. To bring misery on those who have not deserved it, is part of the aggregated guilt of rebellion.

THAT governours have been sometimes given them only that a great man might get ease from importunity, and that they have had judges not always of the deepest learning, or the purest integrity, we have no great reason to doubt, because such misfortunes happen to ourselves. Whoever is governed will sometimes be governed ill, even when he is most concerned in his own government.

THAT improper officers or magistrates are sent, is the crime or folly of those that sent them. When incapacity is discovered, it ought to be removed; if corruption is detected, it ought to be punished. No government could subsist for a day, if single errors could justify defection.

ONE of their complaints is not such as can claim much commiseration from the softest bosom. They tell us, that we have changed our conduct, and that a tax is now laid by Parliament on those which were never taxed by Parliament before. To this we think it may be easily answered, that the longer they have been spared, the better they can pay.

IT is certainly not much their interest to represent innovation as criminal or invidious; for they have introduced into the history of mankind a new mode of disaffection, and have given, I believe, the first example of a proscription published by a Colony against the Mother-country.

To what is urged of new powers granted to the Courts of Admiralty, or the extension of authority conferred on the judges, it may be answered in a few words, that they have themselves made such regulations necessary; that they are established for the prevention of greater evils; at the same time, it must be observed, that these powers have not been extended since the rebellion in America.

ONE mode of persuasion their ingenuity has suggested, which it may perhaps be less easy to resist. That we may not look with indifference on the American contest, or imagine that the struggle is for a claim, which, however decided, is of small importance and remote consequence, the Philadelphian Congress has taken care to inform us, that they are resisting the demands of Parliament, as well for our sakes as their own.

THEIR keenness of perspicacity has enabled them to pursue consequences to a great distance; to see through clouds impervious to the dimness of European sight; and to find, I know not how, that when they are taxed, we shall be enslaved.

THAT slavery is a miserable state we have been often told, and doubtless many a Briton will tremble to find it so near as in America; but how it will be brought hither, the Congress must inform us. The question might distress a common understanding; but the statesmen of the other hemisphere can easily resolve it. Our ministers, they say, are our enemies, and *if they should carry the point of taxation, may with the same army enslave us. It may be said, we will not pay them; but remember,* say the western sages, *the taxes from America, and we may add the men, and particularly the Roman Catholics of this vast continent will then be in the power of your enemies. Nor have you any reason to expect, that after making slaves of us, many of us will refuse to assist in reducing you to the same abject state.*

THESE are dreadful menaces; but suspecting that they have not much the sound of probability, the Congress proceeds: *Do not treat this as chimerical. Know that in less than half a century the quit-rents reserved to the crown from the numberless grants of this vast continent will pour large streams of wealth into the royal coffers. If to this be added the power of taxing America at pleasure, the crown will possess more treasure than may be necessary to purchase* the remains *of liberty in your island.*

ALL this is very dreadful; but amidst the terror that shakes my frame, I cannot forbear to wish that some sluice were opened for these streams of treasure. I should gladly see America return half of what England has expended in her defence; and of the stream that will *flow so largely in less than half a century*, I hope a small rill at least may be found to quench the thirst of the present generation, which seems to think itself in more danger of wanting money than of losing liberty.

IT is difficult to judge with what intention such airy bursts of malevolence are vented: if such writers hope to deceive, let us rather repel them with scorn, than refute them by disputation.

IN this last terrifick paragraph are two positions that, if our fears do not overpower our reflection, may enable us to support life a little longer. We are told by these croakers of calamity, not only that our present ministers design to enslave us, but that the same malignity of purpose is to descend through all their successors, and that the wealth to be poured into England by the Pactolus of America will, whenever it comes, be employed to purchase the remains of liberty.

OF those who now conduct the national affairs we may, without much arrogance, presume to know more than themselves, and of those who shall succeed them, whether minister or king, not to know less.

THE other position is, that the *Crown*, if this laudable opposition should not be successful, *will have the power of taxing America at pleasure*. Surely they think rather too meanly of our apprehensions, when they suppose us not to know what they well know themselves, that they are taxed, like all other British subjects, by Parliament; and that the Crown has not by the new imposts, whether right or wrong, obtained any additional power over their possessions.

It were a curious, but an idle speculation to inquire, what effect these dictators of sedition expect from the dispersion of their letter among us. If they believe their own complaints of hardship, and really dread the danger which they describe, they will naturally hope to communicate their own perceptions to their fellow-subjects. But probably in America, as in other places, the chiefs are incendiaries, that hope to rob in the tumults of a conflagration, and toss brands among a rabble passively combustible. Those who wrote the Address, though they have shown no great extent or profundity of mind, are yet probably wiser than to believe it: but they have been taught by some master of mischief, how to put in motion the engine of political electricity; to attract by the sounds of Liberty and Property, to repel by those of Popery and Slavery; and to give the great stroke by the name of Boston.

When subordinate communities oppose the decrees of the general legislature with defiance thus audacious, and malignity thus acrimonious, nothing remains but to conquer or to yield; to allow their claim of independence, or to reduce them by force to submission and allegiance.

It might be hoped, that no Englishman could be found, whom the menaces of our own Colonists, just rescued from the French, would not move to indignation, like that of the Scythians, who, returning from war, found themselves excluded from their own houses by their slaves.

That corporations constituted by favour, and existing by sufferance, should dare to prohibit commerce with their native country, and threaten individuals by infamy, and societies with at least suspension of amity, for daring to be more obedient to government than themselves, is a degree of insolence, which not only deserves to be punished, but of which the punishment is loudly demanded by the order of life, and the peace of nations.

Yet there have risen up, in the face of the publick, men who, by whatever corruptions or whatever infatuation, have undertaken to defend the Americans, endeavour to shelter them from resentment, and propose reconciliation without submission.

As political diseases are naturally contagious, let it be supposed for a moment that Cornwal, seized with the Philadelphian frenzy, may resolve to separate itself from the general system of the English constitution, and judge of its own rights in its own parliament. A Congress might then meet at Truro, and address the other counties in a style not unlike the language of the American patriots.

"Friends and Fellow-subjects,

"We the delegates of the several towns and parishes of Cornwal, assembled to deliberate upon our own state and that of our constituents, having, after serious debate and calm consideration, settled the scheme of our future conduct, hold it necessary to declare in this publick manner, the resolutions which we think ourselves entitled to form by the immutable laws of Nature, and the unalienable rights of reasonable Beings, and into which we have been at last compelled by grievances and oppressions, long endured by us in patient silence, not because we did not feel, or could not remove them, but because we were unwilling to give disturbance to a settled government, and hoped that others would in time find like ourselves their true interest and their original powers, and all co-operate to universal happiness.

"BUT since having long indulged the pleasing expectation, we find general discontent, not likely to increase, or not likely to end in general defection, we resolve to erect alone the standard of liberty.

"*Know then*, that you are no longer to consider Cornwall as an English county, visited by English judges, receiving law from an English Parliament, or included in any general taxation of the kingdom; but as a state distinct, and independent, governed by its own institutions, administered by its own magistrates, and exempt from any tax or tribute but such as we shall impose upon ourselves.

"WE are the acknowledged descendants of the earliest inhabitants of Britain, of men, who, before the time of history, took possession of the island desolate and waste, and therefore open to the first occupants. Of this descent, our language is a sufficient proof, which, not quite a century ago, was different from yours.

"SUCH are the Cornishmen; but who are you? who but the unauthorised and lawless children of intruders, invaders, and oppressors? who but the transmitters of wrong, the inheritors of robbery? In claiming independence we claim but little. We might require you to depart from a land which you possess by usurpation, and to restore all that you have taken from us.

"INDEPENDENCE is the gift of Nature, bestowed impartially on all her sons; no man is born the master of another. Every Cornishman is a freeman, for we have never resigned the rights of humanity; and he only can be thought free, who is not governed but by his own consent.

"YOU may urge that the present system of government has descended through many ages, and that we have a larger part in the representation of the kingdom, than any other county.

"ALL this is true, but it is neither cogent nor persuasive. We look to the original of things. Our union with the English counties was either compelled by force, or settled by compact.

"THAT which was made by violence, may by violence be broken. If we were treated as a conquered people, our rights might be obscured, but could never be extinguished. The sword can give nothing but power, which a sharper sword can take away.

"IF our union was by compact, whom could the compact bind but those that concurred in the stipulations? We gave our ancestors no commission to settle the terms of future existence. They might be cowards that were frighted, or blockheads that were cheated; but whatever they were, they could contract only for themselves. What they could establish, we can annul.

"AGAINST our present form of government it shall stand in the place of all argument, that we do not like it. While we are governed as we do not like, where is our liberty? We do not like taxes, we will therefore not be taxed; we do not like your laws, and will not obey them.

"THE taxes laid by our representatives are laid, you tell us, by our own consent: but we will no longer consent to be represented. Our number of legislators was originally a burthen imposed upon us by English tyranny, and ought then to have been refused: if it be now considered as a disproportionate advantage, there can be no reason for complaining that we resign it.

"WE shall therefore form a Senate of our own, under a President whom the King shall nominate, but whose authority we will limit, by adjusting his salary to his merit. We will not withhold our share of contribution to the necessary expence of lawful government, but we will decide for ourselves what share we shall pay, what expence is necessary, and what government is lawful.

"TILL the authority of our council is acknowledged, and we are proclaimed independent and unaccountable, we will, after the tenth day of September, keep our Tin in our own hands: you can be supplied from no other place, and must therefore comply at last, or be poisoned with the copper of your own kitchens.

"IF any Cornishman shall refuse his name to this just and laudable association, he shall be tumbled from St. Michael's Mount, or buried alive in a tin-mine; and if any emissary shall be found seducing Cornishmen to their former state, he shall be smeared with tar, and rolled in feathers, and chased with dogs out of our dominions.

From the Cornish Congress at Truro."

OF this memorial what could be said but that it was written in jest, or written by a madman? Yet I know not whether the warmest admirers of Pennsylvanian eloquence can find any argument in the Addresses of the Congress, that is not with greater strength urged by the Cornishman.

THE argument of the irregular troops of controversy, stripped of its colours, and turned out naked to the view, is no more than this. Liberty is the birthright of man, and where obedience is compelled, there is no Liberty. The answer is equally simple. Government is necessary to man, and where obedience is not compelled, there is no government.

IF the subject refuses to obey, it is the duty of authority to use compulsion. Society cannot subsist but by some power; first of making laws, and then of enforcing them.

To one of the threats hissed out by the Congress, I have put nothing similar into the Cornish proclamation; because it is too foolish for buffoonery, and too wild for madness. If we do not withhold our King and his Parliament from taxing them, they will cross the Atlantick and enslave us.

How they will come they have not told us: perhaps they will take wing, and light upon our coasts. When the cranes thus begin to flutter, it is time for pygmies to keep their eyes about them. The Great Orator observes, that they will be very fit, after they have been taxed, to impose chains upon us. If they are so fit as their friend describes them, and so willing as they describe themselves, let us increase our army, and double our militia.

It has been of late a very general practice to talk of slavery among those who are setting at defiance every power that keeps the world in order. If the learned author of the *Reflections on Learning* has rightly observed, that no man ever could give law to language, it will be vain to prohibit the use of the word *slavery*; but I could wish it more discreetly uttered; it is driven at one time too hard into our ears by the loud hurricane of Pennsylvanian eloquence, and at another glides too cold into our hearts by the soft conveyance of a female patriot bewailing the miseries of her *friends and fellow-citizens*.

Such has been the progress of sedition, that those who a few years ago disputed only our right of laying taxes, now question the validity of every act of legislation. They consider themselves as emancipated from obedience, and as being no longer the subjects of the British Crown. They leave us no choice but of yielding or conquering, of resigning our dominion, or maintaining it by force.

From force many endeavours have been used, either to dissuade, or to deter us. Sometimes the merit of the Americans is exalted, and sometimes their sufferings are aggravated. We are told of their contributions to the last war, a war incited by their outcries, and continued for their protection, a war by which none but themselves were gainers. All that they can boast is, that they did something for themselves, and did not wholly stand inactive, while the sons of Britain were fighting in their cause.

If we cannot admire, we are called to pity them; to pity those that shew no regard to their mother country; have obeyed no law which they could violate; have imparted no good which they could withold; have entered into associations of fraud to rob their creditors; and into combinations to distress all who depended on their commerce. We are reproached with the cruelty of shutting one port, where every port is shut against us. We are censured as tyrannical for hindering those from fishing, who have condemned our merchants to bankruptcy and our manufacturers to hunger.

Others persuade us to give them more liberty, to take off restraints, and relax authority; and tell us what happy consequences will arise from forbearance: How their affections will be conciliated, and into what diffusions of beneficence their gratitude will luxuriate. They will love their friends, they will reverence their protectors. They will throw themselves into our arms, and lay their property at our feet. They will buy from no other what we can sell them; they will sell to no other what we wish to buy.

That any obligations should overpower their attention to profit, we have known them long enough not to expect. It is not to be expected from a more liberal people. With what kindness they repay benefits, they are now shewing us, who, as soon as we have delivered them from France, are defying and proscribing us.

BUT if we will permit them to tax themselves, they will give us more than we require. If we proclaim them independent, they will during pleasure pay us a subsidy. The contest is not now for money, but for power. The question is not how much we shall collect, but by what authority the collection shall be made.

THOSE who find that the Americans cannot be shewn in any form that may raise love or pity, dress them in habiliments of terrour, and try to make us think them formidable. The Bostonians can call into the field ninety thousand men. While we conquer all before us, new enemies will rise up behind, and our work will be always to begin. If we take possession of the towns, the Colonists will retire into the inland regions, and the gain of victory will be only empty houses and a wide extent of waste and desolation. If we subdue them for the present, they will universally revolt in the next war, and resign us without pity to subjection and destruction.

To all this it may be answered, that between losing America and resigning it, there is no great difference; that it is not very reasonable to jump into the sea, because the ship is leaky. All those evils may befal us, but we need not hasten them.

THE Dean of Gloucester has proposed, and seems to propose it seriously, that we should at once release our claims, declare them masters of themselves, and whistle them down the wind. His opinion is, that our gain from them will be the same, and our expence less. What they can have most cheaply from Britain, they will still buy, what they can sell to us at the highest price they will still sell.

IT is, however, a little hard, that having so lately fought and conquered for their safety, we should govern them no longer. By letting them loose before the war, how many millions might have been saved. One ridiculous proposal is best answered by another. Let us restore to the French what we have taken from them. We shall see our Colonists at our feet, when they have an enemy so near them. Let us give the Indians arms, and teach them discipline, and encourage them now and then to plunder a Plantation. Security and leisure are the parents of sedition.

WHILE these different opinions are agitated, it seems to be determined by the Legislature, that force shall be tried. Men of the pen have seldom any great skill in conquering kingdoms, but they have strong inclination to give advice. I cannot forbear to wish, that this commotion may end without bloodshed, and that the rebels may be subdued by terrour rather than by violence; and therefore recommend such a force as may take away, not only the power, but the hope of resistance, and by conquering without a battle, save many from the sword.

IF their obstinacy continues without actual hostilities, it may perhaps be mollified by turning out the soldiers to free quarters, forbidding any personal cruelty or hurt. It has been proposed, that the slaves should be set free, an act which surely the lovers of liberty cannot but commend. If they are furnished with fire arms for defence, and utensils for husbandry, and settled in some simple form of government within the country, they may be more grateful and honest than their masters.

FAR be it from any Englishman to thirst for the blood of his fellow-subjects. Those who most deserve our resentment are unhappily at less distance. The Americans, when the Stamp Act was first proposed, undoubtedly disliked it, as every nation dislikes an impost; but they had no thought of resisting it, till they were encouraged and incited by European intelligence from men whom they thought their friends, but who were friends only to themselves.

ON the original contrivers of mischief let an insulted nation pour out its vengeance. With whatever design they have inflamed this pernicious contest, they are themselves equally detestable. If they wish success to the Colonies, they are traitors to this country; if they wish their defeat, they are traitors at once to America and England. To them and them only must be imputed the interruption of commerce, and the miseries of war, the sorrow of those that shall be ruined, and the blood of those that shall fall.

SINCE the Americans have made it necessary to subdue them, may they be subdued with the least injury possible to their persons and their possessions. When they are reduced to obedience, may that obedience be secured by stricter laws and stronger obligations.

NOTHING can be more noxious to society than that erroneous clemency, which, when a rebellion is suppressed, exacts no forfeiture and establishes no securities, but leaves the rebels in their former state. Who would not try the experiment which promises advantage without expence? If rebels once obtain a victory, their wishes are accomplished; if they are defeated, they suffer little, perhaps less than their conquerors; however often they play the game, the chance is always in their favour. In the mean time, they are growing rich by victualing the troops that we have sent against them, and perhaps gain more by the residence of the army than they lose by the obstruction of their port.

THEIR charters being now, I suppose, legally forfeited, may be modelled as shall appear most commodious to the Mother-country. Thus the privileges, which are found by experience liable to misuse, will be taken away, and those who now bellow as patriots, bluster as soldiers, and domineer as legislators, will sink into sober merchants and silent planters, peaceably diligent, and securely rich.

BUT there is one writer, and perhaps many who do not write, to whom the contraction of these pernicious privileges appears very dangerous, and who startle at the thoughts of *England free and America in chains*. Children fly from their own shadow, and rhetoricians are frighted by their own voices. *Chains* is undoubtedly a dreadful word; but perhaps the masters of civil wisdom may discover some gradations between chains and anarchy. Chains need not be put upon those who will be restrained without them. This contest may end in the softer phrase of English Superiority and American Obedience.

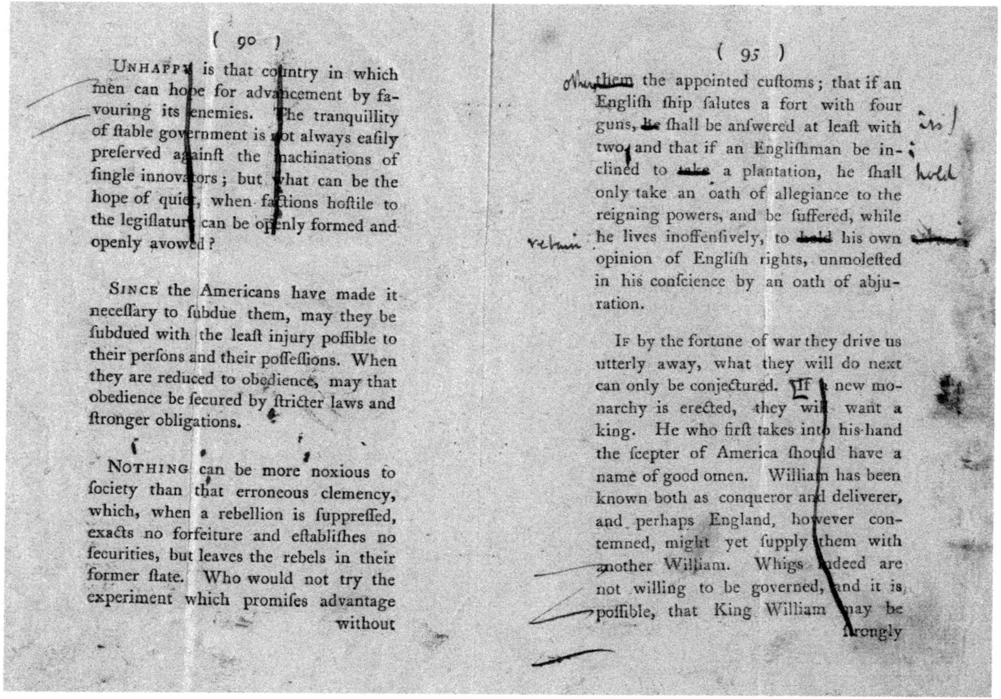

(90)

UNHAPPY is that country in which men can hope for advancement by favouring its enemies. The tranquillity of stable government is not always easily preferred against the machinations of single innovators; but what can be the hope of quiet, when factions hostile to the legislature can be openly formed and openly avowed?

SINCE the Americans have made it necessary to subdue them, may they be subdued with the least injury possible to their persons and their possessions. When they are reduced to obedience, may that obedience be secured by stricter laws and stronger obligations.

NOTHING can be more noxious to society than that erroneous clemency, which, when a rebellion is suppressed, exacts no forfeiture and establishes no securities, but leaves the rebels in their former state. Who would not try the experiment which promises advantage without

(95)

the appointed customs; that if an English ship salutes a fort with four guns, shall be answered at least with two, and that if an Englishman be inclined to a plantation, he shall only take an oath of allegiance to the reigning powers, and be suffered, while he lives inoffensively, to his own opinion of English rights, unmolested in his conscience by an oath of abjuration.

IF by the fortune of war they drive us utterly away, what they will do next can only be conjectured. If new monarchy is erected, they will want a king. He who first takes into his hand the scepter of America should have a name of good omen. William has been known both as conqueror and deliverer, and perhaps England, however contemned, might yet supply them with another William. Whigs indeed are not willing to be governed, and it is, possible, that King William may be strongly

FIGURE 12 Proof page of *Taxation no Tyranny* corrected by the author. Courtesy of Houghton Library, Harvard University.

WE are told, that the subjection of Americans may tend to the diminution of our own liberties: an event, which none but very perspicacious politicians are able to foresee. If slavery be thus fatally contagious, how is it that we hear the loudest yelps for liberty among the drivers of negroes?

BUT let us interrupt a while this dream of conquest, settlement, and supremacy. Let us remember that being to contend, according to one orator, with three millions of Whigs, and according to another, with ninety thousand patriots of Massachusets Bay, we may possibly be checked in our career of reduction. We may be reduced to peace upon equal terms, or driven from the western continent, and forbidden to violate a second time the happy borders of the land of liberty. The time is now perhaps at hand, which Sir Thomas Brown predicted between jest and earnest,

> *When America shall no more send out her treasure,*
> *But spend it at home in American pleasure.*

IF we are allowed upon our defeat to stipulate conditions, I hope the treaty of Boston will permit us to import into the confederated Cantons such products as they do not raise, and such manufactures as they do not make, and cannot buy cheaper from other nations, paying like others the appointed customs; that if an English ship salutes a fort with four guns, it shall be answered at least with two; and that if an Englishman be inclined to hold a plantation, he shall only take an oath of allegiance to the reigning powers, and be suffered, while he lives inoffensively, to retain his own opinion of English rights, unmolested in his conscience by an oath of abjuration.

FINIS.

Diary entry

FRIDAY 14 APRIL 1775

Good Friday, April 14, 1775.

BOSWEL came in before I was up. We breakfasted; I only drank tea, without milk or bread. We went to church, saw Dr. Wetherel in the pew, and, by his desire, took him home with us. He did not go very soon, and Boswel staid. Dilly and Miller called. Boswel and I went to church, but came very late. We then took tea, by Boswel's desire; and I eat one bun, I think, that I might not seem to fast ostentatiously. Boswel sat with me till night; we had some serious talk. When he went, I gave Francis some directions for preparation to communicate. Thus has passed, hitherto, this awful day.

10°.30'. P. M.

WHEN I look back upon resolutions of improvement and amendment, which have year after year been made and broken, either by negligence, forgetfulness, vicious idleness, casual interruption, or morbid infirmity; when I find that so much of my life has stolen unprofitably away, and that I can descry by retrospection scarcely a few single days properly and vigorously employed; why do I yet try to resolve again? I try, because reformation is necessary, and despair is criminal. I try, in humble hope of the help of God.

As my life has, from my earliest years, been wasted in a morning bed, my purpose is from Easter day to rise early, not later than eight.

To Mrs Thrale on her Thirty-fifth Birthday

Oft in Danger yet alive
We are come to Thirty-five;
Long may better Years arrive,
Better Years than Thirty-five;
Could Philosophers contrive
Life to stop at Thirty-five,
Time his Hours should never drive
O'er the Bounds of Thirty-five:
High to soar and deep to dive
Nature gives at Thirty-five;   10
Ladies – stock and tend your Hive,
Trifle not at Thirty-five:
For howe'er we boast and strive,
Life declines from Thirty-five;
He that ever hopes to thrive
Must begin by Thirty-five:
And those who wisely wish to wive,
Must look on Thrale at Thirty-five.

Diary entry for Easter Day

SUNDAY 7 APRIL 1776

EASTER DAY

1776. APR. 7. The time is again at which, since the death of my poor dear Tetty, on whom God have mercy, I have annually commemorated the mystery of Redemption, and annually purposed to amend my life. My reigning sin, to which perhaps many others are appendent, is waste of time, and general sluggishness, to which I was always inclined and in part of my life have been almost compelled by morbid melancholy and disturbance of mind. Melancholy has had in me its paroxisms and remissions, but I have not improved the intervals, nor sufficiently resisted my natural inclination, or sickly habits. I will resolve henceforth to rise at eight in the morning, so far as resolution is proper, and will pray that God will strengthen me. I have begun this morning.

Though for the past week I have had an anxious design of communicating to day, I performed no particular act of devotion, till on Friday I went to Church. My design was to pass part of the day in exercises of piety but Mr Boswel interrupted me; of him however I could have rid myself, but poor Thrale, orbus et exspes, came for comfort and sat till seven when we all went to Church.

In the morning I had at Church some radiations of comfort.

I fasted though less rigorously than at other times. I by negligence poured milk into the tea, and in the afternoon drank one dish of coffee with Thrale yet at night after a fit of drowsiness I felt myself very much disordered by emptiness, and called for tea with peevish and impatient eagerness. My distress was very great.

Yesterday I do not recollect that to go to Church came into my thoughts, but I sat in my chamber, preparing for preparation, interrupted I know not how. I was near two hours at dinner.

I go now with hope

> To rise in the morning at eight
> To use my remaining time with diligence.
> To study more accurately the Christian Religion.

Almighty and most merciful Father, who hast preserved me by thy tender forbearance, once more to commemorate thy Love in the Redemption of the world, grant that I may so live the residue of my days, as to obtain thy mercy when thou shalt call me from the present State. Illuminate my thoughts with knowledge, and inflame my heart with holy desires. Grant me to resolve well, and keep my resolutions. Take not from me thy Holy Spirit, but in life and in death have mercy on me for Jesus Christs sake. Amen.

acts of forgiveness.

P.M. In the pew I read my prayer and commended my friends, and those that θ this year. At the Altar I was generally attentive, some thoughts of vanity came into my mind while others were communicating, but I found when I considered them, that they did not tend to irreverence of God. At the altar I renewed my resolutions. When I received, some tender images struck me. I was so mollified by the concluding address to our Saviour that I could not utter it. The Communicants were mostly women. At intervals I read collects, and recollected, as I could my prayer. Since my return I have said it.

2. P. M.

Lines on Thomas Warton's Poems

1

Wheresoe'er I turn my View,
All is strange, yet nothing new;
Endless Labour all along,
Endless Labour to be wrong;
Phrase that Time has flung away,
Uncouth Words in Disarray:
Trickt in Antique Ruff and Bonnet,
Ode and Elegy and Sonnet.

2

Hermit hoar, in solemn cell,
    Wearing out life's evening gray;
Smite thy bosom, sage, and tell,
    Where is bliss? and which the way?

Thus I spoke; and speaking sigh'd;
    Scarce repress'd the starting tear; –
When the smiling sage reply'd –
    Come, my lad, and drink some beer.

Diary entry

FRIDAY 28 MARCH 1777

March 28.

THIS day is Good Friday. It is likewise the day on which my poor Tetty was taken from me.

My thoughts were disturbed in bed. I remembered that it was my wife's dying day, and begged pardon for all our sins, and commended her; but resolved to mix little of my own sorrows or cares with the great solemnity. Having taken only tea without milk, I went to church; had time, before service, to commend my wife, and wished to join quietly in the service, but I did not hear well, and my mind grew unsettled and perplexed. Having rested ill in the night, I slumbered at the sermon, which, I think, I could not, as I sat, perfectly hear.

I returned home, but could not settle my mind. At last I read a chapter. Then went down, about six or seven, and eat two cross-buns, and drank tea. Fasting for some time has been uneasy, and I have taken but little.

At night I had some ease. L. D. I had prayed for pardon and peace.
I slept in the afternoon.

Prologue to Hugh Kelly's A Word to the Wise

This night presents a play, which publick rage,
Or right, or wrong, once hooted from the stage;
From zeal or malice now no more we dread,
For English vengeance *wars not with the dead.*
A generous foe regards, with pitying eye,
The man whom fate has laid, where all must lye.
To wit, reviving from its author's dust,
Be kind, ye judges, or at least be just:
Let no resentful petulance invade
Th'oblivious grave's inviolable shade.   10
Let one great payment every claim appease,
And him who cannot hurt, allow to please;
To please by scenes unconscious of offence,
By harmless merriment, or useful sense.
Where aught of bright, or fair, the piece displays,
Approve it only – 'tis too late to praise.
If want of skill, or want of care appear,
Forbear to hiss – the Poet cannot hear.
By all, like him, must praise and blame be found;
At best, a fleeting gleam, or empty sound.   20
Yet then shall calm reflection bless the night,
When liberal pity dignify'd delight;
When pleasure fired her torch at Virtue's flame,
And mirth was bounty with a humbler name.

Letter to William Dodd

THURSDAY 26 JUNE 1777

Dear Sir,   June 26, 1777

That which is appointed to all men is now coming upon you. Outward circumstances, the eyes and the thoughts of men, are below the notice of an
immortal being about to stand the trial for eternity, before the Supreme Judge

of heaven and earth. Be comforted: your crime, morally or religiously considered, has no very deep dye of turpitude. It corrupted no man's principles;
it attacked no man's life. It involved only a temporary and reparable injury. Of
this, and of all other sins, you are earnestly to repent; and may God, who
knoweth our frailty and desireth not our death, accept your repentance, for
the sake of his Son Jesus Christ our Lord.

In requital of those well-intended offices which you are pleased so emphatically to acknowledge, let me beg that you make in your devotions one petition
for my eternal welfare. I am, dear Sir, Your affectionate servant,

SAM. JOHNSON

Letter to Richard Farmer

TUESDAY 22 JULY 1777

Sir: Boltcourt, Fleetstreet, July 22, 1777

The Booksellers of London have undertaken a kind of Body of English
Poetry, excluding generally the dramas, and I have undertaken to put before
each authors works a sketch of his life, and a character of his writings. Of
some, however I know very little, and am afraid I shall not easily supply my
deficiencies. Be pleased to inform me whether among Mr. Bakers manuscripts, or any where else at Cambridge any materials are to be found. If any
such collection can be gleaned, I doubt not of your willingness to direct our
search, and will tell the Booksellers to employ a transcriber. If you think my
inspection necessary, I will come down, for who that has once experienced the
civilities of Cambridge would not snatch the opportunity of another visit?
I am, Sir, Your most humble Servant,

SAM. JOHNSON

An Extempore Elegy

Here's a Woman of the Town,
  Lies as Dead as any Nail!
She was once of high renown, –
  And so here begins my Tale.

She was once as cherry plump
  Red her cheek as Cath'rine Pear,
Toss'd her nose, and shook her Rump,
  Till she made the Neighbours stare.

There she soon became a Jilt,
 Rambling often to and fro'   10
All her life was naught but guilt,
 Till Purse and Carcase both were low.

But there came a country Squire
 He was a seducing Pug!
Took her from her friends and sire,
 To his own House her did lug.

Black her eye with many a Blow,
 Hot her breath with many a Dram,
Now she lies exceeding low,
 And as quiet as a Lamb.   20

A Short Song of Congratulation

Long-expected one and twenty
Ling'ring year at last is flown,
Pomp and Pleasure, Pride and Plenty
Great Sir John, are all your own.

Loosen'd from the Minor's tether,
Free to mortgage or to sell,
Wild as wind, and light as feather
Bid the slaves of thrift farewel.

Call the Bettys, Kates, and Jennys
Ev'ry name that laughs at Care,   10
Lavish of your Grandsire's guineas,
Show the Spirit of an heir.

All that prey on vice and folly
Joy to see their quarry fly,
Here the Gamester light and jolly
There the Lender grave and sly.

Wealth, Sir John, was made to wander,
Let it wander as it will;
See the Jocky, see the Pander,
Bid them come, and take their fill.   20

When the bonny Blade carouses,
Pockets full, and Spirits high,

What are acres? what are houses?
Only dirt, or wet or dry.

If the Guardian or the Mother
Tell the woes of wilful waste,
Scorn their counsel and their pother,
You can hang or drown at last.

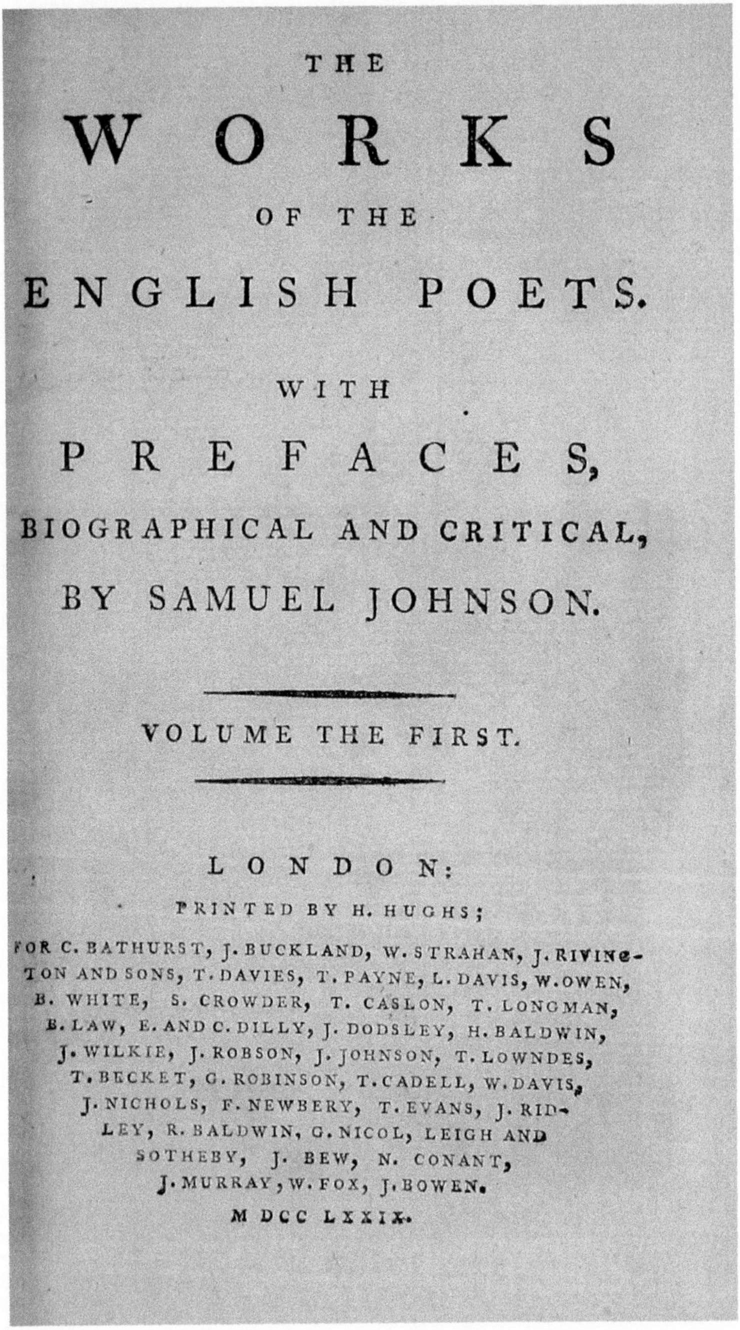

THE

WORKS

OF THE

ENGLISH POETS.

WITH

PREFACES,

BIOGRAPHICAL AND CRITICAL,

BY SAMUEL JOHNSON.

———————

VOLUME THE FIRST.

———————

LONDON:

PRINTED BY H. HUGHS;

FOR C. BATHURST, J. BUCKLAND, W. STRAHAN, J. RIVING-
TON AND SONS, T. DAVIES, T. PAYNE, L. DAVIS, W. OWEN,
B. WHITE, S. CROWDER, T. CASLON, T. LONGMAN,
B. LAW, E. AND C. DILLY, J. DODSLEY, H. BALDWIN,
J. WILKIE, J. ROBSON, J. JOHNSON, T. LOWNDES,
T. BECKET, G. ROBINSON, T. CADELL, W. DAVIS,
J. NICHOLS, F. NEWBERY, T. EVANS, J. RID-
LEY, R. BALDWIN, G. NICOL, LEIGH AND
SOTHEBY, J. BEW, N. CONANT,
J. MURRAY, W. FOX, J. BOWEN.

M DCC LXXIX.

FIGURE 13 *The Works of the English Poets* (1779), title page (Bodl. Dunston B 2008). Courtesy of the Bodleian Library, University of Oxford.

Lives of the Poets

COWLEY

THE Life of Cowley, notwithstanding the penury of English biography, has been written by Dr. Sprat, an author whose pregnancy of imagination and elegance of language have deservedly set him high in the ranks of literature; but his zeal of friendship, or ambition of eloquence, has produced a funeral oration rather than a history: he has given the character, not the life of Cowley; for he writes with so little detail, that scarcely any thing is distinctly known, but all is shewn confused and enlarged through the mist of panegyrick.

ABRAHAM COWLEY was born in the year one thousand six hundred and eighteen. His father was a grocer, whose condition Dr. Sprat conceals under the general appellation of a citizen; and, what would probably not have been less carefully suppressed, the omission of his name in the register of St. Dunstan's parish gives reason to suspect that his father was a sectary. Whoever he was, he died before the birth of his son, and consequently left him to the care of his mother; whom Wood represents as struggling earnestly to procure him a literary education, and who, as she lived to the age of eighty, had her solicitude rewarded by seeing her son eminent, and, I hope, by seeing him fortunate, and partaking his prosperity. We know at least, from Sprat's account, that he always acknowledged her care, and justly paid the dues of filial gratitude.

In the window of his mother's apartment lay Spenser's Fairy Queen; in which he very early took delight to read, till, by feeling the charms of verse, he became, as he relates, irrecoverably a poet. Such are the accidents, which, sometimes remembered, and perhaps sometimes forgotten, produce that particular designation of mind, and propensity for some certain science or employment, which is commonly called Genius. The true Genius is a mind of large general powers, accidentally determined to some particular direction. Sir Joshua Reynolds, the great Painter of the present age, had the first fondness for his art excited by the perusal of Richardson's treatise.

By his mother's solicitation he was admitted into Westminster school, where he was soon distinguished. He was wont, says Sprat, to relate, "That he had this defect in his memory at that time, that his teachers never could bring it to retain the ordinary rules of grammar."

This is an instance of the natural desire of man to propagate a wonder. It is surely very difficult to tell any thing as it was heard, when Sprat could not refrain from amplifying a commodious incident, though the book to which he prefixed his narrative contained its confutation. A memory admitting some things, and rejecting others, an intellectual digestion that concocted the pulp of learning, but refused the husks, had the appearance of an instinctive elegance, of a particular provision made by Nature for literary politeness. But in the author's own honest relation, the marvel vanishes: he was, he says, such "an enemy to all constraint, that his master never could prevail on him to learn the rules without book." He does not tell that he could not learn the rules, but that, being able to perform his exercises without them, and being an "enemy to constraint," he spared himself the labour.

Among the English poets, Cowley, Milton, and Pope, might be said "to lisp in numbers;" and have given such early proofs, not only of powers of language, but of comprehension of things, as to more tardy minds seems scarcely credible. But of the learned puerilities of Cowley there is no doubt, since a volume of his poems was not only written but printed in his thirteenth year; containing, with other poetical compositions, "The tragical History of Pyramus and Thisbe," written when he was ten years old; and "Constantia and Philetus," written two years after.

While he was yet at school he produced a comedy called "Love's Riddle," though it was not published till he had been some time at Cambridge. This comedy is of the pastoral kind, which requires no acquaintance with the living world, and therefore the time at which it was composed adds little to the wonders of Cowley's minority.

In 1636, he was removed to Cambridge, where he continued his studies with great intenseness; for he is said to have written, while he was yet a young student, the greater part of his Davideis; a work of which the materials could not have been collected without the study of many years, but by a mind of the greatest vigour and activity.

Two years after his settlement at Cambridge he published "Love's Riddle," with a poetical dedication to Sir Kenelm Digby; of whose acquaintance all his contemporaries seem to have been ambitious; and "Naufragium Joculare," a comedy written in Latin, but without due attention to the ancient models: for it is not loose verse, but mere prose. It was printed, with a dedication in verse to Dr. Comber, master of the college; but having neither the facility of a popular nor the accuracy of a learned work, it seems to be now universally neglected.

At the beginning of the civil war, as the Prince passed through Cambridge in his way to York, he was entertained with the representation of the "Guardian," a comedy, which Cowley says was neither written nor acted, but rough-drawn by him, and repeated by the scholars. That this comedy was printed during his absence from his country, he appears to have considered as injurious to his reputation; though, during the suppression of the theatres, it was sometimes privately acted with sufficient approbation.

In 1643, being now master of arts, he was, by the prevalence of the parliament, ejected from Cambridge, and sheltered himself at St. John's College in Oxford; where, as is said by Wood, he published a satire called "The Puritan and Papist," which was only inserted in the last collection of his works; and so distinguished himself by the warmth of his loyalty, and the elegance of his conversation, that he gained the kindness and confidence of those who attended the King, and amongst others of Lord Falkland, whose notice cast a lustre on all to whom it was extended.

About the time when Oxford was surrendered to the parliament, he followed the Queen to Paris, where he became secretary to the Lord Jermin, afterwards Earl of St. Albans, and was employed in such correspondence as the royal cause required, and particularly in cyphering and decyphering the letters that passed between the King and Queen; an employment of the highest confidence and honour. So wide was his province of intelligence, that, for several years, it filled all his days and two or three nights in the week.

In the year 1647, his "Mistress" was published; for he imagined, as he declared in his preface to a subsequent edition, that "poets are scarce thought freemen of their company without paying some duties, or obliging themselves to be true to Love."

This obligation to amorous ditties owes, I believe, its original to the fame of Petrarch, who, in an age rude and uncultivated, by his tuneful homage to his Laura, refined the manners of the lettered world, and filled Europe with love and poetry. But the basis of all excellence is truth: he that professes love ought to feel its power. Petrarch was a real lover, and Laura doubtless deserved his tenderness. Of Cowley, we are told by Barnes*, who had means enough of information, that, whatever he may talk of his own inflammability, and the variety of characters by which his heart was divided, he in reality was in love but once, and then never had resolution to tell his passion.

This consideration cannot but abate, in some measure, the reader's esteem for the work and the author. To love excellence, is natural; it is natural likewise for the lover to solicit reciprocal regard by an elaborate display of his own qualifications. The desire of pleasing has in different men produced actions of heroism, and effusions of wit; but it seems as reasonable to appear the champion as the poet of an "airy nothing," and to quarrel as to write for what Cowley might have learned from his master Pindar to call the "dream of a shadow."

It is surely not difficult, in the solitude of a college, or in the bustle of the world, to find useful studies and serious employment. No man needs to be so burthened with life as to squander it in voluntary dreams of fictitious occurrences. The man that sits down to suppose himself charged with treason

* V. Barnesii Anacreontem

or peculation, and heats his mind to an elaborate purgation of his character from crimes which he was never within the possibility of committing, differs only by the infrequency of his folly from him who praises beauty which he never saw, complains of jealousy which he never felt; supposes himself sometimes invited, and sometimes forsaken; fatigues his fancy, and ransacks his memory, for images which may exhibit the gaiety of hope, or the gloominess of despair, and dresses his imaginary Chloris or Phyllis sometimes in flowers fading as her beauty, and sometimes in gems lasting as her virtues.

At Paris, as secretary to Lord Jermin, he was engaged in transacting things of real importance with real men and real women, and at that time did not much employ his thoughts upon phantoms of gallantry. Some of his letters to Mr. Bennet, afterwards Earl of Arlington, from April to December in 1650, are preserved in "Miscellanea Aulica," a collection of papers published by Brown. These letters, being written like those of other men whose mind is more on things than words, contribute no otherwise to his reputation than as they shew him to have been above the affectation of unseasonable elegance, and to have known that the business of a statesman can be little forwarded by flowers of rhetorick.

One passage, however, seems not unworthy of some notice. Speaking of the Scotch treaty then in agitation:

"The Scotch treaty," says he, "is the only thing now in which we are vitally concerned; I am one of the last hopers, and yet cannot now abstain from believing, that an agreement will be made: all people upon the place incline to that of union. The Scotch will moderate something of the rigour of their demands; the mutual necessity of an accord is visible, the King is persuaded of it. And to tell you the truth (which I take to be an argument above all the rest), Virgil has told the same thing to that purpose."

This expression from a secretary of the present time would be considered as merely ludicrous, or at most as an ostentatious display of scholarship; but the manners of that time were so tinged with superstition, that I cannot but suspect Cowley of having consulted on this great occasion the Virgilian lots, and to have given some credit to the answer of his oracle.

Some years afterwards, "business," says Sprat, "passed of course into other hands;" and Cowley, being no longer useful at Paris, was in 1656 sent back into England, that, "under pretence of privacy and retirement, he might take occasion of giving notice of the posture of things in this nation."

Soon after his return to London, he was seized by some messengers of the usurping powers, who were sent out in quest of another man; and, being examined, was put into confinement, from which he was not dismissed without the security of a thousand pounds given by Dr. Scarborow.

This year he published his poems, with a preface, in which he seems to have inserted something, suppressed in subsequent editions, which was interpreted to denote some relaxation of his loyalty. In this preface he declares, that "his desire had been for some days past, and did still very vehemently continue, to retire himself to some of the American plantations, and to forsake this world for ever."

From the obloquy which the appearance of submission to the usurpers brought upon him, his biographer has been very diligent to clear him, and indeed it does not seem to have lessened his reputation. His wish for retirement we can easily believe to be undissembled; a man harrassed in one kingdom, and persecuted in another, who, after a course of business that employed all his days and half his nights in cyphering and decyphering, comes to his own country and steps into a prison, will be willing enough to retire to some place of quiet, and of safety. Yet let neither our reverence for a genius, nor our pity for a sufferer, dispose us to forget that, if his activity was virtue, his retreat was cowardice.

He then took upon himself the character of Physician, still, according to Sprat, with intention "to dissemble the main design of his coming over," and, as Mr. Wood relates, "complying with the men then in power (which was much taken notice of by the royal party), he obtained an order to be created Doctor of Physick, which being done to his mind (whereby he gained the ill-will of some of his friends), he went into France again, having made a copy of verses on Oliver's death."

This is no favourable representation, yet even in this not much wrong can be discovered. How far he complied with the men in power, is to be enquired before he can be blamed. It is not said that he told them any secrets, or assisted them by intelligence, or any other act. If he only promised to be quiet, that they in whose hands he was might free him from confinement, he did what no law of society prohibits.

The man whose miscarriage in a just cause has put him in the power of his enemy may, without any violation of his integrity, regain his liberty, or preserve his life, by a promise of neutrality: for the stipulation gives the enemy nothing which he had not before; the neutrality of a captive may be always secured by his imprisonment or death. He that is at the disposal of another may not promise to aid him in any injurious act, because no power can compel active obedience. He may engage to do nothing, but not to do ill.

There is reason to think that Cowley promised little. It does not appear that his compliance gained him confidence enough to be trusted without security, for the bond of his bail was never cancelled; nor that it made him think himself secure, for at that dissolution of government, which followed the death of Oliver, he returned into France, where he resumed his former station, and staid till the Restoration.

"He continued," says his biographer, "under these bonds till the general deliverance;" it is therefore to be supposed, that he did not go to France, and act again for the King, without the consent of his bondsman; that he did not shew his loyalty at the hazard of his friend, but by his friend's permission.

Of the verses on Oliver's death, in which Wood's narrative seems to imply something encomiastick, there has been no appearance. There is a discourse concerning his government, indeed, with verses intermixed, but such as certainly gained its author no friends among the abettors of usurpation.

A doctor of physick however he was made at Oxford, in December 1657; and in the commencement of the Royal Society, of which an account has been published by Dr. Birch, he appears busy among the experimental philosophers with the title of Doctor Cowley.

There is no reason for supposing that he ever attempted practice; but his preparatory studies have contributed something to the honour of his country. Considering Botany as necessary to a physician, he retired into Kent to gather plants; and as the predominance of a favourite study affects all subordinate operations of the intellect, Botany in the mind of Cowley turned into poetry. He composed in Latin several books on Plants, of which the first and second display the qualities of Herbs, in elegiac verse; the third and fourth the beauties of Flowers in various measures; and in the fifth and sixth, the uses of Trees in heroick numbers.

At the same time were produced from the same university, the two great Poets, Cowley and Milton, of dissimilar genius, of opposite principles; but concurring in the cultivation of Latin poetry, in which the English, till their works and May's poem appeared, seemed unable to contest the palm with any other of the lettered nations.

If the Latin performances of Cowley and Milton be compared, for May I hold to be superior to both, the advantage seems to lie on the side of Cowley. Milton is generally content to express the thoughts of the ancients in their language; Cowley, without much loss of purity or elegance, accommodates the diction of Rome to his own conceptions.

At the Restoration, after all the diligence of his long service, and with consciousness not only of the merit of fidelity, but of the dignity of great abilities, he naturally expected ample preferments; and, that he might not be forgotten by his own fault, wrote a Song of Triumph. But this was a time of such general hope, that great numbers were inevitably disappointed; and Cowley found his reward very tediously delayed. He had been promised by both Charles the first and second the Mastership of the Savoy; but "he lost it," says Wood, "by certain persons, enemies to the Muses."

The neglect of the court was not his only mortification; having, by such alteration as he thought proper, fitted his old Comedy of the Guardian for the stage, he produced it to the publick under the title of the "Cutter of Coleman-street." It was treated on the stage with great severity, and was afterwards censured as a satire on the king's party.

Mr. Dryden, who went with Mr. Sprat to the first exhibition, related to Mr. Dennis, "that when they told Cowley how little favour had been shewn him, he received the news of his ill success, not with so much firmness as might have been expected from so great a man."

What firmness they expected, or what weakness Cowley discovered, cannot be known. He that misses his end will never be as much pleased as he that attains it, even when he can impute no part of his failure to himself; and when the end is to please the multitude, no man perhaps has a right, in things admitting of gradation and comparison, to throw the whole blame upon his judges, and totally to exclude diffidence and shame by a haughty consciousness of his own excellence.

For the rejection of this play, it is difficult now to find the reason: it certainly has, in a very great degree, the power of fixing attention and exciting merriment. From the charge of disaffection he exculpates himself in his preface, by observing how unlikely it is that, having followed the royal family through all their distresses, "he should chuse the time of their restoration to begin a quarrel with them." It appears, however, from the Theatrical Register of Downes the prompter, to have been popularly considered as a satire on the Royalists.

That he might shorten this tedious suspense, he published his pretensions and his discontent, in an ode called "The Complaint;" in which he styles himself the *melancholy* Cowley. This met with the usual fortune of complaints, and seems to have excited more contempt than pity.

These unlucky incidents are brought, maliciously enough, together in some stanzas, written about that time, on the choice of a laureat; a mode of satire, by which, since it was first introduced by Suckling, perhaps every generation of poets has been teazed:

> Savoy-missing Cowley came into the court,
>   Making apologies for his bad play;
> Every one gave him so good a report,
>   That Apollo gave heed to all he could say;
> Nor would he have had, 'tis thought, a rebuke,
>   Unless he had done some notable folly;
> Writ verses unjustly in praise of Sam Tuke,
>   Or printed his pitiful Melancholy.

His vehement desire of retirement now came again upon him. "Not finding," says the morose Wood, "that preferment conferred upon him which he expected, while others for their money carried away most places, he retired discontented into Surrey."

"He was now," says the courtly Sprat, "weary of the vexations and formalities of an active condition. He had been perplexed with a long compliance to foreign manners. He was satiated with the arts of a court; which sort of life, though his virtue made it innocent to him, yet nothing could make it quiet.

Those were the reasons that moved him to follow the violent inclination of his own mind, which, in the greatest throng of his former business, had still called upon him, and represented to him the true delights of solitary studies, of temperate pleasures, and a moderate revenue below the malice and flatteries of fortune."

So differently are things seen, and so differently are they shown; but actions are visible, though motives are secret. Cowley certainly retired; first to Barn-elms, and afterwards to Chertsey, in Surrey. He seems, however, to have lost part of his dread of the *hum of men*. He thought himself now safe enough from intrusion, without the defence of mountains and oceans; and, instead of seeking shelter in America, wisely went only so far from the bustle of life as that he might easily find his way back, when solitude should grow tedious. His retreat was at first but slenderly accommodated; yet he soon obtained, by the interest of the Earl of St. Albans and the duke of Buckingham, such a lease of the Queen's lands as afforded him an ample income.

By the lover of virtue and of wit it will be solicitously asked, if he now was happy. Let them peruse one of his letters accidentally preserved by Peck, which I recommend to the consideration of all that may hereafter pant for solitude.

"To Dr. THOMAS SPRAT

Chertsey, 21 May, 1665.

The first night that I came hither I caught so great a cold, with a defluxion of rheum, as made me keep my chamber ten days. And, two after, had such a bruise on my ribs with a fall, that I am yet unable to move or turn myself in my bed. This is my personal fortune here to begin with. And, besides, I can get no money from my tenants, and have my meadows eaten up every night by cattle put in by my neighbours. What this signifies, or may come to in time, God knows; if it be ominous, it can end in nothing less than hanging. Another misfortune has been, and stranger than all the rest, that you have broke your word with me, and failed to come, even though you told Mr. Bois that you would. This is what they call *Monstri simile*. I do hope to recover my late hurt so farre within five or six days (though it be uncertain yet whether I shall ever recover it) as to walk about again. And then, methinks, you and I and *the Dean* might be very merry upon S. Anne's Hill. You might very conveniently come hither the way of Hampton Town, lying there one night. I write this in pain, and can say no more: *Verbum sapienti*."

He did not long enjoy the pleasure or suffer the uneasiness of solitude; for he died at the Porch-house[†] in Chertsey in 1667, in the 49th year of his age.

He was buried with great pomp near Chaucer and Spenser; and king Charles pronounced, "That Mr. Cowley had not left a better man behind him

---

* L'Allegro of Milton.
† Now in the possession of Mr. Clarke, Alderman of London.

in England." He is represented by Dr. Sprat as the most amiable of mankind; and this posthumous praise may be safely credited, as it has never been contradicted by envy or by faction.

Such are the remarks and memorials which I have been able to add to the narrative of Dr. Sprat; who, writing when the feuds of the civil war were yet recent, and the minds of either party easily irritated, was obliged to pass over many transactions in general expressions, and to leave curiosity often unsatisfied. What he did not tell, cannot however now be known. I must therefore recommend the perusal of his work, to which my narration can be considered only as a slender supplement.

COWLEY, like other poets who have written with narrow views, and, instead of tracing intellectual pleasure to its natural sources in the mind of man, paid their court to temporary prejudices, has been at one time too much praised, and too much neglected at another.

Wit, like all other things subject by their nature to the choice of man, has its changes and fashions, and at different times takes different forms. About the beginning of the seventeenth century appeared a race of writers that may be termed the metaphysical poets; of whom, in a criticism on the works of Cowley, it is not improper to give some account.

The metaphysical poets were men of learning, and to shew their learning was their whole endeavour; but, unluckily resolving to shew it in rhyme, instead of writing poetry, they only wrote verses, and very often such verses as stood the trial of the finger better than of the ear; for the modulation was so imperfect, that they were only found to be verses by counting the syllables.

If the father of criticism has rightly denominated poetry τέχνη μιμητική, *an imitative art*, these writers will, without great wrong, lose their right to the name of poets; for they cannot be said to have imitated any thing; they neither copied nature nor life; neither painted the forms of matter, nor represented the operations of intellect.

Those, however who deny them to be poets, allow them to be wits. Dryden confesses of himself and his contemporaries, that they fall below Donne in wit, but maintains that they surpass him in poetry.

If Wit be well described by Pope, as being, "that which has been often thought, but was never before so well expressed," they certainly never attained, nor ever sought it; for they endeavoured to be singular in their thoughts, and were careless of their diction. But Pope's account of wit is undoubtedly erroneous: he depresses it below its natural dignity, and reduces it from strength of thought to happiness of language.

If by a more noble and more adequate conception that be considered as Wit, which is at once natural and new, that which, though not obvious, is, upon its first production, acknowledged to be just; if it be that, which he that never found it, wonders how he missed; to wit of this kind the metaphysical poets have seldom risen. Their thoughts are often new, but seldom natural;

they are not obvious, but neither are they just; and the reader, far from wondering that he missed them, wonders more frequently by what perverseness
of industry they were ever found.

But Wit, abstracted from its effects upon the hearer, may be more rigorously
and philosophically considered as a kind of *discordia concors*; a combination of
dissimilar images, or discovery of occult resemblances in things apparently
unlike. Of wit, thus defined, they have more than enough. The most heterogeneous ideas are yoked by violence together; nature and art are ransacked for
illustrations, comparisons, and allusions; their learning instructs, and their
subtilty surprises; but the reader commonly thinks his improvement dearly
bought, and, though he sometimes admires, is seldom pleased.

From this account of their compositions it will be readily inferred, that
they were not successful in representing or moving the affections. As they
were wholly employed on something unexpected and surprising, they had
no regard to that uniformity of sentiment which enables us to conceive
and to excite the pains and the pleasure of other minds: they never enquired
what, on any occasion, they should have said or done; but wrote rather as
beholders than partakers of human nature; as Beings looking upon good and
evil, impassive and at leisure; as Epicurean deities making remarks on the
actions of men, and the vicissitudes of life, without interest and without emotion. Their courtship was void of fondness, and their lamentation of sorrow.
Their wish was only to say what they hoped had been never said before.

Nor was the sublime more within their reach than the pathetick; for they
never attempted that comprehension and expanse of thought which at once
fills the whole mind, and of which the first effect is sudden astonishment, and
the second rational admiration. Sublimity is produced by aggregation, and
littleness by dispersion. Great thoughts are always general, and consist in
positions not limited by exceptions, and in descriptions not descending to
minuteness. It is with great propriety that Subtlety, which in its original import
means exility of particles, is taken in its metaphorical meaning for nicety of
distinction. Those writers who lay on the watch for novelty could have little
hope of greatness; for great things cannot have escaped former observation.
Their attempts were always analytick; they broke every image into fragments:
and could no more represent, by their slender conceits and laboured particularities, the prospects of nature, or the scenes of life, than he, who dissects a
sun-beam with a prism, can exhibit the wide effulgence of a summer noon.

What they wanted however of the sublime, they endeavoured to supply by
hyperbole; their amplification had no limits; they left not only reason but
fancy behind them; and produced combinations of confused magnificence,
that not only could not be credited, but could not be imagined.

Yet great labour, directed by great abilities, is never wholly lost: if they frequently threw away their wit upon false conceits, they likewise sometimes
struck out unexpected truth: if their conceits were far-fetched, they were

often worth the carriage. To write on their plan, it was at least necessary to read and think. No man could be born a metaphysical poet, nor assume the dignity of a writer, by descriptions copied from descriptions, by imitations borrowed from imitations, by traditional imagery, and hereditary similies, by readiness of rhyme, and volubility of syllables.

In perusing the works of this race of authors, the mind is exercised either by recollection or inquiry; either something already learned is to be retrieved, or something new is to be examined. If their greatness seldom elevates, their acuteness often surprises; if the imagination is not always gratified, at least the powers of reflection and comparison are employed; and in the mass of materials which ingenious absurdity has thrown together, genuine wit and useful knowledge may be sometimes found, buried perhaps in grossness of expression, but useful to those who know their value; and such as, when they are expanded to perspicuity, and polished to elegance, may give lustre to works which have more propriety though less copiousness of sentiment.

This kind of writing, which was, I believe, borrowed from Marino and his followers, had been recommended by the example of Donne, a man of very extensive and various knowledge; and by Jonson, whose manner resembled that of Donne more in the ruggedness of his lines than in the cast of his sentiments.

When their reputation was high, they had undoubtedly more imitators, than time has left behind. Their immediate successors, of whom any remembrance can be said to remain, were Suckling, Waller, Denham, Cowley, Cleiveland, and Milton. Denham and Waller sought another way to fame, by improving the harmony of our numbers. Milton tried the metaphysick style only in his lines upon Hobson the Carrier. Cowley adopted it, and excelled his predecessors, having as much sentiment, and more musick. Suckling neither improved versification, nor abounded in conceits. The fashionable style remained chiefly with Cowley; Suckling could not reach it, and Milton disdained it.

Critical Remarks are not easily understood without examples; and I have therefore collected instances of the modes of writing by which this species of poets, for poets they were called by themselves and their admirers, was eminently distinguished.

As the authors of this race were perhaps more desirous of being admired than understood, they sometimes drew their conceits from recesses of learning not very much frequented by common readers of poetry. Thus Cowley on *Knowledge*:

> The sacred tree midst the fair orchard grew;
>   The phoenix Truth did on it rest,
>   And built his perfum'd nest,
> That right Porphyrian tree which did true logick shew.
>   Each leaf did learned notions give,

> And th' apples were demonstrative:
> So clear their colour and divine,
> The very shade they cast did other lights outshine.

On Anacreon continuing a lover in his old age:

> Love was with thy life entwin'd,
> Close as heat with fire is join'd,
> A powerful brand prescrib'd the date
> Of thine, like Meleager's fate.
> Th' antiperistasis of age
> More enflam'd thy amorous rage.

In the following verses we have an allusion to a Rabbinical opinion concerning Manna:

> Variety I ask not: give me one
> To live perpetually upon.
> The person Love does to us fit,
> Like manna, has the taste of all in it.

Thus *Donne* shews his medicinal knowledge in some encomiastic verses:

> In every thing there naturally grows
> A Balsamum to keep it fresh and new,
> If 'twere not injur'd by extrinsique blows;
> Your youth and beauty are this balm in you.
> But you, of learning and religion,
> And virtue and such ingredients, have made
> A mithridate, whose operation
> Keeps off, or cures what can be done or said.

Though the following lines of Donne, on the last night of the year, have something in them too scholastick, they are not inelegant:

> This twilight of two years, not past nor next,
> Some emblem is of me, or I of this,
> Who, meteor-like, of stuff and form perplext,
> Whose what and where, in disputation is,
> If I should call me any thing, should miss.

> I sum the years and me, and find me not
> Debtor to th' old, nor creditor to th' new,

That cannot say, my thanks I have forgot,
   Nor trust I this with hopes; and yet scarce true
   This bravery is, since these times shew'd me you.   10
                                        DONNE.

Yet more abstruse and profound is *Donne's* reflection upon Man as a Microcosm:

If men be worlds, there is in every one
Something to answer in some proportion
All the world's riches: and in good men, this
Virtue, our form's form, and our soul's soul is.

OF thoughts so far-fetched, as to be not only unexpected, but unnatural, all their books are full.

To a lady, who wrote poesies for rings.
They, who above do various circles find,
Say, like a ring th' æquator heaven does bind.
When heaven shall be adorn'd by thee,
(Which then more heaven than 'tis, will be)
'Tis thou must write the poesy there,
For it wanteth one as yet,
Though the sun pass through't twice a year,
The sun, which is esteem'd the god of wit.
                                        COWLEY.

The difficulties which have been raised about identity in philosophy, are by Cowley with still more perplexity applied to Love:

Five years ago (says story) I lov'd you,
For which you call me most inconstant now;
Pardon me, madam, you mistake the man;
For I am not the same that I was then;
No flesh is now the same 'twas then in me,
And that my mind is chang'd yourself may see.

The same thoughts to retain still, and intents,
Were more inconstant far; for accidents
Must of all things most strangely inconstant prove,
If from one subject they t'another move: 10
My members then, the father members were
From whence these take their birth, which now are here.

> If then this body love what th'other did,
> 'Twere incest, which by nature is forbid.

The love of different women is, in geographical poetry, compared to travels through different countries:

> Hast thou not found, each woman's breast
>   (The lands where thou hast travelled)
> Either by savages possest,
>   Or wild, and uninhabited?
>   What joy could'st take, or what repose,
> In countries so uncivilis'd as those?
> Lust, the scorching dog star, here
>   Rages with immoderate heat;
> Whilst Pride, the rugged Northern Bear,
>   In others makes the cold too great.   10
> And where these are temperate known,
> The soil's all barren sand, or rocky stone.
>   COWLEY.

A lover, burnt up by his affection, is compared to Egypt:

> The fate of Egypt I sustain,
> And never feel the dew of rain,
> From clouds which in the head appear;
>   But all my too much moisture owe
>   To overflowings of the heart below.
>   COWLEY.

The lover supposes his lady acquainted with the ancient laws of augury and rites of sacrifice:

> And yet this death of mine, I fear,
> Will ominous to her appear:
>   When sound in every other part,
> Her sacrifice is found without an heart.
>   For the last tempest of my death
> Shall sigh out that too, with my breath.

That the chaos was harmonised, has been recited of old; but whence the different sounds arose, remained for a modern to discover:

> Th' ungovern'd parts no correspondence knew,
> An artless war from thwarting motions grew;

Till they to number and fixt rules were brought,
Water and air he for the Tenor chose,
Earth made the Base, the Treble flame arose.

COWLEY.

The tears of lovers are always of great poetical account; but Donne has extended them into worlds. If the lines are not easily understood, they may be read again.

> On a round ball
> A workman, that hath copies by, can lay
> An Europe, Afric, and an Asia,
> And quickly make that, which was nothing, all
>   So doth each tear,
>   Which thee doth wear,
> A globe, yea world, by that impression grow,
> Till thy tears mixt with mine do overflow
> This world, by waters sent from thee my heaven dissolved so.

On reading the following lines, the reader may perhaps cry out—*Confusion worse confounded*.

> Here lies a she sun, and a he moon here,
>   She gives the best light to his sphere,
>   Or each is both, and all, and so
> They unto one another nothing owe.

DONNE.

Who but Donne would have thought that a good man is a telescope?

> Though God be our true glass, through which we see
> All, since the being of all things is he,
> Yet are the trunks, which do to us derive
> Things, in proportion fit, by perspective
> Deeds of good men; for by their living here,
> Virtues, indeed remote, seem to be near.

Who would imagine it possible that in a very few lines so many remote ideas could be brought together?

> Since 'tis my doom, Love's undershrieve,
>   Why this reprieve?
> Why doth my She Advowson fly
>   Incumbency?

To sell thyself dost thou intend
　　By candle's end,
And hold the contrast thus in doubt,
　　Life's taper out?
Think but how soon the market fails,
Your sex lives faster than the males;　　　　　　10
As if to measure age's span,
The sober Julian were th' acount of man,
Whilst you live by the fleet Gregorian.
　　　　　　　　　　　　CLEIVELAND.

OF enormous and disgusting hyberboles, these may be examples:

　　By every wind, that comes this way,
　　Send me at least a sigh or two,
　　Such and so many I'll repay
As shall themselves make winds to get to you.
　　　　　　　　　　　　COWLEY.

　　In tears I'll waste these eyes,
　　By Love so vainly fed;
So lust of old the Deluge punished.
　　　　　　　　　　　　COWLEY.

All arm'd in brass the richest dress of war,
(A dismal glorious fight) he shone afar.
The sun himself started with sudden fright,
To see his beams return so dismal bright.
　　　　　　　　　　　　COWLEY.

An universal consternation:

　　His bloody eyes he hurls round, his sharp paws
　　Tear up the ground; then runs he wild about,
　　Lashing his angry tail and roaring out.
　　Beasts creep into their dens, and tremble there;
　　Trees, though no wind is stirring, shake with fear;
　　Silence and horror fill the place around:
　　Echo itself dares scarce repeat the sound.
　　　　　　　　　　　　COWLEY.

THEIR fictions were often violent and unnatural.

Of his Mistress bathing:

The fish around her crouded, as they do
To the false light that treacherous fishers shew,
And all with as much ease might taken be,
    As she at first took me:
    For ne'er did light so clear
    Among the waves appear,
Though every night the sun himself set there.
                       Cowley.

The poetical effect of a Lover's name upon glass:

    My name engrav'd herein
Doth contribute my firmness to this glass;
    Which, ever since that charm, hath been
As hard as that which grav'd it was.
                       Donne.

Their conceits were sometimes slight and trifling.

On an inconstant woman:

He enjoys thy calmy sunshine now,
    And no breath stirring hears,
In the clear heaven of thy brow,
    No smallest cloud appears.
    He sees thee gentle, fair and gay,
And trusts the faithless April of thy May.
                       Cowley.

Upon a paper written with the juice of lemon, and read by the fire:

    Nothing yet in thee is seen;
    But when a genial heat warms thee within,
A new-born wood of various lines there grows;
    Here buds an L, and there a B,
    Here sprouts a V, and there a T,
And all the flourishing letters stand in rows.
                       Cowley.

As they sought only for novelty, they did not much enquire whether their allusions were to things high or low, elegant or gross; whether they compared the little to the great, or the great to the little.

Physick and Chirurgery for a Lover.

Gently, ah gently, madam, touch
   The wound, which you yourself have made;
That pain must needs be very much,
   Which makes me of your hand afraid.
Cordials of pity give me now,
For I too weak for purgings grow.

COWLEY.

The World and a Clock.

Mahol, th' inferior world's fantastic face,
Through all the turns of matter's maze did trace;
Great Nature's well-set clock in pieces took;
On all the springs and smallest wheels did look
Of life and motion; and with equal art
Made up again the whole of every part.

COWLEY.

A coal-pit has not often found its poet; but, that it may not want its due honour, Cleiveland has paralleled it with the Sun:

The moderate value of our guiltless ore
Makes no man atheist, nor no woman whore;
Yet why should hallow'd vestal's sacred shrine
Deserve more honour than a flaming mine?
These pregnant wombs of heat would fitter be
Than a few embers, for a deity.
   Had he our pits, the Persian would admire
No sun, but warm's devotion at our fire:
He'd leave the trotting whipster, and prefer
Our profound Vulcan 'bove that waggoner.   10
For wants he heat, or light? or would have store
Or both? 'tis here: and what can suns give more?
Nay, what's the sun but, in a different name,
A coal-pit rampant, or a mine on flame!

Then let this truth reciprocally run,
The sun's heaven's coalery, and coals our sun.

Death, a Voyage:

                        No family
Ere rigg'd a soul for heaven's discovery,
With whom more venturers might boldly dare
Venture their stakes, with him in joy to share.
                                    DONNE.

THEIR thoughts and expressions were sometimes grossly absurd, and such as no figures or licence can reconcile to the understanding.

A Lover neither dead nor alive:

Then down I laid my head,
Down on cold earth; and for a while was dead,
And my freed soul to a strange somewhere fled:
    Ah, sottish soul, said I,
    When back to its cage again I saw it fly:
    Fool to resume her broken chain!
    And row her galley here again!
    Fool, to that body to return
Where it condemn'd and destin'd is to burn!
    Once dead, how can it be,   10
Death should a thing so pleasant seem to thee,
That thou should'st come to live it o'er again in me?
                                    COWLEY.

A Lover's heart, a hand grenado.

Wo to her stubborn heart, if once mine come
    Into the self-same room,
    'Twill tear and blow up all within,
Like a grenado shot into a magazin.
Then shall Love keep the ashes, and torn parts,
    Of both our broken hearts:
    Shall out of both one new one make;
From her's th' allay; from mine, the metal take.
                                    COWLEY.

The poetical Propagation of Light:

The Prince's favour is diffus'd o'er all,
From which all fortunes, names, and natures fall;
Then from those wombs of stars, the Bride's bright eyes,
   At every glance a constellation flies,
And sowes the court with stars, and doth prevent
   In light and power, the all-ey'd firmament:
First her eye kindles other ladies' eyes,
   Then from their beams their jewels lustres rise;
And from their jewels torches do take fire,
And all is warmth, and light, and good desire.   10
                                       Donne.

THEY were in very little care to clothe their notions with elegance of dress, and therefore miss the notice and the praise which are often gained by those, who think less, but are more diligent to adorn their thoughts.

That a mistress beloved is fairer in idea than in reality, is by Cowley thus expressed:

Thou in my fancy dost much higher stand,
Than women can be plac'd by Nature's hand;
And I must needs, I'm sure, a loser be,
To change thee, as thou'rt there, for very thee.

That prayer and labour should co-operate, are thus taught by Donne:

In none but us, are such mixt engines found,
As hands of double office: for the ground
We till with them; and them to heaven we raise;
Who prayerless labours, or without this, prays,
Doth but one half, that's none.

By the same author, a common topick, the danger of procrastination, is thus illustrated:

—That which I should have begun
In my youth's morning, now late must be done;
And I, as giddy travellers must do,
Which stray or sleep all day, and having lost
Light and strength, dark and tir'd must then ride post.

All that Man has to do is to live and die; the sum of humanity is comprehended by Donne in the following lines:

> Think in how poor a prison thou didst lie;
> After, enabled but to suck and cry.
> Think, when 'twas grown to most, 'twas a poor inn,
> A province pack'd up in two yards of skin,
> And that usurp'd, or threaten'd with a rage
> Of sicknesses, or their true mother, age.
> But think that death hath now enfranchis'd thee;
> Thou hast thy expansion now, and liberty;
> Think, that a rusty piece discharg'd is flown
> In pieces, and the bullet is his own,   10
> And freely flies: this to thy soul allow,
> Think thy shell broke, think thy soul hatch'd but now.

THEY were sometimes indelicate and disgusting. Cowley thus apostrophises beauty:

> —Thou tyrant, which leav'st no man free!
> Thou subtle thief, from whom nought safe can be!
> Thou murtherer, which hast kill'd, and devil, which
>   would'st damn me.

Thus he addresses his Mistress:

> Thou who, in many a propriety,
> So truly art the sun to me,
> Add one more likeness, which I'm sure you can,
> And let me and my sun beget a man.

Thus he represents the meditations of a Lover:

> Though in thy thoughts scarce any tracts have been
>   So much as of original sin,
> Such charms thy beauty wears as might
> Desires in dying confest saints excite.
>   Thou with strange adultery
> Dost in each breast a brothel keep;
>   A wake, all men do lust for thee,
> And some enjoy thee when they sleep.

The true taste of Tears:

> Hither with crystal vials, lovers, come,
>   And take my tears, which are Love's wine,
> And try your mistress' tears at home;
>   For all are false, that taste not just like mine.
>   DONNE.

This is yet more indelicate:

> As the sweet sweat of roses in a still,
> As that which from chaf'd musk-cat's pores doth trill,
> As the almighty balm of th' early East,
> Such are the sweet drops of my mistress' breast.
> And on her neck her skin such lustre sets,
> They seem no sweat-drops, but pearl coronets:
> Rank sweaty froth thy mistress' brow defiles.
>   DONNE.

THEIR expressions sometimes raise horror, when they intend perhaps to be pathetic:

> As men in hell are from diseases free,
>   So from all other ills am I,
>   Free from their known formality:
> But all pains eminently lie in thee.
>   COWLEY.

THEY were not always strictly curious, whether the opinions from which they drew their illustrations were true; it was enough that they were popular. Bacon remarks, that some falsehoods are continued by tradition, because they supply commodious allusions.

> It gave a piteous groan, and so it broke;
> In vain it something would have spoke:
> The love within too strong for 't was,
> Like poison put into a Venice-glass.
>   COWLEY.

IN forming descriptions, they looked out not for images, but for conceits. Night has been a common subject, which poets have contended to adorn. Dryden's Night is well known; Donne's is as follows:

Thou seest me here at midnight, now all rest:
Time's dead low-water; when all minds divest
To-morrow's business, when the labourers have
Such rest in bed, that their last church-yard grave,
Subject to change, will scarce be a type of this,
Now when the client, whose last hearing is
To-morrow, sleeps; when the condemned man,
Who when he opes his eyes, must shut them then
Again by death, although sad watch he keep,
Doth practise dying by a little sleep,   10
Thou at this midnight seest me.

IT must be however confessed of these writers, that if they are upon common subjects often unnecessarily and unpoetically subtle; yet where scholastick speculation can be properly admitted, their copiousness and acuteness may justly be admired. What Cowley has written upon Hope, shews an unequalled fertility of invention:

Hope, whose weak being ruin'd is,
    Alike if it succeed, and if it miss;
Whom good or ill does equally confound,
And both the horns of Fate's dilemma wound.
    Vain shadow, which dost vanish quite,
    Both at full noon and perfect night!
    The stars have not a possibility
    Of blessing thee;
If things then from their end we happy call,
'Tis Hope is the most hopeless thing of all.   10
    Hope, thou bold taster of delight,
    Who, whilst thou should'st but taste, devour'st it quite!
Thou bring'st us an estate, yet leav'st us poor,
    By clogging it with legacies before!
    The joys which we entire should wed,
    Come deflower'd virgins to our bed;
Good fortunes without gain imported be,
    Such mighty custom's paid to thee:
For joy, like wine, kept close does better taste;
If it take air before, its spirits waste.   20

To the following comparison of a man that travels, and his wife that stays at home, with a pair of compasses, it may be doubted whether absurdity or ingenuity has the better claim:

Our two souls therefore, which are one,
   Though I must go, endure not yet
A breach, but an expansion,
   Like gold to airy thinness beat.

If they be two, they are two so
   As stiff twin-compasses are two,
Thy soul the fixt foot, makes no show
   To move, but doth, if th' other do.

And though it in the centre sit,
   Yet when the other far doth roam,   10
It leans, and hearkens after it,
   And grows erect, as that comes home.
Such wilt thou be to me, who must
   Like th' other foot, obliquely run.
Thy firmness makes my circle just,
   And makes me end where I begun.
                   DONNE.

In all these examples it is apparent, that whatever is improper or vicious, is produced by a voluntary deviation from nature in pursuit of something new and strange; and that the writers fail to give delight, by their desire of exciting admiration.

HAVING thus endeavoured to exhibit a general representation of the style and sentiments of the metaphysical poets, it is now proper to examine particularly the works of Cowley, who was almost the last of that race, and undoubtedly the best.

His Miscellanies contain a collection of short compositions, written some as they were dictated by a mind at leisure, and some as they were called forth by different occasions; with great variety of style and sentiment, from burlesque levity to awful grandeur. Such an assemblage of diversified excellence no other poet has hitherto afforded. To choose the best, among many good, is one of the most hazardous attempts of criticism. I know not whether Scaliger himself has persuaded many readers to join with him in his preference of the two favourite odes, which he estimates in his raptures at the value of a kingdom. I will however venture to recommend Cowley's first piece, which ought to be inscribed *To my muse*, for want of which the second couplet is without reference. When the title is added, there will still remain a defect; for every piece ought to contain in itself whatever is necessary to make it intelligible. Pope has some epitaphs without names; which are therefore epitaphs to be let, occupied indeed for the present, but hardly appropriated.

The ode on Wit is almost without a rival. It was about the time of Cowley that *Wit*, which had been till then used for *Intellection*, in contradistinction to *Will*, took the meaning, whatever it be, which it now bears.

Of all the passages in which poets have exemplified their own precepts, none will easily be found of greater excellence than that in which Cowley condemns exuberance of Wit:

> Yet 'tis not to adorn and gild each part,
>   That shews more cost than art.
> Jewels at nose and lips but ill appear;
>   Rather than all things wit, let none be there.
> Several lights will not be seen,
>   If there be nothing else between.
> Men doubt, because they stand so thick i' th' sky,
>   If those be stars which paint the galaxy.

In his verses to lord Falkland, whom every man of his time was proud to praise, there are, as there must be in all Cowley's compositions, some striking thoughts; but they are not well wrought. His elegy on Sir Henry Wotton is vigorous and happy, the series of thoughts is easy and natural, and the conclusion, though a little weakened by the intrusion of Alexander, is elegant and forcible.

It may be remarked, that in this Elegy, and in most of his encomiastic poems, he has forgotten or neglected to name his heroes.

In his poem on the death of Hervey, there is much praise, but little passion, a very just and ample delineation of such virtues as a studious privacy admits, and such intellectual excellence as a mind not yet called forth to action can display. He knew how to distinguish, and how to commend the qualities of his companion; but when he wishes to make us weep, he forgets to weep himself, and diverts his sorrow by imagining how his crown of bays, if he had it, would *crackle* in the *fire*. It is the odd fate of this thought to be worse for being true. The bay-leaf crackles remarkably as it burns; as therefore this property was not assigned it by chance, the mind must be thought sufficiently at ease that could attend to such minuteness of physiology. But the power of Cowley is not so much to move the affections, as to exercise the understanding.

The *Chronicle* is a composition unrivalled and alone: such gaiety of fancy, such facility of expression, such varied similitude, such a succession of images, and such a dance of words, it is vain to expect except from Cowley. His strength always appears in his agility; his volatility is not the flutter of a light, but the bound of an elastick mind. His levity never leaves his learning behind it; the moralist, the politician, and the critick, mingle their influence even in this airy frolick of genius. To such a performance Suckling could have brought the gaiety, but not the knowledge; Dryden could have supplied the knowledge, but not the gaiety.

The verses to Davenant, which are vigorously begun, and happily concluded, contain some hints of criticism very justly conceived and happily expressed. Cowley's critical abilities have not been sufficiently observed: the few decisions and remarks which his prefaces and his notes on the Davideis supply, were at that time accessions to English literature, and shew such skill as raises our wish for more examples.

The lines from Jersey are a very curious and pleasing specimen of the familiar descending to the burlesque.

His two metrical disquisitions *for* and *against* Reason, are no mean specimens of metaphysical poetry. The stanzas against knowledge produce little conviction. In those which are intended to exalt the human faculties, Reason has its proper task assigned it; that of judging, not of things revealed, but of the reality of revelation. In the verses *for* Reason is a passage which Bentley, in the only English verses which he is known to have written, seems to have copied, though with the inferiority of an imitator.

> The holy Book like the eighth sphere does shine
>   With thousand lights of truth divine,
> So numberless the stars that to our eye
>   It makes all but one galaxy:
> Yet Reason must assist too; for in seas
>   So vast and dangerous as these,
> Our course by stars above we cannot know
>   Without the compass too below,

After this says Bentley:

> Who travels in religious jars,
> Truth mix'd with error, clouds with rays,
> With Whiston wanting pyx and stars,
> In the wide ocean sinks or strays.

Cowley seems to have had, what Milton is believed to have wanted, the skill to rate his own performances by their just value, and has therefore closed his Miscellanies with the verses upon Crashaw, which apparently excel all that have gone before them, and in which there are beauties which common authors may justly think not only above their attainment, but above their ambition.

To the Miscellanies succeed the *Anacreontiques*, or paraphrastical translations of some little poems, which pass, however justly, under the name of Anacreon. Of those songs dedicated to festivity and gaiety, in which even the morality is voluptuous, and which teach nothing but the enjoyment of the present day, he has given rather a pleasing than a faithful representation, having retained their spriteliness, but lost their simplicity. The Anacreon of Cowley, like the Homer of Pope, has admitted the decoration of some modern graces, by which he is undoubtedly made more amiable to common readers, and perhaps, if they would honestly declare their own perceptions, to far the greater part of those whom courtesy and ignorance are content to style the Learned.

These little pieces will be found more finished in their kind than any other of Cowley's works. The diction shews nothing of the mould of time, and the sentiments are at no great distance from our present habitudes of thought. Real mirth must be always natural, and nature is uniform. Men have been wise in very different modes; but they have always laughed the same way.

Levity of thought naturally produced familiarity of language, and the familiar part of language continues long the same: the dialogue of comedy, when it is transcribed from popular manners and real life, is read from age to age with equal pleasure. The artifice of inversion, by which the established order of words is changed, or of innovation, by which new words or new meanings of words are introduced, is practised, not by those who talk to be understood, but by those who write to be admired.

The Anacreontiques therefore of Cowley give now all the pleasure which they ever gave. If he was formed by nature for one kind of writing more than for another, his power seems to have been greatest in the familiar and the festive.

The next class of his poems is called *The Mistress*, of which it is not necessary to select any particular pieces for praise or censure. They have all the same beauties and faults, and nearly in the same proportion. They are written with exuberance of wit, and with copiousness of learning; and it is truly asserted by Sprat, that the plenitude of the writer's knowledge flows in upon his page, so that the reader is commonly surprised into some improvement. But, considered as the verses of a lover, no man that has ever loved will much commend them. They are neither courtly nor pathetick, have neither gallantry nor fondness. His praises are too far-sought, and too hyperbolical, either to express love, or to excite it: every stanza is crouded with darts and flames, with wounds and death, with mingled souls, and with broken hearts.

The principal artifice by which *The Mistress* is filled with conceits is very copiously displayed by Addison. Love is by Cowley, as by other poets, expressed metaphorically by flame and fire; and that which is true of real fire is said of love, or figurative fire, the same word in the same sentence retaining both significations. Thus, "observing the cold regard of his mistress's eyes, and at the same time their power of producing love in him, he considers them as burning-glasses made of ice. Finding himself able to live in the greatest extremities of love, he concludes the torrid zone to be habitable. Upon the dying of a tree, on which he had cut his loves, he observes, that his flames had burnt up and withered the tree."

These conceits Addison calls mixed wit; that is, wit which consists of thoughts true in one sense of the expression, and false in the other. Addison's representation is sufficiently indulgent. That confusion of images may entertain for a moment; but being unnatural, it soon grows wearisome. Cowley delighted in it, as much as if he had invented it; but, not to mention the ancients, he might have found it full-blown in modern Italy. Thus Sanazarro;

Aspice quam variis distringar Vesbia curis,
 Uror, & heu! nostro manat ab igne liquor;
Sum Nilus, sumque Ætna simul; restringite flammas
 O lacrimæ, aut lacrimas ebibe flamma meas.

One of the severe theologians of that time censured him as having published *a book of profane and lascivious Verses*. From the charge of profaneness, the constant tenour of his life, which seems to have been eminently virtuous, and the general tendency of his opinions, which discover no irreverence of religion, must defend him; but that the accusation of lasciviousness is unjust, the perusal of his works will sufficiently evince.

Cowley's *Mistress* has no power of seduction; "she plays round the head, but comes not at the heart." Her beauty and absence, her kindness and cruelty, her disdain and inconstancy, produce no correspondence of emotion. His poetical account of the virtues of plants, and colours of flowers, is not perused with more sluggish frigidity. The compositions are such as might have been written for penance by a hermit, or for hire by a philosophical rhymer who had only heard of another sex; for they turn the mind only on the writer, whom, without thinking on a woman but as the subject for his task, we sometimes esteem as learned, and sometimes despise as trifling, always admire as ingenious, and always condemn as unnatural.

The Pindarique Odes are now to be considered; a species of composition, which Cowley thinks Pancirolus might have counted *in his list of the lost inventions of antiquity*, and which he has made a bold and vigorous attempt to recover.

The purpose with which he has paraphrased an Olympick and Nemeæan Ode, is by himself sufficiently explained. His endeavour was, not to shew *precisely what Pindar spoke, but his manner of speaking*. He was therefore not at all restrained to his expressions, nor much to his sentiments; nothing was required of him, but not to write as Pindar would not have written.

Of the Olympick Ode the beginning is, I think, above the original in elegance, and the conclusion below it in strength. The connection is supplied with great perspicuity, and the thoughts, which to a reader of less skill seem thrown together by chance, are concatenated without any abruption. Though the English ode cannot be called a translation, it may be very properly consulted as a commentary.

The spirit of Pindar is indeed not every where equally preserved. The following pretty lines are not such as his *deep mouth* was used to pour:

Great Rhea's son,
If in Olympus' top where thou
Sitt'st to behold thy sacred show,
If in Alpheus' silver flight,
If in my verse thou take delight,

My verse, great Rhea's son, which is
Lofty as that, and smooth as this.

In the Nemeæan ode the reader must, in mere justice to Pindar, observe
that whatever is said of *the original new moon, her tender forehead and her horns*,
is superadded by his paraphrast, who has many other plays of words and
fancy unsuitable to the original, as,

> The table, free for every guest,
> No doubt will thee admit,
> And feast more upon thee, than thou on it.

He sometimes extends his author's thoughts without improving them. In
the Olympionick an oath is mentioned in a single word, and Cowley spends
three lines in swearing by the *Castalian Stream*. We are told of Theron's
bounty, with a hint that he had enemies, which Cowley thus enlarges in rhyming prose:

> But in this thankless world the giver
> Is envied even by the receiver;
> 'Tis now the cheap and frugal fashion
> Rather to hide than own the obligation:
> Nay, 'tis much worse than so;
> It now an artifice does grow
> Wrongs and injuries to do,
> Lest men should think we owe.

It is hard to conceive that a man of the first rank in learning and wit, when
he was dealing out such minute morality in such feeble diction, could imagine,
either waking or dreaming, that he imitated Pindar.

In the following odes, where Cowley chooses his own subjects, he sometimes rises to dignity truly Pindarick, and, if some deficiencies of language be
forgiven, his strains are such as those of the Theban bard were to his contemporaries:

> Begin the song, and strike the living lyre:
> Lo how the years to come, a numerous and well-fitted quire,
> All hand in hand do decently advance,
> And to my song with smooth and equal measure dance;
> While the dance lasts, how long soe'er it be,
> My musick's voice shall bear it company;
> Till all gentle notes be drown'd
> In the last trumpet's dreadful sound.

After such enthusiasm, who will not lament to find the poet conclude with lines like these!

> But stop, my Muse—
> Hold thy Pindarick Pegasus closely in,
>   Which does to rage begin—
>   —'Tis an unruly and a hard-mouth'd horse—
> 'Twill no unskilful touch endure,
> But flings writer and reader too that sits not sure.

The fault of Cowley, and perhaps of all the writers of the metaphysical race, is that of pursuing his thoughts to their last ramifications, by which he loses the grandeur of generality; for of the greatest things the parts are little; what is little can be but pretty, and by claiming dignity becomes ridiculous. Thus all the power of description is destroyed by a scrupulous enumeration; and the force of metaphors is lost, when the mind by the mention of particulars is turned more upon the original than the secondary sense, more upon that from which the illustration is drawn than that to which it is applied.

Of this we have a very eminent example in the ode intituled *The Muse*, who goes to *take the air* in an intellectual chariot, to which he harnesses Fancy and Judgement, Wit and Eloquence, Memory and Invention: how he distinguished Wit from Fancy, or how Memory could properly contribute to Motion, he has not explained; we are however content to suppose that he could have justified his own fiction, and wish to see the Muse begin her career; but there is yet more to be done.

> Let the *postilion* Nature mount, and let
> The *coachman* Art be set;
> And let the airy *footmen*, running all beside,
> Make a long row of goodly pride;
> Figures, conceits, raptures, and sentences,
> In a well-worded dress,
> And innocent loves, and pleasant truths, and useful lies,
> In all their gaudy *liveries*.

Every mind is now disgusted with this cumber of magnificence; yet I cannot refuse myself the four next lines:

> Mount, glorious queen, thy travelling throne,
>   And bid it to put on;
>   For long though cheerful is the way,
> And life alas allows but one ill winter's day.

In the same ode, celebrating the power of the Muse, he gives her prescience, or, in poetical language, the foresight of events hatching in futurity; but
having once an egg in his mind, he cannot forbear to shew us that he knows
what an egg contains:

> Thou into the close nests of Time dost peep,
>   And there with piercing eye
> Through the firm shell and the thick white dost spy
>   Years to come a-forming lie,
> Close in their sacred secundine asleep.

The same thought is more generally, and therefore more poetically, expressed
by Casimir, a writer who has many of the beauties and faults of Cowley:

> Omnibus mundi Dominator horis
> Aptat urgendas per inane pennas,
> Pars adhuc nido latet, & futuros
>   Crescit in annos.

Cowley, whatever was his subject, seems to have been carried, by a kind of
destiny, to the light and the familiar, or to conceits which require still more
ignoble epithets. A slaughter in the Red Sea, *new dies the waters name*; and
England, during the Civil War, was *Albion no more, nor to be named from white.*
It is surely by some fascination not easily surmounted, that a writer professing to
revive *the noblest and highest writing in verse*, makes this address to the new year:

> Nay, if thou lov'st me, gentle year,
> Let not so much as love be there,
> Vain fruitless love I mean; for, gentle year,
>   Although I fear,
> There's of this caution little need,
>   Yet, gentle year, take heed
>   How thou dost make
>   Such a mistake;
> Such love I mean alone
> As by thy cruel predecessors has been shewn;   10
> For, though I have too much cause to doubt it,
> I fain would try, for once, if life can live without it.

The reader of this will be inclined to cry out with Prior

> —*Ye Criticks, say,*
> *How poor to this was Pindar's style!*

Even those who cannot perhaps find in the Isthmian or Nemeæan songs what Antiquity has disposed them to expect, will at least see that they are ill represented by such puny poetry; and all will determine that if this be the old Theban strain, it is not worthy of revival.

To the disproportion and incongruity of Cowley's sentiments must be added the uncertainty and looseness of his measures. He takes the liberty of using in any place a verse of any length, from two syllables to twelve. The verses of Pindar have, as he observes, very little harmony to a modern ear; yet by examining the syllables we perceive them to be regular, and have reason enough for supposing that the ancient audiences were delighted with the sound. The imitator ought therefore to have adopted what he found, and to have added what was wanting; to have preserved a constant return of the same numbers, and to have supplied smoothness of transition and continuity of thought.

It is urged by Dr. Sprat, that the *irregularity of numbers is the very thing* which makes *that kind of poesy fit for all manner of subjects*. But he should have remembered, that what is fit for every thing can fit nothing well. The great pleasure of verse arises from the known measure of the lines, and uniform structure of the stanzas, by which the voice is regulated, and the memory relieved.

If the Pindarick style be, what Cowley thinks it, *the highest and noblest kind of writing in verse*, it can be adapted only to high and noble subjects; and it will not be easy to reconcile the poet with the critick, or to conceive how that can be the highest kind of writing in verse, which, according to Sprat, *is chiefly to be preferred for its near affinity to prose*.

This lax and lawless versification so much concealed the deficiencies of the barren, and flattered the laziness of the idle, that it immediately overspread our books of poetry; all the boys and girls caught the pleasing fashion, and they that could do nothing else could write like Pindar. The rights of antiquity were invaded, and disorder tried to break into the Latin: a poem on the Sheldonian Theatre, in which all kinds of verse are shaken together, is unhappily inserted in the *Musæ Anglicanæ*. Pindarism prevailed above half a century; but at last died gradually away, and other imitations supply its place.

The Pindarique Odes have so long enjoyed the highest degree of poetical reputation, that I am not willing to dismiss them with unabated censure; and surely though the mode of their composition be erroneous, yet many parts deserve at least that admiration which is due to great comprehension of knowledge, and great fertility of fancy. The thoughts are often new, and often striking; but the greatness of one part is disgraced by the littleness of another; and total negligence of language gives the noblest conceptions the appearance of a fabric august in the plan, but mean in the materials. Yet surely those verses are not without a just claim to praise; of which it may be said with truth, that no man but Cowley could have written them.

The Davideis now remains to be considered; a poem which the author designed to have extended to twelve books, merely, as he makes no scruple of declaring, because the Æneid had that number; but he had leisure or perseverance only to write the third part. Epick poems have been left unfinished by Virgil, Statius, Spenser, and Cowley. That we have not the whole Davideis is, however, not much to be regretted; for in this undertaking Cowley is, tacitly at least, confessed to have miscarried. There are not many examples of so great a work, produced by an author generally read, and generally praised, that has crept through a century with so little regard. Whatever is said of Cowley, is meant of his other works. Of the Davideis no mention is made; it never appears in books, nor emerges in conversation. By the *Spectator* it has once been quoted, by *Rymer* it has once been praised, and by *Dryden*, in Mac Flecknoe, it has once been imitated; nor do I recollect much other notice from its publication till now, in the whole succession of English literature.

Of this silence and neglect, if the reason be inquired, it will be found partly in the choice of the subject, and partly in the performance of the work.

Sacred History has been always read with submissive reverence, and an imagination over-awed and controlled. We have been accustomed to acquiesce in the nakedness and simplicity of the authentick narrative, and to repose on its veracity with such humble confidence, as suppresses curiosity. We go with the historian as he goes, and stop with him when he stops. All amplification is frivolous and vain; all addition to that which is already sufficient for the purposes of religion, seems not only useless, but in some degree profane.

Such events as were produced by the visible interposition of Divine Power are above the power of human genius to dignify. The miracle of Creation, however it may teem with images, is best described with little diffusion of language: *He spake the word, and they were made.*

We are told that Saul *was troubled with an evil spirit*; from this Cowley takes an opportunity of describing hell, and telling the history of Lucifer, who was, he says,

> Once general of a gilded host of sprites,
> Like Hesper leading forth the spangled nights;
> But down like lightning, which him struck, he came,
> And roar'd at his first plunge into the flame.

Lucifer makes a speech to the inferior agents of mischief, in which there is something of heathenism, and therefore of impropriety; and, to give efficacy to his words, concludes by lashing *his breast with his long tail*. Envy, after a pause, steps out, and among other declarations of her zeal utters these lines:

> Do thou but threat, loud storms shall make reply,
> And thunder echo't to the trembling sky.
> Whilst raging seas swell to so bold an height,
> As shall the fire's proud element affright.

> Th' old drudging Sun, from his long-beaten way,
> Shall at thy voice start, and misguide the day.
> The jocund orbs shall break their measur'd pace,
> And stubborn Poles change their allotted place.
> Heaven's gilded troops shall flutter here and there,
> Leaving their boasting songs tun'd to a sphere.   10

Every reader feels himself weary with this useless talk of an allegorical Being.

It is not only when the events are confessedly miraculous, that fancy and fiction lose their effect: the whole system of life, while the Theocracy was yet visible, has an appearance so different from all other scenes of human action, that the reader of the Sacred Volume habitually considers it as the peculiar mode of existence of a distinct species of mankind, that lived and acted with manners uncommunicable; so that it is difficult even for imagination to place us in the state of them whose story is related, and by consequence their joys and griefs are not easily adopted, nor can the attention be often interested in any thing that befals them.

To the subject, thus originally indisposed to the reception of poetical embellishments, the writer brought little that could reconcile impatience, or attract curiosity. Nothing can be more disgusting than a narrative spangled with conceits, and conceits are all that the Davideis supplies.

One of the great sources of poetical delight is description, or the power of presenting pictures to the mind. Cowley gives inferences instead of images, and shews not what may be supposed to have been seen, but what thoughts the sight might have suggested. When Virgil describes the stone which Turnus lifted against Æneas, he fixes the attention on its bulk and weight:

> Saxum circumspicit ingens,
> Saxum antiquum, ingens, campo quod forte jacebat
> Limes agro positus, litem ut discerneret arvis.

Cowley says of the stone with which Cain slew his brother,

> I saw him fling the stone, as if he meant
> At once his murther and his monument.

Of the sword taken from Goliah, he says,

> A sword so great, that it was only fit
> To cut off his great head that came with it.

Other poets describe death by some of its common appearances; Cowley says, with a learned allusion to sepulchral lamps real or fabulous,

> 'Twixt his right ribs deep pierc'd the furious blade,
> And open'd wide those secret vessels where
> Life's light goes out, when first they let in air.

But he has allusions vulgar as well as learned. In a visionary succession of kings:

> Joas at first does bright and glorious show,
> In life's fresh morn his fame does early crow.

Describing an undisciplined army, after having said with elegance,

> His forces seem'd no army, but a crowd
> Heartless, unarm'd, disorderly, and loud;

he gives them a fit of the ague.

The allusions however are not always to vulgar things: he offends by exaggeration as much as by diminution:

> The king was plac'd alone, and o'er his head
> A well-wrought heaven of silk and gold was spread.

Whatever he writes is always polluted with some conceit:

> Where the sun's fruitful beams give metals birth,
> Where he the growth of fatal gold does see,
> Gold, which alone more influence has than he.

In one passage he starts a sudden question, to the confusion of philosophy:

> Ye learned heads, whom ivy garlands grace,
> Why does that twining plant the oak embrace?
> The oak, for courtship most of all unfit,
> And rough as are the winds that fight with it.

His expressions have sometimes a degree of meanness that surpasses expectation:

> Nay, gentle guests, he cries, since now you're in,
> The story of your gallant friend begin.

In a simile descriptive of the Morning:

As glimmering stars just at th' approach of day,
Cashier'd by troops, at last drop all away.

The dress of Gabriel deserves attention:

He took for skin a cloud most soft and bright,
That e'er the midday sun pierc'd through with light,
Upon his cheeks a lively blush he spread,
Wash'd from the morning beauties deepest red;
An harmless flattering meteor shone for hair,
And fell adown his shoulders with loose care;
He cuts out a silk mantle from the skies,
Where the most sprightly azure pleas'd the eyes;
This he with starry vapours sprinkles all,
Took in their prime ere they grow ripe and fall,   10
Of a new rainbow, ere it fret or fade,
The choicest piece cut out, a scarfe is made.

This is a just specimen of Cowley's imagery: what might in general expressions be great and forcible, he weakens and makes ridiculous by branching it into small parts. That Gabriel was invested with the softest or brightest colours of the sky, we might have been told, and been dismissed to improve the idea in our different proportions of conception; but Cowley could not let us go till he had related where Gabriel got first his skin, and then his mantle, then his lace, and then his scarfe, and related it in the terms of the mercer and taylor.

Sometimes he indulges himself in a digression, always conceived with his natural exuberance, and commonly, even where it is not long, continued till it is tedious:

I' th' library a few choice authors stood,
Yet 'twas well stor'd, for that small store was good;
Writing, man's spiritual physic, was not then
Itself, as now, grown a disease of men.
Learning (young virgin) but few suitors knew;
The common prostitute she lately grew,
And with the spurious brood loads now the press;
Laborious effects of idleness.

As the Davideis affords only four books, though intended to consist of twelve, there is no opportunity for such criticisms as Epick poems commonly supply. The plan of the whole work is very imperfectly shewn by the third part. The duration of an unfinished action cannot be known. Of characters either not yet introduced, or shewn but upon few occasions, the full extent and the nice discriminations cannot be ascertained. The fable is plainly implex, formed rather from the Odyssey than the Iliad; and many artifices of diversification are employed, with the skill of a man acquainted with the best models. The past is recalled by narration, and the future anticipated by vision: but he has been so lavish of his poetical art, that it is difficult to imagine how he could fill eight books more without practising again the same modes of disposing his matter; and perhaps the perception of this growing incumbrance inclined him to stop. By this abruption, posterity lost more instruction than delight. If the continuation of the Davideis can be missed, it is for the learning that had been diffused over it, and the notes in which it had been explained.

Had not his characters been depraved like every other part by improper decorations, they would have deserved uncommon praise. He gives Saul both the body and mind of a hero:

> His way once chose, he forward thrust outright,
> Nor turn'd aside for danger or delight.

And the different beauties of the lofty Merab and the gentle Michol are very justly conceived and strongly painted.

Rymer has declared the Davideis superior to the *Jerusalem of Tasso*, "which," says he, "the poet, with all his care, has not totally purged from pedantry." If by pedantry is meant that minute knowledge which is derived from particular sciences and studies, in opposition to the general notions supplied by a wide survey of life and nature, Cowley certainly errs, by introducing pedantry far more frequently than Tasso. I know not, indeed, why they should be compared; for the resemblance of Cowley's work to Tasso's is only that they both exhibit the agency of celestial and infernal spirits, in which however they differ widely; for Cowley supposes them commonly to operate upon the mind by suggestion; Tasso represents them as promoting or obstructing events by external agency.

Of particular passages that can be properly compared, I remember only the description of Heaven, in which the different manner of the two writers is sufficiently discernible. Cowley's is scarcely description, unless it be possible to describe by negatives; for he tells us only what there is not in heaven. Tasso endeavours to represent the splendours and pleasures of the regions of happiness. Tasso affords images, and Cowley sentiments. It happens, however, that Tasso's description affords some reason for Rymer's censure. He says of the Supreme Being,

> Hà sotto i piedi e fato e la natura
> Ministri humili, e'l moto, e ch'il misura.

The second line has in it more of pedantry than perhaps can be found in any other stanza of the poem.

In the perusal of the Davideis, as of all Cowley's works, we find wit and learning unprofitably squandered. Attention has no relief; the affections are never moved; we are sometimes surprised, but never delighted, and find much to admire, but little to approve. Still however it is the work of Cowley, of a mind capacious by nature, and replenished by study.

In the general review of Cowley's poetry it will be found, that he wrote with abundant fertility, but negligent or unskilful selection; with much thought; but with little imagery; that he is never pathetick, and rarely sublime, but always either ingenious or learned, either acute or profound.

It is said by Denham in his elegy,

> To him no author was unknown;
> Yet what he writ was all his own.

This wide position requires less limitation, when it is affirmed of Cowley, than perhaps of any other poet—He read much, and yet borrowed little.

His character of writing was indeed not his own: he unhappily adopted that which was predominant. He saw a certain way to present praise, and not sufficiently enquiring by what means the ancients have continued to delight through all the changes of human manners, he contented himself with a deciduous laurel, of which the verdure in its spring was bright and gay, but which time has been continually stealing from his brows.

He was in his own time considered as of unrivalled excellence. Clarendon represents him as having taken a flight beyond all that went before him; and Milton is said to have declared, that the three greatest English poets were Spenser, Shakspeare, and Cowley.

His manner he had in common with others: but his sentiments were his own. Upon every subject he thought for himself; and such was his copiousness of knowledge, that something at once remote and applicable rushed into his mind; yet it is not likely that he always rejected a commodious idea merely because another had used it: his known wealth was so great, that he might have borrowed without loss of credit.

In his elegy on Sir Henry Wotton, the last lines have such resemblance to the noble epigram of Grotius upon the death of Scaliger, that I cannot but think them copied from it, though they are copied by no servile hand.

One passage in his *Mistress* is so apparently borrowed from Donne, that he probably would not have written it, had it not mingled with his own thoughts, so as that he did not perceive himself taking it from another.

> Although I think thou never found wilt be,
> Yet I'm resolv'd to search for thee;
> The search itself rewards the pains.
> So, though the chymic his great secret miss,
> (For neither it in Art nor Nature is)

Yet things well worth his toil he gains:
And does his charge and labour pay
With good unsought experiments by the way.
                                    COWLEY.

Some that have deeper digg'd Love's mine than I,
Say, where his centric happiness doth lie:
    I have lov'd, and got, and told;
But should I love, get, tell, till I were old,
I should not find that hidden mystery;
    Oh, 'tis imposture all:
And as no chymic yet th' elixir got,
    But glorifies his pregnant pot,
    If by the way to him befal
Some odoriferous thing, or medicinal,   10
    So lovers dream a rich and long delight,
    But get a winter-seeming summer's night.
                                    DONNE.

Jonson and Donne, as Dr. Hurd remarks, were then in the highest esteem.
It is related by Clarendon, that Cowley always acknowledged his obligation
to the learning and industry of Jonson; but I have found no traces of Jonson
in his works: to emulate Donne, appears to have been his purpose; and from
Donne he may have learned that familiarity with religious images, and that
light allusion to sacred things, by which readers far short of sanctity are frequently offended; and which would not be born in the present age, when
devotion, perhaps not more fervent, is more delicate.

Having produced one passage taken by Cowley from Donne, I will recompense him by another which Milton seems to have borrowed from him. He
says of Goliah,

> His spear, the trunk was of a lofty tree,
> Which Nature meant some tall ship's mast should be.

Milton of Satan,

> His spear, to equal which the tallest pine
> Hewn on Norwegian hills, to be the mast
> Of some great admiral, were but a wand,
> He walk'd with.

His diction was in his own time censured as negligent. He seems not to have
known, or not to have considered, that words being arbitrary must owe their
power to association, and have the influence, and that only, which custom has

given them. Language is the dress of thought; and as the noblest mien, or most graceful action, would be degraded and obscured by a garb appropriated to the gross employments of rusticks or mechanicks, so the most heroick sentiments will lose their efficacy, and the most splendid ideas drop their magnificence, if they are conveyed by words used commonly upon low and trivial occasions, debased by vulgar mouths, and contaminated by inelegant applications,

Truth indeed is always truth, and reason is always reason; they have an intrinsick and unalterable value, and constitute that intellectual gold which defies destruction: but gold may be so concealed in baser matter, that only a chymist can recover it; sense may be so hidden in unrefined and plebeian words, that none but philosophers can distinguish it; and both may be so buried in impurities, as not to pay the cost of their extraction.

The diction, being the vehicle of the thoughts, first presents itself to the intellectual eye: and if the first appearance offends, a further knowledge is not often sought. Whatever professes to benefit by pleasing, must please at once. The pleasures of the mind imply something sudden and unexpected; that which elevates must always surprise. What is perceived by slow degrees may gratify us with the consciousness of improvement, but will never strike with the sense of pleasure.

Of all this, Cowley appears to have been without knowledge, or without care. He makes no selection of words, nor seeks any neatness of phrase: he has no elegances either lucky or elaborate; as his endeavours were rather to impress sentences upon the understanding than images on the fancy, he has few epithets, and those scattered without peculiar propriety or nice adaptation. It seems to follow from the necessity of the subject, rather than the care of the writer, that the diction of his heroick poem is less familiar than that of his slightest writings. He has given not the same numbers, but the same diction, to the gentle Anacreon and the tempestuous Pindar.

His versification seems to have had very little of his care; and if what he thinks be true, that his numbers are unmusical only when they are ill read, the art of reading them is at present lost; for they are commonly harsh to modern ears. He has indeed many noble lines, such as the feeble care of Waller never could produce. The bulk of his thoughts sometimes swelled his verse to unexpected and inevitable grandeur; but his excellence of this kind is merely fortuitous: he sinks willingly down to his general carelessness, and avoids with very little care either meanness or asperity.

His contractions are often rugged and harsh:

> One flings a mountain, and its rivers too
> Torn up with't.

His rhymes are very often made by pronouns or particles, or the like unimportant words, which disappoint the ear, and destroy the energy of the line.

His combination of different measures is sometimes dissonant and unpleasing; he joins verses together, of which the former does not slide easily into the latter.

The words *do* and *did*, which so much degrade in present estimation the line that admits them, were in the time of Cowley little censured or avoided; how often he used them, and with how bad an effect, at least to our ears, will appear by a passage, in which every reader will lament to see just and noble thoughts defrauded of their praise by inelegance of language:

> Where honour or where conscience *does* not bind,
>   No other law shall shackle me;
>   Slave to myself I ne'er will be;
> Nor shall my future actions be confin'd
>   By my own present mind.
> Who by resolves and vows engag'd *does* stand
>   For days, that yet belong to fate,
> *Does* like an unthrift mortgage his estate,
>   Before it falls into his hand,
>   The bondman of the cloister so,   10
> All that he *does* receive *does* always owe.
> And still as Time comes in, it goes away,
>   Not to enjoy, but debts to pay!
> Unhappy slave, and pupil to a bell!
> Which his hours' work as well as hours *does* tell:
> Unhappy till the last, the kind releasing knell.

His heroick lines are often formed of monosyllables; but yet they are sometimes sweet and sonorous.

He says of the Messiah,

> *Round the whole earth his dreaded name shall sound,*
> *And reach to worlds that must not yet be found.*

In another place, of David,

> *Yet bid him go securely, when he sends;*
> *'Tis Saul that is his foe, and we his friends.*
> *The man who has his God, no aid can lack;*
> *And we who bid him go, will bring him back.*

Yet amidst his negligence he sometimes attempted an improved and scientifick versification; of which it will be best to give his own account subjoined to this line,

Nor can the glory contain itself in th' endless space.

"I am sorry that it is necessary to admonish the most part of readers, that it is not by negligence that this verse is so loose, long, and, as it were, vast; it is to paint in the number the nature of the thing which it describes, which I would have observed in divers other places of this poem, that else will pass for very careless verses: as before,

> *And over-runs the neighb'ring fields with violent course.*

In the second book;

> *Down a precipice deep, down he casts them all.—*

—And,

> *And fell a-down his shoulders with loose care.*

In the third,

> *Brass was his helmet, his boots brass, and o'er*
> *His breast a thick plate of strong brass he wore.*

In the fourth,

> *Like some fair pineo'er-looking all th' ignobler wood.*

And,

> *Some from the rocks cast themselves down headlong.*

"And many more: but it is enough to instance in a few. The thing is, that the disposition of words and numbers should be such, as that, out of the order and sound of them, the things themselves may be represented. This the Greeks were not so accurate as to bind themselves to; neither have our English poets observed it, for aught I can find. The Latins (*qui musas colunt severiores*) sometimes did it, and their prince, Virgil, always: in whom the examples are innumerable, and taken notice of by all judicious men, so that it is superfluous to collect them."

I know not whether he has, in many of these instances, attained the representation or resemblance that he purposes. Verse can imitate only sound and motion. A *boundless* verse, a *headlong* verse, and a verse of *brass* or of *strong brass*, seem to comprise very incongruous and unsociable ideas. What there is peculiar in the sound of the line expressing *loose care*, I cannot discover; nor why the *pine* is *taller* in an Alexandrine than in ten syllables.

But, not to defraud him of his due praise, he has given one example of representative versification, which perhaps no other English line can equal:

> Begin, be bold, and venture to be wise.
> He who defers this work from day to day,
> Does on a river's bank expecting stay
> Till the whole stream that stopp'd him shall be gone,
> *Which runs, and as it runs, for ever shall run on.*

Cowley was, I believe, the first poet that mingled Alexandrines at pleasure with the common heroick of ten syllables, and from him Dryden borrowed the practice, whether ornamental or licentious. He considered the verse of twelve syllables as elevated and majestick, and has therefore deviated into that measure when he supposes the voice heard of the Supreme Being.

The Author of the Davideis is commended by Dryden for having written it in couplets, because he discovered that any staff was too lyrical for an heroick poem; but this seems to have been known before by *May* and *Sandys*, the translators of the Pharsalia and the Metamorphoses.

In the Davideis are some hemistichs, or verses left imperfect by the author, in imitation of Virgil, whom he supposes not to have intended to complete them: that this opinion is erroneous, may be probably concluded, because this truncation is imitated by no subsequent Roman poet; because Virgil himself filled up one broken line in the heat of recitation; because in one the sense is now unfinished; and because all that can be done by a broken verse, a line intersected by a *cæsura* and a full stop will equally effect.

Of triplets in his Davideis he makes no use, and perhaps did not at first think them allowable; but he appears afterwards to have changed his mind, for in the verses on the government of Cromwell he inserts them liberally with great happiness.

After so much criticism on his Poems, the Essays which accompany them must not be forgotten. What is said by Sprat of his conversation, that no man could draw from it any suspicion of his excellence in poetry, may be applied to these compositions. No author ever kept his verse and his prose at a greater distance from each other. His thoughts are natural, and his style has a smooth and placid equability, which has never yet obtained its due commendation. Nothing is far-sought, or hard-laboured; but all is easy without feebleness, and familiar without grossness.

It has been observed by Felton, in his Essay on the Classicks, that Cowley was beloved by every Muse that he courted; and that he has rivalled the Ancients in every kind of poetry but tragedy.

It may be affirmed, without any encomiastick fervour, that he brought to his poetick labours a mind replete with learning, and that his pages are embellished with all the ornaments which books could supply; that he was the first who imparted to English numbers the enthusiasm of the greater ode, and the gaiety of the less; that he was equally qualified for spritely sallies, and for lofty flights; that he was among those who freed translation from servility, and, instead of following his author at a distance, walked by his side; and that if he left versification yet improvable, he left likewise from time to time such specimens of excellence as enabled succeeding poets to improve it.

MILTON [extract]

IN the examination of Milton's poetical works, I shall pay so much regard to time as to begin with his juvenile productions. For his early pieces he seems to have had a degree of fondness not very laudable: what he has once written he resolves to preserve, and gives to the publick an unfinished poem, which he broke off because he was *nothing satisfied with what he had done*, supposing his readers less nice than himself. These preludes to his future labours are in Italian, Latin, and English. Of the Italian I cannot pretend to speak as a critick; but I have heard them commended by a man well qualified to decide their merit. The Latin pieces are lusciously elegant; but the delight which they afford is rather by the exquisite imitation of the ancient writers, by the purity of the diction, and the harmony of the numbers, than by any power of invention, or vigour of sentiment. They are not all of equal value; the elegies excell the odes; and some of the exercises on Gunpowder Treason might have been spared.

The English poems, though they make no promises of *Paradise Lost*, have this evidence of genius, that they have a cast original and unborrowed. But their peculiarity is not excellence: if they differ from the verses of others, they differ for the worse; for they are too often distinguished by repulsive harshness; the combinations of words are new, but they are not pleasing; the rhymes and epithets seem to be laboriously sought, and violently applied.

That in the early parts of his life he wrote with much care appears from his manuscripts, happily preserved at Cambridge, in which many of his smaller works are found as they were first written, with the subsequent corrections. Such reliques shew how excellence is acquired; what we hope ever to do with ease, we may learn first to do with diligence.

Those who admire the beauties of this great poet, sometimes force their own judgement into false approbation of his little pieces, and prevail upon themselves to think that admirable which is only singular. All that short compositions can commonly attain is neatness and elegance. Milton never learned the art of doing little things with grace; he overlooked the milder excellence of suavity and softness; he was a *Lion* that had no skill *in dandling the Kid*.

One of the poems on which much praise has been bestowed is *Lycidas*; of which the diction is harsh, the rhymes uncertain, and the numbers unpleasing. What beauty there is, we must therefore seek in the sentiments and images. It is not to be considered as the effusion of real passion; for passion runs not after remote allusions and obscure opinions. Passion plucks no berries from the myrtle and ivy, nor calls upon Arethuse and Mincius, nor tells of rough *satyrs* and *fauns with cloven heel*. Where there is leisure for fiction there is little grief.

In this poem there is no nature, for there is no truth; there is no art, for there is nothing new. Its form is that of a pastoral, easy, vulgar, and therefore disgusting: whatever images it can supply, are long ago exhausted; and its inherent improbability always forces dissatisfaction on the mind. When Cowley tells of Hervey that they studied together, it is easy to suppose how much he must miss the companion of his labours, and the partner of his discoveries; but what image of tenderness can be excited by these lines!

> We drove a field, and both together heard
> What time the grey fly winds her sultry horn,
> Battening our flocks with the fresh dews of night.

We know that they never drove a field, and that they had no flocks to batten; and though it be allowed that the representation may be allegorical, the true meaning is so uncertain and remote, that it is never sought because it cannot be known when it is found.

Among the flocks, and copses, and flowers, appear the heathen deities; Jove and Phoebus, Neptune and Æolus, with a long train of mythological imagery, such as a College easily supplies. Nothing can less display knowledge, or less exercise invention, than to tell how a shepherd has lost his companion, and must now feed his flocks alone, without any judge of his skill in piping; and how one god asks another god what is become of Lycidas, and how neither god can tell. He who thus grieves will excite no sympathy; he who thus praises will confer no honour.

This poem has yet a grosser fault. With these trifling fictions are mingled the most awful and sacred truths, such as ought never to be polluted with such irreverend combinations. The shepherd likewise is now a feeder of sheep, and afterwards an ecclesiastical pastor, a superintendent of a Christian flock. Such equivocations are always unskilful; but here they are indecent, and at least approach to impiety, of which, however, I believe the writer not to have been conscious.

Such is the power of reputation justly acquired, that its blaze drives away the eye from nice examination. Surely no man could have fancied that he read *Lycidas* with pleasure, had he not known its author.

Of the two pieces, *L'Allegro* and *Il Penseroso*, I believe opinion is uniform; every man that reads them, reads them with pleasure. The author's design is not, what Theobald has remarked, merely to shew how objects derive their colours from the mind, by representing the operation of the same things upon the gay and the melancholy temper, or upon the same man as he is differently disposed; but rather how, among the successive variety of appearances, every disposition of mind takes hold on those by which it may be gratified.

The *chearful* man hears the lark in the morning; the *pensive* man hears the nightingale in the evening. The *chearful* man sees the cock strut, and hears the horn and hounds echo in the wood; then walks *not unseen* to observe the glory of the rising sun, or listen to the singing milk-maid, and view the labours of the plowman and the mower; then casts his eyes about him over scenes of smiling plenty, and looks up to the distant tower, the residence of some fair inhabitant; thus he pursues rural gaiety through a day of labour or of play, and delights himself at night with the fanciful narratives of superstitious ignorance.

The *pensive* man, at one time, walks *unseen* to muse at midnight; and at another hears the sullen curfew. If the weather drives him home, he sits in a room lighted only by *glowing embers*; or by a lonely lamp outwatches the North Star, to discover the habitation of separate souls, and varies the shades of meditation, by contemplating the magnificent or pathetick scenes of tragick and epic poetry. When the morning comes, a morning gloomy with rain and wind, he walks into the dark trackless woods, falls asleep by some murmuring water, and with melancholy enthusiasm expects some dream of prognostication, or some musick played by aerial performers.

Both Mirth and Melancholy are solitary, silent inhabitants of the breast that neither receive nor transmit communication; no mention is therefore made of a philosophical friend, or a pleasant companion. The seriousness does not arise from any participation of calamity, nor the gaiety from the pleasures of the bottle.

The man of *chearfulness*, having exhausted the country, tries what *towered cities* will afford, and mingles with scenes of splendor, gay assemblies, and nuptial festivities; but he mingles a mere spectator, as, when the learned comedies of Jonson, or the wild dramas of Shakspeare, are exhibited, he attends the theatre.

The *pensive* man never loses himself in crowds, but walks the cloister, or frequents the cathedral. Milton probably had not yet forsaken the Church.

Both his characters delight in musick; but he seems to think that chearful notes would have obtained from Pluto a compleat dismission of Eurydice, of whom solemn sounds only procured a conditional release.

For the old age of Chearfulness he makes no provision; but Melancholy he conducts with great dignity to the close of life. His Chearfulness is without levity, and his Pensiveness without asperity.

Through these two poems the images are properly selected, and nicely distinguished; but the colours of the diction seem not sufficiently discriminated. I know not whether the characters are kept sufficiently apart. No mirth can, indeed, be found in his melancholy; but I am afraid that I always meet some melancholy in his mirth. They are two noble efforts of imagination.

The greatest of his juvenile performances is the *Mask of Comus*; in which may very plainly be discovered the dawn or twilight of *Paradise Lost*. Milton appears to have formed very early that system of diction, and mode of verse, which his maturer judgement approved, and from which he never endeavoured nor desired to deviate.

Nor does *Comus* afford only a specimen of his language; it exhibits likewise his power of description and his vigour of sentiment, employed in the praise and defence of virtue. A work more truly poetical is rarely found; allusions, images, and descriptive epithets, embellish almost every period with lavish decoration. As a series of lines, therefore, it may be considered as worthy of all the admiration with which the votaries have received it.

As a drama it is deficient. The action is not probable. A Masque, in those parts where supernatural intervention is admitted, must indeed be given up to all the freaks of imagination; but, so far as the action is merely human, it ought to be reasonable, which can hardly be said of the conduct of the two brothers; who, when their sister sinks with fatigue in a pathless wilderness, wander both away together in search of berries too far to find their way back, and leave a helpless Lady to all the sadness and danger of solitude. This however is a defect over-balanced by its convenience.

What deserves more reprehension is, that the prologue spoken in the wild wood by the attendant Spirit is addressed to the audience; a mode of communication so contrary to the nature of dramatick representation, that no precedents can support it.

The discourse of the Spirit is too long; an objection that may be made to almost all the following speeches: they have not the spriteliness of a dialogue animated by reciprocal contention, but seem rather declamations deliberately composed, and formally repeated, on a moral question. The auditor therefore listens as to a lecture, without passion, without anxiety.

The song of Comus has airiness and jollity; but, what may recommend Milton's morals as well as his poetry, the invitations to pleasure are so general, that they excite no distinct images of corrupt enjoyment, and take no dangerous hold on the fancy.

The following soliloquies of Comus and the Lady are elegant, but tedious. The song must owe much to the voice, if it ever can delight. At last the Brothers enter, with too much tranquillity; and when they have feared lest their sister should be in danger, and hoped that she is not in danger, the Elder makes a speech in praise of chastity, and the Younger finds how fine it is to be a philosopher.

Then descends the Spirit in form of a shepherd; and the Brother, instead of being in haste to ask his help, praises his singing, and enquires his business in that place. It is remarkable, that at this interview the Brother is taken with a short fit of rhyming. The Spirit relates that the Lady is in the power of Comus; the Brother moralises again; and the Spirit makes a long narration, of no use because it is false, and therefore unsuitable to a good Being.

In all these parts the language is poetical, and the sentiments are generous; but there is something wanting to allure attention.

The dispute between the Lady and Comus is the most animated and affecting scene of the drama, and wants nothing but a brisker reciprocation of objections and replies, to invite attention, and detain it.

The songs are vigorous, and full of imagery; but they are harsh in their diction, and not very musical in their numbers.

Throughout the whole, the figures are too bold, and the language too luxuriant for dialogue. It is a drama in the epic style, inelegantly splendid, and tediously instructive.

The *Sonnets* were written in different parts of Milton's life, upon different occasions. They deserve not any particular criticism; for of the best it can only be said, that they are not bad; and perhaps only the eighth and the twenty-first are truly entitled to this slender commendation. The fabrick of a sonnet, however adapted to the Italian language, has never succeeded in ours, which, having greater variety of termination, requires the rhymes to be often changed.

Those little pieces may be dispatched without much anxiety; a greater work calls for greater care. I am now to examine *Paradise Lost*; a poem, which, considered with respect to design, may claim the first place, and with respect to performance the second, among the productions of the human mind.

By the general consent of criticks, the first praise of genius is due to the writer of an epick poem, as it requires an assemblage of all the powers which are singly sufficient for other compositions. Poetry is the art of uniting pleasure with truth, by calling imagination to the help of reason. Epick poetry undertakes to teach the most important truths by the most pleasing precepts, and therefore relates some great event in the most affecting manner. History must supply the writer with the rudiments of narration, which he must improve and exalt by a nobler art, must animate by dramatick energy, and diversify by retrospection and anticipation; morality must teach him the exact bounds, and different shades, of vice and virtue; from policy, and the practice of life, he has to learn the discriminations of character, and the tendency of the passions, either single or combined; and physiology must supply him with illustrations and images. To put these materials to poetical use, is required an imagination capable of painting nature, and realizing fiction. Nor is he yet a poet till he has attained the whole extension of his language, distinguished all the delicacies of phrase, and all the colours of words, and learned to adjust their different sounds to all the varieties of metrical modulation.

Bossu is of opinion that the poet's first work is to find a *moral*, which his fable is afterwards to illustrate and establish. This seems to have been the process only of Milton; the moral of other poems is incidental and consequent; in Milton's only it is essential and intrinsick. His purpose was the most useful and the most arduous; *to vindicate the ways of God to man;* to shew the reasonableness of religion, and the necessity of obedience to the Divine Law.

To convey this moral, there must be a *fable*, a narration artfully constructed, so as to excite curiosity, and surprise expectation. In this part of his work, Milton must be confessed to have equalled every other poet. He has involved in his account of the Fall of Man the events which preceded, and those that were to follow it: he has interwoven the whole system of theology with such propriety, that every part appears to be necessary; and scarcely any recital is wished shorter for the sake of quickening the progress of the main action.

The subject of an epic poem is naturally an event of great importance. That of Milton is not the destruction of a city, the conduct of a colony, or the foundation of an empire. His subject is the fate of worlds, the revolutions of heaven and of earth; rebellion against the Supreme King, raised by the highest order of created beings; the overthrow of their host, and the punishment of their crime; the creation of a new race of reasonable creatures; their original happiness and innocence, their forfeiture of immortality, and their restoration to hope and peace.

Great events can be hastened or retarded only by persons of elevated dignity. Before the greatness displayed in Milton's poem, all other greatness shrinks away. The weakest of his agents are the highest and noblest of human beings, the original parents of mankind; with whose actions the elements consented; on whose rectitude, or deviation of will, depended the state of terrestrial nature, and the condition of all the future inhabitants of the globe.

Of the other agents in the poem, the chief are such as it is irreverence to name on slight occasions. The rest were lower powers;

> –of which the least could wield
> Those elements, and arm him with the force
> Of all their regions;

powers, which only the controul of Omnipotence restrains from laying creation waste, and filling the vast expanse of space with ruin and confusion. To display the motives and actions of beings thus superiour, so far as human reason can examine them, or human imagination represent them, is the task which this mighty poet has undertaken and performed.

In the examination of epick poems much speculation is commonly employed upon the *characters*. The characters in the *Paradise Lost*, which admit of examination, are those of angels and of man; of angels good and evil; of man in his innocent and sinful state.

Among the angels, the virtue of Raphael is mild and placid, of easy condescension and free communication; that of Michael is regal and lofty, and, as may seem, attentive to the dignity of his own nature. Abdiel and Gabriel appear occasionally, and act as every incident requires; the solitary fidelity of Abdiel is very amiably painted.

Of the evil angels the characters are more diversified. To Satan, as Addison observes, such sentiments are given as suit *the most exalted and most depraved being*. Milton has been censured, by Clarke*, for the impiety which some-times breaks from Satan's mouth. For there are thoughts, as he justly remarks, which no observation of character can justify, because no good man would willingly permit them to pass, however transiently, through his own mind. To make Satan speak as a rebel, without any such expressions as might taint the reader's imagination, was indeed one of the great difficulties in Milton's undertaking, and I cannot but think that he has extricated himself with great happiness. There is in Satan's speeches little that can give pain to a pious ear. The language of rebellion cannot be the same with that of obedience. The malignity of Satan foams in haughtiness and obstinacy; but his expressions are commonly general, and no otherwise offensive than as they are wicked.

The other chiefs of the celestial rebellion are very judiciously discriminated in the first and second books; and the ferocious character of Moloch appears, both in the battle and the council, with exact consistency.

To Adam and to Eve are given, during their innocence, such sentiments as innocence can generate and utter. Their love is pure benevolence and mutual veneration; their repasts are without luxury, and their diligence without toil. Their addresses to their Maker have little more than the voice of admiration and gratitude. Fruition left them nothing to ask, and Innocence left them nothing to fear.

But with guilt enter distrust and discord, mutual accusation, and stubborn self-defence; they regard each other with alienated minds, and dread their Creator as the avenger of their transgression. At last they seek shelter in his mercy, soften to repentance, and melt in supplication. Both before and after the Fall, the superiority of Adam is diligently sustained.

Of the *probable* and the *marvellous*, two parts of a vulgar epic poem, which immerge the critick in deep consideration, the *Paradise Lost* requires little to be said. It contains the history of a miracle, of Creation and Redemption; it displays the power and the mercy of the Supreme Being; the probable therefore is marvellous, and the marvellous is probable. The substance of the narrative is truth; and as truth allows no choice, it is, like necessity, superior to rule. To the accidental or adventitious parts, as to every thing human, some slight exceptions may be made. But the main fabrick is immovably supported.

It is justly remarked by Addison, that this poem has, by the nature of its subject, the advantage above all others, that it is universally and perpetually interesting. All mankind will, through all ages, bear the same relation to

---

* Essay on Study.

Adam and to Eve, and must partake of that good and evil which extend to themselves.

Of the *machinery*, so called from Θεὸς ἀπὸ μηχανῆς, by which is meant the occasional interposition of supernatural power, another fertile topic of critical remarks, here is no room to speak, because every thing is done under the immediate and visible direction of Heaven; but the rule is so far observed, that no part of the action could have been accomplished by any other means.

Of *episodes*, I think there are only two, contained in Raphael's relation of the war in heaven, and Michael's prophetick account of the changes to happen in this world. Both are closely connected with the great action; one was necessary to Adam as a warning, the other as a consolation.

To the compleatness or *integrity* of the design nothing can be objected; it has distinctly and clearly what Aristotle requires, a beginning, a middle, and an end. There is perhaps no poem, of the same length, from which so little can be taken without apparent mutilation. Here are no funeral games, nor is there any long description of a shield: The short digressions at the beginning of the third, seventh, and ninth books, might doubtless be spared; but superfluities so beautiful, who would take away? or who does not wish that the author of the *Iliad* had gratified succeeding ages with a little knowledge of himself? Perhaps no passages are more frequently or more attentively read than those extrinsick paragraphs; and, since the end of poetry is pleasure, that cannot be unpoetical with which all are pleased.

The questions, whether the action of the poem be strictly *one*, whether the poem can be properly termed *heroick*, and who is the hero, are raised by such readers as draw their principles of judgement rather from books than from reason. Milton, though he intituled *Paradise Lost* only a *poem*, yet calls it himself *heroick song*. Dryden, petulantly and indecently, denies the heroism of Adam, because he was overcome; but there is no reason why the hero should not be unfortunate, except established practice, since success and virtue do not go necessarily together. Cato is the hero of Lucan; but Lucan's authority will not be suffered by Quintilian to decide. However, if success be necessary, Adam's deceiver was at last crushed; Adam was restored to his Maker's favour, and therefore may securely resume his human rank.

After the scheme and fabrick of the poem, must be considered its component parts, the sentiments and the diction.

The *sentiments*, as expressive of manners, or appropriated to characters, are, for the greater part, unexceptionably just.

Splendid passages, containing lessons of morality, or precepts of prudence, occur seldom. Such is the original formation of this poem, that as it admits no human manners till the Fall, it can give little assistance to human conduct. Its end is to raise the thoughts above sublunary cares or pleasures. Yet the praise of that fortitude, with which Abdiel maintained his singularity of virtue against the scorn of multitudes, may be accommodated to all times; and

Raphael's reproof of Adam's curiosity after the planetary motions, with the answer returned by Adam, may be confidently opposed to any rule of life which any poet has delivered.

The thoughts which are occasionally called forth in the progress, are such as could only be produced by an imagination in the highest degree fervid and active, to which materials were supplied by incessant study and unlimited curiosity. The heat of Milton's mind might be said to sublimate his learning, to throw off into his work the spirit of science, unmingled with its grosser parts.

He had considered creation in its whole extent, and his descriptions are therefore learned. He had accustomed his imagination to unrestrained indulgence, and his conceptions therefore were extensive. The characteristick quality of his poem is sublimity. He sometimes descends to the elegant, but his element is the great. He can occasionally invest himself with grace; but his natural port is gigantick loftiness.* He can please when pleasure is required; but it is his peculiar power to astonish.

He seems to have been well acquainted with his own genius, and to know what it was that Nature had bestowed upon him more bountifully than upon others; the power of displaying the vast, illuminating the splendid, enforcing the awful, darkening the gloomy, and aggravating the dreadful: he therefore chose a subject on which too much could not be said, on which he might tire his fancy without the censure of extravagance.

The appearances of nature, and the occurrences of life, did not satiate his appetite of greatness. To paint things as they are, requires a minute attention, and employs the memory rather than the fancy. Milton's delight was to sport in the wide regions of possibility; reality was a scene too narrow for his mind. He sent his faculties out upon discovery, into worlds where only imagination can travel, and delighted to form new modes of existence, and furnish sentiment and action to superior beings, to trace the counsels of hell, or accompany the choirs of heaven.

But he could not be always in other worlds: he must sometimes revisit earth, and tell of things visible and known. When he cannot raise wonder by the sublimity of his mind, he gives delight by its fertility.

Whatever be his subject, he never fails to fill the imagination. But his images and descriptions of the scenes or operations of Nature do not seem to be always copied from original form, nor to have the freshness, raciness, and energy of immediate observation. He saw Nature, as Dryden expresses it, *through the spectacles of books*; and on most occasions calls learning to his assistance. The garden of Eden brings to his mind the vale of *Enna*, where Proserpine was gathering flowers. Satan makes his way through fighting elements, like *Argo* between the *Cyanean* rocks, or *Ulysses* between the two

---

* Algarotti terms it *gigantesca sublimita Miltoniana*.

Sicilian whirlpools, when he shunned *Charybdis* on the *larboard*. The mythological allusions have been justly censured, as not being always used with notice of their vanity; but they contribute variety to the narration, and produce an alternate exercise of the memory and the fancy.

His similes are less numerous, and more various, than those of his predecessors. But he does not confine himself within the limits of rigorous comparison: his great excellence is amplitude, and he expands the adventitious image beyond the dimensions which the occasion required. Thus, comparing the shield of Satan to the orb of the Moon, he crouds the imagination with the discovery of the telescope, and all the wonders which the telescope discovers.

Of his moral sentiments it is hardly praise to affirm that they excel those of all other poets; for this superiority he was indebted to his acquaintance with the sacred writings. The ancient epick poets, wanting the light of Revelation, were very unskilful teachers of virtue: their principal characters may be great, but they are not amiable. The reader may rise from their works with a greater degree of active or passive fortitude, and sometimes of prudence; but he will be able to carry away few precepts of justice, and none of mercy.

From the Italian writers it appears, that the advantages of even Christian knowledge may be possessed in vain. Ariosto's pravity is generally known; and though the *Deliverance of Jerusalem* may be considered as a sacred subject, the poet has been very sparing of moral instruction.

In Milton every line breathes sanctity of thought, and purity of manners, except when the train of the narration requires the introduction of the rebellious spirits; and even they are compelled to acknowledge their subjection to God, in such a manner as excites reverence, and confirms piety.

Of human beings there are but two; but those two are the parents of mankind, venerable before their fall for dignity and innocence, and amiable after it for repentance and submission. In their first state their affection is tender without weakness, and their piety sublime without presumption. When they have sinned, they shew how discord begins in mutual frailty, and how it ought to cease in mutual forbearance; how confidence of the divine favour is forfeited by sin, and how hope of pardon may be obtained by penitence and prayer. A state of innocence we can only conceive, if indeed, in our present misery, it be possible to conceive it; but the sentiments and worship proper to a fallen and offending being, we have all to learn, as we have all to practise.

The poet, whatever be done, is always great. Our progenitors, in their first state, conversed with angels; even when folly and sin had degraded them, they had not in their humiliation *the port of mean suitors*; and they rise again to reverential regard, when we find that their prayers were heard.

As human passions did not enter the world before the Fall, there is in the *Paradise Lost* little opportunity for the pathetick; but what little there is has not been lost. That passion which is peculiar to rational nature, the anguish arising from the consciousness of transgression, and the horrours attending the sense of the Divine Displeasure, are very justly described and forcibly impressed. But the passions are moved only on one occasion; sublimity is the general and prevailing quality in this poem; sublimity variously modified, sometimes descriptive, sometimes argumentative.

The defects and faults of *Paradise Lost*, for faults and defects every work of man must have, it is the business of impartial criticism to discover. As, in displaying the excellence of Milton, I have not made long quotations, because of selecting beauties there had been no end, I shall in the same general manner mention that which seems to deserve censure; for what Englishman can take delight in transcribing passages, which, if they lessen the reputation of Milton, diminish in some degree the honour of our country?

The generality of my scheme does not admit the frequent notice of verbal inaccuracies; which Bentley, perhaps better skilled in grammar than in poetry, has often found, though he sometimes made them, and which he imputed to the obtrusions of a reviser whom the author's blindness obliged him to employ. A supposition rash and groundless, if he thought it true; and vile and pernicious, if, as is said, he in private allowed it to be false.

The plan of *Paradise Lost* has this inconvenience, that it comprises neither human actions nor human manners. The man and woman who act and suffer, are in a state which no other man or woman can ever know. The reader finds no transaction in which he can be engaged; beholds no condition in which he can by any effort of imagination place himself; he has, therefore, little natural curiosity or sympathy.

We all, indeed, feel the effects of Adam's disobedience; we all sin like Adam, and like him must all bewail our offences; we have restless and insidious enemies in the fallen angels, and in the blessed spirits we have guardians and friends; in the Redemption of mankind we hope to be included; and in the description of heaven and hell we are surely interested, as we are all to reside hereafter either in the regions of horror or of bliss.

But these truths are too important to be new; they have been taught to our infancy; they have mingled with our solitary thoughts and familiar conversation, and are habitually interwoven with the whole texture of life. Being therefore not new, they raise no unaccustomed emotion in the mind; what we knew before, we cannot learn; what is not unexpected, cannot surprise.

Of the ideas suggested by these awful scenes, from some we recede with reverence, except when stated hours require their association; and from others we shrink with horrour, or admit them only as salutary inflictions, as counterpoises to our interests and passions. Such images rather obstruct the career of fancy than incite it.

Pleasure and terrour are indeed the genuine sources of poetry; but poetical pleasure must be such as human imagination can at least conceive, and poetical terrour such as human strength and fortitude may combat. The good and evil of Eternity are too ponderous for the wings of wit; the mind sinks under them in passive helplessness, content with calm belief and humble adoration.

Known truths, however, may take a different appearance, and be conveyed to the mind by a new train of intermediate images. This Milton has undertaken, and performed with pregnancy and vigour of mind peculiar to himself. Whoever considers the few radical positions which the Scriptures afforded him, will wonder by what energetick operation he expanded them to such extent, and ramified them to so much variety, restrained as he was by religious reverence from licentiousness of fiction.

Here is a full display of the united force of study and genius; of a great accumulation of materials, with judgement to digest, and fancy to combine them: Milton was able to select from nature, or from story, from ancient fable, or from modern science, whatever could illustrate or adorn his thoughts. An accumulation of knowledge impregnated his mind, fermented by study, and exalted by imagination.

It has been therefore said, without an indecent hyperbole, by one of his encomiasts, that in reading *Paradise Lost* we read a book of universal knowledge.

But original deficience cannot be supplied. The want of human interest is always felt. *Paradise Lost* is one of the books which the reader admires and lays down, and forgets to take up again. None ever wished it longer than it is. Its perusal is a duty rather than a pleasure. We read Milton for instruction, retire harrassed and overburdened, and look elsewhere for recreation; we desert our master, and seek for companions.

Another inconvenience of Milton's design is, that it requires the description of what cannot be described, the agency of spirits. He saw that immateriality supplied no images, and that he could not show angels acting but by instruments of action; he therefore invested them with form and matter. This, being necessary, was therefore defensible; and he should have secured the consistency of his system, by keeping immateriality out of sight, and enticing his reader to drop it from his thoughts. But he has unhappily perplexed his poetry with his philosophy. His infernal and celestial powers are sometimes pure spirit, and sometimes animated body. When Satan walks with his lance upon the *burning marle*, he has a body; when, in his passage between hell and the new world, he is in danger of sinking in the vacuity, and is supported by a gust of rising vapours, he has a body; when he animates the toad, he seems to be mere spirit, that can penetrate matter at pleasure; when he *starts up in his own shape*, he has at least a determined form; and when he is brought before Gabriel, he has a *spear and a shield*, which he had the power of hiding in the toad, though the arms of the contending angels are evidently material.

The vulgar inhabitants of Pandæmonium, being *incorporeal spirits*, are *at large, though without number*, in a limited space; yet in the battle, when they were overwhelmed by mountains, their armour hurt them, *crushed in upon*

their substance, now grown gross by sinning. This likewise happened to the uncorrupted angels, who were overthrown *the sooner for their arms, for unarmed they
might easily as spirits have evaded by contraction or remove.* Even as spirits they
are hardly spiritual; for *contraction* and *remove* are images of matter; but if
they could have escaped without their armour, they might have escaped from
it, and left only the empty cover to be battered. Uriel, when he rides on a sun-
beam, is material; Satan is material when he is afraid of the prowess of Adam.

The confusion of spirit and matter which pervades the whole narration of
the war of heaven fills it with incongruity; and the book, in which it is related,
is, I believe, the favourite of children, and gradually neglected as knowledge
is increased.

After the operation of immaterial agents, which cannot be explained, may
be considered that of allegorical persons, which have no real existence. To
exalt causes into agents, to invest abstract ideas with form, and animate them
with activity, has always been the right of poetry. But such airy beings are, for
the most part, suffered only to do their natural office, and retire. Thus Fame
tells a tale, and Victory hovers over a general, or perches on a standard; but
Fame and Victory can do no more. To give them any real employment, or
ascribe to them any material agency, is to make them allegorical no longer,
but to shock the mind by ascribing effects to nonentity. In the *Prometheus* of
Æschylus, we see *Violence* and *Strength*, and in the *Alcestis* of Euripides, we
see *Death*, brought upon the stage, all as active persons of the drama; but no
precedents can justify absurdity.

Milton's allegory of Sin and Death is undoubtedly faulty. Sin is indeed the
mother of Death, and may be allowed to be the portress of hell; but when they
stop the journey of Satan, a journey described as real, and when Death offers
him battle, the allegory is broken. That Sin and Death should have shewn the
way to hell, might have been allowed; but they cannot facilitate the passage by
building a bridge, because the difficulty of Satan's passage is described as real
and sensible, and the bridge ought to be only figurative. The hell assigned to
the rebellious spirits is described as not less local than the residence of man.
It is placed in some distant part of space, separated from the regions of harmony and order by a chaotick waste and an unoccupied vacuity; but *Sin* and
Death worked up a *mole* of *aggregated soil*, cemented with *asphaltus*; a work too
bulky for ideal architects.

This unskilful allegory appears to me one of the greatest faults of the
poem; and to this there was no temptation, but the author's opinion of its
beauty.

To the conduct of the narrative some objections may be made. Satan is
with great expectation brought before Gabriel in Paradise, and is suffered to
go away unmolested. The creation of man is represented as the consequence
of the vacuity left in heaven by the expulsion of the rebels; yet Satan mentions
it as a report *rife in heaven* before his departure.

To find sentiments for the state of innocence, was very difficult; and something of anticipation perhaps is now and then discovered. Adam's discourse of dreams seems not to be the speculation of a new-created being. I know not whether his answer to the angel's reproof for curiosity does not want something of propriety: it is the speech of a man acquainted with many other men. Some philosophical notions, especially when the philosophy is false, might have been better omitted. The angel, in a comparison, speaks of *timorous deer*, before deer were yet timorous, and before Adam could understand the comparison.

Dryden remarks, that Milton has some flats among his elevations. This is only to say, that all the parts are not equal. In every work, one part must be for the sake of others; a palace must have passages; a poem must have transitions. It is no more to be required that wit should always be blazing, than that the sun should always stand at noon. In a great work there is a vicissitude of luminous and opaque parts, as there is in the world a succession of day and night. Milton, when he has expatiated in the sky, may be allowed sometimes to revisit earth; for what other author ever soared so high, or sustained his flight so long?

Milton, being well versed in the Italian poets, appears to have borrowed often from them; and, as every man catches something from his companions, his desire of imitating Ariosto's levity has disgraced his work with the *Paradise of Fools*; a fiction not in itself ill-imagined, but too ludicrous for its place.

His play on words, in which he delights too often; his equivocations, which Bentley endeavours to defend by the example of the ancients; his unnecessary and ungraceful use of terms of art; it is not necessary to mention, because they are easily remarked, and generally censured, and at last bear so little proportion to the whole, that they scarcely deserve the attention of a critick.

Such are the faults of that wonderful performance *Paradise Lost*; which he who can put in balance with its beauties must be considered not as nice but as dull, as less to be censured for want of candour, than pitied for want of sensibility.

Of *Paradise Regained*, the general judgement seems now to be right, that it is in many parts elegant, and every-where instructive. It was not to be supposed that the writer of *Paradise Lost* could ever write without great effusions of fancy, and exalted precepts of wisdom. The basis of *Paradise Regained* is narrow; a dialogue without action can never please like an union of the narrative and dramatic powers. Had this poem been written not by Milton, but by some imitator, it would have claimed and received universal praise.

If *Paradise Regained* has been too much depreciated, *Sampson Agonistes* has in requital been too much admired. It could only be by long prejudice, and the bigotry of learning, that Milton could prefer the ancient tragedies, with their encumbrance of a chorus, to the exhibitions of the French and English stages; and it is only by a blind confidence in the reputation of Milton, that a drama can be praised in which the intermediate parts have neither cause nor consequence, neither hasten nor retard the catastrophe.

In this tragedy are however many particular beauties, many just sentiments and striking lines; but it wants that power of attracting the attention which a well-connected plan produces.

Milton would not have excelled in dramatick writing; he knew human nature only in the gross, and had never studied the shades of character, nor the combinations of concurring, or the perplexity of contending passions. He had read much, and knew what books could teach; but had mingled little in the world, and was deficient in the knowledge which experience must confer.

Through all his greater works there prevails an uniform peculiarity of *Diction*, a mode and cast of expression which bears little resemblance to that of any former writer, and which is so far removed from common use, that an unlearned reader, when he first opens his book, finds himself surprised by a new language.

This novelty has been, by those who can find nothing wrong in Milton, imputed to his laborious endeavours after words suitable to the grandeur of his ideas. *Our language*, says Addison, *sunk under him*. But the truth is, that, both in prose and verse, he had formed his style by a perverse and pedantick principle. He was desirous to use English words with a foreign idiom. This in all his prose is discovered and condemned; for there judgment operates freely, neither softened by the beauty, nor awed by the dignity of his thoughts; but such is the power of his poetry, that his call is obeyed without resistance, the reader feels himself in captivity to a higher and a nobler mind, and criticism sinks in admiration.

Milton's style was not modified by his subject: what is shown with greater extent in *Paradise Lost*, may be found in *Comus*. One source of his peculiarity was his familiarity with the Tuscan poets: the disposition of his words is, I think, frequently Italian; perhaps sometimes combined with other tongues. Of him, at last, may be said what Jonson says of Spenser, that *he wrote no language*, but has formed what *Butler* calls a *Babylonish Dialect*, in itself harsh and barbarous, but made by exalted genius, and extensive learning, the vehicle of so much instruction and so much pleasure, that, like other lovers, we find grace in its deformity.

Whatever be the faults of his diction, he cannot want the praise of copiousness and variety: he was master of his language in its full extent; and has selected the melodious words with such diligence, that from his book alone the Art of English Poetry might be learned.

After his diction, something must be said of his *versification*. *The measure*, he says, *is the English heroick verse without rhyme*. Of this mode he had many examples among the Italians, and some in his own country. The Earl of Surrey is said to have translated one of Virgil's books without rhyme; and, besides our tragedies, a few short poems had appeared in blank verse; particularly one tending to reconcile the nation to Raleigh's wild attempt upon Guiana, and probably written by Raleigh himself. These petty performances cannot be supposed to have much influenced Milton, who more probably took his hint from Trisino's *Italia Liberata*; and, finding blank verse easier than rhyme, was desirous of persuading himself that it is better.

Rhyme, he says, and says truly, *is no necessary adjunct of true poetry*. But perhaps, of poetry as a mental operation, metre or musick is no necessary adjunct: it is however by the musick of metre that poetry has been discriminated in all languages; and in languages melodiously constructed with a due proportion of long and short syllables, metre is sufficient. But one language cannot communicate its rules to another: where metre is scanty and imperfect, some help is necessary. The musick of the English heroick line strikes the ear so faintly that it is easily lost, unless all the syllables of every line co-operate together: this co-operation can be only obtained by the preservation of every verse unmingled with another, as a distinct system of sounds; and this distinctness is obtained and preserved by the artifice of rhyme. The variety of pauses, so much boasted by the lovers of blank verse, changes the measures of an English poet to the periods of a declaimer; and there are only a few skilful and happy readers of Milton, who enable their audience to perceive where the lines end or begin. *Blank verse*, said an ingenious critick, *seems to be verse only to the eye*.

Poetry may subsist without rhyme, but English poetry will not often please; nor can rhyme ever be safely spared but where the subject is able to support itself. Blank verse makes some approach to that which is called the *lapidary style*; has neither the easiness of prose, nor the melody of numbers, and therefore tires by long continuance. Of the Italian writers without rhyme, whom Milton alleges as precedents, not one is popular; what reason could urge in its defence, has been confuted by the ear.

But, whatever be the advantage of rhyme, I cannot prevail on myself to wish that Milton had been a rhymer; for I cannot wish his work to be other than it is; yet, like other heroes, he is to be admired rather than imitated. He that thinks himself capable of astonishing, may write blank verse; but those that hope only to please, must condescend to rhyme.

The highest praise of genius is original invention. Milton cannot be said to have contrived the structure of an epick poem, and therefore owes reverence to that vigour and amplitude of mind to which all generations must be indebted for the art of poetical narration, for the texture of the fable, the variation of incidents, the interposition of dialogue, and all the stratagems that surprise and enchain attention. But, of all the borrowers from Homer, Milton is perhaps the least indebted. He was naturally a thinker for himself, confident of his own abilities, and disdainful of help or hindrance: he did not refuse admission to the thoughts or images of his predecessors, but he did not seek them. From his contemporaries he neither courted nor received support;

there is in his writings nothing by which the pride of other authors might be gratified, or favour gained; no exchange of praise, nor solicitation of support. His great works were performed under discountenance, and in blindness, but difficulties vanished at his touch; he was born for whatever is arduous; and his work is not the greatest of heroick poems, only because it is not the first.

DRYDEN [extract]

DRYDEN may be properly considered as the father of English criticism, as the writer who first taught us to determine upon principles the merit of composition. Of our former poets, the greatest dramatist wrote without rules, conducted through life and nature by a genius that rarely misled, and rarely deserted him. Of the rest, those who knew the laws of propriety had neglected to teach them.

Two *Arts of English Poetry* were written in the days of Elizabeth by Webb and Puttenham, from which something might be learned, and a few hints had been given by Jonson and Cowley; but Dryden's *Essay on Dramatick Poetry* was the first regular and valuable treatise on the art of writing.

He who, having formed his opinions in the present age of English literature, turns back to peruse this dialogue, will not perhaps find much increase of knowledge, or much novelty of instruction; but he is to remember that critical principles were then in the hands of a few, who had gathered them partly from the Ancients, and partly from the Italians and French. The structure of dramatick poems was not then generally understood. Audiences applauded by instinct, and poets perhaps often pleased by chance.

A writer who obtains his full purpose loses himself in his own lustre. Of an opinion which is no longer doubted, the evidence ceases to be examined. Of an art universally practised, the first teacher is forgotten. Learning once made popular is no longer learning; it has the appearance of something which we have bestowed upon ourselves, as the dew appears to rise from the field which it refreshes.

To judge rightly of an author, we must transport ourselves to his time, and examine what were the wants of his contemporaries, and what were his means of supplying them. That which is easy at one time was difficult at another. Dryden at least imported his science, and gave his country what it wanted before; or rather, he imported only the materials, and manufactured them by his own skill.

The dialogue on the Drama was one of his first essays of criticism, written when he was yet a timorous candidate for reputation, and therefore laboured with that diligence which he might allow himself somewhat to remit, when his name gave sanction to his positions, and his awe of the public was abated, partly by custom, and partly by success. It will not be easy to find, in all the opulence of our language, a treatise so artfully variegated with successive representations of opposite probabilities, so enlivened with imagery, so brightened with illustrations. His portraits of the English dramatists are wrought with great spirit and diligence. The account of Shakspeare may stand as a perpetual model of encomiastick criticism; exact without minuteness, and lofty without exaggeration. The praise lavished by Longinus, on the attestation of the heroes of Marathon, by Demosthenes, fades away before it. In a few lines is exhibited a character, so extensive in its comprehension, and so curious in its limitations, that nothing can be added, diminished, or reformed; nor can the editors and admirers of Shakspeare, in all their emulation of reverence, boast of much more than of having diffused and paraphrased this epitome of excellence, of having changed Dryden's gold for baser metal, of lower value though of greater bulk.

In this, and in all his other essays on the same subject, the criticism of Dryden is the criticism of a poet; not a dull collection of theorems, nor a rude detection of faults, which perhaps the censor was not able to have committed; but a gay and vigorous dissertation, where delight is mingled with instruction, and where the author proves his right of judgement, by his power of performance.

The different manner and effect with which critical knowledge may be conveyed, was perhaps never more clearly exemplified than in the performances of Rymer and Dryden. It was said of a dispute between two mathematicians, "malim cum Scaligero errare, quam cum Clavio recte sapere;" that *it was more eligible to go wrong with one than right with the other*. A tendency of the same kind every mind must feel at the perusal of Dryden's prefaces and Rymer's discourses. With Dryden we are wandering in quest of Truth; whom we find, if we find her at all, drest in the graces of elegance; and if we miss her, the labour of the pursuit rewards itself; we are led only through fragrance and flowers: Rymer, without taking a nearer, takes a rougher way; every step is to be made through thorns and brambles; and Truth, if we meet her, appears repulsive by her mien, and ungraceful by her habit. Dryden's criticism has the majesty of a queen; Rymer's has the ferocity of a tyrant.

As he had studied with great diligence the art of poetry, and enlarged or rectified his notions, by experience perpetually increasing, he had his mind stored with principles and observations; he poured out his knowledge with little labour; for of labour, notwithstanding the multiplicity of his productions, there is sufficient reason to suspect that he was not a lover. To write *con amore*, with fondness for the employment, with perpetual touches and retouches, with unwillingness to take leave of his own idea, and an unwearied pursuit of unattainable perfection, was, I think, no part of his character.

His Criticism may be considered as general or occasional. In his general precepts, which depend upon the nature of things, and the structure of the human mind, he may doubtless be safely recommended to the confidence of the reader; but his occasional and particular positions were sometimes interested, sometimes negligent, and sometimes capricious. It is not without reason that Trapp, speaking of the praises which he bestows on Palamon and Arcite, says, "Novimus judicium Drydeni de poemate quodam *Chauceri*, pulchro sane illo, et admodum laudando, nimirum quod non modo vere epicum sit, sed Iliada etiam atque Æneada æquet, imo superet. Sed novimus eodem tempore viri illius maximi non semper accuratissimas esse censuras, nec ad severissimam critices normam exactas: illo judice id plerumque optimum est, quod nunc præ manibus habet, & in quo nunc occupatur."

He is therefore by no means constant to himself His defence and desertion of dramatick rhyme is generally known. *Spence*, in his remarks on Pope's Odyssey, produces what he thinks an unconquerable quotation from Dryden's preface to the Eneid, in favour of translating an epic poem into blank verse; but he forgets that when his author attempted the Iliad, some years afterwards, he departed from his own decision, and translated into rhyme.

When he has any objection to obviate, or any license to defend, he is not very scrupulous about what he asserts, nor very cautious, if the present purpose be served, not to entangle himself in his own sophistries. But when all arts are exhausted, like other hunted animals, he sometimes stands at bay; when he cannot disown the grossness of one of his plays, he declares that he knows not any law that prescribes morality to a comick poet.

His remarks on ancient or modern writers are not always to be trusted. His parallel of the versification of Ovid with that of Claudian has been very justly censured by *Sewel**. His comparison of the first line of Virgil with the first of Statius is not happier. Virgil, he says, is soft and gentle, and would have thought Statius mad if he had heard him thundering out

> Quæ superimposito moles geminata colosso.

Statius perhaps heats himself, as he proceeds, to exaggerations somewhat hyperbolical; but undoubtedly Virgil would have been too hasty, if he had condemned him to straw for one sounding line. Dryden wanted an instance, and the first that occurred was imprest into the service.

What he wishes to say, he says at hazard; he cited *Gorbuduc*, which he had never seen; gives a false account of *Chapman's* versification; and discovers, in the preface to his Fables, that he translated the first book of the Iliad, without knowing what was in the second.

It will be difficult to prove that Dryden ever made any great advances in literature. As having distinguished himself at Westminster under the tuition of Busby, who advanced his scholars to a height of knowledge very rarely attained in grammar-schools, he resided afterwards at Cambridge, it is not to be supposed, that his skill in the ancient languages was deficient, compared

---

* Preface to Ovid's Metamorphoses.

with that of common students; but his scholastick acquisitions seem not proportionate to his opportunities and abilities. He could not, like Milton or Cowley, have made his name illustrious merely by his learning. He mentions but few books, and those such as lie in the beaten track of regular study; from which if ever he departs, he is in danger of losing himself in unknown regions.

In his Dialogue on the Drama, he pronounces with great confidence that the Latin tragedy of Medea is not Ovid's, because it is not sufficiently interesting and pathetick. He might have determined the question upon surer evidence; for it is quoted by Quintilian as the work of Seneca; and the only line which remains of Ovid's play, for one line is left us, is not there to be found. There was therefore no need of the gravity of conjecture, or the discussion of plot or sentiment, to find what was already known upon higher authority than such discussions can ever reach.

His literature, though not always free from ostentation, will be commonly found either obvious, and made his own by the art of dressing it; or superficial, which, by what he gives, shews what he wanted; or erroneous, hastily collected, and negligently scattered.

Yet it cannot be said that his genius is ever unprovided of matter, or that his fancy languishes in penury of ideas. His works abound with knowledge, and sparkle with illustrations. There is scarcely any science or faculty that does not supply him with occasional images and lucky similitudes; every page discovers a mind very widely acquainted both with art and nature, and in full possession of great stores of intellectual wealth. Of him that knows much, it is natural to suppose that he has read with diligence; yet I rather believe that the knowledge of Dryden was gleaned from accidental intelligence and various conversation, by a quick apprehension, a judicious selection, and a happy memory, a keen appetite of knowledge, and a powerful digestion; by vigilance that permitted nothing to pass without notice, and a habit of reflection that suffered nothing useful to be lost. A mind like Dryden's, always curious, always active, to which every understanding was proud to be associated, and of which every one solicited the regard, by an ambitious display of himself, had a more pleasant, perhaps a nearer way, to knowledge than by the silent progress of solitary reading. I do not suppose that he despised books, or intentionally neglected them; but that he was carried out, by the impetuosity of his genius, to more vivid and speedy instructors; and that his studies were rather desultory and fortuitous than constant and systematical.

It must be confessed that he scarcely ever appears to want book-learning but when he mentions books; and to him may be transferred the praise which he gives his master Charles.

> His conversation, wit, and parts,
> His knowledge in the noblest useful arts,
> Were such, dead authors could not give,

But habitudes of those that live;
Who, lighting him, did greater lights receive:
He drain'd from all, and all they knew,
His apprehension quick, his judgement true:
That the most learn'd with shame confess
His knowledge more, his reading only less.

Of all this, however, if the proof be demanded, I will not undertake to give it; the atoms of probability, of which my opinion has been formed, lie scattered over all his works; and by him who thinks the question worth his notice, his works must be perused with very close attention.

Criticism, either didactick or defensive, occupies almost all his prose, except those pages which he has devoted to his patrons; but none of his prefaces were ever thought tedious. They have not the formality of a settled style, in which the first half of the sentence betrays the other. The clauses are never balanced, nor the periods modelled; every word seems to drop by chance, though it falls into its proper place. Nothing is cold or languid; the whole is airy, animated, and vigorous; what is little, is gay; what is great, is splendid. He may be thought to mention himself too frequently; but while he forces himself upon our esteem, we cannot refuse him to stand high in his own. Every thing is excused by the play of images and the spriteliness of expression. Though all is easy, nothing is feeble; though all seems careless, there is nothing harsh; and though, since his earlier works, more than a century has passed, they have nothing yet uncouth or obsolete.

He who writes much, will not easily escape a manner, such a recurrence of particular modes as may be easily noted. Dryden is always *another and the same*, he does not exhibit a second time the same elegances in the same form, nor appears to have any art other than that of expressing with clearness what he thinks with vigour. His style could not easily be imitated, either seriously or ludicrously; for, being always equable and always varied, it has no prominent or discriminative characters. The beauty who is totally free from disproportion of parts and features, cannot be ridiculed by an overcharged resemblance.

From his prose, however, Dryden derives only his accidental and secondary praise; the veneration with which his name is pronounced by every cultivator of English literature, is paid to him as he refined the language, improved the sentiments, and tuned the numbers of English Poetry.

After about half a century of forced thoughts, and rugged metre, some advances towards nature and harmony had been already made by Waller and Denham; they had shewn that long discourses in rhyme grew more pleasing when they were broken into couplets, and that verse consisted not only in the number but the arrangement of syllables.

But though they did much, who can deny that they left much to do? Their works were not many, nor were their minds of very ample comprehension.

More examples of more modes of composition were necessary for the establishment of regularity, and the introduction of propriety in word and thought.

Every language of a learned nation necessarily divides itself into diction scholastick and popular, grave and familiar, elegant and gross; and from a nice distinction of these different parts, arises a great part of the beauty of style. But if we except a few minds, the favourites of nature, to whom their own original rectitude was in the place of rules, this delicacy of selection was little known to our authors; our speech lay before them in a heap of confusion, and every man took for every purpose what chance might offer him.

There was therefore before the time of Dryden no poetical diction, no system of words at once refined from the grossness of domestick use, and free from the harshness of terms appropriated to particular arts. Words too familiar, or too remote, defeat the purpose of a poet. From those sounds which we hear on small or on coarse occasions, we do not easily receive strong impressions, or delightful images; and words to which we are nearly strangers, whenever they occur, draw that attention on themselves which they should transmit to things.

Those happy combinations of words which distinguish poetry from prose, had been rarely attempted; we had few elegances or flowers of speech, the roses had not yet been plucked from the bramble, or different colours had not been joined to enliven one another.

It may be doubted whether Waller and Denham could have over-born the prejudices which had long prevailed, and which even then were sheltered by the protection of Cowley. The new versification, as it was called, may be considered as owing its establishment to Dryden; from whose time it is apparent that English poetry has had no tendency to relapse to its former savageness.

The affluence and comprehension of our language is very illustriously displayed in our poetical translations of Ancient Writers; a work which the French seem to relinquish in despair, and which we were long unable to perform with dexterity. Ben Jonson thought it necessary to copy Horace almost word by word; Feltham, his contemporary and adversary, considers it as indispensably requisite in a translation to give line for line. It is said that Sandys, whom Dryden calls the best versifier of the last age, has struggled hard to comprise every book of his English Metamorphoses in the same number of verses with the original. Holyday had nothing in view but to shew that he understood his author, with so little regard to the grandeur of his diction, or the volubility of his numbers, that his metres can hardly be called verses; they cannot be read without reluctance, nor will the labour always be rewarded by understanding them. Cowley saw that such *copyers* were a *servile race*; he asserted his liberty, and spread his wings so boldly that he left his authors. It was reserved for Dryden to fix the limits of poetical liberty, and give us just rules and examples of translation.

When languages are formed upon different principles, it is impossible that the same modes of expression should always be elegant in both. While they run on together, the closest translation may be considered as the best; but when they divaricate, each must take its natural course. Where correspondence cannot be obtained, it is necessary to be content with something equivalent. *Translation therefore*, says Dryden, *is not so loose as paraphrase, nor so close as metaphrase.*

All polished languages have different styles; the concise, the diffuse, the lofty, and the humble. In the proper choice of style consists the resemblance which Dryden principally exacts from the translator. He is to exhibit his author's thoughts in such a dress of diction as the author would have given them, had his language been English: rugged magnificence is not to be softened: hyperbolical ostentation is not to be repressed, nor sententious affectation to have its points blunted. A translator is to be like his author: it is not his business to excel him.

The reasonableness of these rules seems sufficient for their vindication; and the effects produced by observing them were so happy, that I know not whether they were ever opposed but by Sir Edward Sherburne, a man whose learning was greater than his powers of poetry; and who, being better qualified to give the meaning than the spirit of Seneca, has introduced his version of three tragedies by a defence of close translation. The authority of Horace, which the new translators cited in defence of their practice, he has, by a judicious explanation, taken fairly from them; but reason wants not Horace to support it.

It seldom happens that all the necessary causes concur to any great effect: will is wanting to power, or power to will, or both are impeded by external obstructions. The exigences in which Dryden was condemned to pass his life, are reasonably supposed to have blasted his genius, to have driven out his works in a state of immaturity, and to have intercepted the full-blown elegance which longer growth would have supplied.

Poverty, like other rigid powers, is sometimes too hastily accused. If the excellence of Dryden's works was lessened by his indigence, their number was increased; and I know not how it will be proved, that if he had written less he would have written better; or that indeed he would have undergone the toil of an author, if he had not been solicited by something more pressing than the love of praise.

But as is said by his Sebastian,

What had been, is unknown; what is, appears.

We know that Dryden's several productions were so many successive expedients for his support; his plays were therefore often borrowed, and his poems were almost all occasional.

In an occasional performance no height of excellence can be expected from any mind, however fertile in itself, and however stored with acquisitions. He whose work is general and arbitrary, has the choice of his matter, and takes that which his inclination and his studies have best qualified him to display and decorate. He is at liberty to delay his publication, till he has satisfied his friends and himself; till he has reformed his first thoughts by subsequent examination; and polished away those faults which the precipitance of ardent composition is likely to leave behind it. Virgil is related to have poured out a great number of lines in the morning, and to have passed the day in reducing them to fewer.

The occasional poet is circumscribed by the narrowness of his subject. Whatever can happen to man has happened so often, that little remains for fancy or invention. We have been all born; we have most of us been married; and so many have died before us, that our deaths can supply but few materials for a poet. In the fate of princes the publick has an interest; and what happens to them of good or evil, the poets have always considered as business for the Muse. But after so many inauguratory gratulations, nuptial hymns, and funeral dirges, he must be highly favoured by nature, or by fortune, who says any thing not said before. Even war and conquest, however splendid, suggest no new images; the triumphal chariot of a victorious monarch can be decked only with those ornaments that have graced his predecessors.

Not only matter but time is wanting. The poem must not be delayed till the occasion is forgotten. The lucky moments of animated imagination cannot be attended; elegances and illustrations cannot be multiplied by gradual accumulation: the composition must be dispatched while conversation is yet busy, and admiration fresh; and haste is to be made, lest some other event should lay hold upon mankind.

Occasional compositions may however secure to a writer the praise both of learning and facility; for they cannot be the effect of long study, and must be furnished immediately from the treasures of the mind.

The death of Cromwell was the first publick event which called forth Dryden's poetical powers. His heroick stanzas have beauties and defects; the thoughts are vigorous, and though not always proper, shew a mind replete with ideas; the numbers are smooth, and the diction, if not altogether correct, is elegant and easy.

Davenant was perhaps at this time his favourite author, though Gondibert never appears to have been popular; and from Davenant he learned to please his ear with the stanza of four lines alternately rhymed.

Dryden very early formed his versification: there are in this early production no traces of Donne's or Jonson's ruggedness; but he did not so soon free his mind from the ambition of forced conceits. In his verses on the Restoration, he says of the King's exile,

He, toss'd by Fate—
Could taste no sweets of youth's desired age,
But found his life too true a pilgrimage.

And afterwards, to shew how virtue and wisdom are increased by adversity, he makes this remark:

Well might the ancient poets then confer
On Night the honour'd name of *counsellor*,
Since, struck with rays of prosperous fortune blind,
We light alone in dark afflictions find.

His praise of Monk's dexterity comprises such a cluster of thoughts unallied to one another, as will not elsewhere be easily found:

'Twas Monk, whom Providence design'd to loose
Those real bonds false freedom did impose.
The blessed saints that watch'd this turning scene,
Did from their stars with joyful wonder lean,
To see small clues draw vastest weights along,
Not in their bulk, but in their order strong.
Thus pencils can by one slight touch restore
Smiles to that changed face that wept before.
With ease such fond chimæras we pursue,
As fancy frames for fancy to subdue: 10
But, when ourselves to action we betake,
It shuns the mint like gold that chymists make:
How hard was then his task, at once to be
What in the body natural we see!
Man's Architect distinctly did ordain
The charge of muscles, nerves, and of the brain,
Through viewless conduits spirits to dispense
The springs of motion from the seat of sense.
'Twas not the hasty product of a day,
But the well-ripen'd fruit of wise delay.   20
He, like a patient angler, ere he strook,
Would let them play a-while upon the hook.
Our healthful food the stomach labours thus,
At first embracing what it straight doth crush.
Wise leaches will not vain receipts obtrude,
While growing pains pronounce the humours crude;
Deaf to complaints, they wait upon the ill,
Till some safe crisis authorize their skill.

He had not yet learned, indeed he never learned well, to forbear the improper use of mythology. After having rewarded the heathen deities for their care,

> With *Alga* who the sacred altar strows?
> To all the sea-gods Charles an offering owes;
> A bull to thee, Portunus, shall be slain;
> A ram to you, ye Tempests of the Main.

He tells us, in the language of religion,

> Prayer storm'd the skies, and ravish'd Charles from thence,
> As heaven itself is took by violence.

And afterwards mentions one of the most awful passages of Sacred History. Other conceits there are, too curious to be quite omitted; as,

> For by example most we sinn'd before,
> And, glass-like, clearness mix'd with frailty bore.

How far he was yet from thinking it necessary to found his sentiments on Nature, appears from the extravagance of his fictions and hyperboles:

> The winds, that never moderation knew,
> Afraid to blow too much, too faintly blew;
> Or, out of breath with joy, could not enlarge
> Their straiten'd lungs.—
> It is no longer motion cheats your view;
> As you meet it, the land approacheth you;
> The land returns, and in the white it wears
> The marks of penitence and sorrow bears.

I know not whether this fancy, however little be its value, was not borrowed. A French poet read to Malherbe some verses, in which he represents France as moving out of its place to receive the king. "Though this," said Malherbe, "was in my time, I do not remember it."

His poem on the *Coronation* has a more even tenour of thought. Some lines deserve to be quoted:

> You have already quench'd sedition's brand,
> And zeal, that burnt it, only warms the land;
> The jealous sects that durst not trust their cause
> So far from their own will as to the laws,

> Him for their umpire, and their synod take,
> And their appeal alone to Cæsar make.

Here may be found one particle of that old versification, of which, I believe, in all his works, there is not another:

> Nor is it duty, or our hope alone,
> Creates that joy, but full *fruition*.

In the verses to the lord chancellor Clarendon, two years afterwards, is a conceit so hopeless at the first view, that few would have attempted it; and so successfully laboured, that though at last it gives the reader more perplexity than pleasure, and seems hardly worth the study that it costs, yet it must be valued as a proof of a mind at once subtle and comprehensive:

> In open prospect nothing bounds our eye,
> Until the earth seems join'd unto the sky:
> So in this hemisphere our outmost view
> Is only bounded by our king and you:
> Our sight is limited where you are join'd,
> And beyond that no farther heaven can find.
> So well your virtues do with his agree,
> That, though your orbs of different greatness be,
> Yet both are for each other's use dispos'd,
> His to enclose, and yours to be enclos'd.   10
> Nor could another in your room have been,
> Except an emptiness had come between.

The comparison of the Chancellor to the Indies leaves all resemblance too far behind it:

> And as the Indies were not found before
> Those rich perfumes which from the happy shore
> The winds upon their balmy wings convey'd,
> Whose guilty sweetness first their world betray'd;
> So by your counsels we are brought to view
> A new and undiscover'd world in you.

There is another comparison, for there is little else in the poem, of which, though perhaps it cannot be explained into plain prosaick meaning, the mind perceives enough to be delighted, and readily forgives its obscurity, for its magnificence:

How strangely active are the arts of peace,
Whose restless motions less than wars do cease:
Peace is not freed from labour, but from noise;
And war more force, but not more pains employs:
Such is the mighty swiftness of your mind,
That, like the earth's, it leaves our sense behind,
While you so smoothly turn and rowl our sphere,
That rapid motion does but rest appear.
For as in nature's swiftness, with the throng
Of flying orbs while ours is borne along,   10
All seems at rest to the deluded eye,
Mov'd by the soul of the same harmony:
So carry'd on by our unwearied care,
We rest in peace, and yet in motion share.

To this succeed four lines, which perhaps afford Dryden's first attempt at
those penetrating remarks on human nature, for which he seems to have been
peculiarly formed:

Let envy then those crimes within you see,
From which the happy never must be free;
Envy that does with misery reside,
The joy and the revenge of ruin'd pride.

Into this poem he seems to have collected all his powers; and after this he
did not often bring upon his anvil such stubborn and unmalleable thoughts;
but, as a specimen of his abilities to unite the most unsociable matter, he has
concluded with lines, of which I think not myself obliged to tell the meaning:

Yet unimpair'd with labours, or with time,
Your age but seems to a new youth to climb.
Thus heavenly bodies do our time beget,
And measure change, but share no part of it:
And still it shall without a weight increase,
Like this new year, whose motions never cease.
For since the glorious course you have begun,
Is led by Charles, as that is by the sun,
It must both weightless and immortal prove,
Because the centre of it is above.   10

In the *Annus Mirabilis* he returned to the quatrain, which from that time
he totally quitted, perhaps from this experience of its inconvenience, for

he complains of its difficulty. This is one of his greatest attempts. He had subjects equal to his abilities, a great naval war, and the Fire of London. Battles
have always been described in heroick poetry; but a sea-fight and artillery had
yet something of novelty. New arts are long in the world before poets describe
them; for they borrow every thing from their predecessors, and commonly
derive very little from nature or from life. Boileau was the first French writer
that had ever hazarded in verse the mention of modern war, or the effects of
gunpowder. We, who are less afraid of novelty, had already possession of those
dreadful images: Waller had described a sea-fight. Milton had not yet transferred the invention of fire-arms to the rebellious angels.

This poem is written with great diligence, yet does not fully answer the
expectation raised by such subjects and such a writer. With the stanza of
Davenant he has sometimes his vein of parenthesis, and incidental disquisition, and stops his narrative for a wise remark.

The general fault is, that he affords more sentiment than description, and
does not so much impress scenes upon the fancy, as deduce consequences and
make comparisons.

The initial stanzas have rather too much resemblance to the first lines of
Waller's poem on the war with Spain; perhaps such a beginning is natural,
and could not be avoided without affectation. Both Waller and Dryden might
take their hint from the poem on the civil war of Rome, *Orbem jam totum*, &c.

Of the king collecting his navy, he says,

> It seems as every ship their sovereign knows,
> His awful summons they so soon obey;
> So hear the scaly herds when Proteus blows,
> And so to pasture follow through the sea.

It would not be hard to believe that Dryden had written the two first lines
seriously, and that some wag had added the two latter in burlesque. Who
would expect the lines that immediately follow, which are indeed perhaps
indecently hyperbolical, but certainly in a mode totally different?

> To see this fleet upon the ocean move,
> Angels drew wide the curtains of the skies;
> And heaven, as if there wanted lights above,
> For tapers made two glaring comets rise.

The description of the attempt at Bergen will afford a very compleat
specimen of the descriptions in this poem:

> And now approach'd their fleet from India, fraught
> With all the riches of the rising sun:

And precious sand from southern climates brought,
  The fatal regions where the war begun.

Like hunted castors, conscious of their store,
  Their way-laid wealth to Norway's coast they bring;
Then first the North's cold bosom spices bore,
  And winter brooded on the eastern spring.

By the rich scent we found our perfum'd prey,
  Which, flank'd with rocks, did close in covert lie: 10
And round about their murdering cannon lay,
  At once to threaten and invite the eye.

Fiercer than cannon, and than rocks more hard,
  The English undertake th' unequal war:
Seven ships alone, by which the port is barr'd,
  Besiege the Indies, and all Denmark dare.

These fight like husbands, but like lovers those:
  These fain would keep, and those more fain enjoy:
And to such height their frantic passion grows,
  That what both love, both hazard to destroy: 20

Amidst whole heaps of spices lights a ball,
  And now their odours arm'd against them fly:
Some preciously by shatter'd porcelain fall,
  And some by aromatic splinters die.

And though by tempests of the prize bereft,
  In heaven's inclemency some ease we find:
Our foes we vanquish'd by our valour left,
  And only yielded to the seas and wind.

In this manner is the sublime too often mingled with the ridiculous. The Dutch seek a shelter for a wealthy fleet: this surely needed no illustration; yet they must fly, not like all the rest of mankind on the same occasion, but *like hunted castors*; and they might with strict propriety be hunted; for we winded them by our noses—their *perfumes* betrayed them. The *Husband* and the *Lover*, though of more dignity than the Castor, are images too domestick to mingle properly with the horrors of war. The two quatrains that follow are worthy of the author.

The account of the different sensations with which the two fleets retired, when the night parted them, is one of the fairest flowers of English poetry.

The night comes on, we eager to pursue
  The combat still, and they asham'd to leave:
'Till the last streaks of dying day withdrew,
  And doubtful moon-light did our rage deceive.

In th' English fleet each ship resounds with joy,
  And loud applause of their great leader's fame:
In firy dreams the Dutch they still destroy,
  And, slumbering, smile at the imagin'd flame.

Not so the Holland fleet, who, tir'd and done,
  Stretch'd on their decks like weary oxen lie;   10
Faint sweats all down their mighty members run,
  (Vast bulks, which little souls but ill supply.)

In dreams they fearful precipices tread,
  Or, shipwreck'd, labour to some distant shore:
Or, in dark churches, walk among the dead;
  They wake with horror, and dare sleep no more.

It is a general rule in poetry, that all appropriated terms of art should be
sunk in general expressions, because poetry is to speak an universal language. This rule is still stronger with regard to arts not liberal, or confined to
few, and therefore far removed from common knowledge; and of this kind,
certainly, is technical navigation. Yet Dryden was of opinion that a sea-fight
ought to be described in the nautical language; *and certainly*, says he, *as those
who in a logical disputation keep to general terms would hide a fallacy, so those
who do it in any poetical description would veil their ignorance.*

Let us then appeal to experience; for by experience at last we learn as well
what will please as what will profit. In the battle, his terms seem to have been
blown away; but he deals them liberally in the dock:

So here some pick out bullets from the side,
  Some drive old *okum* thro' each *seam* and rift:
Their left-hand does the *calking-iron* guide,
  The rattling *mallet* with the right they lift.

With boiling pitch another near at hand
  (From friendly Sweden brought) the *seams instops:*
Which, well laid o'er, the salt-sea waves withstand,
  And shake them from the rising beak in drops.

Some the *gall'd* ropes with dawby *marling* blind,
  Or sear-cloth masts with strong *tarpawling* coats: 10
To try new *shrouds* one mounts into the wind,
  And one below, their ease or stiffness notes.

I suppose here is not one term which every reader does not wish away.
His digression to the original and progress of navigation, with his prospect
of the advancement which it shall receive from the Royal Society, then newly

instituted, may be considered as an example seldom equalled of seasonable excursion and artful return.

One line, however, leaves me discontented; he says, that by the help of the philosophers,

> Instructed ships shall sail to quick commerce,
> By which remotest regions are allied.—

Which he is constrained to explain in a note, *By a more exact measure of longitude*. It had better become Dryden's learning and genius to have laboured science into poetry, and have shewn, by explaining longitude, that verse did not refuse the ideas of philosophy.

His description of the Fire is painted by resolute meditation, out of a mind better formed to reason than to feel. The conflagration of a city, with all its tumults of concomitant distress, is one of the most dreadful spectacles which this world can offer to human eyes; yet it seems to raise little emotion in the breast of the poet; he watches the flame coolly from street to street, with now a reflection, and now a simile, till at last he meets the king, for whom he makes a speech, rather tedious in a time so busy; and then follows again the progress of the fire.

There are, however, in this part some passages that deserve attention; as in the beginning:

> The diligence of trades and noiseful gain
> And luxury more late asleep were laid;
> All was the night's, and in her silent reign
> No sound the rest of Nature did invade
> In this deep quiet—

The expression *All was the night's* is taken from Seneca, who remarks on Virgil's line.

> *Omnia noctis erant placida composita quiete,*

that he might have concluded better,

> *Omnia noctis erant.*

The following quatrain is vigorous and animated:

> The ghosts of traytors from the bridge descend
> With bold fanatick spectres to rejoice;
> About the fire into a dance they bend,
> And sing their sabbath notes with feeble voice.

His prediction of the improvements which shall be made in the new city, is elegant and poetical, and, with an event which Poets cannot always boast, has been happily verified. The poem concludes with a simile that might have better been omitted.

Dryden, when he wrote this poem, seems not yet fully to have formed his versification, or settled his system of propriety.

From this time, he addicted himself almost wholly to the stage, *to which*, says he, *my genius never much inclined me*, merely as the most profitable market for poetry. By writing tragedies in rhyme, he continued to improve his diction and his numbers. According to the opinion of *Harte*, who had studied his works with great attention, he settled his principles of versification in 1676, when he produced the play of *Aureng Zebe*; and according to his own account of the short time in which he wrote *Tyrannick Love*, and the *State of Innocence*, he soon obtained the full effect of diligence, and added facility to exactness.

Rhyme has been so long banished from the theatre, that we know not its effect upon the passions of an audience; but it has this convenience, that sentences stand more independent on each other, and striking passages are therefore easily selected and retained. Thus the description of Night in the *Indian Emperor*, and the rise and fall of empire in the *Conquest of Granada*, are more frequently repeated than any lines in *All for Love*, or *Don Sebastian*.

To search his plays for vigorous sallies, and sententious elegances, or to fix the dates of any little pieces which he wrote by chance, or by solicitation, were labour too tedious and minute.

His dramatic labours did not so wholly absorb his thoughts, but that he promulgated the laws of translation in a preface to the English Epistles of Ovid; one of which he translated himself, and another in conjunction with the Earl of Mulgrave.

Absalom and Achitophel is a work so well known, that particular criticism is superfluous. If it be considered as a poem political and controversial, it will be found to comprise all the excellences of which the subject is susceptible; acrimony of censure, elegance of praise, artful delineation of characters, variety and vigour of sentiment, happy turns of language, and pleasing harmony of numbers, and all these raised to such a height as can scarcely be found in any other English composition.

It is not, however, without faults; some lines are inelegant or improper, and too many are irreligiously licentious. The original structure of the poem was defective; allegories drawn to great length will always break; Charles could not run continually parallel with David.

The subject had likewise another inconvenience: it admitted little imagery or description, and a long poem of mere sentiments easily becomes tedious; though all the parts are forcible, and every line kindles new rapture, the reader, if not relieved by the interposition of something that sooths the fancy, grows weary of admiration, and defers the rest.

As an approach to historical truth was necessary, the action and catastrophe were not in the poet's power; there is therefore an unpleasing disproportion between the beginning and the end. We are alarmed by a faction formed out of many sects various in their principles, but agreeing in their purpose of mischief, formidable for their numbers, and strong by their supports, while the king's friends are few and weak. The chiefs on either part are set forth to view; but when expectation is at the height, the king makes a speech, and

> Henceforth a series of new times began.

Who can forbear to think of an enchanted castle, with a wide moat and lofty battlements, walls of marble and gates of brass, which vanishes at once into air, when the destined knight blows his horn before it?

In the second part, written by *Tate*, there is a long insertion, which, for poignancy of satire, exceeds any part of the former. Personal resentment, though no laudable motive to satire, can add great force to general principles. Self-love is a busy prompter.

The *Medal*, written upon the same principles with *Absalom and Achitophel*, but upon a narrower plan, gives less pleasure, though it discovers equal abilities in the writer. The superstructure cannot extend beyond the foundation; a single character or incident cannot furnish as many ideas, as a series of events, or multiplicity of agents. This poem therefore, since time has left it to itself, is not much read, nor perhaps generally understood, yet it abounds with touches both of humorous and serious satire. The picture of a man whose propensions to mischief are such, that his best actions are but inability of wickedness, is very skilfully delineated and strongly coloured.

> Power was his aim: but, thrown from that pretence,
> The wretch turn'd loyal in his own defence,
> And malice reconcil'd him to his Prince.
> Him, in the anguish of his soul, he serv'd;
> Rewarded faster still than he deserv'd:
> Behold him now exalted into trust;
> His counsels oft convenient, seldom just.
> Ev'n in the most sincere advice he gave,
> He had a grudging still to be a knave.
> The frauds he learnt in his fanatic years,   10
> Made him uneasy in his lawful gears;
> At least as little honest as he cou'd:
> And, like white witches, mischievously good.
> To his first bias, longingly, he leans;
> And rather would be great by wicked means.

The *Threnodia*, which, by a term I am afraid neither authorized nor analogical, he calls *Augustalis*, is not among his happiest productions. Its first and
obvious defect is the irregularity of its metre, to which the ears of that age,
however, were accustomed. What is worse, it has neither tenderness nor dignity, it is neither magnificent nor pathetick. He seems to look round him for
images which he cannot find, and what he has he distorts by endeavouring to
enlarge them. He is, he says, *petrified with grief*; but the marble sometimes
relents, and trickles in a joke.

> The sons of art all med'cines try'd,
> And every noble remedy apply'd;
> With emulation each essay'd
> His utmost skill; *nay more they pray'd:*
> Was never losing game with better conduct play'd.

He had been a little inclined to merriment before upon the prayers of a
nation for their dying sovereign, nor was he serious enough to keep heathen
fables out of his religion.

> With him th' innumberable croud of armed prayers
> Knock'd at the gates of heaven, and knock'd aloud;
> *The first well-meaning rude petitioners,*
> All for his life assail'd the throne,
> All would have brib'd the skies by offering up their own.
> So great a throng not heaven itself could bar;
> 'Twas almost borne by force *as in the giants war.*
> The prayers, at least, for his reprieve were heard;
> His death, like Hezekiah's, was deferr'd.

There is throughout the composition a desire of splendor without wealth.
In the conclusion he seems too much pleased with the prospect of the new
reign to have lamented his old master with much sincerity.

He did not miscarry in this attempt for want of skill either in lyrick or
elegiack poetry. His poem *on the death* of Mrs. *Killigrew*, is undoubtedly the
noblest ode that our language ever has produced. The first part flows with a
torrent of enthusiasm. *Fervet immensusque ruit.* All the stanzas indeed are not
equal. An imperial crown cannot be one continued diamond; the gems must
be held together by some less valuable matter.

In his first ode for Cecilia's day, which is lost in the splendor of the second,
there are passages which would have dignified any other poet. The first stanza
is vigorous and elegant, though the word *diapason* is too technical, and the
rhymes are too remote from one another.

From harmony, from heavenly harmony,
  This universal frame began:
When nature underneath a heap of jarring atoms lay,
  And could not heave her head,
The tuneful voice was heard from high,
  Arise ye more than dead.
Then cold and hot, and moist and dry,
In order to their stations leap,
  And musick's power obey.
From harmony, from heavenly harmony,   10
  This universal frame began:
  From harmony to harmony
Through all the compass of the notes it ran,
  The diapason closing full in man.

The conclusion is likewise striking, but it includes an image so awful in itself, that it can owe little to poetry; and I could wish the antithesis of *musick untuning* had found some other place.

As from the power of sacred lays
  The spheres began to move,
And sung the great Creator's praise
  To all the bless'd above.
So when the last and dreadful hour
This crumbling pageant shall devour,
The trumpet shall be heard on high,
The dead shall live, the living die,
And musick shall untune the sky.

Of his skill in Elegy he has given a specimen in his *Eleonora*, of which the following lines discover their author.

Though all these rare endowments of the mind
Were in a narrow space of life confin'd,
The figure was with full perfection crown'd;
Though not so large an orb, as truly round:
As when in glory, through the public place,
The spoils of conquer'd nations were to pass,
And but one day for triumph was allow'd,
The consul was constrain'd his pomp to crowd;
And so the swift procession hurry'd on,
That all, though not distinctly, might be shown: 10

So in the straiten'd bounds of life confin'd,
She gave but glimpses of her glorious mind:
And multitudes of virtues pass'd along;
Each pressing foremost in the mighty throng,
Ambitious to be seen, and then make room
For greater multitudes that were to come.
Yet unemploy'd no minute slipp'd away;
Moments were precious in so short a stay.
The haste of heaven to have her was so great,
That some were single acts, though each compleat;   20
And every act stood ready to repeat.

This piece, however, is not without its faults; there is so much likeness in
the initial comparison, that there is no illustration. As a king would be lamented,
Eleonora was lamented.

As when some great and gracious monarch dies,
Soft whispers, first, and mournful murmurs rise
Among the sad attendants; then the sound
Soon gathers voice, and spreads the news around,
Through town and country, till the dreadful blast
Is blown to distant colonies at last;
Who, then, perhaps, were offering vows in vain,
For his long life, and for his happy reign:
So slowly by degrees, unwilling fame
Did matchless Eleonora's fate proclaim,   10
Till publick as the loss the news became.

This is little better than to say in praise of a shrub, that it is as green as a
tree, or of a brook, that it waters a garden, as a river waters a country.

Dryden confesses that he did not know the lady whom he celebrates; the
praise being therefore inevitably general, fixes no impression upon the reader,
nor excites any tendency to love, nor much desire of imitation. Knowledge of
the subject is to the poet, what durable materials are to the architect.

The *Religio Laici*, which borrows its title from the *Religio Medici* of
Browne, is almost the only work of Dryden which can be considered as a
voluntary effusion; in this, therefore, it might be hoped, that the full effulgence of his genius would be found. But unhappily the subject is rather
argumentative than poetical: he intended only a specimen of metrical disputation.

And this unpolish'd rugged verse I chose,
As fittest for discourse, and nearest prose.

This, however, is a composition of great excellence in its kind, in which the familiar is very properly diversified with the solemn, and the grave with the humorous; in which metre has neither weakened the force, nor clouded the perspicuity of argument; nor will it be easy to find another example equally happy of this middle kind of writing, which, though prosaick in some parts, rises to high poetry in others, and neither towers to the skies, nor creeps along the ground.

Of the same kind, or not far distant from it, is the *Hind and Panther*, the longest of all Dryden's original poems; an allegory intended to comprize and to decide the controversy between the Romanists and Protestants. The scheme of the work is injudicious and incommodious; for what can be more absurd than that one beast should counsel another to rest her faith upon a pope and council? He seems well enough skilled in the usual topicks of argument, endeavours to shew the necessity of an infallible judge, and reproaches the Reformers with want of unity; but is weak enough to ask, why since we see without knowing how, we may not have an infallible judge without knowing where.

The *Hind* at one time is afraid to drink at the common brook, because she may be worried; but walking home with the *Panther*, talks by the way of the *Nicene Fathers*, and at last declares herself to be the Catholic church.

This absurdity was very properly ridiculed in the *City Mouse* and *Country Mouse* of *Montague* and *Prior*; and in the detection and censure of the incongruity of the fiction, chiefly consists the value of their performance, which, whatever reputation it might obtain by the help of temporary passions, seems to readers almost a century distant, not very forcible or animated.

Pope, whose judgment was perhaps a little bribed by the subject, used to mention this poem as the most correct specimen of Dryden's versification. It was indeed written when he had completely formed his manner, and may be supposed to exhibit, negligence excepted, his deliberate and ultimate scheme of metre.

We may therefore reasonably infer, that he did not approve the perpetual uniformity which confines the sense to couplets, since he has broken his lines in the initial paragraph.

> A milk-white Hind, immortal and unchang'd,
> Fed on the lawns, and in the forest rang'd;
> Without unspotted, innocent within,
> She fear'd no danger, for she knew no sin.
> Yet had she oft been chac'd with horns and hounds
> And Scythian shafts, and many winged wounds
> Aim'd at her heart; was often forc'd to fly,
> And doom'd to death, though fated not to die.

These lines are lofty, elegant, and musical, notwithstanding the interruption of the pause, of which the effect is rather increase of pleasure by variety, than offence by ruggedness.

To the first part it was his intention, he says, *to give the majestick turn of heroick poesy*; and perhaps he might have executed his design not unsuccessfully, had not an opportunity of satire, which he cannot forbear, fallen sometimes in his way. The character of a Presbyterian, whose emblem is the *Wolf*, is not very heroically majestick.

> More haughty than the rest, the wolfish race
> Appear with belly gaunt and famish'd face:
> Never was so deform'd a beast of grace.
> His ragged tail betwixt his legs he wears,
> Close clapp'd for shame; but his rough crest he rears,
> And pricks up his predestinating ears.

His general character of the other sorts of beasts that never go to church, though spritely and keen, has, however, not much of heroick poesy.

> These are the chief; to number o'er the rest,
> And stand like Adam naming every beast,
> Were weary work; nor will the Muse describe
> A slimy-born, and sun-begotten tribe;
> Who, far from steeples and their sacred sound,
> In fields their sullen conventicles found.
> These gross, half-animated, lumps I leave;
> Nor can I think what thoughts they can conceive;
> But if they think at all, 'tis sure no higher
> Than matter, put in motion, may aspire;   10
> Souls that can scarce ferment their mass of clay;
> So drossy, so divisible are they,
> As would but serve pure bodies for allay:
> Such souls as shards produce, such beetle things
> As only buz to heaven with evening wings;
> Strike in the dark, offending but by chance;
> Such are the blindfold blows of ignorance.
> They know not beings, and but hate a name;
> To them the Hind and Panther are the same.

One more instance, and that taken from the narrative part, where style was more in his choice, will show how steadily he kept his resolution of heroick dignity.

For when the herd, suffic'd, did late repair
To ferny heaths, and to their forest laire,
She made a mannerly excuse to stay,
Proffering the Hind to wait her half the way:
That, since the sky was clear, an hour of talk
Might help her to beguile the tedious walk.
With much good-will the motion was embrac'd,
To chat awhile on their adventures past:
Nor had the grateful Hind so soon forgot
Her friend and fellow-sufferer in the plot.   10
Yet, wondering how of late she grew estrang'd,
Her forehead cloudy and her count'nance chang'd,
She thought this hour th'occasion would present
To learn her secret cause of discontent,
Which well she hop'd, might be with ease redress'd,
Considering her a well-bred civil beast,
And more a gentlewoman than the rest.
After some common talk what rumours ran,
The lady of the spotted muff began.

The second and third parts he professes to have reduced to diction more familiar and more suitable to dispute and conversation; the difference is not, however, very easily perceived; the first has familiar, and the two others have sonorous, lines. The original incongruity runs through the whole; the king is now *Cæsar*, and now the *Lyon*; and the name *Pan* is given to the Supreme Being.

But when this constitutional absurdity is forgiven, the poem must be confessed to be written with great smoothness of metre, a wide extent of knowledge, and an abundant multiplicity of images; the controversy is embellished with pointed sentences, diversified by illustrations, and enlivened by sallies of invective. Some of the facts to which allusions are made, are now become obscure, and perhaps there may be many satirical passages little understood.

As it was by its nature a work of defiance, a composition which would naturally be examined with the utmost acrimony of criticism, it was probably laboured with uncommon attention; and there are, indeed, few negligences in the subordinate parts. The original impropriety, and the subsequent unpopularity of the subject, added to the ridiculousness of its first elements, has sunk it into neglect; but it may be usefully studied, as an example of poetical ratiocination, in which the argument suffers little from the metre.

In the poem on *the Birth of the Prince of Wales*, nothing is very remarkable but the exorbitant adulation, and that insensibility of the precipice on which the king was then standing, which the laureate apparently shared with the rest of the courtiers. A few months cured him of controversy, dismissed him from court, and made him again a play-wright and translator.

Of Juvenal there had been a translation by Stapylton, and another by Holiday; neither of them is very poetical. Stapylton is more smooth, and Holiday's is more esteemed for the learning of his notes. A new version was proposed to the poets of that time, and undertaken by them in conjunction. The main design was conducted by Dryden, whose reputation was such that no man was unwilling to serve the Muses under him.

The general character of this translation will be given, when it is said to preserve the wit, but to want the dignity of the original. The peculiarity of Juvenal is a mixture of gaiety and stateliness, of pointed sentences and declamatory grandeur. His points have not been neglected; but his grandeur none of the band seemed to consider as necessary to be imitated, except *Creech*, who undertook the thirteenth satire. It is therefore perhaps possible to give a better representation of that great satirist, even in those parts which Dryden himself has translated, some passages excepted, which will never be excelled.

With Juvenal was published Persius, translated wholly by Dryden. This work, though like all the other productions of Dryden it may have shining parts, seems to have been written merely for wages, in an uniform mediocrity, without any eager endeavour after excellence, or laborious effort of the mind.

There wanders an opinion among the readers of poetry, that one of these satires is an exercise of the school. Dryden says that he once translated it at school; but not that he preserved or published the juvenile performance.

Not long afterwards he undertook perhaps the most arduous work of its kind, a translation of Virgil, for which he had shewn how well he was qualified by his version of the Pollio, and two episodes, one of Nisus and Euryalus, the other of Mezentius and Lausus.

In the comparison of Homer and Virgil, the discriminative excellence of Homer is elevation and comprehension of thought, and that of Virgil is grace and splendor of diction. The beauties of Homer are therefore difficult to be lost, and those of Virgil difficult to be retained. The massy trunk of sentiment is safe by its solidity, but the blossoms of elocution easily drop away. The author, having the choice of his own images, selects those which he can best adorn: the translator must, at all hazards, follow his original, and express thoughts which perhaps he would not have chosen. When to this primary difficulty is added the inconvenience of a language so much inferior in harmony to the Latin, it cannot be expected that they who read the Georgick and the Eneid should be much delighted with any version.

All these obstacles Dryden saw, and all these he determined to encounter. The expectation of his work was undoubtedly great; the nation considered its honour as interested in the event. One gave him the different editions of his author, and another helped him in the subordinate parts. The arguments of the several books were given him by Addison.

The hopes of the publick were not disappointed. He produced, says Pope, *the most noble and spirited translation that I know in any language*. It certainly excelled whatever had appeared in English, and appears to have satisfied his friends, and, for the most part, to have silenced his enemies. Milbourne, indeed, a clergyman, attacked it; but his outrages seem to be the ebullitions of a mind agitated by stronger resentment than bad poetry can excite, and previously resolved not to be pleased.

His criticism extends only to the Preface, Pastorals, and Georgicks; and, as he professes, to give his antagonist an opportunity of reprisal, he has added his own version of the first and fourth Pastorals, and the first Georgick. The world has forgotten his book; but since his attempt has given him a place in literary history, I will preserve a specimen of his criticism, by inserting his remarks on the invocation before the first Georgick, and of his poetry, by annexing his own version.

Ver. 1. "*What makes a plenteous harvest, when to turn, The fruitful soil, and when to sow the corn*—It's *unlucky*, they say, *to stumble at the threshold*, but what has a *plenteous harvest* to do here? *Virgil* would not pretend to prescribe *rules* for *that* which depends not on the *husbandman's* care, but the *disposition of Heaven* altogether. Indeed, the *plenteous crop* depends somewhat on the *good method of tillage*, and where the *land's* ill manur'd, the *corn*, without a miracle, can be but *indifferent*; but the *harvest* may be *good*, which is its *properest* epithet, tho' the *husbandman's skill* were never so *indifferent*. The next *sentence* is *too literal*, and *when to plough* had been *Virgil's* meaning, and intelligible to every body; and *when to sow the corn*, is a needless *addition*."

Ver. 3. "*The care of sheep, of oxen, and of kine, And when to geld the lambs, and sheer the swine*, would as well have fallen under the *cura boum, qui cultus habendo sit pecori*, as Mr. *D's* deduction of particulars."

Ver. 5. "*The birth and genius of the frugal bee, I sing*, Mæcenas, *and I sing to thee.* —But where did *experientia* ever signify *birth and genius*? or what ground was there for such a *figure* in this place? How much more manly is Mr. *Ogylby's* version!

> What makes rich grounds, in what celestial signs,
> 'Tis good to plough, and marry elms with vines.
> What best fits cattle, what with sheep agrees,
> And several arts improving frugal bees,
> I sing, *Mœcenas*.

Which four lines, tho' faulty enough, are yet much more to the purpose than Mr. *D's* six."

Ver. 22. "*From fields and mountains to my song repair. For patrium linquens nemus, saltusque Lycœi*—Very well explained!"

Ver. 23, 24. "*Inventor Pallas, of the fattening oil, Thou founder of the plough, and ploughman's toil!* Written as if *these* had been *Pallas's invention. The ploughman's toil's* impertinent."

Ver. 25. "—*The shroud-like cypress*—Why *shroud-like?* Is a *cypress* pulled up by the *roots*, which the *sculpture* in the *last Eclogue* fills *Silvanus's* hand with, so very like a *shroud?* Or did not Mr. *D.* think of that kind of *cypress* us'd often for *scarves and hatbands* at funerals formerly, or for *widow's vails*, &c. if so, 'twas a *deep good thought.*"

Ver. 26. "—*That wear the royal honours, and increase the year*—What's meant by *increasing the year?* Did the *gods* or *goddesses* add more *months*, or *days*, or *hours* to it? Or how can *arva tueri*—signify to *wear rural honours?* Is this to *translate*, or *abuse* an *author?* The next *couplet* are borrow'd from *Ogylby*, I suppose, because *less to the purpose* than ordinary."

Ver 33. "*The patron of the world, and* Rome's *peculiar guard*—*Idle*, and none of *Virgil's*, no more than the sense of the *precedent couplet*; so again, he *interpolates Virgil* with that and *the round circle of the year to guide powerful of blessings, which thou strew'st around*. A ridiculous *Latinism*, and an *impertinent addition*; indeed the whole *period* is but one piece of *absurdity* and *nonsense*, as those who lay it with the *original* must find."

Ver. 42, 43. "*And* Neptune *shall resign the fasces of the sea*. Was he *consul* or *dictator* there? *And watry virgins for thy bed shall strive*. Both absurd *interpolations*."

Ver. 47, 48. "*Where in the void of heaven a place is free*. Ah happy *D—n*, were *that place* for thee! But where is *that void?* Or what does our *translator* mean by it? He knows what *Ovid* says *God* did, to prevent such a *void* in heaven; perhaps, this was then forgotten: but *Virgil* talks more sensibly."

Ver. 49. "*The scorpion ready to receive thy laws*. No, he would not then have *gotten out of his way* so fast."

Ver. 56. "*The Proserpine affects her silent seat*—What made *her* then so *angry* with *Ascalaphus*, for preventing her return? She was now mus'd to *Patience* under the *determinations of Fate*, rather than *fond* of her *residence*."

Ver. 61, 2, 3. "*Pity the poet's, and the ploughman's cares, Interest thy greatness in our mean affairs. And use thyself betimes to hear our prayers*. Which is such a wretched *perversion* of *Virgil's* noble thought as *Vicars* would have blush'd at; but Mr. *Ogylby* makes us some amends, by his better lines:

> O wheresoe'er thou art, from thence incline,
> And grant assistance to my bold design!

Pity with me, poor husbandmen's affairs,
And now, as if translated, hear our prayers.

This is *sense*, and *to the purpose*: the other, poor *mistaken stuff*."

Such were the strictures of Milbourne, who found few abettors; and of whom it may be reasonably imagined, that many who favoured his design were ashamed of his insolence.

When admiration had subsided, the translation was more coolly examined, and found like all others, to be sometimes erroneous, and sometimes licentious. Those who could find faults, thought they could avoid them; and Dr. Brady attempted in blank verse a translation of the Eneid, which, when dragged into the world, did not live long enough to cry. I have never seen it; but that such a version there is, or has been, perhaps some old catalogue informed me.

With not much better success, Trapp, when his Tragedy and his Prelections had given him reputation, attempted another blank version of the Eneid; to which, notwithstanding the slight regard with which it was treated, he had afterwards perseverance enough to add the Eclogues and Georgicks. His book may continue its existence as long as it is the clandestine refuge of schoolboys.

Since the English ear has been accustomed to the mellifluence of Pope's numbers, and the diction of poetry has become more splendid, new attempts have been made to translate Virgil; and all his works have been attempted by men better qualified to contend with Dryden. I will not engage myself in an invidious comparison by opposing one passage to another; a work of which there would be no end, and which might be often offensive without use.

It is not by comparing line with line that the merit of great works is to be estimated, but by their general effects and ultimate result. It is easy to note a weak line, and write one more vigorous in its place; to find a happiness of expression in the original, and transplant it by force into the version: but what is given to the parts, may be subducted from the whole, and the reader may be weary, though the critick may commend. Works of imagination excel by their allurement and delight; by their power of attracting and detaining the attention. That book is good in vain, which the reader throws away. He only is the master, who keeps the mind in pleasing captivity; whose pages are perused with eagerness, and in hope of new pleasure are perused again; and whose conclusion is perceived with an eye of sorrow, such as the traveller casts upon departing day.

By his proportion of this predomination I will consent that Dryden should be tried; of this, which, in opposition to reason, makes Ariosto the darling and the pride of Italy; of this, which, in defiance of criticism, continues Shakspeare the sovereign of the drama.

His last work was his *Fables*, in which he gave us the first example of a mode of writing which the Italians call *refaccimento*, a renovation of ancient writers, by modernizing their language. Thus the old poem of *Boiardo* has been new-dressed by *Domenichi* and *Berni*. The works of Chaucer, upon which this kind of rejuvenescence has been bestowed by Dryden, require little criticism. The tale of the Cock seems hardly worth revival; and the story of *Palamon* and *Arcite*, containing an action unsuitable to the times in which it is placed, can hardly be suffered to pass without censure of the hyperbolical commendation which Dryden has given it in the general Preface, and in a poetical Dedication, a piece where his original fondness of remote conceits seems to have revived.

Of the three pieces borrowed from Boccace, *Sigismunda* may be defended by the celebrity of the story. *Theodore* and *Honoria*, though it contains not much moral, yet afforded opportunities of striking description. And *Cymon* was formerly a tale of such reputation, that, at the revival of letters, it was translated into Latin by one of the *Beroalds*.

Whatever subjects employed his pen, he was still improving our measures and embellishing our language.

In this volume are interspersed some short original poems, which, with his prologues, epilogues, and songs, may be comprised in Congreve's remark, that even those, if he had written nothing else, would have entitled him to the praise of excellence in his kind.

One composition must however be distinguished. The ode for *St. Cecilia's* Day, perhaps the last effort of his poetry, has been always considered as exhibiting the highest flight of fancy, and the exactest nicety of art. This is allowed to stand without a rival. If indeed there is any excellence beyond it, in some other of Dryden's works that excellence must be found. Compared with the Ode on *Killigrew*, it may be pronounced perhaps superiour in the whole; but without any single part, equal to the first stanza of the other.

It is said to have cost Dryden a fortnight's labour; but it does not want its negligences: some of the lines are without correspondent rhymes; a defect, which I never detected but after an acquaintance of many years, and which the enthusiasm of the writer might hinder him from perceiving.

His last stanza has less emotion than the former; but is not less elegant in the diction. The conclusion is vicious; the musick of *Timotheus*, which *raised a mortal to the skies*, had only a metaphorical power; that of *Cecilia*, which *drew an angel down*, had a real effect: the crown therefore could not reasonably be divided.

IN a general survey of Dryden's labours, he appears to have had a mind very comprehensive by nature, and much enriched with acquired knowledge. His compositions are the effects of a vigorous genius operating upon large materials.

The power that predominated in his intellectual operations, was rather strong reason than quick sensibility. Upon all occasions that were presented, he studied rather than felt, and produced sentiments not such as Nature enforces, but meditation supplies. With the simple and elemental passions, as they spring separate in the mind, he seems not much acquainted; and seldom describes them but as they are complicated by the various relations of society, and confused in the tumults and agitations of life.

What he says of love may contribute to the explanation of his character:

> Love various minds does variously inspire;
> It stirs in gentle bosoms gentle fire,
> Like that of incense on the altar laid;
> But raging flames tempestuous souls invade;
> A fire which every windy passion blows,
> With pride it mounts, or with revenge it glows.

Dryden's was not one of the *gentle bosoms*: Love, as it subsists in itself, with no tendency but to the person loved, and wishing only for correspondent kindness; such love as shuts out all other interest; the Love of the Golden Age, was too soft and subtle to put his faculties in motion. He hardly conceived it but in its turbulent effervescence with some other desires; when it was inflamed by rivalry, or obstructed by difficulties: when it invigorated ambition, or exasperated revenge.

He is therefore, with all his variety of excellence, not often pathetick; and had so little sensibility of the power of effusions purely natural, that he did not esteem them in others. Simplicity gave him no pleasure; and for the first part of his life he looked on *Otway* with contempt, though at last, indeed very late, he confessed that in his play *there* was *Nature, which is the chief beauty*.

We do not always know our own motives. I am not certain whether it was not rather the difficulty which he found in exhibiting the genuine operations of the heart, than a servile submission to an injudicious audience, that filled his plays with false magnificence. It was necessary to fix attention; and the mind can be captivated only by recollection, or by curiosity; by reviving natural sentiments, or impressing new appearances of things: sentences were readier at his call than images; he could more easily fill the ear with some splendid novelty, than awaken those ideas that slumber in the heart.

The favourite exercise of his mind was ratiocination; and, that argument might not be too soon at an end, he delighted to talk of liberty and necessity, destiny and contingence; these he discusses in the language of the school with so much profundity, that the terms which he uses are not always understood. It is indeed learning, but learning out of place.

When once he had engaged himself in disputation, thoughts flowed in on either side: he was now no longer at a loss; he had always objections and solutions at command; *verbaque provisam rem*—give him matter for his verse, and he finds without difficulty verse for his matter.

In Comedy, for which he professes himself not naturally qualified, the mirth which he excites will perhaps not be found so much to arise from any

original humour, or peculiarity of character nicely distinguished and diligently pursued, as from incidents and circumstances, artifices and surprizes;
from jests of action rather than of sentiment. What he had of humorous or
passionate, he seems to have had not from nature, but from other poets; if not
always as a plagiary, at least as an imitator.

Next to argument, his delight was in wild and daring sallies of sentiment,
in the irregular and excentrick violence of wit. He delighted to tread upon
the brink of meaning, where light and darkness begin to mingle; to approach
the precipice of absurdity, and hover over the abyss of unideal vacancy. This
inclination sometimes produced nonsense, which he knew; as,

> Move swiftly, sun, and fly a lover's pace,
> Leave weeks and months behind thee in thy race.
> > Amariel flies
> To guard thee from the demons of the air;
> My flaming sword above them to display,
> All keen, and ground upon the edge of day.

And sometimes it issued in absurdities, of which perhaps he was not conscious:

> Then we upon our orb's last verge shall go,
> > And see the ocean leaning on the sky;
> From thence our rolling neighbours we shall know,
> > And on the lunar world securely pry.

These lines have no meaning; but may we not say, in imitation of Cowley on
another book,

> 'Tis so like *sense* 'twill serve the turn as well?

This endeavour after the grand and the new, produced many sentiments
either great or bulky, and many images either just or splendid:

> I am as free as Nature first made man,
> Ere the base laws of servitude began,
> When wild in woods the noble savage ran.

> —'Tis but because the Living death ne'er knew,
> They fear to prove it as a thing that's new:
> Let me th' experiment before you try,
> I'll show you first how easy 'tis to die.

> —There with a forest of their darts he strove,
> And stood like *Capaneus* defying Jove;
> With his broad sword the boldest beating down,   10

While Fate grew pale lest he should win the town,
And turn'd the iron leaves of his dark book
To make new dooms, or mend what it mistook.

—I beg no pity for this mouldering clay;
For if you give it burial, there it takes
Possession of your earth;
If burnt, and scatter'd in the air, the winds
That strew my dust diffuse my royalty,
And spread me o'er your clime; for where one atom
Of mine shall light, know there Sebastian reigns.

Of these quotations the two first may be allowed to be great, the two latter only tumid.

Of such selection there is no end. I will add only a few more passages; of which the first, though it may perhaps not be quite clear in prose, is not too obscure for poetry, as the meaning that it has is noble:

No, there is a necessity in Fate,
Why still the brave bold man is fortunate;
He keeps his object ever full in sight,
And that assurance holds him firm and right;
True, 'tis a narrow way that leads to bliss,
But right before there is no precipice;
Fear makes men look aside, and so their footing miss.

Of the images which the two following citations afford, the first is elegant, the second magnificent; whether either be just, let the reader judge:

What precious drops are these,
Which silently each other's track pursue,
Bright as young diamonds in their infant dew?

—Resign your castle—
—Enter, brave Sir; for when you speak the word,
The gates shall open of their own accord;
The genius of the place its Lord shall meet,
And bow its towery forehead at your feet.

These bursts of extravagance, Dryden calls the *Dalilahs* of the Theatre; and owns that many noisy lines of Maximin and Almanzor call out for vengeance upon him; but I *knew*, says he, *that they were bad enough to please, even when I wrote them.* There is surely reason to suspect that he pleased himself as well as his audience; and that these, like the harlots of other men, had his love, though not his approbation.

He had sometimes faults of a less generous and splendid kind. He makes, like almost all other poets, very frequent use of mythology, and sometimes connects religion and fable too closely without distinction.

He descends to display his knowledge with pedantick ostentation; as when, in translating Virgil, he says, *tack to the larboard*—and *veer starboard*; and talks, in another work, of *virtue spooming before the wind*. His vanity now and then betrays his ignorance:

> They Nature's king through Nature's opticks view'd;
> Revers'd they view'd him lessen'd to their eyes.

He had heard of reversing a telescope, and unluckily reverses the object.

He is sometimes unexpectedly mean. When he describes the Supreme Being as moved by prayer to stop the Fire of London, what is his expression?

> A hollow crystal pyramid he takes,
>   In firmamental waters dipp'd above,
> Of this a broad *extinguisher* he makes,
>   And *hoods* the flames that to their quarry strove.

When he describes the Last Day, and the decisive tribunal, he intermingles this image:

> When rattling bones together fly,
> From the four quarters of the sky.

It was indeed never in his power to resist the temptation of a jest. In his Elegy on Cromwell:

> No sooner was the Frenchman's cause embrac'd,
> Than the *light Monsieur* the *grave Don* outweigh'd;
> His fortune turn'd the scale—

He had a vanity, unworthy of his abilities, to shew, as may be suspected, the rank of the company with whom he lived, by the use of French words, which had then crept into conversation; such as *fraicheur* for *coolness, fougue* for *turbulence*, and a few more, none of which the language has incorporated or retained. They continue only where they stood first, perpetual warnings to future innovators.

These are his faults of affectation; his faults of negligence are beyond recital. Such is the unevenness of his compositions, that ten lines are seldom found together without something of which the reader is ashamed. Dryden was no rigid judge of his own pages; he seldom struggled after supreme excellence, but snatched in haste what was within his reach; and when he could content others, was himself contented. He did not keep present to his mind, an idea of pure perfection; nor compare his works, such as they were, with what they might be made. He knew to whom he should be opposed. He had more musick than Waller, more vigour than Denham, and more nature than Cowley; and from his contemporaries he was in no danger. Standing therefore in the highest place, he had no care to rise by contending with himself; but while there was no name above his own, was willing to enjoy fame on the easiest terms.

He was no lover of labour. What he thought sufficient, he did not stop to make better; and allowed himself to leave many parts unfinished, in confidence that the good lines would overbalance the bad. What he had once written, he dismissed from his thoughts; and, I believe, there is no example to be found of any correction or improvement made by him after publication. The hastiness of his productions might be the effect of necessity; but his subsequent neglect could hardly have any other cause than impatience of study.

What can be said of his versification, will be little more than a dilatation of the praise given it by Pope.

> Waller was smooth; but Dryden taught to join
> The varying verse, the full-resounding line,
> The long majestick march, and energy divine.

Some improvements had been already made in English numbers; but the full force of our language was not yet felt; the verse that was smooth was commonly feeble. If Cowley had sometimes a finished line, he had it by chance. Dryden knew how to chuse the flowing and the sonorous words; to vary the pauses, and adjust the accents; to diversify the cadence, and yet preserve the smoothness of his metre.

Of Triplets and Alexandrines, though he did not introduce the use, he established it. The triplet has long subsisted among us. Dryden seems not to have traced it higher than to Chapman's Homer; but it is to be found in Phaer's Virgil, written in the reign of Mary, and in Hall's Satires, published five years before the death of Elizabeth.

The Alexandrine was, I believe, first used by Spenser, for the sake of closing his stanza with a fuller sound. We had a longer measure of fourteen syllables, into which the Eneid was translated by Phaer, and other works of the ancients by other writers; of which Chapman's Iliad was, I believe, the last.

The two first lines of *Phaer's* third Eneid will exemplify this measure:

> When Asia's state was overthrown, and Priam's kingdom stout,
> All giltless, by the power of gods above was rooted out.

As these lines had their break, or *cæsura*, always at the eighth syllable, it was thought, in time, commodious to divide them; and quatrains of lines, alternately consisting of eight and six syllables, make the most soft and pleasing of our lyrick measures; as,

> Relentless Time, destroying power,
>   Which stone and brass obey,
> Who giv'st to every flying hour
>   To work some new decay.

In the Alexandrine, when its power was once felt, some poems, as *Drayton's Polyolbion*, were wholly written; and sometimes the measures of twelve and fourteen syllables were interchanged with one another. Cowley was the first that inserted the Alexandrine at pleasure among the heroick lines of ten syllables, and from him Dryden professes to have adopted it.

The Triplet and Alexandrine are not universally approved. *Swift* always censured them, and wrote some lines to ridicule them. In examining their propriety, it is to be considered that the essence of verse is regularity, and its ornament is variety. To write verse, is to dispose syllables and sounds harmonically by some known and settled rule; a rule however lax enough to substitute similitude for identity, to admit change without breach of order, and to relieve the ear without disappointing it. Thus a Latin hexameter is formed from dactyls and spondees differently combined; the English heroick admits of acute or grave syllables variously disposed. The Latin never deviates into seven feet, or exceeds the number of seventeen syllables; but the English Alexandrine breaks the lawful bounds, and surprises the reader with two syllables more than he expected.

The effect of the Triplet is the same: the ear has been accustomed to expect a new rhyme in every couplet; but is on a sudden surprized with three rhymes together, to which the reader could not accommodate his voice, did he not obtain notice of the change from the braces of the margins. Surely there is something unskilful in the necessity of such mechanical direction.

Considering the metrical art simply as a science, and consequently excluding all casualty, we must allow that Triplets and Alexandrines, inserted by caprice, are interruptions of that constancy to which science aspires. And though the variety which they produce may very justly be desired, yet to make our poetry exact, there ought to be some stated mode of admitting them.

But till some such regulation can be formed, I wish them still to be retained in their present state. They are sometimes grateful to the reader, and sometimes convenient to the poet. *Fenton* was of opinion that Dryden was too liberal and Pope too sparing in their use.

The rhymes of Dryden are commonly just, and he valued himself for his readiness in finding them; but he is sometimes open to objection.

It is the common practice of our poets to end the second line with a weak or grave syllable:

> Together o'er the Alps methinks we fly,
> Fill'd with ideas of fair *Italy*.

Dryden sometimes puts the weak rhyme in the first:

> Laugh all the powers that favour *tyranny*,
> And all the standing army of the sky.

Sometimes he concludes a period or paragraph with the first line of a couplet, which, though the French seem to do it without irregularity, always displeases in English poetry.

The Alexandrine, though much his favourite, is not always very diligently fabricated by him. It invariably requires a break at the sixth syllable; a rule which the modern French poets never violate, but which Dryden sometimes neglected:

> And with paternal thunder vindicates his throne.

Of Dryden's works it was said by Pope, that *he could select from them better specimens of every mode of poetry than any other English writer could supply*. Perhaps no nation ever produced a writer that enriched his language with such variety of models. To him we owe the improvement, perhaps the completion of our metre, the refinement of our language, and much of the correctness of our sentiments. By him we were taught *sapere & fari*, to think naturally and express forcibly. Though Davis has reasoned in rhyme before him, it may be perhaps maintained that he was the first who joined argument with poetry. He shewed us the true bounds of a translator's liberty. What was said of Rome, adorned by Augustus, may be applied by an easy metaphor to English poetry embellished by Dryden, *lateritiam invenit, marmoream reliquit*, he found it brick, and he left it marble.

ADDISON

JOSEPH ADDISON was born on the first of May, 1672, at Milston, of which his father, Lancelot Addison, was then rector, near Ambrosbury in Wiltshire, and appearing weak and unlikely to live, he was christened the same day. After the usual domestick education, which, from the character of his father, may be reasonably supposed to have given him strong impressions of piety, he was committed to the care of Mr. Naish at Ambrosbury, and afterwards of Mr. Taylor at Salisbury.

Not to name the school or the masters of men illustrious for literature, is a kind of historical fraud, by which honest fame is injuriously diminished: I would therefore trace him through the whole process of his education. In 1683, in the beginning of his twelfth year, his father being made dean of Lichfield, naturally carried his family to his new residence, and, I believe, placed him for some time, probably not long, under Mr. Shaw, then master of the school at Lichfield, father of the late Dr. Peter Shaw. Of this interval his biographers have given no account, and I know it only from a story of a *barring-out*, told me, when I was a boy, by Andrew Corbet of Shropshire, who had heard it from Mr. Pigot his uncle.

The practice of *barring-out*, was a savage license, practised in many schools to the end of the last century, by which the boys, when the periodical vacation drew near, growing petulant at the approach of liberty, some days before the time of regular recess, took possession of the school, of which they barred the doors, and bade their master defiance from the windows. It is not easy to suppose that on such occasions the master would do more than laugh; yet, if tradition may be credited, he often struggled hard to force or surprise the garrison. The master, when Pigot was a schoolboy, was *barred-out* at Lichfield, and the whole operation, as he said, was planned and conducted by Addison.

To judge better of the probability of this story, I have enquired when he was sent to the Chartreux; but, as he was not one of those who enjoyed the Founder's benefaction, there is no account preserved of his admission. At the school of the Chartreux, to which he was removed either from that of Salisbury or Lichfield, he pursued his juvenile studies under the care of Dr. Ellis, and contracted that intimacy with Sir Richard Steele, which their joint labours have so effectually recorded.

Of this memorable friendship the greater praise must be given to Steele. It is not hard to love those from whom nothing can be feared, and Addison never considered Steele as a rival; but Steele lived, as he confesses, under an habitual subjection to the predominating genius of Addison, whom he always mentioned with reverence, and treated with obsequiousness.

Addison*, who knew his own dignity, could not always forbear to shew it, by playing a little upon his admirer; but he was in no danger of retort: his jests were endured without resistance or resentment.

But the sneer of jocularity was not the worst. Steele, whose imprudence of generosity, or vanity of profusion, kept him always incurably necessitous, upon some pressing exigence, in an evil hour, borrowed an hundred pounds of his friend, probably without much purpose of repayment; but Addison, who seems to have had other notions of a hundred pounds, grew impatient of delay, and reclaimed his loan by an execution. Steele felt with great

* Spence.

sensibility the obduracy of his creditor; but with emotions of sorrow rather than of anger.

In 1687 he was entered into Queen's College in Oxford, where, in 1689, the accidental perusal of some Latin verses gained him the patronage of Dr. Lancaster, afterwards provost of Queen's College; by whose recommendation he was elected into Magdalen College as a Demy, a term by which that society denominates those which are elsewhere called Scholars; young men, who partake of the founder's benefaction, and succeed in their order to vacant fellowships.*

Here he continued to cultivate poetry and criticism, and grew first eminent by his Latin compositions, which are indeed entitled to particular praise. He has not confined himself to the imitation of any ancient author, but has formed his style from the general language, such as a diligent perusal of the productions of different ages happened to supply.

His Latin compositions seem to have had much of his fondness; for he collected a second volume of the *Musæ Anglicanæ*, perhaps for a convenient receptacle, in which all his Latin pieces are inserted, and where his Poem on the Peace has the first place. He afterwards presented the collection to Boileau, who from that time *conceived*, says Tickell, *an opinion of the English genius for poetry*. Nothing is better known of Boileau, than that he had an injudicious and peevish contempt of modern Latin, and therefore his profession of regard was probably the effect of his civility rather than approbation.

Three of his Latin poems are upon subjects on which perhaps he would not have ventured to have written in his own language. *The Battle of the Pigmies and Cranes; The Barometer;* and *a Bowling-green.* When the matter is low or scanty, a dead language, in which nothing is mean because nothing is familiar, affords great conveniences; and by the sonorous magnificence of Roman syllables, the writer conceals penury of thought, and want of novelty, often from the reader, and often from himself.

In his twenty-second year he first shewed his power of English poetry, by some verses addressed to Dryden; and soon afterwards published a translation of the greater part of the Fourth Georgick upon Bees; after which, says Dryden, *my latter swarm is hardly worth the hiving.*

About the same time he composed the arguments prefixed to the several books of Dryden's Virgil; and produced an Essay on the Georgicks, juvenile, superficial, and uninstructive, without much either of the scholar's learning or the critick's penetration.

His next paper of verses contained a character of the principal English poets, inscribed to Henry Sacheverell, who was then, if not a poet, a writer of verses; as is shewn by his version of a small part of Virgil's Georgicks, published in the Miscellanies, and a Latin encomium on queen Mary, in the Musæ

---

* He took the degree of M. A. Feb. 14, 1693.

Anglicanæ. These verses exhibit all the fondness of friendship; but on one side or the other, friendship was afterwards too weak for the malignity of faction.

In this poem is a very confident and discriminative character of Spenser, whose work he had then never read*. So little sometimes is criticism the effect of judgement. It is necessary to inform the reader, that about this time he was introduced by Congreve to Montague, then Chancellor of the Exchequer: Addison was then learning the trade of a courtier, and subjoined Montague as a poetical name to those of Cowley and of Dryden.

By the influence of Mr. Montague, concurring, according to Tickell, with his natural modesty, he was diverted from his original design of entering into holy orders. Montague alleged the corruption of men who engaged in civil employments without liberal education; and declared, that, though he was represented as an enemy to the Church, he would never do it any injury but by withholding Addison from it.

Soon after (in 1695) he wrote a poem to king William, with a rhyming introduction addressed to lord Somers. King William had no regard to elegance or literature; his study was only war; yet by a choice of ministers, whose disposition was very different from his own, he procured, without intention, a very liberal patronage to poetry. Addison was caressed both by Somers and Montague.

In 1697 appeared his Latin verses on the peace of Ryswick, which he dedicated to Montague, and which was afterwards called by Smith *the best Latin poem since the Æneid*. Praise must not be too rigorously examined; but the performance cannot be denied to be vigorous and elegant.

Having yet no publick employment, he obtained (in 1699) a pension of three hundred pounds a year, that he might be enabled to travel. He staid a year at Blois†, probably to learn the French language; and then proceeded in his journey to Italy, which he surveyed with the eyes of a poet.

While he was travelling at leisure, he was far from being idle; for he not only collected his observations on the country, but found time to write his Dialogues on Medals, and four Acts of Cato. Such at least is the relation of Tickell. Perhaps he only collected his materials, and formed his plan.

Whatever were his other employments in Italy, he there wrote the letter to lord Halifax, which is justly considered as the most elegant, if not the most sublime, of his poetical productions. But in about two years he found it necessary to hasten home; being, as Swift informs us, distressed by indigence, and compelled to become the tutor of a travelling Squire, because his pension was not remitted.

At his return he published his Travels, with a dedication to lord Somers. As his stay in foreign countries was short, his observations are such as might

* Spence.   † Spence.

be supplied by a hasty view, and consist chiefly in comparisons of the present face of the country with the descriptions left us by the Roman poets, from whom he made preparatory collections, though he might have spared the trouble, had he known that such collections had been made twice before by Italian authors.

The most amusing passage of his book, is his account of the minute republick of San Marino; of many parts it is not a very severe censure to say that they might have been written at home. His elegance of language, and variegation of prose and verse, however, gains upon the reader; and the book, though a while neglected, became in time so much the favourite of the publick, that before it was reprinted it rose to five times its price.

When he returned to England (in 1702), with a meanness of appearance which gave testimony of the difficulties to which he had been reduced, he found his old patrons out of power, and was therefore for a time at full leisure for the cultivation of his mind, and a mind so cultivated gives reason to believe that little time was lost.

But he remained not long neglected or useless. The victory at Blenheim (1704) spread triumph and confidence over the nation; and lord Godolphin lamenting to lord Halifax, that it had not been celebrated in a manner equal to the subject, desired him to propose it to some better poet. Halifax told him that there was no encouragement for genius; that worthless men were unprofitably enriched with publick money, without any care to find or employ those whose appearance might do honour to their country. To this Godolphin replied, that such abuses should in time be rectified; and that if a man could be found capable of the task then proposed, he should not want an ample recompense. Halifax then named Addison; but required that the Treasurer should apply to him in his own person. Godolphin sent the message by Mr. Boyle, afterwards lord Carleton; and Addison having undertaken the work, communicated it to the Treasurer, while it was yet advanced no further than the simile of the Angel, and was immediately rewarded by succeeding Mr. Locke in the place of *Commissioner of Appeals*.

In the following year he was at Hanover with lord Halifax; and the year after was made under-secretary of state, first to Sir Charles Hedges, and in a few months more to the earl of Sunderland.

About this time the prevalent taste for Italian operas inclined him to try what would be the effect of a musical Drama in our own language. He therefore wrote the opera of Rosamond, which, when exhibited on the stage, was either hissed or neglected; but trusting that the readers would do him more justice, he published it, with an inscription to the dutchess of Marlborough; a woman without skill, or pretensions to skill, in poetry or literature. His dedication was therefore an instance of servile absurdity, to be exceeded only by Joshua Barnes's dedication of a Greek Anacreon to the Duke.

His reputation had been somewhat advanced by *The Tender Husband*, a comedy which Steele dedicated to him, with a confession that he owed to him several of the most successful scenes. To this play Addison supplied a prologue.

When the marquis of Wharton was appointed lord lieutenant of Ireland, Addison attended him as his secretary; and was made keeper of the records in Birmingham's Tower, with a salary of three hundred pounds a year. The office was little more than nominal, and the salary was augmented for his accommodation.

Interest and faction allow little to the operation of particular dispositions, or private opinions. Two men of personal characters more opposite than those of Wharton and Addison, could not easily be brought together. Wharton was impious, profligate, and shameless, without regard, or appearance of regard, to right and wrong: whatever is contrary to this, may be said of Addison; but as agents of a party they were connected, and how they adjusted their other sentiments we cannot know.

Addison must however not be too hastily condemned. It is not necessary to refuse benefits from a bad man, when the acceptance implies no approbation of his crimes; nor has the subordinate officer any obligation to examine the opinions or conduct of those under whom he acts, except that he may not be made the instrument of wickedness. It is reasonable to suppose that Addison counteracted, as far as he was able, the malignant and blasting influence of the Lieutenant, and that at least by his intervention some good was done, and some mischief prevented.

When he was in office, he made a law to himself, as Swift has recorded, never to remit his regular fees in civility to his friends: "For," said he, "I may have a hundred friends; and, if my fee be two guineas, I shall, by relinquishing my right, lose two hundred guineas, and no friend gain more than two; there is therefore no proportion between the good imparted and the evil suffered."

He was in Ireland when Steele, without any communication of his design, began the publication of the Tatler; but he was not long concealed: by inserting a remark on Virgil, which Addison had given him, he discovered himself. It is indeed not easy for any man to write upon literature, or common life, so as not to make himself known to those with whom he familiarly converses, and who are acquainted with his track of study, his favourite topicks, his peculiar notions, and his habitual phrases.

If Steele desired to write in secret, he was not lucky; a single month detected him. His first Tatler was published April 22 (1709), and Addison's contribution appeared May 26. Tickell observes, that the Tatler began and was concluded without his concurrence. This is doubtless literally true; but the work did not suffer much by his unconsciousness of its commencement, or his absence at its cessation; for he continued his assistance to December 23, and the paper stopped on January 2. He did not distinguish his pieces by any signature; and I know not whether his name was not kept secret, till the papers were collected into volumes.

To the Tatler, in about two months, succeeded the Spectator; a series of essays of the same kind, but written with less levity, upon a more regular plan, and published daily. Such an undertaking shewed the writers not to distrust their own copiousness of materials or facility of composition, and their performance justified their confidence. They found, however, in their progress, many auxiliaries. To attempt a single paper was no terrifying labour: many pieces were offered, and many were received.

Addison had enough of the zeal of party, but Steele had at that time almost nothing else. The Spectator, in one of the first papers, shewed the political tenets of its authors; but a resolution was soon taken, of courting general approbation by general topicks, and subjects on which faction had produced no diversity of sentiments; such as literature, morality, and familiar life. To this practice they adhered with very few deviations. The ardour of Steele once broke out in praise of Marlborough; and when Dr. Fleetwood prefixed to some sermons a preface, overflowing with whiggish opinions, that it might be read by the Queen, it was reprinted in the Spectator.

To teach the minuter decencies and inferior duties, to regulate the practice of daily conversation, to correct those depravities which are rather ridiculous than criminal, and remove those grievances which, if they produce no lasting calamities, impress hourly vexation, was first attempted by *Casa* in his book of *Manners*, and *Castiglione* in his *Courtier*; two books yet celebrated in Italy for purity and elegance, and which, if they are now less read, are neglected only because they have effected that reformation which their authors intended, and their precepts now are no longer wanted. Their usefulness to the age in which they were written, is sufficiently attested by the translations which almost all the nations of Europe were in haste to obtain.

This species of instruction was continued, and perhaps advanced, by the French; among whom *La Bruyere's* Manners of the Age, though, as Boileau remarked, it is written without connection, certainly deserves great praise, for liveliness of description and justness of observation.

Before the Tatler and Spectator, if the writers for the theatre are excepted, England had no masters of common life. No writers had yet undertaken to reform either the savageness of neglect, or the impertinence of civility; to shew when to speak, or to be silent; how to refuse, or how to comply. We had many books to teach us our more important duties, and to settle opinions in philosophy or politicks; but an *Arbiter elegantiarum*, a judge of propriety, was yet wanting, who should survey the track of daily conversation, and free it from thorns and prickles, which teaze the passer, though they do not wound him.

For this purpose nothing is so proper as the frequent publication of short papers, which we read not as study but amusement. If the subject be slight, the treatise likewise is short. The busy may find time, and the idle may find patience.

This mode of conveying cheap and easy knowledge began among us in the Civil War, when it was much the interest of either party to raise and fix the prejudices of the people. At that time appeared Mercurius Aulicus, Mercurius Rusticus, and Mercurius Civicus. It is said, that when any title grew popular, it was stolen by the antagonist, who by this stratagem conveyed his notions to those who would not have received him had he not worn the appearance of a friend. The tumult of those unhappy days left scarcely any man leisure to treasure up occasional compositions; and so much were they neglected, that a complete collection is no where to be found.

These Mercuries were succeeded by L'Estrange's Observator, and that by Lesley's Rehearsal, and perhaps by others; but hitherto nothing had been conveyed to the people, in this commodious manner, but controversy relating to the Church or State; of which they taught many to talk, whom they could not teach to judge.

It has been suggested that the Royal Society was instituted soon after the Restoration, to divert the attention of the people from publick discontent. The Tatler and Spectator had the same tendency: they were published at a time when two parties, loud, restless, and violent, each with plausible declarations, and each perhaps without any distinct termination of its views, were agitating the nation; to minds heated with political contest, they supplied cooler and more inoffensive reflections; and it is said by Addison, in a subsequent work, that they had a perceptible influence upon the conversation of that time, and taught the frolick and the gay to unite merriment with decency; an effect which they can never wholly lose, while they continue to be among the first books by which both sexes are initiated in the elegances of knowledge.

The Tatler and Spectator adjusted, like Casa, the unsettled practice of daily intercourse by propriety and politeness; and, like La Bruyere, exhibited the *Characters and Manners of the Age*. The personages introduced in these papers were not merely ideal; they were then known, and conspicuous in various stations. Of the Tatler this is told by Steele in his last paper, and of the Spectator by Budgell in the Preface to Theophrastus; a book which Addison has recommended, and which he was suspected to have revised, if he did not write it. Of those portraits, which may be supposed to be sometimes embellished, and sometimes aggravated, the originals are now partly known, and partly forgotten.

But to say that they united the plans of two or three eminent writers, is to give them but a small part of their due praise; they superadded literature and criticism, and sometimes towered far above their predecessors; and taught, with great justness of argument and dignity of language, the most important duties and sublime truths.

All these topicks were happily varied with elegant fictions and refined allegories, and illuminated with different changes of style and felicities of invention.

It is recorded by Budgell, that of the characters feigned or exhibited in the Spectator, the favourite of Addison was Sir Roger de Coverley, of whom he had formed a very delicate and discriminated idea, which he would not suffer to be violated; and therefore when Steele had shewn him innocently picking up a girl in the Temple, and taking her to a tavern, he drew upon himself so much of his friend's indignation, that he was forced to appease him by a promise of forbearing Sir Roger for the time to come.

The reason which induced Cervantes to bring his hero to the grave, *para mi sola nacio Don Quixote, y yo para el*, made Addison declare, with an undue vehemence of expression, that he would kill Sir Roger; being of opinion that they were born for one another, and that any other hand would do him wrong.

It may be doubted whether Addison ever filled up his original delineation. He describes his Knight as having his imagination somewhat warped; but of this perversion he has made very little use. The irregularities in Sir Roger's conduct, seem not so much the effects of a mind deviating from the beaten track of life, by the perpetual pressure of some overwhelming idea, as of habitual rusticity, and that negligence which solitary grandeur naturally generates.

The variable weather of the mind, the flying vapours of incipient madness, which from time to time cloud reason, without eclipsing it, it requires so much nicety to exhibit, that Addison seems to have been deterred from prosecuting his own design.

To Sir Roger, who, as a country gentleman, appears to be a Tory, or, as it is gently expressed, an adherent to the landed interest, is opposed Sir Andrew Freeport, a new man, a wealthy merchant, zealous for the moneyed interest, and a Whig. Of this contrariety of opinions, it is probable more consequences were at first intended, than could be produced when the resolution was taken to exclude party from the paper. Sir Andrew does but little, and that little seems not to have pleased Addison, who, when he dismissed him from the club, changed his opinions. Steele had made him, in the true spirit of unfeeling commerce, declare that he *would not build an hospital for idle people*; but at last he buys land, settles in the country, and builds not a manufactory, but an hospital for twelve old husbandmen, for men with whom a merchant has little acquaintance, and whom he commonly considers with little kindness.

Of essays thus elegant, thus instructive, and thus commodiously distributed, it is natural to suppose the approbation general and the sale numerous. I once heard it observed, that the sale may be calculated by the product of the tax, related in the last number to produce more than twenty pounds a week, and therefore stated at one and twenty pounds, or three pounds ten shillings a day: this, at a half-penny a paper, will give sixteen hundred and eighty for the daily number.

This sale is not great; yet this, if Swift be credited, was likely to grow less; for he declares that the Spectator, whom he ridicules for his endless mention of the *fair sex*, had before his recess wearied his readers.

The next year (1713), in which Cato came upon the stage, was the grand climacterick of Addison's reputation. Upon the death of Cato, he had, as is said, planned a tragedy in the time of his travels, and had for several years the four first acts finished, which were shewn to such as were likely to spread their admiration. They were seen by Pope, and by Cibber; who relates that Steele, when he took back the copy, told him, in the despicable cant of literary modesty, that, whatever spirit his friend had shewn in the composition, he doubted whether he would have courage sufficient to expose it to the censure of a British audience.

The time however was now come, when those who affected to think liberty in danger, affected likewise to think that a stage-play might preserve it: and Addison was importuned, in the name of the tutelary deities of Britain, to shew his courage and his zeal by finishing his design.

To resume his work he seemed perversely and unaccountably unwilling; and by a request, which perhaps he wished to be denied, desired Mr. Hughes to add a fifth act. Hughes supposed him serious; and, undertaking the supplement, brought in a few days some scenes for his examination; but he had in the mean time gone to work himself, and produced half an act, which he afterwards completed, but with brevity irregularly disproportionate to the foregoing parts; like a task performed with reluctance, and hurried to its conclusion.

It may yet be doubted whether Cato was made publick by any change of the author's purpose; for Dennis charged him with raising prejudices in his own favour by false positions of preparatory criticism, and with *poisoning the town* by contradicting in the Spectator the established rule of poetical justice, because his own hero, with all his virtues, was to fall before a tyrant. The fact is certain; the motives we must guess.

Addison was, I believe, sufficiently disposed to bar all avenues against all danger. When Pope brought him the prologue, which is properly accommodated to the play, there were these words, *Britons, arise, be worth like this approved*; meaning nothing more than, Britons, erect and exalt yourselves to the approbation of public virtue. Addison was frighted lest he should be thought a promoter of insurrection, and the line was liquidated to *Britons, attend*.

Now, *heavily in clouds came on the day, the great, the important day*, when Addison was to stand the hazard of the theatre. That there might, however, be left as little to hazard as was possible, on the first night Steele, as himself relates, undertook to pack an audience. This, says Pope*, had been tried for

---

* Spence.

the first time in favour of the Distrest Mother; and was now, with more effi-cacy, practised for Cato.

The danger was soon over. The whole nation was at that time on fire with faction. The Whigs applauded every line in which Liberty was mentioned, as a satire on the Tories; and the Tories echoed every clap, to shew that the satire was unfelt. The story of Bolingbroke is well known. He called Booth to his box, and gave him fifty guineas for defending the cause of Liberty so well against a perpetual dictator. The Whigs, says Pope, design a second present, when they can accompany it with as good a sentence.

The play, supported thus by the emulation of factious praise, was acted night after night for a longer time than, I believe, the publick had allowed to any drama before; and the author, as Mrs. Porter long afterwards related, wandered through the whole exhibition behind the scenes with restless and unappeasable solicitude.

When it was printed, notice was given that the Queen would be pleased if it was dedicated to her; *but as he had designed that compliment elsewhere, he found himself obliged*, says Tickell, *by his duty on the one hand, and his honour on the other, to send it into the world without any dedication.*

Human happiness has always its abatements; the brightest sun-shine of success is not without a cloud. No sooner was Cato offered to the reader, than it was attacked by the acute malignity of Dennis, with all the violence of angry criticism. Dennis, though equally zealous, and probably by his temper more furious than Addison, for what they called liberty, and though a flatterer of the Whig ministry, could not sit quiet at a successful play; but was eager to tell friends and enemies, that they had misplaced their admirations. The world was too stubborn for instruction; with the fate of the censurer of Corneille's Cid, his animadversions shewed his anger without effect, and Cato continued to be praised.

Pope had now an opportunity of courting the friendship of Addison, by vilifying his old enemy, and could give resentment its full play without appearing to revenge himself. He therefore published *A Narrative of the mad-ness of John Dennis*; a performance which left the objections to the play in their full force, and therefore discovered more desire of vexing the critick than of defending the poet.

Addison, who was no stranger to the world, probably saw the selfishness of Pope's friendship; and, resolving that he should have the consequences of his officiousness to himself, informed Dennis by Steele, that he was sorry for the insult; and that whenever he should think fit to answer his remarks, he would do it in a manner to which nothing could be objected.

The greatest weakness of the play is in the scenes of love, which are said by Pope* to have been added to the original plan upon a subsequent review, in

* Spence.

compliance with the popular practice of the stage. Such an authority it is hard to reject; yet the love is so intimately mingled with the whole action, that it cannot easily be thought extrinsick and adventitious; for if it were taken away, what would be left? or how were the four acts filled in the first draught?

At the publication the Wits seemed proud to pay their attendance with encomiastick verses. The best are from an unknown hand, which will perhaps lose somewhat of their praise when the author is known to be Jeffreys.

Cato had yet other honours. It was censured as a party-play by a *Scholar of Oxford*, and defended in a favourable examination by Dr. Sewel. It was translated by Salvini into Italian, and acted at Florence; and by the Jesuits of St. Omer's into Latin, and played by their pupils. Of this version a copy was sent to Mr. Addison: it is to be wished that it could be found, for the sake of comparing their version of the soliloquy with that of Bland.

A tragedy was written on the same subject by Des Champs, a French poet, which was translated, with a criticism on the English play. But the translator and the critick are now forgotten.

Dennis lived on unanswered, and therefore little read: Addison knew the policy of literature too well to make his enemy important, by drawing the attention of the publick upon a criticism, which, though sometimes intemperate, was often irrefragable.

While Cato was upon the stage, another daily paper, called *The Guardian*, was published by Steele. To this, Addison gave great assistance, whether occasionally or by previous engagement is not known.

The character of Guardian was too narrow and too serious: it might properly enough admit both the duties and the decencies of life, but seemed not to include literary speculations, and was in some degree violated by merriment and burlesque. What had the Guardian of the Lizards to do with clubs of tall or of little men, with nests of ants, or with Strada's prolusions?

Of this paper nothing is necessary to be said, but that it found many contributors, and that it was a continuation of the Spectator, with the same elegance, and the same variety, till some unlucky sparkle from a Tory paper set Steele's politicks on fire, and wit at once blazed into faction. He was soon too hot for neutral topicks, and quitted the *Guardian* to write the *Englishman*.

The papers of Addison are marked in the Spectator by one of the Letters in the name of *Clio*, and in the Guardian by *a hand*; whether it was, as Tickell pretends to think, that he was unwilling to usurp the praise of others, or as Steele, with far greater likelihood, insinuates, that he could not without discontent impart to others any of his own. I have heard that his avidity did not satisfy itself with the air of renown, but that with great eagerness he laid hold on his proportion of the profits.

Many of these papers were written with powers truly comick, with nice discrimination of characters, and accurate observation of natural or accidental deviations from propriety; but it was not supposed that he had tried a comedy on the stage, till Steele, after his death, declared him the author of the *Drummer*; this however Steele did not know to be true by any direct testimony; for when Addison put the play into his hands, he only told him, it was the work of a *Gentleman in the Company*; and when it was received, as is confessed, with cold disapprobation, he was probably less willing to claim it. Tickell omitted it in his collection; but the testimony of Steele, and the total silence of any other claimant, has determined the publick to assign it to Addison, and it is now printed with his other poetry. Steele carried the *Drummer* to the playhouse, and afterwards to the press, and sold the copy for fifty guineas.

To the opinion of Steele may be added the proof supplied by the play itself, of which the characters are such as Addison would have delineated, and the tendency such as Addison would have promoted. That it should have been ill received would raise wonder, did we not daily see the capricious distribution of theatrical praise.

He was not all this time an indifferent spectator of publick affairs. He wrote, as different exigences required (in 1707), *The present State of the War, and the Necessity of an Augmentation*; which, however judicious, being written on temporary topicks, and exhibiting no peculiar powers, laid hold on no attention, and has naturally sunk by its own weight into neglect. This cannot be said of the few papers entitled *The Whig Examiner*, in which is employed all the force of gay malevolence and humorous satire. Of this paper, which just appeared and expired, Swift remarks, with exultation, that *it is now down among the dead men*. He might well rejoice at the death of that which he could not have killed. Every reader of every party, since personal malice is past, and the papers which once inflamed the nation are read only as effusions of wit, must wish for more of the *Whig Examiners*; for on no occasion was the genius of Addison more vigorously exerted, and on none did the superiority of his powers more evidently appear. His *Trial of Count Tariff*, written to expose the Treaty of Commerce with France, lived no longer than the question that produced it.

Not long afterwards an attempt was made to revive the *Spectator*, at a time indeed by no means favourable to literature, when the succession of a new family to the throne filled the nation with anxiety, discord, and confusion; and either the turbulence of the times, or the satiety of the readers, put a stop to the publication, after an experiment of eighty numbers, which were afterwards collected into an eighth volume, perhaps more valuable than any one of those that went before it. Addison produced more than a fourth part, and the other contributors are by no means unworthy of appearing as his associates. The time that had passed during the suspension of the *Spectator*, though it had not lessened his power of humour, seems to have increased his disposition to seriousness: the proportion of his religious to his comick papers is greater than in the former series.

The *Spectator*, from its recommencement, was published only three times a week; and no discriminative marks were added to the papers. To Addison Tickell has ascribed twenty-three*.

The *Spectator* had many contributors; and Steele, whose negligence kept him always in a hurry, when it was his turn to furnish a paper, called loudly for the Letters, of which Addison, whose materials were more, made little use; having recourse to sketches and hints, the product of his former studies, which he now reviewed and completed: among these are named by Tickell the *Essays* on *Wit*, those on the *Pleasures* of the *Imagination*, and the *Criticism* on *Milton*.

When the House of Hanover took possession of the throne, it was reasonable to expect that the zeal of Addison would be suitably rewarded. Before the arrival of king George, he was made secretary to the regency, and was required by his office to send notice to Hanover that the Queen was dead, and that the throne was vacant. To do this would not have been difficult to any man but Addison, who was so overwhelmed with the greatness of the event, and so distracted by choice of expression, that the lords, who could not wait for the niceties of criticism, called Mr. Southwell, a clerk in the house, and ordered him to dispatch the message. Southwell readily told what was necessary, in the common style of business, and valued himself upon having done what was too hard for Addison.

He was better qualified for the *Freeholder*, a paper which he published twice a week, from Dec 23, 1715, to the middle of the next year. This was undertaken in defence of the established government, sometimes with argument, sometimes with mirth. In argument he had many equals; but his humour was singular and matchless. Bigotry itself must be delighted with the Tory Fox-hunter.

There are however some strokes less elegant, and less decent; such as the Pretender's Journal, in which one topick of ridicule is his poverty. This mode of abuse had been employed by Milton against king Charles II,

————— *Jacobæi*
Centum exulantis viscera Marsupii regis.

And Oldmixon delights to tell of some alderman of London, that he had more money than the exiled princes; but that which might be expected from Milton's savageness, or Oldmixon's meanness, was not suitable to the delicacy of Addison.

---

* Numb. 556. 557. 558. 559. 561. 562. 565. 567. 568. 569. 571. 574. 575. 579. 580. 582. 583. 584. 585. 590. 592. 598. 600.

Steele thought the humour of the *Freeholder* too nice and gentle for such noisy times; and is reported to have said that the ministry made use of a lute, when they should have called for a trumpet.

This year (1716*) he married the countess dowager of Warwick, whom he had solicited by a very long and anxious courtship, perhaps with behaviour not very unlike that of Sir Roger to his disdainful widow; and who, I am afraid, diverted herself often by playing with his passion. He is said to have first known her by becoming tutor to her son†. "He formed," said Tonson, "the design of getting that lady, from the time when he was first recommended into the family." In what part of his life he obtained the recommendation, or how long, and in what manner he lived in the family, I know not. His advances at first were certainly timorous, but grew bolder as his reputation and influence increased; till at last the lady was persuaded to marry him, on terms much like those on which a Turkish princess is espoused; to whom the Sultan is reported to pronounce, "Daughter, I give thee this man for thy slave." The marriage, if uncontradicted report can be credited, made no addition to his happiness; it neither found them nor made them equal. She always remembered her own rank, and thought herself entitled to treat with very little ceremony the tutor of her son. Rowe's ballad of the *Despairing Shepherd* is said to have been written, either before or after marriage, upon this memorable pair; and it is certain that Addison has left behind him no encouragement for ambitious love.

The year after (1717) he rose to his highest elevation, being made secretary of state. For this employment he might be justly supposed qualified by long practice of business, and by his regular ascent through other offices; but expectation is often disappointed; it is universally confessed that he was unequal to the duties of his place. In the house of commons he could not speak, and therefore was useless to the defence of the government. In the office, says Pope§, he could not issue an order without losing his time in quest of fine expressions. What he gained in rank, he lost in credit; and, finding by experience his own inability, was forced to solicit his dismission, with a pension of fifteen hundred pounds a year. His friends palliated this relinquishment, of which both friends and enemies knew the true reason, with an account of declining health, and the necessity of recess and quiet.

He now returned to his vocation, and began to plan literary occupations for his future life. He purposed a tragedy on the death of Socrates; a story of which, as Tickell remarks, the basis is narrow, and to which I know not how love could have been appended. There would however have been no want either of virtue in the sentiments, or elegance in the language.

---

* August 2.   † Spence.   § Spence.

He engaged in a nobler work, a defence of the *Christian Religion*, of which part was published after his death; and he designed to have made a new poetical version of the Psalms.

These pious compositions Pope imputed* to a selfish motive, upon the credit, as he owns, of Tonson; who having quarrelled with Addison, and not loving him, said, that, when he laid down the secretary's office, he intended to take orders, and obtain a bishoprick; *for*, said he, *I always thought him a priest in his heart.*

That Pope should have thought this conjecture of Tonson worth remembrance is a proof, but indeed so far as I have found, the only proof, that he retained some malignity from their ancient rivalry. Tonson pretended but to guess it; no other mortal ever suspected it; and Pope might have reflected, that a man who had been secretary of state, in the ministry of Sunderland, knew a nearer way to a bishoprick than by defending Religion, or translating the Psalms.

It is related that he had once a design to make an English Dictionary, and that he considered Dr. Tillotson as the writer of highest authority. There was formerly sent to me by Mr. Locker, clerk of the Leathersellers Company, who was eminent for curiosity and literature, a collection of examples selected from Tillotson's works, as Locker said, by Addison. It came too late to be of use, so I inspected it but slightly, and remember it indistinctly. I thought the passages too short.

Addison however did not conclude his life in peaceful studies; but relapsed, when he was near his end, to a political dispute.

It so happened that (1718–19) a controversy was agitated, with great vehemence, between those friends of long continuance, Addison and Steele. It may be asked, in the language of Homer, what power or what cause could set them at variance. The subject of their dispute was of great importance. The earl of Sunderland proposed an act called the *Peerage Bill*, by which the number of peers should be fixed, and the king restrained from any new creation of nobility, unless when an old family should be extinct. To this the lords would naturally agree; and the king, who was yet little acquainted with his own prerogative, and, as is now well known, almost indifferent to the possessions of the Crown, had been persuaded to consent. The only difficulty was found among the commons, who were not likely to approve the perpetual exclusion of themselves and their posterity. The bill therefore was eagerly opposed, and among others by Sir Robert Walpole, whose speech was published.

The lords might think their dignity diminished by improper advancements, and particularly by the introduction of twelve new peers at once, to produce a majority of Tories in the last reign; an act of authority violent enough, yet certainly legal, and by no means to be compared with that

---

* Spence.

contempt of national right, with which some time afterwards, by the instigation of Whiggism, the commons, chosen by the people for three years, chose themselves for seven. But, whatever might be the disposition of the lords, the people had no wish to increase their power. The tendency of the bill, as Steele observed in a letter to the earl of Oxford, was to introduce an Aristocracy; for a majority in the house of lords, so limited, would have been despotick and irresistible.

To prevent this subversion of the ancient establishment, Steele, whose pen readily seconded his political passions, endeavoured to alarm the nation by a pamphlet called *The Plebeian*; to this an answer was published by Addison, under the title of *The Old Whig*, in which it is not discovered that Steele was then known to be the advocate for the commons. Steele replied by a second *Plebeian*; and, whether by ignorance or by courtesy, confined himself to his question, without any personal notice of his opponent. Nothing hitherto was committed against the laws of friendship, or proprieties of decency; but controvertists cannot long retain their kindness for each other. The *Old Whig* answered the *Plebeian*, and could not forbear some contempt of 'little *Dicky*, whose trade it was to write pamphlets.' Dicky however did not lose his settled veneration for his friend; but contented himself with quoting some lines of Cato, which were at once detection and reproof. The bill was laid aside during that session, and Addison died before the next, in which its commitment was rejected by two hundred sixty-five to one hundred seventy-seven.

Every reader surely must regret that these two illustrious friends, after so many years past in confidence and endearment, in unity of interest, conformity of opinion, and fellowship of study, should finally part in acrimonious opposition. Such a controversy was *Bellum plusquam civile*, as Lucan expresses it. Why could not faction find other advocates? But, among the uncertainties of the human state, we are doomed to number the instability of friendship.

Of this dispute I have little knowledge but from the *Biographia Britannica*. The *Old Whig* is not inserted in Addison's works, nor is it mentioned by Tickell in his Life; why it was omitted the biographers doubtless give the true reason; the fact was too recent, and those who had been heated in the contention were not yet cool.

The necessity of complying with times, and of sparing persons, is the great impediment of biography. History may be formed from permanent monuments and records; but Lives can only be written from personal knowledge, which is growing every day less, and in a short time is lost for ever. What is known can seldom be immediately told; and when it might be told, it is no longer known. The delicate features of the mind, the nice discriminations of character, and the minute peculiarities of conduct, are soon obliterated; and it is surely better that caprice, obstinacy, frolick, and folly, however they might delight in the description, should be silently forgotten, than that, by wanton merriment and unseasonable detection, a pang should be given to a widow, a daughter, a brother, or a friend. As the process of these narratives is now bringing me among my contemporaries, I begin to feel myself *walking upon ashes under which the fire is not extinguished*, and coming to the time of which it will be proper rather, to say *nothing that is false, than all that is true*.

The end of this useful life was now approaching.—Addison had for some time been oppressed by shortness of breath, which was now aggravated by a dropsy; and, finding his danger pressing, he prepared to die conformably to his own precepts and professions.

During this lingering decay, he sent, as Pope relates*, a message by the earl of Warwick to Mr. Gay, desiring to see him: Gay, who had not visited him for some time before, obeyed the summons, and found himself received with great kindness. The purpose for which the interview had been solicited was then discovered: Addison told him, that he had injured him; but that, if he recovered, he would recompense him. What the injury was he did not explain, nor did Gay ever know; but supposed that some preferment designed for him, had, by Addison's intervention, been withheld.

Lord Warwick was a young man of very irregular life, and perhaps of loose opinions. Addison, for whom he did not want respect, had very diligently endeavoured to reclaim him; but his arguments and expostulations had no effect. One experiment, however, remained to be tried: when he found his life near its end, he directed the young lord to be called; and when he desired, with great tenderness, to hear his last injunctions, told him, *I have sent for you that you may see how a Christian can die*. What effect this awful scene had on the earl I know not; he likewise died himself in a short time.

In Tickell's excellent Elegy on his friend are these lines:

> He taught us how to live; and, oh! too high
> The price of knowledge, taught us how to die.

In which he alludes, as he told Dr. Young, to this moving interview.

Having given directions to Mr. Tickell for the publication of his works, and dedicated them on his death-bed to his friend Mr. Craggs, he died June 17, 1719, at Holland-house, leaving no child but a daughter.

Of his virtue it is a sufficient testimony, that the resentment of party has transmitted no charge of any crime. He was not one of those who are praised only after death; for his merit was so generally acknowledged, that Swift, having observed that his election passed without a contest, adds, that if he had proposed himself for king, he would hardly have been refused.

His zeal for his party did not extinguish his kindness for the merit of his opponents: when he was secretary in Ireland, he refused to intermit his acquaintance with Swift.

* Spence.

Of his habits, or external manners, nothing is so often mentioned as that timorous or sullen taciturnity, which his friends called modesty by too mild a name. Steele mentions with great tenderness "that remarkable bashfulness, which is a cloak that hides and muffles merit;" and tells us, that "his abilities were covered only by modesty, which doubles the beauties which are seen, and gives credit and esteem to all that are concealed." Chesterfield affirms, that "Addison was the most timorous and aukward man that he ever saw." And Addison, speaking of his own deficience in conversation, used to say of himself, that, with respect to intellectual wealth, "he could draw bills for a thousand pounds, though he had not a guinea in his pocket."

That he wanted current coin for ready payment, and by that want was often obstructed and distressed; that he was oppressed by an improper and ungraceful timidity, every testimony concurs to prove; but Chesterfield's representation is doubtless hyperbolical. That man cannot be supposed very unexpert in the arts of conversation and practice of life, who, without fortune or alliance, by his usefulness and dexterity, became secretary of state; and who died at forty-seven, after having not only stood long in the highest rank of wit and literature, but filled one of the most important offices of state.

The time in which he lived, had reason to lament his obstinacy of silence; "for he was," says Steele, "above all men in that talent called humour, and enjoyed it in such perfection, that I have often reflected, after a night spent with him apart from all the world, that I had had the pleasure of conversing with an intimate acquaintance of Terence and Catullus, who had all their wit and nature, heightened with humour more exquisite and delightful than any other man ever possessed." This is the fondness of a friend; let us hear what is told us by a rival. "Addison's conversation*," says Pope, "had something in it more charming than I have found in any other man. But this was only when familiar: before strangers, or perhaps a single stranger, he preserved his dignity by a stiff silence."

This modesty was by no means inconsistent with a very high opinion of his own merit. He demanded to be the first name in modern wit; and, with Steele to echo him, used to depreciate Dryden, whom Pope and Congreve defended against them†. There is no reason to doubt that he suffered too much pain from the prevalence of Pope's poetical reputation; nor is it without strong reason suspected, that by some disingenuous acts he endeavoured to obstruct it; Pope was not the only man whom he insidiously injured, though the only man of whom he could be afraid.

His own powers were such as might have satisfied him with conscious excellence. Of very extensive learning he has indeed given no proofs. He seems to have had small acquaintance with the sciences, and to have read little except Latin and French; but of the Latin poets his *Dialogues on Medals* shew

---

* Spence.   † Tonson and Spence.

that he had perused the works with great diligence and skill. The abundance of his own mind left him little need of adventitious sentiments; his wit always could suggest what the occasion demanded. He had read with critical eyes the important volume of human life, and knew the heart of man from the depths of stratagem to the surface of affectation.

What he knew he could easily communicate. "This," says Steele, "was particular in this writer, that, when he had taken his resolution, or made his plan for what he designed to write, he would walk about a room, and dictate it into language with as much freedom and ease as any one could write it down, and attend to the coherence and grammar of what he dictated."

Pope*, who can be less suspected of favouring his memory, declares that he wrote very fluently, but was slow and scrupulous in correcting; that many of his Spectators were written very fast, and sent immediately to the press; and that it seemed to be for his advantage not to have time for much revisal.

"He would alter," says Pope, "any thing to please his friends, before publication; but would not retouch his pieces afterwards: and I believe not one word in Cato, to which I made an objection, was suffered to stand."

The last line of Cato is Pope's, having been originally written

> And, oh! 'twas this that ended Cato's life.

Pope might have made more objections to the six concluding lines. In the first couplet the words *from hence* are improper; and the second line is taken from Dryden's Virgil. Of the next couplet, the first verse being included in the second, is therefore useless; and in the third *Discord* is made to produce *Strife*.

Of the course of Addison's familiar day†, before his marriage, Pope has given a detail. He had in the house with him Budgell, and perhaps Philips. His chief companions were Steele, Budgell, Philips, Carey, Davenant, and colonel Brett. With one or other of these he always breakfasted. He studied all morning; then dined at a tavern, and went afterwards to Button's.

Button had been a servant in the countess of Warwick's family, who, under the patronage of Addison, kept a coffee-house on the south-side of Russel-street, about two doors from Covent-garden. Here it was that the wits of that time used to assemble. It is said, that when Addison had suffered any vexation from the countess, he withdrew the company from Button's house.

From the coffee-house he went again to a tavern, where he often sat late, and drank too much wine: In the bottle, discontent seeks for comfort, cowardice for courage, and bashfulness for confidence. It is not unlikely that Addison was first seduced to excess by the manumission which he obtained from the servile timidity of his sober hours. He that feels oppression from the presence of those to whom he knows himself superior, will desire to set loose

---

* Spence.   † Spence.

his powers of conversation; and who, that ever asked succour from Bacchus, was able to preserve himself from being enslaved by his auxiliary?

Among those friends it was that Addison displayed the elegance of his colloquial accomplishments, which may easily be supposed such as Pope represents them. The remark of Mandeville, who, when he had passed an evening in his company, declared that he was a parson in a tye-wig, can detract little from his character; he was always reserved to strangers, and was not incited to uncommon freedom by a character like that of Mandeville.

From any minute knowledge of his familiar manners, the intervention of sixty years has now debarred us. Steele once promised Congreve and the publick a complete description of his character; but the promises of authors are like the vows of lovers. Steele thought no more on his design, or thought on it with anxiety that at last disgusted him, and left his friend in the hands of Tickell.

One slight lineament of his character Swift has preserved. It was his practice when he found any man invincibly wrong, to flatter his opinions by acquiescence, and sink him yet deeper in absurdity. This artifice of mischief was admired by Stella; and Swift seems to approve her admiration.

His works will supply some information. It appears from his various pictures of the world, that, with all his bashfulness, he had conversed with many distinct classes of men, had surveyed their ways with very diligent observation, and marked with great acuteness the effects of different modes of life. He was a man in whose presence nothing reprehensible was out of danger; quick in discerning whatever was wrong or ridiculous, and not unwilling to expose it. *There are*, says Steele, *in his writings many oblique strokes upon some of the wittiest men of the age.* His delight was more to excite merriment than detestation, and he detects follies rather than crimes.

If any judgement be made, from his books, of his moral character, nothing will be found but purity and excellence. Knowledge of mankind indeed, less extensive than that of Addison, will shew, that to write, and to live, are very different. Many who praise virtue, do no more than praise it. Yet it is reasonable to believe that Addison's professions and practice were at no great variance, since, amidst that storm of faction in which most of his life was passed, though his station made him conspicuous, and his activity made him formidable, the character given him by his friends was never contradicted by his enemies: of those with whom interest or opinion united him, he had not only the esteem, but the kindness; and of others, whom the violence of opposition drove against him, though he might lose the love, he retained the reverence.

It is justly observed by Tickell, that he employed wit on the side of virtue and religion. He not only made the proper use of wit himself, but taught it to others; and from his time it has been generally subservient to the cause of reason and of truth. He has dissipated the prejudice that had long connected gaiety with vice, and easiness of manners with laxity of principles. He has restored virtue to its dignity, and taught innocence not to be ashamed. This is an elevation of literary character, *above all Greek, above all Roman fame*. No greater felicity can genius attain than that of having purified intellectual pleasure, separated mirth from indecency, and wit from licentiousness; of having taught a succession of writers to bring elegance and gaiety to the aid of goodness; and, if I may use expressions yet more awful, of having *turned many to righteousness*.

ADDISON, in his life, and for some time afterwards, was considered by the greater part of readers as supremely excelling both in poetry and criticism. Part of his reputation may be probably ascribed to the advancement of his fortune: when, as Swift observes, he became a statesman, and saw poets waiting at his levee, it is no wonder that praise was accumulated upon him. Much likewise may be more honourably ascribed to his personal character: he who, if he had claimed it, might have obtained the diadem, was not likely to be denied the laurel.

But time quickly puts an end to artificial and accidental fame; and Addison is to pass through futurity protected only by his genius. Every name which kindness or interest once raised too high, is in danger, lest the next age should, by the vengeance of criticism, sink it in the same proportion. A great writer has lately styled him *an indifferent poet, and a worse critick*.

His poetry is first to be considered; of which it must be confessed that it has not often those felicities of diction which give lustre to sentiments, or that vigour of sentiment that animates diction: there is little of ardour, vehemence, or transport; there is very rarely the awfulness of grandeur, and not very often the splendour of elegance. He thinks justly; but he thinks faintly. This is his general character; to which, doubtless, many single passages will furnish exceptions.

Yet, if he seldom reaches supreme excellence, he rarely sinks into dulness, and is still more rarely entangled in absurdity. He did not trust his powers enough to be negligent. There is in most of his compositions a calmness and equability, deliberate and cautious, sometimes with little that delights, but seldom with any thing that offends.

Of this kind seem to be his poems to Dryden, to Somers, and to the King. His ode on St. Cecilia has been imitated by Pope, and has something in it of Dryden's vigour. Of his Account of the English Poets, he used to speak as a *poor thing**; but it is not worse than his usual strain. He has said, not very judiciously, in his character of Waller:

> Thy verse could shew ev'n Cromwell's innocence,
> And compliment the storms that bore him hence.
> O! had thy Muse not come an age too soon,
> But seen great Nassau on the British throne,
> How had his triumph glitter'd in thy page!—

* Spence.

What is this but to say that he who could compliment Cromwell had been the proper poet for king William? Addison however never printed the piece.

The Letter from Italy has been always praised, but has never been praised beyond its merit. It is more correct, with less appearance of labour, and more elegant, with less ambition of ornament, than any other of his poems. There is however one broken metaphor, of which notice may properly be taken:

> Fir'd with that name—
> I bridle in my struggling Muse with pain,
> That longs to launch into a nobler strain.

To *bridle a goddess* is no very delicate idea; but why must she be *bridled?* because she *longs to launch*; an act which was never hindered by a *bridle:* and whither will she *launch?* into a *nobler strain.* She is in the first line a *horse*, in the second a *boat*; and the care of the poet is to keep his *horse* or his *boat* from *singing.*

The next composition is the far-famed Campaign, which Dr. Warton has termed a *Gazette in Rhyme*, with harshness not often used by the good-nature of his criticism. Before a censure so severe is admitted, let us consider that War is a frequent subject of Poetry, and then enquire who has described it with more justness and force. Many of our own writers tried their powers upon this year of victory, yet Addison's is confessedly the best performance; his poem is the work of a man not blinded by the dust of learning: his images are not borrowed merely from books. The superiority which he confers upon his hero is not personal prowess, and *mighty bone*, but deliberate intrepidity, a calm command of his passions, and the power of consulting his own mind in the midst of danger. The rejection and contempt of fiction is rational and manly.

It may be observed that the last line is imitated by Pope;

> Marlb'rough's exploits appear divinely bright—
> Rais'd of themselves, their genuine charms they boast,
> And those that paint them truest, praise them most.

This Pope had in his thoughts; but, not knowing how to use what was not his own, he spoiled the thought when he had borrowed it:

> The well-sung woes shall soothe my ghost;
> He best can paint them who shall feel them most.

Martial exploits may be *painted*; perhaps *woes* may be *painted*; but they are surely not *painted* by being *well-sung*: it is not easy to paint in song, or to sing in colours.

No passage in the Campaign has been more often mentioned than the simile of the Angel, which is said in the Tatler to be *one of the noblest thoughts that ever entered into the heart of man*, and is therefore worthy of attentive consideration. Let it be first enquired whether it be a simile. A poetical simile is the discovery of likeness between two actions, in their general nature dissimilar, or of causes terminating by different operations in some resemblance of effect. But the mention of another like consequence from a like cause, or of a like performance by a like agency, is not a simile, but an exemplification. It is not a simile to say that the Thames waters fields, as the Po waters fields; or that as Hecla vomits flames in Iceland, so Ætna vomits flames in Sicily. When Horace says of Pindar, that he pours his violence and rapidity of verse, as a river swoln with rain rushes from the mountain; or of himself, that his genius wanders in quest of poetical decorations, as the bee wanders to collect honey; he, in either case, produces a simile; the mind is impressed with the resemblance of things generally unlike, as unlike as intellect and body. But if Pindar had been described as writing with the copiousness and grandeur of Homer, or Horace had told that he reviewed and finished his own poetry with the same care as Isocrates polished his orations, instead of similitude he would have exhibited almost identity; he would have given the same portraits with different names. In the poem now examined, when the English are represented as gaining a fortified pass, by repetition of attack and perseverance of resolution; their obstinacy of courage, and vigour of onset, is well illustrated by the sea that breaks, with incessant battery, the dikes of Holland. This is a simile: but when Addison, having celebrated the beauty of Marlborough's person, tells us that *Achilles thus was formed with every grace*, here is no simile, but a mere exemplification. A simile may be compared to lines converging at a point, and is more excellent as the lines approach from greater distance: an exemplification may be considered as two parallel lines which run on together without approximation, never far separated, and never joined.

Marlborough is so like the angel in the poem, that the action of both is almost the same, and performed by both in the same manner. Marlborough *teaches the battle to rage*; the angel *directs the storm*: Marlborough is *unmoved in peaceful thought*; the angel is *calm and serene*: Marlborough stands *unmoved amidst the shock of hosts*; the angel rides *calm in the whirlwind*. The lines on Marlborough are just and noble; but the simile gives almost the same images a second time.

But perhaps this thought, though hardly a simile, was remote from vulgar conceptions, and required great labour of research, or dexterity of application. Of this, Dr. Madden, a name which Ireland ought to honour, once gave me his opinion. *If I had set*, said he, *ten school-boys to write on the battle of* Blenheim, *and eight had brought me the Angel, I should not have been surprised*.

The opera of Rosamond, though it is seldom mentioned, is one of the first of Addison's compositions. The subject is well-chosen, the fiction is pleasing, and the praise of Marlborough, for which the scene gives an opportunity, is, what perhaps every human excellence must be, the product of good-luck improved by genius. The thoughts are sometimes great, and sometimes tender; the versification is easy and gay. There is doubtless some advantage in the shortness of the lines, which there is little temptation to load with expletive epithets. The dialogue seems commonly better than the songs. The two comick characters of Sir Trusty and Grideline, though of no great value, are yet such as the poet intended. Sir Trusty's account of the death of Rosamond is, I think, too grossly absurd. The whole drama is airy and elegant; engaging in its process, and pleasing in its conclusion. If Addison had cultivated the lighter parts of poetry, he would probably have excelled.

The tragedy of Cato, which, contrary to the rule observed in selecting the works of other poets, has by the weight of its character forced its way into the late collection, is unquestionably the noblest production of Addison's genius. Of a work so much read, it is difficult to say any thing new. About things on which the public thinks long, it commonly attains to think right; and of Cato it has been not unjustly determined, that it is rather a poem in dialogue than a drama, rather a succession of just sentiments in elegant language, than a representation of natural affections, or of any state probable or possible in human life. Nothing here *excites or assuages emotion*; here is *no magical power of raising phantastick terror or wild anxiety*. The events are expected without solicitude, and are remembered without joy or sorrow. Of the agents we have no care: we consider not what they are doing, or what they are suffering; we wish only to know what they have to say. Cato is a being above our solicitude; a man of whom the gods take care, and whom we leave to their care with heedless confidence. To the rest, neither gods nor men can have much attention; for there is not one amongst them that strongly attracts either affection or esteem. But they are made the vehicles of such sentiments and such expression, that there is scarcely a scene in the play which the reader does not wish to impress upon his memory.

When Cato was shewn to Pope*, he advised the author to print it, without any theatrical exhibition; supposing that it would be read more favourably than heard. Addison declared himself of the same opinion; but urged the importunity of his friends for its appearance on the stage. The emulation of parties made it successful beyond expectation, and its success has introduced or confirmed among us the use of dialogue too declamatory, of unaffecting elegance, and chill philosophy.

The universality of applause, however it might quell the censure of common mortals, had no other effect than to harden Dennis in fixed dislike; but his dislike was not merely capricious. He found and shewed many faults: he shewed them indeed with anger, but he found them with acuteness, such as ought to rescue his criticism from oblivion; though, at last, it will have no other life than it derives from the work which it endeavours to oppress.

Why he pays no regard to the opinion of the audience, he gives his reason, by remarking, that

"A deference is to be paid to a general applause, when it appears that that applause is natural and spontaneous; but that little regard is to be had to it, when it is affected and artificial. Of all the tragedies which in his memory have had vast and violent runs, not one has been excellent, few have been tolerable, most have been scandalous. When a poet writes a tragedy, who knows he has judgement, and who feels he has genius, that poet presumes upon his own merit, and scorns to make a cabal. That people come coolly to the representation of such a tragedy, without any violent expectation, or delusive imagination, or invincible prepossession; that such an audience is liable to receive the impressions which the poem shall naturally make in them, and to judge by their own reason, and their own judgements, and that reason and judgement are calm and serene, not formed by nature to make proselytes, and to controul and lord it over the imaginations of others. But that when an author writes a tragedy, who knows he has neither genius nor judgement, he has recourse to the making a party, and he endeavours to make up in industry what is wanting in talent, and to supply by poetical craft the absence of poetical art: that such an author is humbly contented to raise men's passions by a plot without doors, since he despairs of doing it by that which he brings upon the stage. That party and passion, and prepossession, are clamorous and tumultuous things, and so much the more clamorous and tumultuous by how much the more erroneous: that they domineer and tyrannize over the imaginations of persons who want judgement, and sometimes too of those who have it; and, like a fierce outrageous torrent, bear down all opposition before them."

He then condemns the neglect of poetical justice; which is always one of his favourite principles.

"'Tis certainly the duty of every tragick poet, by the exact distribution of poetical justice, to imitate the Divine Dispensation, and to inculcate a particular Providence. 'Tis true, indeed, upon the stage of the world, the wicked sometimes prosper, and the guiltless suffer. But that is permitted by the Governor of the world, to shew, from the attribute of his infinite justice, that there is a compensation in futurity, to prove the immortality of the human soul, and the certainty of future rewards and punishments. But the poetical persons in tragedy exist no longer than the reading, or the representation; the whole extent of their entity is circumscribed by those; and therefore, during that reading or representation, according to their merits or demerits, they must be punished or rewarded. If this is not done, there is no impartial distribution of poetical justice, no instructive lecture of a particular Providence, and no imitation of the Divine Dispensation. And yet the author of this tragedy does not only run counter to this, in the fate of his principal character;

but every where, throughout it, makes virtue suffer, and vice triumph: for not only Cato is vanquished by Cæsar, but the treachery and perfidiousness of Syphax prevails over the honest simplicity and the credulity of Juba; and the sly subtlety and dissimulation of Portius over the generous frankness and open-heartedness of Marcus."

Whatever pleasure there may be in seeing crimes punished and virtue rewarded, yet, since wickedness often prospers in real life, the poet is certainly at liberty to give it prosperity on the stage. For if poetry has an imitation of reality, how are its laws broken by exhibiting the world in its true form? The stage may sometimes gratify our wishes; but, if it be truly the *mirror of life*, it ought to shew us sometimes what we are to expect.

Dennis objects to the characters that they are not natural, or reasonable; but as heroes and heroines are not beings that are seen every day, it is hard to find upon what principles their conduct shall be tried. It is, however, not useless to consider what he says of the manner in which Cato receives the account of his son's death.

"Nor is the grief of Cato, in the fourth act, one jot more in nature than that of his son and Lucia in the third. Cato receives the news of his son's death not only with dry eyes, but with a sort of satisfaction; and in the same page sheds tears for the calamity of his country, and does the same thing in the next page upon the bare apprehension of the danger of his friends. Now, since the love of one's country is the love of one's countrymen, as I have shewn upon another occasion, I desire to ask these questions: Of all our countrymen, which do we love most, those whom we know, or those whom we know not? And of those whom we know, which do we cherish most, our friends or our enemies? And of our friends, which are the dearest to us? those who are related to us, or those who are not? And of all our relations, for which have we most tenderness, for those who are near to us, or for those who are remote? And of our near relations, which are the nearest, and consequently the dearest to us, our offspring or others? Our offspring, most certainly; as nature, or in other words Providence, has wisely contrived for the preservation of mankind. Now, does it not follow, from what has been said, that for a man to receive the news of his son's death with dry eyes, and to weep at the same time for the calamities of his country, is a wretched affectation, and a miserable inconsistency? Is not that, in plain English, to receive with dry eyes the news of the deaths of those for whose sake our country is a name so dear to us, and at the same time to shed tears for those for whose sakes our country is not a name so dear to us?"

But this formidable assailant is least resistible when he attacks the probability of the action, and the reasonableness of the plan. Every critical reader must remark, that Addison has, with a scrupulosity almost unexampled on the English stage, confined himself in time to a single day, and in place to rigorous unity. The scene never changes, and the whole action of the play passes in the great hall of

Cato's house at Utica. Much therefore is done in the hall, for which any other place had been more fit; and this impropriety affords Dennis many hints of merriment, and opportunities of triumph. The passage is long; but as such disquisitions are not common, and the objections are skilfully formed and vigorously urged, those who delight in critical controversy will not think it tedious.

"Upon the departure of Portius, Sempronius makes but one soliloquy, and immediately in comes Syphax, and then the two politicians are at it immediately. They lay their heads together, with their snuffboxes in their hands, as Mr. Bayes has it, and league it away. But, in the midst of that wise scene, Syphax seems to give a seasonable caution to Sempronius:

> *Syph.* But is it true, Sempronius, that your senate
> Is call'd together? Gods! thou must be cautious,
> Cato has piercing eyes.

There is a great deal of caution shewn indeed, in meeting in a governor's own hall to carry on their plot against him. Whatever opinion they have of his eyes, I suppose they had none of his ears, or they would never have talked at this foolish rate so near:

> Gods! thou must be cautious.

Oh! yes, very cautious: for if Cato should overhear you, and turn you off for politicians, Cæsar would never take you; no, Cæsar would never take you.

"When Cato, Act II. turns the senators out of the hall, upon pretence of acquainting Juba with the result of their debates, he appears to me to do a thing which is neither reasonable nor civil. Juba might certainly have better been made acquainted with the result of that debate in some private apartment of the palace. But the poet was driven upon this absurdity to make way for another; and that is, to give Juba an opportunity to demand Marcia of her father. But the quarrel and rage of Juba and Syphax, in the same Act, the invectives of Syphax against the Romans and Cato; the advice that he gives Juba, in her father's hall, to bear away Marcia by force; and his brutal and clamorous rage upon his refusal, and at a time when Cato was scarce out of sight, and perhaps not out of hearing; at least, some of his guards or domesticks must necessarily be supposed to be within hearing; is a thing that is so far from being probable, that it is hardly possible.

"Sempronius, in the second Act, comes back once more in the same morning to the governor's hall, to carry on the conspiracy with Syphax against the governor, his country, and his family; which is so stupid, that it is below the wisdom of the O—'s, the Mac's, and the Teague's; even Eustace Commins himself would never have gone to Justice-hall, to have conspired again the government. If officers at Portsmouth should lay their heads together, in order to the carrying off J—G—'s niece or daughter, would they meet in J—G—'s hall, to carry on that conspiracy? There would be no necessity for their meeting there, at least till they came to the execution of their plot, because there would be other places to meet in. There would be no probability that they should meet there, because there would be places more private and more commodious. Now there ought to be nothing in a tragical action but what is necessary or probable.

"But treason is not the only thing that is carried on in this hall: that and love, and philosophy, take their turns in it, without any manner of necessity or probability occasioned by the action, as duly and as regularly, without interrupting one another, as if there were a triple league between them, and a mutual agreement that each should give place to and make way for the other, in a due and orderly succession.

"We come now to the third Act. Sempronius, in this Act, comes into the governor's hall, with the leaders of the mutiny: but as soon as Cato is gone, Sempronius, who but just before had acted like an unparalleled knave, discovers himself, like an egregious fool, to be an accomplice in the conspiracy.

> *Semp.* Know, villains, when such paltry slaves presume
> To mix in treason, if the plot succeeds,
> They're thrown neglected by: but if it fails,
> They're sure to die like dogs, as you shall do.
> Here, take these factious monsters, drag them forth
> To sudden death.—

'Tis true, indeed, the second leader says, there are none there but friends: but is that possible at such a juncture? Can a parcel of rogues attempt to assassinate the governor of a town of war, in his own house, in mid-day, and after they are discovered and defeated? Can there be none near them but friends? Is it not plain from these words of Sempronius,

> Here, take these factious monsters, drag them forth
> To sudden death—

and from the entrance of the guards upon the word of command, that those guards were within ear-shot? Behold Sempronius then palpably discovered. How comes it to pass, then, that, instead of being hanged up with the rest, he remains secure in the governor's hall, and there carries on his conspiracy against the government, the third time in the same day, with his old comrade Syphax? who enters at the same time that the guards are carrying away the leaders, big with the news of the defeat of Sempronius; though where he had his intelligence so soon is difficult to imagine. And now the reader may expect a very extraordinary scene: there is not abundance of spirit indeed, nor a great deal of passion, but there is wisdom more than enough to supply all defects.

> *Syph.* Our first design, my friend, has prov'd abortive;
> Still there remains an after-game to play:
> My troops are mounted, their Numidian steeds
> Snuff up the winds, and long to scour the desart:
> Let but Sempronius lead us in our flight,
> We'll force the gate, where Marcus keeps his guard,
> And hew down all that would oppose our passage;
> A day will bring us into Cæsar's camp.
>   *Semp.* Confusion! I have fail'd of half my purpose;
> Marcia, the charming Marcia's left behind.   10

Well! but though he tells us the half-purpose that he has fail'd of, he does not tell us the half that he has carried. But what does he mean by

> Marcia, the charming Marcia's left behind?

He is now in her own house; and we have neither seen her nor heard of her any where else since the play began. But now let us hear Syphax:

> What hinders then, but that thou find her out,
> And hurry her away by manly force?

But what does old Syphax mean by finding her out? They talk as if she were as hard to be found as a hare in a frosty morning.

> *Semp.* But how to gain admission?

Oh! she is found out then, it seems.

> But how to gain admission? for access
> Is giv'n to none, but Juba and her brothers.

But, raillery apart, why access to Juba? For he was owned and received as a lover neither by the father nor by the daughter. Well! but let that pass. Syphax puts Sempronius out of pain immediately; and, being a Numidian, abounding in wiles, supplies him with a stratagem for admission, that, I believe, is a non-pareille:

> *Syph.* Thou shalt have Juba's dress, and Juba's guards;
> The doors will open, when Numidia's prince
> Seems to appear before them.

"Sempronius is, it seems, to pass for Juba in full day at Cato's house, where they were both so very well known, by having Juba's dress and his guards: as if one of the marshals of France could pass for the duke of Bavaria, at noon-day, at Versailles, by having his dress and liveries. But how does Syphax pretend to help Sempronius to young Juba's dress? Does he serve him in a double capacity, as general and master of his wardrobe? But why Juba's guards? For the devil of any guards has Juba appeared with yet. Well! though this is a mighty politick invention, yet, methinks, they might have done without it: for, since the advice that Syphax gave to Sempronius was,

> To hurry her away by manly force,

in my opinion, the shortest and likeliest way of coming at the lady was by demolishing, instead of putting on an impertinent disguise to circumvent two or three slaves. But Sempronius, it seems, is of another opinion. He extols to the skies the invention of old Syphax:

> *Sempr.* Heavens! what a thought was there!

"Now I appeal to the reader, if I have not been as good as my word. Did I not tell him, that I would lay before him a very wise scene?

"But now let us lay before the reader that part of the scenery of the Fourth Act, which may shew the absurdities which the author has run into, through the indiscreet observance of the Unity of Place. I do not remember that Aristotle has said any thing expressly concerning the Unity of Place. 'Tis true, implicitly he has said enough in the rules which he has laid down for the Chorus. For, by making the Chorus an essential part of Tragedy, and by bringing it on the stage immediately after the opening of the scene, and retaining it there till the very catastrophe, he has so determined and fixed the place of action, that it was impossible for an author on the Grecian stage to break through that unity. I am of opinion, that if a modern tragic poet can preserve the unity of place, without destroying the probability of the incidents, 'tis always best for him to do it; because, by the preservation of that unity, as we have taken notice above, he adds grace, and cleanness, and comeliness, to the representation. But since there are no express rules about it, and we are under no compulsion to keep it, since we have no Chorus as the Grecian poet had; if it cannot be preserved, without rendering the greater part of the incidents unreasonable and absurd, and perhaps sometimes monstrous, 'tis certainly better to break it.

"Now comes bully Sempronius, comically accoutred and equipped with his Numidian dress and his Numidian guards. Let the reader attend to him with all his ears; for the words of the wise are precious:

> *Sempr.* The deer is lodg'd, I've track'd her to her covert.

"Now I would fain know why this deer is said to be lodged, since we have not heard one word, since the play began, of her being at all out of harbour:

and if we consider the discourse with which she and Lucia begin the Act, we have reason to believe that they had hardly been talking of such matters in the street. However, to pleasure Sempronius, let us suppose, for once, that the deer is lodged:

> The deer is lodg'd, I've track'd her to her covert.

"If he had seen her in the open field, what occasion had he to track her, when he had so many Numidian dogs at his heels, which, with one halloo, he might have set upon her haunches? If he did not see her in the open field, how could he possibly track her? If he had seen her in the street, why did he not set upon her in the street, since through the street she must be carried at last? Now here, instead of having his thoughts upon his business, and upon the present danger; instead of meditating and contriving how he shall pass with his mistress through the southern gate, where her brother Marcus is upon the guard, and where she would certainly prove an impediment to him, which is the Roman word for the *baggage*; instead of doing this, Sempronius is entertaining himself with whimsies:

> *Sempr.* How will the young Numidian rave to see
> His mistress lost! If aught could glad my soul,
> Beyond th' enjoyment of so bright a prize,
> 'Twould be to torture that young gay Barbarian.
> But hark! what noise? Death to my hopes, 'tis he,
> 'Tis Juba's self! There is but one way left!
> He must be murder'd, and a passage cut
> Through those his guards.

"Pray, what are *those his guards?* I thought at present, that Juba's guards had been Sempronius's tools, and had been dangling after his heels.

"But now let us sum up all these absurdities together. Sempronius goes at noon-day, in Juba's clothes, and with Juba's guards, to Cato's palace, in order to pass for Juba, in a place where they were both so very well known: he meets Juba there, and resolves to murder him with his own guards. Upon the guards appearing a little bashful, he threatens them:

> Hah! Dastards, do you tremble!
> Or act like men, or by yon azure heav'n!

But the guards still remaining restive, Sempronius himself attacks Juba, while each of the guards is representing Mr. Spectator's sign of the Gaper, awed, it seems, and terrified by Sempronius's threats. Juba kills Sempronius, and takes his own army prisoners, and carries them in triumph away to Cato.

Now I would fain know, if any part of Mr. Bayes's tragedy is so full of absurdity as this?

"Upon hearing the clash of swords, Lucia and Marcia come in. The question is, why no men came in upon hearing the noise of swords in the governor's hall? Where was the governor himself? Where were his guards? Where were his servants? Such an attempt as this, so near the person of a governor of a place of war, was enough to alarm the whole garrison: and yet, for almost half an hour after Sempronius was killed, we find none of those appear, who were the likeliest in the world to be alarmed; and the noise of swords is made to draw only two poor women thither, who were most certain to run away from it. Upon Lucia and Marcia's coming in, Lucia appears in all the symptoms of an hysterical gentlewoman:

> *Luc.* Sure 'twas the clash of swords! my troubled heart
> Is so cast down, and sunk amidst its sorrows,
> It throbs with fear, and akes at every sound!

And immediately her old whimsy returns upon her:

> O Marcia, should thy brothers, for my sake—
> I die away with horror at the thought.

She fancies that there can be no cutting-of-throats, but it must be for her. If this is tragical, I would fain know what is comical. Well! upon this they spy the body of Sempronius; and Marcia, deluded by the habit, it seems, takes him for Juba; for, says she,

> The face is muffled up within the garment.

Now how a man could fight, and fall with his face muffled up in his garment, is, I think, a little hard to conceive! Besides, Juba, before he killed him, knew him to be Sempronius. It was not by his garment that he knew this; it was by his face then: his face therefore was not muffled. Upon seeing this man with the muffled face, Marcia falls a-raving; and, owning her passion for the supposed defunct, begins to make his funeral oration. Upon which Juba enters listening, I suppose on tip-toe: for I cannot imagine how any one can enter listening, in any other posture. I would fain know how it came to pass, that during all this time he had sent nobody, no not so much as a candle-snuffer, to take away the dead body of Sempronius. Well! but let us regard him listening. Having left his apprehension behind him, he, at first, applies what Marcia says to Sempronius. But finding at last, with much ado, that he himself is the happy man, he quits his eves-dropping, and discovers himself just time enough to prevent his being cuckolded by a dead man, of whom the moment before he had appeared so jealous; and greedily intercepts the bliss, which was fondly designed for one who could not be the better for it. But here I must ask a question: how comes Juba to listen here, who had not listened before throughout the play? Or, how comes he to be the only person of this tragedy who listens, when love and treason were so often talked in so publick a place as a hall? I am afraid the author was driven upon all these absurdities only to introduce this miserable mistake of Marcia; which, after all, is much below the dignity of tragedy, as any thing is which is the effect or result of trick.

"But let us come to the scenery of the Fifth Act. Cato appears first upon the scene, sitting in a thoughtful posture; in his hand Plato's treatise on the Immortality of the Soul, a drawn sword on the table by him. Now let us consider the place in which this sight is presented to us. The place, forsooth, is a long hall. Let us suppose, that any one should place himself in this posture, in the midst of one of our halls in London; that he should appear *solus*, in a sullen posture, a drawn sword on the table by him; in his hand Plato's treatise on the Immortality of the Soul, translated lately by Bernard Lintot: I desire the reader to consider, whether such a person as this would pass with them who beheld him, for a great patriot, a great philosopher, or a general, or for some whimsical person who fancied himself all these; and whether the people, who belonged to the family, would think that such a person had a design upon their midrifs or his own?

"In short, that Cato should sit long enough, in the aforesaid posture, in the midst of this large hall, to read over Plato's treatise on the Immortality of the Soul, which is a lecture of two long hours; that he should propose to himself to be private there upon that occasion; that he should be angry with his son for intruding there; then, that he should leave this hall upon the pretence of sleep, give himself the mortal wound in his bedchamber, and then be brought back into that hall to expire, purely to shew his good-breeding, and save his friends the trouble of coming up to his bedchamber; all this appears to me to be improbable, incredible, impossible."

Such is the censure of Dennis. There is, as Dryden expresses it, perhaps *too much horse-play in his raillery*; but if his jests are coarse, his arguments are strong. Yet as we love better to be pleased than to be taught, Cato is read, and the critick is neglected.

Flushed with consciousness of these detections of absurdity in the conduct, he afterwards attacked the sentiments of Cato; but he then amused himself with petty cavils, and minute objections.

Of Addison's smaller poems, no particular mention is necessary; they have little that can employ or require a critick. The parallel of the Princes and Gods, in his verses to Kneller, is often happy, but is too well known to be quoted.

His translations, so far as I have compared them, want the exactness of a scholar. That he understood his authors cannot be doubted; but his versions will not teach others to understand them, being too licentiously paraphrastical.

They are however, for the most part, smooth and easy; and, what is the first excellence of a translator, such as may be read with pleasure by those who do not know the originals.

His poetry is polished and pure; the product of a mind too judicious to commit faults, but not sufficiently vigorous to attain excellence. He has sometimes a striking line, or a shining paragraph; but in the whole he is warm rather than fervid, and shews more dexterity than strength. He was however one of our earliest examples of correctness.

The versification which he had learned from Dryden, he debased rather than refined. His rhymes are often dissonant; in his Georgick he admits broken lines. He uses both triplets and alexandrines, but triplets more frequently in his translations than his other works. The mere structure of verses seems never to have engaged much of his care. But his lines are very smooth in Rosamond, and too smooth in Cato.

Addison is now to be considered as a critick; a name which the present generation is scarcely willing to allow him. His criticism is condemned as tentative or experimental, rather than scientifick, and he is considered as deciding by taste rather than by principles.

It is not uncommon for those who have grown wise by the labour of others, to add a little of their own, and overlook their masters. Addison is now despised by some who perhaps would never have seen his defects, but by the lights which he afforded them. That he always wrote as he would think it necessary to write now, cannot be affirmed; his instructions were such as the character of his readers made proper. That general knowledge which now circulates in common talk, was in his time rarely to be found. Men not professing learning were not ashamed of ignorance; and in the female world, any acquaintance with books was distinguished only to be censured. His purpose was to infuse literary curiosity, by gentle and unsuspected conveyance, into the gay, the idle, and the wealthy; he therefore presented knowledge in the most alluring form, not lofty and austere, but accessible and familiar. When he shewed them their defects, he shewed them likewise that they might be easily supplied. His attempt succeeded; enquiry was awakened, and comprehension expanded. An emulation of intellectual elegance was excited, and from his time to our own, life has been gradually exalted, and conversation purified and enlarged.

Dryden had, not many years before, scattered criticism over his Prefaces with very little parsimony; but, though he sometimes condescended to be somewhat familiar, his manner was in general too scholastick for those who had yet their rudiments to learn, and found it not easy to understand their master. His observations were framed rather for those that were learning to write, than for those that read only to talk.

An instructor like Addison was now wanting, whose remarks being superficial, might be easily understood, and being just, might prepare the mind for more attainments. Had he presented *Paradise Lost* to the publick with all the pomp of system and severity of science, the criticism would perhaps have been admired, and the poem still have been neglected; but by the blandishments of gentleness and facility, he has made Milton an universal favourite, with whom readers of every class think it necessary to be pleased.

He descended now and then to lower disquisitions; and by a serious display of the beauties of *Chevy Chase*, exposed himself to the ridicule of Wagstaff, who bestowed a like pompous character on *Tom Thumb*; and to the contempt of Dennis, who, considering the fundamental position of his criticism, that *Chevy Chase* pleases, and ought to please, because it is natural, observes, "that there is a way of deviating from nature, by bombast or tumour, which soars above nature, and enlarges images beyond their real bulk; by affectation, which forsakes nature in quest of something unsuitable; and by imbecillity, which degrades nature by faintness and diminution, by obscuring its appearances, and weakening its effects." In *Chevy Chase* there is not much of either bombast or affectation; but there is chill and lifeless imbecillity. The story cannot possibly be told in a manner that shall make less impression on the mind.

Before the profound observers of the present race repose too securely on the consciousness of their superiority to Addison, let them consider his Remarks on Ovid, in which may be found specimens of criticism sufficiently subtle and refined; let them peruse likewise his Essays on *Wit*, and on the *Pleasures of Imagination*, in which he founds art on the base of nature, and draws the principles of invention from dispositions inherent in the mind of man, with skill and elegance, such as his contemners will not easily attain.

As a describer of life and manners, he must be allowed to stand perhaps the first of the first rank. His humour, which, as Steele observes, is peculiar to himself, is so happily diffused as to give the grace of novelty to domestick scenes and daily occurrences. He never *outsteps the modesty of nature*, nor raises merriment or wonder by the violation of truth. His figures neither divert by distortion, nor amaze by aggravation. He copies life with so much fidelity, that he can be hardly said to invent; yet his exhibitions have an air so much original, that it is difficult to suppose them not merely the product of imagination.

As a teacher of wisdom, he may be confidently followed. His religion has nothing in it enthusiastick or superstitious: he appears neither weakly credulous nor wantonly sceptical; his morality is neither dangerously lax, nor impracticably rigid. All the enchantment of fancy, and all the cogency of argument, are employed to recommend to the reader his real interest, the care of pleasing the Author of his being. Truth is shewn sometimes as the phantom of a vision, sometimes appears half-veiled in an allegory; sometimes attracts regard in the robes of fancy, and sometimes steps forth in the confidence of reason. She wears a thousand dresses, and in all is pleasing.

Mille habet ornatus, mille decenter habet.

His prose is the model of the middle style; on grave subjects not formal, on light occasions not grovelling; pure without scrupulosity, and exact without apparent elaboration; always equable, and always easy, without glowing words or pointed sentences. Addison never deviates from his track to snatch a grace; he seeks no ambitious ornaments, and tries no hazardous innovations. His page is always luminous, but never blazes in unexpected splendour.

It was apparently his principal endeavour to avoid all harshness and severity of diction; he is therefore sometimes verbose in his transitions and connections, and sometimes descends too much to the language of conversation; yet if his language had been less idiomatical, it might have lost somewhat of its genuine Anglicism. What he attempted, he performed; he is never feeble; and he did not wish to be energetick; he is never rapid, and he never stagnates. His sentences have neither studied amplitude, nor affected brevity: his periods, though not diligently rounded, are voluble and easy. Whoever wishes to attain an English style, familiar but not coarse, and elegant but not ostentatious, must give his days and nights to the volumes of Addison.

PRIOR

MATTHEW PRIOR is one of those that have burst out from an obscure original to great eminence. He was born July 21, 1664, according to some, at Winburne in Dorsetshire, of I know not what parents; others say that he was the son of a Joiner of London: he was perhaps willing enough to leave his birth unsettled*, in hope, like Don Quixote, that the historian of his actions might find him some illustrious alliance.

He is supposed to have fallen, by his father's death, into the hands of his uncle, a vintner near Charing-cross, who sent him for some time to Dr. Busby at Westminster; but, not intending to give him any education beyond that of the school, took him, when he was well advanced in literature, to his own house; where the earl of Dorset, celebrated for patronage of genius, found him by chance, as Burnet relates, reading Horace, and was so well pleased with his proficiency, that he undertook the care and cost of his academical education.

He entered his name in St. John's College at Cambridge in 1682, in his eighteenth year; and it may be reasonably supposed that he was distinguished

---

* The difficulty of settling Prior's birth-place is great. In the register of his College he is called, at his admission by the President, *Matthew Prior of Winburn in Middlesex*; by himself next day, *Matthew Prior of Dorsetshire*, in which county, not in Middlesex, *Winborn*, or *Wimborne*, as it stands in the *Villare*, is found. When he stood candidate for his fellowship, five years afterwards, he was registered again by himself as of *Middlesex*. The last record ought to be preferred, because it was made upon oath. It is observable, that, as a native of *Winborne*, he is stiled *Filius Georgii Prior, generosi*; not consistently with the common account of the meanness of his birth.

among his contemporaries. He became a Bachelor, as is usual, in four years; and two years afterwards wrote the poem on the *Deity*, which stands first in his volume.

It is the established practice of that College to send every year to the earl of Exeter some poems upon sacred subjects, in acknowledgement of a benefaction enjoyed by them from the bounty of his ancestor. On this occasion were those verses written, which, though nothing is said of their success, seem to have recommended him to some notice; for his praise of the countess's music, and his lines on the famous picture of Seneca, afford reason for imagining that he was more or less conversant with that family.

The same year he published the *City Mouse and Country Mouse*, to ridicule Dryden's *Hind and Panther*, in conjunction with Mr. Montague.

There is a story* of great pain suffered, and of tears shed, on this occasion, by Dryden, who thought it hard that *an old man should be so treated by those to whom he had always been civil*. By tales like these is the envy raised by superior abilities every day gratified: when they are attacked, every one hopes to see them humbled; what is hoped is readily believed, and what is believed is confidently told. Dryden had been more accustomed to hostilities, than that such enemies should break his quiet; and if we can suppose him vexed, it would be hard to deny him sense enough to conceal his uneasiness.

The *City Mouse and Country Mouse* procured its authors more solid advantages than the pleasure of fretting Dryden; for they were both speedily preferred. Montague, indeed, obtained the first notice, with some degree of discontent, as it seems, in Prior, who probably knew that his own part of the performance was the best. He had not, however, much reason to complain; for he came to London, and obtained such notice, that (in 1691) he was sent to the Congress at The Hague as secretary to the embassy. In this assembly of princes and nobles, to which Europe has perhaps scarcely seen any thing equal, was formed the grand alliance against Lewis; which at last did not produce effects proportionate to the magnificence of the transaction.

The conduct of Prior, in this splendid initiation into public business, was so pleasing to king William, that he made him one of the gentlemen of his bedchamber; and he is supposed to have passed some of the next years in the quiet cultivation of literature and poetry.

The death of Queen Mary (in 1695) produced a subject for all the writers: perhaps no funeral was ever so poetically attended. Dryden, indeed, as a man discountenanced and deprived, was silent; but scarcely any other maker of verses omitted to bring his tribute of tuneful sorrow. An emulation of elegy was universal. Maria's praise was not confined to the English language, but fills a great part of the *Musæ Anglicanæ*.

* Spence.

Prior, who was both a poet and a courtier, was too diligent to miss this opportunity of respect. He wrote a long ode, which was presented to the king, by whom it was not likely to be ever read.

In two years he was secretary to another embassy at the treaty of Ryswick (in 1697); and next year had the same office at the court of France, where he is said to have been considered with great distinction.

As he was one day surveying the apartments at Versailles, being shewn the Victories of Lewis, painted by Le Brun, and asked whether the king of England's palace had any such decorations; *The monuments of my Master's actions*, said he, *are to be seen everywhere but in his own house.* The pictures of Le Brun are not only in themselves sufficiently ostentatious, but were explained by inscriptions so arrogant, that Boileau and Racine thought it necessary to make them more simple.

He was in the following year at Loo with the king; from whom, after a long audience, he carried orders to England, and upon his arrival became under-secretary of state in the earl of Jersey's office; a post which he did not retain long, because Jersey was removed; but he was soon made commissioner of Trade.

This year (1700) produced one of his longest and most splendid compositions, the *Carmen Seculare*, in which he exhausts all his powers of celebration. I mean not to accuse him of flattery; he probably thought all that he writ, and retained as much veracity as can be properly exacted from a poet professedly encomiastic. King William supplied copious materials for either verse or prose. His whole life had been action, and none ever denied him the resplendent qualities of steady resolution and personal courage. He was really in Prior's mind what he represents him in his verses; he considered him as a hero, and was accustomed to say, that he praised others in compliance with the fashion, but that in celebrating king William he followed his inclination. To Prior gratitude would dictate praise, which reason would not refuse.

Among the advantages to arise from the future years of William's reign, he mentions *Societies for useful Arts*, and among them

> Some that with care true eloquence shall teach,
> And to just idioms fix our doubtful speech;
> That from our writers distant realms may know
> The thanks we to our monarch owe,
> And schools profess our tongue through every land,
> That has invok'd his aid, or bless'd his hand.

Tickell, in his *Prospect of Peace*, has the same hope of a new academy:

> In happy chains our daring language bound,
> Shall sport no more in arbitrary sound.

Whether the similitude of those passages which exhibit the same thought on the same occasion proceeded from accident or imitation, is not easy to determine. Tickell might have been impressed with his expectation by Swift's *Proposal for ascertaining the English Language*, then lately published.

In the parliament that met in 1701, he was chosen representative of East Grinstead. Perhaps it was about this time that he changed his party; for he voted for the impeachment of those lords who had persuaded the king to the Partition-treaty, a treaty in which he had himself been ministerially employed.

A great part of queen Anne's reign was a time of war, in which there was little employment for negotiators, and Prior had therefore leisure to make or to polish verses. When the battle of Blenheim called forth all the verse-men, Prior, among the rest, took care to shew his delight in the increasing honour of his country by an Epistle to Boileau.

He published, soon afterwards, a volume of poems, with the encomiastic character of his deceased patron the duke of Dorset: it began with the College Exercise, and ended with the *Nut-brown Maid*.

The battle of Ramillies soon afterwards (in 1706) excited him to another effort of poetry. On this occasion he had fewer or less formidable rivals; and it would be not easy to name any other composition produced by that event which is now remembered.

Every thing has its day. Through the reigns of William and Anne no prosperous event passed undignified by poetry. In the last war, when France was disgraced and overpowered in every quarter of the globe, when Spain, coming to her assistance, only shared her calamities, and the name of an Englishman was reverenced through Europe, no poet was heard amidst the general acclamation; the fame of our counsellors and heroes was intrusted to the Gazetteer.

The nation in time grew weary of the war, and the queen grew weary of her ministers. The war was burdensome, and the ministers were insolent. Harley and his friends began to hope that they might, by driving the Whigs from court and from power, gratify at once the queen and the people. There was now a call for writers, who might convey intelligence of past abuses, and shew the waste of public money, the unreasonable *Conduct of the Allies*, the avarice of generals, the tyranny of minions, and the general danger of approaching ruin.

For this purpose a paper called the *Examiner* was periodically published, written, as it happened, by any wit of the party, and sometimes as is said by Mrs. Manley. Some are owned by Swift; and one, in ridicule of Garth's verses to Godolphin upon the loss of his place, was written by Prior, and answered by Addison, who appears to have known the author either by conjecture or intelligence.

The Tories, who were now in power, were in haste to end the war; and Prior, being recalled (1710) to his former employment of making treaties, was sent

(July 1711) privately to Paris with propositions of peace. He was remembered at the French court; and, returning in about a month, brought with him the Abbé Gaultier, and M. Mesnager, a minister from France, invested with full powers.

This transaction not being avowed, Macky the master of the Dover packet-boat, either zealously or officiously, seized Prior and his associates at Canterbury. It is easily supposed that they were soon released.

The negotiation was begun at Prior's house, where the Queen's ministers met Mesnager (September 20, 1711), and entered privately upon the great business. The importance of Prior appears from the mention made of him by St. John in his Letter to the Queen.

"My Lord Treasurer moved, and all my Lords were of the same opinion, that Mr. Prior should be added to those who are empowered to sign; the reason for which is, because he, having personally treated with Monsieur de Torcy, is the best witness we can produce of the sense in which the general preliminary engagements are entered into: besides which, as he is the best versed in matters of trade of all your Majesty's servants who have been trusted in this secret, if you shall think fit to employ him in the future treaty of commerce, it will be of consequence that he has been a party concerned in concluding that convention, which must be the rule of this treaty."

The assembly of this important night was in some degree clandestine, the design of treating not being yet openly declared, and, when the Whigs returned to power, was aggravated to a charge of high treason; though, as Prior remarks in his imperfect answer to the Report of the *Committee of Secrecy*, no treaty ever was made without private interviews and preliminary discussions.

My business is not the history of the peace, but the life of Prior. The conferences began at Utrecht on the first of January (1711–12), and the English plenipotentiaries arrived on the fifteenth. The ministers of the different potentates conferred and conferred; but the peace advanced so slowly, that speedier methods were found necessary, and Bolingbroke was sent to Paris to adjust differences with less formality; Prior either accompanied him or followed him; and after his departure had the appointments and authority of an ambassador, though no public character.

By some mistake of the Queen's orders, the court of France had been disgusted; and Bolingbroke says in his Letter, "Dear Mat, hide the nakedness of thy country, and give the best turn thy fertile brain will furnish thee with to the blunders of thy countrymen, who are not much better politicians than the French are poets."

Soon after the duke of Shrewsbury went on a formal embassy to Paris. It is related by Boyer, that the intention was to have joined Prior in the same commission, but that Shrewsbury refused to be associated with a man so meanly born. Prior therefore continued to act without a title till the duke returned next year to England, and then he assumed the style and dignity of embassador.

But, while he continued in appearance a private man, he was treated with confidence by Lewis, who sent him with a letter to the Queen, written in favour of the elector of Bavaria. "I shall expect," says he, "with impatience, the return of Mr. Prior, whose conduct is very agreeable to me." And while the Duke of Shrewsbury was still at Paris, Bolingbroke wrote to Prior thus: "Monsieur de Torcy has a confidence in you; make use of it, once for all, upon this occasion, and convince him thoroughly, that we must give a different turn to our parliament and our people, according to their resolution at this crisis."

Prior's public dignity and splendour commenced in August 1713, and continued till the August following; but I am afraid that, according to the usual fate of greatness, it was attended with some perplexities and mortifications. He had not all that is customarily given to ambassadors: he hints to the Queen, in an imperfect poem, that he had no service of plate; and it appeared, by the debts which he contracted, that his remittances were not punctually made.

On the first of August 1714, ensued the downfall of the Tories and the degradation of Prior. He was recalled; but was not able to return, being detained by the debts which he had found it necessary to contract, and which were not discharged before March, though his old friend Montague was now at the head of the treasury.

He returned then as soon as he could, and was welcomed on the 25th of March by a warrant, but was, however, suffered to live in his own house, under the custody of the messenger, till he was examined before a committee of the Privy Council, of which Mr. Walpole was chairman, and lord Coningsby, Mr. Stanhope, and Mr. Lechmere, were the principal interrogators; who, in this examination, of which there is printed an account not unentertaining, behaved with the boisterousness of men elated by recent authority. They are represented as asking questions sometimes vague, sometimes insidious, and writing answers different from those which they received. Prior, however, seems to have been overpowered by their turbulence; for he confesses that he signed what, if he had ever come before a legal judicature, he should have contradicted or explained away. The oath was administered by Boscawen, a Middlesex justice, who at last was going to write his attestation on the wrong side of the paper.

They were very industrious to find some charge against Oxford, and asked Prior, with great earnestness, who was present when the preliminary articles were talked of or signed at his house? He told them, that either the earl of Oxford or the duke of Shrewsbury was absent, but he could not remember which; an answer which perplexed them, because it supplied no accusation against either. "Could any thing be more absurd," says he, "or more inhuman, than to propose to me a question, by the answering of which I might, according to them, prove myself a traitor? And notwithstanding their solemn promise, that nothing which I could say should hurt myself, I had no reason to trust them: for they violated that promise about five hours after. However, I owned I was there present. Whether this was wisely done or no, I leave to my friends to determine."

When he had signed the paper, he was told by Walpole, that the committee were not satisfied with his behaviour, nor could give such an account of it to the Commons as might merit favour; and that they now thought a stricter confinement necessary than to his own house. "Here" says he, "Boscawen played the moralist, and Coningsby the christian, but both very aukwardly." The messenger, in whose custody he was to be placed, was then called, and very decently asked by Coningsby, *if his house was secured by bars and bolts?* The messenger answered, *No*, with astonishment; at which Coningsby very angrily said, *Sir, you must secure this prisoner; it is for the safety of the nation: if he escape, you shall answer for it.*

They had already printed their report; and in this examination were endeavouring to find proofs.

He continued thus confined for some time; and Mr. Walpole (June 10, 1715) moved for an impeachment against him. What made him so acrimonious does not appear: he was by nature no thirster for blood. Prior was a week after committed to close custody, with orders that *no person should be admitted to see him without leave from the Speaker.*

When, two years after, an Act of Grace was passed, he was excepted, and continued still in custody, which he had made less tedious by writing his *Alma.* He was, however, soon after discharged.

He had now his liberty, but he had nothing else. Whatever the profit of his employments might have been, he had always spent it; and at the age of fifty-three was, with all his abilities, in danger of penury, having yet no solid revenue but from the fellowship of his college, which, when in his exaltation he was censured for retaining it, he said, he could live upon at last.

Being however generally known and esteemed, he was encouraged to add other poems to those which he had printed, and to publish them by subscription. The expedient succeeded by the industry of many friends, who circulated the proposals*, and the care of some, who, it is said, withheld the money from him, lest he should squander it. The price of the volume was two guineas; the whole collection was four thousand, to which lord Harley, the son of the earl of Oxford, to whom he had invariably adhered, added an equal sum for the purchase of Down-hall, which Prior was to enjoy during life, and Harley after his decease.

He had now, what wits and philosophers have often wished, the power of passing the day in contemplative tranquillity. But it seems that busy men seldom live long in a state of quiet. It is not unlikely that his health declined. He complains of deafness; *for*, says he, *I took little care of my ears while I was not sure if my head was my own.*

---

* Swift obtained *many* subscriptions for him in Ireland.

Of any occurrences in his remaining life I have found no account. In a letter to Swift, "I have," says he, "treated lady Harriot at Cambridge. A Fellow of a College treat! and spoke verses to her in a gown and cap! What, the plenipotentiary, so far concerned in the damned peace at Utrecht! the man that makes up half the volume of terse prose, that makes up the report of the committee, speaking verses! *Sic est, homo sum.*"

He died at *Wimpole*, a seat of the earl of Oxford, on the eighteenth of September 1721, and was buried in Westminster; where on a monument, for which, as the *last piece of human vanity*, he left five hundred pounds, is engraven this epitaph:

Sui Temporis Historiam meditanti,
Paulatim obrepens Febris
Operi simul & Vitæ filum abrupit,
Sept. 18. An. Dom. 1721. Ætat. 57.
H. S. E.
Vir Eximius
Serenissimis
Regi GULIELMO Reginæque MARIÆ
In Congressione Fœderatorum
Hagæ anno 1690 celebrata,
Deinde Magnæ Britanniæ Legatis
Tum iis,
Qui anno 1697 Pacem RYSWICKI confecerunt,
Tum iis,
Qui apud Gallos annis proximis Legationem obierunt;
Eodem etiam anno 1697 in Hibernia
SECRETARIUS;
Nec non in utroque Honorabili confessu
Eorum,
Qui anno 1700 ordinandis Commercii negotiis,
Quique anno 1711 dirigendis Portorii rebus,
Præsidebant,
COMMISSIONARIUS;
Postremo
Ab ANNA
Felicissimæ memoriæ Reginâ
Ad LUDOVICUM XIV. Galliæ Regem
Missus anno 1711
De Pace stabilienda,
(Pace etiamnum durante
Diuque ut boni jam omnes sperant duratura)
Cum summa potestate Legatus.

MATTHÆUS PRIOR Armiger;
Qui
Hos omnes, quibus cumulatus est, Titulos
Humanitatis, Ingenii, Eruditionis laude
Superavit;
Cui enim nascenti faciles arriserant Musæ.
Hunc Puerum Schola hic Regia perpolivit;
Juvenem in Collegio Sti. Johannis
Cantabrigia optimis Scientiis instruxit;
Virum denique auxit; & perfecit
Multa cum viris Principibus consuetudo;
Ita natus, ita institutus,
A Vatum Choro avelli nunquam potuit,
Sed solebat sæpe rerum Civilium gravitatem
Amœniorum Literarum Studiis condire:
Et cum omne adeo Poetices genus
Haud infeliciter tentaret,
Tum in Fabellis concinne lepideque texendis
Mirus Artifex
Neminem habuit parem.
Hæc liberalis animi oblectamenta;
Quam nullo Illi labore constiterint,
Facile ii perspexere, quibus usus est Amici;
Apud quos Urbanitatum & Leporum plenus
Cum ad rem, quæcunque forte inciderat,
Aptè variè copiosèque alluderet,
Interea nihil quæsitum, nihil vi expressum
Videbatur,
Sed omnia ultro effluere,
Et quasi jugi è fonte affatim exuberare,
Ita Suos tandem dubios reliquit,
Essetne in Scriptis, Poeta Elegantior,
An in Convictu, Comes Jucundior.

Of Prior, eminent as he was, both by his abilities and station, very few memorials have been left by his contemporaries; the account therefore must now be destitute of his private character and familiar practices. He lived at a time when the rage of party detected all which it was any man's interest to hide; and as little ill is heard of Prior, it is certain that not much was known. He was not afraid of provoking censure; for when he forsook the Whigs*,

* Spence.

under whose patronage he first entered the world, he became a Tory so ardent and determinate, that he did not willingly consort with men of different opinions. He was one of the sixteen Tories who met weekly, and agreed to address each other by the title of *Brother*; and seems to have adhered, not only by concurrence of political designs, but by peculiar affection, to the earl of Oxford and his family. With how much confidence he was trusted, has been already told.

He was however, in Pope's* opinion, fit only to make verses, and less qualified for business than Addison himself. This was surely said without consideration. Addison, exalted to a high place, was forced into degradation by the sense of his own incapacity; Prior, who was employed by men very capable of estimating his value, having been secretary to one embassy, had, when great abilities were again wanted, the same office another time; and was, after so much experience of his knowledge and dexterity, at last sent to transact a negotiation in the highest degree arduous and important; for which he was qualified, among other requisites, in the opinion of Bolingbroke, by his influence upon the French minister, and by skill in questions of commerce above other men.

Of his behaviour in the lighter parts of life, it is too late to get much intelligence. One of his answers to a boastful Frenchman has been related, and to an impertinent he made another equally proper. During his embassy, he sat at the opera by a man, who, in his rapture, accompanied with his own voice the principal singer. Prior fell to railing at the performer with all the terms of reproach that he could collect, till the Frenchman, ceasing from his song, began to expostulate with him for his harsh censure of a man who was confessedly the ornament of the stage. "I know all that," says the ambassador, "*mais il chante si haut, que je ne sçaurois vous entendre.*"

In a gay French company, where every one sung a little song or stanza, of which the burden was, *Bannissons la Melancholie*; when it came to his turn to sing, after the performance of a young lady that sat next him, he produced these extemporary lines:

> Mais cette voix, et ces beaux yeux,
> Font Cupidon trop dangereux,
> Et je suis triste quand je crie
> Bannissons la Melancholie.

Tradition represents him as willing to descend from the dignity of the poet and the statesman to the low delights of mean company. His Chloe probably was sometimes ideal; but the woman with whom he cohabited was a despicable

---

* Spence.

drab* of the lowest species. One of his wenches, perhaps Chloe, while he was absent from his house, stole his plate, and ran away; as was related by a woman who had been his servant. Of this propensity to sordid converse I have seen an account so seriously ridiculous, that it seems to deserve insertion†.

"I have been assured that Prior, after having spent the evening with Oxford, Bolingbroke, Pope, and Swift, would go and smoke a pipe, and drink a bottle of ale, with a common soldier and his wife, in Long-Acre, before he went to bed; not from any remains of the lowness of his original, as one said, but, I suppose, that his faculties

—Strain'd to the height,
In that celestial colloquy sublime,
Dazzled and spent, sunk down, and sought repair."

Poor Prior! why was he so *strained*, and in such *want* of *repair*, after a conversation with men not, in the opinion of the world, much wiser than himself? But such are the conceits of speculatists, who *strain* their *faculties* to find in a mine what lies upon the surface.

His opinions, so far as the means of judging are left us, seem to have been right; but his life was, it seems, irregular, negligent, and sensual.

PRIOR has written with great variety, and his variety has made him popular. He has tried all styles, from the grotesque to the solemn, and has not so failed in any as to incur derision or disgrace.

His works may be distinctly considered as comprising Tales, Love-verses, Occasional Poems, Alma, and Solomon.

His Tales have obtained general approbation, being written with great familiarity and great spriteliness: the language is easy, but seldom gross, and the numbers smooth, without appearance of care. Of these Tales there are only four. The *Ladle*; which is introduced by a Preface, neither necessary nor pleasing, neither grave nor merry. *Paulo Purganti*; which has likewise a Preface, but of more value than the Tale. *Hans Carvel*, not over-decent; and *Protogenes* and *Apelles*, an old story, mingled, by an affectation not disagreeable, with modern images The *Young Gentleman in Love* has hardly a just claim to the title of *a Tale*. I know not whether he be the original author of any Tale which he has given us. The Adventure of *Hans Carvel* has passed through many successions of merry wits; for it is to be found in Ariosto's Satires, and is perhaps yet older. But the merit of such stories is the art of telling them.

In his Amorous Effusions he is less happy; for they are not dictated by nature or by passion, and have neither gallantry nor tenderness. They have the coldness of Cowley, without his wit, the dull exercises of a skilful versifyer,

---

* Spence.　　† Richardsoniana.

resolved at all adventures to write something about Chloe, and trying to be amorous by dint of study. His fictions therefore are mythological. Venus, after the example of the Greek Epigram, asks when she was seen *naked and bathing*. Then *Cupid* is *mistaken*; then *Cupid* is *disarmed*; then he loses his darts to *Ganymede*; then *Jupiter* sends him a summons by *Mercury*. Then *Chloe* goes a-hunting, with an *ivory quiver graceful at her side*; Diana mistakes her for one of her nymphs, and Cupid laughs at the blunder. All this is surely despicable; and even when he tries to act the lover, without the help of gods or goddesses, his thoughts are unaffecting or remote. He talks not *like a man of this world*.

The greatest of all his amorous essays is *Henry* and *Emma*; a dull and tedious dialogue, which excites neither esteem for the man nor tenderness for the woman. The example of Emma, who resolves to follow an outlawed murderer wherever fear and guilt shall drive him, deserves no imitation; and the experiment by which Henry tries the lady's constancy, is such as must end either in infamy to her, or in disappointment to himself.

His occasional Poems necessarily lost part of their value, as their occasions, being less remembered, raised less emotion. Some of them, however, are preserved by their inherent excellence. The burlesque of Boileau's Ode on Namur has, in some parts, such airiness and levity as will always procure it readers, even among those who cannot compare it with the original. The Epistle to Boileau is not so happy. The Poems to the King are now perused only by young students, who read merely that they may learn to write; and of the *Carmen Seculare*, I cannot but suspect that I might praise or censure it by caprice, without danger of detection; for who can be supposed to have laboured through it? Yet the time has been when this neglected work was so popular, that it was translated into Latin by no common master.

His Poem on the battle of Ramillies is necessarily tedious by the form of the stanza: an uniform mass of ten lines, thirty-five times repeated, inconsequential and slightly connected, must weary both the ear and the understanding. His imitation of Spenser, which consists principally in *I ween* and *I weet*, without exclusion of later modes of speech, makes his poem neither ancient nor modern. His mention of *Mars* and *Bellona*, and his comparison of Marlborough to the Eagle that bears the thunder of *Jupiter*, are all puerile and unaffecting; and yet more despicable is the long tale told by *Lewis* in his despair, of *Brute* and *Troynovante*, and the teeth of *Cadmus*, with his similies of the raven and eagle, and wolf and lion. By the help of such easy fictions, and vulgar topicks, without acquaintance with life, and without knowledge of art or nature, a poem of any length, cold and lifeless like this, may be easily written on any subject.

In his Epilogues to *Phædra* and to *Lucius*, he is very happily facetious; but into the Prologue before the Queen, the pedant has found his way, with Minerva, Perseus, and Andromeda.

His Epigrams and lighter pieces are, like those of others, sometimes elegant, sometimes trifling, and sometimes dull; among the best are the *Camelion*, and the epitaph on *John* and *Joan*.

Scarcely any one of our poets has written so much, and translated so little: the version of Callimachus is sufficiently licentious; the paraphrase on St. Paul's Exhortation to Charity is eminently beautiful.

Alma is written in professed imitation of Hudibras, and has at least one accidental resemblance: Hudibras wants a plan, because it is left imperfect; Alma is imperfect, because it seems never to have had a plan. Prior appears not to have proposed to himself any drift or design, but to have written the casual dictates of the present moment.

What Horace said when he imitated Lucilius, might be said of Butler by Prior, his numbers were not smooth or neat: Prior excelled him in versification, but he was, like Horace, *inventore minor*; he had not Butler's exuberance of matter and variety of illustration. The spangles of wit which he could afford, he knew how to polish; but he wanted the bullion of his master. Butler pours out a negligent profusion, certain of the weight, but careless of the stamp. Prior has comparatively little, but with that little he makes a fine shew. Alma has many admirers, and was the only piece among Prior's works of which Pope said that he should wish to be the author.

Solomon is the work to which he entrusted the protection of his name, and which he expected succeeding ages to regard with veneration. His affection was natural; it had undoubtedly been written with great labour, and who is willing to think that he has been labouring in vain? He had infused into it much knowledge and much thought; had often polished it to elegance, often dignified it with splendour, and sometimes heightened it to sublimity: he perceived in it many excellences, and did not discover that it wanted that without which all others are of small avail, the power of engaging attention and alluring curiosity.

Tediousness is the most fatal of all faults; negligences or errors are single and local, but tediousness pervades the whole; other faults are censured and forgotten, but the power of tediousness propagates itself. He that is weary the first hour, is more weary the second; as bodies forced into motion, contrary to their tendency, pass more and more slowly through every successive interval of space.

Unhappily this pernicious failure is that which an author is least able to discover. We are seldom tiresome to ourselves; and the act of composition fills and delights the mind with change of language and succession of images; every couplet when produced is new, and novelty is the great source of pleasure. Perhaps no man ever thought a line superfluous when he first wrote it, or contracted his work till his ebullitions of invention had subsided. And even if he should controul his desire of immediate renown, and keep his work *nine years* unpublished, he will be still the author, and still in danger of deceiving himself; and if he consults his friends, he will probably find men who have more kindness than judgement, or more fear to offend than desire to instruct.

The tediousness of this poem proceeds not from the uniformity of the subject, for it is sufficiently diversified, but from the continued tenour of the narration; in which Solomon relates the successive vicissitudes of his own mind, without the intervention of any other speaker, or the mention of any other agent, unless it be Abra; the reader is only to learn what he thought, and to be told that he thought wrong. The event of every experiment is foreseen, and therefore the process is not much regarded.

Yet the work is far from deserving to be neglected. He that shall peruse it will be able to mark many passages, to which he may recur for instruction or delight; many from which the poet may learn to write, and the philosopher to reason.

If Prior's poetry be generally considered, his praise will be that of correctness and industry, rather than of compass of comprehension, or activity of fancy. He never made any effort of invention: his greater pieces are only tissues of common thoughts; and his smaller, which consist of light images or single conceits, are not always his own. I have traced him among the French Epigrammatists, and have been informed that he poached for prey among obscure authors. The *Thief and the Cordelier* is, I suppose, generally considered as an original production; with how much justice this Epigram may tell, which was written by Georgius Sabinus, a poet now little known or read, though once the friend of Luther and Melancthon:

> De Sacerdote Furem consolante.
>
> Quidam sacrificus furem comitatus euntem
> Huc ubi dat sontes carnificina neci.
> Ne sis mœstus, ait; summi conviva Tonantis
> Jam cum cœlitibus (si modo credis) eris.
> Ille gemens, si vera mihi solatia præbes,
> Hospes apud superos sis meus oro, refert.
> Sacrificus contra; mihi non convivia fas est
> Ducere, jejunans hac edo luce nihil.

What he has valuable he owes to his diligence and his judgement. His diligence has justly placed him amongst the most correct of the English poets; and he was one of the first that resolutely endeavoured at correctness. He never sacrifices accuracy to haste, nor indulges himself in contemptuous negligence, or impatient idleness; he has no careless lines, or entangled sentiments; his words are nicely selected, and his thoughts fully expanded. If this part of his character suffers any abatement, it must be from the disproportion of his rhymes, which have not always sufficient consonance, and from the admission of broken lines into his *Solomon*; but perhaps he thought, like Cowley, that hemistichs ought to be admitted into heroic poetry.

He had apparently such rectitude of judgement as secured him from every thing that approached to the ridiculous or absurd; but as laws operate in civil agency not to the excitement of virtue, but the repression of wickedness, so judgement in the operations of intellect can hinder faults, but not produce excellence. Prior is never low, nor very often sublime. It is said by Longinus of Euripides, that he forces himself sometimes into grandeur by violence of effort, as the lion kindles his fury by the lashes of his own tail. Whatever Prior obtains above mediocrity seems the effort of struggle and of toil. He has many vigorous but few happy lines; he has every thing by purchase, and nothing by gift; he had no *nightly visitations* of the Muse, no infusions of sentiment or felicities of fancy.

His diction, however, is more his own than that of any among the successors of Dryden; he borrows no lucky turns, or commodious modes of language, from his predecessors. His phrases are original, but they are sometimes harsh; as he inherited no elegances, none has he bequeathed. His expression has every mark of laborious study; the line seldom seems to have been formed at once; the words did not come till they were called, and were then put by constraint into their places, where they do their duty, but do it sullenly. In his greater compositions there may be found more rigid stateliness than graceful dignity.

Of versification he was not negligent: what he received from Dryden he did not lose; neither did he increase the difficulty of writing, by unnecessary severity, but uses Triplets and Alexandrines without scruple. In his Preface to *Solomon* he proposes some improvements, by extending the sense from one couplet to another, with variety of pauses. This he has attempted, but without success; his interrupted lines are unpleasing, and his sense as less distinct is less striking.

He has altered the Stanza of Spenser, as a house is altered by building another in its place of a different form. With how little resemblance he has formed his new Stanza to that of his master, these specimens will shew.

Spenser.

> She flying fast from heaven's hated face,
> And from the world that her discover'd wide,
> Fled to the wasteful wilderness apace,
> From living eyes her open shame to hide,
> And lurk'd in rocks and caves long unespy'd.
> But that fair crew of knights, and Una fair,
> Did in that castle afterwards abide,
> To rest themselves, and weary powers repair,
> Where store they found of all, that dainty was and rare.

Prior.

To the close rock the frighted raven flies,
Soon as the rising eagle cuts the air:
The shaggy wolf unseen and trembling lies,
When the hoarse roar proclaims the lion near.
Ill-starr'd did we our forts and lines forsake,
To dare our British foes to open fight:
Our conquest we by stratagem should make:
Our triumph had been founded in our flight.
'Tis ours, by craft and by surprise to gain:
'Tis theirs, to meet in arms, and battle in the plain.　　10

By this new structure of his lines he has avoided difficulties; nor am I sure
that he has lost any of the power of pleasing; but he no longer imitates Spenser.

Some of his poems are written without regularity of measures; for, when
he commenced poet, we had not recovered from our Pindarick infatuation;
but he probably lived to be convinced that the essence of verse is order and
consonance.

His numbers are such as mere diligence may attain; they seldom offend the
ear, and seldom sooth it; they commonly want airiness, lightness, and facility;
what is smooth, is not soft. His verses always roll, but they seldom flow.

A survey of the life and writings of Prior may exemplify a sentence which
he doubtless understood well, when he read Horace at his uncle's; *the vessel
long retains the scent which it first receives.* In his private relaxation he revived
the tavern, and in his amorous pedantry he exhibited the college. But on higher
occasions, and nobler subjects, when habit was overpowered by the necessity
of reflection, he wanted not wisdom as a statesman, nor elegance as a poet.

BLACKMORE

SIR RICHARD BLACKMORE is one of those men whose writings have attracted
much notice, but of whose life and manners very little has been communicated, and whose lot it has been to be much oftener mentioned by enemies
than by friends.

He was the son of Robert Blackmore of Corsham in Wiltshire, styled
by Wood *Gentleman*, and supposed to have been an attorney: having been
for some time educated in a country-school, he was sent at thirteen to
Westminster; and in 1668 was entered at Edmund-Hall in Oxford, where he
took the degree of M. A. June 3, 1676, and resided thirteen years; a much
longer time than it is usual to spend at the university; and which he seems to
have passed with very little attention to the business of the place; for in his

poems, the ancient names of nations or places, which he often introduces, are pronounced by chance. He afterwards travelled: at Padua he was made doctor of physick; and, after having wandered about a year and a half on the Continent, returned home.

In some part of his life, it is not known when, his indigence compelled him to teach a school; an humiliation with which, though it certainly lasted but a little while, his enemies did not forget to reproach him, when he became conspicuous enough to excite malevolence; and let it be remembered for his honour, that to have been once a school-master is the only reproach which all the perspicacity of malice, animated by wit, has ever fixed upon his private life.

When he first engaged in the study of physic, he enquired, as he says, of Dr. Sydenham what authors he should read, and was directed by Sydenham to Don Quixote; *which*, said he, *is a very good book; I read it still.* The perverseness of mankind makes it often mischievous in men of eminence to give way to merriment. The idle and the illiterate will long shelter themselves under this foolish apophthegm.

Whether he rested satisfied with this direction, or sought for better, he commenced physician, and obtained high eminence and extensive practice. He became Fellow of the College of Physicians, April 12, 1687, being one of the thirty which, by the new charter of king James, were added to the former Fellows. His residence was in Cheapside, and his friends were chiefly in the city. In the early part of Blackmore's time, a citizen was a term of reproach; and his place of abode was another topick to which his adversaries had recourse, in the penury of scandal.

Blackmore, therefore, was made a poet not by necessity but inclination, and wrote not for a livelihood but for fame; or, if he may tell his own motives, for a nobler purpose, to engage poetry in the cause of Virtue.

I believe it is peculiar to him, that his first publick work was an heroick poem. He was not known as a maker of verses, till he published (in 1695) *Prince Arthur*, in ten books, written, as he relates, *by such catches and starts, and in such occasional uncertain hours as his profession afforded, and for the greatest part in coffee-houses, or in passing up and down the streets.* For the latter part of this apology he was accused of writing *to the rumbling of his chariot-wheels.* He had read, he says, *but little poetry throughout his whole life; and for fifteen years before had not written an hundred verses, except one copy of Latin verses in praise of a friend's book.*

He thinks, and with some reason, that from such a performance perfection cannot be expected; but he finds another reason for the severity of his censurers, which he expresses in language such as Cheapside easily furnished. *I am not free of the Poets Company, having never kissed the governor's hands: mine is therefore not so much as a permission-poem, but a downright interloper. Those gentlemen who carry on their poetical trade in a joint stock, would certainly do what they could to sink and ruin an unlicensed adventurer, notwithstanding I disturbed none of their factories, nor imported any goods they had ever dealt in.* He had lived in the city till he had learned its note.

That *Prince Arthur* found many readers, is certain; for in two years it had three editions; a very uncommon instance of favourable reception, at a time when literary curiosity was yet confined to particular classes of the nation. Such success naturally raised animosity; and Dennis attacked it by a formal criticism, more tedious and disgusting than the work which he condemns. To this censure may be opposed the approbation of Locke and the admiration of Molineux, which are found in their printed Letters. Molineux is particularly delighted with the song of *Mopas*, which is therefore subjoined to this narrative.

It is remarked by Pope, that what *raises the hero often sinks the man.* Of Blackmore it may be said, that as the poet sinks, the man rises; the animadversions of Dennis, insolent and contemptuous as they were, raised in him no implacable resentment: he and his critick were afterwards friends; and in one of his latter works he praises Dennis as *equal to Boileau in poetry, and superior to him in critical abilities.*

He seems to have been more delighted with praise than pained by censure, and, instead of slackening, quickened his career. Having in two years produced ten books of *Prince Arthur*, in two years more (1697) he sent into the world *King Arthur* in twelve. The provocation was now doubled, and the resentment of wits and criticks may be supposed to have increased in proportion. He found, however, advantages more than equivalent to all their outrages; he was this year made one of the physicians in ordinary to king William, and advanced by him to the honour of knighthood, with a present of a gold chain and a medal.

The malignity of the wits attributed his knighthood to his new poem; but king William was not very studious of poetry, and Blackmore perhaps had other merit: for he says, in his Dedication to *Alfred*, that *he had a greater part in the succession of the house of Hanover than ever he had boasted.*

What Blackmore could contribute to the Succession, or what he imagined himself to have contributed, cannot now be known. That he had been of considerable use, I doubt not but he believed, for I hold him to have been very honest; but he might easily make a false estimate of his own importance: those whom their virtue restrains from deceiving others, are often disposed by their vanity to deceive themselves. Whether he promoted the Succession or not, he at least approved it, and adhered invariably to his principles and party through his whole life.

His ardour of poetry still continued; and not long after (1700) he published a *Paraphrase on the Book of Job*, and other parts of the Scripture. This performance Dryden, who pursued him with great malignity, lived long enough to ridicule in a Prologue.

The wits easily confederated against him, as Dryden, whose favour they almost all courted, was his professed adversary. He had besides given them reason for resentment, as, in his Preface to *Prince Arthur*, he had said of the Dramatick Writers almost all that was alleged afterwards by Collier; but Blackmore's censure was cold and general, Collier's was personal and ardent; Blackmore taught his reader to dislike, what Collier incited him to abhor.

In his Preface to *King Arthur* he endeavoured to gain at least one friend, and propitiated Congreve by higher praise of his *Mourning Bride* than it has obtained from any other critick.

The same year he published a *Satire on Wit*; a proclamation of defiance which united the poets almost all against him, and which brought upon him lampoons and ridicule from every side. This he doubtless foresaw, and evidently despised; nor should his dignity of mind be without its praise, had he not paid the homage to greatness which he denied to genius, and degraded himself by conferring that authority over the national taste, which he takes from the poets, upon men of high rank and wide influence, but of less wit, and not greater virtue.

Here is again discovered the inhabitant of Cheapside, whose head cannot keep his poetry unmingled with trade. To hinder that intellectual bankruptcy which he affects to fear, he will erect a *Bank for Wit*.

In this poem he justly censured Dryden's impurities, but praised his powers; though in a subsequent edition he retained the satire and omitted the praise. What was his reason I know not; Dryden was then no longer in his way.

His head still teemed with heroick poetry, and (1705) he published *Eliza* in ten books. I am afraid that the world was now weary of contending about Blackmore's heroes; for I do not remember that by any author, serious or comical, I have found *Eliza* either praised or blamed. She *dropped*, as it seems, *dead-born from the press*. It is never mentioned, and was never seen by me till I borrowed it for the present occasion. Jacob says, *it is corrected, and revised for another impression*; but the labour of revision was thrown away.

From this time he turned some of his thoughts to the celebration of living characters; and wrote a poem on the *Kit-cat Club*, and *Advice to the Poets how to celebrate the Duke of Marlborough*; but on occasion of another year of success, thinking himself qualified to give more instruction, he again wrote a poem of *Advice to a Weaver of Tapestry*. Steele was then publishing the *Tatler*; and looking round him for something at which he might laugh, unluckily lighted on Sir Richard's work, and treated it with such contempt, that, as Fenton observes, he put an end to the species of writers that gave *Advice to Painters*.

Not long after (1712) he published *Creation, a philosophical Poem*, which has been, by my recommendation, inserted in the late collection. Whoever judges of this by any other of Blackmore's performances, will do it injury. The praise given it by Addison (*Spec.* 339) is too well known to be transcribed; but some notice is due to the testimony of Dennis, who calls it a "philosophical Poem, which has equalled that of Lucretius in the beauty of its versification, and infinitely surpassed it in the solidity and strength of its reasoning."

Why an author surpasses himself, it is natural to enquire. I have heard from Mr. Draper, an eminent bookseller, an account received by him from Ambrose Philips, "That Blackmore, as he proceeded in this poem, laid his manuscript from time to time before a club of wits with whom he associated; and that every man contributed, as he could, either improvement or correction; so that," said Philips, "there are perhaps no where in the book, thirty lines together that now stand as they were originally written."

The relation of Philips, I suppose, was true; but when all reasonable, all credible allowance is made for this friendly revision, the author will still retain an ample dividend of praise; for to him must always be assigned the plan of the work, the distribution of its parts, the choice of topicks, the train of argument, and what is yet more, the general predominance of philosophical judgement and poetical spirit. Correction seldom effects more than the suppression of faults: a happy line, or a single elegance, may perhaps be added; but of a large work the general character must always remain; the original constitution can be very little helped by local remedies; inherent and radical dullness will never be much invigorated by extrinsick animation.

This poem, if he had written nothing else, would have transmitted him to posterity among the first favourites of the English Muse; but to make verses was his transcendent pleasure, and as he was not deterred by censure, he was not satiated with praise.

He deviated, however, sometimes into other tracks of literature, and condescended to entertain his readers with plain prose. When the *Spectator* stopped, he considered the polite world as destitute of entertainment; and in concert with Mr. Hughes, who wrote every third paper, published three times a week the *Lay Monastery*, founded on the supposition that some literary men, whose characters are described, had retired to a house in the country to enjoy philosophical leisure, and resolved to instruct the public, by communicating their disquisitions and amusements. Whether any real persons were concealed under fictitious names, is not known. The hero of the club is one Mr. Johnson; such a constellation of excellence, that his character shall not be suppressed, though there is no great genius in the design, nor skill in the delineation.

"The first I shall name is Mr. Johnson, a gentleman that owes to Nature excellent faculties and an elevated genius, and to industry and application many acquired accomplishments. His taste is distinguishing, just and delicate; his judgement clear, and his reason strong, accompanied with an imagination full of spirit, of great compass, and stored with refined ideas. He is a critick of the first rank; and, what is his peculiar ornament, he is delivered from the ostentation, malevolence, and supercilious temper, that so often blemish men of that character. His remarks result from the nature and reason of things, and are formed by a judgement free, and unbiassed by the authority of those who have lazily followed each other in the same beaten track of thinking, and are arrived only at the reputation of acute grammarians and commentators; men, who have been copying one another many hundred years, without any improvement; or, if they have ventured farther, have only applied in a mechanical manner the rules of antient criticks to modern writings, and with great labour discovered nothing but their own want of judgement and capacity. As Mr. Johnson penetrates to the bottom of his subject, by which means his observations are solid and natural, as well as delicate, so his design is always to bring to light something useful and ornamental; whence his character is the reverse to theirs, who have eminent abilities in insignificant knowledge, and a great felicity in finding out trifles. He is no less industrious to search out the merit of an author, than sagacious in discerning his errors and defects; and takes more pleasure in commending the beauties than exposing the blemishes of a laudable writing: like Horace, in a long work, he can bear some deformities, and justly lay them on the imperfection of human nature, which is incapable of faultless productions. When an excellent *Drama* appears in publick, and by its intrinsick worth attracts a general applause, he is not stung with envy and spleen; nor does he express a savage nature, in fastening upon the celebrated author, dwelling upon his imaginary defects, and passing over his conspicuous excellences. He treats all writers upon the same impartial foot; and is not, like the little criticks, taken up entirely in finding out only the beauties of the ancient, and nothing but the errors of the modern writers. Never did any one express more kindness and good nature to young and unfinished authors; he promotes their interests, protects their reputation, extenuates their faults, and sets off their virtues, and by his candour guards them from the severity of his judgement. He is not like those dry criticks, who are morose because they cannot write themselves, but is himself master of a good vein in poetry; and though he does not often employ it, yet he has sometimes entertained his friends with his unpublished performances."

The rest of the *Lay Monks* seem to be but feeble mortals, in comparison with the gigantic Johnson; who yet, with all his abilities, and the help of the fraternity, could drive the publication but to forty papers, which were afterwards collected into a volume, and called in the title *A Sequel to the Spectators.*

Some years afterwards (1716 and 1717) he published two volumes of Essays in prose, which can be commended only as they are written for the highest and noblest purpose, the promotion of religion. Blackmore's prose is not the prose of a poet; for it is languid, sluggish, and lifeless; his diction is neither daring nor exact, his flow neither rapid nor easy, and his periods neither smooth nor strong. His account of *Wit* will shew with how little clearness he is content to think, and how little his thoughts are recommended by his language.

"As to its efficient cause, *Wit* owes its production to an extraordinary and peculiar temperament in the constitution of the possessor of it, in which is found a concurrence of regular and exalted ferments, and an affluence of animal spirits, refined and rectified to a great degree of purity; whence, being endowed with vivacity, brightness, and celerity, as well in their reflexions as direct motions, they become proper instruments for the spritely operations of the mind; by which means the imagination can with great facility range the wide field of Nature, contemplate an infinite variety of objects, and, by observing the similitude and disagreement of their several qualities, single out and abstract, and then suit and unite those ideas which will best serve its purpose. Hence beautiful allusions, surprising metaphors, and admirable sentiments, are always ready at hand: and while the fancy is full of images collected from innumerable objects and their different qualities, relations, and habitudes, it can at pleasure dress a common notion in a strange but becoming garb; by which, as before observed, the same thought will appear a new one, to the great delight and wonder of the hearer. What we call *genius* results from this particular happy complexion in the first formation of the person that enjoys it, and is Nature's gift, but diversified by various specifick characters and limitations, as its active fire is blended and allayed by different proportions of phlegm, or reduced and regulated by the contrast of opposite ferments. Therefore, as there happens in the composition of a facetious genius a greater or less, though still an inferior, degree of judgement and prudence, one man of wit will be varied and distinguished from another."

In these Essays he took little care to propitiate the wits; for he scorns to avert their malice at the expence of virtue or of truth.

"Several, in their books, have many sarcastical and spiteful strokes at religion in general; while others make themselves pleasant with the principles of the Christian. Of the last kind, this age has seen a most audacious example in the book intituled, *A Tale of a Tub.* Had this writing been published in a pagan or popish nation, who are justly impatient of all indignity offered to the established religion of their country, no doubt but the author would have received the punishment he deserved. But the fate of this impious buffoon is very different; for in a protestant kingdom, zealous of their civil and religious immunities, he has not only escaped affronts and the effects of publick resentment, but has been caressed and patronized by persons of great figure, and of all denominations. Violent party-men, who differed in all things besides, agreed in their turn to shew particular respect and friendship to this insolent derider of the worship of his country, till at last the reputed writer is not only gone off with impunity, but triumphs in his dignity and preferment. I do not know that any inquiry or search was ever made after this writing, or that any reward was ever offered for the discovery of the author, or that the infamous book was ever condemned to be burnt in publick: whether this proceeds from the excessive esteem and love that men in power, during the late reign, had for wit, or their defect of zeal and concern for the Christian Religion, will be determined best by those who are best acquainted with their character."

In another place he speaks with becoming abhorrence of a *godless author* who has burlesqued a Psalm. This author was supposed to be Pope, who published a reward for any one that would produce the coiner of the accusation, but never denied it; and was afterwards the perpetual and incessant enemy of Blackmore.

One of his Essays is upon the Spleen, which is treated by him so much to his own satisfaction, that he has published the same thoughts in the same words; first in the *Lay Monastery*; then in the Essay; and then in the Preface to a Medical Treatise on the Spleen. One passage, which I have found already twice, I will here exhibit, because I think it better imagined, and better expressed, than could be expected from the common tenour of his prose:

"—As the several combinations of splenetic madness and folly produce an infinite variety of irregular understanding, so the amicable accommodation and alliance between several virtues and vices produce an equal diversity in the dispositions and manners of mankind; whence it comes to pass, that as many monstrous and absurd productions are found in the moral as in the intellectual world. How surprising is it to observe among the least culpable men, some whose minds are attracted by heaven and earth, with a seeming equal force; some who are proud of humility; others who are censorious and uncharitable, yet self-denying and devout; some who join contempt of the world with sordid avarice; and others, who preserve a great degree of piety, with ill-nature and ungoverned passions: nor are instances of this inconsistent mixture less frequent among bad men, where we often, with admiration, see persons at once generous and unjust, impious lovers of their country, and flagitious heroes, good-natured sharpers, immoral men of honour, and libertines who will sooner die than change their religion; and though it is true that repugnant coalitions of so high a degree are found but in a part of mankind, yet none of the whole mass, either good or bad, are intirely exempted from some absurd mixture."

He about this time (Aug. 22, 1716) became one of the *Elects* of the College of Physicians; and was soon after (Oct. 1) chosen *Censor*. He seems to have arrived late, whatever was the reason, at his medical honours.

Having succeeded so well in his book on *Creation*, by which he established the great principle of all Religion, he thought his undertaking imperfect, unless he likewise enforced the truth of Revelation; and for that purpose added another poem on *Redemption*. He had likewise written, before his *Creation*, three books on the *Nature of Man*.

The lovers of musical devotion have always wished for a more happy metrical version than they have yet obtained of the book of Psalms; this wish the piety of Blackmore led him to gratify, and he produced (1721) *a new Version of the Psalms of* David, *fitted to the Tunes used in Churches;* which, being recommended by the archbishops and many bishops, obtained a licence for its admission into publick worship; but no admission has it yet obtained, nor has it any right to come where Brady and Tate have got possession. Blackmore's name must be added to those of many others, who, by the same attempt, have obtained only the praise of meaning well.

He was not yet deterred from heroick poetry; there was another monarch of this island, for he did not fetch his heroes from foreign countries, whom he considered as worthy of the Epic muse, and he dignified Alfred (1723) with twelve books. But the opinion of the nation was now settled; a hero introduced by Blackmore was not likely to find either respect or kindness; *Alfred* took his place by *Eliza* in silence and darkness: benevolence was ashamed to favour, and malice was weary of insulting. Of his four Epic Poems, the first had such reputation and popularity as enraged the criticks; the second was at least known enough to be ridiculed; the two last had neither friends nor enemies.

Contempt is a kind of gangrene, which if it seizes one part of a character corrupts all the rest by degrees. Blackmore, being despised as a poet, was in time neglected as a physician; his practice, which was once invidiously great, forsook him in the latter part of his life; but being by nature, or by principle, averse from idleness, he employed his unwelcome leisure in writing books on physick, and teaching others to cure those whom he could himself cure no longer. I know not whether I can enumerate all the treatises by which he has endeavoured to diffuse the art of healing; for there is scarcely any distemper, of dreadful name, which he has not taught his reader how to oppose. He has written on the small-pox, with a vehement invective against inoculation; on consumptions, the spleen, the gout, the rheumatism, the king's-evil, the dropsy, the jaundice, the stone, the diabetes, and the plague.

Of those books, if I had read them, it could not be expected that I should be able to give a critical account. I have been told that there is something in them of vexation and discontent, discovered by a perpetual attempt to degrade physick from its sublimity, and to represent it as attainable without much previous or concomitant learning. By the transient glances which I have thrown upon them, I have observed an affected contempt of the Ancients, and a supercilious derision of transmitted knowledge. Of this indecent arrogance the following quotation from his Preface to the Treatise on the Small-pox will afford a specimen; in which, when the reader finds, what I fear is true, that when he was censuring Hippocrates he did not know the difference between *aphorism* and *apophthegm,* he will not pay much regard to his determinations concerning ancient learning.

"As for this book of Aphorisms, it is like my lord Bacon's of the same title, a book of jests, or a grave collection of trite and trifling observations; of which though many are true and certain, yet they signify nothing, and may afford diversion, but no instruction; most of them being much inferior to the say-ings of the wise men of Greece, which yet are so low and mean, that we are entertained every day with more valuable sentiments at the table-conversation of ingenious and learned men."

I am unwilling, however, to leave him in total disgrace, and will therefore quote from another Preface a passage less reprehensible.

"Some gentlemen have been disingenuous and unjust to me, by wresting and forcing my meaning in the Preface to another book, as if I condemned and exposed all learning, though they knew I declared that I greatly honoured and esteemed all men of superior literature and erudition; and that I only undervalued false or superficial learning, that signifies nothing for the service of mankind; and that, as to physick, I expressly affirmed that learning must be joined with native genius to make a physician of the first rank; but if those talents are separated, I asserted, and do still insist, that a man of native sagacity and diligence, will prove a more able and useful practiser, than a heavy notional scholar, encumbered with a heap of confused ideas."

He was not only a poet and a physician, but produced likewise a work of a different kind, *A true and impartial History of the Conspiracy against King William, of glorious Memory, in the Year* 1695. This I have never seen, but suppose it at least compiled with integrity. He engaged likewise in theological controversy, and wrote two books against the Arians; *Just Prejudices against the Arian Hypothesis*; and *Modern Arians unmasked*. Another of his works is *Natural Theology, or Moral Duties considered apart from Positive; with some Observations on the Desirableness and Necessity of a Supernatural Revelation*. This was the last book that he published. He left behind him *The accomplished Preacher, or an Essay upon Divine Eloquence*; which was printed after his death by Mr. White of Nayland in Essex, the minister who attended his death-bed, and testified the fervent piety of his last hours. He died on the eighth of October, 1729.

BLACKMORE, by the unremitted enmity of the wits, whom he provoked more by his virtue than his dulness, has been exposed to worse treatment than he deserved; his name was so long used to point every epigram upon dull writers, that it became at last a bye-word of contempt: but it deserves observation, that malignity takes hold only of his writings, and that his life passed without reproach, even when his boldness of reprehension naturally turned upon him many eyes desirous to espy faults, which many tongues would have made haste to publish. But those who could not blame, could at least forbear to praise, and therefore of his private life and domestick character there are no memorials.

As an author he may justly claim the honours of magnanimity. The incessant attacks of his enemies, whether serious or merry, are never discovered to have disturbed his quiet, or to have lessened his confidence in himself; they neither awed him to silence nor to caution; they neither provoked him to petulance, nor depressed him to complaint. While the distributors of literary fame were endeavouring to depreciate and degrade him, he either despised or defied them, wrote on as he had written before, and never turned aside to quiet them by civility, or repress them by confutation.

He depended with great security on his own powers, and perhaps was for that reason less diligent in perusing books. His literature was, I think, but small. What he knew of antiquity, I suspect him to have gathered from modern compilers: but though he could not boast of much critical knowledge, his mind was stored with general principles, and he left minute researches to those whom he considered as little minds.

With this disposition he wrote most of his poems. Having formed a magnificent design, he was careless of particular and subordinate elegances; he studied no niceties of versification; he waited for no felicities of fancy; but caught his first thoughts in the first words in which they were presented: nor does it appear that he saw beyond his own performances, or had ever elevated his views to that ideal perfection which every genius born to excel is condemned always to pursue, and never overtake. In the first suggestions of his imagination he acquiesced; he thought them good, and did not seek for better. His works may be read a long time without the occurrence of a single line that stands prominent from the rest.

The poem on *Creation* has, however, the appearance of more circumspection; it wants neither harmony of numbers, accuracy of thought, nor elegance of diction: it has either been written with great care, or, what cannot be imagined of so long a work, with such felicity as made care less necessary.

Its two constituent parts are ratiocination and description. To reason in verse, is allowed to be difficult; but Blackmore not only reasons in verse, but very often reasons poetically; and finds the art of uniting ornament with strength, and ease with closeness. This is a skill which Pope might have condescended to learn from him, when he needed it so much in his Moral Essays.

In his descriptions both of life and nature, the poet and the philosopher happily co-operate; truth is recommended by elegance, and elegance sustained by truth.

In the structure and order of the poem, not only the greater parts are properly consecutive, but the didactick and illustrative paragraphs are so happily mingled, that labour is relieved by pleasure, and the attention is led on through a long succession of varied excellence to the original position, the fundamental principle of wisdom and of virtue.

As the heroick poems of Blackmore are now little read, it is thought proper to insert, as a specimen from *Prince Arthur*, the song of *Mopas* mentioned by Molineux.

> But that which Arthur with most pleasure heard,
> Were noble strains, by Mopas sung the bard,
> Who to his harp in lofty verse began,
> And through the secret maze of Nature ran.
> He the great Spirit sung, that all things fill'd,
> That the tumultuous waves of Chaos still'd,

Whose nod dispos'd the jarring seeds to peace,
And made the wars of hostile Atoms cease.
All Beings we in fruitful Nature find,
Proceeded from the great Eternal Mind;   10
Streams of his unexhausted spring of power,
And cherish'd with his influence, endure.
He spread the pure cerulean fields on high,
And arch'd the chambers of the vaulted sky,
Which he, to suit their glory with their height,
Adorn'd with globes, that reel, as drunk with light.
His hand directed all the tuneful spheres,
He turn'd their orbs, and polish'd all the stars.
He fill'd the Sun's vast lamp with golden light,
And bid the silver Moon adorn the night,   20
He spread the airy Ocean without shores,
Where birds are wafted with their feather'd oars.
Then sung the bard how the light vapours rise
From the warm earth, and cloud the smiling skies
He sung how some, chill'd in their airy flight,
Fall scatter'd down in pearly dew by night.
How some, rais'd higher, sit in secret steams
On the reflected points of bounding beams;
Till, chill'd with cold, they shade th' etherial plain,
Then on the thirsty earth descend in rain.   30
How some, whose parts a slight contexture show,
Sink hovering through the air, in fleecy snow.
How part is spun in silken threads, and clings
Entangled in the grass in glewy strings.
How others stampt to stones, with rushing sound
Fall from their crystal quarries to the ground.
How some are laid in trains, that kindled fly
In harmless fires by night, about the sky.
How some in winds blow with impetuous force,
And carry ruin where they bend their course: 40
While some conspire to form a gentle breeze,
To fan the air, and play among the trees.
How some, enrag'd, grow turbulent and loud,
Pent in the bowels of a frowning cloud;
That cracks, as if the axis of the world
Was broke, and heaven's bright towers were downwards
    hurl'd.
He sung how earth's wide ball, at Jove's command,
Did in the midst on airy columns stand.
And how the soul of plants, in prison held,

And bound with sluggish fetters, lies conceal'd,   50
Till with the Spring's warm beams, almost releast
From the dull weight, with which it lay opprest,
Its vigour spreads, and makes the teeming earth
Heave up, and labour with the sprouting birth:
The active spirit freedom seeks in vain,
It only works and twists a stronger chain.
Urging its prison's sides to break away,
It makes that wider, where 'tis forc'd to stay:
Till, having form'd its living house, it rears
Its head, and in a tender plant appears.   60
Hence springs the oak, the beauty of the grove,
Whose stately trunk fierce storms can scarcely move.
Hence grows the cedar, hence the swelling vine
Does round the elm its purple clusters twine.
Hence painted flowers the smiling gardens bless,
Both with their fragrant scent and gaudy dress.
Hence the white lily in full beauty grows,
Hence the blue violet, and blushing rose.
He sung how sun-beams brood upon the earth,
And in the glebe hatch such a numerous birth;   70
Which way the genial warmth in Summer storms
Turns putrid vapours to a bed of worms;
How rain, transform'd by this prolifick power,
Falls from the clouds an animated shower.
He sung the embryo's growth within the womb,
And how the parts their various shapes assume.
With what rare art the wondrous structure's wrought,
From one crude mass to such perfection brought;
That no part useless, none misplac'd we see,
None are forgot, and more would monstrous be."   80

SWIFT

AN Account of Dr. Swift has been already collected, with great diligence and
acuteness, by Dr. Hawkesworth, according to a scheme which I laid before
him in the intimacy of our friendship. I cannot therefore be expected to say
much of a life, concerning which I had long since communicated my thoughts
to a man capable of dignifying his narration with so much elegance of language and force of sentiment.

JONATHAN SWIFT was, according to an account said to be written by himself,
the son of Jonathan Swift, an attorney, and was born at Dublin on St.
Andrew's day, 1667: according to his own report, as delivered by Pope to

Spence, he was born at Leicester, the son of a clergyman, who was minister of a parish in Herefordshire*. During his life the place of his birth was undetermined. He was contented to be called an Irishman by the Irish; but would occasionally call himself an Englishman. The question may, without much regret, be left in the obscurity in which he delighted to involve it.

Whatever was his birth, his education was Irish. He was sent at the age of six to the school at Kilkenny, and in his fifteenth year (1682) was admitted into the University of Dublin.

In his academical studies he was either not diligent or not happy. It must disappoint every reader's expectation, that, when at the usual time he claimed the Bachelorship of Arts, he was found by the examiners too conspicuously deficient for regular admission, and obtained his degree at last by *special favour*; a term used in that university to denote want of merit.

Of this disgrace it may be easily supposed that he was much ashamed, and shame had its proper effect in producing reformation. He resolved from that time to study eight hours a-day, and continued his industry for seven years, with what improvement is sufficiently known. This part of his story well deserves to be remembered; it may afford useful admonition and powerful encouragement to men, whose abilities have been made for a time useless by their passions or pleasures, and who, having lost one part of life in idleness, are tempted to throw away the remainder in despair.

In this course of daily application he continued three years longer at Dublin; and in this time, if the observation and memory of an old companion may be trusted, he drew the first sketch of his *Tale of a Tub*.

When he was about one-and-twenty (1688), being by the death of Godwin Swift his uncle, who had supported him, left without subsistence, he went to consult his mother, who then lived at Leicester, about the future course of his life, and by her direction solicited the advice and patronage of Sir William Temple, who had married one of Mrs. Swift's relations, and whose father Sir John Temple, Master of the Rolls in Ireland, had lived in great familiarity of friendship with Godwin Swift, by whom Jonathan had been to that time maintained.

Temple received with sufficient kindness the nephew of his father's friend, with whom he was, when they conversed together, so much pleased, that he detained him two years in his house. Here he became known to King William, who sometimes visited Temple when he was disabled by the gout, and, being attended by Swift in the garden, shewed him how to cut asparagus in the Dutch way.

King William's notions were all military; and he expressed his kindness to Swift by offering to make him a captain of horse.

---

* Spence's Anecdotes, vol. II. p. 273.

When Temple removed to Moor-park, he took Swift with him; and when he was consulted by the Earl of Portland about the expedience of complying with a bill then depending for making parliaments triennial, against which King William was strongly prejudiced, after having in vain tried to shew the Earl that the proposal involved nothing dangerous to royal power, he sent Swift for the same purpose to the King. Swift, who probably was proud of his employment, and went with all the confidence of a young man, found his arguments, and his art of displaying them, made totally ineffectual by the pre-determination of the King; and used to mention this disappointment as his first antidote against vanity.

Before he left Ireland he contracted a disorder, as he thought, by eating too much fruit. The original of diseases is commonly obscure. Almost every boy eats as much fruit as he can get, without any great inconvenience. The disease of Swift was giddiness with deafness, which attacked him from time to time, began very early, pursued him through life, and at last sent him to the grave, deprived of reason.

Being much oppressed at Moor-park by this grievous malady, he was advised to try his native air, and went to Ireland, but, finding no benefit, returned to Sir William, at whose house he continued his studies, and is known to have read, among other books, *Cyprian* and *Irenæus*. He thought exercise of great necessity, and used to run half a mile up and down a hill every two hours.

It is easy to imagine that the mode in which his first degree was conferred left him no great fondness for the University of Dublin, and therefore he resolved to become a Master of Arts at Oxford. In the testimonial which he produced, the words of disgrace were omitted, and he took his Master's degree (July 5, 1692) with such reception and regard as fully contented him.

While he lived with Temple, he used to pay his mother at Leicester an yearly visit. He travelled on foot, unless some violence of weather drove him into a waggon, and at night he would go to a penny lodging, where he purchased clean sheets for sixpence. This practice Lord Orrery imputes to his innate love of grossness and vulgarity: some may ascribe it to his desire of surveying human life through all its varieties; and others, perhaps with equal probability, to a passion which seems to have been deep fixed in his heart, the love of a shilling.

In time he began to think that his attendance at Moor-park deserved some other recompence than the pleasure, however mingled with improvement, of Temple's conversation; and grew so impatient, that (1694) he went away in discontent.

Temple, conscious of having given reason for complaint, is said to have made him Deputy Master of the Rolls in Ireland; which, according to his kinsman's account, was an office which he knew him not able to discharge. Swift therefore resolved to enter into the Church, in which he had at first no higher hopes than of the chaplainship to the Factory at Lisbon; but being recommended to Lord Capel, he obtained the prebend of *Kilroot* in *Connor*, of about a hundred pounds a year.

But the infirmities of Temple made a companion like Swift so necessary, that he invited him back, with a promise to procure him English preferment, in exchange for the prebend which he desired him to resign. With this request Swift complied, having perhaps equally repented their separation, and they lived on together with mutual satisfaction; and, in the four years that passed between his return and Temple's death, it is probable that he wrote the *Tale of a Tub* and the *Battle of the Books*.

Swift began early to think, or to hope, that he was a poet, and wrote Pindarick Odes to Temple, to the King, and to the Athenian Society, a knot of obscure men, who published a periodical pamphlet of answers to questions, sent, or supposed to be sent, by Letters. I have been told that Dryden, having perused these verses, said, "Cousin Swift, you will never be a poet;" and that this denunciation was the motive of Swift's perpetual malevolence to Dryden.

In 1699 Temple died, and left a legacy with his manuscripts to Swift, for whom he had obtained, from King William, a promise of the first prebend that should be vacant at Westminster or Canterbury.

That this promise might not be forgotten, Swift dedicated to the King the posthumous works with which he was intrusted; but neither the dedication, nor tenderness for the man whom he once had treated with confidence and fondness, revived in King William the remembrance of his promise. Swift awhile attended the Court; but soon found his solicitations hopeless.

He was then invited by the Earl of Berkeley to accompany him into Ireland, as his private secretary; but after having done the business till their arrival at Dublin, he then found that one *Bush* had persuaded the Earl that a Clergyman was not a proper secretary, and had obtained the office for himself. In a man like Swift, such circumvention and inconstancy must have excited violent indignation.

But he had yet more to suffer. Lord Berkeley had the disposal of the deanery of Derry, and Swift expected to obtain it; but by the secretary's influence, supposed to have been secured by a bribe, it was bestowed on somebody else; and Swift was dismissed with the livings of *Laracor* and *Rathbeggin* in the diocese of Meath, which together did not equal half the value of the deanery.

At Laracor he increased the parochial duty by reading prayers on Wednesdays and Fridays, and performed all the offices of his profession with great decency and exactness.

Soon after his settlement at Laracor, he invited to Ireland the unfortunate Stella, a young woman whose name was Johnson, the daughter of the steward of Sir William Temple, who, in consideration of her father's virtues, left her a thousand pounds. With her came Mrs. Dingley, whose whole fortune was twenty-seven pounds a year for her life. With these Ladies he passed his hours of relaxation, and to them he opened his bosom; but they never resided in the same house, nor did he see either without a witness. They lived at the Parsonage, when Swift was away; and when he returned, removed to a lodging, or to the house of a neighbouring clergyman.

Swift was not one of those minds which amaze the world with early pregnancy: his first work, except his few poetical Essays, was the *Dissentions in Athens and Rome*, published (1701) in his thirty-fourth year. After its appearance, paying a visit to some bishop, he heard mention made of the new pamphlet that Burnet had written, replete with political knowledge. When he seemed to doubt Burnet's right to the work, he was told by the Bishop, that he was *a young man*; and, still persisting to doubt, that he was *a very positive young man*.

Three years afterward (1704) was published *The Tale of a Tub*: of this book charity may be persuaded to think that it might be written by a man of a peculiar character, without ill intention; but it is certainly of dangerous example. That Swift was its author, though it be universally believed, was never owned by himself, nor very well proved by any evidence; but no other claimant can be produced, and he did not deny it when Archbishop Sharpe and the Duchess of Somerset, by shewing it to the Queen, debarred him from a bishoprick.

When this wild work first raised the attention of the publick, Sacheverell, meeting Smalridge, tried to flatter him, by seeming to think him the author; but Smalridge answered with indignation, "Not all that you and I have in the world, nor all that ever we shall have, should hire me to write the *Tale of a Tub*."

The digressions relating to Wotton and Bentley must be confessed to discover want of knowledge, or want of integrity; he did not understand the two controversies, or he willingly misrepresented them. But Wit can stand its ground against Truth only a little while. The honours due to learning have been justly distributed by the decision of posterity.

The Battle of the Books is so like the *Combat des Livres*, which the same question concerning the Ancients and Moderns had produced in France, that the improbability of such a coincidence of thoughts without communication is not, in my opinion, balanced by the anonymous protestation prefixed, in which all knowledge of the French book is peremptorily disowned.

For some time after Swift was probably employed in solitary study, gaining the qualifications requisite for future eminence. How often he visited England, and with what diligence he attended his parishes, I know not. It was not till about four years afterwards that he became a professed author, and then one year (1708) produced *The Sentiments of a Church-of-England Man*; the ridicule of Astrology, under the name of *Bickerstaff*; the *Argument against abolishing Christianity*; and the defence of the *Sacramental Test*.

The Sentiments of a Church-of-England Man is written with great coolness, moderation, ease, and perspicuity. The *Argument against abolishing Christianity* is a very happy and judicious irony. One passage in it deserves to be selected.

"If Christianity were once abolished, how could the free-thinkers, the strong reasoners, and the men of profound learning, be able to find another subject so calculated, in all points, whereon to display their abilities? What wonderful productions of wit should we be deprived of from those, whose genius, by continual practice, hath been wholly turned upon raillery and invectives against religion, and would therefore never be able to shine, or distinguish themselves, upon any other subject? We are daily complaining of the great decline of wit among us, and would take away the greatest, perhaps the only, topick we have left. Who would ever have suspected Asgill for a wit, or Toland for a philosopher, if the inexhaustible stock of Christianity had not been at hand to provide them with materials? What other subject, through all art or nature, could have produced Tindal for a profound author, or furnished him with readers? It is the wise choice of the subject that alone adorns and distinguishes the writer. For had an hundred such pens as these been employed on the side of religion, they would have immediately sunk into silence and oblivion."

The reasonableness of a *Test* is not hard to be proved; but perhaps it must be allowed that the proper test has not been chosen.

The attention paid to the papers published under the name of *Bickerstaff,* induced Steele, when he projected the *Tatler,* to assume an appellation which had already gained possession of the reader's notice.

In the year following he wrote a *Project for the Advancement of Religion,* addressed to Lady Berkeley; by whose kindness it is not unlikely that he was advanced to his benefices. To this project, which is formed with great purity of intention, and displayed with spriteliness and elegance, it can only be objected, that, like many projects, it is, if not generally impracticable, yet evidently hopeless, as it supposes more zeal, concord, and perseverance, than a view of mankind gives reason for expecting.

He wrote likewise this year a *Vindication of Bickerstaff;* and an explanation of an *Ancient Prophecy,* part written after the facts, and the rest never completed, but well planned to excite amazement.

Soon after began the busy and important part of Swift's life. He was employed (1710) by the primate of Ireland to solicit the Queen for a remission of the First Fruits and Twentieth parts to the Irish Clergy. With this purpose he had recourse to Mr. Harley, to whom he was mentioned as a man neglected and oppressed by the last ministry, because he had refused to co-operate with some of their schemes. What he had refused, has never been told; what he had suffered was, I suppose, the exclusion from a bishoprick by the remonstrances of Sharpe, whom he describes as *the harmless tool of others hate,* and whom he represents as afterwards *suing for pardon.*

Harley's designs and situation were such as made him glad of an auxiliary so well qualified for his service; he therefore soon admitted him to familiarity, whether ever to confidence some have made a doubt, but it would have been difficult to excite his zeal without persuading him that he was trusted, and not very easy to delude him by false persuasions.

He was certainly admitted to those meetings in which the first hints and original plan of action are supposed to have been formed; and was one of the sixteen Ministers, or agents of the Ministry, who met weekly at each other's houses, and were united by the name of *Brother*.

Being not immediately considered as an obdurate Tory, he conversed indiscriminately with all the wits, and was yet the friend of Steele; who, in the *Tatler*, which began in 1710, confesses the advantages of his conversation, and mentions something contributed by him to his paper. But he was now immerging into political controversy; for the same year produced the *Examiner*, of which Swift wrote thirty-three papers. In argument he may be allowed to have the advantage; for where a wide system of conduct, and the whole of a publick character, is laid open to enquiry, the accuser having the choice of facts, must be very unskilful if he does not prevail; but with regard to wit, I am afraid none of Swift's papers will be found equal to those by which Addison opposed him.

Early in the next year he published a *Proposal for correcting, improving, and ascertaining the English Tongue*, in a Letter to the Earl of Oxford; written without much knowledge of the general nature of language, and without any accurate enquiry into the history of other tongues. The certainty and stability which, contrary to all experience, he thinks attainable, he proposes to secure by instituting an academy; the decrees of which every man would have been willing, and many would have been proud to disobey, and which, being renewed by successive elections, would in a short time have differed from itself.

He wrote the same year a *Letter to the October Club*, a number of Tory Gentlemen sent from the country to Parliament, who formed themselves into a club, to the number of about a hundred, and met to animate the zeal and raise the expectations of each other. They thought, with great reason, that the Ministers were losing opportunities; that sufficient use was not made of the ardour of the nation; they called loudly for more changes, and stronger efforts; and demanded the punishment of part, and the dismission of the rest, of those whom they considered as publick robbers.

Their eagerness was not gratified by the Queen, or by Harley. The Queen was probably slow because she was afraid, and Harley was slow because he was doubtful; he was a Tory only by necessity, or for convenience; and when he had power in his hands, had no settled purpose for which he should employ it; forced to gratify to a certain degree the Tories who supported him, but unwilling to make his reconcilement to the Whigs utterly desperate, he corresponded at once with the two expectants of the Crown, and kept, as has been observed, the succession undetermined. Not knowing what to do, he did nothing; and with the fate of a double-dealer, at last he lost his power, but kept his enemies.

Swift seems to have concurred in opinion with the *October Club*; but it was not in his power to quicken the tardiness of Harley, whom he stimulated as much as he could, but with little effect. He that knows not whither to go, is in no haste to move. Harley, who was perhaps not quick by nature, became yet more slow by irresolution; and was content to hear that dilatoriness lamented as natural, which he applauded in himself as politick.

Without the Tories, however, nothing could be done; and as they were not to be gratified, they must be appeased; and the conduct of the Minister, if it could not be vindicated, was to be plausibly excused.

Swift now attained the zenith of his political importance: he published (1712) the *Conduct of the Allies*, ten days before the Parliament assembled. The purpose was to persuade the nation to a peace; and never had any writer more success. The people, who had been amused with bonfires and triumphal processions, and looked with idolatry on the General and his friends, who, as they thought had made England the arbitress of nations, were confounded between shame and rage, when they found that *mines had been exhausted, and millions destroyed*, to secure the Dutch or aggrandize the emperor, without any advantage to ourselves; that we had been bribing our neighbours to fight their own quarrel; and that amongst our enemies we might number our allies.

That is now no longer doubted, of which the nation was then first informed, that the war was unnecessarily protracted to fill the pockets of Marlborough; and that it would have been continued without end, if he could have continued his annual plunder. But Swift, I suppose, did not yet know what he has since written, that a commission was drawn which would have appointed him General for life, had it not become ineffectual by the resolution of Lord Cowper, who refused the seal.

Whatever is received, say the schools, *is received in proportion to the recipient*. The power of a political treatise depends much upon the disposition of the people; the nation was then combustible, and a spark set it on fire. It is boasted, that between November and January eleven thousand were sold; a great number at that time, when we were not yet a nation of readers. To its propagation certainly no agency of power or influence was wanting. It furnished arguments for conversation, speeches for debate, and materials for parliamentary resolutions.

Yet, surely, whoever surveys this wonder-working pamphlet with cool perusal, will confess that its efficacy was supplied by the passions of its readers; that it operates by the mere weight of facts, with very little assistance from the hand that produced them.

This year (1712) he published his *Reflections on the Barrier Treaty*, which carries on the design of his *Conduct of the Allies*, and shews how little regard in that negotiation had been shewn to the interest of England, and how much of the conquered country had been demanded by the Dutch.

This was followed by *Remarks on the Bishop of Sarum's Introduction to his third Volume of the History of the Reformation*; a pamphlet which Burnet published as an alarm, to warn the nation of the approach of Popery. Swift, who seems to have disliked the Bishop with something more than political aversion, treats him like one whom he is glad of an opportunity to insult.

Swift, being now the declared favourite and supposed confidant of the Tory Ministry, was treated by all that depended on the Court with the respect which dependents know how to pay. He soon began to feel part of the misery of greatness; he that could say he knew him, considered himself as having fortune in his power. Commissions, solicitations, remonstrances, crowded about him; he was expected to do every man's business, to procure employment for one, and to retain it for another. In assisting those who addressed him, he represents himself as sufficiently diligent; and desires to have others believe, what he probably believed himself, that by his interposition many Whigs of merit, and among them Addison and Congreve, were continued in their places. But every man of known influence has so many petitions which he cannot grant, that he must necessarily offend more than he gratifies, because the preference given to one affords all the rest a reason for complaint. *When I give away a place*, said Lewis XIV. *I make an hundred discontented, and one ungrateful.*

Much has been said of the equality and independence which he preserved in his conversation with the Ministers, of the frankness of his remonstrances, and the familiarity of his friendship. In accounts of this kind a few single incidents are set against the general tenour of behaviour. No man, however, can pay a more servile tribute to the Great, than by suffering his liberty in their presence to aggrandize him in his own esteem. Between different ranks of the community there is necessarily some distance: he who is called by his superior to pass the interval, may properly accept the invitation; but petulance and obtrusion are rarely produced by magnanimity; nor have often any nobler cause than the pride of importance, and the malice of inferiority. He who knows himself necessary may set, while that necessity lasts, a high value upon himself; as, in a lower condition, a servant eminently skilful may be saucy; but he is saucy only because he is servile. Swift appears to have preserved the kindness of the great when they wanted him no longer; and therefore it must be allowed, that the childish freedom, to which he seems enough inclined, was overpowered by his better qualities.

His disinterestedness has been likewise mentioned; a strain of heroism, which would have been in his condition romantick and superfluous. Ecclesiastical benefices, when they become vacant, must be given away; and the friends of Power may, if there be no inherent disqualification, reasonably expect them. Swift accepted (1713) the deanery of St. Patrick, the best preferment that his friends could venture to give him. That Ministry was in a great degree supported by the Clergy, who were not yet reconciled to the author of the *Tale of a Tub*, and would not without much discontent and indignation have born to see him installed in an English Cathedral.

He refused, indeed, fifty pounds from Lord Oxford; but he accepted afterwards a draught of a thousand upon the Exchequer, which was intercepted by the Queen's death, and which he resigned, as he says himself, *multa gemens, with many a groan.*

In the midst of his power and his politicks, he kept a journal of his visits, his walks, his interviews with Ministers, and quarrels with his servant, and transmitted it to Mrs. Johnson and Mrs. Dingley, to whom he knew that whatever befel him was interesting, and no accounts could be too minute. Whether these diurnal trifles were properly exposed to eyes which had never received any pleasure from the presence of the Dean, may be reasonably doubted: they have, however, some odd attraction; the reader, finding frequent mention of names which he has been used to consider as important, goes on in hope of information; and, as there is nothing to fatigue attention, if he is disappointed he can hardly complain. It is easy to perceive, from every page, that though ambition pressed Swift into a life of bustle, the wish for a life of ease was always returning.

He went to take possession of his deanery, as soon as he had obtained it; but he was not suffered to stay in Ireland more than a fortnight before he was recalled to England, that he might reconcile Lord Oxford and Lord Bolingbroke, who began to look on one another with malevolence, which every day increased, and which Bolingbroke appeared to retain in his last years.

Swift contrived an interview, from which they both departed discontented: he procured a second, which only convinced him that the feud was irreconcileable; he told them his opinion, that all was lost. This denunciation was contradicted by Oxford, but Bolingbroke whispered that he was right.

Before this violent dissension had shattered the Ministry, Swift had published, in the beginning of the year (1714), *The publick Spirit of the Whigs*, in answer to *The Crisis*, a pamphlet for which *Steele* was expelled from the House of Commons. Swift was now so far alienated from *Steele* as to think him no longer entitled to decency, and therefore treats him sometimes with contempt, and sometimes with abhorrence.

In this pamphlet the Scotch were mentioned in terms so provoking to that irritable nation, that, resolving *not to be offended with impunity*, the Scotch

Lords in a body demanded an audience of the Queen, and solicited reparation. A proclamation was issued, in which three hundred pounds was offered for discovery of the author. From this storm he was, as he relates, *secured by a sleight*; of what kind, or by whose prudence, is not known; and such was the increase of his reputation, that the Scottish *Nation applied again that he would be their friend.*

He was become so formidable to the Whigs, that his familiarity with the Ministers was clamoured at in Parliament, particularly by two men, afterwards of great note, *Aislabie* and *Walpole.*

But, by the disunion of his great friends, his importance and his designs were now at an end; and seeing his services at last useless, he retired about June (1714) into Berkshire, where, in the house of a friend, he wrote what was then suppressed, but has since appeared under the title of *Free Thoughts on the present State of Affairs.*

While he was waiting in this retirement for events which time or chance might bring to pass, the death of the Queen broke down at once the whole system of Tory Politicks; and nothing remained but to withdraw from the implacability of triumphant Whiggism, and shelter himself in unenvied obscurity.

The accounts of his reception in Ireland, given by Lord Orrery and Dr. Delany, are so different, that the credit of the writers, both undoubtedly veracious, cannot be saved, but by supposing, what I think is true, that they speak of different times. When Delany says that he was received with respect, he means for the first fortnight, when he came to take legal possession; and when Lord Orrery tells that he was pelted by the populace, he is to be understood of the time when, after the Queen's death, he became a settled resident.

The Archbishop of Dublin gave him at first some disturbance in the exercise of his jurisdiction; but it was soon discovered, that between prudence and integrity he was seldom in the wrong; and that, when he was right, his spirit did not easily yield to opposition.

Having so lately quitted the tumults of a party and the intrigues of a court, they still kept his thoughts in agitation, as the sea fluctuates a while when the storm has ceased. He therefore filled his hours with some historical attempts, relating to the *Change of the Ministers* and *the Conduct of the Ministry*. He likewise is said to have written a *History of the Four last Years of Queen Anne*, which he began in her lifetime, and afterwards laboured with great attention, but never published. It was after his death in the hands of Lord Orrery and Dr. King. A book under that title was published, with Swift's name, by Dr. Lucas; of which I can only say, that it seemed by no means to correspond with the notions that I had formed of it, from a conversation which I once heard between the Earl of Orrery and old Mr. Lewis.

Swift now, much against his will, commenced Irishman for life, and was to contrive how he might be best accommodated in a country where he considered himself as in a state of exile. It seems that his first recourse was to piety. The thoughts of death rushed upon him, at this time, with such incessant importunity, that they took possession of his mind, when he first waked, for many years together.

He opened his house by a publick table two days a week, and found his entertainments gradually frequented by more and more visitants of learning among the men, and of elegance among the women. Mrs. Johnson had left the country, and lived in lodgings not far from the deanery. On his publick days she regulated the table, but appeared at it as a mere guest, like other Ladies.

On other days he often dined, at a stated price, with Mr. Worral, a clergyman of his cathedral, whose house was recommended by the peculiar neatness and pleasantry of his wife. To this frugal mode of living, he was first disposed by care to pay some debts which he had contracted, and he continued it for the pleasure of accumulating money. His avarice, however, was not suffered to obstruct the claims of his dignity; he was served in plate, and used to say that he was the poorest gentleman in Ireland that eat upon plate, and the richest that lived without a coach.

How he spent the rest of his time, and how he employed his hours of study, has been enquired with hopeless curiosity. For who can give an account of another's studies? Swift was not likely to admit any to his privacies, or to impart a minute account of his business or his leisure.

Soon after (1716), in his forty-ninth year, he was privately married to Mrs. Johnson by Dr. Ashe, Bishop of Clogher, as Dr. Madden told me, in the garden. The marriage made no change in their mode of life; they lived in different houses, as before; nor did she ever lodge in the deanery but when Swift was seized with a fit of giddiness. "It would be difficult," says Lord Orrery, "to prove that they were ever afterwards together without a third person."

The Dean of St. Patrick's lived in a private manner, known and regarded only by his friends, till, about the year 1720, he, by a pamphlet, recommended to the Irish the use, and consequently the improvement, of their manufacture. For a man to use the productions of his own labour is surely a natural right, and to like best what he makes himself is a natural passion. But to excite this passion, and enforce this right, appeared so criminal to those who had an interest in the English trade, that the printer was imprisoned; and, as Hawkesworth justly observes, the attention of the publick being by this outrageous resentment turned upon the proposal, the author was by consequence made popular.

In 1723 died Mrs. Van Homrigh, a woman made unhappy by her admiration of wit, and ignominiously distinguished by the name of *Vanessa*, whose conduct has been already sufficiently discussed, and whose history is too well known to be minutely repeated. She was a young woman fond of literature, whom *Decanus* the *Dean*, called *Cadenus* by transposition of the letters, took pleasure in directing and instructing; till, from being proud of his praise, she grew fond of his person. Swift was then about forty-seven, at an age when vanity is strongly excited by the amorous attention of a young woman. If it be said that Swift should have checked a passion which he never meant to gratify, recourse must be had to that extenuation which he so much despised, *men are but men*: perhaps however he did not at first know his own mind, and, as he represents himself, was undetermined. For his admission of her courtship, and his indulgence of her hopes after his marriage to Stella, no other honest plea can be found, than that he delayed a disagreeable discovery from time to time, dreading the immediate bursts of distress, and watching for a favourable moment. She thought herself neglected, and died of disappointment; having ordered by her will the poem to be published, in which *Cadenus* had proclaimed her excellence, and confessed his love. The effect of the publication upon the Dean and Stella is thus related by Delany.

"I have good reason to believe, that they both were greatly shocked and distressed (though it may be differently) upon this occasion. The Dean made a tour to the South of Ireland, for about two months, at this time, to dissipate his thoughts, and give place to obloquy. And Stella retired (upon the earnest invitation of the owner) to the house of a cheerful, generous, good-natured friend of the Dean's, whom she also much loved and honoured. There my informer often saw her; and, I have reason to believe, used his utmost endeavours to relieve, support, and amuse her, in this sad situation.

"One little incident he told me of, on that occasion, I think I shall never forget. As her friend was an hospitable, open-hearted man, well-beloved, and largely acquainted, it happened one day that some gentlemen dropt in to dinner, who were strangers to Stella's situation; and as the poem of *Cadenus and Vanessa* was then the general topic of conversation, one of them said, 'Surely that Vanessa must be an extraordinary woman, that could inspire the Dean to write so finely upon her.' Mrs. Johnson smiled, and answered, "that she thought that point not quite so clear; for it was well known the Dean could write finely upon a broomstick.""

The great acquisition of esteem and influence was made by the *Drapier's Letters* in 1724. One Wood of Wolverhampton in Staffordshire, a man enterprising and rapacious, had, as is said, by a present to the Duchess of Munster, obtained a patent, empowering him to coin one hundred and eighty thousand pounds of halfpence and farthings for the kingdom of Ireland, in which there was a very inconvenient and embarrassing scarcity of copper coin; so that it was possible to run in debt upon the credit of a piece of money; for the cook or keeper of an alehouse could not refuse to supply a man that had silver in his hand, and the buyer would not leave his money without change.

The project was therefore plausible. The scarcity, which was already great, Wood took care to make greater, by agents who gathered up the old halfpence; and was about to turn his brass into gold, by pouring the treasures of his new mint upon Ireland, when Swift, finding that the metal was debased to an enormous degree, wrote Letters, under the name of *M. B. Drapier*, to shew the folly of receiving, and the mischief that must ensue, by giving gold and silver for coin worth perhaps not a third part of its nominal value.

The nation was alarmed; the new coin was universally refused: but the governors of Ireland considered resistance to the King's patent as highly criminal; and one Whitshed, then Chief Justice, who had tried the printer of the former pamphlet, and sent out the Jury nine times, till by clamour and menaces they were frighted into a special verdict, now presented the *Drapier*, but could not prevail on the Grand Jury to find the bill.

Lord Carteret and the Privy Council published a proclamation, offering three hundred pounds for discovering the author of the Fourth Letter. Swift had concealed himself from his printers, and trusted only his butler, who transcribed the paper. The man, immediately after the appearance of the proclamation, strolled from the house, and staid out all night, and part of the next day. There was reason enough to fear that he had betrayed his master for the reward; but he came home, and the Dean ordered him to put off his livery, and leave the house; "for," says he, "I know that my life is in your power, and I will not bear, out of fear, either your insolence or negligence." The man excused his fault with great submission, and begged that he might be confined in the house while it was in his power to endanger his master; but the Dean resolutely turned him out, without taking farther notice of him, till the term of information had expired, and then received him again. Soon afterwards he ordered him and the rest of the servants into his presence, without telling his intentions, and bade them take notice that their fellow-servant was no longer Robert the butler; but that his integrity had made him Mr. Blakeney, verger of St. Patrick's; an officer whose income was between thirty and forty pounds a year: yet he still continued for some years to serve his old master as his butler.

Swift was known from this time by the appellation of *The Dean*. He was honoured by the populace, as the champion, patron, and instructor of Ireland; and gained such power as, considered both in its extent and duration, scarcely any man has ever enjoyed without greater wealth or higher station.

He was from this important year the oracle of the traders, and the idol of the rabble, and by consequence was feared and courted by all to whom the kindness of the traders or the populace was necessary. The *Drapier* was a sign; the *Drapier* was a health; and which way soever the eye or the ear was turned, some tokens were found of the nation's gratitude to the *Drapier*.

The benefit was indeed great; he had rescued Ireland from a very oppressive and predatory invasion; and the popularity which he had gained he was diligent to keep, by appearing forward and zealous on every occasion where the publick interest was supposed to be involved. Nor did he much scruple to boast his influence; for when, upon some attempts to regulate the coin,

Archbishop Boulter, then one of the Justices, accused him of exasperating the people, he exculpated himself by saying, "If I had lifted up my finger, they would have torn you to pieces."

But the pleasure of popularity was soon interrupted by domestic misery. Mrs. Johnson, whose conversation was to him the great softener of the ills of life, began in the year of the Drapier's triumph to decline; and two years afterwards was so wasted with sickness, that her recovery was considered as hopeless.

Swift was then in England, and had been invited by Lord Bolingbroke to pass the winter with him in France; but this call of calamity hastened him to Ireland, where perhaps his presence contributed to restore her to imperfect and tottering health.

He was now so much at ease, that (1727) he returned to England; where he collected three volumes of Miscellanies in conjunction with Pope, who prefixed a querulous and apologetical Preface.

This important year sent likewise into the world *Gulliver's Travels*, a production so new and strange, that it filled the reader with a mingled emotion of merriment and amazement. It was received with such avidity, that the price of the first edition was raised before the second could be made; it was read by the high and the low, the learned and illiterate. Criticism was for a while lost in wonder; no rules of judgement were applied to a book written in open defiance of truth and regularity. But when distinctions came to be made, the part which gave least pleasure was that which describes the *Flying Island*, and that which gave most disgust must be the history of the *Houyhnhnms*.

While Swift was enjoying the reputation of his new work, the news of the king's death arrived; and he kissed the hands of the new King and Queen three days after their accession.

By the Queen, when she was Princess, he had been treated with some distinction, and was well received by her in her exaltation; but whether she gave hopes which she never took care to satisfy, or he formed expectations which she never meant to raise, the event was, that he always afterwards thought on her with malevolence, and particularly charged her with breaking her promise of some medals which she engaged to send him.

I know not whether she had not, in her turn, some reason for complaint. A Letter was sent her, not so much entreating as requiring her patronage of Mrs. Barber, an ingenious Irishwoman, who was then begging subscriptions for her Poems. To this Letter was subscribed the name of *Swift*, and it has all the appearances of his diction and sentiments; but it was not written in his hand, and had some little improprieties. When he was charged with this Letter, he laid hold of the inaccuracies, and urged the improbability of the accusation; but never denied it: he shuffles between cowardice and veracity, and talks big when he says nothing.

He seemed desirous enough of recommencing courtier, and endeavoured to gain the kindness of Mrs. Howard, remembering what Mrs. Masham had performed in former times; but his flatteries were, like those of the other wits, unsuccessful; the Lady either wanted power, or had no ambition of poetical immortality.

He was seized not long afterwards by a fit of giddiness, and again heard of the sickness and danger of Mrs. Johnson. He then left the house of Pope, as it seems, with very little ceremony, finding that *two sick friends cannot live together*; and did not write to him till he found himself at Chester.

He returned to a home of sorrow: poor Stella was sinking into the grave, and, after a languishing decay of about two months, died in her forty-fourth year, on January 28, 1728. How much he wished her life, his papers shew; nor can it be doubted that he dreaded the death of her whom he loved most, aggravated by the consciousness that himself had hastened it.

Beauty and the power of pleasing, the greatest external advantages that woman can desire or possess, were fatal to the unfortunate Stella. The man whom she had the misfortune to love was, as Delany observes, fond of singularity, and desirous to make a mode of happiness for himself, different from the general course of things and order of Providence. From the time of her arrival in Ireland he seems resolved to keep her in his power, and therefore hindered a match sufficiently advantageous, by accumulating unreasonable demands, and prescribing conditions that could not be performed. While she was at her own disposal he did not consider his possession as secure; resentment, ambition, or caprice, might separate them; he was therefore resolved to make *assurance double sure*, and to appropriate her by a private marriage, to which he had annexed the expectation of all the pleasures of perfect friendship, without the uneasiness of conjugal restraint. But with this state poor Stella was not satisfied; she never was treated as a wife, and to the world she had the appearance of a mistress. She lived sullenly on, in hope that in time he would own and receive her; but the time did not come till the change of his manners and depravation of his mind made her tell him, when he offered to acknowledge her, that *it was too late*. She then gave up herself to sorrowful resentment, and died under the tyranny of him, by whom she was in the highest degree loved and honoured.

What were her claims to this excentrick tenderness, by which the laws of nature were violated to retain her, curiosity will enquire; but how shall it be gratified? Swift was a lover; his testimony may be suspected. Delany and the Irish saw with Swift's eyes, and therefore add little confirmation. That she was virtuous, beautiful, and elegant, in a very high degree, such admiration from such a lover makes it very probable; but she had not much literature, for she could not spell her own language; and of her wit, so loudly vaunted, the smart sayings which Swift himself has collected afford no splendid specimen.

The reader of Swift's *Letter to a Lady on her Marriage*, may be allowed to doubt whether his opinion of female excellence ought implicitly to be admitted; for if his general thoughts on women were such as he exhibits, a very little sense in a Lady would enrapture, and a very little virtue would astonish him. Stella's supremacy, therefore, was perhaps only local; she was great, because her associates were little.

In some Remarks lately published on the Life of Swift, this marriage is mentioned as fabulous, or doubtful; but, alas! poor Stella, as Dr. Madden told me, related her melancholy story to Dr. Sheridan, when he attended her as a clergyman to prepare her for death; and Delany mentions it not with doubt, but only with regret. Swift never mentioned her without a sigh.

The rest of his life was spent in Ireland, in a country to which not even power almost despotick, nor flattery almost idolatrous, could reconcile him. He sometimes wished to visit England, but always found some reason of delay. He tells Pope, in the decline of life, that he hopes once more to see him; *but if not*, says he, *we must part, as all human beings have parted.*

After the death of Stella, his benevolence was contracted, and his severity exasperated; he drove his acquaintance from his table, and wondered why he was deserted. But he continued his attention to the publick, and wrote from time to time such directions, admonitions, or censures, as the exigency of affairs, in his opinion, made proper; and nothing fell from his pen in vain.

In a short poem on the Presbyterians, whom he always regarded with detestation, he bestowed one stricture upon Bettesworth, a lawyer eminent for his insolence to the clergy, which, from very considerable reputation, brought him into immediate and universal contempt. Bettesworth, enraged at his disgrace and loss, went to Swift, and demanded whether he was the author of that poem? "Mr. Bettesworth," answered he, "I was in my youth acquainted with great lawyers, who, knowing my disposition to satire, advised me, that, if any scoundrel or blockhead whom I had lampooned should ask, *Are you the author of this paper?* I should tell him that I was not the author; and therefore I tell you, Mr. Bettesworth, that I am not the author of these lines."

Bettesworth was so little satisfied with this account, that he publickly professed his resolution of a violent and corporal revenge; but the inhabitants of St. Patrick's district embodied themselves in the Dean's defence. Bettesworth declared in Parliament, that Swift had deprived him of twelve hundred pounds a year.

Swift was popular a while by another mode of beneficence. He set aside some hundreds to be lent in small sums to the poor, from five shillings, I think, to five pounds. He took no interest, and only required that, at repayment, a small fee should be given to the accomptant; but he required that the day of promised payment should be exactly kept. A severe and punctilious temper is ill qualified for transactions with the poor; the day was often broken, and the loan was not repaid. This might have been easily foreseen; but for this Swift had made no provision of patience or pity. He ordered his debtors to be sued. A severe creditor has no popular character; what then was likely to be said of him who employs the catchpoll under the appearance of charity? The clamour against him was loud, and the resentment of the populace outrageous; he was therefore forced to drop his scheme, and own the folly of expecting punctuality from the poor.

His asperity continually increasing, condemned him to solitude; and his resentment of solitude sharpened his asperity. He was not, however, totally deserted: some men of learning, and some women of elegance, often visited him; and he wrote from time to time either verse or prose; of his verses he willingly gave copies, and is supposed to have felt no discontent when he saw them printed. His favourite maxim was *vive la bagatelle*; he thought trifles a necessary part of life, and perhaps found them necessary to himself. It seems impossible to him to be idle, and his disorders made it difficult or dangerous to be long seriously studious, or laboriously diligent. The love of ease is always gaining upon age, and he had one temptation to petty amusements peculiar to himself; whatever he did, he was sure to hear applauded; and such was his predominance over all that approached, that all their applauses were probably sincere. He that is much flattered, soon learns to flatter himself: we are commonly taught our duty by fear or shame, and how can they act upon the man who hears nothing but his own praises?

As his years increased, his fits of giddiness and deafness grew more frequent, and his deafness made conversation difficult; they grew likewise more severe, till in 1736, as he was writing a poem called *The Legion Club*, he was seized with a fit so painful, and so long continued, that he never after thought it proper to attempt any work of thought or labour.

He was always careful of his money, and was therefore no liberal entertainer; but was less frugal of his wine than of his meat. When his friends of either sex came to him, in expectation of a dinner, his custom was to give every one a shilling, that they might please themselves with their provision. At last his avarice grew too powerful for his kindness; he would refuse a bottle of wine, and in Ireland no man visits where he cannot drink.

Having thus excluded conversation, and desisted from study, he had neither business nor amusement; for having, by some ridiculous resolution or mad vow, determined never to wear spectacles, he could make little use of books in his later years: his ideas, therefore, being neither renovated by discourse, nor increased by reading, wore gradually away, and left his mind vacant to the vexations of the hour, till at last his anger was heightened into madness.

He however permitted one book to be published, which had been the production of former years; *Polite Conversation*, which appeared in 1738. The *Directions for Servants* was printed soon after his death. These two performances shew a mind incessantly attentive, and, when it was not employed upon great things, busy with minute occurrences. It is apparent that he must have had the habit of noting whatever he observed; for such a number of particulars could never have been assembled by the power of recollection.

He grew more violent; and his mental powers declined till (1741) it was found necessary that legal guardians should be appointed of his person and fortune. He now lost distinction. His madness was compounded of rage and fatuity. The last face that he knew was that of Mrs. Whiteway, and her he ceased to know in a little time. His meat was brought him cut into mouthfuls; but he would never touch it while the servant staid, and at last, after it had stood perhaps an hour, would eat it walking; for he continued his old habit, and was on his feet ten hours a-day.

Next year (1742) he had an inflammation in his left eye, which swelled it to the size of an egg, with boils in other parts; he was kept long waking with the pain, and was not easily restrained by five attendants from tearing out his eye.

The tumour at last subsided; and a short interval of reason ensuing, in which he knew his physician and his family, gave hopes of his recovery; but in a few days he sunk into lethargick stupidity, motionless, heedless, and speechless. But it is said, that, after a year of total silence, when his housekeeper, on the 30th of November, told him that the usual bonfires and illuminations were preparing to celebrate his birth-day, he answered, *It is all folly; they had better let it alone.*

It is remembered that he afterwards spoke now and then, or gave some intimation of a meaning; but at last sunk into perfect silence, which continued till about the end of October 1744, when, in his seventy-eighth year, he expired without a struggle.

WHEN Swift is considered as an author, it is just to estimate his powers by their effects. In the reign of Queen Anne he turned the stream of popularity against the Whigs, and must be confessed to have dictated for a time the political opinions of the English nation. In the succeeding reign he delivered Ireland from plunder and oppression; and shewed that wit, confederated with truth, had such force as authority was unable to resist. He said truly of himself, that Ireland *was his debtor*. It was from the time when he first began to patronize the Irish, that they may date their riches and prosperity. He taught them first to know their own interest, their weight, and their strength, and gave them spirit to assert that equality with their fellow-subjects to which they have ever since been making vigorous advances, and to claim those rights which they have at last established. Nor can they be charged with ingratitude to their benefactor; for they reverenced him as a guardian, and obeyed him as a dictator.

In his works, he has given very different specimens both of sentiment and expression. His *Tale of a Tub* has little resemblance to his other pieces. It exhibits a vehemence and rapidity of mind, a copiousness of images, and vivacity of diction, such as he afterwards never possessed, or never exerted. It is of a mode so distinct and peculiar, that it must be considered by itself; what is true of that, is not true of any thing else which he has written.

In his other works is found an equable tenour of easy language, which rather trickles than flows. His delight was in simplicity. That he has in his works no metaphor, as has been said, is not true; but his few metaphors seem to be received rather by necessity than choice. He studied purity; and though perhaps all his structures are not exact, yet it is not often that solecisms can be found; and whoever depends on his authority may generally conclude himself safe. His sentences are never too much dilated or contracted; and it will not be easy to find any embarrassment in the complication of his clauses, any inconsequence in his connections, or abruptness in his transitions.

His style was well suited to his thoughts, which are never subtilised by nice disquisitions, decorated by sparkling conceits, elevated by ambitious sentences, or variegated by far-sought learning. He pays no court to the passions; he excites neither surprise nor admiration; he always understands himself: and his reader always understands him: the peruser of Swift wants little previous knowledge; it will be sufficient that he is acquainted with common words and common things; he is neither required to mount elevations, nor to explore profundities; his passage is always on a level, along solid ground, without asperities, without obstruction.

This easy and safe conveyance of meaning it was Swift's desire to attain, and for having attained he deserves praise, though perhaps not the highest praise. For purposes merely didactick, when something is to be told that was not known before, it is the best mode, but against that inattention by which known truths are suffered to lie neglected, it makes no provision; it instructs, but does not persuade.

By his political education he was associated with the Whigs; but he deserted them when they deserted their principles, yet without running into the contrary extreme; he continued throughout his life to retain the disposition which he assigns to the *Church-of-England Man*, of thinking commonly with the Whigs of the State, and with the Tories of the Church.

He was a churchman rationally zealous; he desired the prosperity, and maintained the honour of the Clergy; of the Dissenters he did not wish to infringe the toleration, but he opposed their encroachments.

To his duty as Dean he was very attentive. He managed the revenues of his church with exact œconomy; and it is said by Delany, that more money was, under his direction, laid out in repairs than had ever been in the same time since its first erection. Of his choir he was eminently careful; and, though he neither loved nor understood musick, took care that all the singers were well qualified, admitting none without the testimony of skilful judges.

In his church he restored the practice of weekly communion, and distributed the sacramental elements in the most solemn and devout manner with his own hand. He came to church every morning, preached commonly in his turn, and attended the evening anthem, that it might not be negligently performed.

He read the service *rather with a strong nervous voice than in a graceful manner; his voice was sharp and high-toned, rather than harmonious.*

He entered upon the clerical state with hope to excel in preaching; but complained, that, from the time of his political controversies, *he could only preach pamphlets.* This censure of himself, if judgement be made from those sermons which have been published, was unreasonably severe.

The suspicions of his irreligion proceeded in a great measure from his dread of hypocrisy; instead of wishing to seem better, he delighted in seeming worse than he was. He went in London to early prayers, lest he should be seen at church; he read prayers to his servants every morning with such dexterous secrecy, that Dr. Delany was six months in his house before he knew it. He was not only careful to hide the good which he did, but willingly incurred the suspicion of evil which he did not. He forgot what himself had formerly asserted, that hypocrisy is less mischievous than open impiety. Dr. Delany, with all his zeal for his honour, has justly condemned this part of his character.

The person of Swift had not many recommendations. He had a kind of muddy complexion, which, though he washed himself with oriental scrupulosity, did not look clear. He had a countenance sour and severe, which he seldom softened by any appearance of gaiety. He stubbornly resisted any tendency to laughter.

To his domesticks he was naturally rough; and a man of a rigorous temper, with that vigilance of minute attention which his works discover, must have been a master that few could bear. That he was disposed to do his servants good, on important occasions, is no great mitigation; benefaction can be but rare, and tyrannick peevishness is perpetual. He did not spare the servants of others. Once, when he dined alone with the Earl of Orrery, he said, of one that waited in the room, *That man has, since we sat to the table, committed fifteen faults.* What the faults were, Lord Orrery, from whom I heard the story, had not been attentive enough to discover. My number may perhaps not be exact.

In his œconomy he practised a peculiar and offensive parsimony, without disguise or apology. The practice of saving being once necessary, became habitual, and grew first ridiculous, and at last detestable. But his avarice, though it might exclude pleasure, was never suffered to encroach upon his virtue. He was frugal by inclination, but liberal by principle; and if the purpose to which he destined his little accumulations be remembered, with his distribution of occasional charity, it will perhaps appear that he only liked one mode of expence better than another, and saved merely that he might have something to give. He did not grow rich by injuring his successors, but left both Laracor and the Deanery more valuable than he found them.

—With all this talk of his covetousness and generosity, it should be remembered that he was never rich. The revenue of his Deanery was not much more than seven hundred a year.

His beneficence was not graced with tenderness or civility; he relieved without pity, and assisted without kindness, so that those who were fed by him could hardly love him.

He made a rule to himself to give but one piece at a time, and therefore always stored his pocket with coins of different value.

Whatever he did, he seemed willing to do in a manner peculiar to himself, without sufficiently considering that singularity, as it implies a contempt of the general practice, is a kind of defiance which justly provokes the hostility of ridicule; he therefore who indulges peculiar habits is worse than others, if he be not better.

Of his humour, a story told by Pope may afford a specimen.

*"Dr. Swift has an odd, blunt way, that is mistaken, by strangers, for ill-nature. —'Tis so odd, that there's no describing it but by facts. I'll tell you one that first comes into my head. One evening, Gay and I went to see him: you know how intimately we were all acquainted. On our coming in, 'Heyday, gentlemen (says the Doctor), what's the meaning of this visit? How came you to leave all the great Lords, that you are so fond of, to come hither to see a poor Dean?'—Because we would rather see you than any of them.—'Ay, any one that did not know so well as I do, might believe you. But since you are come, I must get some supper for you, I suppose.' No, Doctor, we have supped already.—'Supped already? that's impossible! why, 'tis not eight o'clock yet.— That's very strange; but, if you had not supped, I must have got something for you.—Let me see, what should I have had? A couple of lob-sters; ay, that would have done very well; two shillings—tarts, a shilling: but you will drink a glass of wine with me, though you supped so much before your usual time only to spare my pocket?'—No, we had rather talk with you than drink with you.—'But if you had supped with me, as in all reason you ought to have done, you must then have drunk with me.—A bottle of wine, two shillings—two and two is four, and one is five: just two-and-six-pence a-piece. There, Pope, there's half a crown for you, and there's another for you, Sir; for I won't save any thing by you, I am determined.'—This was all said and done with his usual seriousness on such occasions; and, in spite of every thing we could say to the contrary, he actually obliged us to take the money."

In the intercourse of familiar life, he indulged his disposition to petulance and sarcasm, and thought himself injured if the licentiousness of his raillery, the freedom of his censures, or the petulance of his frolicks, was resented or repressed. He predominated over his companions with very high ascendency, and probably would bear none over whom he could not predominate. To give him advice was, in the style of his friend Delany, *to venture to speak to him.* This customary superiority soon grew too delicate for truth; and Swift, with all his penetration, allowed himself to be delighted with low flattery.

* Spence.

On all common occasions, he habitually affects a style of arrogance, and dictates rather than persuades. This authoritative and magisterial language he expected to be received as his peculiar mode of jocularity; but he apparently flattered his own arrogance by an assumed imperiousness, in which he was ironical only to the resentful, and to the submissive sufficiently serious.

He told stories with great felicity, and delighted in doing what he knew himself to do well. He was therefore captivated by the respectful silence of a steady listener, and told the same tales too often.

He did not, however, claim the right of talking alone; for it was his rule, when he had spoken a minute, to give room by a pause for any other speaker. Of time, on all occasions, he was an exact computer, and knew the minutes required to every common operation.

It may be justly supposed that there was in his conversation, what appears so frequently in his Letters, an affectation of familiarity with the Great, an ambition of momentary equality sought and enjoyed by the neglect of those ceremonies which custom has established as the barriers between one order of society and another. This transgression of regularity was by himself and his admirers termed greatness of soul. But a great mind disdains to hold any thing by courtesy, and therefore never usurps what a lawful claimant may take away. He that encroaches on another's dignity, puts himself in his power; he is either repelled with helpless indignity, or endured by clemency and condescension.

Of Swift's general habits of thinking if his Letters can be supposed to afford any evidence, he was not a man to be either loved or envied. He seems to have wasted life in discontent, by the rage of neglected pride, and the languishment of unsatisfied desire. He is querulous and fastidious, arrogant and malignant; he scarcely speaks of himself but with indignant lamentations, or of others but with insolent superiority when he is gay, and with angry contempt when he is gloomy. From the Letters that pass between him and Pope it might be inferred that they, with Arbuthnot and Gay, had engrossed all the understanding and virtue of mankind, that their merits filled the world; or that there was no hope of more. They shew the age involved in darkness, and shade the picture with sullen emulation.

When the Queen's death drove him into Ireland, he might be allowed to regret for a time the interception of his views, the extinction of his hopes, and his ejection from gay scenes, important employment, and splendid friendships; but when time had enabled reason to prevail over vexation, the complaints, which at first were natural, became ridiculous because they were useless. But querulousness was now grown habitual, and he cried out when he probably had ceased to feel. His reiterated wailings persuaded Bolingbroke that he was really willing to quit his deanery for an English parish; and Bolingbroke procured an exchange, which was rejected, and Swift still retained the pleasure of complaining.

The greatest difficulty that occurs, in analysing his character, is to discover by what depravity of intellect he took delight in revolving ideas, from which almost every other mind shrinks with disgust. The ideas of pleasure, even when criminal, may solicit the imagination; but what has disease, deformity, and filth, upon which the thoughts can be allured to dwell? Delany is willing to think that Swift's mind was not much tainted with this gross corruption before his long visit to Pope. He does not consider how he degrades his hero, by making him at fifty-nine the pupil of turpitude, and liable to the malignant influence of an ascendant mind. But the truth is, that Gulliver had described his *Yahoos* before the visit, and he that had formed those images had nothing filthy to learn.

I have here given the character of Swift as he exhibits himself to my perception; but now let another be heard, who knew him better; Dr. Delany, after long acquaintance, describes him to Lord Orrery in these terms:

"My Lord, when you consider Swift's singular, peculiar and most variegated vein of wit, always rightly intended (although not always so rightly directed), delightful in many instances, and salutary, even where it is most offensive; when you consider his strict truth, his fortitude in resisting oppression and arbitrary power; his fidelity in friendship, his sincere love and zeal for religion, his uprightness in making right resolutions, and his steadiness in adhering to them; his care of his church, its choir, its œconomy, and its income; his attention to all those that preached in his cathedral, in order to their amendment in pronunciation and style; as also his remarkable attention to the interest of his successors, preferably to his own present emoluments; invincible patriotism, even to a country which he did not love; his very various, well-devised, well-judged, and extensive charities, throughout his life, and his whole fortune (to say nothing of his wife's) conveyed to the same Christian purposes at his death; charities from which he could enjoy no honour, advantage or satisfaction of any kind in this world. When you consider his ironical and humorous, as well as his serious schemes, for the promotion of true religion and virtue; his success in soliciting for the First Fruits and Twentieths, to the unspeakable benefit of the established Church of Ireland; and his felicity (to rate it no higher) in giving occasion to the building of fifty new churches in London.

"All this considered, the character of his life will appear like that of his writings; they will both bear to be re-considered and re-examined with the utmost attention, and always discover new beauties and excellences upon every examination.

"They will bear to be considered as the sun, in which the brightness will hide the blemishes; and whenever petulant ignorance, pride, malice, malignity, or envy, interposes to cloud or sully his fame, I will take upon me to pronounce that the eclipse will not last long.

"To conclude—no man ever deserved better of any country than Swift did of his. A steady, persevering, inflexible friend; a wise, a watchful, and a faithful counsellor, under many severe trials and bitter persecutions, to the manifest hazard both of his liberty and fortune.

"He lived a blessing, he died a benefactor, and his name will ever live an honour to Ireland."

IN the Poetical Works of Dr. Swift there is not much upon which the critick can exercise his powers. They are often humorous, almost always light, and have the qualities which recommend such compositions, easiness and gaiety. They are, for the most part what their author intended. The diction is correct, the numbers are smooth, and the rhymes exact. There seldom occurs a hard-laboured expression, or a redundant epithet; all his verses exemplify his own definition of a good style, they consist of *proper words in proper places*.

To divide this Collection into classes, and shew how some pieces are gross, and some are trifling, would be to tell the reader what he knows already, and to find faults of which the author could not be ignorant, who certainly wrote often not to his judgement, but his humour.

It was said, in a Preface to one of the Irish editions, that Swift had never been known to take a single thought from any writer, ancient or modern. This is not literally true; but perhaps no writer can easily be found that has borrowed so little, or that in all his excellences and all his defects has so well maintained his claim to be considered as original.

POPE [extract]

THE person of Pope is well known not to have been formed by the nicest model. He has, in his account of the *Little Club*, compared himself to a spider, and by another is described as protuberant behind and before. He is said to have been beautiful in his infancy; but he was of a constitution originally feeble and weak; and as bodies of a tender frame are easily distorted, his deformity was probably in part the effect of his application. His stature was so low, that, to bring him to a level with common tables, it was necessary to raise his seat. But his face was not displeasing, and his eyes were animated and vivid.

By natural deformity, or accidental distortion, his vital functions were so much disordered, that his life was a *long disease*. His most frequent assailant was the headach, which he used to relieve by inhaling the steam of coffee, which he very frequently required.

Most of what can be told concerning his petty peculiarities was communicated by a female domestick of the Earl of Oxford, who knew him perhaps after the middle of life. He was then so weak as to stand in perpetual need of female attendance; extremely sensible of cold, so that he wore a kind of fur doublet, under a shirt of very coarse warm linen with fine sleeves. When he rose, he was invested in boddice made of stiff canvass, being scarce able to hold himself erect till they were laced, and he then put on a flannel waistcoat.

One side was contracted. His legs were so slender, that he enlarged their bulk with three pair of stockings, which were drawn on and off by the maid; for he was not able to dress or undress himself, and neither went to bed nor rose without help. His weakness made it very difficult for him to be clean.

His hair had fallen almost all away; and he used to dine sometimes with Lord Oxford, privately, in a velvet cap. His dress of ceremony was black with a tye-wig, and a little sword.

The indulgence and accommodation which his sickness required, had taught him all the unpleasing and unsocial qualities of a valetudinary man. He expected that every thing should give way to his ease or humour, as a child, whose parents will not hear her cry, has an unresisted dominion in the nursery.

> C'est que l'enfant toûjours est homme,
> C'est que l'homme est toûjours enfant.

When he wanted to sleep he *nodded in company*; and once slumbered at his own table while the Prince of Wales was talking of poetry.

The reputation which his friendship gave, procured him many invitations; but he was a very troublesome inmate. He brought no servant, and had so many wants, that a numerous attendance was scarcely able to supply them. Wherever he was, he left no room for another, because he exacted the attention, and employed the activity of the whole family. His errands were so frequent and frivolous, that the footmen in time avoided and neglected him; and the Earl of Oxford discharged some of the servants for their resolute refusal of his messages. The maids, when they had neglected their business, alleged that they had been employed by Mr. Pope. One of his constant demands was of coffee in the night, and to the woman that waited on him in his chamber he was very burthensome; but he was careful to recompense her want of sleep; and Lord Oxford's servant declared, that in a house where her business was to answer his call, she would not ask for wages.

He had another fault, easily incident to those who, suffering much pain, think themselves entitled to whatever pleasures they can snatch. He was too indulgent to his appetite; he loved meat highly seasoned and of strong taste; and, at the intervals of the table, amused himself with biscuits and dry conserves. If he sat down to a variety of dishes, he would oppress his stomach with repletion, and though he seemed angry when a dram was offered him, did not forbear to drink it. His friends, who knew the avenues to his heart, pampered him with presents of luxury, which he did not suffer to stand neglected. The death of great men is not always proportioned to the lustre of their lives. Hannibal, says Juvenal, did not perish by a javelin or a sword; the slaughters of Cannæ were revenged by a ring. The death of Pope was imputed by some of his friends to a silver saucepan, in which it was his delight to heat potted lampreys.

That he loved too well to eat, is certain; but that his sensuality shortened his life will not be hastily concluded, when it is remembered that a conformation so irregular lasted six and fifty years, notwithstanding such pertinacious diligence of study and meditation.

In all his intercourse with mankind, he had great delight in artifice, and endeavoured to attain all his purposes by indirect and unsuspected methods. *He hardly drank tea without a stratagem.* If, at the house of his friends, he wanted any accommodation, he was not willing to ask for it in plain terms, but would mention it remotely as something convenient; though, when it was procured, he soon made it appear for whose sake it had been recommended. Thus he teized Lord Orrery till he obtained a screen. He practised his arts on such small occasions, that Lady Bolingbroke used to say, in a French phrase, that *he plaid the politician about cabbages and turnips.* His unjustifiable impression of the *Patriot King*, as it can be imputed to no particular motive, must have proceeded from his general habit of secrecy and cunning; he caught an opportunity of a sly trick, and pleased himself with the thought of outwitting Bolingbroke.

In familiar or convivial conversation, it does not appear that he excelled. He may be said to have resembled Dryden, as being not one that was distinguished by vivacity in company. It is remarkable, that, so near his time, so much should be known of what he has written, and so little of what he has said: traditional memory retains no sallies of raillery, nor sentences of observation; nothing either pointed or solid, either wise or merry. One apophthegm only stands upon record. When an objection raised against his inscription for Shakspeare was defended by the authority of *Patrick*, he replied—*horresco referens*—that *he would allow the publisher of a Dictionary to know the meaning of a single word, but not of two words put together.*

He was fretful, and easily displeased, and allowed himself to be capriciously resentful. He would sometimes leave Lord Oxford silently, no one could tell why, and was to be courted back by more letters and messages than the footmen were willing to carry. The table was indeed infested by Lady Mary Wortley, who was the friend of Lady Oxford, and who, knowing his peevishness, could by no intreaties be restrained from contradicting him, till their disputes were sharpened to such asperity, that one or the other quitted the house.

He sometimes condescended to be jocular with servants or inferiors; but by no merriment, either of others or his own, was he ever seen excited to laughter.

Of his domestick character, frugality was a part eminently remarkable. Having determined not to be dependent, he determined not to be in want, and therefore wisely and magnanimously rejected all temptations to expence unsuitable to his fortune. This general care must be universally approved; but it sometimes appeared in petty artifices of parsimony, such as the practice of writing his compositions on the back of letters, as may be seen in the remaining copy of the *Iliad*, by which perhaps in five years five shillings were saved; or in a niggardly reception of his friends, and scantiness of entertainment, as, when he had two guests in his house, he would set at supper a single pint upon the table; and having himself taken two small glasses would retire, and say, *Gentlemen, I leave you to your wine.* Yet he tells his friends, that *he has a heart for all, a house for all, and, whatever they may think, a fortune for all.*

He sometimes, however, made a splendid dinner, and is said to have wanted no part of the skill or elegance which such performances require. That this magnificence should be often displayed, that obstinate prudence with which he conducted his affairs would not permit; for his revenue, certain and casual, amounted only to about eight hundred pounds a year, of which however he declares himself able to assign one hundred to charity.

Of this fortune, which as it arose from publick approbation was very honourably obtained, his imagination seems to have been too full: it would be hard to find a man, so well entitled to notice by his wit, that ever delighted so much in talking of his money. In his Letters, and in his Poems, his garden and his grotto, his quincunx and his vines, or some hints of his opulence, are always to be found. The great topick of his ridicule is poverty; the crimes with which he reproaches his antagonists are their debts, their habitation in the Mint, and their want of a dinner. He seems to be of an opinion not very uncommon in the world, that to want money is to want every thing.

Next to the pleasure of contemplating his possessions, seems to be that of enumerating the men of high rank with whom he was acquainted, and whose notice he loudly proclaims not to have been obtained by any practices of meanness or servility; a boast which was never denied to be true, and to which very few poets have ever aspired. Pope never set his genius to sale; he never flattered those whom he did not love, or praised those whom he did not esteem. Savage however remarked, that he began a little to relax his dignity when he wrote a distich for *his Highness's dog.*

His admiration of the Great seems to have increased in the advance of life. He passed over peers and statesmen to inscribe his *Iliad* to Congreve, with a magnanimity of which the praise had been compleat, had his friend's virtue been equal to his wit. Why he was chosen for so great an honour, it is not now possible to know; there is no trace in literary history of any particular intimacy between them. The name of Congreve appears in the Letters among those of his other friends, but without any observable distinction or consequence.

To his latter works, however, he took care to annex names dignified with titles, but was not very happy in his choice; for, except Lord Bathurst, none of his noble friends were such as that a good man would wish to have his intimacy with them known to posterity: he can derive little honour from the notice of Cobham, Burlington, or Bolingbroke.

Of his social qualities, if an estimate be made from his Letters, an opinion too favourable cannot easily be formed; they exhibit a perpetual and unclouded effulgence of general benevolence, and particular fondness. There is nothing but liberality, gratitude, constancy, and tenderness. It has been so long said as to be commonly believed, that the true characters of men may be found in their Letters, and that he who writes to his friend lays his heart open before him. But the truth is, that such were simple friendships of the *Golden Age*, and are now the friendships only of children. Very few can boast of hearts which they dare lay open to themselves, and of which, by whatever accident exposed, they do not shun a distinct and continued view; and, certainly, what we hide from ourselves we do not shew to our friends. There is, indeed, no transaction which offers stronger temptations to fallacy and sophistication than epistolary intercourse. In the eagerness of conversation the first emotions of the mind often burst out, before they are considered; in the tumult of business, interest and passion have their genuine effect; but a friendly Letter is a calm and deliberate performance, in the cool of leisure, in the stillness of solitude, and surely no man sits down to depreciate by design his own character.

Friendship has no tendency to secure veracity; for by whom can a man so much wish to be thought better than he is, as by him whose kindness he desires to gain or keep? Even in writing to the world there is less constraint; the author is not confronted with his reader, and takes his chance of approbation among the different dispositions of mankind; but a Letter is addressed to a single mind, of which the prejudices and partialities are known; and must therefore please, if not by favouring them, by forbearing to oppose them.

To charge those favourable representations, which men give of their own minds, with the guilt of hypocritical falshood, would shew more severity than knowledge. The writer commonly believes himself. Almost every man's thoughts, while they are general, are right; and most hearts are pure, while temptation is away. It is easy to awaken generous sentiments in privacy; to despise death when there is no danger; to glow with benevolence when there is nothing to be given. While such ideas are formed they are felt, and self-love does not suspect the gleam of virtue to be the meteor of fancy.

If the Letters of Pope are considered merely as compositions, they seem to be premeditated and artificial. It is one thing to write because there is something which the mind wishes to discharge, and another, to solicit the imagination because ceremony or vanity requires something to be written. Pope confesses his early Letters to be vitiated with *affectation and ambition*: to know whether he disentangled himself from these perverters of epistolary integrity, his book and his life must be set in comparison.

One of his favourite topicks is contempt of his own poetry. For this, if it had been real, he would deserve no commendation, and in this he was certainly not sincere; for his high value of himself was sufficiently observed, and of what could he be proud but of his poetry? He writes, he says, when *he has just nothing else to do*; yet Swift complains that he was never at leisure for conversation, because he *had always some poetical scheme in his head*. It was punctually required that his writing-box should be set upon his bed before he rose; and Lord Oxford's domestick related, that, in the dreadful winter of Forty, she was called from her bed by him four times in one night, to supply him with paper, lest he should lose a thought.

He pretends insensibility to censure and criticism, though it was observed by all who knew him that every pamphlet disturbed his quiet, and that his extreme irritability laid him open to perpetual vexation; but he wished to despise his criticks, and therefore hoped that he did despise them.

As he happened to live in two reigns when the Court paid little attention to poetry, he nursed in his mind a foolish disesteem of Kings, and proclaims that *he never sees Courts*. Yet a little regard shewn him by the Prince of Wales melted his obduracy; and he had not much to say when he was asked by his Royal Highness, *how he could love a Prince while he disliked Kings?*

He very frequently professes contempt of the world, and represents himself as looking on mankind, sometimes with gay indifference, as on emmets of a hillock, below his serious attention; and sometimes with gloomy indignation, as on monsters more worthy of hatred than of pity. These were dispositions apparently counterfeited. How could he despise those whom he lived by pleasing, and on whose approbation his esteem of himself was superstructed? Why should he hate those to whose favour he owed his honour and his ease? Of things that terminate in human life, the world is the proper judge; to despise its sentence, if it were possible, is not just; and if it were just, is not possible. Pope was far enough from this unreasonable temper; he was sufficiently *a fool to Fame*, and his fault was that he pretended to neglect it. His levity and his sullenness were only in his Letters; he passed through common life, sometimes vexed, and sometimes pleased, with the natural emotions of common men.

His scorn of the Great is repeated too often to be real; no man thinks much of that which he despises; and as falsehood is always in danger of inconsistency, he makes it his boast at another time that he lives among them.

It is evident that his own importance swells often in his mind. He is afraid of writing, lest the clerks of the Post-office should know his secrets; he has many enemies; he considers himself as surrounded by universal jealousy; *after many deaths, and many dispersions, two or three of us*, says he, *may still be brought together, not to plot, but to divert ourselves, and the world too, if it pleases*; and they can live together, and *shew what friends wits may be, in spite of all the fools in the world*. All this while it was likely that the clerks did not know his hand; he certainly had no more enemies than a publick character like his inevitably excites, and with what degree of friendship the wits might live, very few were so much fools as ever to enquire.

Some part of this pretended discontent he learned from Swift, and expresses it, I think, most frequently in his correspondence with him. Swift's resentment was unreasonable, but it was sincere; Pope's was the mere mimickry of his friend, a fictitious part which he began to play before it became him. When he was only twenty-five years old, he related that *a glut of study and retirement had thrown him on the world*, and that there was danger lest *a glut of the world should throw him back upon study and retirement*. To this Swift answered with great propriety, that Pope had not yet either acted or suffered enough in the world to have become weary of it. And, indeed, it must be some very powerful reason that can drive back to solitude him who has once enjoyed the pleasures of society.

In the Letters both of Swift and Pope there appears such narrowness of mind, as makes them insensible of any excellence that has not some affinity with their own, and confines their esteem and approbation to so small a number, that whoever should form his opinion of the age from their representation, would suppose them to have lived amidst ignorance and barbarity, unable to find among their contemporaries either virtue or intelligence, and persecuted by those that could not understand them.

When Pope murmurs at the world, when he professes contempt of fame, when he speaks of riches and poverty, of success and disappointment, with negligent indifference, he certainly does not express his habitual and settled sentiments, but either wilfully disguises his own character, or, what is more likely, invests himself with temporary qualities, and sallies out in the colours of the present moment. His hopes and fears, his joys and sorrows, acted strongly upon his mind; and if he differed from others, it was not by carelessness; he was irritable and resentful; his malignity to Philips, whom he had first made ridiculous, and then hated for being angry, continued too long. Of his vain desire to make Bentley contemptible, I never heard any adequate reason. He was sometimes wanton in his attacks; and, before Chandos, Lady Wortley, and Hill, was mean in his retreat.

The virtues which seem to have had most of his affection were liberality and fidelity of friendship, in which it does not appear that he was other than he describes himself. His fortune did not suffer his charity to be splendid and conspicuous; but he assisted Dodsley with a hundred pounds, that he might open a shop; and of the subscription of forty pounds a year that he raised for Savage, twenty were paid by himself. He was accused of loving money, but his love was eagerness to gain, not solicitude to keep it.

In the duties of friendship he was zealous and constant: his early maturity of mind commonly united him with men older than himself, and therefore, without attaining any considerable length of life, he saw many companions of his youth sink into the grave; but it does not appear that he lost a single friend by coldness or by injury; those who loved him once, continued their kindness. His ungrateful mention of Allen in his will, was the effect of his adherence to one whom he had known much longer, and whom he naturally loved with greater fondness. His violation of the trust reposed in him by Bolingbroke could have no motive inconsistent with the warmest affection; he either thought the action so near to indifferent that he forgot it, or so laudable that he expected his friend to approve it.

It was reported, with such confidence as almost to enforce belief, that in the papers intrusted to his executors was found a defamatory Life of Swift, which he had prepared as an instrument of vengeance to be used, if any provocation should be ever given. About this I enquired of the Earl of Marchmont, who assured me that no such piece was among his remains.

The religion in which he lived and died was that of the Church of Rome, to which in his correspondence with Racine he professes himself a sincere adherent. That he was not scrupulously pious in some part of his life, is known by many idle and indecent applications of sentences taken from the Scriptures; a mode of merriment which a good man dreads for its profaneness, and a witty man disdains for its easiness and vulgarity. But to whatever levities he has been betrayed, it does not appear that his principles were ever corrupted, or that he ever lost his belief of Revelation. The positions which he transmitted from Bolingbroke he seems not to have understood, and was pleased with an interpretation that made them orthodox.

A man of such exalted superiority, and so little moderation, would naturally have all his delinquences observed and aggravated: those who could not deny that he was excellent, would rejoice to find that he was not perfect.

Perhaps it may be imputed to the unwillingness with which the same man is allowed to possess many advantages, that his learning has been depreciated. He certainly was in his early life a man of great literary curiosity; and when he wrote his *Essay on Criticism* had, for his age, a very wide acquaintance with books. When he entered into the living world, it seems to have happened to him as to many others, that he was less attentive to dead masters; he studied in the academy of Paracelsus, and made the universe his favourite volume. He gathered his notions fresh from reality, not from the copies of authors, but the originals of Nature. Yet there is no reason to believe that literature ever lost his esteem; he always professed to love reading; and Dobson, who spent some time at his house translating his *Essay on Man*, when I asked him what learning he found him to possess, answered, *More than I expected*. His frequent references to history, his allusions to various kinds of knowledge, and his images selected from art and nature, with his observations on the operations of the mind and the modes of life, shew an intelligence perpetually on the wing, excursive, vigorous, and diligent, eager to pursue knowledge, and attentive to retain it.

From this curiosity arose the desire of travelling, to which he alludes in his verses to Jervas, and which, though he never found an opportunity to gratify it, did not leave him till his life declined.

Of his intellectual character, the constituent and fundamental principle was Good Sense, a prompt and intuitive perception of consonance and propriety.

He saw immediately, of his own conceptions, what was to be chosen, and what to be rejected; and, in the works of others, what was to be shunned, and what was to be copied.

But good sense alone is a sedate and quiescent quality, which manages its possessions well, but does not increase them; it collects few materials for its own operations, and preserves safety, but never gains supremacy. Pope had likewise genius; a mind active, ambitious, and adventurous, always investigating, always aspiring; in its widest searches still longing to go forward, in its highest flights still wishing to be higher; always imagining something greater than it knows, always endeavouring more than it can do.

To assist these powers, he is said to have had great strength and exactness of memory. That which he had heard or read was not easily lost; and he had before him not only what his own meditation suggested, but what he had found in other writers, that might be accommodated to his present purpose.

These benefits of nature he improved by incessant and unwearied diligence; he had recourse to every source of intelligence, and lost no opportunity of information; he consulted the living as well as the dead; he read his compositions to his friends, and was never content with mediocrity when excellence could be attained. He considered poetry as the business of his life, and however he might seem to lament his occupation, he followed it with constancy; to make verses was his first labour, and to mend them was his last.

From his attention to poetry he was never diverted. If conversation offered any thing that could be improved, he committed it to paper; if a thought, or perhaps an expression more happy than was common, rose to his mind, he was careful to write it; an independent distich was preserved for an opportunity of insertion, and some little fragments have been found containing lines, or parts of lines, to be wrought upon at some other time.

He was one of those few whose labour is their pleasure: he was never elevated to negligence, nor wearied to impatience; he never passed a fault unamended by indifference, nor quitted it by despair. He laboured his works first to gain reputation, and afterwards to keep it.

Of composition there are different methods. Some employ at once memory and invention, and, with little intermediate use of the pen, form and polish large masses by continued meditation, and write their productions only when, in their own opinion, they have completed them. It is related of Virgil, that his custom was to pour out a great number of verses in the morning, and pass the day in retrenching exuberances and correcting inaccuracies. The method of Pope, as may be collected from his translation, was to write his first thoughts in his first words, and gradually to amplify, decorate, rectify, and refine them.

With such faculties, and such dispositions, he excelled every other writer in *poetical prudence;* he wrote in such a manner as might expose him to few hazards. He used almost always the same fabrick of verse; and, indeed, by those few essays which he made of any other, he did not enlarge his reputation.

Of this uniformity the certain consequence was readiness and dexterity. By perpetual practice, language had in his mind a systematical arrangement; having always the same use for words, he had words so selected and combined as to be ready at his call. This increase of facility he confessed himself to have perceived in the progress of his translation.

But what was yet of more importance, his effusions were always voluntary, and his subjects chosen by himself. His independence secured him from drudging at a task, and labouring upon a barren topick: he never exchanged praise for money, nor opened a shop of condolence or congratulation. His poems, therefore, were scarce ever temporary. He suffered coronations and royal marriages to pass without a song, and derived no opportunities from recent events, nor any popularity from the accidental disposition of his readers. He was never reduced to the necessity of soliciting the sun to shine upon a birth-day, of calling the Graces and Virtues to a wedding, or of saying what multitudes have said before him. When he could produce nothing new, he was at liberty to be silent.

His publications were for the same reason never hasty. He is said to have sent nothing to the press till it had lain two years under his inspection: it is at least certain, that he ventured nothing without nice examination. He suffered the tumult of imagination to subside, and the novelties of invention to grow familiar. He knew that the mind is always enamoured of its own productions, and did not trust his first fondness. He consulted his friends, and listened with great willingness to criticism; and, what was of more importance, he consulted himself, and let nothing pass against his own judgement.

He professed to have learned his poetry from Dryden, whom, whenever an opportunity was presented, he praised through his whole life with unvaried liberality; and perhaps his character may receive some illustration, if he be compared with his master.

Integrity of understanding and nicety of discernment were not allotted in a less proportion to Dryden than to Pope. The rectitude of Dryden's mind was sufficiently shewn by the dismission of his poetical prejudices, and the rejection of unnatural thoughts and rugged numbers. But Dryden never desired to apply all the judgement that he had. He wrote, and professed to write, merely for the people; and when he pleased others, he contented himself. He spent no time in struggles to rouse latent powers; he never attempted to make that better which was already good, nor often to mend what he must have known to be faulty. He wrote, as he tells us, with very little consideration; when occasion or necessity called upon him, he poured out what the present moment happened to supply, and, when once it had passed the press, ejected it from his mind; for when he had no pecuniary interest, he had no further solicitude.

Pope was not content to satisfy; he desired to excel, and therefore always endeavoured to do his best: he did not court the candour, but dared the judgement of his reader, and, expecting no indulgence from others, he shewed none to himself. He examined lines and words with minute and punctilious observation, and retouched every part with indefatigable diligence, till he had left nothing to be forgiven.

For this reason he kept his pieces very long in his hands, while he considered and reconsidered them. The only poems which can be supposed to have been written with such regard to the times as might hasten their publication, were the two satires of *Thirty-eight*; of which Dodsley told me, that they were brought to him by the author, that they might be fairly copied. "Almost every line," he said, "was then written twice over; I gave him a clean transcript, which he sent some time afterwards to me for the press, with almost every line written twice over a second time."

His declaration, that his care for his works ceased at their publication, was not strictly true. His parental attention never abandoned them; what he found amiss in the first edition, he silently corrected in those that followed. He appears to have revised the *Iliad*, and freed it from some of its imperfections; and the *Essay on Criticism* received many improvements after its first appearance. It will seldom be found that he altered without adding clearness, elegance, or vigour. Pope had perhaps the judgement of Dryden; but Dryden certainly wanted the diligence of Pope.

In acquired knowledge, the superiority must be allowed to Dryden, whose education was more scholastick, and who before he became an author had been allowed more time for study, with better means of information. His mind has a larger range, and he collects his images and illustrations from a more extensive circumference of science. Dryden knew more of man in his general nature, and Pope in his local manners. The notions of Dryden were formed by comprehensive speculation, and those of Pope by minute attention. There is more dignity in the knowledge of Dryden, and more certainty in that of Pope.

Poetry was not the sole praise of either; for both excelled likewise in prose; but Pope did not borrow his prose from his predecessor. The style of Dryden is capricious and varied, that of Pope is cautious and uniform; Dryden obeys the motions of his own mind, Pope constrains his mind to his own rules of composition. Dryden is sometimes vehement and rapid; Pope is always smooth, uniform, and gentle. Dryden's page is a natural field, rising into inequalities, and diversified by the varied exuberance of abundant vegetation; Pope's is a velvet lawn, shaven by the scythe, and levelled by the roller.

Of genius, that power which constitutes a poet; that quality without which judgement is cold and knowledge is inert; that energy which collects, combines, amplifies, and animates; the superiority must, with some hesitation, be allowed to Dryden. It is not to be inferred that of this poetical vigour Pope had only a little, because Dryden had more; for every other writer since Milton must give place to Pope; and even of Dryden it must be said, that if he has brighter paragraphs, he has not better poems. Dryden's performances were always hasty, either excited by some external occasion, or extorted by domestick necessity; he composed without consideration, and published without correction. What his mind could supply at call, or gather in one excursion, was all that he sought, and all that he gave. The dilatory caution of Pope enabled him to condense his sentiments, to multiply his images, and to accumulate all that study might produce, or chance might supply. If the flights of Dryden therefore are higher, Pope continues longer on the wing. If of Dryden's fire the blaze is brighter, of Pope's the heat is more regular and constant. Dryden often surpasses expectation, and Pope never falls below it. Dryden is read with frequent astonishment, and Pope with perpetual delight.

This parallel will, I hope, when it is well considered, be found just; and if the reader should suspect me, as I suspect myself, of some partial fondness for the memory of Dryden, let him not too hastily condemn me; for meditation and enquiry may, perhaps, shew him the reasonableness of my determination.

THE Works of Pope are now to be distinctly examined, not so much with attention to slight faults or petty beauties, as to the general character and effect of each performance.

It seems natural for a young poet to initiate himself by Pastorals, which, not professing to imitate real life, require no experience, and, exhibiting only the simple operation of unmingled passions, admit no subtle reasoning or deep enquiry. Pope's Pastorals are not however composed but with close thought; they have reference to the times of the day, the seasons of the year, and the periods of human life. The last, that which turns the attention upon age and death, was the author's favourite. To tell of disappointment and misery, to thicken the darkness of futurity, and perplex the labyrinth of uncertainty, has been always a delicious employment of the poets. His preference was probably just. I wish, however, that his fondness had not overlooked a line in which the *Zephyrs* are made *to lament in silence*.

To charge these Pastorals with want of invention, is to require what never was intended. The imitations are so ambitiously frequent, that the writer evidently means rather to shew his literature than his wit. It is surely sufficient for an author of sixteen not only to be able to copy the poems of antiquity with judicious selection, but to have obtained sufficient power of language, and skill in metre, to exhibit a series of versification, which had in English poetry no precedent, nor has since had an imitation.

The design of *Windsor Forest* is evidently derived from *Cooper's Hill*, with some attention to Waller's poem on *The Park*; but Pope cannot be denied to excel his masters in variety and elegance, and the art of interchanging description, narrative, and morality. The objection made by Dennis is the want of plan, of a regular subordination of parts terminating in the principal and original design. There is this want in most descriptive poems, because as the scenes, which they must exhibit successively, are all subsisting at the same time, the order in which they are shewn must by necessity be arbitrary, and more is not to be expected from the last part than from the first. The attention, therefore, which cannot be detained by suspense, must be excited by diversity, such as this poem offers to its reader.

But the desire of diversity may be too much indulged; the parts of *Windsor Forest* which deserve least praise, are those which were added to enliven the stillness of the scene, the appearance of Father Thames, and the transformation of *Lodona*. Addison had in his *Campaign* derided the *Rivers* that *rise from their oozy beds* to tell stories of heroes, and it is therefore strange that Pope should adopt a fiction not only unnatural but lately censured. The story of *Lodona* is told with sweetness; but a new metamorphosis is a ready and puerile expedient; nothing is easier than to tell how a flower was once a blooming virgin, or a rock an obdurate tyrant.

The *Temple of Fame* has, as Steele warmly declared, *a thousand beauties*. Every part is splendid; there is great luxuriance of ornaments; the original vision of Chaucer was never denied to be much improved; the allegory is very skilfully continued, the imagery is properly selected, and learnedly displayed: yet, with all this comprehension of excellence, as its scene is laid in remote ages, and its sentiments, if the concluding paragraph be excepted, have little relation to general manners or common life, it never obtained much notice, but is turned silently over, and seldom quoted or mentioned with either praise or blame.

That the *Messiah* excels the *Pollio* is no great praise, if it be considered from what original the improvements are derived.

The *Verses on the unfortunate Lady* have drawn much attention by the illaudable singularity of treating suicide with respect; and they must be allowed to be written in some parts with vigorous animation, and in others with gentle tenderness; nor has Pope produced any poem in which the sense predominates more over the diction. But the tale is not skilfully told; it is not easy to discover the character of either the Lady or her Guardian. History relates that she was about to disparage herself by a marriage with an inferior; Pope praises her for the dignity of ambition, and yet condemns the unkle to detestation for his pride; the ambitious love of a niece may be opposed by the interest, malice, or envy of an unkle, but never by his pride. On such an occasion a poet may be allowed to be obscure, but inconsistency never can be right.

The *Ode for St. Cecilia's Day* was undertaken at the desire of Steele: in this the author is generally confessed to have miscarried, yet he has miscarried only as compared with Dryden; for he has far outgone other competitors. Dryden's plan is better chosen; history will always take stronger hold of the attention than fable: the passions excited by Dryden are the pleasures and pains of real life, the scene of Pope is laid in imaginary existence; Pope is read with calm acquiescence, Dryden with turbulent delight; Pope hangs upon the ear, and Dryden finds the passes of the mind.

Both the odes want the essential constituent of metrical compositions, the stated recurrence of settled numbers. It may be alleged, that Pindar is said by Horace to have written *numeris lege solutis*: but as no such lax performances have been transmitted to us, the meaning of that expression cannot be fixed; and perhaps the like return might properly be made to a modern Pindarist, as Mr. Cobb received from Bentley, who, when he found his criticisms upon a Greek Exercise, which Cobb had presented, refuted one after another by Pindar's authority, cried out at last, *Pindar was a bold fellow, but thou art an impudent one.*

If Pope's ode be particularly inspected, it will be found that the first stanza consists of sounds well chosen indeed, but only sounds.

The second consists of hyperbolical common-places, easily to be found, and perhaps without much difficulty to be as well expressed.

In the third, however, there are numbers, images, harmony, and vigour, not unworthy the antagonist of Dryden. Had all been like this—but every part cannot be the best.

The next stanzas place and detain us in the dark and dismal regions of mythology, where neither hope nor fear, neither joy nor sorrow can be found: the poet however faithfully attends us; we have all that can be performed by elegance of diction, or sweetness of versification; but what can form avail without better matter?

The last stanza recurs again to common-places. The conclusion is too evidently modelled by that of Dryden; and it may be remarked that both end with the same fault, the comparison of each is literal on one side, and metaphorical on the other.

Poets do not always express their own thoughts; Pope, with all this labour in the praise of Musick, was ignorant of its principles, and insensible of its effects.

One of his greatest though of his earliest works is the *Essay on Criticism*, which, if he had written nothing else, would have placed him among the first criticks and the first poets, as it exhibits every mode of excellence that can embellish or dignify didactick composition, selection of matter, novelty of arrangement, justness of precept, splendour of illustration, and propriety of digression. I know not whether it be pleasing to consider that he produced this piece at twenty, and never afterwards excelled it: he that delights himself with observing that such powers may be so soon attained, cannot but grieve to think that life was ever after at a stand.

To mention the particular beauties of the Essay would be unprofitably tedious; but I cannot forbear to observe, that the comparison of a student's progress in the sciences with the journey of a traveller in the Alps, is perhaps the best that English poetry can shew. A simile, to be perfect, must both illustrate and ennoble the subject; must shew it to the understanding in a clearer view, and display it to the fancy with greater dignity; but either of these qualities may be sufficient to recommend it. In didactick poetry, of which the great purpose is instruction, a simile may be praised which illustrates, though it does not ennoble; in heroicks, that may be admitted which ennobles, though it does not illustrate. That it may be complete, it is required to exhibit, independently of its references, a pleasing image; for a simile is said to be a short episode. To this antiquity was so attentive, that circumstances were sometimes added, which, having no parallels, served only to fill the imagination, and produced what Perrault ludicrously called *comparisons with a long tail*. In their similies the greatest writers have sometimes failed; the ship-race, compared with the chariot-race, is neither illustrated nor aggrandised; land and water make all the difference: when Apollo, running after Daphne, is likened to a greyhound chasing a hare, there is nothing gained; the ideas of pursuit and flight are too plain to be made plainer, and a god and the daughter of a god are not represented much to their advantage, by a hare and dog. The simile of the Alps has no useless parts, yet affords a striking picture by itself; it makes the foregoing position better understood, and enables it to take faster hold on the attention; it assists the apprehension, and elevates the fancy.

Let me likewise dwell a little on the celebrated paragraph, in which it is directed that *the sound should seem an echo to the sense*; a precept which Pope is allowed to have observed beyond any other English poet.

This notion of representative metre, and the desire of discovering frequent adaptations of the sound to the sense, have produced, in my opinion, many wild conceits and imaginary beauties. All that can furnish this representation are the sounds of the words considered singly, and the time in which they are pronounced. Every language has some words framed to exhibit the noises which they express, as *thump, rattle, growl, hiss*. These however are but few, and the poet cannot make them more, nor can they be of any use but when sound is to be mentioned. The time of pronunciation was in the dactylick measures of the learned languages capable of considerable variety; but that variety could be accommodated only to motion or duration, and different degrees of motion were perhaps expressed by verses rapid or slow, without much attention of the writer, when the image had full possession of his fancy; but our language having little flexibility, our verses can differ very little in their cadence. The fancied resemblances, I fear, arise sometimes merely from the ambiguity of words; there is supposed to be some relation between a *soft* line and a *soft* couch, or between *hard* syllables and *hard* fortune.

Motion, however, may be in some sort exemplified; and yet it may be suspected that even in such resemblances the mind often governs the ear, and the sounds are estimated by their meaning. One of the most successful attempts has been to describe the labour of Sisyphus:

> With many a weary step, and many a groan,
> Up a high hill he heaves a huge round stone;
> The huge round stone, resulting with a bound,
> Thunders impetuous down, and smoaks along the ground.

Who does not perceive the stone to move slowly upward, and roll violently back? But set the same numbers to another sense;

> While many a merry tale, and many a song.
> Chear'd the rough road, we wish'd the rough road long.
> The rough road then, returning in a round,
> Mock'd our impatient steps, for all was fairy ground.

We have now surely lost much of the delay, and much of the rapidity.

But to shew how little the greatest master of numbers can fix the principles of representative harmony, it will be sufficient to remark that the poet, who tells us, that

> When Ajax strives—the words move slow.
> Not so when swift Camilla scours the plain,
> Flies o'er th' unbending corn, and skims along the main;

when he had enjoyed for about thirty years the praise of Camilla's lightness of foot, tried another experiment upon *sound* and *time*, and produced this memorable triplet;

> Waller was smooth; but Dryden taught to join
> The varying verse, the full resounding line,
> The long majestick march, and energy divine.

Here are the swiftness of the rapid race, and the march of slow-paced majesty, exhibited by the same poet in the same sequence of syllables, except that the exact prosodist will find the line of *swiftness* by one time longer than that of *tardiness*.

Beauties of this kind are commonly fancied; and when real, are technical and nugatory, not to be rejected, and not to be solicited.

To the praises which have been accumulated on *The Rape of the Lock* by readers of every class, from the critick to the waiting-maid, it is difficult to make any addition. Of that which is universally allowed to be the most attractive of all ludicrous compositions, let it rather be now enquired from what sources the power of pleasing is derived.

Dr. Warburton, who excelled in critical perspicacity, has remarked that the preternatural agents are very happily adapted to the purposes of the poem.

The heathen deities can no longer gain attention: we should have turned away from a contest between Venus and Diana. The employment of allegorical persons always excites conviction of its own absurdity; they may produce effects, but cannot conduct actions; when the phantom is put in motion, it dissolves; thus *Discord* may raise a mutiny, but *Discord* cannot conduct a march, nor besiege a town. Pope brought into view a new race of Beings, with powers and passions proportionate to their operation. The sylphs and gnomes act at the toilet and the tea-table, what more terrifick and more powerful phantoms perform on the stormy ocean, or the field of battle, they give their proper help, and do their proper mischief.

Pope is said, by an objector, not to have been the inventer of this petty nation; a charge which might with more justice have been brought against the author of the *Iliad*, who doubtless adopted the religious system of his country; for what is there but the names of his agents which Pope has not invented? Has he not assigned them characters and operations never heard of before? Has he not, at least, given them their first poetical existence? If this is not sufficient to denominate his work original, nothing original ever can be written.

In this work are exhibited, in a very high degree, the two most engaging powers of an author. New things are made familiar, and familiar things are made new. A race of aerial people, never heard of before, is presented to us in a manner so clear and easy, that the reader seeks for no further information, but immediately mingles with his new acquaintance, adopts their interests, and attends their pursuits, loves a sylph, and detests a gnome.

That familiar things are made new, every paragraph will prove. The subject of the poem is an event below the common incidents of common life; nothing real is introduced that is not seen so often as to be no longer regarded, yet the whole detail of a female-day is here brought before us invested with so much art of decoration, that, though nothing is disguised, every thing is striking, and we feel all the appetite of curiosity for that from which we have a thousand times turned fastidiously away.

The purpose of the Poet is, as he tells us, to laugh at *the little unguarded follies of the female sex*. It is therefore without justice that Dennis charges the *Rape of the Lock* with the want of a moral, and for that reason sets it below the *Lutrin*, which exposes the pride and discord of the clergy. Perhaps neither Pope nor Boileau has made the world much better than he found it; but if they had both succeeded, it were easy to tell who would have deserved most from publick gratitude. The freaks, and humours, and spleen, and vanity of women, as they embroil families in discord, and fill houses with disquiet, do more to obstruct the happiness of life in a year than the ambition of the clergy in many centuries. It has been well observed, that the misery of man proceeds not from any single crush of overwhelming evil, but from small vexations continually repeated.

It is remarked by Dennis likewise, that the machinery is superfluous; that, by all the bustle of preternatural operation, the main event is neither hastened nor retarded. To this charge an efficacious answer is not easily made. The sylphs cannot be said to help or to oppose, and it must be allowed to imply some want of art, that their power has not been sufficiently intermingled with the action. Other parts may likewise be charged with want of connection; the game at *ombre* might be spared, but if the Lady had lost her hair while she was intent upon her cards, it might have been inferred that those who are too fond of play will be in danger of neglecting more important interests. Those perhaps are faults; but what are such faults to so much excellence!

The Epistle of *Eloise to Abelard* is one of the most happy productions of human wit: the subject is so judiciously chosen, that it would be difficult, in turning over the annals of the world, to find another which so many circumstances concur to recommend. We regularly interest ourselves most in the fortune of those who most deserve our notice. Abelard and Eloise were conspicuous in their days for eminence of merit. The heart naturally loves truth. The adventures and misfortunes of this illustrious pair are known from undisputed history. Their fate does not leave the mind in hopeless dejection; for they both found quiet and consolation in retirement and piety. So new and so affecting is their story, that it supersedes invention, and imagination ranges at full liberty without straggling into scenes of fable.

The story, thus skilfully adopted, has been diligently improved. Pope has left nothing behind him, which seems more the effect of studious perseverance and laborious revisal. Here is particularly observable the *curiosa felicitas*, a fruitful soil, and careful cultivation. Here is no crudeness of sense, nor asperity of language.

The sources from which sentiments, which have so much vigour and efficacy, have been drawn, are shewn to be the mystick writers by the learned author of the *Essay on the Life and Writings of Pope*; a book which teaches how the brow of Criticism may be smoothed, and how she may be enabled, with all her severity, to attract and to delight.

The train of my disquisition has now conducted me to that poetical wonder, the translation of the *Iliad*; a performance which no age or nation can pretend to equal. To the Greeks translation was almost unknown; it was totally unknown to the inhabitants of Greece. They had no recourse to the Barbarians for poetical beauties, but sought for every thing in Homer, where, indeed, there is but little which they might not find.

The Italians have been very diligent translators; but I can hear of no version, unless perhaps Anguillara's Ovid may be excepted, which is read with eagerness. The *Iliad* of Salvini every reader may discover to be punctiliously exact; but it seems to be the work of a linguist skilfully pedantick, and his countrymen, the proper judges of its power to please, reject it with disgust.

Their predecessors the Romans have left some specimens of translation behind them, and that employment must have had some credit in which Tully and Germanicus engaged; but unless we suppose, what is perhaps true, that the plays of Terence were versions of Menander, nothing translated seems ever to have risen to high reputation. The French, in the meridian hour of their learning, were very laudably industrious to enrich their own language with the wisdom of the ancients; but found themselves reduced, by whatever necessity, to turn the Greek and Roman poetry into prose. Whoever could read an author, could translate him. From such rivals little can be feared.

The chief help of Pope in this arduous undertaking was drawn from the versions of Dryden. Virgil had borrowed much of his imagery from Homer, and part of the debt was now paid by his translator. Pope searched the pages of Dryden for happy combinations of heroic diction; but it will not be denied that he added much to what he found. He cultivated our language with so much diligence and art, that he has left in his *Homer* a treasure of poetical elegances to posterity. His version may be said to have tuned the English tongue; for since its appearance no writer, however deficient in other powers, has wanted melody. Such a series of lines so elaborately corrected, and so sweetly modulated, took possession of the publick ear; the vulgar was enamoured of the poem, and the learned wondered at the translation.

But in the most general applause discordant voices will always be heard. It has been objected by some, who wish to be numbered among the sons of learning, that Pope's version of Homer is not Homerical; that it exhibits no resemblance of the original and characteristick manner of the Father of Poetry, as it wants his awful simplicity, his artless grandeur, his unaffected majesty. This cannot be totally denied; but it must be remembered that *necessitas quod cogit defendit*; that may be lawfully done which cannot be forborn. Time and place will always enforce regard. In estimating this translation, consideration must be had of the nature of our language, the form of our metre, and, above all, of the change which two thousand years have made in the modes of life and the habits of thought. Virgil wrote in a language of the same general fabrick with that of Homer, in verses of the same measure, and in an age nearer to Homer's time by eighteen hundred years; yet he found, even then, the state of the world so much altered, and the demand for elegance so much increased, that mere nature would be endured no longer; and perhaps, in the multitude of borrowed passages, very few can be shewn which he has not embellished.

There is a time when nations emerging from barbarity, and falling into regular subordination, gain leisure to grow wise, and feel the shame of ignorance and the craving pain of unsatisfied curiosity. To this hunger of the mind plain sense is grateful; that which fills the void removes uneasiness, and to be free from pain for a while is pleasure; but repletion generates fastidiousness;

a saturated intellect soon becomes luxurious, and knowledge finds no willing reception till it is recommended by artificial diction. Thus it will be found, in the progress of learning, that in all nations the first writers are simple, and that every age improves in elegance. One refinement always makes way for another, and what was expedient to Virgil was necessary to Pope.

I suppose many readers of the English *Iliad*, when they have been touched with some unexpected beauty of the lighter kind, have tried to enjoy it in the original, where, alas! it was not to be found. Homer doubtless owes to his translator many *Ovidian* graces not exactly suitable to his character; but to have added can be no great crime, if nothing be taken away. Elegance is surely to be desired, if it be not gained at the expence of dignity. A hero would wish to be loved, as well as to be reverenced.

To a thousand cavils one answer is sufficient; the purpose of a writer is to be read, and the criticism which would destroy the power of pleasing must be blown aside. Pope wrote for his own age and his own nation: he knew that it was necessary to colour the images and point the sentiments of his author; he therefore made him graceful, but lost him some of his sublimity.

The copious notes with which the version is accompanied, and by which it is recommended to many readers, though they were undoubtedly written to swell the volumes, ought not to pass without praise: commentaries which attract the reader by the pleasure of perusal have not often appeared; the notes of others are read to clear difficulties, those of Pope to vary entertainment.

It has however been objected, with sufficient reason, that there is in the commentary too much of unseasonable levity and affected gaiety; that too many appeals are made to the Ladies, and the ease which is so carefully preserved is sometimes the ease of a trifler. Every art has its terms, and every kind of instruction its proper style; the gravity of common criticks may be tedious, but is less despicable than childish merriment.

Of the *Odyssey* nothing remains to be observed: the same general praise may be given to both translations, and a particular examination of either would require a large volume. The notes were written by Broome, who endeavoured not unsuccessfully to imitate his master.

Of the *Dunciad* the hint is confessedly taken from Dryden's *Mac Flecknoe*; but the plan is so enlarged and diversified as justly to claim the praise of an original, and affords perhaps the best specimen that has yet appeared of personal satire ludicrously pompous.

That the design was moral, whatever the author might tell either his readers or himself, I am not convinced. The first motive was the desire of revenging the contempt with which Theobald had treated his *Shakspeare*, and regaining the honour which he had lost, by crushing his opponent. Theobald was not of bulk enough to fill a poem, and therefore it was necessary to find other enemies with other names, at whose expence he might divert the publick.

In this design there was petulance and malignity enough; but I cannot think it very criminal. An author places himself uncalled before the tribunal of Criticism, and solicits fame at the hazard of disgrace. Dulness or deformity are not culpable in themselves, but may be very justly reproached when they pretend to the honour of wit or the influence of beauty. If bad writers were to pass without reprehension, what should restrain them? *impune diem consumpserit ingens Telephus*; and upon bad writers only will censure have much effect. The satire which brought Theobald and Moore into contempt, dropped impotent from Bentley, like the javelin of Priam.

All truth is valuable, and satirical criticism may be considered as useful when it rectifies error and improves judgement; he that refines the publick taste is a publick benefactor.

The beauties of this poem are well known; its chief fault is the grossness of its images. Pope and Swift had an unnatural delight in ideas physically impure, such as every other tongue utters with unwillingness, and of which every ear shrinks from the mention.

But even this fault, offensive as it is, may be forgiven for the excellence of other passages; such as the formation and dissolution of Moore, the account of the Traveller, the misfortune of the Florist, and the crouded thoughts and stately numbers which dignify the concluding paragraph.

The alterations which have been made in the *Dunciad*, not always for the better, require that it should be published, as in the last collection, with all its variations.

The *Essay on Man* was a work of great labour and long consideration, but certainly not the happiest of Pope's performances. The subject is perhaps not very proper for poetry, and the poet was not sufficiently master of his subject; metaphysical morality was to him a new study, he was proud of his acquisitions, and, supposing himself master of great secrets, was in haste to teach what he had not learned. Thus he tells us, in the first Epistle, that from the nature of the Supreme Being may be deduced an order of beings such as mankind, because Infinite Excellence can do only what is best. He finds out that these beings must be *somewhere*, and that *all the question is whether man be in a wrong place*. Surely if, according to the poet's Leibnitian reasoning, we may infer that man ought to be, only because he is, we may allow that his place is the right place, because he has it. Supreme Wisdom is not less infallible in disposing than in creating. But what is meant by *somewhere* and *place*, and *wrong place*, it had been vain to ask Pope, who probably had never asked himself.

Having exalted himself into the chair of wisdom, he tells us much that every man knows, and much that he does not know himself; that we see but little, and that the order of the universe is beyond our comprehension; an opinion not very uncommon; and that there is a chain of subordinate beings *from infinite to nothing*, of which himself and his readers are equally ignorant.

But he gives us one comfort, which, without his help, he supposes unattainable, in the position *that though we are fools, yet God is wise.*

This Essay affords an egregious instance of the predominance of genius, the dazzling splendour of imagery, and the seductive powers of eloquence. Never were penury of knowledge and vulgarity of sentiment so happily disguised. The reader feels his mind full, though he learns nothing; and when he meets it in its new array, no longer knows the talk of his mother and his nurse. When these wonder-working sounds sink into sense, and the doctrine of the Essay, disrobed of its ornaments, is left to the powers of its naked excellence, what shall we discover? That we are, in comparison with our Creator, very weak and ignorant; that we do not uphold the chain of existence, and that we could not make one another with more skill than we are made. We may learn yet more; that the arts of human life were copied from the instinctive operations of other animals; that if the world be made for man, it may be said that man was made for geese. To these profound principles of natural knowledge are added some moral instructions equally new; that self-interest, well understood, will produce social concord; that men are mutual gainers by mutual benefits; that evil is sometimes balanced by good; that human advantages are unstable and fallacious, of uncertain duration, and doubtful effect; that our true honour is, not to have a great part, but to act it well: that virtue only is our own; and that happiness is always in our power.

Surely a man of no very comprehensive search may venture to say that he has heard all this before; but it was never till now recommended by such a blaze of embellishment, or such sweetness of melody. The vigorous contraction of some thoughts, the luxuriant amplification of others, the incidental illustrations, and sometimes the dignity, sometimes the softness of the verses, enchain philosophy, suspend criticism, and oppress judgement by overpowering pleasure.

This is true of many paragraphs; yet if I had undertaken to exemplify Pope's felicity of composition before a rigid critick, I should not select the *Essay on Man*; for it contains more lines unsuccessfully laboured, more harshness of diction, more thoughts imperfectly expressed, more levity without elegance, and more heaviness without strength, than will easily be found in all his other works.

The *Characters of Men and Women* are the product of diligent speculation upon human life; much labour has been bestowed upon them, and Pope very seldom laboured in vain. That his excellence may be properly estimated, I recommend a comparison of his *Characters of Women* with Boileau's Satire; it will then be seen with how much more perspicacity female nature is investigated, and female excellence selected; and he surely is no mean writer to whom Boileau shall be found inferior. The *Characters of Men*, however, are written with more, if not with deeper, thought, and exhibit many passages exquisitely beautiful. The *Gem and the Flower* will not easily be equalled.

In the women's part are some defects; the character of *Attossa* is not so neatly finished as that of *Clodio*; and some of the female characters may be found perhaps more frequently among men; what is said of *Philomede* was true of *Prior*.

In the Epistles to Lord Bathurst and Lord Burlington, Dr. Warburton has endeavoured to find a train of thought which was never in the writer's head, and, to support his hypothesis, has printed that first which was published last. In one, the most valuable passage is perhaps the Elogy on *Good Sense*, and the other the *End of the Duke of Buckingham*.

The Epistle to Arbuthnot, now arbitrarily called the *Prologue to the Satires*, is a performance consisting, as it seems, of many fragments wrought into one design, which by this union of scattered beauties contains more striking paragraphs than could probably have been brought together into an occasional work. As there is no stronger motive to exertion than self-defence, no part has more elegance, spirit, or dignity, than the poet's vindication of his own character. The meanest passage is the satire upon *Sporus*.

Of the two poems which derived their names from the year, and which are called the *Epilogue to the Satires*, it was very justly remarked by Savage, that the second was in the whole more strongly conceived, and more equally supported, but that it had no single passages equal to the contention in the first for the dignity of Vice, and the celebration of the triumph of Corruption.

The Imitations of Horace seem to have been written as relaxations of his genius. This employment became his favourite by its facility; the plan was ready to his hand, and nothing was required but to accommodate as he could the sentiments of an old author to recent facts or familiar images; but what is easy is seldom excellent; such imitations cannot give pleasure to common readers; the man of learning may be sometimes surprised and delighted by an unexpected parallel; but the comparison requires knowledge of the original, which will likewise often detect strained applications. Between Roman images and English manners there will be an irreconcileable dissimilitude, and the work will be generally uncouth and party-coloured; neither original nor translated, neither ancient nor modern.

Pope had, in proportions very nicely adjusted to each other, all the qualities that constitute genius. He had *Invention*, by which new trains of events are formed, and new scenes of imagery displayed, as in the *Rape of the Lock*; and by which extrinsick and adventitious embellishments and illustrations are connected with a known subject, as in the *Essay on Criticism*. He had *Imagination*, which strongly impresses on the writer's mind, and enables him to convey to the reader, the various forms of nature, incidents of life, and energies of passion, as in his *Eloisa*, *Windsor Forest*, and the *Ethick Epistles*. He had *Judgement*, which selects from life or nature what the present purpose requires, and, by separating the essence of things from its concomitants, often makes the representation more powerful than the reality: and he had colours of language always before him, ready to decorate his matter with every grace of elegant expression, as when he accommodates his diction to the wonderful multiplicity of Homer's sentiments and descriptions.

Poetical expression includes sound as well as meaning; *Musick*, says Dryden, *is inarticulate poetry*; among the excellences of Pope, therefore, must be mentioned the melody of his metre. By perusing the works of Dryden, he discovered the most perfect fabrick of English verse, and habituated himself to that only which he found the best; in consequence of which restraint, his poetry has been censured as too uniformly musical, and as glutting the ear with unvaried sweetness. I suspect this objection to be the cant of those who judge by principles rather than perception: and who would even themselves have less pleasure in his works, if he had tried to relieve attention by studied discords, or affected to break his lines and vary his pauses.

But though he was thus careful of his versification, he did not oppress his powers with superfluous rigour. He seems to have thought with Boileau, that the practice of writing might be refined till the difficulty should overbalance the advantage. The construction of his language is not always strictly grammatical; with those rhymes which prescription had conjoined he contented himself, without regard to Swift's remonstrances, though there was no striking consonance; nor was he very careful to vary his terminations, or to refuse admission at a small distance to the same rhymes.

To Swift's edict for the exclusion of Alexandrines and Triplets he paid little regard; he admitted them, but, in the opinion of Fenton, too rarely; he uses them more liberally in his translation than his poems.

He has a few double rhymes; and always, I think, unsuccessfully, except once in the *Rape of the Lock*.

Expletives he very early ejected from his verses; but he now and then admits an epithet rather commodious than important. Each of the six first lines of the *Iliad* might lose two syllables with very little diminution of the meaning; and sometimes, after all his art and labour, one verse seems to be made for the sake of another. In his latter productions the diction is sometimes vitiated by French idioms, with which Bolingbroke had perhaps infected him.

I have been told that the couplet by which he declared his own ear to be most gratified was this:

> Lo, where Mœotis sleeps, and hardly flows
> The freezing Tanais through a waste of snows.

But the reason of this preference I cannot discover.

It is remarked by Watts, that there is scarcely a happy combination of words, or a phrase poetically elegant in the English language, which Pope has not inserted into his version of Homer. How he obtained possession of so many beauties of speech, it were desirable to know. That he gleaned from authors, obscure as well as eminent, what he thought brilliant or useful, and preserved it all in a regular collection, is not unlikely. When, in his last years, Hall's Satires were shewn him, he wished that he had seen them sooner.

New sentiments and new images others may produce; but to attempt any further improvement of versification will be dangerous. Art and diligence have now done their best, and what shall be added will be the effort of tedious toil and needless curiosity.

After all this, it is surely superfluous to answer the question that has once been asked, Whether Pope was a poet? otherwise than by asking in return, If Pope be not a poet, where is poetry to be found? To circumscribe poetry by a definition will only shew the narrowness of the definer, though a definition which shall exclude Pope will not easily be made. Let us look round upon the present time, and back upon the past; let us enquire to whom the voice of mankind has decreed the wreath of poetry; let their productions be examined, and their claims stated, and the pretensions of Pope will be no more disputed. Had he given the world only his version, the name of poet must have been allowed him: if the writer of the *Iliad* were to class his successors, he would assign a very high place to his translator, without requiring any other evidence of Genius.

THOMSON

JAMES THOMSON, the son of a minister well esteemed for his piety and diligence, was born September 7, 1700, at Ednam, in the shire of Roxburgh, of which his father was pastor. His mother, whose name was Hume, inherited as co-heiress a portion of a small estate. The revenue of a parish in Scotland is seldom large; and it was probably in commiseration of the difficulty with which Mr. Thomson supported his family, having nine children, that Mr. Riccarton, a neighbouring minister, discovering in James uncommon promises of future excellence, undertook to superintend his education, and provide him books.

He was taught the common rudiments of learning at the school of Jedburg, a place which he delights to recollect in his poem of *Autumn*; but was not considered by his master as superior to common boys, though in those early days he amused his patron and his friends with poetical compositions; with which however he so little pleased himself, that on every new-year's day he threw into the fire all the productions of the foregoing year.

From the school he was removed to Edinburgh, where he had not resided two years when his father died, and left all his children to the care of their mother, who raised upon her little estate what money a mortgage could afford, and, removing with her family to Edinburgh, lived to see her son rising into eminence.

The design of Thomson's friends was to breed him a minister. He lived at Edinburgh, as at school, without distinction or expectation, till, at the usual time, he performed a probationary exercise by explaining a psalm. His diction was so poetically splendid, that Mr. Hamilton, the professor of Divinity, reproved him for speaking language unintelligible to a popular audience, and he censured one of his expressions as indecent, if not profane.

This rebuke is reported to have repressed his thoughts of an ecclesiastical character, and he probably cultivated with new diligence his blossoms of poetry, which however were in some danger of a blast; for, submitting his productions to some who thought themselves qualified to criticise, he heard of nothing but faults, but, finding other judges more favourable, he did not suffer himself to sink into despondence.

He easily discovered that the only stage on which a poet could appear, with any hope of advantage, was London; a place too wide for the operation of petty competition and private malignity, where merit might soon become conspicuous, and would find friends as soon as it became reputable to befriend it. A lady, who was acquainted with his mother, advised him to the journey, and promised some countenance or assistance, which at last he never received; however, he justified his adventure by her encouragement, and came to seek in London patronage and fame.

At his arrival he found his way to Mr. Mallet, then tutor to the sons of the duke of Montrose. He had recommendations to several persons of consequence, which he had tied up carefully in his handkerchief; but as he passed along the street, with the gaping curiosity of a new-comer, his attention was upon every thing rather than his pocket, and his magazine of credentials was stolen from him.

His first want was of a pair of shoes. For the supply of all his necessities, his whole fund was his *Winter*, which for a time could find no purchaser; till, at last, Mr. Millan was persuaded to buy it at a low price; and this low price he had for some time reason to regret; but, by accident, Mr. Whatley, a man not wholly unknown among authors, happening to turn his eye upon it, was so delighted that he ran from place to place celebrating its excellence. Thomson obtained likewise the notice of Aaron Hill, whom, being friendless and indigent, and glad of kindness, he courted with every expression of servile adulation.

Winter was dedicated to Sir Spencer Compton, but attracted no regard from him to the author; till Aaron Hill awakened his attention by some verses addressed to Thomson, and published in one of the newspapers, which censured the great for their neglect of ingenious men. Thomson then received a present of twenty guineas, of which he gives this account to Mr. Hill:

"I hinted to you in my last, that on Saturday morning I was with Sir Spencer Compton. A certain gentleman, without my desire, spoke to him concerning me; his answer was, that I had never come near him. Then the gentleman put the question, If he desired that I should wait on him? he returned, he did. On this, the gentleman gave me an introductory Letter to him. He received me in what they commonly call a civil manner; asked me some common-place questions, and made me a present of twenty guineas. I am very ready to own that the present was larger than my performance deserved; and shall ascribe it to his generosity, or any other cause, rather than the merit of the address."

The poem, which, being of a new kind, few would venture at first to like, by degrees gained upon the publick; and one edition was very speedily succeeded by another.

Thomson's credit was now high, and every day brought him new friends; among others Dr. Rundle, a man afterwards unfortunately famous, sought his acquaintance, and found his qualities such, that he recommended him to the lord chancellor Talbot.

Winter was accompanied, in many editions, not only with a preface and a dedication, but with poetical praises by Mr. Hill, Mr. Mallet (then *Malloch*), and *Mira*, the fictitious name of a lady once too well known. Why the dedications are, to *Winter* and the other seasons, contrarily to custom, left out in the collected works, the reader may enquire.

The next year (1727) he distinguished himself by three publications; of *Summer*, in pursuance of his plan; of *a Poem on the Death of Sir Isaac Newton*, which he was enabled to perform as an exact philosopher by the instruction of Mr. Gray; and of *Britannia*, a kind of poetical invective against the ministry, whom the nation then thought not forward enough in resenting the depredations of the Spaniards. By this piece he declared himself an adherent to the opposition, and had therefore no favour to expect from the Court.

Thomson, having been some time entertained in the family of the lord Binning, was desirous of testifying his gratitude by making him the patron of his *Summer*; but the same kindness which had first disposed lord Binning to encourage him, determined him to refuse the dedication, which was by his advice addressed to Mr. Doddington; a man who had more power to advance the reputation and fortune of a poet.

Spring was published next year, with a dedication to the countess of Hertford; whose practice it was to invite every Summer some poet into the country, to hear her verses, and assist her studies. This honour was one Summer conferred on Thomson, who took more delight in carousing with lord Hertford and his friends than assisting her ladyship's poetical operations, and therefore never received another summons.

Autumn, the season to which the *Spring* and *Summer* are preparatory, still remained unsung, and was delayed till he published (1730) his works collected.

He produced in 1727 the tragedy of *Sophonisba*, which raised such expectation, that every rehearsal was dignified with a splendid audience, collected to anticipate the delight that was preparing for the publick. It was observed however that nobody was much affected, and that the company rose as from a moral lecture.

It had upon the stage no unusual degree of success. Slight accidents will operate upon the taste of pleasure. There was a feeble line in the play;

O Sophonisba, Sophonisba, O!

This gave occasion to a waggish parody;

O, Jemmy Thomson, Jemmy Thomson, O!

which for a while was echoed through the town.

I have been told by Savage, that of the Prologue to *Sophonisba* the first part was written by Pope, who could not be persuaded to finish it, and that the concluding lines were added by Mallet.

Thomson was not long afterwards, by the influence of Dr. Rundle, sent to travel with Mr. Charles Talbot, the eldest son of the Chancellor. He was yet young enough to receive new impressions, to have his opinions rectified, and his views enlarged; nor can he be supposed to have wanted that curiosity which is inseparable from an active and comprehensive mind. He may therefore now be supposed to have revelled in all the joys of intellectual luxury; he was every day feasted with instructive novelties; he lived splendidly without expence, and might expect when he returned home a certain establishment.

At this time a long course of opposition to Sir Robert Walpole had filled the nation with clamours for liberty, of which no man felt the want, and with care for liberty, which was not in danger. Thomson, in his travels on the continent, found or fancied so many evils arising from the tyranny of other governments, that he resolved to write a very long poem, in five parts, upon Liberty.

While he was busy on the first book, Mr. Talbot died; and Thomson, who had been rewarded for his attendance by the place of secretary of the Briefs, pays in the initial lines a decent tribute to his memory.

Upon this great poem two years were spent, and the author congratulated himself upon it as his noblest work; but an author and his reader are not always of a mind. *Liberty* called in vain upon her votaries to read her praises and reward her encomiast: her praises were condemned to harbour spiders, and to gather dust; none of Thomson's performances were so little regarded.

The judgement of the publick was not erroneous; the recurrence of the same images must tire in time; an enumeration of examples to prove a position which nobody denied, as it was from the beginning superfluous, must quickly grow disgusting.

The poem of *Liberty* does not now appear in its original state; but when the author's works were collected, after his death, was shortened by Sir George Lyttelton, with a liberty which, as it has a manifest tendency to lessen the confidence of society, and to confound the characters of authors, by making one man write by the judgement of another, cannot be justified by any supposed propriety of the alteration, or kindness of the friend.—I wish to see it exhibited as its author left it.

Thomson now lived in ease and plenty, and seems for a while to have suspended his poetry; but he was soon called back to labour by the death of the Chancellor, for his place then became vacant; and though the lord Hardwicke delayed for some time to give it away, Thomson's bashfulness, or pride, or some other motive perhaps not more laudable, withheld him from soliciting; and the new Chancellor would not give him what he would not ask.

He now relapsed to his former indigence; but the prince of Wales was at that time struggling for popularity, and by the influence of Mr. Lyttelton professed himself the patron of wit: to him Thomson was introduced, and being gaily interrogated about the state of his affairs, said, *that they were in a more poetical posture than formerly*; and had a pension allowed him of one hundred pounds a year.

Being now obliged to write, he produced (1738) the tragedy of *Agamemnon*, which was much shortened in the representation. It had the fate which most commonly attends mythological stories, and was only endured, but not favoured. It struggled with such difficulty through the first night, that Thomson, coming late to his friends with whom he was to sup, excused his delay by telling them how the sweat of his distress had so disordered his wig, that he could not come till he had been refitted by a barber.

He so interested himself in his own drama, that, if I remember right, as he sat in the upper gallery he accompanied the players by audible recitation, till a friendly hint frighted him to silence. Pope countenanced *Agamemnon*, by coming to it the first night, and was welcomed to the theatre by a general clap; he had much regard for Thomson, and once expressed it in a poetical Epistle sent to Italy, of which however he abated the value, by transplanting some of the lines into his Epistle to *Arbuthnot*.

About this time the Act was passed for licensing plays, of which the first operation was the prohibition of *Gustavus Vasa*, a tragedy of Mr. Brooke, whom the publick recompensed by a very liberal subscription; the next was the refusal of *Edward and Eleonora*, offered by Thomson. It is hard to discover why either play should have been obstructed. Thomson likewise endeavoured to repair his loss by a subscription, of which I cannot now tell the success.

When the publick murmured at the unkind treatment of Thomson, one of the ministerial writers remarked, that *he had taken a* Liberty *which was not agreeable to* Britannia *in any* Season.

He was soon after employed, in conjunction with Mr. Mallet, to write the masque of *Alfred*, which was acted before the Prince at Cliefden-house.

His next work (1745) was *Tancred and Sigismunda*, the most successful of all his tragedies; for it still keeps its turn upon the stage. It may be doubted whether he was, either by the bent of nature or habits of study, much qualified for tragedy. It does not appear that he had much sense of the pathetick, and his diffusive and descriptive style produced declamation rather than dialogue.

His friend Mr. Lyttelton was now in power, and conferred upon him the office of surveyor-general of the Leeward Islands; from which, when his deputy was paid, he received about three hundred pounds a year.

The last piece that he lived to publish was the *Castle of Indolence*, which was many years under his hand, but was at last finished with great accuracy. The first canto opens a scene of lazy luxury, that fills the imagination.

He was now at ease, but was not long to enjoy it; for, by taking cold on the water between London and Kew, he caught a disorder, which, with some careless exasperation, ended in a fever that put an end to his life, August 27, 1748. He was buried in the church of Richmond, without an inscription; but a monument has been erected to his memory in Westminster-abbey.

Thomson was of stature above the middle size, and *more fat than bard beseems*, of a dull countenance, and a gross, unanimated, uninviting appearance; silent in mingled company, but chearful among select friends, and by his friends very tenderly and warmly beloved.

He left behind him the tragedy of *Coriolanus*, which was, by the zeal of his patron Sir George Lyttelton, brought upon the stage for the benefit of his family, and recommended by a Prologue, which Quin, who had long lived with Thomson in fond intimacy, spoke in such a manner as shewed him *to be*, on that occasion, *no actor*. The commencement of this benevolence is very honourable to Quin; who is reported to have delivered Thomson, then known to him only for his genius, from an arrest, by a very considerable present; and its continuance is honourable to both; for friendship is not always the sequel of obligation. By this tragedy a considerable sum was raised, of which part discharged his debts, and the rest was remitted to his sisters, whom, however removed from them by place or condition, he regarded with great tenderness, as will appear by the following Letter, which I communicate with much pleasure, as it gives me at once an opportunity of recording the fraternal kindness of Thomson, and reflecting on the friendly assistance of Mr. Boswell, from whom I received it.

"Hagley in Worcestershire,
October the 4th, 1747.

"My dear Sister,

"I thought you had known me better than to interpret my silence into a decay of affection, especially as your behaviour has always been such as rather to increase than diminish it. Don't imagine, because I am a bad correspondent, that I can ever prove an unkind friend and brother. I must do myself the justice to tell you, that my affections are naturally very fixed and constant; and if I had ever reason of complaint against you (of which by the bye I have not the least shadow), I am conscious of so many defects in myself, as dispose me to be not a little charitable and forgiving.

"It gives me the truest heart-felt satisfaction to hear you have a good kind husband, and are in easy contented circumstances; but were they otherwise, that would only awaken and heighten my tenderness towards you. As our good and tender-hearted parents did not live to receive any material testimonies of that highest human gratitude I owed them (than which nothing could have given me equal pleasure), the only return I can make them now is by kindness to those they left behind them: would to God poor Lizy had lived longer, to have been a farther witness of the truth of what I say, and that I might have had the pleasure of seeing once more a sister, who so truly deserved my esteem and love. But she is happy, while we must toil a little longer here below: let us however do it chearfully and gratefully, supported by the pleasing hope of meeting yet again on a safer shore, where to recollect the storms and difficulties of life will not perhaps be inconsistent with that blissful state. You did right to call your daughter by her name; for you must needs have had a particular tender friendship for one another, endeared as you were by nature, by having passed the affectionate years of your youth together; and by that great softner and engager of hearts, mutual hardship. That it was in my power to ease it a little, I account one of the most exquisite pleasures of my life.—But enough of this melancholy though not unpleasing strain.

"I esteem you for your sensible and disinterested advice to Mr. Bell, as you will see by my Letter to him: as I approve entirely of his marrying again, you may readily ask me why I don't marry at all. My circumstances have hitherto been so variable and uncertain in this fluctuating world, as induce to keep me from engaging in such a state: and now, though they are more settled, and of late (which you will be glad to hear) considerably improved, I begin to think myself too far advanced in life for such youthful undertakings, not to mention some other petty reasons that are apt to startle the delicacy of difficult old batchelors. I am, however, not a little suspicious that was I to pay a visit to Scotland (which I have some thoughts of doing soon) I might possibly be tempted to think of a thing not easily repaired if done amiss. I have always been of opinion that none make better wives than the ladies of Scotland; and yet, who more forsaken than they, while the gentlemen are continually running abroad all the world over? Some of them, it is true, are wise enough to return for a wife. You see I am beginning to make interest already with the Scots ladies.—But no more of this infectious subject.—Pray let me hear from you now and then; and though I am not a regular correspondent, yet perhaps I may mend in that respect. Remember me kindly to your husband, and believe me to be.

"Your most affectionate brother,
JAMES THOMSON."
(Addressed) "To Mrs. Thomson in Lanark."

The benevolence of Thomson was fervid, but not active; he would give, on all occasions, what assistance his purse would supply; but the offices of intervention or solicitation he could not conquer his sluggishness sufficiently to perform. The affairs of others, however, were not more neglected than his own. He had often felt the inconveniences of idleness, but he never cured it; and was so conscious of his own character, that he talked of writing an Eastern Tale of *the Man who loved to be in Distress*.

Among his peculiarities was a very unskilful and inarticulate manner of pronouncing any lofty or solemn composition. He was once reading to Doddington, who, being himself a reader eminently elegant, was so much provoked by his odd utterance, that he snatched the paper from his hand, and told him that he did not understand his own verses.

The biographer of Thomson has remarked, that an author's life is best read in his works: his observation was not well-timed. Savage, who lived much with Thomson, once told me, how he heard a lady remarking that she could gather from his works three parts of his character, that he was a *great Lover, a great Swimmer*, and *rigorously abstinent*; but, said Savage, he knows not any love but that of the sex; he was perhaps never in cold water in his life; and he indulges himself in all the luxury that comes within his reach. Yet Savage always spoke with the most eager praise of his social qualities, his warmth and constancy of friendship, and his adherence to his first acquaintance when the advancement of his reputation had left them behind him.

As a writer, he is entitled to one praise of the highest kind: his mode of thinking, and of expressing his thoughts, is original. His blank verse is no more the blank verse of Milton, or of any other poet, than the rhymes of Prior are the rhymes of Cowley. His numbers, his pauses, his diction, are of his own growth, without transcription, without imitation. He thinks in a peculiar train, and he thinks always as a man of genius; he looks round on Nature and on Life, with the eye which Nature bestows only on a poet; the eye that distinguishes, in every thing presented to its view, whatever there is on which imagination can delight to be detained, and with a mind that at once comprehends the vast, and attends to the minute. The reader of the *Seasons* wonders that he never saw before what Thomson shews him, and that he never yet has felt what Thomson impresses.

His is one of the works in which blank verse seems properly used; Thomson's wide expansion of general views, and his enumeration of circumstantial varieties, would have been obstructed and embarrassed by the frequent intersections of the sense, which are the necessary effects of rhyme.

His descriptions of extended scenes and general effects bring before us the whole magnificence of Nature, whether pleasing or dreadful. The gaiety of *Spring*, the splendour of *Summer*, the tranquillity of *Autumn*, and the horror of *Winter*, take in their turns possession of the mind. The poet leads us through the appearances of things as they are successively varied by the vicissitudes of the year, and imparts to us so much of his own enthusiasm, that our thoughts expand with his imagery, and kindle with his sentiments. Nor is the naturalist without his part in the entertainment; for he is assisted to recollect and to combine, to arrange his discoveries, and to amplify the sphere of his contemplation.

The great defect of the *Seasons* is want of method; but for this I know not that there was any remedy. Of many appearances subsisting all at once, no rule can be given why one should be mentioned before another; yet the memory wants the help of order, and the curiosity is not excited by suspense or expectation.

His diction is in the highest degree florid and luxuriant, such as may be said to be to his images and thoughts *both their lustre and their shade*; such as invests them with splendour, through which perhaps they are not always easily discerned. It is too exuberant, and sometimes may be charged with filling the ear more than the mind.

These Poems, with which I was acquainted at their first appearance, I have since found altered and enlarged by subsequent revisals, as the author supposed his judgement to grow more exact, and as books or conversation extended his knowledge and opened his prospects. They are, I think, improved in general; yet I know not whether they have not lost part of what Temple calls their *race*; a word which, applied to wines, in its primitive sense, means the flavour of the soil.

Liberty, when it first appeared, I tried to read, and soon desisted. I have never tried again, and therefore will not hazard either praise or censure.

The highest praise which he has received ought not to be supprest; it is said by Lord Lyttelton in the Prologue to his posthumous play, that his works contained

No line which, dying, he could wish to blot.

WATTS

THE Poems of Dr. WATTS were by my recommendation inserted in the late Collection; the readers of which are to impute to me whatever pleasure or weariness they may find in the perusal of Blackmore, Watts, Pomfret, and Yalden.

ISAAC WATTS was born July 17, 1674, at Southampton, where his father, of the same name, kept a boarding-school for young gentlemen, though common report makes him a shoemaker. He appears, from the narrative of Dr. Gibbons, to have been neither indigent nor illiterate.

Isaac, the eldest of nine children, was given to books from his infancy; and began, we are told, to learn Latin when he was four years old, I suppose, at home. He was afterwards taught Latin, Greek, and Hebrew, by Mr. Pinhorne, a clergyman, master of the Free-school at Southampton, to whom the gratitude of his scholar afterwards inscribed a Latin ode.

His proficiency at school was so conspicuous, that a subscription was proposed for his support at the University; but he declared his resolution to take his lot with the Dissenters. Such he was as every Christian Church would rejoice to have adopted.

He therefore repaired in 1690 to an academy taught by Mr. Rowe, where he had for his companions and fellow-students Mr. Hughes the poet, and Dr. Horte, afterwards Archbishop of Tuam. Some Latin Essays, supposed to have been written as exercises at this academy, shew a degree of knowledge, both philosophical and theological, such as very few attain by a much longer course of study.

He was, as he hints in his Miscellanies, a maker of verses from fifteen to fifty, and in his youth he appears to have paid attention to Latin poetry. His verses to his brother, in the *glyconick* measure, written when he was seventeen, are remarkably easy and elegant. Some of his other odes are deformed by the Pindarick folly then prevailing, and are written with such neglect of all metrical rules as is without example among the ancients; but his diction, though perhaps not always exactly pure, has such copiousness and splendour, as shews that he was but at a very little distance from excellence.

His method of study was to impress the contents of his books upon his memory by abridging them, and by interleaving them to amplify one system with supplements from another.

With the congregation of his tutor Mr. Rowe, who were, I believe, Independents, he communicated in his nineteenth year.

At the age of twenty he left the academy, and spent two years in study and devotion at the house of his father, who treated him with great tenderness; and had the happiness, indulged to few parents, of living to see his son eminent for literature and venerable for piety.

He was then entertained by Sir John Hartopp five years, as domestick tutor to his son; and in that time particularly devoted himself to the study of the Holy Scriptures; and being chosen assistant to Dr. Chauncey, preached the first time on the birth-day that compleated his twenty-fourth year; probably considering that as the day of a second nativity, by which he entered on a new period of existence.

In about three years he succeeded Dr. Chauncey; but, soon after his entrance on his charge, he was seized by a dangerous illness, which sunk him to such weakness, that the congregation thought an assistant necessary, and appointed Mr. Price. His health then returned gradually, and he performed his duty, till (1712) he was seized by a fever of such violence and continuance, that, from the feebleness which it brought upon him, he never perfectly recovered.

This calamitous state made the compassion of his friends necessary, and drew upon him the attention of Sir Thomas Abney, who received him into his house; where, with a constancy of friendship and uniformity of conduct not often to be found, he was treated for thirty-six years with all the kindness that friendship could prompt, and all the attention that respect could dictate. Sir

Thomas died about eight years afterwards; but he continued with the lady and her daughters to the end of his life. The lady died about a year after him.

A coalition like this, a state in which the notions of patronage and dependence were overpowered by the perception of reciprocal benefits, deserves a particular memorial; and I will not withhold from the reader Dr. Gibbons's representation, to which regard is to be paid as to the narrative of one who writes what he knows, and what is known likewise to multitudes besides.

"Our next observation shall be made upon that remarkably kind Providence which brought the Doctor into Sir Thomas Abney's family, and continued him there till his death, a period of no less than thirty-six years. In the midst of his sacred labours for the glory of God, and good of his generation, he is seized with a most violent and threatening fever, which leaves him oppressed with great weakness, and puts a stop at least to his publick services for four years. In this distressing season, doubly so to his active and pious spirit, he is invited to Sir Thomas Abney's family, nor ever removes from it till he had finished his days. Here he enjoyed the uninterrupted demonstrations of the truest friendship. Here, without any care of his own, he had every thing which could contribute to the enjoyment of life, and favour the unwearied pursuit of his studies. Here he dwelt in a family, which, for piety, order, harmony, and every virtue, was an house of God. Here he had the privilege of a country recess, the fragrant bower, the spreading lawn, the flowery garden, and other advantages, to sooth his mind and aid his restoration to health; to yield him, whenever he chose them, most grateful intervals from his laborious studies, and enable him to return to them with redoubled vigour and delight. Had it not been for this most happy event, he might, as to outward view, have feebly, it may be painfully, dragged on through many more years of languor, and inability for publick service, and even for profitable study, or perhaps might have sunk into his grave under the overwhelming load of infirmities in the midst of his days; and thus the church and world would have been deprived of those many excellent sermons and works, which he drew up and published during his long residence in this family. In a few years after his coming hither, Sir Thomas Abney dies; but his amiable consort survives, who shews the Doctor the same respect and friendship as before, and most happily for him and great numbers besides; for, as her riches were great, her generosity and munificence were in full proportion; her thread of life was drawn out to a great age, even beyond that of the Doctor's; and thus this excellent man, through her kindness, and that of her daughter, the present Mrs. Elizabeth Abney, who in a like degree esteemed and honoured him, enjoyed all the benefits and felicities he experienced at his first entrance into this family, till his days were numbered and finished, and, like a shock of corn in its season, he ascended into the regions of perfect and immortal life and joy."

If this quotation has appeared long, let it be considered that it comprises an account of six-and-thirty years, and those the years of Dr. Watts.

From the time of his reception into this family, his life was no otherwise diversified than by successive publications. The series of his works I am not able to deduce; their number, and their variety, shew the intenseness of his industry, and the extent of his capacity.

He was one of the first authors that taught the Dissenters to court attention by the graces of language. Whatever they had among them before, whether of learning or acuteness, was commonly obscured and blunted by coarseness and inelegance of style. He shewed them, that zeal and purity might be expressed and enforced by polished diction.

He continued to the end of his life the teacher of a congregation, and no reader of his works can doubt his fidelity or diligence. In the pulpit, though his low stature, which very little exceeded five feet, graced him with no advantages of appearance, yet the gravity and propriety of his utterance made his discourses very efficacious. I once mentioned the reputation which Mr. Foster had gained by his proper delivery to my friend Dr. Hawkesworth, who told me, that in the art of pronunciation he was far inferior to Dr. Watts.

Such was his flow of thoughts, and such his promptitude of language, that in the latter part of his life he did not precompose his cursory sermons; but having adjusted the heads, and sketched out some particulars, trusted for success to his extemporary powers.

He did not endeavour to assist his eloquence by any gesticulations; for, as no corporeal actions have any correspondence with theological truth, he did not see how they could enforce it.

At the conclusion of weighty sentences he gave time, by a short pause, for the proper impression.

To stated and publick instruction he added familiar visits and personal application, and was careful to improve the opportunities which conversation offered of diffusing and increasing the influence of religion.

By his natural temper he was quick of resentment; but, by his established and habitual practice, he was gentle, modest, and inoffensive. His tenderness appeared in his attention to children, and to the poor. To the poor, while he lived in the family of his friend, he allowed the third part of his annual revenue, though the whole was not a hundred a year; and for children, he condescended to lay aside the scholar, the philosopher, and the wit, to write little poems of devotion, and systems of instruction, adapted to their wants and capacities, from the dawn of reason through its gradations of advance in the morning of life. Every man, acquainted with the common principles of human action, will look with veneration on the writer who is at one time combating Locke, and at another making a catechism for children in their fourth year. A voluntary descent from the dignity of science is perhaps the hardest lesson that humility can teach.

As his mind was capacious, his curiosity excursive, and his industry continual, his writings are very numerous, and his subjects various. With his theological works I am only enough acquainted to admire his meekness of opposition, and his mildness of censure. It was not only in his book but in his mind that *orthodoxy* was *united* with *charity*.

Of his philosophical pieces, his Logick has been received into the universities, and therefore wants no private recommendation: if he owes part of it to Le Clerc, it must be considered that no man who undertakes merely to methodise or illustrate a system, pretends to be its author.

In his metaphysical disquisitions, it was observed by the late learned Mr. Dyer, that he confounded the idea of *space* with that of *empty space*, and did not consider that though space might be without matter, yet matter being extended, could not be without space.

Few books have been perused by me with greater pleasure than his *Improvement of the Mind*, of which the radical principles may indeed be found in Locke's *Conduct of the Understanding*, but they are so expanded and ramified by Watts, as to confer upon him the merit of a work in the highest degree useful and pleasing. Whoever has the care of instructing others, may be charged with deficience in his duty if this book is not recommended.

I have mentioned his treatises of Theology as distinct from his other productions; but the truth is, that whatever he took in hand was, by his incessant solicitude for souls, converted to Theology. As piety predominated in his mind, it is diffused over his works: under his direction it may be truly said, *Theologiæ Philosophia ancillatur*, philosophy is subservient to evangelical instruction; it is difficult to read a page without learning, or at least wishing, to be better. The attention is caught by indirect instruction, and he that sat down only to reason is on a sudden compelled to pray.

It was therefore with great propriety that, in 1728, he received from Edinburgh and Aberdeen an unsolicited diploma, by which he became a Doctor of Divinity. Academical honours would have more value, if they were always bestowed with equal judgement.

He continued many years to study and to preach, and to do good by his instruction and example; till at last the infirmities of age disabled him from the more laborious part of his ministerial functions, and, being no longer capable of publick duty, he offered to remit the salary appendant to it; but his congregation would not accept the resignation.

By degrees his weakness increased, and at last confined him to his chamber and his bed; where he was worn gradually away without pain, till he expired Nov. 25, 1748, in the seventy-fifth year of his age.

Few men have left behind such purity of character, or such monuments of laborious piety. He has provided instruction for all ages, from those who are lisping their first lessons, to the enlightened readers of Malbranche and Locke; he has left neither corporeal nor spiritual nature unexamined; he has taught the art of reasoning, and the science of the stars.

His character, therefore, must be formed from the multiplicity and diversity of his attainments, rather than from any single performance; for it would not be safe to claim for him the highest rank in any single denomination of literary dignity; yet perhaps there was nothing in which he would not have excelled, if he had not divided his powers to different pursuits.

As a poet, had he been only a poet, he would probably have stood high among the authors with whom he is now associated. For his judgement was exact, and he noted beauties and faults with very nice discernment; his imagination, as the *Dacian Battle* proves, was vigorous and active, and the stores of knowledge were large by which his fancy was to be supplied. His ear was well-tuned, and his diction was elegant and copious. But his devotional poetry is, like that of others, unsatisfactory. The paucity of its topicks enforces perpetual repetition, and the sanctity of the matter rejects the ornaments of figurative diction. It is sufficient for Watts to have done better than others what no man has done well.

His poems on other subjects seldom rise higher than might be expected from the amusements of a Man of Letters, and have different degrees of value as they are more or less laboured, or as the occasion was more or less favourable to invention.

He writes too often without regular measures, and too often in blank verse; the rhymes are not always sufficiently correspondent. He is particularly unhappy in coining names expressive of characters. His lines are commonly smooth and easy, and his thoughts always religiously pure; but who is there that, to so much piety and innocence, does not wish for a greater measure of spriteliness and vigour? He is at least one of the few poets with whom youth and ignorance may be safely pleased; and happy will be that reader whose mind is disposed by his verses, or his prose, to imitate him in all but his non-conformity, to copy his benevolence to man, and his reverence to God.

COLLINS

WILLIAM COLLINS was born at Chichester on the twenty-fifth of December, about 1720. His father was a hatter of good reputation. He was in 1733, as Dr. Warton has kindly informed me, admitted scholar of Winchester College, where he was educated by Dr. Burton. His English exercises were better than his Latin.

He first courted the notice of the publick by some verses to a *Lady weeping*, published in *The Gentleman's Magazine*.

In 1740, he stood first in the list of the scholars to be received in succession at New College; but unhappily there was no vacancy. This was the original misfortune of his life. He became a Commoner of Queen's College, probably with a scanty maintenance; but was in about half a year elected a *Demy* of

Magdalen College, where he continued till he had taken a Bachelor's degree, and then suddenly left the University; for what reason I know not that he told.

He now (about 1744) came to London a literary adventurer, with many projects in his head, and very little money in his pocket. He designed many works; but his great fault was irresolution, or the frequent calls of immediate necessity broke his schemes, and suffered him to pursue no settled purpose. A man, doubtful of his dinner, or trembling at a creditor, is not much disposed to abstracted meditation, or remote enquiries. He published proposals for a History of the Revival of Learning; and I have heard him speak with great kindness of Leo the Tenth, and with keen resentment of his tasteless successor. But probably not a page of the History was ever written. He planned several tragedies, but he only planned them. He wrote now-and-then odes and other poems, and did something, however little.

About this time I fell into his company. His appearance was decent and manly; his knowledge considerable, his views extensive, his conversation elegant, and his disposition chearful. By degrees I gained his confidence; and one day was admitted to him when he was immured by a bailiff, that was prowling in the street. On this occasion recourse was had to the booksellers, who, on the credit of a translation of Aristotle's Poeticks, which he engaged to write with a large commentary, advanced as much money as enabled him to escape into the country. He shewed me the guineas safe in his hand. Soon afterwards his uncle, Mr. Martin, a lieutenant-colonel, left him about two thousand pounds; a sum which Collins could scarcely think exhaustible, and which he did not live to exhaust. The guineas were then repaid, and the translation neglected.

But man is not born for happiness. Collins, who, while he *studied to live*, felt no evil but poverty, no sooner *lived to study* than his life was assailed by more dreadful calamities, disease and insanity.

Having formerly written his character, while perhaps it was yet more distinctly impressed upon my memory, I shall insert it here.

"Mr. Collins was a man of extensive literature, and of vigorous faculties. He was acquainted not only with the learned tongues, but with the Italian, French, and Spanish languages. He had employed his mind chiefly upon works of fiction, and subjects of fancy; and, by indulging some peculiar habits of thought, was eminently delighted with those flights of imagination which pass the bounds of nature, and to which the mind is reconciled only by a passive acquiescence in popular traditions. He loved fairies, genii, giants, and monsters; he delighted to rove through the meanders of inchantment, to gaze on the magnificence of golden palaces, to repose by the waterfalls of Elysian gardens.

"This was however the character rather of his inclination than his genius; the grandeur of wildness, and the novelty of extravagance, were always desired by him, but were not always attained. Yet as diligence is never wholly lost; if his efforts sometimes caused harshness and obscurity, they likewise produced in happier moments sublimity and splendour. This idea which he had formed of excellence, led him to oriental fictions and allegorical imagery; and perhaps, while he was intent upon description, he did not sufficiently cultivate sentiment. His poems are the productions of a mind not deficient in fire, nor unfurnished with knowledge either of books or life, but somewhat obstructed in its progress by deviation in quest of mistaken beauties.

"His morals were pure, and his opinions pious: in a long continuance of poverty, and long habits of dissipation, it cannot be expected that any character should be exactly uniform. There is a degree of want by which the freedom of agency is almost destroyed; and long association with fortuitous companions will at last relax the strictness of truth, and abate the fervour of sincerity. That this man, wise and virtuous as he was, passed always unentangled through the snares of life, it would be prejudice and temerity to affirm; but it may be said that at least he preserved the source of action unpolluted, that his principles were never shaken, that his distinctions of right and wrong were never confounded, and that his faults had nothing of malignity or design, but proceeded from some unexpected pressure, or casual temptation.

"The latter part of his life cannot be remembered but with pity and sadness. He languished some years under that depression of mind which enchains the faculties without destroying them, and leaves reason the knowledge of right without the power of pursuing it. These clouds which he perceived gathering on his intellects, he endeavoured to disperse by travel, and passed into France; but found himself constrained to yield to his malady, and returned. He was for some time confined in a house of lunaticks, and afterwards retired to the care of his sister in Chichester, where death in 1756 came to his relief.

"After his return from France, the writer of this character paid him a visit at Islington, where he was waiting for his sister, whom he had directed to meet him: there was then nothing of disorder discernible in his mind by any but himself; but he had withdrawn from study, and travelled with no other book than an English Testament, such as children carry to the school: when his friend took it into his hand, out of curiosity to see what companion a Man of Letters had chosen, *I have but one book*, said Collins, *but that is the best.*"

Such was the fate of Collins, with whom I once delighted to converse, and whom I yet remember with tenderness.

He was visited at Chichester, in his last illness, by his learned friends Dr. Warton and his brother; to whom he spoke with disapprobation of his Oriental Eclogues, as not sufficiently expressive of Asiatick manners, and called them his Irish Eclogues. He shewed them, at the same time, an ode inscribed to Mr. John Hume, on the superstitions of the Highlands; which they thought superior to his other works, but which no search has yet found.

His disorder was not alienation of mind, but general laxity and feebleness, a deficiency rather of his vital than intellectual powers. What he spoke wanted neither judgement nor spirit; but a few minutes exhausted him, so that he was forced to rest upon the couch, till a short cessation restored his powers, and he was again able to talk with his former vigour.

The approaches of this dreadful malady he began to feel soon after his uncle's death; and, with the usual weakness of men so diseased, eagerly snatched that temporary relief with which the table and the bottle flatter and seduce. But his health continually declined, and he grew more and more burthensome to himself.

To what I have formerly said of his writings may be added, that his diction was often harsh, unskilfully laboured, and injudiciously selected. He affected the obsolete when it was not worthy of revival; and he puts his words out of the common order, seeming to think, with some later candidates for fame, that not to write prose is certainly to write poetry. His lines commonly are of slow motion, clogged and impeded with clusters of consonants. As men are often esteemed who cannot be loved, so the poetry of Collins may sometimes extort praise when it gives little pleasure.

Mr. Collin's first production is added here from the *Poetical Calendar*:

To Miss Aurelia C—R,

ON HER WEEPING AT HER SISTER'S WEDDING.

Cease, fair Aurelia, cease to mourn;
    Lament not Hannah's happy state;
You may be happy in your turn,
    And seize the treasure you regret.

With Love united Hymen stands,
    And softly whispers to your charms;
"Meet but your lover in my bands,
    You'll find your sister in his arms."

GRAY

THOMAS GRAY, the son of Mr. Philip Gray, a scrivener of London, was born in Cornhill, November 26, 1716. His grammatical education he received at Eton under the care of Mr. Antrobus, his mother's brother, then assistant to Dr. George; and when he left school, in 1734, entered a pensioner at Peterhouse in Cambridge.

The transition from the school to the college is, to most young scholars, the time from which they date their years of manhood, liberty, and happiness; but Gray seems to have been very little delighted with academical gratifications;

he liked at Cambridge neither the mode of life nor the fashion of study, and lived sullenly on to the time when his attendance on lectures was no longer required. As he intended to profess the Common Law, he took no degree.

When he had been at Cambridge about five years, Mr. Horace Walpole, whose friendship he had gained at Eton, invited him to travel with him as his companion. They wandered through France into Italy; and Gray's Letters contain a very pleasing account of many parts of their journey. But unequal friendships are easily dissolved: at Florence they quarrelled, and parted; and Mr. Walpole is now content to have it told that it was by his fault. If we look however without prejudice on the world, we shall find that men, whose consciousness of their own merit sets them above the compliances of servility, are apt enough in their association with superiors to watch their own dignity with troublesome and punctilious jealousy, and in the fervour of independance to exact that attention which they refuse to pay. Part they did, whatever was the quarrel, and the rest of their travels was doubtless more unpleasant to them both. Gray continued his journey in a manner suitable to his own little fortune, with only an occasional servant.

He returned to England in September 1741, and in about two months afterwards buried his father; who had, by an injudicious waste of money upon a new house, so much lessened his fortune, that Gray thought himself too poor to study the law. He therefore retired to Cambridge, where he soon after became Bachelor of Civil Law; and where, without liking the place or its inhabitants, or professing to like them, he passed, except a short residence at London, the rest of his life.

About this time he was deprived of Mr. West, the son of a chancellor of Ireland, a friend on whom he appears to have set a high value, and who deserved his esteem by the powers which he shews in his Letters, and in the Ode to *May*, which Mr. Mason has preserved, as well as by the sincerity with which, when Gray sent him part of *Agrippina*, a tragedy that he had just begun, he gave an opinion which probably intercepted the progress of the work, and which the judgement of every reader will confirm. It was certainly no loss to the English stage that *Agrippina* was never finished.

In this year (1742) Gray seems first to have applied himself seriously to poetry; for in this year were produced the *Ode to Spring*, his *Prospect of Eton*, and his *Ode to Adversity*. He began likewise a Latin poem, *de Principiis cogitandi*.

It may be collected from the narrative of Mr. Mason, that his first ambition was to have excelled in Latin poetry: perhaps it were reasonable to wish that he had prosecuted his design; for though there is at present some embarrassment in his phrase, and some harshness in his Lyrick numbers, his copiousness of language is such as very few possess; and his lines, even when imperfect, discover a writer whom practice would quickly have made skilful.

He now lived on at Peterhouse, very little solicitous what others did or thought, and cultivated his mind and enlarged his views without any other purpose than of improving and amusing himself; when Mr. Mason, being elected fellow of Pembroke-hall, brought him a companion who was afterwards to be his editor, and whose fondness and fidelity has kindled in him a zeal of admiration, which cannot be reasonably expected from the neutrality of a stranger and the coldness of a critick.

In this retirement he wrote (1747) an ode on the *Death of Mr. Walpole's Cat*; and the year afterwards attempted a poem of more importance, on *Government and Education*, of which the fragments which remain have many excellent lines.

His next production (1750) was his far-famed *Elegy in the Church-yard*, which, finding its way into a Magazine, first, I believe, made him known to the publick.

An invitation from lady Cobham about this time gave occasion to an odd composition called *a Long Story*, which adds little to Gray's character.

Several of his pieces were published (1753), with designs, by Mr. Bentley; and, that they might in some form or other make a book, only one side of each leaf was printed. I believe the poems and the plates recommended each other so well, that the whole impression was soon bought. This year he lost his mother.

Some time afterwards (1756) some young men of the college, whose chambers were near his, diverted themselves with disturbing him by frequent and troublesome noises, and, as is said, by pranks yet more offensive and contemptuous. This insolence, having endured it a while, he represented to the governors of the society, among whom perhaps he had no friends; and, finding his complaint little regarded, removed himself to Pembroke-hall.

In 1757 he published *The Progress of Poetry* and *The Bard*, two compositions at which the readers of poetry were at first content to gaze in mute amazement. Some that tried them confessed their inability to understand them, though Warburton said that they were understood as well as the works of Milton and Shakspeare, which it is the fashion to admire. Garrick wrote a few lines in their praise. Some hardy champions undertook to rescue them from neglect, and in a short time many were content to be shewn beauties which they could not see.

Gray's reputation was now so high, that, after the death of Cibber, he had the honour of refusing the laurel, which was then bestowed on Mr. Whitehead.

His curiosity, not long after, drew him away from Cambridge to a lodging near the Museum, where he resided near three years, reading and transcribing; and, so far as can be discovered, very little affected by two odes on *Oblivion* and *Obscurity*, in which his Lyrick performances were ridiculed with much contempt and much ingenuity.

When the Professor of Modern History at Cambridge died, he was, as he says, *cockered and spirited up*, till he asked it of lord Bute, who sent him a civil refusal; and the place was given to Mr. Brocket, the tutor of Sir James Lowther.

His constitution was weak, and believing that his health was promoted by exercise and change of place, he undertook (1765) a journey into Scotland, of which his account, so far as it extends, is very curious and elegant; for as his comprehension was ample, his curiosity extended to all the works of art, all the appearances of nature, and all the monuments of past events. He naturally contracted a friendship with Dr. Beattie, whom he found a poet, a philosopher, and a good man. The Mareschal College at Aberdeen offered him the degree of Doctor of Laws, which, having omitted to take it at Cambridge, he thought it decent to refuse.

What he had formerly solicited in vain, was at last given him without solicitation. The Professorship of History became again vacant, and he received (1768) an offer of it from the duke of Grafton. He accepted, and retained it to his death; always designing lectures, but never reading them; uneasy at his neglect of duty, and appeasing his uneasiness with designs of reformation, and with a resolution which he believed himself to have made of resigning the office, if he found himself unable to discharge it.

Ill health made another journey necessary, and he visited (1769) Westmoreland and Cumberland. He that reads his epistolary narration wishes, that to travel, and to tell his travels, had been more of his employment; but it is by studying at home that we must obtain the ability of travelling with intelligence and improvement.

His travels and his studies were now near their end. The gout, of which he had sustained many weak attacks, fell upon his stomach, and, yielding to no medicines, produced strong convulsions, which (July 30, 1771) terminated in death.

His character I am willing to adopt, as Mr. Mason has done, from a Letter written to my friend Mr. Boswell, by the Rev. Mr. Temple, rector of St. Gluvias in Cornwall; and am as willing as his warmest well-wisher to believe it true.

"Perhaps he was the most learned man in Europe. He was equally acquainted with the elegant and profound parts of science, and that not superficially but thoroughly. He knew every branch of history, both natural and civil; had read all the original historians of England, France, and Italy; and was a great antiquarian. Criticism, metaphysics, morals, politics, made a principal part of his study; voyages and travels of all sorts were his favourite amusements; and he had a fine taste in painting, prints, architecture, and gardening. With such a fund of knowledge, his conversation must have been equally instructing and entertaining; but he was also a good man, a man of virtue and humanity. There is no character without some speck, some imperfection; and I think the greatest defect in his was an affectation in delicacy, or rather effeminacy, and a visible fastidiousness, or contempt and disdain of his inferiors in science. He also had, in some degree, that weakness which disgusted Voltaire so much in Mr. Congreve: though he seemed to value others chiefly according to the progress they had made in knowledge, yet he could not bear to be considered himself merely as a man of letters; and though without birth, or fortune, or station, his desire was to be looked upon as a private independent gentleman, who read for his amusement. Perhaps it may be said, What signifies so much knowledge, when it produced so little? Is it worth taking so much pains to leave no memorial but a few poems? But let it be considered that Mr. Gray was, to others, at least innocently employed; to himself, certainly beneficially. His time passed agreeably; he was every day making some new acquisition in science; his mind was enlarged, his heart softened, his virtue strengthened; the world and mankind were shewn to him without a mask; and he was taught to consider every thing as trifling, and unworthy of the attention of a wise man, except the pursuit of knowledge and practice of virtue, in that state wherein God hath placed us."

To this character Mr. Mason has added a more particular account of Gray's skill in zoology. He has remarked, that Gray's effeminacy was affected most *before those whom he did not wish to please*; and that he is unjustly charged with making knowledge his sole reason of preference, as he paid his esteem to none whom he did not likewise believe to be good.

What has occurred to me, from the slight inspection of his Letters in which my undertaking has engaged me, is, that his mind had a large grasp; that his curiosity was unlimited, and his judgement cultivated; that he was a man likely to love much where he loved at all, but that he was fastidious and hard to please. His contempt however is often employed, where I hope it will be approved, upon scepticism and infidelity. His short account of Shaftesbury I will insert.

"You say you cannot conceive how lord Shaftesbury came to be a philosopher in vogue; I will tell you: first, he was a lord; secondly, he was as vain as any of his readers; thirdly, men are very prone to believe what they do not understand; fourthly, they will believe any thing at all, provided they are under no obligation to believe it; fifthly, they love to take a new road, even when that road leads no where; sixthly, he was reckoned a fine writer, and seems always to mean more than he said. Would you have any more reasons? An interval of above forty years has pretty well destroyed the charm. A dead lord ranks with commoners: vanity is no longer interested in the matter; for a new road is become an old one."

Mr. Mason has added, from his own knowledge, that though Gray was poor, he was not eager of money; and that, out of the little that he had, he was very willing to help the necessitous.

As a writer he had this peculiarity, that he did not write his pieces first rudely, and then correct them, but laboured every line as it arose in the train of composition; and he had a notion not very peculiar, that he could not write but at certain times, or at happy moments; a fantastick foppery, to which my kindness for a man of learning and of virtue wishes him to have been superior.

GRAY's Poetry is now to be considered; and I hope not to be looked on as an enemy to his name, if I confess that I contemplate it with less pleasure than his life.

His ode on *Spring* has something poetical, both in the language and the thought; but the language is too luxuriant, and the thoughts have nothing new. There has of late arisen a practice of giving to adjectives, derived from substantives, the termination of participles; such as the *cultured* plain, the *dasied* bank; but I was sorry to see, in the lines of a scholar like Gray, the *honied* Spring. The morality is natural, but too stale; the conclusion is pretty.

The poem on the *Cat* was doubtless by its author considered as a trifle, but it is not a happy trifle. In the first stanza *the azure flowers* that *blow*, shew resolutely a rhyme is sometimes made when it cannot easily be found. *Selima*, the *Cat*, is called a nymph, with some violence both to language and sense; but there is good use made of it when it is done; for of the two lines,

> What female heart can gold despise?
> What cat's averse to fish?

the first relates merely to the nymph, and the second only to the cat. The sixth stanza contains a melancholy truth, that *a favourite has no friend*; but the last ends in a pointed sentence of no relation to the purpose; if *what glistered* had been *gold*, the cat would not have gone into the water; and, if she had, would not less have been drowned.

The *Prospect of Eton College* suggests nothing to Gray, which every beholder does not equally think and feel. His supplication to father *Thames*, to tell him who drives the hoop or tosses the ball, is useless and puerile. Father *Thames* has no better means of knowing than himself. His epithet *buxom health* is not elegant; he seems not to understand the word. Gray thought his language more poetical as it was more remote from common use: finding in Dryden *honey redolent of Spring*, an expression that reaches the utmost limits of our language, Gray drove it a little more beyond common apprehension, by making *gales* to be *redolent of joy and youth*.

Of the *Ode on Adversity*, the hint was at first taken from *O Diva, gratum quæ regis Antium*; but Gray has excelled his original by the variety of his sentiments, and by their moral application. Of this piece, at once poetical and rational, I will not by slight objections violate the dignity.

My process has now brought me to the *wonderful Wonder of Wonders*, the two Sister Odes; by which, though either vulgar ignorance or common sense at first universally rejected them, many have been since persuaded to think themselves delighted. I am one of those that are willing to be pleased, and therefore would gladly find the meaning of the first stanza of the *Progress of Poetry*.

Gray seems in his rapture to confound the images of *spreading sound* and *running water*. A *stream of musick* may be allowed; but where does *Musick*, however *smooth and strong*, after having visited the *verdant vales*, *rowl down the steep amain*, so as that *rocks and nodding groves rebellow to the roar*? If this be said of *Musick*, it is nonsense; if it be said of *Water*, it is nothing to the purpose.

The second stanza, exhibiting Mars's car and Jove's eagle, is unworthy of further notice. Criticism disdains to chase a schoolboy to his common places.

To the third it may likewise be objected, that it is drawn from Mythology, though such as may be more easily assimilated to real life. Idalia's *velvet-green* has something of cant. An epithet or metaphor drawn from Nature ennobles Art; an epithet or metaphor drawn from Art degrades Nature. Gray is too fond of words arbitrarily compounded. *Many-twinkling* was formerly censured as not analogical; we may say *many-spotted*, but scarcely *many-spotting*. This stanza, however, has something pleasing.

Of the second ternary of stanzas, the first endeavours to tell something, and would have told it, had it not been crossed by Hyperion: the second describes well enough the universal prevalence of Poetry; but I am afraid that the conclusion will not rise from the premises. The caverns of the North and the plains of Chili are not the residences of *Glory* and *generous Shame*. But that Poetry and Virtue go always together is an opinion so pleasing, that I can forgive him who resolves to think it true.

The third stanza sounds big with *Delphi*, and *Egean*, and *Ilissus*, and *Meander*, and *hallowed fountain* and *solemn sound*; but in all Gray's odes there is a kind of cumbrous splendor which we wish away. His position is at last false: in the time of Dante and Petrarch, from whom he derives our first school of Poetry, Italy was over-run by *tyrant power* and *coward vice*; nor was our state much better when we first borrowed the Italian arts.

Of the third ternary, the first gives a mythological birth of Shakspeare. What is said of that mighty genius is true; but it is not said happily: the real effects of this poetical power are put out of sight by the pomp of machinery. Where truth is sufficient to fill the mind, fiction is worse than useless; the counterfeit debases the genuine.

His account of Milton's blindness, if we suppose it caused by study in the formation of his poem, a supposition surely allowable, is poetically true, and happily imagined. But the *car* of Dryden, with his *two coursers*, has nothing in it peculiar; it is a car in which any other rider may be placed.

The Bard appears, at the first view, to be, as Algarotti and others have remarked, an imitation of the prophecy of Nereus. Algarotti thinks it superior to its original; and, if preference depends only on the imagery and animation of the two poems, his judgement is right. There is in *The Bard* more force, more thought, and more variety. But to copy is less than to invent, and the copy has been unhappily produced at a wrong time. The fiction of Horace was to the Romans credible; but its revival disgusts us with apparent and unconquerable falsehood. *Incredulus odi.*

To select a singular event, and swell it to a giant's bulk by fabulous appendages of spectres and predictions, has little difficulty, for he that forsakes the probable may always find the marvellous. And it has little use; we are affected only as we believe; we are improved only as we find something to be imitated or declined. I do not see that *The Bard* promotes any truth, moral or political.

His stanzas are too long, especially his epodes; the ode is finished before the ear has learned its measures, and consequently before it can receive pleasure from their consonance and recurrence.

Of the first stanza the abrupt beginning has been celebrated; but technical beauties can give praise only to the inventor. It is in the power of any man to rush abruptly upon his subject, that has read the ballad of *Johnny Armstrong*,

Is there ever a man in all Scotland—

The initial resemblances, or alliterations, *ruin, ruthless, helm nor hauberk,* are below the grandeur of a poem that endeavours at sublimity.

In the second stanza the *Bard* is well described; but in the third we have the puerilities of obsolete mythology. When we are told that *Cadwallo hush'd the stormy main,* and that *Modred* made *huge Plinlimmon bow his cloud-top'd head,* attention recoils from the repetition of a tale that, even when it was first heard, was heard with scorn.

The *weaving* of the *winding sheet* he borrowed, as he owns, from the northern Bards; but their texture, however, was very properly the work of female powers, as the art of spinning the thread of life in another mythology. Theft is always dangerous; Gray has made weavers of his slaughtered bards, by a fiction outrageous and incongruous. They are then called upon to *Weave the warp, and weave the woof,* perhaps with no great propriety; for it is by crossing the *woof* with the *warp* that men *weave* the *web* or piece; and the first line was dearly bought by the admission of its wretched correspondent, *Give ample room and verge enough.* He has, however, no other line as bad.

The third stanza of the second ternary is commended, I think, beyond its merit. The personification is indistinct. *Thirst* and *Hunger* are not alike; and their features, to make the imagery perfect, should have been discriminated. We are told, in the same stanza, how *towers* are *fed.* But I will no longer look for particular faults; yet let it be observed that the ode might have been concluded with an action of better example; but suicide is always to be had, without expence of thought.

These odes are marked by glittering accumulations of ungraceful ornaments; they strike, rather than please; the images are magnified by affectation; the language is laboured into harshness. The mind of the writer seems to work with unnatural violence. *Double, double, toil and trouble.* He has a kind of strutting dignity, and is tall by walking on tiptoe. His art and his struggle are too visible, and there is too little appearance of ease and nature.

To say that he has no beauties, would be unjust: a man like him, of great learning and great industry, could not but produce something valuable. When he pleases least, it can only be said that a good design was ill directed.

His translations of Northern and Welsh Poetry deserve praise; the imagery is preserved, perhaps often improved; but the language is unlike the language of other poets.

In the character of his Elegy I rejoice to concur with the common reader; for by the common sense of readers uncorrupted with literary prejudices, after all the refinements of subtilty and the dogmatism of learning, must be finally decided all claim to poetical honours. The *Church-yard* abounds with images which find a mirrour in every mind, and with sentiments to which every bosom returns an echo. The four stanzas beginning *Yet even these bones*, are to me original: I have never seen the notions in any other place; yet he that reads them here, persuades himself that he has always felt them. Had Gray written often thus, it had been vain to blame, and useless to praise him.

Letter to Thomas Lawrence

THURSDAY 17 JANUARY 1782

Sir: Jan. 17, 1782

Our old Friend Mr. Levett, who was last night eminently cheerful, died this morning. The man who lay in the same room hearing an uncommon noise got up; and tried to make him speak, but without effect, he then called Mr. Holder the apothecary, who though, when he came, he thought him dead, opened a vein but could draw no blood. So has ended the long life of a very useful, and very blam[e]less man. I am, Sir, Your most humble Servant,

SAM. JOHNSON

Diary entry

SUNDAY 20 JANUARY 1782

JANUARY 20, SUNDAY. Robert Levett was buried in the church-yard of Bridewell, between one and two in the afternoon. He died on Thursday 17, about seven in the morning, by an instantaneous death. He was an old and faithful friend; I have known him from about 46. *Commendavi*. May God have had mercy on him. May he have mercy on me.

Letter to Thomas Lawrence

WEDNESDAY 1 MAY 1782

T. Laurentio Medico. S   Maijs calendis, 1782

Novum frigus, nova tussis, nova spirandi difficultas, novam sanguinosi missionem suadent, quam tamen te inconsulto nolim fieri. Ad te venire vix possum, nec est cur ad me venias. Licere vel non licere uno verbo dicendum est; cætera mihi et Holdero reliqueris. Si per te licet, imperetur nuncio Holderum ad me deducere.

Postquam tu discesseris quo me vertam?

Letter to James Boswell

SATURDAY 7 SEPTEMBER 1782

Dear Sir, London, Sept. 7, 1782

I have struggled through this year with so much infirmity of body, and such strong impressions of the fragility of life, that death, wherever it appears, fills me with melancholy; and I cannot hear without emotion, of the removal of any one, whom I have known, into another state.

Your father's death had every circumstance that could enable you to bear it; it was at a mature age, and it was expected; and as his general life had been pious, his thoughts had doubtless for many years past been turned upon eternity. That you did not find him sensible must doubtless grieve you; his disposition towards you was undoubtedly that of a kind, though not of a fond father. Kindness, at least actual, is in our power, but fondness is not; and if by negligence or imprudence you had extinguished his fondness, he could not at will rekindle it. Nothing then remained between you but mutual forgiveness of each other's faults, and mutual desire of each other's happiness.

I shall long to know his final disposition of his fortune.

You, dear Sir, have now a new station, and have therefore new cares, and new employments. Life, as Cowley seems to say, ought to resemble a well ordered poem; of which one rule generally received is, that the exordium should be simple, and should promise little. Begin your new course of life with the least show, and the least expence possible; you may at pleasure encrease both, but you cannot easily diminish them. Do not think your estate your own, while any man can call upon you for money which you cannot pay; therefore, begin with timorous parsimony. Let it be your first care not to be in any man's debt.

When the thoughts are extended to a future state, the present life seems hardly worthy of all those principles of conduct, and maxims of prudence, which one generation of men has transmitted to another; but upon a closer view, when it is perceived how much evil is produced, and how much good is impeded by embarrassment and distress, and how little room the expedients of poverty leave for the exercise of virtue; its sorrows manifest that the boundless importance of the next life, enforces some attention to the interests of this.

Be kind to the old servants, and secure the kindness of the agents and factors; do not disgust them by asperity, or unwelcome gaiety, or apparent suspicion. From them you must learn the real state of your affairs, the characters of your tenants, and the value of your lands.

Make my compliments to Mrs. Boswell; I think her expectations from air and exercise are the best that she can form. I hope she will live long and happily.

I forget whether I told you that Rasay has been here; we dined cheerfully together. I entertained lately a young gentleman from Coriatachat.

I received your letters only this morning. I am, dear Sir, yours, etc.

SAM. JOHNSON

On the Death of Dr Robert Levet

Condemn'd to hope's delusive mine,
    As on we toil from day to day,
By sudden blasts, or slow decline,
    Our social comforts drop away.

Well tried through many a varying year,
    See LEVET to the grave descend;
Officious, innocent, sincere,
    Of ev'ry friendless name the friend.

Yet still he fills affection's eye,
    Obscurely wise, and coarsely kind;   10
Nor, letter'd arrogance, deny
    Thy praise to merit unrefin'd.

When fainting nature call'd for aid,
    And hov'ring death prepar'd the blow,
His vig'rous remedy display'd
    The power of art without the show.

In misery's darkest cavern's known,
    His useful care was ever nigh,
Where hopeless anguish pour'd his groan,
    And lonely want retir'd to die.   20

No summons mock'd by chill delay,
    No petty gain disdain'd by pride,
The modest wants of ev'ry day
    The toil of ev'ry day supplied.

His virtues walk'd their narrow round,
    Nor made a pause, nor left a void;
And sure th' Eternal Master found
    The single talent well employ'd.

The busy day, the peaceful night,
   Unfelt, uncounted, glided by;   30
His frame was firm, his powers were bright,
   Tho' now his eightieth year was nigh.

Then with no throbbing fiery pain,
   No cold gradations of decay,
Death broke at once the vital chain,
   And free'd his soul the nearest way.

Letter to Hester Thrale

FRIDAY 2 JULY 1784

Madam: July 2, 1784

If I interpret your letter right, You are ignominiously married, if it is yet undone, let us once talk together. If You have abandoned your children and your religion, God forgive your wickedness; if you have forfeited your Fame, and your country, may your folly do no further mischief.

If the last act is yet to do, I, who have loved you, esteemed you, reverenced you, and served you, I who long thought you the first of humankind, entreat that before your fate is irrevocable, I may once more see You. I was, I once was, Madam, most truly yours,

SAM. JOHNSON

I will come down if you permit it.

Letter to Hester Maria Thrale

SATURDAY 3 JULY 1784

Dear Madam: London, July 3, 1784

In telling You that I sincerely pity You, and that I approve your Conduct I tell You only what will be said by all Mankind. What I think of your Mothers conduct I cannot express, but by words which I cannot prevail upon myself to use.

Your Guardians, I suppose, have been now with You; I am sorry that I am not with You too. But they have more power to help you than I, and not less inclination. We all compassionate and love You and your Sisters, and I hope by our Friendship, and Your own Virtue, Prudence, and Piety, You may, though thus unworthily deserted, pass a life of security, Happiness, and honour. I am, Dearest Love, your most humble servant,

SAM. JOHNSON

Letter to Hester Maria Thrale

TUESDAY 6 JULY 1784

Dear Madam: London, July 6, 1784

Mr. Cruchley gave me an account of your interview, and of the plan which is for the present exigence settled between You and your Friends. But I either misunderstood him or you, for the two accounts seem very different.

If you comply for the time with proposals not very agreeable, You know that any necessity of compliance can be but short. You will soon be mistress of Yourself. Do your best; and be not discouraged. Serve God; read, and pray. You have in your hand all that the world considers as materials of happiness. You have riches, Youth, and Hea[l]th, all which I shall delight to see You enjoy. But believe a Man whose experience has been long, and who can have no wish to deceive you and who now tells you that the highest honour, and most constant pleasure this life can afford, must be obtained by passing it with attention fixed upon Eternity. The longest life soon passes away. You that are blooming in all the gayety of youth, will be, before You are aware, as old as he that has now the honour of being, Madam, your most humble servant,

SAM. JOHNSON

Letter to Hester Thrale

THURSDAY 8 JULY 1784

Dear Madam: London, July 8, 1784

What You have done, however I may lament it, I have no pretence to resent, as it has not been injurious to me. I therefore breathe out one sigh more of tenderness perhaps useless, but at least sincere.

I wish that God may grant you every blessing, that You may be happy in this world for its short continuance, and eternally happy in a better State. And whatever I can contribute to your happiness, I am very ready to repay for that kindness which soothed twenty years of a life radically wretched.

Do not think slightly of the advice which I now presume to offer. Prevail upon Mr. Piozzi to settle in England. You may live here with more dignity than in Italy, and with more security. Your rank will be higher, and your fortune more under your own eye. I desire not to detail all my reasons; but every argument of prudence and interest is for England, and only s<ome> phantoms of imagination seduce you to Italy.

I am afraid, however, that my counsel is vain, yet I have eased my heart by giving it.

When Queen Mary took the resolution of sheltering herself in England, the Archbishop of St. Andrew's attempting to dissuade her, attended on her journey and when they came to the irremeable Stream that separated the two kingdoms, walked by her side into the water, in the middle of which he seized her bridle, and with earnestness proportioned to her danger and his own affection, pressed her to return. The Queen went forward. —If the parallel reaches thus far; may it go no further. The tears stand in my eyes.

I am going into Derbyshire, and hope to be followed by your good wishes, for I am with great affection, Your most humble servant,

SAM. JOHNSON

Any letters that come for me hither, will be sent me.

Letter to Lord Thurlow

THURSDAY 9 SEPTEMBER 1784

My Lord: [Ashbourne]

After a long and attentive observation of Mankind, the generosity of your Lordship's offer excites in me no less wonder than gratitude. Bounty, so liberally bestowed (if my condition made it necessary) (I should gladly receive,) for to such a Mind who would [not] be proud to own his obligations? But it has pleased God to restore me such a measure of health, that if I should now appropriate so much of a fortune destined to do good I should not escape from myself the charge of advancing a false claim.

My journey to the Continent though I once thought it necessary was never much encouraged by my Physicians, and I was very desirous that your Lordship be told of it by Sir Joshua Reynolds as an event very uncertain; for if I grew much better I should not be willing, if much worse, I should not be able, to migrate.

Your Lordship was solicited without my knowledge, but when I was told that You were pleased to honour me with your patronage, I did not expect to hear of a refusal. Yet as I had little time to form hopes, and have not rioted in imaginary opulence, the cold reception has been scarce a disappointment. And from your Lordship's kindness I have received a benefit which only Men like You can bestow, I shall live *mihi carior* with a higher opinion of my own merit. I am.

Translation of Horace, Odes, *IV.vii (Diffugere nives)*

The snow dissolv'd no more is seen,
The fields, and woods, behold, are green,
The changing year renews the plain
The rivers know their banks again
The spritely Nymph and naked Grace
The mazy dance together trace.
The changing year's successive plan
Proclaims mortality to Man.
Rough Winter's blasts to Spring give way
Spring yields to Summer's sovereign ray   10
Then Summer sinks in Autumn's reign
And Winter chills the World again
Her losses soon the Moon supplies
But wretched Man, when once he lies
Where Priam and his Sons are laid
Is nought but Ashes and a Shade.
Who knows if Jove who counts our Score
Will toss us in a morning more?
What with your friend you nobly share
At least you rescue from your heir.   20
Not you, Torquatus, boast of Rome,
When Minos once has fix'd your doom,
Or Eloquence, or splendid birth
Or Virtue shall replace on earth.
Hyppolytus unjustly slain
Diana calls to life in vain,
Nor can the might of Theseus rend
The chains of hell that hold his friend.

Prayer

SUNDAY 5 DECEMBER 1784

[The following Prayer was composed and used by Doctor Johnson previous
to his receiving the Sacrament of the Lord's Supper, on Sunday December
5, 1784.]

———

Almighty and most merciful Father, I am now, as to human eyes it seems, about to commemorate, for the last time, the death of thy Son Jesus Christ our Saviour and Redeemer. Grant, O Lord, that my whole hope and confidence may be in his merits, and thy mercy; enforce and accept my imperfect repentance; make this commemoration available to the confirmation of my faith, the establishment of my hope, and the enlargement of my charity; and make the death of thy Son Jesus Christ effectual to my redemption. Have mercy upon me, and pardon the multitude of my offences. Bless my friends; have mercy upon all men. Support me, by thy Holy Spirit, in the days of weakness, and at the hour of death; and receive me, at my death, to everlasting happiness, for the sake of Jesus Christ. Amen.

APPENDIX A

Johnson's prayer on beginning *The Rambler*

Almighty God, the giver of all good things, without whose help all Labour is ineffectual, and without whose grace all wisdom is folly, grant, I beseech Thee, that in this my undertaking thy Holy Spirit may not be withheld from me, but that I may promote thy glory, and the Salvation both of myself and others, – Grant this O Lord for the sake of Jesus Christ. Amen. Lord bless me. So be it.

(Taken from *Diaries*, p. 43.)

APPENDIX B

Parallel texts of the original and revised states of *The Rambler,* no. 1

First edition (1750)

Cur tamen hoc libeat potiùs decurrere campo,
Per quem magnus equos Auruncæ flexit Alumnus,
Si vacat, et placidi rationem admittitis, edam.
Juv.

THE Difficulty of the first Address, on any new Occasion, is felt by every Man in his Transactions with the World, and confessed by the settled and regular Forms of Salutation, which Necessity has introduced into all Languages. Judgment was wearied with the inextricable Perplexity of being forced upon Choice, where there was often no Motive to Preference; and it was found convenient that some easy Method of Introduction should be established, which, if it wanted the Allurement of Novelty, might enjoy in its place the Security of Prescription.

Perhaps few Authors have presented themselves before the Publick, without wishing that such ceremonial Modes of Entrance had been anciently established, as might have freed us from the Dangers, which the too ardent Desire of pleasing is certain to produce; and precluded the vain Expedients of softening Censure by Apologies, and of rousing Attention by Abruptness.

Fourth edition (1756)

Cur tamen hoc libeat potius decurrere campo,
Per quem magnus equos Auruncæ flexit alumnus,
Si vacat, et placidi rationem admittitis, edam.
Juv.
Why to expatiate in this beaten field,
Why arms, oft us'd in vain, I mean to wield;
If time permit, and candour will attend,
Some satisfaction this essay may lend.
ELPHINSTON.

THE difficulty of the first address on any new occasion, is felt by every man in his transactions with the world, and confessed by the settled and regular forms of salutation which necessity has introduced into all languages. Judgment was wearied with the perplexity of being forced upon choice, where there was no motive to preference; and it was found convenient that some easy method of introduction should be established, which, if it wanted the allurement of novelty, might enjoy the security of prescription.

PERHAPS few authors have presented themselves before the public, without wishing that such ceremonial modes of entrance had been anciently established, as might have freed them from those dangers which the desire of pleasing is certain to produce, and precluded the vain expedients of softening censure by apologies, or rousing attention by abruptness.

The Epic Writers, indeed, have found the proemial Part of the Poem such an Addition to their laborious Undertaking, that they have almost unanimously adopted the first Lines of *Homer*, and the Reader needs only be informed of the Subject to know in what Manner the Scene will open.

But this solemn Repetition has been hitherto the peculiar Distinction of Heroic Poetry, and has never been legally extended to the lower Orders of Literature, and seems to be considered as an hereditary Privilege, to be enjoyed only by those who can claim it from their Alliance to the Genius of *Homer*.

The Rules, which long Observation of the injudicious Use of this Prerogative suggested to *Horace*, may, indeed, be applied to the Direction of Candidates for inferior Fame; and it may be proper for all to remember, that they ought not to raise Expectation which it is not in their power to satisfy, and that it is more pleasing to see Smoke gradually brightening into Flame, than Flame sinking into Smoke.

Yet though this Precept has been long received, both from regard to the Authority of his that delivered it, and its Conformity to the general Opinion of the World, as well since as before his Time, there have been some, who have thought it no Deviation from Modesty, to recommend their own Labours, and imagined themselves entitled, by indisputable Merit, to an Exemption from general Restraints, and to Elevations not allowed in common Life. They, perhaps, believed, that when, like *Thucydides*, they bequeathed to Mankind χλημα ες αει, *an Estate for ever*, it was an additional Favour to inform them of its Value.

THE epic writers have found the proemial part of the poem such an addition to their undertaking, that they have almost unanimously adopted the first lines of Homer, and the reader needs only be informed of the subject to know in what manner the poem will begin.

BUT this solemn repetition is hitherto the peculiar distinction of heroic poetry; it has never been legally extended to the lower orders of literature, but seems to be considered as an hereditary privilege, to be enjoyed only by those who claim it from their alliance to the genius of Homer.

THE rules which the injudicious use of this prerogative suggested to Horace, may indeed be applied to the direction of candidates for inferior fame; it may be proper for all to remember, that they ought not to raise expectation which it is not in their power to satisfy, and that it is more pleasing to see smoke brightening into flame, than flame sinking into smoke.

This precept has been long received both from regard to the authority of Horace and its conformity to the general opinion of the world, yet there have been always some, that thought it no deviation from modesty to recommend their own labours, and imagined themselves entitled by indisputable merit to an exemption from general restraints, and to elevations not allowed in common life. They, perhaps, believed that when, like Thucydides, they bequeathed to mankind χλημα ες αει, *an estate for ever*, it was an additional favour to inform them of its value.

It may, indeed, be no less dangerous to claim, on some Occasions, too little than too much. There is something captivating in Spirit and Intrepidity, to which we often yield, as to a resistless Power; nor can he reasonably expect the Confidence of others, who, too apparently, distrusts himself.

Plutarch, in his Enumeration of the various Occasions on which a Man may, without just Offence, proclaim his own Excellencies, has, I think, omitted the Case of an Author entering the World; unless it may be comprehended under his general Position, that a Man may lawfully praise himself for those Qualities which cannot be known, but from his own Mouth; as when he is among Strangers, and can probably have no Opportunity of an actual Exertion of his Powers. That the Case of an Author is parallel, will scarcely be granted, because he necessarily discovers the Degree of his Merit to the Judges, when he solicits their Suffrages. But it should be remembered, that unless his Judges be prejudiced in his Favour, they will not be persuaded to hear the Cause.

In Love, the State which fills the Heart with a Degree of Solicitude next that of an Author, it has been held a Maxim, that Success is more easily obtained by indirect and concealed Approaches; he who too soon professes himself a Lover, raises Obstacles to his own Wishes, and those whom Disappointments have taught Experience, endeavour to conceal their Passion till they believe their Mistress wishes for the Discovery. The same Method, if it were practicable to Writers, would save many Complaints of the Partiality of the World, the Severity of

It may, indeed, be no less dangerous to claim, on certain occasions, too little than too much. There is something captivating in spirit and intrepidity, to which we often yield, as to a resistless power; nor can he reasonably expect the confidence of others, who too apparently distrusts himself.

Plutarch, in his enumeration of the various occasions, on which a man may without just offence proclaim his own excellencies, has omitted the case of an author entering the world; unless it may be comprehended under his general position, that a man may lawfully praise himself for those qualities which cannot be known but from his own mouth; as when he is among strangers, and can have no opportunity of an actual exertion of his powers. That the case of an author is parallel will scarcely be granted, because he necessarily discovers the degree of his merit to his judges, when he appears at his trial. But it should be remembered, that unless his judges are inclined to favour him, they will hardly be persuaded to hear the cause.

In love, the state which fills the heart with a degree of solicitude next that of an author, it has been held a maxim, that success is most easily obtained by indirect and unperceived approaches; he who too soon professes himself a lover, raises obstacles to his own wishes, and those whom disappointments have taught experience, endeavour to conceal their passion till they believe their mistress wishes for the discovery. The same method, if it were practicable to writers, would save many complaints of the severity of the age, and the caprices of criticism. If a man could glide the Age, and the Caprices of Criticism. If a Man could glide imperceptibly into the Favour of the Publick, and only proclaim his Pretensions to literary Honours, when he is sure of not being rejected, he might commence Author with better Hopes, as his Failings might escape Contempt, though he shall never attain Excellence sufficient to excite much regard.

But since the Publick supposes every Man that writes ambitious of Applause; as some Ladies have taught themselves to believe that every Man intends Love, who expresses Civility, the Miscarriage of any new Endeavour in Learning raises an unbounded Contempt, which is indulged by most Minds without scruple, as an honest Triumph over unjust Claims, and exorbitant Expectations. The Artifices of those who put themselves in this hazardous State, have therefore been multiplied in proportion to their Fear as well as their Ambition; and are to be looked upon with more Indulgence, as they result from complicated Passions, and are incited at once by the two great Movers of the human Mind, the Desire of Good, and the Fear of Evil. For who can wonder that, thus allured on one Side, and frighted on the other, some Men should endeavour to gain Favour by bribing the Judge with an Appearance of Respect which they do not feel, to excite Compassion by confessing Weakness of which they are not convinced, or to attract Regard by a Shew of Openness and Magnanimity, by a daring Profession of their own Deserts, and a publick Challenge of Honours and Rewards.

imperceptibly into the favour of the publick, and only proclaim his pretensions to literary honours when he is sure of not being rejected, he might commence author with better hopes, as his failings might escape contempt, though he shall never attain much regard.

But since the world supposes every man that writes ambitious of applause, as some ladies have taught themselves to believe that every man intends love, who expresses civility, the miscarriage of any endeavour in learning raises an unbounded contempt, indulged by most minds without scruple, as an honest triumph over unjust claims, and exorbitant expectations. The artifices of those who put themselves in this hazardous state, have therefore been multiplied in proportion to their fear as well as their ambition; and are to be looked upon with more indulgence, as they are incited at once by the two great movers of the human mind, the desire of good, and the fear of evil. For who can wonder that, allured on one side, and frightned on the other, some should endeavour to gain favour by bribing the judge with an appearance of respect which they do not feel, to excite compassion by confessing weakness of which they are not convinced, and others to attract regard by a shew of openness and magnanimity, by a daring profession of their own deserts, and a publick challenge of honours and rewards.

The ostentatious and haughty Display of themselves has been the usual Refuge of diurnal Writers, in vindication of whose Practice it may be said, that what it wants in Prudence is supplied by Sincerity, and who, at least, may plead, that if their Boasts deceive any into the Perusal of their Performances, they defraud them of but little Time.

----- *Quid enim? Concurritur --- Horæ Momento cita Mors venit, aut Victoria læta.*

The Question concerning the Merit of the Day is soon decided, and we are not condemned to toil through half a Folio, to be convinced that the Writer has broke his Promise.

It is one among many Reasons for which I purpose to endeavour the Entertainment of my Countrymen, by a short Essay on *Tuesdays* and *Saturdays*, that I hope not much to tire those whom I shall not happen to please; and if I am not commended for the Beauty of my Works, to be at least pardoned for their Brevity. But whether my Expectations are most fixed on Pardon or Praise, I think it not necessary to discover; for, having accurately weighed the Reasons for Arrogance and Submission, I find them so nearly equiponderant, that my Impatience to try the Event of my first Performance will not suffer me to attend any longer the Trepidation of the Balance.

THE ostentatious and haughty display of themselves has been the usual refuge of diurnal writers, in vindication of whose practice it may be said, that what it wants in prudence is supplied by sincerity, and who at least may plead, that if their boasts deceive any into the perusal of their performances, they defraud them of but little time.

----- *Quid enim? Concurritur --- horæ Momento cita mors venit, aut victoria læta.*

The battle joins, and, in a moment's flight,
Death, or a joyful conquest, ends the fight.

FRANCIS.

The question concerning the merit of the day is soon decided, and we are not condemned to toil thro' half a folio, to be convinced that the writer has broke his promise.

IT is one among many reasons for which I purpose to endeavour the entertainment of my countrymen by a short essay on Tuesday and Saturday, that I hope not much to tire those whom I shall not happen to please; and if I am not commended for the beauty of my works, to be at least pardoned for their brevity. But whether my expectations are most fixed on pardon or praise, I think it not necessary to discover; for having accurately weighed the reasons for arrogance and submission, I find them so nearly equiponderant, that my impatience to try the event of my first performance will not suffer me to attend any longer the trepidations of the balance.

There are, indeed, many Conveniences almost peculiar to this Method of Publication, which may naturally flatter the Author, whether he be confident or timorous. The Man to whom the Extent of his Knowledge, or the Sprightliness of his Imagination, has, in his own Opinion, already secured the Praises of the World, willingly takes that Way of displaying his Abilities, which will soonest give him an Opportunity of hearing the Voice of Fame, and it heightens his Alacrity to think in how many Places he shall hear what he is now writing, read with Ecstasies to morrow. He will often please himself with reflecting, that the Author of a large Treatise must proceed with Anxiety, lest, before the Completion of his Work, the Attention of the Publick may have changed its Object; but that he who is confined to no single Subject, may follow the national Taste through all its Variations, and catch the *Aura popularis*, the Gale of Favour, from what Point soever it shall blow.

Nor is the Prospect less likely to ease the Doubts of the Cautious, and allay the Terrours of the Fearful, for to such the Shortness of every single Paper is a powerful Encouragement. He that questions his Abilities to arrange the dissimilar Parts of an extensive Plan, or fears to be lost in a complicated System, may yet hope to adjust a few Pages without Perplexity; and if, when he turns over the Repositories of his Memory, he finds his Collection too small for a Volume, he may yet have enough to furnish out an Essay. He that is afraid of laying out too much Time upon an Experiment of which he fears

THERE are, indeed, many conveniences almost peculiar to this method of publication, which may naturally flatter the author, whether he be confident or timorous. The man to whom the extent of his knowledge, or the sprightliness of his imagination, has, in his own opinion, already secured the praises of the world, willingly takes that way of displaying his abilities which will soonest give him an opportunity of hearing the voice of fame; it heightens his alacrity to think in how many places he shall hear what he is now writing, read with ecstasies to morrow. He will often please himself with reflecting, that the author of a large treatise must proceed with anxiety, lest, before the completion of his work, the attention of the publick may have changed its object; but that he who is confined to no single topick, may follow the national taste through all its variations, and catch the *Aura popularis*, the gale of favour, from what point soever it shall blow.

NOR is the prospect less likely to ease the doubts of the cautious, and the terrours of the fearful, for to such the shortness of every single paper is a powerful encouragement. He that questions his abilities to arrange the dissimilar parts of an extensive plan, or fears to be lost in a complicated system, may yet hope to adjust a few pages without perplexity; and if, when he turns over the repositories of his memory, he finds his collection too small for a volume, he may yet have enough to furnish out an essay. He that would fear to lay out too much time upon an experiment of which he knows not the

the Event, persuades himself that a few
Days will shew him what he is to expect
from his Learning and his Genius. If he
thinks his own Judgment not sufficiently
enlightened, he may, by attending the
Remarks which every Paper will
produce, inform himself of his Mistakes,
rectify his Opinions, and extend his
Views. If he suspects that he may with
too little Premeditation entangle himself
in an unweildy Subject, he may quit it
without confessing his Ignorance, and
pass to other Topicks less dangerous, or
more tractable. And if he finds, with all
his Industry, and all his Artifices, that he
cannot deserve Regard, or cannot attain
it, he may let the Design fall at once, and,
without Injury to others, or himself,
retire to Amusements of greater Pleasure,
or to Studies of better Prospect.

event, persuades himself that a few days
will shew him what he is to expect from
his learning and his genius. If he thinks
his own judgment not sufficiently
enlightned, he may, by attending the
remarks which every paper will produce,
rectify his opinions. If he should with
too little premeditation encumber
himself by an unweildly subject, he can
quit it without confessing his ignorance,
and pass to other topicks less dangerous,
or more tractable. And if he finds, with
all his industry, and all his artifices, that
he cannot deserve regard, or cannot
attain it, he may let the design fall at
once, and, without injury to others or
himself, retire to amusements of greater
pleasure, or to studies of better
prospect.

APPENDIX C

Bonnell Thornton's parody of *The Rambler*

ΓΝΩΘΙ ΣΕΑΥΤΟΝ
Expatiate free o'er all this Scene of MAN,
A might Maze, but not without a Plan.
POPE.

WHILE capricious CURIOSITY persuades the youth of *Great-Britain* to relish no scenes but those that are extraneous; while the fashionable practice so extensively prevails of visiting distant countries, and in short of cultivating any thing but what is truly *British* and domestic; I shall beg leave to look at home, and take a survey of what more properly may be said to be our own; accurately to delineate the topography of the human body, and enumerate it's respective inhabitants.

First of all, let us investigate the BRAIN, where the MIND sits sceptered and enthroned, and from this eminent situation, like an absolute monarch, regulates and dispenses her commands over the whole subject system of the body.

As soon as we emerge from these obscure regions, the first object that exhibits itself to the attentive examiner is ASSURANCE, high-plumed on the smooth and unembarrassed surface of the FOREHEAD. Observe with what an obstinate and immoveable gaze she stares on every thing around her, and how she glories in her brazen bulwark of countenance. Sublime on the ridgy hillocks of the EYE-BROWS is seated VANITY, and near her PRIDE contracts his face into frowns, and fiercely casts down his eye beneath with a disdainful leer.

As you descend lower, you may observe the FIELDS styled in poetical language, the LAUGHING FIELDS displaying themselves over either JAW. Here every thing wears a brighter and more joyous aspect; here LAUGHTER disports in a thousand wanton wiles, and scatters sleek dimples over the adjacent CHEEKS. — And yet is not this climate always cloudless and serene. ANXIETY is no stranger to these regions; he often bids the salt torrent stream from the swelling eyes, while GRIEF holds out the ready hand to rend the flowing tresses. So close is the neighbourhood between PLEASURE and PAIN!

In the middle of these plains arises a prominence, which mortals have named the NOSE. JESTS wanton on it's summit, and TAUNTS in various shapes sport around it's brow. It must not be forgot, that the top of this hill is sometimes possessed by that savage and implacable fury ANGER.

Nor far off are the roseate LIPS, where Pallas keeps her nectar, and from which distil the streams of ELOQUENCE and PERSUASION in gentle dews, or pour down in fuller and more vehement tides. But near the interior caverns of the THROAT a magnificent Queen, called LUXURY, holds her high-arched palace. And in this neighbourhood ENVY infects the TEETH with her venomous and corrosive gall.

After leaving the declivities of the HEAD, and the rugged ridges of the CHIN, we arrive at the vallies of the NECK. Here VIRTUE, the sister of LIBERTY, resides; here she maintains her unshaken inflexibility, in which she is often assisted by STRENGTH who keeps his *Herculian* fortress on the muscular vigour of the BACK and manly BREAST.

Let us now march by a narrow path down the descent of the ARMS, and we shall find SLOTH reclined on the bend of the ELBOW, while CONTEMPT stands erect and unabashed on the tip of the FOREFINGER. Nor seldom does AVARICE and the insatiable DESIRE OF GAIN tempt the insidious hand to clandestine deeds of theft.

We will now cross over that part, where the trepidating LUNGS receive and give back the vital inspiration in alternate heavings, and where the RIBS confine the VISCERA within their concave circle. Here meek CLEMENCY has chosen her station; here she breathes sigh for sigh, and returns sorrow for sorrow. Hail, tenderest inmate of the HEART! in whatsoever BREAST thou art now compassionating human misfortunes, whatsoever BOWELS are now struggling beneath thy influence, - adieu! - we are reluctantly summoned to proceed farther, and as we descend lower, arrive at - but MODESTY turns away her blushing countenance from this detested seat, this habitation of that impure dæmon LUST.

Not far hence in a desponding condition (and indeed it may be superfluous to remark that the joys of VENUS are ever attended by a dreary train of CARES) REPENTANCE appears, whose business it is to supple the knees to adoration. Behold him prostrate, as in the monastic cloyster, or the desolate cavern, and mixing a flood of tears with a storm of sighs.

Our journey is at length almost consummated; and having now passed the perpendicular declivity of the legs, we shall find FLIGHT and SWIFTNESS situated in the FEET. Nor is every one endued with the same degree of swiftness: cast your eyes from *Pyrenæan* cliffs! Examine the nations of either side! Here you will perceive the slow *Spaniard* stalking with stiff and stately steps; there the *Frenchman* practising every art of agility, cutting everlasting capers, and leaping through life. Nay, so eminently does this volatile people excel in dancing and running away, that some philosophers imagine all that strength, which in others is proportionably diffused over the whole body, to be in them concentred in their heels.

(Taken from Isaac Reed, *The Repository: A Select Collection of Fugitive Pieces of Wit and Humour, in Prose and Verse. By the Most Eminent Writers*. The Second Edition. 4 vols [London, 1790], vol. III, pp. 216-20.)

NOTES

EARLY POETRY AND PROSE TO 1750

Translation of Horace, Odes, I.xxii

Text: *Life*, p. 33.
Date: pre-1725.
According to Boswell, Johnson translated this poem while at school. Johnson also told Boswell that 'Horace's Odes were the compositions in which he took most delight' (*Life*, p. 44).
  l. 7. *Hydaspes*: the Jhelum River, in the Punjab.
  l. 21. *burning line*: the equator.

Translation of Horace, Epodes, II

Text: MS, Hyde Collection, Houghton Library, Harvard.
Date: probably 1726.
Probably a school exercise.
  l. 29. *Ilex*: the holm oak.
  l. 79. *sets it out*: i.e. lends it out at interest.

Translation of Horace, Odes, II.xiv

Text: MS, Johnson Birthplace Museum, Lichfield.
Date: probably 1726.
Probably a school exercise.
  l. 10. *the haughty King below*: i.e. Pluto, the god of the underworld.
  l. 16. *Sirius*: the dog star; associated with ill-health.
  l. 19. *Danaus*: Danaus's daughters killed their husbands on their wedding night.
  l. 24. *Cypress*: traditionally the tree of mourning and funerals.

Translation of Horace, Odes, II.xx

Text: MS, Hyde Collection, Houghton Library, Harvard.
Date: probably 1726.
Probably a school exercise.
  l. 2. *double-form'd*: both man and swan.

l. 7. *Mæcenas*: Horace's patron, and a close associate of the emperor Augustus.

l. 20. *Phasis*: the Rioni River, on the Black Sea; near the ancient Greek colony of Phasis.

Festina Lente

Text: MS, Hyde Collection, Houghton Library, Harvard.
Date: probably late 1726.

The Young Author

Text: *Gentleman's Magazine*, vol. XIII (1743), p. 378.
Date: first published in July, 1743, but here positioned according to its attested date of composition, 1729. Edmund Hector (1708–94), a lifelong friend of Johnson, told Boswell that Johnson wrote this poem 'in his 20th Year' (i.e. 1729).

l. 24. *Settle*: Elkanah Settle (1648–1724); playwright.

l. 24. *Ogilby*: John Ogilby (1600–76); poet, translator, and geographer.

Annals

Text: Wright.
Date: 1734.
First published in 1805; unknown to both Sir John Hawkins and James Boswell.

p. 10. *touched for the evil*: i.e. scrofula; then thought to be curable by the royal touch.

p. 10. *jack-weight*: part of the mechanism for turning a spit.

p. 11. *dear Tetty*: Johnson's wife, Elizabeth (1689–1752).

p. 11. *Quae Genus*: a grammatical exercise involving the declension of nouns.

p. 11. *As in Praesenti*: a grammatical exercise involving the conjugation of verbs.

p. 11. *Accidence*: i.e. the rudiments of grammar.

p. 11. *Propria quae Maribus*: a grammatical exercise involving the declension of nouns.

p. 11. *Syntaxis*: another section of the grammar.

p. 13. *inliciturus*: not a word in classical Latin.

p. 14. *Uvae Crispae*: gooseberries.

Letter to Edward Cave

Text: Redford, vol. I, pp. 5–7.
Date: 25 November 1734.
Edward Cave (1691–1754) was the editor of the *Gentleman's Magazine*, which he had founded in 1731.

Preface to Lobo's Voyage to Abyssinia

Text: *A Voyage to Abyssinia by Father Jerome Lobo, A Portuguese Jesuit* (1735)
Date: 1 February 1735.

p. 15. *Basilisks*: a fabulous reptile, which could kill with its breath or with its look.

p. 15. *without Tears*: the crocodile was said to allure its prey by means of feigned weeping.

p. 15. *Hottentots*: literally, a native inhabitant of the Cape; by extension, an uncultured savage.

p. 16. *Dr. Geddes*: Michael Geddes (*c*.1647–1713); clergyman and author of *The Church-History of Ethiopia* (1696).

p. 16. *Mr. Le Grand*: Joachim le Grand (1653–1733); French historian and diplomat, and the translator of Lobo's narrative.

p. 16. *the patriarch Oviedo*: Andrés de Oviedo (1518–80); first leader of the Jesuit mission to Abyssinia.

p. 17. *the great Ludolfus*: Hiob Ludolf (1624–1704), a German Lutheran who had defended the Abyssinian church against the allegations of the Jesuits.

Letter to Edward Cave

Text: Redford, vol. I, pp. 12–13.
Date: 12 July 1737.
The *Historia del Concilio Tridentino* by Paolo Sarpi (1552–1623) had been published in 1619. A French translation by Pierre François Le Courayer (1681–1776) had been published in 1736.

p. 19. *one of their best translators*: a version of Sarpi's history by Abraham Nicolas Amelot de la Houssaye (1634–1706) had been published in 1683.

London: A Poem

Text: first edition of 12 May 1738. Johnson later revised the poem; for details, see Fleeman, *Poems*, p. 196.
Date: 12 May 1738.

p. 18. *Quis…teneat se?*: 'Who can be so tolerant of this monstrous city? Who can be so iron-willed as to contain himself?' (Juvenal, I.30–1).

l. 2. *Thales*: identified by Sir John Hawkins as Richard Savage.

l. 59. *our silenc'd Stage*: Johnson later revised this phrase to read 'a licens'd Stage'. The Licensing Act had been passed in 1737. Johnson would mock it again in his *A Compleat Vindication of the Licensers of the Stage* (1739).

l. 72. *Gazetteer*: the *Daily Gazetteer*, founded in 1735, was the newspaper of the administration.

l. 150. *Balbo's Eloquence*: *balbus* is the Latin word for one who stammers or stutters.

l. 211. *of Severn or of Trent*: rivers which traditionally mark the boundaries between, respectively, England and Wales, and the south and north of England.

l. 245. *Ways and Means*: the parliamentary term for the raising of money for public projects.

l. 252. *Special Juries*: juries made up of those with substantial property; widely thought to be oppressive and likely to convict.

Debates in the Senate of Magna Lilliputia

Text: *Gentleman's Magazine*, vol. VIII (1738), pp. 283–7.

Date: June 1738.

In the eighteenth century it was forbidden directly to report debates in Parliament before the establishment in 1774 of the *Journal of the House of Commons* (commonly known as *Hansard*, after its publisher Luke Hansard). To evade this prohibition, Johnson made use of the framework of the first part of Swift's *Gulliver's Travels* (1726). Although Johnson would in March 1775 disparage this book ('When once you have thought of big men and little men, it is very easy to do all the rest': *Life*, p. 434), his earlier adaptation of Swift's text suggests a more sympathetic engagement with its blend of imaginative fantasy and political satire.

p. 26. *his Design...unknown Country*: in chapter 4 of Part I of *Gulliver's Travels*, Gulliver says that his 'general Description of this Empire' is 'almost ready for the Press' (*GT*, p. 68).

p. 26. *Numa*: legendary king of Rome and lawgiver.

p. 26. *Lycurgus*: legendary legislator of Sparta.

p. 26. *Cadmus*: hero of Greek mythology.

p. 26. *Theseus*: hero of Greek mythology.

p. 26. *Felix...Argumentum*: 'Happy the wit which has so great a subject; happy the subject that finds so great a wit.' Untraced in classical Latin; possibly Johnson's own composition.

p. 26. *the late Resolution of the House of Commons*: on 13 April 1738 the House of Commons had discussed the propriety or otherwise of the reporting of parliamentary debates (*The History and Proceedings of the House of Commons from the Restoration to the Present Time*, vol. IX (1742), pp. 278–87). The speakers were Sir William Yonge, Sir William Windham, Thomas Winnington, William Pulteney, and Sir Robert Walpole (see below, p. 1174, note to p. 99). Although members were conscious of the need to defend the liberty of the press, they were greatly concerned by the effect that misrepresentation might have on the public character of individual members, and on the standing of the House of Commons as a whole. Walpole spoke most forcibly to this point: 'I have read some Debates of this House, Sir, in which I have been made to speak the very reverse of what I meant. I have read others of them wherein all the Wit, the Learning, and the Argument has been thrown into one Side, and on the other nothing but what was low, mean, and ridiculous; and yet when it comes to the Question, the Division has gone against the Side, which upon the Face of the Debate had Reason and Justice to support it. So that, Sir, had I been a Stranger to the Proceedings and to the Nature of the Arguments themselves, I must have thought this to have been one of the most contemptible Assemblies on the Face of the Earth' (p. 285). As a result of the debate, the House resolved 'That it is a high Indignity to, and a notorious Breach of the Privilege of this House, for any News-Writer, in Letters or other Papers, (as Minutes, or under any other Denomination) or for any Printer or Publisher, of any printed News Paper of any Denomination, to presume to insert in the said Letters or Papers, or to give therein any Account of the Debates, or other Proceedings of this House, or any Committee thereof, as well during the Recess, as the Sitting of Parliament; and that this House will proceed with the utmost Severity against such Offenders' (p. 287).

p. 27. *the Man-Mountain*: the English translation of the Lilliputian name for Gulliver, 'Quinbus Flestrin' (*GT*, p. 50).

p. 27. *Mildendo*: the capital of Lilliput.

p. 28. *Blefuscu*: the rival nation to Lilliput.

p. 28. *Degul*: cf. *GT*, pp. 34 and 37.

p. 30. *Lighters*: flat-bottomed barges used in a harbour to transport people or merchandise to larger vessels (*OED*).

p. 30. *they seiz'd*: Johnson here disguises, under Lilliputian terminology, the provocations which in 1739 would lead to the War of Jenkins' Ear between Great Britain and Spain.

p. 30. *Hurgos*: cf. *GT*, p. 36.

p. 26. *Clinabs*: a word of Johnson's invention not found in *Gulliver's Travels*.

p. 31. *Mulgo Malvin*: not a character in *Gulliver's Travels*.

p. 31. *7 Moons*: thus paralleling the provisions of the Septennial Act of 1716, which had established the maximum length of a Parliament at seven years.

p. 31. *while the Government...primitive Constitution*: a mordant sarcasm.

p. 32. *Belfaborac*: the location of the imperial palace in Lilliput (*GT*, p. 65); corresponding therefore to Westminster.

A Prayer on my Birth-Day

Text: MS, Pembroke College, Oxford.
Date: 7 September 1738.

On Gay's Epitaph

Text: *Gentleman's Magazine*, vol. VIII (1738), pp. 536–7.
Date: October 1738.

p. 33. Παντα...μηδεν: 'All is laughter, all is dust, all is nothingness' (*Greek Anthology*).

p. 33. *Let...learn to be pious*: Herodotus attributes this sentiment to Sethos (II.141).

p. 34. *Was Laius...in Hell*: Dryden, *Oedipus*, III.i.485–8.

The Life of Dr Herman Boerhaave

Text: *Gentleman's Magazine*, vol. IX (1739), pp. 37–8, 72–3, 114–16, and 172–6. Johnson revised the text for volume I of Robert James's *Medicinal Dictionary* (1743); *sub* 'Boerhaave'. The divisions between the original instalments are marked in this edition by three asterisks.

Date: January 1739.

p. 37. *Epicurus*: Epicurus (341–270 BC); atomistic philosopher whose teachings were hostile to ideas of the supernatural and to superstitious religion.

p. 37. *Hobbes*: Thomas Hobbes (1588–1679); philosopher whose writings were thought to be implicitly subversive of both Christianity and political liberty.

p. 37. *Spinosa*: Baruch de Spinoza (1632–77); philosopher whose pantheist doctrines were widely condemned as tending towards atheism.

p. 37. *Clemens Romanus*: St Clement I, byname Clement of Rome (or Clemens Romanus) (d. late 1st or early 2nd cent. AD); first Apostolic Father; Pope from 88 to 97, or from 92 to 101; supposedly the third successor of St Peter.

p. 38. *Vesalius*: André Vesale (1514–64); Belgian anatomist.

p. 38. *Bartholine*: Erasmus Bartholinus (1625–98); German doctor, mathematician, jurist, and scholar.

p. 38. *Fallopius*: Gabriele Fallopio (1523–62); Italian anatomist and surgeon.

p. 38. *Nuck*: Anton Nuck (*d.* 1692); German surgeon.

p. 38. *Hippocrates*: Hippocrates (*b. c.* 460 BC); great Greek physician who emphasized the importance of careful observation.

p. 39. *Sydenham*: Thomas Sydenham (1624–89); physician who moved the practice of medicine away from theory and towards remedies founded on clinical observation.

p. 39. *de utilitate…ut signorum*: 'On the Usefulness of the Examination of the Excrements of the Sick, as Symptoms'.

p. 41. *de commendando Studio Hippocratico*: 'In Praise of the Study of Hippocrates'

p. 41. *Paracelsus*: the byname of Philippus Aureolus Theophrastus Bombastus von Hohenhelm (1493–1541); German-Swiss physician and alchemist.

p. 41. *Helmont*: Jan Baptista van Helmont (1580–1644); Flemish physician, philosopher, mystic, and chemist.

p. 42. *Des Cartes*: René Descartes (1596–1650); French philosopher and mathematician who sought certainty through deduction, rather than through the induction characteristic of experimental science.

p. 43. *Count Marsigli*: Luigi Ferdinando Marsili (1658–1730); Italian count; soldier, diplomat, traveller, scholar, mathematician, scientist, and writer.

p. 43. *De…expurgante*: 'On the Purging of Chemistry from its Errors'.

p. 43. *Pythagoreans of old*: followers of Pythagoras (*b. c.* 580 BC), a philosopher and mathematician, some of whose doctrines assumed the character of secret wisdom.

p. 44. *simple Medicines*: i.e. medicines made from simples, or medicinal herbs.

p. 44. *the Stoick Schools*: a school of Greek philosophy, founded at Athens *c.* 315 BC by Zeno of Citium, which taught that happiness was to be found in detachment from, and independence of, the outer world.

p. 44. *Seneca*: Lucius Annaeus Seneca (4 BC – AD 65); Stoic philosopher and tutor to the emperor Nero.

p. 44. *Cato*: probably Marcus Porcius Cato (95–46 BC), 'Cato the Younger'; famous for his unbending rectitude, and for his resistance to Julius Caesar. Cato's last stand at Utica in North Africa had provided the subject for Addison's wildly popular tragedy *Cato* (1713).

p. 44. *Patientia Christiana*: i.e. Christian patience.

p. 44. *Lipsius*: Joest Lips (or Lipsius) (1547–1606); Flemish humanist and political philosopher.

p. 45. *an Account written by himself*: compare the accounts of his illness composed in Latin which Johnson sent his physician, Thomas Lawrence, in May 1782: Redford, vol. IV, pp. 34 and 39; *Life*, pp. 844–5; above, pp. 1144–5. Johnson's final illness had points of similarity with that of Boerhaave.

p. 46. *Mr Schultens*: Albert Schultens (1686–1750); Hebraist.

p. 48. *the precept of Moses*: Deuteronomy 30:19–20.

A Compleat Vindication of the Licensers of the Stage

Text: *A Compleat Vindication of the Licensers of the Stage*, first edition (1739).
Date: May 1739.
In 1739 Henry Brooke's play *Gustavus Vasa*, which used recent Scandinavian history to reflect critically on the England of George II and Sir Robert Walpole, had been refused a licence by the Lord Chamberlain. Brooke then published the play, prefaced by an indignant defence of his conduct. In the *Compleat Vindication* Johnson assumes the *persona* of a court sycophant.

p. 51. *L— and P—*: George Lyttelton (1709–73) and William Pitt the Elder (1708–78); both prominent in the opposition to Sir Robert Walpole.

p. 52. *special Jury*: see above, p. 1166, note to l. 252.

p. 52. *Levees*: the morning assemblies held by a prince or nobleman.

p. 52. *Who bade...Age*: cf. *Gustavus Vasa* (1739), 'Prologue'.

p. 54. *Boni Judicis...auctoritatem*: 'It is the part of a good judge to enlarge his authority'; traditional legal maxim.

p. 54. *I waited...an Answer*: words apparently put into the mouth of Brooke by Johnson.

p. 55. *maintain a Standing Army*: the Bill of Rights of 1689 had declared it illegal for a standing army to be maintained in England without the permission of Parliament. The maintenance of standing forces by the crown had been the source of great controversy at the end of the 1690s, and to a lesser extent in the 1720s. At the time Johnson composed this pamphlet Parliament gave permission for the maintenance of standing forces by the annual passage of the Mutiny Act.

p. 55. *for fear of the Plague*: following the outbreak of plague in Marseilles in 1720, the Quarantine Act of 1721 had provided for the construction of barracks. In *Gulliver's Travels* (1726) the cipher used in the Academy of Lagado for a standing army is 'the plague' (*GT*, p. 283).

p. 56. *Great Nature's... unletter'd Mind*: cf. *Gustavus Vasa* (1739), 'Prologue'.

p. 57. *Anderson*: a character in *Gustavus Vasa*, and a supporter of the hero.

p. 57. *O Sweden... save thee*: cf. *Gustavus Vasa* (1739), p. 4.

p. 57. *Base Fear... in their Fears*: cf. *Gustavus Vasa* (1739), p. 6.

p. 58. *Yes, my Arvida... Freedom*: cf. *Gustavus Vasa* (1739), p. 8.

p. 59. *an Index Expurgatorius*: i.e. a list of all passages to be removed because of their supposedly seditious tendency.

p. 60. *Imprimatur*: literally, 'let it be printed'; hence the name given to a licence to publish.

p. 60. *Halcyon-days*: a period of calm.

Prologue to Garrick's Lethe

Text: MS, Folger Shakespeare Library.

Date: April 1740.

Garrick has annotated the MS: 'Prologue by Mr Sam: Johnson for Lethe when first it was wrote for Drury Lane at Giffard's Benefit.' Henry Giffard's benefit night was 15 April 1740.

l. 7. *our Bard*: in this instance, David Garrick.

An Epitaph on Claudy Philips, a Musician

Text: *Gentleman's Magazine*, vol. X (1740), p. 464.

Date: September 1740.

Philips was an itinerant violinist who had died in poverty in 1739.

An Essay on Epitaphs

Text: *Gentleman's Magazine*, vol. X (1740), pp. 593–6.

Date: December 1740.

p. 63. *as the Word itself implies*: *epitaph* is derived from two Greek words, επι meaning *upon* and ταφιος meaning *gravestone*.

p. 63. *Picus of Mirandola*: Giovanni Pico della Mirandola (1463–94); Italian scholar and Platonist philosopher.

p. 63. *Hic Situs... Antipodes*: 'Here lies Picus Mirandola: the rest of his story is known on the Tagus and the Ganges, and even the Antipodes.'

p. 64. *Germanicus... Illyricus*: in Latin the suffix '-icus' denotes 'slayer of'; hence, in these examples, 'slayer of Germans', 'slayer of Dacians', 'slayer of Illyrians'.

p. 64. *Isaacus... quiescit*: 'Here rests Isaac Newton, who investigated the laws of nature.'

p. 64. *Stones by the Highway*: Johnson alludes to the Latin custom of beginning such an inscription with the phrase 'Sta, viator...' ('Pause, traveller...').

p. 64. *Minutius Felix*: Marcus Minucius Felix (*d. c.*250); early Christian apologist.

p. 64. *Cowley*: Abraham Cowley (1618–67); English poet.

pp. 64–5. *Aurea...Saxum*: 'Divine poet, while your golden writings fly far and wide throughout the world and while you live in eternal fame, here may you rest in peace: may grey-haired Faith guard your urn, and may the Muses keep watch with their undying torch! May this place be holy, and may no one be so rash as to dare disturb with sacrilegious hand this venerable bust. May the ashes of Cowley remain untouched; may they endure through kindly ages; and may they keep the tombstone unmoved.'

p. 65. *Charon*: in classical mythology, the boatman who ferried the souls of the dead over the river Styx to Hades.

p. 65. *Angelo*: Michelangelo di Lodovico Buonarroti Simoni (1475–1564); Italian sculptor, painter, architect, and poet.

p. 65. *Sannazarius*: Jacopo Sannazaro (*pseud.* 'Actius Sincerus Sannazarius') (1458–1530); Italian pastoral poet. His tomb in Naples was originally flanked by statues of Apollo and Minerva, which were subsequently re-named David and Judith.

p. 65. *Passeratius*: Jean Passerat (1534–1602); French poet.

p. 65. *Henry...Clement the Monk*: on 1 August 1589 Jacques Clément, a fanatical friar, stabbed to death Henri III, king of France.

p. 65. *Adsta...vices*: 'Pause, traveller, and shed a tear for the fates of kings. Beneath this marble lies the heart of a king who gave laws alike to the French and the Poles. A murderer hidden beneath the cowl of a monk laid him low. Pass on, traveller, and shed a tear for the fates of kings.' Henri III was king of Poland as well as of France.

p. 65. *Orate...Peccatoris*: 'Pray for the soul of —, a most miserable sinner.'

p. 66. *Ennius*: Quintus Ennius (239–169 BC); Roman epic poet, dramatist, and satirist.

p. 66. *Nemo...virum*: 'Let no one honour me with tears, and let me not be buried with weeping. Why? I fly alive through the mouths of the living.'

p. 66. *Mæcenas*: Gaius Maecenas (70–8 BC); Roman diplomat and politician; counsellor to Augustus; patron of poets such as Virgil and Horace.

p. 66. *Augustus*: Gaius Julius Caesar Octavianus (63 BC – AD 14); the first Roman emperor.

p. 67. *The Poor cease...at rest*: a conflation of Matthew 11: 28 and Job 3:17.

p. 67. *Epictetus*: Epictetus (60–140); Stoic philosopher.

Review of the Memoirs of the Duchess of Marlborough

Text: *Gentleman's Magazine*, vol. XII (1742), pp. 128–31.

Date: March 1742.

The *Memoirs* of Sarah, dowager Duchess of Marlborough, provoked great interest when they were published in 1742 because of the candid portrait they contained of the secret history of the reign of Queen Anne.

p. 69. *King William*: i.e. William III (1650–1702); king of England, Scotland, and Ireland from 1689.

p. 70. *the House of Bourbon*: i.e. the French royal house.

p. 70. *Queen Mary*: Mary II (1662–1694); queen of England, Scotland, and Ireland from 1689; daughter of James II; wife of William III.

p. 70. *wanted bowels*: i.e. lacked pity or compassion (*OED*, 'bowel', 3 a).

p. 71. *Harley*: Robert Harley (1661–1724); first earl of Oxford; statesman and leader of the ministry from 1710 to 1714.

Proposal for the Harleian Miscellany

Text: *Proposals for Printing, by Subscription, the Two First Volumes of Bibliotheca Harleiana* (1742).

Date: November 1742.

In 1741 the bookseller Thomas Osborne (?1704–1767) bought for £13,000 the great library collected by the earls of Oxford, and employed Johnson and William Oldys to prepare a catalogue of the library to attract potential purchasers. The relationship between Johnson and Osborne soon soured, however, and Johnson would describe Osborne in his 'Life of Pope' as 'intirely destitute of shame' (Lonsdale, vol. IV, p. 50).

p. 71. *Thuanian... Barberinian Libraries*: the libraries of, respectively: Jacques-Auguste de Thou (1553–1617), French statesman and historian; Nicolaus Heinsius (1620–81); Dutch scholar; Antonio Barberini the Younger (1607–71); Italian cardinal and bibliophile; whose collection was later digested into the still more magnificent library of his brother, Francesco Barberini (1597–1679).

p. 72. *Bodleian Library*: the university library of the University of Oxford.

p. 72. *the learned Fabricius*: Johann Albert Fabricius (1668–1736); German classical scholar and bibliographer; compiler of the *Bibliotheca Graeca* (1705–28).

p. 77. *Vossius's Collection*: Gerhard Johann Voss (1577–1649); Dutch theologian and scholar.

Letter to Edward Cave

Text: Redford, vol. I, pp. 34–6.

Date: autumn 1743.

p. 77. *our Historical Design*: apparently an historical account of the British Parliament (*Life*, p. 89), which either was never completed, or has not survived.

p. 78. *Emptoris sit eligere*: 'It falls to the buyer to choose.'

p. 78. *great Primer... Pica*: both fonts in use at the time.

p. 78. *the debates*: the accounts of events in Parliament which Johnson wrote up as 'Debates in the Senate of Magna Lilliputia'.

p. 78. *The Plain Dealer*: a magazine published by Aaron Hill (not the play by Wycherley).

An Account of the Life of Mr Richard Savage

Text: *An Account of the Life of Mr. Richard Savage, Son of the Earl of Rivers* (1744).
Date: 11 February 1744.
Johnson published this life of his friend, the minor poet Richard Savage, anonymously on 11 February 1744. For a very full commentary, see Lonsdale, vol. III, pp. 381–425.

p. 82. *Author... Wanderer*: both poems by Savage; *An Author To be Lett* (1729) and *The Wanderer* (1729).

p. 82. *amused*: i.e. deceived.

p. 84. *the Bangorian Controversy*: a controversy of the 1710s, stirred up by Benjamin Hoadly (1676–1761), bishop of Bangor, who wished to extend within the Church of England the rights of private conscience against ecclesiastical authority.

p. 84. *published a Poem against the Bishop*: *The Convocation: Or, A Battle of the Pamphlets* (1717).

p. 84. *Sir Richard Steele, and Mr. Wilks*: Sir Richard Steele (1672–1729); playwright and occasional writer. Robert Wilks (*c*.1665–1732); actor.

p. 85. *Liveries*: i.e. footmen or other retainers of a household (*OED*, 3 b).

p. 86. *that Condition*: i.e. the profession of being an actor.

p. 86. *the South-Sea Traffick*: the South Sea Bubble of 1720.

p. 87. *Mrs. Oldfield*: Anne Oldfield (1683–1730); actress.

p. 87. *those Faults*: an allusion to Mrs. Oldfield's promiscuity.

p. 87. *the Advantage of a Benefit*: a performance of a play in which the receipts are given to a particular person (*OED*, 4 a).

p. 88. *Sir Thomas Overbury*: Sir Thomas Overbury (1581–1613); poisoned in the Tower of London for his opposition to the marriage of Robert Carr to the divorced Countess of Essex.

p. 88. *Mr. Cibber*: Colley Cibber (1671–1757); manager of the Drury Lane Theatre.

p. 89. *Mr. Hill*: Aaron Hill (1685–1750); dramatist and journalist.

p. 89. *Mr. Theophilus Cibber*: Theophilus Cibber (1703–58); actor and playwright; son of Colley Cibber.

p. 91. *the Gatehouse*: a prison in Westminster.

p. 91. *the Press-Yard*: a part of Newgate which provided separate cells for individual prisoners.

p. 92. *Mr. Page*: Sir Francis Page (*c*.1661–1741); known as the 'hanging judge' for his brutality.

p. 94. *the Front*: i.e. effrontery.

p. 94. *the Countess of Hertford*: Frances Seymour (1699–1754).

p. 95. *a short Account*: the anonymous *Life* of Savage published in 1727.

p. 95. *Collector of Antegua*: James Gregory had become Collector of Customs in Antigua in January 1743.

p. 97. *Lord Tyrconnel*: Sir John Brownlow (1690–1754), viscount Tyrconnel.

p. 99. *the Bathos*: i.e. Alexander Pope, *The Art of Sinking in Poetry* (1728).

p. 99. *Dennis*: John Dennis (1657–1734); poet, dramatist, and critic.

p. 99. *Sir Robert Walpole*: Sir Robert Walpole (1676–1745), first Earl of Orford; Whig politician and statesman; First Lord of the Treasury (i.e. Prime Minister), 1715–17 and 1721–42.

p. 108. *The Bastard*: in fact, published in 1728, seven years before Savage's rupture with Tyrconnel.

p. 110. *Eusden*: Laurence Eusden (1688–1730); Poet Laureate since 1718.

p. 111. *Colly Cibber*: see above, p. 1173, note to p. 88.

p. 115. *Dispute...Chancellor*: a dispute between Edmund Gibson, bishop of London, and the Lord Chancellor, Charles Talbot, over the proposed elevation of Thomas Rundle, suspected of heterodoxy, to the bishopric of Gloucester.

p. 115. *Mr. Foster and Mr. Thompson*: Dr. James Foster (1697–1753); dissenter. James Thomson (1700–48); poet.

p. 116. *The Progress of a Divine*: published in 1735.

p. 116. *Sir Philip Yorke*: Sir Philip Yorke (1690–1764); later Lord Chancellor and earl of Hardwick.

p. 118. *the Ministry...Queen Anne*: a Tory ministry led by Harley and Bolingbroke.

p. 118. *Lord Bolingbroke*: Henry St. John (1678–1751); first viscount Bolingbroke; politician, diplomat, and author.

p. 118. *a Poem...public Works*: the enlarged title of the 1737 second edition of a poem originally published in 1736 as *A Poem on the Birth-Day of the Prince of Wales*.

p. 120. *a Man...his Country*: Stephen Duck (1705–56), rural poet, had in 1735 by the Queen been made Keeper of Merlin's Cave in Richmond Park.

p. 121. *a Bulk*: a framework projecting from the front of a shop, or a stall (*OED*).

p. 123. *Mr. Millar*: James Miller (1706–44); playwright and satirist. The character of the poor and quarrelsome poet 'Bays' in Miller's *The Coffee-House* (1737) was thought to be a portrait of Savage.

p. 124. *subscribed...Duck*: Stephen Duck's *Poems on Several Occasions* (1736) had been printed by subscription.

p. 125. *Duke of Chandos*: James Brydges (1674–1744); duke of Chandos.

p. 126. *Death of the Queen*: Queen Caroline died on 20 November 1737.

p. 127. *Levee*: see above, p. 1169, note to p. 52.

p. 128. *A Letter*: the author was Alexander Pope.

p. 129. *Sir William Lemon*: Sir William Leman (1685–1741); a relative by marriage to Savage.

p. 131. *Mr. Powel and Mrs. Jones*: John Powell (1705–69); barrister. Bridget Jones (1713–80); widow.

p. 131. *Mr. Mallet*: David Mallet (1701/2–1765); poet, freethinker, and author.

p. 131. *Leading-strings*: strings with which children used to be guided and supported when learning to walk (*OED*).

p. 137. *Epictetus*: see above, p. 1171, note to p. 67.

p. 140. *Mr. Woolaston*: William Wollaston (1659–1724); philosopher and freethinker; author of *The Religion of Nature Delineated* (1722).

Introduction to the Harleian Miscellany

Text: *Harleian Miscellany*, vol. I (1744), pp. i–viii.
Date: April 1744.

p. 148. *the Rebels of Devonshire*: in the summer of 1549 popular discontent with the new English Prayer Book imposed by Edward VI had led to armed uprisings in Devon and Cornwall.

p. 149. *the first secret Press*: used to produce the 'Martin Marprelate' tracts.

p. 149. *Mr. Rawlinson*: Thomas Rawlinson (1681–1725); book-collector and antiquarian.

p. 149. *the Popish Controversy*: i.e. the so-called Popish Plot of 1678, fabricated by Titus Oates (1649–1705).

p. 150. *Photius*: St. Photius (*b. c.*820); patriarch of Constantinople; compiler of the *Myriobiblon*, an anthology of Greek prose literature.

To Miss — on Her Playing upon the Harpsichord in a Room Hung with Some Flower-Pieces of Her Own Painting

Text: *The Museum*, November 1747.
Date: 1746?

Prologue Spoken by Mr Garrick

Text: *Prologue and Epilogue Spoken at the Opening of the Theatre in Drury-Lane 1747* (1747), pp. 3–7.
Date: September 1747.
The Drury Lane Theatre opened under Garrick's management on 15 September 1747.

l. 9. *Johnson*: i.e. Ben Jonson (1572/3–1637); poet and playwright.

l. 17. *Charles*: i.e. Charles II, who reigned from 1660 to 1685.

l. 36. *great Faustus*: a common subject of farces.

l. 42. *Behns*: Aphra Behn (1640–89); playwright, author, and poet.

l. 42. *Durfeys*: Thomas D'Urfey (1653–1723); poet, playwright, and balladeer.

The Vision of Theodore, the Hermit of Teneriffe, found in his Cell

Text: *The Preceptor*, vol. II (1748), pp. 520–30.
Date: 7 April 1748.

p. 155. *Summit of Teneriffe*: the north-eastern part of the island of Tenerife rises to a jagged volcanic ridge.

The Vanity of Human Wishes: The Tenth Satire of Juvenal

Text: *The Vanity of Human Wishes. The Tenth Satire of Juvenal, Imitated by Samuel Johnson* (1749).

Date: 9 January 1749.

Johnson's most celebrated poem, composed probably in 1748. In 1766, in conversation with Goldsmith, Johnson discussed his method of poetic composition with reference to this poem: 'When composing, I have generally had them [verses] in my mind, perhaps fifty at a time, walking up and down in my room; and then I have written them down, and often, from laziness, have written only half lines. I have written a hundred lines in a day. I remember I wrote a hundred lines of *The Vanity of Human Wishes* in a day' (*Life*, p. 268). Johnson later revised the poem for Dodsley's *Collection* (1755) and tinkered with it at other times. The copy-text for this edition is the unrevised text of 1749.

l. 34. *bonny Traytor*: the Scotch idiom evokes the recent executions of Kilmarnock, Balmerino and Lovat following the failed Jacobite rebellion of 1745.

l. 49. *Democritus*: Greek philosopher (*fl.* 5th cent. BC) who taught that happiness results from the moderation of desire.

l. 50. *chearful Wisdom and instructive Mirth*: Democritus is sometimes referred to as the 'laughing philosopher'.

l. 84. *Palladium*: a statue of Pallas, said to be the safeguard of Troy.

l. 97. *Septennial*: see above, p. 1167, note to p. 31.

l. 99. *Wolsey*: Thomas Wolsey (1470/1–1530); royal minister, archbishop of York, and cardinal; finally disgraced for his failure to obtain a divorce for Henry VIII.

l. 124. *Trent*: see above, p. 1166, note to l. 211.

l. 129. *Villiers*: George Villiers (1592–1628), first duke of Buckingham; royal favourite; assassinated by John Felton, a disgruntled soldier who had formerly served under Buckingham.

l. 130. *Harley*: see above, p. 1172, note to p. 71.

l. 131. *Wentworth*: Thomas Wentworth (1593–1641), first earl of Strafford; lord lieutenant of Ireland; an object of parliamentary resentment because of his thorough enforcement of the interests and policies of Charles I, to whom he became chief councillor; eventually abandoned by Charles, impeached, and executed.

l. 131. *Hyde*: Edward Hyde (1609–74), first earl of Clarendon; politician and historian; chief councillor to Charles II; fell from favour in 1667, and was impeached and exiled.

l. 139. *Bodley's Dome*: see above, p. 1172, note to p. 72.

l. 140. *Bacon's Mansion*: a structure in Oxford on Folly Bridge supposedly once inhabited by the medieval scholar Roger Bacon. The legend states that, if a scholar greater than Bacon were to pass under it, it would collapse.

l. 164. *Lydiat*: Thomas Lydiat (1572–1646); scholar and chronologist who suffered from persecution during the Civil War, and also from poverty.

l. 164. *Galileo*: Galileo Galilei (1564–1642); Italian mathematician, astronomer, and scientist; prosecuted by the Inquisition for his defence of the Copernican theory of the solar system.

l. 168. *Laud*: William Laud (1573–1645), archbishop of Canterbury; religious adviser to Charles I, whose promotion of measures deemed to be neo-Catholic by Puritans led to his being accused of high treason and executed.

l. 179. *the rapid Greek*: Alexander the Great (356–323 BC), king of Macedon, who in the space of eleven years overran the Persian empire and extended Greek military power to the confines of modern-day India.

l. 182. *the Danube or the Rhine*: the scenes of British military action during the War of the Spanish Succession (1702–14).

l. 192. *Swedish Charles*: Charles XII (1682–1718), king of Sweden from 1697; charismatic leader whose invasion of Russia (1707–9), however, was the death-knell of Swedish military power.

l. 210. *Pultowa*: the decisive engagement of Charles XII's Russian campaign, fought on 8 July 1709, in which the Swedish attack on a Russian fortified camp eventuated in the surrender of the majority of the Swedish army three days later.

l. 224. *Persia's Tyrant*: Xerxes the Great, king of Persia.

l. 224. *Bavaria's Lord*: Karl Albrecht (1697–1745), elector of Bavaria; crowned as Emperor Charles VII in 1742, but deposed shortly afterwards by Austria.

l. 227. *Great Xerxes*: see above, note to l. 224.

l. 241. *bold Bavarian*: see above, note to l. 224.

l. 242. *Cesarean Pow'r*: since Roman times the name Caesar had been associated with imperial power.

l. 266. *Luxury*: here, lasciviousness or lust (*OED*, 1).

l. 268. *Lenitives*: that which softens or alleviates.

l. 270. *Orpheus*: legendary pre-Homeric poet, who was supposed to be able to enchant wild beasts with his song.

l. 313. *Lydia's Monarch*: Croesus (560–546 BC), the last king of Lydia, whose wealth was proverbial.

l. 314. *Solon*: Solon (*c.*640–*c.*558 BC); Athenian statesman and poet; on being asked by Croesus to name the happiest of men, he cited some humble Greeks to the irritation of the king, whom he then warned concerning the uncertainty of life and the resentment of the gods.

l. 317. *Marlb'rough*: John Churchill (1650–1722), first duke of Marlborough; suffered a stroke in 1716 from which he never recovered.

l. 318. *Swift*: Jonathan Swift (1667–1745); Irish clergyman and satirist; afflicted with senile dementia for the final three years of his life.

l. 321. *Vane*: Anne Vane (*d.*1736); mistress of first John Hervey, and then Frederick, Prince of Wales.

l. 322. *Sedley*: Catharine Sedley (1657–1717); mistress of James II.

The Vanity of Wealth: An Ode

Text: *Gentleman's Magazine*, vol. XX (1750), p. 85.
Date: February 1750.

'DICTIONARY' JOHNSON

The Rambler

Text: *The Rambler* (1756).

Date: 1750–2.

Johnson began composing *The Rambler* in March 1750; and the spirit in which he did so is suggested by the prayer reprinted in Appendix A. The first paper was published anonymously on Tuesday 20 March, and subsequently one appeared each Saturday and Tuesday, until the final paper was published on Saturday 14 March 1752. The publishers were John Payne, Joseph Bouquet, and Edward Cave. They paid Johnson two guineas per paper, and on 1 April 1751 Johnson assigned the copyright to Edward Cave. According to Arthur Murphy, the circulation of *The Rambler* never rose above five hundred copies. Nevertheless, the papers were soon reprinted in collected editions, and Johnson took advantage of the opportunity represented by these early reprintings to revise his text. Something of the scale and direction of these acts of revision is suggested by the parallel texts of *Rambler*, no. 1 reprinted here in Appendix B. After the fourth collected edition of 1756, however, the incidence of revision subsides.

NO. 1

p. 177. *Cur tamen... edam*: Juvenal, I.19–21.

p. 178. *Horace*: Johnson has in mind 'non fumum ex fulgore, sed ex fumo dare lucem | cogitat', 'he aims to produce, not smoke out of light, but light from smoke' (*Ars Poetica*, ll. 143–4).

p. 178. *an estate for ever*: Thucydides, *History*, I.xxii.4.

p. 178. *powers*: 'On Praising Oneself Inoffensively', Plutarch, *Moralia*, 539A–547F.

p. 179. *Quid enim? laeta*: Horace, *Satires*, I.i.7–8.

p. 180. *Aura popularis*: cf. Horace, *Odes*, III.ii.20.

NO. 2

p. 180. *Stare... campsum*: 'such misery it is to be rooted to the spot—miles are lost before they begin, and their hooves re-echo across the deserted plain'; Statius, *Thebaid*, VI.400–1.

p. 180. *Th'impatient... lost*: Pope, *Windsor Forest*, ll. 151–4.

p. 181. *hope to hope*: a sentiment with parallels in *Rasselas*, where in chapter 3 Rasselas himself regrets that 'I have already enjoyed too much; give me something to desire', and where in chapter 47 Nekayah observes that 'none are happy but by the anticipation of change: the change itself is nothing; when we have made it, the next wish is to change again. The world is not yet exhausted; let me see something to morrow which I never saw before' (above, pp. 641 and 706). Johnson mistrusted

Hobbes, remarking to Thomas Tyers that 'when I published my Dictionary I might have quoted *Hobbes* as an authority in language, as well as many other writers of his time: but I scorned, sir, to quote him at all; because I did not like his principles' (*Early Biographies*, p. 82). But nevertheless his understanding of man as driven more by hope than by gratification is compatible with a notorious passage of *Leviathan*: 'the Felicity of this life, consisteth not in the repose of a mind satisfied. For there is no such *Finis ultimus*, (utmost ayme,) nor *Summum Bonum*, (greatest Good,) as is spoken of in the Books of the old Morall Philosophers. Nor can a man any more live, whose Desires are at an end, than he, whose Senses and Imaginations are at a stand. Felicity is a continuall progresse of the desire, from one object to another; the attaining of the former, being still but the way to the later' (chapter 11).

p. 182. *inadequate*: Cervantes, *Don Quixote*, pt. 1, chs. 7, 15, and 21.

p. 182. *Laudis...libello*: Horace, *Epistles*, I.i.36–7.

p. 183. *Epictetus*: 'Keep before your eyes day by day death and exile, and everything that seems terrible, but most of all death; and then you will never have any abject thought, nor will you yearn for anything immoderately' (*Enchiridion*, c. 21).

p. 183. *I nunc...canoros*: Horace, *Epistles*, II.ii.76.

NO. 4

p. 184. *Simul... Vitæ*: Horace, *Ars Poetica*, l. 334.

p. 184. *works of fiction*: according to Arthur Murphy, Johnson had in mind Smollett's *Roderick Random* (1748) and Fielding's *Tom Jones* (1749).

p. 184. *Pontanus*: Julius Caesar Scaliger (1484–1558); French classical scholar; his *Poetics* (1561) imparted a neo-classical flavour to the literary criticism of the early modern period, and were particularly important for reinforcing the authority of Aristotle. Pontano, Giovanni (or Jovianus Pontanus) (1426–1503); Italian poet, man of letters, and statesman; one of the finest Latin prose stylists of the Renaissance. Scaliger, *Poetics*, VI.4.

p. 184. *plus oneris...minus*: Horace, *Epistles*, II.i.170.

p. 184. *Apelles*: Apelles (*fl.* 4th cent. BC); the greatest painter of antiquity. It is said that a cobbler criticized the drawing of a sandal in a picture by Apelles. Apelles altered the sandal in deference to the cobbler's opinion, but when the next day the cobbler criticized the drawing of the leg, Apelles replied 'ne sutor supra crepidam', 'a cobbler should not judge of anything above the sole', or as we say, 'let the cobbler stick to his last' (Pliny, *Natural History*, XXXV.xxxvi.85).

p. 185. *chastity of thought*: 'Plurima sunt, Fuscine, et fama digna sinistra | et nitidis maculam haesuram figentia rebus, | quae monstrant ipsi pueris traduntque parentes'; 'Fuscinus, there are many infamous things—things capable of besmirching even the most brilliant lives—which parents themselves point out and pass on to their sons' (Juvenal, XIV.1–3).

p. 185. *power of example...effects*: for another instance of Johnson's concern over the receptiveness of the imagination, and the consequent need for only uplifting or strengthening examples to be placed before it by literature, see his comments on the ending of *King Lear* (*Shakespeare*, pp. 238–41).

p. 186. *grateful... resentful*: *Miscellanies* (1727), vol. II, p. 354.

p. 187. *content... but feared*: an allusion to the principle of Caligula, 'oderint, dum metuant', 'let them hate, so long as they fear' (Suetonius, *Caligula*, XXX.1).

NO. 6

p. 187. *strenua... æquus*: Horace, *Epistles*, I.ii.28–30.

p. 188. *sapientia insaniens*: 'crazy wisdom' (Horace, *Odes*, I.xxxiv.2).

p. 188. *Ni... ortum*: Boethius, *Consolatio*, III.metr.6.9.

p. 188. *canine madness*: rabies.

p. 189. *My desire... philosophy*: Cowley, *Works* (1669), sig. C1ʳ (slightly misquoted and abbreviated).

p. 190. *new persuit*: again, there is a parallel with Rasselas's regret that 'I have already enjoyed too much; give me something to desire' (above, p. 641).

NO. 7

pp. 190–1. *O qui... idem*: Boethius, *Consolatio*, III. metr. 9.1–2, 25–8.

p. 191. *no man... master*: Plutarch, *Moralia*, 780c.

p. 191. *a king... geometry*: the king was Ptolemy I; see Proclus, *In primum Euclidis Elementorum librum commentarii* (1560), Book 2, ch. 4, p. 39.

p. 192. *now especially*: i.e. at Easter.

NO. 8

p. 194. *patitur... habet*: Juvenal, XIII.208–10.

p. 195. *Media... vacævi*: Lucan, *Pharsalia*, X.185–6.

p. 195. *crime to do... think*: Aquinas, *Summa*, I–II, Q. 74, a. 8; Q. 108, a. 3.

p. 196. *Μηδ'... Τέρπου*: *Aurea Carmina*, ll. 40–4.

p. 197. *Evil... behind*: Milton, *Paradise Lost*, V.117–19.

NO. 9

p. 198. *Quod... malis*: Martial, X.xlvii.12.

p. 199. *I laugh... upon him thus*: Addison, *Cato*, II.vi.48–50.

p. 199. *late successes at sea*: a reference to actions in the War of the Austrian Succession (1740–8). In 1747 two French fleets convoying merchantmen to the colonies had been successfully attacked; these victories were a consequence of the policy of Admiral Edward Vernon, who in the 1740s had established the Western Squadron, commanded by Admiral George Anson.

NO. 13

p. 200. *Commissumque...irâ*: Horace, *Epistles*, I.xviii.38.

p. 201. *not to speak*: Quintus Curtius, *History of Alexander*, IV.vi.5–6.

p. 202. *a man...virtually the same*: said of Sarah Churchill, the Duchess of Marlborough; cf. *An Account of the Conduct of the Dowager Duchess of Marlborough* (1742), p. 222 for an expression of her friendship for Anne. In 'De l'Amitié', Montaigne describes his friendship with La Boëtie as one in which 'souls are mingled and confounded in so universal a blending that they efface the seam which joins them together so that it cannot be found' (Montaigne, pp. 211–12). For Johnson's review, see above, pp. 68–71.

NO. 14

p. 204. *Nil...sibi*: Horace, *Satires*, I.iii.18–19.

p. 204. *in a letter...procured him*: to Emeric Bigot, 24 March 1656/57 (*The Works of John Milton*, vol. XII (New York: Columbia University Press, 1936), p. 84).

p. 204. *officer...in their work*: Diodorus Siculus, *Bibliotheca Historica*, II.xxiv.4.

p. 206. *Bacon...attainable*: Bacon, *Historia Naturalis*, in *Works*, ed. Spedding, Ellis, and Heath (1857), vol. II, p. 38.

p. 206. *It is recorded...disgrace*: 'From the first time that the Impressions of Religion setled deeply in his Mind, He used great caution to conceal it:...for he said he was afraid, he should at some time or other, do some enormous thing, which if he were look't on as a very Religious Man, might cast a reproach on the profession of it, and give great advantages to impious Men, to blaspheme the name of God' (Gilbert Burnet, *Life and Death of Sir Matthew Hale, Kt.* (1682), pp. 141–2).

NO. 16

p. 207. *Multis...facundia*: Juvenal, X.9–10.

p. 207. *a late paper*: *Rambler* no. 10.

p. 208. *Facilis...Ditis*: Virgil, *Aeneid*, VI.126–7. A favourite quotation of Johnson's: cf. *The Rambler*, no. 155 and *The Adventurer*, no. 34.

p. 210. *profit of their works*: *Miscellanies* (1727), 'Preface'.

NO. 17

p. 211. *Me non...facit*: Lucan, *Pharsalia*, IX.582–3.

p. 211. *Let those...freed*: N. Rowe, *Lucan's Pharsalia* (1718), IX.1000–3, p. 385; capitalization altered.

p. 211. *thou shalt die*: a commonplace, but see e.g. Herodotus, II.78.

p. 211. *Keep... end of life*: *Greek Anthology*, IX.366.

p. 211. οὐδὲν... τινός: *Enchiridion*, c. 21; cf. also above, p. 1179, note to p. 183.

p. 213. *Ridetque... trunci*: Lucan, *Pharsalia*, IX.14.

p. 214. *art is long... short*: Hippocrates, *Aphorisms*, I.i.

NO. 18

p. 214. *Illic matre... castitas*: Horace, *Odes*, III.xxiv.17–23.

p. 215. *deities... on the other*: an allusion to the celebrated sentiment 'Victrix causa deis placuit, sed victa Catoni', 'the victorious side enjoyed the favour of the gods, but the defeated enjoyed that of Cato' (Lucan, *Pharsalia*, I.128).

NO. 22

p. 218. *Ego nec... amice*: Horace, *Ars Poetica*, ll. 409–11.

p. 218. *unextinguishable merriment*: 'And unquenchable laughter arose among the blessed gods, as they saw Hephaestus puffing through the palace' (Homer, *Iliad*, I.599–600).

NO. 23

p. 221. *Tres mihi... palato*: Horace, *Epistles*, II.ii.61–2.

p. 222. *younger Pliny*: 'Praeterea suae quisque inventioni favet, et quasi fortissimum amplectitur, cum ab alio dictum est quod ipse praevidit'; 'Moreover, everyone favours his own powers of invention, and will be most persuaded by what matches his own conclusion' (Pliny, *Epistles*, I.xx.13).

p. 223. *like the Spectator... physiognomy*: see *The Spectator*, no. 1 (1 March 1711).

NO. 24

p. 224. *Nemo... descendere*: Persius, *Satires*, IV.23.

p. 224. *Lacedemon*: 'know thyself' (*Greek Anthology*, IX.366); cf. Johnson's poem of the same title (above, pp. 791–92).

p. 225. *Gelidus... deep researches*: Mrs. Thrale states that the character of Gelidus was based on that of John Colson, the Lucasian Professor of Mathematics at Cambridge.

p. 226. *dramatick reputation*: see Lonsdale, vol. II, p. 197 (Garth) and vol. III, p. 70 (Congreve). Congreve's alleged negligence of his achievements as a dramatist stems from Voltaire's account of his meeting with the aged playwright, then 'almost at death's door': 'he had one failing, which was that he did not rank high enough his first profession, that of a writer, which had made his reputation and his fortune. He spoke of his works as trifles beneath him, and in our first conversation he told me to think of him as a gentleman who lived very simply. I answered him that if he had had the misfortune of being just a gentleman like any other I would never have come to see him, and I was very shocked at such misplaced vanity' (Voltaire, *Letters on England*, tr. L. Tancock (Harmondsworth: Penguin Books, 1980), pp. 99–100).

NO. 25

p. 227. *Possunt...videntur*: Virgil, *Aeneid*, V.231. Dryden had also used this well-known tag in a footnote to the second edition of his *1 Conquest of Granada* (1670), II.iii.

p. 227. *right path...error*: 'virtus est medium vitiorum et utrimque reductum', 'virtue is found between vices, and shuns extremes' (Horace, *Epistles*, I.xviii.9). This is also an Aristotelian idea of virtue: cf. *Nicomachean Ethics*, II.6.

p. 229. *Infantes barbati*: the tag is ambiguous, being capable of meaning both 'bearded children' and 'dumb philosophers'.

NO. 28

p. 230. *Illi mors...sibi*: Seneca, *Thyestes*, ll. 401–3.

p. 230. *Cowley*: from Cowley's 'Of Solitude'.

p. 230. *late essay*: *The Rambler*, no. 24.

p. 232. *wise friend...sincerity*: cf. Bacon, who in his essay 'Of Frendship' admires 'the wisest and most politic [princes] that ever reigned' for their practice of joining 'to themselves, some of their Servants; Whom both Themselves have called *Frends*; And allowed Others likewise to call them in the same manner; Using the Word which is received between Private Men' (Bacon, *Essayes*, p. 82).

p. 233. *some time...his death*: Alfonso de Valdés (1490–1532), Latin secretary to Charles V. Johnson probably learnt of the anecdote from Izaak Walton's life of Herbert, where the resolution is more pithily expressed as 'there ought to be a vacancy of time, betwixt fighting and dying' (Izaak Walton, *Lives*, ed. G. Saintsbury (Oxford: Oxford University Press, 1927), pp. 312–13).

p. 233. *consider...ourselves*: William Chillingworth, sermon IV, sects. 12 and 15, in *Nine Sermons* (1664), pp. 52–3.

p. 233. *commune...and be still*: Psalm 4:4.

p. 233. *Death...to himself*: Johnson refers to the Senecan epigraph of this paper.

p. 233. *Pontanus*: Giovanni Pontano (1426–1503); Italian humanist, statesman, and man of letters. The quotation (which Johnson slightly misquotes) is from Sir Thomas Pope Blount's *Censura Celebriorum Authorum* (1690), p. 354.

NO. 29

p. 233. *Prudens... trepidet*: Horace, *Odes*, III.xxix.29–32.

p. 235. *never surprised*: a reference to the Horatian maxim 'nil admirari' (Horace, *Epistles*, I.vi.1).

p. 236. *old Cornaro*: Luigi Cornaro (*c.*1467–1566); see his *La Vita Sobria* (1558), p. 25.

p. 236. *when God sends... strength*: 'be satisfied with thus much, that your present strength is sufficient for any present trial; and when a greater comes, God hath promised to give you more strength when you shall have need of more' (Jeremy Taylor, *The Worthy Communicant* (1660), ch. 2, sect. 3, p. 153).

NO. 31

p. 237. *Non ego... meis*: Ovid, *Amores*, II.iv.1–2.

p. 237. *one of the philosophers*: Lochagus the Spartan, as reported in Plutarch, *Moralia*, 225F. Compare also *The Rambler*, no. 32 (above, pp. 240–44), and the portrait of the affected Stoic in *Rasselas*, ch. 18 (above, pp. 664–66).

p. 238. *refused... were confuted*: said of Julius Libri, who rejected Galileo's theories out of hand.

p. 238. *I follow... persue*: from *The Indian Emperor* (1665), IV.iii.3.

p. 238. *Et se... fugitque*: not in fact in Virgil, but in Ovid, *Metamorphoses*, IV.461.

p. 238. *Here, says he... to find it*: Johnson is here misquoting from memory. In the 'Preface' to *Tyrannick Love* (1670), Dryden in fact says: 'Some foole... had charg'd me in the *Indian Emperour* with nonsense in these words, And follow fate which does too fast pursue; which was borrow'd from *Virgil* in the XIth of his *Æneids*, *Eludit gyro inferior, sequiturque sequentem*. I quote not these to prove that I never writ Nonsense, but onely to show that they are so unfortunate as not to have found it' (*The Works of John Dryden*, vol. X, ed. M. Novak (Los Angeles: University of California Press, 1970), p. 113; italic and roman reversed).

p. 240. *So much... character*: Celsus, *De Medicina*, VIII.iv.4.

NO. 32

p. 240. Ὅσσά τε... δύνῃ: Pythagoras, *Aurea Carmina*, ii.17–19.

p. 241. *Zeno*: Zeno of Citium (*c.*335–*c.*263 BC); founder of the school of Stoic philosophy, which taught a doctrine of detachment from the outside world.

p. 241. *he now... an evil*: said in fact of Dionysius, who suffered from ophthalmia, not gout; cf. Diogenes Laertius, *Lives*, VII.37. c. 1.

p. 242. *Leniter... ferendum est*: Ovid, *Heroides*, V.7.

p. 242. *not to spend... repair it*: Henri de la Tour d'Auvergne (1611–75), vicomte de Turenne; French military commander during the reign of Louis XIV. The advice was given by the Duc de Weymar, the guiding principles of whose conduct Turenne recalled in these words: 'ce Général...ne s'enorgueillissoit point de ses succès; que, lorsqu'il avoit du malheur, il ne songeoit pas tant à se plaindre, qu'à s'en relever; qu'il aimoit mieux se laisser blâmer injustement, que de s'excuser aux dépens de ses amis qui avoient manqué dans l'action; qu'il étoit plus occupé à réparer ses fautes, qu'à perdre son tems en apologies' (Andrew Ramsay, *Histoire du Vicomte de Turenne* (La Haye, 1736), vol. I, pp. 108–9).

p. 244. *bless the name...takes away*: Job 1:21.

NO. 33

p. 244. *Quod caret...est*: Ovid, *Heroides*, IV.89.

NO. 36

p. 247. Ἄμ' ἕποντο...προνόησαν: Homer, *Iliad*, XVIII.525–6.

p. 247. *original pair...Maker*: Milton, *Paradise Lost*, V.153–208.

p. 248. *numbers without number*: Milton, *Paradise Lost*, III.346.

p. 249. *Sannazarius*: Jacopo Sannazzaro (1458–1530); Neapolitan poet and celebrant of rustic life; author of a series of verse eclogues published in 1504 as *Arcadia*, and of piscatory eclogues.

p. 249. *metrical geography of Dionysius*: the *Periegesis* of Dionysius.

NO. 37

p. 250. *Canto quæ...Dircæus*: Virgil, *Eclogues*, II.23–4.

p. 250. *Theocritus*: Theocritus (*fl. c.*270 BC); Doric poet, considered to be the father of pastoral.

p. 251. *Anaximander...apprehension*: Anaximander of Miletus (*fl.* early 6th cent. BC); scientist, philosopher, constructor of the sun dial, and alleged to have compiled a map of the world; said to be the first writer of Greek prose; cf. *Eclogues*, III.40–1. Pope, *Pastorals*, 'Spring', l. 38 and note, where Pope claims that 'the Shepherd's hesitation at the name of the Zodiac, imitates that in Virgil'.

p. 252. *Diggon...wretched wight*: Spenser, *Shepheardes Calendar*, 'September', ll. 1–4.

p. 252. *Nunc scio...edunt*: Virgil, *Eclogues*, VIII.43–5.

p. 252. *I know thee, Love...born!*: Pope, 'Autumn', ll. 89–92.

p. 253. *Pollio*: Gaius Asinius Pollio (76 BC – AD 5); associate of Catullus, Julius Caesar and Mark Antony; consul, 40 BC; the first to recognize the genius of Virgil, and of practical assistance to the poet when his farm near Mantua was seized as war booty after Philippi. Virgil celebrates Pollio in the eighth and fourth eclogues; Johnson here refers to the fourth. Because this poem is a vision of a golden age inaugurated by the birth of a child, it was for many years given a Christian interpretation, although it is more likely that Virgil refers to the son of Pollio himself, who was born in the year of his father's consulship.

p. 253. *Silenus*: Silenus was a satyr, sometimes said to be the son of Pan, and a companion of Dionysus; he was frequently depicted as elderly and drunken, and there are often said to be many Sileni, not just one Silenus. Johnson refers to the tenth eclogue of Virgil.

p. 253. *Gallus*: Gaius Cornelius Gallus (69–26 BC); poet and soldier; first prefect of Egypt under Augustus; eventually committed suicide, having fallen from favour; praised by Virgil in the sixth and tenth eclogues; see especially *Eclogues* X.2–3 and 72–3.

p. 253. *harvests*: 'frugibus alternis, non consule computat annum: | autumnum pomis, ver sibi flore notat'; 'For him the returning seasons, not the consuls, mark the year: he knows autumn by her fruits, spring by her flowers' (Claudian, 'Felix, qui propriis aevum transegit in arvis').

NO. 39

p. 253. *Infelix...marito*: 'Unhappy woman—a worthy wife to a worthless husband'. Untraced in the poems of Ausonius; but possibly an inverted recollection of a line in Ovid, 'Felix Andromache, certo bene nupta marito' ('Happy Andromache, the worthy consort of a faithful spouse') (*Epistulae*, V.105), fused with the mournful sense of l. 27 of Ausonius's 'Cupido Cruciatur' ('Cupid in Torment'), 'infelix nato nec fortunata marito' ('unhappy in her son and luckless in her husband'; said of Eriphyle).

NO. 41

p. 256. *Nulla recordanti...frui*: Martial, X.xxiii.5–8.

p. 257. *the fool's...pride*: Prior, *Solomon*, I.236.

p. 258. *in the sacred treasure of the past*: apparently a misremembering of Dryden's *Hind and the Panther*, I.258.

p. 258. *vexit*: Horace, *Odes*, III.xxix.45–8.

p. 259. *Vitæ...longam*: Horace, *Odes*, I.iv.15.

p. 260. *Petite...canis*: Persius, *Satires*, V.64–5.

NO. 45

p. 260. Ἧπερ μεγίστη...πάντα: Euripides, *Medea*, ll. 14–16.

p. 260. *dissertations*: earlier *Ramblers* on the subject of marriage are nos. 18, 35, and 39.

p. 261. *The merchant...crouds*: Horace, *Satires*, I.i.4–12.

NO. 47

p. 263. *Quanquam...egere*: Pliny, *Epistles*, VIII.16. The translation comes from John Boyle's *Letters of Pliny the Younger* (1751), vol. II, p. 231; punctuation slightly changed.

p. 263. *king Pyrrhus...devotion*: Plutarch, *Lives*, 'Pyrrhus', XIV.

p. 264. *vulnerary herbs*: herbs said to possess the power to heal wounds; typically, arnica. See Virgil, *Aeneid*, XII.411 ff. and Claudius Aelianus, *Varia Historia*, I.x: 'The Cretans are excellent Archers; they shoot the Goats which feed on the tops of mountains, which being hurt, immediately eat of the herb Dittany, which as soon as they have tasted, the Arrow drops out' (*Claudius Aelianus his Various History*, tr. Thomas Stanley (1666), p. 5).

p. 266. *Grotius*: Hugo Grotius (1583–1645); Dutch statesman and jurist. The quotation comes from his 'Consolatoria ad Patrem', in *Poemata Collecta* (1617), p. 457, where however the text runs: 'Non cedit Natura morae, si tempore reddi | Pax animo tranquilla potest, tu sperne morari: | Qui sapiet, sibi tempus erit'. Johnson was perhaps quoting from memory.

NO. 49

p. 266. *Non omnis...recens*: Horace, *Odes*, III.xxx.6–8.

p. 267. *first man...the world*: Plutarch, *Lives*, 'Caesar', XI.2.

p. 268. *Anacreon...tomb*: *Anacreontica*, IV.

p. 268. *When Themistocles...same cause*: Plutarch, *Lives*, 'Themistocles', III.3–4.

pp. 268–9. *Cæsar...country*: Plutarch, *Lives*, 'Caesar', XI.3; cf. also Dio Cassius, XXXVII.lii.2 and Suetonius, 'Divo Iulio', VII.1.

p. 269. Πολλὰ...'Ρόδιος: *Greek Anthology*, VIII.348.

NO. 60

p. 269. *Quid sit...dicit*: Horace, *Epistles*, I.ii.3–4.

p. 270. *Parva...quotidie*: Pliny, *Epistles*, III.i.

p. 271. *cujus...miraturi*: Jacques-Auguste de Thou (1553–1617); French statesman and historian. The quotation comes from 'Viri Illustris Jac. Aug. Thuani...Commentariorum de Vita Sua Libri Sex', in *Historiarum Sui Temporis* (1733), VII, pt. iv, p. 3 n. Johnson slightly misquotes. In the original the final word is 'cognituri', which trims the boastfulness of the sentiment.

p. 271. *his walk...again slow*: 'citus modo modo tardus incessus'; Sallust, *De Coniuratione Catilinae*, XV.5.

p. 271. *idleness of suspense*: Joachim Camerarius, *Vita Melancthonis* (1777), ch. XVII, p. 62, where the text is: 'Usque adeo vero indiserta, confusa, vaga, indefinita, inexplicataque auersabatur, ut, quoties cum aliquibus de tempore esset constituendum, semper momentum horae iuberet nominari.'

p. 271. *careful . . . his life*: Sir William Temple, 'Essay on the Cure of the Gout by Moxa', in *Works* (1757), vol. III, p. 244.

p. 271. *the irregularity . . . pulse*: 'Preface' to the *Works of Addison* (1721), vol. I, p. xvi.

p. 271. *sense of both*: Honorat de Beuil, 'Mémoires pour la vie de Malherbe'.

p. 272. *Let me remember . . . due to the country*: untraced in Burnet's life of Hale; but perhaps a recollection of the tenth item in Hale's list of 'Things Necessary to be Continually had in Remembrance': 'X. That I be not biassed with Compassion to the Poor, or favour to the Rich, in point of Justice' (Gilbert Burnet, *Life and Death of Sir Matthew Hale, Kt.* (1682), p. 59).

NO. 63

p. 272. *Habebat sæpe . . . queat*: Horace, *Satires*, I.iii.11–15.

pp. 272–3. *no man . . . deliberation*: Horace, *Satires*, I.i.1–3.

p. 274. *Hermetick philosophy*: so-called after Hermes Trismegistus, an aspect of the Egyptian god Thoth and author of all mystical doctrines, including that of alchemy, to which Johnson here refers.

NO. 64

p. 275. *Idem velle . . . est*: Sallust, *De Coniuratione Catilinae*, XX.4.

p. 275. *When Socrates . . . real friends*: Phaedrus, *Fabulae Aesopiae*, III.9.

p. 278. *precepts of Horace*: 'audebit, quaecumque parum splendoris habebunt / et sine pondere erunt et honore indigna ferentur, | verba movere loco, quamvis invita rededant'; 'he will dare to revise, no matter how reluctantly, if his words are dull, or slight, or low' (Horace, *Epistles*, II.ii.111–13).

NO. 70

p. 278. *Argentea . . . ære*: Ovid, *Metamorphoses*, I.114–15.

pp. 278–9. *The first place . . . use or value*: Hesiod, *Works and Days*, ll. 293–7.

p. 280. *roll down . . . custom*: cf. 'Must helpless Man, in Ignorance sedate, | Roll darkling down the Current of his Fate' (*Vanity of Human Wishes*, ll. 347–8, above, p. 172).

NO. 71

p. 281. *Vivere . . . satis*: Martial, II.xc.3–4.

p. 281. *their souls . . . understand them*: an obscure reference, but cf. Aristotle, *De Anima*, II.i.412 b, 5–6.

p. 282. *dilator, spe longus*: Horace, *Ars Poetica*, l. 172.

p. 282. Τὸ ῥόδον...αλλα βάτον: *Greek Anthology*, XI.53. The translation is Johnson's own: cf. *Poems*, p. 98.

p. 282. *Baxter*: Richard Baxter (1615–91); Puritan divine; imprisoned, 1685–6. Edmund Calamy, *Abridgement of Mr. Baxter's... Life and Times* (1702), pp. 596–7.

p. 283. *Hearne*: Thomas Hearne (1678–1735); antiquary and non-juror. The *Reliquiae Hearnianae*, the most likely source for a judgement such as this, were published from Hearne's notebooks by Philip Bliss only in 1857, and so could not be known to Johnson. I have not been able to trace this remark in those works of Hearne's that Johnson could have read. It may depend on oral tradition.

p. 283. *value of life*: actuarial science advanced significantly during the eighteenth century, particularly at the hands of Richard Price (1723–91), although his most influential writings on this subject were published after *The Rambler*.

NO. 72

p. 284. *Omnis Aristippum...æquum*: Horace, *Epistles*, I.xvii.23–4.

p. 284. *balm of being*: cf. Milton, *Paradise Lost*, XI.546.

p. 286. *he could...better man*: *1 Henry IV*, V.iv.103.

NO. 73

p. 286. *Stulte quid...dies*: Ovid, *Tristia*, III.viii.11–12.

p. 287. *Tudors and Plantagenets*: both royal dynasties which had occupied the throne of England.

p. 288. *escutcheons and white gloves*: both tokens of aristocracy.

NO. 76

p. 290. *Silvis ubi...partibus*: Horace, *Satires*, II.iii.48–51.

p. 291. *lenitive*: a palliative, or soothing, medicine.

NO. 77

p. 292. *Os dignum...vocem*: Prudentius, *Contra Symmachi Orationem*, I.635–7.

p. 294. *albus an ater*: literally, white or black.

p. 295. *his death...for his country*: 'Catilina long a suis inter hostium cadavera repertus est, pulcherrima morte, si pro patria sic concidisset'; 'Catiline was discovered far from his comrades amidst the corpses of his enemies—a fine death, if he had fallen for his homeland' (Florus, *Epitomae Bellorum*, II.xii.12).

p. 295. *Of him... much shall be required*: Luke 12:48.

NO. 79

p. 296. *Tam sæpe... est*: Martial, XII.51.

p. 296. *he who believes... himself to be perjured*: Antiphanes, fragment 241.

p. 297. *to save life... would live*: Juvenal, VIII.84.

p. 297. *Camerarius*: Joachim Camerarius (1500–74); German classical scholar and theologian, who sought to reconcile Catholics and Protestants. The anecdote however is not to be found in his works.

NO. 85

p. 299. *Otia si tollas... faces*: Ovid, *Remedia Amoris*, ll. 139–40.

p. 299. *mural or civick garlands*: mural honours were awarded in the Roman army to the first soldier to scale the walls of a besieged town; by extension, any military or civic honours.

p. 300. *Ludere... Coronæ*: Horace, *Ars Poetica*, ll. 379–81.

p. 301. *System of Education*: John Locke, *Some Thoughts Concerning Education* (1693), §§ 201–6.

p. 301. *Nero*: Nero, who was Roman emperor AD 54–68, was notorious for his affectation of artistic talent, and for singing while watching Rome burn.

p. 302. *loom and the distaff*: Ovid, *Ars Amatoria*, I.359–60; Homer, Iliad, VI.490–91.

p. 302. *peripatetick*: the peripatetic school of philosophy was founded by Aristotle, and was so called because of his habit of teaching his students while walking through the Lyceum; hence, Aristotelian.

NO. 87

p. 302. *Invidus... aurem*: Horace, *Epistles*, I.i.38–40.

p. 303. *the catharticks of the soul*: cf. Addison, *The Spectator*, no. 507 (11 October 1712); 'The Platonists have so just a Notion of the Almighty's Aversion to every thing which is false and erroneous, that they looked upon Truth as no less necessary than Virtue, to qualifie an Human Soul for the Enjoyment of a separate State. For this Reason, as they recommended Moral Duties to qualifie and season the Will for a future Life, so they prescribed several Contemplations and Sciences to rectifie the Understanding. Thus Plato has called Mathematical Demonstrations the Catharticks or Purgatives of the Soul, as being the most proper Means to cleanse it from Error, and to give it a Relish of Truth, which is the natural Food and Nourishment of the Understanding, as Virtue is the Perfection and Happiness of the Will.'

p. 303. *Tentanda ... per ora:* Virgil, *Georgics,* III.8–9.

p. 304. *dead counsellors are safest:* the saying is reported in Melchior de Santa Cruz de Dueñas, *Floresta Española* (1578), I.25, sig. C5ᵛ: 'Dezia el rey den Alonso de Aragon, que ningũo auia de to mar cõsejo cõ los viuos, sino cõ los muertos. Entendiendo por los libros, porque siu amore ni temor siempre dizen la verdad.'

p. 304. *The preacher ... fill up his hour:* untraced.

p. 305. *Tully:* i.e. Cicero.

NO. 90

p. 305. *In tenui labor:* Virgil, *Georgics,* IV.6.

p. 306. *invenias ... membra poetæ:* Horace, *Satires,* I.iv.62; 'you may find the limbs of a poet, albeit a dismembered one.'

p. 306. *Hypocrites ... free to all: Paradise Lost,* IV.744 and 746–7.

p. 307. *Eyes ... Leucothea wak'd: Paradise Lost,* XI.130 and 131–5.

p. 307. *He ended ... His trumpet: Paradise Lost,* XI.72–4.

p. 307. *First in his east ... sweet influence: Paradise Lost,* VII.370–5.

p. 307. *The race ... thee implores: Paradise Lost,* VII.33–8.

p. 307. *He, with his ... Torments him: Paradise Lost,* I.51–6.

pp. 307–8. *God ... train ascending: Paradise Lost,* VII.569 and 571–4.

p. 308. *The evil ... With blessedness: Paradise Lost,* VII.56–9.

p. 308. *What we by day ... to wild: Paradise Lost,* IX.209–12.

p. 308. *The paths ... Assist us: Paradise Lost,* IX.244–7.

p. 308. *Beast now ... him passing: Paradise Lost,* X.710–14.

p. 308. *But now ... chaos to retire: Paradise Lost,* II.1034–8.

p. 309. *Before the hills ... celestial song: Paradise Lost,* VII.8–12.

p. 309. *Or other worlds ... not to inquire: Paradise Lost,* III.567–71.

p. 309. *He blew ... general doom: Paradise Lost,* XI.73–6.

NO. 93

p. 309. *Experiar ... Latinâ:* Juvenal, I.170–1.

p. 310. *Baillet:* Adrien Baillet (1649–1706); French cleric, scholar, and man of letters. For Baillet's indeed lengthy catalogue of the 'préjugés' which can impede the reception of criticism, see his *Jugemens des Sçavans* (Amsterdam, 1725), I.i.118–572.

p. 310. *reach of human abilities:* Johnson may here be confusing some lines from the 'Epilogue' to Congreve's *The Way of the World* ('And sure he must have more than mortal skill | Who pleases anyone against his will') with Dryden's comment in the 'Preface' to *Absalom and Achitophel,* that 'no man can be heartily angry with him, who pleases him against his will'.

p. 310. *Euclid or Archimedes:* Euclid (*fl. c.*300 BC); pre-eminent Greek mathematician and geometrician. Archimedes (*c.*287–212 BC); the most complete scientific genius of antiquity, who made enduring advances in the fields of mathematics, mechanics, physics, and astronomy.

p. 310. *Una tantum... Sæpe et nulla*: Seneca, *Apocolocyntosis*, XII.21–2.

p. 310. *Langbaine, Borrichitus or Rapin*: Gerard Langbaine (1656–92); dramatic critic; author of *An Account of the English Dramatic Poets* (Oxford, 1691) and *Momus Triumphans: or, the Plagiaries of the English Stage* (1688), in which prodigious reading is displayed. Olaus Borch, or Borrichius (not Borrichitus) (1626–90); Danish philologist and scientist; librarian of the University of Copenhagen. René Rapin (1621–87); French poet, critic and theologian; influential in imparting a neo-classical and Aristotelian quality to literary criticism in France and elsewhere during the later seventeenth century.

p. 310. *in a good cause*: cf. *The Spectator*, no. 40 (16 April 1711).

p. 311. *Scaliger*: Joseph Justus Scaliger (1540–1609); the greatest literary scholar of the Renaissance; like his father, the physician, polemicist, and philosopher Julius Cæsar Scaliger (1484–1558), he hailed from Lake Garda, and claimed descent from the noble Italian Della Scala family.

p. 312. *cannot be wounded*: cf. Virgil, *Aeneid*, VI.290–4.

p. 312. *beauties rather than faults*: cf. *The Spectator*, no. 291 (2 February 1712).

NO. 101

p. 312. *Mella jubes... api*: Martial, XI.xlii.3–4.

NO. 106

p. 315. *Opinionum... confirmat*: Cicero, *De Natura Deorum*, II.ii.5.

p. 316. *monuments... more conspicuous than pyramids*: Horace, *Odes*, III.30.

p. 316. *Non unquam... Starent superbi*: Seneca, *Troades*, ll .4–6.

p. 317. *Granvilles, Montagues, Stepneys and Sheffields*: all minor poets of the later seventeenth and early eighteenth centuries. George Granville, Lord Lansdowne (1667–1735); statesman, poet, and dramatist; suspected Jacobite; early patron of Pope. Charles Montagu, first earl of Halifax (1661–1715); one of the signatories of the letter of invitation to William of Orange; prime architect, with John Somers, of William III's financial policy in the 1690s; founder of the Bank of England. George Stepney, (1663–1707); poet; Whig diplomat; associate of Halifax and Marlborough. John Sheffield, third earl of Mulgrave and later first duke of Buckingham and Normanby (1648–1721); patron of Dryden and friend of Pope.

p. 317. *Parnassus*: a mountain north of Delphi in Greece; associated with the worship of Apollo and the muses; poetically, the home of the muses.

p. 318. *Boyle's discovery... air*: Robert Boyle (1627–91); experimental scientist and man of letters; assisted by Robert Hooke he performed the experiments on the qualities of air which led to the formulation of Boyle's Law.

p. 318. *as long as books last*: Sir Francis Bacon (1561–1626); lawyer, statesman, philosopher and essayist. The quotation is taken from the 'Dedication' to the *Essays*, although there Bacon's confidence in the *Essays*' longevity seems to be based more on the fact of their existing in a Latin version ('being in the universal language') than on the perennial human centrality of their subject matter.

NO. 108

p. 318. *Sapere aude… ævum*: Horace, *Epistles*, I.ii.40–3.

p. 319. *its greater part… accommodation of man*: Lucretius, *De Rerum Natura*, V.200–9.

p. 321. *Erasmus*: Desiderius Erasmus (1467–1536); humanist, scholar, and man of letters.

p. 321. *without regard to literature*: Erasmus, μωρίας ενκομιον (Basel, 1515), sig. ai^v.

p. 321. *time was his estate*: said of Girolamo Cardano (1501–76); Italian philosopher, doctor, and mathematician.

NO. 113

p. 321. *Uxorem… colubris?*: Juvenal, VI.28–9.

p. 322. *Horace*: 'hic murus aeneus esto, | nil conscire sibi, nulla pallescere culpa' (Horace, *Epistles*, I.i.60–61); 'may this be to us as a wall of bronze—to have no uneasy conscience, no sense of guilt to make us blanch.'

p. 324. *another letter*: The *Rambler*, no. 115, below.

NO. 114

p. 325. *Audi… longa est*: Juvenal, VI.220–1.

p. 325. *Roman satirist… in his hands*: Juvenal, X.96–7.

p. 325. *Boerhaave*: Herman Boerhaave (1668–1738); Dutch physician and professor of medicine. Cf. Johnson's 'Life of Boerhaave' (above, pp. 35–50).

p. 326. τὸ… φοβερώτατον: Aristotle, *Nicomachean Ethics*, III.vi.2.

p. 328. *Sir Thomas More*: Sir Thomas More (1478–1535); lawyer, statesman and humanist; Lord Chancellor 1529–32; friend of Erasmus. Johnson alludes to a passage in Book One of *Utopia* (1516), in which a character, Raphael Hythlodaeus (and thus not More himself), advocates a policy of controlling crime, not by the threat of ever more savage punishments, but by mitigating the poverty which leads people to commit crimes.

NO. 115

p. 328. *Quædam parva... maritis*: Juvenal, VI.184.

p. 329. *Plato... woman*: reported in Lactantius, *Divinae Institutiones*, III.19.

p. 329. *higher species of monkies*: *Letter to a Young Lady on Her Marriage* (1723), in *The Prose Works of Jonathan Swift*, ed. H. Davis et al. (Oxford: Basil Blackwell, 1939–68), vol. IX, pp. 83–94.

NO. 121

p. 332. *O imitatores, servum pecus!*: Horace, *Epistles*, I.xix.19.

p. 333. *great Mantuan poet*: i.e. Virgil.

p. 333. *infernal regions*: *Odyssey*, book XI.

p. 334. *Æneas... to the shades*: *Aeneid*, book VI.

p. 334. *directions to a painter*: a reference to the seventeenth-century vogue, initiated by Waller's panegyrical 'Instructions to a Painter' and sustained in Marvell's satirical 'Last Instructions to a Painter', of composing poems in the form of guidance to a painter.

p. 334. *to have written no language*: a reference to the comment in Ben Jonson's *Timber, or Discoveries* (1640), that 'Spencer, in affecting the Ancients, writ no Language: Yet I would have him read for his matter; but as Virgil read Ennius' (*Ben Jonson*, ed. C.H. Herford and P. and E. Simpson, volume VIII, 'The Poems. The Prose Works' (Oxford: Clarendon Press, 1947), p. 618).

p. 335. *observed by Milton*: a reference to the 'Preface' to *Paradise Lost* and Milton's notorious justification of his own choice of 'English heroic verse without rhyme' for that poem by reference to what he calls 'the troublesome and modern bondage of rhyming'.

p. 335. *imitators of Spenser*: a reference to eighteenth-century imitations of Spenser, of which perhaps the best-known is James Thomson's *The Castle of Indolence* (1748).

p. 335. *in the play*: Shakespeare, *Troilus and Cressida*, II.ii.166.

NO. 129

p. 335. *Nunc, o nunc... meo*: Ovid, *Ars Amatoria*, II.33–8.

p. 337. *Power... from necessity*: *Aurea Carmina*, l. 8.

NO. 134

p. 338. *Quis scit... superi!*: Horace, *Odes*, IV.vii.17–18.

p. 339. *Tantalus*: in Greek mythology, Tantalus was the father of Pelops and Niobe. He was punished in Hades by having the water and food he craved always just out of reach.

p. 340. *Palladio*: Andrea Palladio (1508–80); Italian neo-classical architect of the late Renaissance.

NO. 135

p. 340. *Cœlum…mutant*: Horace, *Epistles*, I.xi.27.

p. 341. *man is an imitative being*: Aristotle, *Poetics*, ch. 1 (1448b 4; *ALC*, p. 94).

p. 342. *the society of solitude*: Milton, *Paradise Lost*, IX.249.

p. 342. *Ptolemaick and Copernican system*: Ptolemy, or Claudius Ptolemaeus (*fl.* 2nd cent. AD), an Alexandrian astronomer, developed a theory of planetary motion which placed the earth in a stationary, central position. This theory held the field until Copernicus, or Nicolas Koppernik (1473–1543), a Polish astronomer, propounded the rival theory that the planets, including the earth, move in orbits around the sun.

p. 342. *Milton justly observes*: Milton, *Paradise Lost*, IX.445–51.

p. 343. *Dryads*: in classical mythology, nymphs associated with trees.

NO. 137

p. 343. *Dum vitant…currunt*: Horace, *Satires*, I.ii.24.

p. 344. *Divide and conquer*: a proverbial saying, dating in English from the early seventeenth century, translating the Latin tag 'divide et impera'.

p. 344. *as Locke has observed*: John Locke, *Of the Conduct of the Understanding*, § 28.

p. 345. *Books…the use of books*: Johnson slightly misremembers a passage from Bacon's essay 'Of Studies': 'Crafty Men Contemne *Studies*; Simple Men Admire them; and Wise Men Use them; For they teach not their owne Use; But that is a Wisdome without them, and above them, won by Observation' (Bacon, *Essayes*, p. 153).

p. 346. *the simile of Longinus*: 'Longinus', *On the Sublime*, IX.13.

NO. 142

p. 346. Ἔνθα δ' ἀνὴρ…σιτοφάγῳ: Homer, *Odyssey*, IX.187–91.

p. 348. *Drake*: Sir Francis Drake (1540?–1596); sailor and circumnavigator of the globe.

p. 349. *replevin*: in law, the restoration to a person of goods taken from him, provided that he undertakes to have the matter tried in a court of law, and to return the goods should the judgement go against him.

p. 349. *if he is hated, he is likewise feared*: an allusion to the saying of the emperor Caligula, who was fond of quoting a line from the tragic poet Accius, 'Oderint, dum metuant'; 'Let them hate me, as long as they also fear me' (Suetonius, 'Gaius Caligula', XXX.2).

NO. 145

p. 350. *Non si priores... Camœnæ*: Horace, *Odes*, IV.ix.5–8. Pindar (*c.*520–*c.*440 BC); major Greek lyric poet. Alcaeus (*fl.* 7–6th cent. BC); Greek lyric poet. Stesichorus (*c.*640–*c.*555 BC); Greek lyric poet.

p. 351. *several thousands*: presumably a reference to the 'Preface' to Swift's *Tale of a Tub*, in which he proposes the erection of a 'large Academy... capable of containing nine thousand seven hundred forty and three Persons; which by modest Computation is reckoned to be pretty near the current Number of Wits in this Island' (Jonathan Swift, *A Tale of a Tub*, ed. A. C. Guthkelch and D. Nichol Smith, 2nd edn (Oxford: Clarendon Press, 1958), p. 41).

p. 352. *hackneyed in the ways of men*: cf. *1 Henry IV*, III.ii.40.

p. 352. *Ephemeræ*: literally, insects which live for only one day; therefore, metaphorically, transient and trifling works.

NO. 146

p. 352. *Sunt illic... Incitato*: Martial, XI.i.13–16.

p. 353. *Crab or Childers*: both the names of race horses of the time.

p. 353. *supplying no children to the commonwealth*: perhaps a confusion in Johnson's mind between the response of the Roman matrons to the attempted violation of Verginia by Appius (Livy, *Ab Urbe Condita*, III.48), and the plot of Aristophanes' *Lysistrata*.

p. 354. *a turtle feast*: a particularly lavish city feast, at which turtle (proverbially a favourite food of aldermen) would be served.

p. 354. *the monument*: the monument to the Great Fire of London; cf. Pope, *Epistle to Bathurst*, ll. 339–40.

NO. 148

pp. 355–6. *Me pater... releget*: Horace, *Odes*, III.xi.45–8.

p. 356. *from the parent to the magistrate*: cf. the Pompeian and Cornelian laws *de sicariis* and *de parricidis*.

p. 357. *the government... naturally monarchical*: Aristotle, *Politics*, I.ii.21.

NO. 151

p. 359. Ἀμφὶ... τυχεῖν: Pindar, *Olympia*, VII.44–8.

p. 359. *climatericks*: a critical or fatal period of life, at which the vital forces begin to decline.

NO. 156

p. 362. *Nunquam aliud...dicit*: Juvenal, XIV.321.

p. 362. *original constitution*: a glance at the Machiavellian doctrine of the *ricorso*.

p. 362. *vacant to her slaves*: Herodotus, IV.i–iv.

p. 363. *only three...upon the stage*: Horace, *Ars Poetica*, l. 192.

p. 363. *Bacchus*: another name for Dionysus; in Greek mythology the son of Zeus and Semele; his cult incorporated elements of ecstasy and mysticism, and he was closely associated with tragedy.

NO. 158

p. 365. *Grammatici certant...lis est*: Horace, *Ars Poetica*, l. 78.

p. 365. *the Meonian eagle*: i.e. Homer.

p. 366. *Ciceronians of the sixteenth century*: a reference to those, such as Roger Ascham (1515–68), who modelled their style on that of Cicero (106–43 BC), the Roman statesman, philosopher, and man of letters. Johnson composed an anonymous 'Life' of Ascham for the 1761 edition of his works.

p. 366. *are perhaps...precept of Horace*: The Spectator, no. 303.

p. 367. *Speciosa... Cyclope Charybdim*: Horace, *Ars Poetica*, ll. 144–5.

p. 367. Ἄνδρα...και ἥμιν: Homer, *Odyssey*, I.1–10.

NO. 159

p. 368. *Sunt verba...partem*: Horace, *Epistles*, I.i.34–5.

p. 368. *Verecundulus*: the author of the letter in *The Rambler*, no. 157.

p. 369. *few have repented...speak*: untraced.

p. 369. *frigorifick*: cooling.

p. 369. *powerful fascination*: Socrates prepares Alcibiades for public life in *Alcibiades I*; cf. especially 105E and 106C.

NO. 161

p. 370. Οἴη γαρ...Ἄνδρων: Homer, *Iliad*, VI.146.

p. 371. *the tomb of Archimedes*: Cicero, *Tusculan Disputations*, V.xxiii.64.

p. 371. *the Conqueror's survey*: the Domesday Book, a register of property compiled on the order of William the Conqueror.

p. 371. *Quantulacunque...magna voco*: Ovid, *Amores*, III.xv.14.

p. 372. *a cousin in Cheapside*: in other words, she was a kept woman.

p. 373. Ὅς...ναίει: Hesiod, *Works and Days*, l. 8.

p. 373. *the observation of Juvenal*: Juvenal, XIII.159–60.

NO. 165

pp. 373–4. Ἦν νέος...τότ' ἔχω: Antiphilus, *Greek Anthology*, IX.138.

NO. 167

p. 377. *Candida perpetuo...anus*: Martial, IV.xiii.7–10.

p. 379. *concordia discors*: 'harmony of dissonance', Horace, *Epistles*, I.xii.19.

NO. 168

p. 380. *Decipit...angulo*: Phædrus, *Fabulae Aesopiae*, IV.ii.5–7.

p. 380. *a mean or common thought...to examine things*: Johnson has in mind this passage, from the opening to 'Reflexion IX' of *Reflexions critiques sur quelques passages du rheteur Longin*: 'Il n'y a rien qui avilisse davantage un discours que les mots bas. On souffrira plutost, generalement parlant, une pensée basse exprimée en termes nobles, que la pensée la plus noble exprimée en termes bas. La raison de cela est, que tout le monde ne peut pas juger de la justesse & de la force d'une pensée: mais qu'il n'y a presque personne, sur tout dans les Langues vivantes, qui ne sente la bassesse des mots' (Nicolas Boileau Despreaux, *Oeuvres de Nicolas Boileau Despreaux*, 'Nouvelle Edition', première partie (Paris, 1713), p. 550).

p. 381. *Come, thick night!...To cry, hold, hold!*: *Macbeth*, I.v.48–52, where the lines are spoken by Lady Macbeth.

p. 382. δόρυ μαίνεται: Homer, *Iliad*, VIII.111.

p. 382. *Si robora...membra secures*: Lucan, *Pharsalia*, III.430–1.

p. 382. *success of Æneas...preternatural beauty*: Virgil, *Aeneid*, I.586–93.

NO. 170

p. 383. *Confiteor...delicta fateri*: Ovid, *Amores*, II.iv.3.

p. 383. *some natural tears...wiped them soon*: Milton, *Paradise Lost*, XII.645.

p. 385. *mercer*: a dealer in silks or velvets.

NO. 171

p. 386. *Tædet cæli convexa tueri*: Virgil, *Aeneid*, IV.451.

p. 388. *pent-house*: 'A shed hanging out aslope from the main wall' (Johnson).

NO. 176

p. 389. *Naso suspendere adunco*: Horace, *Satires*, I.vi.5.

p. 390. *the boar of Erymanth...the lion of Nemea*: two of the six labours of Hercules.

p. 391. *exultations of his antagonist*: Marco Girolamo Vida (1485–1566); Renaissance Latin poet; author of *De Arte Poetica* (1527), influential in eighteenth-century England through the editions by Basil Kennett (Oxford, 1701) and Thomas Tristram (Oxford, 1723), as well as the translation by Christopher Pitt (1725; 2nd edn, 1742). *De Arte Poetica*, III.469–72.

p. 391. *sinistrous*: malicious or prejudiced.

NO. 181

p. 392. *Neu fluitem...horæ*: Horace, *Epistles*, I.xviii.110.

NO. 183

p. 395. *Nulla fides...erat*: Lucan, *Pharsalia*, I.92–3.

p. 396. *ships are but boards*: *Merchant of Venice*, I.iii.20.

NO. 184

p. 397. *Permittes ipsis...nostris*: Juvenal, X.347–8.

NO. 188

p. 400. *Si te colo...non amabo*: Martial, II.lv.3.

p. 401. *Sardinian Laughter*: Homer, *Odyssey*, XX.302 (where it is characterized by a mixture of wrath and scorn).

p. 402. *not always necessary to be reverenced*: a reproof of the Machiavellian doctrine, that it is better for a prince to be feared than loved; see *The Prince*, ch. 17.

NO. 191

p. 403. *Cereus in Vitium...asper.*: Horace, *Ars Poetica*, l. 163.

p. 403. *flambeaus*: large torches; here by extension the bearers of such torches.

p. 404. *leading-strings*: strings with which children are guided and supported when learning to walk.

NO. 196

p. 406. *Multa ferunt... adimunt*: Horace, *Ars Poetica*, ll. 175–6.

p. 406. *Baxter... disposed him to change*: Richard Baxter (1615–91); puritan divine. The reference is to his *Reliquiae Baxterianae*, ed. M. Sylvester (1696), vol. I, pp. 124–38, where the section begins: 'Because it is Soul-Experiments which those that urge me to this kind of Writing, do expect that I should especially communicate to others, and I have said little of God's dealing with my Soul since the time of my younger Years, I shall only give the Reader so much Satisfaction, as to acquaint him truly what Change God hath made upon my Mind and Heart since those unriper times, and wherein I now differ in Judgment and Disposition from my self'.

NO. 207

p. 408. *Solve senescentem... ridendus*: Horace, *Epistles*, I.i.8–9.

p. 409. *the first and the last*: attributed to Palladas, *Greek Anthology*, XI.381.

p. 409. *in procinctu*: to be in readiness.

p. 410. *supervenient*: occurring subsequent to something else.

NO. 208

p. 411. Ἡράκλειτος ἐγώ... Περσεφόνῃ: Diogenes Laertius, *Greek Anthology*, VII.128.

p. 413. *confers a right... known*: Baldassare Castiglione (1478–1529), Italian humanist. *Book of the Courtier*, II.11.

p. 413. *irregular combinations*: here the congruence of *The Rambler* with the *Dictionary* is apparent.

p. 414. Αὐτῶν ἐκ μακάρων... αμοιβή: Dionysius Periegetes, l. 1186.

The Life of Dr Francis Cheynel

Text: *The Student, or, the Oxford and Cambridge Monthly Miscellany*, vol. II (Oxford, 1751), pp. 260–9, 290–4, and 331–4.

Date: July 1751.

p. 414. *Hammond*: Henry Hammond (1605–60); Church of England clergyman and theologian; chaplain to Charles I; canon of Christ Church, Oxford.

p. 414. *Chillingworth*: William Chillingworth (1602–44); theologian; notorious for the volatility of his beliefs.

p. 415. *Dr. Abbot*: Robert Abbot (1559/60–1618); bishop of Salisbury.

p. 415. *Dr. Brent*: Sir Nathanael Brent (1573/74–1652); ecclesiastical lawyer; warden of Merton College, Oxford.

p. 415. *centum...concoquere*: 'to endure a hundred blows with Spartan nobility'; cf. Petronius, *Satyricon*, 105, for the original Latin phrase to which Cheynel is alluding, and which he is embellishing, here ('Et ego quidem *tres* plagas Spartana nobilitate concoxi').

p. 415. *commendam*: the custody of an ecclesiastical benefice in the absence of a regular incumbent (*OED*, 2 a).

p. 416. *Laud*: see above, p. 1177, note to l. 168.

p. 416. *Calamy*: Edmund Calamy (1671–1732); presbyterian minister, historian, and biographer of the dissenting ministers ejected from their livings as a result of the Act of Uniformity (1662).

p. 417. *Colchester*: a slip for Chichester.

p. 417. *Dr. Maizeaux*: Pierre des Maizeaux (1672/73–1745); biographer and journalist.

p. 419. *Wood*: Anthony Wood (or 'à Wood') (1632–95); antiquary.

p. 419. *William Earbury*: William Earbury (1604/5–1654); clergyman.

p. 421. *General Fairfax*: Thomas Fairfax (1612–71), third Lord Fairfax of Cameron; parliamentarian army officer.

p. 421. *Walker*: Anthony Walker (1622–92); clergyman.

p. 421. *Dr. Fell*: Samuel Fell (1584–1649); dean of Christ Church.

p. 422. *Earl of Pembroke*: Philip Herbert (1584–1650), fourth earl of Pembroke; Chancellor of the University of Oxford.

p. 422. *Dr. Bailey*: Richard Baylie (1586–1667); President of St John's College, Oxford (expelled, 1648; restored, 1660); chaplain to Charles I and to archbishop Laud.

p. 423. *Mr. Rouse*: probably Francis Rous (1580/81–1659); religious writer and politician; Speaker in Barebones Parliament; provost of Eton College.

p. 423. *solemn League and Covenant*: an agreement between the English and Scots under which the Scots agreed to support the English Parliamentarians in their disputes with the royalists in return for an undertaking to create a presbyterian and parliamentarian civil and religious union of England, Scotland, and Ireland.

p. 423. *the negative oath*: an oath never to bear arms against Parliament, imposed from 1647 on Royalist gentry who wished to compound for their estates.

p. 423. *Socinian*: followers of Fausto Sozzini (1539–1604), whose teachings undermined the doctrine of the Trinity by denying the divinity of Jesus.

p. 423. *John Fry*: John Fry (*c.*1609–1656/7); religious controversialist.

p. 423. *the engagement*: the oath of loyalty to the Commonwealth imposed in 1651.

p. 424. *the restoration*: of Charles II, in 1660.

Sermon for the Funeral of his Wife

Text: *A Sermon Written by the Late Samuel Johnson...for the Funeral of his Wife* (1788). *Date*: probably March 1752.

Tetty Johnson died on 17 March 1752 OS, and her death cast Johnson into profound grief.

p. 425. *valley of the shadow of death*: cf. Psalm 23:4.

p. 426. *continual contemplation of matter*: Locke had suggested in the *Essay Concerning Human Understanding* (1690) that God could impart to matter the power of thought. The resulting controversy, to which Johnson here alludes, is described and analysed by John Yolton, *Thinking Matter: Materialism in Eighteenth-Century Britain* (Minneapolis: University of Minnesota Press, 1983).

p. 427. *laid up stores for ourselves*: cf. 1 Timothy 6:19.

p. 430. *the night cometh, when no man can work*: cf. John 9:4.

Prayers Composed on the Death of My Wife

Text: taken from the second 1785 edition (pp. 10–13), and the third 1796 edition (p. 15), of *Prayers and Meditations*.

Date: 24 April – 6 May 1752.

p. 431. *Deus exaudi. — Heu!*: 'O Lord, hear — Alas!'

p. 432. *whatever things are true…think upon*: cf. Philippians 4:8.

p. 432. Μακαριοι…απαρτι: 'Blessed are the dead which die in the Lord from henceforth' (Revelation 14:13).

Prayer on Easter Day

Text: *Prayers and Meditations* (1785), pp. 13–14.

Date: 22 April 1753.

Diary entry

Text: *Diaries*, p. 52.

Date: 22 April 1753.

p. 433. *a new wife*: not conclusively identified, but possibly Hill Boothby; see Donald and Mary Hyde, *Dr. Johnson's Second Wife* (Princeton: Princeton University Press, 1953).

Diary entry

Text: *Diaries*, pp. 52–3.

Date: 23 April 1753.

p. 433. *larme à l'oeil*: 'with a tear in my eye'.

p. 433. *Fluunt lachrymae*: 'tears flowed'.

Diary entry

Text: *Diaries*, pp. 53–4.
Date: 29 April 1753.
p. 434. *intenerate*: to make tender or soften (*OED*).

The Adventurer

Text: *The Adventurer* (1754).
Date: 1752–4.
Johnson contributed twenty-nine essays to *The Adventurer*, which ran from 7 November 1752 to 9 March 1754. The publisher was John Payne, one of the triumvirate who had published *The Rambler*. The text for this edition is based on the 'second' edition of 1754, after which Johnson seems to have made no substantive changes to the wording of the essays. He signed his contributions to *The Adventurer* as 'T'.

NO. 39

p. 434. Ὀδυσεύς...χαμάτοιο: Homer, *Odyssey*, V.491–3.

p. 434. *Pallas pour'd...woes*: slightly misquoted. It should read: 'Till *Pallas* pour'd soft slumbers on his eyes; | And golden dreams (the gift of sweet repose) | Lull'd all his cares, and banish'd all his woes' (Pope, *Odyssey*, V.635–7).

p. 434. *Fontenelle*: Bernard le Bovier de Fontenelle (1667–1757); French man of letters. Johnson is thinking of the following conversation, from the 'Premier Soir' of the *Entretiens sur la pluralité des mondes*, in which the character of Fontenelle is speaking to 'la Marquise': 'J'ai toûjours senti ce que vous me dites, reprit-elle, j'aime les Etoiles, & je me plaindrois volontiers du Soleil qui nous les efface. Ah! m'écriai-je, je ne puis lui pardonner de me faire perdre de vûë tous ces Mondes.... je me suis mis dans la tête que chaque Etoile pourroit bien être un Monde' (*Entretiens sur la Pluralité des Mondes*, 'Nouvelle Edition' (La Haye, 1733), p.15).

p. 435. *the pleasant...the silent*: Milton, *Paradise Lost*, V.38–9.

p. 435. *more shadowy...things*: Milton, *Paradise Lost*, V.43.

p. 435. *Ramazzini*: Bernardino Ramazzini (1633–1714); Italian physician.

p. 435. *Alexander declared...without Sleep*: Plutarch, *Lives*, 'Alexander', XXII.

p. 435. *Clelia*: the romance by Madeleine de Scudéry, *Clélie* (1654–61).

p. 435. *supremely cursed with immortality*: a reference to the Struldbrugs, in Part III of Swift's *Gulliver's Travels* (1726).

p. 435. *Phæacia.*: cf. the motto for this paper.

p. 435. *Barretier*: perhaps Barezzi (*fl.* early 17th cent.); Italian printer and savant.

p. 436. *dragg...along*: Pope, *An Essay on Criticism*, l. 357.

p. 436. *waking nights*: Publius Papinius Statius (*c*.40–96 AD); Roman epic and miscellaneous poet. *Sylvae*, V.4.

p. 437. *Cowley*: *Sex Libri Plantarum*, IV.49–60.

p. 438. *that I dare . . . my prayers*: Sir Thomas Browne (1605–82); doctor and prose writer; author of *Religio Medici* (1643). *Religio Medici*, II.12.

NO. 45

p. 438. *Nulla fides . . . erit*: Lucan, *Pharsalia*, I.92–3.

p. 438. *Pereant . . . ungula campum*: Statius, *Thebaid*, VI.400–1.

p. 438. *Hills, vales . . . lost*: Pope, *Windsor Forest*, ll. 153–4.

p. 439. *There never appear . . . before them*: Johnson here is misremembering the comment Swift made in a letter to Pope of 20 September 1723; 'I have often endeavoured to establish a Friendship among all Men of Genius, and would fain have it done. they are seldom above three or four Cotemporaries and if they could be united would drive the world before them'.

NO. 50

p. 441. *Quicunque turpi . . . fidem*: Phaedrus, I.x.1–2.

p. 441. *not to be credited . . . truth*: Diogenes Laertius, *Lives*, 'Aristotle', XI.

p. 441. *The devils . . . without it*: for Browne, see above, note to p. 438. *Pseudodoxia Epidemica*, I.xi.16.

p. 442. *that every man . . . they have not seen*: Sir Kenelm Digby (1603–65); author, sailor, and diplomat. Quotation untraced.

NO. 67

p. 444. *Inventas . . . per artes*: Virgil, *Aeneid*, VI.663.

p. 445. *how many things . . . I do not want!*: Diogenes Laertius, *Lives*, 'Socrates', IX.

NO. 69

p. 448. *Ferè libenter . . . credunt*: Caesar, *Gallic War*, III.18.

p. 448. *for another year*: Cicero, *De Senectute*, VII.24.

p. 449. *floats lazily down the stream*: cf. ll. 347–48 of *The Vanity of Human Wishes* for another, although slightly differing, use of this metaphor (above, p. 172).

NO. 84

p. 452. *Tolle periclum…remotis*: Horace, *Satires*, II.vii.73–4.

p. 452. *the rest of the world*: Sir William Temple, 'Of Poetry', in his *Works* (1757), vol. III, p. 425.

p. 452. *Don Quixote's inn*: Cervantes, *Don Quixote*, pt. 1, chs. 32–47.

p. 455. *Viator*: i.e. traveller.

NO. 85

p. 455. *Qui cupit…puer*: Horace, *Ars Poetica*, ll. 412–13.

p. 455. *observed by Bacon*: in 'Of Studies' (Bacon, *Essayes*, p. 153); cf. above, p. 1195, note to p. 345, for another reference by Johnson to this essay in *The Rambler*.

p. 456. *opinion has of late been*: Johnson here caricatures and attacks some of the attitudes associated most notoriously with French philosophers such as D'Alembert, who in the 'Discours Préliminaire' to the *Encyclopédie* had recently disparaged scholarship.

p. 457. *knowledge…to possess it*: Persius, I.27.

p. 457. *as Pope expresses it*: Pope, *The Dunciad*, III.182.

p. 457. *Boerhaave complains*: cf. above, p. 1193, note to p. 325. *Elementa Chemiæ* (1733), I. 'Propositum'.

NO. 95

p. 459. *Dulcique…tenebo*: Ovid, *Metamorphoses*, IV.284.

p. 459. *equal readiness*: cf. Johnson's comment about his own *Rasselas* and Voltaire's *Candide*, 'that if they had not been published so closely one after the other that there was not time for imitation, it would have been in vain to deny that the scheme of that which came latest was taken from the other' (*Life*, p. 182).

p. 461. *discovered by Sir Isaac Newton*: Newton's work on colour, including the demonstration of the seven primary colours, was the subject of experiments he performed in 1665 and 1666. These experiments later formed the basis of a paper he delivered at the Royal Society in 1672 (subsequently published in the *Philosophical Transactions* for that year), and for the first book of his *Opticks* (1704).

NO. 99

p. 462. *Magnis…ausis* : Ovid, *Metamorphoses*, II.328.

p. 462. *he who can…fortunate*: Sir William Temple, 'Of Heroick Virtue', in his *Works* (1757), vol. III, p. 306, where Temple in fact says that the 'excellency of genius' necessary for heroic virtue 'must be assisted by fortune, to preserve it to maturity'.

p. 463. *that he always...could think*: *Coriolanus*, IV.v.167–8.

p. 463. *traitors and incendiaries*: Machiavelli, *Discorsi*, I.x.

p. 463. *Alexander the Great*: cf. *The Vanity of Human Wishes*, l. 179 (above, p. 168). For another instance of contemporary disparagement of Alexander the Great, see Alexander Pope, *An Essay on Man*, IV.217–20.

p. 464. *to learn...the art of war*: cf. *The Vanity of Human Wishes*, l. 210 (above, p. 169).

p. 465. *the Orrery*: a clockwork mechanism designed to show the movement of the planets around the sun. The actual inventor was George Graham (1673–1711), John Rowley being the instrument-maker who realized his design.

p. 465. *Boyle*: Robert Boyle (1627–91); experimental scientist; founder of the Boyle Lectures, of which the purpose was to demonstrate the congruence of natural and revealed religion.

p. 465. *immoderata...semper cupiebat*: 'his soul craved the excessive, the incredible, the gigantic'; Sallust, *Catiline*, V.5.

p. 465. *union of the Thames and Severn by a canal*: such a canal was in fact constructed and opened in 1789.

p. 465. *turning the Nile into the Red Sea*: in 1513 Afonso de Albuquerque (1453–1515), the Portuguese viceroy, proposed such a scheme for the reduction of Egypt.

NO. 102

p. 466. *Quid tam...peracti*: Juvenal, X.5–6.

p. 466. *fining for Sheriff*: that is, paying a fine in lieu of shouldering the office.

p. 467. *to tell him...how I hate his beams*: Milton, *Paradise Lost*, IV.37.

p. 468. *corruption of his countrymen*: Marcus Tullius Cicero (106–43 BC) and Demosthenes (383–322 BC), both great orators of respectively republican Rome and ancient Athens; Hannibal (247–182 BC), supreme military commander of the Carthaginians, whose audacious invasion of Italy during the Second Punic War ended in retreat, attributed by some to Hannibal's own reluctance to pursue an advantage, by others to the enervating effects of Italian luxury on the morale of his troops.

p. 469. *Mercator*: i.e. merchant.

NO. 107

p. 469. *Sub judice lis est*: Horace, *Ars Poetica*, l. 78.

p. 470. *a general...fit for tillage*: for Sir Kenelm Digby, see above, p. 1204, note to p. 442. Johnson is here paraphrasing the end of his *Observations upon Religio Medici* (1643).

p. 471. *Through which...to lose it*: *Greek Anthology*, IX.epigr.359.

p. 471. *You may pass...its felicity*: *Greek Anthology*, IX.epigr.360.

NO. III

p. 472. *Quæ non...voco*: Ovid, *Metamorphoses*, XIII.140–1.

p. 473. *a tragic poet*: Seneca, *Troades*, l. 1023.

p. 474. *res non parta...themselves*: Martial, X.xlvii.3.

p. 475. *says South*: Robert South (1634–1716); court preacher favoured by Charles II, and who specialized in attacking Dissenters. The reference is to South's sermon on Proverbs 3:17, 'Her Wayes are Wayes of Pleasantness', in which however Johnson has substituted idleness for South's pleasure as the thing men eventually shun: 'The most Voluptuous, and loose person breathing, were he but tyed to follow his Hawks, and his Hounds, his Dice, and his Courships every day, would find it the greatest Torment, and Calamity that could befal him; he would flie to the *Mines* and the *Gallyes* for his Recreation, and to the Spade and the Mattock for a Diversion from the misery of a Continuall un-intermitted Pleasure' (Robert South, *Sermons Preached Upon Several Occasions* (Oxford, 1679), p. 190).

p. 476. *Permittes...homo quam sibi.*: Juvenal, X.347–8, 350.

NO. 119

p. 476. *Latiùs regnes...Serviat uni*: Horace, *Odes*, II.ii.9–12.

p. 476. *which of mortal men...fewest things*: Diogenes Laertius, *Lives*, 'Socrates', XI.

p. 476. *to be Diogenes*: Plutarch, *Lives*, 'Alexander', XIV.

p. 478. *virtuosos*: a connoisseur or savant in the realm of the fine arts, antiquities or natural curiosities; but with overtones of dilettanteism and shallowness.

p. 479. *tears on other occasions*: related of M. L. Crassus by Plutarch (*Moralia*, 89, 811, and 976), and of Hortensius by Pliny (*Natural History*, IX.172).

p. 479. *he that...blood of a man*: Iamblichus, *Life of Pythagoras*, XXX.

p. 479. *How many things...I do not want*: Diogenes Laertius, *Lives*, 'Socrates', IX.

NO. 126

p. 479. *Steriles...pulvere verum*: Lucan, *Pharsalia*, IX.576–7.

p. 481. *when he conferred with Egeria*: Plutarch, *Lives*, 'Numa', IV.

p. 482. *to pass through...things eternal*: cf. 2 Corinthians 4:18.

NO. 137

p. 482. Τίδ'ἔρεξα: Pythagoras, *Aurea Carmina*, XLII.

p. 483. *shackle the torrent*: Xerxes, when a bridge of ships thrown across the Hellespont to enable him to invade Greece had been destroyed by a storm, had chains thrown over the sea, as a symbol of his mastery; cf. *The Vanity of Human Wishes*, l. 232 (above, p. 169).

    p. 484. *the rearward of the fashion*: 2 *Henry IV*, III.ii.339.

NO. 138

    p. 486. *Quid purè … vitæ?*: Horace, *Epistles*, I.xviii.102–3.

    p. 487. *by Horace*: 'cui lecta potenter erit res, | nec facundia deseret hunc nec lucidus ordo' (Horace, *Ars Poetica*, ll. 40–1).

Letter to Thomas Warton

Text: Redford, vol. I, pp. 81–2.

Date: 16 July 1754.

Thomas Warton (1728–90); poet and scholar; fellow of Trinity College, Oxford; first historian of English poetry.

    p. 489. *the book … favour me*: Warton's *Observations on The Faerie Queene of Spenser* (1754).

    p. 489. *Hughes*: John Hughes (1677–1720); historian, poet, and translator.

    p. 489. *my book*: i.e. the *Dictionary*, which would be published in 1755.

A Dictionary of the English Language: Preface

Text: *A Dictionary of the English Language*, vol. I (1755), sigs. A1^r – C2^v.

Date: 15 April 1755.

    p. 492. *Quid te … una?*: 'What benefit is it to you to remove one amongst many thorns?' (Horace, *Epistles*, II.ii.212).

    p. 493. *Hammond*: see above, p. 1200, note to p. 414.

    p. 493. *Hooker*: Richard Hooker (1554–1600); theologian and philosopher. Johnson is thinking of the following sentence, from Book IV of the *Lawes of Ecclesiastical Polity*: 'But true withal it is, that Alteration, though it be from worse to better, hath in it inconveniencies, and those weighty; …' (Hooker, pp. 181–2).

    p. 494. *words are … sons of heaven*: cf. Genesis 6:4. Samuel Madden's *Boulter's Monument* (1745) contains the line '*Words* are *Mens* Daughters, but GOD's Sons are *Things*' (l. 377), which in a footnote is glossed as '*A famous Axiom of the great* Hippocrates' (p. 40).

    p. 495. *Junius and Skinner*: both notable philologists. Francis Junius (or Du Jon) (1591–1677), whose *Etymologicon Anglicanum* was published posthumously in 1743. Stephen Skinner (1623–67), whose *Etymologicon Linguae Anglicanae* was published in 1671.

    p. 497. *Bailey, Ainsworth, Philips*: Nathan Bailey (1691–1742); lexicographer and schoolmaster. Robert Ainsworth (1660–1743); lexicographer and schoolmaster. Edward Phillips (1630–96?); writer and biographer.

p. 499. *Tully*: Marcus Tullius Cicero (106–43 BC); Roman statesman, lawyer, scholar, and writer. *Tusculan Disputations*, II.xxiii.55.

p. 499. *Aristotle*: cf. *Iliad* X.84.

p. 501. *before the restoration*: i.e. of Charles II in 1660.

p. 501. *the wells of English undefiled*: in *The Faerie Queene* Spenser praises 'Dan *Chaucer*, well of English vndefyled' (IV.ii.32).

p. 501. *Sidney*: Sir Philip Sidney (1554–86); author, soldier, and courtier.

p. 501. *the time of Elizabeth*: Elizabeth I reigned from 1558 to 1603.

p. 502. *Bacon*: Francis Bacon (1561–1626); lord chancellor, politician, and philosopher.

p. 502. *Raleigh*: Sir Walter Ralegh (1554–1618); courtier, explorer, and author.

p. 502. *Spenser*: Edmund Spenser (1552?–1599); poet and colonial administrator.

p. 504. *the first inhabitants of Arcadia*: in Renaissance mythology, Arcadia is the imaginary location of a life of innocence lived according to the principles of the Golden Age.

p. 504. *academicians della Crusca*: the Accademia della Crusca was founded in Florence in 1582 for the purpose of purifying and stabilizing the Tuscan dialect. Their official dictionary, the *Vocabolario degli Accademici della Crusca*, was first published in 1612.

p. 504. *Buonaroti*: see above, p. 1171, note to p. 65.

p. 506. *to lash the wind*: an allusion to the petulance of Xerxes; cf. above, pp. 1207–8, note to p. 483, and *The Vanity of Human Wishes*, l. 232 (above, p. 169). Note, however, that Xerxes chained the sea, not the wind.

p. 506. *The French language...the academy*: the Académie française was established by Cardinal Richelieu in 1634, and was entrusted with the defence of literary taste and the fixing of French literary language.

p. 506. *Amelot...father Paul...Le Courayer*: see above, p. 1165, notes to p. 19.

p. 506. *un peu passé*: a little old-fashioned.

p. 506. *Boccace*: Giovanni Boccaccio (1313–75); Italian poet and scholar.

p. 506. *Machiavel*: Niccolo Machiavelli (1469–1527); Italian statesman, writer, and political theorist; secretary of the Florentine republic.

p. 506. *Caro*: Annibale Caro (1507–66); Italian poet, translator, and ambassador.

p. 506. *the revolutions...of the tide*: cf. the insane astronomer in chap. XLI of *Rasselas* who believes he controls 'the regulation of weather, and the distribution of the seasons' (above, p. 697).

p. 507. *Swift...English language*: *A Proposal for Correcting, Improving and Ascertaining the English Tongue* (1712).

p. 508. *Boyle*: possibly Roger Boyle (1621–79), first earl of Orrery; politician and writer; more probably, Robert Boyle (1627–91); natural philosopher.

p. 508. *Scaliger*: for Scaliger, see above, p. 1192, note to p. 311. See Johnson's repetition of this anecdote in Γνωθι σεαυτον, the poem he composed on completing the revision of the *Dictionary* (above, pp. 791–92).

p. 509. *Beni*: Paolo Beni (1552–1625); Italian jesuit, orator, theologian, poet, and philosopher. Beni's attack on the *Vocabolario degli Accademici della Crusca*, the

Anticrusca overo il Paragone dell'italiana lingua, was also published in 1612 (while bearing the date 1613).

Letter to the Earl of Chesterfield

Text: Redford, vol. I, pp. 94–7.

Date: 7 February 1755.

Philip Dormer Stanhope (1694–1773), fourth earl of Chesterfield; politician and man of letters. Johnson had dedicated his *Plan of a Dictionary* to Chesterfield in 1747. Chesterfield affected to be so unconcerned by this letter that he displayed a copy of it on his hall table for visitors to inspect and admire.

  p. 509. *the Proprietor… Lordship*: Chesterfield's papers praising the *Dictionary* had appeared in nos. 100 and 101 of *The World*.

  p. 509. *Le Vainqueur… de la Terre*: 'the conqueror of the conqueror of the world'; a slight misquotation of a line from Scudéry's *Alaric*, which had been quoted by Boileau in his *Art poétique* (III.272).

  p. 509. *Seven years*: a mordant echo of Horace, *Satires*, II.vi.40–2.

  p. 509. *The Shepherd… Rocks*: a reference to Virgil, *Eclogues*, VIII.43–4.

Letter to Bennet Langton

Text: Redford, vol. I, pp. 105–7.

Date: 6 May 1755.

Bennet Langton the Younger (1737–1801); man of letters who cultivated the friendship of Johnson.

  p. 510. *my Book*: see above, p. 1208, note to p. 489.

  p. 510. *your Father*: Bennet Langton the Elder (1696–1769); Sheriff of Lincolnshire.

Letter to Miss Hill Boothby

Text: Redford, vol. I, pp. 119–21.

Date: 31 December 1755.

Hill Boothby (1708–56); spinster known to Johnson since 1739.

  p. 511. *your book*: unidentified, but evidently a theological work. Though pious, Hill Boothby's religious opinions did not entirely coincide with those of Johnson.

  p. 511. *scruples*: a scruple is one twenty-fourth of an ounce.

  p. 512. *A Dieu… commende*: 'I commend you to God'.

  p. 512. *Miss*: Selina Fitzherbert (*d.*1823); protégée of Hill Boothby.

Letter to Miss Hill Boothby

Text: Redford, vol. I, p. 121.
Date: 8 January 1756.

Letter to Samuel Richardson

Text: Redford, vol. I, p. 132.
Date: 16 March 1756.
Samuel Richardson (1689–1761); printer and author. Richardson's nephew, William, sent Johnson six guineas (i.e. £6. 6s, and thus 8s more than Johnson requested) on receipt of this letter.

An Introduction to the Political State of Great-Britain

Text: *The Literary Magazine*, vol. I (1756), pp. 2–9.
Date: 15 May 1756.
Between April and either October or November of 1756 Johnson was the founding editor of *The Literary Magazine, or Universal Review*, to which he also contributed many articles. 'An Introduction to the Political State of Great Britain' shows Johnson offering a sceptical analysis of the history of the interactions and colonial ambitions of the European powers, and of the political developments which had led Britain to the threshold of the Seven Years' War. Although this conflict would end gloriously for Great Britain, its early phases were littered with reversal and catastrophe.

p. 513. *a compact*: the Treaty of Tordesillas (1494).

p. 516. *relieve Rochelle*: in 1627.

p. 517. *Pen and Venables*: Sir William Penn (1621–70); admiral and founder of Pennsylvania. Robert Venables (1612/13–1687); parliamentarian army officer.

p. 519. *the narrow seas*: i.e. the Channel and the North Sea.

p. 519. *the ministry of Colbert*: Jean-Baptiste Colbert (1619–83); adviser to Louis XIV and controller general of the royal finances from 1665 to 1683.

p. 521. *at La Hogue*: in 1692.

p. 522. *A peace was at length made*: by the Treaty of Ryswick in 1697.

p. 522. *the then darling of England*: cf. Johnson's bitter assessment of Anne as 'little more than the slave of the Marlborough family' (above, p. 71).

p. 522. *war against France*: the War of the Spanish Succession (1702–14).

p. 522. *those ... most loudly against it*: i.e. the Whigs.

p. 523. *benefit of England*: Cabot's expedition occurred in 1497.

p. 524. *dishonourably defeated*: in July 1755.

Review of An Essay on the Writings and Genius of Pope

Text: *The Literary Magazine*, vol. I (1756), pp. 35–8.

Date: 15 May 1756.

Joseph Warton (1722–1800); poet and literary critic; elder brother of Thomas Warton (see above, p. 1208, headnote to *Letter to Thomas Warton*). His *An Essay on the Writings and Genius of Pope* was published in 1756, and would be supplemented by a second volume in 1782. Warton praises Pope, but also wishes to enforce his opinion that the kind of poetry in which Pope excelled was not the highest kind of poetry.

p. 526. *Somerville*: William Somervile (1675–1742); poet. His most famous poem, *The Chace*, had been published in 1735.

p. 527. *Mr. Spence*: Joseph Spence (1699–1768); literary scholar and anecdotist.

p. 528. *Flatman*: Thomas Flatman (1635–88); painter and poet.

p. 528. *Baillet*: Adrien Baillet, *Des Enfans devenus célèbres par leurs études et par leurs écrits* (1688).

p. 529. *Sternhold and Hopkins*: Thomas Sternhold (*d.*1549) and John Hopkins (1520/21–1570); metrical translators of the Psalms.

p. 529. *Tassoni*: Alessandro Tassoni (1565–1635); Italian satirist, literary critic, and political writer; author of *La Secchia Rapita* ('The Rape of the Bucket').

p. 529. *Boileau*: Nicolas Boileau (1636–1711); poet and literary critic; author of *Le Lutrin*.

p. 529. *Garth*: Sir Samuel Garth (1660/61–1719); physician and poet; author of *The Dispensary*.

p. 529. *Cato*: *Cato* (1713), a tragedy on the subject of the death at Utica of Cato the Younger, was written by Joseph Addison (1672–1719), poet and politician.

p. 530. *Rowe*: Nicholas Rowe (1674–1718); playwright and poet.

Review of Thomas Blackwell, Memoirs of the Court of Augustus

Text: *The Literary Magazine*, vol. I (1756), pp. 41–2 and 239–40.

Date: 15 May 1756.

Thomas Blackwell (1701–57); classical scholar and historian. His *Memoirs of the Court of Augustus*, published in three volumes between 1753 and 1763, were an attempt to apply the nascent Scottish 'science of man' to ancient history. Johnson's antipathy to the book reveals his suspicions of the intellectual innovations characteristic of the Scottish Enlightenment.

p. 531. *magnificent promises*: cf. Horace, *Ars Poetica*, ll. 138–9.

p. 532. *Horace...Sabinum*: 'You will drink cheap Sabine wine' (Horace, *Odes*, I.xx.1); Horace's self-deprecating opening to a poetic invitation to his rich patron, Maecenas (see above, p. 1171, note to p. 66).

Observations on the Present State of Affairs

Text: *The Literary Magazine*, vol. I (1756), pp. 161–5.
Date: 15 August 1756.
A continuation to the 'Introduction to the Political State of Great-Britain' (above, pp. 513–25).

p. 538. *the last war*: the War of the Austrian Succession (1740–8), which had been concluded by the Treaty of Aix-la-Chapelle.

p. 539. *New-Scotland*: i.e. Nova Scotia.

p. 540. *the alliance of a nation*: i.e. France.

p. 540. *Dettingen…Fontenoy…Val*: battles in the War of the Austrian Succession, fought in, respectively, 1743, 1745, and 1747.

p. 542. *(To be continued.)*: there was in the event no continuation.

Review of Jonas Hanway, An Essay on Tea

Text: *The Literary Magazine*, vol. II (1757), pp. 161–7.
Date: 15 May 1757.

p. 544. *what Shakespeare ascribes to the concealment of love*: possibly thinking of *Titus Andronicus*, II.iv.36–7: 'Sorrow conceal̀d, like an oven stopped | Doth burn the heart to cinders where it is.'

p. 545. *Athenian cicuta*: hemlock, a vigorous poison.

p. 545. *copperas*: ferrous sulphate, commonly known as green vitriol; used in dyeing, tanning, and making ink (*OED*).

p. 545. *Paulli*: Simon Paulli (1603–80); botanist. His *Commentarius de abusi tabaci et herbae theae* had been published in 1666.

p. 547. *Bedlam*: the common name for the Hospital of St Mary of Bethlehem, a London lunatic asylum which in 1676 was relocated from Bishopsgate to London Wall.

Review of Soame Jenyns, A Free Inquiry

Text: *The Literary Magazine*, vol. II (1757), pp. 171–5, 251–3, and 301–6.
Date: 15 May 1757.
Soame Jenyns (1704–87), writer and politician, published his *A Free Enquiry into the Nature and Origin of Evil* in 1757. Its rationalist theodicy was an affront to Johnson's more traditional Christian beliefs.

p. 549. *while we see but in part*: cf. 1 Corinthians 13:12.

p. 550. *the Manichean system*: a religious system with Christian, Gnostic, and pagan elements, widespread in the Roman Empire and Asia, based on the supposed primeval conflict between light and darkness, and representing Evil as coeternal with God; (more generally) dualism (*OED*).

p. 550. *the system of Mr. Pope*: as expressed in *An Essay on Man* (1733–4); for Johnson's low opinion of this poem, see above, pp. 1116–17.

p. 551. *cut the Gordian knot*: it was a superstition of the Phrygians that whoever could unloose the complicated knot whereby their king Gordius had fastened the yoke to the pole of his wagon would gain the empire of Asia. On being told this, Alexander the Great cut the knot with his sword.

p. 551. *the system of subordination*: cf. A. O. Lovejoy, *The Great Chain of Being* (1936).

p. 553. *Cheyne*: George Cheyne (1671–1743); physician and philosopher.

p. 553. *Qui pauca considerat, facile pronunciat*: 'He who considers few things finds it easy to decide'. A proverbial general rule often quoted in the earlier eighteenth century: cf., e.g., Anon., *Scrinia Reclusa* (1709), p. 125.

p. 555. *a little learning...a dangerous thing*: Pope, *An Essay on Criticism* (1711), l. 215.

p. 558. *the latter end...beginning*: cf. Shakespeare, *The Tempest*, II.i.155.

p. 559. *For fools...fear to tread*: Pope, *An Essay on Criticism* (1711), l. 625.

p. 559. *To die... 'tis o'er*: Sir Samuel Garth, *The Dispensary* (1699), Canto III, ll. 225–7; cf. above, p. 1212, note to p. 529.

p. 561. *Blenheim...Prague*: the battles of Blenheim (1704) and Prague (1757) were both notorious for heavy casualties.

p. 565. *Si sic omnia dixisset!*: 'If only all he said were like this!'

p. 566. *And found...mazes lost*: Milton, *Paradise Lost*, II.561.

p. 568. *Chrysippus's untractableness of matter*: Chrysippus (*fl.* 3rd century BC); Stoic philosopher. The Stoics believed that the creator of the world was unable to disregard or overcome the nature of the matter he had employed.

p. 568. *the hand...temple*: Johnson has misremembered and embellished a phrase in William Burton's *An Account of the Life and Writings of Herman Boerhaave* (1743), p. 133.

Of the Duty of a Journalist

Text: Payne's *Universal Chronicle*, no. 1, 8 April 1758, pp. 1–2.
Date: 8 April 1758.

The Idler

Text: *The Idler* (1761).
Date: between 8 April 1758 and 1760.
Lighter in tone and shorter in length than both *The Rambler* and *The Adventurer*, these essays were published as leading articles in *Payne's Universal Chronicle*, a new weekly newspaper. Johnson, then occupied in his edition of Shakespeare, had been

induced to contribute to the newspaper by the promise of a share in the profits. The text for this edition has been taken from the second edition of 1761.

NO. 1

p. 570. *Vacui...lusimus*: Horace, *Odes*, I.xxxii.1–2.

p. 571. *to beg a name*: Johnson refers to the *Universal Spectator* (1728–46), the *Female Spectator* (1744–6), the *Spectator* (1753–4), and the *Tatler Revived* (1750).

NO. 5

p. 572. Κάλλος...ἀπάντων: *Carmina Anacreontea*, XXIV.9–11. The whole of the short lyric from which Johnson quotes the penultimate sentence may be translated as follows: 'Nature gave horns to bulls, hooves to horses, swiftness to hares, a wide mouth full of teeth to lions, the power of swimming to fish, flight to birds, wisdom to men. But for women she had nothing left. And so? She gives them beauty, strong as any shield, strong as any sword. A beautiful woman prevails over even steel or flame.'

p. 573. *the Salic law*: the alleged fundamental law of the French monarchy, which excluded females from the succession; cf. Shakespeare, *Henry V*, I.ii.33–95.

p. 574. *defeated by women*: on 9 July 1755, at Fort Duquesne.

p. 574. *Minorca*: surrendered to the French on 28 June 1756.

p. 574. *return in safety*: the expedition against Rochefort had been launched in September 1756, and had been a fiasco.

NO. 10

p. 574. *Cartesian*: that is, a follower of René Descartes (1596–1650), French philosopher and mathematician, whose dualistic philosophy in which mind and body were rigidly separated enabled the denial of finer sensations to animals.

p. 574. *Disciple of Malebranche*: Nicolas Malebranche (1638–1715); French theologian and philosopher who expounded the doctrine of Cartesian dualism.

p. 574. *Follower of Berkley*: George Berkeley (1685–1753); notorious, because much misunderstood, immaterialist philosopher. Boswell records a famous incident when Johnson, challenged to refute Berkeley's philosophy, 'answered, striking his foot with mighty force against a large stone, till he rebounded from it, "I refute it *thus*" ' (*Life*, p. 248).

p. 575. *the ruin of England*: Tom Tempest interprets recent English history as a conspiracy carried on by the Hanoverians and their adherents against the Stuarts. His beliefs comprise a caricatured Jacobite creed.

p. 576. *never be a Papist*: Jack Sneaker is the obverse of Tom Tempest, and subscribes to a caricatured Whig creed.

NO. 17

p. 577. *Leeuwenhoeck*: Antoine van Leeuwenhoek (1632–1723); Dutch microscopist; the first man to observe bacteria.

p. 577. *would pass for a Philosopher*: Richard Mead, *Of the Small-Pox and Measles* (1747), 'Preface', pp. v–vi. Mead is discussing '*a malevolent sort of men, who endeavour all they can to villify and depreciate other people's works, as if they added to their own reputation in proportion as they detracted from others*' (p. v), and for Mead the '*chief among them was* John Woodward, *Gresham professor, who serv'd an apprenticeship to a Linnen Draper, and afterwards from having got together an heap of shells, pebbles, and such like fossells, would pass for a Philosopher*' (p. vi).

NO. [22]

p. 578. *9 September 1758*: this essay was not included by Johnson in the collected edition of *The Idler*, presumably on account of the sombreness of its vision.

NO. 27

p. 585. *He that endeavours…slow advances*: Bacon, *Essayes*, 'Of Nature in Men', where however the text reads 'Hee that seeketh Victory over his *Nature*, let him not set Himselfe too great, nor too small Tasks: For the first, will make him dejected by often Faylings; And the Second will make him a small Proceeder, though by often Prevailings' (Bacon, *Essayes*, p. 119).

p. 585. *Pauci…æthera virtus*: Virgil, *Aeneid*, VI.129–30.

NO. 30

p. 586. *Sir Henry Wotton's*: Sir Henry Wotton (1568–1639); Provost of Eton, 1624–39; diplomat and man of letters. The definition was written by Wotton in the commonplace book of a friend; cf. Logan Pearsall Smith, *Life and Letters of Sir Henry Wotton* (Oxford: Clarendon Press, 1907), vol. II, pp. 9–11.

NO. 31

p. 587. *lustre and its shade*: a slight misquotation of Samuel Butler, *Hudibras*, II.i.905–8.

p. 587. *Busiris…calls himself the Proud*: Edward Young, *Busiris, King of Egypt. A Tragedy* (1719), I.i.13, p. 2, where Syphaces says of Busiris 'He calls himself the *Proud*, and Glories in it.'

p. 587. *tell him how they hate his beams*: Milton, *Paradise Lost*, IV.37.

NO. 32

p. 589. *levelled by Death*: Claudian, *De raptu Proserpinæ*, II.302.
p. 589. *necessity of Sleep*: Plutarch, *Lives*, 'Alexander', XXII.3–4.

NO. 36

p. 591. *shortest train of intermediate propositions*: Richard Cumberland (1631–1718); bishop of Peterborough; adversary of Hobbes (which no doubt recommended him to Johnson). The passage Johnson has in mind is the following: 'such Acts which, in the shortest Method, produce the principal Effect as their chief End, are, in their own Nature, Acts strait and right, upon account of that natural Similitude which they bear to a right Line; which Line, between any two given Points, is always the shortest. These very same Acts, however, when they come afterwards to be compared with any Law (whether natural or instituted) as the Rule of Action; and , when such Acts are found to agree, and are conformable to such a *Law* or *Rule*, they then are called *morally good*, or exactly strait and right, *i.e.* they are well and exactly fitted to such a Rule. For, the Rule itself is called strait and right, because it directs and shews the shortest Way to the End proposed' (*Philosophical Enquiry into the Laws of Nature* (1750), 'Prolegomena', sect. xvi, pp. xlv–xlvi).

p. 591. *to drink Tea by stratagem*: *Hudibras*, I.i.125–6; *Satires*, VI.188.

p. 592. *the Ares… to the west*: John Petvin, *Letters Concerning Mind* (1750), pp. 40–1 (with some trivial deviations from Petvin's actual words).

NO. 40

p. 596. *took Dieskaw*: Louis-Auguste Dieskau (1701–67); soldier, German by birth; entered into French service as the aide-de-camp of the maréchal de Saxe; commander of the French troops in Canada, 1755. He was taken prisoner at the Battle of Lake George, 8 September 1755.

p. 596. *Eau de Luce*: a mixture of alcohol, ammonia, and amber, which was used in India as a cure for snake-bites, and in England as smelling-salts.

NO. 41

p. 597 *At tu quisquis eris… morsque gradu*: these verses were composed by Johnson himself on the death of his mother (*Poems*, pp. 146 and 230–1). 'But you, whoever you may be, you who thought the untimely death of an unhappy poet worthy of your tears; may this be your last time to weep, and may life and death for you flow smoothly on with an even pace.'

p. 598. *says Tully*: 'nemo enim est tam senex qui se annum non putet posse vivere' (Cicero, *De Senectute*, VII.24).

p. 598. *There is joy . . . one sinner that repenteth*: Luke 15:10.

p. 599. *Life and Immortality to light*: 2 Timothy 1:10.

p. 599. *cannot assuage it*: Epicurus (341–270 BC) and Zeno of Citium (*c*.335–*c*.263 BC), both ancient Greek philosophers, of whose doctrines Johnson here supplies succinct accounts.

p. 599. *wiped from the eyes*: Revelation 21:4.

NO. 44

p. 600. *art of Forgetfulness*: Themistocles (*fl*. early 5th cent. BC); Athenian statesman and commander. Cicero, *De Finibus*, II.xxxii.104.

NO. 48

p. 601. *Tom Distich*: a comic name for a follower of the theatre.

p. 601. *Malouin privateer*: a pirate based in the port of St. Malo, in Brittany.

NO. 49

p. 602. *king of Prussia*: Frederick II, or the Great (1712–86).

p. 604. *Serbonian . . . have sunk*: Milton, *Paradise Lost*, II.592–4.

p. 604. *Egre of the Severn*: a tidal wave of unusual height, now more usually referred to when it occurs on the Severn as a 'bore'.

NO. 50

p. 604. *seven stages of life*: as related by Jaques, in *As You Like It*, II.vii.142–66.

p. 605. *Pictures of Raphael*: Raffaello Sanzio (1483–1520); Italian painter of the high Renaissance.

p. 605. *Versailles*: the lavish palace of the French monarch, built by Louis XIV just outside Paris.

p. 605. *ejulations*: sounds of wailing or lamentation.

NO. 51

p. 606. *instigation of a harlot*: Alexander is said to have burnt the palace of Xerxes at Persepolis at the suggestion of Thais, a courtesan; cf. Quintus Curtius, *History of Alexander*, V.vii.1–7 and VIII.i.50–2.

p. 606. *subjection to his wife*: John Churchill (1650–1722); first duke of Marlborough; the greatest military commander of the late seventeenth and early eighteenth centuries. He was never forgiven by some for his desertion of James II in 1688, and the charges of avarice and domination by his wife Sarah (1660–1744), through whom he enjoyed the favour of Queen Anne, were in large measure the creation of his Jacobite and Tory enemies.

p. 607. *that he was a Man*: Juvenal, X.41–2.

NO. 59

p. 611. *the Poem of Hudibras*: a satire by Samuel Butler (1613–80), published in three parts between 1663 and 1680. One of its main targets was religious dissent.

NO. 60

p. 612. *every piece...nine years*: Horace, *Ars Poetica*, l. 388.

p. 613. *His opinion was*: there follows a series of critical commonplaces.

p. 614. *Phædra and Hippolitus*: Edmund Smith, *Phædra and Hippolitus* (1707).

p. 614. *rest of the world together*: cf. above, p. 1205, note to p. 452.

p. 614. *Barbarossa*: John Brown, *Barbarossa* (1754).

p. 614. *the author of Cleone*: Robert Dodsley (1758).

p. 615. *the Sound an Echo to the Sense*: Pope, *Essay on Criticism*, l. 365.

p. 615. *When Pulpit...instead of a stick*: Butler, *Hudibras*, I.i.11–12.

p. 615. *Honour...find out why*: Butler, *Hudibras*, II.ii.385–8.

NO. 61

p. 615. *some tribunal*: the project for a British Academy, in emulation of the French Academy established by Cardinal de Richelieu, was frequently discussed after the Restoration, although it seems never to have enjoyed the support of Johnson, who in his 'Life' of Roscommon wrote that 'such a society might, perhaps, without much difficulty, be collected; but that it would produce what is expected from it, may be doubted' (Lonsdale, vol. II, p. 19). Cf. also Johnson's comments on academies in the 'Preface' to the *Dictionary* (above, pp. 506–7).

p. 616. *ornamental luxuriance*: an echo perhaps of the critical views of John Dennis (1657–1734), whose pungently Whiggish outlook would have done little to recommend him to Johnson.

p. 616. *monkish barbarity of rhyme*: cf. Milton, *Paradise Lost*, 'Preface'.

p. 616. *perpetual variation of the numbers*: cf. *The Rambler*, no. 88, in which Johnson praises Milton's versification in similar terms.

p. 616. *the ground...of fire*: Milton, *Paradise Lost*, II.594–5.

p. 616. *So thick...these orbs*: Milton, *Paradise Lost*, III.25.

NO. 65

p. 617. *sequel of Clarendon's History*: Johnson refers to *The Life of Edward, Earl of Clarendon... Being a Continuation of the History of the Grand Rebellion* (1759).

p. 618. *whole winter's fuel*: Nicolas-Claude Fabri de Peiresc (1580–1637); antiquarian, philologist, astronomer; on account of both his humane learning and his wealth, accounted the Mæcenas of his age. The anecdote is related by Gilles Ménage, *Ménagiana* (1693).

p. 618. *Bishop Lloyd*: William Lloyd (1627–1717); bishop of St. Asaph, Lichfield and Coventry, and Worcester; opponent of Charles II; upholder of revolution principles after 1688; eventually driven insane by his remorseless study of the Book of Revelation.

p. 618. *will easily conceive*: cf. Gilbert Burnet, *Life and Death of Sir Matthew Hale* (1682).

p. 618. *Burnet's History... never given*: copies of the first edition of this work usually bear the following MS inscription on the reverse of the title page of volume II: 'The Original Manuscript of both Volumes of this History will be deposited in the Cotton Library by T Burnett'.

p. 618. *two lowest of all human beings*: i.e. John Oldmixon (1673–1742) and George Duckett (*d*.1732).

p. 619. *Lloyd did not lay out... laid it in*: Burnet's character of Lloyd is as follows: 'He was so exact in every thing he set about, that he never gave over any part of study, till he had quite mastered it. But when that was done, he went to another subject, and did not lay out his learning with the diligence with which he laid it in' (Gilbert Burnet, *History of his Own Time*, 2 vols (1724, 1734), vol. I, p. 190).

p. 619. *could never be perfected*: Thomas Baker (1656–1740); author and antiquary; non-juror; friend of Matthew Prior.

NO. 66

p. 619. *Alexandrian library... Palatine repositories*: both great libraries of antiquity. The Alexandrian library was founded by Ptolemy I. At the time of Callimachus (*b*.310 BC) it held 400,000 volumes, and by the 1st century AD had expanded to 700,000 volumes. Ptolemy III is said to have deposited in the library the official, Athenian, copy of the works of Aeschylus, Sophocles, and Euripides. It was for long thought that the library had been burnt in 642 by Amrou, the general of the caliph Omar, but this is now discredited. The Palatine is the hill in Rome on which the imperial palace of the Caesars was constructed.

p. 619. *Sophocles and Euripides... Menander*: Sophocles (496–406 BC); Greek tragedian; said to be the author of some 120 plays, only seven of which have survived. Euripides (480–406 BC); Greek tragedian; said to have written some eighty or ninety plays, nineteen of which have survived (although one, 'Rhesus', is of doubtful authenticity). Menander (*c*.342–292 BC); comic playwright; said to have written in the region of 100 plays, of which substantial fragments of four plays, and shorter fragments of many more, have survived.

p. 620. *Malbranche and Locke*: Nicolas Malebranche (1638–1715); French philosopher. John Locke (1632–1704); English philosopher.

NO. 72

p. 621. *Themistocles*: Themistocles (*c*.524–*c*.460 BC); Athenian politician and naval strategist; victor of the battle of Salamis in 480 BC.

p. 621. *art of Forgetfulness*: cf. *The Idler*, no. 44 (above, pp. 599–600).

NO. 81

p. 622. *towards Quebec*: Quebec had been taken by the English on 13 September 1759.

NO. 84

p. 624. *That no man... his chamber*: usually attributed to Louis II de Bourbon (1621–86), prince de Condé; French soldier, statesman, and patron of the arts.

p. 625. *a real Character*: a reference to the title of the celebrated work by John Wilkins (1614–72), whose *An Essay towards a Real Character and a Philosophical Language* (1668) was an attempt to overcome the deficiencies of natural languages.

p. 627. *with Applause*: Suetonius, 'Divus Augustus', XCIX.

NO. 103

p. 631. *Respicere... ultima vitæ*: Juvenal, X.275.

p. 632. *that solemn week*: i.e. Easter.

Letter to Sarah Johnson

Text: Redford, vol. I, pp. 177–8.
Date: 20 January 1759.
Sarah Johnson, Johnson's mother, died probably on 21 January 1759.

p. 632. *omitted to do well*: cf. the general confession in the order for morning prayer in the *Book of Common Prayer*: 'We have left undone those things which we ought to have done, And we have done those things which we ought not to have done.'

Letter to William Strahan

Text: Redford, vol. I, pp. 178–9.

Date: 20 January 1759.

p. 633. *little Pompadour*: Johnson is probably referring to his translation of a French work, *The History of the Marchioness de Pompadour* (1758).

p. 633. *Mr. Johnston*: William Johnston (*fl.* 1748–74); bookseller.

p. 633. *not print my name*: i.e. on the title page of *Rasselas*, which was indeed published anonymously.

Letter to Lucy Porter

Text: Redford, vol. I, pp. 179–80.

Date: 23 January 1759.

p. 633. *Kitty*: Catherine Chambers (1708–67); Sarah Johnson's maid.

Diary entry and prayer

Text: *Prayers and Meditations* (1785), pp. 31–3.

Date: 23 January 1759.

Rasselas

Text: *The Prince of Abissinia. A Tale. In Two Volumes*, 2 vols (1759).

Date: 26 June 1759.

Johnson composed *Rasselas* during his mother's final illness (as the preceding items show) and while under the most pressing need for ready cash; according to Boswell, Johnson would later tell Reynolds that he 'composed it in the evenings of one week, sent it to the press in portions as it was written, and had never since read it over' (*Life*, p. 182). However, it is also clear that *Rasselas* gathers into itself many of the moral questions which had been preoccupying Johnson since the interesting turn away from topics of immediate political resonance in the early 1740s: questions about happiness, about human restlessness, about hope and fear, about delusions. The text reprinted here is that of the second edition. Readers who wish to consider Johnson's second thoughts about some details of wording and the consequent changes which were made to the text of the first edition of 19 or 20 April 1759 should consult Tom Keymer's 'World's Classics' edition (2009). This is also the most fully-annotated edition, and includes an excellent introduction.

p. 637. *prince of Abissinia*: Johnson had translated Lobo's *A Voyage to Abyssinia* (1735); cf. above, pp. 15–17.

p. 637. *the Father of waters*: i.e. the Nile.

p. 640. *quicken my attention*: cf. *The Adventurer*, no. 102 (above, pp. 466–69).

p. 640. *before he can be happy*: cf. *The Rambler*, no. 41 (above, pp. 256–60).

p. 641. *disease*: here meaning something closer to 'unease', and without any necessary connotation of actual illness.

p. 643. *left nothing real behind it*: cf. *The Adventurer*, no. 137 (above, pp. 482–86).

p. 644. *eagle in a grate*: i.e. in a cage. A tethered eagle is a traditional symbol of yearning.

p. 644. *the blessing of hope*: for Johnson on hope, see *The Rambler*, nos. 67 and 203; and *The Idler*, no. 58 (above, pp. 610–11).

p. 646. *tenuity*: i.e. thinness.

p. 646. *must be first overcome*: cf. *The Adventurer*, no. 99 (above, pp. 462–65).

p. 646. *volant*: i.e. flying.

p. 647. *Imlac*: on the spelling of this name, see Johnson's comments to Boswell (*Life*, p. 779).

p. 647. *rehearsed*: i.e. recited.

p. 648. *the business of a scholar*: cf. *The Adventurer*, no. 85 (above, pp. 455–59).

p. 648. *spoiled*: i.e. despoiled, or pillaged.

p. 648. *Subordination*: for Johnson's comments on the concept of subordination, which was of great interest and importance to him, see *Life*, pp. 217, 233, 236, 257, 267, 376–7, 390–1, 400, 438, 532, 546, 665, 715, 730.

p. 650. *Surat*: an Indian port.

p. 650. *world of waters*: cf. *Paradise Lost*, III.11.

p. 651. *dignity of instructing*: cf. *The Adventurer*, no. 126 (above, pp. 479–82).

p. 652. *always the same*: cf. *The Adventurer*, no. 99 (above, pp. 462–65).

p. 652. *inexhaustible variety*: cf. *The Adventurer*, no. 95 (above, pp. 459–62).

p. 653. *not the individual, but the species*: cf. 'Preface' to Shakespeare (above, p. 729).

p. 654. *the remotest parts of the globe*: a reminder that *Rasselas* was published at the height of the Seven Years' War (1756–63), and before the tide of events had turned in Britain's favour.

p. 654. *the unsearchable will of the Supreme Being*: for Johnson's later endorsement of this comment, see *Life*, p. 829.

p. 655. *much is to be endured, and little to be enjoyed*: a judgement which echoes a comment by Johnson himself in his review of Soame Jenyns (see above, pp. 549–68).

p. 655. *the choice of life*: entertained by Johnson as a possible title for the novel; see the letter to Strahan of 20 January 1759 (above, p. 632).

p. 657. *combine at pleasure*: cf. *The Idler*, no. 101.

p. 658. *the coney*: i.e. the rabbit.

p. 659. *not by strength but perseverance*: cf. *The Rambler*, no. 43.

p. 661. *eat the fruits*: i.e. ate the fruits.

p. 661. *the ruggedness of the commercial race*: cf. Johnson's similar comment on the booksellers of London in his 'Life of Dryden' (above, pp. 974–1009).

p. 663. *inquiring and deliberating*: cf. *The Rambler*, no. 63 (above, pp. 272–75).

p. 663. *I have here the world before me*: cf. *Paradise Lost*, XII.646.

p. 664. *the government of the passions*: a stance typical of Stoicism.

p. 666. *against calamity*: cf. *The Rambler*, no. 32 (above, pp. 240–44).

p. 666. *pastoral simplicity*: cf. the similar delusions about country life nurtured by Richard Savage (above, p. 128).

p. 667. *Bassa*: i.e. pasha, a Turkish magistrate.

p. 670. *but by his own fault*: Johnson would return to this wording to express religious consolation in *The Adventurer*, no. 120.

p. 670. *shall alternately prescribe*: this paragraph and the paragraph following contain a number of echoes of the language and argumentation used by the English deists, particularly Matthew Tindal and Thomas Chubb.

p. 672. *Janisaries*: originally the bodyguard of the Sultan, the Janissaries had by this time become an unruly standing army.

p. 673. *some fury*: in the first edition this read 'some fiend'.

p. 673. *conceal their indigence from the rest*: cf. *The Adventurer*, no. 120.

p. 673. *hope of other favours*: the end of chapter 25 marks the end of the first volume.

p. 673. *exposed to revolutions*: cf. *The Rambler*, no. 148 (above, pp. 356–58).

p. 674. *colours of life…spring and winter*: cf. *The Rambler*, no. 69.

p. 675. *celibacy has no pleasures*: cf. *Life*, pp. 327–8 and *The Rambler*, nos. 18, 45, and 115 (above, pp. 214–17, 260–63, and 328–31).

p. 675. *will be always discontented*: cf. the similar comment in the 'Life of Swift' (above, p. 1080).

p. 676. *a siege like that of Jerusalem*: by the Romans in AD 70, during which the besieged suffered greatly.

p. 677. *its wonted revolutions*: cf. the later, similar, comment by Gibbon; 'The splendid days of Augustus and Trajan were eclipsed by a cloud of ignorance; and the Barbarians subverted the laws and palaces of Rome. But the scythe, the invention or emblem of Saturn, still continued annually to mow the harvests of Italy; and the human feasts of the Læstrigons have never been renewed on the coast of Campania' (*DF*, vol. II, p. 516).

p. 678. *CHAP. XXIX*: misnumbered 'XXVIII' in the first edition, with consequential misnumberings of later chapters.

p. 679. *Long customs…labours in vain*: cf. Johnson's similar thought in 'The Vision of Theodore' (above, pp. 154–62).

p. 681. *my business is with man*: cf. *The Idler*, no. 97.

p. 681. *the revolutions of the intellectual world*: cf. Johnson's similar comment on the 'intellectual revolutions of the world' in his account of the Harleian Library (above, p. 73).

p. 683. *not related and believed*: for other comments by Johnson on the belief in ghosts, see *Life*, pp. 215–16, 347, 355, and 648.

p. 683. *except the wall of China*: for Johnson's admiration for this structure, see *Life*, p. 668.

p. 685. *sunk down*: i.e. sank down.

p. 689. *the suspension of her sorrows*: cf. *The Rambler*, no. 47 (above, pp. 263–66).

p. 689. *the lower country*: i.e. northern Egypt.

p. 691. *denied to justice*: cf. Gibbon's observation that among the Arabs it is believed that 'the posterity of the outlaw Ismael might recover, by fraud or force, the portion of inheritance of which he had been unjustly deprived' (*DF*, vol. III, p. 162).

p. 693. *river-horses*: i.e. hippopotamuses.

p. 696. *the practice of virtue is commanded*: cf. the similar sentiment in the 'Life of Milton' (above, pp. 958–74).

p. 697. *the crab*: i.e. the constellation Cancer, associated with summer heat.

p. 699. *the uncertain continuance of reason*: a fear to which Johnson himself was particularly prone, according to Sir John Hawkins.

p. 699. *recollected*: i.e. recovered her composure.

p. 700. *feasts…bitterness of truth*: cf. the similar phrasing in the 'Preface' to Shakespeare (above, p. 736).

p. 702. *which here I could not find*: cf. the closing lines of *The Vanity of Human Wishes* (above, p. 173).

p. 706. *the gloom that has so long surrounded me*: for a similar sentiment from Johnson, see *Life*, p. 235.

p. 707. *may properly retreat*: a judgement echoed by Johnson to Boswell many years later (*Hebrides*, pp. 59–60).

p. 707. *laborious duties of society*: cf. *The Idler*, no. 38 (above, pp. 593–95).

p. 707. *harmless pleasures*: cf. *Life*, p. 732.

The Bravery of the English Common Soldiers

Text: The British Magazine (1760), pp. 37–9.
Date: January 1760.

p. 711. *perverse Cartesians*: a critical glance at the Cartesian doctrine that animals are insensate; cf. *Idler*, no. 17.

p. 711. *Russian Empress, and Prussian Monarch*: Tsarina Elizabeth (1709–62) and Frederick II, or the Great (1712–86).

p. 712. *French Count*: Lancelot, comte Turpin de Cressé (1715–95), French soldier and tactician; author of the *Essai sur l'art de la guerre* (1754).

Review of William Tytler, Mary Queen of Scots

Text: Gentleman's Magazine, vol. XXX (1760), pp. 453–6.
Date: October 1760.
William Tytler (1711–92); lawyer and historian. His *An historical and critical enquiry into the evidence produced by the earls of Murray and Morton against Mary, queen of Scots* had been published earlier in 1760.

p. 714. *Mr Goodall*: Walter Goodall (1706–66); historian. His *An examination of the letters said to have been written by Mary queen of Scots to James, earl of Bothwell*, 2 vols (1754) is an attempt to exonerate Mary.

p. 714. *Dr Robertson*: William Robertson (1721–93); historian and Moderator of the general assembly of the Church of Scotland. In his *History of Scotland* (1759) he had considered the letters as genuine.

p. 714. *Mr Hume*: David Hume (1711–76); historian and philosopher. In his *The History of England, Under the House of Tudor* (1759) he too had accepted the genuineness of the letters.

THE GREAT CHAM OF LITERATURE

Letter to Giuseppe Baretti

Text: Redford, vol. I, pp. 196–201.

Date: 10 June 1761.

Giuseppe Marc'Antonio Baretti (1719–89); writer.

p. 722. *Mr. Southwell*: Baretti was acting as tutor to Edward Southwell, of Wisbech Castle, Cambridgeshire.

p. 722. *a new King*: George III had acceded to the throne on 25 October 1760.

p. 722. *Fitzherbert*: William Fitzherbert (1712–72); member of parliament and suicide; friend of Johnson's.

p. 722. *Reynolds*: Sir Joshua Reynolds (1723–92); painter and art theorist.

p. 722. *The Jealous Wife*: a farce by George Colman, which had opened at Drury Lane on 12 February 1761.

Letter to James Boswell

Text: Redford, vol. I, pp. 237–40.

Date: 8 December 1763.

James Boswell (1740–95); lawyer, diarist, and biographer.

p. 724. *your father*: Alexander Boswell (1707–82), Lord Auchinleck; judge of the Scots Court of Session.

p. 725. *the Seven Provinces*: i.e. the northern provinces of the Netherlands—Holland, Friesland, Groningen, Drenthe, Utrecht, Gelderland, and Overijssel.

Diary entry

Text: *Prayers and Meditations* (1785), pp. 45–7.

Date: 21 April 1764.

A Reply to Impromptu Verses by Baretti

Text: MS, Baretti's Commonplace Book, Furness Collection, University of Pennsylvania.

Date: 1765?

The Plays of Shakespeare: Preface

Text: *The Plays of William Shakespeare*, 8 vols (1765), vol. I, pp. v–lxxii.
Date: 10 October 1765.

p. 728. *Pythagorean scale of numbers*: cf. Aristotle, *Metaphysics*, I.5.

p. 728. *outlived his century*: Horace, *Epistles*, II.i.39; cf. Pope, 'To Augustus', ll. 55–68.

p. 729. *Euripides...precept*: Cicero, *Ad Familiares*, XVI.8.

p. 729. *pedant in Hierocles*: Hierocles of Alexandria (*fl.* 5th cent. AD), a neo-platonist philosopher, who wrote a commentary on Pythagoras in which this anecdote appears. For Johnson's interest in Hierocles, see *Life*, p. 976, n. a.

p. 730. *any other place*: cf. Petronius, *Satyricon*, 1.

p. 730. *I will not say with Pope*: in his 'Preface' to Shakespeare of 1725, Pope says of Shakespeare's plays that 'had all the Speeches been printed without the very names of the Persons, I believe one might have apply'd them with certainty to every speaker' (Nichol Smith, p. 45).

p. 731. *Dennis*: see above, p. 1173, note to p. 99. The allusion is to his 'On the Genius and Writings of Shakespeare' (1712) (Nichol Smith, p. 31).

p. 731. *Rhymer*: Thomas Rymer (1642/43–1713); literary critic and historian. Johnson refers to his 'A Short View of Tragedy' (1693).

p. 731. *Voltaire*: François Marie Arouet de Voltaire (1694–1778); dramatist, poet, historian, and philosopher. His Shakespeare criticism is to be found in *L'Appel à toutes les nations de l'Europe* (1761) and *Dissertation sur la tragédie ancienne et moderne* (1748).

p. 732. *The players, who in their edition*: the actors John Heminges (1566–1630) and Henry Condell (1576?–1627) had published the first folio of Shakespeare in 1623.

p. 733. *led him to comedy*: cf. Rymer's 'A Short View of Tragedy' (1693).

p. 735. *Pope...interpolators*: cf. Nichol Smith, p. 53.

p. 735. *Sidney*: see above, p. 1209, note to p. 501.

p. 737. *Aristotle...and an end*: in his *Poetics* (*ALC*, p. 100).

p. 737. *Corneille*: Pierre Corneille (1606–84); French dramatist and critic.

p. 737. *the dragons of Medea*: in Greek mythology when Medea had killed two of her children she fled in a chariot drawn by dragons.

p. 738. *Pharsalia...Granicus*: the sites of battles.

p. 738. *calenture*: an illness affecting sailors in hot climates, who become subject to delusions.

p. 739. *soliloquy of Cato*: see above, p. 1212, note to p. 529. The famous soliloquy is the speech Addison gives to Cato on the immortality of the soul (V.i.1–40).

p. 739. *Non usque...a Cæsare tolli*: 'The passage of time has not yet brought about such confusion that the laws would not rather be annulled by Caesar than rescued by the voice of Metellus' (Lucan, *Pharsalia*, III.138–40).

p. 740. *as Æneas...besiegers*: cf *Aeneid*, II.610–15.

p. 740. *Lilly*: William Lily (1468?–1522); grammarian.

p. 740. *Linacer*: Thomas Linacre (1460?–1524); physician and humanist.

p. 740. *More*: Sir Thomas More (1478–1535); Lord Chancellor, humanist, and author of Utopia (1516).

p. 740. *Pole*: Reginald Pole (1500–58); scholar and statesman.

p. 740. *Cheke*: Sir John Cheke (1514–57); tutor to Edward VI.

p. 740. *Gardiner*: Stephen Gardiner (*c.*1483–1555); theologian, scholar, and bishop of Winchester.

p. 740. *Smith*: Sir Thomas Smith (1514–77); scholar.

p. 740. *Clerk*: John Clerk (*d.*1541); chaplain to Cardinal Wolsey, and bishop of Bath and Wells.

p. 740. *Haddon*: Walter Haddon (1516–72); scholar.

p. 740. *Ascham*: Roger Ascham (1515–68); tutor to Elizabeth I; humanist and author of *The Scholemaster* (1570).

p. 741. *The Death of Arthur*: Sir Thomas Malory, *Le Morte d'Arthur* (1485).

p. 741. *Palmerin and Guy of Warwick*: chivalric romances.

p. 741. *Chaucer's Gamelyn*: *The Tale of Gamelyn* is now regarded as an apocryphal text, but it was included in editions of Chaucer until 1775.

p. 741. *old Mr. Cibber*: see above, p. 1173, note to p. 88.

p. 741. *Plutarch...North*: Sir Thomas North's translation of Plutarch's *Lives* had been published in 1579.

p. 742. *Voltaire...Cato*: in *L'Appel à toutes les nations de l'Europe* (1761).

p. 742. *Johnson*: see above, p. 1175, note to l. 9. The comment about Shakespeare's lack of learning comes from Jonson's verses on Shakespeare printed with the first folio.

p. 743. *I have found...sequar*: Johnson refers to Zachary Grey, *Critical, Historical, and Explanatory Notes on Shakespeare* (1754), vol. II, p. 53; cf. *Richard III*, I.i.144 and Terence, *Andria*, l. 171.

p. 743. *Caliban...same occasion*: cf. *The Tempest*, III.ii.141.

p. 743. *then in English*: in fact, *The Comedy of Errors* was composed before William Warner's translation of the *Menaechmi* was published in 1595.

p. 743. *knowledge of the original*: Shakespeare could read Italian, as his use of Cinthio's then untranslated *Gli Hecatommithi* for *Othello* reveals.

p. 743. *justly observed by Pope*: cf. Nichol Smith, p. 49.

p. 744. *Rowe*: see above, p. 1212, note to p. 530. These remarks are taken from Rowe's 'Some Account of the Life' which he included in his 1709 edition of Shakespeare (Nichol Smith, p. 4).

p. 745. *Boyle...access*: cf. Thomas Birch, *The Life of Robert Boyle* (1744), pp. 18–19.

p. 745. *dewdrops from a lion's mane*: cf. *Troilus and Cressida*, III.iii.223.

pp. 745–6. *He seems...common conversation*: Nichol Smith, p. 24.

p. 746. *Gorboduc*: a play by Thomas Norton and Thomas Sackville acted in 1561.

p. 746. *Hieronnymo*: Thomas Kyd, *The Spanish Tragedy* (1592).

p. 746. *Spenser*: see above, p. 1209, note to p. 502.

p. 746. *some modern critick*: John Upton, *Critical Observations on Shakespeare* (1746), pp. 284–328.

p. 747. *two are concluded*: i.e. *The Old Batchelor* (1693) and *Love for Love* (1695).

p. 747. *declined into the vale of years*: cf. *Othello*, III.iii.269–70.

p. 747. *late revisers*: i.e. recent editors.

p. 747. *In this state . . . unregarded*: Warburton, in the 'Preface' to his 1747 edition of Shakespeare, suggests that the 'stubborn Nonsense, with which he was incrusted, occasioned his lying long neglected amongst the common Lumber of the Stage' (Nichol Smith, p. 89).

p. 747. *an edition was undertaken by Rowe*: in 1709.

p. 748. *when Mr. Pope made them acquainted*: in 1725.

p. 748. *more of amputation than of cure*: for Pope's editorial procedures and presentational conventions, see Nichol Smith, p. 57.

p. 748. *commended by Dr. Warburton*: see Nichol Smith, p. 90.

p. 748. *the dull duty of an editor*: see Nichol Smith, p. 57.

p. 748. *hostility with verbal criticism*: primarily in *The Dunciad*, of which the 'hero' of the first version is Theobald. On verbal criticism, see particularly IV.149–88.

p. 749. *Theobald*: Lewis Theobald (1688–1744); literary editor and writer; author of *Shakespeare Restored* (1726), an attack on Pope's edition, before publishing his own edition of Shakespeare in 1733.

p. 749. *Sir Thomas Hanmer*: Sir Thomas Hanmer (1677–1746); politician and man of letters.

p. 750. *the last editor*: William Warburton (1698–1779); bishop of Gloucester (1760), scholar, and controversialist.

p. 751. *How canst . . . Achilles?*: cf. *Iliad*, XXI.99–114.

p. 751. *His chief assailants are the authours*: Thomas Edwards (*d*.1757) and Benjamin Heath (1704–66).

p. 751. *Coriolanus*: cf. IV.iv.5–6.

p. 751. *Macbeth*: cf. II.iv.12–13.

p. 752. *Mr. Upton*: John Upton (1707–60); clergyman and literary scholar, whose *Critical Observations on Shakespeare* had been first published in 1746. A second edition in 1748 had addressed Warburton's edition.

p. 752. *Dr. Grey*: Zachary Grey (1688–1766); clergyman and scholar whose *Critical, Historical, and Explanatory Notes on Shakespeare* (2 vols, 1754) upheld the earlier work of Theobald and Hanmer against the school of Pope and Warburton.

p. 752. *small things make mean men proud*: cf. *2 Henry VI*, IV.i.105.

p. 755. *Huetius*: Pierre Huet (1630–1721); critic and scholar. Johnson is recalling Huet's *De Interpretatione* (1661), a copy of which he owned.

p. 757. *quod dubitas ne feceris*: 'when in doubt, don't' (Pliny, *Epistles*, I.xviii).

p. 757. *Criticks . . . first behind*: Pope, *The Temple of Fame* (1715), ll. 37–40.

p. 757. *the Bishop of Aleria*: Joannes Andreas (1417–*c*.1480); scholar and secretary to the Vatican library.

p. 757. *English Bentley*: Richard Bentley (1662–1742); master of Trinity College, Cambridge; pre-eminent classical scholar.

p. 758. *Illudunt . . . incidimus*: 'Our conjectures make us look foolish, make us blush, when afterwards we come across better manuscripts' (Joseph Scaliger, *Epistolae* (Leyden, 1627), p. 534; to Claudius Salmasius, 14 July 1608, letter 248).

p. 758. *Ut olim... laboratur*: 'As once we toiled over corruptions, so now we toil over corrections' (Justus Lipsius, *Ad Annales Cornelii Taciti Liber Commentarius sive Notae* (Antwerp, 1581), 'Ad Lectorem').

p. 759. *Dryden...cupressi*: the quotation comes from Dryden's *An Essay of Dramatick Poesy* (1668). The line of Latin means 'as the cypress rises above the pliant osiers' (Virgil, *Eclogues*, I.25).

Diary entry

Text: *Prayers and Meditations* (1785), p. 62.
Date: 1 January 1766.

The Fountains: A Fairy Tale

Text: Anna Williams, *Miscellanies in Prose and Verse* (1766), pp. 111–41.
Date: 1 April 1766.
Anna Williams (1706–83); blind Welsh poet and member of Johnson's household. Johnson assisted her in the augmentation of her narrow income, and composed *The Fountains* to bulk out her own writings, which would otherwise have been too meagre to justify separate publication. Mrs. Piozzi recalled the impulse which led to its composition: 'Come Mistress, now *I'll* write a tale and your character shall be in it'. Floretta is a portrait of Mrs. Piozzi.

p. 760. *Felix...lucidum*: Boethius, *Consolation of Philosophy*, III.xii.1–2. Translated by Johnson himself as: 'Happy he, whose eyes have view'd | The transparent Fount of Good'.

p. 760. *Plinlimmon*: a mountain in Wales, Anna Williams's native country.

p. 765. *termagant*: a virago or shrew (*OED*, 2 b).

p. 769. *not perpetual health*: cf. Swift's portrait of the Struldbrugs in chapter ten of Part III of *Gulliver's Travels* (*GT*, pp. 309–21).

p. 769. *dropped one by one*: cf. *The Vanity of Human Wishes*, ll. 305–8 (above, p. 171).

Letter to James Boswell

Text: Redford, vol. I, pp. 328–9.
Date: 9 September 1769.

p. 769. *Brighthelmston*: i.e. Brighton.

p. 769. *Account of Corsica*: Boswell's *Account of Corsica* had been published on 18 February 1768.

p. 769. *History...journal*: the first part of Boswell's *Account* is a derivative survey of the history and geography of Corsica; the second part is a journal of Boswell's visit to the island, and his encounters with the Corsican leader, General Paoli.

p. 771. *going to be married*: Boswell would marry his cousin, Margaret Montgomerie, on 25 November 1769.

The False Alarm

Text: *The False Alarm* (1770).

Date: 16 January 1770.

We learn from Mrs. Piozzi that Johnson composed this pamphlet on 10 and 11 January 1770. The 'false alarm' of its title is the claim, loudly made by supporters of John Wilkes, that the exclusion of Wilkes from the House of Commons following his election in March 1768 for the county of Middlesex (the House of Commons had declared Wilkes incapable of sitting as a member on 17 February 1769) represented an assault on the liberties of the subject and on the constitution itself. As the Wilkesites repeatedly said, this was an 'alarming crisis'.

p. 772. *Non de...capellis*: 'I have gone to law, not about assault or killing with a weapon or poisoning, but about three goats' (Martial, VI.xix.1–2).

p. 773. *five members in the long parliament*: a reference to the attempt made by Charles I on 4 January 1642 to arrest five members of the House of Commons (Pym, Hampden, Hollis, Strode, and Haselrig).

p. 773. *expelled a member*: Arthur Hall, member for Grantham.

p. 776. *Selden*: John Selden (1584–1654); lawyer and scholar.

p. 778. *subscribing the test*: i.e. the Test Act (1673), which required the holders of public office to repudiate the Catholic doctrine of transubstantiation, and to receive communion in the Church of England.

p. 779. *If infatuation be...destruction*: a reference to a Latin tag which, however, expresses an ancient Greek sentiment, 'quem Juppiter vult perdere, dementat prius'; 'the man whom Jupiter wishes to destroy, he first makes mad' (*Quotations*, 129.11 and cf. 13.8).

p. 779. *South Sea directors*: at the time of the South Sea Bubble in 1720 a number of the directors of the South Sea Company who were also members of the House of Commons were expelled.

p. 780. *to make a House*: i.e. to make a quorum.

p. 780. *Supporters of the Bill of Rights*: the Society for the Defence of the Bill of Rights had been formed in February 1769 by John Horne Tooke and Serjeant John Glynn. The Bill of Rights (1689) itself had been drawn up in the aftermath of the revolution of 1688.

p. 782. *an honest alehouse*: the London Tavern.

p. 782. *he trusts...good as he*: a quotation from the ballad *Chevy Chase*, as cited by Addison in *The Spectator*, no. 70 (21 May 1711).

p. 782. *sound of places*: in later editions Johnson revised this to read 'sound of pensions and places', no doubt as a defiance to those supporters of Wilkes who had cited Johnson's own pension as the explanation for his defence of the ministry.

p. 783. *the three brothers*: Richard Grenville (1711–79), George Grenville (1712–70), and their brother-in-law, William Pitt the Elder (1708–78); all vigorous opponents of the current ministry.

p. 785. *resigned for seven*: the Septennial Act (1716) had fixed the maximum length of a parliament at seven years.

p. 785. *great engine...as before*: cf. *Paradise Lost*, VI.621–7.

p. 785. *took arms in their hands*: a reference to the Jacquerie of 1358.

p. 786. *the cabinet of Naseby*: after the battle of Naseby in 1645 the parliamentarian army captured Charles I's cabinet of secret papers, which they then used to embarrass and damage the royalist cause.

p. 786. *Catilinarian conspiracy*: Lucius Sergius Catilina (*d.* 62 BC), an impoverished patrician, formed a conspiracy to seize power in Rome in 63 BC which was frustrated by Cicero.

p. 786. *Tiler*: Wat Tyler (*d.*1381); leader of the Peasants' Revolt.

p. 786. *Ket*: Robert Kett (*c.*1492–1549); leader of Kett's Rebellion (1549).

p. 786. *an exiled king*: i.e. James II (who had however died in 1701, before Anne ascended the throne).

p. 786. *Fiunt...patellae*: 'they are making pipkins, basins, frying pans, and slop buckets' (Juvenal, X.64). Juvenal is commenting on the sordid purposes to which the metal from melted busts of the disgraced favourite of Tiberius, Sejanus, is being put.

Prayer on Easter Day

Text: *Prayers and Meditations* (1785), pp. 97–8.
Date: 31 March 1771.

Parodies of Bishop Percy's Hermit of Warkworth

Text: a) Boswell's *Journal* for 7 April 1773; b) *Thraliana*, p. 398; c) *St James's Chronicle*, 13 January 1785.
Date: summer 1771?
Percy's imitation ballad, *The Hermit of Warkworth*, was published in March 1771, and Johnson parodied it affectionately on several occasions.

Γνωθι σεαυτον

Text: MS, Beinecke Library, Yale.
Date: 12 December 1772.
Johnson began to correct and revise his *Dictionary* in the summer of 1771, and the work had been completed by the middle of October 1772 (see his letter to William Strahan of 8 October 1772: Redford, vol. I, p. 397). He then took a holiday, visiting his friend John Taylor in Derbyshire, and composed this poem the day following his return to London. On the general theme of 'knowing thyself', see the opening of *The Rambler*, no. 24 (above, p. 224). The phrase Γνωθι σεαυτον itself was written as an admonition in the temple of Apollo at Delphi.

p. 791. *Scaliger*: see above, p. 1192, note to p. 311.

p. 791. *discordia concors*: cf. Horace, *Epistles*, I.xii.19, and Johnson's own 'Life of Cowley' (above, p. 924).

p. 792. *Res angusta domi*: cf. Juvenal, III.164–5, and Johnson's own version of this idea in *London*, l. 177 (above, p. 23).

Know Thyself

(After the Revision and Correction of the English Dictionary)

When Scaliger after long struggle finally finished his dictionary, thoroughly bored with the slender achievement, indignant at the worthless study and the irksome trifles, he groaned in hatred, and specified the writing of dictionaries for condemned criminals, as one punishment in place of all other punishments.

He was indeed correct, that sublime, learned, and sharp-witted man; who was fit for greater works and should have attempted greater tasks; who had treated now the deeds of ancient generals, now the poems of ancient bards; and whatever Virtue had accomplished, whatever Wisdom had uttered; and had fathomed with his intellect the rise and fall of empire, the movements of the heavens, and the cycle of the ages.

We are deceived by examples; the lowest crowd of scholars rashly believes that your anger is also permitted to them, Scaliger. Let each man know his measure. It was not granted to me by fate that I should hope to rival you in scholarship, first of men, or to dare to equal you in complaints, whether because the chills of sluggish blood or lying too long in idleness stand in the way, or because Nature has made me pusillanimous.

Once you had finished your fruitless labour, once you had safely struggled through the rough roads of words, divine Wisdom received you into the reaches of clear upper air; every Art gave you its friendly applause; and the discord of tongues in every land, now reconciled, with manifold voices sounded around you, the master who led them back from exile.

As for me, though now freed from my task, I am become my own master, the harsh lot of slothful idleness awaits me, and black and gloomy leisure, more burdensome than any labour, and the tedium of sluggish living. Worries give rise to worries, and a pestering company of troubles harass me, and the bad dreams of an empty mind. Now the noisy enjoyments of late-night dinners are my delight, now solitary places are my pleasure; in vain, kindly Sleep, I call on you, as I lie down, impatient of the night and fearful of the day. In trembling I rush through everything, I wander round everything, to see if anywhere a path to a better life opens up. But I am at a loss for what to do, meditating on grand schemes, and I am forced to know myself better and confess to an uncouth heart and a mind that boasts of itself with empty strength. A mind, unless Learning provides it with material, lies idle, just as when the supply of marble is wanting, the fertile power of Phidias's chisel languishes. Whatever I do, wherever I am taken, my narrow means and the poverty of a meagre mind hamper me.

The Spirit, now reviewing its gains, does not see the wealth of Intellect accumulated and admire itself in them, nor does the almighty master from his high tower command the presence of what daily life demands for itself from the treasure; it does not enjoy, as it counts the serried years, its serried works, things of the past, nor, its own judge, does it accept gratifying honours, the rewards of a well-spent life; but seeing its own kingdom, it shudders at the wide regions silent in darkness, where empty appearances and fleeting shadows and thin shapes of things flit through the void.

What shall I do? Is it left to me to condemn my sluggish old age to darkness? Or should I gird myself boldly for weightier studies? Or, if this is too much, should I ask at last for new dictionaries?

Letter to James Boswell

Text: Redford, vol. II, p. 7-10.
Date: 24 February 1773.
    p. 792. *Dr. Beattie*: Dr. James Beattie (1735-1803); poet and philosopher.
    p. 793. *new edition*: the fourth folio edition of the *Dictionary* was published in March 1773.
    p. 793. *Baretti*: see above, p. 1226, headnote to *Letter to Giuseppe Baretti*.
    p. 793. *Davies*: Thomas Davies (c.1712-1785); bookseller and actor.
    p. 793. *Goldsmith*: Oliver Goldsmith (1730-74); Irish poet, playwright, novelist, essayist, and critic.
    p. 793. *No name is yet given it*: the play was advertised as *The Mistakes of a Night*, and acquired its eventual title, *She Stoops to Conquer*, only on the eve of performance.
    p. 793. *your cause of Intromission*: cf. *Life*, pp. 363-7.
    p. 793. *Lord Auchinleck*: i.e. Boswell's father.

Diary entry

Text: *Prayers and Meditations* (1785), pp. 123-5.
Date: 22 July 1773.
    p. 794. *catharticks*: a purgative or laxative (*OED*).

Diary entries

Text: MS British Library; *Diaries*, pp. 174-5.
Date: 25 and 26 July 1774.
    p. 794 *Ilam*: the seat of the Port family, in Staffordshire. Johnson had visited the estate on 11 July 1774.
    p. 795. *Parnel*: Thomas Parnell (1679-1718); poet and essayist.

The Patriot

Text: *The Patriot. Addressed to the Electors of Great Britain* (1774).
Date: 12 October 1774.

Composed on 1 or 8 October for the general election of 1774, *The Patriot* gave satisfying expression to Johnson's contempt for the whiggish language of patriotism, by which is meant not disinterested love of one's country, but rather a tendency towards agitating disaffection and a suspicion of the role of the Crown in the constitution.

p. 795. *They bawl . . . wise and good*: Milton, Sonnet XII, 'I did but prompt the age to quit their clogs', ll. 9–12.

p. 795. *every seven years*: see above, p. 1167, note to p. 31.

p. 795. *sooner than it could be claimed*: a general election was not positively required until 1775, since the previous one had been held in 1768.

p. 796. *this degenerate age*: cf. Pope, *The Dunciad*, II.39–40.

p. 796. *many, made for one*: Pope, *An Essay on Man*, III.242.

p. 797. *Mr. Wilkes*: see above, p. 1231, headnote to *The False Alarm*.

p. 797. *secret satire*: an allusion to the biting satires which had been recently published under the pseudonym of Junius.

p. 797. *their own laws*: the Quebec Act of 1774 allowed the continuance of French law in the province of Quebec, and provided for a limited toleration of Roman Catholicism.

p. 797. *his dragoons and his gallies*: after the revocation of the Edict of Nantes in 1685, and the consequent removal of toleration of Protestantism, Louis XIV had persecuted his Protestant subjects by means of 'dragonnades', and by sentencing them to serve as galley slaves.

p. 798. *was stipulated*: by the Treaty of Paris (1763), which ended the Seven Years' War.

p. 798. *surrender of Limeric*: the Treaty of Limerick (1691) extended a measure of religious toleration to Irish Catholics.

p. 798. *who enjoy a toleration*: i.e. the English Dissenters.

p. 798. *burning a boot*: a popular form of protest against the earl of Bute, a close adviser to George III.

p. 798. *the meeting at Mile-end*: the Assembly-room at Mile End was a favourite rendezvous for supporters of John Wilkes.

p. 798. *the Lumber-troop*: a club of supporters of Wilkes.

p. 799. *what they called their own*: a reference to the Falkland Islands incident of June 1770, when Spanish forces had seized the Falkland Islands and had claimed them for the Spanish crown. Johnson had written on this episode in his *Thoughts on Falkland's Islands* (1771).

p. 800. *the poor Bostonians*: after the 'Boston Tea Party' of 1773 the port of Boston had been closed.

p. 800. *the new judicature instituted for the trial of elections*: by the Elections Act of 1770.

p. 801. *raised by merit to this bad eminence*: cf. Milton, *Paradise Lost*, II.5–6.

A Journey to the Western Islands of Scotland

Text: *A Journey to the Western Islands of Scotland*, first edition (1775).
Date: 18 January 1775.
Johnson travelled to Scotland in August 1773, returning to London on 26 November of that year. He immediately began collecting materials for an account of his trip; but according to Thomas Campbell the actual composition of the narrative took only twenty days in May and June of 1774. The manuscript was delivered to the printer, William Strahan, on 20 June 1774, and printing was complete by mid-December. There is an excellent modern edition by J. D. Fleeman (Oxford: Clarendon Press, 1985).

p. 802. *another gentleman*: William Nairne, advocate.

p. 803. *archiepiscopal*: i.e. containing the residence of an archbishop.

p. 803. *Buchanan*: George Buchanan (1506–82); poet, historian, and humanist. For Johnson's reading of and admiration for Buchanan, see *Life*, pp. 242, 309, 866.

p. 803. *Knox's reformation*: John Knox (*c.*1514–1572); religious reformer. In June 1559 Knox had preached inflammatory sermons in St Andrews, as a consequence of which the cathedral was attacked and damaged.

p. 803. *Cardinal Beatoun*: David Beaton (1494?–1546); cardinal and archbishop of St Andrews; assassinated 29 May 1546 by a group of disaffected Fife lairds, enraged by Beaton's trial and execution of a reformer, George Wishart.

p. 803. *trade and intercourse with England*: following the Act of Union of 1707.

p. 805. *in our Liturgy*: in the Litany of the Book of Common Prayer.

p. 805. *the irruptions of Alaric and the Goths*: Alaric (*c.*370–410); chief of the Visigoths, and leader of the Gothic army which sacked Rome in August 410.

p. 806. *as a horse in Venice*: presumably because the canal system of Venice rendered a horse useless as a mode of transport.

p. 806. *Davies observes... orchard*: Sir John Davies, *Discoverie of the True Causes* (1612), p. 170.

p. 807. *Sir Alexander Gordon*: seventh baronet of Lismore.

p. 808. *Hector Boece*: Hector Boece (*c.*1465–1536); historian and college head.

p. 808. *Erasmus*: Desiderius Erasmus (1467–1536); humanist and theologian.

p. 808. *Roger Ascham*: Roger Ascham (1514/15–1568); author and royal tutor.

p. 808. *Arthur Johnston*: Arthur Johnston (*c.*1579–1641); poet and rector of King's College, Aberdeen.

p. 808. *Leonardus Aretinus*: Leonardo Bruni (also called Leonardo Aretino) (*c.*1370–1444); Italian humanist and scholar.

p. 809. *Victorius*: Pietro Vettori the elder (1499–1585).

p. 809. *Lambinus*: Denis Lambin (1520–72).

p. 810. *an estate was overwhelmed and lost*: the parish of Forvie.

p. 811. *an imperfect constitution*: for the revision of the text at this point which Johnson made in proof, suppressing a harsh comment about the re-roofing of Lichfield Cathedral, see *Journey*, p. 164, n. 1.

p. 812. *kail*: i.e. cabbage.

p. 812. *Deliciae Poetarum Scotorum*: *Delitiae Poetarum Scotorum*, ed. Arthur Johnston, 2 vols (Amsterdam, 1637). For Johnston, see above, p. 1236, note to p. 808.

p. 812. *May's Supplement*: Thomas May (*c.*1596–1650); poet and historian. His *Supplementum Lucani Libri Septem* was published at Leyden in 1640. For Johnson's admiration for May as a Latin poet, see the comments in his 'Life of Cowley' (above, p. 920).

p. 816. *Prideaux's Connection*: Humphrey Prideaux (1648–1724); dean of Norwich and writer on religious subjects. His *Old and New Testament Connected* (1716–18) was much reprinted in the eighteenth century, and is a history of the Jewish people from 747 BC to AD 33.

p. 816. *mien*: i.e. facial appearance (*OED* 3).

p. 817. *a book, which I happened to have about me*: Edward Cocker (1631/2–1676); calligrapher and arithmetician. His *Arithmetick* was first published in 1678, and had reached its fifty-first edition by 1769. It is not known which edition Johnson presented to this anonymous Highland woman.

p. 817. *Of the hills…waving their leaves*: cf. *Iliad*, VIII.47 and 117 (Mount Ida) and *Iliad*, II.757 and *Odyssey*, XI.316 (Mount Pelion).

p. 819. *the ridges of Taurus*: a range of mountains in Turkey.

p. 821. *Proctors*: the two principal disciplinary officers of the University of Oxford, who are elected annually for a term of one year.

p. 821. *the Trent*: see above, p. 1166, note to l. 211.

p. 821. *described by Thucydides*: cf. *Peloponnesian War*, I.vi.3.

p. 822. *before they were disarmed*: as part of the measures of pacification adopted by the British government after the suppression of the Jacobite Rebellion of 1745–6.

p. 824. *black as a Cyclops from the forge*: cf. *Aeneid*, VIII.416–53.

p. 824. *Mr. Janes the fossilist*: John Jeans.

p. 824. *Dr. Campbell…state of Britain*: John Campbell (1708–75); historian. His *Political Survey of Britain* had been published in two volumes in 1774. For Johnson's admiration of Campbell, see *Life*, pp. 221 and n. a, 222, 289, 375, 430, 503, and 655 and n. a.

p. 826. *the same word which signified a gown signified peace*: i.e. toga; cf. Cicero, *De Oratore*, III.xlii.167.

p. 826. *Coriatachan*: more properly, Corichatachan, as Boswell corrected Johnson.

p. 828. *sooner than Apicius would prescribe*: Quintus Gavius Apicius, a celebrated epicure of antiquity who lived during the reign of Tiberius; cf. *Life*, p. 503. Meat which has not been hung for the right period of time tends to be tough.

p. 828. *empyreumatick*: tasting or smelling of burnt organic matter (*OED*).

p. 829. *a French author*: untraced.

p. 829. *the last conquest, and the subsequent laws*: see above, note to p. 822. The principal piece of legislation was *An Act for the more effectual Disarming the Highlands in Scotland…and for restraining the Use of the Highland Dress* (1746).

p. 831. *emersion*: the action of coming out, or issuing (*OED*, 2 a).

p. 831. *He acknowledges…preeminence*: an error on Johnson's part, concerning which Macleod complained to Boswell, and which Johnson retracted; see *Journey*, p. 184, n. 3, and plates 4 and 5 on pp. 185 and 186.

p. 832. *in a famine*: in 1764.

p. 832. *brought from China*: tea was not imported from India or Africa in 1775.

p. 832. *as England from wolves*: cf. *Life*, p. 507.

p. 833. *proceleusmatick*: something that causes or engenders excitement or enthusiasm; encouraging, animating (*OED*, 2; citing this passage).

p. 833. *Mr. Banks*: Sir Joseph Banks (1743–1820), baronet; naturalist and patron of science; PRS, 1778–1820. Banks had sailed with Captain Cook on the great expedition to the South Seas of 1768–71.

p. 834. *told by Martin...erect a cross*: Martin Martin (*c.* 1660–1719); traveller and author.

p. 835. *Ulysses...Phœacia*: in the *Odyssey*, Odysseus is taken in by Alcinous, king of Phœacia (*Odyssey*, VI–VIII).

p. 850. *the American war*: i.e. the Seven Years' War (1756–63).

p. 865. *bends a keener eye on vacancy*: cf. *Hamlet*, III.iv.117–19.

p. 865. *the American campaign*: see above, note to p. 850.

p. 866. *feculent*: polluted with filth or faeces (*OED*, 1).

p. 866. *mensuration*: i.e. measurement (*OED*, 1 a).

p. 867. *conglobated*: gathered into a ball, rounded (*OED*, a).

p. 867. *Wheeler and Spon*: Sir George Wheler (1651–1724); clergyman, traveller, botanist, and scholar. In Venice in 1675 Wheler met Jacob Spon, with whom he travelled in Greece during 1675 and 1676. On their return they both published accounts of their travels.

p. 868. *the plain of Marathon*: the site in north-eastern Attica of a momentous victory of the Athenians over an invading Persian army in 490 BC.

p. 868. *Mr. Pennant*: Thomas Pennant (1726–98); naturalist, traveller, and writer. The reference is to Pennant's *A Tour in Scotland* (Chester, 1774), p. 246.

p. 877. *whose name is Braidwood*: Thomas Braidwood (1715–1806); teacher of deaf people.

p. 877. *Wallis and Holder*: John Wallis (1616–1703), FRS. William Holder (1616–98), FRS.

p. 877. *Mr. Baker*: Henry Baker (1698–1774); natural philosopher and teacher of deaf people.

p. 877. *Burnet*: Gilbert Burnet (1643–1715); bishop of Salisbury and historian. In his *Some Letters, containing, An Account of what seemed most remarkable in Switzerland, Italy, etc.* (Rotterdam, 1686) Burnet described a deaf Genevan girl who could understand her sister by placing her hand on her sister's mouth.

Letter to James Macpherson

Text: Redford, vol. II, pp. 168–9.
Date: 20 January 1775.
James Macpherson (1736–96) had published what he claimed to be fragments of ancient Scottish poetry between 1760 and 1763. In his *Journey to the Western Islands of Scotland* Johnson had expressed his disbelief in the genuineness of these poems

(*Journey*, pp. 97–8; cf. *Life*, pp. 210, 420–4, 428–9, and 678). On 15 January 1775 Macpherson had written to the publisher of the *Journey*, William Strahan, demanding a retraction. Macpherson also wrote to Johnson using insulting language, and thereby provoked Johnson to the composition of this memorable letter of defiance.

p. 878. *since your Homer*: Macpherson had published a translation of the *Iliad* in 1773.

Taxation No Tyranny

Text: *Taxation no Tyranny; An Answer to the Resolutions and Address of the American Congress* (1775).

Date: 8 March, 1775.

Johnson composed *Taxation no Tyranny* at the request of Lord North's administration and as a reply to the 'resolves' of the American Continental Congress, which had met in Philadelphia from 5 September to 26 October 1774.

p. 881. *dropping...from our hands*: cf. *London*, l. 251 (above, p. 25).

p. 882. *the Hydra*: in Greek mythology, a poisonous water-snake with many heads, killed by Heracles in the second of his twelve labours.

p. 882. *the great actor of patriotism*: i.e. William Pitt the Elder; see above, p. 1169, note to p. 51.

p. 883. *profuse...with delight*: Joseph Addison, *A Letter from Italy* (1701), ll. 119–20.

p. 883. *recusants*: those who refuse to acknowledge authority or to comply with a command or regulation (*OED*, 2).

p. 884. *adopt the opinion*: untraced.

p. 886. *the same year*: 1498, when Columbus discovered Venezuela, and when Vasco de Gama reached India.

p. 886. *Stukeley of London*: Thomas Stukeley or Stucley (*c.*1520–1578); soldier and adventurer.

p. 888. *to bind them in all cases whatsoever*: a quotation from the Declaratory Act (1766).

p. 888. *for the purpose of raising a revenue*: a quotation from the Revenue Act (1767).

p. 889. *the fanciful Montesquieu*: Charles-Louis de Secondat (1689–1755), baron de Montesquieu; philosophe and historian. The quotation comes from his most important work, *De l'Esprit des Loix* (1748), Book XI, chapter 6 (on the subject of the English constitution).

p. 889. *That they are...consent*: *V&P*, p. 4 (Resolution 1).

p. 890. *their ancestors...realm of England*: *V&P*, p. 4 (Resolution 2).

p. 890. *they were...and enjoy*: *V&P*, p. 4 (Resolution 3).

p. 890. *no longer possible*: in 1776 Johnson added a footnote here attributing some of the credit for this argument to Sir John Hawkins.

p. 891. *Doris...undam*: 'May briny Doris not mingle her waves with yours' (Virgil, *Eclogues*, X.5). Virgil is addressing the river Arethusa. Doris is the consort of the sea-god Nereus.

p. 891. *ubi imperator, ibi Roma*: 'wherever the emperor is, there is Rome'.

p. 891. *As the English Colonists...without their consent*: *V&P*, pp. 4–5 (Resolution 4).

p. 892. *Mr. Cushing*: Thomas Cushing, the Speaker of the General Court of Massachusetts.

p. 892. *his majesty's...provincial laws*: *V&P*, pp. 5–6 (Resolution 7).

p. 892. *lay a cess*: impose an assessment, tax, or levy (particularly a land-tax) (*OED*, 1).

p. 892. *Dr. Tucker*: Josiah Tucker (1713–99); clergyman, economist, and political writer.

p. 892. *no exemption from Parliamentary Taxes*: a reference to a footnote in Tucker's *Four Tracts* (1774), pp. 97–8.

p. 892. *Davenant*: Charles Davenant (1656–1714); government official and political economist. The reference is to his *An Essay on the Probable Methods of Making a People Gainers in the Balance of Trade* (1699).

p. 892. *Molyneux*: William Molyneux (1656–98); experimental philosopher and constitutional writer. Johnson refers to his *The Case of Ireland's Being Bound by Acts of Parliament Stated* (1698).

p. 893. *particular representatives*: many major British cities were without parliamentary representation until the Great Reform Bill of 1832.

p. 893. *the Old Member*: the author of *An Appeal to the Justice and Interests of the People of Great Britain* (1774) is generally thought to have been Arthur Lee, but the attribution is not secure. The quotation occurs on pp. 44–5.

p. 895. *and as...punishable by law*: in the second edition Johnson exchanged 'conventicle' for the less offensive word 'meeting'; and in later editions he removed this inflammatory phrase altogether.

p. 896. *the sagacity of Frenchmen*: see *V&P*, p. 76.

p. 896. *a religion fraught...impious tenets*: see *V&P*, p. 28.

p. 896. *from the liberality...low-minded infirmities*: see *V&P*, p. 79.

p. 896. *guarrantied by...English Sovereigns*: see *V&P*, p. 27.

p. 896. *Mr. Mauduit*: Israel Mauduit (1708–87); colonial official and political writer. Johnson refers to Mauduit's *A Short View of the History of the Colony of Massachusetts Bay* (1769), a work which was in its third edition by 1774.

p. 897. *what he has already seen*: untraced.

p. 898. *if they should...same abject state*: see *V&P*, p. 39.

p. 898. *Do not treat...in your island*: see *V&P*, pp. 39–40.

p. 898. *flow so...less than half a century*: see *V&P*, p. 39.

p. 898. *Pactolus*: in Greek mythology, the river in which Midas bathed, and which in consequence became gold-bearing.

p. 898. *taxing America at pleasure*: see *V&P*, p. 40.

p. 899. *imposts*: i.e. taxes.

p. 899. *some master of mischief*: a satirical reference to the colonial leader Benjamin Franklin (1706–90), who had made electrical experiments.

p. 899. *the Scythians...by their slaves*: see Herodotus, IV.1.

p. 902. *cranes...pygmies*: a reference to the Greek myth of the war between the cranes and the pygmies. As a boy Johnson had translated Addison's Latin poem on the subject.

p. 902. *Great Orator*: William Pitt the Elder; see above, p. 1169, note to p. 51.

p. 902. *law to language*: a reference to Thomas Baker, *Reflections Upon Learning* (1699), p. 11.

p. 902. *a female patriot*: Catharine Macaulay (1731–91); historian and polemicist. She frequently uses the quoted phrase in her *An Address to the People of England, Scotland and Ireland, on the Present Important Crisis of Affairs* (1775).

p. 903. *The Dean of Gloucester*: i.e. Josiah Tucker; see above, p. 1240, note to p. 892. The reference is to the argument of *Four Tracts* (1774), 'Tract IV', pp. 143–216. Cf. *Othello*, III.iii.266–7.

p. 905. *Sir Thomas Brown*: Sir Thomas Browne, *Certain Miscellany Tracts* (1683), 'The Prophecy', p. 183.

p. 906. *an oath of abjuration*: such as had been imposed by the Hanoverians on English office holders in respect of the exiled house of Stuart.

Diary entry

Text: MS Pembroke College, Oxford; *Prayers and Meditations* (1785), pp. 132–3.
Date: 14 April 1775.

p. 906. *Dr. Wetherel*: Nathan Wetherell (1726–1807); master of University College, Oxford.

p. 906. *Dilly*: Edward Dilly (1732–79); bookseller and publisher.

p. 906. *Miller*: John Miller (*fl.* 1771); printer of the *London Evening Post*.

p. 906. *Francis*: Francis Barber, Johnson's black manservant.

To Mrs Thrale on her Thirty-Fifth Birthday

Text: MS, John Rylands Library, Manchester.
Date: 24 January, 1776.
The manuscript is in Mrs. Thrale's hand, and was made at Johnson's dictation. Mrs. Thrale recorded a secret satisfaction Johnson took in the rhymes of this poem: 'And now (said he, as I was writing them down), you may see what it is to come for poetry to a Dictionary-maker; you may observe that the rhymes run in alphabetical order exactly' (*Anecdotes*, p. 165; however, note that 'drive' in l. 7 precedes 'dive' in l. 9).

p. 906. *in Danger*: as a result of pregnancy.

p. 907. *Life declines from Thirty-five*: because after thirty-five one is entering the second half of man's allotted span of seventy years.

Diary entry

Text: MS, Pembroke College, Oxford; *Prayers and Meditations* (1785), pp. 139–43; *Diaries*, pp. 257–60.
Date: 7 April 1776.

p. 907. *orbus et exspes*: bereft and hopeless. Thrale's son had recently died.

p. 908. Θ: the first letter of Θανατος, the Greek word for death; hence, shorthand for those who have died.

Lines on Thomas Warton's Poems

Texts: *Thraliana*, p. 209; *Life*, p. 608.
Date: early 1777?
Thomas Warton's poems were published in January 1777. Johnson was fond of Warton, but thought his poetic manner unnatural—'a bad style of poetry' (cf. *Life*, p. 608). These two short poems strike a fine balance between mockery and affection.

Diary entry

Text: MS, Pembroke College, Oxford; *Prayers and Meditations* (1785), pp. 147–8; *Diaries*, p. 263.
Date: 28 March 1777.
   p. 909. *L. D.*: 'laus deo', or 'praise be to God'.

Prologue to Hugh Kelly's A Word to the Wise

Text: *Public Advertiser*, 31 May 1777.
Date: 29 May 1777.
Hugh Kelly (1739–77), writer, dramatist, and attorney, died on 3 February 1777 following an unsuccessful operation. Kelly's second play, *A Word to the Wise* (1770) had caused riots when Garrick attempted to stage it, because Kelly was known to be a writer for the ministry who had written against the radical cause associated with John Wilkes (see above, p. 1231, headnote to *The False Alarm*; and cf. *Life*, pp. 581–2). Johnson's poem was composed as the prologue to the performance of *A Word to the Wise* given for the benefit of Kelly's widow and children on 29 May 1777.
   p. 909. *wars not with the dead*: cf. Pope, *Iliad*, VII.485.

Letter to William Dodd

Text: Redford, vol. III, pp. 32–3.
Date: 26 June 1777.
William Dodd (1729–77); clergyman and forger. Dodd had forged a bill of exchange for £4,200. Despite popular agitation for his pardon, he was hanged at Tyburn on 27 June.

Letter to Richard Farmer

Text: Redford, vol. III, p. 43.

Date: 22 July 1777.

Richard Farmer (1735–97); master of Emmanuel College, Cambridge, and literary scholar.

p. 911. *character of his writings*: here Johnson announces the project which would become the *Lives of the Poets*.

p. 911. *Mr. Baker*: Thomas Baker (1656–1740); antiquarian and biographer.

p. 911. *the civilities of Cambridge*: Johnson had visited Cambridge with Topham Beauclerk in the early months of 1765 (*Life*, p. 256).

An Extempore Elegy

Text: MS, Berg Collection, New York Public Library

Date: ?1778

According to Fanny Burney, this poem was composed in turns by Johnson, Mrs. Thrale, and Fanny Burney herself.

p. 911. *Pug*: as explained by Johnson in the *Dictionary*, a term of endearment for 'any thing tenderly loved'.

p. 912. *Dram*: a measure of strong liquor.

A Short Song of Congratulation

Text: MS, Huntington Library.

Date: sent to Mrs. Thrale in August 1780.

Sir John Lade was Mrs. Thrale's nephew. He led a dissipated life, which however he managed to prolong until 1838.

p. 912. *Free to mortgage or to sell*: as one was not free to do before attaining one's majority.

p. 912. *Joy to see their quarry fly*: because it is then 'fair game' and can be shot at.

Lives of the Poets

Text: *The Lives of the Most Eminent English Poets*, 4 vols (1783).

Date: composed, 1777–9; first published as a free-standing collection of essays in June 1781; second, revised edition in February 1783.

On 29 March 1777, Johnson was approached by three London booksellers (Thomas Cadell, Thomas Davies, and William Strahan) with a proposal that he should compose biographical prefaces for an ambitious project to publish *The Works of the English Poets* (*Life*, p. 579; note Boswell's misreading of 'May' for 'Mar'). Johnson accepted the proposal with pleasure, perhaps because it permitted him to act on a suggestion made by George III in 1767, that he should undertake 'the literary biography of this country' (*Life*, p. 284). A very full account of the conception, prosecution, printing, and publication of the *Lives of the Poets* is to be found in Lonsdale, vol. I, pp. 1–185. This edition also offers a rich and precise commentary on the individual lives.

Cowley

p. 915. *Dr. Sprat*: Thomas Sprat (1635–1713); bishop of Rochester; FRS and historian of the Royal Society. Sprat's 'Life' of Cowley was prefaced to Cowley's *Works* (1668).

p. 915. *Wood*: see above, p. 1201, note to p. 419.

p. 915. *Sir Joshua Reynolds... Richardson's treatise*: for Reynolds, see above, p. 1226, note to p. 722. Jonathan Richardson (1667?–1745); portrait painter. Richardson wrote two treatises on painting: an *Essay on the Theory of Painting* (1715) and *Two Discourses on the Art of Criticism as it relates to Painting* (1719). It is not clear which of these made such an impact on Reynolds.

p. 916. *Sir Kenelm Digby*: Sir Kenelm Digby (1603–65); author, diplomat, FRS.

p. 916. *"Naufragium Joculare"*: i.e. 'The Comic Shipwreck'.

p. 916. *Dr. Comber*: Thomas Comber (1575–1654); master of Trinity College, Cambridge from 1631 to 1644.

p. 917. *Lord Falkland*: Lucius Cary (1609/10–1643), second viscount Falkland; politician and author.

p. 917. *Lord Jermin*: Henry Jermyn (1605–84), earl of St Albans; courtier and government official.

p. 917. *Petrarch*: Francesco Petrarca (1304–74); Italian poet.

p. 917. *Barnes*: Joshua Barnes (1654–1712); professor of Greek at Cambridge. Johnson refers to a comment in the 'Preface' to Barnes's edition of Anacreon, published in 1705.

p. 917. *an "airy nothing"*: cf. *A Midsummer Night's Dream*, V.i.16.

p. 917. *the "dream of a shadow"*: a phrase from Cowley's 'Life and Fame', l. 7.

p. 918. *Mr. Bennet*: Henry Bennet (1618–85), first earl of Arlington; politician.

p. 918. *the Virgilian lots*: the 'sortes Virgilianae', that is to say the random selection of lines from Virgil, which are then taken to be prognostications.

p. 918. *Dr. Scarborow*: Charles Scarborough (1616–94); physician.

p. 919. *Oliver's death*: i.e. the death of Oliver Cromwell, the Lord Protector, which occurred on 3 September 1658.

p. 920. *Dr. Birch*: Thomas Birch (1705–66); historian and biographer; secretary to the Royal Society. Birch's *The History of the Royal Society* had been published in four volumes in 1756–7.

p. 920. *May I hold to be superior to both*: for May, see above, p. 1237, note to p. 812.

p. 920. *Mastership of the Savoy*: the Savoy at this time was a charity hospital in the Strand.

p. 920. *Mr. Dennis*: see above, p. 1173, note to p. 99.

p. 921. *the Theatrical Register of Downes the prompter*: John Downes (*d.*1712?); theatre prompter and historian. Downes's *Roscius Anglicanus, or, An Historical Review of the English Stage* had been published in 1708. Downes said of Cowley's play that it was 'not a little injurious to the Cavalier Indigent Officers' (p. 25, n.).

p. 921. *Suckling*: Sir John Suckling (1609–1641?); poet.

p. 922. *hum of men*: Milton, 'L'Allegro', l. 118.

p. 922. *Peck*: Francis Peck (1692–1743); antiquary.

p. 922. *Monstri simile*: 'like a wonder'.

p. 922. *Verbum sapienti*: 'a word to the wise'.

p. 923. *an imitative art*: cf. Aristotle, *Poetics*, ch. VIII.

p. 923. *If Wit…so well expressed*": a surprisingly unmetrical misquotation of Pope's actual couplet: 'True Wit is Nature to Advantage drest, | What oft was Thought, but ne'er so well Exprest' (*An Essay on Criticism*, ll. 297–8). Note Johnson's comment later in this 'Life' that 'Language is the dress of thought' (above, p. 954).

p. 924. *discordia concors*: a Pythagorean notion of harmonious discord. For another Johnsonian usage of the phrase, see Γνωθι σεαυτον, l. 22 (above, p. 791).

p. 924. *exility*: thinness, slenderness, meagreness (*OED*, 1 a).

p. 925. *Marino*: Giambattista Marino (or Marini) (1569–1625); Italian poet and founder of the poetical school of 'Marinism', which was characterized by elaborate word play and complicated metaphors.

p. 925. *Donne*: John Donne (1572–1631); clergyman and poet.

p. 925. *Jonson*: Ben Jonson (1572–1637); poet and playwright.

p. 925. *Waller*: Edmund Waller (1606–87); poet and politician.

p. 925. *Denham*: Sir John Denham (1614/15–1669); poet and courtier.

p. 925. *Cleiveland*: John Cleveland (1613–1658); poet.

p. 925. *lines upon Hobson the Carrier*: two early short poems by Milton grouped under the title 'On the University Carrier'.

p. 929. *Confusion worse confounded*: Paradise Lost, II.996.

p. 938. *Scaliger himself*: for J. C. Scaliger, see above, p. 1192, note to p. 311. Cf. his *Poetices* (1561), p. 339.

p. 939. *Sir Henry Wotton*: Sir Henry Wotton (1568–1639); diplomat and writer.

p. 939. *Hervey*: William Hervey (*d.*1642), baron; naval officer.

p. 939. *Davenant*: Sir William Davenant (1606–68); poet, playwright, and theatre manager.

p. 940. *Bentley*: see above, p. 1229, note to p. 757.

p. 940. *Crashaw*: Richard Crashaw (1612/13–1648); poet.

p. 941. *displayed by Addison*: in his various remarks on 'false wit', most conveniently to be found in *The Spectator*, nos. 58–62.

p. 941. *Sanazarro*: Giacomo Sannazaro (1458–1530); Italian poet. The quotation comes from 'Ad Vesbiam', in Sannazaro's *Opera Omnia* (Venice, 1535), vol. II, p. 43. Cf. *The Rambler*, no. 36 (above, p. 247).

p. 942. *"she plays… not at the heart"*: Pope, *Essay on Man*, IV.254.

p. 942. *Pancirolus*: Guido Panciroli (1523–99); Italian jurist and writer.

p. 945. *Casimir*: Mathias Casimir (1595–1640); poet. The quotation comes from Casimir's *Libri Lyricorum* (1625), and translates as follows: 'The lord of the world equips all hours with vigorous wings to drive them through empty space; some remain yet hidden in the nest, to grow in future years.'

p. 945. *cry out with Prior*: for Prior, see the 'Life' above (pp. 1045–60). The quoted lines come from his *An English Ballade... on the Taking of Namure* (1695), ll. 95–6.

p. 947. *Rymer*: see above, p. 1227, note to p. 731.

p. 947. *He spake the word, and they were made*: Psalm 148:5.

p. 947. *troubled with an evil spirit*: 1 Samuel 16:14.

p. 948. *When Virgil...discerneret arvis*: 'Then he spies a great stone, a great and ancient stone which lay by chance upon the plain, and which was placed as a boundary, to keep conflict from the fields' (Virgil, *Aeneid*, XII.896–8).

p. 951. *implex*: involved or possessing a complicated plot (*OED*, citing this passage).

p. 951. *the Jerusalem of Tasso*: Torquato Tasso (1544–95); Italian poet. His heroic epic poem, *Gerusalemme liberata* was published in 1581, and narrates the capture of Jerusalem during the First Crusade.

p. 951. *Hà sotto...il misura*: 'He has beneath his feet fate and nature, his humble ministers, and movement, and that which measures it' (*Gerusalemme liberata*, IX.lvi.7–8).

p. 952. *Denham*: see above, p. 1245, note to p. 925. The quotation comes from Denham's 'On Mr. Cowley His Death', ll. 7–8.

p. 952. *Clarendon*: Edward Hyde (1609–74), first earl of Clarendon; politician and historian. The praise of Cowley occurs in Clarendon's *Life* (Oxford, 1759), p. 16.

p. 952. *Grotius*: see above, p. 1187, note to p. 266.

p. 953. *Dr. Hurd*: Richard Hurd (1720–1808); literary critic and clergyman; bishop of Worcester. For Johnson's opinion of Hurd, see *Life*, p. 868.

p. 956. *qui musas colunt severiores*: 'who cultivate the more severe Muses' (an adaptation of Martial, *Epigrams*, IX.xi.17)

p. 957. *May and Sandys*: for May, see above, p. 1237, note to p. 812. George Sandys (1578–1644); writer and traveller.

p. 957. *Felton*: Henry Felton (1679–1740); clergyman and scholar; principal of St Edmund Hall, Oxford. Felton's commendation of Cowley occurs in his *Dissertation on Reading the Classics* (1713), pp. 35–6.

Milton [extract]

p. 958. *nothing satisfied with what he had done*: a slight misquotation from Milton's note to 'The Passion' (1630?), where the wording is: 'nothing satisfied with what was begun'.

p. 958. *a man well qualified*: probably Giuseppe Baretti; see above, p. 1226, headnote to *Letter to Giuseppe Baretti*.

p. 958. *Lion...dandling the kid*: cf. *Paradise Lost*, IV.343–4.

p. 959. *When Cowley tells of Hervey*: a reference to Cowley's 'On the Death of Mr William Hervey'.

p. 959. *what Theobald has remarked*: in the prefatory essay to his *Works of Shakespeare* (1733), vol. I, pp. xix–xx. For Theobald, see above, p. 1229, note to p. 749.

p. 960. *Pluto... Eurydice... conditional release*: in Greek mythology Eurydice was the wife of the legendary poet and musician Orpheus. On her death Orpheus descended to the underworld, and by the beauty of his music prevailed on Persephone (the companion of Pluto) to release her. The condition of Eurydice's release was that Orpheus should not look back at her as she followed him out of Hades. On the verge of the land of the living, Orpheus forgot the condition, glanced back, and Eurydice vanished.

p. 962. *Bossu is of opinion*: René le Bossu (1631–80), whose *Traité du poème épique* (Paris, 1675) had asserted that the choice of the 'moral' (p. 15) was the first task of an epic poet.

p. 963. *to vindicate... man*: a significant misquotation of *Paradise Lost*, I.26, where Milton in fact says that his purpose is to 'justify the ways of God to men'. Cf. *Rambler*, no. 94 and Pope, *An Essay on Man*, I.16.

p. 964. *To Satan... depraved being*: cf. *The Spectator*, no. 303.

p. 964. *Clarke*: a reference to John Clarke's *Essay Upon Study* (1731), pp. 204–7.

p. 964. *justly remarked by Addison*: cf. *The Spectator*, no. 273.

p. 965. *Of the machinery*: 'the god in the machine' (Aristotle, *Poetics*, XV).

p. 965. *funeral games... long description of a shield*: elements in *The Iliad* (XXIII – funeral games, and XVIII – the shield of Achilles) and *The Aeneid* (V – funeral games).

p. 965. *Cato... Lucan... Quintilian*: Cato the younger (see above, p. 1169, note to p. 44), whom Lucan praises in his *Pharsalia*, IX.18; cf. Quintilian, X.i.90.

p. 966. *through the spectacles of books*: a phrase taken from Dryden's *Of Dramatick Poesie* (1667), where Shakespeare is praised for not requiring the spectacles of books to see nature.

p. 967. *Ariosto... Deliverance of Jerusalem*: see below, p. 1246, note to p. 951.

p. 967. *the port of mean suitors*: cf. *Paradise Lost*, XI.8–9.

p. 968. *Bentley*: for Richard Bentley, see above, p. 1229, note to p. 757. In his edition of *Paradise Lost* (1732) Bentley had freely corrected what he asserted to be errors in the text of the poem, introduced as he supposed by the person to whom the blind poet had entrusted the manuscript and the correction of proof.

p. 969. *one of his encomiasts*: Samuel Barrow (1625?–1683); physician and lawyer to the army. Barrow's Latin poem in praise of *Paradise Lost*, 'In Paradisum Amissum' was prefixed to the second, 1674, edition of the poem.

p. 972. *Our language... under him*: cf. *The Spectator*, no. 297.

p. 972. *Jonson... no language*: a reference to a judgement on Spenser in Jonson's *Discoveries*.

p. 972. *Butler... Babylonish Dialect*: cf. *Hudibras*, I.i.93.

p. 972. *The Earl of Surrey*: Henry Howard (1517?–1547), earl of Surrey, whose translations of books II and IV of *The Aeneid* are the earliest blank verse poems in English.

pp. 972–3. *one tending... upon Guiana*: George Chapman's 'De Guiana, Carmen Epicum' (1596).

p. 973. *Trisino's Italia Liberata*: Giangiorgio Trissino (1478–1550), whose *Italia liberata dai Goti* had been published in 1547–8.

p. 973. *he says, and says truly*: in 'The Verse', the short essay of one paragraph prefixed to *Paradise Lost*.

p. 973. *Blank verse...to the eye*: William Locke (1732–1810), as identified by Boswell; see *Life*, p. 786.

p. 973. *lapidary style*: i.e. suited to a monumental inscription. Note Charles Burney's recollection of Johnson's *obiter dictum*: 'In lapidary inscriptions a man is not upon oath' (*Life*, p. 480).

Dryden [extract]

p. 974. *father of English criticism*: in his 'Life of Cowley' Johnson had acknowledged Aristotle to be the father of criticism *tout court* (above, p. 923).

p. 974. *Webb*: William Webbe, *A Discourse of English Poetrie* (1586).

p. 974. *Puttenham*: George Puttenham, *The Arte of English Poesie* (1589).

p. 974. *hints...by Jonson*: presumably in his *Timber* (1640).

p. 975. *praise lavished by Longinus*: see *On the Sublime*, ch. XVI (*ALC*, pp. 480–1).

p. 975. *Rymer*: see above, p. 1227, note to p. 731.

p. 975. *malim...recte sapere*: 'I would rather be wrong with Scaliger, than right with Clavius'.

p. 975. *con amore*: with love.

p. 976. *Trapp*: Joseph Trapp (1679–1747); clergyman and literary scholar. Trapp was Professor of Poetry at Oxford from 1708 to 1718, and Johnson quotes from the text of his lectures: *Praelectiones Poeticae*, 3 vols (Oxford, 1711–19), vol. III, p. 122. The translation published in 1742 reads: 'We know our Countryman, Mr. *Dryden*'s Judgment, about a Poem of *Chaucer*'s, truly beautiful, and worthy of Praise; namely, that it was not only equal, but even superior to the *Iliad* and *Aeneid*: But we know, likewise, that his Opinion was not always the most accurate, nor form'd upon the severest Rules of Criticism. What was in Hand, was generally most in Esteem; if it was uppermost in his Thoughts, it was so in his Judgment too.'

p. 976. *Spence*: Joseph Spence, *An Essay on Pope's Odyssey* (1726), pp. 121–2.

p. 976. *Sewel*: George Sewell, 'Preface' to Ovid's *Metamorphoses* (1717), pp. xix–xx.

p. 976. *Gorboduc*: Thomas Sackville and Thomas Norton, *The Tragedy of Gorboduc* (1563).

p. 976. *Westminster...Busby*: Richard Busby (1606–95); schoolmaster, whose period as headmaster of Westminster (from 1638) was celebrated, and whose pupils included (as well as Dryden), John Locke, Matthew Prior, and Sir Christopher Wren.

p. 977. *Quintilian...Seneca*: Quintilian, *Institutio Oratoria*, IX.ii.9 and VIII.v.6.

p. 977. *the praise which he gives his master Charles*: see Dryden, *Threnodia Augustalis*, ll. 337–45.

p. 978. *another and the same*: see Dryden, 'Of the Pythagorean Philosophy', ll. 580–1.

p. 978. *Waller*: see above, p. 1245, note to p. 925.

p. 978. *Denham*: see above, p. 1245, note to p. 925.

p. 979. *Feltham*: Owen Feltham (1602?–1668); Johnson refers to his *Resolves Or, Excogitations* (1628), sig. A2ᵛ.

p. 979. *Sandys*: see above, p. 1246, note to p. 957.

p. 979. *Holyday*: Barten Holyday (1593–1661); clergyman and poet. Johnson alludes probably to Holyday's translation of Persius's *Satires* (1616), which had reached its fifth edition by 1650.

p. 979. *copyers were a servile race*: cf. Dryden, 'The First Book of Homer's *Ilias*', l. 191 for his use of the phrase 'servile race'. Both Dryden and Johnson are recalling Horace's 'O imitatores, servum pecus' (*Epistles*, I.xix.19). Johnson had used this as the motto for *Rambler* no. 121 (above, p. 332).

p. 980. *Translation…metaphrase*: taken from the 'Dedication' to the *Aeneid* (1697).

p. 980. *Sir Edward Sherburne*: Sir Edward Sherburne (1618–1702); translator and poet. Johnson refers to Sherburne's 'A Brief Discourse Concerning Translation', in his *The Tragedies of…Seneca* (1702), pp. xxxvi–xxxix.

p. 980. *authority of Horace*: see Horace, *Ars Poetica*, l. 133.

p. 980. *Poverty…too hastily accused*: and occasionally so by Johnson himself; cf. *London*, l. 177 (above, p. 23).

p. 980. *by his Sebastian*: *Don Sebastian*, II.iii.586.

p. 981. *Virgil…fewer*: this tradition concerning Virgil's habits of composition goes back to Donatus. For an earlier eighteenth-century version of it, see Joseph Warton *et al.*, *The Works of Virgil*, 4 vols (1753), vol. I, p. 32. Johnson also recalls this tradition in his 'Life of Pope' (above, p. 1104).

p. 981. *death of Cromwell*: Cromwell died on 3 September 1658. Dryden's celebration of the Lord Protector, 'Heroique Stanza's', was published in 1659.

p. 981. *Davenant*: see above, p. 1245, note to p. 939.

p. 981. *verses on the Restoration*: *Astraea Redux* (1660).

p. 982. *Monk's dexterity*: George Monck (1608–70), first duke of Albemarle; army officer and naval officer. Monck's combination of shrewdness and audacity as he led his forces south from Scotland was vital in facilitating the Restoration.

p. 983. *Malherbe*: François de Malherbe (1555–1628); French writer. For the anecdote, see A. H. de Sallengre, *Mémoires de littérature*, 2 vols (The Hague, 1715–17), vol. II, pp. 72–3.

p. 983. *poem on the Coronation*: *To His Sacred Majesty* (1661), quoting ll. 79–84.

p. 984. *lord chancellor Clarendon*: see above, p. 1176, note to l. 131.

p. 986. *Boileau*: in his 'Epître IV' (1672), ll. 119–24.

p. 986. *Waller*: in his 'Of a War with Spain, and a Fight at Sea'.

p. 986. *Milton had not yet transferred*: cf. *Paradise Lost*, VI.469–627.

p. 986. *Waller's poem on the war with Spain*: see above, note to p. 986.

p. 986. *Orbem jam totum*: cf. Petronius, *Satyricon*, 119, l. 1.

p. 988. *an universal language*: for Johnson's aversion to specialist vocabularies, see the 'Preface' to the *Dictionary* (above, p. 505) and his review of Thomas Blackwell's *Memoirs of the Court of Augustus* (above, pp. 532–33).

p. 988. *the Royal Society, then newly instituted*: the Royal Society had been founded in November 1660, and had received its royal charter of incorporation in 1662. Dryden was elected FRS on 19 November 1662.

p. 989. *taken from Seneca*: Seneca, *Controversiae*, VII.i.27.

p. 990. *the opinion of Harte*: Walter Harte (1709–74); poet, clergyman, and valetudinarian.

p. 990. *the Earl of Mulgrave*: John Sheffield (1647–1721), third earl of Mulgrave, first duke of Buckingham and Normanby; poet and politician.

p. 991. *written by Tate*: Nahum Tate (*c*.1652–1715); poet, playwright, and translator. Dryden contributed several hundred lines to Tate's *The Second Part of Absalom and Achitophel* (1682).

p. 992. *Fervet immensusque ruit*: 'he foams, and rushes on unrestrained' (Horace, *Odes*, IV.ii.7; comparing Pindar to a mountain stream).

p. 992. *diapason*: a musical term of various, and variously precise, meanings; but used here probably in the sense of a melodious succession of notes, a melody, a strain; a swelling sound, as of a grand burst of harmony (*OED*, 3 b).

p. 994. *Browne*: Sir Thomas Browne (1605–82); physician and author. His *Religio Medici* was composed in 1635–6, published twice surreptitiously in 1642, and first published in an authorized edition in 1643.

p. 995. *Montague and Prior*: see the account in the 'Life of Prior' (above, pp. 1045–60); and see below, p. 1251, note to p. 1012.

p. 998. *Stapylton*: Sir Robert Stapylton (1607/9?–1669); translator and playwright. Stapylton's complete translation of the satires of Juvenal had been published in 1647, and had been preceded by a translation of only the first six in 1644.

p. 998. *Holiday*: for Holyday, see above, p. 1249, note to p. 979. Holyday's *Juvenal and Persius Translated and Illustrated* had been published in 1673.

p. 998. *Creech*: Thomas Creech (1659–1700); poet and translator.

p. 999. *says Pope*: a quotation from the 'Preface' to Pope's translation of the *Iliad*.

p. 999. *Milbourne*: Luke Milbourne (1649–1720); clergyman and poet. Milbourne's sharply critical *Notes on Dryden's Virgil* had been published in 1698.

p. 1001. *Dr. Brady*: Nicholas Brady (1659–1726); clergyman and poet. Brady's translation of the *Aeneid* came out in instalments (1714; 1716–17; 1726).

p. 1001. *Trapp*: see above, p. 1248, note to p. 976.

p. 1001. *Ariosto*: Ludovico Ariosto (1474–1533); Italian poet.

p. 1001. *refaccimento*: more correctly, *rifacimento*.

p. 1002. *Boiardo*: Matteo Maria Boiardo (1434–94); Italian poet, scholar, and translator.

p. 1002. *Domenichi*: Lodovico Domenichi (1515–64); Italian jurist, translator, and writer.

p. 1002. *Berni*: Francesco Berni (*c*.1497–1535); Italian poet.

p. 1002. *Boccace*: Giovanni Boccaccio (1313–75); Italian poet and scholar. Dryden's *Fables* (1700) contains versions of three tales taken from Boccaccio's *Decameron* (1348–53).

p. 1002. *one of the Beroalds*: in fact, Filippo Beroaldo the Elder (1453–1505).

p. 1003. *Otway*: Thomas Otway (1652–85); playwright.

p. 1003. *verbaque provisam rem*: 'once matter is provided, words will follow' (Horace, *Ars Poetica*, l. 311).

p. 1005. *Dryden calls…even when I wrote them*: Johnson quotes from the 'Preface' to *The Spanish Fryar* (1681).

p. 1007. *Waller... energy divine*: Pope, *Ep. II.i*, ll. 267–69.

p. 1007. *Chapman's Homer*: George Chapman (1559/60–1634); poet, playwright, and translator. Chapman's translation of Homer had been published in 1598.

p. 1007. *Phaer's Virgil*: Thomas Phaer, *The Seven First Bookes of the Eneidos of Virgill* (1558).

p. 1007. *Hall's Satires*: Joseph Hall, *Virgidemiarum* (1597–8).

p. 1007. *the death of Elizabeth*: in 1603.

p. 1008. *Drayton's Polyolbion*: Michael Drayton, *Polyolbion* (1612–22).

p. 1008. *Swift... ridicule them*: Swift, 'A Description of a City Shower' (1710), ll. 61–3.

p. 1008. *Fenton*: Elijah Fenton (1683–1730); poet.

p. 1009. *Davis*: Sir John Davies (1569–1626); poet and lawyer. Johnson has in mind Davies's *Nosce Teipsum*, a poem on the immortality of the soul and its relation to the body composed *c.*1594 and first published in 1599.

p. 1009. *What was said of Rome... marble*: Suetonius, 'Divus Augustus', XXIX.

Addison

p. 1010. *the school at Lichfield*: also attended by Johnson himself.

p. 1010. *the Chartreux*: i.e. Charterhouse, a famous public school then occupying a site in London.

p. 1010. *Sir Richard Steele*: see above, p. 1173, note to p. 84.

p. 1011. *Tickell*: Thomas Tickell (1685–1740); poet and government official.

p. 1011. *Boileau*: see above, p. 1212, note to p. 529.

p. 1011. *Henry Sacheverell*: Henry Sacheverell (1674–1724); Church of England clergyman and polemicist; darling of the ultra High Church wing.

p. 1012. *Montague*: Charles Montagu (1661–1715), first earl of Halifax; politician, financial innovator, and minor poet.

p. 1012. *lord Somers*: John Somers (1651–1715), baron Somers; politician and statesman.

p. 1013. *lord Godolphin*: Sidney Godolphin (1645–1712), first earl of Godolphin; politician and statesman.

p. 1014. *marquis of Wharton*: Thomas Wharton (1648–1715), first marquess of Wharton; politician.

p. 1015. *Dr. Fleetwood*: William Fleetwood (1656–1723), bishop of St. Asaph and subsequently Ely.

p. 1015. *Casa in his book of Manners*: Giovanni della Casa, *Il Galateo* (1558).

p. 1015. *Castiglione in his Courtier*: Baldassare Castiglione, *Il libro del cortegiano* (1528).

p. 1015. *La Bruyere's Manners of the Age*: Jean de la Bruyère, *Les Caractères de Theophraste... avec les caractères ou les mœurs de ce siècle* (1688).

p. 1017. *Cervantes... para el*: 'for me alone was Don Quixote born, and I for him'.

p. 1018. *Mr. Hughes*: John Hughes (1678?–1720); dramatist, musician, poet, and librettist.

p. 1018. *Dennis*: see above, p. 1173, note to p. 99.

p. 1019. *Bolingbroke*: see above, p. 1174, note to p. 118.

p. 1019. *the fate of... Cid*: a reference to the unavailing censure passed on Corneille's *Le Cid* (1637) by Cardinal Richelieu; cf. Boileau, *Satire* IX.231–2.

p. 1020. *Jeffreys*: George Jeffreys (1678–1755).

p. 1020. *of the Lizards*: cf. *The Guardian*, nos. 5 and 6.

p. 1021. *the succession of a new family to the throne*: i.e. the accession of the House of Hanover, in 1714.

p. 1022. *Milton... regis*: Johnson quotes an epigram from Milton's *Defensio Pro Populo Anglicano* in which the author mocks 'the hundred Jacobuses which were the substance of an exiled king'. A Jacobus was a gold coin, originally worth 20s, first struck in the reign of James I.

p. 1023. *Tonson*: Jacob Tonson the Elder (1655/56–1736); bookseller and literary entrepreneur.

p. 1024. *Dr. Tillotson*: John Tillotson (1630–1694); archbishop of Canterbury.

p. 1025. *chose themselves for seven*: on the Septennial Act, see above, p. 1231, note to p. 785.

p. 1025. *Bellum plusquam civile*: 'a more than civil war' (Lucan, *Pharsalia*, I.1).

p. 1026. *Dr. Young*: Edward Young (1683–1765); clergyman and poet.

p. 1027. *Chesterfield*: see above, p. 1210, headnote to *Letter to the Earl of Chesterfield*.

p. 1029. *Mandeville*: Bernard Mandeville (1670–1733); physician and political writer; author of *The Fable of the Bees* (1714).

p. 1030. *a great writer*: William Warburton (see above, p. 1229, note to p. 750).

p. 1031. *Dr. Warton*: Joseph Warton (see above, p. 1212, headnote to *Review of* An Essay on the Writings and Genius of Pope).

p. 1032. *Dr. Madden*: Samuel Madden (1686–1765); clergyman and author.

p. 1035. *Whatever pleasure... to expect*: cf. Johnson's comments on the conclusion of *King Lear* (Shakespeare, pp. 239–40).

p. 1044. *Mille... habet*: Tibullus III.viii.14. Johnson supplies a translation of the Latin immediately before the quotation.

Prior

p. 1045. *Dr. Busby at Westminster*: see above, p. 1248, note to p. 976.

p. 1045. *earl of Dorset*: Charles Sackville (1643–1706), sixth earl of Dorset and first earl of Middlesex; poet and politician.

p. 1045. *Burnet*: see above, p. 1238, note to p. 877.

p. 1046. *Mr. Montague*: see above, p. 1251, note to p. 1012.

p. 1046. *the grand alliance against Lewis*: an alliance comprising principally England, the United Provinces of the Netherlands, and the Austrian Hapsburgs, which resisted the expansionist plans of Louis XIV of France in the War of the Grand Alliance (1689–97) (also sometimes referred to as the War of the League of Augsburg).

p. 1047. *the treaty of Ryswick*: see above, p. 1211, note to p. 522.

p. 1047. *Le Brun*: Charles le Brun (1619–90); principal French painter and designer of the reign of Louis XIV.

p. 1047. *Boileau*: see above, p. 1212, note to p. 529.

p. 1047. *Racine*: Jean Racine (1639–99); French dramatic poet and historiographer, particularly celebrated for his classical tragedies.

p. 1047. *Loo*: Het Loo, William III's country house in the east central Netherlands, near Apeldoorn.

p. 1047. *Tickell*: see above, p. 1251, note to p. 1011.

p. 1048. *Swift's Proposal*: i.e. *A Proposal for Correcting, Improving and Ascertaining the English Tongue* (1712).

p. 1048. *the Partition-treaty*: the First Treaty of Partition (1698) had stipulated that on the death of Charles II of Spain the Spanish crown should go to Prince Joseph Ferdinand, son of the elector of Bavaria (thus preventing the possible unification of the crowns of Spain and France under a Bourbon). The death of Joseph Ferdinand in February 1699 required a Second Treaty of Partition (1699), and this stipulated that the Spanish crown should go to the Archduke Charles, second son of the Emperor Leopold I. When Charles II died in November 1700, he bequeathed the Spanish crown to the Duc d'Anjou, the grandson of Louis XIV. Louis accepted the bequest, and so the War of the Spanish Succession (1701–14) was fought in order to prevent Bourbon hegemony in southern Europe.

p. 1048. *Blenheim*: an engagement of the War of the Spanish Succession fought on the Danube in Bavaria on 13 August 1704, in which the army of the Grand Alliance under John Churchill (later duke of Marlborough) defeated a numerically superior French force under Tallard.

p. 1048. *the last war*: i.e. the Seven Years' War (1756–63).

p. 1048. *the Gazetteer*: the ministerial newspaper of record.

p. 1048. *Harley*: see above, p. 1172, note to p. 71.

p. 1048. *Conduct of the Allies*: the title of a famously effective anti-war pamphlet by Swift, published in 1711.

p. 1048. *Mrs. Manley*: Delarivier Manley (*c.*1670–1724); novelist, playwright, and miscellaneous writer.

p. 1049. *Abbé Gaultier*: abbé François Gaultier (*d.*1720).

p. 1049. *M. Mesnager*: Nicolas Le Baillif (1658–1714), comte de Saint-Jean Le Mesnager; diplomat.

p. 1049. *Macky*: John Macky (*d.*1726); writer, spy, and government agent.

p. 1049. *Monsieur de Torcy*: Jean-Baptiste Colbert (1665–1746), marquis de Torcy; diplomat and foreign minister.

p. 1049. *Bolingbroke*: see above, p. 1174, note to p. 118.

p. 1049. *duke of Shrewsbury*: Charles Talbot (1660–1718), duke of Shrewsbury; politician.

p. 1049. *Boyer*: Abel Boyer (1667?–1729); lexicographer, historian, and journalist.

p. 1050. *Mr. Walpole*: i.e. Robert Walpole; see above, p. 1174, note to p. 99.

p. 1050. *lord Coningsby*: Thomas Coningsby (1657–1729), first earl of Coningsby; politician.

p. 1050. *Mr. Stanhope*: James Stanhope (1673–1721), first earl Stanhope; army officer, diplomat, and politician.

p. 1050. *Mr. Lechmere*: Nicholas Lechmere (1675–1727), baron Lechmere; politician and lawyer.

p. 1050. *Boscawen*: Hugh Boscawen (*c.* 1680–1734), first viscount Falmouth; politician and courtier.

p. 1050. *Oxford*: i.e. Robert Harley.

p. 1051. *the Speaker*: i.e. the Speaker of the House of Commons.

p. 1052. *Sic est, homo sum*: 'thus it is, I am a man.'

p. 1052. *engraven this epitaph*: the following translation by Samuel Humphreys was published in the third edition of Prior's *Poems on Several Occasions* (1733), vol. III, pp xxx–xxxii; 'Whilst he was Writing | The *History* of *his Own Time*, | A lingering Fever | Snapt the Thread of his Work and his Life together, | On the 17th Day of *Sept.* 1721. | In the 57th Year of his Age. | Here lies interred | That excellent Man. | He was Secretary to their most Serene Majesties | King WILLIAM and Queen MARY, | At the Congress of the *Allies* held at the *Hague*, 1690. | He was thence | Appointed Secretary | To those Ambassadors of *Great Britain* | Who concluded the Peace of *Reswick*, 1697. | He was likewise Secretary | To the Two succeeding Embassies in *France*. | And also in the Year 1697, | Secretary of State in the Kingdom of *Ireland*. | In the Year 1700, | He was appointed one of the Lords Commissioners | Of *Trade* and *Plantations*. | And in the year 1711, | Made one of the *Commissioners* of the *Customs*; | And lastly, | Sent by Her Majesty Queen ANNE, | (Of blessed Memory) | In the Year 1711. | Plenipotentiary-Minister to *LEWIS* XIV, King of *France*, | With the fullest Powers to establish the *Peace*. | (A *Peace* to this Day *Lasting*, | And which, | That it may long *Last*, | Is the Wish of all good Men.) | MATTHEW PRIOR, *Esq*; | Surpassed all the Characters | With which he was invested, | By the Force of his Genius, | And the Politeness of his Erudition; | At whose Birth the gentle Muses | Smiled propitious. | The *Literature* of this *Royal Foundation* [i.e. Westminster School]| Trained up, and embellished him while a *Boy*: | St. JOHN's College in *Cambridge* | Endowed and furnished his *ripening Years* | With its brightest Sciences; | And at last, | A long and intimate Conversation | With the most illustrious Persons | Improved and finished the *Man*. | Thus Born, thus Educated, | He could never be withdrawn | From the *Choir* of the *Muses*; | But was often accustomed | To alleviate and sweeten | The Fatigue of his *public Employments*, | By a Retreat to Studies | More inviting and delightsom: | And after performing almost | Every *Species* of *Poetry* with Success: | In the agreeable and happy Manner | Of contriving and delivering *his Tales*, | This *wonderful Artist* found no Equal. | The unlaboured Delicacy, | With which he toyed in these Amusements, | Was easily observed by all | Whom he received into his Friendship: | In whose Company | If any Subject of Humour casually occurred, | He would treat it, | Being full of Wit and Pleasantry, | With the most Copious, Suitable, Sprightly, | And Beautiful Turns, | Nothing appearing to be either studies or forced, | But all freely rising from his Invention, | And flowing, as from an inexhaustible Fountain: | So, that among his Acquaintance, | It is a Matter of Doubt, | Whether in his *Writings*, | He was the more elegant *Poet*: | Or, in his *Conversation*, | The more facetious *Companion*.'

p. 1054. *one of the sixteen Tories... Brother*: the Brothers' Club included Harley and Swift, and eventually numbered over twenty 'men of wit or men of interest', as Swift characterized the membership to Stella. See the brief remarks in Johnson's 'Life of Swift' (above, p. 1078).

p. 1054. *"mais il... vous entendre"*: 'but he was singing so loud, that I was unable to hear you.'

p. 1054. *Bannissons la Melancholie*: 'let us banish melancholy.'

p. 1054. *Mais cette... la Melancholie*: 'But that voice, and those fine eyes make Cupid too dangerous, and I am sad when I cry, 'let us banish melancholy'.

p. 1055. *Strain'd... sought repair*: *Paradise Lost*, VIII.454–5, 457.

p. 1055. *Ariosto's Satires*: see above, p. 1250, note to p. 1001. Ariosto's seven satires, modelled on Horace, were composed between 1517 and 1525. Ariosto's fifth satire is a possible source for Prior's 'Hans Carvel', although its outlines are to be found in much early modern Italian literature.

p. 1057. *Hudibras*: see above, p. 1219, note to p. 611.

p. 1057. *Horace... when he imitated Lucilius*: cf. Horace, *Satires*, I.iv.8–13 and I.x. The quotation ('inferior to the inventor') comes from I.x.48.

p. 1057. *nine years*: cf. Horace, *Ars Poetica*, l. 388.

p. 1058. *Georgius Sabinus*: Georg Sabinus (1508–60); German poet, philologist, and teacher.

p. 1058. *Luther*: Martin Luther (1483–1546); German theologian and religious reformer.

p. 1058. *Melancthon*: Philipp Melanchthon (1497–1560); German humanist, reformer, theologian, and educator. Friend of Martin Luther.

p. 1058. *De Sacerdote... luce nihil*: 'On a Priest Consoling a Thief. A certain priest accompanied a thief when he was handed over to the hangman for execution. 'Do not be sad,' said the priest. 'If you only have faith, in an instant you will be feasting with God and the heavenly host.' The thief replied with a groan, 'If you would truly comfort me, I beg that you would be the guest of those above.' The priest demurred; 'It is not fitting for me to revel – I am fasting, and this day I eat nothing.'

p. 1059. *said by Longinus of Euripides*: Longinus, *On the Sublime*, ch. XV (*ALC*, pp. 477–8).

p. 1059. *nightly visitations*: *Paradise Lost*, IX.22.

p. 1060. *the vessel... first receives*: cf. Horace, *Epistles*, I.ii.69.

Blackmore

Blackmore was included at Johnson's insistence (see the opening of the 'Life of Watts', above, p. 1128).

p. 1060. *Wood*: see above, p. 1201, note to p. 419.

p. 1061. *Dr. Sydenham*: see above, p. 1168, note to p. 39.

p. 1061. *the rumbling of his chariot-wheels*: an allusion to Dryden, 'Prologue' to *The Pilgrim* (1700), ll. 41–2.

p. 1062. *Dennis*: see above, p. 1173, note to p. 99.

p. 1062. *Molineux*: William Molyneux (1656–98); experimental philosopher and political writer.

p. 1062. *Boileau*: see above, p. 1212, note to p. 529.

p. 1062. *ridicule in a Prologue*: the 'Prologue' to *The Pilgrim* (1700).

p. 1063. *alleged afterwards by Collier*: Jeremy Collier (1650–1726); non-juring clergyman and anti-theatrical polemicist. Collier's *A Short View of the Immorality and Profaneness of the English Stage* (1698) had attacked what he saw as the mischievous moral influence of the drama.

p. 1063. *dropped... dead-born from the press*: an allusion to Pope, *Epilogue to the Satires* 2, l. 226.

p. 1063. *the Kit-cat Club*: an early eighteenth-century literary club of a pronounced Whiggish character.

p. 1063. *Steele*: see above, p. 1173, note to p. 84.

p. 1063. *Fenton*: see above, p. 1251, note to p. 1008.

p. 1064. *Mr. Draper*: Somerset Draper (d. 1756); bookseller and partner to Jacob Tonson.

p. 1064. *Ambrose Philips*: Ambrose Philips (1674–1749); poet and playwright.

p. 1064. *Mr. Hughes*: see above, p. 1252, note to p. 1018.

p. 1066. *A Tale of a Tub*: the first major work by Swift, first published anonymously in 1704, and never explicitly acknowledged by Swift to be his work; see Johnson's comment on this in his 'Life of Swift' (above, p. 1076).

p. 1068. *Brady and Tate*: Nicholas Brady (1659–1726), poet and clergyman; and Nahum Tate (*c.*1652–1715), poet, playwright, and translator. Brady and Tate's *A New Version of the Psalms of David* was first published in 1696, revised in 1698, and extended in 1700.

p. 1068. *Hippocrates*: Hippocrates (*c.*460–*c.*375 BC); ancient Greek physician regarded as the father of medicine.

p. 1068. *aphorism and apophthegm*: Aphorism; any principle or precept expressed in few words; a short pithy sentence containing a truth of general import; a maxim (*OED*, 2). Apophthegm; a terse, pointed saying, embodying an important truth in few words; a pithy or sententious maxim (*OED*). Perhaps, therefore, a forgiveable confusion on Blackmore's part.

Swift

p. 1072. *Dr. Hawkesworth*: John Hawkesworth (1720–73); writer; editor of Swift's *Works* (1755).

p. 1073. *Sir William Temple*: Sir William Temple (1628–99); politician, diplomat, and author.

p. 1074. *Earl of Portland*: Hans Willem Bentinck (1649–1709), first earl of Portland; diplomat and politician; close and trusted associate of William III.

p. 1074. *a disorder*: Ménière's disease; Swift's succumbing to this disease was perfectly unrelated to his diet.

p. 1074. *Lord Orrery*: John Boyle (1707–62), fifth earl of Cork and fifth earl of Orrery; Jacobite politician and biographer of Swift.

p. 1075. *Lord Capel*: Henry Capel (1639–96), baron Capel of Tewkesbury; politician and government official; one of the three Lord Justices in Ireland.

p. 1075. *prebend*: originally the estate or portion of land from which a stipend is derived to support a canon of a cathedral or collegiate church; by extension, the tenure of this as a benefice, or the right to an equivalent share in the revenues of such a church (*OED*, 1 a).

p. 1075. *Earl of Berkeley*: Charles Berkeley (1649–1710), second earl of Berkeley; politician and Lord Justice of Ireland.

p. 1075. *the unfortunate Stella*: Esther or Hester Johnson (1681–1728); daughter of Sir William Temple's steward, Edward Johnson.

p. 1075. *Mrs. Dingley*: Rebecca Dingley (*c.*1665–1743); dependent relative of Sir William Temple.

p. 1076. *Archbishop Sharpe*: John Sharp (1645–1717); archbishop of York.

p. 1076. *the Duchess of Somerset*: Elizabeth Seymour (1667–1722), duchess of Somerset.

p. 1076. *Sacheverell*: see above, p. 1251, note to p. 1011.

p. 1076. *Smalridge*: George Smalridge (1663–1719); dean of Christ Church, Oxford; bishop of Bristol.

p. 1076. *Wotton*: William Wotton (1666–1727); linguist and theologian; Wotton's *Reflections Upon Ancient and Modern Learning* (1694) launched the English phase of the 'querelle' between the ancients and moderns.

p. 1076. *Bentley*: see above, p. 1229, note to p. 757.

p. 1077. *Asgill*: John Asgill (1659–1738); member of parliament, deist, and author.

p. 1077. *Toland*: John Toland (1670–1722); freethinker and philosopher.

p. 1077. *Tindal*: Matthew Tindal (1657–1733); freethinker and religious controversialist.

p. 1077. *reasonableness of a Test*: the Test Act obliged those who held public office to receive the sacrament according to the rites of the Church of England. It was thus the principal instrument of religious conformity in England, and was staunchly defended by Swift.

p. 1077. *Mr. Harley*: see above, p. 1172, note to p. 71.

p. 1078. *by the name of Brother*: see above, p. 1255, note to p. 1054.

p. 1078. *Steele*: see above, p. 1173, note to p. 84.

p. 1079. *he published (1712) the Conduct of the Allies*: in fact, 1711.

p. 1079. *mines had been exhausted, and millions destroyed*: a reformulation of phrases taken from Tickell's *Poem on the Prospect of Peace* (1712), ll. 55–6.

p. 1079. *Lord Cowper*: William Cowper (1665–1723), Lord Chancellor.

p. 1079. *Whatever is received…recipient*: a scholastic commonplace; cf., e.g., Aquinas, *Summa Contra Gentiles*, II.79.

p. 1079. *not yet a nation of readers*: an interesting aside which hints at the transformation in British literary culture which occurred in Johnson's lifetime.

p. 1080. *When I give away…ungrateful*: for the original remark, see Voltaire, *Siècle de Louis Quatorze*, ch. XXVI, para. 3: 'Le roi…dit qu'il avait cherché des amis, et qu'il n'avait trouvé que des intrigants. Cette connaissance malheureuse des hommes, qu'on acquiert trop tard, lui faisait dire aussi: "Toutes les fois que je donne une place vacante, je fais cent mécontents et un ingrat." '

p. 1081. *a journal of his visits*: the text which is now known as the *Journal to Stella*; in fact, a series of letters, many of which were written over several days and which therefore read like a journal.

p. 1081. *not to be offended with impunity*: a translation of the old Scotch motto, 'Nemo me impune lacessit' ('No one who offends me goes unpunished').

p. 1082. *secured by a sleight…their friend*: adaptations of some lines of Swift's; 'The Author Upon Himself', ll. 57–70.

p. 1082. *Aislabie*: John Aislabie (1670–1742); politician; chancellor of the exchequer; related by marriage to John Sharp (above, p. 1257, note to p. 1076).

p. 1082. *Walpole*: see above, p. 1174, note to p. 99.

p. 1082. *into Berkshire*: more precisely, to Letcombe Bassett.

p. 1082. *a friend*: the Rev. John Geree.

p. 1082. *Dr. Delany*: Patrick Delany (1685/6–1768); clergyman of the Church of Ireland and writer; his riposte to Orrery's biography of Swift was published in 1754.

p. 1082. *Archbishop of Dublin*: William King (1650–1729), archbishop of Dublin.

p. 1082. *Dr. King*: William King (1685–1763); principal of St Mary Hall, Oxford; Jacobite sympathizer.

p. 1082. *Dr. Lucas*: Dr. Charles Lucas (1713–71); physician.

p. 1082. *Mr. Lewis*: Erasmus Lewis (1670–1754); government official.

p. 1083. *Mr. Worral*: John Worrall (*c.*1666–1751); choirmaster at St. Patrick's.

p. 1083. *he was privately married*: a point of great controversy in Swift scholarship. The current consensus is that, in the absence of documentary evidence, it is safer to assume that Swift did not marry Stella.

p. 1083. *Dr. Ashe*: St. George Ashe (*c.*1658–1718); Swift's former tutor; bishop of, in succession, Clone, Clogher, and Derry.

p. 1083. *Dr. Madden*: Samuel Madden (1686–1765); clergyman and writer.

p. 1083. *by a pamphlet*: i.e. *A Proposal for the Universal Use of Irish Manufacture* (1720).

p. 1083. *Mrs. Van Homrigh*: Esther or Hester Vanhomrigh (1688–1723); pronounced 'vannummery'. For Swift's poetic description of their relationship, cf. *Cadenus and Vanessa* (Dublin, 1726).

p. 1084. *men are but men*: proverbial; cf. Aubrey's recollection of a saying of General Lambert, that 'the best of men are but men at the best' (*Brief Lives*, p. 109).

p. 1084. *Wood of Wolverhampton*: William Wood (1671–1730); ironmonger.

p. 1084. *Duchess of Munster*: Melusine von der Schulenburg (1667–1743), duchess of Kendal and duchess of Munster; mistress of George I.

p. 1085. *one Whitshed*: William Whitshed (*c.*1656–1727); Lord Chief Justice of the King's Bench in Ireland.

p. 1085. *Lord Carteret*: John Carteret (1690–1763), second earl Granville; politician; Lord Lieutenant of Ireland.

p. 1086. *Archbishop Boulter*: Hugh Boulter (1672–1742); archbishop of Armagh.

p. 1086. *Lord Bolingbroke*: see above, p. 1174, note to p. 118.

p. 1086. *three volumes of Miscellanies*: the four volumes were published in 1727 (vols 1 and 2), 1728 ('The Last'), and 1732 (as vol. 3).

p. 1086. *the Flying Island*: i.e. Part III.

p. 1086. *the history of the Houyhnhnms*: i.e. Part IV.

p. 1086. *Mrs. Barber*: Mary Barber (*c.*1690–1757), wife of a Dublin woollen-draper.

p. 1086. *Mrs. Howard*: Henrietta Howard (*c.*1688–1767); mistress of George II; subsequently countess of Suffolk.

p. 1086. *Mrs. Masham*: Abigail Masham (1670?–1734); lady-in-waiting to Queen Anne.

p. 1087. *two sick friends cannot live together*: slightly misquoted from Swift's letter to Pope of 12 October 1727.

p. 1087. *make assurance double sure*: *Macbeth*, IV.i.83.

p. 1088. *Dr. Sheridan:* Thomas Sheridan (1687–1738); clergyman and schoolteacher.

p. 1088. *Bettesworth:* Richard Bettesworth (*c.* 1689–1741); Irish member of parliament and Sergeant-at-Law. Cf. Swift's poem 'On the Words—Brother Protestants, and Fellow Christians', ll. 25–8.

p. 1088. *catchpoll:* a contemptuous term for a warrant-officer who arrests for debt (*OED,* 2 a).

p. 1089. *vive la bagatelle:* a bagatelle is a trifle or thing of no importance. Cf. Pope, *Ep. I.vi,* l. 128.

p. 1090. *Mrs. Whiteway:* Martha Whiteway (1690–1768); Swift's widowed cousin on whom he increasingly relied as he became more senile.

p. 1092. *hypocrisy... than open impiety:* in his *Project for the Advancement of Religion and Manners* (1709), Swift wrote: 'Hypocrisy is much more eligible than open Infidelity and Vice: It wears the Livery of Religion, it acknowledges her Authority'.

p. 1094. *Arbuthnot:* John Arbuthnot (1667–1735); physician and satirist.

p. 1096. *proper words in proper places:* a quotation from Swift's *A Letter to a Young Gentleman* (1720).

p. 1096. *never been known to take a single thought from any writer:* cf. the 'Apology' to *A Tale of a Tub,* and Swift's *Verses on the Death of Dr. Swift,* ll. 317–18. Paradoxically the claim to independence echoes a line in Cowley's elegy on Denham.

Pope

p. 1096. *his account of the Little Club:* in *The Guardian,* nos. 91 and 92.

p. 1096. *long disease:* see Pope's *Epistle to Arbuthnot,* l. 132.

p. 1097. *C'est que... enfant:* 'The fact is that the child is still a man, and the man is still a child'. Johnson had recently quoted this line of the French author Antoine Houdar de la Motte in a letter to Mrs. Thrale (Redford, vol. III, p. 282).

p. 1097. *nodded in company:* cf. Pope. *Sat. II.i,* l. 13.

p. 1097. *Hannibal, says Juvenal:* Juvenal, X.164–6.

p. 1098. *He hardly... a stratagem:* cf. Young, *The Love of Fame,* VI.190.

p. 1098. *Lord Orrery:* see above, p. 1256, note to p. 1074.

p. 1098. *he plaid... turnips:* cf. *Life,* p. 698.

p. 1098. *Patriot King:* a political tract by Bolingbroke, entrusted to Pope before publication so that a handful of presentation copies could be printed, but of which with Pope's approval a full edition of fifteen hundred copies was made in 1738.

p. 1098. *Bolingbroke:* see above, p. 1174, note to p. 118.

p. 1098. *Patrick:* Samuel Patrick (1684–1748); editor of dictionaries.

p. 1098. *horresco referens:* 'I shudder as I mention it' (*Aeneid,* II.204).

p. 1098. *Lady Mary Wortley:* Lady Mary Wortley Montagu (1689–1762); writer and traveller. Cf. Pope, *Sat. II.i,* ll. 83–4, where Lady Mary is disguised as 'Sappho'.

p. 1099. *Gentlemen... fortune for all:* the anecdote derives ultimately from Swift; cf. Patrick Delany, *Observations upon... Swift* (1754), p. 181.

p. 1099. *a distich for his Highness's dog:* cf. Pope's 'Epigram. Engraved on the Collar of a Dog which I gave to his Royal Highness' (composed 1737).

p. 1099. *Lord Bathurst:* Allen Bathurst (1684–1775), first earl Bathurst; politician.

p. 1099. *Cobham*: Richard Temple (1675–1749), first viscount Cobham; politician and landowner.

p. 1099. *Burlington*: Richard Boyle (1694–1753), third earl of Burlington and fourth earl of Cork; architect, collector, and patron of the arts.

p. 1100. *the Golden Age*: in classical mythology and poetry, the age when Saturn ruled the world; a period of innocent happiness, when men lived without violence, labour, and injustice, and when the earth yielded its fruits abundantly and spontaneously.

p. 1100. *affectation and ambition*: Pope admits this in the 'Preface' to the 1737 edition of his *Letters*.

p. 1101. *he has just nothing else to do*: as Pope admitted in a letter to Richardson of February or March 1732.

p. 1101. *he had always…in his head*: a quotation from Swift's letter to Mrs Caesar of 30 July 1733.

p. 1101. *in two reigns*: i.e. those of George I (1714–27) and George II (1727–60).

p. 1101. *he never sees Courts*: cf. the letter from Pope to Swift of 20 April 1733.

p. 1101. *how he…disliked Kings?*: in fact, Pope had a very good reply; 'I consider royalty under that noble and authorised type of the Lion; while he is young, and before his nails are grown, he may be approached, and caressed with safety and pleasure' (Owen Ruffhead, *The Life of Alexander Pope* (1769), p. 535, n. †). The encounter with the Prince of Wales occurred in 1735. Cf. *Life*, p. 790 for a slightly different version of Pope's riposte, which Boswell received from John Wilkes.

p. 1101. *emmets*: a poetic or archaic word for ants (*OED*, 1, quoting this passage).

p. 1101. *a fool to Fame*: see Pope's *Epistle to Arbuthnot*, l. 127.

p. 1101. *after many…fools in the world*: a series of phrases taken from Pope's correspondence.

p. 1102. *Philips*: Ambrose Philips (1674–1749); poet and playwright. Mocked by Pope in the course of an essay on pastoral in *The Guardian*, no. 40 (27 April 1713).

p. 1102. *Bentley*: see above, p. 1229, note to p. 757.

p. 1102. *Chandos*: James Brydges (1674–1744), first duke of Chandos; politician and patron of music.

p. 1102. *Hill*: see above, p. 1173, note to p. 89.

p. 1102. *Dodsley*: Robert Dodsley (1704–64); bookseller.

p. 1102. *Allen*: Ralph Allen (1693–1764); entrepreneur and philanthropist.

p. 1103. *Earl of Marchmont*: Hugh Hume Campbell (1708–94), third earl of Marchmont; politician. Johnson had an interview with Marchmont, whom Pope had admired and liked, on 1 May 1779.

p. 1103. *Racine*: see above, p. 1253, note to p. 1047.

p. 1103. *the academy of Paracelsus*: i.e. nature.

p. 1103. *Dobson*: William Dobson, whose Latin translation of Milton had been published in 1750–3.

p. 1103. *verses to Jervas*: the 'Epistle to Mr. Jervas'; cf. ll. 23–8.

p. 1104. *It is related of Virgil*: recalled also in Johnson's 'Life of Dryden'; see above, p. 981, and p. 1249, note to p. 981.

p. 1106. *the two satires of Thirty-eight*: i.e. the two poems now more commonly referred to as the 'Epilogues to the Satires'.

p. 1107. *Waller's poem on The Park*: *A Poem on St. James's Park, as Lately Improved by His Majesty* (1661).

p. 1107. *Dennis*: see above, p. 1173, note to p. 99.

p. 1108. *Steele*: see above, p. 1173, note to p. 84.

p. 1109. *numeris lege solutis*: 'in metre freed from rule', Horace's comment on Pindar's irregular poetic measures (*Odes*, IV.ii.11–12).

p. 1109. *Mr. Cobb… an impudent one*: Samuel Cobb (1675–1713); poet and critic, and a student at Trinity College, Cambridge, where Bentley was master.

p. 1110. *Perrault… with a long tail*: cf. Charles Perrault, *Parallèle des anciens et des modernes* (1693), vol. II, p. 41.

p. 1110. *the celebrated paragraph*: *An Essay on Criticism*, ll. 337–83.

p. 1111. *With many… along the ground*: *Odyssey*, XI.735–8.

p. 1111. *When Ajax… along the main*: *An Essay on Criticism*, ll. 370–3.

p. 1111. *Waller… energy divine*: *Ep. II.i*, ll. 267–9.

p. 1111. *nugatory*: trifling or insignificant. Cf. *The Idler*, no. 40 (above, pp. 595–97).

p. 1111. *Dr. Warburton*: see above, p. 1229, note to p. 750.

p. 1112. *the little unguarded follies of the female sex*: cf. the first paragraph of Pope's 'Dedication' of the *Rape of the Lock* to Arabella Fermor.

p. 1112. *the Lutrin*: Nicolas Boileau, *Le Lutrin* (1674), an anti-clerical mock-heroic poem.

p. 1113. *the game at ombre*: *Rape of the Lock*, II.19–100.

p. 1113. *curiosa felicitas*: 'studied felicity' (Petronius, *Satyricon*, 118).

p. 1113. *the learned author… Writings of Pope*: Joseph Warton; for Johnson's review, see above, pp. 525–31.

p. 1113. *Anguillara's Ovid*: Giovanni Andrea Anguillara (*c*.1517–1574); Italian poet and dramatist. His translation of Ovid's *Metamorphoses* was published in 1584.

p. 1113. *Salvini*: Antonio Maria Salvini (1653–1729); Italian jurist, philologist, and professor of Greek literature. His translation of the *Iliad* was published in 1723.

p. 1114. *Tully and Germanicus*: Cicero translated Aratus, as did Nero Claudius Germanicus.

p. 1114. *necessitas quod cogit defendit*: 'what necessity compels, necessity extenuates' (Seneca, *Controversiae*, IX.iv.5).

p. 1115. *Broome*: William Broome (1689–1745); clergyman, poet, and translator.

p. 1116. *Theobald*: see above, p. 1229, note to p. 749.

p. 1116. *impune diem consumpserit ingens Telephus*: 'will [*a tragedy on*] great Telephus consume a day without redress?' (Juvenal, I.4–5). Juvenal is complaining about tedious and bombastic tragic drama.

p. 1116. *Moore*: James Moore Smythe (1702–34); cf. *The Dunciad*, II.35–50 and 109–20.

p. 1116. *the javelin of Priam*: cf. *Aeneid*, II.544–6.

p. 1116. *Leibnitian reasoning*: Gottfried Wilhelm Leibniz (1646–1716); mathematician and philosopher, whose *Théodicée* (1710) contended that men lived in the best of all possible worlds, a view mocked in Voltaire's *Candide* (1759). For Johnson's deep-seated hostility to such extenuations of evil, see his review of Soame Jenyns (above, pp. 549–68).

p. 1117. *with Boileau's Satire*: i.e. 'Satire' X.

p. 1118. *Arbuthnot*: see above, p. 1259, note to p. 1094.

p. 1118. *the satire upon Sporus*: *An Epistle from Mr. Pope, to Dr. Arbuthnot*, ll. 305–33.

p. 1119. *Musick...inarticulate poetry*: in the 'Preface' to *Tyrannick Love* (1669).

p. 1119. *Fenton*: see above, p. 1251, note to p. 1008.

p. 1119. *Lo,...waste of snows*: *The Dunciad*, III.87–8.

p. 1120. *Hall's Satires*: see above, p. 1251, note to p. 1007.

Thomson

p. 1121. *Mr. Mallet*: David Mallet (formerly 'Malloch') (1701/2?–1765); poet and man of letters.

p. 1121. *Sir Spencer Compton*: Spencer Compton (*c.* 1674–1743), earl of Wilmington; politician and (briefly) prime minister.

p. 1121. *Aaron Hill*: Aaron Hill (1685–1750); writer and entrepreneur.

p. 1122. *Dr. Rundle*: Thomas Rundle (*c.* 1688–1743); chaplain to William Talbot, bishop of Durham; later accused of heresy.

p. 1122. *lord chancellor Talbot*: Charles Talbot (1685–1737); barrister, politician, and Lord Chancellor.

p. 1122. *Mr. Gray*: Thomas Gray (1716–71); poet and literary scholar.

p. 1122. *lord Binning*: Charles Hamilton (1697–1732), lord Binning; landowner.

p. 1122. *Mr. Doddington*: George Bubb Dodington (1690/91–1762), baron Melcombe; politician and diarist.

p. 1123. *Sir Robert Walpole*: see above, p. 1174, note to p. 99.

p. 1123. *Sir George Lyttelton*: George Lyttelton (1709–73), first baron Lyttelton; politician and writer.

p. 1124. *lord Hardwicke*: Philip Yorke (1690–1764), first earl of Hardwicke; barrister, politician, and Lord Chancellor.

p. 1124. *the Act was passed for licensing plays*: for Johnson's contribution to this episode in the history of censorship, see his *Compleat Vindication of the Licensers of the Stage* (above, pp. 50–61).

p. 1125. *more fat than bard beseems*: a quotation from canto I, stanza lxviii, l. 604 of Thomson's *The Castle of Indolence*.

p. 1125. *Quin*: James Quin (1693–1766); actor.

p. 1128. *both their lustre and their shade*: Samuel Butler, *Hudibras*, II.i.907–8; cf. also *The Idler*, no. 31 (above, pp. 587–89).

p. 1128. *Temple*: for Temple, see above, p. 1256, note to p. 1073. Johnson is probably thinking of a phrase from Temple's notorious 'An Essay Upon the Ancient and Modern Learning': 'more Race, more Spirit, more Force of Wit and Genius' (Temple, *Works*, 2 vols (1720), vol. I, p. 166).

Watts

p. 1128. *Dr. Gibbons*: Thomas Gibbons (1720–85); Independent minister and diarist.

p. 1129. *Mr. Rowe*: Thomas Rowe (1657–1705); Independent minister and schoolmaster.

p. 1129. *Mr. Hughes*: John Hughes (see above, p. 1252, note to p. 1018).

p. 1129. *the glyconick measure*: a lyric metre in which each line consists of three trochees and a dactyl (*OED*, quoting this passage).

p. 1132. *Malbranche*: Nicolas Malebranche (1638–1715); French philosopher.

Collins

p. 1133. *Dr. Warton*: Joseph Warton; see above, p. 1212, headnote to *Review of* An Essay on the Writings and Genius of Pope.

p. 1134. *Leo the Tenth*: Pope Leo X (1475–1521); patron of the arts. He was succeeded by Pope Adrian VI (1459–1523).

p. 1134. *formerly written his character*: this character of Collins was first published in the *Poetical Calendar*, XII (December 1763), and subsequently in the *Gentleman's Magazine* (January 1764).

p. 1135. *Mr. John Hume*: John Home (1722–1808); dramatist.

Gray

p. 1136. *November 26, 1716*: in fact, Gray was born on 26 December 1716.

p. 1137. *Horace Walpole*: Horace Walpole (1717–97); son of Sir Robert Walpole; novelist, dilettante, and man of letters.

p. 1137. *Mr. West*: Richard West (1717–42).

p. 1137. *Mr. Mason*: William Mason (1725–97); poet and garden designer.

p. 1138. *Mr. Bentley*: Richard Bentley (1708–82); writer and artist; son of the classical scholar (for whom, see above, p. 1229, note to p. 757).

p. 1138. *Warburton*: see above, p. 1229, note to p. 750.

p. 1138. *Cibber*: see above, p. 1173, note to p. 88.

p. 1138. *Mr. Whitehead*: William Whitehead (1715–85); poet and playwright.

p. 1138. *the Museum*: i.e. the British Museum.

p. 1138. *cockered and spirited up*: i.e. encouraged to apply.

p. 1139. *Dr. Beattie*: James Beattie (1735–1803); professor of Moral Philosophy at Aberdeen.

p. 1139. *Voltaire...Mr. Congreve*: in his *Letters on England* (1733) Voltaire expressed his dismay at the assumed gentility of William Congreve, who when Voltaire called upon him, affected to believe that his writings were beneath the dignity of a gentleman.

p. 1141. *O Diva...Antium*: 'O Goddess that rules pleasant Antium' (Horace, *Odes*, I.xxxv.1).

p. 1142. *ternary*: a set or group of three (*OED*, B 1 a, quoting this passage).

p. 1142. *Algarotti*: Francesco Algarotti (1712–1764); Italian author.

p. 1142. *Incredulus odi*: 'I disbelieve, and so detest' (Horace, *Ars Poetica*, l. 188).

p. 1143. *Double, double, toil and trouble*: Macbeth, IV.i.10.

Letter to Thomas Lawrence

Text: Redford, vol. IV, p. 6.

Date: 17 January 1782.

    p. 1144. Robert Levett (or Levet, or Levit) (1705–82); surgeon and apothecary; member of Johnson's household from 1756 until his death. For Johnson's elegy on his death, see above, pp. 1146–7.

Diary entry

Text: Hawkins, p. 554; *Diaries*, p. 311.

Date: 20 January 1782.

    p. 1144 *Commendavi*: both 'I have entrusted [i.e. Levett to God]' and 'I have praised [Levett]. Hawkins mistakenly prints 'Commendari'. For Johnson's use of the English word 'commended' in these senses, see his diary entry for 28 March 1777 (above, pp. 909–10).

Letter to Thomas Lawrence

Text: Redford, vol. IV, p. 34.

Date: 1 May 1782.

Thomas Lawrence was Johnson's physician at the end of his life, and was also (so Johnson told Boswell) 'one of the best men whom I have known' (*Life*, p. 844). When writing to Lawrence about his health it was Johnson's custom to do so in Latin, a practice which perhaps shows the influence of Boerhaave: see above, p. 1169, note to p. 45.

'To Dr. Lawrence. A fresh chill, a fresh cough, and a fresh difficulty in breathing call for a fresh letting of blood. Without your advice, however, I would not submit to the operation. I cannot well come to you, nor need you come to me. Say yes or no in one word, and leave the rest to Holder and to me. If you say yes, tell the messenger to send Holder. May 1, 1782. When you have left, to whom shall I turn?'

Letter to James Boswell

Text: Redford, vol. IV, pp. 71–3.

Date: 7 September 1782.

    p. 1145. *into another state*: Boswell's father had died on 30 August 1782.

    p. 1145. *a well ordered poem*: in his 'Ode Upon Liberty'.

    p. 1146. *Rasay*: i.e. John Macleod (*c.*1714–1786), eleventh laird of Raasay. Johnson had made his acquaintance during his tour of Scotland in 1773.

    p. 1146. *Coriatachat*: i.e. Corichatachan, Skye; see above, p. 1237, note to p. 826.

On the Death of Dr Robert Levet

Text: *Gentleman's Magazine*, vol. LIII (1783), pp. 695–6.

Date: August 1783.

For Levett, see above, p. 1264, note to p. 1144. For Johnson's view of the pitfalls surrounding elegy as a poetic form, see his critical comments on 'Lycidas' in his 'Life of Milton' (above, pp. 958–59).

l. 1. *Condemn'd to hope's delusive mine*: being condemned to labour in the mines was a punishment in ancient Rome.

l. 7. *Officious*: i.e. attending to his duties; here used without any pejorative connotation.

l. 20. *And lonely want retir'd to die*: originally 'And Labour steals an hour to die' (*Life*, p. 841, n. c)

l. 28. *single talent*: cf. Matthew 25:14–30.

Letter to Hester Thrale

Texts: Redford, vol. IV, pp. 338.

Date: 2 July 1784.

Hester Lynch Thrale (1741–1821); married first the brewer Henry Thrale in 1763, and subsequently, in the teeth of Johnson's opposition, the musician Gabriel Piozzi in 1784; author of *Anecdotes of the Late Samuel Johnson* (1786). On 30 June 1784, Hester Thrale had notified Johnson that she intended to marry Piozzi. The marriage ceremonies (one Roman Catholic, the other Church of England) would occur on 23 and 25 July respectively.

Letter to Hester Maria Thrale

Texts: Redford, vol. IV, pp. 339.

Date: 3 July 1784.

Hester Maria Elphinstone (1764–1857), Viscountess Keith; eldest daughter of Henry and Hester Thrale; favourite of Samuel Johnson; student of Hebrew and mathematics; married Admiral George Elphinstone, Baron Keith, in 1808; widowed in 1823.

Letter to Hester Maria Thrale

Texts: Redford, vol. IV, pp. 339–40.

Date: 6 July 1784.

Letter to Hester Thrale

Texts: Redford, vol. IV, pp. 343–4.
Date: 8 July 1784.
    p. 1149. *Queen Mary*: i.e. Mary Stuart, Queen of Scots.
    p. 1149. *irremeable*: admitting of no return (*OED*).

Letter to Lord Thurlow

Text: Redford, vol. IV, pp. 399–400.
Date: 9 September 1784.
Lord Thurlow had petitioned the King that Johnson's pension might be increased to allow him to travel to Italy. The request had been refused, and Lord Thurlow had offered to provide Johnson with funds out of his own pocket.
    p. 1149. *mihi carior*: literally 'dearer to myself', or as we might say, 'higher in my own estimation'.

Translation of Horace, Odes, *IV.vii (Diffugere nives)*

Text: MS, Hyde Collection, Houghton Library, Harvard.
Date: November 1784.
    l. 28. *his friend*: i.e. Pirithous, king of the Lapithae. In Greek mythology Theseus and Pirithous descended to Hades to try to carry off Persephone.

Prayer

Text: MS Yale; *Diaries*, pp. 417–18.
Date: 5 December 1784.
Johnson died on 13 December 1784.

CONTENTS BY GENRE

b) Moral Essays

c) Political Essays

d) Literary Essays, Works of Scholarship, and Reviews

INDEX OF FIRST LINES

INDEX OF PROPER NAMES